AZTECS

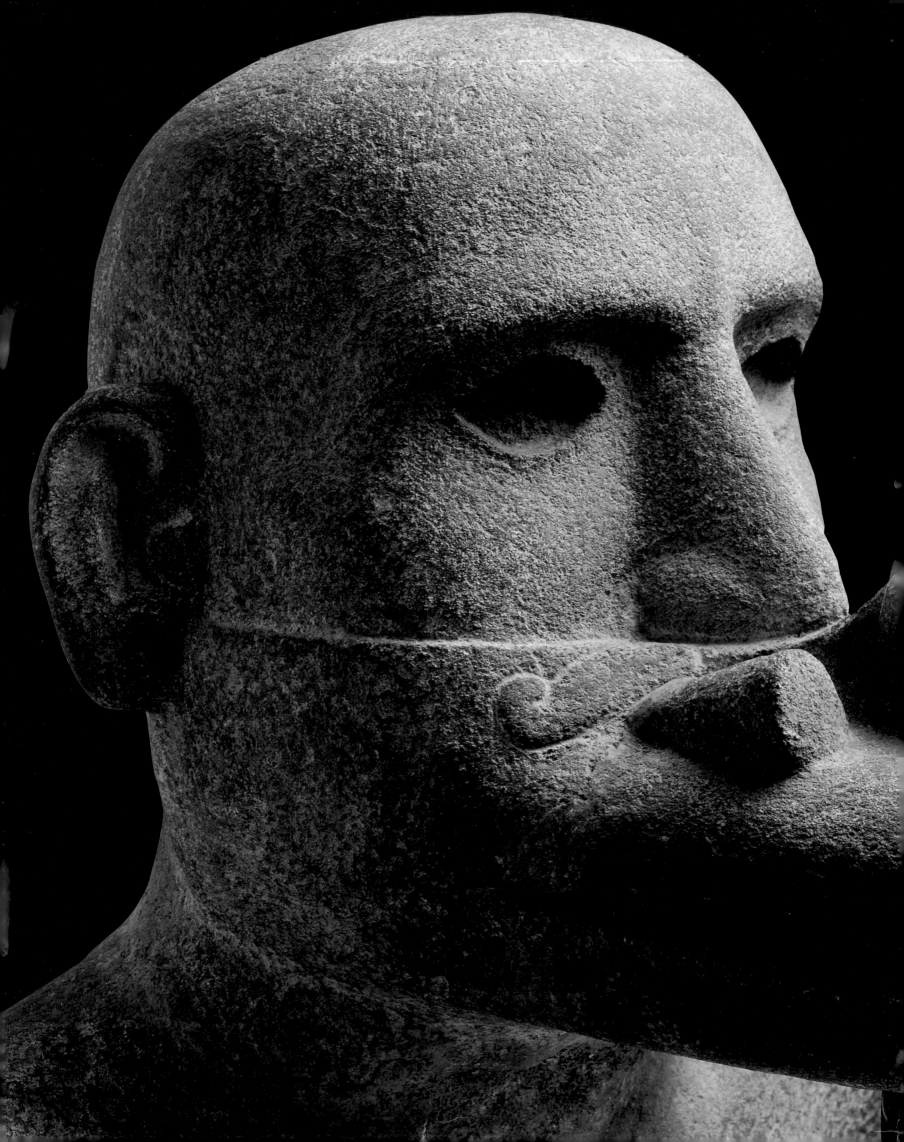

AZTECS

First published on the occasion
of the exhibition 'Aztecs'
Royal Academy of Arts, London
16 November 2002 – 11 April 2003

The Royal Academy of Arts is grateful to
Her Majesty's Government for agreeing to indemnify
this exhibition under the National Heritage Act 1980,
and to Resource, The Council for Museums, Archives
and Libraries, for its help in arranging the indemnity.

Supported by

Generous support has also been received
from Virginia and Simon Robertson.

EXHIBITION CURATORS, MEXICO CITY
Eduardo Matos Moctezuma
Felipe Solís Olguín

ROYAL ACADEMY OF ARTS, LONDON
Tom Phillips RA, *Chairman of Exhibitions Committee*
Norman Rosenthal, *Exhibitions Secretary*
Adrian Locke, *Aztec Exhibition Curator*
Isabel Carlisle, *Curator*

EXHIBITION ORGANISATION
Emeline Max, *Head of Exhibitions Organisation*
Lucy Hunt, *Exhibition Organiser*
Hillary Taylor, *Assistant Exhibition Organiser*

PHOTOGRAPHIC AND COPYRIGHT COORDINATION
Andreja Brulc
Roberta Stansfield

CATALOGUE
Royal Academy Publications
David Breuer
Harry Burden
Carola Krueger
Fiona McHardy
Peter Sawbridge
Nick Tite

CONSULTING EDITOR
Warwick Bray

COPY-EDITING AND PROOFREADING
Michael Foster

TRANSLATION
Translate-A-Book, Oxford

BOOK AND MAP DESIGN
Isambard Thomas

PICTURE RESEARCH
Julia Harris-Voss with Celia Dearing

SPECIAL PHOTOGRAPHY
Michel Zabé

ILLUSTRATIONS
Russell Bell
Roger Taylor

COLOUR ORIGINATION
Robert Marcuson Publishing Services

Printed in Madrid by Turner at Artes Gráficas
Palermo, S.L., and bound at Hermanos Ramos

British Library Cataloguing-in-Publication Data

A catalogue record for this book is available
from the British Library

ISBN 1–903973–22–8 (paperback)
ISBN 1–903973–13–9 (hardback)
D. L.: M-46.614-2002

Distributed outside the United States and Canada
by Thames & Hudson Ltd, London
Distributed in the United States and Canada
by Harry N. Abrams, Inc., New York

EDITORIAL NOTE
All measurements are given in centimetres,
height before width before depth

The Royal Academy of Arts acknowledges with
gratitude the assistance of CONACULTA-INAH
in organising the loans from Mexico.

CONTENTS

I am very glad to have the opportunity and honour to welcome this exhibition of Mexican artefacts to the United Kingdom. I am delighted that it is being officially opened by my friend and colleague President Vicente Fox of Mexico, at the Royal Academy of Arts.

I believe this exhibition will be a milestone in cultural relations between Mexico and the United Kingdom. I would like to acknowledge Mexico's great generosity in allowing so many wonderful works of art and treasured objects to come from its museums to London.

The era of the Aztecs represents one of the great historic milestones in human history, contributing richly to the modern world we know today. The first European encounter with this civilisation can only have been one of awe.

I was able to visit Mexico myself in August 2001. It became clear to me then that Mexico today is an exciting cosmopolitan country with a rich cultural heritage – a fine example of peoples from many races coming together to make one of the most vibrant countries in the world.

From all I saw during my time in Mexico, I do not doubt that the exhibition will be a great success.

Tony Blair
Prime Minister of Great Britain

The cultural legacy of Mexico is extraordinarily rich and varied: the imprint of Europe is everywhere apparent; echoes of Asia and Africa are easily discernible; and the Arab and Jewish worlds – through the medium of Spain – have also left their mark.

But the civilisations that flourished in Pre-Hispanic Mexico, before the arrival of the Europeans, occupy an especially prominent place within this vast heritage. The Mexica – or Aztecs – were one of the most highly developed among these civilisations. From inauspicious beginnings they built an empire that spanned central and southern Mexico, from the Atlantic to the Pacific. Their complex society displayed remarkable artistic and technical accomplishments, as well as customs that can seem, to contemporary eyes, harsh or violent.

The first Europeans to see the Aztec capital were amazed by its splendour. And although the civilisation that inspired this wonderment was ultimately to fall to Hernán Cortés, and, in the process, give rise to a new country, it has lost none of its fascination. The achievements of the Aztecs continue to excite the curiosity of scholars in Mexico and abroad. Recent decades have seen great advances in our understanding of the Aztec world, thanks to the discovery of the monumental disc of the goddess Coyolxauhqui in 1978 and the excavations of the ambitious Templo Mayor project in Mexico City.

The people and government of Mexico are thus proud to present this major exhibition at the Royal Academy of Arts. Although Britain has made an outstanding contribution to the study and conservation of the world's cultural heritage, it remains relatively unfamiliar with the rich legacy of the indigenous cultures of the Americas. We hope that this exhibition, together with the opening of the Mexican Gallery at the British Museum, will enhance interest in and awareness of the achievements of the civilisations that flourished in the Americas before the advent of the Europeans.

'Aztecs' at the Royal Academy will stand as a milestone in the dissemination of the achievements of the Pre-Hispanic world. Never before have so many major pieces been brought together. Many, indeed, are being exhibited for the first time. Our deepest gratitude and appreciation goes to the Royal Academy of Arts for providing such a splendid setting for this exhibition, with the support of the following Mexican institutions: the Consejo Nacional para la Cultura y las Artes (CONACULTA), the Instituto Nacional de Antropología e Historia (INAH), the Mexican Tourism Board, the Secretaría de Relaciones Exteriores and Petróleos Mexicanos (Pemex).

The display of Mexico's cultural legacy is a powerful means for us to let others see us as we truly are, fostering mutual understanding and strengthening ties of friendship. This is our ultimate purpose in bringing the unique heritage of the Aztecs to London.

Vicente Fox
President of Mexico

It is always an honour as well as a joyous responsibility to share the glories of Mexican culture and history with other nations. We are convinced that there is no better dialogue than that generated by the interchange of artistic expressions between peoples. For this we celebrate the presence of the Aztecs in the United Kingdom.

This exhibition, presented by the Royal Academy of Arts, shows the world of the Aztecs as a splendid crucible in which all aspects of their society, arts and culture are brought together. From the time of their arrival in the basin of Mexico and the foundation of their magnificent city of Tenochtitlan in 1325, the Aztecs built a civilisation whose influence spread across most of Mesoamerica.

Through the artistic and plastic properties of the works included in this exhibition, it is possible to glimpse the aesthetic values inherent in all aspects of Aztec life. Each one of these objects is an example of the conception they had of the world, the gods, and of themselves.

The knowledge we have of the Aztecs has been considerably enriched by research undertaken over the past 25 years, particularly by the excavations made at the Templo Mayor in Mexico City. Many of the subsequent finds are included in this exhibition.

We live in a world where there is increasing interest in the identity and culture particular to each nation. A growing fascination with pre-Hispanic Mexico, and in particular the world of the Aztecs, is a case in point. For this reason it is an honour for the Mexican people and the Consejo Nacional para la Cultura y las Artes (CONACULTA) to celebrate this exhibition which allows us to share our historical patrimony in such a rewarding way.

As a Nahua song collected in the seventeenth century reads, 'while the world lasts, the fame and glory of Tenochtitlan will never be lost'.

Sari Bermúdez
President, Consejo Nacional para la Cultura y las Artes (CONACULTA)

The ancient Nahuas wrote 'Oh my friends! I wish that we were immortal. Oh friends! Where is the land where one cannot die?' Today more than two million descendants of the Aztec people, dispersed across Mexico, use this language of jade and turquoise to convey their experiences, desires and hopes. The poetic talent of these people is reflected in their culture, a product of an evolutionary and well-maintained social, military, religious, artistic and economic society.

The Aztecs, one of the seven tribes that left the mythic land of Aztlan, followed the signs of their tutelary god, Huitzilopochtli, and based the foundation and development of a vast empire, the greatest of pre-Hispanic North America, on his prophecy. Their authority allowed them to dominate and impose a way of life over a large part of Mesoamerica. In the same way, the grandeur of their civilisation was built on elements they integrated from their predecessors' cultures.

The Consejo Nacional para la Cultura y las Artes (CONACULTA) and the Instituto Nacional de Antropología e Historia (INAH) joined forces with various cultural and educational organizations in Mexico to give rise to, and lay the foundations for, this exhibition. This show, comprised in large part of objects from Mexican museums, constitutes a recognition of the universality of Aztec civilisation as world heritage. The curatorial work undertaken by two important Mexican archaeologists stands out: Eduardo Matos Moctezuma, Co-ordinator of the Proyecto Templo Mayor, and Felipe Solís Olguín, Director of the Museo Nacional de Antropología.

Certainly, on looking at these pieces it is possible to hear the Nahua voice of 'he who speaks with understanding'. In communicating their immortal message regarding the customs and cosmovision of the Aztec people to an appreciative British public, these works reinforce the fraternal links between two countries already joined together through culture and art.

Sergio Raúl Arroyo García
General Director, Instituto Nacional de Antropología e Historia (INAH)

The encounter between Mexico and Spain in the early sixteenth century was an event which changed world history for ever. It brought together two sophisticated cultures previously unknown to each other: the Aztecs, the latest in a long line of extraordinary Mexican civilisations, and Europe, as represented by the Spanish conquistadors. Although it is widely thought that after the fall of their magnificent capital Tenochtitlan, in 1521, the Aztecs were a vanquished society, they remained a potent force in the subsequent development of the art and architecture of Mexico, then called New Spain. A new culture emerged, reflecting aspects of both America and Europe in much the same manner that the Aztecs had absorbed previous cultures like Teotihuacan and Tula.

The last time an exhibition dedicated to the art and culture of the Aztecs was shown in London, the Royal Academy was fifty-six years old and the distinguished painter Sir Thomas Lawrence (1769–1830) its fifth President. It is somehow fitting that the Aztecs should return to Piccadilly since it was in the Egyptian Hall, almost directly opposite Burlington House, in 1824, that William Bullock showed off the collection of Mexican objects that he had collected on his travels the previous year. The Egyptian Hall is sadly no more and almost two centuries have passed since that show, the first exhibition of Mexican pre-Columbian art in the world. Mexican culture is now familiar to many, and times have changed from those early days when a real 'live' Mexican formed part of Bullock's display. Recent great exhibitions on the cultures of the Olmec and Maya have paved the way for this ambitious presentation of the art and culture of the Aztecs. Many collections in Mexico, the USA, and Europe have generously agreed to lend their treasures to this exhibition which will provide an extraordinary glimpse into the world of the Aztecs.

The Royal Academy of Arts has worked very closely with the Mexican government on the preparation of this exhibition and owes a huge debt of gratitude to Sari Bermúdez, President of the Consejo Nacional para la Cultura y las Artes (CONACULTA), Sergio Raúl Arroyo García, General Director of the Instituto Nacional de Antropología e Historia (INAH), Jaime Nualart, Director General for International Affairs (CONACULTA) and José Enrique Ortiz Lanz, Co-ordinator for Museums and Exhibitions (INAH), for facilitating the loan of these treasures of Mexico's national heritage. Three Ambassadors of the Republic of Mexico have worked tirelessly to make this exhibition possible: Ambassador Jorge Alberto Lozoya, Ambassador Andrés Rozental, and Ambassador Alma Rosa Moreno. It is a measure of the importance of this exhibition that the President of Mexico, Vicente Fox, will do us the enormous honour of officially opening 'Aztecs'. Our thanks also extend to the distinguished Mexican Aztec scholars Eduardo Matos Moctezuma, Co-ordinator of the Proyecto Templo Mayor and Felipe Solís Olguín, Director of the Museo Nacional de Antropología who have curated this exhibition with the greatest skill and understanding. The Academy also acknowledges the help afforded by Her Majesty's Ambassadors to the Republic of Mexico, namely Ambassador Adrian Thorpe, and Ambassador Denise Holt. Tom Phillips, Chairman of the Exhibitions Committee, and many members of staff at the Royal Academy, including Norman Rosenthal, Isabel Carlisle, Adrian Locke and Emeline Max, have worked over several years to make it possible to realise this show. The exhibition has been designed with imagination and skill by Ivor Heal. Lastly I should like to extend the thanks of the Royal Academy to David Gordon, now Director of the Milwaukee Museum of Art, who worked tirelessly on this exhibition during his tenure as Secretary of the Royal Academy of Arts and to Peter Sawbridge who has edited the catalogue with great dedication and skill.

Ambitious loan exhibitions are increasingly impossible without generous subvention and therefore I would like to acknowledge the supporters for this exhibition, particularly the Mexico Tourism Board and Pemex. In addition I would like to thank Virginia and Simon Robertson for their generous donation, and also BAT for their support.

Phillip King
President of the Royal Academy of Arts

USA

MEXICO

● TAMPICO

HUASTECS

METZTITLAN

● TUXPAN

CHICHIMECA

TOTONACA

METLATOYUCA ●

● METZTITLAN

● PACHUCA

OCOTLAN ●

● XALAPA

TIZAPAN ●

TULA ● ● OTUMBA

TLAXCALA

TECALCO ●

TETZCOCO ●

CALIXTLAHUACA ●

● VERACRUZ

TENOCHTITLAN
(MEXICO CITY) ●

MATLALCUETETL ●

● TLÁHUAC

TARASCANS

● HUEXOTZINGO

TOLUCA ●

CHOLULA ●

XOCHICALCO ●

TENANGO ● ● TLAMANALCO

PUEBLA ●

TEOTITLAN

TEPOZTLAN ● SAN RAFAEL

MALINALCO ● ● CUERNAVACA

TECAMACHALCO ●

COATEPEC HARINAS ●

TOCHTEPEC ●

COATZACOALCOS

CIHUATLAN ●

TEHUACAN ●

MORELOS

TUXTEPEC ●

● CHALCATZINGO

GUERRERO

● TELOLOAPAN

TEOTITLAN ●

YOPITZINCO

ZAPIT

OAXACA ●

● MITLA

MONTE ALBÁN ●

OAXACA

TEHUANTEPE

ZAACHILA ●

TEQUIZISTLAN ●

TOTOTEPEC

COATLICAMAC

● MANIALTEPEC

Gulf of
Tehuantepe

EXTENT OF AZTEC EMPIRE

**DETAILED MAPS OF TENOCHTITLAN
AND THE VALLEY OF MEXICO
ARE FOUND ON PAGE 16**

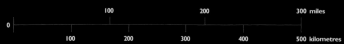

100   200   300 miles

0

100   200   300   400   500 kilometres

Gulf of Mexico

HAVANA

CUBA

Yucatan Channel

Bay of
Campeche

ISLA DE
MUJERES

ACANCÉH

COZUMEL

CHICHÉN ITZÁ

YUCATAN
PENINSULA

CAMPECHE

CHAMPOTON

DZIBALCHEN

Gulf of Honduras

QUECHOLAC
VILLAHERMOSA

TIKAL

CHIAPAS

GUATEMALA

HONDURAS

EL SALVADOR

NICARAGUA

INTRODUCTION

Eduardo Matos Moctezuma and Felipe Solís Olguín

… and you, Tenoch, will see that a cactus has grown over there that is the heart of Copil; on it is perched an eagle holding a serpent in its claws which it rips apart and devours. You are that cactus, Tenoch, and I am the eagle, and that will be our glory, as while the world lasts, the fame and glory of Tenochtitlan will never be lost.

Codex Chimalpahin[1]

SYMBOL OF A NATION

At the beginning of the fourteenth century, after two hundred years of migration, a group of Mexica watched an eagle devour a serpent on a prickly-pear cactus and knew that their journey was at an end (fig. 1). According

to legend, the cactus had grown where the heart of their enemy Copil, torn out after a battle at Chapultepec and thrown across the waters of the lake, had landed. This was the long-awaited sign from their patron god, Huitzilopochtli, that they had reached the site of their city, Tenochtitlan. Over the next two centuries, their simple settlement on a swampy island in Lake Tetzcoco was to grow into a great metropolis, the most important in Mesoamerica,[2] and a seat of power from which they set out to conquer the world.

Even though the Spanish conquistadors captured and destroyed Tenochtitlan in 1521, the sixteenth-century coat of arms of colonial New Spain boasted a crenellated tower with two broken

Fig. 1
An eagle devours a serpent on a prickly-pear cactus, Huitzilopochtli's sign to the Mexica that their migration was at an end. Folio 6 of the Codex Durán, 1579–81 (cat. 343).

Biblioteca Nacional, Madrid

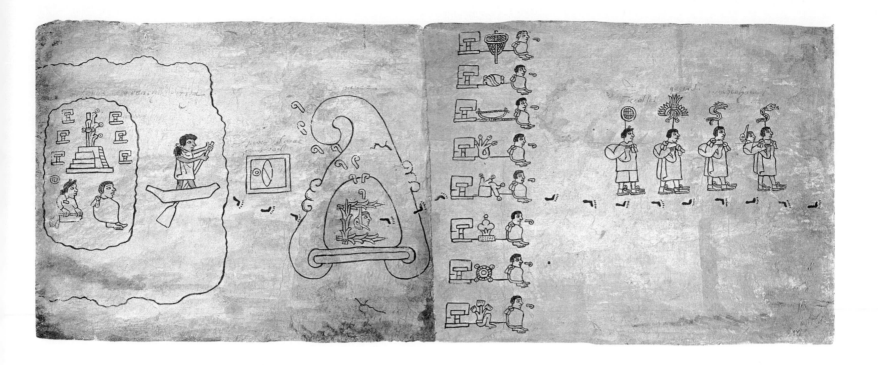

Fig. 2

The first two pages of the Codex Boturini, the Tira de la Peregrinación, depicting the Mexica migration from Aztlan, sixteenth century.

Biblioteca Nacional de Antropología e Historia, Mexico City

bridges, symbols of the causeways that joined Tenochtitlan to the mainland. A cactus was used as a decorative element in the band that framed the coat of arms of the colonial capital. By the eighteenth century, the emblem of the metropolis was still an eagle perching on a cactus, although it wore an imperial crown. From the early nineteenth-century struggle for Mexican independence to the present day, the same emblem has dominated the national coat of arms as the symbol of Mexican identity.

AZTECS, MEXICA AND TENOCHCAS

The people to whom we owe the foundation of Huitzilopochtli's city are historically known by three names in Nahuatl, their original language: Aztecs, Mexicas and Tenochcas.

The first links them to the place they left at the beginning of the twelfth century. The chronicler Hernando Alvarado de Tezozómoc, in his *Crónica mexicáyotl*, records that 'their home is called Aztlan and that is why they are called Aztecs'.[3] Although we cannot be sure that Aztlan ever existed, it is described as an island and shown as such in the Codex Boturini (fig. 2). Alvarado de Tezozómoc tells that Huitzilopochtli gave them a new name, saying: 'You will no longer be called Aztecs: you are now Mexica.' The origin of this second name is obscure, although it is thought to have been derived from Mexi, a secret name for the patron deity. 'Tenochcas' is derived from the name Tenoch, the leader who successfully guided them through the last stages of their migration from Aztlan.

Although Huitzilopochtli's predictions had foretold greatness and power for them, the Aztecs had many sufferings and trials to bear before they could enjoy the power and riches brought by an empire on the scale of that discovered by the Spanish. Aztec history falls into two great episodes: the foundation of Tenochtitlan at a time when the Tepanec city of Atzcapotzalco ruled the lake area; and the military conquests of the Aztecs, which brought them inexhaustible riches from subjugated provinces. This second period saw their capital, Tenochtitlan, flourish under the successive governments of *tlatoque*, the Aztec rulers.

A HOME FOR THE EAGLE

After Tenoch had carried out the foundation ritual in the year 2-house, or 1325, he distributed the population around the island in a pattern designed to imitate that of the Aztec universe, dividing the reedbeds into four sectors with canals or ditches that marked the four quarters of the city.

Tenoch died in 1363. Some years later, the council of elders elected Acamapichtli, a young prince of Toltec lineage from nearby Culhuacan, as the first *tlatoani*; he governed from 1375 to 1395. Acamapichtli married Ilancueitl, who descended from an old Aztec family, in a union which mystically personified them as the deities Xiuhtecuhtli and Coatlicue. To institute a new nobility and create a royal family for Tenochtitlan, Acamapichtli was given twenty young women of the leading families from whom future rulers would descend. Acamapichtli was succeeded as *tlatoani* by his son Huitzilihuitl (1396–1417), who

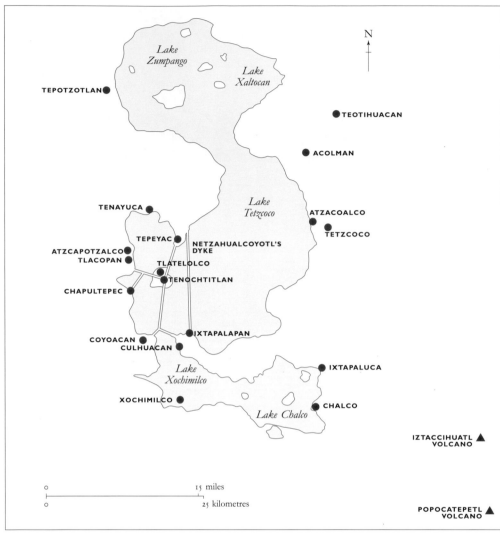

Fig. 3
The Basin of Mexico.

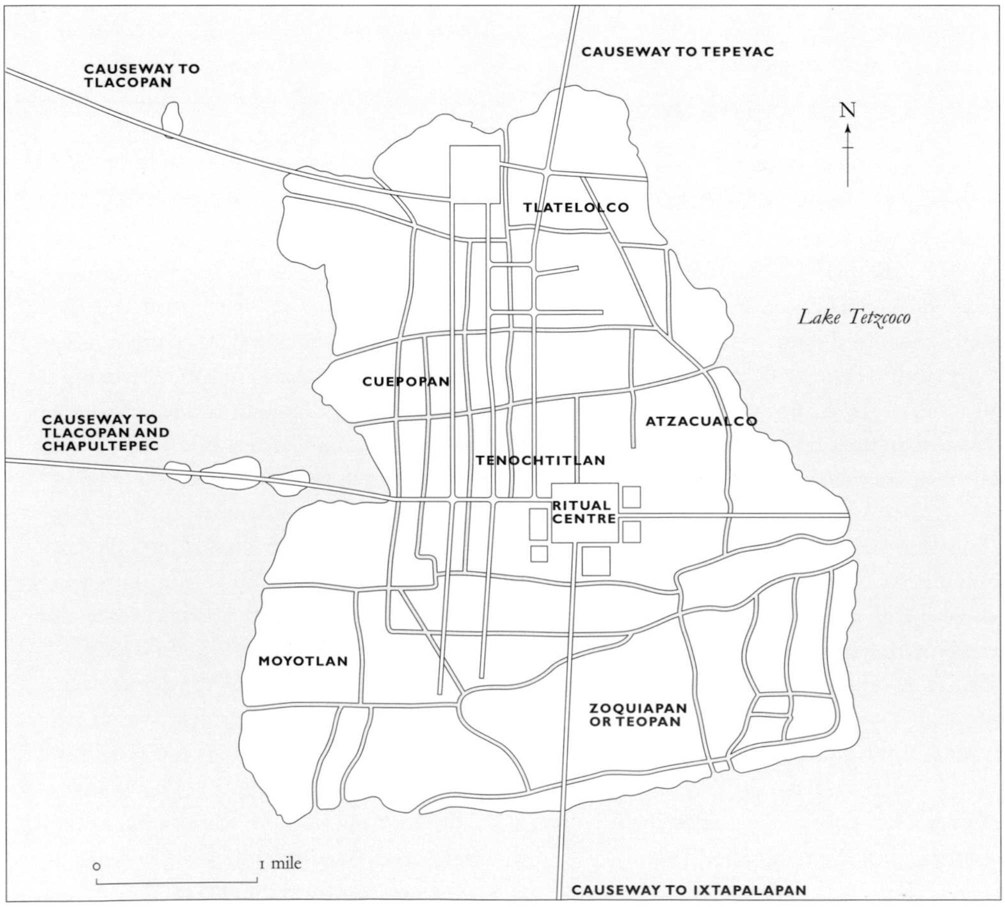

Fig. 4
Tenochtitlan and Tlatelolco.

in turn was followed by Chimalpopoca (1417–27). Because the lake territories remained subject to the military authority of Atzcapotzalco, these first three rulers of Tenochtitlan worked as mercenaries for the Tepanecs, conquering lakeside communities and extending their victories as far as the tropical valleys of Cuernavaca and Oaxtepec.

The principal duty of each *tlatoani* was to enlarge the temple to the supreme deities first constructed by Tenoch, following the example of the double pyramid at Tenayuca. Huitzilopochtli's first pyramid was built of earth and wood at a time when houses in Tenochtitlan were made of mud and thatch. This was the construction that would one day grow into the magnificent Templo Mayor, the building at the heart of the ritual precinct in Tenochtitlan. Chimalpopoca (grandson of Tezozomoc, one of the greatest kings of Atzcapotzalco) began a programme of improvement works in his capital, particularly the renovation of the drinking-water aqueduct that came from Chapultepec. But the death of Tezozomoc brought these plans to an abrupt halt: the young Aztec king was assassinated by Maxtla, his uncle and the usurper of the Tepanec throne.

The threat of war brought about the election of Itzcoatl as the fourth *tlatoani* (1427–40). A charismatic warrior, he negotiated the so-called Triple Alliance with Netzahualcoyotl, leader of the Acolhuas of Tetzcoco, and a dissident group of Tepanecs from Tlacopan. That coalition triumphed in 1428 with the crushing defeat of the city of Atzcapotzalco and was consolidated three years later with the death of Maxtla, his heart torn out by Netzahualcoyotl in a ritual killing, and the reconquest of Tetzcoco.

Now free to act, the Aztecs and their allies began the conquest of settlements in the Basin of Mexico (fig. 3). Tenochtitlan was strengthened as a political capital, while Tetzcoco became a centre for the arts and culture. It was there, indeed, that the most important sculpture workshops flourished. After the conquest of the Xochimilcas, the southern causeway leading to the mainland was built to allow armies to advance towards the valleys of Morelos and the south (fig. 4). The alliance between gods and kings had been reinforced: Itzcoatl enlarged the temple in gratitude to Huitzilopochtli for his guidance and protection in battle.

THE FLIGHT OF THE LEFT-SIDED HUMMINGBIRD

By now the Aztecs' power was widely respected throughout Mesoamerica. Their patron god Huitzilopochtli, the 'left-sided hummingbird', guided their armies wherever they went. Motecuhzoma Ilhuicamina ruled as fifth *tlatoani* from 1440 to 1469. Tlacaelel, a peerless strategist who had done much during the struggle against Maxtla and the Tepanecs, assisted him greatly in the expansion of the empire, which by this time extended to Oaxaca, the centre of Veracruz and the Huasteca. The 'flowery wars' against Tlaxcala and Huexotzingo, ritual encounters whose purpose was the capture of sacrificial victims, were staged during this period. Tlacaelel helped Motecuhzoma to beautify Tenochtitlan, and, with the support of Netzahualcoyotl, they rebuilt the great double aqueduct from Chapultepec and a flood barrier to protect the city.

Fig. 5
The Sun Stone, Late Postclassic.
Basalt, diameter 360 cm.
Museo Nacional de Antropología,
Mexico City

Fig. 6
The Tizoc Stone, Late Postclassic.
Stone, height 94 cm, diameter
265 cm.
Museo Nacional de Antropología,
Mexico City

Motecuhzoma Ilhuicamina was succeeded by three of his grandsons: Axayacatl (1469–81), Tizoc (1481–86) and Ahuizotl (1486–1502). Axayacatl defeated Tlatelolco, neighbour and twin city of Tenochtitlan and a threat because of its commercial power and famous market. He conquered 37 towns, many in the Toluca valley, but the bellicose Purepecha (Tarascan) people of Michoacán halted his advance. It is believed that the Sun Stone (fig. 5), a carved representation of the five Aztec world-eras, was carved during his reign. Although Tizoc is said to have captured fourteen towns, his short reign suggests that he was eliminated for not complying with the expansionist policies of the empire. The stone that bears his name (fig. 6) is one of the most important artefacts of Pre-Hispanic Mexico. Ahuizotl brought 45 towns, from Guerrero to Guatemala, under the sway of Tenochtitlan. His armies subjugated Soconusco, bringing the Aztecs control of the valuable cacao grown in that province. In Oaxaca he unleashed his fury on the Mixtecs and the Zapotecs from Mitla and Tehuantepec.

The ninth *tlatoani*, Motecuhzoma Xocoyotzin, ruled from 1502 to 1520. In 1507 he organised the last New Fire ceremony, whose rites marked the turn of a 52-year cycle in the Aztec calendar, with a lavish splendour that reflected the greatness and size of the empire, which by now extended from Michoacán, Bajío and the Huasteca in the north to the frontier of the Maya territories in the south. Tenochtitlan prided itself upon the splendour of its ceremonial precinct, whose latest phases of construction had raised the main pyramids so far above the horizon that they could be seen from the far shores of the lake (fig. 7).

The sumptuousness of the Aztec capital and its imperial riches gave rise to innumerable descriptions,[4] mainly the accounts of Spanish soldiers. Some likened it to Venice with its characteristic walks and canals. Bernal Díaz del Castillo saw it as an enchanted city, something from a fairytale.

In 1521 the Spanish destroyed the great city without mercy. Figures of the gods were vandalised or at best buried by natives to hide them from the inquisitorial gaze of the Catholic Church. Treasures were melted down and turned into ingots to be taken to Europe to finance wars. Pyramids and palaces were demolished and used as rubble in the foundations of the buildings of the emerging New Spain.

In the early days of colonialism some fragments of the glory of Tenochtitlan must still have been visible, but by the end of the sixteenth century the city's appearance had been all but forgotten. The maps and plans that attempted to represent it were merely fantastic, stylised drawings (fig. 8). In the wider Aztec territories, abandoned towns disappeared or, as at Tenochtitlan, were replaced with new settlements built on the ruins of the past.

All that remained of the splendour of Aztec court life and their complex religious rituals were indigenous accounts recorded by chroniclers, mostly missionaries trying to eradicate Aztec systems of belief. Young Indians educated at Spanish schools learnt to write in Nahuatl as well as Spanish and Latin, and wrote down the oral histories of their families and people in codices (manuscript texts which were frequently illustrated). During three centuries of Spanish rule the efforts of the viceroys and the Church were directed towards the elimination of every vestige of the Aztec world. In the Mexican countryside nature reclaimed her territory, covering magnificent monuments in vegetation.

Fig. 7
Ignacio Marquina,
Reconstruction of the Templo
Mayor, Tenochtitlan, 1951.

American Museum of Natural History,
New York

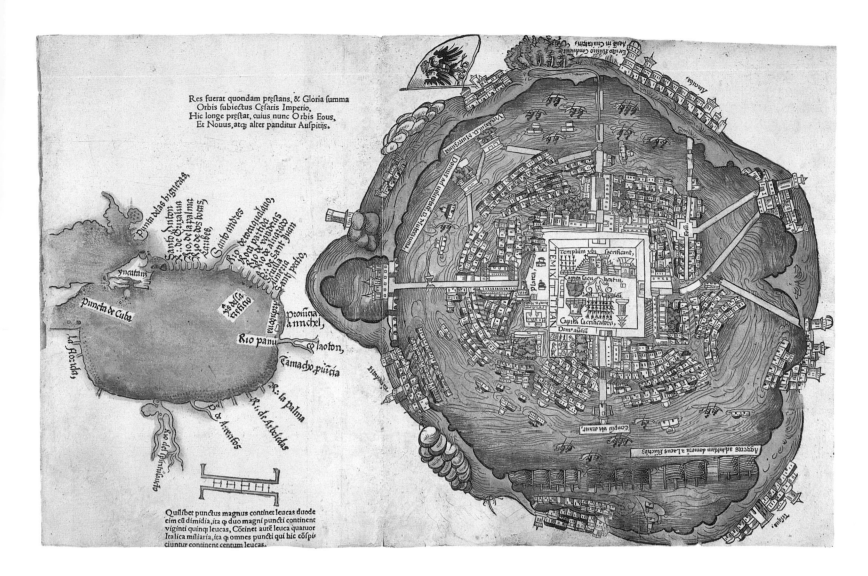

Res fuerat quondam præstans, & Gloria summa
Orbis subiectus Cesaris Imperio,
Hic longe præstat, cuius nunc Orbis Eous,
Et Nouus, atq; alter panditur Auspitijs.

Quilibet punctus magnus continet leucas duode
cim cū dimidia, ita φ duo magni puncti continent
viginti quinq; leucas. Cōtinet autē leuca quatuor
Italica miliaria, ita φ omnes puncti qui hic cōspi
ciuntur continent centum leucas.

Fig. 8

Map of Tenochtitlan and the Gulf
of Mexico, from Hernán Cortés's
*Praeclara de Nova Maris Oceani
Hyspania Narratio...*, Nuremberg,
1524. Handcoloured woodcut,
31 × 46.5 cm.

Newberry Library, Chicago

THE GODS WHO REFUSED TO DIE

A discovery of great importance took place in
1790, when a sculpture of the deity Coatlicue
(fig. 9) and the Sun Stone were discovered while
flagstones were being laid in the main square
in Mexico City, formerly Tenochtitlan and in
colonial times the capital of New Spain. The great
Coatlicue was sent for safekeeping to the Royal
and Pontifical University of Mexico, and the Sun
Stone was placed on one of the towers of the
Metropolitan Cathedral to be viewed by the
public.[5] Various archaeological objects were
displayed from 1790 onwards in a corner of the
main entrance to the university. Despite its
simplicity, the site became the first exhibition
area for Pre-Hispanic art. Images drawn by Pedro
Gualdi show the huge figure of Coatlicue and the
Tizoc Stone placed behind a simple wooden
trellis.[6] Many years were to pass before they were
celebrated as the artistic expression of Amerindian
societies and not as primitive carvings.[7]

In 1825, shortly after the first federal republic
of Mexico was founded, the National Museum
at the university was established. W. Franck
illustrated much of the museum's collection and

his unpublished drawings are kept in the library of
the British Museum, London.[8] These early visual
records include objects discovered on the
Island of Sacrifices in the Gulf of Mexico, some
remaining items from the holdings of the notable
Italian collector Lorenzo Boturini, and, most
particularly, finds from central Mexico, largely
from the capital. In addition to the large
sculptures, there were objects found by Captain
Guillermo Dupaix,[9] who travelled across much of
New Spain to gather archaeological information,
and private donations, the most interesting of
which came from ruined houses and discoveries
made during public works carried out in Mexico
City. From the outset, the museum displayed
Aztec art to the public through archaeology.

We know the condition of these objects and
how they were exhibited from descriptions
provided by European travellers,[10] who recounted
seeing the large figures in the patio of the museum.
Minor works, particularly smaller sculptures,
pottery, greenstone ornaments, weapons and
projectile points, were kept in poorly lit and even
more poorly ventilated rooms on the top floor of
the university, placed together haphazardly with

ethnographic objects and historical testimonies of the colonial era. This was the birthplace of Mexican museology.[11]

During the first half of the nineteenth century, travellers and artists disseminated these early images of Pre-Hispanic art in various ways. In 1824 London hosted the first exhibition of Mexican art, which consisted mainly of objects from the Aztec era.[12] Engravings were used to illustrate albums and books. Carl Nebel published an album in Paris in 1836 showing the Coatlicue, the Sun Stone and the Tizoc Stone. These gigantic sculptures were accompanied by diminutive clay figurines – images of the Aztec deities – and by models of pyramids and temples which expressed the popular traditions of the people of Tenochtitlan.[13]

In 1854 José Fernando Ramírez further developed our knowledge of ancient Mexican art by describing the most important pieces in the National Museum's collection, illustrating his historical and aesthetic text with a beautiful engraving showing the monoliths, the commemorative tombstone from the Templo Mayor, the ball-game ring with the relief of the decapitating warrior, a 'year bundle' (a stone carving of a bundle of 52 reeds, each representing a year in the Aztec cycle), and sculptures of gods and sacred animals, principally the plumed serpent.[14] The engraving also shows smaller objects, such as wooden musical instruments, feathered objects, pipes and the usual figurines and models of temples.

During the reign of the Habsburg Emperor Maximilian (1864–67), the archaeological collection was transferred from the university to a building that had previously served as a mint. The completion of this monumental task coincided with the triumph of the republican government. In what was now a burgeoning new institution, large works of sculpture were again exposed to the elements in the middle of the patio, surrounded by the vegetation that decorated the building.[15]

A solemn bond between the Aztecs and the public at large was established in 1888, with the opening of the museum's Hall of Monoliths. The hall triumphantly exhibited the Sun Stone, which had been at the mercy of the elements at the Metropolitan Cathedral for nearly a hundred years.[16] Works could finally be appreciated by those interested in the artistic creations of the Pre-Hispanic world, particularly the legacy of Tenochtitlan. During the second half of the nineteenth century, many research projects were carried out at the museum. The most notable were the studies of Aztec monumental sculpture published in the institution's first series of *Annals*.

At the same time, the first catalogues of the various collections were published.[17]

With the new century came the extraordinary discoveries made in the Calle de las Escalerillas in 1900 while a deep-drainage trench was being cut across the Mexican capital from east to west. At last, archaeological finds could be related to their original contexts. The discovery of this complex, excavated by Leopoldo Batres, permitted the exact positioning of finds in the plan, thereby allowing their cultural and historical associations to be established.[18]

The first Mexica Hall in the museum was installed in the late 1940s and displayed objects from the Aztec capital and its empire. Unlike the Hall of Monoliths, in which sculptures had been arranged according to size, the Mexica Hall showed the art and culture of the Aztec civilisation in an ordered thematic sequence.[19] In 1964 a new building was inaugurated to house the museum's collections.

At around midnight on 21 February 1978, a team of archaeologists finished clearing away the debris which for hundreds of years had covered the monumental disc of the goddess Coyolxauhqui (fig. 10), sister and adversary of Huitzilopochtli. The monument had remained hidden from the Spanish and its discovery launched a new era in Aztec studies, providing

Fig. 9

The great Coatlicue, earth mother and goddess of life and death, Late Postclassic. Stone, height 257 cm.

Museo Nacional de Antropología, Mexico City

Fig. 10

The dismemberment of Coyolxauhqui, goddess of the moon, Late Postclassic. Stone, diameter 300 cm.

Museo del Templo Mayor, Mexico City

scope for a new generation of researchers to work with established academics to test earlier theories and put forward new interpretations that would shape the modern understanding of Aztec culture. Throughout the twentieth century, major excavations took place to discover the origins of Mexico City and to find evidence of the ancient Aztec empire, a process which led to the research and discoveries being made today in the context of the Proyecto Templo Mayor.

The study of Pre-Hispanic art continues to develop as research provides a modern understanding of indigenous aesthetics.

The most select objects from museums in Mexico and around the world are shown together once more in this exhibition, in acknowledgement of the boundless creativity of the Aztec civilisation. Thus Huitzilopochtli's plan to conquer the hearts of people in every corner of the globe will be fulfilled. The Aztec gods re-emerge, but without ceremony; this time they open the door to the study of the society, the culture and the art of their time.[20]

It faced the west and on a plain that stretched in front of this temple, there was another smaller temple [...] on which was another idol a little smaller than the first one, called Mictlanteuctli, which means 'Lord of Hell'. [...] A little further, toward the north, was another temple slightly smaller than the first, which was called 'the hill of the Moon', on top of which was another idol [...], which was called the Moon. All around it were many temples, in one of which (the largest of them) there were six other idols, who were called Brothers of the Moon, [and] the priests of Montezuma, lord of Mexico, came with this Montezuma, every twenty days to [offer] sacrifices to all of them.[8]

Other Pre-Hispanic activities, however, did leave an indelible mark on archaeological sites. The first group of these we might define as additive, because they resulted in new elements being added to the ruins. Such interventions were carried out by many different people at different times and practically everywhere in Mesoamerica. A clear example of this can be found in the Preclassic settlement of Cerro Chalcatzingo, Morelos.[9] On the sides of this sacred mountain sufficient evidence exists for us to state that the Olmec-like reliefs sculpted there between 700 and 500 BC were venerated two thousand years later. In fact, around the thirteenth century AD, the Tlahuicas who lived in the immediate surroundings built a series of wide stairways and platforms which led to a place of worship. These structures allowed people to ascend 30 metres with ease and perform ceremonies in front of the relief known as Monument 2.

Other additions include offerings and corpses buried inside destroyed buildings, indicating the way in which ruins were regarded as sacred. Both practices were widespread during the Postclassic period. Examples are the Mayan effigy censers that were buried as propitiatory gifts or as symbols of gratitude in the collapsed temples of the Late Classic period in Dzibanché, Quintana Roo;[10] the sumptuous Mixtec funerary offerings deposited in Tomb 7 at Monte Albán, Oaxaca;[11] and the mortal remains of two individuals with Aztec and Tetzcocan pottery placed in Structure 1-R of the Ciudadela in Teotihuacan.[12]

However, it is the ruins of Tula which provide the most evidence. As a consequence of two decades of excavations in the main square, the archaeologist Jorge R. Acosta recovered huge quantities of so-called Aztec pottery, unquestionable proof of three hundred years of human activity taking place directly over the ruins of the city.[13] Unfortunately it has been impossible to determine exactly who brought this pottery here because we know it was made in at least four different zones of the Basin of Mexico: Tenochtitlan, Tetzcoco, Chalco and the far western end of the Ixtapalapan peninsula. We can establish with accuracy, however, the type of additive activities which these groups engaged in. Large quantities of offerings are buried inside the ruins of the main buildings of the Toltec golden age, including the Central Shrine, Buildings B and C, and the Burnt Palace. Fewer in number are the tombs of individuals of all ages, almost always buried with very humble funerary offerings, discovered in Building B, Building 4 and the Burnt Palace. It is also worth mentioning the construction of religious buildings and sumptuous residences over the ruins of the ancient ceremonial centre. Examples of this include the residential complex erected over Building K, the shrine attached to the north-west corner of Building C and the pyramidal plinth placed over the Burnt Palace.

Another additive activity engaged in by carriers of Aztec pottery, albeit of a different nature, relates to the creation of sculptures in the immediate surroundings of the main plaza, specifically the reliefs of Cerro de la Malinche, created at the end of the fifteenth century in the purest Aztec style.[14] This unique group, which consists of the effigies of Ce Acatl Topiltzin Quetzalcoatl and Chalchiuhtlicue, has been interpreted both as an Aztec homage to the deities inherited from their Toltec forefathers[15] and as a 'retrospective historical image' of Ce Acatl – the most famous ruler of Tula – validating the Aztec tradition of sculpting portraits of their rulers on the rocks of Chapultepec hill.[16]

The Dominican friar Diego Durán recounts one of the last recorded additive activities.[17] He states that in 1519, while still at the coast of the Gulf of Mexico, Hernán Cortés sent Motecuhzoma Xocoyotzin a gift of wine and biscuits. On receiving the gifts in Tenochtitlan, the Aztec *tlatoani* (ruler) refused to consume them – whether because he found them strange or because of the way they looked after having travelled across the ocean we shall never know – and stated that they 'belonged to the gods'. He gave orders for his priests to take them all to the ruins of Tula 'with great solemnity and to bury them in the temple of Quetzalcoatl, whose sons had arrived'.

AZTEC REMOVALS FROM ARCHAEOLOGICAL SITES
Archaeology and history also provide much evidence of activities we could define as subtractive. Naturally they include the excavation of buildings to extract architectural elements, sculptures, offerings and bones, all actions that

Fig. 13
Fragment of a Teotihuacan mask,
AD 150–650, found in Chamber III,
a very rich Aztec offering in the
north-western corner of Stage IV(a)
of the Templo Mayor. Greenstone,
covered by the Aztecs with a layer
of tar, 16.7 × 7.7 × 5.7 cm.

Museo del Templo Mayor, Mexico City

Fig. 14
Offering 82, found in the south-
eastern corner of the Templo
Mayor, contained, among other
things, the skull of a decapitated
individual, a Teotihuacan mask
(cat. 260), and an Aztec
travertine mask.

Museo del Templo Mayor, Mexico City

many modern authors have defined pejoratively as sacking and pillage. Most of these operations, however, were clearly not carried out for profit but only to recover useful construction materials or objects that were appreciated for their aesthetic beauty, particularly because they were considered to be the work of gods, giants or almost mythical people.

In the case of Teotihuacan, a simple bowl – a fragment of an Aztec container found at the entrance to a large man-made cave over which the Pyramid of the Sun was built – could be a clue to planned excavations having taken place just before the arrival of the Spanish. When archaeologists entered this sacred space in the early 1970s, they found that the walls that sealed access along the tunnel had been knocked down, and that in the four-lobed chamber at the end there were no traces of offerings or burials. According to some researchers, unless it was accidentally left there in recent times, the fragment of pottery would suggest that the people who broke in were the Aztecs themselves.[18]

Historical sources from the sixteenth century provide firmer evidence. For example, the indigenous informants of Friar Bernardino de Sahagún describe the procedures individuals had to perform to acquire precious stones:

And those of experience, the advised, these look for it [the precious stone]. In this manner [they see,] they know where it is: they can see that it is breathing [smoking], giving off vapour. Early, at early dawn, when [the sun] comes up. They find where to place themselves, where to stand; they face the sun [...] Wherever they can see that something like a little smoke [column] stands, that one of them is giving off vapour, this one is the precious stone [...] They take it up; they carry it away. And if they are not successful, if it is only barren where the little [column of] smoke stands, thus they know that the precious stone is there in the earth.

Then they dig. There they see, there they find the precious stone, perhaps already well formed, perhaps already burnished. Perhaps they see something buried there either in stone, or in a stone bowl, or in a stone chest; perhaps it is filled with precious stones. This they claim there.[19]

The same work contains a more explicit mention, and talks not only about the profound knowledge Aztecs had of the vestiges of Tula but also of the way they went exploring underground in search of antiquities:

Because verily they [the Toltecs] there [in Tula-Xicocotitlan] resided together, they there dwelt, so also many are their traces which they produced. And they left behind that which today is there, which is to be seen, which they did not finish – the so-called serpent column. [...] And the Tolteca

mountain is to be seen; and the Tolteca pyramids, the mounds, and the surfacing of Tolteca [temples]. And Tolteca potsherds are there to be seen. And Tolteca bowls, Tolteca ollas are taken from the earth. And many times Tolteca jewels – armbands, esteemed greenstones, fine turquoise, emerald-green jade – are taken from the earth.[20]

Various people who lived at the same time as the Aztecs were also involved in taking Toltec antiquities. There is credible testimony that, after they had been exhumed, old sculptures were taken to various destinations, one of which was the city of Tlaxcala, capital of the Aztec empire's greatest enemies. According to Friar Toribio de Benavente (Motolinía),[21] a mask and a small image brought from Tula were venerated in the main pyramid of this city, together with the sculpture of the fire god Camaxtli. Another destination was Tlatelolco, as described in a short passage of *Historia de los mexicanos por sus pinturas* (*A History of the Mexicans Through Their Paintings*):

In the year 99 [AD 1422] the people of Tlatilulco went to Tula and since [the Toltecs] had died and left their god there, whose name was Tlacahuepan, they took him and brought him back to Tlatilulco.[22]

These activities, which had been carried out intensively since at least the thirteenth century, had a devastating effect from an archaeological point of view. In fact no records exist whatsoever of the massive, if not total, loss of sculptures and covering stones.

RECOVERY OF A GLORIOUS PAST: REUSE

These additive and subtractive activities not only had a serious impact on archaeological sites but also affected the populations responsible for them. Relics recovered during planned excavations, as well as those discovered accidentally and handed down from generation to generation,[23] were reused as worthy relics of vanished worlds.[24] The high quality of the raw materials and manufacture of these objects certainly had an influence on their value, but the allegedly supernatural origin of these items, which were thought to have been created by powerful beings, convinced their owners to wear them as amulets or to re-bury them inside temples and palaces as part of dedicatory and funerary offerings. Furthermore, as is often the case with all kinds of relic, fragments were also venerated. This would explain why these offerings include so many broken bits and pieces (fig. 13).[25]

The Aztecs were not the first Mesoamerican people to reuse antiquities to establish a direct connection with their ancestors and gods.

Evidence of this practice has been found in many other Mesoamerican regions. Examples include numerous anthropomorphic and zoomorphic figurines, masks, pendants, ritual spoons, miniature canoes, celts and self-sacrifice instruments all made of greenstone and produced by both the Olmecs and their contemporaries of the Middle Preclassic period (1200–400 BC) which have been found by modern archaeologists in Protoclassic (100 BC–AD 200) and Classic (AD 200–900) sites. The most notable finds were made at Cerro de las Mesas, Veracruz;[26] Dzibilchaltún and Chacsinkín, Yucatan;[27] Cozumel, Quintana Roo;[28] Laguna Francesa, Chiapas;[29] and Uaxactún and Tikal, Guatemala.[30] Similar objects have also been found at Postclassic (900–1521) sites, including Mayapán, Yucatan,[31] and San Cristóbal Verapaz, Guatemala.[32] To this list we could add the Olmec pieces found in the sacred well at Chichén Itzá, which may have been thrown into the water by the Maya during the Classic and Postclassic periods.[33]

Although we lack any contextual archaeological information, other Olmec works of art were clearly reused as amulets by dignitaries of the Protoclassic and Classic periods, as is demonstrated by the presence of Mayan inscriptions on their surfaces.

Examples include the ritual spoon in the Museum of San José, Costa Rica,[34] and the greenstone pendants in the shape of a human face in the Brooklyn Museum of Art,[35] the British Museum[36] and at Dumbarton Oaks.[37] Around 50 BC, an effigy and an inscription in the early Mayan style were engraved on the back of this Dumbarton Oaks piece which appeared to allude to the enthronement of a ruler called 'sky-moan bird'.

Although these activities were commonplace throughout the vast Mesoamerican territory, Tenochtitlan was the centre when it came to reusing antiquities. A century of archaeological excavation in the Aztec capital has unearthed hundreds of relics in the main religious buildings (fig. 14). Items made of greenstone predominate, although there are also beautiful ceramic and basalt objects. Most notable are a mask, a pendant and various fragments of figurines made by the Olmecs and other Middle Preclassic societies;[38] hundreds of masks, and anthropomorphic and zoomorphic figurines, in addition to a model of a temple, Mezcala-style objects, all of them ranging from the Middle Preclassic to the Epiclassic periods;[39] various pendants that may date back to the Classic Mayan period; tens of masks, anthropomorphic

Fig. 15
An Early Postclassic Toltec *chacmool*. Stone, 49 × 106 × 46 cm. Found in the colonial building known as the Casa del Marqués del Apartado, located in front of the ruins of the Templo Mayor.

Museo del Templo Mayor, Mexico City

Fig. 16
Front and rear views of a mask made in the Mezcala region, AD 150–650. Greenstone, 11 × 9.5 × 3.9 cm. From Chamber III of the Templo Mayor. The Aztecs added the image of a person playing a horizontal drum.

Museo del Templo Mayor, Mexico City

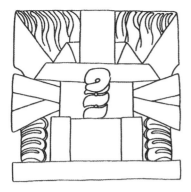

Fig. 17
Line drawing of a stone discovered in front of the Pyramid of the Sun at Teotihuacan showing the symbol of the *xiuhmolpilli*, or cycle of 52 years.

Fig. 18
La Chinola, *c.* 1500. Volcanic stone, 107 × 40 × 10 cm. Discovered at Cerro de la Chinola in the late nineteenth century. This Aztec-style slab seems to represent Chalchiuhtlicue, the water goddess, wearing an archaic headdress in the shape of the Teotihuacan symbol of the *xiuhmolpilli*, or cycle of 52 years.

Museo Nacional de Antropología, Mexico City

figurines, nose-plugs in the shape of snake rattles and containers dating back to the Teotihuacan Classic period;[40] and a *plumbate* vessel made in the eastern part of Soconusco during the Early Postclassic period.[41] Strangely, only one antiquity which is undeniably Toltec has been unearthed to date: a decapitated *chacmool* which was discovered in the foundations of the colonial Casa del Marqués del Apartado, opposite the ruins of the Templo Mayor in Mexico City (fig. 15).[42] The piece's typically Toltec features, in terms of raw material, size, proportions, style and iconography, make its origin unquestionable.

Interestingly, the Aztecs did not bury all relics just as they found them.[43] They altered quite a number, adding paint or tar to accentuate their original religious significance or to confer new meaning upon them. Thus, for example, Tlaloc jars from Teotihuacan retained their pluvial symbolism by being painted blue or with tar. Many Mezcala human masks and figurines, however, were transformed into divinities by having the faces of Xiuhtecuhtli or Tlaloc painted on them. As if that were not enough, the inside of tens of Mezcala masks were decorated with aquatic glyphs and human figures (fig. 16).

RECOVERY OF A GLORIOUS PAST: IMITATION

Tenochtitlan was the main centre of imitation in Mesoamerica. Aztec exploration was sufficiently intensive for the island's artists to have the opportunity of copying ancient styles of sculpture, painting and architecture, as well as completing iconographic scenes. It is well known that Aztecs used alien artistic types in their capital, often without being particularly faithful to their original form and meaning.[44] We might say that their imitations reinterpreted the past, eclectically combining the ancient with the modern. Their archaisms were therefore fragmentary evocations of times gone by, rather than identical and integral copies of specific artistic creations.

As examples of these, the Aztec sculptures based on the effigies from Teotihuacan could be mentioned. One of them is the image of the old fire god, found near the North Red Temple at Tenochtitlan (cf. cat. 5).[45] The Aztec sculptor was faithful to the Teotihuacan models in copying the round-shouldered posture of the deity as well as the position of his hands and feet, but he added new iconographic attributes – connected with water and the underworld – such as the fangs, the rectangular plates over the eyes and mouth, a huge brazier and terrestrial figureheads. A different example is the famous stone of La Chinola, an Aztec-style slab discovered near the site of Castillo de Teayo, Veracruz (fig. 18). Everything seems to indicate that the front side of the monument represents Chalchiuhtlicue – the water goddess – emerging from or descending into the jaws of a terrestrial monster. On the back, however, are four flying *tlaloque* (assistants of the rain god Tlaloc) making rain fall with their jugs of water. Intriguingly, the main divinity wears an archaic headdress[46] in the shape of the Teotihuacan symbol of the *xiuhmolpilli*, a composite bundle representing the cycle of 52 years (fig. 17).[47] It is extremely likely that the Postclassic artist knew the meaning of this ancient symbol and sculpted it to allude to one of the first four eras of humanity, which was ruled by Chalchiuhtlicue and ended with a flood.

As regards Epiclassic art, we know of only one Aztec greenstone plaque inspired by the Temple of the Plumed Serpents at Xochicalco, and a sculptural complex at Tenochtitlan, consisting of three fire-serpent heads with calendar dates in the Xochicalcan style.[48] It is also worth mentioning the many evocations of Tula sculpture. Contrary to what happened with the religious images of Teotihuacan and Xochicalco, the Aztecs copied practically every Toltec vestige that met their eyes, particularly braziers with the face of Tlaloc, telamons, standard-bearers, colossal

Fouilles de Teotihuaco.

plumed serpents, as well as reliefs showing people bearing arms, undulating serpents, birds of prey, felines and the so-called man-bird serpents.[49]

Imitation extended, even more effectively, to religious architecture. At the end of the fifteenth century, the sacred precincts of Tenochtitlan and Tlatelolco included several buildings which revived the forgotten shapes of Teotihuacan. Known as the Red Temples, five small shrines harmoniously combine the typical Teotihuacan *talud-tablero* (a rectangular panel [*tablero*] sitting on a sloping panel [*talud*]), a structure that had not been built for several centuries, with decorative Aztec elements fashionable at the time of construction.[50] Even though the builders of the Red Temples undoubtedly used local materials and applied their own architectural techniques, they took special care to reproduce the ancient proportions and, in particular, to re-create the mural paintings of the Classic period (fig. 19).[51] In so doing, they copied various Teotihuacan symbols on red backgrounds following repetitive patterns: storm god masks, trilobes (water droplets), elongated eyes (flowing water) and cut shells

(wind?; fig. 21). To these motifs they added the red and white stripes and knots that distinguish Xochipilli, the Aztec god of music and dance (fig. 20). These elements, and boxes found inside the shrines, filled with musical instruments, demonstrate that the Red Temples were used to worship Xochipilli.[52]

Finally, mention should be made of the House of Eagles, a fifteenth-century religious building located to the north of the Templo Mayor in Tenochtitlan. The design of this building is vaguely reminiscent of the Toltec hypostyle halls, but its iconographic and decorative programme revives Tula in all its splendour. Braziers with the face of Tlaloc, benches with undulating serpents and processions of armed men, and mural paintings with multi-coloured friezes decorate interiors to convey the living image of a glorious past. Petrographic, chemical, technological, iconographic and stylistic studies[53] have shown that these decorative elements are local copies that illustrate a kind of Neo-Toltequism in the art of the Aztec capital.[54] There is, therefore, much evidence to support the observation made by the

Fig. 19
E. L. Méhédin, Detail of a temple in Teotihuacan excavated by Longpérier in 1865. Watercolour, 20 × 36 cm. The proportions and mural paintings of this temple may have inspired the Aztecs when they built the North Red Temple at Tenochtitlan.

Collection Agence Régionale de l'Environnement de Haute-Normandie, Rouen

Fig. 20
Building L of Tlatelolco was
excavated in 1963–64. Its mural
paintings, with Xochipilli's stripes
and knots, are very similar to those
of the South Red Temple at
Tenochtitlan.

Fig. 21
Certain decorative elements of the
North Red Temple, among them
cut shells and aquatic currents in
the shape of an eye, are identical
to those of the Teotihuacan temple
excavated by Longpérier.

Mexican poet Octavio Paz, who commented
that 'if Tula was a rustic version of Teotihuacan,
México-Tenochtitlan was an imperial version
of Tula'.[55]

THE FUNCTIONS OF THE PAST
The reuse of relics, the imitation of ancient
sculptures and the construction of archaic
buildings in Tenochtitlan and Tlatelolco coincided
with the period of maximum integration,
consolidation and expansion of the Aztec empire.
The recovery and ennoblement of extinct
civilisations in this particular historical context
should perhaps be seen as one of the many
strategies adopted by Aztec rulers to sustain a new,
dominant position in the eyes of both kindred and
strangers. As the centuries passed, these
antiquities, making direct allusion to a grandiose
past and genealogically legitimising the actions
of their belligerent users,[56] no doubt became the
ultimate sacred symbols.

COSMOVISION, RELIGION AND THE CALENDAR OF THE AZTECS

Alfredo López Austin

EXODUS AND SETTLEMENT

Through 'official' histories, we have become familiar with the subject of native peoples and their origins. Although our interest in these origins is at times overshadowed by a metaphysical search for 'true ethnic identity', many of the issues it raises are fundamental to our understanding of the historical development of human societies.

The Aztecs referred to their origins obsessively in abundant, detailed, sometimes contradictory tales. Some were more concerned with human events; others focused on the presence of gods in the life of men. A concise summary of the numerous versions highlights a number of important aspects in these tales.

The Aztecs identified themselves as *chichimecas*[1] from a city called Aztlan,[2] situated to the north-east of the Basin of Mexico. Aztlan was a lacustrine city inhabited by a powerful civilisation that the Aztecs served as fishermen and bird-hunters, work assigned to them by their patron god, Huitzilopochtli. In the early years of the twelfth century, by express and miraculous order of Huitzilopochtli, the Aztecs left Aztlan in search of their promised land. Guided by their god, whose image was carried on the shoulders of a priest, the Aztecs began a punishing two-hundred-year migration (fig. 22) that was to be interrupted only by brief periods of settlement in favourable sites. In Coatepec, north of the Basin of Mexico, the Aztecs believed that they had found their goal and settled, building the artificial lake they needed to carry out their work. Soon

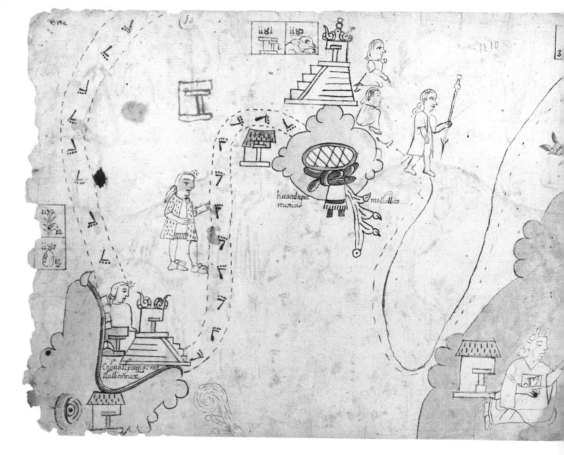

afterwards, however, convinced now that they were mistaken, they left and travelled onwards to the Basin of Mexico, a densely populated area at that time. On arrival, they encountered hostility from the inhabitants. Finally, the gods spoke to them on an islet in Lake Tetzcoco. A majestic eagle alighted on a prickly-pear cactus to show them that they had found the place chosen by Huitzilopochtli. They settled, founding Tenochtitlan (*c.* 1325) and Tlatelolco (*c.* 1338), twin towns, and political adversaries, on islands protected by the waters of the lake. Settlement and development were made possible by the use of complex techniques to drain marshes to create farming plots called *chinampas* (fig. 71).

Even in this brief summary a significant contradiction exists: how could nomads (by definition *chichimecas*) have once lived in a city? How had they acquired the skills to drain and cultivate marshland? The question has divided historians. Some argue that the Aztecs began a process of adaptation, learning and cultural appropriation that very quickly led them to the pinnacle of political power. Others prefer the idea of a gradual march by a poor Mesoamerican people to a position of hegemony.[3] This second theory takes into account the dual meaning of the term *chichimeca*: hunter-gatherer and rustic man of the north. The Aztecs saw themselves as rough men of the north, but never as real nomads. Whatever the case, the Aztecs were a marginalised group from the frontier of civilised Mesoamerica, although they had always participated in the maize-growing traditions of the settled farmers.

The second theory supports the idea of a common history of people striving to better themselves but provides no explanation for the prodigious historical and cultural development achieved by the Aztecs. Not only does this second theory allow us to understand the position of the Aztecs in Mesoamerican culture, but it also permits the migration to be interpreted from a different point of view. The short historical time-depth of the story, the *chichimeca* origin, the fact that the place of departure is close to Chicomoztoc ('the place of the seven caves')[4] or is identified with such a place, the guidance given by a patron god leading them to a promised land, the existence of a founding miracle and many other fascinating episodes which took place during the journey are not specific to the Aztec migration but typical of similar tales told by other Mesoamerican peoples, from the Basin of Mexico to the remote highlands of Guatemala. We should assume, therefore, that the Aztecs were already part of the great Mesoamerican tradition before their migration.

THE AZTEC VIEW OF THE COSMOS

The Mesoamerican view of the cosmos belongs to an ancient tradition shared by farmers from very different ethnic groups and linguistic families who lived in environments ranging from semi-desert to rainforest, from sea level to snow-covered mountains, all with different levels of social and political complexity, and with many different local and regional histories. Obviously, such diversity gave rise to local peculiarities and slight differences over time and in each cultural area. But the thinking they jointly developed over 41 centuries (25 before Christ's birth and 16 afterwards) in the vast territory of Mesoamerica was based on a set of core ideas that allowed them to perceive situations, conceive ideas and explain their surroundings in a similar way. These ideas covered various fields of thought and action: perception of time and space, man's relationship with nature, the treatment and care of the human body, basic principles of social organisation, religion, mythology, ritual, magic, medicine and the calendar.

The Mexica shared with their contemporaries their deepest and most organisational thinking, based on a dualism that saw the whole of existence as consisting of substances in balanced opposition. This manifested itself in many different, binary oppositions. The first group contained life, heat, light, dryness, height, masculinity, strength, daytime, while the other contained death, darkness, dampness, smallness, femininity, weakness, night-time and other correspondences. When two opposites were combined, the proportion or dominance of one over the other determined the nature of each being and its inherent properties. The same law also applied to gods, who belonged to one or other opposing camp of the cosmos to a greater or lesser extent, but who had a dual nature which could be expressed as a divine couple.

Within the geometry of the cosmos, various natural and supernatural components circulated. There were three vertical levels, comprising a set of nine celestial planes (Topan), the surface of the earth with the four closest celestial planes (Tlalticpac), and the nine planes of the underworld, or place of death (Mictlan). The middle section, surrounded by the sea, was inhabited by men, animals and plants, but also by meteorological phenomena and the astral bodies which travelled through the sky. The earth's plane was divided into quadrants and represented as a surface on which there were five points, often depicted as five trees (fig. 23), corresponding to the *axis mundi* and four pillars which separated Topan and Mictlan. The central tree, the *axis mundi*, was rooted in the world of the dead but as tall as the highest skies. The pillars were extensions of the central tree in the four extremities of the world. At the foot of each of the five trees stood a hollow hill. Inside the trees, which were also hollow, flowed the forces of the Topan and Mictlan, which permitted the cyclical movement of time, life and death, meteorological phenomena, astral bodies and sustenance. If the trees were broken or the wall around their petrified bases knocked down, the forces poured out over Tlalticpac to return in the following cycle. The beings that inhabited Tlalticpac (including objects created by men) were part of the divinity of nature and constituted an animated environment in which men could communicate and establish relationships.

THE MYTH OF THE FIVE SUNS

Although rituals and iconography are vital to our understanding of the Aztec view of the cosmos, our best source is undoubtedly mythology. Interpretation of Aztec mythology can be

considerably enriched by making comparisons with that of other Mesoamerican peoples and even that of the indigenous people of today, their descendants, who have preserved copious amounts of tales in the southern half of Mexico and western Central America.

The principal myths allow us to reconstruct the process of the creation of the world. The father and mother of the gods[5] faced a revolt by their children, whom they punished for wanting to be worshipped or for violating the celestial prohibition of picking flowers from the cosmic trees or breaking their branches. Those who refused to comply were condemned to populate the earth and the underworld. One of them, the proto-Sun,[6] rose to supremacy with his self-sacrifice, thus establishing the fate of his fellow-gods by his example. After his death, he rose in the east as a creature: the star that would rule the world. However, before he would consent to begin his journey, the Sun imposed the condition that all the expelled gods should offer themselves for sacrifice. By dying, the victims gave birth to the various creatures of the world. For example, when he was beheaded, the god Yappan became the first dark scorpion, while the god Xolotl became the amphibian called *ajolote*. It was thought that every terrestrial being consisted of a divine part, which was imperceptible but gave it its 'soul' and essential characteristics, and a worldly part, similar to a hard shell which grew, deteriorated and destroyed itself with the passage of time. The archetypal death of the Sun and his siblings not only gave birth to creatures but also started the cyclical journey which was the fate of the gods. Their existence was divided between their transitory appearance on earth in the form of creatures, and their period of rest in the world of the dead.

Not all of the myths refer to the origin of worldly beings. Others describe the structure of the cosmos. One of the most important is the myth of the cosmogonic eras, or suns, which tells how various gods succeeded one another in ruling the world until it reached its definitive form. Major versions of the myth speak of five successive eras,[7]

Fig. 23
The cosmic trees.

Fig. 24
The third world-era, presided over by Chiconahui Ollin. Folio 6v of the Codex Ríos, c. 1570–95 (cat. 346).

Biblioteca Apostolica Vaticana, Vatican City

each ruled by a god who performed the functions of the Sun (fig. 24). The stability of the eras was interrupted by an attack from an opposing god, the weakening of the ruling god and a chaotic cataclysm. The fifth and final era is presided over by Nahui Ollin ('4-movement'). This era, during which human beings and maize took shape, is destined to end at the termination of one of the 52-year cycles at which time Nahui Ollin will be attacked by the dark god of destiny, Tezcatlipoca. Terrible earthquakes will destroy

the world and its creatures will perish in an ensuing famine.

The various versions of the myth associate each era with a colour; these colours reflect the horizontal divisions of the earth's surface. One of the symbols of the earth's surface was a four-petalled flower in which the centre, quadrants and trees were all of different colours. In the versions which refer to four eras, the myth can be interpreted as the successive establishment of the four quadrants of the world and of the function of its pillars. Where five eras are mentioned – as in a number of Aztec versions – in addition to the above quadrants there is the establishment of the central tree and the beginning of the cosmic processes of the *axis mundi*. The erection of the cosmic trees marks the beginning of the ordered passage of time, in other words the order of the calendar.

THE AZTEC CALENDAR

The Mesoamerican calendar is a system which includes cycles of different sizes and their respective combinations. Some cycles were based on the movement of the astral bodies; others were merely based on numeric values. Regardless of its structure in the general calendar system, each cycle had its own specific mechanism and functions. Thus, for example, the cycle of 365 days – sometimes called *xihuitl* – consisted of 18 'months' of 20 days each, plus five fateful days, giving a total that corresponds to the days of the common solar year. This cycle was essentially religious, because it established the order of the most important feasts dedicated to the gods, and work-related, since it linked human activities to the seasons.[8]

Alongside this cycle ran the *tonalpohualli*, which consisted of a combination of 13 numerical symbols (1 to 13) with 20 non-numerical symbols (fig. 25), corresponding to animals, elements, gods and artificial objects (crocodile, wind, house, lizard, snake and death etc.). The 260 possible combinations result in a cycle of 260 days. The *tonalpohualli* is out of step with the solar calendar and was essentially divinatory, although some of its days indicated the celebration of important religious feasts. Thus the fortune of the day *chicome ácatl* ('7-reed') was told by referring to the specific positive or negative influences of the number 7, of the *ácatl* symbol and of the day which preceded the *trecena* (a period of thirteen days which started whenever the number one recurred). The combination of these influences was thought to affect significantly the lives of wordly beings.

Other cycles included those of the Moon, Venus and the Nine Lords of the Night. These

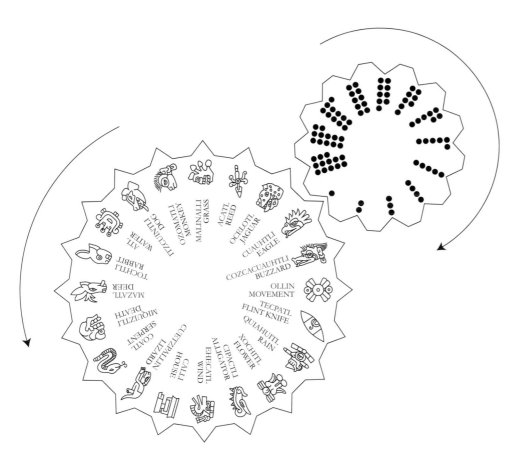

Fig. 25
Combination of the 13 numerical symbols and the 20 non-numerical symbols of the *tonalpohualli*.

combinations formed higher cycles, which were also charged with divine influences. For example, the *xihuitl* and the *tonalpohualli* formed 18,980 unrepeatable compounds, which gave rise to the 'century' or *xiuhmolpilli*, a period which consisted of 52 *xihuitl* years, equivalent to 73 turns of the *tonalpohualli* wheel.

Time was considered a sacred substance. Days, months, years and centuries were not only protected by specific gods, but were part of the gods themselves, who influenced creatures. Men received these influences daily and did their best to benefit from the positive ones and lessen the blow of the negative. Time, dictated by the gods, was ordered mathematically to flow inside the four pillars at the extremities of the cosmos and over the world through the eastern, northern, western and southern trees, circulating anticlockwise.

THE GODS

The Aztecs believed that time was the gods themselves, but what were the gods? Essentially, the Aztecs – like all Mesoamerican peoples – believed them to be entities, made of a substance imperceptible to humans,[9] who acted on the world that humans could perceive and whose origin predated the creation of that world. These beings could be likened to the supernatural in European thinking. For the Aztecs, the gods were supernatural beings who had power, will and personality in a similar way to men. Because the gods were transformed into worldly beings, the

Aztec cosmos was full of divinity. At one end there was the One God, union and source of all the gods,[10] and at the other an extraordinary multiplicity of the divine existed, which filtered into even the humblest of insects, blades of grass and particles of rock.

Between these two extremes was a crowded pantheon of gods, all of whom had well-defined strengths and powers, despite the fact that they could easily merge with one another or divide into others. The most important Mexican gods included Tezcatlipoca (night and destiny), Huitzilopochtli (a solar deity), Xiuhtecuhtli (fire; fig. 26), Tlaloc (rain), Quetzalcoatl (deliverer of the goods of the gods), Chicomecoatl (maize), Tlaltecuhtli (earth), Cihuacoatl (mother goddess and also goddess of the earth), Chalchiuhtlicue (water), Toci (childbirth), Mictlantecuhtli (death), Tlazolteotl (love), Xolotl (transformations), Xochipilli (flowers, music and song) and Xipe Totec (oppositions and transitions). One example of division is that of Tlaloc, who divided into four *tlaloque*,[11] each a different colour, who created various kinds of rain and each of whom was situated in one of the cosmic trees. Another is that of Quetzalcoatl, who manifested himself as Ehecatl (wind) or Tlahuizcalpantecuhtli (dawn; fig. 26).

The plurality of the gods reflected the diversity of the cosmos, and the interaction between complementary forces or the conflict that men believed they could perceive in nature. Throughout the eighteen twenty-day periods of

Fig. 26
Xiuhtecuhtli, god of fire, and
Tlahuizcalpantecuhtli, god of dawn,
on page 8 of the Codex
Borbonicus, sixteenth century.

Bibliothèque de l'Assemblée Nationale
Française, Paris

the year a succession of feasts honoured the gods, who successively exercised their influence on the world.

The various peoples of Mesoamerica chose to descend from and be protected by a particular god, creating a cult around him and often assigning him a unique, familiar name. Each of these peoples considered their patron god the being who had created their remote ancestors and given them their language, customs, profession and characteristics. The Aztecs believed that their patron, Huitzilopochtli, was a sun-god who had

assigned them the tasks of fishing and other waterborne activities, which were represented by a spear-thrower (*átlatl*), a harpoon or a trident (*minacachalli*) and a net in which to load the catch. As the Aztecs became a powerful and militarised civilisation they came to see their god as an increasingly aggressive being, interpreting the *átlatl* and the *minacachalli* as offensive weapons. The initial promise which Huitzilopochtli had made to them – a lacustrine settlement where they would develop by dint of labour – also became a prediction of the glory they would

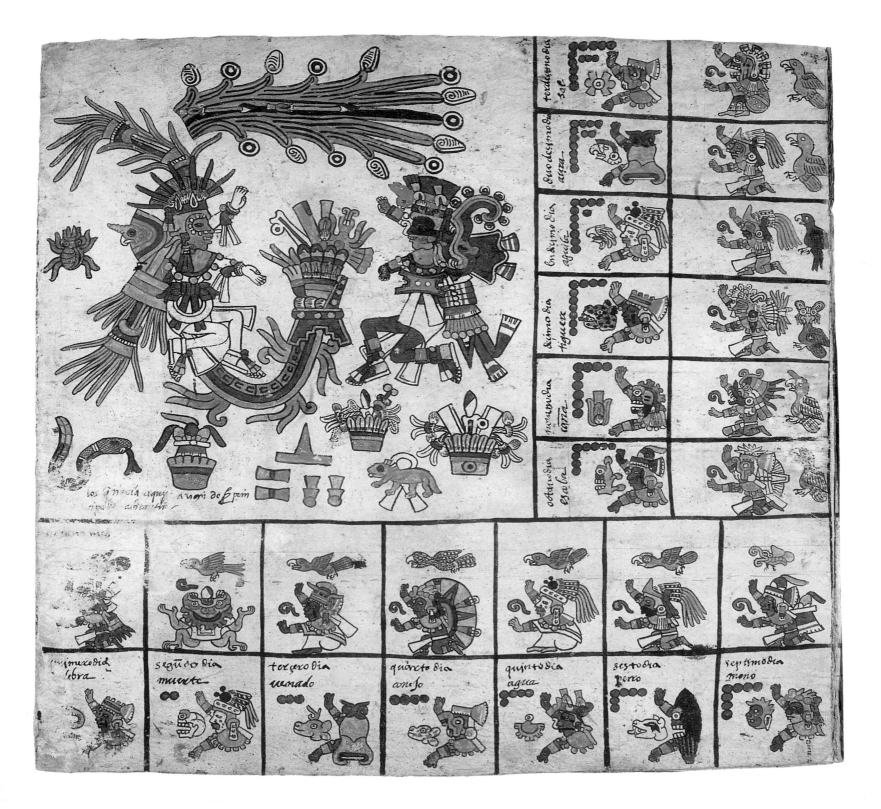

achieve as conquerors, forcing their enemies to acknowledge the supremacy of their god and to pay high taxes to the Aztec state.

A PIOUS SOCIETY AND STATE

From the first quarter of the fifteenth century to the time of the Spanish conquest, the Aztecs lived in a permanent state of religious and military fervour. Children and young people – both male and female – were taught to connect their devotion to the gods with a passion for war. All members of society were priests at least in the first stages of their lives, since children were offered to the temple soon after birth and their parents committed them to serve its gods once they had reached the age of reason (fig. 27). Therefore, education associated priesthood with a career in the army. Child priests (*tlamacaztoton*) rose through the ranks until they became military men forged on the field of battle. Even when they left school to marry, young people would leave behind an amulet as security, which contained part of their soul and ensured that the link between themselves as adults and the institution would never be broken.

The fusion between the divine order and the political order meant that each official was responsible for executing the plans of the gods, particularly those of the patron god. The ruler (*tlatoani*) was the image of divine power in the eyes of his people, although his representation favoured the celestial and masculine part of the cosmos. At his side, an assistant (*cihuacoatl*) dealt with matters that related to the underworld, including fiscal ones.[12] Both these leaders were the highest authorities in politics, religion, the army, worship, administration and trade. Such public positions reproduced the duality of the cosmos.[13]

The whole apparatus of state was directed, by divine design, towards hegemonic expansion and the subjugation and plundering of conquered peoples.

Priests, of whom there were many, were responsible for worshipping the gods, educating children and young people (a task in which they were assisted by the army), advising rulers, administering the property of the temple, caring for the faithful, and predicting the future. The clergy consisted of both men and women, although the main functions were performed by men. They were assisted in their activities, which were highly specialised and organised by hierarchy, by numerous devotees who had promised to serve the gods for a certain number of years.

MILITARISM, RELIGION AND HUMAN SACRIFICE

As can be imagined, the militaristic ideology of the Aztecs considerably influenced their beliefs, mythology and ritual. Personal, family, community and religious matters were conditioned by the interests of the ruling élite and all benefited from war.

One of the most important feasts of the Aztec cult was the binding of the years into a *xiuhmolpilli*, a bundle of 52 reeds (fig. 28). Every 52 years saw the end of the 18,980-day cycle produced by the combination of the *xihuitl* and the *tonalpohualli*. All fires were extinguished and the world was temporarily at risk of being ruled by the terrifying beings of the night. Domestic objects, including representations of deities, millstones and grinding stones, were destroyed for fear of their sacred essence rebelling at a critical time of darkness and exacting revenge for daily abuse and mistreatment. The main worry, however, was that the Fifth Sun – Nahui Ollin – would be extinguished forever. During the night, on Mount Huixachtepetl, south-

Fig. 27
A father takes his son to school. Vol. 1, folio 232v, of the Florentine Codex, 1575–77 (cat. 344).
Biblioteca Medicea Laurenziana, Florence

Fig. 28
The Aztecs celebrate the binding of the years during their sojourn in Apazco. Page 10 of the Codex Boturini, the Tira de la Peregrinación, sixteenth century.
Biblioteca Nacional de Antropología e Historia, Mexico City

Fig. 29

A human sacrifice. Folio 70r
of the Codex Magliabechiano,
sixteenth century (cat. 342).

Biblioteca Nazionale Centrale di Firenze,
Florence

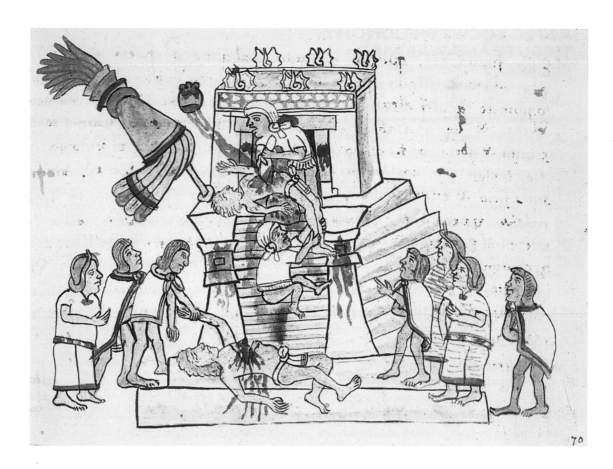

east of Tenochtitlan, a priest placed the fire-drill[14] on the chest of a sacrificed enemy and lit a new flame there. The new fire began to glow, to great public jubilation, and every home was filled with light and heat. From that moment, to prevent the weakened Sun from extinguishing itself forever at the end of the next 52 years, humankind was obliged to strengthen the god by providing him with suitable nutrition: human blood and hearts.

The practice of human sacrifice had been common among sedentary farmers for a thousand years and remained one of the main rituals of Mesoamerican religion (fig. 29). However, the number of ritual murders increased to untold proportions when militarism developed in civilisations such as those of the Aztecs and the Tarascans in the years leading up to the Spanish conquest, and at certain times among the northern Maya.

The type of victim varied according to the specific deity and ceremony. One important feast required the sacrifice of a mature woman from a noble family of Aztec descent. The Aztecs believed that the rain gods, the *tlaloque*, required children who had two cowlicks in their hair for sacrifice. Furthermore, to prevent damage to the Sun during eclipses, the god was strengthened by the sacrifice of albinos, people full of light. With military expansion, the majority of victims came to be enemies captured in battle who were so numerous

that they had to be divided among the various districts of the city for their keepers to feed them until the time came for them to be delivered to the gods.

These ritual murders had different meanings. Some victims were considered to be sources of energy for the gods who drank their blood and devoured their hearts; but there were also the so-called *in teteo imixiptlahuan*, human beings chosen to receive the fire of the gods in their bodies, as if they were vessels of divinity. They were killed on the feast day of the god they impersonated in the belief that the god would be freed of its host and, thus rejuvenated, could enter the body of another man who could contain its strength until the next feast day.

The Aztecs, heirs of an ancient cultural tradition, lived in and developed a shared view of the cosmos, stamping upon it their own conceptions of their history. Their primary view of themselves as farmers, hunters, fishermen and lacustrine gatherers changed considerably when it had to fulfil the requirements of hegemonic expansion.

affairs. Similarly, artisans making precious stone ornaments, gold and silver jewellery, and featherwork accoutrements lived in exclusive *calpulli*. Some were in the employ of specific rulers or nobles, but others produced more generally for the market. In either case, the consumers of their exquisite products were nobles and demand was high, with the result that these artisans became quite wealthy. They enjoyed political and social rights denied to other commoners, but were at pains to hide their considerable wealth from the possibly jealous eyes of the nobles. They were a vigorous force in an increasingly commercialised economy.

In theory, some avenues of mobility existed in this apparently rigid society. The most important of these was personal achievement on the battlefield. A primary goal of warfare was the capture of enemy warriors for ritual sacrifice; each capture enhanced the captor's status and rewards.

However, as the empire expanded, rifts developed between nobles and commoners, perhaps predictably, in view of the increasing number of noble children being born and the relatively slower expansion in the number of noble-level occupations available.

ECONOMIC PRODUCTION

The large populations and complex specialisations of Aztec Mexico were supported by extensive agricultural surpluses (fig. 30). Intensive cultivation of maize, beans, chillis, squashes, tomatoes and other vegetables provided sustenance for noble and commoner alike. In the Basin of Mexico and other lacustrine areas, abundant aquatic resources and migratory birds supplemented this diet. In drier environments, prickly-pear cactuses supplied reliable foods, and maguey plants provided *octli* (*pulque* in Spanish), a fermented beverage made

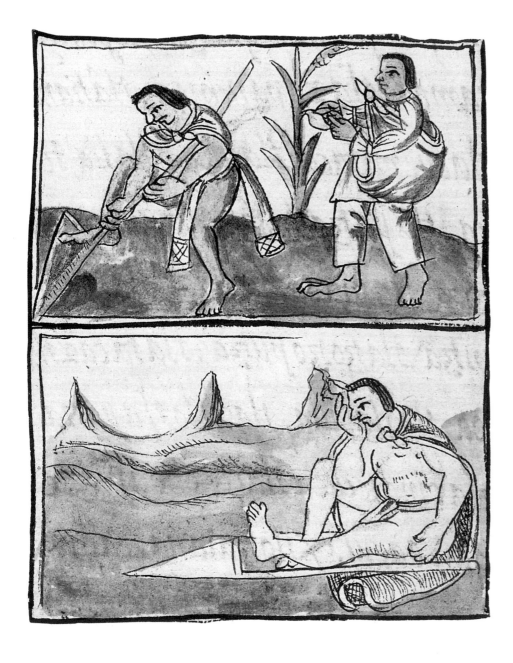

Fig. 30
Farmers at work in the fields.
Vol. 3, folio 30*v*, of the Florentine Codex, 1575–77 (cat. 344).

Biblioteca Medicea Laurenziana, Florence

from the heart of the plant.[4] Salt, a dietary essential, was extracted along the shores of lakes and ocean coastlines. Cacao (chocolate) was grown in humid, tropical regions, and animals such as deer and rabbits were hunted in wild habitats. Prominent among the few domesticated animals were the dog and the turkey, both of which were eaten. Horses, cattle, sheep, pigs and goats were all introduced by the Spanish.

The Mexica and their neighbours were accomplished horticulturists, and devised many ingenious means of increasing food production. They terraced highland slopes, and controlled water courses through the construction of irrigation canals and check dams.[5] Perhaps most important for the urban development of the Basin of Mexico were the *chinampas*, more commonly known today as 'floating gardens' (fig. 71). These high-yield plots increased the land area available for cultivation, and served as settlement extensions of lakeside cities. Tenochtitlan would never have attained its estimated population of 250,000 on its original small island, and numerous other cities expanded in the same fashion.[6]

Chinampas, remarkably productive tracts of land built up in the shallow beds of freshwater lakes, were constructed from alternate layers of mud and vegetation which were secured by posts and the roots of willow trees. Plots were systematically planned and arranged in the lake, and each was typically bordered on one side by a canal and on the other by a footpath adjacent to another field (see fig. 71). Fertility was enhanced by intensive cultivation techniques: water for irrigation was supplied by dipping into adjacent canals, a process which also dredged the canals and kept them clear for canoe transport. Cultivation was accomplished by the effective use of seedbeds, thus allowing for continuous planting and harvesting of crops. Although the fecundity of these fields was remarkable, Edward Calnek has suggested that about 500 square metres of this type of land would be required to support one person.[7] In that Tenochtitlan *chinampas* ranged in size from 100 to 850 square metres and were cultivated by an average of 10 to 15 persons each, Calnek maintains that these fields were not self-sufficient and were not capable of producing a substantial surplus for sale to the urban population. Perhaps their value lay more in their ability to produce high yields of the garden vegetables and aromatic flowers essential for the endless round of flamboyant rituals and political displays.

Many farmers maintained fields comparable to kitchen gardens, planted with foods, herbs and medicines. But some cultivators and other food producers grew more specialised crops in suitable environments. As we have seen, *chinampa* horticulturists may have concentrated upon vegetable and flower cultivation. Chalco (in the south-eastern Basin of Mexico) and Tlaxcala (east of the Basin of Mexico) were known as maize 'breadbaskets'; Tochtepec near the coast of the Gulf of Mexico was famous for its cacao; northern Yucatan was the source of the finest salt; and other city-states gained reputations for producing high-quality chillis, cacao and chia.[8]

Non-food crops were also grown in abundance throughout the Aztec world. In drier environments, as well as providing a desirable (but normally prohibited) beverage, maguey, an agave plant, yielded cloth and net fibres, its sharp spines providing sewing needles and its sap offering medicines. Similarly, the prickly-pear cactus (a source of food from its pads, fruit and flowers) provided a habitat for the small insects which gave prized red cochineal dyes. The cultivation of

Fig. 31
Featherworkers.
Vol. 2, folio 371r, of the Florentine Codex, 1575–77 (cat. 344).

Biblioteca Medicea Laurenziana, Florence

cotton, a particularly significant product, was restricted to lowland areas, although cotton clothing was woven by both highland and lowland women. Other raw materials included obsidian from volcanic zones, gold from certain rivers, reeds from lake shores, wood from forests, shells from marine environments, paper from forests with the appropriate trees, and exotic feathers and jaguar pelts from tropical zones. Clays, mineral dyes, jade, turquoise, glues and assorted other materials were found in dispersed areas.

Aztec consumers had access to an impressive array of products. Raw materials were transformed into usable and exotic goods by a myriad of artisans who specialised in their manufacture. Specialised artisans were concentrated in the large Basin of Mexico cities, but were also dispersed throughout the Aztec domain and beyond. Although there appears to have been minimal state control over artisans making utilitarian objects,[9] a more formalised organisation was instituted for the luxury crafts. The fine art of featherworking, for instance, was carried out by accomplished, meticulous craftsmen in a particular *calpulli* of Tlatelolco. These featherworkers (fig. 31) crafted elaborate mosaic shields, flowing headdresses and decorative banners, overseeing their own affairs with their own officials and worshipping a specific patron deity. Artisans working with precious metals and stones established a similar guild-like system; they were localised in their own *calpulli* and exercised control over training, manufacture and production quality. Similar types of item were made all over the Aztec empire and beyond, and warriors from all regions charged onto the battlefield flaunting their splendid paraphernalia. It is not known if such artisans enjoyed special attention and privileges in more remote cities, but given their importance to the nobility it appears likely.

Not all specialist workers produced material goods. The complexity of an urban society demanded the full attention of administrative and bureaucratic officials (from rulers to tax-collectors and scribes), and the Aztecs' elaborate polytheistic religion required an extensive retinue of priests, priestesses and temple-workers. Commerce, too, was highly developed in Aztec Mexico, and, as we shall see, professional merchants gained a lucrative livelihood.

TRADE AND MARKETS

Specialisation requires some type of exchange system to allow distribution of utilitarian products, exotic goods and necessary or desired services. Among the Aztecs and their neighbours,

distribution took several forms: market exchange, long-distance commerce by professional merchants, tribute, and reciprocity among élites. Tribute and élite reciprocity were essentially political institutions, and will be discussed in the final section of this essay.

The most common mode of economic distribution in the Aztec domain was market exchange (fig. 33). Virtually every community of any size held a market either daily or in rotation with neighbouring communities. The outdoor marketplace, or *tianquiztli*, was undoubtedly the liveliest spot in a town. Not only the setting for trade in a wide range of goods, it also served as the venue for circulation of the latest news among kin and acquaintants.

Marketplaces varied considerably in scale, depending on city size, location, reputation and specialisation. The grandest marketplace in Aztec Mexico, at Tlatelolco, reportedly offered virtually everything produced in the known world, from a wide selection of foodstuffs, to medicines, cooking vessels, lumber, clothing and fancy adornments. Vendors ranged from commoner-producers of small garden surpluses (a few chillis or tomatoes), to regional merchants carrying products such as cotton or cacao from market to market (fig. 32), to professional luxury merchants trafficking in expensive exotic goods such as tropical feathers and jadeite ornaments.

Other marketplaces were smaller and their produce often reflected their environment. Coyoacan's market, for instance, was known for wood products from its nearby forested hinterland, and Cholula's was famed for its locally produced

Fig. 32
Travelling merchants.
Vol. 2, folio 316r, of the Florentine Codex, 1575–77 (cat. 344).

Biblioteca Medicea Laurenziana, Florence

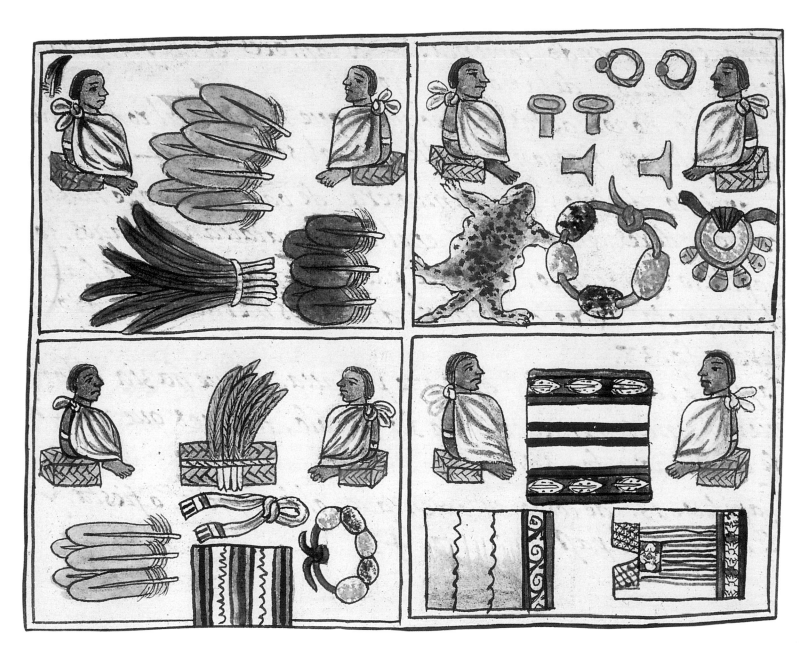

Fig. 33

Merchants selling their wares.
Vol. 2, folio 308v, of the Florentine
Codex, 1575–77 (cat. 344).

Biblioteca Medicea Laurenziana, Florence

and well-reputed chillis and maguey honey.[10]
Aztec consumers knew that it was best to go to
the Acolman market for a wide selection of dogs,
to the Tetzcoco market for ceramics, cloth and
fine gourds, or to the markets at Atzcapotzalco
or Itzocan for slaves.

Barter was the usual means of exchange in
Aztec marketplaces. But exchanges were facilitated
by the use of commonly accepted currency,
especially cacao beans and large cotton cloaks.
Cacao beans served as 'small change' and were
valuable enough to engage the energies of
counterfeiters, who would remove the chocolate
from the outer husk and replace it with sand or
ground avocado stones. Individual cacao beans
carried little value: in early Colonial times one
cacao bean was equivalent to a large tomato or a
tamale, three cacao beans could purchase a turkey
egg or a newly picked avocado, 30 cacao beans
would buy a small rabbit, while 200 were required

to purchase a turkey cock.[11] Large, white cotton
cloaks served as higher-value media of exchange;
depending on the respective qualities of bean and
garment, values ranged from 65 to 300 cacao beans
for one cloak.[12] As a measure of standard of living,
twenty cloaks (of unstated quality) could support
a person, probably a commoner, for a year.[13]

Marketplaces attracted *pochteca*, who traded
their expensive merchandise both inside and
outside the Aztec imperial domain, often
becoming quite wealthy in the process. As will
be recalled, well-established *pochteca* also served
as city-state and imperial emissaries, formally
trading their ruler's goods for the goods of a
foreign ruler. Some specialised *pochteca* (known as
oztomeca) served as spies by disguising themselves
and gathering current news in outlying
marketplaces. Known as political as well as
economic agents, *pochteca* risked assault and
assassination on the road (fig. 34).

Marketplace exchange and long-distance trading enterprises moved a vast array of goods from region to region and from hand to hand. These activities evened out regional availabilities, seasonal fluctuations and specialised manufacture. Exchanges were not strictly economic events, but were intimately tied to social and political networks: friendships were established, news was exchanged, spying was carried out and alliances were forged.

DAILY LIFE

Standards of living varied considerably across the Aztec social scheme. Everyone lived in houses, but their size and quality were a measure of status. At one end of the scale were the royal palaces. Motecuhzoma's palace in Tenochtitlan was not just a residence but also a government building; it contained courthouses, warriors' council chambers, tribute storage rooms (including two armouries), rooms for bureaucratic officials and visiting dignitaries, a library, an aviary, a zoo, and various courtyards, gardens and ponds.[14] The palace of Netzahualcoyotl[15] (fig. 35) in neighbouring Tetzcoco reportedly covered over 200 acres.[16] Wealthy merchants and luxury artisans enjoyed quality housing, but on a much smaller scale. Commoners' houses were more modest still, although they varied with the economic circumstances of each household. Some were made of adobe and consisted of a number of rooms surrounding a central patio. Rooms tended to be small and windowless, and most daily living seems to have taken place outside on the patio. Others were constructed of wattle and daub, wooden planks or stone. The houses of Mexica from all backgrounds contained few furnishings and household possessions.

Diet was another dimension of life separating noble from commoner. The Mexica ruler was reportedly presented with two thousand kinds of food each day: 'hot tortillas, white tamales with beans forming a sea shell on top; red tamales; the main meal of roll-shaped tortillas and many [foods]: sauces with turkeys, quail, venison, rabbit, hare, rat, lobster, small fish, large fish; then all [manner of] sweet fruits'.[17] Contrast this with a commoner's mid-day meal of *atolli* (maize gruel) and a later meal of tortillas with a chilli sauce, beans and other vegetables, with meat only on special occasions. In between these extremes, professional merchants and luxury artisans apparently ate quite well and were able to afford to host lavish feasts.

Clothing tended to advertise social and economic status. Cotton was more prestigious than the coarser maguey fibre, and elaborate designs carried special meanings. Successful warriors, for instance, were awarded cloaks of specific designs to signal their achievements. Nonetheless, clothing was relatively simple, with men wearing loincloths and capes, and women wearing tunics and skirts.

Daily work in Aztec Mexico was labour-intensive. Women-commoners' work was physically demanding and time-consuming. All clothing was woven on backstrap looms by women who also spun thread for weaving by hand. Women spent hours at the *metate*, grinding maize for the day's tortillas. They prepared special tamales and other foods for ceremonial occasions, and devoted considerable time to childcare. They were periodically called upon to labour in a noble's palace. Their men worked long hours in the fields cultivating crops with hoes and digging sticks, on lakes catching fish with nets, or at home making pottery or obsidian blades by hand. Men were also subject to military or labour conscription. Noble occupations generally required less physical effort, but often carried heavy responsibilities. Professional merchants trekked difficult and treacherous trails, and luxury artisans spent long hours in their meticulous arts.

Despite their differences, noble, merchant and commoner alike were subject to the same cultural mores and legal codes. The virtues of 'the exemplary life', representing 'obedience, honesty, discretion, respect, moderation, modesty and energy',[18] were extolled. Individuals were expected to work hard (and not to sleep long hours),

Fig. 34
The funeral of a wealthy merchant. Folio 68r of the Codex Magliabechiano, sixteenth century (cat. 342).

Biblioteca Nazionale Centrale di Firenze, Florence

Fig. 35
Netzahualcoyotl, King of Tetzcoco. Folio 106r of the Codex Ixtlilxochitl, sixteenth century.

Bibliothèque Nationale de France, Paris

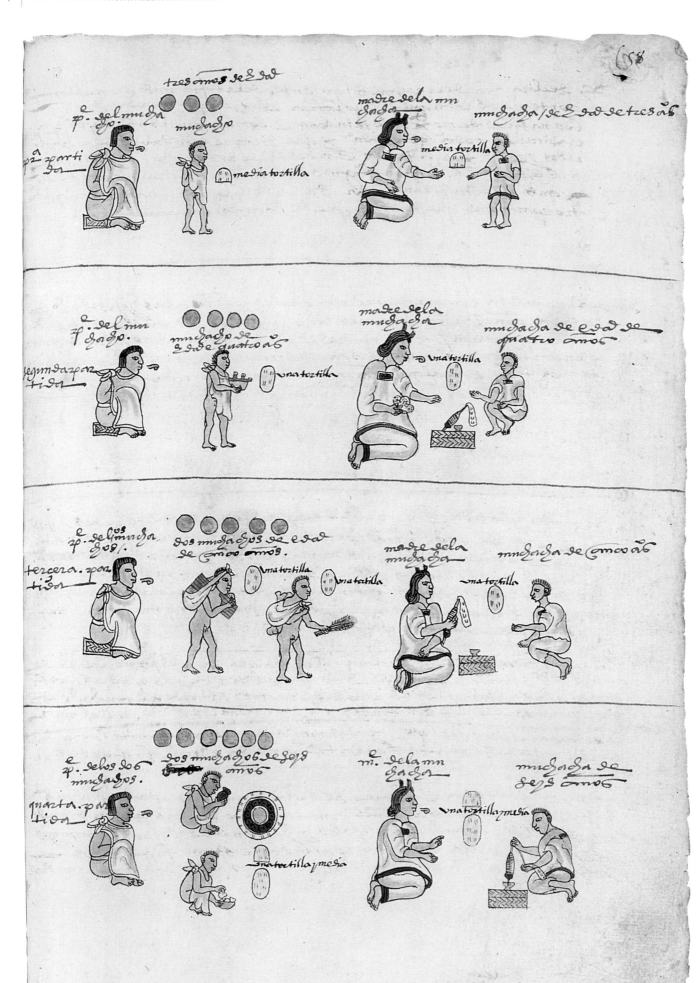

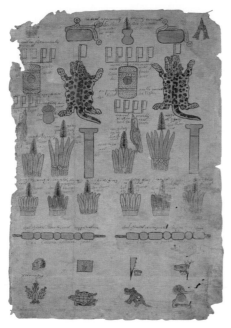

Fig. 37

A register of tribute paid by the province of Xoconochco on the Pacific coast. Folio 13r of the Matrícula de Tributos, early sixteenth century.

Biblioteca Nacional de Antropología e Historia, Mexico City

Fig. 36

The instruction of Aztec children aged between three and six. Folio 58r of the Codex Mendoza, c. 1541 (cat. 349).

Bodleian Library, University of Oxford

to dress modestly, to eat quietly and speak thoughtfully. Children were explicitly taught these rules along with practical skills (fig. 36), and discipline was severe for those who did not comply.[19] Legal codes were in place to direct and punish those who infringed these rules. Punishments tended to be more severe for nobles than for commoners; because they carried more responsibility, it was thought that nobles should be held more accountable for the consequences of their actions. Ceremonial events called for participation by both noble and commoner, with each performing complementary roles. Participation in such events welded noble and peasant into a common cultural milieu.

WARFARE AND THE AZTEC EMPIRE

In 1430 the Aztec empire took form, based on the Triple Alliance between the city-states of Tenochtitlan, Tetzcoco and Tlacopan. This militarily aggressive coalition had conquest as its primary goal. Over the 91 years in which it held sway, the Triple Alliance conquered numerous city-states in central and southern Mexico, ranging from areas to the north of the Basin of Mexico to present-day Guatemala, and from the Pacific coast to the coast of the Gulf of Mexico.

Conquest and empire-building relied on successful military engagements. The goals of warfare were essentially twofold: to capture enemy warriors for sacrifice, and to conquer other polities for the extraction of tribute. As we have seen, enemy captures on the battlefield were a measure of a warrior's personal achievements. Significant rewards and renown awaited the courageous warrior, important incentives in motivating a fighting force that engaged essentially in hand-to-hand combat. To this end, the Mexica arranged military engagements called 'flowery wars', scheduled battles with long-term enemies such as the Tlaxcalans. Each city-state used these encounters as training grounds for neophyte warriors as well as a convenient source of sacrificial victims. These goals aside, however, it seems that the battles were fought in earnest and that conquests were indeed sought.

Although the warriors of the Triple Alliance did not always emerge victorious,[20] on balance they were the dominant military force in Mesoamerica during their 91-year heyday. In the course of imperial growth, they dealt with subjugated city-states by establishing 'strategic provinces' and 'tributary provinces'.[21] Strategic provinces were formed more through alliance than conquest, and involved gift-exchanges among élites rather than outright tribute payments. These provinces were

located in hostile borderlands, at important resource sites, or along major transport routes. Tributary provinces experienced military conquest and were required to pay an established tribute on a predetermined schedule. The style of imperial management of these conquered polities was hegemonic; following conquest, a city-state was permitted to retain rulership as long as tributes were paid on time.

Typically, tribute payments were required in goods readily available to the conquered subjects: wood products from forested regions; maguey cloth from drier northern areas; and shimmering feathers, jaguar pelts and cacao beans from tropical lowland environments (fig. 37). Cotton clothing was paid by all but two tributary provinces, demonstrating its widespread use and generalised demand. Staple foodstuffs such as maize and beans, being heavy and bulky, were given in large quantities by provinces close to the imperial capitals.

Tribute demands were carefully planned by the imperial powers. They ranged from subsistence staples to store against famine, to decorated clothing and costumes for awards to valiant warriors, to precious gold and jadeite ornaments for élite display. As the empire expanded in the later years of its growth, more and more tributes took the form of fancy, élite goods. This in part indicates the availability of these precious materials in distant regions, but undoubtedly also represents the expansion of the nobility and a growth in its taste for extravagance.

Although the loose, hegemonic style of imperial administration was an inexpensive strategy for the Mexica, it was ultimately to be their undoing. As Hernán Cortés sought to defeat Motecuhzoma Xocoyotzin of Tenochtitlan, he engaged as allies the many disenchanted conquered and unconquered city-states whose dynasties, resources and fighting forces remained intact despite continued demands and pressures from the powerful Triple Alliance. With the arrival of the Spanish, the tide of conquest turned on the powerful Mexica.

5

THE TEMPLO MAYOR, THE GREAT TEMPLE OF THE AZTECS
Eduardo Matos Moctezuma

The night after the Mexicans had finished repairing the chapel of their god, having blocked off most of the lagoon and created the base on which the houses would be built, Huitzilopochtli spoke to the priest and said: 'Tell the Mexican congregation that they must split up, with each nobleman taking his relatives, friends and those closest to him, into four main districts around the house you have built for me to rest in…'[1]

Thus Friar Diego Durán described how the god Huitzilopochtli ordered the construction of the city of Tenochtitlan in 1325, leading to the establishment of the two areas of the city: the sacred and the profane. The first is where the Templo Mayor and its surrounding buildings were constructed within the ceremonial precinct (fig. 38), the ultimate sacred site inhabited by the gods. This was to become the absolute centre of the city and within it the Templo Mayor occupied the most sacred space: the centre of centres, the place from which you could ascend to the sky or descend to the underworld, the point from which the four directions of the universe began. For all these reasons, the Templo Mayor was hugely important; it lay at the heart of the Aztec universe, where the various forces of their cosmos met. The profane space, as the god explained, was destined to house the Aztec community, divided into four districts or *calpullis*. The rapid enlargement of the city led these *calpullis* to proliferate; at the time of its greatest splendour, Tenochtitlan numbered some 250,000 inhabitants.

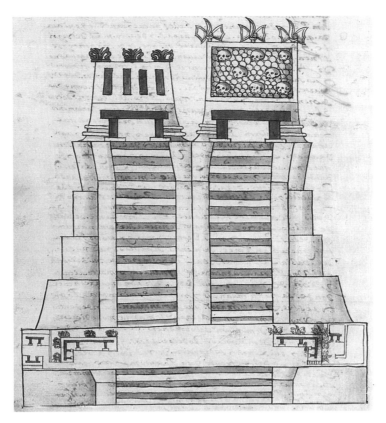

A review, based both on archaeological evidence and on historical sources, of the various stages of the Templo Mayor's construction follows, as well as a discussion of the elements associated with each stage. Archaeology has provided much new information after five years of digging in the heart of Mexico City. It is well known that what is now Mexico City covers various Pre-Hispanic cities and towns which existed at the time of the Spanish conquest in the area of Lake Tetzcoco. Both Tenochtitlan and Tlatelolco, its twin city, were situated in the middle of the lake. The first was linked to the mainland by the Tacuba causeway to the west, the Ixtapalapan causeway to the south, and the Tepeyac causeway to the north. Reports also exist of a fourth causeway leading eastwards. These wide causeways led from the ceremonial precinct out along the four directions of the universe, according to the Aztec view of the cosmos.

Historical sources provide a great deal of information on the Templo Mayor. Various chroniclers of the sixteenth and seventeenth centuries left records stating that the temple was dedicated to two gods: Tlaloc, god of water, rain and fertility, and Huitzilopochtli, god of the sun and war. Various pictures of the temple survive (fig. 39), showing its stairways leading to the upper part and the two dedicated shrines at the top of the building where the figures of the gods stood.

All this information led to the setting up of the Proyecto Templo Mayor under the auspices of the Mexican Instituto Nacional de Antropología

e Historia (INAH), which, following the chance discovery of a sculpture of the goddess Coyolxauhqui (fig. 10) in 1978, carried out archaeological work with an interdisciplinary team consisting of archaeologists, biologists, chemists, historians and physical anthropologists who worked hard over the next five years to understand the Templo Mayor and the Aztecs themselves.

STAGE I:

CONSTRUCTION OF THE FIRST TEMPLE (1325)

Archaeologists have not reached the site of the first shrine built in Huitzilopochtli's honour. The only information we have lies in historical sources, which say that the god ordered the first temple to be built of wood, reeds and mud. Friar Diego Durán describes how this temple was erected. As his account shows, it must have been very small:

...let us all go, and, in that place where the prickly-pear cactus grows, build a small chapel where our god may now rest; though it cannot be made of stone let it be made of wattle and daub, since that is all we can do for the time being. Then everyone went very willingly to the place where the prickly-pear cactus grew and cutting down thick grasses from the reeds that grew next to the cactus, they built a square base, which was to serve as the foundation of the chapel for the god to rest in; and so they built a poor but pretty little house...covered with the reeds they gathered from the water itself...they were so poor, destitute and fearful that they built even that small mud hut in which to place their god in fear and trepidation.[2]

contained a large quantity of Mezcala-style masks. In Chamber I, on the Huitzilopochtli side, was found a figure identified as Mayahuel, god of *pulque*, made from a large piece of greenstone that undoubtedly came from the south of Mesoamerica. Another important offering was Chamber III, on the Tlaloc side, which contained two multi-coloured pots with images of Chicomecoatl, the goddess of foodstuffs and sustenance (cat. 284). The remains of feline bones were found between the two pots, in addition to a large quantity of objects and animals from both the coast and the highlands.

STAGE IV(B) (*c.* 1469)

This stage represents a partial extension to the western side of the Templo Mayor which is attributed to Axayacatl, who came to the throne of Tenochtitlan during 1469 and remained in power until 1481. The empire conquered several regions and was defeated only when it tried to overcome the Tarascans of Michoacán. One of the most significant of its conquests was that of the twin city of Tlatelolco in 1473; their neighbours' remarkable commercial success must have made Tlatelolco a tempting prospect for the people of Tenochtitlan.

During this period, the main façade of the Templo Mayor was extended. The architectural remains consist of the main platform on which the temple base sat. This platform has five steps leading up from the ceremonial square, which consists of a paved surface. The stairway has no central division, as can be seen on those leading to the upper part of the temple. It is interrupted only by a small altar, in line with the centre of the Tlaloc side, which is known as the Altar of the Frogs because it is decorated with two of these animals linked to the god of water. On the Huitzilopochtli side, towards the middle of the steps, an enormous sculpture of Coyolxauhqui (fig. 10) was found. Various offerings with rich contents are associated with this goddess, among them two funerary urns, made of orange clay and covered with lids (offerings 10 and 14), which contained the cremated bones of two adult males (cat. 279). Tests carried out on the bones showed that they may have belonged to people involved in military activities, given the clear evidence of musculature on the bones. From the moment of the discovery of these urns it was suggested that they might be those of high-ranking soldiers injured in the war against the people of Michoacán and brought to Tenochtitlan to die, because of

Fig. 42
Shrine B, from Stage VI, is decorated with 240 stucco-covered stone skulls.

their placement beneath the platform on the side of the temple dedicated to Huitzilopochtli and very close to the sculpture of Coyolxauhqui, a goddess who died in combat. Furthermore, the urns were decorated with two figures of gods armed with spear-throwers and spears. Their location suggests that the urns date from the time when Axayacatl was ruler, as shown by the '3-house' glyph placed south of the Huitzilopochtli side, which gives 1469, the year of this ruler's accession. Under Axayacatl's rule the Aztecs suffered defeat at the hands of the people of Michoacán.

To continue with our description of the main platform, on both sides of the two stairways leading to the shrines of Tlaloc and Huitzilopochtli, the heads of four serpents rest on the platform. The two on the side devoted to the water god differ from those on the side of the war god. In between the two central heads are offerings, two of which stand out from the others because they were placed in stone boxes with lids. Inside each of the offerings were thirteen Mezcala-style figures arranged in a row facing south, in addition to greenstone beads. This is significant because the southward direction of the universe was ruled by the god Huitzilopochtli, who was closely connected to this quadrant because of the movement of the sun.[6]

The north and south ends of the platform have chambers with floors paved with marble. Two enormous serpent bodies meet on the platform, one looking northwards and the other southwards. Between them is a serpent's head. The three snakes still bear some of their original painted decoration.

Interestingly, Stage IV(b) is the stage in which most offerings were found, showing that Tenochtitlan was at the zenith of its success and in full military expansion at this time. The number of tributary towns had increased and the contents of the offerings demonstrated this expansion, both in the types of animal sacrificed and in the objects deposited. The Templo Mayor had increased in size and splendour, reflecting the military might of Tenochtitlan in other regions.

STAGE V (c. 1482)

All that remains of this stage is the part of the main platform upon which the Templo Mayor sat. It retains some of the stucco that covered it. Four offerings were found. This stage may correspond to the government of Tizoc, who ruled Tenochtitlan from 1481 to 1486. This may also be the period during which the building known as the House of Eagles was constructed, north of the Templo Mayor, in which superb clay sculptures

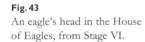

Fig. 43
An eagle's head in the House of Eagles, from Stage VI.

of eagle men (cat. 228) were found as well as sculptures of skeletons and two life-size representations of the god Mictlantecuhtli, lord of the underworld (cat. 233).[7] The building consists of a vestibule area, with pillars supporting the roof, which leads into a rectangular chamber. A short corridor leads to an internal patio with rooms at the north and south ends. The whole complex has stone benches decorated with processions of warriors, still in their original colours (fig. 44). Various studies have been carried out to determine where rituals were carried out. The clay sculptures of eagle men, the skeletons and the gods of the underworld are all associated with war.[8]

STAGE VI (c. 1486)

This stage may be attributable to Ahuizotl, who ruled from 1486 to 1502. The building was extended on all four sides; among the excavated remains is the main platform supporting the temple. This is characterised by decoration on the balustrades of the east-facing stairway, consisting of a moulding made up of three elements. This stage is important because it brought to light various shrines surrounding the Templo Mayor. Each of these will be described in turn.

The Red Temples, the two shrines found on the north and south side of the Templo Mayor respectively, are east-facing and have a vestibule with a circular altar at the centre. The vestibule is made up of two walls that are bordered by two stone hoops painted red. Their stairways face east and the walls are decorated with paint. An offering, containing a considerable number of musical instruments, both real and in the form of small representative sculptures, was found on the upper part of the south side. Among other items discovered were large, painted ceremonial knives. A study carried out on these shrines showed that they were related to the god Macuilxochitl. The Red Temple on the north side was aligned with Shrines A and B, and is also known as Shrine C.

Shrines A and B lie to the north of the Templo Mayor and are aligned with the wall of the main platform, standing on a paved stone floor which forms the floor of the ceremonial square. Shrine A has two stairways, one facing west and the other east. There is no particular decoration on its walls. Shrine B (fig. 42), however, has a west-facing stairway and is decorated on its three remaining walls with 240 stucco-covered stone skulls arranged close together like a *tzompantli* (a wooden rack on which the skulls of sacrificial victims were displayed). This shrine may have indicated the northern sector of the universe, given that this region was related to death, being the territory of

Mictlampa. On the upper part there are offerings, one of which contains felines and objects connected with Tlaloc (fig. 45).

Shrine D is a west-facing building which also lies to the north of the Templo Mayor. It is well preserved and has a recess in the floor of its upper storey, indicating that it once housed a circular sculpture, which was not found during the excavation.

The House of Eagles, with its magnificent clay sculptures of warriors, skeletons and the gods of the underworld, has been mentioned in connection with the previous stage. During Stage VI it was covered by another, similar building. Only the platform was found, on top of which was a colonial-style patio which must have belonged to one of Cortés's captains, an example of a Pre-Hispanic structure being used as the foundations for a house for conquistadors. The platform has a west-facing stairway and is decorated at the ends with bird heads which still have yellow paint on their beaks as well as black-and-white feathers on their heads (fig. 43). To the north it turns a corner and the House of Eagles runs westwards to another stairway.

Recent excavations have uncovered part of the stairway that led to the main platform. It was found to be in good condition and various offerings were discovered on it. These correspond to the next stage of construction.

STAGE VII (c. 1502)

All that remains of this stage is the main platform on which the Templo Mayor stood. Attributed to Motecuhzoma Xocoyotzin (1502–20), this was the stage which the Spaniards saw and razed to the ground in the sixteenth century. By that time, the building was around 82 metres square and is estimated to have been 45 metres high. Destroying this architectural mass, of which only the platform exists, must have presented a formidable challenge to the Spaniards. We have already mentioned the various offerings found in the filling that covered Stage VI and lay beneath Stage VII. Offering 102 was particularly important because it contained pieces of paper made from *amate*-tree bark and well-preserved fabrics which seemed to form part of the garb of a priest who worshipped Tlaloc.

Almost two centuries passed between 1325, the date of Tenochtitlan's supposed foundation, and 1521, the date of the destruction of the Templo Mayor by the Spaniards and their indigenous allies. Having followed the course of the building's development from its beginnings to the grandeur it had attained just before the Spanish

Fig. 44
The painted benches in the House of Eagles.

conquest, we should now turn our attention to the symbolism of the Templo Mayor, and to the reasons why it was the most important building in the ceremonial complex.

THE SYMBOLISM OF THE TEMPLO MAYOR

To begin with, it should be remembered that the Templo Mayor was the very centre of the Aztec universe. According to the cosmovision of the Aztecs and other Mesoamerican peoples, the universe was divided into three levels, of which the central level, the terrestrial zone, was inhabited by man. Above it were 13 planes, or skies, the last being Omeyocan, the place of duality. Below it was the underworld, consisting of nine planes, the deepest of which was Mictlan, inhabited by the couple formed by Mictlantecuhtli and Mictlancihuatl, the discarnate deities who ruled the world of the dead.

Four universal directions coincided with the cardinal points. Each direction was identified by a god, a plant, a bird, a colour and a glyph. The north was the direction of death and cold. It was known as Mictlampa, or the region of death. Its glyph was a sacrificial knife and it was associated with the colours black and yellow. The tree which symbolised it was a xerophyte, a plant native to these regions. It was ruled by the god Tezcatlipoca. The south was the region of dampness; it was identified by the colour blue and ruled by the god Huitzilopochtli. Its glyph was a rabbit, the symbol of fertility and abundance. The east, where the sun rose, was the masculine quadrant of the universe and was the path along which warriors, killed in combat or by sacrifice, travelled to accompany the sun from dawn until midday. It corresponded to the red Tezcatlipoca or Xipe Totec and was identified by this colour. Its glyph was a reed. The west was the female sector of the universe. Women who had died in childbirth – considered a battle by the Aztecs – accompanied the sun from midday to dusk, when the sun was devoured by the earth (Tlaltecuhtli) and passed through the world of the dead until the earth goddess (Coatlicue) gave birth to it again the next morning in the east. Its colour was white, its glyph was a house and it corresponded to the god Quetzalcoatl.

The centre of this vision of the cosmos was the Templo Mayor, the centre of centres, the most sacred place, the universal *axis mundi*. It was crossed by both the ascendant and descendant forces and from it departed the four directions of the universe, with the result that it contained the forces of each.

As we have seen, the Templo Mayor was split into two parts: one dedicated to the god of war and the other dedicated to the god of water. The Aztecs were extremely concerned to portray these deities, both in the architecture of the building and in the elements that surround it: from the sculptures with serpent's heads to the braziers that adorned the great platform on which stood the four structures that formed the pyramidal platform, to the upper shrines dedicated to Huitzilopochtli and Tlaloc, each painted specific colours (red and black for Huitzilopochtli, blue for Tlaloc) to show that they were two separate entities. Each part corresponded to a hill. The Huitzilopochtli side was Coatepec, the place where Coatlicue, the earth goddess, had given birth to the Aztecs' patron god to fight her enemies. The Tlaloc side was Tonacatepetl, the hill where the grains of maize that the gods give to men were stored. These two entities formed a single unit, the *axis mundi* of the Aztecs' universal conception. Furthermore, ceremonies were performed in them that were dedicated to these gods and recalled the myths associated with each part of the building. The Templo Mayor expressed the ultimate duality, the duality of life and death.

By analysing the temple we can see how the main platform on which it stands corresponds to the terrestrial level. Throughout excavations, this is where most offerings have been found. The presence, on the platform at the foot of the temple-hill, of the sculpture of the goddess Coyolxauhqui, goddess of the moon, against whom the sun god Huitzilopochtli battled, is very significant. In the myth that recounts the story of this battle, the gods fight at the top of Coatepec. Coyolxauhqui is captured by Huitzilopochtli, who beheads her and throws her body over the side of

the hill. As it falls, the body is dismembered and ends up at the foot of the hill. This is what the Aztecs intended to reproduce in the Templo Mayor on the Huitzilopochtli side: the victor at the top of the temple-hill and the vanquished goddess, beheaded and dismembered, lying on the ground (the main platform).

The four tiers of the Templo Mayor's pyramidal platform may represent celestial levels. At the top, the two shrines dedicated to each of the gods are the clearest representation of the life and death duality: on one side is the god of the sun and war; on the other is the god of water, fertility and life. This reflects the essential needs of the Aztecs: war as an economic necessity which provided Tenochtitlan with tax from the conquered regions, and the overriding requirement for agricultural produce. Furthermore, each side of the building was identified with the places where people went after death. Warriors who died in battle or sacrifice accompanied the sun along part of its path, and are therefore associated with Huitzilopochtli. People who died in water (as a result of a waterborne disease, drowning or being struck by lightning) had to go to Tlalocan, the place of eternal summer ruled by the god of water. The two sacred hills or mountains represented by the Templo Mayor were one of the first steps one had to take to reach Mictlan, the place to which those who died of all other causes were destined. An old poem speaks of the places where people would go after death:

Oh, where will I go?
Where will I go?
Where is the duality?…Difficult, oh so difficult!
Perhaps everyone's home is there,
where those who no longer have a body live,
inside the sky,
or perhaps the place for those who
no longer have a body is here on earth!
We will all go, all go completely.
No one will remain on the earth!
Who would say: 'Where are our friends?'
Rejoice!

Thus the Templo Mayor was the focal point of the Aztec view of the cosmos: the survival of the Aztec people, the order of the universe and the unimpeded daily progress of heavenly bodies, including the sun, relied on what it represented.

Fig. 45
Offering H, found in the upper part of Shrine B, contained remains of felines and objects associated with Tlaloc.

6

ART AT THE TIME OF THE AZTECS

Felipe Solís Olguín

Aztec monumental art reached a pinnacle of splendour and brought the period of indigenous Pre-Hispanic art to a dazzling conclusion, not only because of its proportions and masterly technique, but also, and predominantly, because of its overwhelming sculptural power, its sense of melodrama and its masculine and distinctive style.
Miguel Covarrubias[1]

TOLTECAYOTL

The Toltecs, inhabitants of Tollan (Tula), were the inspiration behind the Aztecs' creation of 'prime, polished and striking' works of art. The name Toltec is the origin of the Nahuatl descriptive term *tolteca*, or 'prime official artist', and the root of the word *toltecayotl*, whose meaning is close to our concept of artistic sensitivity.[2]

The link between Tula and Tenochtitlan was established in the initial migration from Aztlan. The Aztecs describe a period spent among the abandoned ruins of Tula, the ancestral city founded by Quetzalcoatl, the man-god or 'plumed serpent'. They gazed in wonder at pillars shaped like serpents and other material testimonies of bygone glory, attributing the origin of *toltecayotl* to Quetzalcoatl.

Following in the footsteps of his teacher Ángel María Garibay Kintana, Miguel León-Portilla, a well-known expert on Nahuatl literature and philosophy, has delved more deeply into the meaning of *toltecayotl* by studying texts collected by Friar Bernardino de Sahagún.[3]

His analysis demonstrates the esteem in which the creators of valuable objects were held in the Aztec world. Various expressions existed for artists, such as *yolteotl*, 'god in his heart', to describe the inspiration which the god gives the artist; *tlayolteuhuiani*, 'he who puts the deified heart into objects', to describe the action of introducing divine breath into the material the artist will work in; and *moyolnonotzani*, 'he who confers with his heart', to describe those who feel the divine touch and shape it into a work of art.[4]

The Franciscan friar's Indian informants attributed the origin of the manual trades to the Toltecs, classifying artists according to the importance of their works: *amantecas*, who invented the art of feathers; *tlacuiloque*, painter-scribes specifically dedicated to creating codices; and the artisans who worked so masterfully with jade, turquoise and other semi-precious stones (fig. 46). These were followed by craftsmen: carpenters, bricklayers, whitewashers, potters, spinners and weavers. Also defined as *tolteca* were goldsmiths and silversmiths, whose ingenuity allowed them to discover the secrets of metallurgy, and herbalist doctors, who knew the secrets of plants. The Toltecs were also credited with the development of the first calendars, the result of their accurate observations of the stars.[5]

THE CHARACTERISTIC FEATURES OF AZTEC ART

Although the modern Western world accepts the existence of art for its own sake, it must be remembered that in Aztec Mesoamerica sculpture could not be disassociated from the ideological concepts, whether religious, economic, political or social, that had characterised the cultural development of the area before the arrival of the Spaniards. For the citizens of Tenochtitlan, and indeed for all the peoples of ancient Mexico, art was a material manifestation of their vision of the universe. Its symbols, its association with real and imaginary nature, and its visual language allowed them to create parallel realities in which the human and the divine expressed the sacred messages associated with the cosmogonic concepts that determined their perception of the world around them. The act of creating images of men, animals, plants and supernatural beings reinforced the magic of the genesis of the universe, in which the destiny of each was established in a primordial pact with the gods. Flora and fauna symbolise the power and strength of the deities, personifying their actions in the cosmos. Supernatural beings display the true function of indigenous sculpture, giving physical form to fears and anxieties and invoking the forces of the unknown by means of symbols that are repeated like prayers and chants.

No surviving original texts attest to the value placed by Aztec society on artistic creations. The only remaining examples that mention the arts, mainly those collected by Sahagún, do so indirectly. Sahagún contrasts a good artist with one who does not do his work properly. One is dedicated, careful and able to achieve perfection; the other is careless and does not apply his skills properly.[6] The end of the reign of the fifth *tlatoani* of Tenochtitlan most clearly demonstrates the Aztec civilisation's appreciation of sculptural work. A native account of this time was recorded

by Diego Durán. In his twilight years, Motecuhzoma discussed with his brother Tlacaelel the need to perpetuate his memory in scenes to be carved in the rock of Chapultepec hill. Stone-cutters and quarrymen were ordered to select the most suitable rock surfaces.[7] Motecuhzoma was so pleased with the carving that he rewarded the sculptors with clothes described as 'embroidered cloths' and 'honourable garments'.[8]

Scarce information exists about the worth of artistic works in Pre-Hispanic times. Durán's text states that the means of payment varied according to the recipient. Valuable objects were usually used for this purpose, such as the cotton textiles with painted designs shown in the Codex Magliabechiano (cat. 342), the Matrícula de Tributos (fig. 37) and the Codex Mendoza (cat. 349); jewellery set with semi-precious stones, jade, rock crystal and obsidian; feathered ornaments (figs 47, 51); and cacao beans and powdered gold.

AZTEC ARCHITECTURE AND TOWN-PLANNING
The style of Aztec ritual architecture evolved principally in Tenayuca, where archaeologists discovered substructures from earlier periods beneath a mound of rubble. The site illustrates the genesis of the double pyramid typical of Tenochtitlan, and was the earliest example found in Mesoamerica of this innovative structure, which unites two pyramidal bases supporting a pair of twin temples.[9] This successful architectural formula was adopted by the Aztecs and their neighbours in buildings designed for the worship of their own supreme deities.

The origins of the pyramid of circular plan, such as that used at the Aztec temple of the wind god Ehecatl, can be recognised at Calixtlahuaca in

Fig. 46
Double-headed serpent pectoral, 1400–1521. Wood, turquoise and shell, 20.5 × 43.3 cm.
British Museum, London

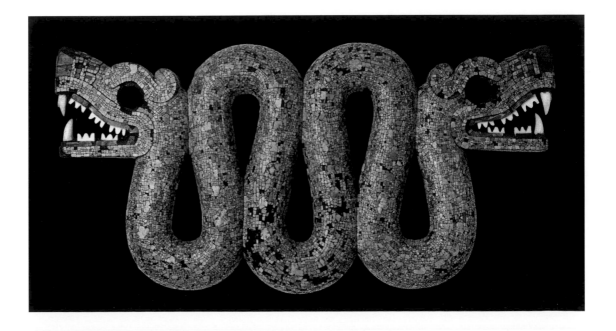

Fig. 47
Feather fan, early sixteenth century.
Quetzal feathers and gold appliqué,
height 119 cm, diameter 68 cm.

Museum für Völkerkunde, Vienna

the Valley of Toluca,[10] although the beginnings of the form are much older and lie in the distant Mayan territories, particularly in the Yucatan Peninsula. Various stages of construction have been detected at Calixtlahuaca. These recur, with stylistic variations, in the sacred dwelling of the god of the wind in the Aztec world, a circular-based building that combines a rectangular façade for the access stairway with the curved temple wall and conical roof. The characteristic Aztec ball-game courts (fig. 48) must have originated in Tula, Xochicalco or Teotenango.[11] The architectural benches in various buildings in Tenochtitlan that portray processions of richly attired warriors originated in Chichén Itzá, via Tula.[12]

The steep platform façades and the enormous temples that dominated Huitzilopochtli's capital and other cities of the Aztec world, with rooms

built one on top of another serving as storerooms for vestments, offerings and treasures of the gods, were all characterised by verticality. Studies of Pre-Hispanic architecture identify the Late Postclassic construction period with the so-called architectural dado, an element which finishes off the upper part of the balustrades and is used as the base for ceremonial braziers, and with the moulding that decorates the uppermost tier of the platform, whose purpose was to accentuate the verticality of the structures.[13]

The layout of Tenochtitlan, the island city whose beauty so impressed the Spanish conquistadors, is a model of the indigenous view of the universe, a vision of the cosmos that dates from the time of the Olmecs. Essentially, it is a four-sided shape whose diagonals meet at the very centre of the creation of the gods. The design appears in pictographical manuscripts such as the Codex Tro-Cortesianus from the Postclassic Mayan period, and the Codex Fejérváry-Mayer (cat. 341), produced by artists in Puebla and Oaxaca states. In both, an illustration shows the four-sided shape, locating the patron gods of the four directions and the one who governs the centre of the universe (fig. 54).[14] An early image of the Aztec capital on the first folio of the Codex Mendoza (cat. 349; of indigenous authorship) tells how the city of Huitzilopochtli was founded. Again this shows the four cardinal divisions corresponding to the main districts. In the central area, where the magnificent Templo Mayor was later to be built, appears the sign awaited by the Aztecs on their sacred migration from Aztlan, an eagle on a prickly-pear cactus (see p. 14).

Tenochtitlan was based on the Aztecs' memories of the city they had left behind. Aztlan, an island city situated in an aquatic environment, probably a lake, was shown on the first pages of the Codex Boturini, known as the Tira de la Peregrinación (fig. 2), a text that chronicles the wanderings of the Aztecs before the foundation of their island capital. The island of Aztlan is pictured as having six houses, which were probably intended to represent the six original divisions of the town. The people of four of these divisions migrated, and two probably decided to stay where they were. Tenochtitlan was divided into four main districts in which the indigenous families lived: Teopan, Moyotlan, Atzacualco and Cuepopan (fig. 4). The central area of the island was occupied by the four-sided Templo Mayor complex, a sacred precinct which contained numerous buildings associated with religious rites, the largest of which was the great double pyramid. Tenochtitlan was connected to the mainland by three causeways which were centred on the ceremonial precinct. A detailed description of the Aztec capital was made by Hernán Cortés in his second report to the Spanish king Charles I.

Records describe the difficulties encountered by the Aztecs as they struggled to expand their new capital. We have a description of the indigenous city from the later period, when Tenochtitlan was at the height of its splendour. By then the island city covered a wide area which had grown through the creation of *chinampas*, artificial islands that served both as dwellings and as fields for farmers to grow their crops, as depicted in the so-called maguey-paper plan (fig. 71).[15]

THE MONUMENTAL SCULPTURES
The artistic creations that best define the Aztec world are its sculptures, whose style extended throughout the Central Highlands. The gigantic monoliths carved throughout the Late Postclassic period took their inspiration from Teotihuacan and Tula, where huge figures survived, such as the image of the water-goddess or the so-called atlantes (stone columns in human form that supported the roofs of temples; fig. 11).[16]

The colossal scale of the sculptures in Tenochtitlan reinforced the power of the Aztec gods and the strength of the natural elements that were thought to be governed by the creators of the universe. The devotion and the Messianic character of the Aztec people led them to sculpt

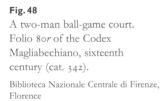

Fig. 48
A two-man ball-game court. Folio 8*or* of the Codex Magliabechiano, sixteenth century (cat. 342).

Biblioteca Nazionale Centrale di Firenze, Florence

monuments that represented the cosmos and to place themselves at the centre of creation.[17] Conspicuous among these monuments are the great Coatlicue (fig. 9) and Yolotlicue, which represent the earth goddess, sustainer of humanity and source of all life but also ruler of the ultimate destination of the dead. Both carvings show the symbols of life and death united. For its part, the Sun Stone (fig. 5) recounts the sequence of the cosmogonic suns, an eternal cycle of creation and destruction. The sequence speaks eloquently of the Aztecs' concept of time and was indeed the basis of their calendar.[18] The sculptural art of the Late Postclassic period is characterised by date-glyphs which are carved into the reliefs to mark historical and mythological events (fig. 50).[19]

Monuments dedicated to the solar cult that show Aztec military conquests alongside the sun's image were the greatest contribution made by the inhabitants of Tenochtitlan to Mesoamerican art. These monoliths give physical form to the religious ideology of the Aztecs, who followed the instructions of Huitzilopochtli and imposed their military might on the known universe. Indigenous chroniclers tell of the sacred obligation of each *tlatoani* (ruler), from Motecuhzoma Ilhuicamina onwards, to order the carving of these *temalácatl-cuauhxicalli*, which celebrated their military victories and those of their ancestors. The surviving sculptures include one ordered by Motecuhzoma Ilhuicamina (fig. 49), and that of his grandson Tizoc (fig. 6), which was known as the Sacrificial Stone for a long time because it was used in the Tlacaxipehualiztli ceremony, a springtime rite signifying renewal. The Sun Stone mentioned above is another example of this type of monument, but it is incomplete and is thought to have been made around the time of Axayacatl.

Monumental sculptures and those on a smaller scale were displayed during public celebrations in open spaces or on the altars of temples and palaces. Those with a human appearance – deities, priests or the people themselves – represent the inhabitants of the sacred universe created by the gods. Figures of plants and animals, both naturalistic and anthropomorphic, link the world of nature to the cosmic order of creation.

Clay sculptures, covered with plaster and garishly coloured, probably came from the coast of the Gulf of Mexico, where they were popular during Classic times.[20] Discoveries made at the site of the Templo Mayor have brought to light important pieces made of this fragile material, including works with great visual impact, such as the eagle men (cat. 228) and the two statues of Mictlantecuhtli (cat. 233), lord of the dead, that marked the entrances to the House of Eagles.[21]

THE MINOR ARTS

Tenochtitlan and its twin city and enemy Tlatelolco have yielded many archaeological objects which demonstrate that many differences in lifestyle existed between the commoners, or *macehualtin*, and the *pipiltin*, the nobility.

Humble peasants lived in individual family huts and had only the essentials: woven mats made from plant fibres, on which they worked, sat and slept, and diminutive images of deities and of temples where they were worshipped, made of clay and intended for family altars. The most abundant objects in their homes were ceramic vessels, mostly large, monochrome pots used to store liquids and grains, and containers used for daily cooking. Distinctive pieces from the Late Postclassic period include jugs, plates and grinding stones called *molcajetes*, which were used to prepare sauces and tend to be decorated with black geometric or naturalistic representations of plants and animals.

Life was very different for members of the Aztec nobility. The Spanish conquerors, who were accommodated with great courtesy by indigenous rulers, described the splendour of their reception with astonishment. Palaces contained vast, porticoed rooms arranged around the four sides of patios, representing the four-sided vision of the Aztec universe. Only one palace precinct of a ceremonial character remains from Tenochtitlan, within the complex of the Templo Mayor. Known as the House of Eagles, it is profusely decorated with wall paintings and sculptures.[22]

Fig. 49
Cuauhxicalli of Motecuhzoma Ilhuicamina, showing scenes of conquest. Late Postclassic. Basalt, height 76 cm, diameter 224 cm.

Museo Nacional de Antropología, Mexico City

Fig. 50
Teocalli of the Sacred War, commemorating the New Fire ceremony of 1507. Late Postclassic. Basalt, 123 × 92 × 99 cm. Date-glyphs appear on either side of the 'stairway' at the lower front.

Museo Nacional de Antropología, Mexico City

Fig. 51

A large feather headdress of the type worn by Aztec priests representing deities in the early sixteenth century. 450 quetzal feathers, gold appliqué and fibre net, 116 × 175 cm.

Museum für Völkerkunde, Vienna

In order to gauge the dimensions of Aztec palaces, we can compare them with the housing complexes unearthed in Teotihuacan, which must have been similar in many ways, or analyse the details of the palace of Netzahualcoyotl at Tetzcoco, reproduced in the Codex Quinatzin (Bibliothèque Nationale de France, Paris).

For decoration, the austerity of dwellings characterised by plain plastering was softened by murals or stone reliefs of sacred images or geometric motifs, particularly the rhythmic repetition of stepped fretwork known as *xicalcoliuhqui*. There was little furniture, apart from the seats or thrones used exclusively by the ruler. These were made of sculpted wood or woven reeds and covered with jaguar skins. In some areas, benches were placed against the walls. These were variously decorated and used for solemn meetings, such as the performance of specific rites for rulers and deities.

The pottery vessels used for rulers' banquets, which were also used to make sacred offerings and during the burial of high-ranking individuals, came mainly from the workshops of the Tetzcoco region. Highly polished red containers were the most popular during this period. For the purposes of trade, the nobility also ordered garish multicoloured ceramics from Cholula and the Mixtec region of Oaxaca.[23]

Various musical instruments were used on feast days, particularly vertical drums called *huehuetl*, made from tree-trunks and covered with jaguar skin (see cat. 156). Horizontal *teponaxtli* (cats 126, 157–58, 338), xylophones with a double tongue, were decorated with images related to the rites and ceremonies for which they were used. As an accompaniment to the drums and xylophones, the musicians played flutes, whistles and trumpets made from clay or sea shells. Rattles made of clay contained little stones to produce harmonious sounds. A characteristic feature of Aztec feasts was the *omexicahuaztli*, a special notched rasp made of a human femur or animal horn which produced unique musical sounds when scraped with a shell.[24]

Clothing was another expression of differences in lifestyle: commoners were limited to textiles made of cactus fibres, whereas members of the nobility wore cotton fabrics, dyed in bright colours and decorated with a multitude of naturalistic and geometrical designs, occasionally with feathers, gold or shell plaques and jade beads sewn or woven into them.[25] As well as social rank, clothing distinguished gender in Aztec society. Men covered their genitals with a *máxtlatl*, a long strip of cloth which passed between the legs and around the waist and was then knotted at the front and held by straps. The back and torso were covered by a *tílmatl*, a long cape generally knotted over one shoulder. Women wore a skirt called a *cúeitl*, simply a long piece of cloth wrapped around the body and held in place by a sash. The women of Tenochtitlan traditionally wore the *huipil*, a type of long shirt, while women in other regions of the Central Highlands and on the coast of the Gulf of Mexico wore the *quechquémitl*, a rhomboid cape-type garment that covered the torso, or simply wore nothing on the upper part of their bodies.

The nobility wore *cacli* (sandals) made of animal skins or woven plant fibres, while commoners went barefoot. Only rulers wore the *xicolli*, a type of highly decorated waistcoat, while warriors were identified by a triangular cloth worn like an apron. Like many Mesoamerican civilisations, the Aztecs liked to wear animal skins, particularly those of jaguars, and elaborate ornaments made from vividly coloured feathers. A rare survival is the so-called headdress of Motecuhzoma (fig. 51).[26]

The fabulous riches of the Aztec rulers – masks covered with turquoise mosaics (fig. 52), gold and silver jewellery, and jade and rock-crystal ornaments – complete this vision of art and culture in Tenochtitlan at the time of the European conquest. Objects scattered around collections in Mexico, Europe and the United States stand as silent witnesses to the greatness of the empire that succumbed to the conquest of Hernán Cortés and his army at the beginning of the sixteenth century.

Fig. 52
Mask of Quetzalcoatl, Late Postclassic. Turquoise, mother-of-pearl, jade, shell, 25 × 15 cm.

Museo Nazionale Preistorico-Etnografico 'L. Pigorini', Rome

Miguel León-Portilla

Fig. 53
A representation of the Aztec underworld. Folio *2r* of the Codex Ríos, *c.* 1570–95 (cat. 346).

Biblioteca Apostolica Vaticana, Vatican City

Monuments in stone, mural paintings, codices (books of paintings and glyphs), and the oral tradition of the ancient Mexicans are the conduits through which we can gain an understanding of their religious beliefs, ritual practices, world-view, history, and social, economic and political organisation. Although the Spanish conquest brought about the destruction of much material, some small consolation can be derived from the fact that, as a direct result of it, many new records came into being. Some of these were the fruit of enquiries carried out by missionary friars anxious to find out more about indigenous culture and thus identify the idolatries that they sought to suppress. Others were the product of the diligent efforts of surviving natives who were determined to preserve the memory of their past and the core of their culture. By studying both the surviving material remains, and, with their inevitable shortcomings, the Post-Conquest sources, an appreciation of Aztec codices, literature and philosophy can be pieced together.

Codices are one of the prime sources for the study of Aztec literature and philosophy. Some texts in Nahuatl from the native oral tradition are literary productions; others convey the doubts, reflections and wisdom of philosophers, or *tlamatinime*, 'those who know something'. By correlating these texts with the codices and the results of archaeological findings we can begin to glimpse some of the more refined aspects of the spiritual culture that flourished in ancient Mexico.

CODICES

Much discussion has centred upon the debate about whether at least one Pre-Hispanic Aztec codex survives. Three possible candidates – the Codex Borbonicus (fig. 57), the Matrícula de Tributos (fig. 37) and the Codex Boturini (fig. 2) – exist. Most interesting in the context of this essay is the Codex Borbonicus, which deals with many aspects of Aztec spiritual culture. Even if it is not Pre-Hispanic, it conveys indigenous concepts in accordance with ancient tradition.

Similar Aztec codices with parallel contents were produced after the Conquest. Among these the Ríos (cat. 346) and the Telleriano-Remensis (cat. 348) stand out. They include a *tonalamatl*, a book of the destinies of each day, a presentation of the feasts throughout the solar year, and a historical section which embraces a lengthy time-span. In addition, the Ríos contains a sort of cosmological treatise. Five other codices, which, if not properly Aztec, are certainly closely related to that culture and are Pre-Hispanic in origin, have survived: the Borgia and the Vaticanus B (Biblioteca Apostolica Vaticana, Vatican City), the Cospi (cat. 340), the Laud (Bodleian Library, Oxford) and the Fejérváry-Mayer (cat. 341).

The cosmological ideas of Aztec *tlamatinime* can be studied in depictions such as those on the Aztec Sun Stone (fig. 5) and in the Ríos. The cosmic eras which preceded the present – that of the sun which was brought into being on the day known as Nahui Ollin ('4-movement') – are represented in these.[1] Besides these representations

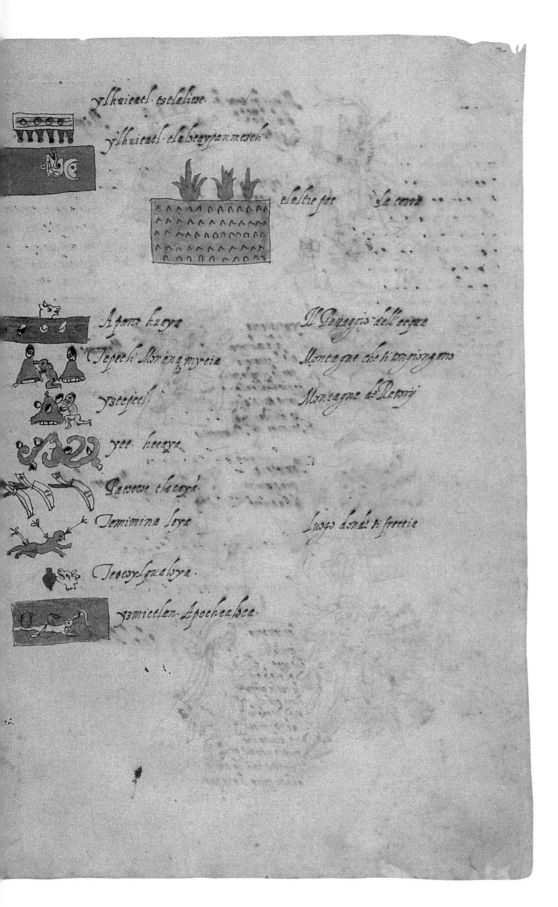

of cosmic time, images of both horizontal and vertical cosmic space appear in the codices Fejérváry-Mayer and Ríos.

The Ríos depicts the thirteen planes of the heavens, the surface of the earth and the nine planes of the underworld (fig. 53).[2] In the uppermost plane, Ometeotl, the supreme god of duality, presides over the world. In a parallel role, Xiuhtecuhtli, god of fire and time, is represented at the centre of the horizontal image of the universe. A text in Nahuatl, which belongs to a *huehuehtlahtolli*, or 'ancient word', obtained by Friar Bernardino de Sahagún from Aztec elders, tells us that Xiuhtecuhtli is none other than the father and mother of the gods, the ultimate He-She, the dual-god Ometeotl, who resides in the navel of the earth.[3] Aztec beliefs concerning the afterlife are depicted in the nine planes of the underworld. Texts in Nahuatl, testimonies of the ancient oral tradition, explain in detail the fate that awaits those going to Mictlan, the region of the dead.[4]

On the first page of the Codex Fejérváry-Mayer (fig. 54) we see a horizontal image of the world, with the five great cosmic sections: east, north, west, south and centre. Each has its own colour, gods, cosmic bird and tree.[5] As if to confirm the idea that Mesoamericans were deeply concerned with knowing their destinies, both collective and individual, two counts of the destinies of each day (*tonalpohualli*) appear in the same image of horizontal cosmic space, permeating everything that exists. Time is a recurrent theme in both literary and philosophical texts.

Several Aztec codices of the type known as *xiuhamatl*, or 'papers of the years' (among them the Codex Azcatitlan [cat. 355], the Codex Mexicanus [Bibliothèque Nationale de France, Paris] and the Codex Aubin [cat. 354]), record happenings, many of which were considered manifestations of the *tonalli*, or destinies, of individuals and peoples in general. Some expressions of the oral tradition in Nahuatl are commentaries on the scenes depicted in the paintings. A dramatic example of this occurs in the Florentine Codex (cat. 344), in which anguished words concerning the omens which anticipated the arrival of the Spaniards were recorded by the assistants of Friar Bernardino de Sahagún.

LITERATURE

The survival of ancient indigenous Aztec literature is due to the process of collaboration that took place between Spanish friars and native Americans. Sometimes working together and sometimes independently, they drew on the oral tradition and

Fig. 54

The Aztec world-view. Page 1
of the Codex Fejérváry-Mayer,
before 1521 (cat. 341).

National Museums and Galleries
on Merseyside (Liverpool Museum)

the contents of books of paintings and characters as their ultimate sources. The native elders agreed, after lengthy deliberations, to communicate to the friars what they knew of their past and culture, and showed them codices made of *amate*-tree bark, deerskin or cotton, with the proviso that these were to remain in their possession. Following the contents of the codices, as they did in their *calmecac* (priestly schools), the elders recited commentaries on the meanings of paintings and glyphs. Young Aztecs who had mastered the European alphabet transcribed the elders' commentaries or readings. As early as 1531, Friar Andrés de Olmos was assisted by native elders knowledgeable about their antiquities and young scribes who had been their disciples; Friar Bernardino de Sahagún received the same assistance from 1545 to 1565.

Similar procedures were also followed, but independently, by surviving elders and sages interested in the preservation of their culture. An example of this is the alphabetic transcript of the Nahuatl text known as the 'Legend of the Suns', an account of the cosmogonies and other portentous happenings related to the Aztec past. In the 'Legend', written in 1558, the presence of phrases such as 'here is', 'here we see' and 'this follows' indicates that the scribe had a codex before him from which text was being extracted.[6]

Although the Aztecs had not developed an alphabetic form of writing, some of their compositions, drawing on both oral traditions and manuscript codices, are true works of literature. In these compositions, as in other cultural productions, the inspiration of the *toltecayotl* – summing up the great achievement of the Toltecs under the wise guidance of the culture-hero Quetzalcoatl – is manifest, and these works show great dexterity. Such is the case with Aztec temples and palaces, paintings, sculptures and all sorts of jewels. Archaeology gives ample testimony to this. The uncovered remains of mural paintings and fine sculptures in stone and clay from the Aztec Templo Mayor in Tenochtitlan reveal something of its former splendour. For their part, the pages of the Codex Borbonicus and other indigenous manuscripts speak eloquently of the adroitness of the *tlacuiloque* (painter-scribes) who produced them. The same can be said about their literature. Extant compositions in the Nahuatl language compare very favourably with those preserved from Classic cultures of antiquity, as a few examples with a commentary will demonstrate.

Sacred hymns, epic and lyric poetry, chronicles, history and other forms of prose are the main genres. Hymns are known to have been intoned in honour of the gods at great religious ceremonies. Some were in the form of entreaty to Tlaloc, the god of rain; Centeotl and Chicomecoatl, gods of maize; Huitzilopochtli, a solar deity and god of war; and to several goddesses. This is the hymn to Huitzilopochtli, the patron god of the Aztecs:

Huitzilopochtli, the young warrior,
he who acts above, moving along his way.

'Not in vain did I take the raiment of yellow plumage,
for it is I who makes the sun appear.'

Portentous one, who inhabits the region of clouds,
you have but one foot!
Inhabiter of the cold region of wings,
you have opened your hand!

Near the wall of the region that burns,
feathers come forth.
The Sun spreads out,
there is a war cry.
My god is called Protector of Men.
Oh, now he advances, comes well adorned with paper,
he who inhabits the region that burns,
in the dust, in the dust, he gyrates.

Our enemies are those of Amantla;
come adhere to us!
War is made with combat,
come adhere to us!

Our enemies are those of Pipiltlan:
come adhere to us!
War is made with combat,
come adhere to us![7]

The hymn to the young warrior was probably intoned in the form of a dialogue. A singer begins by referring to Huitzilopochtli, the sun which follows its path in the heavens. The god answers in the voice of a chorus saying that he is the one who has made the sun appear. Again, the singer exalts the magnificence of the one who inhabits the clouds. The last part, again chanted by the chorus, praises the god and ends with warlike exclamations. Stylistically, repeated phrases and numerous metaphors enhance the hymn's effect.

Examples of epic poetry can be identified in compositions that recall the beginnings and violent destructions of the cosmic eras; the cycle of the culture-hero Quetzalcoatl; and the birth of Huitzilopochtli. Poems of great force, they bring forth key concepts of the Aztec world-view. In the one which deals with Huitzilopochtli's birth, the key was found to the meaning of the great bas-relief unearthed in the Templo Mayor (fig. 10). The goddess Coyolxauhqui, Huitzilopochtli's sister, was beheaded by him; her body, as the poem tells, fell to the bottom of the Snake Mountain which much later was transformed into the Templo Mayor.

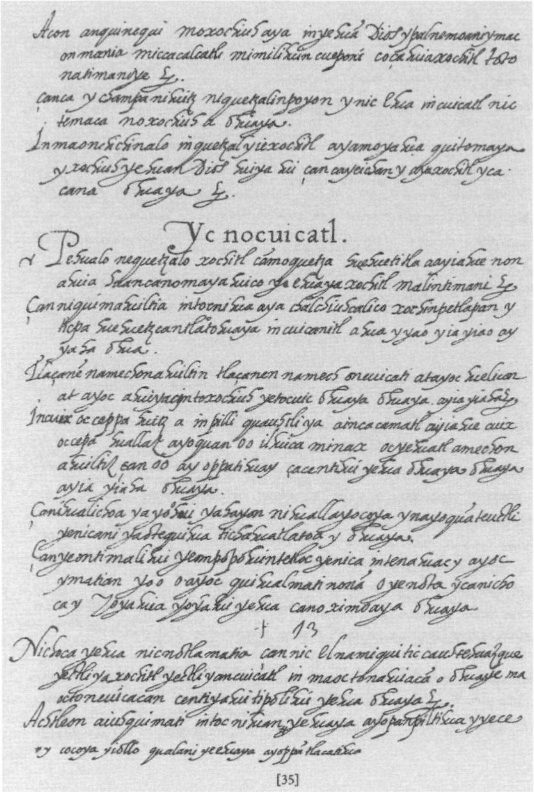

Lyric poetry, intoned at feasts with music and dance, is the best-preserved literary genre. Among its most common stylistic characteristics, the repetition of ideas and expression of sentiments stand out. A frequently appearing device consists of uniting two words which complement each other, either because they are synonyms or because they metaphorically evoke a third idea: 'flower and song' mean poetry, art and symbolism; 'arrow and shield' stand for war; 'seat and mat' suggest authority and power; and 'skirt and blouse' evoke woman in her sexual aspect.

Lyric compositions embraced a number of subgenres known as *xochicuicatl*, flowery chants; *xopancuicatl*, songs of springtime; *yaocuicatl*, songs of war; and *icnocuicatl*, songs of orphanhood and vehicles for philosophical reflection. The following is an example of a *xochicuicatl*:

At last my heart knows it,
I hear a song.
I contemplate a flower,
would they will not wither! [8]

A *xopancuicatl*, a song of the springtime composed by Tecayehuatzin, ruler of Huexotzingo by the end of the fifteenth century, exalts above all the value of friendship on earth:

Now, oh, friends,
listen to the words of a dream,
each spring brings us life,
the golden corn refreshes us,
the pink corn becomes a necklace.
At last we know,
the hearts of our friends are true! [9]

Songs of war, *yaocuicatl*, abound, confirming the belligerent inclinations of the Aztec nation:

Do not fear, my heart!
In the midst of the plain
my heart craves death
by the obsidian edge.
Only this my heart craves:
death in war. [10]

Examples of *icnocuicatl*, songs of orphanhood, appear below in a discussion of Aztec philosophy.

Chronicles, historical accounts and legends also make up a part of ancient Mexican literature. Most of these compositions have a parallel in the *xiuhamatl*, 'books of years' or pictoglyphic annals. Numerous examples exist of this genre. Among them the Historia Tolteca-Chichimeca (cat. 345), accompanied by some paintings and glyphs, stands out. Covering a long period, this book describes

Fig. 55

An *icnocuicatl*, or poem of orphanhood. Folio 35r of the Cantares Mexicanos, transcribed in the sixteenth century.

From a facsimile edition, 1994, published by the Universidad Nacional Autónoma de México, Mexico City

the events that followed the collapse of the Toltec metropolis until several decades after the arrival of the Spaniards. [11]

Other manuscripts of historical interest include the Annals of Cuauhtitlan and those of the cities of Tlatelolco, Tecamachalco, Puebla-Tlaxcala and Quecholac. The Codex Aubin, for its part, was produced by a painter-scribe who placed images next to one another, accompanied by the glyphs of the corresponding years and an explanatory text in Nahuatl. In most of these manuscripts, accounts exist of how the Aztecs viewed the Spanish invasion of their land, and the drama of the conquest. Particular mention should be made of the Nahuatl texts of the Florentine Codex and of the Codex Tlatelolco (Museo Nacional de Antropología, Mexico City), which give extensive accounts from the viewpoint of the vanquished.

The existence of *xiuhamatl*, such as the Codex Azcatitlan (cat. 355), the Codex Tlatelolco, the Codex Mexicanus and others, permits an approach to the way in which books of years were conceived and produced. All in all, notwithstanding the losses that followed the conquest, surviving Aztec historical manuscripts represent a rich corpus.

Other texts in prose, such as *huehuehtlahtolli*, testimonies of the ancient word, exist. Expressed in the form of discourses and long prayers, these cover a variety of subjects. Friar Bernardino de Sahagún transcribed forty, describing their contents as compositions in which the Aztecs 'displayed their rhetoric and moral philosophy'. [12] We will turn our attention to these next.

PHILOSOPHY

Some scholars maintain that to speak of an Aztec philosophy is to exaggerate greatly. Nevertheless, texts related to the problems of human life do exist, and they reveal a restlessness of spirit. It is true that such texts were transcribed after the Conquest, but independent native sources exist which concur with them.

Some collections of poems, songs and discourses in Nahuatl have been preserved. Strange as it may appear to modern people used to encountering philosophy as a solitary exposition in written form, the questions, doubts and assertions of *tlamatinime* regarding humanity, the world and the gods were often expressed in public ceremonies in a sort of open-air philosophical discourse. Examples of this are provided by several *icnocuicatl* and the *huehuehtlahtolli* (fig. 56). A relation can be perceived in them with the contents of some *tonalamatl*, which display a concern for human destiny (fig. 57).

Netzahualcoyotl (1402–72; fig. 35), a famous poet and sage, expressed a keen awareness of the change and destruction wrought by time. The Nahuatl word for time is *cahuitl*, 'that which leaves us'. Everything on earth appears and in a brief while disappears:

I, Netzahualcoyotl, ask this:
is it true that one lives on the earth?
What is it that has roots here?
Not forever on earth,
only a brief while here.
Although it were jade,
it will be broken;
although it were turquoise,
it will be shattered
as if it were just quetzal feathers.
Not forever on earth,
only a brief while here.[13]

The assertion about the evanescence of all things terrestrial is repeated many times in the texts. As we have seen, expressions of this concern were often heard at feasts. There, *icnocuicatl* (fig. 55), songs of orphanhood, were intoned in the open air, accompanied by the music of flutes and drums:

One day we must go,
one night we will descend
into the region of mystery.
Here we only come to know ourselves;
only in passing are we on earth.[14]

As if to compensate for the sadness that the idea of our inescapable end provokes, the song continues with an invitation that would touch the hearts of participants in the feast:

Let us spend our lives
in peace and pleasure.
Come, let us enjoy ourselves!
This is not for us, wrath,
the earth is vast indeed!
Would that one could live forever,
that we were not to die![15]

Again, mention should be made of the *tonalpohualli*, the count of the destinies of each day.

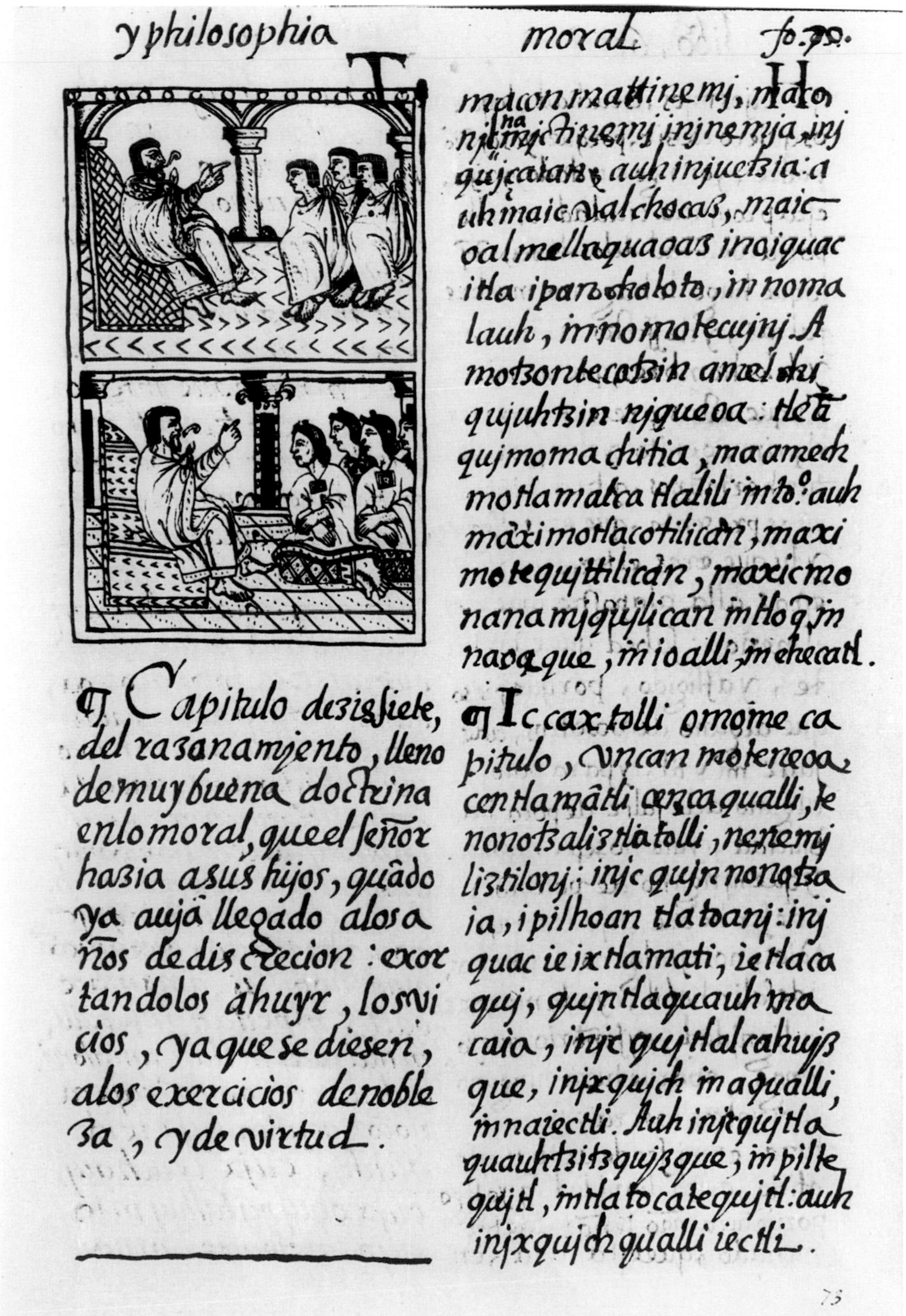

Fig. 56

A *huehuehtlahtolli* in which an Aztec father admonishes his sons and daughters. Vol. 2, folio 73r, of the Florentine Codex, 1575–77 (cat. 344).

Biblioteca Medicea Laurenziana, Florence

Sages believed that it was a means, if not to escape transience and death, at least to foresee and interpret the destinies built into all the segments of time. Although the *tonalpohualli* could not allay fears and anxieties about the human condition, it afforded the possibility of divining the most suitable response to the complex omens, good or bad, converging at given moments and places in the world. We should recall at this point the horizontal image of the world in the Codex Fejérváry-Mayer (fig. 54) where the development of two counts of the destinies of each day permeates whatever exists in the four quadrants and the centre of the earth.

The author of a *huehuehtlahtolli* puts these words into the mouth of an Aztec father addressing his daughter about her destiny on earth:

Here you are, my little girl, my necklace of precious stones, my plumage. You are my blood, my colour, my image [...] Here on earth is the place of much wailing, the place where our strength is worn out, where we are well-acquainted with bitterness and discouragement. A wind blows, sharp as obsidian it slides over us. They say that we are burned by the force of the sun and wind. This in the place where one almost perishes of thirst and hunger. This is the way here on earth [...]

But the elders have also said: 'So that we should not go always moaning, that we should not be filled with sadness, the one who is near and close has given us laughter, sleep, food, our strength and fortitude and also the act by which we propagate.'

All this sweetens life on earth so that we are not always moaning. But even though it be like this, though it be true that there is only suffering, and this were the way things are on earth, even so, should we always be afraid? Should we always be fearful? Must we live weeping?[16]

These courageous words recognise that not only the awareness of transience and death afflicts human beings but also that life itself, with its 'bitterness' and 'much wailing', is a challenge. Besides expressions like these, some texts reflect the doubts of the sages on other crucial subjects. One text questions the truth of anything seen or spoken on earth. Addressing himself to the supreme dual god Ometeotl, also known as Ipalnemohuani, the 'giver of life', and Tloque Nahuaque, 'the one who is near and close', a sage asks:

Do we speak true words here, giver of life? We merely dream, we only rise from a dream. All is like a dream. No one speaks here of truth.[17]

Singing at a feast, a dancer intones the deep reflection of a sage:

Does man possess any truth? If not, our song is no longer true. Is anything stable and lasting? What reaches its aim?[18]

In a social and political context in which religious beliefs were firmly established, we might not expect utterances of doubt about the ultimate realities. Nevertheless there were questions along these lines: if Ometeotl really exists, how is it possible to speak the truth about him? Is it possible to discover a path to approach him?

Where shall I go? Oh, where shall I go? The path of the god of duality Is your home in the place of the dead? In the interior of the heavens? Or only here on earth is the abode of the dead?[19]

Questions like these, which imply some distrust of established beliefs, resemble those put forward at different times and places by persons known as philosophers. In ancient Mexico those who posed them were called *tlamatinime*, 'those who know something'.

Fig. 57
Page 4 of the Codex Borbonicus, a page from the *tonalamatl*, depicting the water-goddess Chalchiuhtlicue, sixteenth century.

Bibliothèque de l'Assemblée Nationale Française, Paris

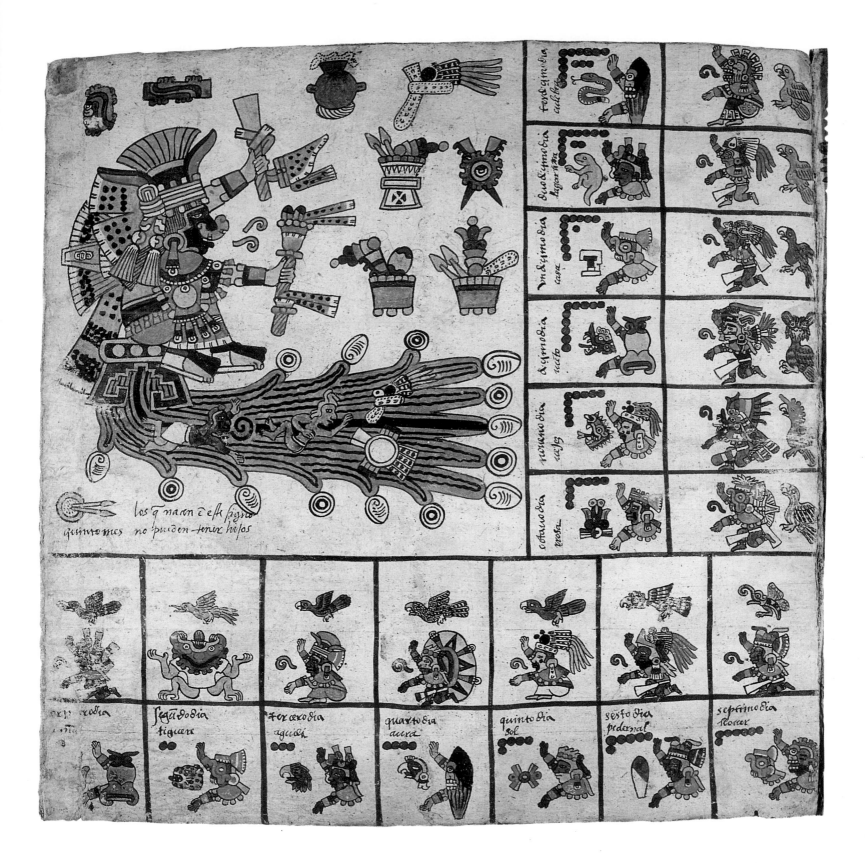

EARLY CONTACT

In 1500 the empire of the Aztecs, or, as we are learning to call them, the Mexica, constituted the paramount power in what is now known as Mesoamerica.[1] Their beautiful capital, Tenochtitlan, dominated the Basin of Mexico. True, to the west, the monarchs of Michoacán had, because of their use of copper weapons, been able to put a rude end to the Mexica's expansion. In the temperate land to the east of the volcano Popocatepetl, the city-state of Tlaxcala was an enclave whose inhabitants the rulers of Tenochtitlan alternately teased and fought. In the east and the south, the declining Maya principalities, like several polities in central America, remained independent but traded with the Mexica. The Mexica held sway over a large number of tributaries, whose contributions were skilfully and interestingly recorded for the Spanish in the Codex Mendoza (cat. 349).

The Mexica believed, as their ruler Motecuhzoma Xocoyotzin (in the past often Europeanised as 'Montezuma') is reported to have said, that they were the 'masters of the world'.[2] But they did not concern themselves much with what lay beyond the wild tribes whom they called the Chichimeca in the north, and the Maya in the south, although their merchants certainly knew that beyond the Chichimeca turquoise could be obtained for use in mosaic such as that so wonderfully represented in the Mexican room at the British Museum, London. South of the Maya lived peoples who traded in jade and, further on,

in emeralds and gold, which some of the Mexica's tributaries learned to work with incomparable skill. From both north and south, too, slaves were obtained by the rulers of Tenochtitlan.

Equally, the Mexica had no interest in what happened beyond the Eastern Sea, which we now think of as the Gulf of Mexico, though legend told that the intellectual and reforming god Quetzalcoatl (fig. 58) had vanished there. Cuba is only 125 miles from Yucatan, but the currents between the two are strong. Some believe that the long, Mexican-style drums found in Cuba derive from some kind of commerce with Mexico, but it is more likely that their presence can be explained by a canoe shipwreck. Later there were rumours in Cuba of trading connections with the 'north-west', but these did not amount to much. On the other hand, the Western Sea, or the Southern Sea (as the Spaniards at first called the Pacific), seemed to the Mexica to mark the end of the world.

From about 1500 onwards, strange rumours came to Tenochtitlan from the east. In 1502, for example, some indigenous merchants, perhaps Jicaques or Payas, met Columbus, then on his fourth voyage, somewhere off the islands now called the Bay Islands in the Gulf of Honduras; and presumably descriptions of bearded Europeans were carried back to the Maya authorities as they were to the ruler of the Mexica in Tenochtitlan. Columbus is said to have thought that he had discovered a 'land called Maya'.[3] Then, in 1508, two master sailors from Seville, Vicente

Fig. 58
The god Quetzalcoatl in human–animal form, probably fifteenth century. Red porphyry, 44 × 25 × 23 cm.

Musée du Louvre, Paris

Yáñez Pinzón, who had been captain of the carabel *Pinta* on Columbus's first voyage, and Juan Díaz de Solís, who was later to discover the River Plate, seem to have made landfall in Yucatan. They found nothing interesting, but possibly their journey led to the depiction by a Mexican merchant about that time of what looked like three temples floating in the sea on large canoes. The sketch was sent up to Tenochtitlan, where Motecuhzoma consulted both advisers and priests.[4] A little later a trunk was washed up on the Gulf of Mexico near Xicallanco, a Mexica trading outpost near what is now Campeche. Inside were several suits of European clothes, some jewels and a sword. No one there had ever seen such things before. Whose possessions were these? Motecuhzoma is said to have divided the trunk's contents with his cousins the kings of Tetzcoco and Tacuba.

A Spanish settlement was established in 1510 at Darién in Panama, at first directed by Vasco Núñez de Balboa, the first European to see the Pacific, and afterwards by Pedrarias Dávila. Darién was the first Spanish colony in the mainland of the New World. The conquistadors' brutalities under the leadership of Pedrarias would have made it likely that some rumour of what was happening reached the Mexica. Indeed, a magician in Tenochtitlan, later known to the Spaniards as Martín Ocelotl, predicted the arrival of 'men with beards coming to this land'.[5]

In 1511 Diego de Nicuesa, a merchant-explorer sailing from Darién to Santo Domingo, was wrecked off Yucatan. Several Spanish sailors survived, and two of these, Gonzalo Guerrero and Jerónimo de Aguilar, were for some years Maya prisoners, the former openly siding with his captors (the latter would later be a useful interpreter to Hernán Cortés).

Another Spanish landing probably took place in 1513, when Juan Ponce de León stopped in Yucatan on his return from an unsuccessful journey to Florida on a quest to find the Fountain of Eternal Youth. Several Maya texts seem to speak of that landing.[6] In 1515 another curious contact between Spain and the Mesoamerican world occurred: a judge named Corrales in the Spanish colony in Darién reported that he had met a 'refugee from the interior provinces of the West'. This man had observed the judge reading a document and asked, 'You too have books? You also understand the signs by which you talk to the absent?'.[7] Although Mexican painted books were very different to their European counterparts they had the same purpose.

The last years of old Mexico were full of legends and stories of comets, predictions and

ACALEI. YCUITLATLATI. CAPITA.

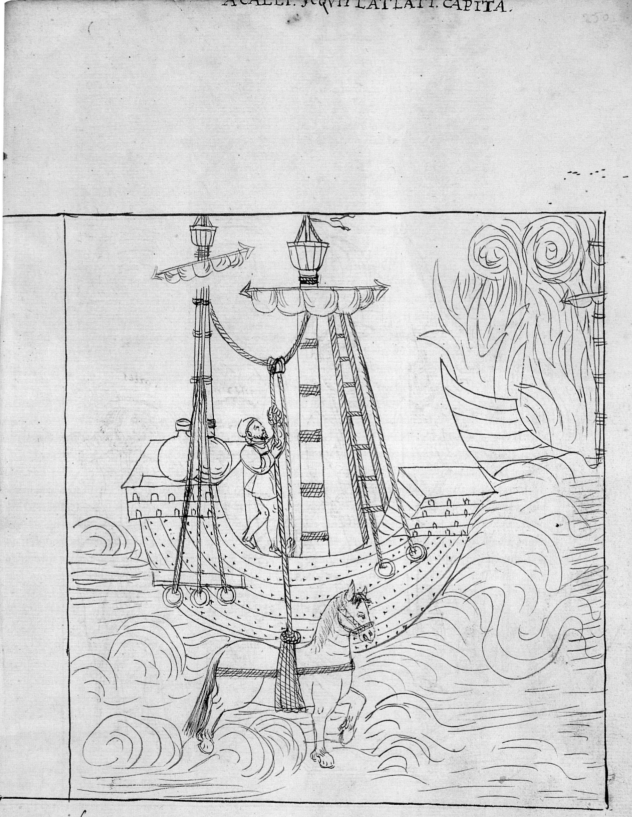

La llegada de Cortes al puerto de Cempuala de la nueua España, con su
armada y gente, y quando hiso barrenar los nauios y hechar los a fondo /

Fig. 62

A horse is lowered into the waves from a Spanish ship moored off the coast of the Gulf of Mexico. Folio 250r of Diego Muñoz Camargo's *Descripción de la ciudad y provincia de Tlaxcala...*, 1581–84 (cat. 356).

MS Hunter 242, Special Collections Department, Glasgow University Library

The Spaniards established a base near Veracruz, in defiance of the wishes of Diego Velázquez, Governor of Cuba. There Cortés left about a hundred of his men, while he led the rest up to Tenochtitlan. The Mexica seem to have confused him with the lost god Quetzalcoatl; or perhaps it suited some in Motecuhzoma's court to argue that this was the case. Quetzalcoatl, god of learning and the wind, was supposed to have been opposed to human sacrifice. It appears that Motecuhzoma accorded him special devotion. The god was said to have vanished several hundred years before in the Eastern Sea, the Gulf of Mexico, but was expected to return. As if to confirm this Mexica belief, Cortés's landfall was made at exactly the location of Quetzalcoatl's departure and in a year '1-reed', the prophesied year of the god's return. Cortés and his army were received as guests by Motecuhzoma, who was soon seized and held captive in the lodgings that had been allocated to the Spaniards. For a time, Motecuhzoma continued to rule Mexico, while Cortés ruled Motecuhzoma; a style of rule which, ironically, echoed in some ways that of the Mexica towards their tributaries.

This period came to an end in April 1520 when about a thousand Spaniards, led by a veteran conquistador, Pánfilo de Narváez, landed at Veracruz determined to capture or kill Cortés and restore the authority of the Governor of Cuba. Cortés left his deputy Pedro de Alvarado, who had been with Grijalva in 1518, in Tenochtitlan and set off for the coast, where he surprised his fellow Spaniards in a night attack. Then he returned to Tenochtitlan, his forces enlarged by some newcomers who had switched their allegiance. In the meantime the rash Alvarado, fearing an attack, had, in what modern strategists would term a pre-emptive strike, massacred much of the Mexican

nobility and was being besieged. Cortés sought to raise the siege but could not do so and decided, with Alvarado, to leave the city by night. They were surprised and in a fierce battle on the city's causeways on the night of 30 July 1520, the so-called 'Noche Triste', lost a great many men. The Spaniards regrouped in the town of Tacuba and were then able to recover in the city-state of Tlaxcala where the indigenous enemies of the Mexica welcomed and succoured them, in return for a treaty which gave them authority in the Basin of Mexico. Tlaxcala was the leading city-state to have successfully resisted incorporation into the Mexican empire. Other peoples had been conquered and forced into resentful submission, and some of these saw the Spaniards' arrival as a heaven-sent opportunity to recover their independence, but the Tlaxcalans viewed the Spaniards as mercenaries from whose help they might benefit, and drove a hard bargain with Cortés in return for their support.

Cortés regrouped, and devoted several months to the brutal conquest of minor cities of the Mexican empire to the east of the capital. Next, his army, much enhanced both by the help of indigenous allies and by new Spanish volunteers from Santo Domingo, set about besieging Tenochtitlan. Cortés was able to attack Tenochtitlan from its lake (fig. 63) by commissioning twelve brigantines from Martín López which were built at Tlaxcala and then carried over the hills in separate pieces to be assembled on Lake Tetzcoco, an astonishing feat.

The siege, a long and bloody battle, brought many setbacks for both sides. It led to the destruction of the city and the death from starvation of many Mexica. Motecuhzoma had been killed, probably by a stone thrown by one of his own people, in June 1520 (the story that

Fig. 63

The Spaniards approach the coast of Mexico. Folio 197 of the Codex Durán, 1579–81 (cat. 343).

Biblioteca Nacional, Madrid

EXHIBITIONS AND COLLECTORS
OF PRE-HISPANIC MEXICAN ARTEFACTS IN BRITAIN

Adrian Locke

British involvement with, and interest in, the archaeology of Pre-Hispanic Mexico spans more than four hundred years. In Europe the collecting of artefacts other than books began in earnest during the sixteenth century with the so-called 'cabinets of curiosities' assembled by individuals who sought to understand better the world in which they lived. Hernán Cortés sent several objects back to Spain in the first shipment from Mexico in 1519 but these were subject to the aesthetics of the time; as Anthony A. Shelton explains, 'the New World's material products that most attracted the Spaniards were items that closely corresponded with the canons of taste they had inherited from medieval thought'.[1] Although much was lost through ignorance or greed in those early days of collecting, significant numbers of objects exist in museum collections outside Mexico, especially in Europe and the United States of America. Early collections, however, such as that formed by Archduke Ferdinand II of Tyrol (1529–1595) and now housed at the Museum für Völkerkunde in Vienna, are exceptional: most collections of Mexican artefacts date from the nineteenth century.

In general terms the English have been interested in Mexico since its discovery in the early part of the sixteenth century and its subsequent annexation by the Spanish crown. The apparent wealth of the Spanish colonies in the Americas generated great curiosity and fuelled economic rivalries as European nation states competed in the race for betterment. Spain jealously guarded her richest colonies of Mexico, then known as Nueva España (New Spain), and Peru, refusing to permit any country to trade with her American colonies or to allow non-Spaniards to enter or travel within them. There was an enormous desire to understand, and exploit, economic opportunities in Mexico, in the light of the large shipments of gold and silver that were regularly sent back across the Atlantic (and intercepted by pirates from, among other countries, England, France and the Netherlands) and the arrival of such previously unknown natural products as tobacco, potatoes, tomatoes, maize and chocolate. The mineral and natural wealth of the Americas was all too evident.

The Americas in general continued to pose a serious intellectual question to the Europeans' world-view, since the continent was not mentioned in the Bible and was absent from all medieval maps.[2] Despite the immediate wealth provided by objects made of precious metals, the codices, often referred to as 'painted books', attracted great interest in England because, remarkably, they were recognised early on as literary texts by three seventeenth-century collectors: William Laud (1573–1645, Archbishop of Canterbury under Charles I), Sir Thomas Bodley (1545–1613, a scholar and diplomat), and John Selden (1584–1654, a jurist and scholar).[3] Indeed the earliest-known English connection with these books was in 1588 when the geographer Richard Hakluyt (c. 1552–1616) acquired the Codex Mendoza (cat. 349) from André Thevet

Fig. 65
The title page of the Codex Mendoza (see p. 358), reproduced as a woodcut in Hakluyt's *Haklvytvs Posthvmvs; or Pvrchas his Pilgrimes*, London, 1624.

British Library, London

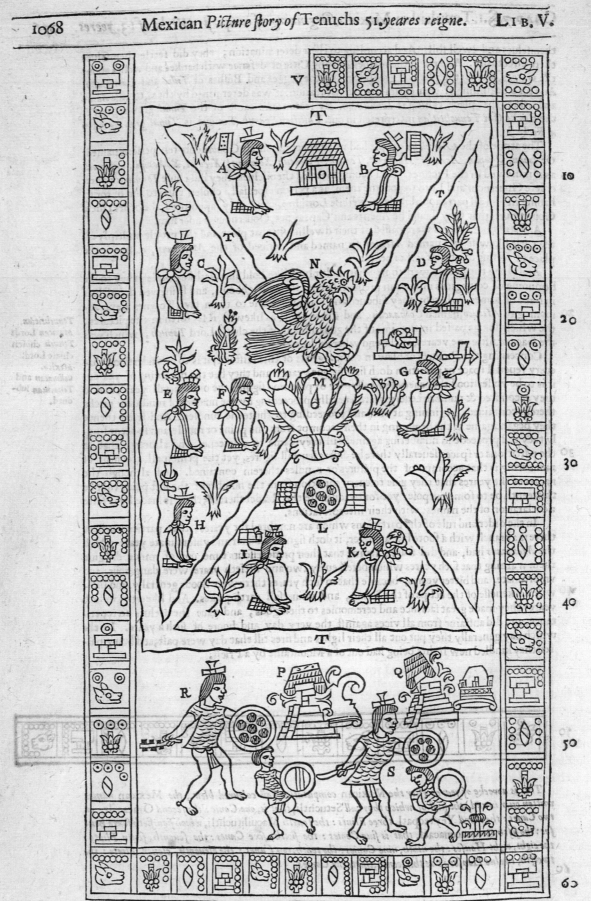

This Picture presents the number of 51. yeares: that is, the time of Tenuchs reigne: in this wheele or square (which, as all the like representing yeares, are in the originall picture coloured blew.) The pictures of men signifie the ten Lords or Gouernours before mentioned; their names are inscribed in the originall pictures, which here we haue by the letters annexed directly to a following glosse. A. Acacitli. B Quapan. C Ocelopan. D Aguexotl. E Tecineuh. F Tenuch. G Xominitl. H Xocoyol. I Xiuhcaqui.

Thomas Athol Joyce, the British Museum's Keeper of Ethnography. This was followed in 1947 by 'Art of Ancient America' organised at the Berkeley Galleries by Irwin Bullock and G. H. S. Bushnell (Curator of the Museum of Archaeology and Ethnography at the University of Cambridge). Catalogues were produced for both exhibitions. In the meantime, attention was drawn to the celebrated collection of originals and casts made by Maudslay on his numerous expeditions to Mexico and Central America. Maudslay's collection, which included the Yaxchilan lintels now at the British Museum, reflects his particular interest in the Maya. His work was included in the *Biologia Centrali-Americana*.[23]

From 4 March to 3 May 1953 the Tate Gallery in London hosted the monumental 'Exhibition of Mexican Art from Pre-Columbian Times to the Present Day'. With some thirteen hundred objects divided into three principal sections (ancient, colonial and republican), this was the largest exhibition of its kind mounted to date in Great Britain (fig. 69).[24] The exhibition, previously displayed in Paris and at the Statens Etnografiska Museum, Stockholm, was nearly not held in London as had been arranged. On 3 January 1953 the London press, following an official announcement made the previous day, reported that the exhibition had been cancelled without reason by the Mexican government despite the

success it had already generated. The American leg of the tour, scheduled for the Metropolitan Museum of Art in New York, was also withdrawn. Then, in what was reported as a gesture of friendship to Great Britain, President Adolfo Ruiz Cortines of Mexico revoked the decision and agreed to hold the exhibition as arranged.[25]

In a letter to Sir John Rothenstein, Director and Keeper of the Tate Gallery, Susana Gamboa, General Secretary of the Mexican Exhibition, testified to the huge popularity of the show in Stockholm, where it had attracted 182,000 paying visitors who bought 32,000 copies of the catalogue.[26] Despite the complex logistics of bringing all the works to London, and a River Thames flood warning which delayed the opening, the exhibition was a huge success. It was widely reported in the press throughout the country where it attracted much attention and received numerous reviews. There was a marked tendency among the reporters to emphasise the concept of sacrifice and the headlines were often shocking. Nevertheless reports reveal the degree of fascination exerted on the postwar British public by the Mexican culture on display. The press described 'Mexican Art' as 'the most ghastly, horrifying and exciting exhibition London has ever seen',[27] 'one of the most extraordinary exhibitions ever seen in London',[28] and 'the most gripping, emotional experience ever offered the inhabitants of the Old World by the New'.[29] On 4 March 1953 the *Evening Standard* captured the excitement generated by the exhibition in reporting the huge turn-out of nearly a thousand visitors for a private view organised by the Contemporary Arts Society, despite thick fog.

'Mexican Art', at the time the largest exhibition ever mounted by the Arts Council of Great Britain, was a great success. The Tate Gallery was open seven days a week with late openings every weekday until 9 pm, including a special reduced admission fee after 6 pm, to satisfy demand. The exhibition, originally intended to close on 26 April, was extended for a week. On 4 May the *Manchester Guardian* reported that 'Mexican Art' had received a total of 121,520 visitors.[30] The catalogue reveals that there were several non-Mexican lenders to the exhibition, such as the British Museum, Mr Robert Woods Bliss (whose collection is now at Dumbarton Oaks, Washington DC), the Philadelphia Museum of Art and the Art Institute of Chicago. 'An Exhibition of Pre-Columbian Art' (1958) at Gimpel Fils reveals a continuing interest in the subject in London.

Since 'Mexican Art', a number of smaller exhibitions in Britain have included Mexican

Fig. 68
A newspaper advertisement announces the exhibition of two 'Aztecs' from Ixamaya at the Egyptian Hall, Piccadilly, in 1853.

Guildhall Library, Corporation of London

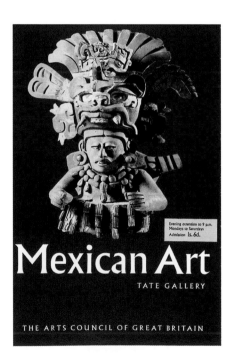

Fig. 69
The poster for the Tate Gallery's 'Exhibition of Mexican Art from Pre-Columbian Times to the Present Day', 1953.

Tate Archive, London

archaeological objects, although not always exclusively. At the centre of these exhibitions was the Museum of Mankind in Burlington Gardens, which until recently housed the ethnographic collections of the British Museum. The inauguration of the Mexican Gallery at the British Museum in 1994 signalled a decision to unite all of the museum's ethnography collections at its Bloomsbury site.[31] The project was a collaboration between the Consejo Nacional para la Cultura y las Artes (CNCA), the Instituto Nacional de Antropología e Historia (INAH) and the British Museum. The gallery, designed by the Mexican architect Teodoro González de León, provides a permanent exhibition space for the museum's Mexican artefacts, demonstrating their importance within the whole collection. Exhibitions at the Museum of Mankind included 'Maya Sculpture and Pottery from Mexico: The Manuel Barbachano Ponce Collection' (1971),[32] 'The British and the Maya' (1973), 'The Other America: Native Artefacts from the New World' (1982), 'Lost Magic Kingdoms and Six Paper Moons from Nahuatl' (1985), and 'The Skeleton at the Feast: The Day of the Dead in Mexico' (1991).

'Lost Magic Kingdoms and Six Paper Moons from Nahuatl' was particularly innovative since it was the first time that the Museum of Mankind had directly involved a major contemporary artist in the creation of an exhibition. In a sense, the exhibition, curated by the distinguished British sculptor Eduardo Paolozzi (b. 1924), followed the publication of *Henry Moore at the British Museum* (1981), in which Paolozzi's fellow British sculptor Henry Moore (1898–1986) appraised the qualities of the museum's collection of statuary. Moore believed that people needed to be able to examine the back of sculpture, especially that of the Aztecs, which he found extremely relaxed and expressive.[33] Paolozzi chose to display a variety of objects from the ethnographic collections which he juxtaposed with his own work. The title of the exhibition and, for example, the papier-mâché copy of the celebrated Tlazoteotl from the Dumbarton Oaks collection (cat. 320) that he made for the exhibition reflect Paolozzi's interest in Mexico: '"Six Paper Moons" is a metaphor for the way the Aztec looked at the moon: according to them, the moon was a mother, the sun a father, and the stars were their children' (fig. 70).[34]

Several exhibitions outside London have incorporated Mexican archaeological objects, such as 'Ancient American Art' at the Royal Scottish Museum, Edinburgh (1971), which included some items owned by Cowdray, and 'Men and Gods of Ancient America: An Exhibition of Treasures from Mexico and Peru' at the Liverpool Museum (1973). 'The Art of Ruins: Adela Breton and the Temples of Mexico' at the Bristol Museums and Art Gallery (1989) highlighted the museum's extensive collection of watercolours of Mexico and Central America by Adela Breton (1849–1923) and included part of her collection of artefacts. Born in Bath, Breton made numerous trips to Mexico between 1894 and 1923 and developed a passionate interest in the Pre-Hispanic architecture of the region. She is best known for her paintings and sketches of the Mayan sites of Chichén Itzá and Acancéh in the Yucatan. Indeed her representations of Acancéh have become an important archaeological record of the now-deteriorated reliefs at the site.[35] In 1908 she produced a copy of the 'Plano en papel de maguey' (fig. 71) (now part of the collection of codices at the Museo Nacional de Antropología, Mexico City) for Maudslay's English translation of the classic *Historia verdadera de la conquista de la Nueva España* by Bernal Díaz del Castillo, one of Cortés's footsoldiers. The original map, first published in Bullock's *Six Months' Residence and Travel in Mexico*, was exhibited at the Egyptian Hall in 1824.

Fig. 70
An array of objects featured in 'Lost Magic Kingdoms and Six Paper Moons from Nahuatl', an exhibition curated by Eduardo Paolozzi at the Museum of Mankind, London. Tlazolteotl, the Aztec goddess of filth, derived from cat. 320, was sculpted in papier mâché by Paolozzi himself.

Fig. 71

A *chinampa* district, probably located in the outskirts of north-western Tenochtitlan. Detail of Adela Breton's 1908 copy of the 'Plano en papel de maguey' (*c.* 1523–25; Museo Nacional de Antropología, Mexico City). Maguey paper, *c.* 215 × 150 cm.

Bristol Museums and Art Gallery

A number of exhibitions in Britain, such as 'Sañuq and Toltecatl: Pre-Columbian Arts of Middle and South America' at the Manchester Museum (1992), commemorated the quincentenary of Columbus's 'discovery' of the Americas in 1492. 'Painted Books of Mexico' at the British Museum (1992) reunited many of the codices in British collections. In addition, three manuscripts from the British Museum, the Metlatoyuca Map, the Itzcuintepec Codex and the Itzcuintepec Roll, were included in the exhibition 'Mapping the Americas' at the University Gallery of the University of Essex, Colchester (1992), which was part of the acclaimed Fourth World conference.

Numerous large-scale survey exhibitions have taken place around the world over the last hundred years. These have included 'Les Arts anciens de l'Amérique: exposition organisée au Musée des Arts Décoratifs' at the Palais du Louvre, Paris (1928); 'Twenty Centuries of Mexican Art' at the Museum of Modern Art, New York (1940); 'Master Works of Mexican Art from Pre-Columbian Times to the Present' at the Los Angeles County Museum of Art (1963); 'Before Cortés: Sculpture of Middle America' at the Metropolitan Museum of Art, New York (1970); 'México antiguo' at the Museo de América, Madrid (1986); 'Mexico: Splendors of Thirty Centuries' at the Metropolitan Museum of Art, New York (1990); 'L'America prima di Colombo: arte precolombino dal 2000 a.C. agli Aztechi' at the Castello di Lerici, Milan (1990); 'Circa 1492: Art in the Age of Exploration' at the National Gallery of Art, Washington DC (1991); and 'Arte precolombino en la colección Barbier-Mueller' at the Casa de América, Madrid (1994). More recent exhibitions include 'Soleils mexicains' at the Petit Palais, Paris (2000); 'The Journey to Aztlan: Art from a Mythic Homeland' at the Los Angeles County Museum of Art (2001); and 'Art Treasures from Ancient Mexico: Journey to the Land of the Gods' at the Nieuwe Kerk, Amsterdam (2002).[36]

A number of more specifically Aztec exhibitions are also worthy of mention: 'Aztec Stone Sculpture' at the Centre for Inter-American Relations, New York (1976); 'Mexique d'hier et d'aujourd'hui: découverte du Templo Mayor de Mexico; artistes contemporains' at the Ministère des Relations Extérieures, Paris (1981); 'Art of Aztec Mexico: Treasures of Tenochtitlan' at the National Gallery of Art, Washington DC (1983); 'Glanz und Untergang des alten Mexiko: Die Azteken und ihre Vorläufer' at the Roemer– und Pelizaeus-Museum, Hildesheim (1986); 'Die Azteken: Maisbauern und Krieger' at the Museum für Völkerkunde, Basle (1986); and

'Azteca-Mexica: las culturas del México antiguo' at the Sociedad Estatal Quinto Centenario, Madrid (1992).

'The Art of Ancient Mexico' at the Hayward Gallery, London (1992), was the most recent and largest exhibition specifically dedicated to Mexican archaeology to be held in Britain. The show, which toured extensively before arriving in London, was a major collaboration with the British Museum, which lent many of its holdings;[37] indeed Joanna Drew, Director of the Hayward Gallery, described the exhibition in the catalogue acknowledgements as 'in a small but important way a collaboration between the national museums in both countries'. A complete survey of Mexican archaeology from the Preclassic through to the Postclassic period, including the coast of the Gulf of Mexico, Oaxaca, Yuacatan and Chiapas, Teotihuacan, Tula, Tenochtitlan, as well as northern and western Mexico, the exhibition proved to be very popular.

Although library holdings were formed much earlier, the great collections of Mexican archaeology in Britain were formed during the nineteenth century. The Ethnography Department of the British Museum, which acquired many of these objects, has been at the heart of all the great twentieth-century exhibitions of Mexican archaeological objects in Britain, either as a lender or an organiser. This position has been consolidated through the inauguration of the permanent Mexican Gallery. However, the British Museum's important role does not diminish the achievements of numerous museums throughout Britain with significant holdings of ancient Mexican artefacts that have organised innovative exhibitions and have many objects on permanent display. Together these institutions demonstrate the international importance of British collections of Mexican art, and illustrate the long tradition of exhibitions of Mexican artefacts in Britain, of which 'Aztecs' at the Royal Academy is the latest chapter.

15 Netzahualcoyotl was not only a ruler but also a poet and philosopher. He enjoyed a lengthy reign, from 1418 to 1472.

16 Alva Ixtlilxochitl 1975–77, vol. 2, pp. 92–100.

17 Sahagún 1950–82, vol. 8, p. 39.

18 Berdan 1982, p. 73.

19 Codex Mendoza 1992.

20 Their most disastrous defeat came at the hands of the powerful Tarascans to the west. Of the untold thousands of Triple Alliance warriors who fought, a mere 200 stumbled home to Tenochtitlan (see Durán 1964, p. 167).

21 Berdan et al. 1996.

5 THE TEMPLO MAYOR, THE GREAT TEMPLE OF THE AZTECS

01 Durán 1951, p. 42.

02 Durán 1951, pp. 40–41.

03 Chávez Balderas 2002.

04 Matos Moctezuma, Broda and Carrasco 1987.

05 López Austin and López Luján 2001.

06 Matos Moctezuma 1993.

07 López Luján forthcoming.

08 López Luján 1994.

6 ART AT THE TIME OF THE AZTECS

01 Covarrubias 1961, p. 348.

02 Codex Matritense 1907, fol. 144r.

03 León-Portilla 2002, pp. 49–53.

04 Manrique 1960.

05 Sahagún 1988, vol. 2, pp. 652–53.

06 Codex Matritense 1907, fols 117v and 172v–176r.

07 Durán 1995, vol. 1, p. 299.

08 Ibid., p. 300.

09 Marquina 1951, pp. 187–89.

10 García Payón 1979.

11 Taladoire 1981, pp. 283–92.

12 Architectural benches decorated with processions of warriors marching towards the zacatapayolli, the ball of straw set with bloody thorns, the supreme symbol of self-sacrifice, were found both on the north and the south sides of the Templo Mayor. Beyer 1955.

13 Pasztory 1983, plate 22, which represents the precinct of the 'First Memorials' at the Templo Mayor, shows the stylistic unity of the sacred buildings with the presence of the architectural dado and the moulding on the bases and the walls of the temples.

14 Codex Tro-Cortesianus 1967, plates 75–76. Codex Fejérváry-Mayer 1971, page 1.

15 This pictorial document represents a section of an indigenous city, probably Tenochtitlan, and shows the boundaries of the land owned by each family, the fields of crops and houses as well as the pyramidal base that corresponds to the local temple, also showing the irrigation ditches and the earth streets. Toussaint, Gómez de Orozco and Fernández 1938, pp. 49–84.

16 Kubler 1986, pp. 64 and 85–89.

17 Townsend 1979, pp. 40–43.

18 Caso 1967, pp. 1–41.

19 Umberger 1981.

20 Solís Olguín 1992, pp. 101–08.

21 López Luján 1995.

22 In the northern area of the Templo Mayor, a courtly precinct was excavated whose architectural plan repeated a Toltec pattern; in the internal and external part of the entrance to the vestibule were located the pair of eagle men (cat. 228) that

corresponded to a pair of figures, unfortunately very fragmented and incomplete, of the god Mictlantecuhtli (cat. 233). Matos Moctezuma 1989, pp. 64–71.

23 In the former Volador, Eduardo Noguera discovered a pyramid filled with more than a thousand ceramic vessels from various traditions. Containers made in Cholula and in the Mixtec area were mixed with Aztec pottery, which proves that they existed at the same time. Solís Olguín and Morales Gómez 1991.

24 Information provided by clay models of bone rasps, discovered during excavation work in Calle de las Escalerillas shows that musicians produced sound using cut-down snail shells joined together with string tied to the ends of the bone. Castillo Tejero and Solís Olguín 1975, p. 13, pl. XII.

25 In the Cave of the Carafe, in Chiapas, textiles were found with Mexican-style multicoloured decoration showing images of deities, particularly Tezcatlipoca. Landa et al. 1988, pp. 18–182.

26 The headdress, or quetzalapanecayotl, kept at the Museum für Völkerkunde in Vienna was part of the Ambras Treasure. A 1596 inventory described 15 feathered objects as part of the Austrian empire's treasure. Anders 1970, pp. 32–34.

7 AZTEC CODICES, LITERATURE, POETRY AND PHILOSOPHY

01 Codex Vaticanus 3738 1979, fols 3v–7r.

02 Codex Vaticanus 3738 1979, fols 1v–2r.

03 Sahagún 1979, vol. 2, book 6, fol. 34r.

04 Sahagún 1979, vol. 1, book 3, fols 25r–26r.

05 Codex Fejérváry-Mayer 1971, page 1. See also Alfredo López Austin (p. 33) and Eduardo Matos Moctezuma (pp. 54–55) in this volume.

06 'Legend of the Suns' 1992, pp. 142–62.

07 Sahagún 1979, vol. 1, book 2, fol. 137r.

08 Romances de los Señores 1964, fol. 39v.

09 Cantares Mexicanos 1994, fol. 11v.

10 Cantares Mexicanos 1994, fol. 9r.

11 Historia Tolteca-Chichimeca 1976.

12 Sahagún 1979, vol. 2, book 6, fol. 1r.

13 Cantares Mexicanos 1994, fol. 17r.

14 Cantares Mexicanos 1994, fol. 26r.

15 Ibid.

16 Sahagún 1979, vol. 2, book 6, fols 74v–75v.

17 Cantares Mexicanos 1994, fol. 5v.

18 Cantares Mexicanos 1994, fol. 10v.

19 Cantares Mexicanos 1994, fol. 35v.

8 THE CONQUEST

01 The people whom we know as the Aztecs were described as the 'Mexica' during the fifteenth and sixteenth centuries. The word 'Aztec' seems to come from Aztlan, the city in what is now north-west Mexico from which the Aztecs' patron god, Huitzilopochtli, urged them to depart in search of the site of a settlement of their own. The name 'Aztec' first began to be attached to them in the eighteenth century.

02 Durán 1967, vol. 2, p. 128.

03 Colección de documentos ineditos 1864, vol. 39, p. 415: 'A certain Benito González, a Valencian, said in 1515 "que el dicho

almirante el postrimero viaje que fizo descobrió una tierra dicha Maya…"'.

04 Toribio de Benavente (Motolinía) in García Icazbalceta 1980, vol. 1, p. 65; Sahagún 1950–82, vol. 1, p. 341.

05 Klor de Alva 1981.

06 Closs 1976.

07 Anglería 1989, p. 241, letter to Pope Leo X: 'Eh, tambien vosotros teneis libros? ¡Cómo! Tambien vosotros usáis de caracteres con los cuales os entendéis estando ausentes.' The judge must have been Rodrigo de Corrales from Valladolid.

08 Alvarado de Tezozómoc 1987, pp. 684ff.

09 Ibid.

10 'Otras tierras en el mundo no se habían descubierto mejores', in Díaz del Castillo 1984, vol. 2, p. 321.

11 See the introduction to my Who's Who of the Conquistadors, London, 2000.

12 The name Malinche signifies Cortés himself, for it means 'master of Malinalli', but it has often been falsely used to indicate Marina.

13 Díaz del Castillo 1984, vol. 2, p. 515.

14 I am indebted to Teresa Castelló Iturbide's brilliant El arte plumaria en México, Mexico City, 1993.

9 EXHIBITIONS AND COLLECTORS OF PRE-HISPANIC MEXICAN ARTEFACTS IN BRITAIN

01 Shelton 1994, p. 190.

02 Brotherston 1979, p. 13.

03 Brotherston 1995, p. 18.

04 Harwood 2002, pp. 25–29. These woodcuts were included in part III, book V, chapter VII, pp. 1066–117 of Purchas 1624.

05 See Brotherston 1995 and Berger 1998 for more details on codices in British collections. Recent facsimiles of codices include Codex Zouche-Nuttall 1992; Códice Fejérváry-Mayer 1994; and Códice Laud 1994. A new facsimile edition of the Codex Aubin, currently being prepared by the University of Oklahoma with a commentary by J. Richard Andrews and Ross Hassig, is expected to be published in 2003.

06 See the transcription of a letter from Captain Nepean to the Earl of Aberdeen, President of the Society of Antiquaries of London, dated 11 July 1842, in Society of Antiquaries of London 1844, pp. 138–43. I am grateful to Clara Bezanilla, Research Assistant at the British Museum, for sharing her research on Captain Nepean with me.

07 The Pitt Rivers collection was originally offered to the British Museum before becoming the Pitt Rivers Museum at the University of Oxford in 1884. The Wellcome Trust distributed their extensive American archaeological collection to numerous British museums, including large donations in 1951 and 1982 to Birmingham Museums and Art Gallery, the British Museum, the Hancock Museum (Newcastle-upon-Tyne), Ipswich Borough Council Museums and Galleries, National Museums of Scotland and the Pitt Rivers Museum. The British Museum purchased 22 objects from the Cowdray collection at auction in London (Sotheby's). These were accessioned in 1946.

08 Graham 1993, p. 62.

09 Agustín de Iturbide (1783–1824) declared himself Emperor of Mexico in 1821. The United States of Mexico was proclaimed a federal republic in 1824. Bullock, on landing in Veracruz in 1823, was granted free passage to Mexico City by Antonio López de Santa Anna, an anti-monarchist fighting for the establishment of a republic.

10 Six Months' Residence and Travel in Mexico, Containing Remarks on the Present State of New Spain, London, 1824.

11 Alexander 1985, p. 143.

12 Graham 1993, p. 55.

13 The galleries were situated on the south side of Piccadilly facing Old Bond Street and the Burlington Arcade. Their façade was reputedly inspired by the Temple of Hat-hor at Dendera (Graham 1993, p. 56). They remained a landmark of London entertainment until its demolition in 1905. Egyptian House, 170–173 Piccadilly, was built on its site (Honour 1954, p. 39).

14 Both of these objects are illustrated in Bullock 1824, as are some of the other objects in the British Museum collection, including stone sculptures of Chalchiuhtlicue and Xochipilli.

15 These casts were later donated to the Society of Antiquaries of Scotland by E. W. A. Drummond Hay (Graham 1993, p. 63).

16 Among the exhibits were a number of original codices that Bullock had borrowed from the Mexican government. An enlarged copy of the Codex Boturini (which recounts the migration of the Mexica from their mythical home of Aztlan to the foundation of Tenochtitlan) was produced for Bullock by Agostino Aglio (1777–1857), who also produced engravings of the exhibition for the catalogue. These were seen by Edward King, Lord Kingsborough (1795–1837), who later commissioned Aglio to reproduce a number of codices for his monumental nine-volume publication The Antiquities of Mexico, Comprising Facsimiles of Ancient Mexican Painting and Hieroglyphs, London, 1831–48.

17 Many items were purchased by the Reverend Professor William Buckland, Dean of Westminster and Professor of Geology at the University of Oxford, and donated to the British Museum.

18 See John Lloyd Stephens and Frederick Catherwood, Views of Ancient Monuments in Central America, Chiapas and Yucatan, London, 1844, and the same authors' Incidents of Travel in Central America, Chiapas and Yucatan…Illustrated by Numerous Engravings… Twelfth Edition, London, 1854.

19 See Mexico City 1996 and King 1996 for more details on these and other artists.

20 Stocking 1985, p. 5.

21 'Additions of the British Museum', Illustrated London News, no. 257, vol. 10, 3 April 1847.

22 As can be seen in Sotheby and Wilkinson 1859, these three objects were in the collection formed by the German Bram Hertz, a long-time resident of London, and sold by Joseph Mayer (1803–1886), who acquired the collection through Sotheby and Wilkinson of the Strand as part of a nine-day sale. Christy paid a total of £113 for lots 1,834 (inlaid mosaic mask: £32), 1,835 (mosaic sacrificial knife: £41), and 1,836 (decorated human skull: £40) on 16 February 1859.

23 Maudslay contributed the six-volume section 'Archaeology' to the comprehensive Biologia Centrali-Americana. With his wife, Anne Cary Maudslay, he published A Glimpse at Guatemala… as a more accessible account of their seven voyages between 1881 and 1894. The casts were originally displayed and stored at the Victoria & Albert Museum in London before being integrated into the British Museum's collections. Copies of the casts were made for the Trocadéro Museum, Paris, and the American Museum of Natural History, New York.

24 The catalogue (London 1953) lists 1,243 objects, excluding the popular art section, of which 101 were classified as Aztec. Thirteen objects in this section were on loan from the British Museum.

25 Ruiz Cortines, like his predecessor, Miguel Alemán, 'pledged to foster economic growth in general and large-scale industrialisation in particular' (Meyer and Sherman 1979, p. 639) and no doubt used the exhibition to increase Mexico's international profile in the postwar years.

26 Tate Gallery Archive: TG92/97/1, p. 5.

27 Bernard Denvir, Daily Herald, 4 March 1953.

28 London Evening News, 3 March 1953.

29 Pierre Jeannerat, Daily Mail, 4 March 1953.

30 As a consequence Fernando Gamboa, director of the exhibition, and Dr Andrés Iduarte, Director of the Instituto Nacional de Bellas Artes (INBA), were awarded the CBE, and Susana Gamboa, and Luis Aveleyra Arroyo de Anda, of the Instituto Nacional de Antropología e Historia (INAH), the OBE. The honours were conferred by the British ambassador on 14 August 1953 in Mexico City. Tate Gallery Archive: TG92/97/1, p. 100.

31 This ambitious programme has recently seen the opening of the North American and African galleries at Bloomsbury, and the current renovation of the King's Library following the transfer of its contents to the British Library at St Pancras.

32 This loan exhibition, arranged in collaboration with the Mexican National Tourist Council, was also shown at the Museum für Völkerkunde, Frankfurt am Main (1972), and the Nationalmuseum, Stockholm (1973).

33 Moore 1981, p. 73.

34 London 1985, p. 9.

35 McVicker 1989, p. 16.

36 Antwerp 1992 and Brooklyn 1996 examined the art of the early colonial period more specifically.

37 Held from 17 September to 6 December 1992, 'The Art of Ancient Mexico' had visited venues in Venice, Paris, Madrid, Berlin and Tokyo over a period of two years before arriving in London. See Oriana Baddeley's supplement to the catalogue (London 1992) for details of the 56 objects from the British Museum included in the exhibition.

Det

4 Goblet

c. 1100, Maya
Fired clay, height 31 cm,
diameter 12.5 cm

Museo Regional de Antropología
Carlos Pellicer, Villahermosa, 64

3 Plaque in the form
of a Maya warrior

c. 250–700, Maya
Shell, 9.5 × 5.8 × 0.8 cm

Collections of The Field Museum,
Chicago, 95075

5 Huehueteotl

c. 450, Teotihuacan
Stone, height 74.5 cm, diameter 80 cm

Museo Nacional de Antropología,
Mexico City, CONACULTA-INAH, 10-79920

7 Standing goddess

c. 250–650, Teotihuacan
Volcanic stone and traces of paint,
height 91.4 cm

Philadelphia Museum of Art, The Louise and Walter
Arensberg Collection, 1950, 1950-134-282

6 Urn

c. 400, Teotihuacan
Greenstone, 24.5 × 14 cm

Museo Nacional de Antropología, Mexico City,
CONACULTA-INAH, 10-9626

9 Tripod vessel

c. 500, Teotihuacan
Fired clay and stucco, height 25 cm,
diameter 28 cm

Museo de Sitio de Teotihuacan,
CONACULTA-INAH, 10-336713

8 Tripod bowl

c. 450, Teotihuacan
Fired clay, stucco and paint,
height 15 cm, diameter 16.5 cm

Museo Nacional de Antropología, Mexico City,
CONACULTA-INAH, 10-79930

10 Mask

c. 450–650, Teotihuacan
Stone, 22.5 × 28 cm

Museo Nacional de Antropología,
Mexico City, CONACULTA-INAH,
10-9628

13 Mask

c. 450, Teotihuacan
Stone, turquoise, obsidian
and shell, 21.5 × 20 cm

Museo Nacional de Antropología,
Mexico City, CONACULTA-INAH, 10-9630

11 Mask

c. 250–600, Teotihuacan
Granitic stone, iron pyrite
and shell inlay,
21.6 × 24 × 10 cm

Philadelphia Museum of Art,
The Louise and Walter Arensberg
Collection, 1950, 1950-134-947

12 Mask

c. 250–600, Teotihuacan
Greenstone,
15.8 × 17.3 × 5 cm

Museo degli Argenti, Florence,
Gemme 824

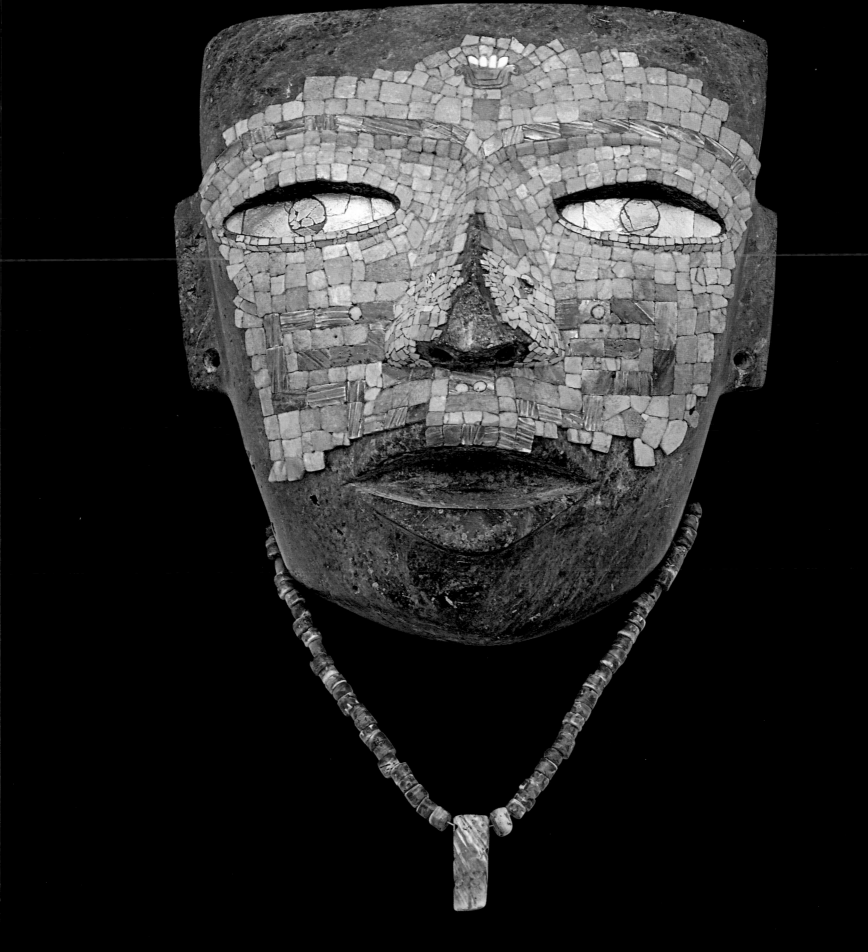

14 Plaque with an image of a
goddess with a reptile-eye glyph

c. 250–700, Teotihuacan
Pale green, translucent onyx,
29 × 16 × 3 cm

Collections of The Field Museum, Chicago,
23913

15 Anthropomorphic figure

c. 400, Teotihuacan
Greenstone, 25.5 × 10 cm

Museo Nacional de Antropología, Mexico City,
CONACULTA-INAH, 10-2562

16 Anthropomorphic figure

c. 400–600, Teotihuacan
Serpentine, height 34 cm

Museum für Völkerkunde, Hamburg, B264

17 Mythological feline

c. 400, Teotihuacan
Volcanic stone, stucco and paint,
96.5 × 97.5 × 74.5 cm

Museo Nacional de Antropología,
Mexico City, CONACULTA-INAH, 10-626269 0/10

18 Offering vessel in the form
of an ocelot

c. 400–600, Teotihuacan
Calcite onyx, 16 × 31 × 33.5 cm

Trustees of the British Museum, London,
Ethno. 1926-22

20 *Chacmool*

c. 1100, Toltec
Stone, 85 × 120 × 54 cm

Museo de Sitio de Tula,
CONACULTA-INAH, 10-215198

21   Vessel

c. 950–1150, Toltec
Fired clay, height 24.5 cm,
diameter 19 cm

Museum für Völkerkunde Wien
(Kunsthistorisches Museum mit MVK und
ÖTM), Vienna, 60.303, Becker Collection

22   Vessel

c. 1250–1521, Toltec–Mixtec
Fired clay, height 24.7 cm,
diameter 15.3 cm

Museum für Völkerkunde Wien
(Kunsthistorisches Museum mit MVK und
ÖTM), Vienna, 14.698, Bilimek Collection

23   Atlantean figure

c. 950–1150, Toltec
Volcanic stone and paint,
81 × 36 × 31 cm

Museum für Völkerkunde Wien
(Kunsthistorisches Museum mit MVK und
ÖTM), Vienna, 59.143, Becker Collection

24   Atlantean figure

c. 1100, Toltec
Stone and paint, 94.5 × 38.5 × 34 cm

Museo de Sitio de Tula, CONACULTA-INAH,
10-215119

25   Eagle reliefs

c. 1000–1300, Toltec
Volcanic stone (andesite/dacite)
and remains of paint,
69.8 × 74.9 cm and 69.8 × 77.5 cm

Lent by The Metropolitan Museum of Art,
New York, Gift of Frederic E. Church, 1893,
93.27.1, 2

27 Deified warrior

c. 1500, Aztec
Stone, 119 × 48 × 34.5 cm

Museo Nacional de Antropología,
Mexico City, CONACULTA-INAH,
10-48555

26 Plaque with an image
of a bleeding heart

c. 1100, Toltec
Stone and stucco, 61.5 × 60 × 7 cm

Museo Nacional de Antropología, Mexico City,
CONACULTA-INAH, 10-81752

28–31 Deified warriors

c. 1500, Aztec
Stone, 120 × 42 × 37 cm,
120 × 41 × 39 cm,
119 × 38 × 34 cm and
122 × 42 × 39 cm

Museo Nacional de Antropología,
Mexico City, CONACULTA-INAH,
10-81768, 10-9774, 10-81769
and 10-81767

For the Aztecs, religious power could be exercised through bodily transformation. This central tenet of Aztec belief is shown most vividly in the codices, where priests elaborately dressed as gods assume the attributes of the deities they represent. The hand gestures, grave facial expressions and controlled bodily stance of small votive statues can in this context be read as an expression of their religious role as mediators between the people and their gods. They were almost certainly placed in domestic shrines, in public spaces and alongside principal routes, much as is seen in Catholic countries today.

Physical beauty was held to be a sign of favour from the gods. The Franciscan friar Bernardino de Sahagún recorded that it marked out individuals as candidates for human sacrifice to the gods. What was given had to be returned in the cycle of death and rebirth: 'For he who was chosen was of fair countenance, of good understanding and quick, of clean body – slender like a reed; long and thin like a stout cane; well built; not of overfed body, not corpulent, and neither very small nor exceedingly tall…like something smoothed, like a tomato, or like a pebble, as if hewn of wood. [He did] not [have] curly hair, [but] straight, long hair; no scabs, pustules or boils on the forehead, nor large-headed…' (Sahagún 1950–82, vol. 2, pp. 64, 66).

This, then, is the ideal type depicted in the masks and in the statues of youths and men, their faces emphasised by being made larger than the rest of their bodies. What seems to have been valued in art, more than ideal form, was an appearance of vitality, of the divine spark of life. The Aztecs' quest for realism in their art distinguishes their representation of the human form from that of their predecessors, the Olmecs, the Toltecs and the people of Teotihuacan. It was an impetus that challenged sculptors to depict the different ages of man from youth to old age.

The old men, with their furrowed brows and prominent ribcages, may be representations of the fire god Xiuhtecuhtli. One of his personifications was as Huehueteotl ('old, old god'), who is shown with a brazier on his head, as in the figure found at Teotihuacan (cat. 5). Indeed, an alternative reading of the more youthful figures is as gods rather than guardians, in this case goddesses of maize shown with anthropomorphic features. The exceptionally finely carved standing goddess with her tasselled headdress (cat. 38) has a folded paper fan at the back of her head. Unlike the other maize goddesses with their large paper headdresses resembling houses or granaries, her diamond-patterned skirt is fastened with a serpent belt.

Very little Aztec sculpture in wood has survived the alternating wet and dry seasons of Mesoamerica. Quite exceptional therefore is the standing fertility goddess (cat. 41) who still has remains of the shell inlays used for her eyes and teeth. Her hands, cupped under her breasts, have beautifully carved fingers and fingernails. The so-called Venus of Tetzcoco (cat. 40) is unique. Nearly 1.5 metres tall, she is the only known extant standing female nude in Aztec art. Her flexed knees and open mouth suggest tension, if not suffering. In common with some other statues (see cats 36, 43) there is a cavity in her chest that probably held a precious stone secured by paste. Again, it is likely that she was dressed in a costume.

Together with these statues, mainly carved of the volcanic rock native to the Basin of Mexico, are shown masks of precious greenstone, obsidian, alabaster and gilded wood (cats 49–53). As Esther Pasztory has pointed out: 'These masks represent the Aztec facial ideal: a long head, wide mouth, straight nose, and eyebrows set close to the eyes. In all cases the ears are carefully detailed with a spiral form and the lobes have holes for the insertion of ornaments' (Pasztory 1983, p. 257). The eye-sockets will originally have contained inlays. Doubtless based on human features although they almost certainly depict gods, these masks bring us close to an encounter with Aztec faces. Poignantly, they recall the Nahuatl poem about the afterlife:

Will I have to go like the flowers that perish?
Will nothing remain of my name?
Nothing of my fame here on earth?
At least my flowers, at least my songs!
Earth is the region of the fleeting moment.
Is it also thus in the place
where in some way one lives?
Is there joy there, is there friendship?
Or is it only here on earth
we come to know our faces?

(León-Portilla 1969, pp. 81–82)

32 Ehecatl-Quetzalcoatl

c. 1500, Aztec
Basalt, 176 × 56 × 50 cm

Instituto Mexiquense de Cultura:
Museo de Antropología e
Historia del Estado de México,
Toluca, A-36229 10-109262

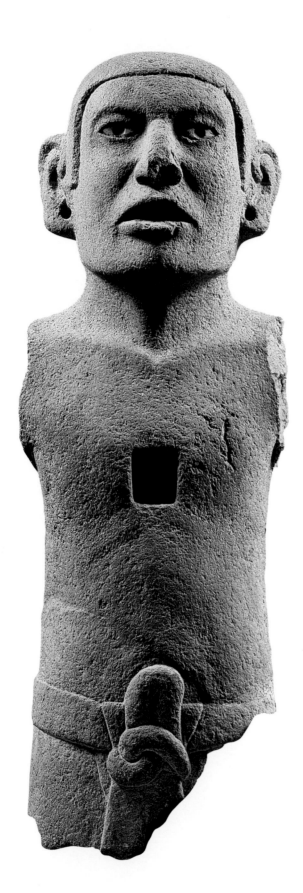

36 Male head and torso

c. 1500, Aztec
Stone and white shell, 63 × 20 cm

Museo Nacional de Antropología, Mexico City,
CONACULTA-INAH, 10-40607

37 Huehueteotl

c. 1500, Aztec
Stone, 48 × 23 cm

Museo Nacional de Antropología,
Mexico City, CONACULTA-INAH,
10-220145

42   Xiuhtecuhtli

c. 1500, Aztec
Stone, 80 × 32 × 18 cm

Museo Nacional de Antropología,
Mexico City, CONACULTA-INAH,
10-81575

44 Hunchback

c. 1500, Aztec
Stone, 33 × 16 × 12 cm

Museo Nacional de Antropología,
Mexico City, CONACULTA-INAH, 10-97

43 Young man

c. 1500, Aztec
Stone, 63 × 20 cm

Museo Nacional de Antropología, Mexico City,
CONACULTA-INAH, 10-620964

48 Head of a youth

c. 1500, Aztec
Stone, red shell and obsidian,
19.5 × 15.5 cm

Museo Nacional de Antropología,
Mexico City, CONACULTA-INAH, 10-92

49 Mask

c. 1450–1521, Aztec
Stone, 20 × 17 × 8 cm

American Museum of Natural History,
New York, 30/11847

III | THE NATURAL WORLD

Like the other indigenous peoples of Mesoamerica, the Aztecs were immersed in a nature that they believed was infused with spirit. Every species, animal or vegetable, every mineral, heavenly body or element was created by a deity out of his or her own essence, so that divinity and creation shared the same substance. Although in such creations the divine essence was thought to be partly concealed by a solid and dense material layer, beneath this lay a network of invisible links that demanded acknowledgement. For that reason the Aztecs needed to approach these creations not only with the traditional knowledge of the correct way to exploit resources, but also with the consideration of someone dealing with other animate individuals. Before taking the life of a vegetable or an animal, a man would apologise to it for his action, explaining that he was obliged to kill it for his own survival and that his attack on its species would be strictly limited to the satisfaction of his needs.

Documentary evidence of this conception of the world is not unusual: asking bees respectfully for honey; persuading fish to enter the net; courteous treatment of a tree felled by an axe; or saying to maize you are about to eat: 'Don't be insulted, I will draw sustenance from you, you will keep me alive.' Many sources illustrate this view of nature, among them carvings, pottery, murals, pictograms and books dating to earliest colonial times. Notable among these is Book XI of *Historia general de las cosas de Nueva España* ('*General History of the Things of New Spain*') by Bernardino de Sahagún, which contains the text of the Franciscan's interviews with natives in Nahuatl along with a Spanish translation and beautiful drawings of animals, plants and minerals. Also particularly important are *Historia natural de la Nueva España* ('*The Natural History of New Spain*') by Francisco Hernández, Philip II's principal physician, and the *Libellus de medicinalibus indorum herbis* ('*Book of Indian Medicinal Herbs*'), written by the native doctor Martín de la Cruz and translated

55 Cihuacoatl

c. 1500, Aztec
Stone, 61 × 44.5 × 15 cm

Museo Nacional de Antropología,
Mexico City, CONACULTA-INAH,
10-81787

56 Casket

c. 1500, Aztec
Stone, jade, stucco and paint,
19.5 × 20 × 20 cm

Museo Nacional de Antropología, Mexico City,
CONACULTA-INAH, 10–280180/2

57 Life–death figure

c. 1200–1521, Aztec
Volcanic stone, 26.7 × 14 × 15.6 cm

Brooklyn Museum of Art, Purchased with
funds given by The Henfield Foundation,
64.50

59 Toad with an image
of Chalchihuitl

c. 1500, Aztec
Stone, 19 × 51 × 34 cm

Museo Nacional de Antropología,
Mexico City, CONACULTA-INAH, 10-1097

58 Figure representing the duality

c. 1500, Aztec
Greenstone, 9.5 × 8 × 9 cm

Museo Nacional de Antropología,
Mexico City, CONACULTA-INAH, 10-9683

66 Squash

c. 1300–1521, Aztec
Aragonite, 12 × 8 cm

Trustees of the British Museum, London,
Ethno. 1952 Am 18.1

67 Pumpkin

c. 1500, Aztec
Diorite, 16 × 36 × 17 cm

Museo Nacional de Antropología, Mexico City,
CONACULTA-INAH, 10-392922

68 Cactus

c. 1500, Aztec
Stone, 99 × 28 cm

Museo Nacional de Antropología,
Mexico City, CONACULTA-INAH,
10-220928

Below: underside of cat. 68,
showing a relief of Tenoch,
founder of Tenochtitlan

70 Dog

c. 1500, Aztec
Stone, 47.5 × 20 × 29 cm

Museo Regional de Puebla,
CONACULTA-INAH, 10-203439

69 Feathered coyote

c. 1500, Aztec
Stone, 38 × 17 × 13 cm

Museo Nacional de Antropología,
Mexico City, CONACULTA-INAH, 10-47

71 Reclining jaguar

c. 1440–1521, Aztec
Volcanic stone,
12.5 × 14.5 × 28 cm

Brooklyn Museum of Art,
Carll H. de Silver Fund, 38.45

72 Rabbit

c. 1500, Aztec
Stone, 33 × 22 × 24 cm

Museo Nacional de Antropología,
Mexico City, CONACULTA-INAH,
10-81666

73 Insect

c. 1500, Aztec
Stone, 22 × 21.5 × 36.5 cm

Museo Nacional de Antropología,
Mexico City, CONACULTA-INAH, 10-594039

74 Insect

c. 1500, Aztec
Stone, 13.5 × 9.5 × 18 cm

Museum für Völkerkunde Wien
(Kunsthistorisches Museum mit MVK und
ÖTM), Vienna, 6.450, Bilimek Collection

75 Grasshopper

c. 1500, Aztec
Cornelian, 19.5 × 16 × 47 cm

Museo Nacional de Antropología,
Mexico City, CONACULTA-INAH, 10-220929

76 Fish

c. 1500, Aztec
Volcanic stone, 26.3 × 58.6 × 10.5 cm

Laboratoire d'Ethnologie, Musée de
l'Homme, Paris, M.H.87.155.17

77 Plaque with an image of a lizard

c. 1325–1520, Aztec
Stone, 24 × 15 × 8 cm

Musées Royaux d'Art et d'Histoire, Brussels,
AAM 3480

83 Eagle

c. 1500, Aztec
Stone, 41 × 20 cm

Museo Regional de Puebla,
CONACULTA-INAH, 10-203440

82 Relief of an eagle

c. 1300–1521, Aztec
Andesite, 20 × 28 × 8 cm

Trustees of the British Museum, London, Ethno. 8624

91 Vessel with an image
   of a centipede

1400, Totonac
Fired clay and paint,
height 16 cm, diameter 19 cm

Museo Nacional de Antropología,
Mexico City, CONACULTA-INAH, 10-78683

89 Plate

c. 1500, Aztec
Fired clay and paint, height 4.5 cm,
diameter 31 cm

Museo Nacional de Antropología,
Mexico City, CONACULTA-INAH, 10-116416

90 Two-tiered tripod plate

c. 1500, Aztec
Fired clay and paint,
height 6 cm, diameter 22.5 cm

Museo Nacional de Antropología,
Mexico City, CONACULTA-INAH, 10-1049

also included their own specific gods. Chief among these was Huitzilopochtli ('left-sided hummingbird'), a legendary figure attributed with guiding the migration of the Aztecs on their mythical journey from Aztlan to the site of Tenochtitlan over a period of some two hundred years. It was Huitzilopochtli who foresaw their final destination as the place where an eagle would be seen perched on a cactus growing out of a stone. Images of the god are rare and known mainly through representations in painted books, including the Florentine Codex (cat. 344); sculptures of him, made from organic materials such as amaranth seeds, copal and resin, have not survived, although this type of object is represented by a similar sculpture of Tlaloc (cat. 241).

The Aztecs boasted a large number of gods, many of whom had more than one aspect. They were represented in various media, including painted books, polychrome ceramics and free-standing three-dimensional sculptures in stone (which was then covered in stucco and painted), wood and other organic substances, and precious materials, among them turquoise, jade and gold. Virtually every aspect of human culture and nature was represented by a god, although generally they were organised around a small number of central themes such as creation, death, agriculture, rain and war. Sculptural representations of deities were ritually interred as offerings to the gods, especially the fire god Xiuhtecuhtli (cats 244–46), who is specifically linked to such offerings at the Templo Mayor. Others were deliberately encased during the building stages of the Templo Mayor (cat. 265). Xiuhtecuhtli is closely associated with Huehueteotl ('old, old god'), whose likeness is to be found on Teotihuacan braziers (cat. 5). He was re-created by Aztec stonemasons (cat. 229), although they portrayed him as a youthful god instead of as an old man. Sculptures were also used to decorate the exterior of temples; restrictions of interior space meant that public rituals took place outside.

Most gods were perceived as having human form and animal counterparts. For this reason, many sculptural representations of deities appear to be individuals, most probably priests, who are impersonating the gods, whereas those depicted in the Pre-Hispanic codices are often more conceptual and less obviously human. Examples of the former include the large representation of Ehecatl, god of wind (cat. 103), or the cross-legged image of Xochipilli, god of flowers and poetry, seated on his throne (cat. 105). Elaborate costumes were prepared for deity impersonators and these are captured in the realistic form of Aztec sculpture, especially the large temple headdresses made of paper worn by Chicomecoatl ('seven serpent'), goddess of seed corn (cat. 109). Religious ritual was accompanied by music performed on drums, seen here copied in stone and ceramic (cats 125–26), and flutes (cats 159–62), and by dancing. Chalchiuhtlicue ('she of the jade skirt'; cats 120–22), goddess of water (precious liquid), was associated with agriculture and human birth and is here represented as a kneeling woman with a tasselled headdress.

In some cases the gods were interchangeable with animal counterparts, which were also used to represent them. A clear example is that of Ehecatl, who is often shown as a monkey wearing either a characteristic 'beak' (cat. 102) or a shell pendant (cat. 100). Ehecatl was one of the aspects of Quetzalcoatl, 'the feathered serpent' (cat. 114), one of the creator-gods who is also associated with Teotihuacan and the Toltecs of Tula (where he was priest-ruler). Tezcatlipoca ('smoking mirror') was an omnipotent god of rulers, characterised by bands across his face (seen on a fine turquoise mosaic mask [cat. 304]) and by one leg ending in a protruding shinbone. He was associated with the jaguar and, like Quetzalcoatl, was a creator-god; the two fought during the creation of the world.

92 Xipe Totec

c. 1350–1521, Aztec
Volcanic stone and paint,
46 × 26.3 × 27.4 cm

Museum der Kulturen Basel, Basle,
IVb 647

93 Xipe Totec

c. 1500, Aztec
Fired clay, 15 × 4 × 6.5 cm

Museo Nacional de Antropología,
Mexico City, CONACULTA-INAH, 10-333885

94 Xipe Totec

c. 1500, Aztec
Fired clay, 15.5 × 5 × 3 cm

Museo Nacional de Antropología,
Mexico City, CONACULTA-INAH,
10-333856

95 Xipe Totec

c. 1500, Aztec
Fired clay, 14.5 × 6 × 3.5 cm

Museo Nacional de Antropología,
Mexico City, CONACULTA-INAH,
10-116779

96 Xipe Totec

c. 1500, Aztec
Fired clay, 12 × 5.5 × 8 cm

Museo Nacional de Antropología,
Mexico City, CONACULTA-INAH,
10-116778 2/2

99 Xipe Totec

c. 1500, Aztec
Fired clay and paint,
97 × 43 × 20 cm

Museo Regional de Puebla,
CONACULTA-INAH, 10-203061

97 Container for flayed skin

c. 1500, Aztec
Fired clay, height 25 cm,
diameter 48.5 cm

Museo Nacional de Antropología,
Mexico City, CONACULTA-INAH, 10-594908

98 Brazier with an image
of Xipe Totec

c. 1500, Aztec
Fired clay, 36 × 40 cm

Museo Nacional de Antropología,
Mexico City, CONACULTA-INAH, 10-220143

100 Spider monkey with ornaments relating to Ehecatl-Quetzalcoatl

c. 1500, Aztec
Volcanic stone,
43.5 × 24.6 × 24.4 cm

Laboratoire d'Ethnologie, Musée de l'Homme, Paris, M.H.78.1.89

101 Spider monkey with ornaments relating to Xochipilli

c. 1500, Aztec
Volcanic stone, 19.5 × 18.5 × 8.5 cm

Laboratoire d'Ethnologie, Musée de l'Homme, Paris, M.H.87.159.143

102 Dancing monkey

c. 1500, Aztec
Stone, 60 × 37 × 33 cm

Museo Nacional de Antropología, Mexico City, CONACULTA-INAH, 10-116784

103 Ehecatl-Quetzalcoatl

c. 1480–1519, Aztec
Andesite, 195 × 40 × 50 cm

Rautenstrauch-Joest-Museum,
Cologne, Ludwig Collection, SL CVII

104 Mask with an image
of Ehecatl-Quetzalcoatl

c. 1350–1521, Aztec
Stone, 14 × 14 × 10 cm

Staatliche Museen zu Berlin:
Preußischer Kulturbesitz,
Ethnologisches Museum,
IV Ca 26077

105 Xochipilli

c. 1500, Aztec
Stone, 115 × 53 × 43 cm

Museo Nacional de Antropología,
Mexico City, CONACULTA-INAH,
10-222116 0/2

106 Xochipilli

c. 1500, Aztec
Fine-grained volcanic stone,
74.5 × 31 × 26 cm

Völkerkundliche Sammlungen Reiss-
Engelhorn-Museen, Mannheim, V Am 1085

107 Figure with flowers and maize

c. 1325–1521, Aztec
Stone and traces of paint,
27.7 × 25.2 × 29.9 cm

The Cleveland Museum of Art,
The Norweb Collection, 1949.555

108 Xilonen

c. 1500, Aztec
Stone, 52 × 20 cm

Museo Nacional de Antropología,
Mexico City, CONACULTA-INAH, 10-82209

109 Chicomecoatl

c. 1350–1521, Aztec
Stone, 68 × 27 × 14 cm

Staatliche Museen zu Berlin:
Preußischer Kulturbesitz,
Ethnologisches Museum,
IV Ca 46167

110 Brazier in the form
of Chalchiuhtlicue

c. 1500, Aztec
Fired clay and paint,
54.5 × 64 × 55 cm

Museo Nacional de Antropología,
Mexico City, CONACULTA-INAH, 10-1125

111 Plaque representing the
Ochpaniztli festival

c. 1500, Aztec
Fired clay and paint, 32 × 29 × 12.5 cm

Museo Nacional de Antropología, Mexico City,
CONACULTA-INAH, 10-1069

113 Tlaloc

c. 1500, Mixtec–Istmeña (Huave)
Fired clay, height 88 cm,
diameter 37.5 cm

Museo Nacional de Antropología,
Mexico City, CONACULTA-INAH,
10-76360

112 Tlaloc

c. 1350–1521, Aztec
Stone, 40 × 27 × 22 cm

Staatliche Museen zu Berlin: Preußischer Kulturbesitz,
Ethnologisches Museum, IV Ca 3721

114 Serpent

c. 1250–1521, Aztec
Reddish stone, 53 × 24 × 25 cm

Vatican Museums, Vatican City, AM 3296

115 Feathered serpent with
an image of Tlaltecuhtli

c. 1500, Aztec
Stone, 28 × 45 × 45 cm

Museo Nacional de Antropología,
Mexico City, CONACULTA-INAH, 10-81678

116 Tripod incense burner

c. 1500, Aztec
Fired clay, height 10.5 cm,
diameter 10 cm

Museo Nacional de Antropología,
Mexico City, CONACULTA-INAH,
10-78292

117–18 Pipes in the form of macaws

c. 1500, Aztec
Fired clay, 12 × 17.5 × 5.5 cm
and 14 × 21 × 5.5 cm

Museo Nacional de Antropología,
Mexico City, CONACULTA-INAH, 10-79956
and 10-223669

119   Vessel in the form of a rabbit

c. 1500, Aztec
Fired clay, 24 × 27 × 42.5 cm

Museo Nacional de Antropología,
Mexico City, CONACULTA-INAH, 10-564023

120 Chalchiuhtlicue

c. 1500, Aztec
Fine-grained volcanic stone,
53 × 25 × 20 cm

Völkerkundliche Sammlungen
Reiss-Engelhorn-Museen,
Mannheim, V Am 1084

121 Chalchiuhtlicue

c. 1300–1521, Aztec
Andesite, 37 × 19.5 × 20 cm

Trustees of the British Museum, London,
Ethno. St. 373

122 Chalchiuhtlicue

c. 1500, Aztec
Stone, 32 × 20 × 15 cm

Museo Nacional de Antropología, Mexico City,
CONACULTA-INAH, 10-1103

124 Slab with an image
of Chalchiuhtlicue

c. 1500, Aztec
Volcanic stone,
107 × 40 × 10 cm

Museo Nacional de Antropología,
Mexico City, CONACULTA-INAH,
10-613348

123 Mask of Chalchiuhtlicue

c. 1500, Aztec
Diorite, 33 × 17.5 × 10 cm

Museo Nacional de Antropología,
Mexico City, CONACULTA-INAH, 10-15717

125 Vessel in the form of a drum

c. 1500, Aztec
Fired clay, 15.5 × 25 × 10.5 cm

Museo Nacional de Antropología, Mexico
City, CONACULTA-INAH, 10-116789

126 Votive drum

c. 1500, Aztec
Stone, 35 × 72 × 26 cm

Museo Nacional de Antropología,
Mexico City, CONACULTA-INAH,
10-78329

127 Mirror with a depiction
of Ehecatl-Quetzalcoatl

c. 1500, Aztec
Pyrite, 6 × 5.5 × 3 cm

Laboratoire d'Ethnologie, Musée de l'Homme,
Paris, M.H.78.1.61

128 Huitzilopochtli

c. 1500, Aztec
Greenstone,
6.7 × 4.1 × 4.7 cm

Laboratoire d'Ethnologie,
Musée de l'Homme, Paris,
M.H.30.100.43

129 Solar ray

c. 1500, Aztec
Basalt, 110 × 26.5 × 15 cm

Instituto Mexiquense de Cultura:
Museo Arqueológico del Estado
de México 'Dr Román Piña Chan',
Teotenango, A-52215

V | GODS OF DEATH

The concept of death and its representation in art played a central role in Aztec religion and culture. 'Death's head', for example, was one of the twenty multivalent signs associated with the 260-day ritual calendar, the *tonalpohualli*. The 365-day Aztec yearly calendar, the *xiuhpohualli*, comprised eighteen 'months' of twenty days, each of which was celebrated every year with a specific festival. Huey Miccailhuitl ('great feast of the dead'), celebrated from 13 August to 1 September, included sacrifices to fire, to Huehueteotl ('old, old god') and to the fire god Xiuhtecuhtli. The correlation of fire with death relates to the origins of the Fifth Sun, or fifth world-era, of the Aztecs, as recorded by the Franciscan friar Bernardino de Sahagún. At a ceremony held at Teotihuacan in the darkness of a world without a sun, Nanauatzin, an impoverished deity, and Tecuciztecatl, a wealthy deity, immolated themselves in an act of supreme self-sacrifice in order to bring the sun and moon into being. The remaining gods followed them into the fire and, with the aid of Ehecatl, god of wind, gave the hitherto stationary sun and moon movement. In another account of the creation, chronicled by Gerónimo de Mendieta, Quetzalcoatl, the feathered serpent of whom Ehecatl is one aspect, descended into Mictlan, the underworld, accompanied by the dog Xolotl, whose colossal head can be seen here (cat. 140), to collect the bones of past generations, which he then ground and mixed with his own blood to create a new human race. There is, therefore, a strong association among the Aztecs between death and rebirth and regeneration. For this reason, skulls or skull masks, like those decorating the pair of polychrome goblets (cat. 134), can often be seen with bright shining eyes, representing the continuity of life after death.

The presence of life in death can be seen in the magnificent representations of the *cihuateteo* (sing. *cihuateotl*; cats 143–45), female spirits associated with the west, place of the sunset. These were women who died in childbirth and were equivalent to male warriors who lost their lives on the battlefield. As demons of the night, they stole children and induced men to commit adultery. They are menacingly portrayed as kneeling women with skull heads, complete with large bright eyes, and outstretched arms. Another, more complex sculpture shows a kneeling woman wearing a necklace of alternating skulls and hands (as well as a crown of skulls) similar to those of the monumental sculpture of Coatlicue ('serpent skirt'), mother of the supreme Aztec deity Huitzilopochtli. These features also appear on the intricate piece once known as the 'Coatlicue of the Metro' (cat. 132) and now thought to represent the earth monster Tlaltecuhtli ('earth lord or lady'). The seated, cross-legged figure leans her head back and braces her arms as if she were supporting the world's surface. Tlaltecuhtli was invoked by women during difficult labour and can be found represented on the bases of many sculptures, where they made unseen contact with the earth. The presence of skulls on images of Tlaltecuhtli is perhaps indicative of her mediation between the worlds of the living and the dead. A fine stone representation of Teteoinnan-Toci (cat. 135), goddess of the earth, stands erect with shell inlays representing her eyes.

The Aztecs believed that the nine planes of Mictlan ('place of the dead') were presided over by gods associated with death. The first plane was Tlalticpac, the surface of the world, which was mediated by Tlaltecuhtli. The journey to Mictlan was a dangerous one with many obstacles to overcome. The dead carried with them the objects with which they had been buried. They offered these on arrival to Mictlantecuhtli ('lord of Mictlan') and his consort. Mictlantecuhtli is usually represented with a skeletal head and the characteristic 'living' eyes. He wears vestments of paper, like those depicted on the small greenstone vessel excavated from the Templo Mayor (cat. 141). The underworld was associated with dogs and Mictlantecuhtli was the patron of the day *itzcuintli* ('dog', like 'death's head', one of the twenty signs), one of only two animals domesticated by the Aztecs (the other was the turkey). Dogs accompanied the dead on their journey to Mictlan, acting as protectors and guides. Although the Spanish associated Mictlan with the Christian concept of Hell, it was not a place of punishment for immoral or evil people, but rather the destination of all those who died a natural death. Those who died unnaturally, such as warriors, entered one of the thirteen planes of the upper world, of which Omeyocan, the place of duality presided over by Ometeotl, was uppermost.

The striking, finely carved greenstone *pulque* vessel (cat. 142) is thought to have been made for a specific historical event. Its combination of a skeletal head with the earth monster has strong links with death. What is perhaps the ultimate symbol of death, the skull and crossed bones, which is also featured on Aztec ceramics, is seen on the base. Opposing skulls are also encountered on several *cuauhxicalli*, ceremonial receptacles associated with human sacrifice (cat. 151).

The altar decorated on four sides with spider, scorpion, bat and owl (cat. 131) – creatures all associated with darkness, such as the night or solar eclipse – has a base similarly decorated with Tlaltecuhtli. Collectively referred to as the *tzitzinime*, the star demons of darkness were among the most feared of all supernaturals. The most important of them was Itzpapalotl, the obsidian moth. These creatures of destruction were thought to be stars and constellations that transformed themselves into demons during certain calendrical and celestial events and descended from the sky to wreak havoc. *Tzitzinime* was another name for the *cihuateteo*, who were transformed into spectres equivalent to the living dead.

130 Figure with three faces

c. 250–700, Teotihuacan (?)
Fired clay and traces of paint,
18 × 22 × 9 cm

Col. Museo Universitario de Ciencias
y Arte, Universidad Nacional
Autónoma de México, Mexico City,
08-741814

131 Altar of nocturnal animals

c. 1500, Aztec
Stone, 56 × 67 × 62 cm

Museo Nacional de Antropología,
Mexico City, CONACULTA-INAH,
10-220921

132 Tlaltecuhtli

c. 1500, Aztec
Stone, 93 × 57 × 34 cm

Museo Nacional de Antropología,
Mexico City, CONACULTA-INAH, 10-81265

133 Brazier

c. 1500, Aztec
Fired clay, height 45.5 cm,
diameter 45 cm

Museo Nacional de Antropología,
Mexico City, CONACULTA-INAH, 10-223665

134 Goblets with images of skulls

c. 1500, Mixtec
Fired clay and paint,
height 30 cm each,
diameter 12.5 cm each

Museo Nacional de Antropología,
Mexico City, CONACULTA-INAH, 10-77820,
10-3344

143 *Cihuateotl*

c. 1300–1521, Aztec
Andesite, 74 × 45 × 42 cm

Trustees of the British Museum, London,
Ethno. 1990. Am. 10.1

144 *Cihuateotl*

c. 1500, Aztec
Stone, 73 × 48 × 43 cm

Museo Nacional de Antropología, Mexico City,
CONACULTA-INAH, 10-220920

145 *Cihuateotl*

c. 1500, Aztec
Stone, 112 × 53 × 53 cm

Museo Nacional de Antropología,
Mexico City, CONACULTA-INAH, 10-9781

147 Ehecatl-Quetzalcoatl

c. 1500, Aztec
Stone and obsidian, 41 × 23 × 18 cm

Museo Nacional de Antropología,
Mexico City, CONACULTA-INAH, 10-48

148 Macuilxochitl

c. 1500, Aztec
Stone, 36 × 43 × 54 cm

Museo Nacional de Antropología,
Mexico City, CONACULTA-INAH, 10-1102

149 Tonatiuh

c. 1350–1521, Aztec
Volcanic stone and traces of paint,
31.5 × 16.2 × 24.5 cm

Museum der Kulturen Basel, Basle, IVb 634

150 *Cuauhxicalli*

Late fifteenth or early sixteenth
century, Aztec
Greenstone, height 6.4 cm,
diameter 15.5 cm

Museum für Völkerkunde Wien
(Kunsthistorisches Museum mit MVK und
ÖTM), Vienna, 59.896, Becker Collection

153 Sacrificial knife

c. 1500, Aztec
Wood and flint, 7 × 31 × 5 cm

Museo Nacional de Antropología,
Mexico City, CONACULTA-INAH,
10-559650

151 *Cuauhxicalli*

c. 1500, Aztec
Stone, height 17.5 cm,
diameter 40 cm

Museo Nacional de Antropología,
Mexico City, CONACULTA-INAH,
10-220916

152 *Cuauhxicalli*

c. 1500, Aztec
Basalt, height 56 cm,
diameter 30 cm

Trustees of the British Museum,
London, Ethno. +6185

154 Heart

c. 1500, Aztec
Greenstone, 24 × 20 × 11 cm

Museo Nacional de Antropología,
Mexico City, CONACULTA-INAH,
10-392930

155 *Téchcatl*

c. 1500, Aztec
Stone, 94 × 80 × 28 cm

Museo Nacional de Antropología,
Mexico City, CONACULTA-INAH, 10-81578

163 Brazier

c. 1500, Aztec
Fired clay and paint,
12 × 23.5 × 20 cm

Museo Nacional de
Antropología, Mexico City,
CONACULTA-INAH, 10-78081

164 Vessel with stepped pattern

c. 1500, Aztec
Stone, height 40 cm,
diameter 81 cm

Museo Nacional de Antropología,
Mexico City, CONACULTA-INAH, 10-1091

166 Two-handled bowl

c. 900–1521, Mixtec
Fired clay and paint,
23.5 × 38 cm

Didrichsen Art Museum, Helsinki,
acc. no. 822

165 Urn

c. 1250–1550, Totonac (?)
Fired clay and paint, height 41.5 cm,
diameter 47 cm

Fowler Museum of Cultural History, UCLA,
Anonymous gift, X75.1531

167 Two-handled polychrome urn

c. 1500, Mixtec
Fired clay and paint,
35.5 × 40 cm

Colección Fundación Televisa, Mexico City,
Reg. 21 pj. 35

170 Altar of the 52-year
calendrical cycle

c. 1500, Aztec
Stone, 38.3 × 30 × 22.3 cm

Colección Fundación Televisa,
Mexico City, 21 Pj.9

171 *Xiuhmolpilli*

c. 1500, Aztec
Stone, length 61 cm,
diameter 26 cm

Museo Nacional de Antropología,
Mexico City, CONACULTA-INAH,
10-220917

174 Calendar stone

c. 1500, Aztec
Stone, 24 × 24 × 9.5 cm

Museo Nacional de Antropología,
Mexico City, CONACULTA-INAH,
10-223606

172 Calendar stone

c. 1500, Aztec
Stone, 31 × 37 × 15 cm

Museo Nacional de Antropología,
Mexico City, CONACULTA-INAH, 10-46541

173 Date stone

c. 1469, Aztec
Volcanic stone, 33 × 32 × 7.6 cm

Philadelphia Museum of Art: The Louise and Walter
Arensberg Collection, 1950, 1950-134-374

VII | GOLD AND SYMBOLS OF STATUS

During its transformation from wandering tribe to imperial power, the original Aztec community of farmers and fishermen developed into a hierarchical society in which power and wealth were concentrated in the hands of a hereditary nobility, the *pipiltin*. Under the patronage of the ruler, the *pipiltin* monopolised the important positions in the army, the civil service and the priesthood, and their ostentatious lifestyle set them apart from the commoners, in death as in life (cat. 201). Most of the objects in this section can be linked with the nobility, either in their private lives or, indirectly, through their public roles as administrators, warriors and priests. To emphasise their status they demanded expensive and exotic materials (gold, jade, tropical feathers, turquoise, jaguar skins) and also the highest quality of craftsmanship.

The ruling élite employed various stratagems to distance itself from the rest of the people, and class distinctions were rigidly enforced. The law code of Motecuhzoma I prohibited, on pain of death, all commoners from wearing sandals in the city, using cotton clothing or wearing expensive jewellery. This simplicity contrasts with the extravagance of aristocratic dress. Bernardino de Sahagún lists some of the items of dance attire stored in the royal treasury: artefacts of jade and amber, a cylindrical lip-plug of crystal with cotinga feathers in a gold setting (cat. 187), a greenstone eagle set in gold (cat. 192), a gold-mounted turquoise disc and gold representations of pelicans, eagles, fire serpents and plants. The pictorial manuscripts show that gold, coloured stones, patterned textiles and iridescent feathers were used in combination to create 'multimedia' costumes for both men and gods, and these costumes are also represented in sculpture (see, for example, cats 200 and 205, both of which wear necklace discs engraved with the symbol for gold).

183 Pendant bell

c. 1500, Aztec
Gold, 9 × 7.5 × 3.8 cm

The State Hermitage Museum, St Petersburg, DM 321

184 Pectoral with an
image of Xiuhtecuhtli

c. 1500, Mixtec
Gold, 10.5 × 7.5 × 2 cm

Museo Nacional de Antropología,
Mexico City, CONACULTA-INAH,
10-9676

185 Pendant depicting a
warrior-ruler with ritual regalia

c. 1200–1521, Mixtec
Cast gold, 8 × 4.5 × 1.5 cm

Trustees of the British Museum, London,
Ethno. +7834

186 Warrior

After 1325, Aztec
Cast gold-silver-copper
alloy, 11.2 × 6.1 cm

The Cleveland Museum of Art,
Leonard C. Hanna, Jr Fund,
1984.37

198 Fan

Grip *c.* 1500, Aztec; feathers 1999
Wood with parakeet and
hummingbird feathers,
40 × 10.5 × 4.5 cm

Museo Nacional de Antropología,
Mexico City, CONACULTA-INAH, 10-393455

197 Plaque or pectoral

c. 800–1000, Mixtec
Jade, 17 × 8 cm

Didrichsen Art Museum, Helsinki, acc. no. 822

202 Head of a feathered serpent

c. 1500, Aztec
Stone, 54 × 55 × 61 cm

Museo Nacional de Antropología, Mexico
City, CONACULTA-INAH, 10-81558

203 Plaque with an image of an *ahuizotl*

c. 1500, Aztec
Stone, 73.5 × 72 × 24 cm

Museo Nacional de Antropología,
Mexico City, CONACULTA-INAH, 10-81550

208 Round shield

c. 1350–1521, Aztec
Stone, diameter 17 cm,
thickness 5.5 cm

Staatliche Museen zu Berlin: Preußischer
Kulturbesitz, Ethnologisches Museum,
IV Ca 3982a

209 *Temelácatl*

c. 1500, Aztec
Stone, height 24 cm,
diameter 92 cm

Museo Nacional de Antropología,
Mexico City, CONACULTA-INAH,
10-46485

220 Plate

Fifteenth or sixteenth century, Mixtec
Fired clay and paint, diameter 21.7 cm

Staatliches Museum für Völkerkunde,
Munich, 10.3565

221–22 Two tripod plates

c. 1500, Aztec
Fired clay and paint,
heights 7 cm and 4 cm,
diameters 32 cm and 22 cm

Museo Nacional de Antropología, Mexico,
CONACULTA-INAH, 10-223671, 10-116504

227 Altar of the four suns

c. 1500, Aztec
Stone, 60 × 63 × 59 cm

Museo Nacional de Antropología,
Mexico City, CONACULTA-INAH, 10-46617

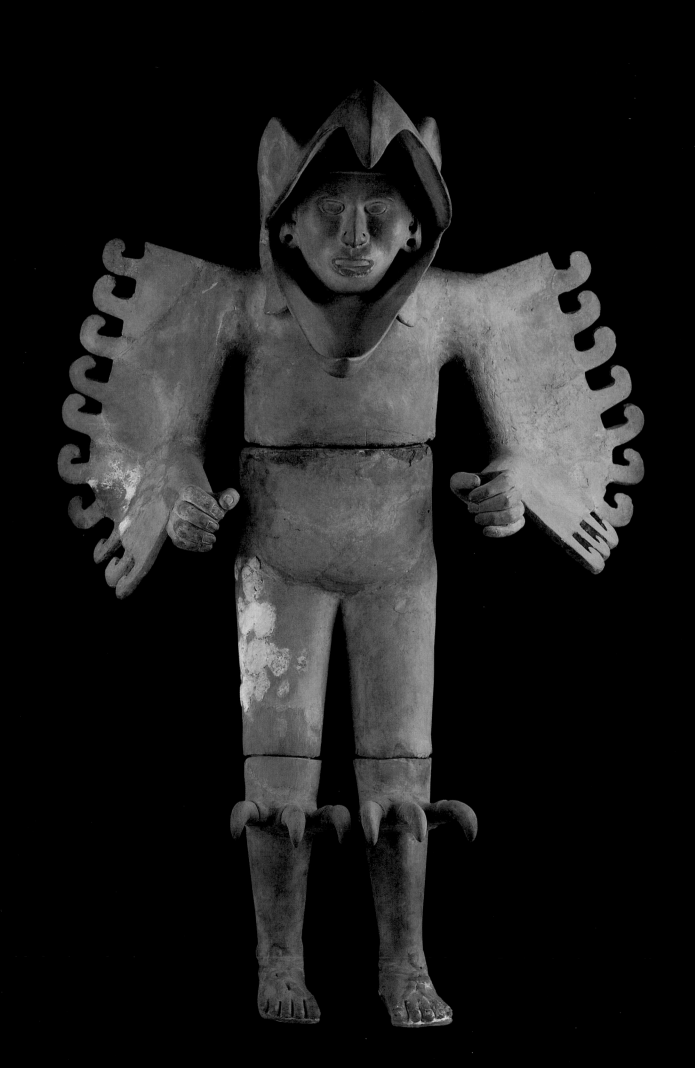

228 Eagle man

c. 1440–69, Aztec
Fired clay, stucco and paint,
170 × 118 × 55 cm

Museo del Templo Mayor, Mexico City,
CONACULTA-INAH, 10-220366

230 Seated god

c. 1350–1521, Aztec
Basalt, 34 × 21.6 × 24.5 cm

Museum der Kulturen Basel,
Basle, IVb 649

229 Huehueteotl

c. 1486–1502, Aztec
Basalt, 66 × 57.3 × 56 cm

Museo del Templo Mayor, Mexico City,
CONACULTA-INAH, 10-212978

233 Mictlantecuhtli

c. 1480, Aztec
Fired clay, stucco and paint,
176 × 80 × 50 cm

Museo del Templo Mayor, Mexico City,
CONACULTA-INAH, 10-264984

234 Votive vessel with an image
of Chicomecoatl

c. 1500, Aztec
Fired clay and paint,
106 × 74 × 51 cm

Museo Nacional de Antropología,
Mexico City, CONACULTA-INAH, 10-571544

235 Votive vessel with an image
of Xilonen

c. 1500, Aztec
Fired clay and paint,
99 × 65 × 49 cm

Museo Nacional de Antropología,
Mexico City, CONACULTA-INAH, 10-583437

238 Vessel with a mask of Tlaloc

c. 1440–69, Aztec
Fired clay and paint, 35 × 35.5 cm,
diameter including the mask 31.5 cm

Museo del Templo Mayor, Mexico City,
CONACULTA-INAH, 10-220302

239 Tlaloc

c. 1469–81, Aztec
Greenstone, obsidian and shell,
32 × 19.5 × 16 cm

Museo del Templo Mayor, Mexico City,
CONACULTA-INAH, 10-168826

240 Lidded pot with an image of Tlaloc

c. 1469–81, Aztec
Basalt and traces of paint, height 28 cm,
diameter 24.5 cm

Museo del Templo Mayor, Mexico City,
CONACULTA-INAH, 10-219815 1/2

241 Tlaloc

c. 1500, Aztec
Wood, resin and copal,
34 × 19 × 20.5 cm

Museo Nacional de Antropología,
Mexico City, CONACULTA-INAH,
10-392920

247 *Pulque* deity

c. 1469–81, Aztec
Basalt and traces of paint,
36.5 × 23 × 20 cm

Museo del Templo Mayor, Mexico City,
CONACULTA-INAH, 10-162940

244–46 Xiuhtecuhtli

c. 1469–81, Aztec
Basalt, 36.6 × 21.9 × 21.2 cm,
37 × 21.8 × 20 cm and
31.5 × 19 × 19 cm

Museo del Templo Mayor,
Mexico City, CONACULTA-INAH,
10-220304, 10-220305 and 10-220357

248 Relief with an image
of an eagle and a snake

c. 1450–1521, Aztec
Olivine basalt, 59 × 27 × 12 cm

Museum der Kulturen Basel, Basle, IVb 732

251 Serpent's head

c. 1500, Aztec
Stone, 90 × 92 × 155 cm

Museo Nacional de Antropología,
Mexico City, CONACULTA-INAH,
10-280936

249 *Cuauhxicalli*

c. 1502–20, Aztec
Basalt, 139 × 82 × 76 cm

Museo del Templo Mayor, Mexico City,
CONACULTA-INAH, 10-252747

250 Snail shell

c. 1500, Aztec
Stone and traces of stucco and paint,
105 × 75.5 cm

Museo Nacional de Antropología,
Mexico City, CONACULTA-INAH, 10-213080

252 Coatlicue

c. 1500, Aztec
Stone, red shell, turquoise and traces of paint,
115 × 40 × 35 cm

Museo Nacional de Antropología, Mexico City,
CONACULTA-INAH, 10-8534

253 Xiuhtecuhtli-Huitzilopochtli

c. 1500, Aztec
Stone, white shell and obsidian,
112 × 38 × 31 cm

Museo Nacional de Antropología, Mexico City,
CONACULTA-INAH, 10-9785

255 Head of Coyolxauhqui

c. 1500, Aztec
Diorite, 80 × 85 × 68 cm

Museo Nacional de Antropología,
Mexico City, CONACULTA-INAH,
10-2209118

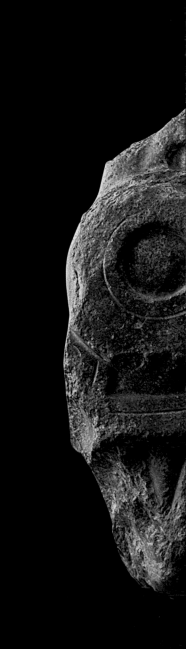

254 Mask of Coyolxauhqui

c. 1500, Aztec
Greenstone, 10.5 × 14.5 × 4 cm

Peabody Museum of Archaeology and Ethnology,
Harvard University, Anonymous gift, 28-40-20/C10108

262 Pectoral with an image of a moth

c. 1500, Aztec
Greenstone, diameter 13.5 cm

Museo Nacional de Antropología,
Mexico City, CONACULTA-INAH,
10-162943

265 Offering 106

c. 1325–1502, Aztec
Various materials and dimensions

Museo del Templo Mayor, Mexico City,
CONACULTA-INAH, 10-252003

263 Figurine

c. 1200–1481, Mezcala
Greenstone and paint,
25.4 × 5.7 × 4.2 cm

Museo del Templo Mayor, Mexico City,
CONACULTA-INAH, 10-220316

264 Figurine

c. 1469–81, Mixtec
Greenstone, 11.25 × 3.38 × 3.03 cm

Museo del Templo Mayor, Mexico City,
CONACULTA-INAH, 10-168804

272 Nose-ring in the form
of a butterfly

c. 1500, Aztec
Gold, 7.5 × 7.5 × 0.1 cm

Museo Nacional de
Antropología, Mexico City,
CONACULTA-INAH, 10-220922

275 *Chicahuaztli*

c. 1469–81, Aztec
Alabaster, 11.9 × 2.6 × 0.9 cm

Museo del Templo Mayor, Mexico City,
CONACULTA-INAH, 10-266040

276 Staff in the form
of a deer's head

c. 1469–81, Aztec
Alabaster, 9.4 × 3.2 × 0.9 cm

Museo del Templo Mayor, Mexico City,
CONACULTA-INAH, 10-265825

277 Knife blades with
an image of a face

c. 1325–1521, Aztec
Coffee-coloured and white flint
and green obsidian,
23 × 6.3 × 1 cm,
23.2 × 6.7 × 1.2 cm,
26.5 × 7.3 × 1.1 cm,
23.1 × 7.3 × 0.9 cm,
16.5 × 6.4 × 4.4 cm
and 15 × 5 × 3.9 cm

Museo del Templo Mayor, Mexico City,
CONACULTA-INAH, 10-220282, 10-220280,
10-220284, 10-220291 and 10-253024

273–74 *Xiuhcoatl*

c. 1500, Aztec
Gold, both 16 × 1 cm

Museo Nacional de Antropología,
Mexico City, CONACULTA-INAH, 10-594810
and 10-3302

279 Funerary urn with an image of Tezcatlipoca

c. 1470, Aztec
Fired clay, height 53 cm,
diameter 17 cm

Museo del Templo Mayor, Mexico City,
CONACULTA-INAH, 10-168823 0/2

278 Votive pot with images
of Xiuhtecuhtli and
Tlahuizcalpantecuhtli

c. 1500, Aztec
Fired clay and paint, height 25.5 cm,
diameter 22.5 cm

Museo Nacional de Antropología, Mexico City,
CONACULTA-INAH, 10-10918

287–88, 291 Models of temples

c. 1500, Aztec–Mixtec
Fired clay and paint, 39.5 × 23 cm,
28 × 14.5 cm and 39 × 24 × 15.5 cm

Museo Regional de Puebla, CONACULTA-INAH,
10-496916; Museo Nacional de Antropología,
Mexico City, CONACULTA-INAH, 10-496914 and
10-496915

290 Model of a temple

c. 1500, Aztec
Fired clay and traces of paint,
32 × 15.5 × 19.5 cm

Museo Nacional de Antropología,
Mexico City, CONACULTA-INAH,
10-223673

289 Model of a twin temple

c. 1350–1521, Aztec
Fired clay, 20 × 18.2 × 17.2 cm

Staatliche Museen zu Berlin: Preußischer Kulturbesitz,
Ethnologisches Museum, IV Ca 2429

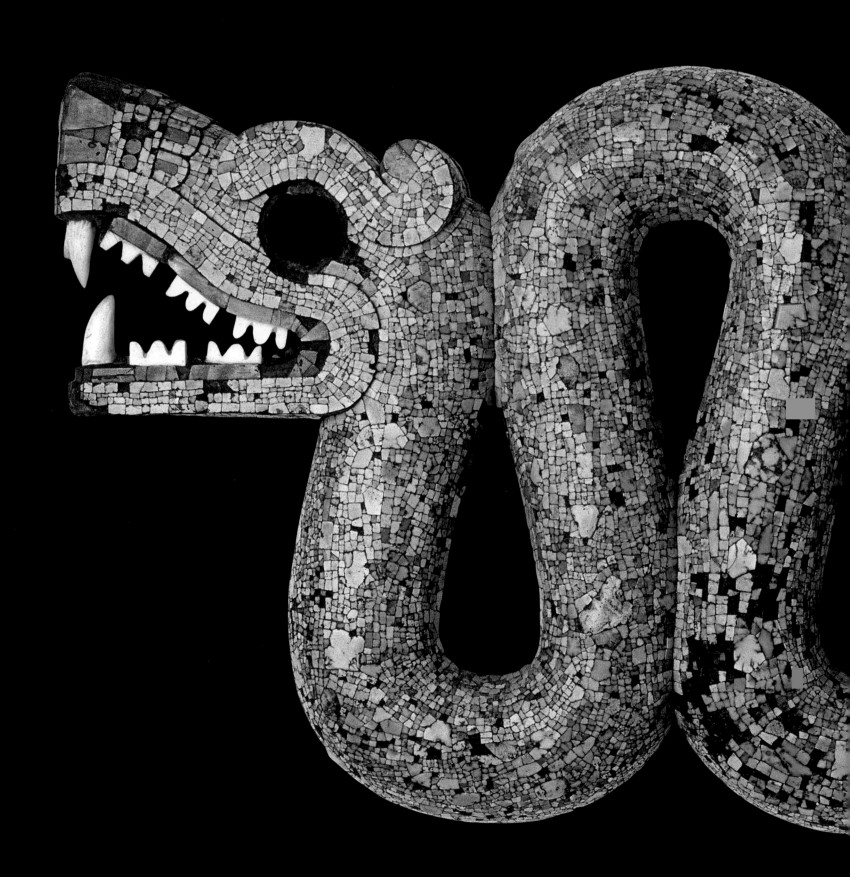

295 Handle of a sacrificial knife

c. 1500–21, Aztec–Mixtec
Wood, turquoise, malachite,
mother-of-pearl and shell, 5 × 12.5 cm

Museo Nazionale Preistorico-Etnografico
'L. Pigorini', Rome, inv. no. 4216

297 Tlaloc (?)

c. 1500, Aztec–Mixtec (?)
Wood, turquoise, jade,
malachite, mother-of-pearl
and red and white shell,
29 × 12 × 17 cm

The National Museum of Denmark,
Copenhagen, Department of
Ethnography, ODIh.41

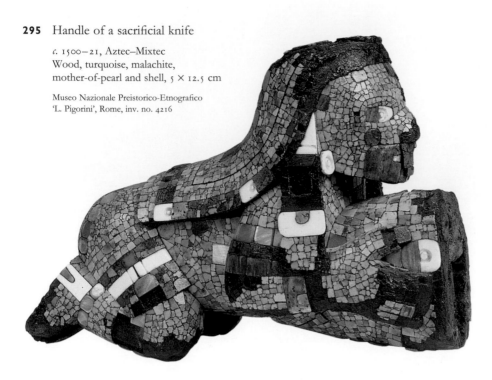

296 Sacrificial knife

c. 1400–1521, Aztec–Mixtec
Wood, turquoise, shell and
chalcedony, height 9.3 cm,
length 31.7 cm

Trustees of the British Museum,
London, Ethno. St. 399

299 Shield

c. 1500, Aztec
Feathers, sheet-gold, agave
paper, leather and reed,
diameter 70 cm

Museum für Völkerkunde Wien
(Kunsthistorisches Museum mit
MVK und ÖTM), Vienna, 43.380,
Ambras Collection

298 Shield with mosaic decoration

c. 1250–1521, Mixtec
Wood, turquoise and shell,
diameter 45.5 cm

Musées Royaux d'Art et d'Histoire,
Brussels, AAM 68.11

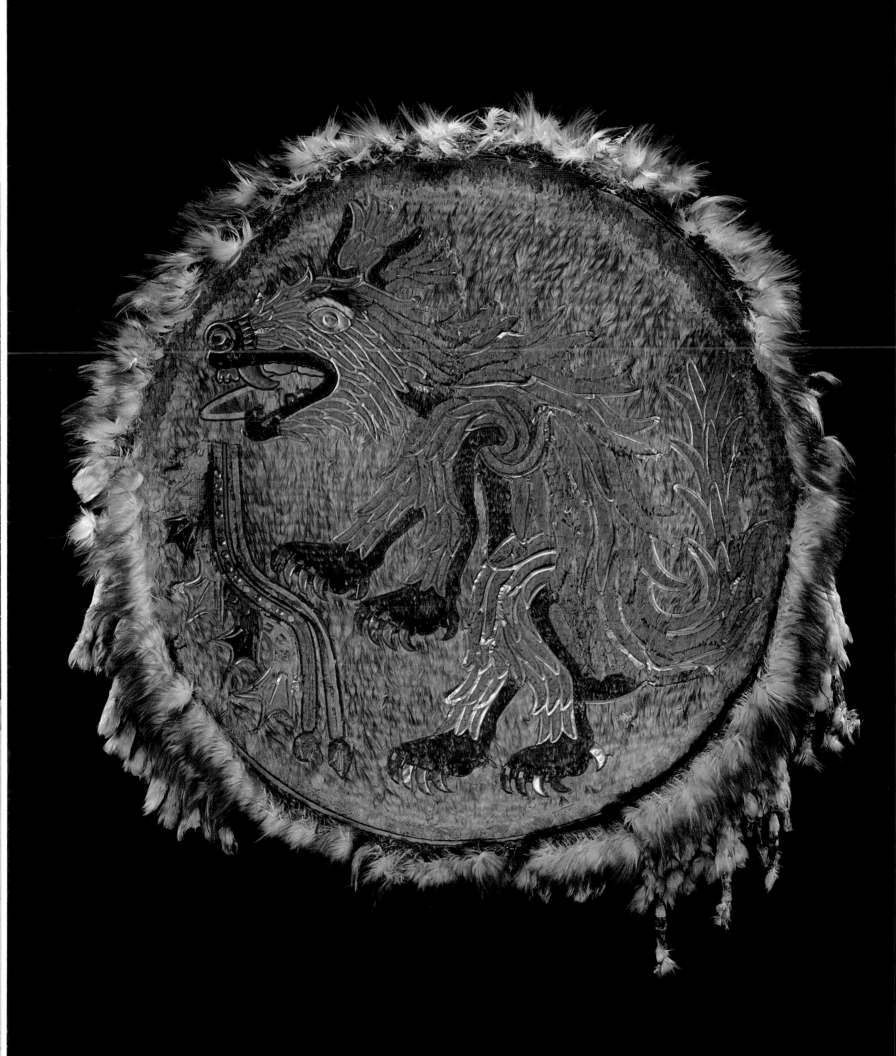

310 Pectoral

c. 1500, Aztec
Greenstone, 8 × 4.5 × 0.5 cm

Museo Nacional de Antropología,
Mexico City, CONACULTA-INAH, 10-8153

312 Mirror frame

c. 1500, Huexotzingo
Obsidian, 9.8 × 9.8 × 7.1 cm

Museum für Völkerkunde Wien
(Kunsthistorisches Museum mit
MVK und ÖTM), Vienna, 59.253,
Becker Collection

311 Pectoral or pendant
with engraved images

c. 1500, Aztec
White shell, 3.5 × 12 × 0.3 cm

Museo Nacional de Antropología,
Mexico City, CONACULTA-INAH, 10-275

313 Mask

c. 1500, Aztec
Greenstone, 21.5 × 19.5 × 10.5 cm

Museum für Völkerkunde Wien (Kunsthistorisches
Museum mit MVK und ÖTM), Vienna, 12.415

314 Pendant

c. 1300–1521, Aztec
Spondylus shell, 5.5 × 4.6 × 3 cm

Dumbarton Oaks Research Library and Collections,
Washington DC, B-82

315 *Átlatl*

c. 1500, Mixtec
Wood and traces of paint,
length 57.5 cm

Staatliches Museum für
Völkerkunde, Munich, 27-12-1

319 Human hand holding
a deer's head

c. 1500, Aztec
Deer's antler,
21.2 × 9.6 × 7.9 cm

Laboratoire d'Ethnologie,
Musée de l'Homme, Paris,
M.H. 87.101.714

316 Drumstick

c. 1350–1521, Aztec
Deer's antler,
length 22 cm

Staatliche Museen zu Berlin:
Preußischer Kulturbesitz,
Ethnologisches Museum,
IV Ca 41046

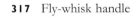

317 Fly-whisk handle

c. 1500, Aztec
Bone, 12 × 2 × 3 cm

Museo Nacional de
Antropología, Mexico City,
CONACULTA-INAH, 10-81623

318 Femur with
inscriptions

c. 1500, Aztec
Bone, 35 × 4.8 cm

Museo Nacional de
Antropología, Mexico City,
CONACULTA-INAH, 10-594025

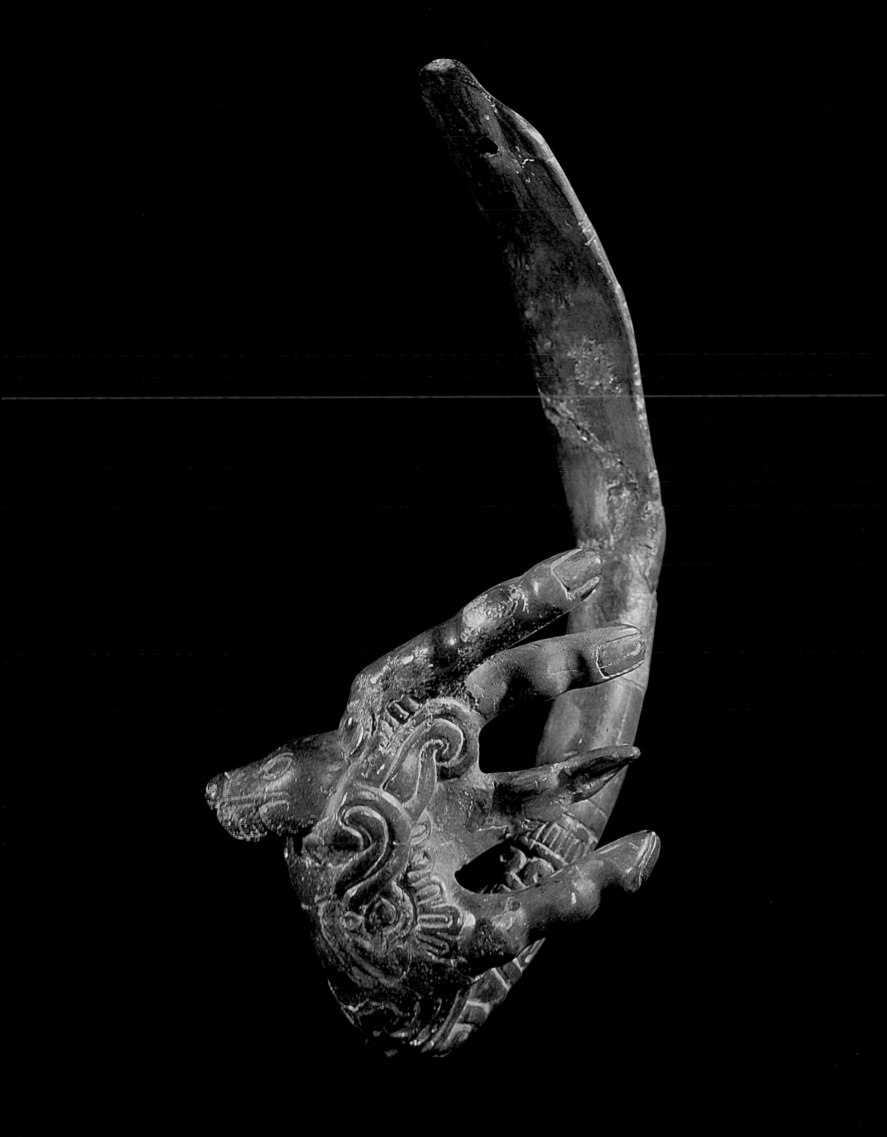

X | CONTACT: INDO-CHRISTIAN ART

If the pictorial writing systems of the Aztecs survived the Spanish conquest – albeit in a much changed form – other areas of artistic endeavour were less fortunate. This is especially true in the religious sphere: native architecture and imagery were wholly unacceptable to the Catholic Church, not just because of their close associations with the old religion, but also at the level of aesthetics. However, the invaders were not slow to recognise the potential of the technical skills behind their production. Special workshops were established to train native artists and artisans in the principles of Renaissance art and to impose on them the iconography of the Christian tradition. The models from which they worked were, in the main, engravings and woodcuts appearing as illustrations in bibles and similar imported theological works. Innovation was discouraged, above all in thematic art (portraits of the Saints or the Holy Family, representations of Christ's Passion and other biblical stories), in which, through error or intent, the 'signs of the Devil' might appear.

The greater part of surviving examples of contact native artwork comes in architectural sculpture and mural painting, which still grace churches and monastery buildings. The large stone crosses carved with the symbols of Christ's Passion that stood at the centre of their courtyards are also not uncommon. Portable objects, such as silver-, gold– and feather-worked crucifixes, chalices, wall hangings, altar cloths and ecclesiastical apparel, complemented these permanent fixtures not only in terms of workmanship, but also in that they were quite obviously the trappings of Christianity. As such, these edifices and the symbols and accessories that they housed might appear to announce a cultural and religious point of no return for Aztec 'art' and its executors, those scribes of old whose task was to 'write' the sacred, rather than illustrate or beautify it.

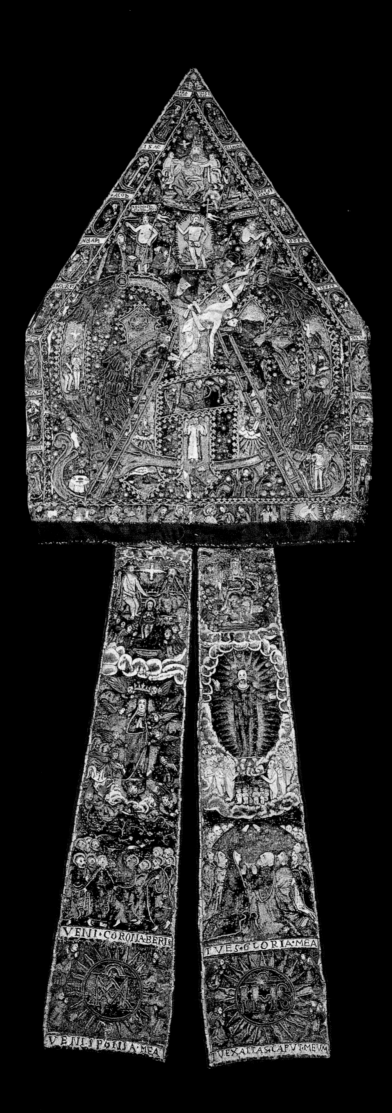

323 Mitre

Second third of the sixteenth century,
colonial
Feather mosaic on maguey paper
and cotton fabric, 82.5 × 28.5 cm

Patrimonio Nacional, Monasterio de
San Lorenzo de El Escorial, 10050202

324 Triptych

Late sixteenth century, colonial
Silver gilt, boxwood and hummingbird feathers, 8 × 8 × 0.5 cm

Victoria and Albert Museum, London,
226-1866

328 Chalice cover

c. 1540, colonial
Feathers and bark,
diameter 28 cm

Museo Nacional de Antropología,
Mexico City, CONACULTA-INAH,
10-220923

327 Chalice

c. 1575–78, colonial
Silver-gilt, rock crystal,
boxwood and hummingbird
feathers, height 33 cm

Los Angeles County Museum
of Art, William Randolph Hearst
Collection, 48.24.20

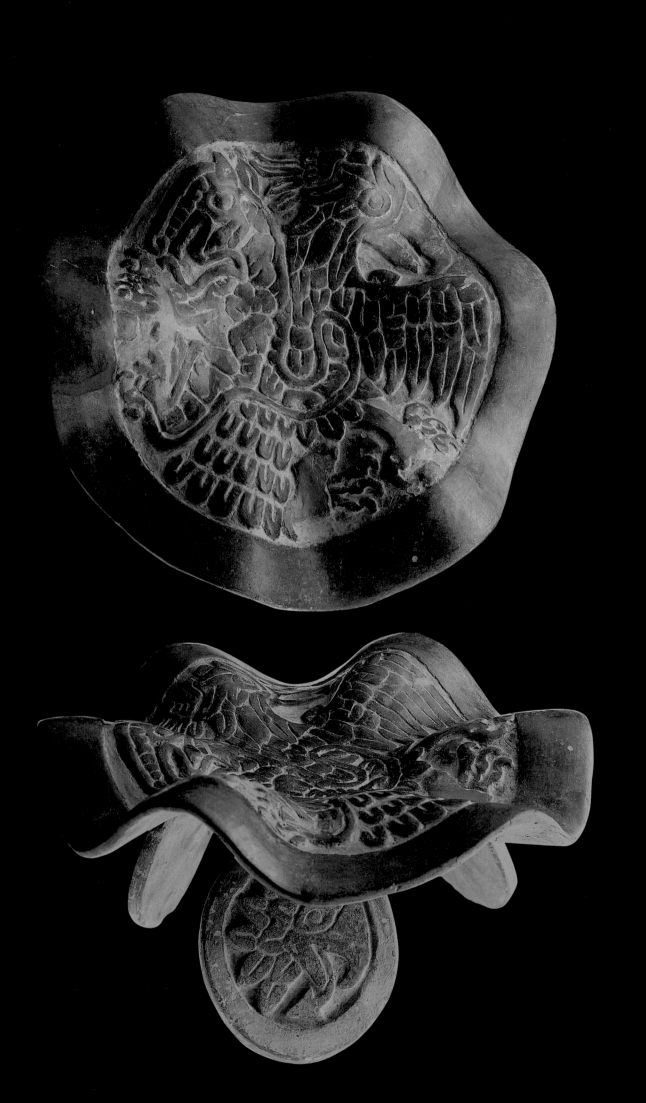

337 Tripod ceremonial plate

c. 1530, Aztec
Fired clay, height 10 cm,
diameter 23.5 cm

Museo Nacional de Antropología,
Mexico City, CONACULTA-INAH,
10-81584

338 Drum

c. 1521, early colonial
Chicozapote wood and animal molars,
22 × 88 × 25 cm

Museo Nacional de Antropología, Mexico City,
CONACULTA-INAH, 10-220924

339 Column base with an
image of Tlaltecuhtli

Image *c.* 1500, Aztec;
base *c.* 1650, colonial
Stone, 84 × 75 × 76 cm

Museo Nacional de Antropología,
Mexico City, CONACULTA-INAH, 10-46679

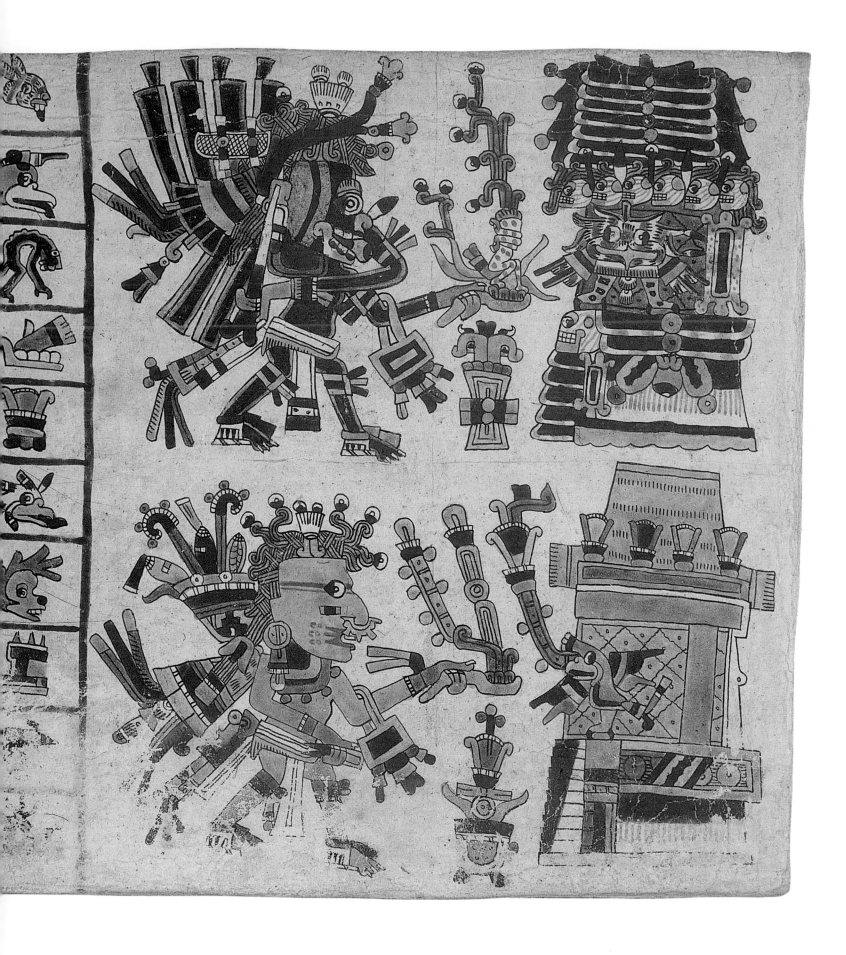

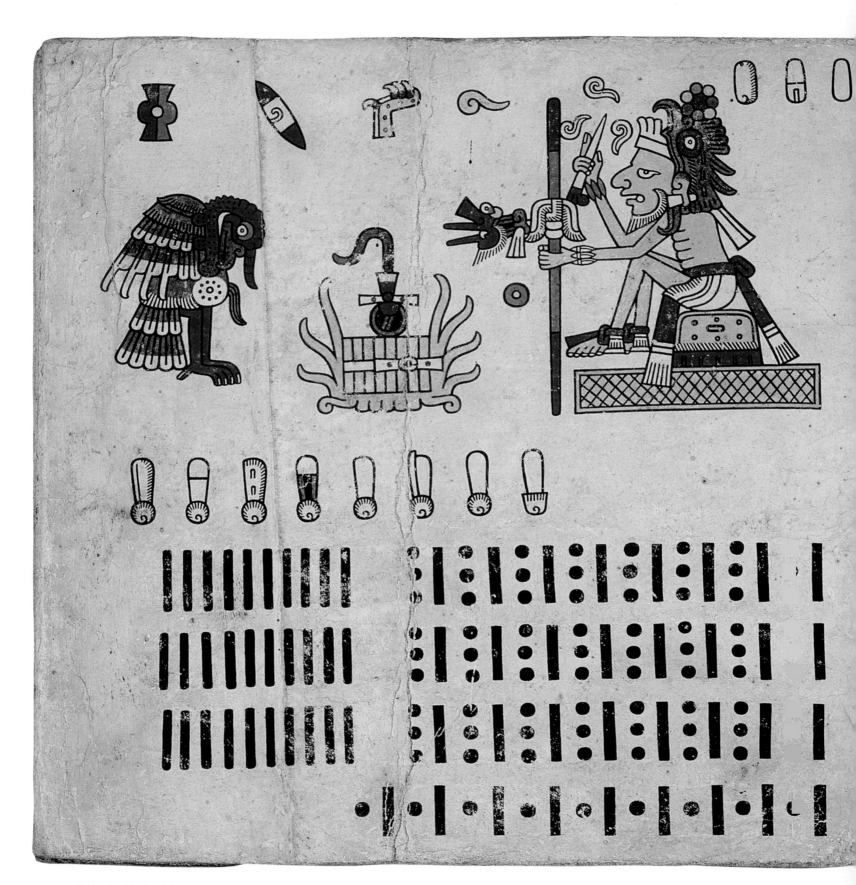

341 Codex Fejérváry-Mayer

Before 1521, Mixtec style with Aztec
and Gulf of Mexico influence
Screenfold codex, four strips of animal skin
glued together, covered with white lime (gesso)
and painted, 22 double-sided pages plus covers,
each page 17.5 × 17.5 cm, full length 403 cm

OPENING ILLUSTRATED:
pages 6–5

✝

¶ Este es vn diablo muy solemizado en sus rritos / el qual siempre tenja gran sed por sã[gre]
vmana y asi cada y quando q se le frecia tiempo o por tunidad pa ser adorado no avi[a]
de aver njngun ympedimento / y ase denotar q juntamente cõ ser comun a to[dos]
las oras este sacrificio deste de monjo avia vna lei q njnguno avia de entrar en su te[m]
plo sino sacrificaba vna escudilla de sangre vmana y juntamente cõ esto abia dell[os]
bar en san grentada la mano derecha el ydolo yva a sacrificar / y esto hazian por q este di[a]
les fuese faborable al tpo de su muerte en cuia memoria ponian a sus pies des te demor[te]
muchas cala vernjas y guesos de muertos signjficando q era señor de la muer[te]
y en estando ofrecida esta sangre ponjan vn escalera de rras del y subian por ella y o[t]
tra mas vanzela en cima de la cabeça en señal q recebia y ponja sobre su cabeça este sa[cri]
ficio para no lo olvidar al tpo de la muerte de aquel ydolo ofrecia // el tener la boca abierta y
la lengua sacada y encarnjçada signjfica jamas dezir de no a sacrificio q les frecieseñ

342   Codex Magliabechiano
Libro de la vida que los Yndios antiguamente
hazian y supersticiones y malos ritos que
tenian y guardavan

Sixteenth century, colonial
Codex, 92 folios, European paper,
16.5 × 22.5 cm

Biblioteca Nazionale Centrale di Firenze,
Florence, BR 232 (Magl. XIII, 3)

OPENING ILLUSTRATED: folios 87v–88r

88

343 Codex Durán
Diego Durán, *Historia de las Indias de Nueva España e Islas de Tierra Firme*

1579–81
Codex, 344 folios, European paper, 28 × 19 cm; nineteenth-century leather binding

Biblioteca Nacional, Madrid, Vit. 26-11

OPENINGS ILLUSTRATED:
folios 91*v*–92*r*, detail of folio 208*v*

se ponga por obra y juntamente señaleys
el año de otros rey donde empeço la gi
han obra passada y luego buscaron la piedra
que mejor les paresçiere para el efeto y res
pondieron los canteros que les plaçia de en
tera voluntad haçer aque se les manda
ua diçiendo que aquella sea su sepultura y lo
que perduran que les dessauan las me
orias y ello y salidos de su presençia fueron
se sin ninguna dilaçion al cerro de cha
pultepeç y vista la piedra ser muy apropia
da para el efeto enpeçaron la alabear y
a esculpir en ella la figura de los dos herma
nos las quales esculpieron muy al propio
y con tanta presteça que cassi no fue sentido
cauadas las figuras vinieron al rey a da
lle notiçia de como las figuras eran aca
badas diçiendole de esta manera poderoso se
ñor a esta tus siervos y vassallos les fue
mandado esculpir tu real figura y la de
tu hermano tlacaellel las quales estan
as estan hechas y acauadas con toda la per
fecion que hemos podido aunque no confor
me a tu merecimiento si fueres servido de los
yr a ver podras todas las veçes que quisie
res el rey se espanto de la brevedad con
que se auia hecho una obra que al principio
les se le haçia dificultossa y agradeçiendo
selo les mando vestir y dar algunas pre
seas de honrra en pago de su trabajo y soli
çitud y les dio dictados de honrra como entre
ellos asta el dia de oy duran tlacaellel di
xo al rey señor vros vassallos han hechos lo
que les mandaste justo sera que bamos a ver
nuestras estatuas la hechura que tienen
y una mañana sin ser vistos de nadie y sin

ninguna conpania salieron de la ciudad
y se fueron al cerrado de chapultepeç a ver
y consideran las estatuas y hallaron que
estavan muy al propio assi en el adereço
como en el modo de sus personas y asi dixo
el rey hermano tlacaellel contentadome
han estas figuras las quales sean me
moria perpetua de nra grandeça como tene
mos memoria de que tzacoate y de tupil
tzin de los quales esta escrito que quan
do se fueron dexaron esculpidas sus figu
ras en palos y en piedras en quien ado
ran la gente comun y sauemos que se
ran hombres como nosotros llevemos
nos nosotros esta gloria por delante
y bueltos a la ciudad estandolos dos
hermanos juntos sin ser visto de nadie
dixo el rey hermano yo quiero haçer un
concierto contigo y es que pues ambos
a dos hemos gobernado y sustentado es
ta naçion mexicana y la hemos en gran
deçido que si yo muriere primero que tu
que te quedes por rey de la tierra pues
fue hecho tan antigos lo mereçen y que
ningun hijo mio ni hermano ni deudo cer
cano lo pueda pretender pues lo tienes
tan merecido y si tu muriere primer
o quiero yo lo here de uno de tus hijos
el que tu señalares y que el se siente en
la silla y trono de nuestros antepasa
dos el rey acamapich vitzilivitl chi
malpopoca y çeuate tleyca y señores
de este mundo a tan grande de chessa
memoria los quales con no menos tra
bajos fundaron esta ciudad y la en
no eligieron derramando su sangre en

344 Florentine Codex
Bernardino de Sahagún,
*Historia general de las cosas
de Nueva España*

1575–77, colonial
3 vols, 353, 375 and 495 folios,
paper, 31.8 × 21 cm;
contemporary Spanish binding

Biblioteca Medicea Laurenziana,
Florence, Mediceo Palatino 218–220

OPENINGS ILLUSTRATED:
vol. 1, folios 73v–74r,
vol. 2, folios 369v–370r

libro. 2   *de las cerimonjas.*

qujtoznequj, amo mictlan iao
yoan ipampa inqujtzoncuja, y
mopialtiaia ynitzon: ichica a
oqujmomaceuj, inmavizcotl,
zuchitl ynietl, intilmatli: y
amo can nenpoliuiz itiaicau
io: iuhqujnma ic contleiocuj
aia malli. Auh intlamanj v
pa muchichioa intecanma,
nochtitla, iztac totolihujtl, y
mopotonja, injuh omoteneu
ipan quaujtleoa. Auh invn
momanaia tototecti, tecpanti m
vipantimanj ticapan, anoço c
pan: ipampa caticatl antoca in
can momanaia. Auh incana a
petl ipan, çacatl motzetzeloa, y
pan qujnoalmana, qujnoalque
qujnoalteitititia: tlaixco qujnoaln
na inxipeme, ynonmaqujaia ti
eoatl. Auh ynaqujque, mih
vintia, iauhtaueliloque, mixtlap
loanj, acan ixmauhque, iollo
paltique, iollochicaoaque, qujp
anj ynjntiacauhio, moqujchne
quj, qujmonpepeoaltia, qujmon
hecalhuja, oiaiaopeoa, qujnmo
iaopeoaltia. Auh inic vel qujn
uelcujtiaia, ynic vel qujmolin
ia, ynic vel intlauel, inguala
qujcuja, qujmonxiccuja, quj
xiccuj, qujmonxiccotona: ic n
man in xipeme tlapaynaltiaia
ymjcampa inteputzco icatiuh e

totec, itoca iooallaoan, qujntoca
qujntlaiehecalhujtiuh, in mu
chintin tototecti: ic njman in
tech ietiqujça, qujntlalochtoca,
qujniaochiuhtiuj, qujma aciti
uj, qujn mamacujtiuj, iuhqjn
in cotztitech ietiuj, intecaloanj:
auh oalmocueptiuj, oalmomala
cachotiuj, ocoquauhtica quin
oallaheecalhujtiuj. Auh intla
ceme anoia, intecaloanj, qujn
ujujtequj inxipeme, inchicaoaz
tica qujxixilia, vel. qujncocoltia.
Auh iopico conujcaia, amo can
nen oalqujçaia, amo can nen
caoaloia, itla ic moqujxtiaia,
itla iconanoia, aço totoli, aço qua
chtli qujtemacaia. &c. Ynoiuh
mito ipan itlatollo xippe, çanie
noiuh mochioaia: çatepan,
inonte totocaque, ynonteauj
eltique, ynontlapactique toto
tecti, xipeme: njman ic peoa
intlaoaoano, tecpantimanj in
mamalti, qujnnanamjctima
ti, qujujujcatimanj intlamanj:
njman no oalqujça intlaoaoan
que, yiacatiujtz, qeyiacatiti
ujtz, inteiacantiujtz occelutl
ipan qujztiujtz, conjttitia, conj
aujlia ynichimal, ynimaqua

Capitulo veinte, de los instrumentos, con que labran los officiales de la pluma,

E nesta letra, se ponen todos los instrumentos, que vsauan estos officiales, de la pluma: y tambien agora los vsan; donde quijera, que estan : por esso no se declara, en la Lengua española : quien quisiere ver los, y saber sus nombres, delos mesmos officiales, lo podra saber, y ver los con sus ojos.

tomecahoan mochiuhque puch
teca, inic iancuican qui petlaqui
anaoaca tlalli, icoac quinnoiuia
quineztique quiiocusque quinene
milique.

¶ Inic cempoalli capitulo:
itechpa tlatoa inic tlachichi
oa iniehoantin amanteca
in tlachichiuhque inqui
chioa ihuitl inic tlachi
chioa

¶ Inisquich intlachichioa
ia: intepuzuictli, tepuztlateco
m, inic motequi ihuitl, ioan ino
mihuictli inicmocaloa, ioan in
tlacuiloloni, in tlapalcaxitl inic
quicuiloa, quitlilania inin machi
ouh, ioan inquauhtlateconi ini
pan motequi ihuitl quinamicti
que intepuztli tlaquaoac qua
uitl intla tlauhqui. Auh inie
quine uelueis tultecaiotl: inih
uitlacuilolli iemochioa, quin ipã
inmotecuçoma: ipampa inicac
tlatocatia, ieuel ipan totocac, inic
oallacia quetzalli; ioan inie

mochi tlaço ihuitl uel ipan tlapiuis.
ic nonqua quintecac, quincalten cen
tetl calli quinmacac iniscoian iiania
tecahoan catca imtech pouia: nepanis
toca in tenochtitlan amanteca ioan
im tlatilulco amanteca. Auh miehoan
tinjz, canquiscahuiaia m quichioaia
jtlatqui Vitzilobuchtli inquitoca
iotiaia teuquemitl, quetzalquemitl
uitzitzilquemitl, xiuhtotoquemitl,
ic tlatlacuilolli, ic tlatlatlamachilli
im iemochi iniz quican icac tlaçoih-
uitl. yoan quichioaia iniscoian
jtlatqui motecuçoma: inquin maca-
ia, m quin tlauhtiaia icoahoan in
altepetl ipan tlatoque, ic monotzaia
motenehoaia tecpan amanteca
jtultecahoan in tlacatl. Auh in ce
quintin, motenehoaia calpiscan
amanteca, itechpouia iniz quitetl
icaca icalpiscacal motecuçoma:
iehoatl quichioaia, intlein imaceh
uallatqui motecuçoma inipan ma
cehoaia, mitotiaia: inicoac ilhuitl
quiçaia, quitlatlattitia, quitlane
nectiaia, mçaço catlehoatl queleuiz
inipan mitotiz: ca ceen tlamantli
iecauia, cerentlamantli quichioaia

345 Historia Tolteca-Chichimeca

1550–70, Cuauhtinchan,
Puebla
Codex, 50 folios,
European paper,
31.5 × 22.5 cm; modern
parchment binding

Bibliothèque Nationale de
France, Paris, MS Mexicain
46–58

OPENING ILLUSTRATED:
folios 15r and 16r

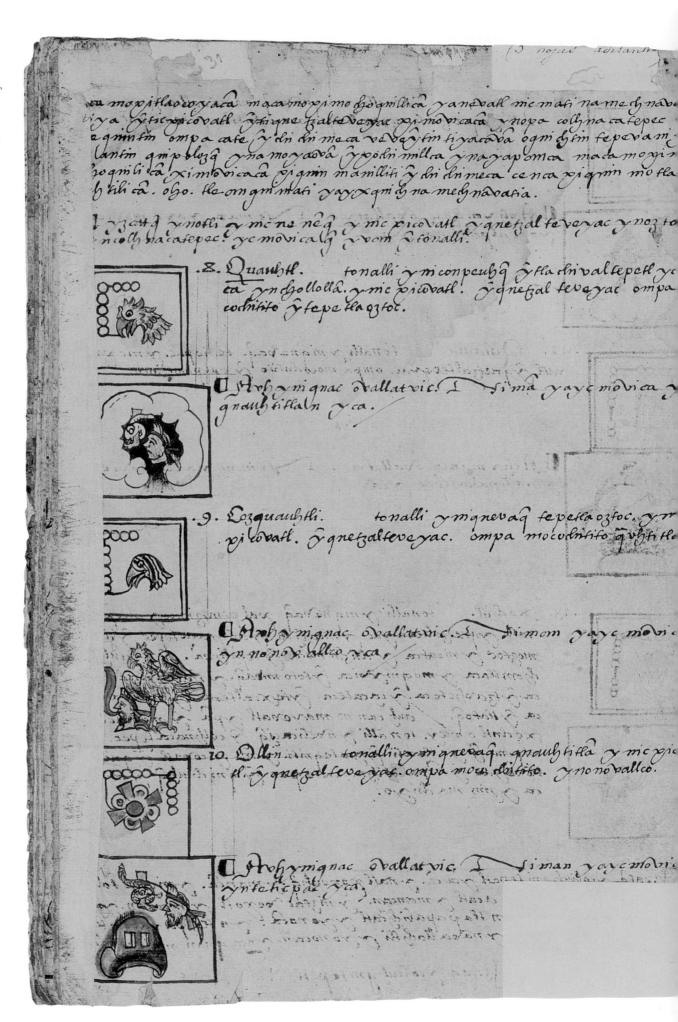

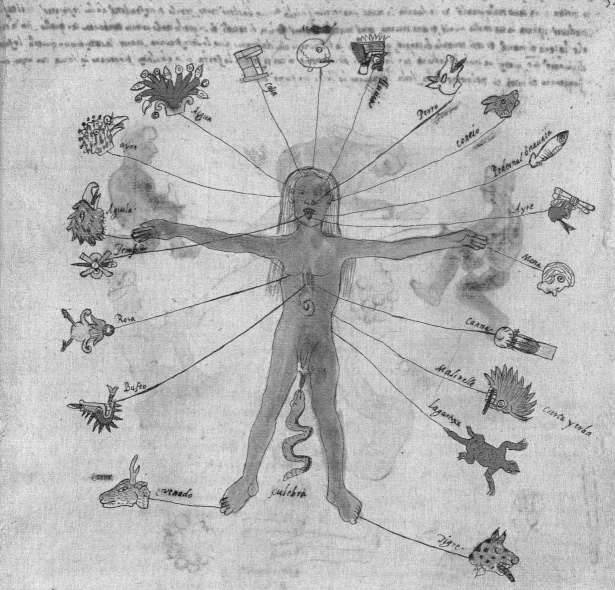

Queste sono le xx sorti ò figure le quali eglino usauano, per nar i lor numeri, le quali dicono ch'è teniano dominio soura
gli huomini, come qui si rappresenta: et di questo modo lor medicauano, gn alcuni s'ammalaua, o veramente le dolia qualche parte del corpo
Bufeo soura il fegado. Rosa nelle mamelle, temblor nella lingua, Aguila nel braccio destro, Ayra nell'uchio destro, conejo nell'uchio sinistro
Pederual ne denti, ayre nel pian, Mona nel braccio sinistro, cane nel cuore, Malinalle nelli odelli, lagartixa nella madrice delle donne, Tigre
la culebra, da qual suogha parte ch'ella uenga per il maggior auguriò di tutti ghaltri: et così ancora i medij usauano questa figura gn curauano
cosa si conosce che questa gente non era così bestiale, come alcuni la faceuano; poiche teniano tanto conto et ordine nelle cose loro, et usauano
il medesimo mezo che usano gli astrologi, et i medici fra noi altri, che ancora si tiene questa figura, et così si trouera ne refersy

346 Codex Ríos ('Codex
Vaticanus Latinus A',
'Codex Vaticanus
3738')

c. 1570–95, Rome
95 folios, European paper,
approx. 46.5 × 29.5 cm
each; red leather binding
(replacing original black
leather), 1869–89

Biblioteca Apostolica Vaticana,
Vatican City, A3738

OPENING ILLUSTRATED: folio 54*r*

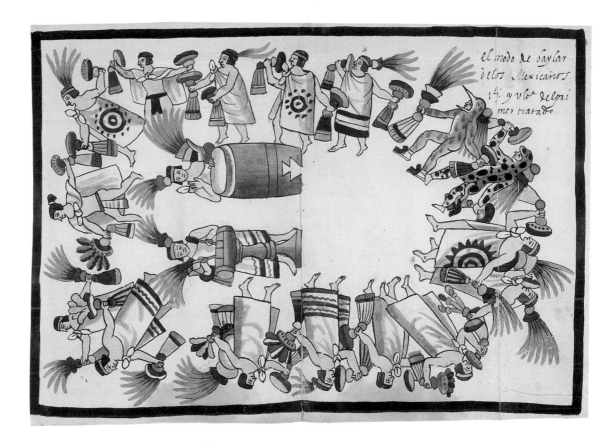

347 Juan de Tovar, *Relación del origen de
los Yndios que havitan en esta Nueva
España según sus historias*

1583–87, colonial
Ink and watercolour on European
paper, 21.2 × 15.6 cm

The John Carter Brown Library at Brown
University, Providence, Rhode Island

OPENINGS ILLUSTRATED: folios 119 and 134

349 Codex Mendoza

c. 1541, Aztec

71 folios, European paper,
30–31.5 × 21–21.5 cm;
seventeenth-century binding

Bodleian Library, University of Oxford,
Ms Arch. Selden A.1

OPENING ILLUSTRATED: folios 24*v*–25*r*

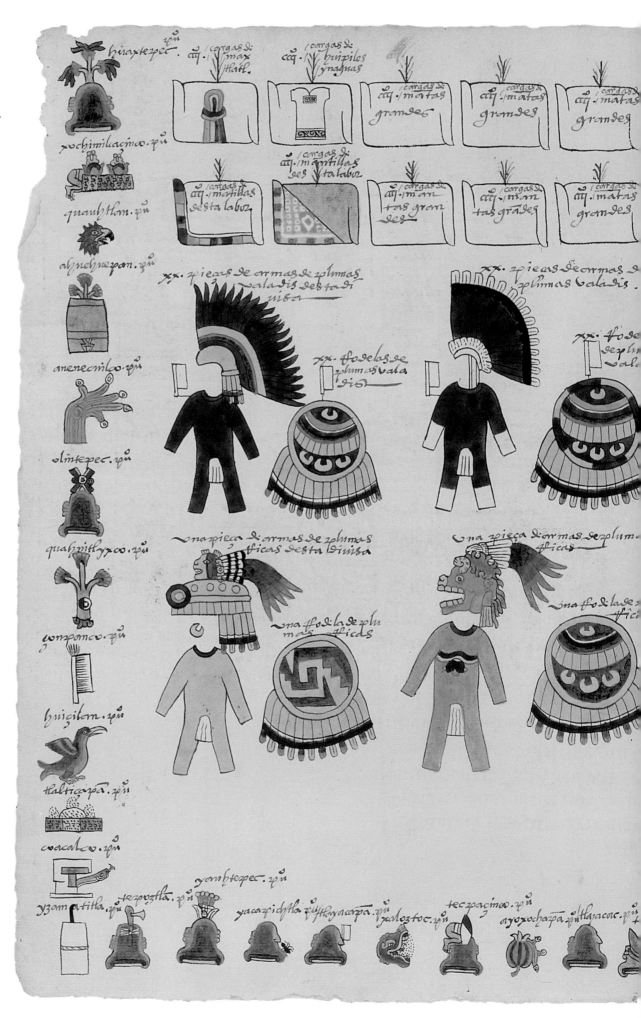

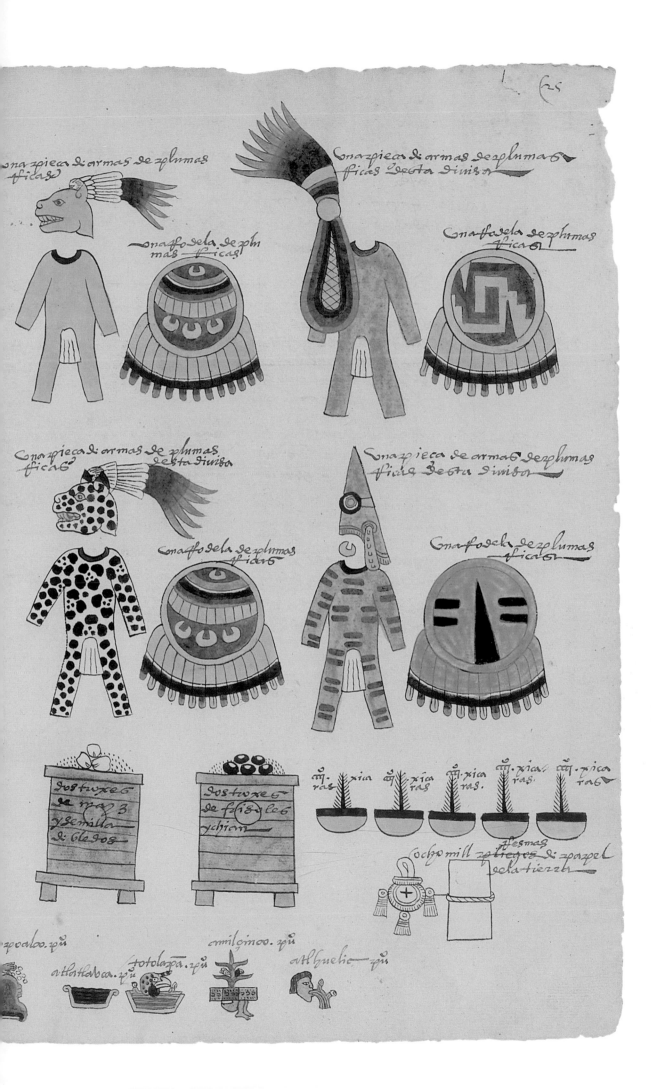

350 Codex Tepotzotlan

c. 1555–56, Tepotzotlan
Amatl paper, 40 × 110 cm

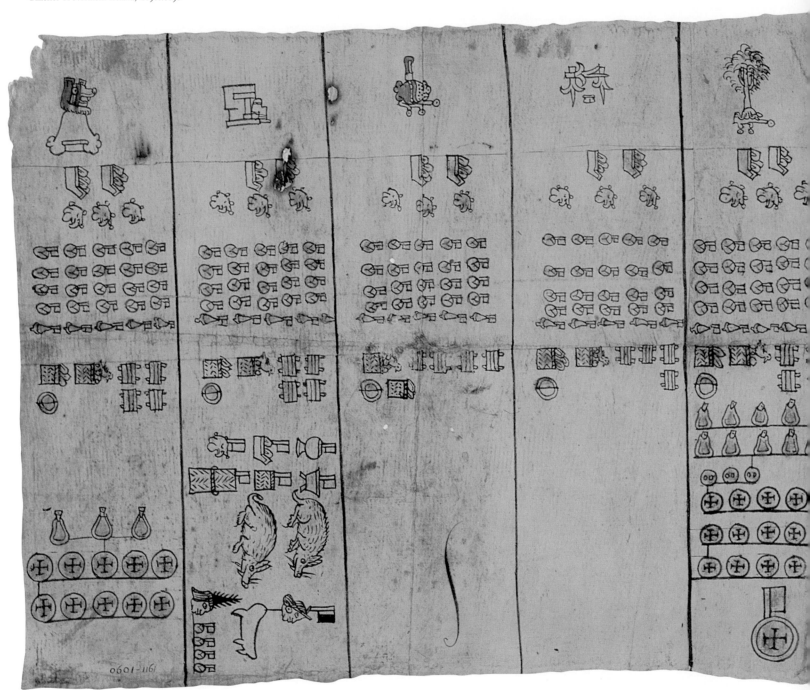

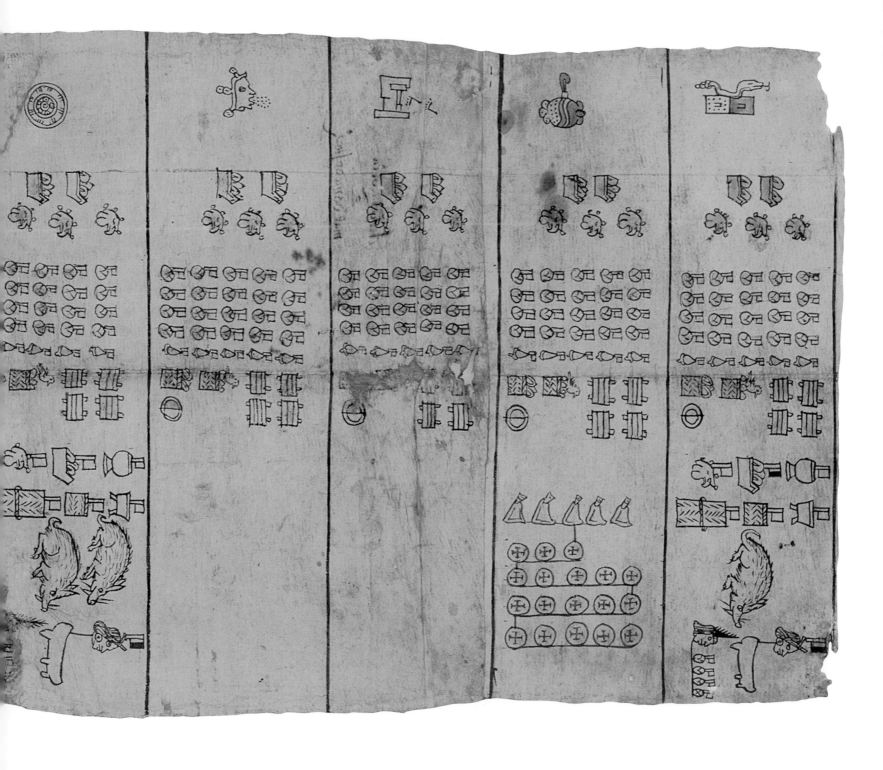

352 Lienzo of Quetzpalan

Second half of sixteenth
century, colonial
Paint on fabric,
154 × 183 cm

Colección Fundación Televisa,
Mexico City, 403

351 Codex Tepetlaoztoc

c. 1555, colonial
72 folios, European paper,
29.8 × 21.5 cm; unbound

Trustees of the British Museum,
Add. Ms 43795 (part)

OPENING ILLUSTRATED: folios 214*v*–215*r*

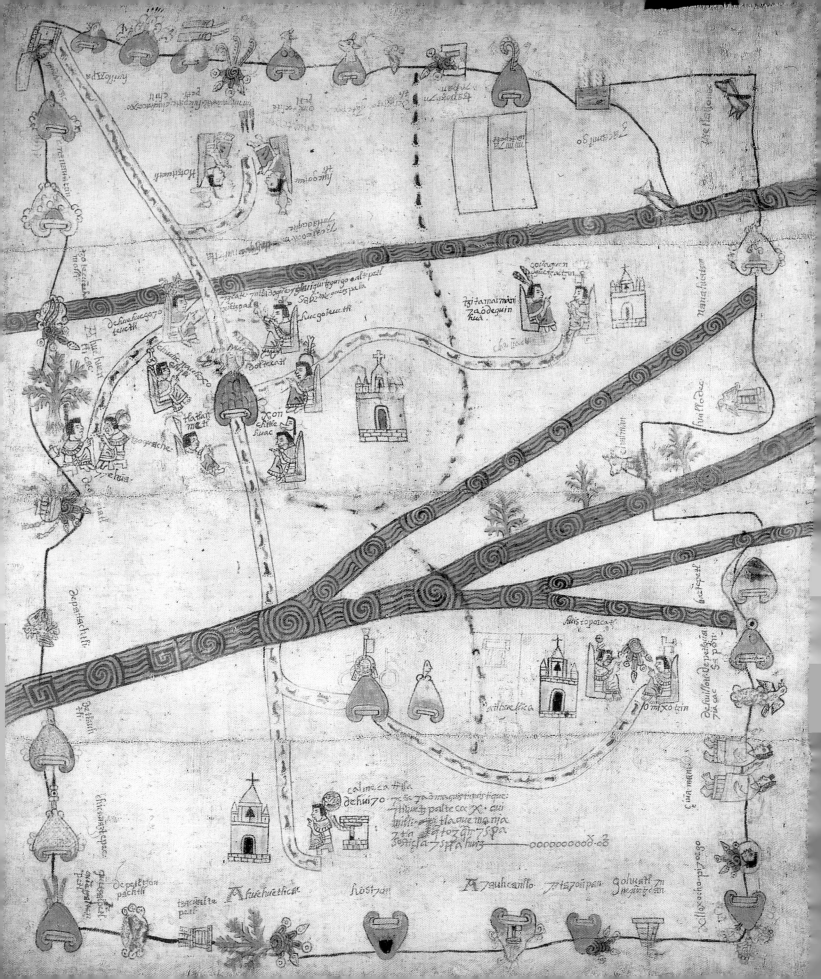

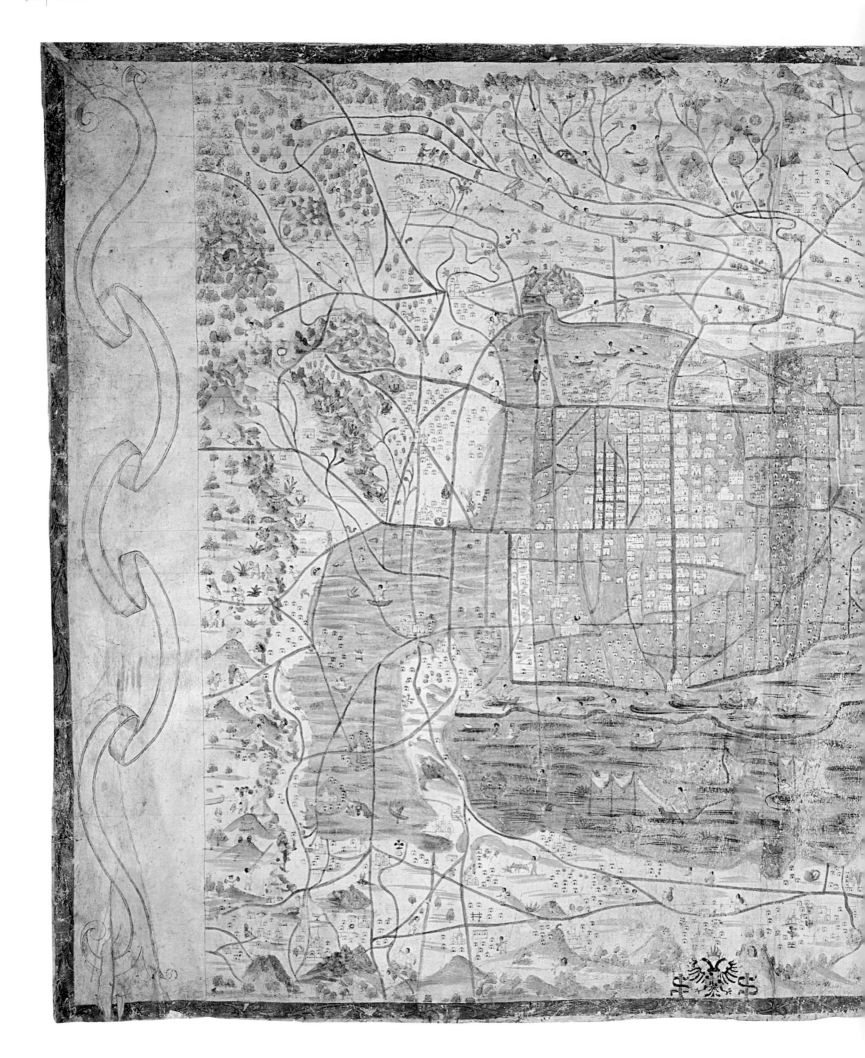

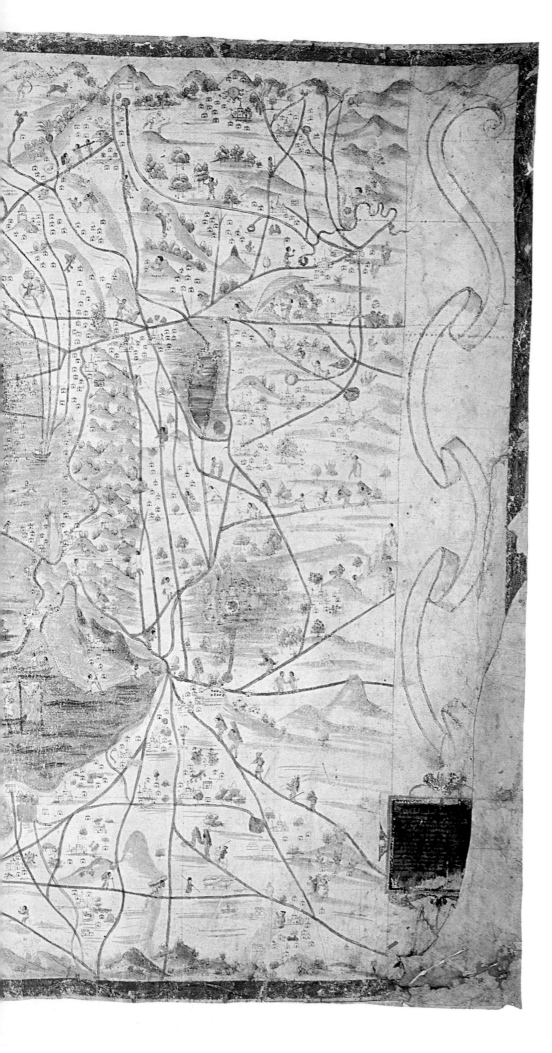

353 Digital representation
of the Map of Mexico City

Original: 1550s, Spanish
Ink and watercolour on
parchment (two sheets),
75 × 114 cm

Uppsala University Library

354 Codex Aubin

c. 1576–96, 1608, colonial
81 folios, European paper,
15 × 11 cm; red leather binding

OPENINGS ILLUSTRATED: main picture,
folios 58*v*–59*r*; bottom left, folios
25*v*–26*r*; bottom right, folios 41*v*–42*r*

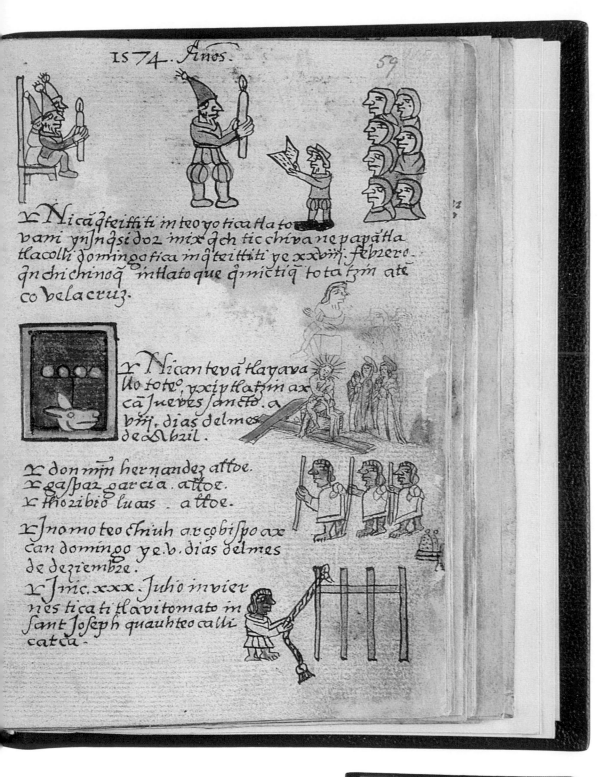

1574. Años.   59

↑ Nicã qteittiti in teoyotica tla to
vani ynInqsidoz mix qch tic chiva ne papātla
tlacolli domingo tica mq teittiti ye xxviij. febzero
qn chichinoq intlatoque qmictiq totatzin ate
co velacruz.

↑ Nican tevã tlayava
llo toteo, yxciptlatzin ax
cã jueves sancto. a
viij. dias delmes
de Abzil.

↑ don mjn hernandez altoe.
↑ gaspaz garcia. altoe.
↑ thozibio lucas. altoe.

↑ Jnomo teochiuh arçobispo ax
can domingo ye.v. dias delmes
de deziembze.

↑ Jnic. xxx. Julio invier
nes tica ti tlavitomato in
sant Joseph quauhteocalli
catca.

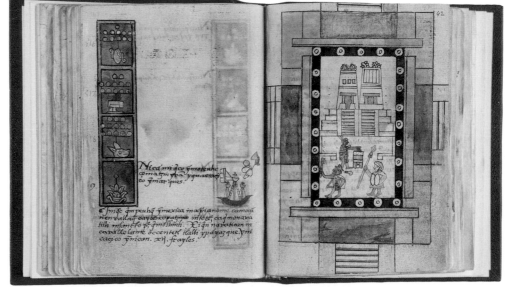

355 Codex Azcatitlan

Late sixteenth century, colonial
25 folios, European paper, 22.5 × 29.5 cm;
modern red demi-shagreen binding

Bibliothèque Nationale de France, Paris,
MS Mexicain 59-64

OPENING ILLUSTRATED: folios 22v–23r

356 Diego Muñoz
Camargo

*Descripción de la ciudad y
provincia de Tlaxcala de las
Yndias y del Mar Océano
para el buen gobierno y
ennoblecimiento dellas*
1581–84
Codex, 327 folios,
European paper,
29 × 21 × 3.5 cm;
original binding
of limp vellum

Special Collections Department,
Glasgow University Library,
MS Hunter 242 (U.3.15)

OPENING ILLUSTRATED:
folios 241*v*–242*r*

ymican. quintlahtique. tlatlacatecollo teopisque.

Incendio de todas las ropas y libros y atauios de los sacerdotes idolatricos
que se los quemaron los frayles.

357 Cochineal Treatise

c. 1599, colonial
4 folios, European paper,
29.8 × 21.5 cm, unbound

Trustees of the British Museum,
London, Add. Ms 13964, ff.
129–202

LEFT: Scene 3, *'Estas son nuevas plantas puestas de las que seccan ha podaron han se de poner por diciembre y enero para que con la primavera se lo nescan'* and scene 4, *'Aquí se pone la cochinilla en las nuevas plantas passados seis meses y más que se plantaron la semilla se pone por marzo y abril a los árboles viejos que a los nuevos, es bien no poner se la hasta que tengan más edad de seis meses o un año'*

RIGHT: *'Relacion de la Plata Reales Oro Joias que se a llevado a su magestad desta Nueva España a los Reinos d. Castilla desde el año de mil quinientos y vein y dos que fue recien descubierta y ganada esta tierra hasta el año presente de mil quinientos y noventa y nueve ques quando este memorial se haze &'*

Relacion dela

Plata Reales oro Ioias que se alleuado a su
magestad desta nueua españa alos Reinos d
Castilla desdeel año demil y quinientos y vein
y dos que fue rreciendescubierta y ganada es
ta tierra hasta el año presente demil y quinie
tos y nouenta y nueue ques quando este me
morial se haze &

ANOS	TESORO
Gouernando Hernando Cortes EMBIO IUD.XXII Años	Lij UDCC.IX.Pš.iiij Tš.IX.Gr.
IUD.XXIII.ANOS	No se lleuo nada.
IUD.XXIIII. años	xcix Ucc.Lxiiii Pš.v.Tš.viii.Gr.
IUD.XX.V.años	xxx UDcc.Lxxx vi.Pš.
ORO EN OIA	— UDCCXXXVIII Pš.II.Tš.
ORO EN IOIAS	— UD XC.II.Pš.
ORO SIN LEY	— UC.xL.v.Pš.II Tš
Gouerná do Alon so deestra da emvio IUD.XX.vi Años Oro sin Ley.	xx Ucc Lxxx vii Pš.i Tš.i.Gr. VUD.xL.II.Pš.
IUD.XXVII. oro Sin LEY. Oro en Ioyas	xlvii UD—v.Pš.vi Tš.vii Gr xvi U—XLIX Pš.iiii Tš. — Ucc xxx.Pš
Gouernan do la Real Audiencia IUD.XX viii. Oro sin Ley.	xxxiii U—x.v Pš.iii Tš.vj Gr. xvi UD.Lviii Pš.

358 Doctrina Cristiana

c. 1714, colonial
30 leaves (15 double folios),
European paper, 24 × 16.5 cm;
skin binding

Trustees of the British Museum, London,
Egerton Ms. 2898

OPENINGS ILLUSTRATED: leaves 4, 10 and 19

359 Christoph Weiditz,
Trachtenbuch

1529–30
Codex, 154 folios, paper,
19.4 × 14.5 cm; twentieth-century
leather binding

Leihgabe, Germanisches
Nationalmuseum, Nuremberg, Hs 22474

OPENINGS ILLUSTRATED: folios 12*v*–13*r*
and 9*r*

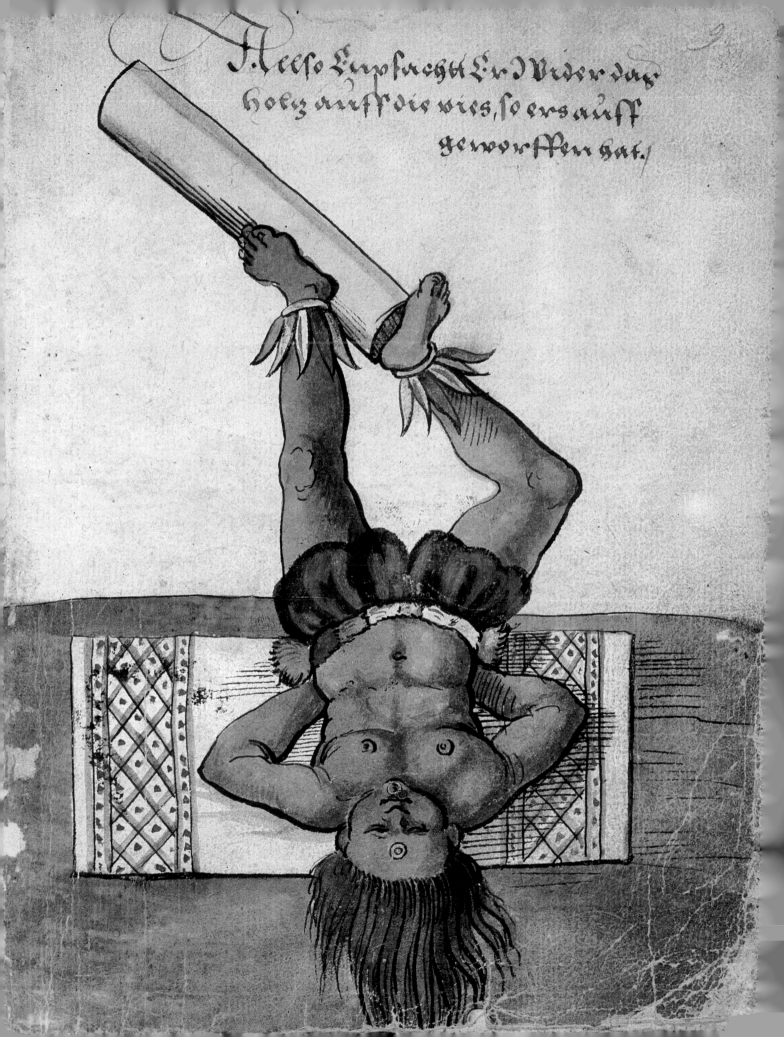

Also leysackt er d vider das
holz auff die vies, so ers auff
geworssen hat.

CATALOGUE

CONTRIBUTORS

AB	*Alexander Brust*
AG	*Angel Gallegos*
AL	*Adrian Locke*
BD	*Berete Due*
CE	*Christina Elson*
CK	*Cecelia Klein*
CMcE	*Colin McEwan*
CN	*Carlo Nobile*
CP	*Carla Pinzauti*
CR	*Corinna Raddatz*
DC	*David Carrasco*
DGV	*Daniel Granados Vázquez*
DW	*David Weston*
DZ	*Daniela Zanin*
EMH	*Ellen M. Hoobler*
EMM	*Eduardo Matos Moctezuma*
ES	*Eberhard Slenczka*
FFJ	*Fabien Ferrer-Joly*
FS	*Felipe Solís*

GC	*Giorgio Careddu*
GGG	*Gillet G. Griffin*
GMF	*Gary M. Feinman*
GvB	*Gerard van Bussel*
HK	*Heidi King*
IGR	*Ida Giovanna Rao*
JH	*Joanne Harwood*
JLVM	*José Luis Valverde Merino*
JO	*Joanna Ostapkowicz*
JT	*Jyrki Talvitie*
JWN	*John W. Nunley*
LDK	*Lily Díaz-Kommonen*
LK	*Lily Kassner*
LLL	*Leonardo López Luján*
LM	*Linda Manzanilla*
LOL	*Lars-Olof Larsson*
LT	*Loa Traxler*
MAM	*Martín Antonio Mondragón*
MCe	*Massimo Ceresa*
MCo	*Monique Cohen*
MD	*Mariam Dandamayeva*

MDC	*Michael D. Coe*
MFFB	*Marie-France Fauvet-Berthelot*
MG	*Maria Gaida*
MM	*Marilena Mosco*
MT	*Michael Tellenbach*
NJS	*Nicholas J. Saunders*
NR	*Nancy Rosoff*
PHA	*Pilar Hernández Aparicio*
RDT	*Rita De Tata*
RFT	*Richard F. Townsend*
RML	*Ruben Morante López*
RVA	*Roberto Velasco Alonso*
SEB	*Susan E. Bergh*
SH	*Sabine Heym*
SM	*Sonja Marzinzik*
SP	*Sergio Purin*
ST	*Stefanie Teufel*
UKR	*Ursula Kubach-Reutter*
VF	*Virginia Fields*
WG	*Winifred Glover*
WLF	*William L. Fash*

I ANTECEDENTS

1

Anthropomorphic figure

c. 800 BC, Olmec

Jade and cinnabar, 52 × 29 cm

Museo Regional de Puebla,
CONACULTA-INAH, 10-203321

PROVENANCE: probably Puebla State;
José Luis Bello collection, deposited with
the Banco de Comercio; passed to the state
government and the Puebla museum, 1970

SELECTED REFERENCES: Berdan et al. 1996,
pp. 208 09; Amsterdam 2002, p. 86 87,
no. 3

In the nineteenth century this sculpture belonged to José Luis Bello, an avid collector from Puebla who devoted a large part of his considerable fortune to acquiring paintings, furniture, glass, weapons and other items. His house near the main square of the city of Puebla became an informal museum, visited by travellers and other interested people. Bello considered the figure to be of Chinese origin, because it has full cheeks and because it is made of jade, a material thought to be especially abundant in the Far East. In his day little if anything was known of Olmec culture. When its specific characteristics eventually came to be recognised, at the round-table meeting of the Mexican Society of Anthropology in 1940, the present piece was added to the collection of Puebla's Museo Regional and became one of its most important items.

The sculpture depicts a high-ranking person, robust in stature and with the angular cranium typical of Olmec figures. He wears a short skirt held in place by a wide belt, a strip of which hangs down at the front. Among the symbols engraved in the clothing are a torch, which has been interpreted as an emblem of status, and signs standing for the four cardinal directions.
FS, RVA

2

Mask

c. 900–400 BC, Olmec

Jade, 15.5 × 13 × 7 cm

Museo de Antropología de Xalapa
de la Universidad Veracruzana, Veracruz,
Reg. Pj. 49-4013

PROVENANCE: Arroyo Pesquero, Veracruz,
1969; donated to the museum, 1969

SELECTED REFERENCES: Medellín Zenil 1983,
p. 63; Coe 1992, p. 62; Berdan et al. 1996,
pp. 235–37, no. 77; Amsterdam 2002,
pp. 177–78

The mask, with its half-open mouth and empty eyes, has a number of motifs engraved in its lower section. They relate to a mythical toad-like animal whose eyes contain a St Andrew's cross. This symbol, widely used by the Olmecs, has been interpreted as representing solstitial points on the horizon. Above the 'toad' are four motifs recalling Olmec images of infants, who were depicted with an incision in their skull and were possibly connected with maize deities.

Such masks fulfilled three functions. Initially worn in rituals, they were placed over the face of their owner when he died and buried with him. Centuries later, they could be recovered and used as offerings in shrines at springs, streams and mountain localities.

The mask was among a major deposit of archaeological objects discovered in 1969 at Arroyo Pesquero, near Las Choapas in south-east Veracruz. The find included other masks, figurines and axes, all finely carved from hard stones such as serpentine and jade. RML

3

Plaque in the form of a Maya warrior

c. 250–700, Maya

Shell, 9.5 × 5.8 × 0.8 cm

Collections of The Field Museum,
Chicago, 95075

PROVENANCE: Tula, Hidalgo; purchased
from the Antonio Peñafiel collection
by Frederick Starr, who sold the piece
to the museum in 1905

SELECTED REFERENCES: Charnay 1885;
Fort Worth 1986, pp. 78, 89;
Chicago 1993, pp. 67, 83;
McVicker and Palka 2001

This carved and incised plaque of Pacific pearl oyster (*Pinctada mazatlanica*) was first published in 1885 by Charnay, who noted that it had been found at Tula, Hidalgo, in central Mexico. The piece shows an elaborately attired and seated Maya lord on one side and Late Classic-period Maya hieroglyphs on the reverse. The few readable glyphs may refer to specific individuals.

The glyphs and the iconography make this the only definitively lowland Maya artefact found at Tula. Stylistically, the piece most resembles a number of small carved jade plaques depicting Maya lords that were crafted in the Usumacinta area but then exchanged, perhaps as gifts to seal alliances among the social élite. Many such items have been found far away from their likely place of manufacture. This plaque appears to have been carved more than once, possibly because it changed hands several times before reaching Tula. GMF

4

Goblet

c. 1100, Maya

Fired clay, height 31 cm, diameter 12.5 cm

Museo Regional de Antropología Carlos
Pellicer, Villahermosa, 64

PROVENANCE: Emiliano Zapata,
Tabasco, first half of the twentieth century

SELECTED REFERENCE: Amsterdam 2002,
p. 270, no. 235

The Chontales, also called Putunes, were a Tabasco-based group of Mayan people who dominated an extensive area of the coastal region of the Gulf of Mexico between Veracruz and Yucatan from the end of the Classic to the Early Postclassic period (900–1250). In the wake of several important military victories they established a complex trading network and introduced to central Mexico numerous features of the culture prevailing in the south-east. Among these were elegant 'orange' ceremonial vessels, notably goblets with straight sides and truncated conical bases. The surfaces of these vessels bear relief decoration, sometimes impressed using moulds, that depicts mythological scenes centring on rulers and warriors. The present example shows a warrior with a clay nose-ring and pendant with the glyph *ahau*, which denoted a lord in the Mayan world. Among the Toltecs such vessels were much sought after as status symbols, and tradition has it that the Aztecs commissioned a pair to commemorate the creation of the monolith of the goddess Coyolxauhqui (fig. 10) during Stage IV(b) in the construction of the Templo Mayor in Tenochtitlan, along with images of their principal war deities, notably Tezcatlipoca. FS, RVA

5

Huehueteotl

*c.*450, Teotihuacan

Stone, height 74.5 cm, diameter 80 cm

Museo Nacional de Antropología, Mexico City, CONACULTA-INAH, 10-79920

PROVENANCE: Teotihuacan, Mexico State, 1963

SELECTED REFERENCE: Bernal and Simoni-Abbat 1986, p. 148

From the beginnings of civilisation in Mesoamerica, Huehueteotl ('old, old god') was worshipped as the deity of fire and the heat of the earth. The earliest physical evidence of this cult dates from the times of Cuicuilco in the Late Preclassic era (600–100 BC), but the definitive iconography of the deity was not established until the Teotihuacan era (AD 200–750). Sculptures of the god show him seated crossed-legged with both hands resting on his knees, one clenched, the other palm up. Resting on his head and arched back is a large brazier decorated with four vertical bars and four rhomboid shapes, symbols associated with fire and the cardinal directions. He has the face of an old man, with wrinkled skin and only two teeth. His body, however, is full of vigour, indicating his commitment to keep alight forever the fire that illuminates the earth. FS, AG

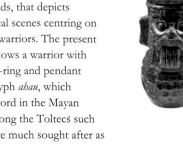

6

Urn

*c.*400, Teotihuacan

Greenstone, 24.5 × 14 cm

Museo Nacional de Antropología, Mexico City, CONACULTA-INAH, 10-9626

PROVENANCE: Nanchititlán, Mexico State; purchased by the museum from the first collection of Francisco Plancarte y Navarrete, first half of the twentieth century

SELECTED REFERENCES: Pijoán 1946, p. 104, no. 165; Bernal 1967, p. 87, no. 49; Solís Olguín 1991B, p. 56, no. 71

The rain-god cult was a constant feature of Mesoamerican cultures from the Classic period (*c.*250–900) onwards, when the region's chief cities were Teotihuacan and Monte Albán. Images of the deity showed a fantastical face with rings and bands around the eyes, prominent jaws and threatening fangs. Nahuatl-speakers called the god 'Tlaloc', the Zapotecs of Oaxaca 'Cocijo'. In the early years of the twentieth century the present ritual urn was given by a peasant to Francisco Plancarte y Navarrete (1856–1920), Archbishop of Monterrey and the possessor of a vast collection of archaeological artefacts. It would appear to combine the two iconographical traditions in the depiction of the rain god, those of Teotihuacan and the Zapotec region. The spherical body and the high neck recall the Tlaloc vessels characteristic of the Central Highlands (see cat. 243). The face of the god has bulging eyes and the eyebrows intertwine to form the nose in the Teotihuacan manner. On the other hand, the face-mask is similar to those found on urns from the early Classic period in Monte Albán and the most striking feature, the projecting fangs, likewise recalls urns with images of Cocijo. Another element alien to Teotihuacan is the bar across the forehead, a distinctive feature of the Oaxacan numbering system. FS, RVA

7

Standing goddess

*c.*250–650, Teotihuacan

Volcanic stone and traces of paint, height 91.4 cm

Philadelphia Museum of Art, The Louise and Walter Arensberg Collection, 1950, 1950-134-282

PROVENANCE: Louise and Walter Arensberg collection, 1950

SELECTED REFERENCES: Santa Barbara 1942, no. 137; Philadelphia 1954, no. 2; Townsend 1992, pp. 140, 142; Uriarte 1994, p. 113

The standing goddess is very similar to the monumental statue from Teotihuacan now in the Museo Nacional de Antropología, Mexico City. However, the present figure is much smaller and not as finely detailed, and was perhaps intended for devotional use by a small group, such as the inhabitants of one of Teotihuacan's apartment complexes. The basic iconography of the two figures is the same: the large square headdress identifies her as the deity of water, which was crucial to a large urban area that depended on rainfall for successful crops and could be devastated by drought. Her benevolence and generosity are indicated by the large, open, outstretched hands. The sculpture bears traces of red and green paint. These colours, with black and white, are typical of Teotihuacan fresco panels and ceramics. The art of Teotihuacan tends to emphasise abstract visual formulas, and here this creates a pleasing contrast between the blocky form of the figure and the curves of her ear-spools, eyes and fingers.

The Arensbergs probably acquired the figure from the dealer Earl Stendahl, between *c.*1935 and 1950. They enjoyed juxtaposing Pre-Hispanic and modern works, and displayed the goddess in their home as a counterpoint to the rounded forms of sculptures by Constantin Brancusi. EMH

8

Tripod bowl

*c.*450, Teotihuacan

Fired clay, stucco and paint, height 15 cm, diameter 16.5 cm

Museo Nacional de Antropología, Mexico City, CONACULTA-INAH, 10-79930

PROVENANCE: grave 14, Tetitla palace, Teotihuacan, Mexico State, late 1950s

SELECTED REFERENCES: Séjourné 1966, pp.108–17, nos 75, 92; San Francisco 1993, p.252; Amsterdam 2002, pp.100–01, no.20

The residential precincts of Teotihuacan, called palaces, were multi-family dwellings whose occupants participated in the main religious, political and economic activities of the capital. Artefacts found among ritual offerings in the palaces provide a wealth of information on the life of the inhabitants. The present tripod bowl, for example, discovered by the archaeologist Laurette Séjourné in the late 1950s, represents a prime piece of evidence for the importance of sacrifice and self-sacrifice in the Teotihuacan period (*c.*200–750). The vessel was painted in a technique similar to that used for murals. A thin layer of stucco mixed with an adhesive substance, often sap from the nopal tree, was applied to the wall of the vessel. The design was then drawn on the stucco, which was dampened to receive the painting. The figure of a walking priest, his apparel notable for its abundance of blue feathers, appears twice on the vessel. He wears goggles, linking him with Tlaloc, the god of rain, and he carries a large curved obsidian knife, holding its point at a human heart that drips three streams of blood. A scroll (the symbol for speech or song) evokes the sacrificial chant. FS, RVA

9

Tripod vessel

*c.*500, Teotihuacan

Fired clay and stucco, height 25 cm, diameter 28 cm

Museo de Sitio de Teotihuacan, CONACULTA-INAH, 10-336713

PROVENANCE: San Francisco Mazapa, Teotihuacan, 1984

SELECTED REFERENCES: New York 1990, p.108; Mexico City 1995, pp.169–70

This tripod vessel was found during excavations directed by the archaeologist Patricia Cruz in the village of San Francisco Mazapa, in the immediate vicinity of the archaeological zone of Teotihuacan. It contained the bones of a child and must therefore have been a funerary urn. The most striking feature of the decoration incised on this highly polished, coffee-coloured vessel is the face of a man with puffed-out cheeks and half-closed eyes – a sign relating to death in Mesoamerican art. Scholars specialising in the religion of the Teotihuacan era recognise in the face the 'god with puffed-out cheeks', a deity associated with plenty and thus with agricultural feasts. Ceramic vessels continued to be used as funerary urns in the Aztec era, the finest example being the pair of fine orange urns from Stage IV(b) in the construction of the Templo Mayor that contained the cremated bones of those sacrificed in honour of the gods of Tenochtitlan. FS, RVA

10

Mask

*c.*450–650, Teotihuacan

Stone, 22.5 × 28 cm

Museo Nacional de Antropología, Mexico City, CONACULTA-INAH, 10-9628

PROVENANCE: probably Teotihuacan

SELECTED REFERENCE: San Francisco 1993, pp.184–85

The artefacts produced at Teotihuacan, approximately 35 km north-east of Tenochtitlan, embodied the ideals of a pre-Aztec society in Mesoamerica during the Classic period (200–650). Extant masks, all of them depicting the face of a young, presumably male, adult, give sophisticated expression to those ideals (see also cat.12). Holes at the sides and the top enabled the masks to be attached to mortuary bundles containing the remains of the deceased: a clay model of such a bundle has survived that shows how the masks were positioned. For these masks, Teotihuacan sculptors favoured hard or semi-precious stones, which might be very highly polished. Examples are known in basalt, diorite serpentine and alabaster, and some bear traces of the original red paint on a stucco ground. The eye-sockets of the present mask contain remnants of the glue used to attach inlays, probably of shell. FS, RVA

11

Mask

*c.*250–600, Teotihuacan

Granitic stone, iron pyrite and shell inlay, 21.6 × 24 × 10 cm

Philadelphia Museum of Art, The Louise and Walter Arensberg Collection, 1950, 1950-134-947

PROVENANCE: Louise and Walter Arensberg collection, 1950

SELECTED REFERENCE: Philadelphia 1954, no.18

This mask, with its extremely simplified facial features, is typical of the Teotihuacan aesthetic. Such square masks of approximately the same size have been found in large numbers. The present example is remarkable in that it retains the inlays in its eyes, softening its features and giving it an almost personal quality.

Masks like this may have been attached to mortuary bundles (see cat.10) or they may have been placed on ceramic busts used as devotional objects by the inhabitants of Teotihuacan. They have holes for the attachment of ear-spools and could have been adorned with the salient features of different deities as desired.

The Aztecs considered Teotihuacan a sacred place. Centuries after its fall they scavenged objects there for ritual use in their capital, Tenochtitlan. Hence, masks of this kind have been found in many of the caches of ritual offerings discovered on the site of Teotihuacan's Templo Mayor.

The clean lines and smooth, glossy surfaces of these masks appealed to Western collectors in the nineteenth and twentieth centuries. Walter Arensberg owned more than a dozen, yet was far from their most prolific collector at the time. The present piece is probably the mask purchased by Arensberg from the dealer Josef Smilovits on 11 December 1950. EMH

12

Mask

*c.*250–600, Teotihuacan

Greenstone, 15.8 × 17.3 × 5 cm

Museo degli Argenti, Florence, Gemme 824

PROVENANCE: Grand Dukes of Tuscany, passed to the museum, 1921

SELECTED REFERENCES: Heikamp 1972, pp.25, 48, figs 54, 55; Guarnotta 1980, p.170, fig. 314; Florence 1997, p.127, no. 90

This mask dates from the third phase of Teotihuacan civilisation. The forehead shows a horizontal incision along the upper edge; the eyes will originally have been inlaid with white shells for the whites and black obsidian for the pupils. The mouth is half open, allowing a glimpse of white painted teeth and of the inside of the mouth, which is painted red. The left ear is pierced for the attachment of an ornament. A similar Teotihuacan mask is in the Birmingham Museum of Art, Alabama (see also cat. 10).

Like other Pre-Hispanic artefacts in the Medici collections, this piece was no doubt found by gold-seekers in the Central Highlands of Mexico. It appears as 'a mask of jade stone' in the inventory made at the death of Antonio de' Medici, the son of Francesco I, Grand Duke of Tuscany, in 1621 (Archivio di Stato, Florence, Guardaroba medicea 39, c. 30r). The mask must therefore have been in Antonio's residence, the Casino di San Marco, by the first decades of the seventeenth century. It passed to the Uffizi in 1723, and to the Museo degli Argenti in 1921. MM

13

Mask

*c.*450, Teotihuacan

Stone, turquoise, obsidian and shell, 21.5 × 20 cm

Museo Nacional de Antropología, Mexico City, CONACULTA-INAH, 10-9630

PROVENANCE: Malinaltepec, Guerrero, 1921–22

SELECTED REFERENCES: Pijoán 1946, pp.106–08, nos 168–69; Soustelle 1969, p.53; Solís Olguín 1991B, p.59, no. 79

When this mask was discovered between August 1921 and January 1922 its unusualness and excellent state of preservation led some scholars to doubt its authenticity. Eventually, it was acknowledged as one of the great treasures of Pre-Hispanic art in Mesoamerica. Its formal qualities link it with the style of Teotihuacan, and it was probably carried from there to its findspot near the Pacific coast by traders or by members of religious or military expeditions. The piece owes its compelling power to inlays of shell and obsidian in the eyes and to the blue of the turquoise that covers most of the face. Red *Spondylus* shell was used for the nose-ring (shaped like a geometrical *greca* pattern), the curved line of the eyebrows and part of the glyph on the forehead. This last feature, comprising what seems to be a vessel with four white, feather-like protuberances made of shell, no doubt relates to the identity of the personage depicted, which has not been established. According to those who discovered the mask, it graced a funerary image and the red shell necklace formed part of the deceased's adornments. FS, RVA

14

Plaque with an image of a goddess with a reptile-eye glyph

*c.*250–700, Teotihuacan

Pale green, translucent onyx, 29 × 16 × 3 cm

Collections of The Field Museum, Chicago, 23913

PROVENANCE: unearthed during construction of an irrigation canal in Ixtapaluca near Chalco in the Basin of Mexico; sold by W.W. Blake as part of a collection purchased for the museum by A.V. Armour, 1897

SELECTED REFERENCES: Holmes 1897, pp.304–09; Berlo 1992; Chicago 1993, pp.1–2, 23, 78; San Francisco 1993, pp.274–75

This engraved onyx plaque was first published by William H. Holmes, who described a series of biconical perforations along the upper margin. Despite these holes, Holmes reasoned that the piece was too large to have been worn regularly as a pendant and may have had a more special use. When first unpacked in Chicago more than a century ago, the plaque was found to be broken. A longitudinal perforation exposed in section by the fracture revealed the end of a tubular bone drill used to make the holes.

Although polished on all sides, the plaque is engraved on only one face. The engraving depicts a figure in a fully frontal pose wearing an elaborate headdress, ear ornaments and a nose-bar. Both hands are open. Images of this type have been noted with emblematic regularity at Teotihuacan and are thought to represent a key female supernatural being, denoted by a reptile-eye glyph, with fertility associations. GMF

15

Anthropomorphic figure

*c.*400, Teotihuacan

Greenstone, 25.5 × 10 cm

Museo Nacional de Antropología, Mexico City, CONACULTA-INAH, 10-2562

PROVENANCE: Covarrubias collection, donated to the museum, first half of the twentieth century

SELECTED REFERENCES: Lothrop 1964, p.43; Solís Olguín 1991B, p.57, no. 73

In the 1940s many intellectuals and show-business personalities in Mexico began collecting items of Pre-Hispanic art, impressed by their appearance, rare materials or unusual shapes. The present figure, for example, was acquired, reportedly in Guerrero or Oaxaca, by Miguel Covarrubias, a famous caricaturist who became a leading authority on Pre-Hispanic art and the author of a classic book on the subject. The medium-sized sculpture, carved from veined greenstone, probably depicts a naked man. The sculptor shaped the parts of the figure with great subtlety, softening the facial features and body and emphasising the collarbone and eyelids by incisions. The holes on the cheekbones formerly held inlays, the large cavity in the belly a small piece of jade symbolising the figure's heart. Although the sculpture has been attributed to Teotihuacan, its formal qualities do not conform to the classical canons of the Teotihuacan style.

FS, RVA

16

Anthropomorphic figure

c. 400–600, Teotihuacan

Serpentine, height 34 cm

Museum für Völkerkunde, Hamburg, B264

PROVENANCE: donated to the museum by C. W. Lüders, 1880

SELECTED REFERENCE: Hildesheim 1986, vol. 2, p. 126

Tool marks on the head of this standing figure indicate that the sculpture is unfinished. The two holes in the right leg were probably for attaching a foot. The right ear has been broken off. The figure was no doubt buried in this state as an offering, either in a tomb or as part of a deposit in, say, the floor of a building.

The figure dates from the Xolalpan phase of Teotihuacan culture, but the glyphs incised in its breast – '1-flint' and '3-movement' – were probably added in Aztec times. The first date relates to the year of birth of Huitzilopochtli, the patron god of the Aztecs, who evidently valued this product of an earlier culture.

CR

17

Mythological feline

c. 400, Teotihuacan

Volcanic stone, stucco and paint, 96.5 × 97.5 × 74.5 cm

Museo Nacional de Antropología, Mexico City, CONACULTA-INAH, 10-626269 0/10

PROVENANCE: Xalla compound, Teotihuacan, Mexico State, 2001

SELECTED REFERENCES: Benson 1972; Winning 1987, vol. 1, pp. 97–109; Saunders 1998; López Luján and Manzanilla 2001

The jaguar and the puma were of deep political and religious significance from the time of the Olmecs to that of the Aztecs. Mesoamericans symbolically linked felines with the night, the underworld, the earth and fertility because of their nocturnal habits, with war and sacrifice because of their ferocity and with magic and sorcery because of their furtive manner and their excellent night-time vision. For this last reason, the jaguar was considered the most effective ally of transforming shamans and, by extension, the ultimate patron and symbol of élites and governments.

The sculpture depicts a mythical feline emerging from a doorway that is decorated with starfishes, zigzag patterns signifying light and fringe feathers. The image symbolises the passage from the 'other world'. It was discovered in 2001 by members of the Xalla project in the ruins of what appears to be a gigantic palace situated north of the Pyramid of the Sun. The feline's head has bird's eyes: round, feathered, with serrated edges. The block supporting the head is missing, but similar representations suggest that the feline originally had the forked tongue of a serpent. The paws have large claws, hooked and extremely sharp. Two additional slabs show scrolls and flowers sprouting from the doorway. In Teotihuacan iconography mythical felines often emerge from water and are frequently associated with the storm god, the emblem of the city and its power. Similar felines and portals were found in the Pyramid of the Sun, indicating a close relationship between this building and the Xalla compound.

LLL, LM, WLF

18

Offering vessel in the form of an ocelot

c. 400–600, Teotihuacan

Calcite onyx, 16 × 31 × 33.5 cm

Trustees of the British Museum, London, Ethno. 1926-22

PROVENANCE: purchased with the Christy Fund from Miss L. H. Wake, 1926

SELECTED REFERENCE: McEwan 1994, p. 69

Ceremonial vessels and other objects were sculpted in stone that was carefully selected for its visual qualities and symbolic value. This striking vessel is carved from translucent white stone called *tecalli* (calcite onyx in this case) that was quarried in the town of Tecalco in the Mexican Highlands. It is fashioned in the form of an ocelot (*Panthera pardalis*), a species of feline native to highland Mexico that has a distinctive spotted pelt. Like the larger and much-feared jaguar, this creature habitually emerges at dusk to hunt its prey by night. The marked rectangular geometry of the vessel emphasises the planar surfaces and formal elements evident in public architecture at Teotihuacan. Even the outstretched front and rear paws of the animal obey this rigid symmetry. The same aesthetic is expressed in the impassive features of large stone masks (cats 10, 12) and imparts a distinctive 'corporate' style to Teotihuacan sculpture. The eyes and mouth were probably once inlaid with semi-precious shell or stone, and the two depressions hollowed in the back were used to place offerings. CMcE

19

Model of a temple

c. 1500, Aztec

Fired clay and stucco, 31.5 × 35 × 23 cm

Museo de Sitio de Tula, CONACULTA-INAH, 10-215143

PROVENANCE: Tula, Hidalgo, 1947–48

Archaeological excavations of the Burnt Palace in Tula (see cat. 20) provided important evidence of the Aztec reoccupation of the ancient Toltec city after it had been abandoned for a long time. In the main room of the palace

27

Deified warrior

c. 1500, Aztec

Stone, 119 × 48 × 34.5 cm

Museo Nacional de Antropología,
Mexico City, CONACULTA-INAH, 10-48555

PROVENANCE: Ceremonial Precinct of the
Templo Mayor, Mexico City, 1944

28

Deified warrior

c. 1500, Aztec

Stone, 120 × 42 × 37 cm

Museo Nacional de Antropología,
Mexico City, CONACULTA-INAH, 10-81768

PROVENANCE: Ceremonial Precinct of the
Templo Mayor, Mexico City, 1944

29

Deified warrior

c. 1500, Aztec

Stone, 120 × 41 × 39 cm

Museo Nacional de Antropología,
Mexico City, CONACULTA-INAH, 10-9774

PROVENANCE: Ceremonial Precinct of the
Templo Mayor, Mexico City, 1944

30

Deified warrior

c. 1500, Aztec

Stone, 119 × 38 × 34 cm

Museo Nacional de Antropología,
Mexico City, CONACULTA-INAH, 10-81769

PROVENANCE: Ceremonial Precinct of the
Templo Mayor, Mexico City, 1944

31

Deified warrior

c. 1500, Aztec

Stone, 122 × 42 × 39 cm

Museo Nacional de Antropología,
Mexico City, CONACULTA-INAH, 10-81767

PROVENANCE: Ceremonial Precinct of the
Templo Mayor, Mexico City, 1944

SELECTED REFERENCES: Townsend 1979,
p. 18; Pasztory 1983, p. 178, pl. 144;
Umberger 1987, pp. 75–76; Bernal and
Simoni-Abbat 1986, p. 264; Solís Olguín
1991, pp. 60–92

In Tenochtitlan there must have
existed a sacred building
representing the Aztec vision of
the cosmos, and no doubt these
five sculptures, depicting the
warriors who support the gods'
creation by their military actions,
formed part of it. A building of
this type survives in the Plaza de
la Luna in front of the Pyramid of
the Sun in Teotihuacan and may
have provided the Aztecs with a
model. Four of the sculptures are
male, the fifth (cat. 29) female.
Three of the male figures possibly
mark the cardinal points east,
north and south, their female
counterpart west, the 'place of
women'. The bearded figure
(cat. 27) would then indicate the
centre of the universe, the
'crossroads' of the four directions.
As on the Tizoc Stone (fig. 6),
these images of deified warriors
supporting the sun in its celestial
plane wear stylised butterfly
pectorals of Toltec origin, a
pattern repeated on their helmets.
The male figures' military vocation
is indicated not only by their
spear-throwers (see cat. 315) and
spears, but also by the triangular
cloth worn over their loincloth
and by their clay nose-bars. The
woman wears an unusual skirt
made of interwoven arrows. The
four warriors are holding sacrificial
knives, while the female warrior
brandishes a *tzotzopaztli* (weaving
batten), emblem of her femininity.
FS, RVA

II THE HUMAN FIGURE

32

Ehecatl-Quetzalcoatl

c. 1500, Aztec

Basalt, 176 × 56 × 50 cm

Instituto Mexiquense de Cultura: Museo de Antropología e Historia del Estado de México, Toluca, A-36229, 10-109262

PROVENANCE: Calixtlahuaca, Mexico State, 1938

SELECTED REFERENCES: Pijoán 1946, pp. 26–28; García Payón 1979, p. 200; Bernal and Simoni-Abbat 1986, p. 320; Solís Olguín 1991, pp. 86–87

One of the most important Aztec gods, Quetzalcoatl took several guises. As a deity of duality (expressed in his name, which means 'feathered serpent'), he became the main symbol of fertility. As an image of the planet Venus, he was Tlahuizcalpantecuhtli, the morning star, and Xolotl, the evening star. Depicted as Ehecatl Quetzalcoatl, as in the sculpture shown here, he was the god of wind, capable of blowing storm clouds to produce the rain that fertilised the fields. The chief attribute of Ehecatl-Quetzalcoatl is the bird-like mask, commonly painted in red, with its beak half opened to reveal the tongue. Here, the mask covers the mouth and nose of a virtually naked young man, who wears the dress of a *macehual* (commoner): a *máxtlatl* (loincloth) and *huaraches* (sandals).

The sculpture was found among the debris inside a round temple at Calixtlahuaca. MAM

33

Young man

c. 15, Aztec

Stone, 55 × 20 × 15 cm

Museo Nacional de Antropología, Mexico City, CONACULTA-INAH, 10-1121

PROVENANCE: Tetzcoco, Mexico State; Augusto Genin collection, donated to the museum in the nineteenth century

SELECTED REFERENCES: Pijoán 1946, p. 152; Bernal 1967, p. 161, no. 87; Solís Olguín 1991, p. 78; Mexico City 1995, p. 42, no. 16

This sculpture of a young man with an erect penis is among the extremely rare examples of erotic sculpture in Pre-Hispanic Mesoamerica. Very few instances of completely naked figures are known in Aztec art (they include cats 35 and 40), which suggests, on the one hand, that the present figure was clothed with real garments and ornaments (as indicated by the perforations in the ears) during certain ceremonies and, on the other, that it was intended to celebrate the transition from childhood to adulthood. Between the ages of fifteen and twenty, young people were separated from their family and lived in schools run by the state. During this period, men learned to become active members of society. The erect member symbolises their fertility in the cosmic scheme of things. FS, RVA

34

Young man

c. 1500, Aztec

Stone, 80 × 28 × 19 cm

Museo Nacional de Antropología, Mexico City, CONACULTA-INAH, 10-220926

PROVENANCE: Mexico City, first half of the twentieth century

SELECTED REFERENCES: Alcina Franch 1983, no. 296; Washington 1983, pp. 80–81; Solís Olguín 1991, pp. 80–81, no. 45a, b

During the reign of Motecuhzoma II (1502–21) commoners (*macehualtin*) wore clothes made solely from the fibre of the henequen, a plant of the agave family. They were forbidden to wear sandals and to own or decorate themselves with jewels made of precious metals and jade, so they generally adorned themselves with simple clay ear ornaments and necklaces. The present figure is considered to exemplify Aztec ideals of the *macehual*, the male commoner: young and strong, he was responsible for sustaining the Aztec world with his might. The Indian artist, who produced a simplified image, also fulfilled an apparent aesthetic requirement – that the head of an individual be one quarter of his overall height.

Such figures functioned as mannequins, clothed and adorned with feathers and real jewels (see also cat. 35). FS, AG

35

Standing male nude

c. 1400–1521, Aztec

Grey basalt, height 107.5 × 37 × 25 cm

Peabody Museum of Natural History, Yale University, New Haven, ANT.008525 (Avery Judd Skilton collection)

PROVENANCE: purchased, 1881

Nudity of any sort is very rare in Aztec art, so this naturalistic image of a boy or adolescent male may well have been dressed and fitted with a distinguishing headdress during festivals. It may even have functioned as a kind of mannequin for various male gods. The faintly visible black stripes passing vertically through the eyes suggest that at its last appearance in public rituals the figure represented Xipe Totec ('our flayed lord'), a god of springtime and the renewal of vegetation at the start of the rainy season who was impersonated each year by priests wearing the skins of flayed captives. The ears are pierced for attaching ornaments, and the partly open mouth indicates that the figure is singing. Originally, the eyes will have been inlaid with shell for the whites and jet or obsidian for the pupils. The figure possibly held banners or flowers in his hands.

The sculpture once belonged to Avery Judd Skilton, US Consul in Mexico, and was reportedly collected in 'the mountains of Puebla'. It was purchased by the Peabody Museum in 1881, with a partial donation from Julius A. Skilton. According to accession records, some of Avery Skilton's statues had been in the private collection of Maximilian, Emperor of Mexico from 1864 to 1867. MDC

45

Seated male figure

c. 1350–1521, Aztec

Basalt, 31 × 21.5 × 18 cm

Museum der Kulturen Basel, Basle, IVb 627

PROVENANCE: Lukas Vischer collection, donated to the museum, 1844

SELECTED REFERENCES: Basle 1985, p.61; Bankmann and Baer 1990, p.130; Miller and Taube 1993, p.92

The sculpture is thought to represent Huehueteotl, the 'old, old god' of the Aztecs. The iconography of Huehueteotl, a god of fire, changed very little from the first millennium BC to the end of Aztec culture. He is depicted here seated and leaning slightly forward, his hands resting on his bent knees. He wears only a loincloth. His forehead and cheeks are covered with wrinkles. Both ear lobes are pierced. The mouth is open and the slightly damaged lower lip has an incision in the middle, which may be a perforation for a lip-plug. The right eye retains its white inlay. Anatomical details, including the collarbone, the wrists and ankle joints, are depicted with the realism typical of Aztec sculpture. The spine, too, is clearly delineated and is curved as a sign of the god's advanced age. AB

46

Kneeling woman

c. 1250–1521, Aztec

Stone and traces of paint, 54 × 34 × 22 cm

American Museum of Natural History, New York, 30.1/1201

PROVENANCE: Ixtapalapan, Mexico; purchased from Lawrence Higgins, 1931

SELECTED REFERENCE: Durán 1971, pp.221–28

The statue, said to represent a maize goddess, comes from the Aztec town of Ixtapalapan, located on the southern lake shore of the Basin of Mexico. Deities personifying maize appeared in several forms. Xilonen ('young maize ear'), for example, was associated with the first tender corn of the harvest season, Chicomecoatl ('seven serpent') with dried seed corn. According to the sixteenth-century Franciscan

friar Diego Durán, adolescent girls were chosen to represent the maize goddess in celebrations that took place in September. In the temple of Chicomecoatl in Tenochtitlan the goddess was represented as an adolescent with open arms. The cheeks of the statue were coloured red and it was richly robed in bright red, finely made garments and adorned with gold and featherwork.

George Vaillant, curator and an early expert on the Aztecs, acquired this statue for the museum while directing archaeological fieldwork in Mexico in June 1931. CE

47

Seated male figure

c. 1350–1521, Aztec

Stone, 30.5 × 19 × 15.5 cm

Staatliche Museen zu Berlin: Preußischer Kulturbesitz, Ethnologisches Museum, IV Ca 4401

PROVENANCE: Carl Uhde collection, purchased by the museum, 1862

SELECTED REFERENCES: Washington 1983, pp.82–83; Solís Olguín 1993, pp.69–74

The Aztecs, masters of stonework, created an unmistakable image of the human form. Along with deities they sculpted figures such as this *macehual* (commoner; see also cat. 43), obviously guided by a need to convey an idealised image of vigorous, youthful members of their society.

The unadorned figure, wearing only the characteristic loincloth, is seated on the ground. His left hand rests on the knee of his left leg, which is bent inwards; he appears to be holding an object in his other hand. His facial expression is rigid and expressionless. This no doubt reflects the strict upbringing of young Aztecs, who were prepared in schools for a life as fierce warriors and active members of society. MG

48

Head of a youth

c. 1500, Aztec

Stone, red shell and obsidian, 19.5 × 15.5 cm

Museo Nacional de Antropología, Mexico City, CONACULTA-INAH, 10-92

PROVENANCE: Mexico City, 1940

SELECTED REFERENCES: Caso 1950, p.8; Toscano 1940, pp.86–89; Madrid 1992, p.191

Two similar sculptures depicting the heads of young Aztecs were discovered by chance in 1940 during the construction of a building in the historic quarter of Mexico City. Both pieces, of which this is one, have the original pyrite, red and white shell inlays, which accentuate the vivid representation of men in a state of drunkenness. *Pulque*, a mildly alcoholic beverage made from the sap of the maguey cactus mixed with psychotropic plants, is known to have been consumed during certain festivities. An incision in the base of the neck permitted both sculptures to be attached to the body. Hence, they were probably used as substitutes for living victims in ceremonial decapitation rituals. FS, RVA

49

Mask

c. 1450–1521, Aztec

Stone, 20 × 17 × 8 cm

American Museum of Natural History, New York, 30/11847

PROVENANCE: collected by Teobert Maler in the vicinity of Castillo de Teayo, Veracruz, 1903; given to the museum by the Duke of Loubat

SELECTED REFERENCES: Ekholm 1970, p.61; Matos Moctezuma 1988, p.112

Ethnohistorical accounts of Aztec religious practices document the pervasive use of masks in temple ceremonies. Masks made of stone or clay have been preserved from Pre-Hispanic times, but many others were probably made of wood or other perishable materials and have not survived. Masks no doubt played a central role in ceremonies involving deity impersonation. The present example does not have perforated eyes, making it unlikely that it was worn, but it does have holes drilled in the back for hanging. In addition, the ears are perforated so that ornaments could have been attached to the lobes. Stone masks similar to this have been found among offerings in the Aztec Templo Mayor in Mexico City. CE

50

Anthropomorphic mask

*c.*1500, Aztec

Obsidian, 15 × 13.5 × 11 cm

Museo Nacional de Antropología, Mexico City, CONACULTA-INAH, 10-9681

51

Anthropomorphic mask

*c.*1500, Aztec

Obsidian, 20.5 × 17 × 9 cm

Museo Nacional de Antropología, Mexico City, CONACULTA-INAH, 10-96

52

Anthropomorphic mask

*c.*1500, Aztec

Alabaster, 22 × 23 × 11 cm

Museo Nacional de Antropología, Mexico City, CONACULTA-INAH, 10-223664

PROVENANCE: probably Basin of Mexico and Mexico City, nineteenth and twentieth centuries

SELECTED REFERENCES: Caso 1950; Bernal 1967, no. 120; Solís Olguín 1991B, p.250, no. 379; Belém 1995, pp.94–95

Masks carved from semi-precious stones are among the innovations in Mesoamerican art introduced towards the end of the Aztec empire. Examples in jade and greenstone (particularly diorite) have survived along with the present pieces, made of obsidian and alabaster. Such objects have traditionally been connected with funerals, related to certain passages in chronicles and to images in codices indicating that the deceased wore masks. The masks survived the cremation of the dead, giving them an eternal face. Like most Aztec masks, these are notably realistic. The sculptor has depicted the face of a strong young man, with wide nostrils and pronounced cheekbones that emphasise the lines from the nostrils to the mouth. The polished surfaces contrast with the cavities representing the eyes and mouth, which were designed to be inlaid with shell and obsidian. FS, RVA

53

Mask

*c.*1500, Aztec

Wood and traces of stucco and gold leaf, 20 × 20.5 × 11.4 cm

Princeton University Art Museum, Gift of Mrs Gerard B. Lambert, Y 1970-111

PROVENANCE: museum purchase, gift of Mrs Gerard B. Lambert, 1970

This may be the only surviving wooden mask in pure Aztec, rather than Mixtec, style. The mask is not made for wearing: neither the eyes nor the mouth are punctured, nor is the back hollowed to fit a human face. It does not represent a deity, but possibly a noble, which is unusual.

In its original form the mask certainly had inlaid eyes of shell and obsidian and shell teeth. There are traces of gold leaf over a thin coating of stucco. The ear lobes have platforms, which undoubtedly supported ear-flares of stone or gold.

Such a mask may have been placed over the face of the deceased in a tomb or it may have been displayed in a sanctuary. It is said to have been found in a dry cave in the Mexican state of Oaxaca, the homeland of Mixtec culture. Most surviving wooden masks are of Mixtec style and are often covered with mosaic designs. It is remarkable that the only wooden mask in pure Aztec style should have been found in Mixtec territory. GGG popular at all levels of society, and decoration produced by means of them must have played a considerable part in the various annual festivals. Some *pintaderas* were cylindrical, rolled on the fabric or skin. Others were curved, used to decorate thighs and legs (cats 63–65). The motifs on these became extremely stylised, depicting interlaced flowers, eagle heads, snakes and monkeys dancing in pairs to some irresistible rhythm. Perhaps the most attractive are the flat stamps that show images of animals, such as the two snakes included here, one of which (cat. 61) represents the *xiuhcoatl* ('fire serpent'), its tail taking the form of a sun disc with rays. FS, RVA

66
Squash

c. 1300–1521, Aztec

Aragonite, 12 × 8 cm

Trustees of the British Museum, London, Ethno. 1952 Am 18.1

PROVENANCE: reportedly a grave at Mitla, Oaxaca; bequeathed to the museum by Miss Amy Drucker, 1952

SELECTED REFERENCES: New York 1970, p. 289; Washington 1983, p. 114, pl. 41

Among the naturalistic stone sculptures fashioned by Aztec artisans are a few that accurately represent important staple fruits and vegetables. In this example, the lifelike rendering of a particular variety of squash (*Cucurbita mixta*) reflects an intense interest in the cultivation of such crops. In the course of thousands of years of experimentation and innovation indigenous people accumulated the blend of deep knowledge and practical skills to plant, harvest and process corn, beans, squash, avocados, chillis, tomatoes, cacao and a host of other crops. Along with maize and beans, various species of squash, including the common Mexican pumpkin (*Cucurbita pepo*), comprised a significant part of the Aztec diet. Squash seeds could be stewed or parched and count among the most common items of food tribute. These formed part of an impressive

arsenal of staple cultigens as well as more exotic seeds, fruits and spices upon which Pre-Hispanic Mesoamerican societies depended. In due course they came to play an integral role in myths, rituals, calendars, customs and performances in Aztec life. There is very little direct information about the functions and uses of vegetative sculptures. They may have served as offerings dedicated to agricultural deities. CMcE

67
Pumpkin

c. 1500, Aztec

Diorite, 16 × 36 × 17 cm

Museo Nacional de Antropología, Mexico City, CONACULTA-INAH, 10-392922

PROVENANCE: unknown

SELECTED REFERENCES: New York 1970, p. 305, no. 288; Kubler 1985, p. 221, no. III-12; Amsterdam 2002, p. 240, no. 195

Along with maize, the staple foods of the Aztecs and other Mesoamerican peoples included chillis, beans and gourds, which were esteemed for their nutritional value. The present sculpture is a faithful representation of the pumpkin variety *Cucurbita pepo* in which the sculptor has made skilful use of diorite, a very hard stone of a greenish colour with veins that look like the marks on the skin of a pumpkin. FS, RVA

68
Cactus

c. 1500, Aztec

Stone, 99 × 28 cm

Museo Nacional de Antropología, Mexico City, CONACULTA-INAH, 10-220928

PROVENANCE: Mexico City; Alfredo Chavero collection, donated to the museum in the nineteenth century

SELECTED REFERENCES: New York 1970, no. 287; Amsterdam 2002, p. 240, no. 194; Solís Olguín forthcoming

The *marginatus* variety of *Cereuss* cactus has been used since time immemorial by various peoples to create natural fences or walls. In sculpted form, it was employed by the Aztecs to mark the boundary between the capital, Tenochtitlan, and the

neighbouring town of Tlatelolco. The present example reproduces faithfully the elongated shape of the plant and depicts its roots. On the base is a relief of Tenoch, founder of Tenochtitlan, who, according to legend, had been guided to the site by the Aztecs' patron god, Huitzilopochtli. Other, similar sculptures have survived, four of which may have marked the sacred precincts of the capital. FS, RVA

69
Feathered coyote

c. 1500, Aztec

Stone, 38 × 17 × 13cm

Museo Nacional de Antropología, Mexico City, CONACULTA-INAH, 10-47

PROVENANCE: unknown

SELECTED REFERENCES: Pijoán 1946, pp. 158–64; Amsterdam 2002, p. 251, no. 212

The coyote was considered the most sexually potent of animals in the Pre-Hispanic Nahuatl world and was associated with Tezcatlipoca, god of masculinity and of war. Aztec men prayed to Huehuecoyotl ('old coyote') for health and long life. The present sculpture shows the dog sitting on its hindquarters and covered in a thick fur of plumes that imitates feathers in motion. FS, RVA

70
Dog

c. 1500, Aztec

Stone, 47.5 × 20 × 29 cm

Museo Regional de Puebla, CONACULTA-INAH, 10-203439

PROVENANCE: Ruiz de Tepeaca collection, acquired by the Puebla State government, nineteenth century; Museo de la Universidad, Puebla, 1939; Museo Regional de Puebla, 1976

SELECTED REFERENCES: New York 1970, p. 300, no. 279; Washington 1983, pp. 120–21; Mexico City 1995, p. 171

In ancient Mesoamerica dogs were prized for their closeness to humankind, their loyalty and their watchfulness, which helped protect homes and crops. Moreover, they were closely associated with rituals relating to fire and the sun's rays.

The sculpture shows the dog in a characteristic position, sitting on its hind legs, supporting itself on its front legs and raising its head as if to look at its master. Although its mouth is closed, some scholars believe the animal may be howling at the moon.

The Aztecs and other Nahuatl-speakers called all species of dog known to them *itzcuintli*. It has been claimed that they also referred to dogs affectionately as *xochcóyotl, tehuitzotl, tetlami, tehui* and *chichi*. *Itzcuintli* was one of the twenty glyphs in the Mesoamerican agricultural calendar (the *xiuhpohualli*), while the fourteenth thirteen-day period in the ritual calendar (*tonalpohualli*) began with the glyph *ce izcuintli* ('1-dog'). It was thought that people born during this period would be lucky, especially if they were rulers. FS, RVA

Michael D. Coe (in Washington 1991) suggests that, while we do not know why or for whom naturalistic representations of animals and plants were carved, they may have been placed in temples, palaces or the homes of élite families. He also proposes that the present sculpture may have adorned a military academy at which jaguar warriors were trained.

The Brooklyn Museum's archives state that, like cat. 39, the sculpture was purchased in 1938 from Mr G. M. Echániz, a dealer who owned an antiquarian bookstore and gallery in Mexico City. NR

73

Insect

c. 1500, Aztec

Stone, 22 × 21.5 × 36.5 cm

Museo Nacional de Antropología, Mexico City, CONACULTA-INAH, 10-594039

PROVENANCE: Mexico City, nineteenth century.

SELECTED REFERENCES: Covarrubias 1961, pp. 366–67; Pasztory 1983, p. 234, pl. 230

In their art the Aztecs meticulously reproduced the salient features of the plants and animals that formed part of their natural surroundings. The present sculpture, for example, which probably depicts a flea, includes the mouth part that the insect uses to suck blood from humans and other mammals. Among the insects represented in Aztec art are some that have been identified as water-fleas, animals associated with the gods of rain and flowing water, Tlaloc and Chalchiuhtlicue. FS, RVA

72

Rabbit

c. 1500, Aztec

Stone, 33 × 22 × 24 cm

Museo Nacional de Antropología, Mexico City, CONACULTA-INAH, 10-81666

PROVENANCE: possibly Mexico City

SELECTED REFERENCES: Bernal 1967, p. 164, no. 93; Solís Olguín 1991, pp. 112–13; Mexico City 1995, p. 138, no. 146

Among Nahuatl-speakers the rabbit (*tochtli*) was closely associated with the moon and with the intoxicating effects of *pulque*. These peoples explained the silhouette of a rabbit seen on the moon's surface with reference to the punishment that Tecuciztecatl (the god who became the moon) was thought to have received for his cowardice when he did not instantly perform the self-sacrifice necessary for him to become the sun: a rabbit was flung in his face. Ome Tochtli ('2-rabbit') was god of drunkenness and commander of the Centzon Totochtin ('400 rabbits'), i.e. the countless attitudes that drunkards adopt as they run the gamut from happiness to sadness and from lechery to madness. This remarkably naturalistic sculpture depicts a graceful creature, hunched up with its front paws raised, alert to danger. FS, RVA

71

Reclining jaguar

c. 1440–1521, Aztec

Volcanic stone, 12.5 × 14.5 × 28 cm

Brooklyn Museum of Art, Carll H. de Silver Fund, 38.45

PROVENANCE: purchased from G. M. Echániz, Mexico City, with funds from the Carll H. de Silver Fund, 1938

SELECTED REFERENCES: Brooklyn 1938–41; Pasztory 1983, p. 233, pl. 214; Washington 1991, pp. 569–70, pl. 402; Smith 1996, p. 266, fig. 10.9; Brooklyn 1997, pp. 81–82

This reclining jaguar is an excellent example of Aztec naturalistic sculpture. Every part of the animal is carefully rendered, including the underside, where the paw pads are carved in low relief. To the Aztecs, the jaguar symbolised power, courage and war. Hence the highest-ranking warriors were called either jaguar or eagle warriors, and rulers associated themselves with Tezcatlipoca ('smoking mirror'), a deity who sometimes took the guise of this predator. Rulers were also depicted wearing and sitting on jaguar skins. In addition, the jaguar, as a night hunter, was associated with danger and darkness.

74

Insect

c. 1500, Aztec

Stone, 13.5 × 9.5 × 18 cm

Museum für Völkerkunde Wien (Kunsthistorisches Museum mit MVK und ÖTM), Vienna, 6.450, Bilimek Collection

PROVENANCE: Dominik Bilimek collection, acquired by the museum, 1878

SELECTED REFERENCE: Vienna 1992, no. 158

The sculpture has been thought to depict a grasshopper, fly or cicada, but the species of insect cannot be established beyond doubt. Its symbolic meaning is almost equally obscure. The 'shell' decoration on the chest is a characteristic of Quetzalcoatl, a god whom several creation myths describe as having dealings with insects, including bees, ants and butterflies, and with spiders.

Close to Tenochtitlan, the Aztec capital, lay Chapultepec ('grasshopper hill'), where the Mexica-Aztecs first tried to found their capital. This was also where Topiltzin, the *quetzalcoatl*, or priest-ruler, of the Toltecs, resided for a while after abandoning the Toltec capital, Tula. The present piece may possibly be an image of Chapultepec. GvB

75

Grasshopper

c. 1500, Aztec

Cornelian, 19.5 × 16 × 47 cm

Museo Nacional de Antropología,
Mexico City, CONACULTA-INAH, 10-220929

PROVENANCE: Chapultepec, Mexico City,
nineteenth century

SELECTED REFERENCES: Pasztory 1983, p.234,
pl. 231; Kubler 1985, p.222, no. III-13;
Solís Olguín 1991, p.116

The Aztecs migrated from Aztlan
to the Basin of Mexico and settled
on the hill called Chapultepec.
Pictograms show this with a
grasshopper on its summit and it
is therefore known as 'grasshopper
hill'. A sweet-water spring on the
mountain was later channelled
to provide Tenochtitlan with
drinking water. In Chapultepec the
Aztecs built a system of reservoirs
and canals. A sculpture of a
grasshopper was discovered
in the main reservoir towards the
end of the nineteenth century.
Grasshoppers are abundant in the
fields in Mesoamerica after the
rainy season.

The present piece was carved
in a red volcanic rock called
cornelian. The creature is depicted
in all its anatomical detail and its
legs are flexed as if it is ready to
jump. FS, RVA

76

Fish

c. 1500, Aztec

Volcanic stone, 26.3 × 58.6 × 10.5 cm

Laboratoire d'Ethnologie, Musée de
l'Homme, Paris, M.H.87.155.17

PROVENANCE: Latour Allard collection,
on loan from the Musées nationaux

SELECTED REFERENCES: Nicholson 1971,
p.129, fig. 45; Pasztory 1983, p.234, pl. 229;
Baquedano 1984, p.77, fig. 48; López Luján
1991, pp.219–20; Espinosa Pineda 1996,
pp.115–29; Seler 1996, pp.305–09

This sculpture and a bas-relief
in the British Museum (Ethno.
St. 371) are among the few
representations of fish in Aztec
sculpture. Fish are rare in Aztec
art as a whole and difficult to
identify in taxonomic terms.
The present example has a round
eye, an open mouth and large
hexagonal scales, along with two
fins on the back, one on the chest,
one at the front of the pelvis and

one at the anus. The number and
position of the fins correspond to
the species *Chirostoma jordani* and
Chirostoma regani (*charal*), which are
some 5 cm long, and *Chirostoma
humboldtianum* (*pescado blanco*),
which is approximately 16 cm in
length. Once common in the lakes
of Mexico, these fish were staples
of the Aztec diet. The biologist
Ana Fabiola Guzmán has pointed
out, however, that the proportions
of the scales indicate that the
sculptor intended to represent
a saltwater fish. The piece might
therefore depict a *tlacamichi*, an
edible sea fish described by
the Spanish chronicler Friar
Bernardino de Sahagún in the
sixteenth century.

For the Aztecs, fish symbolised
the world of water and fertility.
They were associated with the
gods Chalchiuhtlicue, Cipactli,
Mayahuel, Quetzalcoatl, Xochipilli
and Xochiquetzal. At the end of
the fourth world-era, Nahui Atl
('4-water'), all human beings were
thought to have been turned into
fish following a flood. LLL, MFFB

77

Plaque with an image of a lizard

c. 1325–1520, Aztec

Stone, 24 × 15 × 8 cm

Musées Royaux d'Art et d'Histoire,
Brussels, AAM 3480

PROVENANCE: gift of Auguste Génin, 1930

SELECTED REFERENCE: Lavachery and
Minnaert 1931, p. 25

The shape and dimensions of the
plaque would seem to suggest that
it was the lid of a receptacle, yet
the majority of surviving
decorative motifs on Aztec stone
receptacles are executed in low
relief. The object was collected by
Auguste Génin on his travels in
Mexico during the rush to acquire
Pre-Hispanic works in the first
quarter of the twentieth century,
but the notes he made at the time
have been lost, so no clue as to
its function can be gained from
that quarter.

In Mexica iconography the
lizard occurs only in connection
with the *tonalpohualli*, the sacred
or ritual calendar, where it is one

of the twenty day-signs that are
grouped with the numbers 1 to 13
as a means of indicating the time
of the year. In the Florentine
Codex (cat. 344), by the chronicler
Friar Bernardino de Sahagún,
it features prominently on
pl. XXI–5, where it is associated
with the number 11. Sahagún calls
it *cuetzpali* or *cuetzpallin*.

Auguste Génin's donation
formed the basis for the Mexican
collections at the Musées Royaux
d'Art et d'Histoire in Brussels. SP

78

Feathered serpent

c. 1500, Aztec

Stone, 50 × 45 × 52 cm

Colección Fundación Televisa, Mexico City,
Reg. 21 pj. 8

PROVENANCE: unknown, acquired
through Manuel Reyero, late 1960s

SELECTED REFERENCE: Reyero 1978,
pp.143–44

Quetzalcoatl, the mythical
'feathered serpent', was among
the most important Pre-Hispanic
deities in Mesoamerica. The
present sculpture of the coiled
reptile shows the rings that allow
it to slither over the ground and
its skin covered in long quetzal
feathers. The oldest known image
of Quetzalcoatl comes from
Tlatilco and dates from *c.* 800 BC.
Later, in Teotihuacan, his cult
grew in importance and he was
associated with the fertilising
power of water. A sculpture of
him adorned the main pyramid
of the Ciudadela (citadel) there.
The Toltecs believed that this
supernatural reptile protected
processions of warriors, as can
be seen in images surviving on
benches in Teotihuacan. The
Aztecs considered his image to
be divine and the counterpart
of Quetzalcoatl as a man. FS, RVA

79

Serpent

c. 1500, Aztec

Stone, 31 × 82 × 80 cm

Museo Nacional de Antropología,
Mexico City, CONACULTA-INAH, 10-220933

PROVENANCE: probably Basin of Mexico, first half of the twentieth century

SELECTED REFERENCES: Garibay Kintana 1964, p. 314; Washington 1983, p. 138

The serpent played a versatile and crucial role in the mythology of ancient Mexico. It is identified both with the sun's rays, which are the weapons of the *xiuhcoatl* ('fire serpent'), and with driving rain, which resembles water-snakes falling from the sky during heavy storms. Moreover, the earth itself is Cihuacoatl ('serpent woman'), the creative female force. The present sculpture shows a further aspect of serpents: their mysteriousness. The artist has captured the sense of power emanating from a coiled rattlesnake, its muscular tension and its intimidating effect as it shakes its rattle and shows its forked tongue. FS, RVA

80

Snake

c. 1500, Aztec

Stone, 31 × 44 × 24 cm

Museo Nacional de Antropología, Mexico City, CONACULTA-INAH, 10 220932

PROVENANCE: unknown

SELECTED REFERENCES: Westheim et al. 1969, p. 162; Kubler 1985, p. 222, no. III-9; Solís Olguín 1991, pp. 105–06

Today snakes generally arouse feelings of terror and revulsion, but for the people of ancient Mesoamerica, not least the Aztecs, they symbolised fertility and plenty. The fact that snakes reproduce especially abundantly led people to believe that the top layer of the earth consisted of interlaced snakes, forming a sacred 'carpet' from which men, plants and other animals had grown.

The body of the snake depicted here engulfs itself, conveying a sense of the animal as a life-generating nucleus. The dynamic movement that informs the entire body comes to a halt at the head: the snake looks at the spectator, hypnotising him with eyes that are now missing their shell inlays. The oversized forked tongue

contrasts with the realistic dimensions of the rest of the animal. FS, RVA

81

Coiled rattlesnake

c. 1300–1521, Aztec

Granite and traces of paint, height 36 cm, diameter 53 cm

Trustees of the British Museum, London, Ethno. 1849.6-29.1

PROVENANCE: ex-González Carvajal and Wetherell collections, purchased by the museum, 1849

SELECTED REFERENCES: Joyce 1912, pl. Ve; Washington 1983, pp. 154–55; Baquedano 1984, p. 72, pl. 41; McEwan 1994, p. 69

The Aztecs carved naturalistic sculptures of reptiles, birds and insects, suggesting that they observed the life cycles and habits of these creatures closely. The imposing presence of this rattlesnake (*Crotalus horridus*) is enhanced by the foreshortening of the coiled body compared to the size of its head and rattle. Key anatomical details, such as the fangs and bifurcated tongue, are accurately recorded. Small circular cavities on either side of the head between the nostrils and the eyes are the external openings to highly effective heat sensors, enabling the snake to locate and strike at prey in complete darkness. The hole visible on the floor of the mouth is the trachea. In snakes these are movable, so that when they are digesting their prey, the trachea moves forward to enable them to continue to breathe. The traces of red pigment on the right nostril and mouth and the red dots on the surfaces of the ventral coils on the underside of the sculpture may allude to the coloured skin of some species of rattlesnake. The rattle itself consists of successive segments, a new one being produced each year when the snake sheds its skin, reaching, in the present case, a total of thirteen. This is perhaps not coincidental, since the 260-day ritual calendar in Mesoamerica is based on a cycle of thirteen day-numbers and twenty day-names. CMcE

82

Relief of an eagle

c. 1300–1521, Aztec

Andesite, 20 × 28 × 8 cm

Trustees of the British Museum, London, Ethno. 8624

PROVENANCE: ex-Uhde collection, Museum für Völkerkunde, Berlin, acquired by exchange, 1872

SELECTED REFERENCES: Pasztory 1983, p. 283, pl. 223; Baquedano 1984, p. 74, pl. 44

The eagle (*cuauhtli*) was linked to the solar deity Tonatiuh and was widely used among the Aztecs to symbolise the qualities and attributes of this most important of celestial objects. According to myth, the golden eagle had a special role in the legendary founding of the Aztec capital, Tenochtitlan (see p. 14). In Nahuatl the terms for ascending eagle (*cuauhtlehuanitl*) and descending eagle (*cuauhtemoc*) referred to the archetypal diurnal movements of the sun in its daily emergence from and return to the depths of the underworld. The eagle exemplified the aggressive power to strike that inspired the military order of eagle warriors and was identified with human sacrifice. Large sculptures of eagles with circular cavities in their backs, as well as special ceremonial 'eagle vessels' (*cuauhxicalli*; see cat. 152), served as receptacles for blood offerings as nourishment for the solar deity. While much Aztec sculpture is renowned for its volumetric qualities and arresting presence, the present piece is modest in size and sculpted in low relief. The backward glance of the head is a novelty that defies the usual conventions. CMcE

83

Eagle

c. 1500, Aztec

Stone, 41 × 20 cm

Museo Regional de Puebla, CONACULTA-INAH, 10-203440

PROVENANCE: Puebla State, nineteenth century

SELECTED REFERENCE: Solís Olguín 1991, pp. 100–23

The patron gods of the supreme rulers (*tlatoque*) of the Aztec empire were the deities associated with the sun and with war, principally Xiuhtecuhtli and Huitzilopochtli. Hence, the animals who symbolised these gods were intimately linked with the *tlatoque*. The eagle was one of them. The present sculpture depicts an eagle standing on a rectangular base, the sides of which show the wickerwork characteristic of the *tlatoani*'s throne (*icpalli*) in Tenochtitlan. The hieratic image is a metaphor of the power and sovereignty of the *tlatoani*. The eagle stands erect on its base, its wings held close to its body, in the way that the *tlatoani*, the living representative of the sun and of fire, appeared before his people on the *icpalli*. Traces of the original stucco can be seen around the eyes and on parts of the plumage. FS, RVA

84
Vessel in the shape of a deer's head

*c.*1250–1521, Mixteca–Puebla

Fired clay and paint, 29 × 26 × 22 cm, diameter of spout 9.5 cm

Rautenstrauch-Joest-Museum, Cologne, Ludwig Collection, SL XCVI

PROVENANCE: Ludwig collection, donated 1983 to the Rautenstrauch-Joest-Museum

SELECTED REFERENCES: Bolz-Augenstein 1975, nos 96, 97; Hildesheim 1986, no. 237; Nuremberg 1993, p.42, no. 11

The vessel is shaped as a deer's head with a cylindrical spout at the top. The ears of the roe-deer are white and its eyes are depicted in a fairly realistic manner. Similar images of such *mazatl* ('deer') with antlers suggest that they represent the white-tailed deer (*Odocoileus virginianus mexicanus*).

The deer was associated in Mesoamerican mythology with the female deity Quilaztli or Cihuacoatl ('woman serpent'), who was worshipped at Colhuacan on Lake Xochimilco, south of Tenochtitlan. In the form of a double-headed deer she was said to have been killed by the hunting god Mixcoatl ('cloud serpent'). Promptly changing into a woman, she was impregnated by Mixcoatl and gave birth to the hero Quetzalcoatl ('feathered serpent').

The present vessel may have been used in rituals devoted to Quilaztli.

Although it is not known where the vessel was found, the style of the painted decoration is typical of Postclassic ceramics from Cholula and its environs. ST

85
Pipe in the form of a dog

*c.*1500, Aztec

Fired clay, 7.5 × 24.5 cm

Museo Nacional de Antropología, Mexico City, CONACULTA-INAH, 10-79507

PROVENANCE: Tlatelolco, Mexico City

86
Pipe in the form of a duck

*c.*1500, Aztec

Fired clay, 9 × 19 cm

Museo Nacional de Antropología, Mexico City, CONACULTA-INAH, 10-116576

PROVENANCE: Tlatelolco, Mexico City

87
Pipe

*c.*1500, Aztec

Fired clay, 12.5 × 28 × 4 cm

Museo Nacional de Antropología, Mexico City, CONACULTA-INAH, 10-220130

PROVENANCE: Tlatelolco, Mexico City

SELECTED REFERENCE: Porter 1948, pp.206–08, nos 18–20

Two varieties of tobacco were cultivated in Mexico: *Nicotiana tabacum* and *Nicotiana rustica*. The Aztecs and other Nahuatl-speaking people called it *yetl*. They considered tobacco to be a sacred plant created for the enjoyment of the gods and they venerated it for what appeared to be its magical powers. They either rolled the leaves into cylinders and smoked them like a modern cigar or shredded and pounded them for smoking in pipes like those shown here. Tobacco pipes were usually made of clay, and their bowls took a great variety of shapes. Archaeological excavations in Tlatelolco have unearthed large numbers of pipes, which suggests that smoking was very popular in the Aztec world. Some of the most elegant pipes have plain cylindrical bowls that are covered in red pigment and burnished to a high gloss (cat. 87). Others are shaped in the form of animals, and

these were probably used by priests devoted to the deity whose *nahual* (spirit twin) was a particular animal. Such examples are the pipes shaped like a dog (cat. 85), an animal associated with Xolotl, god of monsters; like a duck (cat. 86) and like macaws (cats 117–18), birds that brought memories of ancestors, the effect that smoking tobacco produced in the minds of the Aztecs. FS, RVA

88
Flute in the form of a macaw

*c.*1300–1521, Aztec

Fired clay and traces of paint, 8.3 × 11 × 14 cm

Trustees of the British Museum, London, Ethno. 1865.6-10.9

PROVENANCE: purchased from Charles Farris, 1865

SELECTED REFERENCE: Smith 1996, pp.272–73

Vivid first-hand accounts as well as pictorial records preserved in codices offer glimpses of the kind of energetic communal Aztec celebrations in which music, song and dance played an indispensable role. Rhythmic chanting and drumming formed a key element in much ritual performance and were accompanied by a range of wind and percussion instruments, including flutes, whistles, drums and rattles. The sounds and cries of birds and animals could also be mimicked both by vocalisation and by playing appropriate instruments. This ceramic flute of the kind known as an *ocarina* is fashioned in the form of a macaw or parrot identified by its distinctive curved upper beak and modelled eye. It is played by blowing through an aperture at the end of the bird's tail, with the body acting as a sound chamber. The arrangement of four other openings on its back enables dextrous fingers to conjure up a haunting, melodious sound. Such instruments were thought to become animate objects when played and contributed to the cacophony of sounds, movement and colour that once characterised the seasonal festivals in the Aztec calendrical round. CMcE

89

Plate

c. 1500, Aztec

Fired clay and paint, height 4.5 cm,
diameter 31 cm

Museo Nacional de Antropología,
Mexico City, CONACULTA-INAH, 10-116416

PROVENANCE: Tlatelolco, Mexico City, 1964

SELECTED REFERENCE: Vega Sosa 1975

The decoration of the plate is full of symbolism relating to the sun god, Tonatiuh. His *nahual* (spirit twin) is the eagle, which appears in the centre of the plate with wings and tail outstretched, as if in full flight. Decorated with sacrificial feathers, its tongue hangs out in allusion to its thirst for blood. Pointing in the cardinal directions, four symbols are arranged like shells around the central disc, alternating with the *tonallo* (four circles associated with heat) and the many-petalled *chimalxóchitl* (sunflower), which some believe to be the image of the full sun. As a whole, the design represents the passage of the sun from east to west, emphasising its position at midday, when it provides maximum light and heat. Thirteen bands with various geometric and linear motifs indicating the celestial planes appear around the central design, reinforcing its astronomic and calendrical character. The first band, with 29 circles, represents the plane of the moon, while the third, with the *xicalcoliuhqui* (stepped pattern), refers to the plane on which the sun moves, shown as twenty spirals (the number of signs denoting the days of the indigenous calendar). The fifth band is associated with fire, as indicated by its 50 circles, i.e. ten times the quincunx. FS, RVA

90

Two-tiered tripod plate

c. 1500, Aztec

Fired clay and paint, height 6 cm,
diameter 22.5 cm

Museo Nacional de Antropología,
Mexico City, CONACULTA-INAH, 10-1049

PROVENANCE: Mexico City, 1966

SELECTED REFERENCES: Bernal 1967, p. 197,
no. 132; Solís Olguín 1991B, p. 260, no. 401

Among the everyday ceramics typical of Tenochtitlan were vessels made of yellowish and coffee-coloured clay, burnished to produce a polished surface. Before firing they were decorated with motifs painted with very fine brushes. The present example served a secular rather than religious purpose, its two tiers designed to keep wet food separate from dry. The decoration features the head of a spider monkey with the half-mask in the shape of a bird's beak that identifies the figure as Ehecatl-Quetzalcoatl, god of wind. He wears the feathered attire of sacrificial victims, the *cuauhpiyolli* headdress of great warriors and the ear ornament known as an *oyohualli*. The rim is adorned with lines indicating precious liquid – blood – with *chalchihuitl* (symbols for jade). FS, RVA

91

Vessel with an image
of a centipede

1400, Totonac

Fired clay and paint, height 16 cm,
diameter 19 cm

Museo Nacional de Antropología,
Mexico City, CONACULTA-INAH, 10-78683

PROVENANCE: Los Otates, Veracruz, Mexico

SELECTED REFERENCES: Lothrop 1964, p. 37;
Bernal and Simoni-Abbat 1986, p. 242

In the course of their travels throughout Mesoamerica, the Aztec army and *pochteca* (professional merchants) acted as a channel for the dissemination of cultural influence from the capital, Tenochtitlan. The clearest evidence of this are the ceramics dating from the Late Postclassic period (1250–1521) that have been found at various points along military and commercial routes. The present vessel was discovered at Los Otates, in the coastal region of the Gulf of Mexico. Stylistically, it is closely related to illustrations in codices, particularly those produced by the Mixtecs. The elegant, realistically depicted centipede (*petlazolcoatl*) is painted in orange and yellow. The Aztecs associated centipedes with the earth, night and the powers of darkness, and in some reliefs from Tenochtitlan they can be seen among the tangled locks of Tlaltecuhtli, the 'earth lord'. FS, RVA

IV GODS OF LIFE

92

Xipe Totec

c. 1350–1521, Aztec

Volcanic stone and paint,
46 × 26.3 × 27.4 cm

Museum der Kulturen Basel, Basle, IVb 647

PROVENANCE: near Tetzcoco, before *c.* 1830;
Lukas Vischer collection, donated to the
museum, 1844

SELECTED REFERENCES: Nebel 1963, pl. 48;
Basle 1985, p. 77; Bankmann and Baer 1990,
p. 122; Miller and Taube 1993, p. 188

The cult of Xipe Totec ('our flayed
lord') was prominent in several
Postclassic Mesoamerican cultures
since it related to the earth,
vegetation and agricultural
renewal. During the
Tlacaxipehualiztli festival, held
before the rainy season, captives
or slaves were sacrificed by having
their hearts removed. The corpses
were then flayed and priests wore
the skins for twenty days.

The sculpture depicts Xipe
Totec wearing flayed skin, the
open mouth and the eyes revealing
those of the figure beneath.
Originally, the oval hollows of the
eyes probably contained inlays.
The ears are pierced to take
ornaments. The mask is tied with
cords at the back of the head, over
plaited hair. Human skin hangs
from the neck to the upper part of
the thighs. The long vertical cut at
the back, the pieces sewn together
in two places, indicates where the
body was flayed, while a horizontal
seam at the chest marks the point
where the skin was sewn together
after the extraction of the heart.
The skin leaves the hands
uncovered. Resting on the knees,
they are carved as hollow fists and
may have held insignia of some
kind. The hands of the flayed skin
dangle from the wrists. The legs
are bent upwards and the ankles
crossed. Those parts of the body
not covered by the skin, such as
the neck, legs and hands, are
painted red.

Carl Nebel made a drawing
of the sculpture *c.* 1830.
He mentioned that it had been
found near Tetzcoco. AB

93

Xipe Totec

c. 1500, Aztec

Fired clay, 15 × 4 × 6.5 cm

Museo Nacional de Antropología,
Mexico City, CONACULTA-INAH, 10-333885

PROVENANCE: Tlatelolco, Mexico City, 1968

94

Xipe Totec

c. 1500, Aztec

Fired clay, 15.5 × 5 × 3 cm

Museo Nacional de Antropología,
Mexico City, CONACULTA-INAH, 10-333856

PROVENANCE: Tlatelolco, Mexico City, 1968

95

Xipe Totec

c. 1500, Aztec

Fired clay, 14.5 × 6 × 3.5 cm

Museo Nacional de Antropología,
Mexico City, CONACULTA-INAH, 10-116779

PROVENANCE: Tlatelolco, Mexico City, 1968

96

Xipe Totec

c. 1500, Aztec

Fired clay, 12 × 5.5 × 8 cm

Museo Nacional de Antropología,
Mexico City, CONACULTA-INAH,
10-116778 2/2

PROVENANCE: Tlatelolco, Mexico City, 1968

SELECTED REFERENCES: Solís Olguín 1991B,
p. 259, no. 396; Seville 1997, pp. 136–37;
Guilliem 1999, pp. 97–102, 302–04; Mexico
City 2001, p. 359

The four sculptures from
Tlatelolco – the twin city of
Tenochtitlan, now part of Mexico
City – re-create the rites associated
with the god Xipe Totec, a god
of spring and the patron of
goldsmiths. The figurines
represent the god's impersonators,
who may have been priests,
warriors or commoners. They all
wear the flayed skins of captives
sacrificed during the ceremonies,
which took place in the 'month' of
Tlacaxipehualiztli ('flaying of men
in honour of Xipe'). The festivities
culminated in the hand-to-hand
combat called *tlauauaniliztli*, in
which five Mexica warriors – two
each from the jaguar and eagle
orders and a fifth who had to be
left-handed – wielded *macáhuitl*
(swords with obsidian-edged
blades) against prisoners taken
in battle, all of whom ended their

days on the sacrificial stone.
The Spanish dubbed this warlike
ceremony the 'gladiatorial
sacrifice'.

Two figures in the group are
seated on a small bench (cats 93,
96). These are high-ranking
warriors. Their headdresses bear
a large copper axe on top and they
are notable for small, removable
face masks. One of them (cat. 93)
wears a lip-plug . The other pair
of figures (cats 94–95), shown in
a processional pose, wear the
flayed skin of a victim, with a
clearly visible suture on the chest
indicating that the heart has been
removed. One of the headdresses
is conical, the other curves in the
shape of a hoop. The swallow-
tailed ear ornaments resemble the
obsidian items found among the
offerings at the Templo Mayor in
Mexico City and are a distinctive
feature of Xipe Totec
iconography. FS, RVA, AG

97

Container for flayed skin

c. 1500, Aztec

Fired clay, height 25 cm, diameter 48.5 cm

Museo Nacional de Antropología,
Mexico City, CONACULTA-INAH, 10-594908

PROVENANCE: Calle de las Escalerillas,
Mexico City, 1900

SELECTED REFERENCES: Batres 1902, p. 25;
Amsterdam 2002, p. 235, no. 189

The Tlacaxipehualiztli ceremony
took place during the second
twenty-day period of the Aztec
year. The present container was
among objects used in connection
with these rites that were
discovered in the Calle de las
Escalerillas in Mexico City, in
the area of the Templo Mayor,
proving that the temple was linked
with the Yopico, a ritual building
dedicated to the worship of Xipe
Totec ('our flayed lord'). The
exterior surface of the container
is puckered like flayed human skin,
a reference to the ceremonially
flayed skins of human sacrifices
that were worn by priests and
other devotees of Xipe Totec. The
Spanish chronicler Bernardino de
Sahagún described how, during
the Tlacaxipehualiztli ceremony,

they wore the skins over their body and face for twenty days in order to resemble the god, then removed them and stored them in a chamber beneath the temple. Containers such as the present item were probably used for this purpose, since they have tight-fitting lids that would have prevented the stench of the rotting skins from escaping. FS, RVA

98
Brazier with an image of Xipe Totec

c. 1500, Aztec

Fired clay, 36 × 40 cm

Museo Nacional de Antropología, Mexico City, CONACULTA-INAH, 10-220143

PROVENANCE: Mexico City, 1982

SELECTED REFERENCE: Mexico City 1995, p. 123, no. 110

Atzcapotzalco, the part of Mexico City where the brazier was found, was once the capital of the Tepanecs, from whose yoke the Aztecs freed themselves by defeating the Tepanec ruler Maxtla to gain control of the Basin of Mexico. Following the instructions of Huitzilopochtli, the Aztecs proceeded further on their 'sacred mission' by conquering the surrounding villages. The brazier once formed part of the decoration of the ceremonial centre of Atzcapotzalco. It bears an image of a triumphant warrior dressed as Xipe Totec, who was believed by the Aztecs to have invented war. Impersonating the god, the warrior has covered his face with a mask of human skin and has adorned himself with vertical strips of paper ending in the swallow-tail design exclusive to the iconography of Xipe Totec. He wears a crenellated headdress, decorated with small bows and held in place by a band of discs like those associated with Xiuhtecuhtli, the god of fire. On his back is a large strip of bark-paper, curved and gleaming and decorated with rosettes of pleated paper. The warrior holds a round shield, which would originally have been yellow, and a sceptre, which is broken. FS, RVA

99
Xipe Totec

c. 1500, Aztec

Fired clay and paint, 97 × 43 × 20 cm

Museo Regional de Puebla, CONACULTA-INAH, 10-203061

PROVENANCE: Tepeji el Viejo, Puebla, 1975

SELECTED REFERENCES: Madrid 1990, pp. 111–12, no. 46; Mexico City 1995, p. 122

In 1975 the Mexican historian Eduardo Merlo carried out excavations at Tepeji el Viejo, an ancient fortified city in the mountains of southern Puebla State. Before it was conquered by the Aztecs, this region had been inhabited by the Popolocas, a people related to the Mixtecs. First expeditions to the area, undertaken at the behest of Charles IV of Spain in 1805 by the army officer Captain Guillermo Dupaix, brought to light a fragment of a *temalácatl* (see cat. 209) that showed evidence of having been used during Tlacaxipehualiztli, the ceremony associated with the god Xipe Totec. This was confirmed in 1975 by the discovery of an offering containing the bones of warriors or victims sacrificed to Xipe Totec along with the present striking image of a priest in the service of the god, which had also been 'sacrificed' by being broken into pieces. Despite this, the sculpture is especially well preserved. FS, RVA

100
Spider monkey with ornaments relating to Ehecatl-Quetzalcoatl

c. 1500, Aztec

Volcanic stone, 43.5 × 24.6 × 24.4 cm

Laboratoire d'Ethnologie, Musée de l'Homme, Paris, M.H.78.1.89

PROVENANCE: Eugène Boban collection; Alphonse Pinart collection, donated to the Musée d'Ethnographie du Trocadéro, 1878

SELECTED REFERENCES: Hamy 1897, pp. 25–26, pl. 13, no. 37; Basler and Brumer 1928, pl. 104A; Pasztory 1983, p. 234, pl. 224; Washington 1983, pp. 126–27, no. 48; Gendrop and Díaz Balerdi 1994, p. 90, fig. 103; Espinosa Pineda 2001, p. 262, fig. 13

The Aztecs associated the spider monkey (*Ateles geoffroyi*), along with the opossum and certain species of duck, spider, ant and snail, with

Ehecatl-Quetzalcoatl, the god of wind. They connected this animal with air currents and whirlwinds because of its great agility, its incessant swinging through trees and its long, prehensile, spiral-shaped tail. According to Aztec cosmogony, at the end of the world-era known as Nahui Ehecatl ('4-wind') human beings were turned into monkeys as a result of violent gales.

The present sculpture, which belonged to the nineteenth-century collector and antique dealer Eugène Boban and was shown at the Exposition Universelle in Paris in 1878, depicts a monkey squatting on a quadrangular base. Its legs, adorned with knotted ribbons, rest beside its characteristically large belly; its hands, likewise decorated with knotted ribbons, are laid on its shoulders. The curled tail lies against the bottom of its back. The head, with its tuft of hair, is turned slightly upwards, and the cheeks are inflated as if the creature were blowing vigorously. Some features of the sculpture relate specifically to Ehecatl-Quetzalcoatl: the tubular nose ornament, the curved ear adornments (*epcololli*) made of shell, obsidian and pyrite, and the spiral-shaped pendant (*ehecacozcatl*) created from a sliced *Strombus* conch. LLL, MFFB

101
Spider monkey with ornaments relating to Xochipilli

c. 1500, Aztec

Volcanic stone, 19.5 × 18.5 × 8.5 cm

Laboratoire d'Ethnologie, Musée de l'Homme, Paris, M.H.87.159.143

PROVENANCE: donated by M. Franck, lent by the Musées nationaux

SELECTED REFERENCES: Nicholson 1971, p. 129, fig. 42; Manrique 1988, pp. 144–45; Seler 1996, pp. 167–73

Aztec sculptors frequently depicted the spider monkey (*Ateles geoffroyi*), one of three monkey species indigenous to Mesoamerica. This fruit-eating, tree-dwelling animal was common in the jungle regions of Maya territory, the Isthmus of

Tehuantepec, the Balsas basin, the mid-Pacific and the coastal areas of Veracruz. For the Aztecs, the good-natured spider monkey, which was regarded as the most vivacious and playful creature in the animal kingdom, symbolised gluttony, sexuality and pleasure in general. Among the deities it was associated with was Xochipilli-Macuilxochitl ('flower prince-five flower'), the god of dance, song, music, games and poetry. It was thought that those born in the thirteen-day period '1-monkey' of the divination calendar would be friendly and cheerful with an aptitude for music, painting and art, while those born on day '5-monkey' would tend to be self-indulgent and fond of joking.

The large-bellied male monkey on this disc-shaped sculpture is crouching with a tropical alcatraz flower and leaf in one hand (species *Philodendron*) and, in the other, what appears to be a sceptre made from the fruit of this climbing plant, one of the spider monkey's favourite foods. The monkey wears a necklace with seven snail shells and ear adornments known as *oyohualli*, which are associated with Xochipilli-Macuilxochitl. On the reverse is a circular mat bearing a checkerboard pattern. LLL, MFFB

102

Dancing monkey

c. 1500, Aztec

Stone, 60 × 37 × 33 cm

Museo Nacional de Antropología, Mexico City, CONACULTA-INAH, 10-116784

PROVENANCE: Pino-Suarez Metro station, Mexico City, 1967

SELECTED REFERENCES: Bernal and Simoni-Abbat 1986, pp. 355–57; Solís Olguín 1991, p. 110

The bird-beak mask and the body twisted in a spiral dancing movement identify this pregnant monkey as Ehecatl-Quetzalcoatl, god of wind. Like the pose, the coils of the serpent creeping up the monkey's leg recall the whirlwinds that announce the arrival of the rainy season. The sculpture was discovered during archaeological excavations

at Pino-Suarez Metro station in Mexico City, where it was found in a 'circular pyramid', a form characteristic of buildings dedicated to Ehecatl-Quetzalcoatl. It had been 'sacrificed' by the Aztecs, who had broken it into several fragments and buried it. FS, RVA

103

Ehecatl-Quetzalcoatl

c. 1480–1519, Aztec

Andesite, 195 × 40 × 50 cm

Rautenstrauch-Joest-Museum, Cologne, Ludwig Collection, SL CVII

PROVENANCE: private collection, Mexico City; purchased from a dealer by Peter and Irene Ludwig, 1966; donated to the Rautenstrauch-Joest-Museum, 2002

SELECTED REFERENCES: Bolz-Augenstein and Disselhoff 1970, pp. 112–14, no. 33; Hildesheim 1986, no. 163; Cologne 1999, p. 186, no. 84

The sculpture represents Quetzalcoatl ('feathered serpent') in his manifestation as the god of wind, Ehecatl ('wind'). This deity played an important role in Aztec creation myths, for he was thought to have set the sun and moon in motion by his blowing. He was also a leading god of agriculture, producing whirlwinds that swept the roads for the rain gods and thus ensuring that the dry season ended.

Ehecatl is identified by the mouth mask, which here resembles a duck's beak and is an integral part of the face. The wide-open nostrils indicate that he is blowing through the mask. Other distinctive features are the curved ear pendant and the conical headdress; a zigzag band with a knot at the front is attached to the latter. The body seems to be formed of a coiled serpent, but the feathers characteristic of Ehecatl-Quetzalcoatl are missing. More probably, the body represents a vortex of the kind produced by the wind on the Mexican plateau before the rainy season.

It is not known where the sculpture was found. It may have come from Tenochtitlan, the Aztec capital, which became a centre of stylistic innovation *c.* 1480. ST

104

Mask with an image of Ehecatl-Quetzalcoatl

c. 1350–1521, Aztec

Stone, 14 × 14 × 10 cm

Staatliche Museen zu Berlin: Preußischer Kulturbesitz, Ethnologisches Museum, IV Ca 26077

PROVENANCE: collected by Eduard Seler, 1905

SELECTED REFERENCES: Seler 1960–61, vol. 2, pp. 953–58; Washington 1983, pp. 103–04; Miller and Taube 1993, pp. 84–85; Solís Olguín 1993, pp. 69, 74

The mask shows the clean-cut features of a youthful face and, on the concave reverse, an image in low relief of the wind god Ehecatl-Quetzalcoatl, distinguished by a conical headdress and a beak-like mouth mask through which he blows the wind that brings rain clouds. Ehecatl-Quetzalcoatl is among the guises assumed by Quetzalcoatl ('feathered serpent'), one of the most important gods in the Aztec pantheon. He is shown here seated cross-legged in a frontal view, but with his head in profile. A large pendant adorns his ear and he wears a necklace. In his hands he holds curved sceptres bearing small circles.

The nine circles above Ehecatl-Quetzalcoatl on the left permit the relief to be read as the date '9-wind', one of the god's calendrical names. Associated with wind, rain and fertility, Ehecatl-Quetzalcoatl was also the patron of the 'wind' day, the second of twenty day-glyphs in the 260-day ritual calendar. In the Aztec creation myths he plays a central role as a divine creator and bringer of culture. During the creation of the earth and the sky Ehecatl-Quetzalcoatl, together with the deity Tetzcatlipoca, rescued the bones of humans from the underworld, thereby creating present-day humankind.

In the early decades of the twentieth century Eduard Seler, who in 1903 became head of the American department at the ethnological museum in Berlin, laid the foundations of Mexican studies in the German capital. He acquired the mask for his collection on one of his six extended visits to America. MG

105
Xochipilli

c. 1500, Aztec

Stone, 115 × 53 × 43 cm

Museo Nacional de Antropología, Mexico City, CONACULTA-INAH, 10-222116 0/2

PROVENANCE: Tlamanalco, Mexico State; Alfredo Chavero collection, donated to the Museo Nacional in the nineteenth century

SELECTED REFERENCES: Peñafiel 1910, p. 15; Pijoán 1946, pp. 143–44; Anton 1969, p. 112, no. 193; Wasson 1983, pp. 89–107

The regenerative force of nature is present in this sculpture of Xochipilli ('flower prince'), the god of flowers and plants and the patron of dance and song. The deity sits cross-legged on a ritual seat sculpted in the form of a flower whose corolla, petals, stamens and pistils spread round all four sides of the throne. Each side shows another fully opened flower with a butterfly drinking nectar at its centre – an image invoking the flowering of the universe. Xochipilli's main item of attire is the sacred mask he wears as god of the feast celebrating the rainy season and the flowering of the earth. He also wears a necklace made of the skin of a jaguar head and a loincloth. Flowers are painted or tattooed on his limbs. Some scholars have identified these as the most important plants used to communicate with supernatural forces, i.e. as plants with hallucinatory properties.

The Mexican dramatist and historian Alfredo Chavero found the sculpture on the outskirts of Tlamanalco, a small village on the slopes of the volcano Iztaccihuatl. FS, RVA

106
Xochipilli

c. 1500, Aztec

Fine-grained volcanic stone, 74.5 × 31 × 26 cm

Völkerkundliche Sammlungen Reiss-Engelhorn-Museen, Mannheim, V Am 1085

PROVENANCE: purchased in Mexico by a Mr Dohrmann, 1830; acquired by Gabriel von Max from the Schilling collection; acquired by the Reiss-Engelhorn-Museen from the Gabriel von Max collection, 1916–17

SELECTED REFERENCES: Krickeberg 1960, p. 1; Pasztory 1983, p. 225

The male figure, seated on a stool with his legs drawn towards him and his arms resting across his knees, wears only a loincloth, sandals and broad leather bands on his forearms and shins. The open helmet framing the face is shaped in the form of the bird known as *quetzalcoxcoxtli*, identifiable by the feather crest as a *tuberquel Hokko*, a tropical species that is the first to sing in the morning. This attribute helps to establish the context in which the figure was viewed, as does the rectangular stool, which in Aztec iconography was the seat of rulers and gods. The thin nose-bar ending on both sides in spheres links the wearer to the sun god, and both the human and the bird's head are adorned with rosette-shaped ear ornaments with bows. Clearly, the sculpture represents a divine being associated with the rising sun. A similar sculpture, surrounded by miniature music instruments, was found in 1900 in the former temple of Xochipilli in the centre of Mexico City, enabling the present figure to be identified as Xochipilli, the god of the rising sun, springtime, flowers and music. MT

107
Figure with flowers and maize

c. 1325–1521, Aztec

Stone and traces of paint, 27.7 × 25.2 × 29.9 cm

The Cleveland Museum of Art, The Norweb Collection, 1949.555

PROVENANCE: donated to the museum by Mrs R. Henry Norweb, 1949

SELECTED REFERENCES: Pasztory 1983, pp. 228–29; Madrid 1992, p. 157; Miller and Taube 1993, pp. 62, 78–79, 88–89, 90–91, 108, 190; Matos Moctezuma 1994, p. 198

Experts usually identify this appealingly expressive male as either Macuilxochitl ('five flower', a calendrical name) or Xochipilli ('flower prince'), two youthful Aztec deities so closely related that they often overlap. The domain of these gods – beauty, the arts and such pleasures as game-playing, dancing and sex – is signalled by their association with flowers: both names incorporate the

Nahuatl word for 'flower', and in one hand the figure holds a cone of flowers, perhaps the blossoming crown of a cactus. For the Aztecs flowers were richly metaphoric, signifying, among other things, beauty and refinement as well as fertility in general and sexuality in particular. The burden of maize cobs on the figure's back may further allude to these gods' creative energies and to Xochipilli's link to the maize god Centeotl, another vibrant young male.

Macuilxochitl and Xochipilli also meted out punishment to those who over-indulged in pleasure. Punishment often took the form of misfortune or disease – the latter, like immoderation, regarded as a dangerous imbalance – that fitted the crime. For instance, both gods sent afflictions of the reproductive organs, such as venereal disease, to those who violated a period of fast by having sex. SEB

108
Xilonen

c. 1500, Aztec

Stone, 52 × 20 cm

Museo Nacional de Antropología, Mexico City, CONACULTA-INAH, 10-82209

PROVENANCE: Teloloapan, Guerrero, Mexico, 1964

SELECTED REFERENCES: Solís Olguín 1991, pp. 90–91, no. 54; Belém 1995, p. 99, no. 12; Amsterdam 2002, p. 198, no. 143

In the mid-fifteenth century the Aztec armies fell like predators on the provinces of Cihuatlan and Tepecuacuilco, territories on the Pacific coast in the present-day Mexican state Guerrero, from which they obtained greenstones, copper axes, cotton, honey, copal resin and red *Spondylus* shells, as well as rich spoils of woven cloaks, military garments and shields. Although the present sculpture of Xilonen, goddess of young maize, was discovered at Teloluapan in Guerrero, the quality of the carving suggests that it was made in a metropolitan workshop. The deity wears a headdress of cotton strips tied at the nape of the neck in a bow from which hang two dedicated to Mictlantecuhtli, the deity of death and the underworld, a statue of whom no doubt stood on top of it. On its four sides are reliefs depicting nocturnal creatures, shown to be conveyors of human sacrifices by the hearts and livers they hold in their paws or claws: a bat (on the front), a scorpion, an owl and a spider. The base bears an image of Tlaltecuhtli ('earth lord') with the symbol of the five parts of the universe, the quincunx, on his stomach. FS, RVA

132

Tlaltecuhtli

c. 1500, Aztec

Stone, 93 × 57 × 34 cm

Museo Nacional de Antropología, Mexico City, CONACULTA-INAH, 10-81265

PROVENANCE: Mexico City, 1968

SELECTED REFERENCES: New York 1970, p. 274; Pasztory 1983, pp. 160–61; Mexico City 1995, p. 184

When the sculpture was found in 1968 during the construction of a Metro line in Mexico City its necklace of severed hands and human hearts led to it being dubbed 'Coatlicue of the Metro'. Subsequent research has corrected this identification: this is the first known three-dimensional depiction of Tlaltecuhtli ('earth lord'), previously familiar only from reliefs and illustrations in codices. His pose, gazing aloft cross-legged with his claw-like hands tilted upwards, characterises him as a devourer of human remains. Like his female counterpart, Coatlicue-Cihuacoatl, he is the embodiment of the earth, the final destination of human beings. His face recalls that at the centre of the so-called Sun Stone (fig. 5), a resemblance that links both sculptures with Tlachi-Tonatiuh ('underground sun'), i.e. the sun on the nocturnal part of its daily journey, when it travels through the earth. FS, RVA

133

Brazier

c. 1500, Aztec

Fired clay, height 45.5 cm, diameter 45 cm

Museo Nacional de Antropología, Mexico City, CONACULTA-INAH, 10-223665

PROVENANCE: acquired 1950

SELECTED REFERENCES: Hildesheim 1986, no. 171; Mexico City 1995, p. 72, no. 53

Ceremonial braziers were closely linked to the ritual architecture of Tenochtitlan, placed in front of the deities' altars or outside temples. Their embers burned offerings of human and animal remains, as well as *copalli* (a kind of aromatic incense) and balls of *hulli* (a rubber latex extracted from the tree *Castilloa elastica*). The pattern of spheres on the edge of the present brazier may refer to its function of burning balls of latex. The dense, very dark smoke this produced was believed magically to blacken the clouds until they resembled those that brought the rain much-awaited by farmers. FS, RVA

134

Goblets with images of skulls

c. 1500, Mixtec

Fired clay and paint, height 30 cm each, diameter 12.5 cm each

Museo Nacional de Antropología, Mexico City, CONACULTA-INAH, 10-77820, 10-3344

PROVENANCE: Mexico City, 1936–37

SELECTED REFERENCES: Westheim 1962, no. 48; Solís Olguín 1991B, pp. 257, 393; Amsterdam 2002, pp. 236–37, nos 190, 191

The goblets were made in the Oaxaca region and are a representative example of Mixtec polychrome ceramics. They were found, however, in Mexico City, among a large offering of vessels excavated to the south of the palace of Motecuhzoma at a place called El Volador, an area that some archaeologists believe once formed part of the palace. The goblets are practically identical. They are shaped like a double cone and have both painted and modelled decoration: three painted celestial bands that show the stars as the 'eyes of night', i.e. as half-closed eyes, and a modelled skull that evokes the rite of Tzompantli,

during which skulls were skewered and displayed in the Templo Mayor. The goblets were used to feed the gods: filled with blood, they were connected to the mouth of the idols by straws called *pópotl* in Nahuatl. FS, RVA

135

Teteoinnan-Toci

c. 1500, Aztec

Stone and shell, 107 × 41 × 26 cm

Museo Nacional de Antropología, Mexico City, CONACULTA-INAH, 10-1077 o/2

PROVENANCE: Tlalmanalco, Mexico State, nineteenth century

SELECTED REFERENCES: Pijoán 1946, p. 95; Bernal and Simoni-Abbat 1986, p. 246

The old goddess Teteoinnan-Toci ('mother of the deities-our grandmother') is identified by her serene countenance, the deep lines of her face and, in particular, the headdress, which consists of a plaited cotton band that fits firmly on the head and is tied at the nape of the neck. Bernardino de Sahagún and other Spanish chroniclers describe the headdress as a complicated cloth structure with knotted ends falling down the back. The pleated paper bow (*tlaquechpányotl*) at the rear is a mark of the goddess's rank and high birth. She also wears a *quechquémitl* (cape), its edge decorated with large cotton tassels, and a *cuéitl* (skirt), on which her calendrical name, '3-monkey', appears within a large square next to a rather comic image of a monkey making a ritual gesture. Although the whites of the eyes retain their original shell inlays, those depicting the irises have disappeared.

Sculptures of this kind were dressed in a variety of clothes, in accordance with the requirements of each feast celebrated at twenty-day intervals. At such times they probably held the *tlachpanoni* (broom) and *chimalli* (round shield) with which they are depicted in manuscripts. FS, RVA

136

Altar of the planet Venus

c. 1500, Aztec

Stone, 58 × 63 × 64 cm

Museo Nacional de Antropología,
Mexico City, CONACULTA-INAH, 10-357224

PROVENANCE: Mexico City, first half of the
twentieth century

SELECTED REFERENCE: Mexico City 1995,
p. 75, no. 59

The thirteen celestial planes that
constituted the firmament of the
Aztec universe were defined as the
field of action of heavenly bodies.
The sun, moon and stars were
believed to move along paths
of stars. Special significance was
attached to Venus because its
synodic span – the Venusian year
of 584 days – includes two periods
when it is invisible and another
two when it is the first star to
appear in the evening or the last
to fade in the morning. On the
present altar Venus is represented
by a three-lobed figure, an icon
that also identifies the planet in
reliefs and in images in codices.
The altar is a four-sided prism.
Its upper band consists of
a sequence of spheres symbolising
the canopy of stars; Venus, with
her nocturnal, half-closed eyes and
monstrous jaws, can be seen in the
lower band. The celestial element
tecpatl ('flint') is flanked and framed
by fantastical faces; two flint
knives commemorate the sacrifice
of Venus, which, according to
legend, was pierced by the sun's
arrow. FS, RVA

137

Brazier with an image
of a dead warrior

c. 1500, Aztec

Fired clay and paint, height 99 cm,
diameter 88 cm

Museo Nacional de Antropología,
Mexico City, CONACULTA-INAH, 10-116586

PROVENANCE: Metro Line 2, Mexico City,
1967

SELECTED REFERENCE: Amsterdam 2002,
pp. 206–07, no. 152

During construction work on
the Metro in Mexico City in the
area of the Templo Mayor, five
ceremonial braziers were found
that bore images of warriors killed
in battle or sacrificed to the sun.

The warriors symbolise the dead
fighters who were thought to
accompany the sun on its daily
path across the firmament. The
soldier depicted on the present
brazier is magnificently attired as
an eagle, the *nahual* (spirit twin) of
the sun, and armed with a *chimalli*
(round shield) and a *macáhuitl*
(obsidian-edged sword), held
aloft in his right hand in a warlike
gesture. He wears a necklace of
hearts and human hands, similar
to that associated with the
goddess Coatlicue, mother of
Huitzilopochtli, the patron deity
of war. The warrior's emaciated
face with vivid, protruding eyes
was intended to breathe new life
into soldiers returning to earth
four years after being sacrificed.
The bone ear ornaments and the
severed hands link him to the
deities of the underworld, while
the headdress, a band of turquoise
crescents and a *xiuhtótol* (blue
bird), also made of turquoise,
symbolises Xiuhtecuhtli, god of
fire, the day and heat. Together,
the attributes suggest opposites,
such as life/death and
light/darkness. The columns of
smoke produced by such ritual
braziers were thought to lead the
tonal (soul) of the deceased to
the celestial battlefield. FS, RVA

138

Anthropomorphic brazier

c. 1500, Aztec

Fired clay and paint, 91 × 76 × 57.5 cm

Museo Nacional del Virreinato, Tepotzotlan,
CONACULTA-INAH, 10-133646

PROVENANCE: Metro Line 2, Mexico City,
1967

SELECTED REFERENCE: Mexico City 1995,
p. 185, no. 218

This is the best-preserved of the
five braziers discovered during
construction of the Metro in
Mexico City in the former precinct
of the Templo Mayor. It depicts
a divine warrior crossing the
threshold of death, either because
he was killed in battle or because
he has been sacrificed to the gods.
The black, red and yellow painting,
particularly the facial paint
consisting of yellow bands on

a black background above the eyes
and mouth, associates him with
Yayauhqui Tezcatlipoca, patron
of youthful energy and military
victory. This sacred receptacle still
preserves long, pointed ornaments
which descend from the rim. We
can clearly see the figure's finery
and ornaments emerging from
its disguise: an enormous eagle
helmet with an open beak. All the
warriors in the group of braziers
wear the headdress characteristic
of the god Xiuhtecuhtli – a band
with turquoise discs bearing an
image of the cotinga bird. The
present figure has a 'halo' of nine
feathers around the upper part
of his face, evoking the planes
of the underworld. He wears a
chest protector with two red strips
from which a pectoral once hung,
the triangular apron-like garment
characteristic of warriors, circular
ear ornaments and a necklace
made up of severed hands,
recalling the sacrifice of war
captives. FS, RVA

139

Coyote

c. 1500, Aztec

Stone, 28 × 46 × 45 cm

Museo Nacional de Antropología,
Mexico City, CONACULTA-INAH, 10-81642

PROVENANCE: Mexico City, first half of the
twentieth century

SELECTED REFERENCES: Kubler 1985,
pp. 220–21, no. III-12; Pasztory 1983,
pp. 234–35; Solís Olguín 1991, pp. 110–11,
no. 72

The coyote, its name derived from
the Nahuatl *coyotl*, is the most
common species of canine
in Mexico. It occupied an
outstanding place among the
animals the Aztecs chose as
patrons and protectors of their
military activities. In the present
sculpture the dog is shown alert,
awaiting his prey with claws at the
ready – a reflection of the ferocity
with which warriors should plunge
into battle. The military insignia of
supreme warriors, *cuauhpiyolli*, and
two white eagle feathers appear
on the coyote's head. The image
is unusual because the back of the
animal is flayed, exposing his
backbone and ribs. This evokes

VI RELIGION

146
Figure

c. 1350–1521, Aztec

Fired clay, height 18 cm

Staatliche Museen zu Berlin, Preußischer Kulturbesitz, Ethnologisches Museum, IV Ca 36407

PROVENANCE: collected by Eduard Seler, 1911

SELECTED REFERENCE: Pasztory 1983, pp. 281–82

The Aztecs are known above all as masters of stone sculpture, but they also produced large numbers of small clay figures, generally made with the help of moulds and representing, among other things, warriors, deities and women. Unlike full-scale stone images of gods, which played a central part in religious celebrations within temple precincts, small clay figures were probably installed in the homes of the lower classes of society and worshipped in connection with the frequent rituals that were a feature of Aztec life. MG

147
Ehecatl-Quetzalcoatl

c. 1500, Aztec

Stone and obsidian, 41 × 23 × 18 cm

Museo Nacional de Antropología, Mexico City, CONACULTA-INAH, 10-48

PROVENANCE: acquired in the first half of the twentieth century

SELECTED REFERENCES: Westheim et. al. 1969, p. 168, no. 194; Bernal and Simoni-Abbat 1986, pp. 319–21, no. 293; Mateos Higuera 1992–94, vol. 2, pp. 185–209, nos 46–48; Mexico City 1995, p. 108, no. 90

By the time the Aztecs reached Mesoamerica in the Late Postclassic period (1250–1521), the deity Quetzalcoatl was also being worshipped in the guise of Ehecatl, god of wind. Farmers waited eagerly for the powerful gales that swept across the country announcing the rains, produced, it was believed, by Ehecatl blowing through the mask shaped like a bird's beak that is the staple item in his iconography. The

present image of the god is remarkable for its naturalism. Ehecatl sits with his legs apart, revealing the details of the loincloth, and places his crossed arms on his knees in a statuesque attitude of contemplation that draws attention to the mask. The obsidian eyes evoke the dark colour of the clouds before they release rain onto the fields. FS, RVA

148
Macuilxochitl

c. 1500, Aztec

Stone, 36 × 43 cm

Museo Nacional de Antropología, Mexico City, CONACULTA-INAH, 10-1102

PROVENANCE: unknown

SELECTED REFERENCES: Castañeda and Mendoza 1933, pp. 209–10; Solís Olguín 1991, pp. 148–49, no. 104a, b

Macuilxochitl ('5-flower') is the calendrical name of Xochipilli, who, in the guise of a turtle, was the god of song, dance, music and the happiness associated with celebrations. Among the musical instruments played on such occasions were turtle shells used as drums, which were struck with deer's antlers (see cat. 316). In the present sculpture the god takes the place of the turtle inside the shell, symbolising his patronage of music. He wears a warrior's nose-bar and characteristic ear ornaments in an inverted drop-shape. On his buttocks is the flower with five pistils signifying '5-flower'. FS, RVA

149
Tonatiuh

c. 1350–1521, Aztec

Volcanic stone and traces of paint, 31.5 × 16.2 × 24.5 cm

Museum der Kulturen Basel, Basle, IVb 634

PROVENANCE: Lukas Vischer collection, donated to the museum, 1844

SELECTED REFERENCES: Basle 1985, pp. 78–79; Bankmann and Baer 1990, p. 124; Miller and Taube 1993, p. 172

The sculpture depicts Tonatiuh, the sun god of Postclassic central Mexico. His arms crossed on his knees, the god sits in a crouching position on two blocks of stone,

his feet resting on one, his buttocks and the solar disc on his back on the other. His head and oval eyes are directed slightly upwards. The front of his diadem has five circular elements representing jewels; at the back are remains of a feather headdress. Especially striking are the circular ear ornaments. Tonatiuh wears a loincloth and sandals; his thighs are decorated with ribbons and circular adornments. The solar disc on the god's back is framed by a large feather crown and reaches down the full length of the figure. The circle in the middle of the disc bears the glyph Ollin and the number Nahui. Nahui Ollin ('4-movement') is the name of the present and final era, or sun, into which Aztec mythology divided the history of the world. The body and the feather crown bear traces of red paint.

Like other items included here (cats 45, 92, 205, 230, 248), the sculpture was donated to the Basle museum in 1844 as part of the estate of the Swiss merchant and traveller Lukas Vischer, who visited Mexico between 1828 and 1837. AB

150
Cuauhxicalli

Late fifteenth or early sixteenth century, Aztec

Greenstone, height 6.4 cm, diameter 15.5 cm

Museum für Völkerkunde Wien (Kunthistorisches Museum mit MVK und ÖTM), Vienna, 59.896, Becker Collection

PROVENANCE: Philipp J. Becker collection, acquired by the museum, 1897

SELECTED REFERENCES: Nowotny 1961, pp. 128–32; Vienna 1992, p. 215

Cuauhxicalli ('eagle vessels') were major items of Aztec material culture (see also cats 151–52, 249). When the Mexica-Aztecs reached Coatepec ('serpent hill') on their mythical journey to their future homeland, their first action was to build both a temple to their patron god, Huitzilopochtli, and a *cuauhxicalli*, either the name of another building or a receptacle for hearts and blood. The eagle was the spirit companion of Huitzilopochtli, the sun, and was therefore associated with warriors. During human sacrifice, the chest of the victim dedicated to the god was opened, the heart – the precious 'eagle cactus fruit' – extracted, offered to the sun and placed in a *cuauhxicalli*. The body was then called 'eagle man'.

The outside of the present *cuauhxicalli* is decorated with a wreath of eagle feathers in reference to the name for the vessel; beneath the feathers is a row of circles indicating preciousness. The underside of the vessel is carved with the image of the earth deity Tlatecuhtli. His mouth, opened to reveal rows of teeth and a sacrificial knife, is directed upwards; his arms and legs are decorated with skulls; his hands and feet have become jaws. A further, larger skull appears on his body. This deity is often depicted on the underside of sculptures: the earth was thought to devour both the sun every night and the dead. The mirror depicted on the inside of the vessel bears a simple, stylised image of Nahui Ollin ('4-movement'; the 4 is missing here), the present world-era, or sun, the fifth in the Aztec creation cycle. Nahui Ollin is the day not only on which the present era began, but also that on which it will be destroyed by earthquakes. The sun sign is surrounded by symbols for jade or preciousness. GvB

151
Cuauhxicalli

c. 1500, Aztec

Stone, height 17.5 cm, diameter 40 cm

Museo Nacional de Antropología, Mexico City, CONACULTA-INAH, 10-220916

PROVENANCE: Tláhuac, Mexico City, 1913

SELECTED REFERENCES: Anton 1969, p. 196; Washington 1983, pp. 38–39; Mexico City 1995, p. 68

Sacred containers such as this, called *cuauhxicalli* ('eagle vessels'), held the food of the gods. While this consisted primarily of the blood and hearts of sacrificial victims, usually captives, all members of Aztec society were

expected to contribute to the maintenance of the universe by sacrificing some of their own blood. The cactus thorns used for such sacrifices were burned in *cuauhxicalli*, a function indicated in the present example by the *zacatapayolli*, the ball of straw into which the instruments of sacrifice were inserted, that is carved in the bottom with two thorns on the sides. An offering of blood was thought to ensure the continuing existence of the universe: the row of skulls on the outside of the vessel evokes the cycle of life and death. FS, RVA

152
Cuauhxicalli

c. 1500, Aztec

Basalt, height 56 cm, diameter 30 cm

Trustees of the British Museum, London, Ethno. +6185

PROVENANCE: reportedly found in a village near Puebla; purchased from Consul Doormann, Hanover, with the Christy Fund, 1893

SELECTED REFERENCES: Joyce 1912, pl. IIb; Pasztory 1983, p. 236, pl. 243; Baquedano 1984, p. 84, pl. 55; McEwan 1994, p. 77; see also Washington 1983, p. 37

The chronicles record how *cuauhxicalli* ('eagle vessels') such as this served as receptacles for sacrificial offerings and were used in the solemn state ceremonies of investiture and enthronement of new rulers. The shape of the vessel echoes that of pottery storage jars used to hold *pulque*. Its upper part is composed of encircling superimposed bands of human hearts, feathers and jade. The front bears a solar disc and the glyph Nahui Ollin ('4-movement'), the symbol for the fifth world-era in the Aztec creation cycle. On the base beneath this is the glyph '1-rain'. On the obverse a symbol for the moon is found together with the glyph '2-rabbit', one of the calendrical names of a *pulque* god. This opposition expresses a deep-rooted Mesoamerican concern with the opposed, complementary forces governing the rhythmic relationship between seasonal change and human affairs. The hollow basin on the top of the vessel and some details of the

exterior surface were never completed. The object also shows signs of intentional defacement, particularly at the sides. This suggests that an unexpected event, perhaps the arrival of the Spanish, intervened before it could be finished. CMcE

153
Sacrificial knife

c. 1500, Aztec

Wood and flint, 7 × 31 × 5 cm

Museo Nacional de Antropología, Mexico City, CONACULTA-INAH, 10-559650

PROVENANCE: Mexico City, first half of the twentieth century

SELECTED REFERENCES: Pazstory 1983, p. 264; Mexico City 1995, p. 67

Sacrificial knives (*tecpatl*) were an essential feature of Aztec rituals, used to cut open the chests of captives and extract their hearts as nourishment for the gods. The hafts of the few surviving examples bear images of the gods symbolised by the knife. The carved figure in the present instance wears the large plume and the circular ear ornaments typical of the sun god Tonatiuh. The arms are supporting the blade, a pose similar to that shown on two further knives, their hafts covered with turquoise mosaic (cats 295–96). Emerging from the top of the head, the *xiuhcoatl* ('fire serpent'), the weapon of Huitzilopochtli, god of the sun and war, bares its fangs. No evidence remains of any further decoration on the knife. The haft was found in the foundations of a colonial building in southern Mexico City. The blade, also Pre-Hispanic, was added in modern times. FS, RVA

154
Heart

c. 1500, Aztec

Greenstone, 24 × 20 × 11 cm

Museo Nacional de Antropología, Mexico City, CONACULTA-INAH, 10-392930

PROVENANCE: Mexico City, 1977

SELECTED REFERENCES: Dahlgren et al. 1982; Solís Olguín 1991, pp. 24–27, no. 7a, b; Solís Olguín 1991B, p. 250, no. 381

Postclassic period that were found at Cholula and neighbouring sites. Since the paintings on the exterior of this urn lack the technical mastery and fine detail seen on the Cholula-style vases, the urn may have been painted in Veracruz by local artists imitating the Cholula polychrome style. The two large, rather carelessly painted eagles that appear on opposite sides of the vessel alternate with two large solar discs containing a seemingly poorly understood version of the *ollin* ('movement', or earthquake) sign as it is represented on an urn from Puebla now in the Museo Nacional de Antropología, Mexico City. Eagles, which were closely associated with the sun in Nahua thought, commonly appear on such urns. The pairs of vertically striped rectangles separating the eagles from the solar discs on the urn shown here may represent *mantas*, multi-purpose pieces of cloth that were used as gifts and ritual offerings. CK

166
Two-handled bowl

*c.*900–1521, Mixtec

Fired clay and paint, 23.5 × 38 cm

Didrichsen Art Museum, Helsinki, acc. no. 822

PROVENANCE: purchased by Gunnar and Marie-Louise Didrichsen from Frank Elmer, New York, 1974

The Postclassic polychrome clay bowl is of Mixtec origin. Although the Mixtecs are best known for their goldwork, they also made a range of attractive pottery, from pitchers with handles to large funerary jars. The present bowl is a fine example. The significance of the decorative motifs has not been established. JT

167
Two-handled polychrome urn

*c.*1500, Mixtec

Fired clay and paint, 35.5 × 40 cm

Colección Fundación Televisa, Mexico City, Reg. 21 pj. 35

PROVENANCE: unknown, acquired through Manuel Reyero, late 1960s

SELECTED REFERENCE: Reyero 1978, p.116

During the Late Postclassic period (1250–1521) a tradition of ritual ceramics developed in the regions of Puebla and Oaxaca that produced polychrome funerary urns with a wide mouth, two handles at the sides and painted decoration. Most of these objects are from the area known as 'Mixtequilla veracruzana', which lies in the south of what is now the state of Veracruz, on the border with Oaxaca. The main decorative motif on the present urn consists of bunches of eagle feathers hanging from a disc with four strips of paper evoking the *zacatapayolli*, the ball of straw into which sacrificial instruments were inserted. At the centre is an ornament with a striped section, showing how the extremities of sacrificial victims were adorned. This culminates in four feathers, recalling the arms and legs severed during the ritual. Finally, there is pendant consisting of large sacrificial feathers and a disc of smaller feathers, next to which appears a cruciform design consisting of strips of paper – a reference to the four cardinal directions. FS, RVA

168
Casket

*c.*1350–1521, Aztec

Stone, 29.5 × 25.5 × 20 cm

Staatliche Museen zu Berlin: Preußischer Kulturbesitz, Ethnologisches Museum, IV Ca 26921 a-b

PROVENANCE: Bauer collection, purchased by the museum, 1904

SELECTED REFERENCES: Washington 1983, p.66; Solís Olguín 1993, p.78

The casket, complete with its lid, is a particularly fine example of Aztec stonework. Two attributes of a Mesoamerican ruler, symbols of his power and sovereignty, are carved on one of the long sides: the diadem known as *xihuitzolli* and a nose ornament. The lid bears the date-glyph '6-reed'. Various ethnohistorical sources state that such stone caskets were used as funerary urns, in which case the date may be that of a ruler's death. MG

169
Tepetlacalli

*c.*1500, Aztec

Stone, 21 × 32 × 32 cm

Museo Nacional de Antropología, Mexico City, CONACULTA-INAH, 10-466061

PROVENANCE: Mexico City; donated by General Riva Palacio, nineteenth century

SELECTED REFERENCES: Galindo y Villa 1903, pp.207–09, no. 2; Madrid 1992, p.213; Amsterdam 2002, p.233, no. 186

Self-sacrifice was widespread throughout Mesoamerica, the ritual of shedding their own blood enabling practitioners to commune with the gods. People learned to draw blood from specific areas of their body in childhood. Carried out with sacred instruments, such as maguey thorns, obsidian knives, sharpened human and jaguar bones, and sting-ray spines, this act of devotion was equivalent to the primordial act of the gods when they created the Fifth Sun and humankind.

The *tepetlacalli*, a stone casket designed to contain items associated with self-sacrifice, bears the image of a richly adorned warrior drawing blood from his ear with a sharpened human bone. The man has a fleshless jaw and is missing his left foot, a possible reference to Huitzilopochtli, the god of war. The *xiuhcoatl* ('fire serpent') behind him underlines his relationship with Huitzilopochtli, for whom the *xiuhcoatl* acts as a weapon. Other identifiable symbolic features on the casket are the *zacatapayolli*, the ball of straw containing two pairs of bloody thorns surrounded by flowers and smoke, and, on the bottom, the figure of Tlaltecuhtli ('earth lord'), who was fed by the ritual of self-sacrifice. FS, RVA

170
Altar of the 52-year calendrical cycle

*c.*1500, Aztec

Stone, 38.3 × 30 × 22.3 cm

Colección Fundación Televisa, Mexico City, 21 Pj.9

PROVENANCE: unknown, acquired through Manuel Reyero, late 1960s

SELECTED REFERENCE: Reyero 1978, pp.150–52

Monuments commemorating the end of the 52-year cycle in the Aztec calendar generally take the form of a cylinder representing a bundle of reeds – 'year bundles' (see cat. 171) – and bearing several numbers, in particular the date '2-reed', the year in which the rites marking the beginning of a new cycle took place. The present cuboid altar also relates to these rites, focusing on the warring actions of the Aztecs to sustain the Fifth Sun (i.e. the present world-era), the provider of light. The reeds of the year bundles have been replaced by arrows. The top of the altar bears the calendrical name of the Fifth Sun, Nahui Ollin ('4-movement'); the date '2-reed' appears on the front.

The Spanish no doubt saw to it that the altar was converted into a simple container. Apparently, those who performed this operation were Indians, for they were careful to open the altar at the bottom, thus preserving its sacred message for posterity – eloquent testimony to the value they attached to it. FS, RVA

171
Xiuhmolpilli

c. 1500, Aztec

Stone, length 61 cm, diameter 26 cm

Museo Nacional de Antropología, Mexico City, CONACULTA-INAH, 10-220917

PROVENANCE: probably Mexico City, nineteenth century

SELECTED REFERENCES: Caso 1967, pp. 129–40; Bernal and Simoni-Abbat 1986, pp. 305–06

Mesoamerican peoples arrived at their calendars by measuring the revolution period of the main heavenly bodies, particularly the sun. Among the Aztecs the most celebrated cycle of time, marked by the New Fire, consisted of 52 years, i.e. thirteen times the journey of the four bearers of the year: *acatl* ('reed'), *tecpatl* ('flint'), *calli* ('house') and *tochtli* ('rabbit'). At the end of this period all fires were extinguished in houses, palaces and temples, for fear that the order established by the gods, and therefore the world as the Aztecs knew it, would collapse.

During the New Fire ceremony, called Toxiomolpilia, a young captive was sacrificed, 52 bundles of reeds were burned and the same number bound together to form a *xiuhmolpilli* ('year bundle'). The present sculpture represents one such *xiuhmolpilli*. The main panel contains the date *ome acatl* ('2-reed'), which indicates the year in which the New Fire rite took place, while the dates '1-death' and '1-flint' appear on the ends along with the mirror that links them with Tezcatlipoca ('smoking mirror'), the god of fate. The last New Fire ceremony took place in 1507, twelve years before the arrival of the Spanish. FS, RVA

172
Calendar stone

c. 1500, Aztec

Stone, 31 × 37 × 15 cm

Museo Nacional de Antropología, Mexico City, CONACULTA-INAH, 10-46541

PROVENANCE: probably Mexico City, nineteenth century

SELECTED REFERENCES: Galindo y Villa 1903, pp. 213–14; Umberger 1981, p. 142

In the 1840s José Fernando Ramírez identified the date commemorated on this calendar stone as the year '3-flint' and the day '12-lizard'. Inside the square is the sacred knife (flint) bearing a ghostly face that seems to emerge from a *cuauhxicalli* (the container used to store the hearts and blood produced by human sacrifices) with an edging of plumes and *chalchihuitl* (symbols for jade). Three strips emerge from the nose, one of them curved in the shape of a comma – perhaps a speech scroll indicating speech or song. The number is indicated by three *chalchihuitl* in a line above and below the strips. On the left, under the knife and smaller in size, is the image of a lizard with twelve *chalchihuitl* giving the number of the day. Some authors believe that the date corresponds to 1456 and commemorates the end of the famine in that year of Motecuhzuma II's reign. FS, RVA

173
Date stone

c. 1469, Aztec

Volcanic stone, 33 × 32 × 7.6 cm

Philadelphia Museum of Art: The Louise and Walter Arensberg Collection, 1950, 1950-134-374

PROVENANCE: Louise and Walter Arensberg collection, 1950

SELECTED REFERENCE: Philadelphia 1954, no. 46

This date stone records the year-name '3-house', depicted by three dots and the glyph for 'house'. It is more finely executed than, but iconographically similar to, a relief set into the Templo Mayor in Mexico City, which apparently commemorated the additions made to the complex upon the accession of Axayacatl as *tlatoani* (ruler) in 1469. It seems probable that other projects sponsored by Axayacatl in the year of his coronation were also symbolically marked by reliefs, including the present piece. Use of the calendar was part of the Aztecs' strategy of legitimising and documenting their domination of central Mexico. They set great store by astrology, and people's destiny and profession were supposedly determined by their birth date. The Aztecs may also have organised rituals and battles on calendrically auspicious days.

The piece is made from the volcanic stone that is common in central Mexico and relatively easy to work. It was carved in three planes, which enabled detail to be added to the house doorway and the crenellation above it.

The Arensbergs probably purchased the stone sometime during the 1940s from their neighbour in Los Angeles and principal dealer in Pre-Hispanic art, Earl Stendhal. EMH sacred sticks which were rubbed together to produce fire. Prominent facial features are the large beard, created in false filigree, and the two fangs, which mark the figure out as a primeval deity, one who has lost his teeth with age. Also notable are the huge circular ear ornaments ending in solar rays, symbols that relate the fire at the centre of the universe to the heat of the sun. FS, RVA

180
Pair of ear ornament frontals

c. 1400–1521, Aztec–Mixtec

Cast gold, height 6 cm

The Metropolitan Museum of Art, The Michael C. Rockefeller Memorial Collection, Purchase, Nelson A. Rockefeller Gift, 1967, 1978. 412.200 a, b

PROVENANCE: The Michael C. Rockefeller Memorial Collection, gift of Nelson A. Rockefeller, 1967

SELECTED REFERENCES: Hildesheim 1986, no. 258; Jones and King 2002, p. 54

Gold ornaments were symbols of power and prestige among many ancient American peoples who worked gold, and wearing them was strictly regulated. In Aztec society only members of the nobility and accomplished warriors were entitled to adorn themselves with necklaces, ear and nose ornaments, and lip-plugs.

The Mixtecs, the most skilled goldworkers in Pre-Hispanic Mexico, cast their gold ornaments by the lost-wax method (see cat. 282) and liked to link a number of dangling elements, which would swing and tinkle with each movement of the wearer. On the present ornaments, originally attached to backings, two bird heads project from stylised solar discs (partly miscast). A series of articulated tassels and small bells hangs from the strong, curved beaks. The heads have three pronged crests and may depict *coxcoxtli*, a species of woodland bird associated with Xochipilli, the god of spring, music, games and pleasure. Since he also had solar associations, his animal symbol is shown emerging from the solar disc.

The bird heads, tassels and bells are hollow cast. Some core material, a mixture of charcoal and clay, remains in places. HK

181
Pendant in the form of an image of Xiuhtecuhtli

c. 1500, Aztec–Mixtec

Gold, 4 × 3.5 × 2 cm

Museo Nacional de Antropología, Mexico City, CONACULTA-INAH, 10-8543

PROVENANCE: Mexico City

SELECTED REFERENCES: Seville 1997, pp. 114–15; Vienna 1997, pp. 69–70

In Pre-Hispanic Mexico gold (*cuitlatl*) was believed to be an excrescence of the sun. Its possession among the Aztecs was restricted to the *tlatoani* (rulers), who made gifts of gold objects to outstanding warriors and to members of the nobility who had otherwise distinguished themselves. Goldsmithing, introduced to Mesoamerica *c.* AD 800, was practised with the greatest skill by the metallurgists of the Mixtec realms. When the Aztecs conquered the Oaxaca region they took many local goldsmiths to Tenochtitlan. Such artisans probably made the present pendant, which was cast by the lost-wax method (see cat. 282). It takes the form of an image of Xiuhtecuhtli, the god of fire, identifiable by his fangs, which accentuate his smiling expression. He has a beard, circular ear ornaments, a headdress of feathers and an unusually prominent nose, which has been damaged. FS, RVA

182
Rattle

c. 1500, Mixtec

Gold, 5.5 × 4.5 cm

Museo de las Culturas de Oaxaca, CONACULTA-INAH, 10-105430

PROVENANCE: Oaxaca State

SELECTED REFERENCE: Solís Olguín and Carmona 1995, pp. 118, 185

Goldsmithing developed late in Mesoamerica compared to South America, where goldworked objects have been discovered that date from earlier than 2000 BC. By *c.* AD 800 metal technology had been introduced from South America into western Mexico and, probably after 1000, metallurgy reached southern and central Mexico as a result of contact with the Isthmus of Central America. Mixtec goldwork belongs to the second tradition, and the Mixtecs became the great metalworkers of southern Mexico, masters of the technology known at the time. The rattle was made by the lost-wax technique (see cat. 282). It combines the image of a bat with a spherical section that contained the clapper. The bat was regarded as a sacred animal because it inhabited caves, anterooms of the underworld. Maize seeds were thought to enter the underworld before growing, which is why the Pre-Hispanic people of Oaxaca associated the bat with the god of maize, whom they called Pitao Cozobi. The face here includes characteristic features of the bat: round eyes, prominent incisors and a spiral between the nose and the forehead that looks like a small horn. FS, RVA

183
Pendant bell

c. 1500, Aztec

Gold, 9 × 7.5 × 3.8 cm

The State Hermitage Museum, St Petersburg, DM 321

PROVENANCE: Stroganoff collection; passed to the Hermitage, 1935

SELECTED REFERENCES: Kinzhalov 1960; New York 1990, pp. 229–31, no. 110

This pendant bell is shaped like a warrior in eagle attire. The two halves of the beak serve as a kind of helmet, opened to reveal a finely modelled, severe-looking human face. The top of the helmet is adorned with feathers. The pear-shaped body is hollow; a copper pellet inside it rattles at every movement. The breast is decorated with a plaque, a delicate golden bow on the reverse indicating that such plaques were attached with a cord. The thin human arms are covered with feathers; the hands hold a kind of a staff, three darts and a small round shield trimmed with feathers. Eagle claws protrude from the lower part of the body. The upper part of the piece is surrounded by a rectangular frame of gold wire with spirals at the edges. Two large loops at the back of the head show that the pendant was worn on a chain or a thick cord. The bell was made by the lost-wax technique (see cat. 282).

Representations of warriors in eagle attire were quite common in Aztec art (see cat. 206), but the present ornament seems to be unique. It is believed to have been worn by a prominent member of the order of eagle warriors, which consisted of representations of aristocratic Aztec families. MD

184

Pectoral with an image of Xiuhtecuhtli

c. 1500, Mixtec

Gold, 10.5 × 7.5 × 2 cm

Museo Nacional de Antropología, Mexico City, CONACULTA-INAH, 10-9676

PROVENANCE: Papantla, Veracruz, nineteenth century

SELECTED REFERENCES: Aguilar et al. 1989, pp. 164, 166; Solís Olguín and Carmona 1995, pp. 58–59; Seville 1997, pp. 110–11

Purchased at Papantla, a coastal town near the ruins of Tajín in Veracruz, this piece of jewellery made by Mixtec metalworkers using the lost-wax technique (see cat. 282) is generally known as the 'Papantla pectoral'. It represents the Aztec god Xiuhtecuhtli, the equivalent of the Mixtec deity Iha Ndikandii, who was worshipped as the sun god in the Oaxaca region. Bearded, he bares his two characteristic fangs. His headdress combines Aztec and Mixtec features, consisting of a band above the forehead with two protruding vertical elements (one is broken) and a large construction, made of false filigree, that includes feathers, rosettes and spirals. The pectoral takes the form of the disc typically worn by warriors. The calendar combination '1-reed' and '4-serpent' appears on the reverse

of the rectangular panels at the bottom.

In 1940 the piece was stolen and broken into two sections. Traces of the rudimentary repair work carried out after its recovery are visible on the reverse. FS, RVA

185

Pendant depicting a warrior-ruler with ritual regalia

c. 1200–1521, Mixtec

Cast gold, 8 × 4.5 × 1.5 cm

Trustees of the British Museum, London, Ethno. +7834

PROVENANCE: San Sebastián, Tehuantepec; purchased with the Christy Fund, 1880

SELECTED REFERENCES: Young-Sánchez 1993, p. 144, fig. 1; McEwan 1994, p. 65

Claims to hereditary nobility depended upon tracing ancestral lineage and proclaiming military prowess in dress and ornament. Mixtec metalsmiths fashioned gold into prestigious objects that signalled their owners' status in life, and upon death accompanied them as tomb offerings. The present image of a warrior-ruler was fashioned by a process of lost-wax casting (see cat. 282) incorporating finely detailed false filigree work that defines the Mixtec gold style. Its relatively small size makes the complexity of detail all the more remarkable. The figure sports a headband with embellishments running round its circumference and is richly adorned with dangling ear ornaments, what appears to be a nose-piece, and pendant plaques strung across his chest. In his left hand he grasps a circular shield and in his right brandishes a serpent-headed sceptre or spear-thrower (see cat. 315). From a lip-plug hangs a disembodied head – perhaps a war trophy – beneath which hang three pendant bells. The whole assemblage was itself apparently worn suspended as a chest or lip ornament. The framing armature may represent a formal backdrop used on ceremonial occasions or have served the more prosaic purpose of facilitating the fabrication and durability of the object. CMcE

186

Warrior

After 1325, Aztec

Cast gold-silver-copper alloy, 11.2 × 6.1 cm

The Cleveland Museum of Art, Leonard C. Hanna, Jr Fund, 1984.37

PROVENANCE: Tetzcoco (?); European private collection, early 1960s; Edward Merrin, 1983; purchased by the museum, 1984

SELECTED REFERENCES: Hassig 1988; Young-Sánchez 1993; Young-Sánchez 1996

Unusual in several respects, including its size and survival, the figurine represents a warrior who clutches a serpent-headed spear-thrower (see cat. 315) in one hand and a shield, darts and banner in the other. His élite status is revealed both by the gold from which he is made and by his accoutrements, especially the jewellery – ear, nose and lower lip ornaments – and sandals, all reserved for nobles or great warriors. As the figurine implies, military accomplishment was prized by the Aztecs, whose imperial expansion was fuelled by political and economic ambition as well as by belief in themselves as a people chosen to uphold cosmic order through war and sacrifice.

The openings in the chest and back of the head remain unexplained; perhaps a precious stone was set in the chest, anchored via a small metal loop inside the body cavity. The eyes may have been inlaid with obsidian and shell. Two stylistically peculiar glyphs on the figure's back can be read as '2-rabbit [or jaguar]' and '3-water'; the glyphs' significance is unclear. Also on the back are two loops from which the figurine may have been suspended as a pendant. A sample of the casting core yielded a thermoluminescence date indicating manufacture some time between 1346 and 1570.

The figurine reportedly belongs to a group of gold objects found in Tetzcoco. The group was photographed and recorded in 1961 and shortly thereafter entered the European private collection from which it was acquired by Edward Merrin in 1983. SEB

PROVENANCE: Ferdinand II, Archduke of Tyrol (1529–1595), Ambras castle near Innsbruck; passed to the Natural History Museum as part of the imperial collections, 1880

SELECTED REFERENCE: Feest 1990, fig. 19

This pendant has the shape of a duck's head. One eye is inlaid with a malachite bead. The Aztecs associated ducks with the rain god, Tlaloc. Attempts to establish the symbolic meaning of Aztec duck images, which have remained inconclusive, have centred on the animal's ability to fly, walk, swim and dive and thus to act as a mediator between three, partly supernatural, spheres and their denizens: the sky, the earth and the world beneath the waters. GvB

194

Ear ornaments

c. 1500, Mixtec

Gold, diameter 3.9 cm, depth 1.3 cm (each)

Museo de las Culturas de Oaxaca, CONACULTA-INAH, 10-105428 0/2

PROVENANCE: Oaxaca State, 1925

SELECTED REFERENCES: Solís Olguín and Carmona 1995, p. 160; Seville 1997, pp. 138–39; Amsterdam 2002, p. 106, no. 26

From Preclassic times (2000–100 BC) members of Mesoamerican village communities had adorned their ears with cylindrical objects made from all kinds of material. In due course, ear ornaments came to serve not simply as decoration but also as signs of status. Commoners wore ear ornaments made of fired clay, wood or bone. Initially, those worn by the supreme ruler, army chiefs, priests and the nobility were made of obsidian, rock crystal or greenstone (including jade). Later, when precious metals began to be worked, such ornaments were produced for these social classes mainly in repoussé sheet gold. Spool-shaped ear ornaments like the pair shown here were inserted in the ear lobes using the groove formed by the two flat sections, flanking the face with two resplendent golden discs. FS, RVA

195

Ear-spool

c. 1300–1521, Aztec

Obsidian and gold, diameter 3.7 cm, depth 1 cm

Dumbarton Oaks Research Library and Collections, Washington DC, B-88

PROVENANCE: acquired from Earl Stendahl, 1941

SELECTED REFERENCES: Washington 1947, no. 118; Lothrop 1957, no. 68, pl. 50; Dumbarton Oaks 1963, no. 118; Hildesheim 1986, no. 261

Aztec mastery of stone and metalworking are combined in this delicate obsidian ear-spool. A flawless piece of obsidian was ground into a thin spool shape and then polished. A hammered disc of gold, attached with an organic adhesive, accentuates the black of the obsidian. The brilliant flash of gold in sunlight was a quality sought by Aztec and Mixtec craftsmen, who fashioned many types of jewellery by juxtaposing gold and other materials. The combination of obsidian and gold in this manner is unusual. Strict sumptuary laws governed Tenochtitlan and ensured that only wealthy nobles and rulers could wear adornments such as this ear-spool, which was probably one of a pair. LT

196

Lip-plugs

c. 1500, Mixtec

Black obsidian, 2.5 × 4.1 × 1.9 cm; black obsidian, 1.6 × 3.2 × 1.6 cm; black obsidian with turquoise inlay, 2.5 × 4.1 × 1.9 cm; and red chert, 2.5 × 4.1 × 1.9 cm

The Saint Louis Art Museum, Gift of Morton D. May, 138:1980, 139:1980, 140:1980 and 141:1980

PROVENANCE: gift of Morton D. May, 1980

SELECTED REFERENCE: Parsons 1980, p. 121

These four stone lip-plugs demonstrate the highest development of the lapidary artistry for which the Mixtecs were well known. Each lip-plug was produced by drilling and cutting with string, using an extremely abrasive sand that may have contained quartz. The slightly trapezoidal hollow cylinders are perfectly round and feel as though they were machine-milled. Each cylinder sits on a slightly bowed

flange platform with elliptical ends. These works are most striking as abstract forms, yet their purpose was not purely aesthetic: they served to convey the power, prestige, spirituality and beauty of the wearer and owner.

The Aztecs saw the world in transformational terms. Nature was governed by shifting, mutable shapes, and all things had multiple personalities and appearances. One of the black obsidian lip-plugs has a turquoise insert in the cylinder, making it in every sense weightier than the other three. Turquoise symbolised water and sky and, by association, the rain god Tlaloc. By wearing this object, its owner may have been revealing his Tlaloc side and rain-god personality. Similarly, the black-rimmed cylinder may have represented his underworld and death aspect. That the other lip-plugs lack a stone inlay makes no aesthetic sense, since without it they would have been largely invisible from the front. These ornaments may have been designed to contain a variety of stones, conveying multiple spiritual aspects of their owners on different occasions. JWN

197

Plaque or pectoral

c. 800–1000, Mixtec

Jade, 17 × 8 cm

Didrichsen Art Museum, Helsinki, acc. no. 822

PROVENANCE: Milton Arno Leof collection (?); purchased by Gunnar and Marie-Louise Didrichsen from Stolper Galleries, Amsterdam, 1967

The Mixtecs were the finest workers of turquoise in ancient Mexico. Greenstone was more precious than gold to the peoples of Mesoamerica, and jade was a coveted material. The present Early Postclassic jade plaque or pectoral, which is preserved intact despite its large size, is one of only a very small number of comparable pieces to have survived. The use of jade, rather than the less highly valued serpentine, and the outstanding workmanship suggest that the item belonged to the ceremonial attire worn by a prominent Mixtec. The seven drilled holes may have formed part of a pattern involving the cord that passed through them to hold the piece in place. The main decorative motif consists of four intertwined serpents. The Musée de l'Homme in Paris and the Ethnologisches Museum in Berlin each possess a similar, though smaller, plaque. JT

198
Fan

Grip c. 1500, Aztec; feathers 1999

Wood with parakeet and hummingbird feathers, 40 × 10.5 × 4.5 cm

Museo Nacional de Antropología, Mexico City, CONACULTA-INAH, 10-393455

PROVENANCE: Mango de Madera, Mexico City, first half of the twentieth century

In Pre-Hispanic times fans were a mark of both the nobility and the high-ranking travelling *pochteca* (professional merchants). The *tlatoani* (rulers) and their families in the major cities were notably elegant and distinguished, finishing touches to their appearance being provided by a bunch of flowers, a mouthpiece to inhale aromatic tobacco smoke, and a fan. The present example, carved from wood with a tip in the form of a richly attired warrior's head, was discovered by chance in Mexico City, in a field to the north of the Tlaloc Pyramid in what had been the sacred precincts of Tenochtitlan. In the course of a recent reorganisation of the Mexica gallery in the Museo Nacional de Antropología it was decided to employ an *amanteca* (featherworker) to restore the fan to its original splendour using new feathers. FS, RVA

199
Lid of a casket with a sculpture of an *ahuizotl*

Late fifteenth century, Aztec

Andesite, 13 × 33 × 30 cm

Staatliche Museen zu Berlin: Preußischer Kulturbesitz, Ethnologisches Museum, IV Ca 3776

PROVENANCE: Carl Uhde collection, purchased by the museum, 1862

SELECTED REFERENCES: Seler 1960–61, vol. 4, pp. 513–18; Pasztory 1983, pp. 164–65

The quasi-mythical animal known as the *ahuizotl* ('water-thorn beast') appears here in a crouching position with its tail coiled and water symbols on its back. The *ahuizotl*, which dwells by watercourses, springs and river banks, was said by the Aztecs to seize people who came too close to the water's edge with its long tail, pull them down into the depths and hold them there until they drowned.

The image of this beast was the glyph of the Aztec ruler who bore its name, Ahuizotl (reigned 1486–1502), who dedicated the new Templo Mayor of Tenochtitlan on day '7-reed' of the year 1487. As this date is carved on the underside of the lid, the stone casket from which it comes may have been deposited, full of sacrificial offerings, in the temple precinct during the dedication. Eduard Seler noted that the cover most probably belongs to a casket in the British Museum (cat. 200). MG

200
Casket

Late fifteenth century, Aztec

Andesite, 23 × 33 × 18 cm

Trustees of the British Museum, London, Ethno. Q82 Am 860

PROVENANCE: presented by A.W. Franks, 1872

SELECTED REFERENCES: Joyce 1912, fig. 9; Pasztory 1983, pls 122, 123, 164; Washington 1983, p. 120; Baquedano 1984, pp. 89–91, pl. 59; López Luján 1994, p. 221

This stone casket bears the image of a quasi-mythical aquatic creature, perhaps a water possum (*ahuizotl*), carved on the inside bottom surface and may once have belonged to the eighth Aztec ruler named Ahuizotl (reigned 1486–1502). This animal was believed to eat the eyes, nails and entrails of people who died by drowning, and Ahuizotl himself is reputed to have drowned in a flood caused by the catastrophic

collapse of the Acuecuexcatl aqueduct. The casket was apparently originally paired with a lid now in Berlin (cat. 199). The uppermost side of the lid bears a three-dimensional sculpture of an *ahuizotl*, while the underside is inscribed with the date '7-reed', which perhaps corresponds to a dedication offering made at the Templo Mayor of Tenochtitlan during Ahuizotl's reign. Ahuizotl was a formidable military leader and ruler. Upon completing each campaign of strategically planned and ruthless conquest, he earned a fearsome reputation for human sacrifice on an unprecedented scale.

On the front of the casket the rain god Tlaloc is shown holding a large jar adorned with the symbol for jade (*chalchihuitl*). Streams of water and ears of maize pour from the vessel, each rivulet terminating in *chalchihuitl* and conch shells offered in propitiation to ensure the continued productivity and fruitfulness of the earth. A pectoral with a symbol for gold hangs from Tlaloc's neck. The casket itself may have been used to hold the special sacrificial instruments used to draw blood offerings to the earth deity who is depicted in reliefs carved on the underside and inside bottom. CMcE

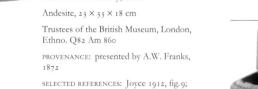

201
Funerary casket

c. 1500, Aztec

Stone, 22 × 24 × 24 cm

Museo Nacional de Antropología, Mexico City, CONACULTA-INAH, 10-223670 0/2

PROVENANCE: probably Tetzcoco, Mexico State, nineteenth century

SELECTED REFERENCES: Peñafiel 1910, pp. 124–26; Umberger 1981; Pasztory 1983, p. 247, pl. 255a,b; Solís Olguín 1991, pp. 152–53; Belém 1995, p. 98

Stone caskets with calendrical inscriptions were a characteristically Aztec creation (see cats 168, 293). They were made either in connection with specific rites for particular deities or, as in the present case, for the use of certain rulers, whose names accounts, around one foot) and fastened to a *temalácatl*, a sacred disc-shaped stone with a hole in the centre for attaching the cord. The present *temalácatl* shows a relief of the sun with four rays interspersed with four spikes and eight *chalchihuitl* (symbols for jade). During the symbolic battle blood flowed from the captives' wounds over the image of the sun. One side of the stone bears a St Andrew's cross repeated four times – the symbol of fire – with two *chalchihuitl* flanking it. The emphasis on the number four and its multiples relates to the Aztecs' conception of the universe as quatripartite. FS, RVA

210
Cup with images of a warrior

c. 1500, Aztec

Fired clay, height 15.5 cm, diameter 15 cm

Museo Nacional de Antropología, Mexico City, CONACULTA-INAH, 10-116788

PROVENANCE: Mexico City, 1967

This cup was among the many objects found during construction of the Metro in Mexico City, one line of which passes through the centre of what had been Tenochtitlan, the Aztec capital. Shaped like the ritual drinking bowl known as a *jícara*, it combines impressed decoration with fine painting, both techniques that originated in the Oaxaca region. The two decorative bands at the top show *ilhuitl*, signs symbolising the day or the daytime sky, alternating with three parallel vertical bars, signifying fire. The lower section bears a *xicalcoliuhqui* – stepped pattern – in the style of Mixtec manuscripts. Of particular note is the raised design repeated four times round the body of the vessel. A heart-shape encloses the upside-down image of a warrior wearing a coyote helmet, feathers and a mask in the form of a bird's beak, features associating him with Tezcatlipoca, god of war at night, and Huitzilopochtli, sun warrior of the day. FS, RVA

211
Pot in the form of a head of Tezcatlipoca

c. 1500, Aztec

Fired clay and paint, height 18 cm, diameter 13 cm

Colección Fundación Televisa, Mexico City, Reg. 21 pj. 71

PROVENANCE: unknown, acquired through Manuel Reyero, late 1960s

SELECTED REFERENCE: Reyero 1978, p.117

The polychrome anthropomorphic pot is the most enigmatic of the few surviving representations of Tezcatlipoca because it shows the deity in a form that combines life and death in a single entity. The face has the characteristic horizontal bands of face paint: three very narrow black bands (one across the chin, one crossing the cheekbones and the tip of the nose, one across the forehead) alternating with two wide sections painted yellowish red. Missing its eyelids and part of its lips, the head shows bulging eyes and both rows of teeth. Other faces in Aztec art, such as those on ceramic braziers and in sculptures of *cihuateteo* from Calixtlahuaca (see cat. 145), are also missing eyelids and lips, which has been interpreted as being the destiny of people who die in childbirth or battle and achieve permanence as a result of their death. The present pot probably exalts the eternal youth granted Tezcatlipoca by the sacrifice of young people, which took place at the end of the year. FS, RVA

212
Cup in the form of a flower

c. 1500, Aztec

Fired clay, height 28.5 cm, diameter 18 cm

Museo Nacional de Antropología, Mexico City, CONACULTA-INAH, 10-116786

PROVENANCE: Mexico City, 1968

SELECTED REFERENCE: Solís Olguín 1991B, p.258, no. 394

The ceremonial cup, discovered during construction of the Metro in Mexico City, is of a unique kind. It evokes the privileged life of the Aztec nobility – particularly the leaders of Tenochtitlan and Tetzcoco – who were said to live

among 'in cuícatl in xóchitl' ('songs and flowers'). Certainly, members of the nobility often held bunches of flowers in their hands in order to enjoy their scent. The grip of the cup consists of four stems. Their spiralling movement ends at the foot of the bowl, which takes on the character of a corolla from which the coloured petals emerge. FS, RVA

213
Cup

c. 1521–1600, colonial

Fired clay and paint, height 16.8 cm, diameter 12.5 cm

Staatliches Museum für Völkerkunde, Munich, 10.3555

PROVENANCE: reportedly found in a grave at Acatzingo, Puebla State; acquired by the museum from the Schenk and Nohl collection, 1910

SELECTED REFERENCES: Munich 1968, p.59, no. 76; Hildesheim 1986, no. 238

The shape of this richly decorated cup with hollow foot is unusual in Mesoamerican pottery. It would seem that a Christian communion cup was copied and adorned with Pre-Hispanic symbols. The inside is painted with two birds and various kinds of flower, which are repeated on the outside. The foot bears ancient geometric patterns, including an S-shaped motif and a design including concentric rings that probably symbolises *chalchihuitl* ('precious greenstone'). The painting is in the Mixteca-Puebla style, although the choice of motifs and the shape of the vessel reveal European influence. Thus the cup probably dates from early colonial times. ST

214
Pitcher

c. 1500, Aztec

Fired clay, paint and wickerwork, height 27 cm, diameter 15 cm

Museo Nacional de Antropología, Mexico City, CONACULTA-INAH, 10-607774

PROVENANCE: Tlateloco, Mexico City, 1993

SELECTED REFERENCE: González Rul 1988, pp.74–77

After the conquest of Tlatelolco by the *tlatoani* Axayacatl in 1473 the Aztecs made it all but impossible for their neighbours in this city to offer the gods objects made of such precious materials as jade, turquoise, gold, silver and so forth. Henceforth ritual burials contained mainly ceramic objects, such as this two-coloured jug with a handle and a tubular spout. The vessel, which was never intended for domestic use, belongs to the Texcocan tradition of 'polished red' pottery and is painted delicately in white with stylised symbols resembling *chalchiuhuitl* and feathers. FS, RVA

215
Pitcher

c. 1500, Aztec

Fired clay and paint, 20.3 × 14.6 × 7.6 cm

The Saint Louis Art Museum, Gift of Morton D. May, 135:1979

PROVENANCE: gift of Morton D. May, 1979

SELECTED REFERENCE: Parsons 1980, p. 123

The pitcher belongs to an Aztec tradition of redware pottery with black designs that originated at Tetzcoco in the Basin of Mexico. The conquistadors who accompanied Hernán Cortés noted beautiful displays of pottery in the great market of Tenochtitlan. Objects such as this pitcher were purchased at markets for home use. The designs on these vessels are generally described as hastily rendered geometric patterns with shell-like forms, yet I believe that in the present instance their iconography relates to the function of the vessel: to pour *pulque*.

The scallop design on one side may well represent a cross-section of a leaf of the maguey, the cactus from which *pulque* is obtained. Moreover, the land snail in the centre of this motif symbolises water and by extension *pulque*. The opposite side of the vessel features four black, comb-like designs that strongly resemble the pistils of the agave, along with curling, tail-like motifs that no doubt refer to the pollen. Hence, the sexuality of the plant is represented on the pitcher. The Aztecs associated the drinking of *pulque* with heightened sexuality.

The front view of the vessel, which is notably phallic in shape, reinforces this sexual reference, as does the phallic allusion in what has been called a double S on this side but may well depict a snake. The artist who decorated this vessel thus employed an iconographical programme that referred to its function of pouring *pulque* and to the sexual benefits accruing to those who drank the beverage. JWN

216
Tripod plate

c. 1500, Aztec

Fired clay and paint, height 15 cm, diameter 27 cm

Museo Nacional de Antropología, Mexico City, CONACULTA-INAH, 10-580947

PROVENANCE: Mexico City, 1967–68

SELECTED REFERENCE: Belém 1995, p. 90

Food was served to the Aztec nobility in the same types of vessel as those used for offerings to the gods and as burial objects. This pottery differed from popular wares in the refinement of its polychrome decoration, in a style derived from the Cholula region of the Mixtec realm. Its most elegant form was a tripod plate supported on discs with painted decoration of flowers with open petals. The stepped patterns on the inside recall those found in manuscripts. The bases were decorated with highly stylised heads of animals important in Mesoamerican mythology, especially eagles and serpents with open beaks and jaws. FS, RVA

217
Tripod plate

c. 1500, Mixtec

Fired clay and paint, height 13.5 cm, diameter 34.6 cm

Museo Nacional de Antropología, Mexico City, CONACULTA-INAH, 79133

PROVENANCE: tombs 1-2, Zaachila, Oaxaca, 1962

SELECTED REFERENCES: Solís Olguín 1991B, p. 166, no. 244; Amsterdam 2002, p. 104, no. 24

Archaeological discoveries in the royal tombs at Zaachila in Oaxaca included a group of polychrome vessels that attest to the high quality of Mixtec ceramic wares. The present tripod plate, its legs in the shape of jaguar claws, was intended to contain precious objects, particularly gold jewellery, as is indicated by the image of a stylised butterfly painted on the floor of the bowl: the Museo Nacional de Antropología, Mexico City, contains items of jewellery similar to this. Polychrome ceramic pieces of this type reached Tenochtitlan via the trading networks maintained by professional Aztec merchants, the *pochtecas*. FS, RVA

218
Tripod bowl

Sixteenth century, Aztec

Fired clay and paint, height 6.2 cm, diameter 18.5 cm

Staatliche Museen zu Berlin: Preußischer Kulturbesitz, Ethnologisches Museum, IV Ca 32143

PROVENANCE: acquired by Eduard and Caecilie Seler in Huexotla for the museum, 1907

SELECTED REFERENCES: Pasztory 1983, pp. 292–99; Washington 1983, p. 163, fig. 77

The motif in the centre of the bowl resembles a many-petalled flower. This rosette is surrounded by two concentric bands. The first contains alternating S- and ring-shaped patterns, the second intertwined S-shaped markings. At the edge of the bowl, separated from the centre by three circular lines, is a flame pattern, a feature suggesting that this piece of black-on-orange pottery dates from the late Aztec era, probably Post-Conquest. The feet of the tripod are painted with horizontal lines and each is divided into three smaller feet bearing stylised floral motifs. MG typical goggle eyes, coiled nose, 'moustache' ornament and fangs. The eyes contain shell and obsidian inlays (one of the irises is missing). The god wears a paper bow at the nape of his neck, a conical hat and ear ornaments.

The sculpture was placed in a stone box in Chamber II of the Templo Mayor of Tenochtitlan as part of an offering to Tlaloc notable for its complexity and richness. The bottom layer consisted of large quantities of greenstone beads and material of marine origin. The second layer revealed 98 complete figurines and 56 masks from the region of Mezcala (including cats 257–59, 261, 263), 57 large conches, numerous pieces of coral, 60 greenstone beads, the remains of a feline with a greenstone sphere in its mouth and many other objects. In the uppermost layer the image of Tlaloc shown here presided over the offering with that of another deity, carved from alabaster. EMM

240
Lidded pot with an image of Tlaloc

c. 1469–81, Aztec

Basalt and traces of paint, height 28 cm, diameter 24.5 cm

Museo del Templo Mayor, Mexico City, CONACULTA-INAH, 10-219815 1/2

PROVENANCE: offering 60, Huitzilopochtli building, Stage IV(b) of the Templo Mayor, Mexico City, 1980

SELECTED REFERENCE: López Luján 1993, pp.323–30

Ometecuhtli, the dual god, created Tlaloc and his companion Chalchiuhtlicue. To the former he assigned water from the sky, to the latter terrestrial water, i.e. that in rivers, lakes, lagoons and the sea. During Alcahualo, the ceremony devoted to Tlaloc, children and young people were sacrificed to these two deities to ensure that rains would fall to provide good harvests. People who drowned or who died from being struck by lightning, and those who suffered from leprosy or other illnesses related to water, were said to pass to Tlalocan, the

place of eternal summer where everything is fertile.

The pot was found in offering 60 of the Templo Mayor. The lowest layer consisted of an irregular arrangement of shells and small conches, greenstone beads, copper rattles and sea urchins. The next layer comprised a variety of marine materials, including red and brain coral, *Xancus* and *Strombus* conches, while the layer after that consisted of osteoderms and crocodile phalanxes, the rostral cartilage of a swordfish, remnants of various species of fish and incomplete remains of the bones of rabbits, pumas, cats and snakes. The final layer contained a *tecpatl* ('flint', i.e. sacrificial knife), five skulls, projectile heads, nine flint knives, fourteen self-sacrifice perforators arranged in a radial pattern, fourteen quails and, among many other objects, two bowls of copal in front of an image of Xiuhtecuhtli and that of Tlaloc shown here. The god has his characteristic 'goggles', coiled nose, 'moustache' ornament and fangs. The lid bears traces of blue pigment. EMM

241
Tlaloc

c. 1500, Aztec

Wood, resin and copal, 34 × 19 × 20.5 cm

Museo Nacional de Antropología, Mexico City, CONACULTA-INAH, 10-392920

PROVENANCE: Iztaccíhuatl, San Rafael, Mexico State, 1959

SELECTED REFERENCE: Navarrete 1968

A fantastical face, ear ornaments and prominent fangs are among the constant features of the varied iconography associated with Tlaloc, god of rain. His characteristic headdress was a kind of crown with points representing the mountains where he kept water. The *tlaquechpányotl*, a folded paper bow on the back of his neck, indicated the god's noble ancestry.

The present sculpture, produced by applying resin and copal to an armature of sticks, was discovered in a cave in Iztaccíhuatl volcano together with an image of Tlaloc's consort, Chalchiuhtlicue. Both

pieces show that not only clay and stone, but also perishable materials were used for images of the gods. It is highly probable that these sculptures were burned after Tlaloc's favour had been gained by intense worship: it was believed that the smoke issuing from the resin and copal would blacken the clouds and cause them to release their fertilising load over the fields. FS, RVA

242
Tepetlacalli

c. 1469–81, Aztec

Basalt, box 69 × 58 × 38.5 cm, lid 67 × 57 × 13 cm

Museo del Templo Mayor, Mexico City, CONACULTA-INAH, 10-168850 0/2

PROVENANCE: offering 41, Tlaloc building, Stage IV(b) of the Templo Mayor, Mexico City, 1980

SELECTED REFERENCE: López Luján 1993, pp.409–12

Most archaeological objects found in the Templo Mayor were housed in offerings. As a form of communication between humankind and the gods, the contents of such offerings fulfilled a specific symbolic function. Archaeologists have grouped the offerings according to the time each was made, its location in the temple, the type and dimensions of the container, the position of the objects and the richness of their materials.

Offering 41 was a box made of blocks of volcanic stone, with a stone slab base and lid. It contained the present *tepetlacalli* (stone casket) surrounded by a large quantity of conches, shells, mother-of-pearl, sea urchin jaws, fragments of greenstone objects and a ceramic pot. The walls of the *tepetlacalli* are painted blue inside and decorated with reliefs outside. Two of the outside faces show a number of half-bent legs, with ornaments round the ankles and sandals on the feet. One of the remaining faces bears the calendar glyphs '13-rain' and '13-reed', the other an unidentified glyph. On the lid is a mask of the rain god Tlaloc, with his characteristic 'goggles', 'moustache' ornament, coiled nose and fangs. Taken together, the lid with the facial features, the box and the two sides with the legs might be interpreted as a complete representation of Tlaloc's body.

Unlike other *tepetlacalli*, the present casket contained no items associated with self-sacrifice, but instead a large number of objects relating to water – beads, small greenstone sculptures, shells, conches, two model canoes, two oars, a rudder – along with things more often included in offerings, such as Mezcala-style figurines and masks. Other notable objects were a spear-thrower (*átlatl*) carved from white stone and some items included elsewhere in this publication (cats 280–81). EMM

243
Votive vessel with an image of Tlaloc

c. 1500, Tepanec

Fired clay and traces of paint, 116.5 × 40 × 47 cm

Museo Nacional de Antropología, Mexico City, CONACULTA-INAH, 10-357182

PROVENANCE: Azcapotzalco, Mexico City, first half of the twentieth century

SELECTED REFERENCE: Solís Olguín 1991B, p. 255, no. 388

Following their victory over the Tepanecs, the Aztecs destroyed virtually all evidence of Tepanec cultural identity, a process continued by the Spaniards during their occupation – the nineteenth in the history of the region. The present vessel bearing an image of the rain god Tlaloc, the best preserved of two found in the area, thus belongs among the few artefacts to have survived from the former Tepanec domain of Azcapotzalco. The ornamentation around the sides of the vessel, which depicts the steam that was thought to have created the clouds in the sky, was made separately and attached to the body after firing. Tlaloc is identified by his characteristic mask. According to myth, he ordered his helpers, the *tlaloque*, to collect water from the mountains in vessels like this: the *tlaloque* raised them to the height of the sky and the precious liquid

poured down. The god's benevolent role is indicated by the beads and pendants on his chest and by the circular plaque symbolising gold. FS, RVA

244
Xiuhtecuhtli

c. 1469–81, Aztec

Basalt, 36.6 × 21.9 × 21.2 cm

Museo del Templo Mayor, Mexico City, CONACULTA-INAH, 10-220304

245
Xiuhtecuhtli

c. 1469–81, Aztec

Basalt, 37 × 21.8 × 20 cm

Museo del Templo Mayor, Mexico City, CONACULTA-INAH, 10-220305

246
Xiuhtecuhtli

c. 1469–81, Aztec

Basalt, 31.5 × 19 × 19 cm

Museo del Templo Mayor, Mexico City, CONACULTA-INAH, 10-220357

PROVENANCE: offerings 17, 20 and 61, between the Tlaloc and Huitzilopochtli buildings (cats 245–46) and Tlaloc building (cat. 244), Stage IV(b) of the Templo Mayor, Mexico City, 1979

SELECTED REFERENCES: Matos Moctezuma 1988, p. 92; López Luján 1993, pp. 172–92

Xiuhtecuhtli, the ancient god of fire, also known as Huehueteotl, was represented as an old, toothless man with blind or closed eyes, sitting with his arms crossed over his knees. Sculptures of this type were found in 26 of the over 120 offerings excavated on the site of the Templo Mayor in Mexico City, most of them near the Tlaloc building, in which gods representing contrary but complementary elements, such as fire and water, were united. Fire was associated with the male and celestial half of the universe, where all is light and warmth, while water was the female side: dark, damp, cold and earthly. Accordingly, Xiuhtecuhtli was the patron of the day called *atl* ('water') and *atl-tlachinolli* ('burnt water') was the symbol of sacred war.

The present images of Xiuhtecuhtli show his main attributes. He is naked but for

a simple loincloth, two rectangular ear ornaments with a pendant in the centre, a paper bow at the nape of the neck (the last two features typical of gods of water and fertility) and a *xiuhuitzolli* diadem decorated with concentric circles, probably representing precious stones, the most distinctive aspect of which is the fire bird (*xiuhtototl*) at centre. Likewise characteristically, the lower half of his face is painted black, the areas around his ears and mouth red. Crowning his head are two protuberances representing the sticks rubbed together to produce fire.

In his guise of 'lord of the year', Xiuhtecuhtli-Huehueteotl ruled over time and the recording of time. He was celebrated during two feasts, Xocolhuetzi and Izcalli, and every 52 years he presided over the New Fire rites. As the god of fire, Xiuhtecuhtli lived at the centre of the universe, from which the three vertical levels and the four horizontal directions started. He was at the centre, just as fire was at the centre of the home and the temple. As 'turquoise lord', he was worshipped for inhabiting the navel of the world, enclosed by turquoises. The attributes of Xiuhtecuhtli are expressed in a song recorded on folio 34 of the Florentine Codex (cat. 345): 'Mother of the gods, father of the gods, the old god / lying in the navel of the earth, / placed in an enclosure of turquoises. / He who is in water the colour of bluebirds, / He who is enclosed in clouds. / The old god, he who lives in the shadows of the region of the dead / The lord of fire and of the year.' EMM

247
Pulque deity

c. 1469–81, Aztec

Basalt and traces of paint, 36.5 × 23 × 20 cm

Museo del Templo Mayor, Mexico City, CONACULTA-INAH, 10-162940

PROVENANCE: offering 6, Huitzilopochtli building, Stage IV(b) of the Templo Mayor, Mexico City, 1978

SELECTED REFERENCE: Nicholson 1991

Her lowered eyelids indicate that she is dead and the two bells on her cheeks linked by an incised band across the nose symbolise her name. Her striated hair, or possibly a head cloth, is studded with down-feather balls that stand for light, sun and sacrifice. She wears ear ornaments consisting of circular and triangular elements from which hang what appear to be trapezoidal year symbols. The two perforations above the ears suggest that the mask was worn as a pectoral during ritual performances. Twelve pairs of perforations on the rear edge of the underside may have been used to hang other miniature objects when the mask was employed as a pectoral. This piece has striking similarities to two other images of Coyolxauhqui: an enormous diorite head unearthed in 1830 in Mexico City (cat. 255) and the colossal circular stone carving found in 1978, also in Mexico City (fig. 10).

Coyolxauhqui plays a major role in the myth of the birth of the Aztec patron deity Huitzilopochtli ('left-sided hummingbird'). She becomes enraged because her mother, Coatlicue ('serpent skirt'), conceives Huitzilopochtli while sweeping out a temple on the sacred mountain Coatepec ('serpent hill'). She leads her brothers, the Centzon Huitznahua ('400 southerners'), to attack their mother after preparing them for war through ritual dance and costuming. When Coyolxauhqui arrives at the top of Coatepec in full battle array, Coatlicue gives birth to Huitzilopochtli, who is fully grown and armed. The young warrior god slays and scatters his siblings by using his magical weapon, the *xiuhcoatl* ('fire serpent'). He then decapitates and dismembers Coyolxauhqui, whose body falls to pieces, rolling down Coatepec. This myth was symbolised in the design and location of certain sculptural objects at the Templo Mayor in Tenochtitlan. DC

255

Head of Coyolxauhqui

c. 1500, Aztec

Diorite, 80 × 85 × 68 cm

Museo Nacional de Antropología, Mexico City, CONACULTA-INAH, 10-2209118

PROVENANCE: Convento de la Concepción, Mexico City, 1830; donated by the convent to the museum, 1830

SELECTED REFERENCES: Peñafiel 1910, p. 52; Washington 1983, pp. 48–50

The sculpture depicts the head of Coyolxauhqui ('the one with bells on her face'), goddess of the moon. Symbols on the ornaments she wears on her face indicate that the bells were made of gold. The circles on her head stand for the feathers that were attached to people about to be sacrificed, recalling the creation myth in which Huitzilopochtli, the warrior sun, decapitated his sister and enemy, the moon (see cat. 254). On the base of the sculpture is a relief of *atl-tlachinolli*, symbol of sacred war, expressed as the union of fire and water, together with date '1-rabbit'. Both elements show that the monument commemorates the earth mother Coatlicue giving birth to Huitzilopochtli.

The sculpture formed part of the Templo Mayor complex and was found in March 1830 in the old Convento de la Concepción near the street of Santa Teresa (now Guatemala Street). FS, RVA

256

Mask

c. 1100–600 BC, Olmec

Greenstone, 10.2 × 8.6 × 3.1 cm

Museo del Templo Mayor, Mexico City, CONACULTA-INAH, 10-168803

PROVENANCE: offering 20, between the Tlaloc and Huitzilopochtli buildings, Stage IV(b) of the Templo Mayor, Mexico City, 1978

SELECTED REFERENCES: Matos Moctezuma 1979; López Luján 1993, pp. 323–30

Approximately 80 per cent of the objects found among offerings in the Templo Mayor in Mexico City came from towns under Tenochtitlan rule, but they included items from earlier civilisations, such as those of Teotihuacan and the Olmecs. Scientific examination of the

present Olmec mask, and the aquiline shape of its nose, suggest that it came from the border area between Guerrero, Oaxaca and Puebla. Some three thousand years old, it evokes the jaguar, a feature typical of the ancient cultures of the Gulf of Mexico, and shows the characteristic V-shaped groove in the upper part. The Aztecs, who clearly recognised the value of the mask, placed it in offering 20. The first layer of this offering contained very fine black sand, the second shells and small conches, greenstone beads, copper rattles, sea urchins and anthropomorphic figurines made of copal. The third layer consisted of larger marine objects: *Strombus* and *Xancus* conches along with 'brain', 'antler' and 'net' types of coral. The fourth layer contained the remains of various animal skins – fish, tortoise shells, rostral swordfish cartilages – and the fifth images of Tlaloc and Xiuhtecuhtli, the Olmec mask shown here, various Mezcala-type greenstone figurines and masks, Mixtec penates, sacrificial knives (*tecpatl*) and inlaid skull masks. The offering was completed by sceptres in the shape of serpents and deer's heads, a *chicahuaztli* staff (see cat. 275), spear points and nine skulls of decapitated human beings. EMM

257

Mask

c. 1200–1481, Mezcala

Greenstone and paint, 15.4 × 14.4 × 4.12 cm

Museo del Templo Mayor, Mexico City, CONACULTA-INAH, 10-220264

258

Mask

c. 1200–1481, Mezcala

Greenstone and paint, 12 × 17.4 × 4.52 cm

Museo del Templo Mayor, Mexico City, CONACULTA-INAH, 10-220266

259

Mask

c. 1200–1481, Mezcala

Greenstone and paint, 19.9 × 18 × 2.9 cm

Museo del Templo Mayor, Mexico City, CONACULTA-INAH, 10-220316-16879

See cat. 261.

260

Mask

c. 300–600, Teotihuacan

Greenstone, shell, obsidian and coral,
21 × 20.5 × 14 cm

Museo del Templo Mayor, Mexico
City, CONACULTA-INAH, 10-220037
(ear ornaments) and 10-220032 (mask)

PROVENANCE: offering 82, Huitzilopochtli
building, Stage IV(b) of the Templo Mayor,
Mexico City, 1981

SELECTED REFERENCES: López Luján 1989;
López Luján 1993, pp. 424–25

This Teotihuacan mask was
already one thousand years old
when the Aztecs used it as an
offering in the Templo Mayor.
The Aztecs sought to link their
own history to that of previous
civilisations, such as those of
Teotihuacan and the Toltecs, in
an attempt to erase their nomadic
origins and their humble cultural
lineage. The discovery of
Teotihuacan objects in offerings
in the Templo Mayor proves
that the Aztecs carried out
excavations there.

The dark green mask retains
the shell and obsidian inlays in
its eyes and the coral used for its
teeth. It was placed in the middle
of the offering and faced south,
the direction associated with
Huitzilopochtli, the Aztec patron
deity. The bottom layer contained
an Aztec mask of white stone and
a series of greenstone objects; the
uppermost included a skull that
showed signs of decapitation.
EMM

261

Mask

c. 1200–1481, Mezcala

Greenstone and paint, 14.8 × 15 × 4.8 cm

Museo del Templo Mayor, Mexico City,
CONACULTA-INAH, 10-220267

PROVENANCE: Chamber II, Tlaloc building,
Stage IV(b) of the Templo Mayor,
Mexico City

SELECTED REFERENCES: González and
Olmedo Vera 1990; Matos Moctezuma
1993

The Mezcala style of sculpture
originated in the early first
century in the vicinity of the River
Mezcala, now in the Mexican state
of Guerrero, and developed
concurrently with the Classic
period of Teotihuacan (200–650).

Among the hallmarks of the
Mezcala style, clearly visible in the
present pieces, are highly abstract
facial features that are simply
suggested by lines and variations
in surface texture. Most of the
Mezcala objects discovered in
the Templo Mayor in Mexico City
are masks, heads and complete
figurines, found in the offerings
and occasionally painted with the
attributes of the rain god Tlaloc.

All the items shown are made
of greenstone. The first mask (cat.
257) shows remains of red and
white paint and has wide oval eyes,
a triangular nose and a large open
mouth – features of the
Teotihuacan style. The second
mask (cat. 258) is notable for a
prominent bar representing the
eyebrows, which are joined to the
nose. The eyes are small and oval
and traces of red paint can be seen
under the mouth. A water-glyph is
drawn in black on the reverse. The
triangular nose and the oval eyes
of the third mask (cat. 259), which
has a rectangular forehead, are
indicated by incisions, as is the
mouth, which is decorated with
vertical bands of red. The fourth
mask (cat. 261) bears traces of
red, white, blue and black paint
and has arched eyebrows, eyes
consisting of circular holes, a
triangular nose and a 'moustache'
ornament painted above its mouth
– an attribute of Tlaloc. The
figurine (cat. 263) has inlaid eyes
and bears traces of white, black,
red and blue pigment on various
parts of the body. The head is
painted with the facial features
of Tlaloc.

Chamber II, from which these
pieces come, was among the
Templo Mayor offerings with the
largest number of Mezcala objects,
including a further 84 masks and
56 complete figures. Since it
contained the greenstone sculpture
of Tlaloc (cat. 239), it is believed
to have been dedicated to the
tlaloque, helpers of Tlaloc who
were responsible for pouring rain
from vessels bearing the image
of the god (see cat. 243). EMM

262

Pectoral with an image of a moth

c. 1500, Aztec

Greenstone, diameter 13.5 cm

Museo Nacional de Antropología,
Mexico City, CONACULTA-INAH, 10-162943

PROVENANCE: Coyolxauhqui monument,
Templo Mayor, Mexico City, 1978

SELECTED REFERENCES: García Cook and
Arana 1978, p. 65, no. 56; Solís Olguín
1991B, p. 261, no. 403; González Rul 1997,
p. 36, fig. 20

This circular pectoral with the
image of a deified moth belonged
to a group of votive objects
discovered on 23 February 1978
on the site of the circular
monument to the goddess
Coyolxauhqui in the Templo
Mayor, Mexico City. It bears
witness to the advanced
technology employed by Aztec
stoneworkers, who in the Late
Postclassic period (1250–1521)
were already using copper and
bronze tools in addition to the
traditional small axes made of hard
stones such as nephrite or basalt.
The moth is flying downwards:
its head, in the lower part, is
covered with white down-feathers,
a symbol of human sacrifice, and
its hands are held in an aggressive
gesture at the sides of the face.
The rest of the disc contains the
extended wings, each of three
lobes. The star-shaped eye, partly
covered by the eyelid, links the
creature with the night. FS, RVA

263

Figurine

c. 1200–1481, Mezcala

Greenstone and paint, 25.4 × 5.7 × 4.2 cm

Museo del Templo Mayor, Mexico City,
CONACULTA-INAH, 10-220316

PROVENANCE: Chamber II, Tlaloc building,
Stage IV(b) of the Templo Mayor,
Mexico City

SELECTED REFERENCES: González and
Olmedo Vera 1990; Matos Moctezuma
1993

See cat. 261.

264

Figurine

c. 1469–81, probably Mixtec

Greenstone, 11.25 × 3.38 × 3.03 cm

Museo del Templo Mayor, Mexico City,
CONACULTA-INAH, 10-168804

PROVENANCE: Chamber II, Tlaloc building,
Stage IV(b) of the Templo Mayor,
Mexico City, 1980

This figurine probably comes from
the Mixtec area, in the modern
states of Puebla and Oaxaca,
which was conquered by the
Aztecs about the second half of
the fifteenth century. This origin
has not been established beyond
doubt, however, for although the
piece has the characteristics typical
of greenstone sculptures from
this region, which show figures
standing or seated, their arms on
their knees or, as here, crossed
over their chest, it is more finely
worked and its features are more
detailed than other examples. The
eyes of the figure are closed and
he wears a large headdress in the
shape of a two-headed serpent. He
is probably dead. The sculpture
was found in Chamber II of the
Templo Mayor along with other
items included here (cats 239,
257–59, 261, 263). EMM

265

Offering 106

c. 1325–1502, Aztec

Various materials and dimensions

Museo del Templo Mayor, Mexico City,
CONACULTA-INAH, 10-252003

PROVENANCE: house of the Ajaracas,
Calle República de Argentina, opposite
the Templo Mayor, Mexico City, 2000

Excavations carried out in 2000
as part of the Urban Archaeology
Programme of the Museo del
Templo Mayor in Mexico City
brought to light seven offerings to
Tlaloc, the god of rain. They were
found in the Calle República de
Argentina, in buildings previously
occupied by the Ajaracas and
Campanas that had been erected
on the remains of a platform
belonging to one of the last stages
(possibly VI) in the construction
of the Templo Mayor.

Among the offerings was
that shown here just as the
archaeologists found it. Aztec

priests had placed a large number
of objects in a box made of
volcanic rock with a stone slab
base. The bottom layer contained
items evoking the sea: corals,
seaweed and the saw of a sawfish.
Above this, were a sculpture of
Xiuhtecuhtli, the god of fire, a
miniature *pulque* vessel, a ceramic
glyph, masks with the face of
Tlaloc, blue flutes bearing the
image of Xochipilli-Macuilxochitl
(the god of dance and music),
copal figures, knives and the
remains of eagle, heron and
quail bones. Along the edge of
the box were flint knives and
representations of drums.
Offerings to the god of rain
frequently contained such
recurrent symbolic references
to music, fertility and plants. EMM

266

Sceptre

c. 1325–1481, Aztec

Obsidian, 55 × 5.86 × 1.7 cm

Museo del Templo Mayor, Mexico City,
CONACULTA-INAH, 10-250354

PROVENANCE: offering 7, Huitzilopochtli
building, Stage IV(b) of the Templo Mayor,
Mexico City, 1980

See cats 268–69.

267

Eccentric flint

c. 1500, Aztec

Flint, 44 × 22.5 × 10 cm

Museo Nacional de Antropología,
Mexico City, CONACULTA-INAH, 10-393945

PROVENANCE: Mexico City, 1940

SELECTED REFERENCES: Solís Olguín 1991B,
p. 262, no. 407; Amsterdam 2002, p. 232,
no. 185

In 1940 two ritual instruments
associated with human sacrifice
were discovered among the
offerings excavated in the area
of the Templo Mayor behind the
Metropolitan Cathedral in Mexico
City. They point to the use of the
tecpatl ('flint', i.e. sacrificial knife)
as a link between life and death.
Of the two, that shown here is
the more finely carved and adds
a 'nose' to what looks like the
profile of a human skull so that
it resembles a second *tecpatl*.

The design recalls the handle and
blade of a sacrificial knife, but the
present object was not actually
used to extract hearts. Rather, its
function was symbolic: to evoke
the god Mictlantecuhtli ('lord of
Mictlan [place of the dead]'), spirit
of the dead and personification of
death, through a depiction of him
and his deadly breath. FS, RVA

268

Serpent's head and rattle

c. 1325–1481, Aztec

Green obsidian, 6.3 × 2.5 × 1.5 cm,
7.3 × 0.9 × 1.3 cm

Museo del Templo Mayor, Mexico City,
CONACULTA-INAH, 10-262756 0/2

PROVENANCE: offering 60, Huitzilopochtli
building, Stage IV(b) of the Templo Mayor,
Mexico City, 1980

269

Two sceptres

c. 1325–1481, Aztec

Green obsidian, 9.4 × 1.9 × 0.9 cm
and 9.2 × 1.8 × 0.9 cm

Museo del Templo Mayor, Mexico City,
CONACULTA-INAH, 10-263826, 10-265172

PROVENANCE: offering 60, Huitzilopochtli
building, Stage IV(b) of the Templo Mayor,
Mexico City, 1980

SELECTED REFERENCE: Matos Moctezuma
1988, p. 97

The Aztecs developed great skill in
fashioning objects from obsidian,
a hard and brittle volcanic glass
that is extremely difficult to work.
It was used in Mesoamerica from
the earliest times and continued
to grow in importance among the
various settlements in the Basin
of Mexico until the Spanish
arrived. Obsidian, which has grey,
green or golden reflections
depending on the type, was
obtained by collecting blocks of
it on the surface of the earth or
extracting it from mines. Large
deposits existed in present-day
Mexico Federal District and in the
federal states Hidalgo and Puebla,
the most important and closest to
Tenochtitlan being those in
Mexico and at Sierra de las
Navajas in Hidalgo. The material
reached the Aztec capital via trade
with these areas and in the form
of tribute paid by them.

Obsidian symbolised the
night and the cold. Tezcatlipoca
('smoking mirror'), the

omnipotent god of fate, was associated with it, one of his attributes being an obsidian mirror that reflected the night (see cat. 279). The stone was also linked to death, to the cold wind of knives that was one of the eight stages the dead had to pass through before reaching the realm of Mictlantecuhtli, lord of the land of the dead.

The offerings excavated from the Templo Mayor in Mexico City contained a vast number of objects made from obsidian, including ear ornaments, nose-rings, miniature and full-scale sceptres of various kinds, an urn bearing the face of a monkey, arrow heads, small knives and so forth. These finds have substantially increased the list of known items made from this stone. The two examples with spherical grips shown here are miniature versions of the sceptre held by Techalotl, a *pulque* deity (see cat. 247). EMM

270–71
Two flutes

c. 1502, Aztec

Fired clay and paint, both 4 × 4 × 13.5 cm

Museo del Templo Mayor, Mexico City, CONACULTA-INAH, 10-219817, 10-252479

PROVENANCE: offering 89, external patio, Stage VI of the Templo Mayor, Mexico City, 1981

SELECTED REFERENCE: López Luján 1993, pp. 353–54

Flutes are among the oldest instruments known to humankind. As in other cultures, Pre-Hispanic Mesoamericans realised that by making a hole in a clay tube or reed the sound produced was higher in pitch. Later, they discovered that by closing the hole they could reproduce the original sound of the tube. After making further holes in the tube it was found that by opening each of them in ascending order the sounds became increasingly high. In Mesoamerica flutes reached a high degree of technical perfection, and both musicians and composers were honoured and respected by the peoples and their rulers. Flutes and other wind

instruments, along with percussion instruments, played an important role in collective rites and ceremonies. The 'flower prince' Xochipilli, also known as Macuilxochitl, was the patron god of music-making and games.

The two flutes shown here were found placed in a box of volcanic rock together with three seashells, eighteen representations of *teponaztli* drums (see cat. 157), thirteen volcanic rock sculptures of *chicahuaztli* staffs (see cat. 275) and a further ten ceramic flutes coloured blue. Completing the offering were a vessel with an image of the rain god, Tlaloc, that contained beads, pieces of greenstone and remains of copal, wood and bone in a poor state of preservation (the offering was found practically immersed in groundwater). The flutes are tubular, with a mouthpiece at one end and a decorative plaque at the other consisting of three circles with a hole in the centre and undulating scrolls – probably a reference to Tlaloc. Both have four circular finger-holes in the body and a square one near the mouthpiece, and both are painted entirely blue, the colour of water. EMM

272
Nose-ring in the form of a butterfly

c. 1500, Aztec

Gold, 7.5 × 7.5 × 0.1 cm

Museo Nacional de Antropología, Mexico City, CONACULTA-INAH, 10-220922

PROVENANCE: Calle de las Escalerillas, Mexico City, 1900

SELECTED REFERENCES: Beyer 1965B, pp. 465, 468, no. 5; Seville 1997, pp. 144–45, no. 37; Vienna 1997, pp. 44–45, no. 13

The nose-ring, a ritual adornment once worn by the image of a deity in the Templo Mayor of Tenochtitlan, is among the very few examples of Aztec goldwork that survived the greed of Spanish soldiers when they discovered the treasure chamber in the palace of Axayacatl and distributed its contents among troops and officers. Found on 16 October 1900 in the course of drainage

construction carried out in Mexico City, it formed part of a find, rescued by Leopoldo Batres, that included solid discs and discs with a circular incision in the centre known as an *anahuatl*, an emblem of the patrons of war or the flowering of the fields. Butterfly-shaped nose-rings, called *yacapapalotl* in Nahuatl, characterised several deities, among them Xochiquetzal and Chalchiuhtlicue, goddesses of flowers and water respectively. The present ornament, however, is topped by the tail of the *xiuhcoatl* ('fire serpent'), evoking the celestial deities who provide light and heat, principally the sun. Hence, the nose-ring may have been an attribute of Coyolxauhqui, who is rendered as rays of light in the sculptures of her that have come down to us. FS, RVA

273–74
Xiuhcoatl

c. 1500, Aztec

Gold, both 16 × 1 cm

Museo Nacional de Antropología, Mexico City, CONACULTA-INAH, 10-594810 and 10-3302

PROVENANCE: Calle de las Escalerillas, Mexico City, 1900

SELECTED REFERENCES: Solís Olguín and Carmona 1995, p. 115, no. 91; Seville 1997, pp. 164–65, no. 54; Vienna 1997, pp. 70–72, no. 61

Gold (*cuzticteocuícatl* in Nahuatl) was thought by the Mexica to be a type of divine excrement, dropped from the sky onto the face of the earth. The goldsmiths of Tenochtitlan fashioned it into bracelets, rings, necklaces, pectorals, ear ornaments and other items of jewellery to be worn only by rulers and high-ranking nobles as a symbol of their power and social status. The supreme Aztec ruler – considered to be the owner of the precious metal – presented it as a gift to warriors who distinguished themselves in battle. The present pair of sheet gold items, discovered on the site of the Templo Mayor in Mexico City, was produced by hammering out a gold nugget until it reached the desired size and thickness.

They portray the *xiuhcoatl* ('fire serpent') in the form of the weapon thought to have been used by Huitzilopochtli, the Aztecs' patron god, i.e. a sword consisting of a reptile covered in flames, its tail a ray of sunlight. FS, RVA, AG

275

Chicahuaztli

c. 1469–81, Aztec

Alabaster, 11.9 × 2.6 × 0.9 cm

Museo del Templo Mayor, Mexico City, CONACULTA-INAH, 10-266040

PROVENANCE: offering 58, Tlaloc building, Stage IV(b) of the Templo Mayor, Mexico City, 1980

SELECTED REFERENCE: López Luján 1993, pp. 258, 340–43

The staff called *chicahuaztli* is an attribute of the god Xipe Totec ('our flayed lord'), who inhabited the eastern – the masculine – part of the universe and was associated with the colour red and the *acatl* ('reed') glyph. Images show him wearing the yellow skin of a sacrificial victim, carrying a shield of the same colour and holding the *chicahuaztli*, in which he keeps seeds. Standing for the surface of the earth and its regenerative powers, Xipe Totec participated in the creative process together with water, seeds and the sun. His festival, Tlacaxipehualiztli ('flaying of men'), was celebrated in March. During it, his priests wore the skins of the sacrificial victims over their own, signifying the renewal that allowed life to continue beyond death.

Chalchiuhtlicue, Xochiquetzal and other gods also hold this type of staff, which has thus generally been associated with deities of fertility and interpreted as symbolising the sun's rays penetrating and fertilising the surface of the earth. This phallic symbolism is clearly reflected in the shape of the staff and its contents. Alfonso Caso extended the range of the staff's applications, claiming that it was carried not only by the gods of water and vegetation, who control the fertility of agricultural land, but also by creation deities, such

as Quetzalcoatl, celestial gods, including Huitzilopochtli (the sun), the god of fire, Xiuhtecuhtli, and even the god of death, Mictlantecuhtli.

The present *chicahuaztli* was found at the bottom of offering 58, together with marine materials, greenstone beads, an animal-head staff, two serpent-shaped staffs, a Xipe Totec nose-ring and an obsidian disc. The seeds in such staffs, which were originally made of wood, produced a rattling sound when the staff was shaken. Rattles of this kind are still used in agricultural ceremonies in Mexico. EMM

276

Staff in the form of a deer's head

c. 1469–81, Aztec

Alabaster, 9.4 × 3.2 × 0.9 cm

Museo del Templo Mayor, Mexico City, CONACULTA-INAH, 10-265825

PROVENANCE: offering 24, Tlaloc building, Stage IV(b) of the Templo Mayor, Mexico City, 1978–79

SELECTED REFERENCE: López Luján 1993, pp. 254–57, 338–39

Deer were associated with the sun and with drought. Staffs in the shape of deer's heads are among the attributes of Xiuhtecuhtli, Xochiquetzal and other gods. The present model staff is made of alabaster, which the Aztecs considered a precious material because of its whiteness and translucency. Alabaster reached Tenochtitlan from Tecalco, a town in the Mixtec area of Puebla that was conquered by the Aztecs at the end of the fifteenth century; hence its Nahuatl name, *tecalli*.

A number of comparable pieces were found among the offerings of the Templo Mayor in Mexico City, complementing other items with wavy contours, which evoked serpents. The staff shown here was found in offering 24, which had six layers. The lowest consisted of a large quantity of small marine items and was followed by another containing larger objects of this kind: the shells of four turtles, mother-of-pearl shells, coral and so forth. Other items included remains of swordfish and white

herons, the skeleton of a puma, greenstone beads, a skull mask, sacrificial knives, a shell necklace, an ear ornament and, at the very top, sculptures of Xiuhtecuhtli and Tlaloc. EMM

277

Knife blades with an image of a face

c. 1325–1521, Aztec

Coffee-coloured and white flint and green obsidian, 23 × 6.3 × 1 cm, 23.2 × 6.7 × 1.2 cm, 26.5 × 7.3 × 1.1 cm, 23.1 × 7.3 × 0.9 cm, 16.5 × 6.4 × 4.4 cm and 15 × 5 × 3.9 cm

Museo del Templo Mayor, Mexico City, CONACULTA-INAH, 10-220282, 10-220280, 10-252376, 10-220284, 10-220291 and 10-253024

PROVENANCE: offering 52, Stage VII of the Templo Mayor, Mexico City, 1980

SELECTED REFERENCE: Matos Moctezuma 1988, p. 97

The Aztecs called the northern part of the universe Mictlampa ('place of the dead'), a dry region where cold winds blew. Identified with Mictlan, the region of fleshless beings, it was associated with the colour black and the glyph *tecpatl* ('flint', i.e. sacrificial knife) and was presided over by the black god Tezcatlipoca, whose attributes included an obsidian knife symbolising black wind.

Two types of knife blade were found in the Templo Mayor in Mexico City. The blade with a face, sometimes set in a copal base so that it could stand upright, represents the glyph *tecpatl*, one of the year-bearers who was considered a deity. The second type of blade is the sacrificial knife, made of flint and with no decoration or apparent grip. Various quantities of these were found in most of the Templo Mayor offerings, some of them in the mouth or nasal passages of skull masks as a symbol of death stopping the flow of air, the element of life. Inlays of white flint, and of white flint and obsidian, on both sides of the face blade shown here simulate teeth and eyes respectively, producing the image of a face seen in profile. EMM

278

Votive pot with images
of Xiuhtecuhtli and
Tlahuizcalpantecuhtli

c. 1500, Aztec

Fired clay and paint, height 25.5 cm,
diameter 22.5 cm

Museo Nacional de Antropología,
Mexico City, CONACULTA-INAH, 10-10918

PROVENANCE: Calle de las Escalerillas,
Mexico City, 1900

SELECTED REFERENCES: Batres 1902,
pp. 17–18; Peñafiel 1910, pp. 11–12,
pls 18–22

This large polychrome votive
vessel in the Cholula style was
discovered at the foot of the steps
of an ancient building in the
grounds of the Templo Mayor
on 16 October 1900, during
excavations in Calle de las
Escalerillas. The find included
another pot and, most notably,
long-handled censers (cat. 285).
The present vessel glorifies the
pair of deities that feature
prominently in the ninth 'week'
of the *tonalpohualli*, the Aztec
divinatory or ritual calendar:
Xiuhtecuhtli, identifiable
by the fact that the lower part of
the face is painted black, and
Tlahuizcalpantecuhtli, whose black
facial painting resembles a mask in
that it covers part of the forehead
and the area around the eyes. The
gods are depicted as busts, the
form in which the rulers of day
and night appear in the *tonalamatl*,
the codices containing the
tonalpohualli calendar (see cats
340–41). They are surrounded
by floral motifs, down-feathers
(the mark of sacrificial victims)
and other signs of a ritual nature.
On the neck of the vessel an icon
of the sun, consisting of rays,
alternates with sacred quills. The
images were formerly identified
as the souls of sacrificed warriors,
yet it has never been doubted that
the purpose of the vessel was to
mark an important thirteen-day
period in the ritual calendar.
FS, RVA

279

Funerary urn with an image
of Tezcatlipoca

c. 1470, Aztec

Fired clay, height 53 cm, diameter 17 cm

Museo del Templo Mayor, Mexico City,
CONACULTA-INAH, 10-168823 o/2

PROVENANCE: offering 14, Huitzilopochtli
building, Stage IV(b) of the Templo Mayor,
Mexico City, 1978

SELECTED REFERENCES: Matos Moctezuma
1983; Fuente, Trejo and Gutiérrez Solana
1988; Mexico City 1995, p. 164

During the Templo Mayor
excavation project (1978–82)
two orange-ware ceramic urns
stylistically typical of the coastal
region of the Gulf of Mexico,
made of clay from the Toluca
Valley and bearing Toltec-style
reliefs, were found a short distance
from the monolith of the goddess
Coyolxauhqui. They contained the
cremated bones of Aztec warriors
who had probably died in battle
against the people of Michoacán
during the reign of Axayacatl
(1469–81). One of them,
shown here, bears an image of
Tezcatlipoca ('smoking mirror'),
the universal god, the invisible
one who had the gift of ubiquity;
patron god of warriors, rulers and
sorcerers; god of the cold who
represented the night sky; and god
of creation who inhabited the
three levels and the four directions
of the universe.

Enclosed in a rectangle,
Tezcatlipoca is surrounded by
a feathered serpent with a forked
tongue emerging from its jaws.
The god is armed for war, his
spear-thrower (see cat. 315) in one
hand, two spears in the other. He
wears a headdress with long eagle
feathers and a huge pectoral
consisting of a four-string necklace
and a central disc – probably an
obsidian mirror – fastened by
a four-pointed bow. His nose-ring
has the shape of a spearhead;
the ear ornament consists of two
concentric discs from which
projects a sequence of one tubular
and three spherical beads. The god
wears a bracelet, and the arm
holding the spears is covered by
a protector of a type familiar from
Toltec images. He has rings
around his ankles and one of his

feet bears his principal attribute,
a smoking mirror. In addition to
ashes, the urn, the lid of which is
undecorated, contained various
obsidian objects, including a
necklace of beads shaped like
duck's heads (see p. 316), a spear
point, two tubular beads and
a bone perforator. EMM

280

Fish

c. 1469–81, Aztec

Greenstone, 3.6 × 15.6 × 3 cm

Museo del Templo Mayor, Mexico City,
CONACULTA-INAH, 10-168782

281

Seven fish

c. 1325–1481, Aztec

Mother-of-pearl (*Pinctada mazatlanica*),
approx. 2 × 6 × 1.5 cm each

Museo del Templo Mayor, Mexico City,
CONACULTA-INAH, 10-252244, 10-263416,
10-263411, 10-263622, 10-263417, 10-263267
and 10-263415

PROVENANCE: offering 41, Tlaloc building,
Stage IV(b) of the Templo Mayor,
Mexico City, 1980

SELECTED REFERENCES: Velázquez Castro
1999, pp. 78–80; Velázquez Castro 2000,
pp. 78–79; Polaco and Guzmán 2001

The shells of various molluscs
from the coasts of the Pacific, the
Mexican Caribbean and the Gulf
of Mexico were highly appreciated
for their value both as generative
symbols and as materials for
works of art. Seven of the fish
sculptures shown here (cat. 281),
all from offering 41 in the Templo
Mayor, were fashioned from
mother-of-pearl. The holes
were no doubt for threading the
individual items onto a necklace
or pectoral. The greenstone piece
(cat. 280), like the others
remarkably naturalistic, bears
traces of bitumen.

The great symbolic value
attached to fish by the Aztecs is
made clear by the fact that most
of the Templo Mayor offerings
contained remains of various
species, both freshwater and
saltwater, from the coasts of
Mexico. These show that Aztec
cultural practice involved cutting
the fish in different ways, including
the elimination of the spine and

321

Figure of Macuilxochitl

c. 1500, Aztec (?)

Wood and traces of paint, 44 × 18 × 15 cm

Museum für Völkerkunde Wien (Kunthistorisches Museum mit MVK und ÖTM), Vienna, 59.866, Becker Collection

PROVENANCE: Tehuacan/Santa Infantita, Puebla; Philipp J. Becker collection, acquired by the museum, 1897

SELECTED REFERENCES: Nowotny 1961, pp. 105–34; Vienna 1992, no. 175

This is a rare specimen of a seated, wooden figure representing the god Macuilxochitl ('five flower'), wearing a loincloth and the crested headdress that is his hallmark. The sculpture was discovered in a cave in which favourable climatic conditions had ensured its preservation. Traces of red paint are still visible. The eyes probably contained inlays and one of Macuilxochitl's important features, a mouth ornament (usually a hand), has likewise disappeared. Macuilxochitl was a god of pleasure, gambling and excess, as well as of music and dance, and was closely related to the deity Xochipilli ('flower prince').

GvB

X CONTACT: INDO-CHRISTIAN ART

322

Cross

c. 1600, colonial

Stone, 156 × 91 × 36 cm

Museo Regional de Tlaxcala, CONACULTA-INAH, 10-341001

PROVENANCE: probably Tlaxcala State

SELECTED REFERENCE: Monterrosa 1967

The spread of Christianity in the New World met with many obstacles arising from the vastly different concepts and practices encountered in the native religion, not least the ritual sacrifice of human beings. Christian missionaries attempted to bridge the cultural gap by depicting Christ's Passion in terms of the pictographic system favoured by the indigenous population. The most characteristic product of this new way of spreading the gospel were crosses such as this, which were placed at church entrances. At the top of the present example from Tlaxcala are the letters INRI (*Iesus Nazarenus Rex Iudaeiorum*, 'Jesus of Nazareth, King of the Jews'), referring to the inscription that was fastened to the cross on which Christ was crucified. At the centre of the cross appears the face of Christ wearing the crown of thorns. On the left is a palm leaf, which stands for Christ's triumph over death, and an open hand, which symbolises the ridicule he suffered; on the right is a vessel, evoking the scene of Pilate washing his hands, and a bag of coins, representing the money Judas was paid for betraying Christ. Below Christ's face is the reed sceptre (in the form of a maize plant) given him during his mockery, followed by the instruments of the Passion: nails, pincers, a ladder and a hammer. A cock, alluding to Peter's three denials of Christ, appears above a sponge (a sponge was soaked in wine and offered to Christ on the cross) and a lance (one of the soldiers present at the

Crucifixion pierced Christ's body with a lance), which form a St Andrew's cross behind the column to which Christ was bound during the Flagellation. Below this is Christ's tunic from the scene of the soldiers dividing his clothes among themselves. At the bottom is a depiction of a bound figure (the face has been destroyed), illustrating the episode of the Mocking of Christ. FS, RVA

323

Mitre

Second third of the sixteenth century, colonial

Feather mosaic on maguey paper and cotton fabric, 82.5 × 28.5 cm

Patrimonio Nacional, Monasterio de San Lorenzo de El Escorial, 10050202

PROVENANCE: Philip II of Spain, donated to the Monastery of El Escorial, 1576

SELECTED REFERENCES: Estrada 1957, Garcia Granados 1946, p. 576; Maza 1971, p. 71; Toussaint 1982, pp. 20–22; Alicante and Murcia 1989, p. 31; New York 1990, p. 243; Martínez de la Torre 1992, p. 17; Checa Cremades 1997, pp. 126–27; El Escorial 1998, p. 545

The mitre symbolises the status and supernatural power of a bishop in a way similar to the plume worn by high-ranking Aztecs. A mosaic of feathers from tzinitzans, white-fronted parrots, cotingas, hummingbirds, spoonbills, starlings and macaws is pasted to a sheet of maguey and cotton. The iconography of this multicoloured composition, which was inspired by a French miniature of *c.* 1500 (Louvre, Paris), revolves around Christ's redemption of humanity. The front, framed by a border containing images of the Apostles and the Fathers of the Church, shows episodes from the Passion of Christ (centred on the Crucifixion), the four Evangelists and the Last Judgement. This compositional scheme is repeated on the reverse, which carries depictions of the genealogy of Christ, various scenes ranging from his descent into hell to his appearances after the Resurrection, and the Holy Trinity. The lappets (*infulae*) contain the Assumption and Coronation of the Virgin Mary and the Ascension of Christ.

The feathers are arranged so as to resemble paint, an effect enhanced by their metallic sheen when struck by light. Europeans were astonished by the skill of Mexican featherworkers, and items decorated in this way soon became collector's pieces. The Bishop of Michoacán, Vasco de Quiroga, promoted this craft, which was described in great detail by Friar Bernardino de Sahagún in the sixteenth century. The bishop's workshops produced various mitres, including this example and others now in Florence, Lyons, Milan, New York, Toledo and Vienna. JLVM

324

Triptych

Late sixteenth century, colonial

Silver gilt, boxwood and hummingbird feathers, 8 × 8 × 0.5 cm

Victoria and Albert Museum, London, 226-1866

PROVENANCE: Lecarpentier sale, Paris, 1866

SELECTED REFERENCES: Oman 1968, no. 104a; Feest 1986, p. 176; Egan 1993, pp. 42–45; London 2000, no. 48

The triptych represents an amalgamation of the artistic skills of the Old and New Worlds. The engraved silver-gilt case and carved boxwood scenes have close parallels in sixteenth-century Europe, but the background of hummingbird feathers draws on Aztec traditions. The *amanteca* (the Nahuatl term for members of the featherworkers' guild) were highly esteemed craftsmen who created garments and objects for ceremonial use by the Aztec élite and military. Miniature boxwood carvings such as this were probably executed by Mexican craftsmen trained by Flemish and Spanish Jeronymite friars in Mexico.

Four of the scenes here are taken from the Passion. The central tableau shows the Deposition, while the wings illustrate the Flagellation, Christ carrying the Cross with the help of Simon of Cyrene, and Christ mocked by a soldier. The fifth, upper right tableau depicts an event not mentioned in the

Gospels that is known as 'Christ on the Cold Stone' or 'Christ at Rest on Calvary'. This motif first appeared in northern Europe in the late Middle Ages and may have been transmitted to Mexico by missionaries.

Similar carvings set on hummingbird feathers are in the collections of the Metropolitan Museum of Art, New York; the Louvre, Paris; the Museo Nacional de Historia, Mexico City; and the Walters Art Gallery, Baltimore. The latter piece contains a Deposition scene almost identical to that on the present triptych. SM

325

The Mass of St Gregory

1539, colonial

Feathers on panel, 68 × 56 cm

Musée des Jacobins, Auch, 986.1.1

PROVENANCE: private collection; acquired by the museum, 1986

SELECTED REFERENCE: Mongne 1994

Pope Gregory I is faced by a gathering of the faithful who question the mystery of the Eucharist. After appealing to God for help, he sees before him a vision of Christ coming forth from his tomb – the scene depicted here. This subject was chosen as an effective means of instructing the native Mexican population in the basics of the Christian faith, for the image provides a summary of the Easter mystery, with all the instruments of the Passion shown in detail and arranged on the picture plane in a manner not unlike Aztec glyphs.

A few years after the Spanish conquest of Mexico, the Franciscan friar Peter of Ghent founded a school of arts and crafts in Mexico City, which at that time was governed by Don Diego Huamitzin, the son-in-law of the last Aztec *tlatoani* (ruler), Motecuhzoma II. Teaching at the school retained indigenous techniques, in particular featherwork, which was the preserve of the native nobility. Hence, the governor of the city may well have taken a personal interest in the production of the

Bernardino de Sahagún (1499–1590), who travelled as a missionary to Mexico after its conquest by Hernán Cortés in 1521. Compiled from 1558 to 1560, Sahagún's work represented an extraordinary attempt at Christianising by means of cultural understanding rather than force. Although the author's signature appears in the lower margin of folio 328r in volume 1, the manuscript was written by various scribes in Tlatelolco from the end of 1575 to the beginning of 1577, in two columns, one in Spanish, the other in Nahuatl, the language spoken most widely among the Toltecs, Chichimecs and Aztecs. The work was carried out at the request of the Franciscan Commissary General, Friar Rodrigo de Sequera, a great admirer of the *Historia*, who was implementing an order given by Juan de Ovando, President of the Council of the Indies, who was keen to discover more about this illustrated encyclopaedia of Mexican civilisation before the Conquest. Philip II of Spain (*reg.* 1556–98) opposed the liberal approach to converting the indigenous peoples and in 1577 required all the *Historia* material to be sent to Spain to prevent its dissemination. De Sequera rescued it by stealing this codex and bringing it to Europe in 1580.

In 1589 the Florentine painter Ludovico Buti (active 1560–1603) painted a ceiling fresco in the Uffizi that was inspired by the illustrations in the manuscript – a clear indication that the codex had already entered the Palatina library (either by purchase or private donation), where it complemented the wealth of Mexican objects in the non-European collections of the Medici Grand Dukes Francis I (1574–87) and Ferdinand I (1587–1609). It was not rediscovered until 1793, when the head of the Biblioteca Medicea, Angelo Maria Bandini (1757–1803), described it in the final volume of his monumental *Catalogus* along with the other codices in the Grand-Ducal library

that had been chosen for inclusion in the Biblioteca Laurenziana by order of Peter Leopold of Lorraine (*reg.* 1765–90). IGR

345

Historia Tolteca-Chichimeca

1550–70, Cuauhtinchan, Puebla

Codex, 50 folios, European paper, 31.5 × 22.5 cm; modern parchment binding

Bibliothèque Nationale de France, Paris, MS Mexicain 46–58

PROVENANCE: Alonso de Castañeda Tezcacoatl and descendants until at least 1718; acquired by Lorenzo Boturini Benaduci (1702–1755), 1737/46; acquired by Joseph Marius Alexis Aubin (1802–1891), 1830/40; Eugène Goupil (1831–1895), 1889; donated to the Bibliothèque Nationale by Goupil's widow, Augustine Elie, 23 April 1898

SELECTED REFERENCES: Glass and Robertson 1975, no. 359; Historia Tolteca-Chichimeca 1976

The Historia Tolteca-Chichimeca, the first item in Lorenzo Boturini Benaduci's *Catalogo del Museo Indiano* (1746), is a major source for the history of Pre-Hispanic central Mexico. It recounts the events of 1116 to 1547. This period saw the migration of the Toltecs, guided by Icxicouatl ('serpent's foot') and Quetzalteueyac ('great green feather'), from their mythical land of origin, Chicomoztoc ('seven caves'), and the destruction in 1168 of their capital, Tula, by the Chichimecs, whom they then followed to the Puebla region. The account moves on to the conquest of Cholula, a city inhabited by the Olmeca-Xicalanca, and the foundation of the city Cuauhtinchan ('eagle house' – the eagle was the totemic animal of the Chichimecs), where the Mexica gained power in 1471. Continuing until 1547, the chronicle gives an unadorned description of events during the early years of the colonial era: the arrival of the Spanish in 1519 (section 423) and of the Franciscans in 1524 (section 427) and the foundation of Puebla in 1531 (section 433).

The Nahuatl text, transcribed in Roman letters with headings, alternates with pictographic notations. Not all of these were

completed, some consisting merely of dates preceding the event reported or of facts recounted 'in pictures'. Others, however, are full painted pages in the tradition of the native *mapas*. One such (fol. 29r) shows a detailed depiction of Chicomoztoc, the 'seven caves' of the seven tribes of Mount Culhuacan. Each tribe is shown inside its cave, designated by its glyph and listed opposite in a Spanish inscription (section 171, fol. 28v): 'On the date 13-flower Icxicouatl [shown lower right on the painted page] and Quetzalteueyac [just above Icxicouatl] left Xalpantzinco to go to Chicomoztoc on Culhuacan, whence the Chichimec tribes had come: the Totomiuacs, the Acolchichimecs, the Cuauhtinchantls, the Moquiuixcs, the Tzauhctecs, the Texcaltecs and the Malpantlaca'. MCo

346

Codex Ríos ('Codex Vaticanus Latinus A', 'Codex Vaticanus 3738')

c. 1570–95, Rome

95 folios, European paper, approx. 46.5 × 29.5 cm each; red leather binding (replacing original black leather), 1869–89

Biblioteca Apostolica Vaticana, Vatican City, A 3738

PROVENANCE: in the Vatican Library by 1596

SELECTED REFERENCES: Codice Vaticano 3738 1900; Glass and Robertson 1975; Codex Vaticanus 3738 1979

The rarity of Pre-Hispanic manuscripts from Mexico is doubtless due to the extensive destruction of Aztec books undertaken during the first phase of the Spanish war on idolatry. Subsequently, the invaders came to realise that conversion of the native population to Christianity would be helped by learning about Aztec religious rites and that indigenous manuscripts were a valuable source of such knowledge. Missionaries enlisted the help of elders and chiefs in explaining the contents of the books, but within only a century of the Conquest very few people still understood the illustrations.

The Codex Ríos (also known as the Codex Vaticanus Latinus A or the Codex Vaticanus 3738) belongs among the rare manuscripts to contain explanations of Aztec myths and religious ceremonies, written by an unknown author in Italian beneath the illustrations. (This commentary is transcribed in its entirety, though not always accurately, in the facsimile edition of the Codex Ríos published in 1900.)

The manuscript acquired its name from Pedro de los Ríos, a Mexican Dominican friar who is twice mentioned as its illustrator (fols 4v, 23r). It is first recorded in the 1596 catalogue of manuscripts in the Vatican Library. Watermarks indicate that it was written, probably in Rome, on paper from Fabriano dating to later than 1570. One passage shows that the text was written after 1566. The manuscript must therefore date from c. 1570–95.

The Codex Ríos consists of four sections. The first is devoted to mythology and cosmology (fols 1r–11v), the second to the calculation of the 260-day ritual calendar (tonalpohualli; fols 12v–33r), of years (calendrical tables for 1558 to 1619; fols 34r–36r) and of 'months' in the solar calendar (xiuhpohualli; fols 42r–51r), the third to rites (comprising ethnographical sections on the day-signs attributed to various body parts, on sacrificial and mortuary customs, portraits of various types of native Mexican and miscellaneous drawings; fols 54r–61r) and the fourth to annals, both with illustrations (fols 66r–94r) and without (fols 94v–95v). The annals illustrations include an image of the Spanish military leader Nuño Beltrán de Guzmán setting off to conquer Jalisco in 1529 and a snake emerging from the sky as a bad omen to the native population, along with earthquakes (under 1530) and an eclipse of the sun (under 1531; fol. 88r). Other drawings relating to the first decades of Spanish rule are the arrival in 1534 of Antonio de

Mendoza as the first viceroy of New Spain (fol. 88v) and the death in 1538 of many Aztecs from smallpox (fol. 90v). The final image in the codex shows the death of the first Bishop of Mexico, Juan de Zumárraga, in 1547 (fol. 94r).

The drawings are very similar, though cruder and less detailed, to those in another Mexican manuscript, the Codex Telleriano-Remensis in Paris (cat. 348). Both manuscripts are considered to derive from a single source, the Vatican codex helping to provide knowledge of parts missing from the Paris volume. MGB

347

Juan de Tovar, *Relación del origen de los Yndios que havitan en esta Nueva España según sus historias*

1583–87, colonial

Ink and watercolour on European paper, 21.2 × 15.6 cm

The John Carter Brown Library at Brown University, Providence, Rhode Island

PROVENANCE: acquired from the collection of Sir Thomas Phillipps, 1946

SELECTED REFERENCES: Tovar 1951; Durán 1964; Tovar 1972

The earliest missionary ethnologists in New Spain after the Conquest, among them Andrés de Olmos, Toribio de Benavente Motolinía and Bernardino de Sahagún, were followed by a generation of historians some of whom had been born in Mexico. This group of scholars included Hernando Alvarado de Tezozómoc, the Dominican Diego Durán and two Jesuits, José de Acosta and Juan de Tovar. With the exception of Acosta, whose knowledge of ancient Mexico seems to have been based entirely on that of Tovar, most of them drew their information from living informants and from old, indigenous chronicles that have not survived.

Juan de Tovar was born in New Spain c. 1543–46, either in Mexico City or Tetzcoco, and died in 1626. He was ordained as a priest in 1570 and entered the Jesuit order three years later, eventually gaining fame as a missionary

preacher. He was fluent in Nahuatl, Otomí and Mazagua. Apparently basing his studies on original sources, Tovar prepared a history of Pre-Hispanic Mexico, now lost, and the work containing the present illustration.

The codex has three parts: an exchange of letters between Acosta and Tovar; a historical text entitled 'Relación del origen de los Yndios', covering Aztec history and the great ceremonies linked to the solar calendar; and the Tovar calendar, with a description of the rites and feasts of the Aztecs, including a correlation with the Christian calendar.

The second part is illustrated by 32 watercolour drawings of Aztec gods and practices. 'The Mexicans' Manner of Dancing', spread across two facing pages, shows a large anticlockwise dance of men to music provided by a horizontal and a vertical drum (*teponaztli*, *huehuetl*; see cats 156–57, 338). All the participants appear to be of very high rank, including the musicians, who wear the headdress insignia of the Aztec ruler on their shoulder. Each of the dancers is attired in a cloak knotted at the shoulder and carries a bouquet in one hand and a device topped with feathers in the other. Among the dancers are a jaguar warrior and an eagle warrior. MDC

348

Codex Telleriano-Remensis

1555–61, Tlatelolco

50 folios, European paper, 31.3 × 22 cm; modern parchment binding

Bibliothèque Nationale de France, Paris, MS Mexicain 385

PROVENANCE: collection of Charles Maurice le Tellier (1642–1710), Archbishop of Reims, donated to the Bibliothèque du roi, 1700, with 500 other MS from his collection

SELECTED REFERENCES: Glass and Robertson 1975, no. 308; Codex Telleriano-Remensis 1995

The manuscript bears striking witness to the rich and subtle pictographic tradition of the Aztecs. It was acquired by one of the great bibliophiles of his time, Charles le Tellier, Archbishop of Reims, who donated it in 1700 to the library of Louis XIV.

The codex consists of three parts. The first is a calendar of the ritual feasts of the eighteen 'months' of twenty-days each, called *veintenas* ('twenty-day periods') by the Spanish, of the solar year (fols 1–7). Ceremonies conducted in honour of the tutelary gods of each *veintena* are shown in all their splendour. The name of each *veintena* is given in both Nahuatl and Spanish, with the corresponding date in the Western calendar also specified. The year ends with the feast of Izcalli ('growth'), held under the aegis of Xiuhtecuhtli ('turquoise lord').

This part is followed by a *tonalamatl* (day book), the manual of divination for the twenty 'weeks', called *trecenas* ('thirteen-day periods') by the Spanish, into which the Aztec sacred year was divided (fols 8–24). Every *trecena* occupies two facing pages, each showing a divinity, one major and one minor. The *yoallitecutin* ('lords of the night') of each day of the *trecena* are shown in profile above that day.

The third section of the manuscript comprises a chronicle of the Aztecs. Events from their mythical migration in 1197 to the end of the first three decades of Spanish presence in 1549 are illustrated; those from the years 1550 to 1561 recounted on the final folios lack images (fols 25–50). The drawings for 1494–96 depict the last victories of Ahuizotl in Oaxaca, along with an earthquake in 1495 and a solar eclipse in 1496 (fols 40v/41r). Ahuizotl, who died following his final conquest in Tehuantepec, was succeeded in 1502 by Motecuhzoma II, the last ruler of the Pre-Hispanic era. Several folios are devoted to Motecuhzoma's military victories from his accession until 1518, yet, oddly, the years from 1519 (when the Spanish arrived in Mexico) to 1528 are missing from the chronicle. MCo

349
Codex Mendoza

c. 1541, Aztec

71 folios, European paper, 30–31.5 × 21–21.5 cm; seventeenth-century binding

Bodleian Library, University of Oxford, Ms Arch. Selden A.1

PROVENANCE: Mexico City; André Thevet, 1553; Richard Hakluyt, *c.* 1588; Samuel Purchas, 1616; John Selden *c.* 1654; entered Bodleian Library, 1659, five years after Selden's death

SELECTED REFERENCES: Glass and Robertson 1975, no. 196; Codex Mendoza 1992; Brotherston 1995; Codex Mendoza 1997; Berger 1998

The Codex Mendoza is one of the best-known early colonial pictorial manuscripts from Mexico. Seventy-two pages of its 71 folios contain Aztec iconic script written by a single, highly skilled indigenous *tlacuilo* (painter-scribe). The pictorial text is annotated with Spanish glosses by a Spanish interpreter versed in Nahuatl and accompanied by 63 pages of more extensive Spanish commentary in the same hand. Another Spanish hand has added headings that divide the manuscript into three sections. The first begins with the foundation of Tenochtitlan by the Mexica in 1325 and continues with an account of the reigns and conquests of nine Mexica rulers, ending with the reign of Motecuhzoma II (1502–20) and brief mention of the pacification of New Spain in 1521. Details of eleven imperial outposts precede the second part, which comprises a list of tribute Motecuhzoma II exacted from areas throughout the Aztec empire, whose subject towns and their tribute obligations are described in great detail. Samuel Purchas, who in 1625 published the earliest edition of the Codex Mendoza, described Part 3 as containing the public and private rites of the Mexicans 'from the grave of the wombe to the wombe of the grave'. More precisely, this section, which includes birth, education, marriage, work and justice, refers to the labour, duty and discipline of the citizens of Tenochtitlan.

Parts 1 and 2 are traditionally thought to be copies of Pre-Hispanic documents, the first an annals-type manuscript and the second a tribute list known as the Matrícula de Tributos. Part 3, by contrast, is generally considered to be a Post-Conquest invention created in response to Spanish questions. Recent studies suggest that all three sections represent adaptations of one or more traditional documents that adhere closely to ancient ideas and modes of expression found in 'ritual' books such as the Codex Fejérváry-Mayer (cat. 341). Scholars have now also questioned the association between the Codex Mendoza and Viceroy Antonio de Mendoza (1535–50), who was thought to have commissioned the manuscript that has come to carry his name. Even if this association is tenuous, it is likely that the Codex Mendoza's indigenous authors and scribe aimed this document at the Spanish authorities, especially the courts of the Real Audiencia, as a means of protesting against the abuses of Spanish *encomenderos* (see cat. 276) entrusted with indigenous land and labour. JH

350
Codex Tepotzotlan

c. 1555–56, Tepotzotlan

Amatl paper, 40 × 110 cm

Collection Ulster Museum, Belfast, by kind permission of the Board of Trustees of the National Museums and Galleries of Northern Ireland, C1911.1090

PROVENANCE: given by Robert McCalmont to the Belfast Natural History & Philosophical Society, 1833; the collections of the BNH&PS passed to the Belfast Museum (now the Ulster Museum) by Deed of Gift, 1910–11

SELECTED REFERENCES: Brotherston and Gallegos 1988; Brotherston 1995, pp. 169–76, 183

This document represents legal evidence in a court case concerning the excessive tribute demanded by Tepotzotlan from three of its tributaries, Xoloc, Cuautlapan and Tepoxaco. Their case was judged by Francisco Maldonado of Chiconautla, appointed by the Real Audiencia, who sided with his fellow Tepotzotlan nobles against the complainants and their wards and treated them brutally. The script and signs are entirely native in style and there is no Spanish gloss. (A European-style copy in Spanish, now called 'Codex Tepotzotlan 2' and preserved in the Archivo General de la Nación in Mexico City, lacks the subtle and succinct information contained in the original.) The verso bears two inscriptions in different hands. One names the judge, 'Maldonado juez Chiconautla', the other, in medieval Spanish, reads: 'A los agravios q a hecho Maldonado. Q Valverde aya informacion ye la embie a esta audiencia' (Let Valverde collect the evidence and send it to the Audiencia about the offences committed by Maldonado).

Each of the ten columns is headed by the place-glyph of a town or a ward. Below this are registered the items of tribute paid by it. The signs indicating quantity – flags for twenty and a fir-tree-like symbol for 400 – are in Pre-Hispanic style. Half a flag blacked represents ten, half a fir tree 200. All places paid a daily tribute of maize, turkeys, cacao, chillis, tortillas, eggs, salt and firewood, but some were required to pay further tribute, in the form of woven mats, cloth, pottery, pesos and reals, boars, male burden-bearers and female corn-grinders. The bearers were paid in cocoa beans, whereas the corn-grinders received no payment.

The codex was given to the Belfast Natural History & Philosophical Society by Robert McCalmont in 1833. He and his brother were stockbrokers in London for 53 years, but the family had a house called Abbeylands in Whiteabbey, Co. Antrim, where Robert lived for several years. Apparently, he did not travel abroad, although in 1853 he donated a drawing of a fish caught in the Bering Straits to the Society. In 1814 a relative of the family, possibly Robert McCalmont's cousin, had been slave owner in the Berbice Colony, British Guiana. This seems to have been the only family link with South America and may have been the source of the codex. Following the transfer of the collections of the Belfast Natural History & Philosophical Society to what is now the Ulster Museum, the codex remained undiscovered for many years until the present writer found it in a box of Peruvian pottery in 1987. WG

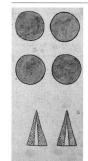

351

Codex Tepetlaoztoc

c. 1555, colonial

72 folios, European paper, 29.8 × 21.5 cm; unbound

Trustees of the British Museum, London, Add. Ms 43795 (part)

PROVENANCE: acquired by the museum from the bookseller Rodd, 11 March 1843

SELECTED REFERENCES: Glass and Robertson 1975, no. 181; Memorial de los Indios de Tepetlaoztoc 1992; Brotherston 1995; Berger 1998, pp. 35–37

The Codex Tepetlaoztoc, also known as the Codex Kingsborough, is named after the town (whose name means 'stone mat cave') to the east of Lake Tetzcoco where it was produced. This stunning pictorial document was painted in the Tetzcocan style, with some European innovations, by an indigenous *tlacuilo* (painter-scribe) whose original tracings are still visible beneath the rich pigments. The Spanish alphabetic glosses and commentary are probably by more than one native hand and the information is organised horizontally across the breadth of two facing pages, instead of vertically down their length.

The codex was commissioned by the inhabitants of Tepetlaoztoc and its indigenous governor, Luis de Tepeda, probably for the Council of the Indies in Spain, which dealt with the affairs of New Spain. It undoubtedly formed part of a lawsuit brought by Tepetlaoztoc against the town's Spanish *encomenderos*, overlords entrusted with converting the native inhabitants to Christianity in return for tribute in the form of services and goods. The Spanish abuse of this system led to many complaints by native communities from the mid-sixteenth century. Tepetlaoztoc's first *encomendero* was Hernán

Cortés. Among Tepetlaoztoc's worst *encomenderos* was Gonzalo de Salazar, whose son, Juan Velázquez de Salazar, was in charge at the time the case was brought. The *tlacuilo*'s portrayal of the Spaniards, who have sickly grey skin, shows versatile command of European drawing techniques.

The Codex Tepetlaoztoc sets the Spaniards' excessive demands within a broader historical context, beginning in the first part with two maps of the town and its surroundings and going on to record the migration of the indigenous population's Chichimec ancestors from Chicomoztoc ('seven caves'). The first section continues with the settlement, foundation and rulers of Tepetlaoztoc and the (more reasonable) tribute exacted by these. The second part lists the daily service and yearly tribute given to the *encomenderos* between 1522–23 and 1555–56. The tribute included precious items, such as gold jewels (fol. 218*r*), obsidian mirrors (fol. 219*v*) and a gold and emerald box (fol. 220*r*), as well as foodstuffs, such as beans (*frijoles*), flour (*harina*) and chickens (*gallinas*) (fol. 214*v*), and services, such as the carrying of goods by male *tamemes*, or porters (fol. 214*v*). Spanish demands and punishment resulted in the death of large numbers of native inhabitants (shown by a horizontal shrouded figure), leading to a rapid decline in the town's population in a few decades. The second section is followed by a summary of tribute, including daily, then weekly accounts, and ends with a petition by the native inhabitants. JH

352

Lienzo of Quetzpalan

Second half of sixteenth century, colonial

Paint on fabric, 154 × 183 cm

Colección Fundación Televisa, Mexico City, 403

PROVENANCE: Quetzpalan, Puebla State; acquired through Manuel Reyero, 1980

SELECTED REFERENCE: Gómez-Haro Desdier 1994

The tradition of pictographic documents characteristic of Mesoamerican culture did not disappear with the Spanish conquest of Mexico. Such documents certainly continued to be produced in the sixteenth century, principally painted on large pieces of cloth and known as *lienzos*. The Lienzo of Quetzpalan provides a geographical, historical and economic survey of the territory occupied by the Quetzpala people, an area in the south of the present-day state of Puebla that lay under Izúcar rule. The document contains 44 place-glyphs, 36 of which mark the territorial boundaries. The glyph for the town of Quetzpala comprises the sign for 'hill' (*altepetl*) and that for 'lizard' (*quetzpallin*, the origin of the place-name). The *lienzo* clearly shows the two main rivers running from north to south, the Atila and the Ahuehuello, the latter taking its name from the ancient, sacred *ahuehuete* (a species of cypress) that still line its banks. In addition to recording the names of indigenous leaders, notably around the central place-glyph, the notes in Nahuatl tell of a dispute involving calico and textiles between the inhabitants of Quetzpala and the neighbouring town of Calmeca.

FS, RVA

353

Digital representation of the Map of Mexico City

Original: 1550s, Spanish

Ink and watercolour on parchment (two sheets), 75 × 114 cm

Uppsala University Library

PROVENANCE: Johan G. Sparwenfeld, donated to the university, early eighteenth century

SELECTED REFERENCES: Dahlgren 1889; Dahlgren 1892; Guzman 1939; Linné 1948; Cuesta Domingo 1983–84; León-Portilla and Aguilera 1986; Woodward and Lewis 1998

This is one of only two maps that give a fairly accurate picture of Mexico City and its surrounding regions in the mid-sixteenth century. It was made by Alonso de Santa Cruz, who from 1526 to 1530 took part as an accountant in

an expedition up the Rio de la Plata in what is now Argentina. Becoming an expert in navigation and map-making, he was later employed as a cosmographer at Seville and in 1536 was appointed Royal Cosmographer. During his period of service he assembled a large collection of maps, which passed to his successor, Juan Lopez de Velasco, at Santa Cruz's death in 1572. Later dispersed, this collection included the present item, which was probably bought by the Swedish linguist and traveller Johan G. Sparwenfeld during his stay in Spain at the end of the seventeenth century.

The map is framed by a border painted in many colours, with ornamental ribbons on the right and left. The damaged cartouche in the lower right corner contains a dedication to Emperor Charles V, whose arms appear in the centre of the frame at the bottom between two pillars with entwined ribbons bearing his motto, 'Plus Ultra'.

The map shows Tenochtitlan surrounded by water and with canals between its buildings. The clearly drawn roads over the mountains to other parts of the country permit us to retrace the routes taken by the Spanish conquerors. The map also gives information about the ethnography and the flora and fauna of the region. The population is shown performing a variety of activities, such as woodcutting, canoeing, hunting and fishing. On the roads files of Indians are transporting heavy loads, driven by their Spanish masters. The approximately 150 glyphs on the map, representing human and animal heads, feet, hands, plants, rings, circles and stars, refer to place names.

The map is shown here in a digital facsimile produced in the Media Lab at the University of Art and Design in Helsinki. An interactive model, it uses digital technology to reconstruct sections of the original by superimposing layers of the facsimile produced by Nordenskjöld and Dahlgren in 1886 and published in 1906.

LOL, LDK

354

Codex Aubin

c. 1576–96, 1608, colonial

81 folios, European paper, 15 × 11 cm; red leather binding

Trustees of the British Museum, London, Add. Ms 31219

PROVENANCE: acquired from M. J. Des Portes, 1880

SELECTED REFERENCES: Glass and Robertson 1975, no. 14; Vollmer 1981; Brotherston 1995, p. 177; Berger 1998, p. 14

The Codex Aubin is named after the French ethnographer Joseph Marius Alexis Aubin, who published a facsimile of the document between 1849 and 1859. Four of its 81 folios are blank. The remaining folios, drawn on both sides, contain coloured pictorial information, outlined in brown ink and painted in traditional iconic script style, and Nahuatl alphabetic text in black ink. More than one indigenous hand appears to be responsible for the alphabetic text. Although adapted to a European format, the codex belongs to the annals-style genre of Pre-Hispanic document known as *xiuhamatls* (books of years). These record events year by year in relation to the *xiuhpohualli* (year count), which approximates our solar year. In these annals, of which there are many types, each year is represented by a square containing one of four year signs – *calli* ('house'), *tochtli* ('rabbit'), *acatl* ('reed'), *tecpatl* ('flint') – and a number from 1 to 13, represented by dots. In the Codex Aubin the corresponding year in the Gregorian calendar is written to the left of each indigenous year-glyph. The relevant pictorial and alphabetic text is placed to the right of the year-glyph.

The codex records the years 1168 to 1608 in Mexica history and can be roughly divided into three parts. The last of these, covering 1596 to 1608, is an addendum notable for the gradual replacement of native pictorial script by alphabetic writing. The first of the other two parts comprising the main document begins with the Aztecs' migration from their island home, Aztlan, in 1108, proceeds to the foundation of Tenochtitlan in 1325 (the same date as that given in the Codex Mendoza [cat. 349]) and, like the Codex Mendoza, then details the reigns and conquests of the Mexica lords until 1519 and the arrival of the Spanish. Unlike the Codex Mendoza, the Codex Aubin records in its second part the events of the colonial period, documenting the introduction of European weapons, diseases, officials and religion. The *tlacuilo* (painter-scribe) invented new iconic signs for Christian symbols, such as a bald-headed figure for a friar, and shows considerable command of European drawing techniques in, for example, the representation of Christ resting while carrying the Cross on folio 59*r*. The authors of the Codex Aubin are unknown, but it is likely to have been commissioned by high-ranking indigenous officials. JH

355

Codex Azcatitlan

Late sixteenth century, colonial

25 folios, European paper, 22.5 × 29.5 cm; modern red demi-shagreen binding

Bibliothèque Nationale de France, Paris, MS Mexicain 59-64

PROVENANCE: Lorenzo Boturini Benaduci (1702–1755), 1746; Joseph Marius Alexis Aubin (1802–1891); Eugène Goupil (1831–1895), 1899; donated to the Bibliothèque nationale by Goupil's widow, Augustine Elie, 23 April 1898

SELECTED REFERENCES: Glass and Robertson 1975, no. 20; Codex Azcatitlan 1995

The uncompleted drawings and glosses of this history of Mexico, given the name Codex Azcatitlan by Robert Barlow in the facsimile edition of the manuscript first published in 1949, features in the first inventory (dating from 1746) of Lorenzo Boturini Benaduci's collection. Its folios, some of which are missing, show the great phases of Aztec history in extensive scenes, each laid out on two facing pages.

At the beginning we see the wanderings of the Mexica after they leave Aztlan, their mythical, paradisiacal land of origin; their subsequent settlement on the high plateaux of Anáhuac; and the foundation of Tenochtitlan, their

capital (fols 1–12). The latter event is depicted as a human sacrifice laid on the altar at the top of a pyramid in the shade of a *nopal* (prickly-pear) cactus in which Huitzilopochtli ('left-sided hummingbird'), the patron god of the Mexica, is hiding.

Ten scenes represent the period of almost two centuries before the Spanish arrived in 1519 (fols 13–22), from the enthronement of the first ruler, which took place in a 'rabbit' year and is portrayed by means of peaceful scenes in the life of the fishermen and hunters of the lakeside region, to that of Motecuhzoma II (1502–20). As one reign follows another, we see a succession of victories and defeats, but also major works of construction, including canals and protective walls. Every reign is represented on a double page, from the accession of the monarch, seated on the royal throne in full regalia, until the end of his life, shown in the form of a burial bundle under his name-glyph. The great reigns of Motecuhzoma I (1440–68), Axayacatl (1469–81) and Ahuizotl (1487–1502) are rich in warrior exploits and military conquests, which are indicated by rows of place-glyphs of the subjugated cities.

The final pages of the manuscript are its best known. In unfinished but vivid scenes they depict the beginnings of the colonial period. Hernán Cortés, having dismounted from his horse, is shown hat in hand as he goes to meet Motecuhzoma II in Mexico; between them, the native woman Malintzin (called 'Marina' by the Spanish) acts as interpreter (fol. 22*v*; the figure of Motecuhzoma is missing). The armour-clad conquistadors bear the banner of the Holy Ghost; the Indian porters are heavily laden with provisions. The next scene, which is missing its left-hand side, takes place in the patio of the Main Palace of Tenochtitlan (fol. 23*r*). It shows the tragic death of the last Aztec ruler, pierced by an arrow while the musicians continue to play.

The closing folios, some of which are mutilated, depict the conversion of the indigenous population to Christianity, including the construction of churches, but they also contain representations of Indian traditions, such as the rite of the *volador*, in which men with their feet tied to a rope attached to the top of a tree trunk spiralled down playing the flute. In addition we see some minor occurrences (thefts and their punishment) and historic events, including the arrival in 1528 of the first Bishop of Mexico, Juan de Zumárraga. MCO

356

Diego Muñoz Camargo, *Descripción de la ciudad y provincia de Tlaxcala de las Indias y del Mar Océano para el buen gobierno y ennoblecimiento dellas*

1581–84

Codex, 327 folios, European paper, 29 × 21 × 3.5 cm; original binding of limp vellum

Special Collections Department, Glasgow University Library, MS Hunter 242 (U.3.15)

PROVENANCE: Real Biblioteca, El Escorial; William Hunter, c. 1768–83

SELECTED REFERENCES: Muñoz Camargo 1984; Berger 1998, pp. 62–66

Diego Muñoz Camargo's *Descripción de la ciudad y provincia de Tlaxcala* (*Description of the City and Province of Tlaxcala*) is an extended *relación geográfica* supplemented here by a pictorial section. The author was an educated *mestizo* whom Alonso de Nava, the *alcalde* (magistrate or mayor) of Tlaxcala, asked to respond to a questionnaire sent to town officials by order of Philip II in 1577. The Tlaxcalans were the fiercest enemies of the Aztecs and subsequently became loyal allies of the Spanish. When Hernán Cortés arrived in Tlaxcala in 1519 he found its inhabitants confined to a small territory, vigorously defending their independence from their powerful neighbours. The codex, in addition to being a major source for Tlaxcalan history, topography and social conditions, is clearly intended to celebrate the Tlaxcalans' role in the conquest of the New World.

Two methods of computing time are described, each illustrated with a calendrical wheel. The pictorial section, the work of an unknown indigenous artist, comprises 157 pen and ink drawings with short Nahuatl captions written above the images; these are glossed in Spanish in a different hand below. Some 80 are almost identical to drawings in the *Lienzo of Tlaxcala*, a large painted cloth (now lost) that may have been a source for the present series. The pictures at the beginning of the manuscript depict the first encounters between the Spanish and the Tlaxcalans: the conversion of the population to Christianity, the destruction of cultic objects and native books, and the punishment of those not conforming to the new order. Also shown are the nine provinces subjugated by the Spanish, with their emblems and episcopal mitres. The remainder of the images includes equestrian portraits of Cortés, Christopher Columbus, Francisco Pizarro, Charles V and Philip II, and spirited evocations of the many victories and conquests of the allied forces.

Muñoz Camargo travelled to Spain in 1584 in the company of other Tlaxcalans as part of a diplomatic mission. The manuscript, which was completed and bound in Madrid, was presented to the king in 1585. It remained in the Biblioteca Real at least until the early seventeenth century, after which its fate is obscure until it was acquired by Dr William Hunter (1718–1783) for his famous museum, established in 1768 in Windmill Street, Glasgow. DW

357

Cochineal Treatise

*c.*1599, colonial

4 folios, European paper, 29.8 × 21.5 cm; unbound

Trustees of the British Museum, London, Add. Ms 13964, ff. 129–202

PROVENANCE: purchased by the museum from the bookseller Rodd, 11 March 1843

SELECTED REFERENCES: Glass and Robertson 1975, no. 128; Brotherston 1995, pp. 177–78; Berger 1998, p. 19

The Cochineal Treatise comprises twelve drawings and explanatory alphabetic Spanish glosses. It forms part of a larger manuscript of 76 folios containing Gonzales Gómez de Cervantes's *Memorial de Gonzalo Gomez de Cervantes para el Doctor Eugenio Salazar, oidor del real consejo de las Indias* (*Report by Gonzalo Gomez de Cervantes for Doctor Eugenio Salazar, judge of the Royal Council of the Indies*), dated 1599. This report includes information about the lives of the indigenous inhabitants of New Spain, about silver and gold mines and, under the heading 'Relación de [lo] que toca la Grana Cochinilla' (fols 129–202), about the production of cochineal.

Cochineal is a red dye obtained from the tiny *cochinilla* beetle (*Dactylopius coccus* or *Coccus cacti*) that feeds on the nopal (prickly-pear) cactus. In the Cochineal Treatise the beetles are referred to as *semilla* ('seed'), although their Nahuatl name is *noch-eztli* ('cactus blood'). In Pre-Hispanic Mesoamerica cochineal was produced in large amounts in the Oaxaca area, which paid the dye as tribute to Tenochtitlan, as recorded in the Codex Mendoza (cat. 349). *Grana cochinilla* ('cochineal red'), as it is referred to in the Cochineal Treatise, was also exported in great quantity by the Spanish during the colonial period.

The twelve scenes in the document show the stages in the cultivation of the *semilla* during the year. The cycle begins in December and January when cuttings are taken from old plants and dried to produce new ones (Scenes 1 and 2). It ends by leaving the nopal to recover for the next season (Scene 11) and showing what happens when it is neglected (Scene 12). Scene 3 depicts the new plants that have been cut, pruned and planted, and Scene 4 shows the new beetles being placed on the new plants, which must be at least six months old. The final image in the document (fol. 202) illustrates the various pests that can destroy the

nopal, with their Nahuatl names. The anonymous creator of the drawings used some European techniques, such as shading, but depicted architecture, dress, hairstyles and plants (with their roots visible) in accordance with native traditions, implying that an indigenous painter-scribe (*tlacuilo*) was involved. JH

358

Doctrina Cristiana

*c.*1714, colonial

30 leaves (15 double folios), European paper, 24 × 16.5 cm; skin binding

Trustees of the British Museum, London, Egerton Ms. 2898

PROVENANCE: purchased by the museum from Ida Bühle, 13 November 1911

SELECTED REFERENCES: Glass and Robertson 1975, no. 813; Galarza 1992, pp. 7, 14; Brotherston 1995, p. 188; Berger 1998, pp. 79–81

The Doctrina Cristiana, also known as BM Egerton Ms 2898, is the finest extant example of a Mexican Testerian manuscript. These documents, around 35 of which remain, were produced by native painter-scribes (*tlacuiloque*, sing. *tlacuilo*) in Mexico from the sixteenth to the eighteenth century to instruct young indigenous neophytes in the doctrine and Catechism of the Catholic Church. The manuscripts are named after Jabobo de Testera, a Franciscan friar who arrived in New Spain in 1529 and who is thought to have invented the pictorial system by which they convey information. This system, which incorporates many Christian symbols, employs pictograms (the depiction of a sword, for example, means 'sword'), ideograms (the cross, for instance, represents Christ) and phonetic signs (the hand, *maitl*, combining, for example, with the flower, *xochitl*, to form the phrase *ma in mochihua*: 'may it be so' or 'amen'). These characteristics and the inclusion of traditional pictorial symbols, such as the lizard/scorpion to represent 'sin', suggest that the system is closely linked to Pre-Hispanic iconic script and was in fact invented by native *tlacuiloque*. The present codex is unusual in that the *tlacuilo*, Lucas Matheo, signed the document (which bears the date 1714) and also because, instead of the more usual Otomi or Mazahua languages, the alphabetic glosses accompanying the images are written in Nahuatl. As in other Testerian manuscripts, the scribe was presumably responsible for the images as well as the glosses. The Doctrina Cristiana is probably a copy of an earlier, sixteenth-century document.

The organisation of information in the Doctrina Cristiana continues to respect indigenous traditions, arranging it across two facing pages that are divided by thick black lines into horizontal registers. The registers are read from left to right and top to bottom. Certain sections (fols 1–7) are numbered internally using the Pre-Hispanic system of dots found in documents such as the Codex Fejérváry-Mayer (cat. 341). The manuscript is also outstanding for the breadth of its content. As well as the Catechism, it contains a full set of the prayers of the Catholic Church (fols 13*v* to 20*r*). JH

359

Christoph Weiditz, Trachtenbuch

1529–30

Codex, 154 folios, paper, 19.4 × 14.5 cm; twentieth-century leather binding

Leihgabe, Germanisches Nationalmuseum, Nuremberg, Hs 22474

PROVENANCE: Presented by Johann N. Egger, Freyung near Passau, 1868

SELECTED REFERENCES: Hampe 1927; Washington 1991, pp. 517, 572, no. 406; Nuremberg 1992, p. 835, no. 5.9; Antwerp 1997, p. 259, no. 32; Ghent 1999, p. 277, no. 168; Weiditz 2001

The coloured drawings in this codex record costumes and scenes from the daily life mainly of humble people, but also of shipowners, burghers and slaves, mostly in Spain but also in other western European countries. They were made by the Augsburg medallist Christoph Weiditz (*c.* 1500–1559) on a trip to Spain via the Netherlands in 1528–29. Weiditz journeyed by sea to the court of Emperor Charles V in order to obtain a licence for the manufacture of medals in the free imperial city of Augsburg. He followed the imperial court around Spain and probably also travelled about the country independently, returning to Germany via southern France and northern Italy.

At the imperial court in Toledo, Weiditz met Hernán Cortés, the conqueror of the Aztecs, who had been summoned by the Emperor to account for his actions in Mexico. Cortés had brought back from the New World eleven Aztec acrobats, who are illustrated on the first folios of the manuscript. Folios 12*v* and 13*r* show two of these Indians playing a game, accompanied by the inscriptions 'These are the Indian people who were brought to His Majesty from India by Hernán Cortés and played thus before His Majesty with wood and ball' (fol. 12*v*) and 'With their fingers they gamble like the Italians' (fol. 13*r*). The game depicted may be *patolli*, an Aztec game similar to Parcheesi, or a kind of mora, using stones and fingers as gambling instruments (see also cat. 310). Folios 8*v* and 9*r* show Aztecs balancing a tree trunk on their feet that is comparable in length and weight to a human being, tossing it into the air and catching it as it falls.

These and the other illustrations in the codex of members of the Aztec party are the earliest known realistic representations by a European of the inhabitants of the New World. They were drawn carefully from life, reproducing the details of their clothing and their characteristic adornments of coloured stone. ES

TABLE OF RULERS

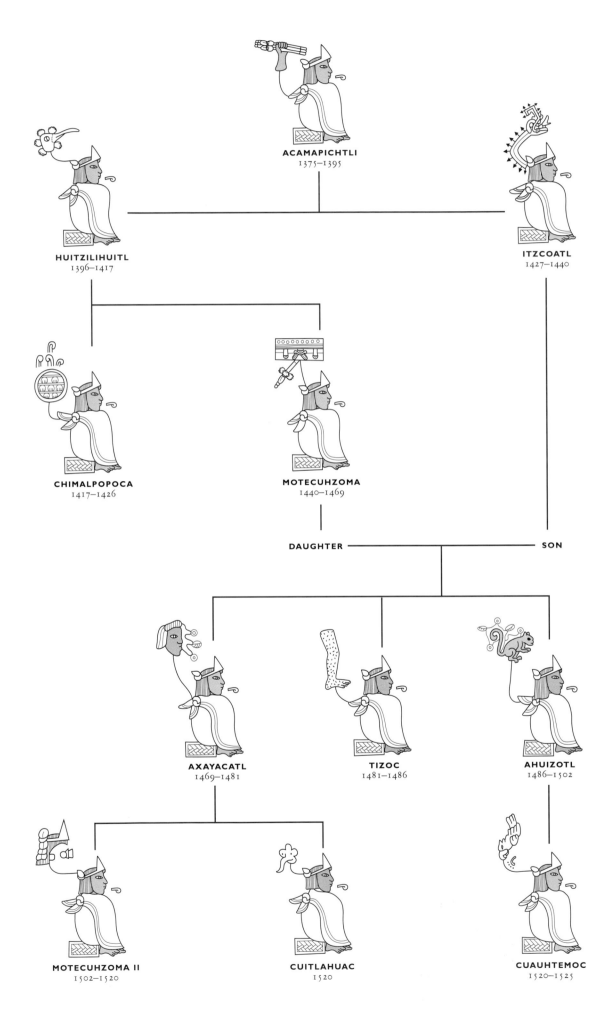

ACAMAPICHTLI
1375–1395

HUITZILIHUITL
1396–1417

ITZCOATL
1427–1440

CHIMALPOPOCA
1417–1426

MOTECUHZOMA
1440–1469

DAUGHTER — SON

AXAYACATL
1469–1481

TIZOC
1481–1486

AHUIZOTL
1486–1502

MOTECUHZOMA II
1502–1520

CUITLAHUAC
1520

CUAUHTEMOC
1520–1525

GUIDE TO GLYPHS

1

5

10

20

400

8000

CAVE
Shown as the jaws of a serpent, the entrance to Mitla

COMET
Shown as a flying serpent

CONQUEST
The burning temple

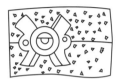

EARTHQUAKE
The sign for *ollin* 'movement' in the midst of the earth

ECLIPSE
The broken sun disk

FAMINE

FERTILE YEAR

FIRE CEREMONY
The fire drill and board used to start a new 52-year cycle

FOOTPRINT
Denoting movement or path

MAT OF POWER
Occupied by the ruler, 'he who speaks'

MARRIAGE CEREMONY
Literally 'tying the knot'

PLACE
Altepetl, literally 'water mountain' or community

PLAGUE

PRICKLY-PEAR CACTUS

RAIN

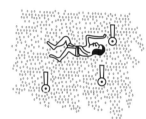

SNOWSTORM

SPEECH, SONG OR SOUND

STARS
Eyes of the night

WAR
Represented by the *chimalli*, a shield with four darts

WATER

GLOSSARY
Adrian Locke

ALTEPETL
Literally 'water mountain'. A term that refers primarily to territory but more specifically to a group of people, usually based on ethnic identity and governed by a ruler, who control a given territory. The amounts of territory varied enormously, ranging from a city-state such as Tenochtitlan to a ward within one. The term also refers specifically to the place itself.

CALMECAC
Special schools run by priests who instructed the sons of the nobility in the ways of Aztec religion, warfare, rulership and other such skills.

CALPULLI
A collective term that refers to the grouping of the lower class, often referred to as 'commoners' or *macehualtin*, into districts, possibly based on kinship which, at the time of the Spanish conquest, centred around a territorial unit such as the ward of a town or a temple from which they worked communal land holdings.

CHACMOOL
From the Yucatec Maya for 'great jaguar paw'. The British-born archaeologist Augustus Le Plongeon (died *c.* 1908) adopted the term in the nineteenth century to describe the three-dimensional sculptures of reclining figures with sacrificial vessels placed on their chests that were discovered at Chichén Itzá. *Chacmools* have been found across Mesoamerica but are particularly associated with Chichén Itzá, Tula and Tenochtitlan.

CHALCHIHUITL
In central Mexico the name given to jade, one of the materials most prized by the Aztecs. Owing to its colour, jade was associated with water and gave its name to Chalchiuhtlicue ('she of the jade skirt'), goddess of springs, rivers, lakes and the sea. Jade was also linked to blood. Thus jade was intimately related to these two liquids, which, because jade symbolises preciousness, were referred to as 'precious liquids'. Droplets, the representation of jade in Aztec art and literature, are therefore multivalent symbols signifying blood, water, greenstone and preciousness in general.

CHICHIMECA
Like the Aztecs, the Nahuatl-speaking Chichimec, 'the dog people', were a nomadic group who migrated southwards into central Mexico, settling in the Toltec region. They brought with them the bow and arrow, as recorded in, for example, the Codex Xolotl and the Mapa Quinatzin. They gave their name to the highland region to the north of Tenochtitlan that is referred to as the Chichimeca. Also used as a generic term for all migrant groups.

CHINAMPA
A system of land reclamation for agricultural use still to be found in the southern part (Xochimilco) of Mexico City. Canals were cut through marshland and artificial islands created. Fertile silt was dredged from the canals and placed on the islands which were stabilised by planting willow trees and using wickerwork fences. The resultant highly productive parcels of land were expanded in size over time.

CIHUACOATL
The title of the secondary ruler of Tenochtitlan who handled the internal affairs of the city. The *cihuacoatl* worked alongside the *tlatoani* (see below). Together they represented both sides of the universe and were the ultimate authorities of all the affairs of the state. Also the name, literally 'snake woman', of one of a number of Aztec goddesses associated with the earth.

COCHINEAL
Natural red pigment obtained from the *cochinilla* beetle, which feeds on the nopal (prickly-pear) cactus, and made into a dye. Cochineal was cultivated by the Aztecs and later, during the colonial period, exported to Spain.

CODEX
Typically the term refers to a manuscript volume but it has come to be associated specifically with the painted books produced in Pre-Hispanic and colonial Mexico. Information was recorded using pictograms and ideograms on prepared animal skin, *amatl* (paper produced from the bark of the fig tree), cotton cloth, or, after the arrival of the Spaniards, European paper. Codices can be single sheets of paper or cotton; numerous sheets gathered together much like conventional European-style books; or screenfolds, which are double-sided books, folded accordion-like.

FLOWERY WARS
Xochiyaotl, or 'flowery wars', were ritual, pre-arranged battles fought between the Triple Alliance and hostile groups such as those found in Tlaxcala, Cholula and Huexotzingo, with the sole aim of capturing enemy warriors for sacrifice. The name comes from the finely dressed warriors who would fall like a rain of blossom on the battlefield.

GLYPH
A symbol used in the writing system of the Aztecs, in which pictograms and ideograms represented concepts or phonetic prompts. Thus, the curling symbol placed in front of the mouth of an individual to represent speech or sound is referred to as the speech glyph. For a basic guide to reading glyphs, see p.497.

HUEHUEHTLAHTOLLI
Traditional speeches given by Aztec elders to accompany important communal occasions such as marriages and funerals.

JADE
Term given to a hard ornamental greenstone of varying hue which refers to both nephrite (a silicate of calcium and magnesium) and jadeite (see below). Greatly prized by the Aztecs and other Mesoamerican cultures, jade was imported from western Mexico. In Nahuatl, *chalchihuitl* referred to both water, 'precious liquid', and jade.

JADEITE
The only type of jade found in Mesoamerica, a silicate of aluminium and sodium.

MACEHUALTIN
See *calpulli*.

MAGUEY
A type of cactus also known as agave, American aloe or century plant. Widespread in Mexico, the maguey continues to be cultivated for its milk (see *pulque*) and fibres. The latter were used to make a type of paper, and maguey cloth for use by commoners.

MAYEQUE
Along with slaves, the lowest social class. Although freemen, *mayeque* were landless peasants who were possibly newcomers to the region, descendants of conquered tribes or those who had fallen from grace. Thought to number up to 30% of the population, they worked on the private lands of the nobility.

MICTLAN

The 'Place of the Dead', or the underworld, was divided into nine planes that were presided over by Mictlantecuhtli, lord of Mictlan (see cat. 233). Those who died a natural death went to Mictlan, the ninth and deepest plane, having to overcome numerous hazardous obstacles to reach their destination.

NAHUATL

A Mesoamerican language adopted by the Aztecs as their *lingua franca*. Long compound forms juxtapose various roots, prefixes, suffixes and infixes, enabling complex forms to be produced. In Pre-Hispanic times, Nahuatl was an oral language but it soon began to be written down in European alphabetic script during the colonial period.

NAHUI OLLIN

Literally '4-movement', Nahui Ollin refers to the fifth and last of the mythological Aztec Suns or world-eras, marked by the creation of maize and men by the gods at Teotihuacan. The four previous Suns ('4-jaguar', '4-wind', '4-rain' and '4-water') all ended violently and it was predicted that 4-movement would end with an earthquake.

NEW FIRE CEREMONY

The New Fire ceremony marked the completion of the 365-day calendar (see *xiuhpohualli*), i.e. 52 years had to pass before it began to repeat itself (13 numbers × 4 year bearers = 52 years). This special occasion was marked by the ceremonial tying of 52 reeds in a bundle (see *xiuhmolpilli*) and the extinguishing of fires. The beginning of the new cycle was marked by a fire-drilling ceremony that provided the spark to light a great new bonfire. Fire was then taken from this and used to light the fires of waiting communities, proclaiming the beginning of a new 52-year cycle.

OBSIDIAN

A vitreous-acid, volcanic, glass-like rock highly prized in Mexico since the Early Formative period for its sharpness and beauty. Although obsidian is largely black in colour, it varies in shades and often contains smoky patterns. Pachuca, near Tula, was known for its highly prized, olive-green obsidian. The material was used in many ways by the Aztecs: opposing blades were set into wooden handles to make swords; thin sharp

blades were fashioned for auto-sacrifice (individuals would draw their own blood as an offering); surfaces were polished to act as mirrors; and for beautifully finished jewellery such as labrets (lip-plugs) and ear-plugs.

OZTOMECA

Vanguard merchants, among the more important of their class, who were also involved in state-sponsored espionage (see *pochteca*).

PIPILTIN

Literally the 'sons of the nobility', the noble class who enjoyed a privileged social position, below the *tlatoani*.

PLUMBATE

A salt of plumbic (lead-based) acid used for decorating pottery. Although it gave a distinctive dark, shiny finish to kiln-fired ceramics, it was not a glaze, a glass technology that the Mexicans never knew.

POCHTECA

Merchants who maintained long-distance trade networks within the tribute empire individually, or on behalf of the Aztec nobility. There were four principal types: administrators (*pochtecatlatoque*), who oversaw the principal marketplace and the actions of other merchants; slave-traders (*tlaltani*); the personal traders of rulers (*tencunenenque*); and *naualoztomeca*, state-sponsored spies. *Pochteca* were assisted by *tlamemes*, individuals who carried goods on their backs like porters. *Pochteca* were highly esteemed and played an important role in the expansionist policies of the state.

PULQUE

Spanish for the Nahuatl *octli*. *Pulque* is a naturally fermented, mildly alcoholic drink made from the sap of the maguey (see above). It is often shown as a frothy brew in painted books such as the Codex Mendoza (cat. 349). The Aztecs had many gods associated with *pulque* who were collectively known as the Centzon Totochtin ('400 rabbits').

TELAMON

Architectural term (from the Greek) to describe a sculpted male figure used as a pillar to support an entablature. The term has been used to describe the atlantean figures associated with the Toltec site of Tula, or those that support altars.

TEZONTL

The name given to the reddish-black volcanic stone widely used throughout

Tenochtitlan for the construction of buildings such as the Templo Mayor. The stone, which has many air holes, was later reused by the Spanish when they rebuilt Tenochtitlan as colonial Mexico City.

TIANQUIZTLI

An open-air marketplace, common to all communities, to which items were brought from outlying regions to be traded by count rather than weight. Such marketplaces were highly planned and administered (see *pochteca*) and also served as important social centres. The principal market was located in Tlatelolco. Up to 50,000 people gathered there and goods from all over the tribute empire were available.

TLACUILOQUE

Plural of *tlacuilo*. The learned native scribes who taught the art of *tlacuilloli*, 'to write-paintings', in the *calmecac* (see above). *Tlacuiloque* were the anonymous authors of Mexican painted books or codices.

TLALOQUE

Plural of Tlaloc. The four Tlalocs, gods of rain, each of whom had a distinctive colour and was specifically associated with one of the four Aztec world directions (often mistakenly referred to as the cardinal points north, south, east and west).

TLAMACAZOTON

Literally 'child priests', the name given to young boys entered into the *calmecac* (see above) by their parents. They went on to become priests or warriors.

TLAMACAZQUI

Head priest who, as well as undertaking religious rituals, instructed sons of the nobility at special schools (see *calmecac*).

TLAMATINIME

Plural of *tlamantini*. Teachers, literally 'wise men', the most venerated of all priests for their ability to offer counsel, interpret codices, compose and recite music, and instruct others in religious matters.

TLATOANI

The Aztec ruler, literally 'he who speaks', who is shown occupying the mat of power in, for example, the Codex Mendoza (cat. 349). Also used to refer to rulers of regions or towns.

TLATOQUE

Plural of *tlatoani* (see above).

TLAXILACALLI

The different districts or wards that made up a town or city.

TLAZOLTEOTL

A central Mexican goddess of purification who is also associated with filth. *Tlazolli* refers to both vices and diseases, especially those brought on through sexual excess or misdeed, for which Tlazolteotl was able to provide cures.

TONALAMATL

The 260-day count (see *tonalpohualli*) recorded as a 'book of days' as part of a codex, which also served as a divinatory almanac.

TONALLI

A highly complex concept intricately related to the *tonalpohualli*, with multiple meanings. It refers, for instance, to a number of cosmic forces, such as solar heat and, by association, the hot, dry summer season, and the solar day. Significantly, it also refers more specifically to individuals through their names, fates and souls. In addition, *tonalli* has links to the act of fire-drilling associated with the New Fire ceremony (see above) and the creation of man.

TONALPOHUALLI

The 260-day count which was composed of 20 signs (such as flint, rabbit, deer, grass, death) and 13 numbers (denoted by dots 1–13). When combined, these produced 260 variations (20 × 13 = 260) before the cycle was completed at the moment when the first pairing recurred. The 260-day count was sub-divided into weeks (see *trecena*). The *tonalpohualli* count was maintained in books (see *tonalamatl*) that were consulted by diviners to make prognostications for newborn children. It has been suggested that the *tonalpohualli* specifically reflected the nine-month period of human gestation. The *tonalpohualli* worked in conjunction with the *xihuitl* (see below and fig. 25).

TRECENA

Spanish term used to describe the division of the *tonalpohualli* into 20 weeks of 13 days each (20 × 13 = 260) after the Nahuatl term was lost. Each 13-day period, or *trecena*, began with the number 1 and the appropriate sign (see *tonalpohualli*) and ended with the number 13. Every combination of the *trecena* was unique, since no day in any week could be confused with that of another within the 260-day cycle. In addition, each *trecena* had its own patron deity, and every day was influenced by one

of the 13 lords of the day and nine lords of the night.

TRIPLE ALLIANCE

The union of three distinct cultural groups that came together in the Basin of Mexico to increase their collective power and influence in the region. Collectively known as the Aztecs, the partners were the Mexica of Tenochtitlan, the Tepanecs of Tlacopan (also known as Tacuba) on the western side of Lake Tetzcoco, and the Acolhuacans of Tetzcoco on the eastern side of Lake Tetzcoco.

TZOMPANTLI

Skull racks, in which the decapitated heads of sacrificial victims were threaded onto wooden poles in great numbers and placed on public view. A more permanent, symbolic *tzompantli*, made of stone skulls, was discovered alongside the Templo Mayor in Tenochtitlan.

XIHUITL

A 365-day yearly calendar which comprised 18 months or feasts of 20 days, known by the Spanish term *veintenas*, with an additional five-day period of inauspicious days known as the *nemontemi* (18 × 20 + 5 = 365). Each feast was celebrated with a public ritual, dedicated to a specific god, that was also directed towards religious, social and religious issues of general importance to the community. The *xihuitl* worked in conjunction with the *tonalpohualli* (see above and fig. 25).

XIUHAMATL

The name given to the Book of Years (see *xiuhpohualli*). These native historical documents were continuous year counts in which each year was represented pictorially by one of four year-bearing signs (reed, rabbit, flint, house) with the events depicted which took place in specific years.

XIUHMOLPILLI

The ritual bundle of 52 reeds which were tied together to mark the 'binding of the years' when the 52-year cycle of the calendar had been completed (see New Fire ceremony). Aztec stone representations of these reed-bundles have been discovered in modern Mexico City (cat. 171).

XIUHPOHUALLI

Another term for *xihuitl*.

BIBLIOGRAPHY

ACOSTA 1956
Jorge R. Acosta, 'El enigma de los chacmooles de Tula', in *Estudios antropológicos publicados en homenaje al doctor Manuel Gamio*, Mexico City, 1956, pp. 159–70

ACOSTA 1956-57
Jorge R. Acosta, 'Interpretación de algunos de los datos obtenidos en Tula relativos a la época tolteca', *Revista Mexicana de Estudios Antropológicos*, 14, 1956–57, pp. 75–110

ACOSTA 1961
Jorge R. Acosta, 'La doceava temporada de exploraciones en Tula, Hidalgo', *Anales del Instituto Nacional de Antropología e Historia*, 6th ser., vol. 13, 1961, pp. 29–58

AGUILAR ET AL. 1989
P. Carlos Aguilar, Beatriz Barba, Román Piña Chan, Luis Torres, Francisca Franco and Guillermo Ahuja, *Orfebrería prehispánica*, Mexico City, 1989

AGUILERA 1985
Carmen Aguilera, *Flora y fauna mexicana*, Mexico City, 1985

ALCINA FRANCH 1978
José Alcina Franch, *L'Art précolombien*, Paris, 1978

ALCINA FRANCH 1983
José Alcina Franch, *Pre-Columbian Art*, New York, 1983

ALCINA FRANCH 1992
José Alcina Franch, *L'arte precolombiana*, Milan, 1992

ALEXANDER 1985
Edward P. Alexander, 'William Bullock: Little-remembered Museologist and Showman', *Curator*, 28, 2, 1985, pp. 117–47

ALICANTE 1989
México colonial, exh. cat., Caja de Ahorros del Mediterráneo, Museo de América y Ministerio de Cultura, Alicante, 1989

ALTICK 1978
Richard D. Altick, *The Shows of London*, Cambridge, Mass., and London, 1978

ALVA IXTLILXOCHITL 1975-77
Fernando de Alva Ixtlilxochitl, *Obras históricas 1600–1640*, 2 vols, Mexico City, 1975–77

ALVARADO DE TEZOZÓMOC 1987
Hernando Alvarado de Tezozómoc, *Crónica méxicana*, Mexico City, 1987

ALVARADO DE TEZOZÓMOC 1998
Hernando Alvarado de Tezozómoc, *Crónica mexicáyotl*, Mexico City, 1998

AMSTERDAM 2002
Art Treasures from Ancient Mexico: Journey to the Land of the Gods, Felipe Solís Olguín and Ted Leyenaar (eds), exh. cat., Nieuwe Kerk, Amsterdam, 2002; State Hermitage Museum, St Petersburg

ANAWALT 1981
Patricia R. Anawalt, *Indian Clothing Before Cortés*, Norman, 1981

ANDERS 1970
Ferdinand Anders, 'Las artes menores', in *Tesoros de México: Arte Plumario y de Mosaico*, *Artes de México*, 137, 1970, pp. 4–45

ANDERS 1978
Ferdinand Anders, 'Der altmexikanische Federmosaikschild in Wien', *Archiv für Völkerkunde*, 32, 1978, pp. 67–88

ANDERS 1992
Ferdinand Anders, 'Huitzilopochtli – Vitzliputzli – Fizlipuzli – Fitzebutz: Das Schicksal eines mexikanischen Gottes in Europa', in Nuremberg 1992, vol. 1, pp. 423–46

ANDERSON, BERDAN AND LOCKHART 1976
Arthur J. O. Anderson, Frances F. Berdan and James Lockhart, *Beyond the Codices: The Nahua View of Colonial Mexico*, Berkeley, 1976

ANDREWS 1987
E. Wyllys Andrews V, 'A Cache of Early Jades from Chacsinkin, Yucatan', *Mexicon*, 9, 1987, pp. 78–85

ANGLERÍA 1989
Pedro Mártir de Anglería, *Decadas del Nuevo Mundo*, Madrid, 1989

ANTIGÜEDADES DE MÉXICO 1964-67
Antigüedades de México, basadas en la recopilación de Lord Kingsborough, 4 vols, Mexico City, 1964–67

ANTON 1969
Ferdinand Anton, *Ancient Mexican Art*, London, 1969

ANTWERP 1992
America: Bride of the Sun. 500 Years of Latin America and the Low Countries, exh. cat., Koninklijk Museum van Schone Kunsten, Antwerp, 1992

ANTWERP 1997
De Kleuren van de Geest: Dans en Trans in Afro-Europese Tradities, Paul Vandenbroeck (ed.), exh. cat., Koninklijk Museum van Schone Kunsten, Antwerp, 1997

APENS 1947
Ola Apens, *Mapas antiguos del Valle de México*, Mexico City, 1947

ARANA 1987
Raúl Martín Arana, 'Classic and Postclassic Chalcatzingo', in *Ancient Chalcatzingo*, D. C. Grove (ed.), Austin, 1987, pp. 386–89, 395

BANDINI 1793
Angelus Maria Bandinius, *Bibliotheca Leopoldina laurentiana seu Catalogus manuscriptorum qui nuper in Laurentianam translati sunt sub auspiciis Ferdinandi III…*, vol. 3, Florence, 1793

BANKMANN AND BAER 1990
Ulf Bankmann and Gerhard Baer, *Altmexikanische Skulpturen der Sammlung Lukas Vischer, Museum für Völkerkunde Basel, Corpus Antiquitatum Americanensium*, Basle, 1990

BAQUEDANO 1984
Elizabeth Baquedano, *Aztec Sculpture*, London, 1984

BARCELONA 1992
El juego de pelota en el México precolombino y su pervivencia en la actualidad, Fernando Jordi (ed.), exh. cat., Museu Etnológic, Barcelona, 1992

BARJAU 1998
Luis Barjau, *El mito mexicano de las edades*, Mexico City, 1998

BASLE 1985
Gerhard Baer, Ulf Bankmann, Susanne Hammacher and Annemarie Seiler-Baldinger, *Die Azteken Maisbauern und Krieger*/ Berthold Reise, *Die Maya*, companion book and exh. cat., Museum für Völkerkunde und Schweizerisches Museum für Volkskunde Basel, Basle, 1985

BASLER AND BRUMER 1928
Adolphe Basler and Ernest Brumer, *L'Art précolombien*, Paris, 1928

BATRES 1902
Leopoldo Batres, *Exploraciones arqueológicas en la Calle de las Escalerillas, año de 1900*, Mexico City, 1902

BATRES 1906
Leopoldo Batres, *Teotihuacan*, Mexico City, 1906

BELÉM 1995
Tejedores de Voces, a Arte do México Antigo, Nuno Saldaña (ed.), exh. cat., Centro Cultural de Belém, Fundáço das Descobertas, Belém, 1995

BENAVENTE 1971
Toribio de Benavente (Motolinía), *Memoriales, o Libro de las cosas de la Nueva España y de los naturales de ella*, Mexico City, 1971

BENSON 1972
The Cult of the Feline, Elizabeth P. Benson (ed.), Washington DC, 1972

BERDAN 1982
Frances F. Berdan, *The Aztecs of Central Mexico: An Imperial Society*, Fort Worth, 1982

BERDAN ET AL. 1996
Frances F. Berdan, Richard E. Blanton, Elizabeth H. Boone, Mary G. Hodge, Michael E. Smith and Emily Umberger, *Aztec Imperial Strategies*, Dumbarton Oaks, Washington DC, 1996

BERGER 1998
Uta Berger, *Mexican Painted Manuscripts in the United Kingdom*, London, 1998

BERLIN 1992
Amerika 1492–1992: Neue Welten – Neue Wirklichkeiten, exh. cat., Martin-Gropius-Bau, Berlin, 1992

BERLO 1992
Art, Ideology, and the City of Teotihuacan, Janet Catherine Berlo (ed.), Washington DC, 1992

BERNAL 1967
Ignacio Bernal, *Museo Nacional de Antropología, Arqueología*, Mexico City, 1967

BERNAL 1979
Ignacio Bernal, *Historia de la arqueología en México*, Mexico City, 1979

BERNAL AND SIMONI-ABBAT 1986
Ignacio Bernal and Mireille Simoni-Abbat, *Le Mexique*, Paris, 1986

BEYER 1924
Hermann Beyer, 'El origen, desarrollo y significado de la greca escalonada', *El México Antiguo*, 2, 1924, pp. 1–13

BEYER 1955
Hermann Beyer, '"La procesión de los señores", decoración del primer teocalli de piedra en México-Tenochtitlán', *El México Antiguo*, 8, 1955, pp. 1–42

BEYER 1965
Hermann Beyer, 'El llamado Calendario Azteca. Descripción e interpretación del cuauhxicalli de la Casa de las Águilas', *El México Antiguo*, 10, 1965, pp. 134–260

BEYER 1965B
Hermann Beyer, *Myth and Symbol of Ancient Mexico: El México antiguo*, Mexico City, 1965

BIERHORST 1990
John Bierhorst, *The Mythology of Mexico and Central America*, New York, 1990

BIERHORST 1992
John Bierhorst, *Codex Chimalpopoca: The Text in Nahuatl with a Glossary and Grammatical Notes; The Codex Chimalpopoca: History and Mythology of the Aztecs*, 2 vols, Tucson and London, 1992

BIOLOGIA CENTRALI-AMERICANA 1889–1902
Biologia Centrali-Americana; or Contributions to the Knowledge of the Fauna and Flora of Mexico and Central America, Frederick Du Cane and Osbert Salvin (eds), London, 1889–1902

BOLOGNA 1667
Breve descrizione del Museo dell'Illustriss. Sig. Cav. Commend. dell'Ordine di S. Stefano Ferdinando Cospi…donato dal medesimo all'Illustriss. Senato, & ora annesso al famoso Cimeliarchio del Celebre Aldrovandi, Bologna, 1667

BOLOGNA 1677
Lorenzo Legati, *Museo Cospiano annesso a quello del famoso Ulisse Aldrovandi e donato alla sua patria dall'illustrissimo signor Ferdinando Cospi…*, Bologna, 1677

BOLZ-AUGENSTEIN 1975
Ingeborg Bolz-Augenstein, *Sammlung Ludwig: Altamerika, Ethnologica*, n.s., vol. 7, Recklinghausen, 1975

BOLZ-AUGENSTEIN AND DISSELHOFF 1970
Ingeborg Bolz-Augenstein and H. D. Disselhoff, *Werke präkolumbianischer Kunst: Die Sammlung Ludwig, Aachen, Monumenta Americana*, vol. 6, Berlin, 1970

BONIFAZ NUÑO 1981
Rubén Bonifaz Nuño, *El arte en el Templo Mayor*, Mexico City, 1981

BOONE 1989
Elizabeth H. Boone, *Incarnations of the Aztec Supernatural: The Image of Huitzilopochtli in Mexico and Europe*, Philadelphia, 1989

BOONE 1993
Collecting the Pre-Columbian Past: A Symposium at Dumbarton Oaks, 6–7 October 1990, Elizabeth H. Boone (ed.), Washington DC, 1993

BOONE 2000
Elizabeth H. Boone, 'Venerable Place of Beginnings: The Aztec Understanding of Teotihuacan', in Carrasco, Jones and Sessions 2000, pp. 371–95

BOSTON 1968
The Gold of Ancient America, Allen Wardwell (ed.), exh. cat., Museum of Fine Arts, Boston, 1968

BRAUN 1993
Barbara Braun, *Pre-Columbian Art and the Post-Columbian World*, New York, 1993

BRAY 1968
Warwick Bray, *Everyday Life of the Aztecs*, London and New York, 1968

BRISTOL 1989
The Art of Ruins: Adela Breton and the Temples of Mexico, Sue Giles and Jennifer Stewart (eds), exh. cat., Bristol Museum and Art Gallery, 1989

BRIZZI 1976
Il Museo Pigorini, B. Brizzi (ed.), Rome, 1976

BRODA 1969
Johanna Broda, *The Mexican Calendar as Compared to Other Mesoamerican Systems*, Vienna, 1969

BROOKLYN 1938–41
Brooklyn Museum of Art Archives, AAPA Records, Objects offered for sale/purchases by Museum [03] (file #33), 1938–39, and [04] (file #33), 1940–41

BROOKLYN 1996
Converging Cultures: Art and Identity in Spanish America, Diana Fane (ed.), exh. cat., Brooklyn Museum, New York, 1996

BROOKLYN 1997
Brooklyn Museum of Art, New York, 1997

BROTHERSTON 1979
Gordon Brotherston, *Images of the New World: The American Continent Portrayed in Native Texts*, London, 1979

BROTHERSTON 1992
Gordon Brotherston, *Mexican Painted Books*, Colchester, 1992

BROTHERSTON 1995
Gordon Brotherston, *Painted Books from Mexico: Codices in UK Collections and the World They Represent*, London, 1995

BROTHERSTON AND GALLEGOS 1988
Gordon Brotherston and Ana Gallegos, 'The Newly-discovered Tepotzotlan Codex: A First Account', in *Recent Studies in Pre-Columbian Archaeology*, Nicholas J. Saunders and Olivier de Montmollin (eds), *British Archaeological Reports: International Series*, vol. 421, Oxford, 1988, pp. 205–27

BRUNDAGE 1979
Burr Cartwright Brundage, *The Fifth Sun: Aztec Gods, Aztec World*, Austin, 1979

BRUNNER 1970
Herbert Brunner, *Schatzkammer der Residenz München: Katalog*, Munich, 1970

BULLOCK 1824
William Bullock, *Six Months' Residence and Travel in Mexico, Containing Remarks on the Present State of New Spain*, London, 1824

BULLOCK 1991
William Bullock, *Catálogo de la Primera Exposición de Arte Prehispánico*, prologue, translation and notes by Begoña Arteta, Mexico City, 1991

CALDERÓN DE LA BARCA 1843
Marquesa de Calderón de la Barca, *Life in Mexico*, London, 1843

CALLEGARI 1924
Guido Valeriano Callegari, 'La raccolta d'oggetti precolombiani del Museo d'Antichità di Torino', *Emporium*, 40, 355, 1924, pp. 450–57

CALNEK 1972
Edward Calnek, 'Settlement Pattern and Chinampa Agriculture at Tenochtitlan', *American Antiquity*, 37, 1972, pp. 104–15

CALNEK 1976
Edward Calnek, 'The Internal Structure of Tenochtitlan', in *The Valley of Mexico: Studies in Pre-Hispanic Ecology and Society*, Eric R. Wolf (ed.), Albuquerque, 1976, pp. 287–302

CANTARES MEXICANOS 1994
Cantares Mexicanos, Miguel León-Portilla and José G. Moreno de Alba (eds), Mexico City, 1994

CARMICHAEL 1970
Elizabeth Carmichael, *Turquoise Mosaics from Mexico*, London, 1970

CARRASCO 1979
Pedro Carrasco, 'Las bases sociales del politeísmo mexicano: los dioses tutelares', in *Actes du XLIIe Congrès International des Américanistes, 1976*, Paris, 1979, pp. 11–17

CARRASCO 1990
David Carrasco, *Religions of Mesoamerica. Cosmovision and Ceremonial Centers*, San Francisco, 1990

CARRASCO 1998
David Carrasco, with Scott Sessions, *Daily Life of the Aztecs, People of the Sun and Earth*, Westport, Conn., and London, 1998

CARRASCO 1999
Aztec Ceremonial Landscapes, David Carrasco (ed.), Niwot, 1999

CARRASCO, JONES AND SESSIONS 2000
Mesoamerica's Classic Heritage: From Teotihuacan to the Aztecs, David Carrasco, Lindsay Jones and Scott Sessions (eds), Boulder, 2000

CASO 1932
Alfonso Caso, 'La Tumba 7 de Monte Albán es mixteca', *Universidad de México*, 26, 1932, pp. 117–50

CASO 1950
Alfonso Caso, 'Una máscara azteca femenina', *México en el Arte*, 9, 1950, pp. 2–9

CASO 1952
Alfonso Caso, 'Un cuauhxicalli del Dios de los Muertos', *Memorias y Revista de la Academia Nacional de Ciencias*, 57, 1–2, 1952, pp. 99–111

CASO 1953
Alfonso Caso, *El pueblo del Sol*, Mexico City, 1953

CASO 1956
Alfonso Caso, 'Los barrios antiguos de Tenochtitlan y Tlatelolco', *Memorias de la Academia Mexicana de la Historia*, 15, 1956, pp. 7–63

CASO 1967
Alfonso Caso, *Los calendarios prehispánicos*, Mexico City, 1967

CASO AND MATEOS HIGUERA 1937
Alfonso Caso and Salvador Mateos Higuera, *Catálogo de la Colección de Monolitos del Museo Nacional de Antropología*, Mexico City, 1937

CASTAÑEDA 1986
Francisco de Castañeda, 'Relación de Tequizistlan y su partido', in *Relaciones geográficas del siglo XVI*, vol. 7, René Acuña (ed.), Mexico City, 1986, pp. 211–51

CASTAÑEDA AND MENDOZA 1933
Daniel Castañeda and Vicente T. Mendoza, *Instrumental Precortesiano*, vol. 1, Museo Nacional de Arqueología, Etnografía e Historia, Mexico City, 1933

CASTELLÓ ITURBIDE 1993
Teresa Castelló Iturbide, *El arte plumaria en México*, Mexico City, 1993

CASTILLO FARRERAS 1971
Víctor M. Castillo Farreras, 'El bisiesto náhuatl', *Estudios de Cultura Náhuatl*, 9, 1971, pp. 75–104

CASTILLO TEJERO AND SOLÍS OLGUÍN 1975
Noemí Castillo Tejero and Felipe Solís Olguín, *Ofrendas mexicas en el Museo Nacional de Antropología*, in *Corpus Antiquitatum Americanensium: México*, vol. 8, Mexico City, 1975

CELORIO 1962
Miguel Celorio, *Presencia del pasado, IV Congreso Mundial de Cardiología, Exposición de arqueología mexicana*, Mexico City, October 1962

CHARNAY 1885
Désiré Charnay, *Les Anciennes Villes du nouveau monde: voyages d'explorations au Mexique et dans l'Amérique centrale*, Paris, 1885

CHAVERO 1958
Alfredo Chavero,
México a través de los siglos,
Mexico City, 1958

CHÁVEZ BALDERAS 2002
Ximena Chávez Balderas,
*Los rituales funerarios del Templo
Mayor de Tenochtitlan*, BA
thesis, Escuela Nacional de
Antropología e Historia,
Mexico City, 2002

CHECA CREMADES 1997
Fernando Checa Cremades,
Las maravillas de Felipe II,
Madrid, 1997

CHEFS-D'ŒUVRE 1947
*Chefs-d'œuvre de l'Amérique
précolombienne*, Paris, 1947

CHEFS-D'ŒUVRE 1965
*Chefs-d'œuvre du Musée de
l'Homme*, Paris, 1965

CHICAGO 1993
México: la visión del cosmos,
Donald McVicker and
Laurene Lambertino-Urquizo
(eds), exh. cat., Mexican Fine
Arts Center Museum,
Chicago, 1993

CLOSS 1976
Michael Closs, 'New
Information on the European
Discovery of Yucatan',
American Antiquity, 41, 1976,
pp. 192–95

CODEX AZCATITLAN 1949
Codex Azcatitlan, facsimile,
Robert H. Barlow (ed.),
*Journal de la Société des
Américanistes*, vol. 38,
Paris, 1949

CODEX AZCATITLAN 1995
Codex Azcatitlan: facsimilé,
Michel Graulich (intro.),
Robert H. Barlow
(commentary), 2 vols,
Paris, 1995

CODEX BORBONICUS 1974
Codex Borbonicus, facsimile,
with a commentary by Karl
Anton Nowotny, Graz, 1974

CODEX CHIMALPAHIN 1997
*Codex Chimalpahin, Volume 1:
Society and Politics in Mexico and
Tenochtitlan, Tlatelolco, Texcoco,
Culhuacan and Other Nahua
Altepetl in Central Mexico*,
Arthur J. O. Anderson
and Susan Schroeder (trans.
and eds), Oklahoma, 1997

CODEX FEJÉRVÁRY-MAYER 1971
*Codex Fejérváry-Mayer (12014-M),
City of Liverpool Museums*,
facsimile, with an
introduction by Cottie A.
Burland, Graz, 1971

CODEX LAUD 1966
*Codex Laud (Ms Laud Misc.
678), Bodleian Library, Oxford*,
facsimile, Graz, 1966

CODEX MAGLIABECHIANO 1903
*The Book of the Life of the
Ancient Mexicans…An
Anonymous Hispano-Mexican
Manuscript*, facsimile,
Zelia Nuttal (trans. and ed.),
Berkeley, 1903

CODEX MAGLIABECHIANO 1970
*Codex Magliabechiano, Cl xiii.
(B.R. 232), Biblioteca Nazionale
Centrale di Firenze*, facsimile,
Ferdinand Anders (intro.
and summary), Graz, 1970

CODEX MAGLIABECHIANO 1983
*The Book of Life of the Ancient
Mexicans…An Anonymous
Hispano-Mexican Manuscript:
Introduction and Facsimile;
The Codex Magliabechiano and
the Lost Prototype of the
Magliabechiano Group: Notes
and Commentary*, Elizabeth H.
Boone (ed.), 2 vols, Berkeley,
1983

CODEX MATRITENSE 1907
*Codex Matritense of the Academy
of History: Texts of the Nahua
Informants of Friar Bernardino de
Sahagún*, facsimile, Francisco
del Paso y Troncoso (ed.),
3 vols, Madrid, 1907

CODEX MENDOZA 1992
The Codex Mendoza, facsimile,
Frances F. Berdan and
Patricia Rieff Anawalt (eds),
4 vols, Berkeley, 1992

CODEX MENDOZA 1997
The Essential Codex Mendoza,
Frances F. Berdan and
Patricia Rieff Anawalt (eds),
Berkeley, 1997

CODEX TELLERIANO-REMENSIS 1995
*Codex Telleriano-Remensis:
Ritual, Divination and History
in a Pictorial Aztec Manuscript*,
facsimile, Eloise Quiñones
Keber (commentary), Austin,
1995

CODEX TRO-CORTESIANUS 1967
*Codex Tro-Cortesianus (Codex
Madrid), Museo de América
Madrid*, facsimile,
introduction and summary
by Ferdinand Anders,
Graz, 1967

CODEX VATICANUS 3738 1979
*Codex Vaticanus 3738 ('Cod.
Vat. A', 'Cod. Ríos') des
Biblioteca Apostolica Vaticana:
Farbereproduktion des Codex in
verkleinertem Format*, facsimile,
commentary by Ferdinand
Anders, Graz, 1979

CODEX ZOUCHE-NUTTALL 1992
*Codex Zouche-Nuttall. Crónica
mixteca: el rey 8 venado. Garra de
Jaguar, y la dinastía Teozacualco-
Zaachila*, facsimile, Ferdinand
Anders, Maarten Jansen and
Gabina Aurora Pérez Jiménez
(eds), Graz and Mexico City,
1992

CÓDICE BORBÓNICO 1979
Códice Borbónico, facsimile,
E.-T. Hamy (ed.), Paris, 1899;
Mexico City, 1979

CÓDICE BORBÓNICO 1993
*Descripción, Historia y
Exposición del Códice Borbónico*,
facsimile, Francisco del Paso
y Troncoso (ed.), 3rd edition,
Mexico City, 1993

CÓDICE BORBÓNICO 1994
*Códice Borbónico. El libro del
Ciuacóatl: homenaje para el año
del Fuego Nuevo*, facsimile,
Ferdinand Anders, Maarten
Jansen and Luis Reyes García
(eds), Mexico City, 1994

CÓDICE BOTURINI 1964
Códice Boturini or *Tira de la
Peregrinación*, facsimile, in
Antigüedades de México
1964–67, vol. 2, pp. 7–29

CÓDICE CHIMALPOPOCA 1945
*Códice Chimalpopoca: anales de
Cuauhtitlan y leyenda de los soles*,
facsimile, Primo Feliciano
Velázquez (ed.), Mexico City,
1945

CODICE COSPI 1992
*Calendario e rituale precolombiani:
Codice Cospi*, L. Laurencich
Minelli (ed.), Milan, 1992

CÓDICE COSPI 1994
*Códice Cospi. Calendario de
pronósticas y ofrendas*. Ferdinand
Anders, Maarten Jansen and
Peter van der Loo, Graz and
Mexico City, 1994

CÓDICE FEJÉRVÁRY-MAYER 1994
*Códice Fejérváry-Mayer. El libro
de Tezcatlipoca, señor del tiempo*,
facsimile, Ferdinand Anders,
Maarten Jansen and Gabina
Aurora Pérez Jiménez (eds),
Graz and Mexico City, 1994

CÓDICE IXTLILXOCHITL 1996
*Códice Ixtlilxochitl. Papeles y
pinturas de un historiador*, Geert
Bastiaan van Doesburg (ed.),
Graz and Mexico City, 1996

CÓDICE LAUD 1994
*Códice Laud. Pintura de la muerte
y los destinos*, facsimile,
Ferdinand Anders, Maarten
Jansen and Alejandra Cruz
Ortiz (eds), Graz and
Mexico City, 1994

CÓDICE MAGLIABECHI 1996
*Códice Magliabechi. Libro de la
vida*, Ferdinand Anders and
Maarten Jansen (eds), Graz
and Mexico City, 1996

CÓDICE MAGLIABECHIANO 1979
*Códice Magliabechiano. Cl xiii.
(B.R. 232) Biblioteca Nazionale
Centrale di Firenze*, facsimile,
Ferdinand Anders (ed.),
Graz, 1979

CÓDICE MATRITENSE 1906
Códice Matritense, Madrid, 1906

CÓDICE MATRITENSE 1907
*Códice Matritense de la Real
Academia de la Historia (textos
en náhuatl de los indígenas
informantes de Sahagún), edición
facsimilar a cargo de Francisco del
Paso y Troncoso*, 3 vols, Madrid,
1907

CÓDICE MENDOCINO 1964
Códice Mendocino, facsimile,
José Corona Núñez (ed.), in
Antigüedades de México
1964–67, vol. 1, pp. 1–149

CÓDICE TELLERIANO-REMENSIS 1964
Códice Telleriano-Remensis,
facsimile, in Antigüedades de
México 1964–67, vol. 1,
pp. 151–338

CODICE VATICANO 3738 1900
*Il manoscritto messicano Vaticano
3738 detto il codice Ríos, riprodotto
in fotomicrografi a spese di sua
eccellenza il duca di Loubat per
cura della Biblioteca Vaticana*,
Franz Ehrle (ed.), Rome,
1900

CÓDICE VATICANO A 1996
*Códice Vaticano A. Religión,
costumbres e historia de los
antiguos mexicanos*, facsimile,
Ferdinand Anders and
Maarten Jansen (eds),
Mexico City, 1996

CÓDICE VATICANO LATINO 1964–67
Códice Vaticano Latino (3738)
or *Códice Ríos* or
Códice Ríos, facsimile, José
Corona Núñez (ed.), in
Antigüedades de México
1964–67, vol. 3, pp. 7–314

COE 1966
Michael D. Coe, *An Early
Stone Pectoral from South-eastern
Mexico*, Washington DC, 1966

COE 1992
Michael D. Coe, *Museo de
Antropología de Xalapa,
Gobierno del Estado de Veracruz*,
Veracruz, 1992

COE 1994
Michael D. Coe, *Mexico*,
London and New York, 1994

COLCHESTER 1992
Pauline Antrobus, Gordon
Brotherston, Valerie Fraser,
Peter Hulme and Jeremy
Theopolis, *Mapping the
Americas*, exh. cat., University
of Essex, Colchester, 1992

**COLECCIÓN DE DOCUMENTOS
INÉDITOS 1864**
*Colección de documentos inéditos
relativos al descubrimiento,
conquista y organización de las
posesiones españolas en
América…*, 42 vols, Madrid,
1864 ff.

COLOGNE 1999
*Kunst der Welt im Rautenstrauch-
Joest-Museum für Völkerkunde,
Köln*, Gisela Vögler (ed.), exh.
cat., Cologne, Rautenstrauch-
Joest-Museum für
Völkerkunde, 1999

CONRAD AND DEMAREST 1984
Geoffrey W. Conrad and
Arthur A. Demarest, *Religion
and Empire: The Dynamics of
Aztec and Inca Expansionism*,
Cambridge, 1984

CORSI 1982
Pietro Corsi, 'Il Codice
Fiorentino: nota storica',
*FMR: mensile d'arte e di cultura
dell'immagine*, 4 June 1982,
pp. 80–83, 134–35

CORTÉS 1963
Hernán Cortés, *Cartas y
documentos*, introduction by
Mario Hernández Sánchez-
Barba, Mexico City, 1963

CORTÉS 1986
Hernán Cortés, *Letters from
Mexico*, Anthony Pagden (ed.),
New Haven and London,
1986

COVARRUBIAS 1957
Miguel Covarrubias, *Indian
Art of Mexico and Central
America*, New York, 1957

COVARRUBIAS 1961
Miguel Covarrubias,
*Arte Indígena de México y
Centroamérica*, Mexico City,
1961

CUESTA DOMINGO 1983–84
Mariano Cuesta Domingo,
*Alonzo de Santa Cruz y su obra
cartográfica*, 2 vols, Madrid,
1983–84

DAHLGREN 1889
Erik Wilhelm Dahlgren,
*Något om det forna och nuvarande
Mexiko*, Stockholm, 1889,
pp. 3–30

DAHLGREN 1892
Erik Wilhelm Dahlgren, *Map
of the World by Alonzo de Santa
Cruz, 1542*, Stockholm, 1892

DAHLGREN ET AL. 1982
Barbara Dahlgren, Emma
Perez-Rocha, Lourdes Suárez
Díez and Perla Valle de
Revueltas, *Corazón de Cópil*,
Mexico City, 1982

**DEPARTAMENTO DEL DISTRITO
FEDERAL 1975**
Departamento del Distrito
Federal, *Memorias de las obras
del Sistema de Drenaje Profundo
del Distrito Federal: Atlas*, vol.
4, Secretaría de Obras y
Servicios del DDF,
Mexico City, 1975

DÍAZ DEL CASTILLO 1956
Bernal Díaz del Castillo,
*The Discovery and Conquest of
New Spain*, Arthur Percival
Maudslay (trans.), New York,
1956

DÍAZ DEL CASTILLO 1984
Bernal Díaz del Castillo,
*Historia verdadera de la conquista
de la Nueva España*, 2 vols,
Miguel León-Portilla (ed.),
Madrid, 1984

DIETSCHY 1941
Hans Dietschy, 'Zwei
altmexikanische Steinbilder
von Sonnengöttern', *Ethnos*,
6, 1–2, 1941, pp. 75–96

DRUCKER 1955
Phillip Drucker, 'The Cerro
de las Mesas Offering of Jade
and Other Materials', *Bulletin
of the Smithsonian Institution of
Washington*, 157, 1955,
pp. 25–68

DUMBARTON OAKS 1963
Handbook of the Robert Woods Bliss Collection of Pre-Columbian Art, Dumbarton Oaks, Washington DC, 1963

DUPAIX 1978
Guillermo Dupaix, *Atlas de las antigüedades mexicanas halladas en el curso de los tres viajes de la Real Expedición de Antigüedades de la Nueva España*, with an introduction and notes by Roberto Villaseñor Espinosa, Mexico City, 1978

DURÁN 1867,1880
Diego Durán, *Historia de las Indias de Nueva España e Islas de Tierra Firme*, 2 vols, Mexico City, 1867, 1880

DURÁN 1951
Diego Durán, *Historia de las Indias de Nueva España e Islas de Tierra Firme*, 3 vols, Mexico City, 1951

DURÁN 1964
Diego Durán, *The Aztecs: The History of the Indies of New Spain (1581)*, Doris Heyden and Fernando Horcasitas (trans. and eds), Ignacio Bernal (intro.), New York, 1964

DURÁN 1967
Diego Durán, *Historia de las Indias de Nueva España e Islas de Tierra Firme*, Ángel María Garibay Kintana (ed.), 2 vols, Mexico City, 1967; 1975

DURÁN 1971
Diego Durán, *Book of the Gods and Rites and the Ancient Calendar*, Fernando Horcasitas and Doris Heyden (trans. and eds), Norman, 1971

DURÁN 1990–91
Diego Durán, *Historia de las Indias de Nueva España e Islas de Tierra Firme*, José Rubén Moreno and Rosa Camelo (intro.), 2 vols, Madrid, 1990–91

DURÁN 1995
Diego Durán, *Historia de las Indias de Nueva España e Islas de Tierra Firme*, Mexico City, 1995

DUYVIS 1935
G. E. G. Duyvis, 'Mexicaansche Mozaiken', *Maandblad voor Beeldenden Kunsten*, 12, 1935, pp. 355–66

DYCKERHOFF 1999
Ursula Dyckerhoff, in Cologne 1999

EDINBURGH 1971
Dale Idiens, *Ancient American Art*, exh. cat., Royal Scottish Museum, Edinburgh, 1971

EDMONSON 1988
Munro S. Edmonson, *The Book of the Year: Middle American Calendrical Systems*, Salt Lake City, 1988

EGAN 1993
Martha J. Egan, *Relicarios: Devotional Miniatures from the Americas*, Santa Fe, 1993

EISLEB 1973
Dieter Eisleb, 'Hundert Jahre Museum für Völkerkunde Berlin: Abteilung Amerikanische Archäologie', *Baessler-Archiv*, n.s., 21, 1973, pp. 175–217

EKHOLM 1970
Gordon Ekholm, *Ancient Mexico and Central America*, Companion Book to the Hall of Mexico and Central America, American Museum of Natural History, New York, 1970

EKHOLM AND BERNAL 1971
Archaeology of Northern Mesoamerica Part 1, Gordon Ekholm and Ignacio Bernal (eds), *Handbook of Middle American Indians*, vol. 10, Robert Wauchope (series ed.), Austin, 1971

EL ESCORIAL 1998
Felipe II: un monarca y su época – la monarquía hispánica, exh. cat., Real Monasterio de San Lorenzo de El Escorial, 1998

ENCISO 1947
Jorge Enciso, *Sellos del México antiguo*, Mexico City, 1947

ESPINOSA PINEDA 1996
Gabriel Espinosa Pineda, *El embrujo del lago: el sistema lacustre de la cuenca de México en la cosmovisión mexica*, Mexico City, 1996

ESPINOSA PINEDA 2001
Gabriel Espinosa Pineda, 'La fauna de Ehécatl: propuesta de una taxonomía a partir de las deidades, o la función de la fauna en el orden cósmico', in González Torres 2001, pp. 255–303

ESTERAS MARTÍN 1989
Cristina Esteras Martín, 'Platería virreinal novohispana: siglos XVI–XIX', in *El arte de la platería mexicana: 500 años*, Lucía García-Noriega y Nieto (ed.), Mexico City, 1989, pp. 152–55

ESTRADA 1937
Genaro Estrada, 'El arte mexicano en España', in *Enciclopedia ilustrada mexicana*, vol. 5, Mexico City, 1937

EZQUERRA 1970
Ramón Ezquerra, 'El viaje de Pinzón y Solís al Yucatán', *Revista de Indias*, 30, 1970, pp. 217–38

FALDINI 1978
Luisa Faldini, 'America', in *Africa, America, Oceania: le collezioni etnologiche del Museo Civico*, Turin, 1978, pp. 53–125

FEEST 1986
Christian F. Feest, 'Koloniale Federkunst aus Mexiko', in *Gold und Macht: Spanien in der Neuen Welt*, Vienna, 1986, pp. 173–78

FEEST 1990
Christian F. Feest, 'Vienna's Mexican Treasures: Aztec, Mixtec and Tarascan Works from Sixteenth-century Austrian Collections', *Archiv für Völkerkunde*, 44, 1990

FERNÁNDEZ 1987
Miguel Ángel Fernández, *Historia de los museos de México*, Mexico City, 1987

FERNÁNDEZ DE OVIEDO 1959
Gonzalo Fernández de Oviedo, *Historia general y natural de las Indias*, Juan Pérez de Tudela Bueso (ed.), 5 vols, Madrid, 1959; 1992

FLORENCE 1997
Christina Acidini Luchinat, Mina Gregori, Detlef Heikamp and Antonio Paolucci, *Magnificenza alla corte dei Medici. Arte a Firenze alla fine del Cinquecento*, exh. cat., Museo degli Argenti, Palazzo Pitti, Florence, 1997

FLORESCANO 1990
Enrique Florescano, 'Mitos e historia en la memoria nahua', *Historia Mexicana*, 155, 1990, pp. 607–62

FORT WORTH 1986
Linda Schele and Mary Ellen Miller, *The Blood of Kings*, exh. cat., Kimbell Art Museum, Fort Worth, 1986

FRANCK 1829
W. Franck, *Catalogue of Drawings of Mexican Antiquities/Description feuille par feuille de la collection de dessins d'antiquités mexicaines*, original manuscript, British Museum, London, 1829

FRANKS 1868
Augustus Wollaston Franks, *Guide to the Christy Collection of Prehistoric Antiquities and Ethnography Temporarily Placed at 103 Victoria Street, Westminster*, London, 1868

FRANKS 1870
Augustus Wollaston Franks, *Catalogue of the Christy Collection of Prehistoric Antiquities and Ethnography Formed by the Late Henry Christy and Presented by the Trustees Under His Will to the British Museum*, London, 1870

FUENTE 1990
Beatriz de la Fuente, 'Escultura en el tiempo: retorno al pasado tolteca', *Artes de México (nueva época)*, 9, 1990, pp. 36–53

FUENTE 2000
Beatriz de la Fuente, 'Rostros: Expresión de vida en la plástica prehispánica', *Arqueología Mexicana*, 6, 2000, pp. 6–11

FUENTE, TREJO AND GUTIÉRREZ SOLANA 1988
Beatriz de la Fuente, Silvia Trejo and Nelly Gutiérrez Solana, *Escultura en piedra de Tula, catálogo*, UNAM, Mexico City, 1988

FUENTES 1964
Patricia Fuentes, *The Conquistadors*, London, 1964

FUMAGALLI 1932
Savina Fumagalli, 'Amuleti e oggetti d'oro della collezione precolombiana di Torino', *Atti della Società Piemontese di Archeologia e Belle Arti*, 13, 1932, pp. 165–95

GALARZA 1992
Joaquín Galarza, *Códices testerianos: catecismos indígenas, el pater noster*, Mexico City, 1992

GALINDO Y VILLA 1897
Jesús Galindo y Villa, *Catálogo del Departamento de Arqueología del Museo Nacional. Primera parte: Galería de monolitos*, 2nd edition, Mexico City, 1897

GALINDO Y VILLA 1903
Jesús Galindo y Villa, 'La escultura nahua', *Anales del Museo Nacional*, 2nd series, 1, 1903, pp. 195–234

GARCÍA COOK AND ARANA 1978
Ángel García Cook and Raúl Martín Arana, *Rescate arqueológico del monolito Coyolxauhqui: informe preliminar*, Mexico City, 1978

GARCÍA GRANADOS 1946
Rafael García Granados, 'El arte plumario', in *México prehispánico*, Mexico City, 1946, pp. 576–82

GARCÍA ICAZBALCETA 1980
Joaquín García Icazbalceta, *Colección de documentos para la historia de México*, Mexico City, 1980

GARCÍA MOLL ET AL. N.D.
Roberto García Moll, Roberto Gallegos, Daniel Juárez, Alfredo Barrera, Felipe Solís Olguín and Olivié y Flores, *Herencia recuperada*, Mexico City, n.d.

GARCÍA PAYÓN 1979
José García Payón, *La zona arqueológica de Tecaxic-Calixtlahuaca y los matlatzincas*, Mexico City, 1936; 1979

GARIBAY KINTANA 1953–54
Ángel María Garibay Kintana, *Historia de la literatura náhuatl*, 2 vols, Mexico City, 1953–54

GARIBAY KINTANA 1964
Ángel María Garibay Kintana, *Flor y canto del arte prehispánico de México*, Mexico City, 1964

GARIBAY KINTANA 1965
Teogonía e historia de los mexicanos. Tres opúsculos del siglo XVI, Ángel María Garibay Kintana (ed.), Mexico City, 1965

GENDROP 1979
Paul Gendrop, *Arte prehispánico en Mesoamérica*, Mexico City, 1979

GENDROP 1981
Paul Gendrop, 'Mesoamérica en imágenes', *Boletín del Museo Universitario de Antropología, México*, 1981

GENDROP AND DÍAZ BALERDI 1994
Paul Gendrop and Iñaki Díaz Balerdi, *Escultura azteca: una aproximación a su estética*, Mexico City, 1994

GENOA 1992
Due 'Mondi' a confronto: i segni della storia, exh. cat., Aurelio Rigoli (ed.), Palazzo Ducale, Genoa, 1992

GERBER AND TALADOIRE 1990
Frédéric Gerber and Eric Taladoire, '1865: Identification of "Newly" Discovered Murals from Teotihuacan', *Mexicon*, 12, 1990, pp. 6–9

GHENT 1999
Carolus: Keizer Karel V 1500–1558, exh. cat., Kunsthal de Sint-Pietersabdij, Ghent, 1999

GLASS AND ROBERTSON 1975
John B. Glass and Donald Robertson, 'A Census of Native Middle American Pictorial Manuscripts', in *Handbook of Middle American Indians*, vol. 14, Austin and London, 1975, pp. 81–252

GLASS AND ROBERTSON 1975B
John B. Glass and Donald Robertson, 'A Census of Middle American Testerian Manuscripts', in *Handbook of Middle American Indians*, vol. 14, Austin and London, 1975, pp. 281–96

GÓMEZ-HARO DESDIER 1994
Germaine Gómez-Haro Desdier, 'Estudio del Lienzo de Quetzpalan', unpublished thesis, Secretaría de Educación Pública, Mexico City, 1994

GONÇALVES DE LIMA 1956
Oswaldo Gonçalves de Lima, *El maguey y el pulque*, Mexico City and Buenos Aires, 1956

GONZÁLEZ AND OLMEDO VERA 1990
Carlos Javier González and Bertina Olmedo Vera, *Esculturas Mezcala en el Templo Mayor*, Mexico City, 1990

GONZÁLEZ RUL 1988
Francisco González Rul, *La cerámica en Tlatelolco*, Mexico City, 1988

GONZÁLEZ RUL 1997
Francisco González Rul, *Matériales líticos y cerámicos encontrados en las cercanías del monolito Coyolxauhqui*, INAH, Serie Arqueología, Mexico City, 1997

GONZÁLEZ TORRES 1985
Yólotl González Torres, *El sacrificio humano entre los mexicas*, Mexico City, 1985

GONZÁLEZ TORRES 1991
Yólotl González Torres, *Diccionario de mitología y religión de Mesoamérica*, Mexico City, 1991

GONZÁLEZ TORRES 2001
Yólotl González Torres, *Animales y plantes en la cosmovisión mesoamericana*, Mexico City, 2001

GONZÁLEZ TORRES 2001B
Yólotl González Torres, 'Huitzilopochtli', in *Oxford Encyclopaedia of Mesoamerican Cultures*, David Carrasco (ed.), Oxford and New York, 2001, vol. 2, pp. 21–23

GRAHAM 1993
Ian Graham, 'Three Early Collectors in Mesoamerica', in Boone 1993, pp. 49–80

GRAHAM 1998
Mark Miller Graham, 'Mesoamerican Jade and Costa Rica', in *Jade in Ancient Costa Rica*, exh. cat., Julie Jones (ed.), The Metropolitan Museum of Art, New York, 1998, pp. 38–57, 105

GRAULICH 1982
Michel Graulich, *Mythes et rituels du Mexique ancien préhispanique*, Brussels, 1982

GRAULICH 1983
Michel Graulich, 'Myths of Paradise Lost in Pre-Hispanic Central Mexico', *Current Anthropology*, 5, 1983, pp. 575–88

GUALDI 1841
Pedro Gualdi, *Monumentos de México tomados del natural y litografiados*, Mexico City, 1841

GUARNOTTA 1980
Antonio Guarnotta, 'Report', in *Palazzo Vecchio: committenza e collezionismo Medicei*, Florence, 1980

GUILLIEM 1999
Salvador Guilliem, *Ofrendas a Ehécatl Quetzalcóatl en México: Tlatelolco*, Mexico City, 1999

GUSSINYER 1969
Jordi Gussinyer, 'Hallazgos en el Metro, conjunto de adoratorios superpuestos en Pino Suárez', *Boletín del INAH*, 36, 1969, pp. 33–37

GUSSINYER 1970
Jordi Gussinyer, 'Un adoratorio dedicado a Tláloc', *Boletín del INAH*, 39, 1970, pp. 7–12

GUSSINYER 1970B
Jordi Gussinyer, 'Un adoratorio azteca decorado con pinturas', *Boletín del INAH*, 40, 1970, pp. 30–35

GUSSINYER AND MARTÍNEZ 1976–77
Jordi Gussinyer and Alejandro Martínez, 'Una figurilla olmeca en un entierro del horizonte clásico', *Estudios de Cultura Maya*, 10, 1976–77, pp. 69–80

GUTIÉRREZ SOLANA 1983
Nelly Gutiérrez Solana, *Objetos ceremoniales en piedra de la cultura mexica*, Mexico City, 1983

GUZMAN 1939
Eulalia Guzman, *The Art of Map-making Among the Ancient Mexicans*, London, 1939, pp. 1–7

HAMPE 1927
Theodor Hampe, *Das Trachtenbuch des Christoph Weiditz*, Berlin, 1927

HAMY 1897
E.-T. Hamy, *Galerie américaine du Musée d'Ethnographie du Trocadéro: choix de pièces archéologiques et ethnographiques*, 2 vols, Paris, 1897

HAMY 1906
E.-T. Hamy, 'Note sur une statuette méxicaine', *Journal de la Société des Américanistes*, 3, 1, 1906, pp. 1–5

HARWOOD 2002
Joanne Harwood, 'Disguising Ritual: A Reassessment of Part 3 of the Codex Mendoza', unpublished PhD thesis, Department of Art History and Theory, University of Essex, 2002

HASSIG 1988
Ross Hassig, *Aztec Warfare: Imperial Expansion and Political Control*, Norman, 1988

HEIKAMP 1970
Detlef Heikamp with Ferdinand Anders, 'Mexikanische Altertümer aus süddeutschen Kunstkammern', *Pantheon*, 28, 1970, pp. 205–20

HEIKAMP 1972
Detlef Heikamp, *Mexico and the Medici*, Florence, 1972

HERNÁNDEZ PONS 1982
Elsa Hernández Pons, 'Sobre un conjunto de esculturas asociadas a las escalinatas del Templo Mayor', in *El Templo Mayor: excavaciones y estudios*, Mexico City, 1982, pp. 221–32

HERNÁNDEZ PONS 1996
Elsa Hernández Pons, 'Xiuhtecuhtli, deidad mexica del fuego', *Arqueología Mexicana*, 4, 20, 1996, pp. 68–70

HERNÁNDEZ PONS 1997
Elsa Hernández Pons, 'La plataforma mexica, las excavaciones de 1901 y los nuevos descubrimientos', in *La antigua Casa del Marqués del Apartado: arqueología e historia*, Mexico City, 1997, pp. 45–71

HERTZ 1851
Bram Hertz, *Catalogue of the Collection of Assyrian, Babylonian, Egyptian, Greek, Etruscan, Roman, Indian, Peruvian and Mexican Antiquities Formed by B. Hertz*, London, 1851

HEYDEN 1973
Doris Heyden, '¿Un Chicomostoc en Teotihuacan? La cueva bajo la pirámide del Sol', *Boletín del INAH (segunda época)*, 6, 1973, pp. 3–18

HEYDEN 1979
Doris Heyden, 'El "Signo del Año" en Tehuacán [*sic*], su supervivencia y el sentido sociopolítico del símbolo', in *Mesoamérica: Homenaje al doctor Paul Kirchhoff*, Barbara Dalhgren (ed.), Mexico City, 1979, pp. 61–86

HILDESHEIM 1986
Glanz und Untergang des Alten Mexiko: Die Azteken und ihre Vorläufer, Eva and Arne Eggebrecht (eds), exh. cat., 2 vols, Roemer- und Pelizaeus-Museum, Hildesheim, 1986; Haus der Kunst, Munich; Oberösterreichisches Landesmuseum, Linz; Louisiana Museum, Humlebæk; Musées Royaux d'Art et d'Histoire, Brussels

HISTORIA DE LOS MEXICANOS POR SUS PINTURAS 1965
Historia de los mexicanos por sus pinturas, in Garibay Kintana 1965, pp. 21–90

HISTORIA DE MÉXICO 1965
Historia de México (Histoire du Mechique), in Garibay Kintana 1965, pp. 91–120

HISTORIA TOLTECA-CHICHIMECA 1976
Historia Tolteca-Chichimeca, Paul Kirchhoff, Lina Odena Güemes and Luis Reyes García (trans. and eds), Mexico City, 1976

HOLMES 1897
William H. Holmes, *Archaeological Studies among the Ancient Cities of Mexico*, Chicago, 1897

HONOUR 1954
Hugh Honour, 'Curiosities of the Egyptian Hall', *Country Life*, 115, 2973, 1954, pp. 38–39

ICAZA Y GONDRA 1827
Isidro Icaza y Gondra, *Colección de las antigüedades mexicanas que existen en el Museo Nacional*, Mexico City, 1827

INAH 1956
Instituto Nacional de Antropología e Historia, *Guía oficial del Museo Nacional de Antropología*, Mexico City, 1956

INFORMACIÓN SOBRE LOS TRIBUTOS 1957
Información sobre los tributos que los indios pagaban a Moctezuma – año de 1554, France V. Scholes and Eleanor B. Adams (eds), Mexico City, 1957

JIMÉNEZ MORENO 1971
Wigberto Jiménez Moreno, '¿Religión o religiones mesoamericanas?', in *Verhandlungen des XXXVIII. Internationalen Amerikanistenkongresses*, vol. 3, Stuttgart and Munich, 1971, pp. 201–06

JONES 1987
Julie Jones, *The Metropolitan Museum of Art: The Pacific Islands, Africa, and the Americas*, New York, 1987

JONES AND KING 2002
Julie Jones and Heidi King, *The Metropolitan Museum of Art: Gold of the Americas*, Spring Bulletin of The Metropolitan Museum of Art, New York, 2002

JOYCE 1912
Thomas Athol Joyce, *A Short Guide to the American Antiquities in the British Museum*, London, 1912

JOYCE 1923
Thomas Athol Joyce, *Guide to the Maudslay Collection of Maya Sculptures (Casts and Originals) from Central America*, London, 1923

JOYCE N.D.
Thomas Athol Joyce, *Catalogue of a Collection of Mexican and Other American Antiquities (Including the Chavero Collection) in the Possession of Viscount Cowdray*, London, n.d.

KELEMEN 1943
Pál Kelemen, *Medieval American Art: A Survey in Two Volumes*, 2 vols, New York, 1943

KIDDER 1947
Alfred V. Kidder, *The Artifacts of Uaxactun, Guatemala*, Washington DC, 1947

KING 1831–48
Edward King, Lord Kingsborough, *The Antiquities of Mexico, Comprising Facsimiles of Ancient Mexican Painting and Hieroglyphs*, 9 vols, London, 1831–48

KING 1996
Jonathan King, 'William Bullock: Showman', in Mexico City 1996, pp. 119–21

KINZHALOV 1960
R. V. Kinzhalov, 'Atstekskoe zolotoe nagrudnoe ukrashenie', *Shornik Muzeia Antropologii I Etnografii*, 19, 1960, pp. 206–20

KLOR DE ALVA 1981
Jorge Klor de Alva, 'Martín Ocelotl, Clandestine Cult Leader', in *Struggle and Survival in Colonial America*, D. G. Sweet and Gary B. Nash (eds), Berkeley, 1981

KRICKEBERG 1960
Walter Krickeberg, 'Xochipilli und Chalchiuhtlicue: Zwei aztekische Steinfiguren in der völkerkundlichen Sammlung der Stadt Mannheim', *Baessler-Archiv: Beiträge zur Völkerkunde*, n.s., 8, 1960, pp. 1–30

KRICKEBERG 1985
Walter Krickeberg, *Mitos y leyendas de los aztecas, incas, mayas y muiscas*, Mexico City, 1985

KUBLER 1963
George Kubler, *The Shape of Time: Remarks on the History of Things*, New Haven and London, 2nd edition, 1963 (1962)

KUBLER 1985
George Kubler, 'The Cycle of Life and Death in Metropolitan Aztec Sculpture', in *Studies in Ancient American and European Art*, Thomas F. Reese (ed.), New Haven and London, 1985, pp. 219–24

KUBLER 1986
George Kubler, *Arte y arquitectura en la América precolonial*, Madrid, 1986

KUBLER 1991
George Kubler, *Esthetic Recognition of Ancient Amerindian Art*, New Haven and London, 1991

LANDA ET AL. 1988
María Elena Landa et al., *La Garrafa*, Mexico City, 1988

LANGLEY 1986
James C. Langley, *Symbolic Notation of Teotihuacan: Elements of Writing in a Mesoamerican Culture of the Classic Period*, Oxford, 1986

LA NIECE AND MEEKS 2000
Susan La Niece and Nigel Meeks, 'Diversity of Goldsmithing Traditions in the Americas and the Old World', in *Pre-Columbian Gold: Technology, Style and Iconography*, Colin McEwan (ed.), London, 2000

LAS CASAS 1986
Bartolomé de las Casas, *Historia de las Indias*, Agustín Millares Carlo (ed.), Mexico City, 1986

LAURENCICH MINELLI 1992
Terra Ameriga. Il Mondo Nuovo nelle collezioni emiliano-romagnole, L. Laurencich Minelli (ed.), Bologna, 1992

LAURENCICH MINELLI AND FILIPETTI 1983
L. Laurencich Minelli and A. Filipetti, 'Per le collezioni americanistiche del Museo Cospiano e dell'Istituto delle Scienze. Alcuni oggetti ritrovati a Bologna', *Archivio per l'Antropologia e l'Etnologia*, 113, pp. 207–25

LAVACHERY AND MINNAERT 1931
Henri Lavachery and Paul Minnaert, 'La Collection d'antiquités mexicaines de M. Aug. Génin', *Bulletin de la Société des Américanistes de Belgique*, 5, 1931

'LEGEND OF THE SUNS' 1992
Anonymous, 'Legend of the Suns', in Bierhorst 1992

LEHMAN 1906
Walter Lehman, 'Die Mexikanischer Grünsteinfigur des Musée Guimet in Paris', *Globus*, 90, 1906, pp. 60–61

LEÓN-PORTILLA 1959
Miguel León-Portilla, *La filosofía náhuatl estudiada en sus fuentes*, Mexico City, 1959

LEÓN-PORTILLA 1962
Miguel León-Portilla, *The Broken Spears: The Aztec Account of the Conquest of Mexico*, Boston, 1962

LEÓN-PORTILLA 1963
Miguel León-Portilla, *Aztec Thought and Culture*, Jack Emory Davis (trans.), Norman, 1963

LEÓN-PORTILLA 2002
Miguel León-Portilla, 'A Nahuatl Concept of Art', in Amsterdam 2002, pp. 46–53

LEÓN-PORTILLA AND AGUILERA 1986
Miguel León-Portilla and Carmen Aguilera, *Mapa de México Tenochtitlan y sus contornos hacia 1550*, Mexico City, 1986

LEÓN Y GAMA 1792
Antonio León y Gama, *Descripción histórica y cronológica de las dos piedras que con ocasión del nuevo empedrado que se está formando en la plaza principal de México, se hallaron en ella el año de 1790*, 1st edition, Mexico City, 1792; 2nd edition, Carlos María de Bustamante (ed.), Mexico City, 1832

'LEYENDA DE LOS SOLES' 1945
Anonymous, 'Leyenda de los soles', in Códice Chimalpopoca 1945, pp. 119–64

LIND 1994
Michael D. Lind, 'Cholula and Mixteca Polychromes: Two Mixteca-Puebla Regional Sub-styles', in *Mixteca-Puebla: Discoveries and Research in Mesoamerican Art and Archaeology*, Henry B. Nicholson and Eloise Quiñones Keber (eds), Culver City, California, 1994, pp. 79–99

LINNÉ 1948
Sigvald Linné, *El Valle y la Ciudad de México en 1550*, Stockholm, 1948

LIVERPOOL 1973
Charles Hunt, *Men and Gods of Ancient America: An Exhibition of Treasures from Mexico and Peru*, exh. cat., Liverpool Museum, 1973

LOCKHART 1992
James Lockhart, *The Nahuas after the Conquest: A Social and Cultural History of the Indians of Central Mexico, Sixteenth through Eighteenth Centuries*, Stanford, 1992

LONDON 1824
William Bullock, *Catalogue of the Exhibition, called Modern Mexico; Containing a Panoramic View of the City, with Specimens of the Natural History of New Spain…Now Open for Public Inspection at the Egyptian Hall, Piccadilly*, exh. cat., London Museum of Natural History and Pantherion, London, 1824

LONDON 1824B
William Bullock, *A Description of the Unique Exhibition, called Ancient Mexico: Collected on the Spot in 1823…and Now Open for Public Inspection at the Egyptian Hall, Piccadilly*, exh. cat., London Museum of Natural History and Pantherion, London, 1824

LONDON 1824C
William Bullock, *A Descriptive Catalogue of the Exhibition, entitled Ancient and Modern Mexico…Now Open…at the Egyptian Hall, etc.*, exh. cat., London Museum of Natural History and Pantherion, London, 1824

LONDON 1920
Thomas Athol Joyce, *Catalogue of an Exhibition of Objects of Indigenous American Art*, exh. cat., Burlington Arts Club, London, 1920

LONDON 1947
Art of Ancient America, with a foreword by Irwin Bullock and G. H. S. Bushnell, exh. cat., Berkeley Galleries, London, June–August 1947

LONDON 1953
Exhibition of Mexican Art from Pre-Columbian Times to the Present Day Organised Under the Auspices of the Mexican Government, The Tate Gallery, London, 4 March to 26 April 1953, exh. cat., Arts Council of Great Britain, Tate Gallery, London, 1953

LONDON 1953B
Mexican Art from 1500 BC to the Present Day. Illustrated Supplement to the Catalogue of an Exhibition at the Tate Gallery, London, 4 March to 26 April 1953, Arts Council of Great Britain, Tate Gallery, London, 1953

LONDON 1958
An Exhibition of Pre-Columbian Art, exh. cat., Gimpel Fils, London, 1958

LONDON 1965
Henry Christy: A Pioneer of Anthropology. An Exhibition in the King Edward VII Gallery, exh. cat., British Museum, London, 1965

LONDON 1971
Manuel Barbachano Ponce, *Maya Sculpture and Pottery from Mexico: The Manuel Barbachano Ponce Collection*, exh. cat., Museum of Mankind, London, 1971; Museum für Völkerkunde, Frankfurt; Nationalmuseum, Stockholm

LONDON 1973
Elizabeth Carmichael, *The British and the Maya*, exh. cat., Museum of Mankind, London, 1973

LONDON 1982
The Other America: Native Artefacts from the New World, Valerie Fraser and Gordon Brotherston (eds), exh. cat., Museum of Mankind, London, 1982

LONDON 1985
Eduardo Paolozzi, *Lost Magic Kingdoms and Six Paper Moons from Nahuatl: An Exhibition at the Museum of Mankind*, exh. cat., Museum of Mankind, London, 1985

LONDON 1986
Lost Magic Kingdoms and Six Paper Moons from Nahuatl: An Exhibition at the Museum of Mankind Created by Eduardo Paolozzi from 28 November 1985, London, 1985

LONDON 1991
Elizabeth Carmichael and Chlöe Sayer, *The Skeleton at the Feast: The Day of the Dead in Mexico*, exh. cat., Museum of Mankind, London, 1991

LONDON 1992
The Art of Ancient Mexico, Marianne Ryan (ed.), exh. cat., Hayward Gallery, London, 1992; Oriana Baddeley, *The Art of Ancient Mexico: Loans from the British Museum. Supplement to the Catalogue*, London, 1992

LONDON 1992B
Gordon Brotherston, *Painted Books of Mexico*, exh. cat., British Museum, London, 1992

LONDON 2000
Gabriele Finaldi, *The Image of Christ*, exh. cat., National Gallery, London, 2000

LÓPEZ AUSTIN 1985
Alfredo López Austin, 'El texto sahaguntino sobre los mexicas', *Anales de Antropología*, 22, 1985, pp. 287–336

LÓPEZ AUSTIN 1990
Alfredo López Austin, 'Del origen de los mexicas: ¿nomadismo o migración?', *Historia Mexicana*, 155, 1990, pp. 663–75

LÓPEZ AUSTIN 1993
Alfredo López Austin, *The Myths of the Opossum: Pathways of Mesoamerican Mythology*, Albuquerque, 1993

LÓPEZ AUSTIN 1994–97
Alfredo López Austin, 'La religione della Mesoamerica', in *Storia delle religioni*, Giovanni Filoramo (ed.), vol. 5, Rome, 1994–97, pp. 5–75

LÓPEZ AUSTIN 1996
Alfredo López Austin, 'La cosmovisión mesoamericana', in *Temas mesoamericanos*, Sonia Lombardo and Enrique Nalda (eds), Mexico City, 1996, pp. 471–507

LÓPEZ AUSTIN 1997
Alfredo López Austin, *Tamoanchan, Tlalocan. Places of Mist*, Niwot, 1997

LÓPEZ AUSTIN AND LÓPEZ LUJÁN 2001
Alfredo López Austin and Leonardo López Luján, 'Los mexicas y el Chac-mool', *Arqueología Mexicana*, 49, 2001, pp. 68–73

LÓPEZ LUJÁN 1989
Leonardo López Luján, *La recuperación mexica del pasado teotihuacano*, Mexico City, 1989

LÓPEZ LUJÁN 1991
Leonardo López Luján, 'Peces y moluscos en el libro undécimo del *Códice Florentino*', in *La fauna en el Templo Mayor*, O. J. Polaco (ed.), Mexico City, 1991, pp. 213–63

LÓPEZ LUJÁN 1993
Leonardo López Luján, *Las ofrendas del Templo Mayor de Tenochtitlan*, Mexico City, 1993

LÓPEZ LUJÁN 1994
Leonardo López Luján, *The Offerings of the Templo Mayor of Tenochtitlan*, Niwot, 1994

LÓPEZ LUJÁN 1995
Leonardo López Luján, 'Guerra y muerte en Tenochtitlán: descubrimientos en el Recinto de los Guerreros Águila', *Arqueología Mexicana*, 2, 12, 1995, pp. 75–77

LÓPEZ LUJÁN 1998
Leonardo López Luján, 'Anthropologie religieuse du Templo Mayor, Mexico: la Maison des Aigles', PhD thesis, University of Paris-X, Nanterre, 1998

LÓPEZ LUJÁN 2001
Leonardo López Luján, 'Arqueología de la arqueología: de la época prehispánica al siglo XVIII', *Arqueología Mexicana*, 52, 2001, pp. 20–27

LÓPEZ LUJÁN FORTHCOMING
Leonardo López Luján, *La Casa de las Águilas: un ejemplo de arquitectura sacra mexica*, Mexico City, in press

LÓPEZ LUJÁN AND MANZANILLA 2001
Leonardo López Luján and Linda Manzanilla, 'Excavaciones en un palacio de Teotihuacan: el Proyecto Xalla', *Arqueología Mexicana*, 50, 2001, pp. 14–15

LÓPEZ LUJÁN AND MERCADO 1996
Leonardo López Luján and Vida Mercado, 'Dos esculturas de Mictlantecuhtli encontradas en el Recinto Sagrado de México-Tenochtitlan', *Estudios de Cultura Náhuatl*, 26, 1996, pp. 41–68

LÓPEZ LUJÁN, NEFF AND SUGIYAMA 2000
Leonardo López Luján, Hector Neff and Saburo Sugiyama, 'The 9-Xi Vase: A Classic Thin Orange Vessel Found at Tenochtitlan', in Carrasco, Jones and Sessions 2000, pp. 219–49

LÓPEZ LUJÁN, TORRES TREJO AND MONTÚFAR 2002
Leonardo López Luján, Jaime Torres Trejo and Aurora Montúfar, 'Los materiales constructivos del Templo Mayor de Tenochtitlan', *Estudios de Cultura Náhuatl*, 33, 2002, in press

LOS ANGELES 1963
Fernando Gamboa, *Master Works of Mexican Art from Pre-Columbian Times to the Present*, exh. cat., Los Angeles County Museum of Art, 1963

LOS ANGELES 2001
The Journey to Aztlan: Art from a Mythic Homeland, Virginia M. Fields and Victor Zamudio-Taylor (eds), exh. cat., Los Angeles County Museum of Art, 2001; Austin Museum of Art; Albuquerque Museum

LOTHROP 1957
S. K. Lothrop, *Robert Woods Bliss Collection: Pre-Columbian Art*, London, 1957

LOTHROP 1964
S. K. Lothrop, *Treasures of Ancient America*, New York, 1964

MACCURDY 1910
George Grant MacCurdy, 'An Aztec "Calendar Stone" in the Yale University Museum', *American Anthropologist*, n.s., 12, 4, 1910, pp. 481–96

MCEWAN 1994
Colin McEwan, *Ancient Mexico in the British Museum*, London, 1994

MCVICKER 1989
Mary Frech McVicker, 'From Parlours to Pyramids', in Bristol 1989, pp. 12–23

MCVICKER AND PALKA 2001
Donald McVicker and Joel W. Palka, 'A Maya Carved Shell Plaque from Tula, Hidalgo, Mexico: Comparative Study', *Ancient Mesoamerica*, 12, 2001, pp. 175–97

MADRID 1986
México antiguo, exh. cat., Museo de América, Madrid, 1986

MADRID 1990
Arte precolombino de México, Roberto García Moll, Beatriz de la Fuente, Sonia Lombardo and Felipe Solís Olguín (eds), exh. cat., Palacio de Velázquez, Madrid, 1990

MADRID 1992
Azteca-Mexica: las culturas del México antiguo, José Alcina Franch, Miguel León-Portilla and Eduardo Matos Moctezuma (eds), exh. cat., Sociedad Estatal Quinto Centenario, Madrid, 1992

MADRID 1994
Jean Paul Barbier, Iris Barry, Michel Butor, Conceição G. Corrêa, Danièle Lavallée, Octavio Paz and Henri Stierlin, *Arte precolombino en la colección Barbier-Mueller*, exh. cat., Casa de América, Madrid, 1994

MANCHESTER 1992
George Bankes and Elizabeth Baquedano, *Sañuq and Toltecatl: Pre-Columbian Arts of Middle and South America*, exh. cat., Manchester Museum, 1992

MANRIQUE 1960
Jorge Manrique, 'Introducir la divinidad en las cosas: finalidad del arte náhuatl', in *Estudios de Cultura Náhuatl*, 2, 1960, pp. 197–207

MANRIQUE 1988
Leonardo Manrique and Jimena Manrique, *Flora y fauna mexicana: panorama actual*, Mexico City, 1988

MANZANILLA AND LÓPEZ LUJÁN 2001
Linda Manzanilla and Leonardo López Luján, 'Exploraciones en un posible palacio de Teotihuacan: el Proyecto Xalla (2000–2001)', *Mexicon*, 23, 2001, pp. 58–61

MARQUINA 1951
Ignacio Marquina, *Arquitectura prehispánica*, Mexico City, 1951

MARQUINA 1960
Ignacio Marquina, *El Templo Mayor de México*, Mexico City, 1960

MARQUINA 1964
Ignacio Marquina, *Arquitectura prehispánica*, 2nd edition, Mexico City, 1964

MARTÍNEZ DE LA TORRE 1992
Cruz Martínez de la Torre, 'Obras de arte americano en el Patrimonio Nacional', *Reales Sitios*, 112, 1992, pp. 17–28

MARTÍNEZ DEL RÍO 1960
Marita Martínez del Río, 'Comentarios sobre el arte plumario durante la colonia', *Artes de México*, 17, 137, 1960, pp. 86–98

MARTÍNEZ MARÍN 1963
Carlos Martínez Marín, 'La cultura de los mexicanos durante su migración. Nuevas ideas', *Cuadernos Americanos*, 4, 1963, pp. 175–83

MATEOS HIGUERA 1992–94
Salvador Mateos Higuera, *Enciclopedia gráfica del México antiguo*, 4 vols, Mexico City, 1992–94

MATOS MOCTEZUMA 1965
Eduardo Matos Moctezuma, 'El adoratorio decorado de las calles de Argentina', *Anales del Instituto Nacional de Antropología e Historia*, 17, 1965, pp. 127–38

MATOS MOCTEZUMA 1979
Eduardo Matos Moctezuma, 'Una máscara olmeca en el Templo Mayor de Tenochtitlan', *Anales de Antropología*, 16, 1979, pp. 11–19

MATOS MOCTEZUMA 1980
Eduardo Matos Moctezuma, 'El arte en el Templo Mayor', in Mexico City 1980, pp. 13–15

MATOS MOCTEZUMA 1981
Eduardo Matos Moctezuma, 'Los hallazgos de la arqueología', in *El Templo Mayor*, Mexico City, 1981

MATOS MOCTEZUMA 1983
Eduardo Matos Moctezuma, 'Notas sobre algunas urnas funerarias del Templo Mayor', *Jahrbuch für Geschichte von Staat, Wirtschaft und Gesellschaft Lateinamerikas*, 20, 1983, pp. 17–32

MATOS MOCTEZUMA 1984
Eduardo Matos Moctezuma, 'Los edificios aledaños al Templo Mayor', *Estudios de Cultura Náhuatl*, 17, 1984, pp. 15–21

MATOS MOCTEZUMA 1986
Eduardo Matos Moctezuma, *Vida y muerte en el Templo Mayor*, Mexico City, 1986

MATOS MOCTEZUMA 1988
Eduardo Matos Moctezuma, *The Great Temple of the Aztecs*, London and New York, 1988

MATOS MOCTEZUMA 1989
Eduardo Matos Moctezuma, *Los aztecas*, Barcelona and Madrid, 1989

MATOS MOCTEZUMA 1990
Eduardo Matos Moctezuma, 'El águila, el jaguar y la serpiente', *Artes de México*, 7, 1990, pp. 54–66

MATOS MOCTEZUMA 1991
Eduardo Matos Moctezuma, 'Las seis Coyolxauhqui: variaciones sobre un mismo tema', *Estudios de Cultura Náhuatl*, 21, 1991, pp. 15–29

MATOS MOCTEZUMA 1993
Eduardo Matos Moctezuma, 'Los mexicas y el rumbo sur del universo', in *El arte de Mezcala*, Mexico City, 1993, pp. 120–39

MATOS MOCTEZUMA 1994
Eduardo Matos Moctezuma, 'Los mexica y llegaron los españoles', in *México en el mundo de las colecciones de arte*, vol. 2, *Mesoamérica*, Mexico City, 1994, pp. 179–243

MATOS MOCTEZUMA 2000
Eduardo Matos Moctezuma, 'Rostros de la muerte', *Arqueología Mexicana*, 6, 2000, pp. 12–17

MATOS MOCTEZUMA, BRODA AND CARRASCO 1987
Eduardo Matos Moctezuma, Johanna Broda and David Carrasco, *The Great Temple of Tenochtitlan*, London and New York, 1987

MATOS MOCTEZUMA AND LÓPEZ LUJÁN 1993
Eduardo Matos Moctezuma and Leonardo López Luján, 'Teotihuacan and Its Mexica Legacy', in San Francisco 1993, pp. 156–65

MATRÍCULA DE TRIBUTOS 1997
Matrícula de Tributos o Códice Moctezuma, Ferdinand Anders, Maarten Jansen and Luis Reyes García (eds), Graz and Mexico City, 1997

MAUDSLAY 1899
Arthur Percival Maudslay and Anne Cary Maudslay, *A Glimpse at Guatemala, and Some Notes on the Ancient Monuments of Central America…with Maps, Plans, Photographs, etc.*, London, 1899

MAYER 1844
Brantz Mayer, *Mexico as It Was and as It Is*, New York, 1844

MAZA 1971
Francisco de la Maza, 'La mitra mexicana de plumas de El Escorial', *Artes de México*, 137, 1971, pp. 71–72

MEDELLÍN ZENIL 1983
Alfonso Medellín Zenil, *Obras maestras del Museo de Xalapa*, Veracruz, 1983

MEMORIAL DE LOS INDIOS DE TEPETLAOZTOC 1992
Memorial de los indios de Tepetlaoztoc o Códice Kingsborough, Perla Valle (ed.), Mexico City, 1992

MENDIETA 1945
Gerónimo de Mendieta, *Historia eclesiástica indiana*, 4 vols, Mexico City, 1945

MERLO 1995
Eduardo Merlo, 'Maquetas prehispánicas de Calipan', *Arqueología Mexicana*, 3, 9, 1995, pp. 60–62

MEXICO CITY 1980
El arte del Templo Mayor, exh. cat., Museo del Palacio de Bellas Artes, Mexico City, 1980

MEXICO CITY 1995
Dioses del México antiguo, Eduardo Matos Moctezuma, Alfredo López Austin, Miguel León-Portilla, Felipe Solís Olguín, Miguel A. Fernández and José Enrique Ortiz Lanz (eds), exh. cat., Antiguo Colegio de San Ildefonso, Mexico City, 1995

MEXICO CITY 1996
European Traveller-artists in Nineteenth-century Mexico, exh. cat., Palacio de Iturbide, Mexico City, 1996

MEXICO CITY 1997
La cerámica de la Ciudad de México (1325–1917), Karina Simpson (ed.), exh. cat., Museo de la Ciudad de México, Mexico City, 1997

MEXICO CITY 2001
Descubridores del pasado en Mesoamérica, exh. cat., Antiguo Colegio de San Ildefonso, Mexico City, 2001

MEYER AND SHERMAN 1979
Michael C. Meyer and William L. Sherman, *The Course of Mexican History*, New York, 1979

MILAN 1990
L'America prima di Colombo: arte precolombiano dal 2000 a.C. agli Aztechi, exh. cat., Castello di Lerici, Milan, 1990

MILLER AND TAUBE 1993
Mary Miller and Karl Taube, *The Gods and Symbols of Ancient Mexico and the Maya: An Illustrated Dictionary of Mesoamerican Religion*, London, 1993

MILNE 1984
Michael George Milne, *Diego Durán: Historia de las Indias de Nueva España*, Ann Arbor, 1984

MONGNE 1994
Pascale Mongne, 'La Messe de Saint Grégoire du Musée d'Auch', *Revue du Louvre*, nos 5–6, 1994, pp. 38–47

MONJARÁS-RUIZ 1987
Mitos cosmogónicos del México indígena, Jesús Monjarás-Ruiz (ed.), Mexico City, 1987

MONTERROSA 1967
Mariano Monterrosa, 'Cruces del siglo XVI', *Boletín del INAH*, 30, 1967, pp. 16–19

MOORE 1981
Henry Moore, *Henry Moore at the British Museum*, London, 1981

MORENO DE LOS ARCOS 1967
Roberto Moreno de los Arcos, 'Los cinco soles cosmogónicos', *Estudios de Cultura Náhuatl*, 7, 1967, pp. 183–210

MÜLHLENPFORDT 1844
D. T. Mülhlenpfordt, *Intento de una descripción exacta de la República de México*, Hanover, 1844

MÜLLER 1970
Florencia Müller, 'La cerámica de Cholula', in *Proyecto Cholula*, Ignacio Marquina (ed.), Mexico City, 1970, pp. 129–42

MUNICH 1958
Präkolumbische Kunst aus Mexiko und Mittelamerika, exh. cat., Haus der Kunst, Munich, 1958

MUNICH 1968
Altamerikanische Kunst: Mexico-Peru, Andreas Lommel (ed.), exh. cat., Staatliches Museum für Völkerkunde, Munich, 1968

MUNICH 2001
Gold: Magie, Mythos, Macht – Gold der Alten und Neuen Welt, Ludwig Wamser and Rupert Gebhard (eds), exh. cat., Archäologische Staatssammlung: Museum für Vor– und Frühgeschichte, Munich, 2001

MUÑOZ CAMARGO 1981
Diego Muñoz Camargo, *Descripción de la ciudad y provincia de Tlaxcala de las Indias y del Mar Océano para el buen gobierno y ennoblecimiento dellas*, René Acuña (ed.), Mexico City, 1981

MUÑOZ CAMARGO 1984
Diego Muñoz Camargo, *Descripción de la ciudad y provincia de Tlaxcala, Relaciones geográficas del siglo XVI, Tlaxcala*, vol. 1, Mexico City, 1984

NALDA AND LÓPEZ CAMACHO 1995
Enrique Nalda and Javier López Camacho, 'Investigaciones arqueológicas en el sur de Quintana Roo', *Arqueología Mexicana*, 14, 1995, pp. 12–27

NAVARRETE 1968
Carlos Navarrete, 'Dos deidades de las aguas, modeladas en resina de árbol', *Boletín del INAH*, 33, 1968, pp. 39–42

NAVARRETE 1995
Carlos Navarrete, 'Anotaciones sobre el reuso de piezas durante el Postclásico mesoamericano', *Utz'ib*, 3, 1995, pp. 22–26

NAVARRETE AND CRESPO 1971
Carlos Navarrete and Ana María Crespo, 'Un atlante mexica y algunas consideraciones sobre los relieves del Cerro de la Malinche, Hidalgo', *Estudios de Cultura Náhuatl*, 9, 1971, pp. 11–15

NEBEL 1963
Carlos Nebel, *Viaje pintoresco y arqueológico sobre la parte más interesante de la República Mexicana, en los años transcurridos desde 1829 hasta 1834*, 2nd edition, Mexico City, 1963

NEW YORK 1940
Alfonso Caso, Antonio Castro Leal, Miguel Covarrubias, Roberto Montenegro and Manuel Toussaint, *Twenty Centuries of Mexican Art*, exh. cat., Museum of Modern Art, New York, 1940; published in conjunction with the Instituto Nacional de Antropología e Historia, Mexico City

NEW YORK 1970
Before Cortés: Sculpture of Middle America, Elizabeth Kennedy Easby and John F. Scott (eds), exh. cat., The Metropolitan Museum of Art, New York, 1970

NEW YORK 1976
Aztec Stone Sculpture, Esther Pasztory (ed.), exh. cat., Center for Inter-American Relations, New York, 1976

NEW YORK 1983
The Vatican Collections: The Papacy and Art, exh. cat., The Metropolitan Museum of Art, New York, 1983

NEW YORK 1990
Mexico: Splendors of Thirty Centuries, John P. O'Neill and Kathleen Howard (eds), exh. cat., The Metropolitan Museum of Art, New York, 1990; San Antonio Museum of Art; Los Angeles County Museum of Art

NICHOLSON 1955
Henry B. Nicholson, 'Native Historical Traditions of Nuclear America and the Problem of Their Archaeological Correlation', *American Anthropologist*, 57, 1955, pp. 594–613

NICHOLSON 1971
Henry B. Nicholson, 'Major Sculpture in Pre-Hispanic Central Mexico City', in Ekholm and Bernal 1971, pp. 92–134

NICHOLSON 1971B
Henry B. Nicholson, 'Religion in Pre-Hispanic Central Mexico', in Ekholm and Bernal 1971, pp. 395–446

NICHOLSON 1979
Henry B. Nicholson, 'Correlating Mesoamerican Historical Traditions with Archaeological Sequence: Some Methodological Considerations', in *Actes du XLIIe Congrès International des Américanistes, 1976*, Paris, 1979, pp. 187–98

NICHOLSON 1988
Henry B. Nicholson, 'The Iconography of the Deity Representations in Fray Bernardino de Sahagún's *Primeros Memoriales*: Huitzilopochtli and Chalchiuhtlicue', in *The Work of Bernardino de Sahagún, Pioneer Ethnographer of Sixteenth-century Aztec Mexico*, Jorge Klor de Alva, Henry B. Nicholson and Eloise Quiñones Keber (eds), New York, 1988, pp. 229–53

NICHOLSON 1991
Henry B. Nicholson, 'The *Octli* Cult in Late Pre-Hispanic Central Mexico', in *To Change Place: Aztec Ceremonial Landscape*, David Carrasco (ed.), Niwot, 1991, pp. 158–87

NICHOLSON 2001
Henry B. Nicholson, *Topiltzin Quetzalcoatl. The Once and Future Lord of the Toltecs*, Boulder, 2001

NOGUERA 1954
Eduardo Noguera, *La cerámica arqueológica de Cholula*, Mexico City, 1954

NOWOTNY 1959
Karl Anton Nowotny, *Americana*, Archiv für Völkerkunde, vol. 14, Vienna, 1959

NOWOTNY 1960
Karl Anton Nowotny, *Mexikanische Kostbarkeiten aus Kunstkammern der Renaissance*, Vienna, 1960

NOWOTNY 1961
Karl Anton Nowotny, *Americana*, Archiv für Völkerkunde, vol. 16, Vienna, 1961

NUREMBERG 1992
Focus Behaim Globus, exh. cat., Germanisches Nationalmuseum, Nuremberg, 2 vols, 1992

NUREMBERG 1993
Ludwigs Lust: Die Sammlung Irene und Peter Ludwig, Michael Eissenhauer (ed.), exh. cat., Germanisches Nationalmuseum, Nuremberg, 1993

OLIVIER 1997
Guilhem Olivier, *Moqueries et métamorphose d'un dieu aztèque. Tezcatlipoca, le 'Seigneur au miroir fumant'*, Paris, 1997

OLMEDO VERA 2001
Bertina Olmedo Vera, 'Mezcala', in *The Oxford Encyclopaedia of Mesoamerican Cultures*, David Carrasco (ed.), Oxford and New York, 2001, vol. 2, pp. 303–05

OLMEDO VERA 2002
Bertina Olmedo Vera, *Los templos rojos del recinto sagrado de Tenochtitlan*, Mexico City, 2002

OMAN 1968
Charles Oman, *The Golden Age of Hispanic Silver 1400–1665*, London, 1968

PARIS 1928
Les Arts anciens de l'Amérique: exposition organisée au Musée des Arts Décoratifs, exh. cat., Palais du Louvre, Paris, 1928

PARIS 1981
Mexique d'hier et d'aujourd'hui: découverte du Templo Mayor de Mexico; artistes contemporains, exh. cat., Ministère des Relations Extérieures, Paris, 1981

PARIS 2000
Esther Acevedo, Teresa del Conde, Eloísa Uribe Hernández, Jacques Lafaye, Carlos Monsiváis, Efraín Castro Morales and Salvador Rueda Smithers, *Soleils mexicains*, exh. cat., Petit Palais, Musée des Beaux-Arts de la Ville de Paris, 2000

PARSONS 1980
Lee Parsons, *Pre-Columbian Art*, New York, 1980

PASZTORY 1983
Esther Pasztory, *Aztec Art*, New York, 1983

PAZ 1989
Octavio Paz, *Los privilegios de la vista. Arte de México*, Mexico City, 1989

PEÑAFIEL 1910
Antonio Peñafiel, *Descripción del Templo Mayor de México antiguo*, Mexico City, 1910

PHILADELPHIA 1954
George Kubler, *The Louise and Walter Arensberg Collection of Pre-Columbian Sculpture*, exh. cat., Philadelphia Museum of Art, 1954

PIJOÁN 1946
José Pijoán, *Arte precolombino, mexicano y maya, Summa Artis: historia general del arte*, vol. 10, Madrid, 1946

PIÑA CHAN 1982
Román Piña Chan, *Los olmecas antiguos*, Mexico City, 1982

POHL 2002
John M. D. Pohl, 'Narrative Art, Craft Production, and Gift Economy in Postclassic Oaxaca and Related Areas of Mexico: Workbook for the Advanced Mixtec Class, Mixtec Workshop at the Maya Meetings, University of Texas', Austin, 2002

POLACO AND GUZMÁN 2001
Óscar Polaco and Ana Fabiola Guzmán, *Los peces arqueológicos de la ofrenda 23 del Templo Mayor*, Mexico City, 2001

PORTER 1948
Muriel N. Porter, 'Pipas precortesianas', *Acta Antropológica*, vol. 3/2, Mexico City, 1948

PREM AND DYCKERHOFF 1986
Hanns J. Prem and Ursula Dyckerhoff, *El antiguo México*, Esplugues de Llobregat, 1986

PROSKOURIAKOFF 1974
Tatiana Proskouriakoff, *Jades from the Cenote of Sacrifice, Chichén Itzá, Yucatan*, Cambridge, Mass., 1974

PURCHAS 1624
Samuel Purchas, *Haklvtvs Posthvmvs; or Pvrchas his Pilgrimes. Contayning a History of the World, in Sea Voyages & lande Travells, by Englifhmen & others. Wherein Gods Wonders in Nature & Providence, The Actes, Arts, Varieties & Vanities of Men, vvᵗʰ a world of the Worlds Rarities are by a world of Eyewitnefse-Authors, Related to the World. Some left written by Mr Hakluyt at his death & perfected. All examined, abreviated, Illvftrated vᵗʰ Notes, Enlarged vᵗʰ Difcourses Adorned vᵗʰ pictures, and Exprefsed in Mapps. In fower Parts Each containing five Bookes*, London, 1624; *Pvrchas his Pilgrimes in Five Bookes…*, London, 1625

QUIÑONES KEBER 1993
Eloise Quiñones Keber, 'Quetzalcoatl as Dynastic Patron: The "Acuecuexatl Stone" Reconsidered', in *The Symbolism in the Plastic and Pictorial Representations of Ancient Mexico: A Symposium of the 46th International Congress of Americanists, Amsterdam, 1988*, Jacqueline de Durand-Forest and Marc Eisinger (eds), Bonn, 1993, pp. 149–55

RAMÍREZ 1844–46
José Fernando Ramírez, 'Descripción de cuatro lápidas monumentales conservadas en el Museo Nacional de México, seguida de un ensayo sobre su interpretación', in *Historia de la conquista de México de William H. Prescott*, Mexico City, 1844–46, pp. 106–24

RAMÍREZ 1864
José Fernando Ramírez, 'Antigüedades mexicanas conservadas en el Museo Nacional de México', in *México y sus Alrededores*, 2nd edition, Mexico, 1864, pp. 48–57

RAMSEY 1975
James Ramsey, 'An Analysis of Mixtec Minor Art, with a Catalogue', 2 vols, PhD thesis, Tulane University, New Orleans, 1975

RATHJE 1973
William L. Rathje, 'El descubrimiento de un jade olmeca en la isla de Cozumel, Quintana Roo, México', *Estudios de Cultura Maya*, 9, 1973, pp. 85–91

REYERO 1978
Manuel Reyero, *Fundación Cultural Televisa: Colección prehispánica*, Mexico City, 1978

RIGOLI 1992
A. Rigoli, *Due 'Mondi' a confronto*, Milan, 1992

ROBERTSON 1959
Donald Robertson, *Mexican Manuscripts of the Early Colonial Period: The Metropolitan Schools*, New Haven, 1959

ROBERTSON 1968
Donald Robertson, 'Paste-over Illustration in the Durán Codex of Madrid', *Tlalocan*, 5, 1968, pp. 340–48

ROMANCES DE LOS SEÑORES 1964
Romances de los Señores de Nueva España, Ángel María Garibay Kintana (trans.), Mexico City, 1964

ROME 1960
Arte Precolombiana del Messico e dell'America Centrale, exh. cat., Centro di Azione Latina, Rome, 1960

ROMERO 1982
Erica Romero, 'Evidencias post-teotihuacanas en el lado este de la Ciudadela', in *Teotihuaca 80–82, primeros resultados*, Rubén Cabrera Castro et al. (eds), Mexico City, 1982, pp. 149–54

ROUSSELL 1957
The National Museum of Denmark, Aage Roussell (ed.), Copenhagen, 1957

SAHAGÚN 1905
Bernardino de Sahagún, *Historia general de las cosas de Nueva España*, Francisco del Paso y Troncoso (ed.), vol. 5, Madrid, 1905

SAHAGÚN 1950–82
Bernardino de Sahagún, *Florentine Codex: A General History of the Things of New Spain, Books 1–12*, Arthur J. O. Anderson and Charles E. Dibble (trans. and eds), Santa Fe, 1950–82

SAHAGÚN 1979
Bernardino de Sahagún, *Códice florentino. Historia general de las cosas de Nueva España*, facsimile, 3 vols, Mexico City, 1979

SAHAGÚN 1988
Bernardino de Sahagún, *Historia General de las cosas de Nueva España*, with introduction, glossary and notes by Alfredo López Austin and Josefina García Quintana, 2 vols, Madrid, 1988

SAHAGÚN 2000
Bernardino de Sahagún, *Historia general de las cosas de Nueva España*, Mexico City, 2000

SANDERS, PARSONS AND SANTLEY 1979
William T. Sanders, Jeffrey R. Parsons and Robert S. Santley, *The Basin of Mexico: Ecological Processes in the Evolution of Civilization*, New York and San Francisco, 1979

SANDOVAL 1945
Fernando B. Sandoval, 'La relación de la conquista de México en la Historia de Fray Diego Durán', in *Estudios de Historiografía de la Nueva España*, Mexico City, 1945, pp. 51–90

SAN FRANCISCO 1993
Teotihuacan: Art from the City of the Gods, Kathleen Berrin and Esther Pasztory (eds), exh. cat., Fine Arts Museums of San Francisco, 1993

SANTA BARBARA 1942
Maurice Ries, *Ancient American Art, 500 BC – AD 1500, The Catalog of an Exhibition of the Art of the Pre-European Americas*, exh. cat., Santa Barbara Museum of Art, 1942

SANTA BARBARA 1992
Cambios: The Spirit of Transformation in Spanish Colonial Art, Gabrielle Palmer and Donna Pierce, exh. cat., Santa Barbara Museum of Art, 1992

SAUNDERS 1998
Icons of Power: Feline Symbolism in the Americas, Nicholas J. Saunders (ed.), London, 1998

SAUNDERS 2001
Nicholas J. Saunders, 'A Dark Light: Reflections on Obsidian in Mesoamerica', *World Archaeology*, 33, 2, 2001, pp. 220–36

SAUNDERS FORTHCOMING
Nicholas J. Saunders, *Mirrors, Aras and Tezcatlipoca: Obsidian Sorcery in a Colonial Landscape*, forthcoming

SAVILLE 1922
Marshall H. Saville, *Turquoise Mosaic Art in Ancient Mexico*, Indian Notes and Monographs, no. 8, Museum of the American Indian, Heye Foundation, New York, 1922

SÉJOURNÉ 1966
Laurette Séjourné, *Arqueología de Teotihuacan, la cerámica*, Mexico City and Buenos Aires, 1966

SELER 1960–61
Eduard Seler, *Gesammelte Abhandlungen zur Amerikanischen Sprach- und Altertumskunde*, 2nd edition, 5 vols, Graz, 1960-61

SELER 1996
Eduard Seler, 'The Animal Pictures of the Mexican and Maya Manuscripts', in Idem, *Collected Works in Mesoamerican Linguistics and Archaeology*, vol. 5, Lancaster, California, pp. 167–340

SERNA ET AL. 1953
Jacinto de la Serna et al., *Tratado de las idolatrías, supersticiones, dioses, ritos, hechicerías y otras costumbres gentílicas de las razas aborígenes*, 1687; 2 vols, Mexico City, 1953

SERRA PUCHE 1994
Mari Carmen Serra Puche, 'Objetos de Obsidiana y otros cristales en el México antiguo', in *Cristales y obsidiana prehispánicos*, Mari Carmen Serra Puche and Felipe Solís Olguín (eds), Mexico City, 1994, pp. 73–216

SEVILLE 1997
Tesoros de México, Paulino Castañeda, Antonio-Miguel Bernal, Felipe Solís Olguín, Martha Carmona, Alma Montero and Pedro Bazán (eds), exh. cat., Real Monasterio de San Clemente, Seville, 1997

SHELTON 1989
Anthony A. Shelton, 'An Aztec Cihuateotl Discovered in Scotland', *Apollo*, vol. 129, no. 326, 1989, pp. 261–62

SHELTON 1992
Anthony A. Shelton, *Anthropology, Art and Aesthetics*, Jeremy Coote (ed.), Oxford, 1992

SHELTON 1994
Anthony A. Shelton, 'Cabinets of Transgression: Renaissance Collections and the Incorporation of the New World', in *The Cultures of Collecting*, John Elsner and Roger Cardinal (eds), London, 1994, pp. 177–203

SMITH 1996
Michael E. Smith, *The Aztecs*, Oxford, 1996

SMITH AND RUPPERT 1953
A. L. Smith and Karl Ruppert, 'Excavations in House Mounds at Mayapán: II', *Current Reports of the Carnegie Institution of Washington*, 1, 1953, pp. 180–206

SOLÍS OLGUÍN 1981
Felipe Solís Olguín, *Catálogo de escultura del Castillo de Teayo, Veracruz, México*, Mexico City, 1981

SOLÍS OLGUÍN 1982
Felipe Solís Olguín, 'The Formal Pattern of Anthropomorphic Sculpture and the Ideology of the Aztec State', in *The Art and Iconography of Late Post-Classic Central Mexico*, Washington DC, 1982, pp. 73–110

SOLÍS OLGUÍN 1991
Felipe Solís Olguín, *Gloria y fama de México Tenochtitlan*, Mexico City, 1991

SOLÍS OLGUÍN 1991B
Felipe Solís Olguín, *Tesoros artísticos del Museo Nacional de Antropología*, Mexico City, 1991

SOLÍS OLGUÍN 1992
Felipe Solís Olguín, 'El Centro de Veracruz', in *Museo de Antropología de Jalapa*, Mexico City, 1992, pp. 76–161

SOLÍS OLGUÍN 1993
Felipe Solís Olguín, 'Aztekische Steinplastik', in *Die Sammlung vorspanischer Kunst und Kultur aus Mexiko im Museum für Völkerkunde, Berlin*, Veröffentlichung des Museums für Völkerkunde Berlin, n.s., 57; *Abteilung Amerikanische Archäologie*, vol. 7, Berlin, 1993, pp. 66–81

SOLÍS OLGUÍN 1997
Felipe Solís Olguín, 'Un hallazgo olvidado: relato e interpretación de los descubrimientos arqueológicos del predio de la calle de Guatemala núm. 12, en el Centro Histórico de la Ciudad de México, en 1944', in *Homenaje al doctor Ignacio Bernal*, Leonardo Manrique and Noemí Castillo Tejero (eds), Mexico City, 1997, pp. 81–93

SOLÍS OLGUÍN 2000
Felipe Solís Olguín, 'La Piedra del Sol', *Arqueología Mexicana*, 7, 41, January–February 2000, pp. 32–39

SOLÍS OLGUÍN 2001
Felipe Solís Olguín, 'La época mexica revelada por los estudios arqueológicos', in Mexico City 2001, pp. 333–67

SOLÍS OLGUÍN FORTHCOMING
Felipe Solís Olguín, 'La imagen de Ténoch en los monumentos conmemorativos de la capital azteca', in *Acercase y mirar. Homenaje a la Dra. Beatriz de la Fuente*, Mexico City, forthcoming

SOLÍS OLGUÍN AND CARMONA 1995
Felipe Solís Olguín and Martha Carmona, *El oro precolombino de México*, Mexico City, 1995

SOLÍS OLGUÍN AND MORALES GÓMEZ 1991
Felipe Solís Olguín and David Morales Gómez, *Rescate de un rescate: colección de objetos arqueológicos de El Volador, Ciudad de México*, Mexico City, 1991

SOTHEBY AND WILKINSON 1859
S. Leigh Sotheby and John Wilkinson, *Catalogue of the Extensive Collection of Assyrian, Babylonian, Egyptian, Greek, Etruscan, Roman, Indian, Peruvian, Mexican, and Chinese Antiquities and Articles of Vertu Formed by B. Hertz, Corresponding Member of the Archaeological Institute at Rome, with the Prices and Purchasers' Names; Preceded by the Descriptive Analysis, Published in the Berlin Archaeologische Zeitung by E. Gerhard*, London, 1859

SOUSTELLE 1940
Jacques Soustelle, *La Pensée cosmologique des anciens mexicains. Représentations du monde et de l'espace*, Paris, 1940

SOUSTELLE 1969
Jacques Soustelle, *El arte del México antiguo*, Barcelona, 1969

SPAGNESI 1993
Enrico Spagnesi, 'Bernardino da Sahagún, la natura in Messico, l'arte a Firenze', *Quaderni di Neotropica*, 1, 1993, pp. 7–24

STEINHAUER 1862
Carl Ludwig Steinhauer, *Catalogue of a Collection of Ancient and Modern Stone Implements, and of Other Weapons, Tools and Utensils of the Aborigines of Various Countries in the Possession of Henry Christy*, London, 1862

STEPHENS AND CATHERWOOD 1844
John Lloyd Stephens and Frederick Catherwood, *Views of Ancient Monuments in Central America, Chiapas and Yucatan*, London, 1844

STEPHENS AND CATHERWOOD 1854
John Lloyd Stephens and Frederick Catherwood, *Incidents of Travel in Central America, Chiapas and Yucatan…Illustrated by Numerous Engravings…Twelfth Edition*, London, 1854

STOCKING 1985
George W. Stocking Jr, 'Essays on Museum and Material Culture', in *Objects and Others: Essays on Museum and Material Culture*, George W. Stocking Jr (ed.), Madison, 1985, pp. 3–14

SWANSEA 1988
Eduardo Paolozzi, *Lost Magic Kingdoms and Six Paper Moons: An Exhibition Created by Eduardo Paolozzi for the Museum of Mankind and Toured by the South Bank Centre*, exh. cat., Glynn Vivian Art

Gallery, Swansea, 1988;
Birmingham City Art Gallery;
Graves Art Gallery, Sheffield;
York City Art Gallery; Bolton
Museum and Art Gallery;
Leeds City Art Gallery

TALADOIRE 1981
Eric Taladoire, *Les Terrains de
Jeu de Balle (Mésoamérique et
Sud-ouest des Etats-Unis)*, in
Etudes Mesoaméricaines, 2, 4,
Mission Archéologique et
Ethnologique Française au
Mexique, Mexico City, 1981

TAUBE 1993
Karl A. Taube, 'The Bilimek
Pulque Vessel: Starlore,
Calendrics and Cosmology
of Late Postclassic Central
Mexico', *Ancient Mesoamerica*,
4, 1, 1993, pp. 1–15

TENA 1987
Rafael Tena, *El calendario
mexica y la cronografía*, Mexico
City, 1987

THOMAS 1993
Hugh Thomas, *The Conquest of
Mexico*, London, 1993

THOMAS 2000
Hugh Thomas, *Who's Who of
the Conquistadors*, London,
2000

**TONALAMATL DE LOS POCHTECAS
1985**
*Tonalamatl de los pochtecas
(Códice Fejérváry-Mayer)*, Miguel
León-Portilla (ed.), Mexico
City, 1985

TOORIANS 1994
Lauran Toorians,
'The Earliest Inventory of
Mexican Objects in Munich,
1572', *Journal of the History of
Collections*, 6, 1, 1994,
pp. 59–67

**TORRES MONTES AND FRANCO
VELÁZQUEZ 1989**
Luis Torres Montes and
Francisca Franco Velázquez,
'La orfebrería prehispánica en
el Golfo de México y el
tesoro del pescador', in
Aguilar et al. 1989,
pp. 219–70

TOSCANO 1940
Salvador Toscano, *Arte y
arqueología en México, hallazgos
en 1940*, 2, 6, *Anales del Instituto
de Investigaciones Estéticas,
Universidad Autónoma de
México*, Mexico City, 1940

TOUSSAINT 1948
Manuel Toussaint,
Arte colonial en México, Mexico
City, 1948

TOUSSAINT 1982
Manuel Toussaint, *Pintura
colonial en México*, Mexico City,
1982

TOUSSAINT 1983
Manuel Toussaint, *Paseos
coloniales*, Mexico City, 1983

**TOUSSAINT, GÓMEZ DE OROZCO AND
FERNÁNDEZ 1938**
Manuel Toussaint, Federico
Gómez de Orozco and
Justino Fernández, *Planos de
la Ciudad de México, Siglos XVI
y XVII*, Instituto de
Investigaciones Estéticas,
Universidad Autónoma de
México, Mexico City, 1938

TOVAR 1951
Juan de Tovar, *The Tovar
Calendar: An Illustrated Mexican
Manuscript, c. 1585*, facsimile,
George Kubler and Charles
Gibson (eds), New Haven,
1951

TOVAR 1972
Juan de Tovar, *Manuscrit
Tovar: origines et croyances des
Indiens du Mexique*, facsimile,
Jacques Lafaye (ed.), Graz,
1972

TOWNSEND 1979
Richard F. Townsend, *State
and Cosmos in the Art of
Tenochtitlan*, Studies in
Pre-Columbian Art and
Archaeology, vol. 20,
Dumbarton Oaks,
Washington DC, 1979

TOWNSEND 1982
Richard F. Townsend,
'Malinalco and the Lords of
Tenochtitlan,' in *The Art and
Iconography of Late Postclassic
Central Mexico*, Elizabeth H.
Boone (ed.), Dumbarton
Oaks, Washington DC, 1982,
pp. 111–40

TOWNSEND 1987
Richard F. Townsend,
'Coronation at Tenochtitlan,'
in *The Aztec Templo Mayor*,
Elizabeth H. Boone (ed.),
Dumbarton Oaks,
Washington DC, 1987,
pp. 371–410

TOWNSEND 1992
Richard F. Townsend,
The Aztecs, London and
New York, 1992

TOWNSEND 2000
Richard F. Townsend,
The Aztecs, London and
New York, revised edition,
2000

TOWNSEND 2000B
Richard F. Townsend, 'The
Renewal of Nature at the
Temple of Tlaloc', in *The
Ancient Americas: Art from
Sacred Landscapes*, exh. cat.,
Richard F. Townsend (ed.),
Art Institute of Chicago,
2000, pp. 171–86

UMBERGER 1981
Emily Good Umberger,
*Aztec Sculptures, Hieroglyphics
and History*, Ann Arbor, 1981

UMBERGER 1987
Emily Good Umberger,
'Antiques, Revivals, and
References to the Past in
Aztec Art', *Res: Anthropology
and Aesthetics*, 13, 1987,
pp. 63–106

URIARTE 1994
Teresa Uriarte, 'Teotihuacan:
el legado de la ciudad de los
dioses', in *México en el Mundo
de las Colecciones de Arte:
Mesoamérica I*, María Luisa
Saban García (ed.), Mexico
City, 1994, pp. 70–129

VAILLANT 1941
George Vaillant, *The Aztecs of
Mexico*, New York, 1941

VARGAS 1989
Ernesto Vargas, *Las máscaras
de la cueva de Santa Ana
Teloxtoc*, Mexico City, 1989

VEGA SOSA 1975
Constanza Vega Sosa, *Forma y
decoración en las vasijas de
tradición azteca*, Mexico City,
1975

VELÁZQUEZ CASTRO 1999
Adrián Velázquez Castro,
*Tipología de los objetos de concha
del Templo Mayor de Tenochtitlan*,
Mexico City, 1999

VELÁZQUEZ CASTRO 2000
Adrián Velázquez Castro,
*Simbolismo de los objetos de concha
encontrados en las ofrendas del
Templo Mayor de Tenochtitlan*,
INAH, Colección Científica,
Serie Arqueología, Mexico
City, 2000

VIENNA 1992
*Das Altertum der Neuen Welt:
Voreuropäische Kulturen
Amerikas*, exh. cat., Museum
für Völkerkunde, Vienna,
1992

VIENNA 1997
*Gold und Silber aus Mexiko:
Präkolumbisches Gold und
koloniales Silber aus dem
anthropologischen
Nationalmuseum und anderen
bedeutenden Sammlungen
Mexikos*, Wilfried Seipel (ed.),
exh. cat., Kunsthistorisches
Museum, Vienna, 1997

VIENNA 2000
*Kaiser Karl V (1500–1558): Macht
und Ohnmacht Europas*,
Wilfried Seipel (ed.), exh. cat.,
Kunsthistorisches Museum,
Vienna, 2000

VIENNA 2001
*Die Entdeckung der Welt,
Die Welt der Entdeckungen:
Österreichische Forscher, Sammler,
Abenteuer*, Wilfried Seipel
(ed.), exh. cat.,
Kunsthistorisches Museum,
Vienna, 2001

VOLLMER 1981
Günter Vollmer (ed.),
*Geschichte der Azteken: Der
Codex Aubin und verwandte
Dokumente*, Berlin, 1981

WALDECK 1866
Jean Frédéric de Waldeck,
*Monuments anciens du Mexique:
Palenque et autres ruines de
l'ancienne civilisation du Mexique;
Collection de vues, bas-reliefs,
morceaux d'architecture, coupes,
vases, terres cuites, cartes et plan –
Dessinés d'après nature et relevés
par M. de Waldeck*, Paris, 1866

WASHINGTON 1947
Robert Woods Bliss,
*Indigenous Art of the Americas:
Collection of Robert Woods Bliss*,
exh. cat., National Gallery of
Art, Washington DC, 1947

WASHINGTON 1983
*Art of Aztec Mexico: Treasures
of Tenochtitlan*, Henry B.
Nicholson and Eloise
Quiñones Keber (eds), exh.
cat., National Gallery of Art,
Washington DC, 1983

WASHINGTON 1991
*Circa 1492: Art in the Age of
Exploration*, Jay A. Levenson
(ed.), exh. cat., National
Gallery of Art, Washington
DC, 1991

WASSON 1983
Gordon Wasson, *El hongo
maravilloso: Teonanácatl*,
Mexico City, 1983

WEIDITZ 2001
Christoph Weiditz, *El Códice
de los trajes/ Trachtenbuch*,
facsimile, 2 vols, Valencia,
2001

WESTHEIM 1962
Paul Westheim, *La cerámica del
México antiguo, fenómeno artístico*,
Mexico City, 1962

WESTHEIM ET AL. 1969
Paul Westheim, Alberto Ruz,
Pedro Armillas, Ricardo de
Robina and Alfonso Caso,
*Cuarenta siglos de plástica
mexicana, arte prehispánico*,
Mexico City, 1969

WETHERELL 1842
John Wetherell, *Catálogo de
una colección de antigüedades
mejicanas con varios idolos,
adornos, y otros artefactos de los
indios, que ecsiste en poder de Don
Juan Wetherel*, Seville, 1842

WINNING 1987
Hasso von Winning,
*La iconografía de Teotihuacan:
los dioses y los signos*, 2 vols,
Mexico City, 1987

WOLF 1999
Eric R. Wolf, *Envisioning
Power*, Berkeley, 1999

WOODWARD AND LEWIS 1998
David Woodward and
Malcolm G. Lewis,
The History of Cartography,
Chicago, 1998, vol. 2, book 3,
pp. 183–247

YOUNG 1855
Charles Bedford Young,
*Descriptive Catalogue of the
Collection of Mexican Antiquities
now Exhibiting at No. 57,
Pall Mall*, Leamington, 1855

YOUNG-SÁNCHEZ 1993
Margaret Young-Sánchez,
'Figurine of a Warrior',
*Bulletin of the Cleveland Museum
of Art*, 80, 4, 1993, pp. 144–47

YOUNG-SÁNCHEZ 1996
Margaret Young-Sánchez,
'An Aztec gold warrior
figurine (from the Cleveland
Museum)', *Res: Anthropology
and Aesthetics*, 29–30, 1996,
pp. 102–26

ZANTWIJK 1985
Rudolph van Zantwijk,
*The Aztec Arrangement: The
Social History of Pre-Spanish
Mexico*, Norman, 1985

ZANTWIJK 1994
Rudolf van Zantwijk,
*Zegevierend met de Zon: Duizend
jaar Azteekse gedichten en
gedachten*, Amsterdam, 1994

**ZANTWIJK, RIDDER AND BRAAKHUIS
1990**
*Mesoamerican Dualism.
Dualismo mesoamericano*, Rudolf
van Zantwijk, Rob de Ridder
and Edwin Braakhuis (eds),
Utrecht, 1990

LIST OF
LENDERS

AUCH
Musée des Jacobins

BASLE
Museum der Kulturen Basel

BELFAST
Ulster Museum

BERLIN
Staatliche Museen zu Berlin:
    Preußischer Kulturbesitz,
    Ethnologisches Museum

BOLOGNA
Biblioteca Universitaria

BRUSSELS
Musées Royaux d'Art et
    d'Histoire

CAMBRIDGE, MASS.
Peabody Museum of
    Archaeology and Ethnology,
    Harvard University

CHICAGO
The Art Institute of Chicago
The Field Museum of Natural
    History

CLEVELAND
Cleveland Museum of Art

COLOGNE
Rautenstrauch-Joest-Museum für
    Völkerkunde

COPENHAGEN
The National Museum
    of Denmark

EL ESCORIAL
Monasterio de San Lorenzo
    de El Escorial

FLORENCE
Biblioteca Medicea Laurenziana
Biblioteca Nazionale Centrale
    di Firenze
Museo degli Argenti

GLASGOW
University Library

HAMBURG
Museum für Völkerkunde
    Hamburg

HELSINKI
Didrichsen Art Foundation

JALAPA
Museo de Antropología de Jalapa

LIVERPOOL
Liverpool Museum

LONDON
British Museum
Victoria and Albert Museum

LOS ANGELES
Los Angeles County Museum
    of Art
Fowler Museum of Cultural
    History, UCLA

MADRID
Biblioteca Nacional

MANNHEIM
Völkerkundlichen Sammlungen
    der Stadt Mannheim im
    Reiss-Museum

MEXICO CITY
Fundación Televisa
Museo Nacional de Antropología
Museo Templo Mayor
Museo Universitario de Ciencias
    y Arte, Universidad Nacional
    Autónoma de México

MUNICH
Schatzkammer der Residenz
    München
Staatliches Museum für
    Völkerkunde

NEW HAVEN
Peabody Museum of Natural
    History, Yale University

NEW YORK
American Museum of Natural
    History
Brooklyn Museum of Art
Metropolitan Museum of Art

NUREMBERG
Germanisches Nationalmuseum
Museen der Stadt Nürnberg

OAXACA
Museo de las Culturas de Oaxaca

OXFORD
Bodleian Library

PARIS
Bibliothèque Nationale
    de France
Musée de l'Homme

PHILADELPHIA
Philadelphia Museum of Art

PRINCETON
The Henry and Rose Pearlman
    Foundation, Princeton
    University Art Museum

PROVIDENCE
The John Carter Brown Library,
    Brown University

PUEBLA
Museo Regional de Antropología
    de Puebla

ROME
Museo Nazionale Preistorico
    ed Etnografico 'Luigi Pigorini'

SAINT LOUIS
The Saint Louis Art Museum

ST PETERSBURG
The State Hermitage Museum

TEOTENANGO
Museo Arqueológico del Estado
    de México 'Dr Román Piña
    Chan'

TEOTIHUACAN
Museo de la Pintura Mural
    Teotihuacana

TEPOTZOTLAN
Museo Nacional del Virreinato

TLAXCALA
Museo Regional de Tlaxcala

TOLUCA
Instituto Mexiquense de Cultura:
    Museo de Antropología
    e Historia del Estado de
    México

TULA
Museo de Sitio de Tula

TURIN
Museo Civico d'Arte Antica,
    e Palazzo Madama

VATICAN CITY
Biblioteca Apostolica Vaticana
Museo Missionario Etnografico

VERACRUZ
Museo Baluarte de Santiago

VIENNA
Museum für Völkerkunde

VILLAHERMOSA
Museo Regional de Antropología
    Carlos Pellicer

WASHINGTON
Dumbarton Oaks Pre-Columbian
    Collection

PHOTO CREDITS

All works of art are reproduced by kind permission of the owners. Special acknowledgements for providing photographs are as follows:

AUCH
Musée des Jacobins, cat. 325

BASEL
© Museum der Kulturen/Peter Horner, cats 45, 92, 149, 205, 230, 248

BELFAST
© Ulster Museum. Photograph reproduced with the kind permission of the Trustees of the Museums & Galleries of Northern Ireland, cat. 350

BERLIN
© Bildarchiv Preussischer Kulturbesitz/Martin Franken, 2002, cats 47, 104, 146, 208, 218, 289; Dietrich Graf, cats 219, 316; W. Schneider-Schütz, cats 109, 112, 168, 199

BOLOGNA
Biblioteca Universitaria, Bologna/Roncaglia, Modena, cat. 340

BRISTOL
Bristol Museums and Art Gallery, fig. 71

BRUSSELS
Musées royaux d'art et d'histoire/Raymond Mommaerts, cats 77, 298

CAMBRIDGE (MA)
© The President and Fellows of Harvard College, cat. 254

CHICAGO
© 2002 The Field Museum/Diane Alexander White, cats 3, 14
© The Art Institute of Chicago. All Rights Reserved, cat. 226
Newberry Library, fig. 8

CLEVELAND
© The Cleveland Museum of Art, cats 107, 186

COLOGNE
Rautenstrauch-Joest-Museum of Anthropology, cats 84, 103

COPENHAGEN
© The National Museum of Denmark, Department of Ethnography/John Lee, cat. 297

FLORENCE
Microfoto s.r.l./Alberto Scardigli, cat. 344
su concessione del Ministero dei Beni e le Attività Culturali. Biblioteca Nazionale Centrale/Microfoto s.r.l., cat. 342; Museo degli Argenti/Studio Fotografico Quattrone, cat. 12

GLASGOW
Glasgow University Library, Department of Special Collections, cat. 356; fig. 62

LIVERPOOL
© The Board of Trustees, National Museums & Galleries on Merseyside, Liverpool Museum, cat. 341; fig. 54

LONDON
The Art Archive/Dagli Orti, figs 2, 10, 42, 44
© British Library, fig. 65
© The British Museum, cats 18, 66, 81, 83, 88, 121, 143, 152, 175, 185, 200, 294, 296, 303, 304, 351, 354, 357, 358; fig. 61; Colin McEwan, fig 46
Guildhall Library, Corporation of London/Geremy Butler, figs 66, 67, 68
Tate, fig. 69
V&A Picture Library/D.P.P. Naish, cat. 324

LOS ANGELES
© 2002 Museum Associates/LACMA. All Rights Reserved, cat. 327
© UCLA Fowler Museum of Cultural History/Don Cole, cat. 165

MADRID
Biblioteca Nacional, cat. 343; figs 1, 63
© Patrimonio Nacional, cat. 323; fig. 64

MANNHEIM
© Reiss-Engelhorn Museen/Jean Christen, cats 106, 120

MEXICO CITY
courtesy CONACULTA – INAH, figs 13, 16, 28, 37, 40, 41/Fernando Carrizosa, fig. 17; Salvador Guilliem, figs 14, 20; Leonardo López Luján, fig. 21; Germán Zúñiga, José Luis Rojas Martínez, fig. 18

MEXICO CITY
Universidad Nacional Autónoma de México, fig. 55

MUNICH
© Bayerische Schlösserverwaltung/Wolf Christian von der Mülbe, Dachau, cat. 177
© Staatliches Museum für Völkerkunde/Alexander Laurenzo, cats 213, 220, 315

NEW HAVEN (CT)
© 2002 Peabody Museum of Natural History, Yale University, cats 35, 224

NEW YORK
© American Museum of Natural History Library, fig. 7; Craig Chesek, cats 46, 49, 158; D. Finnin, cat. 292
Brooklyn Museum of Art/Central Photo Archive, cats 39, 57, 71
© 2002 The Metropolitan Museum of Arts, cats 25, 180; fig. 38

NUREMBERG
Courtesy Germanisches Nationalmuseum, cat. 359
Museen der Stadt Nürnberg, Gemälde und Skulpturen, cat. 336

OXFORD
© The Bodleian Library, University of Oxford, cat. 349; fig 36

PARIS
© Assemblée Nationale Française, figs 26, 57
Bibliothèque Nationale de France, cats 345, 348, 355; figs 22, 35, 39
© Musée de l'Homme/D. Destable, cats 76, 101, 319; fig. 58; M. Delaplanche, cats 127, 128; P. Ponsard, cat. 100

PHILADELPHIA
© Philadelphia Museum of Art/Graydon Wood, 1991, cat. 7; 1995, cat. 225; 2002, cats 11, 173

PRINCETON
© Trustees of Princeton University/Bruce M. White, cat. 53

ROME
IKONA, figs 24, 53; IKONA/Microfoto, figs 27, 29, 30, 31, 32, 33, 34, 48, 56, 59; Museo Pigorini/Damiano Rosa, cat. 295

ROUEN
© 2002 AREHN/Th. Asencio-Parvy, fig. 19

ST LOUIS
The Saint Louis Art Museum, cats 189, 196, 215, 305

ST PETERSBURG
© 2002 The State Hermitage Museum, cat. 183

TURIN
su concessione dei Musei Civici di Torino. Fototeca dei Musei Civici/Ernani Orcorte, cats 176, 188, 190

VATICAN CITY
© Biblioteca Apostolica Vaticana, cat. 346
Musei Vaticani/A Bracchetti, cat. 114

VIENNA
© Museum für Völkerkunde, cats 21, 22, 23, 74, 142, 150, 187, 193, 299, 312, 313, 321, 334; figs 47, 51

WASHINGTON
Dumbarton Oaks Research Library and Collection, Washington, D.C, cats 178, 192, 195, 314, 320, 335

© Yann Arthus-Bertrand/Corbis, fig. 12

© Gianni/Dagli Orti/Corbis, fig. 11

Richard Hurley, cat. 347

Jürgen Liepe, cats 16, 293

© Alfredo López Austin, fig. 23

Eduardo Matos Moctezuma, figs 43, 45

© Marco Antonio Pacheco/Raíces/INAH, fig. 15

Matti Ruotsalainen, cats 166, 197

© Michel Zabé/BMI, figs 5, 6, 9, 49, 50

Michel Zabé, cats 1, 2, 4, 5, 6, 8, 9, 10, 13, 15, 17, 19, 20, 24, 26, 27, 28, 29, 30, 31, 32, 33, 34, 36, 37, 38, 40, 41, 42, 43, 44, 48, 50, 51, 52, 54, 55, 56, 58, 59, 60, 61, 62, 63, 64, 65, 67, 68, 69, 70, 72, 73, 75, 78, 79, 80, 83, 85, 86, 89, 90, 91, 93, 94, 95, 96, 97, 98, 99, 102, 105, 108, 110, 111, 113, 115, 116, 117, 118, 119, 122, 123, 124, 125, 126, 129, 130, 131, 132, 133, 134, 135, 136, 137, 138, 139, 140, 141, 144, 145, 147, 148, 151, 153, 154, 155, 156, 157, 159, 160, 161, 162, 163, 164, 167, 169, 170, 171, 172, 174, 179, 181, 182, 184, 191, 194, 198, 201, 202, 203, 204, 206, 207, 211, 212, 214, 216, 217, 221, 222, 223, 227, 228, 229, 231, 232, 233, 234, 235, 236, 237, 238, 239, 240, 241, 242, 243, 244, 245, 246, 247, 249, 250, 251, 252, 253, 255, 256, 257, 258, 259, 260, 261, 262, 263, 264, 265, 266, 267, 268, 269, 269, 270, 271, 272, 273, 274, 275, 276, 277, 278, 279, 280, 281, 282, 283, 284, 285, 286, 287, 288, 290, 291, 300, 301, 302, 306, 307, 308, 309, 310, 311, 317, 318, 322, 326, 328, 329, 330, 331, 332, 333, 337, 338, 339, 352

ACKNOWLEDGEMENTS

Dawn Ades
Jean-Jacques Aillagon
César J. Aldama Muciño
Richard Alford
Robert Anderson
Chris Anderton
Carmen Aneiros
Franca Arduini
Emilio Azcárraga Jean
Christine Bailey
George Bankes
Bruce Barker-Benfield
Brent R. Benjamin
María Clara Bernal Bermúdez
Marla C. Berns
Clara Bezanilla
Antonino Biancastella
Warwick Bray
Gordon Brotherston
Alexander Brust
Francesco Buranelli
Richard Burger
Reg Carr
Ximena María Chávez Balderas
Mary Clapinson
Carlos A. Córdova
Carlos Córdova-Plaza
Alan Curry
Lily Díaz
Manuel Díaz Cebrián
Peter Didrichsen
Joanne Doornewaard
Beret Due
Brian Durrans
Gregory Eades
Ángeles Espinoza Yglesias
Raffaele Farina
Fabien Ferrer-Joly
Miguel Fernández Félix
Norman Fiering
David Flemming
Antonia Ida Fontana
Teresa Franco
Simonetta Fraquelli
Maria Antonietta Fugazzola Delpino
Ellen V. Futter
Laura Galbán
Mercedes de la Garza Camino
Juliete Giménez Cacho G.
Daniel Goeritz Rodríguez
Heriberto Gómez Ramírez
Blanca González
Claudio X. González
Ulf Göranson

Rosario Granados
Habil G. Ulrich Grossmann
Anne d'Harnoncourt
Joanne Harwood
Allis Helleland
Ian Hughes
Jean-Noël Jeanneney
Mark Jones
Peter Kann
Lily Kassner
Edward L. Keenan
Viola König
Wulf Köpke
Milena Koprivitza Acuña
Rolf Krebs
Ursula Kubach-Reutter
Amelia Lara Tamburino
Arnold Lehman
Roberto López
John Mack
Mauricio Maillé
Juan Manuel Santin
Anna Maris
María Teresa Márquez Díez-Canedo
Monica Martí
Juan Carlos de la Mata González
Irene Martin
Jesús Martínez Arvizu
John W. McCarter, Jr.
Colin McEwan
Rafael Micha
Diana Mogollón González
Martín Antonio Mondragón
Carolina Monroy del Mazo
Rúben B. Morante López
Marilena Mosco
Philippe de Montebello
Claudius Mueller
Lars Munkhammar
Virginia Murrieta
Thomas D. Nicholson
J. C. Nolan
Francis van Noten
Jaime Nualart
Santiago Oñate Laborde
José Enrique Ortíz Lanz
Joanna Ostapkowicz
Ignacio Padilla
Enrica Pagella
Vanessa Paredes
Néstor Paredes C.
María Esther Paredes Solís
Alejandra de la Paz
Rebeca Perales

Mikhail Piotrovsky
Jeffrey Quilter
Luis Racionero Grau
Yolanda Ramos Galicia
Froilán Ramos Pérez
Miguel Ángel Recio Crespo
Katherine Lee Reid
Andrea L. Rich
Catherine Rickman
Pierre Robbe
Miguel Rodríguez-Acosta Carlström
Juan Alberto Román Berrelleza
Rosa María Romo López
Eduardo Rostán
Nancy Rostoff
Sandra Rozental
Mariana Salgado
Juan Manuel Santín
Klaus Schneider
Cristina Serrano Pérez
Marjorie Shiers
Charles Spencer
Annie Starkey
Kate Storey
Robert Tavenor
Keith Taylor
Michael Taylor
Susan Taylor
Michael Tellenbach
Richard Townsend
Loa Traxler
Miguel Ángel Trinidad Meléndez
Ernst W. Veen
Manuel Velasco
Roberto Velasco Alonso
Emilo Velázquez Gallegos
Roxana Velásquez Martínez del Campo
Robert A. Vornis
John Vrieze
Gabriele Weiss
David Weston
Clara Wilpert
Anne Winton
James N. Wood
Greg Youmans
Michel Zabé
Arturo Zárate Ramírez

INDEX

All references are to page numbers; those in **bold** type indicate catalogue entries and those in *italic* type indicate essay illustrations.

Mrs Michael Green
Mr and Mrs Thomas Griffin
Mr and Mrs Clifford J Gundle
The Harris Family
Mr Andrew Hawkins
David and Lesley Haynes
Michael and Morven Heller
Robin Heller Moss
Mrs Margarita Hernandez
Mrs Alexander F Hehmeyer
Mr and Mrs J Hodkinson
Anne Holmes-Drewry
Mr and Mrs Ken Howard
Mrs Sue Howes and Mr Greg Dyke
Mr and Mrs Allan Hughes
Mrs Pauline Hyde
Simone Hyman
Mr Oliver Iny
Mr S Isern-Feliu
Mr and Mrs F Lance Isham
Sir Martin and Lady Jacomb
Mr and Mrs Ian Jay
Harold and Valerie Joels
Sir Paul Judge
Mr and Mrs Richard Kaufman
Mr and Mrs Laurence Kelly
Rona and Robert Kiley
Mr D H Killick
Mr and Mrs James Kirkman
Miss Divia Lalvani
Tom Larsen, Holt Value Associates
L A Tanner & Co, Inc
Mr George Lengvari
Colette and Peter Levy
Sir Christopher and Lady Lewinton
Mrs Rosemary Lieberman
Susan Linaker
Mrs Livingstone
Miss R Lomax-Simpson
Mr and Mrs Mark Loveday
Mr Charles G Lubar
Richard and Rose Luce
Mrs Gertie Lurie
Mrs Marilyn Maklouf
Mr and Mrs Eskandar Maleki
Ms Claudine B Malone
Mr and Mrs Michael (RA)
    and Jose Manser
Mr and Mrs M Margulies
The Lord Marks of Broughton
Marsh Christian Trust
R C Martin
Mr and Mrs Stephen Mather
Mrs M C W McCann
Mr and Mrs Andrew McKinna
Mr and Mrs Bruce McLaren
Sir Kit and Lady McMahon
Mr and Mrs Philip Mengel
The Mercers' Company
Lt Col L S Michael OBE
Mr and Mrs Donald Moore
Mr and Mrs Peter Morgan
Mr and Mrs I Morrison
The Mulberry Trust
Mr and Mrs Carl Anton Muller
N Peal Cashmere
Mr and Mrs Elis Nemes
John Nickson and Simon Rew
Mr and Mrs Simon Oliver
Mr Neil Osborn and Ms Holly Smith
Sir Peter Osborne and Lady Osborne
Mr Michael Palin
Mr and Mrs Vincenzo Palladino
Mr and Mrs Gerald Parkes
Mr and Mrs Stephen Partridge-Hicks
John Pattisson
Mr and Mrs D J Peacock
The Pennycress Trust
Miss Karen Phillipps
Mr David Pike
Mr Godfrey Pilkington
George and Carolyn Pincus
Mr and Mrs William A Plapinger
David and Linda Pohs-Supino
Mr and Mrs John Pomian
John Porter Charitable Trust
Miss Victoria Provis
The Quercus Trust
John and Anne Raisman
Sir David and Lady Ramsbotham
Martin Randall Travel Ltd
Mr T H Reitman
Mrs Clare Rich

Sir John and Lady Riddell
The Roland Group of Companies Plc
Mr and Mrs Ian Rosenberg
Alastair and Sarah Ross Goobey
Mr and Mrs Kerry Rubie
Mr and Mrs Derald H Ruttenberg
The Audrey Sacher Charitable Trust
Dr P B St Leger
Mr and Mrs Victor Sandelson
Mr and Mrs Bryan Sanderson
Mr and Mrs Nicholas Sassow
Mrs Sylvia B Scheuer
Mr and Mrs Stuart L Scott
Dr Lewis Sevitt
The Countess of Shaftesbury
Mr and Mrs Paul Shang
Mr and Mrs Colin Sharman
Mrs Lois Sieff OBE
Mr and Mrs William Sieghart
Mr Peter Simon
Mrs Margaret Simpson
Brian D Smith
Mr and Mrs John Sorrell
Don and Susan Starr
Mrs Jack Steinberg
Mr and Mrs David Stileman
John and Sheila Stoller
Mr and Mrs R W Strang
The Swan Trust
Mr and Mrs David Swift
Mr John Tackaberry
Mr and Mrs John D Taylor
Mrs Jonathan Todhunter
The Hon Barbara S Thomas
Mr and Mrs Julian Treger
Miss Joanna Trollope OBE
Carole Turner Record
Mrs Kathryn Uhde
Miss M L Ulfane
Michael and Yvonne Uva
Visa Lloyds Bank Monte Carlo
Mrs Catherine Vlasto
Mr and Mrs Santo Volpe
Mrs Claire Vyner
Mr and Mrs Ludovic de Walden
Mrs Cynthia Walton
John B Watton
Mr and Mrs Jeffrey M Weingarten
Edna and Willard Weiss
Mrs Gerald Westbury
Mr and Mrs Anthony Williams
Mr Jeremy Willoughby
Mr John D Winter
Miss Caroline Wiseman
The Right Hon and Lady Young
    of Graffham
and others who wish to remain anonymous

SCHOOLS PATRONS GROUP
The Lord Aldington
Arts and Humanities Research Board
The Charlotte Bonham-Carter
    Charitable Trust
Mrs Stephen Boyd
Mr Robert Bullock
The Candide Charitable Trust
Mr Raymond Cazalet
Smadar and David Cohen
Mr Simon Copsey
Keith and Pam Dawson
The Delfont Foundation
The D'Oyly Carte Charitable Trust
Mr Alexander Duma
The Marchioness of Dufferin and Ava
The Gilbert & Eileen Edgar
    Foundation
The Eranda Foundation
Mr Hani Farsi
Jack and Greta Goldhill
The Headley Trust
Fiona Johnstone
The Lark Trust
Lora Lehmann
The Leverhulme Trust
The Loughborough Fellowship
    in Fine Art
Mr John Martin
The Henry Moore Foundation
Robin Heller Moss
The Mulberry Trust
Newby Trust Limited
Miranda Page-Wood
N Peal Cashmere

The Worshipful Company
    of Painter-Stainers
The Stanley Picker Trust
Pickett Fine Leather Ltd
Edith and Ferdinand Porjes
    Charitable Trust
Mr David A Robbie
Mr and Mrs Anthony Salz
Paul Smith and Pauline Denyer Smith
The South Square Trust
Mr and Mrs Michele Sportelli
The Starr Foundation
Mr and Mrs Robert Lee Sterling Jr
The Peter Storrs Trust
Mr and Mrs Denis Tinsley
Mr David Tudor
The Celia Walker Art Foundation
The Harold Hyam Wingate
    Foundation
and others who wish to remain anonymous

GENERAL BENEFACTORS
Mr Keith Bromley
Miss Jayne Edwardes
Catherine Lewis Foundation
Lady Sainsbury
and others who wish to remain anonymous

American Associates

BENEFACTORS
Mrs Deborah Loeb Brice
Mr Francis Finlay
Mrs Melville Wakeman Hall
Mrs Jeanne K Lawrence
Sir Christopher and Lady Lewinton
Ms Brenda Neubauer Straus

SPONSORS
Mrs Jan Cowles
Mrs Katherine D W Findlay
Ms Frances S Hayward
Mr James Kemper Jr
The Honorable and Mrs Philip Lader
Mrs Linda Noe Laine
Mrs Edmond J Safra
Mr Peter Schoenfeld
Mr Arthur O Sulzberger
    and Ms Allison S Cowles
Virgin Atlantic

PATRONS
Ms Helen Harting Abell
Mr and Mrs Steven Ausnit
Mr and Mrs Stephen D Bechtel Jr
Mrs William J Benedict
Mr Donald A Best
Mr and Mrs Henry W Breyer III
Mrs Mildred C Brinn
Dr and Mrs Robert Carroll
Mr and Mrs Benjamin Coates
Ms Anne S Davidson
Ms Zita Davisson
Mr and Mrs Charles Diker
Mrs June Dyson
Mrs John W Embry
Mrs A Barlow Ferguson
Mrs Robert Ferst
Mr Richard E Ford
Mrs William Fox Jr
Mr and Mrs Lawrence S Friedland
Goldman, Sachs & Co
Mrs Betty Gordon
Ms Rachel K Grody
Mr and Mrs Martin D Gruss
Mrs Richard L Harris
Mr and Mrs Gurnee F Hart
Mr Edward H Harte
Mr and Mrs Gustave M Hauser
Dr Bruce C Horten
Mr Robert J Irwin
Ms Betty Wold Johnson
    and Mr Douglas Bushnell
The Honorable and Mrs W Eugene
    Johnston III
Mr William W Karatz
Mr and Mrs Stephen M Kellen
Mr and Mrs Gary A Kraut
William M and Sarah T Lese
    Family Fund

Mr Arthur L Loeb
The Nathan Manilow
    Foundation
Mrs John P McGrath
Mrs Mark Millard
Mrs Barbara T Missett
Mr Paul D Myers
Mr and Mrs Wilson Nolen
Mrs Richard D O'Connor
Mr and Mrs Jeffrey Pettit
Mr Robert S Pirie
Mrs Nanette Ross
Mrs Frances G Scaife
Ms Jan Blaustein Scholes
Mr and Mrs Stanley D Scott
Ms Georgia Shreve
Mr James Sollins
Mrs Frederick M Stafford
Mr and Mrs Stephen Stamas
Elizabeth F Stribling
Mrs Royce Deane Tate
Mrs Britt Tidelius
Mrs Richard B Tullis
Ms Sue Erpf Van de Bovenkamp
Mrs Vincent S Villard Jr
Mr and Mrs Stanford S
    Warshawsky
Mrs Sara E White
Dr and Mrs Robert D Wickham
Mr and Mrs Robert G Wilmers
Mr Robert W Wilson
Mr and Mrs Kenneth Woodcock
and others who wish to remain anonymous

Contributing Friends of the Royal Academy

PATRON FRIENDS
Mrs Yvonne Barlow
Mr and Mrs Sidney Corob
Mr David Ker
Mrs Janet Marsh
Mrs Maureen D Metcalfe
Mr R J Mullis
Mr Robin Symes
and others who wish to remain anonymous

SUPPORTING FRIENDS
Mr Keith G Bennett
Mrs C W T Blackwell
Mr C Boddington
    and Ms R Naylor
Mr Paul Brand
Miss E M Cassin
Mr R A Cernis
Mrs M F Coward
Mrs Nadine Crichton
Mrs Belinda Davie
Mr John Denham
Miss N J Dhanani
Mr Kenneth Edwards
Jack and Irene Finkler
Mrs D Goodsell
Mr Gavin Graham
Miss Karen Harper-Gow
Mr R J Hoare
Mr Christopher Hodsoll
Mrs Manya Igel
Ms Shiblee Jamal
Mrs Jane Jason
Mrs G R Jeffries
Mr and Mrs J Kessler
Mrs L Kosta
Mrs Carol Kroch
Mrs Joan Lavender
Mr Owen Luder CBE PRIBA FRSA
Mr Donald A Main
Mrs Gillian McIntosh
Mrs Barbara Minto
Mr George Moore
Angela Nevill
Mrs Elizabeth M Newell
Miss Kim Nicholson
Mr C Mark Nicolaides
Mrs Elaine Nordby
Mr Ralph Picken
Mr Benjamin Pritchett-Brown
Mrs Elizabeth Ridley
Mr D S Rocklin
Mrs A Rodman

Mr and Mrs O Roux
Lady Sainsbury
The Rt Hon Sir Timothy
    Sainsbury
Mrs D Scott
Mrs Josephine Seaton
Mrs E D Sellick
Mr R J Simmons CBE
Mr John H M Sims
Mr Brian Smith
Mrs K M Söderblom
Mrs J A Tapley
Mrs Claire Weldon
Mrs Jacqueline Williams
and others who wish to remain anonymous

Corporate Membership of the Royal Academy of Arts

Launched in 1988, the Royal
Academy's Corporate Membership
Scheme has proved highly successful.
Corporate membership offers
company benefits to staff and clients
and access to the Academy's facilities
and resources. Each member pays an
annual subscription to be a Member
(£7,000) or Patron (£20,000).
Participating companies recognise the
importance of promoting the visual
arts. Their support is vital to the
continuing success of the Academy.

Corporate Membership Scheme

CORPORATE PATRONS
Ashurst Morris Crisp
Bloomberg LP
BNP Paribas
BP Amoco p.l.c.
Debenhams Retail plc
Deloitte & Touche
Deutsche Bank AG
Ernst and Young
GlaxoSmithKline plc
Granada plc
John Lewis Partnership
Merrill Lynch
Radisson Edwardian Hotels
Royal & Sun Alliance

CORPORATE MEMBERS
Anonymous
Accel Partners
Apax Partners Holding Ltd
Barclays plc
Bear, Stearns International Ltd
BMP DDB Limited
The Boston Consulting Group
Bovis Lend Lease Limited
The British Land Company PLC
BT plc
Bunzl plc
Cantor Fitzgerald
Cazenove & Co
CB Hillier Parker
Christie's
Chubb Insurance Company
    of Europe
Citigroup
CJA (Management Recruitment
    Consultants) Limited
Clifford Chance
Colefax and Fowler Group
Credit Agricole Indosuez
De Beers
Diageo plc
Dresdner Kleinwort Wasserstein
The Economist Group
Eversheds
F&C Management plc
Goldman Sachs International
Govett Investment Management
    Limited
Hay Group

Hewitt, Bacon and Woodrow
H J Heinz Company Limited
HSBC plc
ICI
King Sturge
KPMG
Linklaters & Alliance
Macfarlanes
Man Group plc
Mayer, Brown, Rowe & Maw
Mellon Global Investments
Morgan Stanley
MoMart Ltd
Pearson plc
The Peninsular and Oriental Steam
    Navigation Company
Pentland Group plc
Provident Financial plc
Raytheon Systems Limited
Redwood
Reed Elsevier Group plc
The Royal Bank of Scotland
Schroders & Co
Sea Containers Ltd.
SG
Six Continents PLC
Skanska Construction Group
    Limited
Slaughter and May
The Smith & Williamson Group
Sotheby's
Travelex
Trowers & Hamlins
Unilever UK Limited
UBS AG Private Banking
Vivendi Water

**HONORARY CORPORATE
MEMBERS**
All Nippon Airways Co. Ltd
A.T. Kearney Limited
Derwent Valley Holdings plc
London First
Reuters Limited
Yakult UK Limited

Sponsors of
Past Exhibitions

The President and Council of the
Royal Academy thank sponsors
of past exhibitions for their support.
Sponsors of major exhibitions during
the last ten years have included the
following:

Allied Trust Bank
    Africa: The Art of a Continent,
    1995*
*Anglo American Corporation of South
    Africa*
    Africa: The Art of a Continent,
    1995*
A.T. Kearney
    231st Summer Exhibition, 1999
    232nd Summer Exhibition, 2000
    233rd Summer Exhibition, 2001
    234th Summer Exhibition, 2002
The Banque Indosuez Group
    Pissarro: The Impressionist
    and the City, 1993
Barclays
    Ingres to Matisse: Masterpieces
    of French Painting, 2001
BBC Radio 3
    Paris: Capital of the Arts
    1900–1968. 2001
BMW (GB) Limited
    Georges Rouault: The Early Years,
    1903–1920. 1993
    David Hockney: A Drawing
    Retrospective, 1995*
British Airways Plc
    Africa: The Art of a Continent,
    1995
Cantor Fitzgerald
    From Manet to Gauguin:
    Masterpieces from Swiss Private
    Collections, 1995
    1900: Art at the Crossroads, 2000
The Capital Group Companies
    Drawings from the J Paul Getty
    Museum, 1993
Chase Fleming Asset Management
    The Scottish Colourists
    1900–1930. 2000
Chilstone Garden Ornaments
    The Palladian Revival: Lord
    Burlington and His House and
    Garden at Chiswick, 1995
Christie's
    Frederic Leighton 1830–1896.
    1996
    Sensation: Young British Artists
    from The Saatchi Collection, 1997
Classic FM
    Goya: Truth and Fantasy,
    The Small Paintings, 1994
    The Glory of Venice: Art in the
    Eighteenth Century, 1994
Corporation of London
    Living Bridges, 1996
Country Life
    John Soane, Architect: Master
    of Space and Light, 1999
Credit Suisse First Boston
    The Genius of Rome 1592–1623.
    2000
The Daily Telegraph
    American Art in the 20th Century,
    1993
    1900: Art at the Crossroads, 2000
De Beers
    Africa: The Art of a Continent,
    1995
Debenhams Retail plc
    Premiums and RA Schools Show,
    1999
    Premiums and RA Schools Show,
    2000
    Premiums and RA Schools Show,
    2001
    Premiums and RA Schools Show,
    2002
Deutsche Morgan Grenfell
    Africa: The Art of a Continent,

1995
Diageo plc
    250th Summer Exhibition, 1998
The Drue Heinz Trust
    The Palladian Revival: Lord
    Burlington and His House
    and Garden at Chiswick, 1995
    Denys Lasdun, 1997
    Tadao Ando: Master of
    Minimalism, 1998
The Dupont Company
    American Art in the 20th Century,
    1993
Elf
    Alfred Sisley, 1992
Ernst & Young
    Monet in the 20th Century, 1999
eyestorm
    Apocalypse: Beauty and Horror
    in Contemporary Art, 2000
Fidelity Foundation
    The Dawn of the Floating World
    (1650–1765). Early Ukiyo-e
    Treasures from the Museum
    of Fine Arts, Boston, 2001
Fondation Elf
    Alfred Sisley, 1992
Friends of the Royal Academy
    Victorian Fairy Painting, 1997
Game International Limited
    Forty Years in Print: The Curwen
    Studio and Royal Academicians,
    2001
*The Jacqueline and Michael Gee Charitable
    Trust*
    LIFE? or THEATRE? The Work
    of Charlotte Salomon, 1999
Générale des Eaux Group
    Living Bridges, 1996
Glaxo Wellcome plc
    The Unknown Modigliani,
    1994
Goldman Sachs International
    Alberto Giacometti, 1901–1966.
    1996
    Picasso: Painter and Sculptor
    in Clay, 1998
The Guardian
    The Unknown Modigliani,
    1994
Guinness Peat Aviation
    Alexander Calder, 1992
Guinness PLC (see Diageo plc)
    223rd Summer Exhibition, 1991
    224th Summer Exhibition, 1992
    225th Summer Exhibition, 1993
    226th Summer Exhibition, 1994
    227th Summer Exhibition, 1995
    228th Summer Exhibition, 1996
    229th Summer Exhibition, 1997
Harpers & Queen
    Georges Rouault: The Early Years,
    1903–1920. 1993
    Sandra Blow, 1994
    David Hockney: A Drawing
    Retrospective, 1995*
    Roger de Grey, 1996
The Headley Trust
    Denys Lasdun, 1997
The Henry Moore Foundation
    Alexander Calder, 1992
    Africa: The Art of a Continent,
    1995
Ibstock Building Products Ltd
    John Soane, Architect: Master
    of Space and Light, 1999
The Independent
    Living Bridges, 1996
    Apocalypse: Beauty and Horror
    in Contemporary Art, 2000
International Asset Management
    Frank Auerbach, Paintings
    and Drawings 1954–2001. 2001
Donald and Jeanne Kahn
    John Hoyland, 1999
Land Securities PLC
    Denys Lasdun, 1997
The Mail on Sunday
    Royal Academy Summer Season,
    1992
    Royal Academy Summer Season,

1993
Marks & Spencer
    Royal Academy Schools
    Premiums, 1994
    Royal Academy Schools Final
    Year Show, 1994*
Martini & Rossi Ltd
    The Great Age of British
    Watercolours, 1750–1880. 1993
Paul Mellon KBE
    The Great Age of British
    Watercolours, 1750–1880. 1993
Merrill Lynch
    American Art in the 20th Century,
    1993*
    Paris: Capital of the Arts
    1900–1968. 2002
Midland Bank plc
    RA Outreach Programme,
    1992–1996
    Lessons in Life, 1994
Minorco
    Africa: The Art of a Continent,
    1995
Natwest Group
    Nicolas Poussin 1594–1665.
    1995
The Nippon Foundation
    Hiroshige: Images of Mist, Rain,
    Moon and Snow, 1997
Olivetti
    Andrea Mantegna, 1992
Peterborough United Football Club
    Art Treasures of England:
    The Regional Collections, 1997
*Premiercare (National Westminster
    Insurance Services)*
    Roger de Grey, 1996*
RA Exhibition Patrons Group
    Chagall: Love and the Stage,
    1998
    Kandinsky, 1999
    Chardin 1699–1779. 2000
    Botticelli's Dante: The Drawings
    for The Divine Comedy, 2001
    Return of the Buddha: The
    Qingzhou Discoveries, 2002
Redab (UK) Ltd
    Wisdom and Compassion:
    The Sacred Art of Tibet, 1992
Reed Elsevier plc
    Van Dyck 1599–1641. 1999
    Rembrandt's Women, 2001
Republic National Bank of New York
    Sickert: Paintings, 1992
The Royal Bank of Scotland
    Braque: The Late Works, 1997*
    Premiums, 1997
    Premiums, 1998
    Premiums, 1999
    Royal Academy Schools Final
    Year Show, 1996
    Royal Academy Schools Final
    Year Show, 1997
    Royal Academy Schools Final
    Year Show, 1998
The Sara Lee Foundation
    Odilon Redon: Dreams and
    Visions, 1995
Sea Containers Ltd
    The Glory of Venice: Art in the
    Eighteenth Century, 1994
Silhouette Eyewear
    Wisdom and Compassion:
    The Sacred Art of Tibet, 1992
    Sandra Blow, 1994
    Africa: The Art of a Continent,
    1995
Société Générale, UK
    Gustave Caillebotte: The
    Unknown Impressionist, 1996*
Société Générale de Belgique
    Impressionism to Symbolism:
    The Belgian Avant-garde
    1880–1900. 1994
Spero Communications
    Royal Academy Schools Final
    Year Show, 1992
Thames Water Plc
    Thames Water Habitable Bridge
    Competition, 1996

The Times
    Wisdom and Compassion:
    The Sacred Art of Tibet, 1992
    Drawings from the J Paul Getty
    Museum, 1993
    Goya: Truth and Fantasy,
    The Small Paintings, 1994
    Africa: The Art of a Continent,
    1995
Time Out
    Sensation: Young British Artists
    from The Saatchi Collection, 1997
    Apocalypse: Beauty and Horror
    in Contemporary Art, 2000
Tractabel
    Impressionism to Symbolism:
    The Belgian Avant-garde
    1880–1900, 1994
Union Minière
    Impressionism to Symbolism:
    The Belgian Avant-garde
    1880–1900, 1994
Vistech International Ltd
    Wisdom and Compassion:
    The Sacred Art of Tibet, 1992
Yakult UK Ltd
    RA Outreach Programme,
    1997–2002*
    alive: Life Drawings from the
    Royal Academy of Arts & Yakult
    Outreach Programme

*   Recipients of a Pairing Scheme
    Award, managed by Arts +
    Business. Arts + Business is
    funded by the Arts Council
    of England and the Department
    for Culture, Media and Sport.

Other Sponsors

Sponsors of events, publications
and other items in the past five years:

Carlisle Group plc
Country Life
Derwent Valley Holdings plc
Dresdner Kleinwort Wasserstein
Fidelity Foundation
Foster and Partners
Goldman Sachs International
Gome International
Gucci Group
Rob van Helden
IBJ International plc
John Doyle Construction
Marks & Spencer
Michael Hopkins & Partners
Morgan Stanley Dean Witter
Prada
Radisson Edwardian Hotels
Richard and Ruth Rogers
Strutt & Parker

THE VICTORIA CLIMBIÉ INQUIRY

REPORT OF AN INQUIRY
BY LORD LAMING

*Presented to Parliament by the
Secretary of State for Health and
the Secretary of State for the Home Department
by Command of Her Majesty
January 2003*

Cm 5730

£42.50 inc VAT

THE VICTORIA CLIMBIÉ INQUIRY

Rt Hon Alan Milburn MP
Secretary of State for Health

Rt Hon David Blunkett MP
Home Secretary

Dear Secretaries of State,

In April 2001, you asked me to chair an Independent Statutory Inquiry following the death of Victoria Climbié, and to make recommendations as to how such an event may, as far as possible, be avoided in the future. I am pleased to submit my report to you.

I appointed four expert assessors to assist me in my task. They were Dr Nellie Adjaye, Mr John Fox, Mrs Donna Kinnair and Mr Nigel Richardson.

I take responsibility for this report and I am pleased that my four colleagues who sat with me fully endorse its findings and its recommendations.

Yours sincerely,

LORD LAMING

DR NELLIE ADJAYE

MR JOHN FOX

MRS DONNA KINNAIR

MR NIGEL RICHARDSON

Part one: Background

1 Introduction

"Victoria had the most beautiful smile that lit up the room." Patrick Cameron

1.1 This Report begins and ends with Victoria Climbié. It is right that it should do so. The purpose of this Inquiry has been to find out why this once happy, smiling, enthusiastic little girl – brought to this country by a relative for 'a better life' – ended her days the victim of almost unimaginable cruelty. The horror of what happened to her during her last months was captured by Counsel to the Inquiry, Neil Garnham QC, who told the Inquiry:

> "The food would be cold and would be given to her on a piece of plastic while she was tied up in the bath. She would eat it like a dog, pushing her face to the plate. Except, of course that a dog is not usually tied up in a plastic bag full of its excrement. To say that Kouao and Manning treated Victoria like a dog would be wholly unfair; she was treated worse than a dog."

1.2 On 12 January 2001, Victoria's great-aunt, Marie-Therese Kouao, and Carl John Manning were convicted of her murder.

Abuse and neglect

1.3 At his trial, Manning said that Kouao would strike Victoria on a daily basis with a shoe, a coat hanger and a wooden cooking spoon and would strike her on her toes with a hammer. Victoria's blood was found on Manning's football boots. Manning admitted that at times he would hit Victoria with a bicycle chain. Chillingly, he said, "You could beat her and she wouldn't cry ... she could take the beatings and the pain like anything."

1.4 Victoria spent much of her last days, in the winter of 1999–2000, living and sleeping in a bath in an unheated bathroom, bound hand and foot inside a bin bag, lying in her own urine and faeces. It is not surprising then that towards the end of her short life, Victoria was stooped like an old lady and could walk only with great difficulty.

1.5 When Victoria was admitted to the North Middlesex Hospital on the evening of 24 February 2000, she was desperately ill. She was bruised, deformed and malnourished. Her temperature was so low it could not be recorded on the hospital's standard thermometer. Dr Lesley Alsford, the consultant responsible for Victoria's care on that occasion, said, "I had never seen a case like it before. It is the worst case of child abuse and neglect that I have ever seen."

1.6 Despite the valiant efforts of Dr Alsford and her team, Victoria's condition continued to deteriorate. In a desperate attempt to save her life, Victoria was transferred to the paediatric intensive care unit at St Mary's Hospital Paddington. It was there that, tragically, she died a few hours later, on the afternoon of 25 February 2000.

1.7 Seven months earlier, Victoria had been a patient in the North Middlesex Hospital. Nurse Sue Jennings recalled:

> "Victoria did not have any possessions – she only had the clothes that she arrived in. Some of the staff had brought in dresses and presents for Victoria. One of the nurses had given her a white dress and Victoria found some pink wellingtons which she used to wear with it. I remember Victoria dressed like this, twirling up and down the ward. She was a very friendly and happy child."

Victoria's injuries

1.8 At the end, Victoria's lungs, heart and kidneys all failed. Dr Nathaniel Carey, a Home Office pathologist with many years' experience, carried out the post-mortem examination. What stood out from Dr Carey's evidence was the extent of Victoria's injuries and the deliberate way they were inflicted on her. He said:

> "All non-accidental injuries to children are awful and difficult for everybody to deal with, but in terms of the nature and extent of the injury, and the almost systematic nature of the inflicted injury, I certainly regard this as the worst I have ever dealt with, and it is just about the worst I have ever heard of."

1.9 At the post-mortem examination, Dr Carey recorded evidence of no fewer than 128 separate injuries to Victoria's body, saying, "There really is not anywhere that is spared – there is scarring all over the body."

1.10 Therefore, in the space of just a few months, Victoria had been transformed from a healthy, lively, and happy little girl, into a wretched and broken wreck of a human being.

Abandoned, unheard and unnoticed

1.11 Perhaps the most painful of all the distressing events of Victoria's short life in this country is that even towards the end, she might have been saved. In the last few weeks before she died, a social worker called at her home several times. She got no reply when she knocked at the door and assumed that Victoria and Kouao had moved away. It is possible that at the time, Victoria was in fact lying just a few yards away, in the prison of the bath, desperately hoping someone might find her and come to her rescue before her life ebbed away.

1.12 At no time during the weeks and months of this gruelling Inquiry did familiarity with the suffering experienced by Victoria diminish the anguish of hearing it, or make it easier to endure. It was clear from the evidence heard by the Inquiry that Victoria's intelligence, and the warmth of her engaging smile, shone through, despite the ghastly facts of what she experienced during the 11 months she lived in England. The more my colleagues and I heard about Victoria, the more we came to know her as a lovable child, and our hearts went out to her. However, neither Victoria's intelligence nor her lovable nature could save her. In the end she died a slow, lonely death – abandoned, unheard and unnoticed.

Victoria's parents

1.13 Before moving on to the introductory part of this Report, I wish to pay a warm tribute to Victoria's parents, Francis and Berthe Climbié. They were present for the whole of Phase One of this Inquiry. Their love for Victoria was clear, as were their hopes that she would receive a better education in Europe. In the face of the most disturbing evidence about the treatment of their daughter, they displayed both courage and dignity.

"I have suffered too much grief in setting down these heartrending memories. If I try to describe him, it is to make sure that I shall not forget him."

Jiro Hirabayashi from Yasunori Kawahara's
translation of *The Little Prince* by Antoine de Saint-Exupéry.

This sentiment applies also to Victoria Climbié.
This Report is dedicated to her memory.

Contents

Changes in services to support children

What is wrong with current arrangements?

1.32 Current inter-agency arrangements for protecting children depend very heavily on the key agencies in health, the police and social services working within closely related geographical boundaries. This is no longer the case. Local authorities with responsibility for social services have been reorganised so they are now smaller and more numerous. Indeed, there are now 150 of them in England. In contrast, health authorities are now larger and fewer, numbering only 30. Front-line health services are provided by a growing number of Primary Care Trusts, currently over 300, while 43 police authorities cover England and Wales.

1.33 As a result, Area Child Protection Committees (ACPCs), the organisations with responsibility for co-ordinating child protection services at a local level, have generally become unwieldy, bureaucratic and with limited impact on front-line services. I was told that in the London Metropolitan Police area, there are 33 local authorities with social services responsibilities and 27 Area Child Protection Committees. In Liverpool, there are five ACPCs, while in Essex (with a population of over one million) there is one. Such wide variations in geographical areas and populations served by the ACPCs must inevitably lead to equally wide variations in the co-ordination and quality of services offered to vulnerable children. A new arrangement is needed.

Improvements at a national level

A Children and Families Board

1.34 Therefore, I recommend a fundamental change in the way that services to support children and families are organised and managed. With the support of the Prime Minister, a Children and Families Board should be established at the heart of government. The Board should be chaired by a minister of Cabinet rank and have representatives at ministerial level from each of the relevant government departments. This Inquiry was told that well-intentioned ministerial initiatives are introduced piecemeal, and either do not fulfil their potential or divert staff from other essential front-line work. This Board should be charged with ensuring that the impact of all such initiatives that have a bearing on the well-being of children and families is considered within this forum.

A National Agency for Children and Families

1.35 In addition, a National Agency for Children and Families should be created. The chief executive of this agency – who may have the functions of a Children's Commissioner for England – would be responsible for servicing the Government's Children and Families Board. The National Agency for Children and Families should:

- assess, and advise the Children and Families Board about, the impact on children and families of proposed changes in policy;
- scrutinise new legislation and guidance issued for this purpose;
- advise on the implementation of the UN Convention on the Rights of the Child;
- advise on setting nationally agreed outcomes for children and how they might best be achieved and monitored;
- ensure that policy and legislation are implemented at a local level and are monitored through its regional office network;
- report annually to Parliament on the quality and effectiveness of services to children and families, in particular on the safety of children;
- at its discretion, conduct serious case reviews or oversee the process if this task is carried out by other agencies.

At a local level

1.36 Clearly, it is for central government to make key decisions on overall policy, legislation and the funding of services. However, it is unrealistic for service delivery to be managed centrally. The managers of local services must be given the responsibility to assess local need and to respond accordingly. However, where the care and protection of children and the support of children and families is concerned, this independence must not be pursued to the detriment of effective joint working. I recognise that committee structures and job descriptions vary between local authorities.

1.37 The future lies with those managers who can demonstrate the capacity to work effectively across organisational boundaries. Such boundaries will always exist. Those able to operate flexibly need encouragement, in contrast to those who persist in working in isolation and making decisions alone. Such people must either change or be replaced. The safeguarding of children must not be placed in jeopardy by individual preference. The joint training of staff and the sharing of budgets are likely to ensure an equality of desire and effort to make them work effectively.

Committees for Children and Families

1.38 In order to secure strong local working relationships so that collaboration on the scale of that which I envisage takes place, I propose that each local authority with social services responsibilities should establish a Committee for Children and Families, with members drawn from the relevant committees of the local authority, the police authority and relevant boards and trusts of health services. This committee will oversee the work of a Management Board for Services to Children and Families.

Management Board for Services to Children and Families

1.39 In each local authority, the chief executive should chair a Management Board for Services to Children and Families, made up of chief officers (or very senior officers) from the police, social services, relevant health services, education, housing and the probation service. The Management Board for Services to Children and Families will be required to appoint a director of children and family services at local level. This person will be responsible for ensuring service delivery, including the effectiveness of local inter-agency working, which must also include working with voluntary and private agencies. Each board must also establish a local forum to secure the involvement of voluntary and private agencies, service users, including children, and other contributors as appropriate. Special arrangements will have to be made in London, to take account of the fact there are 33 London authorities.

Accountability

1.40 The relevant government inspectorates should be jointly required to inspect the effectiveness of these arrangements.

1.41 In order to ensure coherence within this proposed structure, it should be a requirement that each Management Board for Services to Children and Families reports to its parent Committee for Children and Families. In turn, the Committee for Children and Families will report through the regional structure to the National Agency for Children and Families. The Children and Families Board should report annually to Parliament on the state of services to children and families.

1.42 The purpose of these proposals is to secure a clear line of accountability for the protection of children and for the well-being of families. Never again should people in senior positions be free to claim – as they did in this Inquiry – ignorance of what was happening to children. These proposals are designed to ensure that those who manage services for children and families are held personally accountable for the effectiveness of these services, and for the arrangements their organisations put in place to ensure that all children are offered the best protection possible.

Improvements to the exchange of information

1.43 Improvements to the way information is exchanged within and between agencies are imperative if children are to be adequately safeguarded. Staff must be held accountable for the quality of the information they provide. Information systems that depend on the random passing of slips of paper have no place in modern services. Each agency must accept responsibility for making sure that information passed to another agency is clear, and the recipients should query any points of uncertainty. In the words of the two hospital consultants who had care of Victoria:

> "I cannot account for the way other people interpreted what I said. It was not the way I would have liked it to have been interpreted."
>
> (Dr Ruby Schwartz)

> "I do not think it was until I have read and re-read this letter that I appreciated quite the depth of misunderstanding."
>
> (Dr Mary Rossiter)

The fact that an elementary point like this has to be made reflects the dreadful state of communications which exposed Victoria to danger.

1.44 There can be no justification for hospitals in close proximity to each other failing to access information about earlier patient contact. In this day and age, it must be reasonable to expect the free exchange of information within the National Health Service. The need for this is all the more critical because experience shows that 'shopping around' the health service is one of the favourite ploys of carers wishing to evade suspicion about their treatment of their children.

1.45 Effective action designed to safeguard the well-being of children and families depends upon sharing relevant information on an inter-agency basis. The following contribution to one of the Phase Two seminars was compelling in this respect:

> "Whenever we do a Part 8 case review ... we have this huge chronology of information made available to the Panel and it is very frustrating to read that ... a long way before that happened, a pattern of things emerging, but knowing that at the time ... separate agencies held those bits of information. So GPs will be seeing things, accident and emergency will be seeing things, the police may be dealing with other aspects of what is going on in that child's life, and nobody is bringing it together."

1.46 However, I was told that the free exchange of information about children and families about whom there are concerns is inhibited by the legislation on data protection and human rights. It appears that, unless a child is deemed to be in need of protection, information cannot be shared between agencies without staff running the risk of contravening this legislation. This has two consequences: either it deters information sharing, or it artificially increases concerns in order that they can be expressed as the need for protection. This is a matter that the Government must address. It is not a matter that can be tackled satisfactorily at local level.

A national children's database

1.47 Those who deliberately harm children have a tendency to cover their tracks. Poor record-keeping, doubts about the exchange of information between services, and inadequate client information systems make that easy. We live in a highly mobile society. Ninety million people pass through our ports of entry each year. Many children experience several moves. I have considered the benefits of establishing a national database on children. In the circumstances set out above, there is much to be said in favour of a database covering all children. I was told that such a database is technically feasible and that there are many much larger systems. The benefit of such a database would be that every new contact with a child by a member of staff from any of the key services would initiate an entry that would build up a picture of the child's health, developmental and educational needs. I have recommended that the Government commission work to look into the feasibility of such a national database, and this may result in pilot studies being carried out.

Action now

1.48 While the introduction of the proposals set out above will require changing the law, the vast majority of recommendations in this Report can be implemented immediately. Some 82 of the 108 recommendations should be implemented within six months. The Inquiry website received around three million hits in the period 30 September 2001 to 30 September 2002, and already a number of the key agencies have reviewed their practices. In this respect, the Inquiry has already had a considerable impact on service delivery. This momentum must be maintained and, where necessary, speeded up, if the unacceptable practice I heard about is to be eliminated. This Report is intended to have an impact on practice **now** – not just some time in the future. Its recommendations cannot be deferred to some bright tomorrow. Robust leadership must replace bureaucratic administration. The adherence to inward-looking processes must give way to more flexible deployment of staff and resources in the search for better results for children and families.

Service funding

1.49 Some elected councillors from Haringey and Brent insisted that the amount of money allocated by central government to their authorities for children's services under the Standard Spending Assessment (SSA) was a result of the distribution formula and did not reflect the needs of the local area. They claimed that because 80 per cent of the funding comes from central government, and because they were being pressed to address central government priorities, they had little scope to influence spending at a local level.

1.50 In this respect, local authorities portrayed themselves as being little more than the agents of central government, rather than being independently elected corporate bodies. If this is correct, it has potentially serious implications for the future of local government in this country. Significantly, at the time that Ealing, Brent and Haringey were spending well below their SSA on services for children, the national picture was quite different, with most local authorities overspending the SSA on services for children and families.

1.51 Nobody from these authorities could give a convincing explanation as to why services for children and families were so significantly underfunded. For example, in 1998/1999 the Brent SSA for children and families was £28 million, whereas the amount spent was just £14.5 million. Since the death of Victoria, Ealing, Brent and Haringey have increased their budgetary provision for children and families. It is my opinion that elected councillors and senior managers in these authorities allowed the services for children and families to become seriously under-funded, and they did not properly consider the impact this would have upon their front-line services.

Eligibility criteria

1.52 The management of the social care of children and families represents one of the most difficult challenges for local government. The variety and range of referrals, together with the degree of risk and urgency, needs strong leadership, effective decision-making, reliable record-keeping, and a regular review of performance.

What went wrong?

1.14   I recognise that those who take on the work of protecting children at risk of deliberate harm face a tough and challenging task. Staff doing this work need a combination of professional skills and personal qualities, not least of which are persistence and courage. Adults who deliberately exploit the vulnerability of children can behave in devious and menacing ways. They will often go to great lengths to hide their activities from those concerned for the well-being of a child. Staff often have to cope with the unpredictable behaviour of people in the parental role. A child can appear safe one minute and be injured the next. A peaceful scene can be transformed in seconds because of a sudden outburst of uncontrollable anger.

1.15   Whenever a child is deliberately injured or killed, there is inevitably great concern in case some important tell-tale sign has been missed. Those who sit in judgement often do so with the great benefit of hindsight. So I readily acknowledge that staff who undertake the work of protecting children and supporting families on behalf of us all deserve both our understanding and our support. It is a job which carries risks, because in every judgement they make, those staff have to balance the rights of a parent with that of the protection of the child.

A lack of good practice

1.16   But Victoria's case was altogether different. Victoria was not hidden away. It is deeply disturbing that during the days and months following her initial contact with Ealing Housing Department's Homeless Persons' Unit, Victoria was known to no less than two further housing authorities, four social services departments, two child protection teams of the Metropolitan Police Service (MPS), a specialist centre managed by the NSPCC, and she was admitted to two different hospitals because of suspected deliberate harm. The dreadful reality was that these services knew little or nothing more about Victoria at the end of the process than they did when she was first referred to Ealing Social Services by the Homeless Persons' Unit in April 1999. The final irony was that Haringey Social Services formally closed Victoria's case on the very day she died. The extent of the failure to protect Victoria was lamentable. Tragically, it required nothing more than basic good practice being put into operation. This never happened.

1.17   In his opening statement to the Inquiry, Neil Garnham QC listed no fewer than 12 key occasions when the relevant services had the opportunity to successfully intervene in the life of Victoria. As evidence to the Inquiry unfolded, several other opportunities emerged. Not one of these required great skill or would have made heavy demands on time to take some form of action. Sometimes it needed nothing more than a manager doing their job by asking pertinent questions or taking the trouble to look in a case file. There can be no excuse for such sloppy and unprofessional performance.

A gross failure of the system

1.18   Not one of the agencies empowered by Parliament to protect children in positions similar to Victoria's – funded from the public purse – emerge from this Inquiry with much credit. The suffering and death of Victoria was a gross failure of the system and was inexcusable. It is clear to me that the agencies with responsibility for Victoria gave a low priority to the task of protecting children. They were under-funded, inadequately staffed and poorly led. Even so, there was plenty of evidence to show that scarce resources were not being put to good use. Bad practice can be expensive. For example, had there been a proper response to the needs of Victoria when she was first referred to Ealing Social Services, it may well be that the danger to her would have been recognised and action taken which may have avoided the need for the later involvement of the other agencies.

2 The Inquiry

Why establish the Inquiry?

2.1   On 25 February 2000, Victoria Adjo Climbié died in the Intensive Care Unit at St Mary's Hospital Paddington. She died as a result of months of appalling ill-treatment at the hands of two individuals who were supposed to be caring for her.

2.2   On 12 January 2001 at the Central Criminal Court, Marie-Therese Kouao and Carl John Manning were convicted of her murder. Both were sentenced to life imprisonment. Victoria had been called 'Anna' by Kouao while she was in this country. I decided early on that this Inquiry would call her by her proper name.

2.3   On 20 April 2001, I was appointed by the Secretary of State for Health and the Secretary of State for the Home Department to conduct three statutory Inquiries. Together they would be known as The Victoria Climbié Inquiry.

2.4   The first Inquiry was established under section 81 of the Children Act 1989. It was concerned with the functions of local authority social services committees and the way they relate to children. The second Inquiry was established under section 84 of the National Health Service Act 1977 and was concerned with matters arising under that Act. The third Inquiry was established under section 49 of the Police Act 1996 and was concerned with policing.

2.5   The Inquiry's Terms of Reference were as follows:

1. *To establish the circumstances leading to and surrounding the death of Victoria Climbié.*

2. *To identify the services sought or required by, or in respect of Victoria Climbié, Marie-Therese Kouao and Carl Manning from local authorities in respect of their social services functions, the Health bodies and the Police between the arrival of Victoria Climbié and Marie-Therese Kouao in England in March 1999 and Victoria Climbié's death in February 2000.*

3. *To examine the way in which local authorities in respect of their social services functions, the health bodies and the police:*

   (i)   responded to those requests, or need for services
   (ii) discharged their functions
   (iii) co-operated with each other
   (iv) co-operated with other services including the local education authorities and the local housing authorities;

   in respect of the three persons named above during the period referred to above and thereafter.

4. *To reach conclusions as to the circumstances leading to Victoria Climbié's death and to make recommendations to the Secretary of State for Health and to the Secretary of State for the Home Department as to how such an event may, as far as possible, be avoided in the future.*

> 5. *To deliver a report of the Inquiry to the Secretary of State for Health and to the Secretary of State for the Home Department, who will then arrange for its publication.*

The Inquiry panel

2.6   I appointed four assessors to help me to consider and analyse the evidence:

- Dr Nellie Adjaye, a Fellow of the Royal College of Paediatrics and Child Health and a consultant paediatrician with the Maidstone and Tunbridge Wells NHS Trust;
- John Fox, a detective superintendent and the head of the Specialist Investigations Department in the Hampshire Constabulary;
- Donna Kinnair, a nurse and health visitor and formerly the strategic commissioner for children's services for the Lambeth, Southwark and Lewisham Health Authority;
- Nigel Richardson, the assistant director of Children and Families for North Lincolnshire Council.

2.7   The assessors gave advice on matters within their areas of expertise throughout the Inquiry. Their knowledge and support were of enormous value and I am very grateful to them, and to their employers for releasing them so that they could take part in this important work.

2.8   We also had very beneficial advice and assistance on housing issues from Mike Smith, head of Community Housing Services, Greenwich Council.

2.9   I appointed Mandy Jacklin as Secretary to the Inquiry. She was responsible for the management of the overall work of the Inquiry. With the consent of the Attorney General, I appointed Neil Garnham QC to be Counsel to the Inquiry, and Caroline Gibson and Neil Sheldon to be junior Counsel to the Inquiry. Their role was to help me in the investigation, advise me on matters of law and evidence, and present the evidence to the Inquiry at its hearings. Michael Fitzgerald acted as Solicitor to the Inquiry. A full list of those who worked on the Inquiry is in Annex 3.

Inquiry accommodation

2.10   The Inquiry was accommodated at Hannibal House, a government building at Elephant and Castle, London. The floors used for Inquiry purposes were substantially refurbished to provide secure accommodation for the Inquiry's offices and a well-equipped Inquiry room for the hearings. These floors were kept entirely separate from the other occupiers of the building.

What form did the Inquiry take?

Public or private?

2.11   The two secretaries of state allowed me to decide whether the Inquiry should be conducted in public or in private. After careful consideration, I decided it would be a public inquiry. However, I reserved the right to hear evidence in private in exceptional circumstances. I exercised that power on just one occasion, when it was necessary for the Inquiry to hear evidence that involved the child of one witness. I took the view that in order to protect the interests of the child, their evidence should be heard in private.

Format?

2.12   I decided that the Inquiry would be divided into two phases. Phase One (Parts one to four of this Report) would be mostly backward-looking. It would try to discover what happened to Victoria while she was in this country and why it happened.

Phase One would address paragraphs 1 to 3 of the Terms of Reference (see paragraph 2.5), and look at the conclusions that could properly be drawn from the evidence on those topics.

2.13   Phase Two (see Part five of this Report) would be forward-looking and examine what recommendations might be made to avoid, as far as possible, a tragedy like this happening again.

Adversarial or inquisitorial?

2.14   There is no statutory entitlement for any person to call witnesses, cross-examine or make submissions in an Inquiry of this sort. However, it was for me to decide what form the Inquiry should take, and I decided the Inquiry would be inquisitorial not adversarial in nature. In Phase One, Counsel to the Inquiry would decide which witnesses it was necessary to call to give evidence, and they would examine them.

Identifying Interested Parties and Represented Witnesses

2.15   A number of bodies and individuals expressed an interest in the work of the Inquiry. Therefore, it was decided to recognise people who had a legitimate interest in the work of the Inquiry as 'Interested Parties'. Also, a number of witnesses not represented as an Interested Party asked to be represented by lawyers at the Phase One hearings. In every case, permission was granted and these witnesses were known as 'Represented Witnesses'. A list of Interested Parties and their representatives and Represented Witnesses and their representatives can be found in Annex 4.

2.16   Most Interested Parties were public bodies or individuals involved with Victoria's case in this country who wished to be involved in Phase One, and who I thought could help the Inquiry with its work. At an early stage, we received an application for Victoria's parents, Francis and Berthe Climbié, to also be granted that status. I decided that it would be right to grant that application, given the obvious human interest any parent would have in an investigation into their child's death. Mr and Mrs Climbié also asked me to recommend to the Government that the cost of their travelling to the UK and their accommodation here throughout Phase One be met from the public purse. After careful reflection, I decided to make those recommendations, and the Government accepted them.

2.17   I decided that, as a general rule, Interested Parties and those acting for Represented Witnesses would not be allowed to call or cross-examine witnesses. I had indicated at the preliminary meeting (described in more detail in paragraph 2.20) that there might be exceptions to this general rule. However, I was only asked to make such an exception once, and I granted the request. Counsel to the Inquiry agreed to consider any requests for them to call additional witnesses and any requests for particular lines of questioning to be put to witnesses. I indicated during the preliminary meeting that if Counsel did not call such witnesses or ask such questions, I would adjudicate on the need to do so. In fact, this was not necessary and I am grateful to Counsel to the Inquiry and all the representatives for their sensible co-operation in this regard.

2.18   Those representing Interested Parties and Represented Witnesses were allowed to re-examine witnesses whom they represented. That re-examination was time limited.

2.19   At the end of oral hearings, representatives of Interested Parties and Represented Witnesses who wished to do so were allowed to make time-limited closing submissions, which could be supplemented with written submissions.

Preparing for the Inquiry

Preliminary meeting

2.20   On 30 May 2001, we held a preliminary meeting at Hannibal House and invited everyone who had expressed an interest in the work of the Inquiry. The meeting was open to the public. We began the meeting by holding a minute's silence in memory of Victoria.

2.21   At the meeting, I set out the arrangements I proposed to make for the running of the Inquiry, and I invited comments on those arrangements. No one suggested then, or in the weeks that followed, that the arrangements should be changed. Therefore, the arrangements proposed at the meeting were put into effect.

Gathering witness statements

2.22   In order to structure the work in Phase One, a list of issues was produced which reflected the Terms of Reference.

2.23   The Solicitor to the Inquiry wrote to everyone who might be able to give relevant evidence, asking them to produce a witness statement. A questionnaire was included that set out matters arising from the list of issues, which it was thought they would be able to speak about. In most cases these requests were made through the Interested Parties, and I am grateful for their assistance with this.

2.24   A bundle of witness statements was prepared by the secretariat and copies were made available to Interested Parties. The Interested Parties made a written statement that they understood they had to keep that material confidential and only use it for the purposes of this Inquiry.

Gathering documents

2.25   The three statutes to which I have referred gave me power to require the production of documents. The secretariat wrote to the relevant public bodies asking them to produce all relevant documents. One of the more difficult tasks that fell to the secretariat was managing the vast amount of documentation that was produced in response.

2.26   This work was made particularly difficult because of the late supply of some relevant material by some of the Interested Parties, and by others. For example, Brent council was late providing some documents and at times I felt material was drip-fed to us. Similarly, at one stage I was unhappy with the NSPCC's provision of documents. Documents which were supposedly lost were suddenly discovered, and on one occasion it was only during witness examinations that it became clear that documents had been given to the Inquiry in an edited form. However, in most cases, including those of Brent and the NSPCC, the problems were temporary and solved quickly due to the good sense and co-operation of those concerned.

2.27   I regret to say this was not always the case with Haringey council. I was so concerned about the way Haringey was responding to requests for documents that I issued a summons, in line with my powers under section 250 of the Local Government Act 1972. The summons was directed to Haringey's director of social services requiring her to produce four identified documents and any other documents relevant to the lessons learned by Haringey as a result of Victoria's death. From then on, there could be no confusion as to what the Inquiry required.

2.28   More than 650 new documents were produced in response to this summons. Several times after this, Haringey produced even more documentation. This was material that should have been produced, at the latest, by the date stated in the summons. I invited Haringey's chief executive to attend the Inquiry and explain Haringey council's conduct. He did so, and expressed his embarrassment at what had happened.

2.29 More material continued to be produced. I found it particularly disturbing that documents directly relevant to Victoria's case were found in a filing cabinet in the office where her case had been handled, and in a locked storage area next to that office. Haringey's Counsel told me that her client's embarrassment about these discoveries was "off the scale". I requested a further explanation from Haringey's chief executive. In the course of that explanation, I was told that to describe him as "absolutely furious" about what had happened would be an understatement.

2.30 I have seriously considered whether Haringey's method of dealing with its documentation was the result of a deliberate attempt to frustrate the Inquiry's work, or simple incompetence. Having considered the observations of Haringey's chief executive, I have concluded it was incompetence.

2.31 The smooth functioning of Inquiries such as this will always depend on the co-operation and assistance of the public bodies involved. The enormous inconvenience that can be caused by the late submission of relevant material was graphically illustrated by a document provided by the Social Services Inspectorate (SSI) after the Phase One hearings had been completed.

2.32 I describe in paragraphs 2.37 to 2.41 the significance of the document in question and the impact that its late submission had on the running of this Inquiry. For present purposes, I simply wish to express my surprise and disappointment that the work of the Inquiry was delayed in this manner.

2.33 The documents were read and assessed by the Inquiry team and bundles of relevant material were produced. Copies of the bundles were made available to Interested Parties in the same way referred to in paragraph 2.24. The material was made available in hard copy form and a searchable, electronic index on disk was produced to accompany the Inquiry bundle.

Phase One proceedings

Opening the Inquiry and hearing evidence

2.34 The hearings began on 26 September 2001, when Counsel to the Inquiry made his opening statement. That statement identified the matters which the Inquiry would need to focus on over the following months. In line with what had been said at the preliminary meeting, a television crew was given access to the Inquiry on that day. The next day, opening statements from the other Interested Parties were received.

2.35 The first witness, Francis Climbié, Victoria's father, was called on 28 September 2001. After this, Counsel to the Inquiry called a further 158 witnesses, all of whom gave their evidence on oath. In the case of four witnesses who had subsequently moved abroad, it was decided that the most convenient and economic method of obtaining their evidence was to use a video link between studios in their present country of residence and a Department of Health building close to the Inquiry's premises. This evidence was recorded and the video recordings were played in the public sessions of the Inquiry. The arrangements worked extremely well.

2.36 The written statements of a further 119 witnesses were put into evidence without the need for them to attend the Inquiry. Most of the oral evidence was completed by 4 February 2002. A list of the witnesses who were called to give evidence and those whose statements were read into the evidence can be found in Annex 2.

Final submissions from the Interested Parties and Counsel to the Inquiry were heard on 18, 19 and 27 February 2002. Proceedings on the first two of those days were also televised.

Reconvening Phase One hearings

2.37 I had expected the final submission on 27 February 2002 to mark the end of the public hearings in Phase One. However, on the advice of Counsel to the Inquiry, I chose not to close Phase One at that point because it was possible that further matters might emerge which would require the taking of additional evidence.

2.38 This advice turned out to be crucial. On 27 February 2002, the SSI gave the Inquiry a report of the Joint Review of Haringey Social Services. The Joint Review had been conducted by the SSI and the Audit Commission and published in November 1999.

2.39 It quickly became obvious that this document was not just relevant but potentially greatly important to Phase One of the Inquiry. It was immediately distributed to the Interested Parties and documents relevant to its preparation were sought from the SSI and the Audit Commission. These documents filled a further six lever-arch files.

2.40 This additional material was read and analysed. Then Counsel to the Inquiry advised that further witness statements should be obtained. The Inquiry was given 14 such statements, which were then circulated to the Interested Parties.

2.41 Having considered these additional statements, I reluctantly came to the view that I had no option but to reconvene the Phase One public hearings in order to take additional oral evidence. As a result, the Inquiry sat for two days on 9 and 10 July 2002. Four witnesses gave oral evidence subject to the same procedures used before. Interested Parties and the SSI were given the opportunity to make closing submissions on the new material, although not all Interested Parties took up that opportunity.

2.42 The three statutes under which the Inquiry was established gave me the power to call witnesses to attend and answer questions. It was necessary for me to exercise that power on only three occasions. The first was in respect of Carole Baptiste, the Haringey social work manager, who refused to agree to attend the Inquiry voluntarily. She also disobeyed the summons I issued and, as a result, criminal proceedings were begun against her. After this, she did attend and answered questions put to her. However, I decided that the criminal proceedings should go ahead.

2.43 I also issued summonses against Kouao and Manning. Kouao, who had refused to co-operate with the Inquiry in any way, was brought from prison to the Inquiry to give evidence in person. At first she refused to answer Counsel's questions. Eventually she was persuaded by him to give answers to some of the matters he raised with her. Manning, by contrast, had co-operated throughout and had given the Inquiry a witness statement when requested. It was arranged that he would give his evidence by video link from the Combined Court Centre in Leeds. That evidence was recorded and then played at the public hearings.

The involvement of broadcasters

2.44 A number of broadcasting organisations applied for access to the video evidence of Manning. At the time of the recording of his evidence, I sought Manning's views on whether I should allow his evidence to be broadcast. He opposed it. Having considered his views and the detailed oral and written submissions from Counsel acting on the broadcasters' behalf and from others, I decided to refuse the application.

Publishing evidence and data protection

2.45 All oral evidence was simultaneously transcripted using a system called Livenote. The system proved very useful.

2.46 I believed it was important that the Inquiry should conduct its work as openly and transparently as possible. I wanted to give those with an interest in the evidence as much access to it as possible, at the same time ensuring the fair conduct of the proceedings. In particular, I wanted those who might be able to contribute to Phase Two to have a convenient way of learning about the issues being raised in Phase One.

2.47 As a result, an Inquiry website was established (**www.victoria-climbie-inquiry.org.uk**). All statements provided to the Inquiry and transcripts of each day's evidence were placed on this website. The website received around three million hits in the period 30 September 2001 to 30 September 2002. The average length of the website's 'visitor sessions' was 20 minutes (compared with an internet average of three minutes). This suggests that members of the public were using the site for detailed reading, rather than out of a passing interest.

2.48 Before statements and transcripts were published in this manner, the Inquiry contacted the assistant data protection commissioner. It was agreed with him that the Inquiry constituted legal proceedings for the purposes of section 35 of the Data Protection Act 1998, and that the Inquiry might lawfully process non-sensitive personal data without the consent of the data subject. It was made clear that telephone numbers, addresses and names of family members would be removed from witness statements before they were placed on the website, and that the security of such information would be strictly maintained by the Inquiry team. It was confirmed that the Inquiry could also lawfully process sensitive personal data without the explicit consent of the person concerned.

2.49 The assistant data protection commissioner agreed that statements and transcripts of the public hearings would be placed on the website but would not contravene the Eighth Data Protection Principle. The Principle restricts the communication of personal information to countries which have adequate protection for personal information in place. It was in the public interest to make this information available, especially to those who would be able to make a contribution to Phase Two of the Inquiry.

Legal expenses

2.50 The Inquiry does not have any power to order payment of legal costs from public funds or by any other party. However, the Government indicated to me that if I made a recommendation that the costs of an Interested Party or Represented Witness should be met out of public funds, then it would be sympathetically considered. I made such a recommendation for one Interested Party and two Represented Witnesses and on each occasion the Government accepted my recommendation.

Dealing with potential criticism

2.51 I made clear at the preliminary meeting that some individuals or organisations could be criticised in this Report, and that out of fairness I would adopt a procedure that allowed those concerned to address any criticism. The procedures for the representation of Interested Parties and Represented Witnesses and the preparation of their statements seemed to me to already meet those requirements. However, I proposed taking an extra step to ensure proceedings were conducted fairly.

2.52 I made it clear that I would make no findings significantly adverse to an individual or organisation without ensuring that they first had a proper opportunity to answer the criticism. Wherever it was possible to do so, the witness would be informed by the Inquiry team of the nature of the potential criticism before they were called to give evidence. Where that was not possible, either because of the time at which grounds for the potential criticism emerged or otherwise, arrangements would be made either for the witness to respond in writing, or for the witness to be recalled so that they could answer the criticism. At the preliminary meeting, I made it clear that I would particularly welcome representations on those procedures. I received no suggestions indicating a need to amend the proposed arrangements and so they were put into practice during the course of the Inquiry.

2.53 Notices of potential criticism were sent to individuals or public bodies where it appeared they may be criticised for their conduct in relation to matters covered by the Inquiry's Terms of Reference. Each witness was given the chance to address these points during the course of their evidence. The Solicitor to the Inquiry wrote to the relevant party afterwards to make sure they felt they had been given a fair chance to respond. No one said that they had not.

Phase Two

Preparing for Phase Two

2.54 The fourth paragraph of our Terms of Reference requires us to make recommendations as to how a tragedy like this could be avoided in the future.

2.55 It was apparent early on that, in responding to this, we were likely to have to consider making two different types of recommendations. The first type would be addressed to the particular circumstances of Victoria's case and to the events that occurred in Ealing, Brent and Haringey while Victoria lived there. The second type would be recommendations with wider potential impact and that might affect relevant agencies across the country.

2.56 In the course of Phase One, we were likely to become familiar with practice and procedure in certain parts of London, but it would be an obvious mistake to assume that these same practices and procedures were necessarily followed elsewhere. We are not charged with conducting a review of the whole child protection system in this country. However, we had to devise a way for a wider audience to test the ideas prompted by Victoria's case so that they could be used elsewhere.

Providing a framework for Phase Two

2.57 Phase Two was designed to be a way for such wider consideration to happen. In order to give some shape to our thinking on these subjects, the Inquiry produced a provisional framework document for Phase Two in late October 2001. That framework was based on our reading of the documents and witness statements gathered for Phase One. It identified broad issues, aspects of which we believed might be worthy of consideration in Phase Two. We asked for comments on the structure and contents of that framework and suggestions for topics that should be considered. We received a large number of responses to that framework document and, in the light of those responses, we drew up a discussion paper, which we published on the website and circulated widely.

2.58 The issues were addressed in two ways. First, we invited written submissions from the public at large. We anticipated that not all of the submissions we received were likely to help us, so we made it clear in the beginning that only those that were relevant and valuable would be treated as evidence to the Inquiry. In fact, out of over 200 submissions we received, we accepted 77 as evidence and published them on the website. I am very grateful to all those who took the trouble to send in written submissions.

2.59   Second, the Inquiry organised a series of five seminars, which were held in March and April 2002. They were conducted in public at the Inquiry's premises at Hannibal House. The seminars covered the following aspects of working with children:

- Ensuring that children and their families receive the full range of services they are entitled to;
- Making sure that children and families in need of extra care and support are identified at an early stage;
- Carrying out a proper assessment of the needs of children and families and developing plans to achieve the best outcomes for them;
- Making sure that key agencies are able to deliver an effective service;
- Monitoring the performance of the key agencies.

2.60   A wide range of people with an interest in our work were invited to the seminars. These included practitioners and managers from social services, the police, health services, academics, lawyers and commentators. They were chosen from those who had responded to our framework document and discussion paper, and from those not previously involved in the Inquiry. A full list of those who took part in the seminars can be found in Annex 5. The seminars were chaired by Neil Garnham QC and attended by the assessors and myself. They were a most valuable source of ideas, and are discussed further in section 17 of this Report. I am most grateful to all those who took part.

Closing the Inquiry

2.61   On 31 July 2002, I formally closed the evidence-gathering process of the Inquiry. No material received by the Inquiry after this date has been considered for the purposes of preparing this Report.

3.8   In the beginning, Kouao seemed prepared to honour her promise to make sure Victoria received a proper education. Shortly after her arrival in France, Victoria was enrolled at the Jean Moulin primary school in Villepinte. However, by December 1998, Kouao began to receive formal warnings from the school about Victoria's absenteeism. The situation became serious enough by February 1999 for the school to issue a Child at Risk Emergency Notification. A social worker became involved and she reported a difficult 'mother and child relationship' between Victoria and Kouao.

3.9   Some of Victoria's absences from school were justified by medical certificates, all of which said she needed to rest. When she was at school, staff worried about Victoria's tendency to fall asleep in class. As a result, the school formed the view that Victoria was clinically unwell and being monitored and treated by doctors. The head teacher, Monsieur Donnet, also recalled Kouao mentioning that Victoria was suffering from some form of dermatological condition.

3.10   Some time in the spring of 1999, Kouao gave the school notice that she was removing Victoria so she could receive "treatment" in London. The home address of Esther Ackah was given as a forwarding address. Ms Ackah was a distant relative of Kouao's and the two had been in intermittent contact for the previous two years. When Victoria went to say goodbye to her classmates on 25 March 1999, Monsieur Donnet noticed that Victoria had a shaven head and was wearing a wig.

3.11   Why Kouao decided to leave France for the UK is unclear. For a long while before leaving, she had been claiming benefits that she was not entitled to. The French benefits agency was trying to recover money for these benefits, and this could have influenced her decision.

Victoria arrives in the UK

3.12   Kouao and Victoria boarded a flight from Paris to London on 24 April 1999. They travelled on Kouao's French passport, in which Victoria was described as her daughter. The picture in the passport was not of Victoria but 'Anna', the child she had replaced. The two children did not look particularly similar so it is likely that Victoria was made to wear a wig so she looked more like the child in the photograph.

3.13   Kouao and Victoria travelled as EU citizens, so no immigration record of their arrival exists. However, the date they travelled can be established by the airline ticket that was later shown to Ealing Social Services by Kouao as proof of her identity. Kouao also presented documentation from the French travel company that arranged the trip.

3.14   When they arrived in the UK, Kouao and Victoria went to Acton and moved into a double room in a bed and breakfast in Twyford Crescent. The reservation had been made in France and lasted until 1 May 1999.

3.15   At about 4.30pm on 25 April 1999, Victoria and Kouao paid an unannounced visit to Ms Ackah. Ms Ackah had just come home from work when she heard the doorbell ring at her house in Hanwell, west London. Victoria was introduced to her as 'Anna'. Despite being somewhat taken aback by their presence, Ms Ackah invited Kouao and Victoria inside.

3.16   The first thing Ms Ackah noticed about Victoria was that she was wearing a wig. This was also remarked upon by Ms Ackah's daughter, Grace Quansah, who joined her in a visit to see Victoria and Kouao later that day. Ms Quansah removed the wig from Victoria's head to discover that she had no hair and her scalp was covered with patchy marks. She also thought Victoria looked rather small and frail, but neither she nor her mother noticed anything inappropriate or disturbing about Victoria's behaviour or her interaction with Kouao at this stage.

3.17   The following day, Kouao and Victoria visited Ealing's Homeless Persons' Unit because they needed somewhere to live when their week in Twyford Crescent ran out. The unit agreed to provide them with accommodation in a hostel situated at Nicoll Road, Harlesden, and they moved in around 1 May 1999.

The first warning signs

3.18   Over the next few weeks, Victoria and Kouao attended Ealing Social Services several times to collect subsistence payments and, on one occasion, to complain about the standard of their accommodation. During this period, concerns first started to emerge. A number of Ealing staff who saw Kouao and Victoria together during May 1999 noticed a marked difference between Kouao's appearance (she was always well dressed) and that of Victoria (who was far scruffier). Deborah Gaunt, who saw the two of them together on 24 May 1999, went as far as to say that she thought Victoria looked like an "advertisement for Action Aid".

3.19   It is unclear how Victoria passed her days during the first month she spent in the Nicoll Road hostel. No effort was made, either by Kouao or by Ealing Social Services, to enrol her in any form of educational or daycare activity, and there is no evidence to indicate she had any friends or playmates.

3.20   On 8 June 1999, Kouao took Victoria to a GP surgery on Acton Lane, Harlesden. Here she was seen by the practice nurse, Grace Moore. Nurse Moore did not carry out a physical examination of Victoria because she was reported not to have any current health problems or complaints. She felt there were "no child protection concerns that required follow up or reporting to other agencies".

3.21   Shortly afterwards, Victoria began to show what may have been early signs of deliberate physical harm. Ms Ackah, who had not seen Victoria since her visit six weeks earlier, bumped into her and Kouao on the street on or around 14 June 1999. Victoria was wearing a dress with long sleeves, leaving only her face and hands exposed. Ms Ackah noticed a fresh scar on Victoria's right cheek, which Kouao told her had been caused when Victoria fell on an escalator.

Victoria meets Manning

3.22   Later that same day, Victoria met Manning for the first time. He had been driving a bus boarded by Kouao four days before and the two had fallen into conversation. According to Manning, he gave Kouao his telephone number and she called him a few days later inviting him to visit her at Nicoll Road. This appears to have been the start of their relationship. It lasted until their arrest just over eight months later.

Anonymous telephone call

3.23   Ms Ackah was sufficiently concerned by what she had seen of Victoria in the street to visit Nicoll Road on 17 June 1999. She thought the accommodation was unsuitable for a child because it was dirty, cramped and ill-equipped. She also thought Victoria had lost weight since she had last seen her. A Ghanaian man was present and he told Ms Ackah he was concerned about the way Kouao treated Victoria. The following day, Ms Ackah made the first of her two anonymous telephone calls to Brent Social Services.

3.38   Due to the infectious nature of scabies, Victoria was nursed in isolation for the rest of her stay on the ward. Victoria was extremely distressed to see Ms Cameron leave earlier that evening, but then seemed to settle down and, apart from wetting the bed, she passed a fairly uneventful night. The next morning, after the police had withdrawn their protection, Kouao returned to the hospital and left with Victoria.

3.39   The first agency they visited on leaving hospital was Ealing Social Services' Acton Area Office. Kouao left Victoria in the waiting room on her own for over an hour, much to the annoyance of a social worker named Pamela Fortune. They spent that night in a hotel in Wembley before returning to Somerset Gardens the next day.

3.40   On the way, they stopped off at the Camerons' house to collect Victoria's clothes. Mrs Cameron tried to speak to Victoria but she would not answer her. Mr Cameron was also there and recalled that Victoria seemed "totally different" from other times he had seen her. She would not smile at him and she did not respond when he said hello to her in French. The clothes were retrieved and Kouao and Victoria left. Apart from one occasion when Mrs Cameron saw Kouao and Victoria walking together down the street, the Camerons never saw either of them again.

Victoria's second visit to hospital

3.41   Just over a week later on 24 July 1999, Victoria was back in hospital. This time it was the North Middlesex Hospital and Kouao who brought her in. Her most urgent injury was a serious scald to the face, which Kouao said was caused by Victoria placing her head under the hot tap in the bathroom to try and relieve the itching caused by scabies. According to one of the versions of events put forward by Kouao, she had been asleep in bed at around midday when a scream from the bathroom woke her up. Victoria's burns were so serious she was admitted to the paediatric ward – known as Rainbow ward – where she stayed for the next 13 nights.

3.42   At about 11pm on 24 July 1999, Dr Simone Forlee, the senior house officer who first examined her, explained the position to Haringey Social Services. A more detailed referral was made three days later by Karen Johns, an Enfield social worker based at the hospital. As a result, a strategy meeting was held at Haringey's offices on 28 July 1999 and Victoria's case was allocated to a social worker – Lisa Arthurworrey.

3.43   A number of medical staff who cared for Victoria during her stay on Rainbow ward noticed marks on her body which they considered were signs of serious deliberate physical harm. Nurse Beatrice Norman saw what she thought was a belt buckle mark on Victoria's shoulder, and Nurse Millicent Graham noticed a mark which made her suspect Victoria had been deliberately burned. Nurse Grace Pereira, who bathed Victoria the following day, saw marks which led her to believe Victoria had been hit with a belt and bitten.

3.44   It seems Victoria had started to suffer serious deliberate harm by late July 1999. This is also indicated by her behaviour when Kouao and Manning came to visit her on the ward. She gave the impression of being frightened of them. When Kouao came onto the ward, Victoria changed from being lively and vivacious to withdrawn and timid, and the relationship between her and Kouao was recorded in the ward's critical incident log as being like that of "master and servant". On one occasion she was seen to wet herself while standing to attention in front of a seated Kouao, who was apparently telling her off.

3.45   Her reaction to Manning when he came to visit seems to have been similar. He said Victoria seemed "wary of his presence" and was anxious to keep her distance from him. Neither he nor Kouao ever brought Victoria anything in the way of clothes, food, toys or treats throughout the fortnight she spent in hospital.

3.46   When Kouao was not around, Victoria seems to have enjoyed her time on Rainbow ward. She certainly became something of a favourite of several of the nurses, including Nurse Lucienne Taub, a French speaker whom Dr Mary Rossiter, the hospital's named doctor for child protection, had asked to befriend Victoria. She liked to dress up and was given clothes to dress up in by the nursing staff. Nurse Taub would take her to see the babies in the neo-natal ward and bought her sweets and treats. According to Dr Rossiter, she was a "little ray of sunshine".

3.47   Apart from Kouao and Manning, the only other visitors Victoria received while in the North Middlesex Hospital were Ms Arthurworrey and PC Karen Jones. They visited on 6 August 1999 and, after speaking briefly to Victoria, decided it would be appropriate for her to be discharged back into Kouao's care.

3.48   The brief interlude in her life in this country during which Victoria was safe, happy and well cared for ended. She left the North Middlesex Hospital with Kouao at approximately 8pm on 6 August 1999. They went straight back to Manning's flat in Somerset Gardens where Victoria was to spend the remaining seven months of her life.

The first social worker visit

3.49   During the course of those seven months, Victoria's contact with the outside world was limited and sporadic. Professionals saw her on only four separate occasions during this period. The first two times were home visits made by Ms Arthurworrey to Somerset Gardens. The other two occasions were at the beginning of November when Kouao took Victoria to Haringey Social Services' North Tottenham District Office. Here Kouao made, then later retracted, allegations that Victoria had been sexually harmed by Manning.

3.50   No representative from the Tottenham Child and Family Centre, to which she had been referred by Haringey Social Services on 5 August 1999, ever visited Victoria at Manning's flat. She was registered in November at the health centre that stands approximately 100 yards from Manning's flat, but she never attended it and none of the medical staff who worked there ever saw her.

3.51   The first of Ms Arthurworrey's two visits to Somerset Gardens took place on 16 August 1999, shortly after Victoria was discharged from the North Middlesex Hospital. She found her to be smartly dressed and well cared for. Victoria spent most of the visit playing with a doll – one of a number of toys seen by Ms Arthurworrey. Although Ms Arthurworrey did not talk to Victoria during the course of this visit, she formed the impression that Victoria was happy and seemed like the "little ray of sunshine" described by the nurses. As far as Ms Arthurworrey was concerned, the priority was to move Kouao and Victoria to alternative accommodation, because she did not think their current living arrangements were satisfactory.

3.52   Ms Arthurworrey did not ask Kouao how Victoria was spending her days at this stage. She was not enrolled in a school and there is no indication she participated in any form of daycare activity. Kouao no longer worked at the Northwick Park Hospital (her employment had been terminated due to prolonged absences) and so Manning's assumption that Kouao and Victoria spent most of their time in his bedsit seems correct.

Mr and Mrs Kimbidima

3.53   Some time in July, probably just before Victoria was admitted to the Central Middlesex Hospital, Kouao approached a man on the street and engaged him in conversation. They discovered that they both spoke French and the man, Julien Kimbidima, invited Kouao back to his house so that she could meet his wife, Chantal. Kouao visited the Kimbidimas again on 2 August 1999 (to celebrate their daughter's birthday) and appears to have struck up a friendship with Mr Kimbidima in particular.

3.54   Shortly after Victoria's discharge from the North Middlesex Hospital, Kouao took her to meet Mr and Mrs Kimbidima for the first time. Victoria appeared quiet and withdrawn, although she started to cry when Kouao told Mrs Kimbidima that Victoria was not her real daughter. Judging by the strength with which Kouao complained to the Kimbidimas, Victoria's incontinence had become serious by this stage.

3.55   The Kimbidimas saw Victoria several times over the following months, and Mrs Kimbidima sometimes looked after Victoria when Kouao was otherwise engaged. When at the Kimbidimas' house, Victoria would, on Kouao's instruction, sit quietly in the corner unless instructed to do otherwise. Once or twice she wet herself while at their house but she was never incontinent of faeces. According to Mrs Kimbidima, Kouao would shout at Victoria all the time and never showed her much affection. At one stage, Kouao told her that Victoria was possessed by an evil spirit.

Victoria and the church

3.56   Kouao visited church towards the end of August and this helps explain why she began to believe Victoria was possessed. Since her arrival in the UK, Kouao had shown an interest in attending church. According to Pat Mensah, a Baptist pastor based at a church in north west London, Kouao started visiting her church on a fairly regular basis from the middle of May 1999. The move to Manning's flat in early July may have prompted her to look elsewhere. On 29 August 1999, Kouao and Victoria attended the Mission Ensemble pour Christ, a church which meets in a hall close to Borough High Street.

3.57   The pastor here was Pascal Orome. He had a detailed recollection of Victoria's appearance at this stage. Despite the season, Victoria was dressed in heavy clothing that covered all of her body apart from her head and hands. He noticed wounds on both and advised Kouao to cut Victoria's hair shorter so that the injuries to her scalp could "breathe". Kouao told him about Victoria's incontinence and he formed the view that she was possessed by an evil spirit. He advised that the problem could be solved by prayer.

3.58   Two weeks after her first visit to his church, Kouao phoned Pastor Orome and told him that, following a brief improvement, Victoria's incontinence had returned. He claims he reproached her for being insufficiently vigilant and allowing the evil spirit to return. Whatever its cause, the incontinence appears to have continued throughout the rest of September because it was in October, according to Manning, that the sofa bed Victoria had been sleeping on was thrown out and she began to spend her nights in the bathroom.

The second social worker visit

3.59   The bathroom in Manning's flat was small and the door opened out onto the living room. There was no window and, although there was a heater, it was either broken or unused. When Victoria was inside, the door was kept closed and the light was switched off. She began to spend her nights alone, cold and in pitch darkness.

3.60   However, Ms Arthurworrey noticed nothing untoward when she made the second of her two pre-announced home visits to Somerset Gardens on 28 October 1999. The purpose of her visit was to explain to Kouao that the housing application, made after the previous visit in August, had been turned down and to discuss the remaining options. Victoria seems to have been all but ignored during this visit as she sat on the floor playing with a doll. The fact that she was still not attending school was raised during the conversation, but no questions seem to have been asked about how Victoria was spending her days.

3.61   At his trial, Manning described this second visit of Ms Arthurworrey's as "a put up job". It seems that the flat had been made especially clean and tidy in preparation for the visit. This seems to be consistent with Ms Arthurworrey's evidence: she said she neither saw nor smelt any evidence of Victoria's incontinence. According to Manning, Victoria was told how to behave in front of Ms Arthurworrey. Victoria was said to be sleeping on the remaining sofa bed, with Manning and Kouao sharing a newly-purchased bed on the other side of the room. At the end of the visit, Victoria suddenly jumped up and shouted at Ms Arthurworrey. She said words to the effect that she did not respect her or her mother, and that they should be given a house. This behaviour surprised Ms Arthurworrey at the time.

3.62   During the course of their conversation, Ms Arthurworrey told Kouao that the council only accommodated children who were "at risk of serious harm" and that, in the council's view, Victoria was not at such risk. It may be no coincidence that within three days of this conversation, Kouao contacted Ms Arthurworrey to make allegations which, if true, would have placed Victoria squarely within that category.

3.63   On 1 November 1999, Kouao telephoned Ms Arthurworrey and told her that Manning had been sexually harming Victoria. Ms Arthurworrey told Kouao to come to her office. Kouao arrived with Victoria and Manning later that morning. Understandably, Ms Arthurworrey thought it would be better if Manning left. Kouao then cited three separate instances of sexual abuse. Victoria was then spoken to alone and repeated what Kouao had said, almost word for word. She appeared very anxious to be believed and both Ms Arthurworrey and the other social worker present, Valerie Robertson, thought she had been coached. However, in Ms Arthurworrey's view, Victoria did not seem to be "a particularly nervous, frightened or fearful child" on this occasion.

3.64   The short-term solution devised by Ms Arthurworrey to deal with the sexual harm allegations was to arrange for somewhere else for Victoria to stay while the allegations were investigated. A call was made to Mrs Kimbidima whom Kouao had identified as a friend who might be willing to help. It is unclear what precisely was agreed to by the Kimbidimas as a result of this telephone call. Mrs Kimbidima, whose English is far from perfect, may have initially agreed but later changed her mind having spoken about the matter to her husband. In any event, the result was that Victoria and Kouao left the office in a taxi bound for the Kimbidimas' house, but by the end of the day they were both back at Somerset Gardens.

3.65   The next day, Victoria and Kouao returned to north Tottenham to withdraw the allegations of sexual harm. They spoke to Rosemarie Kozinos who told Kouao that, despite the retraction, she and Victoria would have to live elsewhere while the matter was investigated. Kouao told Ms Kozinos that she and Victoria could continue to stay with the Kimbidimas. In fact, they simply returned to Somerset Gardens.

3.66   This was the last time any of the professionals involved in Victoria's case saw her before her admission to hospital on the night before her death. This fact, together with the incoherence of much of Kouao's evidence – both at her trial and before the Inquiry – means that any account of the last four months of Victoria's life must partly be guesswork.

Victoria's last four months alive

3.67   It is likely that Victoria spent most of this four-month period in the Somerset Gardens flat. However, there is some evidence to suggest she made two trips to France towards the end of 1999. Manning recalled that he, Kouao and Victoria all went to Paris on or about 11 November. They stayed for a long weekend at Kouao's son's house where Victoria was allowed to sleep in a bed. Manning recalled no particular problems concerning Victoria's incontinence during the visit.

3.68   A second visit to France seems to have been made at the end of November. Following her arrest, a Eurostar ticket in Kouao's name was found at Manning's flat showing that she had travelled to Paris on 29 November 1999 and returned on 12 December 1999. No ticket was found for Victoria, but Manning was clear that she had accompanied Kouao on the trip. As he understood it, they had again stayed with Kouao's son.

3.69   Whatever the nature or purpose of these two visits to France, they appear to have made little difference to the pattern of Victoria's life when she returned to Somerset Gardens. She continued to be forced to sleep in the bath and, from November onwards, she was tied up inside a black plastic sack in an effort to stop her from soiling the bath. We know that these were her circumstances on New Year's Eve due to the disturbing entry in Manning's diary. In it he describes an argument with Kouao which ended by her returning to his flat in order to "release satan from her bag".

3.70   This refinement of the torture meant that Victoria spent extended periods lying in her own urine and faeces. The obviously corrosive effect this was having on her skin may have prompted Kouao and Manning to abandon this policy in January 2000. In his interview with the police, Manning suggested he and Kouao became worried that the condition of Victoria's skin might cause social workers to ask "undue questions". However, in his evidence to the Inquiry he was unable to remember the thinking behind the change.

3.71   Despite no longer being kept in a bag, Victoria began to spend more and more of her time in the bathroom in January 2000. Not only did she continue to sleep in the bath, but she also began to spend some of her days in it as well. This could explain why she was not with Kouao and Manning when they met Mr Kimbidima at a tube station around 16 January 2000. They told him they had left Victoria at home because her incontinence made it difficult to get things done.

3.72   At the start of the new year, Kouao and Manning began to serve Victoria her meals in the bath. This was done by placing the food on a piece of plastic, or a plastic bag, and placing it in the bath next to Victoria. She would generally be given whatever Manning and Kouao had cooked for themselves, but by the time it reached her it was usually cold. Given that her hands were kept bound with masking tape, she was forced to eat by pushing her face towards the food, like a dog.

3.73   As well as being forced to spend much of her time in inhuman conditions, Victoria was also beaten on a regular basis by both Kouao and Manning. According to Manning, Kouao used to strike Victoria on a daily basis, sometimes using a variety of weapons. These included a shoe, a hammer, a coat hanger and a wooden cooking spoon. The forensic examination of the flat after Manning's arrest revealed traces of Victoria's blood on the walls, on his football boots and on the undersole of one of his trainers. He also admitted to sometimes using a bicycle chain.

3.74   It is unclear what Kouao's intentions were at this stage. During the course of Ms Arthurworrey's home visit on 28 October 1999, they discussed the option of returning to France. However, despite the two visits to Paris, Kouao seems to have had little inclination to return permanently. Manning was under the impression that Kouao's intention was to send Victoria back to her parents in the Ivory Coast, but despite his obvious distaste for Victoria, he said he did not push the issue.

3.75   If this was Kouao's plan, she did little to advance it and Victoria's parents were not approached to see if they would be willing to have their daughter back. Instead, Kouao kept them in complete ignorance of Victoria's condition. In early 2000, they received a Christmas card from Kouao containing several photographs of a smiling Victoria. On the back of one photograph was written in French, "She's growing up well and she finds herself … well".

3.76   Given the very limited contact Victoria had with the outside world in the weeks leading up to her death, it is difficult to identify with any accuracy the speed with which her condition deteriorated to the state she was in when admitted to the North Middlesex Hospital on 24 February 2000. The pastor from north west London, Pat Mensah, recalled that Victoria seemed "a bit poorly" when she visited Somerset Gardens on 12 February. Although she neglected to mention it in her statement, during the course of her oral evidence Ms Mensah indicated that she was sufficiently concerned about Victoria's health at this point to advise Kouao to take her to a hospital. She also advised her to take her to a church.

Victoria returns to church

3.77   There is evidence to suggest that by 19 February 2000, Victoria was very ill. On this day, which was a Saturday, Kouao took her to the Universal Church of the Kingdom of God housed in the old Rainbow Theatre on Seven Sisters Road. This was the church recommended to her by Ms Mensah during the course of her visit earlier that month. Audrey Hartley-Martin, who was assisting Pastor Alvaro Lima in the administration of the 3pm service, noticed the two of them coming up the stairs. They were shouting at each other and Victoria seemed to be having difficulty walking.

3.78   Kouao and Victoria were disturbing the service, so Ms Hartley-Martin took Victoria downstairs to the crèche. She noticed Victoria was shivering and she asked her if she was cold. Victoria replied that she was not cold but she was hungry. Ms Hartley-Martin obtained some biscuits for her and Victoria hid them in her pocket when Kouao came down to collect her. Ms Hartley-Martin said in evidence that she did not seek to ensure Victoria received any medical attention because she "was not aware that the child was ill".

3.79   At the end of the service, Pastor Lima spoke to Kouao about the difficulties she said she was having with Victoria, particularly her incontinence. He expressed the view that Victoria's problems were due to her possession by an evil spirit and said he would spend the week fasting on Victoria's behalf. He believes he made it clear that Victoria was not expected to fast herself. Kouao was advised to bring Victoria back to church on the following Friday morning. According to Pastor Lima, Friday was the day on which prayers are said for deliverance from "witchcraft, bad luck and everything bad or evil".

3.80   The events of the next week unfolded as follows. On the Sunday, Kouao and Victoria returned to the church where they were seen by Pastor Celso Junior. Apparently, Victoria was quiet and well-behaved during the visit. On Wednesday, Kouao phoned Pastor Lima in the evening and told him Victoria's behaviour had improved in that she had ceased to cover the flat in excrement. On Thursday, Kouao phoned Ms Hartley-Martin and told her that Victoria had been asleep for two days and had not eaten or drunk anything. By the evening of the same day, Kouao was sufficiently concerned to bring Victoria to the church and ask for help. Pastor Lima advised them to go to the hospital and a mini-cab was called.

Victoria's final visit to hospital

3.81   Mr Salman Pinarbasi, the mini-cab driver, was sufficiently concerned about the condition Victoria was in to take her instead to the nearby Tottenham Ambulance Station. She was then taken by ambulance to the North Middlesex Hospital and admitted to the casualty unit. On arrival, Victoria was unconscious and very cold. Her temperature was 27 degrees Celsius. Initial attempts to warm her up were unsuccessful and a paediatric consultant, Dr Lesley Alsford, was called in to take responsibility for Victoria's treatment.

3.82   Dr Alsford arrived around midnight. Her examination of Victoria was limited because her first wish was to increase Victoria's temperature, which at this point was 28.7 degrees Celsius. In any event, she could not have recorded all the injuries she saw because they were "too numerous". She formed the view that Victoria needed the type of intensive care facilities unavailable at the North Middlesex Hospital. She tried to find space in another hospital and was eventually successful. A team from the paediatric intensive care unit at St Mary's Hospital Paddington arrived at 2.30am.

3.83   Victoria was transferred to St Mary's Hospital Paddington where she remained in a critical condition with severe hypothermia and multi-system failure. The medical staff were unable to straighten her legs. Over the hours that followed, Victoria suffered a number of episodes of respiratory and cardiac arrest. Her respiratory, cardiac and renal systems began to fail. At about 3pm, Victoria went into cardiac arrest for the last time. Cardio-pulmonary resuscitation was attempted but Victoria did not respond. She was declared dead at 3.15pm on 25 February 2000. She was eight years and three months old.

The post-mortem examination

3.84   A post-mortem examination was carried out the following day by Dr Nathaniel Carey, a Home Office-accredited pathologist. He found the cause of death to be hypothermia, which had arisen in the context of malnourishment, a damp environment and restricted movement. He also found 128 separate injuries on Victoria's body, showing she had been beaten with a range of sharp and blunt instruments. No part of her body had been spared. Marks on her wrists and ankles indicated that her arms and legs had been tied together. It was the worst case of deliberate harm to a child he had ever seen.

The arrest

3.85   Kouao was arrested on suspicion of neglect at the hospital around 11.35pm on 25 February 2000. She told the police, "It is terrible, I have just lost my child." Manning was arrested the following afternoon as he returned to his flat. Both were subsequently charged with Victoria's murder and were convicted at the Central Criminal Court on 12 January 2001. Kouao and Manning are currently serving sentences of life imprisonment.

Part two: Social services

4 Ealing Social Services

The managerial context

4.1   Between the end of April and early July 1999, Kouao attended Ealing Social Services on no less than 18 different occasions. She was accompanied by Victoria on at least 10 of these visits. Together they had dealings with six social workers, one group support assistant and one housing officer. Yet by the time Ealing closed Victoria's file on 7 July 1999, they knew virtually no more about Victoria than when Kouao first visited the Ealing Homeless Persons' Unit on 26 April 1999 to seek help with her housing needs.

4.2   Ealing Social Services have acknowledged from the outset that the quality of their social work in Victoria's case was unacceptable. In particular, they "failed to address Victoria's needs as an individual and instead treated her as a part of ... Kouao's homelessness case". To Ealing's credit they did not lay the blame on a lack of resources. Indeed, Judith Finlay, senior commissioning manager at the time, was quite clear when she said, "I cannot say that resources were an issue because we paid more than probably we would have if we had done a proper assessment and we certainly took longer about it."

4.3   Even more disturbing, Ealing could not be sure that the total inadequacy of Victoria's assessment was a one-off because they had no proper systems in place for tracking cases through the referral and assessment stage. This was a serious failing. I strongly believe that Victoria's case could and should have started and finished in Ealing – a conclusion to which I shall return later.

Referral and assessment weaknesses

4.4   To a large extent, the weakness in Ealing's referral and assessment process in early 1999 had been highlighted in a highly critical Social Services Inspectorate (SSI) report that Ealing received in December 1997 relating to the safety of the children they looked after. Ealing Social Services were subsequently placed on special measures in June 1998. Significantly, that report concluded that children in care and on the child protection register "were not considered by any measure to be adequately safeguarded". The SSI commented on the "culture of hopelessness" within the social services department, the serious deficiencies in assessment and care planning, and the fact that 45 per cent of the staff were temporary agency staff.

The need for radical change

4.5   The report led to a radical shake-up of senior management and organisational structures. The director of social services at the time resigned and was replaced, initially on an interim basis, by Norman Tutt in June 1998. Together with a new assistant director for children's services, John Skinner, Mr Tutt oversaw the creation of a new specialist children's team structure by the end of 1998. The team brought together fieldwork and residential and daycare services. However, the housing and social services departments were at that time two separate directorates and were not finally to merge until January 2001.

4.6   Two specialist referral and assessment teams – one in each district office – were established to build up an expertise among staff in short-term assessment work. In addition, there were a number of long-term teams split between the two districts, the most relevant to the Inquiry being the 'child in need' teams, which focused on work with children in need of protection and support services. During the relevant period, Ms Finlay was the operations manager responsible for all children's services provided from the Acton area office.

4.7   In preparation for the restructuring, initiatives were taken to audit 'child protection' and 'looked-after-children' files to assess the quality of work done. Managers who were performing poorly were not reappointed. Any action taken was quick and decisive. "In all, the restructuring took some three months. It was a very difficult and demanding time," said Mr Skinner, "for both the organisation and for staff. A massive amount of change took place within a very condensed timetable". There was "enormous drive to improve standards within children's services". Although the disruption caused by such wholesale restructuring did have an impact on staff morale, Mr Tutt told the Inquiry that he believed the overall effect was positive. He said he targeted those managers whose performance was below standard:

> "They were recognised by their colleagues as not performing, so having somebody deal with it raised morale ... The unions were not at all happy about it ... I made it quite clear that in the light of the SSI report, my job was to make sure children were safe in the borough of Ealing, and if members of staff were not able to be compatible with that aim or objective I was quite happy to defend my position in whatever forum might be appropriate."

4.8   That it was achievable in such a short timescale Mr Tutt put down to political backing: "[The leader of the council] ... met me, I think, on the first day and said that he would back whatever needed to be done."

Evidence of progress

4.9   It paid dividends. A further SSI inspection in March 1999 noted a significant improvement in services, recognised that there was a strategy for development and that basic systems were in place at least for children being looked after. The SSI commented, "We found that the culture of hopelessness we referred to in the previous report had been replaced by one of expectation."

4.10   There had also been an impressive turn around on staff recruitment and retention. According to Mr Tutt, Ealing social workers were paid less than comparable boroughs and they progressed up the salary ladder more slowly. That was addressed in June 1998 and continued to be addressed. By spring 1999, 85 per cent of staff in the department were permanent, and some teams had virtually no agency staff. The referral and assessment team that Victoria was referred to was "a reasonably solid team of social workers". Although there were some locum workers, there was no great turnover and staff sickness was not an issue.

4.11   Mr Tutt attributed the improvement to greater managerial responsibility for employment, improving culture and speeding up the recruitment process. He put great emphasis on the work ethos of the children's services department:

> "The way we have tried to tackle it is by stressing that we believe in a very high standard of work and we do not accept less than that, and most social workers actually want to work in a department which will support them to achieve the best for children."

Improving competence

4.12   However, gaps remained. In particular there were gaps in the competence of staff, problems in the identification of potentially serious child protection matters with further training required, and an "inadequate management information system". Significantly, problems remained with regards to assessment. There were also a number of steps in the authority's action plan, dated March 1999, that were still waiting to be carried out by the time Victoria arrived in Ealing in late April 1999. A review of the deployment of staff in the referral and assessment teams was still incomplete and not all cases held on duty had "a named worker to progress the work within identified timescales". Ms Finlay went on to state:

> "We were working intensively with managers to ensure that cases were allocated quickly. That involved a change in culture and a change in understanding of the work, and we did not get there straightaway ... We should have had work allocated immediately, but we did not."

4.13   In practical terms, Mr Skinner told the Inquiry, he thought it was virtually impossible in the spring of 1999 to have allocated all work coming into the referral and assessment team. He said, "We had a backlog of work and also we were overwhelmed with new referrals, so the possibility of allocating all that work immediately was unrealistic."

4.14   Failure to allocate Victoria's case early was almost certainly to prove critical in contributing to a lack of any clear focus and continuity in handling. Most importantly, and surprisingly, only allocated cases were the subject of supervision. Yet Ms Finlay said that at the time, "We relied on the team managers and senior practitioners to undertake the assessments, to undertake the supervision of social workers and to make sure that the assessments were completed." She admitted that by April 1999 senior managers had not got to the stage of auditing the referral and assessment team. As a result, there were no arrangements in place to ensure that assessments were properly carried out by those teams. Therefore, I make the following recommendation:

> **Recommendation**
> Managers of duty teams must devise and operate a system which enables them immediately to establish how many children have been referred to their team, what action is required to be taken for each child, who is responsible for taking that action, and when that action must be completed.

4.15   Mr Tutt confirmed that assessment processes were poor before the introduction of the National Assessment Framework: "One of the problems until the framework was produced was that there was no clear definition of how assessment should be undertaken at the point of entry." Discussing assessments in April 1999, Ms Fortune said, "To be quite honest with you, we did not have any kind of grounding for assessments."

Practice guidance

4.16   In fact, social workers had little by way of up-to-date manuals to guide them in their day-to-day practice. The fieldwork manual 'current' in early 1999 which dealt with matters other than child protection (and was therefore relevant to Victoria at the time she made contact with Ealing Social Services), amazingly predated the Children Act 1989. Understandably, it was described by Mr Tutt as "grossly inadequate" and "indefensible". This was particularly so in relation to agency staff, who might have expected to place heavy reliance on up-to-date manuals, and to new staff who could not be sure of receiving proper induction training. New child protection procedures were implemented in February 1999 and the eligibility criteria for children's services were being developed, but a manual of child protection practice guidelines, which should have been finalised in April 1999, was marked "interim". Significantly, it was to retain that status through to at least the end of the Phase One hearings of this Inquiry, in February 2002.

Mr Skinner acknowledged that a new member of staff to the Department, such as Sharmain Lawrence in spring 1999, who received no induction training when she arrived, would have had "an incomplete set of procedures" and "would struggle as a consequence". Therefore, I make the following recommendation:

> **Recommendation**
> Directors of social services must ensure that staff in their children and families' intake teams are experienced in working with children and families, and that they have received appropriate training.

4.17   The Area Child Protection Committee (ACPC), chaired by Mr Skinner from January 1999, ought to have been the driving force for regeneration and renewal among the child protection agencies. However, according to Mr Skinner its agenda had been dominated by Part 8 reviews and other responsibilities, and so this received little or no attention. It appears that the ACPC had all but become detached from front-line staff, and its policies, procedures and guidelines were out of date. In fact, it was the social services child protection procedures that were adopted by the ACPC in 1999 as a temporary measure – and there was little or no real investment in developing an effective inter-agency child protection partnership. This was the first of several concerns I was to hear about the ACPC arrangements.

Gaps remained

4.18   When the SSI returned for a follow up children's services inspection in December 1999, some five months after Ealing had closed Victoria's case file, they found that progress had continued but they highlighted, yet again, the need to continue to improve standards in the referral and assessment teams. Initial assessments were seen as being "of variable quality, particularly for lower priority cases".

4.19   It was accepted to be fair criticism. In evidence, Mr Tutt was quite clear that his first and second priority had to be children in need of protection and children looked after because "the most serious criticism of the SSI had been that no child could be guaranteed to be safe in the borough". That meant that other areas, such as referral and assessment team initial services, received a lower priority. As Mr Tutt said, this area of work "was not the highest priority, certainly".

4.20   Along with other social services departments, Ealing struggled with the quality of some of its front-line staff. According to Mr Tutt, "Many of the staff coming into post were relatively inexperienced in that they had not many years post qualification experience and/or were from [overseas]." In the referral and assessment teams, managers knew that "a lot of work had to be done with individual members of staff around core basic skills".

Homeless families

4.21   The intake team was dealing with a wide range of referrals, not least homeless families like Kouao and Victoria, coming from abroad. Mr Tutt told the Inquiry, "They come with a whole range of health and other problems and present in our offices although they have no status legally within our country." Many were asylum seekers. Some, like Kouao, were travellers under the Treaty of Rome – people without a documented history. Pamela Fortune, the social worker eventually allocated to Victoria, thought that perhaps 60 to 70 per cent of referrals came from abroad. The difficulty, according to senior practitioner Ms Lawrence, was that "there were not very clear protocols and guidance for dealing with people that were presenting from abroad and presenting as homeless, and quite often I felt that people were left to rely on ... professional judgement".

4.22   The policy at the time was to give a weekly subsistence sum to those who came from abroad without the means to support themselves. Ms Fortune explained, "If there were issues about accommodation, if they could not get any help via housing services, we would have to offer a service." Financial assistance would continue if they appealed their habitual residency status and those appeals could take years.

Management arrangements

4.23   By 26 April 1999, the Acton referral and assessment team, which consisted of one team manager, Sarah Stollard, one senior practitioner, Ms Lawrence, nine social workers, one social work assistant and three group support assistants, had already received 388 referrals that month. Ms Stollard said:

> "It was a very busy team ... There was varied experience in the team. Some of the social workers had hardly any experience, and some had quite a number of years experience. It was also a new team and a new structure, so people did not have experience of working in a referral and assessment team, necessarily ... when I took over that team, we had a backlog of 200 cases ... we continued to take in cases, so I would say it was a team that was under quite a lot of pressure, and we did have a number of agency staff."

4.24   There were no workload management systems in place in 1999. The general expectation was that social workers would carry between 12 and 15 allocated cases on top of their duty commitments. An audit in July 1999 indicated that staff in the Acton referral and assessment team had on average 11.25 allocated cases. Ms Fortune described workloads as "high but not unmanageable". Deborah Gaunt, another social worker in the Acton referral and assessment team, thought, "The workload was challenging but I felt that it was appropriate for my level of experience and that I could handle it."

Duty rota

4.25   Social workers took turns being on duty for one week in three. In theory, they were supposed to work on duty for the whole week. However, Ms Stollard explained that "reality and practicality dictates that they are not always the same three workers on for the whole week". It was explained that social workers on duty worked on duty cases, assigned daily, downstairs in the Acton office. Social workers not on duty worked upstairs on 'allocated' cases.

4.26   A referral could be by letter, telephone or in person. According to the level of risk or concern, the referral would either be taken straight to the duty manager or would be dealt with on the spot by the duty social worker. If the duty manager was not available, social workers would go to a more senior manager, such as the operations manager (Ms Finlay). If not dealt with immediately (and not urgent), the social worker would write an action plan and leave that, together with the referral form, in a basket on the duty manager's desk.

4.27   Ms Stollard alternated with her senior practitioner, Ms Lawrence, as duty manager on a "one week on, one week off" basis, although she also line managed Ms Lawrence. As a result, accountability for case management decisions was not clear. It was demonstrated in Victoria's case that it was possible for the two managers to take opposed views when it came to their 'turn' to manage the case.

4.28   Ms Stollard summarised the differences in their roles as follows:

> "I was the overall manager ... I suppose the last decision would be mine if it was felt necessary to come to me, to seek my view on something. In terms of ... the practicalities of how it worked, Sharmain was, I suppose, like a deputy team manager ... and I would not get involved in her

decision making unless something was brought to my attention where I thought I needed to, or where she wanted to ask me what I thought about something."

The duty manager

4.29 It was the job of the duty manager to review all the work in the duty basket on a daily basis, but according to Mr Skinner, assistant director of children's services, "That was an aim not always achieved." Regular payments, similar to those made to Kouao, had to be signed off and managers would take the opportunity to consider those cases as the payments fell due – although there was no formal review. However, Ms Stollard acknowledged that some files were not reviewed as regularly as they should have been. The safety net, such as it was, was almost totally reliant on her memory of the case details as well as the paper tracking system that she devised and only she felt fully confident in using. It was certainly no way to run a busy duty system that began the year with a backlog of 200 cases and where case allocation, if it happened at all, was such a hit-and-miss affair.

4.30 If no further action was required for the time being on a particular file it would be stored in the A–Z cabinet. Cases requiring action were placed in the 'pend' cabinet to be allocated to the duty social workers on the relevant dates. Progress was certainly made in moving cases on. Of the backlog of cases Ms Stollard inherited at the beginning of the year, only 30 or so were left on the duty system by the end of 1999. However, there was nothing in place to gauge whether the scope and timeliness of the intervention offered was in any way appropriate to the needs of the children concerned.

4.31 Mr Tutt told the Inquiry that the A–Z system was almost totally reliant on the memory of one manager. Ms Stollard said that the entire system depended on her initiative, intellect, memory and physical review of the files in the cabinet. Although Ms Finlay's understanding was slightly different, the difference was more a matter of semantics. Ultimately in the absence of a proper, electronic tracking system, knowledge of those priorities relied once again on the diligence, hard work and memory of the duty managers.

Use of IT systems

4.32 By December 1999, according to Mr Tutt, an electronic database that could track cases was in place. But in March 1999 Ms Stollard relied on a manual paper system which she had devised and which amounted to no more than "simply a sheet of paper where details of up to 10 cases could be summarised – that is updated on a weekly basis and you hope that cases fall off by the end of the week because they have either been disposed of finally or allocated".

4.33 It was a system described variously as "adequate", "basic and had flaws", "on a basic level ... barely adequate" and "fairly crude". However, Ms Lawrence was quite clear that she did not find it easy to use.

4.34 At the end of the duty week, cases were supposed to be reviewed and possibly closed or allocated. According to Ms Stollard, cases were allocated "if the case was looking more complex or it appeared that a longer piece of work needed to be carried out, or if a case conference was needed or the child became a looked after child".

Staff supervision

4.35 Allocation was the key to whether or not a case was discussed in supervision. Each member of staff in the referral and assessment team was to be supervised once a month as a minimum. Ms Stollard aimed for fortnightly supervision but at least once every three weeks for allocated cases. Supervision records relating to individual cases were placed on each case file. In relation to duty cases, I was told by Ms Finlay that "supervision was informal in that social workers would approach the duty manager to discuss aspects of a duty case upon which **they** [my emphasis] felt they needed support or guidance". That meant there might be no supervision at all if a case was open and shut while a social worker was on duty. Significantly, in Victoria's case it took over two months to allocate her case, and it was subsequently closed one week later. Therefore, there was no formal supervision discussion and no supervision record appears on the file.

4.36   Handover between the two managers at the end of the duty week was only thought necessary for cases that were of particular concern. Where a conversation was not possible, notes would be left or conversations would be had on another day or simply not at all. Nonetheless, Ms Finlay regarded the system as adequate and Ms Lawrence felt the whole process was assisted by her and Ms Stollard's "professionalism".

4.37   But this, too, was to come under some strain during 1999. Ms Stollard had concerns about Ms Lawrence "as a result of [her] poor performance and a lack of commitment". In particular she was concerned about Ms Lawrence's frequent absences, and she felt Ms Lawrence was undermining her as team manager.

4.38   Matters came to a head in September 1999. Ms Stollard returned from annual leave to find the referral and assessment services in what she considered to be a "dangerous state". She pursued the matter with Ms Finlay in writing.

4.39   During the management investigation which lasted from October 1999 to March 2000, Ms Lawrence was removed from her role as senior practitioner and invited to remain at home "in her own interests".

4.40   The outcome of the management investigation led ultimately to Ms Stollard leaving Ealing Social Services in July 2000. Ms Lawrence in the meantime returned to work and was subsequently promoted to the position of team manager.

4.41   It is far from clear what impact the process of investigating these complaints had on service delivery. Ms Stollard said the interviews with the team were lengthy and "very disruptive". She did not think there was any impact on the way service users were dealt with, although she later said:

> "Inevitably team members found the investigation distressing and of interest. It was a matter of significant office gossip and although I never spoke to staff about the investigation, it was a matter of considerable discussion which was a diversion to the task at hand. Time was obviously spent encouraging people to make complaints and all of this would have had an impact on the provision of service to clients."

4.42   Mr Skinner was not aware of any "visible impact" on service delivery, although there was a "degree of tension" among staff as they became more aware of the difficulty.

4.43   All, however, were at pains to point out that the problems between Ms Stollard and Ms Lawrence arose after Victoria's time at Ealing, and so had no adverse impact on the way her case was handled. I am unwilling to accept such firm assurances.

Victoria

4.44   Although Ms Lawrence, as senior practitioner, would not have been the allocated social worker for Victoria, Victoria's case remained on the duty system for some two months. If Ms Lawrence had any concerns about her management of the case, which she undoubtedly did, supervision would have provided the opportunity for her to air those concerns with her team and line manager. But as Ms Lawrence admitted, supervision arrangements with Ms Stollard were a bit "ad hoc" and at least initially were not "adequate". Therefore, it seems possible that the worsening relationship between the two, and which senior managers were certainly aware of from the spring of 1999, might have hindered the effective duty system handover at the end of each week and could have contributed to the prolonged and differing approach that each took in relation to Victoria's case.

4.45   It certainly provided added reason, if reason was needed, to get a management grip of a duty system that was seriously deficient. The senior management team at the time failed to do this. When asked to identify defects in the duty system team, Ms Stollard referred to "changes in plan, different people getting involved ... situations getting slightly lost", while Ms Lawrence said she was "perturbed" by the number of unallocated cases. She thought it was "Very difficult to work with the volume of cases there was on the duty system ... it was difficult to monitor all the cases on duty." Victoria's was just one of those cases.

4.46   There is no excuse for failing to have in place a system for efficiently managing the workload in a social services team dealing with children and families.

Victoria in Ealing

4.47   On 26 April 1999, just two days after Kouao and Victoria arrived in the UK, they attended Ealing Homeless Persons' Unit. Kouao was seen by Julie Winter, a homeless persons' officer, to whom she spoke in English. She indicated that Victoria spoke only French. According to Ms Winter, Kouao preferred to conduct the interview in English because she did not want Victoria to listen in.

4.48   Ms Winter's impression of Kouao was that she appeared "tidy, clean, presentable, not a rough sleeper, not someone who was street homeless".

4.49   However, Ms Winter recalled nothing of Victoria's appearance other than the rather unusual fact that she was wearing a wig. But she made no note of this at the time.

The housing application form

4.50   Together, Kouao and Ms Winter completed a housing application form. Kouao gave her date of birth as 17 July 1956, her age as 43 years old and said that she had lived in France since birth. Initially she said she had three older children with her, but subsequently informed Ms Winter that they were in France, staying with a friend and were being educated there.

4.51   She told Ms Winter both she and Victoria were in good health, that neither of them were registered with a GP and that she was currently unemployed. Kouao said she did not intend to stay in the UK permanently. Her purpose in coming here was to spend a year improving her English. Kouao told Ms Winter that she had made some inquiries with an airline company in France and was advised that if she could communicate well in English, her chances of being offered a job were high. Ms Winter also recorded that while in France, Kouao had been a housewife, and that her husband had died in October 1998 following a road traffic accident. In fact, Kouao divorced her husband, the father of two of her children, in December 1978 and he died in June 1995. She had been evicted from her home because of rent arrears.

4.52 Rather than applying for assistance with rent in some less desirable accommodation in France, Kouao told Ms Winter that she had sought, and been given, assistance with the fare for her and Victoria to come to England. She had obtained seven nights' bed and breakfast accommodation as part of the flight package deal, but had no other accommodation once that period expired at the end of the week, on 30 April 1999.

4.53 Ms Winter did not question that the French authorities apparently had contributed to Kouao and Victoria's fare, although she thought it unusual. She told the Inquiry: "We have no knowledge of how the French authorities work. It seemed a reasonable situation, that she could either have money towards rent or a one-off payment to travel elsewhere ... I had not come across it before, but I had no reason to disbelieve that this was in fact the case."

4.54 Kouao's explanation for why Victoria was wearing a wig, which they discussed while completing the health section of the form, but which was never recorded, was that it was Victoria's choice. It was because she had "short or very short hair". Ms Winter had no concerns about this: "I accepted her reasons – she was a very plausible person." In fact, Ms Winter's overall impression was that Kouao was forthcoming with her answers, she did not appear to be withholding information and the material she provided seemed accurate.

4.55 Ms Winter, not surprisingly, concluded that Kouao was not habitually resident in the UK. Her ties at that stage were with France. She had no settled plans for staying in this country. Kouao had provided documentation to confirm her identification and proof of the date of her arrival into the UK. Although Ms Winter was shown both Kouao's travel documents and her passport, which included Victoria's 'details' and her 'photograph', she paid no further attention to them, believing Kouao's application to be ineligible on the grounds of habitual residence.

4.56 As it happens, it would have been helpful for social services to have sight of the passport, as they may have noted that the photograph was not that of Victoria, as did the police when conducting their murder inquiry following Victoria's death. Detective Inspector Keith Niven said in his statement to the Inquiry that the child on the passport was "clearly not Victoria" and he later confirmed in oral evidence that there "were distinct differences".

Housing application refused

4.57 Ms Winter confirmed her decision with her duty senior and then told Kouao she was not eligible for housing. It was a reasonable decision for the housing department to have come to in all the circumstances. Nevertheless, Kouao was clearly distressed and was emphatic to Ms Winter that she and Victoria would very soon have nowhere to live. It appears that Victoria understood the gist of that response because this was the first time she spoke and implored Ms Winter, in French and referring to her as "Madame" to find "une maison" for her. She was tearful, but Ms Winter did not think Victoria's behaviour was unusual. She said, "Often the children get distressed when they see their parent upset in the interviews."

4.58 Ms Winter advised Kouao that she might obtain assistance from social services under the National Assistance Act 1948, as someone who was destitute and responsible for a dependant child, and she noted in her interview record that an appointment had been arranged for Kouao to attend the social services office on 30 April 1999.

The referral to social services

4.59 In the meantime, she quite properly telephoned the referral across to Ms Fortune, a social worker in Ealing's Acton office referral and assessment team. Although there were forms in use at the time for making such referrals, and Ms Winter 'imagined' there was guidance on how to complete them, she usually preferred not to put her trust on the internal post but to speak directly to an officer. Her lack of confidence in the internal mail is noteworthy. But the net effect was that no written or electronic referral to social services was ever made and no copy of the relevant documentation passed across when it should have. As a result, social services were not in a position to double check inconsistencies in the details Kouao gave about her and Victoria's life either here in England or in France. As a result, I make the following recommendation:

> **Recommendation**
> When a professional makes a referral to social services concerning the well-being of a child, the fact of that referral must be confirmed in writing by the referrer within 48 hours.

4.60 Ms Winter was clear in her evidence that her sole reason for making the referral to social services was that the family were going to become destitute in a matter of days. They had no income and were unlikely to have any in the immediate future. But she told the Inquiry, "She did not place any emphasis on the child's needs." After all, Victoria's circumstances were not unusual: "Cases that are found to be not eligible ... persons from abroad, they have no jobs lined up here, they have only the money they travel with, quite often they are refused benefits because again they are not habitually resident."

4.61 She acknowledged she was not familiar with the Children Act 1989. All she knew was that if the housing department could not assist a family with rehousing and the family was shortly to become 'roofless', then the authority had obligations towards the welfare of the child under the Act. Ms Winter said, "I took that to mean shelter and subsistence." This illustrates well the importance of social services being clear about the responsibilities they carry in law and ensuring other agencies understand this also.

4.62 In evidence, Ms Fortune conceded that from the very start she believed she was being asked to focus on Victoria's needs. On the first level assessment core form she noted, "Ms Winters would like S/S [social services] to undertake an assessment of Ms Kouao and her daughter's needs."

4.63 At the time she understood these centred on the family's housing needs. She also noted down the name of the solicitor that Kouao had already found to act on her behalf. She believed she had been told by Ms Winter that Kouao had enough money until 1 May 1999. But she did not record this on the referral form.

4.64 She recorded the nature of the concern to be assessed by the duty social worker as a "mother and child who were (pending) homeless" and a "child in need". An appointment was made for Kouao to attend social services on 29 April 1999 – not 30 April as noted by Ms Winter – and this information was given to Ms Winter over the phone to pass to Kouao. Nothing else on the first level assessment core form – including the recommendations and management decisions arising from the assessment – was recorded by Ms Fortune that day. She placed the referral form in the duty basket for the duty senior to allocate to a duty social worker on 29 April. Her expectation was that the duty social worker on the day would complete the assessment and record the management decisions on the form. In fact, no such assessment was undertaken on 29 April, or any day thereafter. Ms Fortune, who ultimately became Victoria's allocated case worker, was to have no further contact with Kouao or Victoria until 1 June 1999.

Kouao returns to Ealing Homeless Persons' Unit

4.65   Early in the evening of the following day, 27 April 1999, Kouao and Victoria returned to Ealing Homeless Persons' Unit. Kouao requested money for food and essential items. She was referred to William Martin, an approved social worker under the Mental Health Act 1989, who was working in the out-of-office-hours team. At that time, this team covered both the London boroughs of Ealing and Hounslow. Kouao gave Mr Martin her French social security number and he telephoned the out-of-hours Department of Social Security (DSS) number to request a payment for her, as his team held no funds. The usual procedure, which Mr Martin followed that evening, was to leave Kouao's details, including her telephone contact number and his own, on a recorded message to the DSS. If the DSS had any further queries they would contact Mr Martin in the first instance. No such call was received that evening and Mr Martin assumed that the DSS responded to Kouao's request by contacting her directly.

4.66   Mr Martin also advised Kouao to attend Ealing Social Services the following day, describing Victoria on the out-of-office-hours team referral report as a "child in need".

4.67   When asked why he did this Mr Martin replied, "I used the term as a precautionary measure, more of an alerting mechanism, to ensure that there was some follow up on the following day. I thought that was good practice really. I had no particular concerns at that time."

4.68   Indeed Mr Martin knew very little about Kouao and Victoria. He had been told by Kouao that she needed money to buy food and essential items and she and Victoria were living in temporary accommodation. He said it was not his role to ask Kouao why she was in this position – Mr Martin believed his task as an out-of-office-hours team worker was to deal with the emergency, to "hold things together until the day services can take over". The typical response to an urgent request for cash was via the DSS, and this he pursued. This may well be established practice for out-of-office-hours teams. However, it raises a number of questions about access to services which I return to in Phase Two of this Inquiry.

Kouao returns to Acton area office

4.69   Kouao did as she was advised and returned with Victoria to the social services office the next day on 28 April 1999. She spoke to Godfrey Victor, a social worker on duty in the Acton area office. He recalled that Victoria seemed rather small for her age and described her as "stunted in growth", though he made no record of this in his notes. He could not be sure, but he did not think Victoria was wearing a wig at the time though he remembered that her hair was very short.

4.70   This is the first of numerous observations disclosed as evidence to this Inquiry but not at any time recorded on Victoria's case file. The importance of accurately recording observations about children cannot be over-emphasised. The importance of accurate case recording will form a recommendation for general application later in this Report.

4.71   The interview with Mr Victor lasted 15 to 20 minutes. Mr Victor found on the computer the earlier referral made to Ms Fortune on 26 April 1999 – a hard copy was also in the duty manager's basket. But he did not know about the family's contact with the out-of-office-hours team. This is alarming given Mr Martin's evidence that the role of the out-of-office-hours team was "to hold things together until the day services can take over". Nor did Mr Victor do any other statutory checks because the family had just arrived from France and he presumed such checks would reveal nothing. It is clearly never safe to make such assumptions. Checks against Ealing's own housing department files, as the referrer, may have led to a trail which, if vigorously pursued in France, as it would likely have been if Victoria had come from another part of the UK, may have resulted in information coming to light. Such information did come to light after Victoria's death – she was known to French social services and Victoria's school in Paris had registered a Child at Risk Emergency Notification with the French education authorities on 9 February 1999, because of Victoria's repeated absences from school.

4.72 Kouao again requested financial assistance for food and other essentials for Victoria. She spoke reasonable English. She told Mr Victor that the DSS had refused her benefits because she had failed the habitual residency test. Mr Victor was aware that Kouao had other children in France but she refused to provide any details about them. This did not cause him to be suspicious and he assumed this would be probed further when Kouao returned for a fuller family assessment. His only anxiety was to ensure that Victoria was provided with a service that day.

Accommodation arranged

4.73 Mr Victor spoke to his manager, Ms Stollard, who agreed the provision of short-term financial assistance, amounting to £10 for food for Victoria, until Kouao could return to the office for an assessment on 30 April 1999. In the meantime, bed and breakfast accommodation for the family was arranged at 6–8 Nicoll Road, Harlesden. Mr Victor said he had no reason to believe Nicoll Road was unsuitable for Kouao and Victoria, but he made no checks to find out, and he was not aware of any complaints about the premises. It would seem that Mr Victor was also entirely unaware that Ms Fortune had already arranged for Kouao and Victoria to be assessed just one day earlier, despite the information recorded on the first level assessment core form.

4.74 Ms Stollard's perception of the case from the outset was that Victoria was in need only in so far as she needed food and accommodation. Nothing was brought to her attention at the time to suggest that Victoria might be in need of any other assistance. As no inquiries had been made it is understandable that there was nothing more to share. As a result, neither she, nor any of the six social workers in her team who were to come into contact with Victoria during her time in Ealing, did more than respond at this superficial level. Ms Stollard stated:

"[Victoria] did not present with injuries, she did not present as a child that other agencies were concerned about, it was an accommodation issue and a finance issue and that was how it presented at the time. We did not go looking for child protection issues."

4.75 This ignores the important fact that the only justification for the involvement of social services was Victoria's needs, which were not being assessed.

4.76 Kouao next returned to the office on 30 April 1999. Again Mr Victor saw Kouao and Victoria and he admitted that once again he did not speak to Victoria: "I attempted to speak to her, but mum was always talking to me."

4.77 It was agreed, a decision authorised by senior commissioning manager Judith Finlay, that accommodation costs would be met by social services funding, and that the bed and breakfast accommodation at Nicoll Road, Harlesden would continue until Kouao's habitual residency appeal had been determined. Ms Finlay said she assumed the accommodation was satisfactory because it had been used previously. However, at no stage did she investigate or question whether the accommodation was in fact suitable for Victoria. She accepted that Ealing's approach to determining the suitability of Nicoll Road was not adequate. Therefore, I make the following recommendation:

> **Recommendation**
>
> If social services place a child in temporary accommodation, an assessment must be made of the suitability of that accommodation and the results of that assessment must be recorded on the child's case file. If the accommodation is unsuitable, this should be reported to a senior officer.

4.78   Although Nicoll Road is not far from Ealing's offices, it does in fact fall under Brent council – a fact Mr Victor knew all too well because he had come across the premises when he had been employed by Brent in the early 1990s. Yet it appears that none of the relevant Brent agencies were informed of this placement. This is despite the spirit of a pan-London agreement of social services directors, clearly set out in Ealing's own child protection procedures manual, that states:

> "With families placed in bed and breakfast, it is considered good practice for the placing borough to provide social services support immediately following the placement, until and unless such support is specifically assumed by the receiving borough."

4.79   That was an obligation that Brent, of course, could not possibly have assumed if Ealing decided to cease supporting Kouao and Victoria (which ultimately they did), unless Brent were first made aware of the family's presence within their area.

4.80   However, Mr Victor saw no reason for him to notify Brent because:

> "The child was not at risk, the child was not under child protection. The child was not being looked after. The child was not under a supervision order. It was a case of just placing the family within Brent."

4.81   Ms Finlay believed (wrongly) that the continuing support obligations applied only to children on the child protection register, and while senior managers thought the principle "admirable", they believed it would be impossible to implement. Mr Tutt shared this view and voiced concerns about the sheer quantity of information that would need to be exchanged and the systems needed to support and maintain that process.

4.82   The problem, however, may well get worse as the supply of affordable housing shrinks in parts of London. Unless greater weight is attached to such agreements, the risk of 'losing' vulnerable children somewhere in the system may well increase too. Therefore, I make the following recommendation:

> **Recommendation**
>
> If social services place a child in accommodation in another local authority area, they must notify that local authority's social services department of the placement. Unless specifically agreed in writing at team manager level by both authorities or above, the placing authority must retain responsibility for the child concerned.

4.83   Mr Victor did not manage to complete an assessment of Victoria and Kouao on 30 April 1999. Kouao told him that Victoria had not eaten that day. He said in evidence that "because the department was child centred, we allowed her to go in the belief that she would be back". Kouao and Victoria left, but not before collecting £17.50 subsistence, which was to last until the following Thursday – 6 May 1999.

4.84   It seems probable that Kouao and Victoria moved into Nicoll Road on 1 May 1999 immediately after their bed and breakfast booking at Twyford Crescent in Acton expired.

4.85   Kouao's next two visits to Ealing Social Services were on 7 May 1999, to collect a further payment of £17.50, and again on 11 May. On that second occasion, Ms Stollard agreed further subsistence funding of £64.44 per week – an amount equivalent to 90 per cent of the DSS rate for a mother and child. This appears to have been local policy at the time.

Social services record keeping

4.86   Some time before 24 May 1999, but after Kouao's visit to the area office on 11 May, Ms Lawrence, the duty senior that week, made the following, undated, entry on Victoria's case file. It reads:

"i)   This lady came to England to learn English

ii)   she has no connection with this country and has been found not habitually resident so is entitled to no benefits

iii)   she has a 17yr/16yr and 7yr and she intends to return to France for 2 other children in June

iv)   she has no skills and has made clear she has a 2 yr plan to be in this country

v)   she has not even sought assistance from a solicitor yet ... I advised her to do so yesterday [although had Ms Lawrence taken the trouble to read the First Level Core Assessment form she would have noticed that Ms Fortune had already noted down the details of Kouao's solicitor]

vi)   what do we do with this case, there will inevitably be a long-term financial implication for this department if she remains."

4.87   Ms Lawrence wrote a note to herself to speak to Ms Finlay, the senior commissioning manager, or Mr Skinner, assistant director of children's services, for their view of this case.

4.88   As stated in paragraph 4.21, Ms Fortune thought 60 to 70 per cent of the cases they were seeing on duty at the time were housing type cases. Families coming from abroad and who were ineligible for benefits were not uncommon. Despite this, when asked why this case should have prompted a discussion with senior management, Ms Lawrence said, "There was no specific guidance around how we approached cases or referrals where the presenting issue was homelessness or destitution and there was no particular assessment framework for approaching the case."

4.89   Asked if Victoria's case stood out in any way from the average, she replied, "[Kouao] ... did come from France and she did have a family or part of a family in France." Ms Lawrence thought that needed exploring but was unclear as to how to go about it. She thought an assessment was called for, yet Ms Winter's

recorded referral on 26 April 1999 had already requested that social services do
an assessment of Victoria's need so there was no progress in decision making here.
Ms Lawrence "supposed" the assessment ought to be a full family assessment. In
fact, Ms Lawrence could no longer clearly recall whether that was what she meant
or whether she intended a short assessment in accordance with a format that the
team had devised for dealing with this particular type of case. Nor could she recall
whether she in fact spoke to either Ms Finlay or Mr Skinner. There is no record of a
conversation with either, though she expected she would only have gone to them
directly if Ms Stollard had not been available. According to Ms Lawrence, all cases
with long-term financial implications for the department would have necessitated
discussion with senior managers.

4.90   In the event, whatever assessment Ms Lawrence thought might have been
appropriate, according to her statement to the Inquiry, her discussions with senior
managers were heading in a completely opposite direction and were to culminate in
a "final decision of the social services department ... to withdraw financial support".

Kouao complains about accommodation

4.91   On 24 May 1999, Kouao and Victoria came to the Acton area office without an
appointment. They were interviewed by Ms Gaunt, one of the duty social workers,
who had been in post in Ealing for just four months. She admitted that she knew
very little about the family other than Kouao had failed the habitual residency
test, that she and Victoria were living in Nicoll Road and that they had come from
France. She was not aware that Ealing housing services had already referred the
family for an assessment to be made of Victoria's needs.

4.92   The interview lasted about 20 minutes and was conducted in English, although
Ms Gaunt thought there were sufficient lapses in understanding to have required
an interpreter.

4.93   Kouao voiced a number of complaints about her accommodation in Nicoll Road
which Ms Gaunt recorded. Kouao complained that the rooms were being burgled
and the police were often involved. She complained of the noise, drinking and
"weed smoking", the violence in the corridors and the toilets that were often
vomited in. If true, Nicoll Road could hardly be described as accommodation
suitable for a mother and seven-year-old child, yet Ms Gaunt never alluded to
Victoria in her record of the interview nor to the fact that Victoria was resident in
the hostel.

4.94   Ms Gaunt explained to Kouao that the department would pursue her concerns
and decide whether the bed and breakfast accommodation was indeed suitable for
women and children. She arranged for Kouao to return to the office that afternoon
to collect her subsistence money.

4.95   In the meantime, she telephoned Peter Pandelli of Star Lettings, the letting
agency, to pass on Kouao's complaints in the confident expectation that he would
investigate them with the manager of the accommodation and report back to the
duty team. Although this was the first complaint about temporary accommodation
that Ms Gaunt had dealt with, it did not occur to her that there was anything
inappropriate in leaving the checks for the letting agency to follow up. They clearly
had an interest in maximising the take up of hostel places and ensuring that those
places were suitable for as wide a range of local authority client groups as possible.

4.96   It is, of course, questionable whether social services should be involved in the
management of temporary accommodation. I suggest they should confine their
activities to supporting vulnerable families placed in such accommodation.

4.97   Before leaving the office, Ms Gaunt discussed Victoria's case with Ms Stollard and a decision was made to provide Kouao and Victoria with subsistence and accommodation for one more week, after which they would be invited to return to France. The decision was relayed to Kouao and it was this, according to Ms Gaunt, that prompted Victoria to start crying. She stopped when Kouao gave her some sugar.

4.98   To Ms Gaunt, the whole episode appeared to have been "stage-managed". It seemed odd to her that the prospect of returning to France – where Victoria had other siblings and where life by Kouao's account had been reasonable – should have provoked such a response.

4.99   Sadly, Ms Gaunt made no record of Victoria's reaction, or of her own observations about it, but she was clear that the incident had happened and that she had not, in hindsight, confused this with a similar incident recorded by Bernadette Wilkin later that same day.

4.100   In her evidence, Ms Gaunt made some other observations as to Victoria's appearance and her relationship to Kouao. Had these observations been recorded at the time they might well have prompted closer scrutiny of their true relationship. Ms Gaunt told the Inquiry that there was a marked difference between Kouao's appearance and that of Victoria. Whereas Kouao's hair was well styled, Victoria's was dull, short, unhealthy and generally less well groomed. Victoria's skin colour was also darker than Kouao's and was noticeably blotchy. She vividly described Victoria as looking like one of the "adverts you see for Action Aid".

4.101   To Ms Gaunt's eye there seemed to be no obvious mother/daughter relationship between them. When asked what she thought was lacking specifically, Ms Gaunt replied, "When Victoria began to cry I may have expected a mother to comfort her child in some way and that did not occur."

4.102   This, coupled with the differences in skin colour, led her to doubt whether the two were indeed mother and daughter. But she made no record of any of these observations, nor did they prompt her to initiate any further assessment of Victoria's needs. She said, "I can see in hindsight that it may well have been a truly important piece of assessment, but nevertheless at the time it was not. It did not raise concerns. It did not make me concerned."

4.103   Ms Gaunt said she was sufficiently concerned to raise her doubts with colleagues on her return to the duty room. But she could no longer remember with whom she raised the possibility that Kouao and Victoria were unrelated or what responses she received.

4.104   Unlike some of her colleagues, Ms Gaunt seemed to have a clearer understanding that Victoria was a "child in need" within the meaning of the Children Act 1989, and she knew that the local authority had a duty to complete a full assessment of the family. Ms Gaunt said, "She had no roof over her head, unless we were providing it for her at the time. She had no recourse to public funds, and therefore her health or well-being would have been hampered had we not provided those things."

4.105   Nonetheless she allowed Kouao to leave the office that day knowing that no such assessment had yet been completed, an assessment that she now conceded would "have made the management of the case clearer, earlier".

Kouao continues to collect subsistence

4.106   As instructed, Kouao returned with Victoria to the Acton area office later the same day to collect her subsistence monies. On this occasion she was dealt with by

Ms Wilkin, a support assistant in the referral and assessment team. This was not the first time that Kouao had had her subsistence cash paid out in the reception area by Ms Wilkin. The two women first met on 28 April 1999 when Kouao collected the first of her weekly payments. Ms Wilkin, who had a daughter the same age as Victoria, had also observed the differences between Kouao and Victoria. She told the Inquiry that Kouao "was a very pretty lady with clear shiny skin and well dressed. Victoria was petite with really short hair".

4.107   She observed Victoria a few times wearing little short dresses and a leather jacket which seemed "a bit old fashioned for a little girl. It was burgundy, it was gathered at the waist and it had lapels on it". She also noticed that Victoria always stood very close to Kouao. Ms Wilkin recalled saying "hello" to Victoria but "she just smiled and that was it".

4.108   Ms Wilkin repeated to Kouao what Ms Gaunt had already told her, that this would be her last payment and that the council would pay only for her accommodation until Monday 31 May 1999. It was the first time that Ms Wilkin had had to convey such information to a client. According to her file note, Kouao asked her what she should do. Ms Wilkin explained that it was a management decision and that perhaps she should take legal advice. Kouao proceeded to say something to Victoria at which, for the second time that day, Victoria began to cry. Unlike Ms Gaunt, Ms Wilkin did record this reaction in her file note. She said she also relayed it back to a social worker but she could no longer remember to whom.

Accommodation complaint investigated

4.109   In a late additional statement to the Inquiry, Ms Gaunt recalled another material event that she failed to record at the time and omitted to mention in her original statement for the Inquiry. This concerned her visit to the Nicoll Road premises, which she believed she made some time after Kouao had lodged her complaints on 24 May 1999. It is Ms Gaunt's hazy recollection that she volunteered to do the visit in response to a suggestion by Ms Stollard that she lived in that direction and could pass the address on her way home. The visit, according to Ms Gaunt, was only partly in response to Kouao's complaints. She believed other complaints may have been made about the same premises and she said it was for this reason that no write up of her visit appeared on Victoria's file.

4.110   In the absence of any record, it is difficult to pinpoint exactly when this visit occurred. Ms Stollard told those who conducted Ealing's Part 8 management review following Victoria's death that the visit to Nicoll Road had taken place before Kouao made her complaints. But in evidence to this Inquiry she thought it must have taken place at around the same time. The Part 8 review also noted that Ms Stollard asked "two social workers to make an unannounced visit to the accommodation and inspect it all". In fact, Ms Stollard could only recall with any conviction that an unannounced visit did take place at Nicoll Road and that it happened while Kouao was living there. She thought it was "regrettable" that there was no record of the visit on the case file. When pressed, she could not deny that the only response to Kouao's complaints may well have been the phone call to Mr Pandelli at Star Lettings, as recorded by Ms Gaunt at the time.

4.111   In fact, unbeknown to Ms Gaunt, it appears that another visit was made to Nicoll Road by Ealing Social Services. On this occasion the visit was announced and conducted by two social workers – Ms Fortune and Cecilia Schreuder. I shall return to this later and its implications in the evidence given by Ms Stollard and Ms Gaunt in respect of the visit to Nicoll Road.

4.112   Ms Gaunt said that when she visited the premises she asked the manager whether Kouao and Victoria were in their room but was told they were not. As a result, it was not possible for her to assess the suitability of Room 13 for Victoria. She proceeded, nonetheless, to check out the common parts of the house – the corridors, toilets and bathroom – those areas that Kouao had mentioned specifically. Ms Gaunt found nothing to cause her concern. She came away with the general impression that the accommodation was adequate and she conveyed this to Ms Stollard.

4.113 On 28 May 1999, four days after Kouao had been told that her board and lodging would be paid up until 31 May, Ms Stollard reviewed Victoria's case. She said she may have read through the file but she probably would have been influenced more by the decisions made by the senior practitioner than by what was on the file. Ms Stollard decided to close the case one week later pending any further contact. When asked if she was satisfied that there had been a proper assessment of Victoria's needs she said,

> "I was satisfied we had looked at the accommodation issues ... I have to say that I did not make any of the management decisions on this case. Sharmain [Lawrence] made the decisions [yet it was Ms Stollard who closed the case], and she made them with Judith [Finlay] so the details of the discussion and the assessment did not actually involve me."

4.114 The 'assessment' would not, it would seem, have involved Victoria either. Ms Stollard wrote a brief description of the case on her review note: "French woman homeless over here learning English. Has been told to go back to France."

4.115 Victoria, ostensibly Ealing Social Services' client, did not get a single mention. Nor is it clear from the case file that it was Ms Lawrence who had made the decisions in Victoria's case. Her last recorded, but undated, entry showed that she was anything but certain as to what to do next and needed to discuss the case with senior managers. By contrast, Ms Gaunt's case note for 24 May 1999 shows quite clearly that the decision to offer Kouao board and accommodation for one more week followed from "discussion and decisions with Sarah Stollard".

The involvement of solicitors

4.116 Kouao, in the meantime, had instructed her solicitors and they wrote to Ealing on 27 May 1999. They pointed out that their client had come to the UK in March 1999, although Ealing housing department already knew from Kouao's flight tickets that she had arrived in England in April 1999. They also claimed that Kouao had exhausted her savings as she was required to pay £166 per week for a room for herself and daughter – again an assertion that Ealing could have questioned as they had been funding Kouao's accommodation since the beginning of May. The solicitor restated Kouao's position that she would have nowhere to live from 31 May 1999 as she had been asked to leave the hostel accommodation provided by Ealing. Nor did their client have any money to feed herself and Victoria. They reminded Ealing of their duty under sections 17 and 20 of the Children Act 1989, seeking on Kouao's behalf financial assistance and help with accommodation and care for "her child".

4.117 The letter came to Ms Fortune while on duty on 1 June 1999. She said she was brought up to date on the case in the duty team discussion and knew that Ealing's funding of Kouao's stay at Nicoll Road had come to an end the day before. On reading the solicitor's letter, Ms Fortune said she was anxious to discuss this with her duty manager, Ms Lawrence, and to seek legal advice. If there had been a clear strategy previously to close Victoria's case the solicitor's letter appears to have turned that on its head. Ms Lawrence's unsigned and undated instruction on the case record contact sheet, was to extend the accommodation booking at Nicoll Road and for the case to be allocated for assessment as "no thorough assessment has been carried out as yet". Ms Lawrence also raised the possibility that Ealing could consider paying for return tickets to France.

4.118 Ms Lawrence accepted it was unusual for housing cases to be allocated at all, particularly in the light of Ms Stollard's 'decision' the previous week that Kouao be given one more week's assistance before going back to France. But on this occasion Ms Lawrence said:

> "There appeared to have been some drift in that although there was a process of information gathering and there was information recorded on the file, the assessment format that we were using at the time had not been used, and I felt that it needed to come off the duty system and be given to one worker to carry out the task."

4.119 However, by "thorough assessment", Ms Lawrence said she meant no more than completing the three-sided assessment template for families who have failed the habitual residence test. This is an assessment which she admitted with hindsight could not be described as "thorough". The solicitor's letter, it seems, had merely been the prompt for her to review the case file and ensure that the paperwork was up to date.

4.120 Despite being told that Kouao had no money for food – the last subsistence cheque for £64.44 had been paid on 24 May 1999, just over a week previously, though Ms Fortune did not know this because she did not check – Ms Fortune said she had no concerns as to where Victoria's next meal was to come from because Ms Lawrence had also instructed that the subsistence money should continue for another week. The monies were not paid out, however, until the next day, though nothing was done by Ms Fortune on 1 June 1999 to ensure that Victoria did not go without food.

4.121 Ms Fortune also had the impression that Kouao and Victoria looked very dissimilar:

> "Kouao always dressed immaculately. Her clothing and jewellery seemed expensive and her hair was very well done. She did not in any way look destitute, contrary to what she always claimed. In contrast, Victoria was poorly dressed. I cannot recall exactly what she wore but there were times when she did not seem to be dressed appropriately. She always appeared to look as if she was in hand-me-down clothes. I thought she looked shabbily dressed. I also thought she looked very small for her age. She was very slim and very dark skinned. She had very short dark hair."

4.122 Yet again, none of these observations were recorded by Ms Fortune on the case file. It serves to support the general recommendation I make on the importance of case recording.

4.123 By chance, Kouao's solicitor spoke to Ms Fortune the same day, 1 June, that she received their letter. Apart from reiterating what was in the letter, they told Ms Fortune that Kouao was destitute and that she had asked Brent Social Services for assistance. Brent Social Services asked her to return to the Acton area office.

4.124 Ms Fortune told Kouao's solicitor that "social services had been given variations of her [Kouao's] circumstances" and that social services had a duty to undertake a "thorough" assessment of their client.

4.125 Kouao's solicitor promptly advised Kouao to return to social services and she arrived with Victoria at the Acton area office at about 4.45pm. Kouao was told that she could stay at Nicoll Road one more night and that she would be telephoned the next day and informed whether social services could continue to assist her. Although she agreed to stay at the hostel, according to Ms Fortune, she seemed unhappy at Nicoll Road. Kouao complained that for the last three days she and Victoria had been sleeping in the kitchen area because of water leaking through the ceiling. When she had complained to the manager he had been abusive to her and that had upset Victoria. It had also upset Kouao sufficiently that she took her complaint about the manager to Harlesden police station the next day. She also mentioned again that the place was dirty and the toilets were filled to the rim with vomit and excrement.

4.126 Those complaints notwithstanding, the very next day on 2 June 1999, Ealing Social Services extended Kouao's booking at Nicoll Road for another week until 9 June. An interpreter was also booked and an appointment was made for the assessment interview to take place on 7 June.

Inspection of accommodation

4.127 Asked how she responded to Kouao's complaints about the premises, Ms Fortune said, "I know that there was a phone call made to Nicoll Road and that they said Kouao had ripped up the carpets." In fact, this was a reference to a telephone call received by Ms Wilkin on 4 June 1999 from the accommodation agency through which Kouao and Victoria had been placed in Nicoll Road. The member of staff at Star Lettings, Mr Pandelli, told Ms Wilkin that he had personally inspected the accommodation the previous day and found it adequate. However, he was angry because following Kouao's complaints, she had been moved to a new room the previous night but had removed all the carpets and put them outside her room.

4.128 Ms Fortune told the Inquiry that social services had checked out the premises. She recalled that she herself had made an earlier visit to Nicoll Road – her diary confirmed this visit on 1 March 1999 – and that she had made a second 'announced' visit with another social worker, Ms Schreuder. But, like Ms Gaunt, she could not remember when that was. She thought it was "somewhere between May and June". Ms Fortune stated that she could not remember whether the visit took place before or after her conversation with Kouao. Therefore it is not clear whether the visit was a direct response to Kouao's complaints or complaints by other residents. She made no mention of it in her witness statement and she did not record it on the case file. Asked why not, she said, "I was called to go out with another duty social worker to see another family. I presumed she would have written the information. She obviously presumed I would have."

4.129 She said that if she had recorded her visit she would have noted that the bedrooms and toilets that she saw had basic amenities and were reasonably clean.

4.130 Having heard their evidence and that of Ms Stollard, I am prepared to accept that Ms Fortune and Ms Gaunt probably did visit Nicoll Road on two separate occasions and may well have done so during the time that Kouao and Victoria lived there. However, their and Ms Stollard's recollection as to precisely when these visits occurred was vague and inconsistent. On neither occasion was any serious attempt made to see Kouao's accommodation, particularly in the light of Kouao's complaint on 1 June 1999 that she and Victoria had been forced to sleep in the kitchen area because of a water leak. There was also a failure to record anywhere on the case file the outcomes of these visits. Therefore it seems unlikely that either visit was a direct response to, or was designed to follow up specifically, Kouao's complaints. As a result, Ealing Social Services left unresolved the question of whether the accommodation they were providing at Nicoll Road was in any way suitable for Victoria to live in.

4.131 Kouao and Victoria paid another visit to Ealing Social Services on 4 June 1999 without an appointment. Kouao made further complaints about Nicoll Road to Louise Jones, another social worker in the referral and assessment team who was on duty that day. She complained that there were no carpets in her room and that she had not had a bath for a month because the place was so dirty.

4.132 Ms Jones said she knew that complaints had been made before about the state of Nicoll Road so she asked in the duty room whether anyone had visited. She was told – though she could not remember by whom – that the accommodation had been checked and approved by social workers recently, and she passed on this information to Kouao.

4.133 In her unsigned case file note, Ms Jones recorded that Kouao was due to attend a job interview and that if she was successful she would arrange childcare for Victoria.

4.134 She also noted that Victoria had some rough skin on her arm. Kouao explained that Victoria had eczema and that she was registered with a Dr Emias, but Kouao was unable to give any contact details for Victoria's GP. Ms Jones accepted and recorded these details without question.

4.135 In the meantime, Kouao had instructed her solicitors to write to Ealing a second time which they did on 2 June 1999. Their letter, received in the social services office two days later, noted that Kouao's room in Nicoll Road had flooded on 28 May 1999 as a result of a burst water pipe and that her mattress was sodden – a matter that the manager of the hostel had yet to resolve. They also advised Ealing that neither Kouao nor Victoria had eaten in the last couple of days because Kouao had run out of money. It is not evident that either Ms Jones or anyone else in the Acton area office referral and assessment team ever responded to, or sought to check out, this new information that Victoria was going for long periods of time without food.

4.136 Kouao did not attend her appointment for the assessment interview on 7 June 1999. Instead she turned up again unannounced with Victoria, on 8 June 1999 for her subsistence monies. She explained to Ms Jones that she had missed her appointment the previous day because she had gone for a job interview. She had been successful and was due to start work at Northwick Park Hospital that afternoon. She promised to telephone once she knew her shift rota so that she could fix up a new assessment interview date and an interpreter could be booked. In the meantime, she needed a letter from social services so that she could open a bank account – her first pay cheque was due at the end of the month. Kouao then collected another week's subsistence cheque for £64.44.

4.137 Altogether, Ms Jones's involvement with Kouao and Victoria while on duty amounted to no more than two unannounced office visits, each lasting between 10 and 15 minutes. Yet she too recalled noticing the differences in the appearance of 'mother and daughter', that Kouao "appeared to be well dressed and she had very nice make-up and very nicely presented and [Victoria] by comparison did not seem to be well presented in her clothes and appearance".

4.138 She observed that Victoria appeared to be a little short for her age and that she seemed "to stand quite quietly, a little behind Ms Kouao and to be extremely quiet and reserved". She did not play with the toys in the Wendy house like the other children did. On the second of the two visits, she described Victoria's posture as "submissive, very quiet and timid".

4.139 However, like her colleagues before her, Ms Jones recorded none of these observations about Kouao and Victoria's physical appearance. She told the Inquiry that in a busy duty system, the need to write down events and contacts as they happened did not allow time for proper reflection and evaluation. Nonetheless, she said she discussed what she had seen informally within the team shortly afterwards:

> "We maybe had feelings – a gut feeling about the observations we had made but ... this was not a level of concern that would mean we would instigate child protection procedures, or any level of concern that we felt that we would follow up."

4.140 This cumulative failure to record basic information about Victoria over a period of weeks denied Ealing the benefit of assembling what was becoming a substantial body of information which could and should have been used to inform the assessment of Victoria's needs and future care. By not completing the simple task of assessing Victoria's needs, the original reason for the referral, two and a half months of limited reactive and ineffective social work followed. It was the start of a pattern of response Victoria was to receive in the months ahead. Ms Finlay's admission that less effort may well have been used in completing a basic assessment of Victoria's needs is correct, and it illustrates the degree of disorganisation in the Ealing office at the time and that poor work can waste scarce resources.

4.141 Kouao's next contact with Ealing Social Services was not the telephone call she had promised to make but an early morning unannounced visit on 14 June 1999. She spoke to Ms Wilkin as soon as the office opened to ask whether the department would pay the £30 a week costs of a childminder she had found to look after Victoria while she was at work. It is not clear whether she was given an immediate answer to her question. She did, however, collect her weekly subsistence money and she was given a further assessment interview appointment for 1.30pm on 17 June 1999. She was told that failure to attend on that occasion would cost her her place at Nicoll Road and her financial support would stop.

Kouao turns up for assessment

4.142 On 17 June 1999, Kouao attended Ealing's offices for the assessment. On that occasion, Victoria, who ought to have been the focus of the assessment, did not accompany her. Ms Fortune, as the duty social worker, saw Kouao and was told that Victoria was with a childminder. She was not particularly concerned by this, even though by this stage Victoria had been in the country almost two months and was still not at school. Kouao's explanation was that she wanted to bring over her other children from France, to settle the family's accommodation and then make arrangements for Victoria's schooling.

4.143 Ms Fortune did nothing to alert the education authorities to Victoria's presence in Ealing, nor did she ask any questions to establish whether Victoria was going to a registered childminder. Therefore, I make the following recommendation:

Recommendation
Where, during the course of an assessment, social services establish that a child of school age is not attending school, they must alert the education authorities and satisfy themselves that, in the interim, the child is subject to adequate daycare arrangements.

4.144   According to Ms Fortune, it was a difficult interview. Kouao seemed anxious
and distressed and said that she had only a limited time as she had to be at
work later in the afternoon. Kouao also refused to speak any English and would
only talk to, and allow information to be written down by, the French-speaking
interpreter, Ouafa Choufani. So Ms Choufani, rather than Ms Fortune, completed
the assessment of families who have failed the habitual residence test form. This
was the assessment form that Ms Lawrence had instructed to be completed by an
'allocated social worker'. It is questionable whether Ms Fortune learned anything
new that day – certainly nothing about Victoria – and what she was told bore little
relation to the information Kouao had given in the past.

4.145   Kouao described her previous employment as a "manager at Roissy Airport",
yet she had told Ms Winter that she had been a housewife. She gave the name
and contact details of Dr I Patel as her GP – the same name as she had given to
Ms Winter. She had previously told Ms Jones that Victoria was registered with a
Dr Emias whose address she did not know. In fact, none of these details relating to
the registration of either Victoria or Kouao were entirely correct. When asked about
Victoria's education, she gave details of her own, which included "A levels in science
and three years study at a medical centre". When asked about the general health
of the family, the recorded answer was "none". When asked about her reasons
for coming to the country and staying here, Kouao again provided her French
national insurance card details and repeated her intention to improve her English.
Ms Fortune was able to complete the only remaining details on the form from
information she already knew, namely the name of Kouao's solicitor and that she
had been supported by Ealing Social Services with accommodation and funding.

4.146   Ms Fortune's assessment was limited by the fact that important sections of the
form – her conclusion, assessment and management decisions – were left blank.
Her assessment at best only partially considered Victoria's needs. Ms Fortune told
the Inquiry that it was difficult to undertake an assessment if a person gives various
accounts: "We can only work with the information that we have ... I asked Kouao
to bring Victoria, she did not bring her at all. It was difficult."

4.147   Ms Fortune's case file note of the interview appears in two separate places. The first
note, which appears in chronological date order on the contact sheets for 17 June
1999, outlines Ms Fortune's action points for the next day, 18 June, when she was
away on leave. The action points were:

● to contact Kouao's solicitor to find out when the result of Kouao's habitual
residency test appeal would be known;
● to write to Kouao and arrange a home visit so that the assessment could be
completed;
● to discuss with the duty team manager if financial assistance should continue
pending the outcome of the assessment.

4.148   There is no record on the file to suggest that any manager endorsed Ms Fortune's
action plan. Managers remained unaware that a visit to Victoria in Nicoll Road was
ever made. Ms Fortune said that she later contacted Kouao's solicitor but she did
not receive an answer to her question about Kouao's appeal.

4.149   Ms Fortune's second entry on the case file relating to her interview with Kouao on
17 June 1999 appears on the contact sheets after an entry by her duty manager,
Ms Lawrence, for 30 June. Ms Lawrence's entry instructs Ms Fortune to "complete
the assessment and write to Ms Kouao, invite her into the office to discuss the
management decision". It is in this entry that Ms Fortune describes Kouao's
anxious state and her insistence on only speaking through the interpreter. She
also notes that she explained to Kouao that her financial support would probably

cease as she was now in work – in effect pre-empting the management decision that Ms Lawrence referred to. When Kouao again repeated her request for help with childminding fees, Ms Fortune told her that social services would "probably not assist".

4.150 When asked if she could have written this entry on the case file after 30 June 1999, and indeed after Ms Lawrence's instruction to her, Ms Fortune replied, "It could be. I do not know." In my view, this is the most plausible explanation.

4.151 On 22 June 1999, Ms Fortune discussed the case with her duty manager who informed her that Kouao's accommodation would not be funded after 30 June 1999. The next day Ms Lawrence made an entry on the file to the effect that the duty social worker should contact Kouao's solicitors to check the outcome of what Ms Lawrence called "her housing appeal" (that is, her habitual residency test). That social services should consider paying her return fare to France, that they should withdraw funding once the outcome of the appeal was known and they should write to Kouao informing her of the outcome of the assessment.

4.152 Ms Lawrence said that she could not recall if she ever saw Ms Fortune's assessment. She believed the only reason she recorded "something on the file" was because Ms Fortune brought it to her attention for some direction. She said, "I did not see the assessment. I was given feedback, I was told the assessment had been completed; I did not check it." As a result, I make the following recommendation:

> **Recommendation**
> All social services assessments of children and families, and any action plans drawn up as a result, must be approved in writing by a manager. Before giving such approval, the manager must ensure that the child and the child's carer have been seen and spoken to.

4.153 When asked if it was her responsibility to read the file and to make sure that the case was properly directed, she replied, "Overall responsibility would have been with the team manager. However, I played a part in that I managed duty on a fortnightly basis."

Case allocation

4.154 That same day, Ms Lawrence finally allocated Victoria's case to Ms Fortune, or so she thought. The process involved making the papers up into a file and logging the details on the computer – a task that was to take a week before Ms Fortune finally received the case papers. As a result, the case allocation date was subsequently changed to 30 June 1999 and Ms Fortune was instructed to "complete the assessment".

4.155 It might seem bizarre that the decision to allocate Victoria's case should have come more than two months after Victoria was first referred to Ealing and after an assessment had supposedly been completed which was to lead to Ealing Social Services discontinuing their support to Kouao and Victoria. Ms Lawrence's explanation was "for the assessment that Pamela [Fortune] said she had completed to be put down on paper ... to take it off the duty system, to ensure that that person got it done". It would seem that the process of allocation on this occasion was no more than a vehicle for ensuring that Ms Fortune, the person who conducted the assessment interview such as it was, also wrote it up.

4.156 By "completing the assessment" Ms Lawrence certainly meant no more than that Ms Fortune should write it up. Ms Fortune, on the other hand, believed she was being asked to "complete" the assessment. She said she told Ms Lawrence that she had found the assessment "difficult", which no doubt accounts for why Ms Fortune's account of her interview with Kouao appears after Ms Lawrence's file instruction for 30 June 1999. Ms Fortune also knew that a decision had been made "from quite early on that Mrs Kouao should go back to France or the child should be accommodated".

4.157   Ms Fortune was instructed to write to Kouao to invite her into the office to discuss the decisions that had been reached. The decisions, as they appear on the case file in Ms Lawrence's handwriting, unsigned and undated, were:

"i)   client has no connection with this country, has no significant family/friends

ii)   there has been no appropriate/adequate planning prior to coming to this country

iii)   reasons for coming are weak – to learn English

iv)   she has family/friends in France, has access to housing and state benefits in France

v)   she has children who she left back in France whom she intends to return to France to collect and bring back to this country, who will subsequently become dependent on social services funding

vi)   based on the above the department has decided that we can no longer fund Ms Kouao as it is apparent that she will need intermittent funding for a long period of time. Ms Kouao has left a stable lifestyle to come to this country where she has no recourse to public funds or accommodation and has therefore placed herself in a vulnerable situation. We are in a position to provide Ms Kouao with return tickets for herself and child to France."

4.158   What is extraordinary about these decisions was the basis for making them. As Ms Lawrence recorded, they reflected almost precisely the reasons Ms Winter gave back in April for Kouao failing the habitual residency test. All the emphasis was on Kouao's lack of significant ties in this country, the fact that she had left family and friends in France and that her stay in the country was intended to be short term. There is not a single mention of Victoria. Indeed, there can be no doubt that the "client" referred to was Kouao. Nothing more had been learnt about Kouao, let alone Victoria, in the two months since the case had been referred to Ealing Social Services.

4.159   Ms Lawrence said she fully accepted that the focus of the assessment was on the adult and the presenting issue, which was homelessness. She admitted that she did nothing to assure herself that the assessment was complete, let alone adequate. In fact, she never read Ms Fortune's account of what had happened on 17 June 1999:

"I was not the person who closed the case – perhaps if I had closed the case I would have referred back to the assessment before closing it as I had directed that it be done ... I had been informed by Pamela [Fortune] that it had been carried out and I informed Judith Finlay that it had. I accept that I should have actually looked at that form and signed it off and ensured that it was completed before I reported to Judith Finlay."

4.160   Her only concern, it appears, was that the form had not been properly completed. Asked if a different conclusion might have been reached if someone had read the file from start to finish, Ms Lawrence replied:

"I do not think there would have been a different approach. I think we could have come to the conclusions that we came to at an earlier point in our involvement with the family, but I am not convinced that the outcome would have been different."

4.161 In a telephone call with Ms Lawrence, Ms Finlay ratified the management decisions that had been made. She did not know at the time that Victoria had never been seen or spoken to. She was told that a comprehensive assessment had been undertaken: "My understanding of a comprehensive assessment is that the child is seen and spoken to."

4.162 But she also did nothing to check this was the case. On average, Ms Finlay said she was consulted about once a week on similar cases where the presenting issues were homelessness. Had she known the truth, she said she would not have endorsed the management decisions.

4.163 Kouao returned to the Ealing office on 30 June 1999, again without Victoria. She saw Ms Fortune and told her that Victoria was with the childminder. Ms Fortune gave her a letter setting out the reasons why social services would no longer fund her stay in England. Kouao was told that her accommodation would be paid for until 7 July 1999 and she and Ms Lawrence went through the letter with Kouao. Before leaving the office, Kouao made it clear that she did not want to return to France and that she would be contacting her solicitor. To Ms Lawrence's eye, Kouao appeared "forceful" and "manipulative" and that she seemed to understand only what was being said when it suited her. However, she never recorded these observations on the case file.

Ealing council's legal department

4.164 On advice, Ms Fortune contacted Ealing council's legal department (interestingly the only authority to make use of its legal section) and spoke to Phillip Joseph. Mr Joseph told the Inquiry that he found the circumstances of Victoria's case "slightly bizarre". He said, "It just struck me as peculiar that a lady would come from France with a child and leave her other children in France merely to learn English."

4.165 Regrettably, this was not a perception shared by his social work colleagues, and in particular by Ms Fortune or her managers.

4.166 Mr Joseph was told by Ms Fortune that a section 17 assessment had been done of Victoria's needs. In his view it was perfectly reasonable to fund return tickets to France for Kouao and Victoria if the child's needs could best be met there. He thought there had been some preliminary inquiries as to Kouao's circumstances in France, though he was reliant on what Ms Fortune had told him, and she in turn had simply accepted at face value what Kouao had chosen to tell social services. At no stage had Ealing Social Services attempted to verify independently any aspect of Kouao's life before her arrival in England.

4.167 On 2 July 1999, Mr Joseph had a second telephone conversation with Ms Fortune. Kouao's solicitors had written another letter to Ealing Social Services expressing surprise at the decision to repatriate their "client", and asking them to review that decision or face judicial review proceedings. Mr Joseph repeated his earlier advice and suggested as an alternative to the family returning to France, that social services could offer to accommodate Victoria in their care until Kouao had found full-time work. Ms Fortune passed this on to Kouao's solicitors.

4.168 On 7 July 1999, Kouao again visited the offices alone. She was seen by Ms Fortune who confirmed that social services would no longer pay for her accommodation or continue to offer financial assistance. Kouao, who according to Ms Fortune was quite emotional at the time, was adamant that she would not return to France nor would she agree to Victoria being accommodated separately from her. Ms Fortune advised her to return to her solicitors but Kouao indicated that they were "no good". She also asked if she could have the money for the tickets, but Ms Fortune repeated her offer of purchasing the return tickets if Kouao would give her a travel date. Kouao did not respond and left the office.

The file is closed

4.169 That day, Ealing Social Services closed their files on Kouao and Victoria. They did so in the full knowledge that funding for their accommodation at Nicoll Road would cease the same day and that Kouao had no intention of returning to France. It was a poor decision that lacked any sound professional basis. Ms Fortune said she was not unduly concerned about Victoria because "[Kouao] had a part-time job at that time so I knew she had money to be able to look after her".

4.170 Ms Fortune conceded, however, that by the time Victoria's case was closed, Ealing had done nothing to determine Victoria's future or safeguard and promote her welfare. During the nine or so weeks Victoria had been Ealing's responsibility, none of the social workers who had come into contact with Victoria had got beyond saying "hello" to her. No assessment of her needs had been completed.

Brent Social Services

4.171 On 14 July 1999, barely a week after closing Victoria's case, Ms Fortune learned that her team manager, Ms Stollard, had "received a message from Brent Social Services" to the effect that Victoria had been admitted to the Central Middlesex Hospital with suspected non-accidental injuries. There was also a message to ring Elzanne Smit, a social worker in Brent. Ms Fortune did so the following day. Ms Smit told Ms Fortune that Victoria's childminder had noticed injuries to Victoria's body and had taken her to the hospital. Although admitted with suspected non-accidental injuries, Kouao's explanation that they were self-inflicted had been accepted by another doctor. Victoria was diagnosed as having scabies and the injuries were thought to have been caused by Victoria scratching herself.

4.172 Ms Fortune explained to Ms Smit that Ealing had closed the case. When asked if Ealing could send over a copy of their assessment – an assessment that never of course existed – Ms Fortune said, according to her contact note, that she would speak to her manager and unless there was a problem she would send across a summary. That 'summary', which ought to have chronicled Ealing's involvement with Kouao and Victoria since April and the outcome of their assessment, was no more than a copy of the letter handed over to Kouao on 30 June 1999, which set out Ealing's decision to cease their support for the family and their reasons for coming to that decision.

4.173 Ms Fortune believed that she did pass on more information to Ms Smit over the telephone about Ealing's involvement though she made no record of this. At the very least, according to Ms Smit's record of the conversation on the Brent file, Brent learned that Kouao had come to England in April, that she had been referred to social services by Ealing Homeless Persons' Unit after failing the habitual residency test, that she had sought legal advice and been offered accommodation in Harlesden until 7 July 1999. Indeed, this would have been the first time that Brent had confirmed knowledge of Kouao's placement within their borough. Ms Smit was told that Kouao planned to stay in the UK.

4.174 Kouao returned again to the Acton area office with Victoria later on 15 July 1999, the very same day that Victoria had been discharged from the Central Middlesex Hospital. It seems that Kouao left Victoria alone in the reception area. According to Ms Wilkin she was told by reception staff that Kouao was waiting, but when she went out to tell Kouao that a social worker would be out shortly she found Victoria alone sitting in a chair. Ms Wilkin said she returned several times to check on Victoria. She also told Ms Fortune that Victoria had been left alone.

4.175 Ms Wilkin could no longer recall anything about Victoria's appearance on that occasion. Ms Fortune went out to speak to Victoria and said "hello" just as Kouao ran back in. Ms Fortune noticed at once that Victoria had a rash and blisters on her face and arms. She presumed that this was the scabies that the consultant at the Central Middlesex Hospital had diagnosed the day before. Ms Fortune recalled that she felt quite angry and told Kouao it was unacceptable for her to leave Victoria in the reception area. Kouao said that she had been to the toilet and left Victoria for just five minutes. The reception staff were unable to say how long Victoria had been sitting alone although Ms Wilkin said she was told it could have been up to an hour. Nonetheless, uppermost in Ms Fortune's mind were health and safety concerns for the staff. If, as seemed likely, Victoria had yet to recover from her scabies infection then she should have been at home. But this was not an observation, nor an incident, that Ms Fortune thought worthwhile to mention to Brent Social Services, despite their recent child protection concerns.

4.176 Ms Fortune informed Kouao that her case was closed at Acton and that she would have to return to Brent. She also suggested that Kouao seek independent legal advice from the Acton Law Centre, which was housed in the Acton area office next to the reception area. Ms Fortune's case file note for 15 July 1999 refers to a telephone call that she received from a Mr Armstrong, whom she believed to be from the law centre, asking for information and expressing some concern about Kouao's case. Ms Fortune told him that the case was closed and that Kouao was now being seen by Brent "due to concerns about Anna". Yet these were the very same concerns which, according to Ms Fortune, had all but been dismissed because "the information that we got from Elzanne [Smit] was that it was scabies, and the doctor had made a decision".

4.177 There was therefore no reason, in her view, to let Brent know that Victoria had been left alone in the Ealing Social Services office on the day of her discharge from the Central Middlesex Hospital. I strongly disagree. Ms Fortune knew that as recently as the day before, Brent were investigating potential child protection concerns. The proper course of action for Ms Fortune to have taken, while Kouao and Victoria were still in the Ealing office, was to telephone Brent Social Services there and then to let them know where Victoria was and what had just happened. One telephone call ought to have prompted a discussion about what to do next, leading ultimately to a meeting between social services officers as to who should take on case responsibility in the immediate future. Most likely it would also have been the trigger for Ealing to share all the information they already had about the family, including Kouao's lack of co-operation with the assessment process and the observations of the Ealing staff as to the relationship between Kouao and Victoria.

4.178 Ms Fortune's final action note for 15 July 1999 makes a clear reference to Brent having "resumed the case due to their involvement with 'Anna' when she was admitted to hospital". Thereafter, neither Ms Fortune, nor anyone else from Ealing Social Services, saw Victoria or Kouao again.

4.179 The only reason Kouao was referred to Ealing Social Services was because of Victoria's needs. Yet throughout contact, her needs were largely ignored and instead the focus was on Kouao. Victoria was never seen as the client and never became the focus of the work in Ealing. This was the start of a pattern of social work practice that was to disadvantage Victoria repeatedly over the next 11 months.

Analysis of practice

4.180   This first appearance by Kouao and Victoria at the childcare offices was the start of a process which illustrates just how poorly organised the 'front door' services in Ealing were. The case was passed from worker to worker with differing assumptions being made about who had done what and what remained to be done. The practice ensured that no supervisory overview was given to Victoria, other than a rather brief reactive analysis being offered by the duty senior manager in passing.

Organisational failures

4.181   The capacity of the team to keep track of each of the referrals they were dealing with appears to have been dependent upon the memory and diligence of the senior staff and a defective system involving baskets, books, A–Z cabinets, pending trays, diaries and logs. The case recording throughout was grossly inadequate and the likelihood of cases drifting or being lost was high. Indeed, I wonder what would have happened had Kouao not repeatedly been knocking at the front door of social services? By Ealing's own admission, the threat of legal action was the only reason the case was kept open. Ealing's main intervention was to give money to Kouao for subsistence and to finance her accommodation once she had been deemed ineligible for housing by the housing department. Although this response was under the Children Act 1989, the reality was that the needs of the child, Victoria, were never considered. In fact it was said that homeless families were dealt with administratively and not allocated to a social worker. This is entirely unacceptable and is bad practice.

4.182   I found it hard to understand the evidence I heard from qualified social workers about what they described as a lack of clarity on how they should assess the needs of a child and its family. While the National Assessment Framework was published more recently, and welcomed, I would have expected qualified social workers at the time Victoria needed protection to be capable of completing an assessment of her needs. The Children Act 1989 had been implemented in 1991. The forms for this purpose were available and senior managers accepted that the tasks had been completed. In reality, however, the conversations with Victoria were limited to little more than "hello, how are you?". The only 'assessment' completed involved the writing down of limited and sometimes contradictory information provided by Kouao.

4.183   The overall picture of what happened to Victoria while in Ealing serves to illustrate well the effect of drift in social work. No plan of action was ever devised and no sense of direction could be identified. Little wonder that the information recorded on the file in June 1999 was precisely that which was in the referral two months earlier. This ineffective work was no doubt not helped by the confusion in the managerial responsibilities and the ad hoc weekly handover arrangements and irregular supervision between the team manager and the senior practitioner. This is certainly something which should have been sorted out by senior managers. The decision was made to close Victoria's case without seeing or speaking to Victoria, and without any indication of how her welfare was to be safeguarded or promoted. Therefore, I make the following recommendation:

Recommendation
Directors of social services must ensure that no case involving a vulnerable child is closed until the child and the child's carer have been seen and spoken to, and a plan for the ongoing promotion and safeguarding of the child's welfare has been agreed.

What Ealing Social Services could have recorded

4.184 It is useful to reflect on what Ealing knew, or suspected, about Victoria despite their failure to undertake an assessment of her needs. From the documentary evidence and other evidence put to this Inquiry that did not always find its way onto the case records, the following picture would have emerged under the four areas for concern.

4.185 1: The credibility of the story as told by Kouao:

- Kouao and Victoria arrived in London on a travel package, which included seven days' bed and breakfast accommodation. (I suspect an unusual route by a homeless family.)
- Kouao had no means to support herself and Victoria for more than a few days.
- Within two days, Kouao had presented herself as a homeless person with a young child.
- Kouao said she had left three other children in France, a matter which should have resulted in contact with the French authorities.
- Kouao said the reason she came was to improve her English.
- Kouao made it clear she had no immediate intention of returning to France.
- Kouao provided the Ealing duty team social worker with a French social security number. Had the social worker contacted the authorities in France, they may have heard about the quite serious concerns the school had about the welfare of Victoria.
- Kouao claimed she was given financial assistance by French social security to travel to London with Victoria, which was never checked.
- Kouao gave a different story to different members of staff in housing and social services.

4.186 2: Concerns about Victoria's appearance:

- Victoria was wearing a wig.
- The photograph of Victoria on the passport was a questionable likeness of her.
- Kouao was very well dressed.
- In contrast, Victoria was shabby and resembled one of the "adverts you see for Action Aid".
- Victoria was said to be small and of "stunted growth".
- Kouao and Victoria appeared to have a different skin colour.

4.187 3: Concerns about Victoria's behaviour:

- Kouao was "forceful" and "manipulative" and did not allow Victoria to answer questions staff directed to her.
- Social services believed that Victoria was being coached in her reactions.
- When Victoria cried it seemed to be "stage managed".
- In the office it was noted that Victoria stood silently and did not play with the Wendy house or the toys like the other children.

4.188 4: The apparent lack of Kouao's concern for Victoria's welfare:

- There did not appear to be any parental warmth from Kouao toward Victoria.
- When a meeting was fixed to perform an assessment of Victoria's needs, unusually Kouao attended without Victoria and she was less than co-operative.
- Despite being in this country for some two months, Victoria still had not been registered with a school.

4.189 Each of the above is not of itself a determining factor, but together they indicate that Victoria was probably in need of safeguarding. I accept that in a busy office dealing with a high number and a wide range of referrals, decisions have to be made about likelihood of deliberate harm and urgency. The fact remains that the initial reason for Victoria's referral was for an assessment of her needs and in my view enough was known, or was observed about the family during the months they spent in Ealing, to have triggered a full assessment of those needs. It is a duty placed on social services to assemble and analyse information about children who may need to have their welfare safeguarded and promoted. This needs to be done in a rigorous way, viewed, as far as possible, through the eyes of the child. It certainly needs to be both tough-minded and with an awareness of the ability of some adults to mislead and to use children to satisfy their own needs. Had a proper assessment been done at that point, it is possible that Victoria would have received the necessary protection in Ealing and the other authorities may never have been involved. That being so, I reject the implications of a key conclusion of the Part 8 review, undertaken in response to the death of Victoria, that "staff in Ealing were not aware of any indicators suggesting that Victoria was at risk of serious abuse or any indicators of serious deficits in Kouao's parenting". Ealing were not aware because they undertook no proper assessment of Victoria so that they could become aware of her needs.

4.190   Doing the basic things well saves lives. In my view, Ealing failed to meet even the elementary standards of childcare practice, and as a result Victoria went unprotected. It could have been so different.

5 Brent Social Services

The managerial context

5.1   Brent Social Services had the opportunity to help Victoria on two separate occasions. The first was on receipt of an anonymous telephone call expressing concern about Victoria's safety in June 1999, while Kouao and Victoria were living at 8 Nicoll Road and supported by Ealing Social Services. The second was almost a month later, after Kouao and Victoria had moved in with Carl Manning at 267 Somerset Gardens. This was when Victoria was taken to the Central Middlesex Hospital by her childminder's daughter, Avril Cameron, with suspected non-accidental injuries. Regrettably, at no time during Brent's brief involvement with Victoria did social workers make any connection between these two referrals. Indeed, the first time senior managers acknowledged that there had been two referrals in relation to Victoria was in February 2001, a year after her death and in the month following the criminal trial of Kouao and Manning for her murder. Had the link been made at the relevant time it seems highly likely that events in Victoria's life would have taken a very different turn.

5.2   The two referrals found their way to a duty team. The Social Services Inspectorate (SSI) in May 2000 assessed this team to be "failing to meet basic requirements for an initial response to referrals." They were operating administrative systems the SSI considered to have "broken down" and to be "creating serious risks". Overall, in May 2000 the inspectors found a situation that was "very serious" and a children's services department that "lacked any clear vision or sense of direction". This did not happen overnight.

5.3   Brent has accepted there were serious shortcomings in the practice and in professional judgements made at the time, which resulted in missed opportunities to help Victoria. If the criticism could be fairly made that senior management took its eye off its 'front door' children's services in Ealing, the position in Brent was far more deep-rooted – as the SSI May 2000 inspection was to reveal. Mike Boyle, the director of social services until April 1999, accepted that he had 'taken his eye off the ball' in respect of children's services from 1998.

5.4   In fact, at one stage children were so low in Brent's priorities that children's social work was not even mentioned in the 1999 Corporate Strategy Update. It was not surprising, then, that in May 2000, the SSI could find no up-to-date children's plan. The most recent was dated 1995 and referred to the period 1995–1998. The interim child protection procedures were still considered 'interim', despite being over four years old. Jenny Goodall, Brent's new director of social services appointed in April 2000, went further and said, "I think there was a period when **social services** [my emphasis] somehow slipped below the horizon." Therefore, I make the following recommendation:

> **Recommendation**
> Chief executives and lead members of local authorities with social services responsibilities must ensure that children's services are explicitly included in their authority's list of priorities and operational plans.

5.5 Responsibility for this sorry state of affairs rests squarely with Brent's council members, chief executive Gareth Daniel, and his senior social services officers. Mr Daniel said in evidence both politicians and management accepted that in 1999 they had plainly not done enough for children in Brent. This does little more than state the obvious – especially as the SSI May 2000 inspection was preceded by critical SSI inspections into the safety of children looked after in February 1998 and Brent's child protection services in September 1996. The latter inspection warned of serious deficiencies in child protection practice and urged a "re-prioritising of management endeavour" so as to "increase the level of direct support, advice and direction to team managers and social workers until such time as practice achieves a consistently good standard".

5.6 In 1998, the SSI identified an absence of workload management systems in the social work teams and said workload pressures had worsened. They warned, "These pressures could, if allowed to continue or deteriorate, reduce workers ability to identify and address safety issues for children."

5.7 Mr Daniel, who was appointed to his position in September 1998 after being the acting chief executive from May 1998, said of himself, "I am a general strategic manager for the authority and that is my discrete role. It is not my role to be a surrogate for the people that I directly manage." Mr Daniel then explained that he discharged his responsibilities by "making sure that the resources are available, the proper checks are in place and that we appoint people in whom we have confidence to discharge the statutory responsibilities which I have to reinforce".

5.8 In my view, other parts of the evidence of Mr Daniel cast some doubt on this assertion. Looking specifically at social services and children's social work, Mr Daniel said that he thought the leadership at a high level in the social services department during 1998, 1999 and 2000 was "seriously defective", with staff being "poorly managed and poorly led". He said, "My impression of the social services department from a **professional distance** [my emphasis] in the town hall is [that] there were a lot of good front-line staff working in that department putting in very long hours, and there were senior managers who were certainly doing all of those things, but I did not feel confident that they were providing the strategic leadership for the department that it needs." As to how the lack of good management affected the way children in Brent were looked after and cared for, Mr Daniel said, "I do not think it assisted the process. I mean, I think the endeavours of front-line staff probably rescued us from a lot of crises which may potentially have arisen. We were very heavily dependent on the integrity and the commitment of those front-line staff."

5.9 In my view, the chief executive can exercise considerable influence on the quality and effectiveness of front-line social work, and indeed has a responsibility to do so. In the particular circumstances in which Mr Daniel found himself in Brent, he failed (during the period with which I am concerned) to address the shortage of staff in the children's services and to implement the recommendations of the SSI reports of 1996 and 1998. He also failed to ensure these services were adequately funded. These were all matters which had a major impact on the children's services, for which Mr Daniel must take personal responsibility. Therefore, I make the following recommendation:

Recommendation
The Department of Health should require chief executives of local authorities with social services responsibilities to prepare a position statement on the true picture of the current strengths and weaknesses of their 'front door' duty systems for children and families. This must be accompanied by an action plan setting out the timescales for remedying any weaknesses identified.

5.10 A fair assessment of the performance of front-line staff in Brent at the time Victoria needed protection has to be made against the backdrop of the dysfunctional and administratively chaotic children's service in which they were expected to work.

Structure of children's social work

5.11 In 1999, Brent senior management team was structured as follows:

- Gareth Daniel, chief executive
- Mike Boyle, director of social services (and later Ronald Ludgate)
- Lucille Thomas, director of children's social work services
- Branton Bamford, assistant director for finance and administration
- David Charlett, service manager for the duty team and the child protection and investigation team.

5.12 Brent children's social services had two initial assessment teams. These were the duty team and the child protection investigation and assessment team (child protection team) – and six teams that were allocated cases on a long-term basis. The duty team was the first team to consider referrals received about children, though this was complicated by the fact that many of these came through Brent's One Stop Shops. If the referral raised issues of 'a child in need', the case would remain in the duty team for initial assessment. But if it was agreed that it contained child protection concerns, it would be transferred to the child protection team. Both of these teams were assisted by a duty administrative team, which would log the referrals into a database and complete checks to find out whether the child was known to the borough.

5.13 The duty child protection and duty administrative teams shared an open-plan office on the ground floor of the children's social work building. I heard evidence that the building was "overcrowded", "grotty", and "neglected". The SSI in 2000 said the accommodation for duty work needed to be improved to meet health and safety requirements. The manager of the duty team, Edward Armstrong, and the manager of the child protection team, Tina Roper, shared a small office at the end of the room. The seven duty social workers including Lori Hobbs, Kate Thrift and Yolande Viljoen (née Hurter), worked at one side of the room and the six child protection social workers were stationed at the opposite side of the room.

5.14 At the time Victoria's case was handled by Brent, all the duty social workers had received their training abroad and were on temporary contracts. Several workers in the child protection team were also recruited on a temporary basis. The fact that so many staff in the initial assessment teams were agency staff had important consequences to which I shall return later in paragraphs 5.59 to 5.61. The two duty senior social workers were Monica Bridgeman and Pauline Phillips, and the two child protection seniors were Michelle Hines and Christina Austin. The group administrative officer was Robert Smith. Martin Punch was one of the administrative support workers. Unlike other boroughs, Brent did not deploy any of its social workers at local hospitals.

The duty team

5.15 Mr Boyle was frank in his evidence to the Inquiry on the state of the duty team. Looking back, he said it was clear to him now that "the duty team began to unravel during 1998 and 1999. The attention of senior managers was elsewhere and as a consequence the service declined to a point that was unacceptable". He believed Victoria's case demonstrated "individual, collective and institutional failures in the system [which were] intended to ensure that the needs of the most vulnerable children are met".

Workload

5.16 Counsel for Brent acknowledged that the duty team was undoubtedly "a team under pressure, over busy, very short of permanent and experienced staff" and Mr Armstrong pointed out that in 1999 the pressure was particularly acute because of the increase in the number of asylum seekers. Ms Viljoen described the duty team as "very busy". She said, "The phones would ring constantly." Mr Punch said the duty team was "very, very swamped with work". Mr Armstrong said, "It was concerning to look at working with between 200 to 300-odd cases per week that was in the backlog system." Given the caseload in June and July 1999, he said that he barely had time for lunch, let alone to stand back within his office and look at the systems the duty team worked under.

5.17 Mr Armstrong dated the beginning of the influx of unaccompanied asylum seekers to 1999. By then, he said, **"We lost our ability to be social workers** [my emphasis] because of the time we had to spend dealing with asylum seekers – there were no additional resources to cope with it." Mr Armstrong estimated that in June and July 1999 he was dealing with at least 15 referrals in relation to intentionally homeless people and asylum seekers each week, and that at least 50 per cent of social workers' time would be spent working on cases of unaccompanied minors. By May 2000, the SSI found that duty staff were overwhelmed with cases of homeless people and were required to spend up to 80 per cent of their time working on what might be considered housing and homelessness issues. I can only question, and not for the first time as will become clear, why Brent's senior management team failed to act more quickly to protect the 'front door' of their children's services.

Bottleneck of cases

5.18 Even more significant than the increase in numbers coming through social services' door was the inability of the duty team to pass cases on to the long-term teams, after the initial work had been completed. Mr Armstrong described how every Wednesday morning he would attend allocation meetings with the assistant directors and the child protection team to refer cases for allocation to the long-term teams. He said, "It had become a common theme for me to go to the allocation meeting with cases for allocation to a 'long-term' team, only to return with the same cases because there was insufficient resource availability in long-term teams to deal with the cases." He added, "It was something that went on, not for months, for years." Ms Roper confirmed that the relevant assistant directors and occasionally Ms Thomas would attend the allocation meeting, so they were perfectly well aware of the difficulty and the bottleneck in allocating cases to the long-term teams.

5.19 The effect on the duty team staff was immense. Ms Hobbs said it was a "major problem", which "was frustrating because there was little let-up". This bottleneck of cases meant that duty workers would have to carry out work that should have been done in the long-term teams in addition to each day's new referrals. For Mr Armstrong, the pressures reached such a pitch that he said, "It got to the point where I actually filled the boot of my car every Friday evening to take cases home, in order to get them up to date, bring them up to date and still report to senior management about what was happening." To do this Mr Armstrong said he needed Ms Thomas's permission.

Management knowledge

5.20 Mr Armstrong did not, however, suffer in silence. He raised his concerns about the workload pressures and staffing with his superiors on a number of occasions. He said, "I would mention it to all the senior managers that I came into contact with, but it got to the point where I felt it was because I kept on doing the work, and was not falling off sick or going off sick for months on end, that it became acceptable to senior management." Ms Bridgeman said she also reported her concerns to members of the senior management team on numerous occasions. She said, "We were constantly working in a crisis situation. Senior management knew this."

5.21   Mr Charlett, when discussing the problem of allocating child protection cases to the long-term teams, said, "We could not stop work coming into the office, but on the other hand, it seemed to be blocked at that point, and there was no way I could – I had no authority to order people in the other teams to take on cases." It is difficult to credit a more ineffectual management response, despite Brent's action plan following the 1996 SSI inspection stating that they should take measures to reduce pressures on team managers. Mr Armstrong said, "Nothing was done to relieve the pressure. Instead the pressure increased."

Faxed referrals

5.22   During the summer of 1999, the duty team also appeared to have let slip vital administrative functions. Although the administrative team was a separate unit, there was considerable overlap between the functions and operation of the two teams, and often a confusion as to which team bore the responsibility for particular tasks. One area of contention was the collection and distribution of faxed referrals and other important communications received by the children's social work team. In his evidence, Mr Armstrong painted a graphic picture of faxes at times streaming on the floor and nobody picking them up. It was not a description that others in the duty team recognised, though Ms Bridgeman acknowledged she was aware of significant delays in the distribution of faxes on one or two occasions. When asked why he himself did not do something about it, Mr Armstrong said, "It was not my job to pick up the fax from the fax machine. It was not my role. I had other things to do." He did, however, complain to administrative colleagues about the problem.

Cases going missing

5.23   The evidence relating to the tracking of cases within the duty and administrative teams raised further serious concerns. According to Mr Armstrong, more than one case was going missing every day and it was obviously difficult to monitor what was going on in the missing cases: "Some files were misplaced and some were never found." Mr Smith believed that it had been known for files to go missing and never reappear, though this was not his personal experience. Mr Punch wrote in a later memo: "Retrieving files has become like the 'National Lottery' with the same odds for finding files." It was Mr Punch's view that the high number of systems in use at the time only contributed to the problem. There were just too many routes and locations in which files could be lost.

5.24   There can be little doubt the duty system was in administrative chaos in 1999. Instead of senior management taking urgent steps to remedy the sources of the problems, the duty team was left to devise its own ad hoc solutions that included introducing a number of manual logging systems. Mr Armstrong said there was no way in which information could be matched up between the books they used. For example, the duty book "would not give us as much information as we require, but it will let us know that that file has been in the system, is in the system, but is now missing". Therefore, I make the following recommendation:

> **Recommendation**
> Directors of social services must devise and implement a system which provides them with the following information about the work of the duty teams for which they are responsible:
>
> • number of children referred to the teams;
> • number of those children who have been assessed as requiring a service;
> • number of those children who have been provided with the service that they require;
> • number of children referred who have identified needs which have yet to be met.

Supervision and monitoring

5.25 With the heavy work pressure and the presence of so many agency staff, good supervision and support was essential. The agency social workers spoke highly of the supervision and support they received from their seniors and team manager while at Brent, but this was not carried through at more senior levels. In relation to his supervision of the senior social workers in his team, Mr Armstrong said, "Due to the volume of cases which we were handling, supervision arrangements slipped and certainly did not occur on a monthly basis." He was supposed to have monthly supervision meetings with Mr Charlett but Mr Armstrong said he could not say how often these actually occurred, other than to point out they were less regular than monthly. Ms Roper said she found Mr Charlett's supervision to be supportive, but pointed out that his recent experience of child protection matters was limited.

5.26 In view of the regular turnover of staff, the monitoring of the quality of the work carried out should, in my opinion, have been a top priority. In fact what actually occurred in Brent was just the reverse. As Mr Armstrong pointed out, it was obviously difficult to monitor work in the cases that were lost. In his written statement Mr Charlett said, "Monitoring arrangements included case records monitoring, the system of regular staff/case supervision through the line management system, random monitoring of cases by supervisors/managers, statistical analysis of referrals and caseloads." However, when specifically questioned on this, Mr Charlett made a somewhat unconvincing attempt to outline these processes in practice and it became clear that there were no formal procedures in place, or at least none used by him, to monitor cases. On the other hand, Ms Roper said that she would monitor the progress of cases in the child protection team and that she carried out an audit of cases once every fortnight.

5.27 Despite written procedures in the Brent *Quality Protects Management Action Plan 1999–2000* requiring assistant directors to produce quarterly reports on individual cases, Mr Charlett said he could not recall producing such reports routinely for the director of children's social work. When it was suggested to him that the systems of monitoring and supervision of cases within his department were inadequate, Mr Charlett said that he would have to agree, up to a point. He said, "Certainly they were not what I would have liked, and what would have been desirable, but as I have pointed out, there were lots of difficulties with regard to covering just the day-to-day work." Therefore, I make the following recommendation:

> **Recommendation**
> Directors of social services must ensure that senior managers inspect, at least once every three months, a random selection of case files and supervision notes.

Child protection team

5.28 Despite a very heavy workload and several temporary social workers, in contrast to other teams in the children's social work unit, Mr Charlett observed, "The child protection team was always more stable, it had ... more of a team quality about it, and it was a team where other social workers wanted to join." Mr Charlett said he had a great deal of confidence in Ms Roper and the other workers in the team. Child protection team members themselves said they thought it was a supportive team, with a good manager. Mr Charlett was also of the opinion that the team was capable of managing its workload. This may in part have been because the administrative and the long-term teams would prioritise the cases above those concerning children in need. In fact, Ms Roper said that on occasion she would volunteer at allocation meetings to keep some of her cases, in an effort to allow some duty cases to be allocated.

5.29   Mr Charlett said that all child protection workers were meant to follow a seven-day modular course, but that agency workers were less able to pursue training courses. Although it was not something he agreed with, Mr Charlett said, "There was certainly a feeling that it was sometimes a waste of time training agency staff." Yet these were the very same workers whose task it was to assess the most vulnerable of Brent's children, those for whom it had already been decided, rightly or wrongly, that there were clear child protection concerns.

5.30   Ms Roper said that she would meet with any new worker to the team and talk them through the processes and systems of the child protection team and they would initially co-work with other members of the team. However, there was no formal induction process in place. Ms Hines said she personally had not received any induction and whether or not locum workers who joined more recently received an induction depended upon the staffing of the department at the time. Therefore, I make the following recommendation:

> **Recommendation**
> Directors of social services must ensure that all staff who work with children have received appropriate vocational training, receive a thorough induction in local procedures and are obliged to participate in regular continuing training so as to ensure that their practice is kept up to date.

Effect of workload on administration

5.31   The increased workload in the two initial assessment teams, particularly the duty team, had a knock-on effect on the duty administrative team. Yet Brent's response was to understaff this department as well. According to Mr Bamford, there were three members of the administrative team during the relevant period, but one of these three was off sick. He said that the previous fourth position had been notionally frozen. When the third staff member went on sick leave, Mr Bamford said he discussed whether to get in additional temporary help. But after considering the time it would take to train someone and that they might stay only a short time, Mr Smith agreed to cover until Brent Social Services' Finance and Administration Department had a better idea of the length of the sick leave.

5.32   Mr Bamford said he was unaware of any administration problems at the time, other than the staffing issues. While he acknowledged that "things were not run as smoothly as one would hope", he seemed totally unaware of any backlog at the time in question and thought that if there were any problems these should have been brought to his attention.

5.33   I found Mr Bamford's ignorance of the problems facing the team to be surprising. The administrative problems were numerous and glaring. In addition to the backlog of referral details waiting to be inputted because of staff shortages, the absence of a common database in social services meant that administrative staff had to complete checks on five or more different databases. As the duty administrative team staff did not have direct access to most of these, the time taken to complete a check was unnecessarily lengthened, which just added to the workload. Child protection cases were prioritised but the backlog meant that cases not yet on the system could not be easily searched. Mr Armstrong said referrals that were initially or wrongly categorised as 'child in need' but later transpired to have child protection issues, were almost inevitably caught up in this administrative delay, making it harder and slower to detect and remedy any mistake, as happened in Victoria's case.

Administrative backlog

5.34   According to Mr Punch, "People were struggling in a very difficult environment."
        Ms Hobbs said she could remember cases piled high and thought the
        administration staff were under more stress than anyone. Others described the
        team as "relentlessly overworked" and "overburdened". Records for June 1999, the
        month of Victoria's first referral to Brent, showed that only 107 referrals (42 per
        cent) were logged onto the system within one working week, and 41 (16 per cent)
        took between four and 12 weeks. Mr Armstrong said, "I complained week in, week
        out to the administrative officers about the backlog, about getting people to come
        in and clear the backlog, because the backlog was getting so high it was actually
        hiding the administrative staff from the rest of the team." Nor did this situation
        appear to be temporary either. In May 2000, the SSI inspected a duty area where
        there were "hundreds of case files that had not been administratively processed,
        going back four to five months". Staff, therefore, had to rely on their memories
        to link new contacts with past contacts, and there was no system to ensure that
        repeat contacts were linked and patterns of referrals identified and responded to.

5.35   Other problems relating to the duty administrative team were raised in abundance.
        Ms Bridgeman said that due to work pressures, the administrative team did not
        make up a whole file for the duty workers. Instead they just received the duty
        manager's action sheet, the administrative checks sheet and the referral.

5.36   Mr Punch also identified the problems of inadequate filing space and the unusual
        system of filing by problem type, rather than by the person's name. On the
        basis of the evidence of Mr Armstrong, there appears to have been almost a
        complete absence of filing closed cases. Mr Armstrong said that when a file was
        closed and the administrative officers had input the necessary information on
        the database, "Instead of the files being taken from the duty room direct to the
        archive room, they were just put in a corner or on desks around the office, until
        the administrative officers had time available on their hands to get them up there,
        which could take months. I have known files which took years to get upstairs."

Management responsibility

5.37   As team manager for the duty team, Mr Armstrong was clear that he had no
        management responsibility for the administration team or over its systems, yet he
        was dependent on them for the logging in of referrals, the checking of databases,
        and the issuing of appointments, which were fundamental to the smooth operation
        of his duty team. Mr Armstrong said, "Looking back, maybe I should have taken
        the view to go above the heads of my senior managers, and possibly maybe as far
        as the chief executive."

5.38   I heard much evidence in support of his opinion. Although the administration
        failings in Brent deserve my criticism in full, I do not direct this at the individual
        administration workers. Mr Punch, for one, appears to have been conscientious
        and hard-working and to have tried his best in the impossible situation
        management put him in. Mr Punch considered the position so fragile that even
        as late as September 2000, seven months after Victoria's death, he wrote a
        lengthy plea to Mimi Konigsberg, the new assistant director for children's services,
        Mr Bamford and Mr Smith. He outlined his grave concerns and suggested ways
        in which improvements could be made. In general, he spoke of a particularly
        "difficult, frustrating and depressing period of work" during which he had become
        disheartened because he felt he was part of a function rather than a team. He said,
        "The work of duty admin has generally been under-resourced, unsupported,
        unappreciated and not fully understood by other staff members and even by
        management." It was not until the instigation of this Inquiry, and some 14
        months after he sent his memo, that he finally received a substantive reply from
        Ms Konigsberg. It therefore came as no surprise to me that the SSI wrote in 2000,

"Communication in the past had been too much top down and staff needed to be listened to and their contribution to the development of the department recognised and supported."

Financial pressures

5.39   Part of the explanation of how and why Brent children's social work teams had fallen into such a state of disarray must lie with the legacy of past council decisions, and a corporate structure designed to deal with their persistent financial pressures.

5.40   Mr Daniel said, "I think children's social work was under-funded, I think social services were under-funded, and I think Brent council was under-funded." Mr Boyle believed that the primary difficulties were Brent's historic debt that had to be met from revenue funds, the under-funding by government of adult community care services, the inadequate level of council reserves, and the failure of the government grant to keep pace with the real costs of inflation. As such, Mr Boyle said he thought the council was effectively bankrupt. It had no ability at all to respond to any significant variations in service demands and was managing in a "financially impossible position".

5.41   The implications were severe. In 1997/1998, the overall social services budget was fixed at 4.4 per cent below the Government's Standard Spending Assessment (SSA), while the average total spending on social services in England was 8.3 per cent above the SSA. Brent was the second lowest spending authority in London. Children's services were particularly badly hit. In the financial year 1998/1999, Brent had a children's SSA of £28.12m (as against £26.5m in the previous year), but the actual spend was only about £14.5m, up barely £250,000 on the year before. Mr Boyle, who was the director of social services at the time, said he felt "extreme concern and unhappiness" about only being allowed to spend half the SSA. In 1999/2000, the SSA itself decreased by almost £7.5m to £20.65m as a result of the Government's decision to remove ethnicity from the assessment formula. This sorely affected Brent, which has a substantial ethnic minority population. Mr Daniel described his oversight of the budget as a "baptism of fire" because of the reduction of £7.5m and a budget deficit of £17.5m that he had to try to bridge. Yet he could not dispute that, even with the reduction, the council was still not spending the SSA on children's social work.

5.42   Politicians and management were keen to submit that the SSA was a notional figure or formula for distributing money, rather than being prescriptive as to what the council should spend. Councillor Mary Cribbin said that there was real deprivation in the borough and that the budgeting process was therefore a "balancing act" between competing concerns. As a result, while spending on children's social work was under the SSA, other units were being funded in excess of their designated SSA. I address the issues concerning spending in relation to Government-set SSA's elsewhere in this Report. It is enough to say here that I heard no evidence from Brent's senior managers or lead council members to show that they could justify spending so little on children's services during the relevant period. In fact, it became clear that wherever the money was going, the adequate provision of children's services was certainly not one of the council's priorities.

5.43   The social services committee certainly could not claim it was unaware of the implications of budget decisions or of the problems surfacing in children's social work. Mr Boyle said, "There was a corporate understanding that social services was financially very challenged indeed." There were the critical SSI reports in both 1996 and 1998 and the committee regularly received information from its officers. Mr Boyle, as director of social services, wrote to the social services committee on 4 March 1999. In his letter he outlined the likely impact of the council's decisions, since September 1998, to reduce the spending plans of the committee by £4m.

Mr Boyle pointed out that the managed reduction in spending had resulted in "severe pressures and stresses" including long-term illnesses and absences among a number of service unit directors and front-line staff. He said that social services were carrying vacancies in all teams and the Area Child Protection Committee (ACPC) had been advised for the first time in many years that there were unallocated child protection cases. Mr Boyle's letter continued:

> "Your officers advised that it is not possible for these savings to be achieved from 'salami-slicing' and there will be significant and serious implications for service delivery. I[n] some instances, we may be expecting staff to manage risks which are unacceptable and dangerous. Your officers fully appreciate the circumstances facing the Council but setting unachievable savings targets will not assist you, or the Committee, in meeting the objectives of the Council."

5.44　The message could not have been clearer. However compelling the financial pressures may have been at the time, they could not, in my view, excuse the failure of Brent's council and senior management to address the problems in their children's services that had become so evident in the late 1990s.

Structure and business units

5.45　I was told that alongside the financial pressures, Brent's other legacy from the previous administration was its corporate structure. The council had been split into 'core units' with corporate and strategic responsibilities, 'commissioning units' that dealt with needs analysis and service planning, and most importantly 'business units' that were responsible for service delivery. Ms Goodall said that this structure "did away with everything that I think you would recognise as traditional local government". She said at one point there were nine different business units in children's social work and they were all semi-autonomous, operating without traditional line management responsibilities. Although the new administration sought to alter this framework, Ms Goodall observed: "Brent Social Services really had not sort of thrown off the old business unit culture. And to a great extent there was not a departmental culture, there were lots of separate managers, really, doing their own thing." In Mr Boyle's view, "Many of the difficulties, financial and operational, encountered in later years arose from the inherent weakness in these structures established during 1993/1994 and 1994/1995." He said, "Over a period, the lack of accountability became apparent, complex cases were not dealt with properly, and financially many social services units were not able to make a corporate contribution without compromising the safety of the service."

5.46　A clear example of the failings of the independent business units was the absence of a common database throughout the whole of social services, let alone the whole council. In 1993, the main system in use was the Social Services Information Database (SSID) and this continued to be the predominant database used by adult social services and the One Stop Shops. In May 1996, when Mr Bamford arrived in children's social work, the department had no connection to SSID after a corporate decision had been made to discard it. He believed that parts of social services were meant to make their own alternative arrangements. In so doing, and because SSID was not generally considered by Brent to be an easy system to use nor did it lend itself to reporting information on children, Mr Bamford decided that children's social work would use Filemaker as their primary database. This database was only accessible by administration and not practitioner staff. In addition to Filemaker, Mr Punch, who was responsible for inputting practically all the child protection referrals, had his own system specifically catering for child protection cases. Mr Bamford explained that the operation of five or more different systems in social services "was not an ideal situation", with the consequence that telephone calls would have to be made to different departments to find out whether or not a family was known. Worse still, the out-of-office-hours team, which operated the out-of-office hours social work, could only consult the child protection register and had no access to either the SSID or Filemaker database to find out whether children not on the register were known to Brent. It was not until September 1999 that SSID was actually reintroduced to children's services, and the out-of-office-hours team and practitioner staff could access this information. Therefore, I make the following recommendation:

Recommendation
Local authority chief executives must ensure that only one electronic database system is used by all those working in children and families' services for the recording of information. This should be the same system in use across the council, or at least compatible with it, so as to facilitate the sharing of information, as appropriate.

Staff reductions

5.47 Accompanying the introduction of the business units was a reduction of general, non-operational support services. Mr Daniel described the devolved culture in Brent by saying:

> "On the whole we have a minimalist corporate centre – as a deliberate policy choice between 1991 and 1996, support services in the authority were stripped down to the bare minimum, and that meant quite a lot of central support functions, particularly in areas like HR or information gathering, were either reduced to a skeletal basis or eliminated altogether ... a lot of our capacity to gather information about the organisation became somewhat limited."

At a departmental level, by the late 1990s Mr Ludgate said that social services had lost all of its human resources and training staff.

5.48 According to Mr Boyle, "A further feature of the new arrangements was a general belief that the council, and social services, was over-managed. Consequently, significant reductions were made in non-operational budgets resulting in the loss of a number of key management posts." The effect was to significantly reduce the strategic and management capacity of the organisation. The posts of both senior policy manager for children's services and the service development director were frozen or deleted in late 1997. According to Mr Boyle, by 1997 the effects of this policy prompted the then chief executive to describe the council as suffering from "institutional anorexia". Reductions nevertheless continued and as a result, when practice began to deteriorate, Mr Boyle said, "The management infrastructure was not in place to identify that that was happening."

5.49 Front-line children's services did not escape the cutbacks. Despite increasing pressures on the department, in August 1997, service reductions resulted in 10 children's social work posts being deleted and a further 13 vacancies frozen. The SSI in 1998 recognised that "Staff reductions had had a debilitating effect." From inside, Ms Roper observed, "The whole of Brent children's social work was running with a large number of vacancies." In June 1998, the director of social services reported to the Committee: "Eight social workers have been recruited to ease caseload pressures and to reduce the number of unallocated cases." However, overall that only placed the council, in the words of Councillor Cribbin, "down 23 and up 8".

Difficulties of senior management

5.50　In his evidence, Mr Daniel was critical of the strategic leadership of the directors of social services and of children's social services at the time.

5.51　Certainly Ms Thomas, as director of children's services, held a key position in the management framework. The absence of a witness statement and her inability to give evidence to this Inquiry due to ill health has made it more difficult to assess fairly her contribution to the state of affairs in Brent's children's services. Ms Thomas's ill health also caused her to be absent from work on sick leave for five or six weeks during the summer of 1999. I heard evidence that as non-front-line posts were deleted from children's social work, Ms Thomas, along with other managers, were consequently expected to carry a much larger and more varied workload, in her case a workload that was both strategic and operational. *Brent's Management Action Plan* in mid 1999 was heavily criticised by the SSI, in particular reflecting that the service "lacked any clear vision or sense of direction". The previous post of senior policy officer for children's services had been deleted, and Mr Daniel considered this to have created a "critical weakness" in the senior structure of the department. I can only assume this was a view he held with hindsight, otherwise once again I am left asking why he did nothing about it once in post as chief executive.

5.52　Mr Boyle, talking of his time as director of social services, said, "Throughout 1998/1999, most senior management time was spent on financial matters, either in trying to align actual spending with the budget available, or in making plans to deal with the financial shortfall in 1999/2000." Mr Boyle said that he thought the turning point came in 1998 when "Social services senior managers began to take on more and more work and took their eye off the ball, I think particularly with the director of children's social work services ... because of the extra work that she was required to do ... as a consequence ... strong management attention on the service, which the SSI pointed out in 1996 was required, did not occur and the service deteriorated from that point onwards." Mr Boyle said that he had "very serious concerns" about what was happening in social services in 1998/1999, "not just with children's services ... but also with the increasing effect of concentrating social services provision, both in children and on adults, on those at the most risk". Looking back, he said, "In truth, the funding problems for Brent and in social services were there even before I arrived. I was just unable to stop the position deteriorating year on year."

5.53　Despite his own admission that it took him some time to "come up to speed" with children's social services as it was not his "area", Mr Ludgate (appointed acting director of social services in April 1999) appeared to be well aware of the problems facing children's social services. The level of children's services they were able to provide caused him concern because of:

- the very high proportion of agency and temporary workers;
- the imbalance of too many complicated cases and too few experienced social workers;
- not having the training and development staff to bring locum workers up to speed fast enough on policies and procedures;
- the fact that child protection and children-looked-after cases were being held by teams without appropriate manpower.

Mr Ludgate said, "Managers and social workers were responding to the highest need and highest risk presenting at the time."

Staffing problems

5.54   In March 1999, following a series of meetings between the SSI, council members and senior managers, Brent council accepted proposals involving the release of £170,000 from reserves in 1999/2000 and £250,000 in 2000/2001 into children's social services. The extra funds were in part to improve the infrastructure of children's services, to re-establish the post of assistant director for children's services and positions within human resources, to appoint three family support workers, and to pay for scarcity and honorarium payments. Mr Daniel said, "At the time, I have to say that was a very difficult decision for the members to take, given the overall financial position of the council, and the low level of our reserves, so it was a very significant tide of political commitment, I think, to start at least the process of addressing the problems that were beginning to be identified." In fact, as shall become clear, it was a matter of 'too little too late'.

Recruitment difficulties

5.55   In view of the staffing crisis, Mr Ludgate said that during his tenure as acting director he "was willing to pay for any social worker we could get hold of. So no posts were being frozen in terms of operational staff". But the decision to recruit was only the start. Filling posts was not so simple. Difficulties in recruiting social workers was a London-wide problem, but Brent was particularly badly affected because of the terms and conditions offered. Also, according to Mr Charlett, "There was a residual kind of perception of Brent as not a very attractive place to come to, so I think you were starting with a disadvantage anyway."

5.56   In May 1999, the issue was discussed by the Area Child Protection Committee (ACPC) as the staffing crisis was contributing to the number of unallocated cases. Dr Bridget Edwards, the Brent ACPC vice chair, subsequently wrote to Councillor Cribbin on 8 June 1999 "to express serious concerns about children's social work unit's ability to recruit and retain qualified and experienced social workers". Dr Edwards said:

> "You'll be aware that recruitment and retention of staff in children's social services have been a problem for quite some time now. However, it seems there has been a particularly high level of staff turnover in the past few weeks, not helped I think by the introduction of new pay and conditions of services, on top of the already low level of London weighting payments in Brent."

Dr Edwards continued:

> "As safety of children is an important issue when cases remain to be allocated, I wonder if you would consider improving the existing package of pay and conditions to enable children's social services to attract new staff as well as to keep experienced staff."

Dr Edwards could not recall receiving a reply to her letter. This was further evidence of the lack of impact of ACPCs.

Uncompetitive salaries

5.57   It appears that Brent council did little to help itself ease the problem. In 1999, along with other local authorities across the country, Brent was required to implement the 'single status agreement' which equalised the terms and conditions of existing manual and office staff. However, the decision was taken that new staff coming to Brent should not receive the higher London weighting. Instead the inner-London weighting was preserved for existing staff by way of "honorarium payments". Mr Charlett said, "This was obviously not very attractive to people from outside ... I thought it was plainly ridiculous, but that was part of the council's cost cutting

– saving strategy. So that made it difficult with agencies who frankly told us we were uncompetitive in the job market." He added, "It meant there was a kind of two tier system ... but it also meant that compared to neighbouring boroughs, Brent was paying less money and expecting people to work longer hours, in arguably worse conditions. It seemed to me quite a potent factor, if I had been looking for a job myself." Councillor Cribbin disagreed: "We made a political decision because of financial restraints, and it was a method of saving money." She said that she did not think "that a matter of a few hundred pounds would be a deterrent to a social worker coming to work in a borough".

5.58   Brent was not alone in experiencing problems with the recruitment and retention of social workers. Evidence as to the scale of the problem emerged clearly in Phase Two of this Inquiry, as well as from looking at social services provision in Ealing and Haringey. While pay and conditions were clearly a factor, albeit not the only factor, I question whether this at least might be addressed through the implementation of a national pay structure.

Agency staff

5.59   The approach taken by Brent, ironically designed to save money, led to the recruitment of a large number of agency staff, costing approximately 30 to 40 per cent more per employee than permanent staff. When asked about the recruitment of temporary staff, Councillor Cribbin said, unconvincingly, one of the reasons Brent was not able to fill the vacancies was because "we had decided we were only going to employ the best staff". This was perhaps an unrealistic goal for a council offering among the worst pay and conditions in London. A comprehensive recruitment package was not finalised in Brent until October 2001.

5.60   The teams most affected were the duty and child protection teams because Brent Social Services had made a policy decision in 1996 that in an effort to ensure that all long-term cases were held by permanent social workers, it would manage the initial duty response through agency and temporary staff where necessary. As a result, Mr Armstrong said the duty team he managed, in mid 1999 at a time of high workload pressures and when the two referrals relating to Victoria passed through his team, was staffed entirely by agency workers who had not qualified in England. He agreed it was not acceptable to have people on short-term contracts at the front-line of contact with very vulnerable children but said, "It was what we were doing and what we were working. There were occasions where a person will get off a plane in the morning, arrive in the office just after lunch, be interviewed and start work either in the duty team or the child protection team. It was happening very, very often." Mr Charlett said, "I thought the fundamental problem was there were just not the resources available. There were just not the people there that stayed long enough for the continuity that was desirable, and to familiarise themselves properly with the work, and become a true team ... it seemed to me that there were obvious disadvantages in having a team composed of people who are purely agency staff."

5.61   Mr Charlett's concerns at the time were well justified. Because of the bottleneck in passing cases on to the long-term teams, the very same short-term agency staff were left holding cases on a long-term basis. Also, as agency staff they did not stay long enough to be trained and their induction was varied or non-existent. Inevitably, as both Mr Armstrong and Mr Charlett pointed out, the agency staff were less familiar with the procedures and the local area and therefore took longer to carry out their tasks. Although hesitant on the subject, Mr Charlett said that it was likely that the reliance on agency workers caused the service in the duty team to suffer. Mr Armstrong said that he was told by one of the assistant directors within children's services that the financial cost of a week's worth of induction outweighed the financial cost of the workers being allocated cases immediately.

Poor inductions

5.62   If help was needed, the newly arrived duty workers would and did turn to the support of other staff members and their seniors. Ms Hobbs said that she felt well equipped to do the work, but that was mainly due to the extra support she received from her seniors and manager. She said, "I think they had to provide a lot more than they should have if there had been a more formal induction process." Ms Thrift also spoke very highly of the help from those around her, but said, "I did feel, though, maybe I should get a little bit more time to understand Brent procedures."

5.63   In fact, the length and complexity of the procedures and policies existing at the time, namely the interim child protection periods of 1996 and Volume C of Brent Social Services' *Children's Services Manual of Procedures*, meant they were of limited help. Dr Edwards said the local authorities' child protection procedures and guidance could be voluminous. She found them quite daunting and thought it was "quite difficult to grapple with so many sheets of paper". Ms Hines said she would not say the procedures were "user friendly", while the SSI in 2000 found them to be "inadequate and In need of a major revision".

Conclusion

5.64   Overall, it is difficult to draw any other conclusion than front-line staff in Brent Social Services, whose actions and decisions affected Victoria in mid 1999, were working in an under-resourced, understaffed, under-managed and dysfunctional environment. The SSI in 2000 and again in 2001 remained highly critical about a number of the deep-rooted problems that were apparent in 1999, such as the over-reliance on agency staff, the tracking of cases and the transfer of cases to the long-term teams. Senior managers and elected members were either unaware of or unable to tackle these deep-rooted deficiencies within the organisation, and for that they must take responsibility.

Victoria in Brent

The first referral

5.65   Esther Ackah, a distant relative of Kouao, made the first of two telephone calls to Brent Social Services from a telephone box on the afternoon of Friday 18 June 1999. She gave details about a child called 'Anna'. She said she was aged about seven, her mother's name was Marie-Therese Kouao, their address was Room 10, 8 Nicoll Road, Harlesden, London, and that they were French. She said she was worried about the unfit state of the accommodation that Kouao and 'Anna' were living in, the problems the child was having with incontinence, that she had a scar on her face which her mother had said was due to a fall from an escalator, and that others had expressed concerns about the well-being of 'Anna'. Ms Ackah said at that stage she believed Victoria's life was in danger, not because of physical harm, but due to the dangers posed by her living conditions. She said she made this clear to the person on the other end of the telephone. She wanted social services to make an urgent visit. As the coins for the telephone ran out, Ms Ackah was cut off before she could give, or was asked for, her own name as the referrer.

5.66   Samantha Hunt, a temporary customer services officer in the call centre at the One Stop Shop at Brent House, said she received an anonymous call from a lady concerning a child aged eight years. The caller gave the child's first name as 'Anna' but gave no surname. She described herself as a neighbour and wanted to report her concern about the child.

5.67   The caller said she had seen 'Anna' repeatedly wetting herself and that she had also previously seen her with cuts and bruises to her face, although the mother had said that this was caused when she fell down an escalator. Other neighbours had expressed their concern and had asked this neighbour to call social services. The caller said that as far as she was aware, 'Anna' was not attending school and was living in a home "surrounded by drug addicts". She did not think that 'Anna' was being treated by a doctor. The caller then hung up without giving any further information.

5.68   Ms Hunt believed she made a note of the conversation by hand and typed it up immediately after the telephone call. Although she could no longer remember the conversation, she was confident that if she had been given the child's surname or her place of origin she would have recorded those details. Similarly, if she had been told that the child's life was in danger, that also would have been recorded on the referral.

5.69   Notwithstanding these discrepancies in the detail of the concerns relayed to Brent Social Services about 'Anna', it is clear that the first telephone call made by Ms Ackah and the anonymous telephone referral received by Ms Hunt on 18 June 1999 were one and the same. Whether or not Ms Ackah told Ms Hunt that Victoria's life was in danger, the referral, as Ms Hunt recorded it, was clearly a child protection referral and should have been dealt with as such, even if it did not fully express the weight of Ms Ackah's concerns.

5.70   Ms Hunt responded promptly and did exactly what she was trained to do. She had been told to put all calls regarding children through to the children's social work department. However, at times this would prove impossible because all the lines were busy. In that situation the customer services officers, and she was one of two dealing mainly with social services, were expected to take down the referral details themselves and then pass them on. This is what Ms Hunt did on this occasion.

5.71   One can only speculate about what other potentially important details Ms Hunt might have found if she had had the time to question Ms Ackah further. What is clear is that social services should do as much as possible to access such information at the earliest opportunity, particularly in relation to child protection concerns where these have been relayed by members of the public whose chosen means of communication is by public telephone. I therefore make the following recommendation:

> **Recommendation**
> Local authorities with responsibility for safeguarding children should establish and advertise a 24-hour free telephone referral number for use by members of the public who wish to report concerns about a child. A pilot study should be undertaken to evaluate the feasibility of electronically recording calls to such a number.

5.72   Ms Hunt also checked the client database system for any previous referrals matching the name 'Anna' and the address of 8 Nicoll Road but drew a blank. At 4.21pm that same afternoon, Ms Hunt faxed the referral across to the children's social work department. According to Ms Hunt, all children's social work was deemed as urgent. She said, "It was not for us to ascertain the urgency, so all the children's social work referrals, from what I can remember, were faxed through." There was therefore no need in her mind to attach a cover sheet to Victoria's referral to signify that it was urgent, nor was it the practice to check whether anyone in the children's social work department had received the fax.

5.73   Sadly, nobody picked up Ms Ackah's referral that Friday afternoon and what actually happened to it was to prove the subject of some of the most bizarre and contradictory evidence this Inquiry was to hear.

Logging the referral

5.74   The next agreed sighting of the 18 June referral was some three weeks later on 6 July 1999. Robert Smith, the group administrative officer, undertook the index check for Victoria that day. His team was responsible for completing checks for the duty intake and child protection teams on all new referrals. As the team supervisor, he had stepped out of his usual role on that occasion to assist his staff because the office was understaffed and busy with a backlog of work.

5.75   Notwithstanding these staff shortages, he said it was unusual for a delay of as much as three weeks before a case was logged, although other documentary evidence to the Inquiry clearly suggested the contrary. By way of explanation, Mr Smith thought it possible that if some work had already been done on the case before his office received it, the administrative staff might have only just seen the referral on 6 July 1999.

5.76   That, unfortunately, does not appear to have been the situation in relation to Ms Ackah's referral. Whether the fault lies with the administrative team or the duty team that failed to pass it on, a delay of three weeks in processing any child protection referral can never be acceptable and Brent accepted this. In Victoria's case, inquiries under section 47 of the Children Act 1989 should have begun immediately on 18 June 1999. The failure to do so constituted a significant missed opportunity to protect her.

5.77   To my surprise, Mr Smith and others confirmed that there was no system for ensuring that faxes that arrived in the building went to the people for whom they were intended. In a case such as this, the fax from Ms Hunt should have gone to the duty manager or duty senior social worker, who would log it in the referrals log book and complete the necessary paperwork. They, in turn, would pass it to the administration team who would log it onto the database and complete index checks to find out whether the child was known to Brent. Referrals marked as 'child protection' were usually passed to one particular administrative officer, Mr Punch, for processing.

5.78   Mr Smith entered the details of Ms Hunt's referral onto the database, creating a new, 'unique' record reference number: 1009966. This reference number was important. It contributed the crucial evidence to show that while the social workers involved with Victoria's case may not have made a link between the 18 June 1999 referral and the later referral by the Central Middlesex Hospital, the computer certainly did.

5.79   Mr Smith summarised onto the computer the details of the case as:

> "Sees the child constantly wetting herself and has seen her previously with cuts and bruises around the face. Others have expressed concerns. As far as the referrer knows the child is not attending school."

5.80   Importantly, one printout of the computer record created by Mr Smith as it appears on the case file, and as it might well have been seen by those social workers involved with Victoria, shows no more than the first line of case detail and reads, "Sees the child constantly wetting herself and has seen her." Social workers should, however, also have had access to other records with the complete referral information.

5.81 It is clear that the information inputted by Mr Smith was edited from the details of Ms Hunt's referral. There can therefore be no doubt that it was this referral that was seen by Mr Smith on 6 July 1999. Mr Smith also had sight of a duty manager's action sheet, which enabled him to fill in on the same day and as part of the status section of the same computer record the following facts:

- the initial action date as 21 June 1999
- the duty manager's name as Eddie Armstrong
- the action to be taken as a home visit on 14 July
- the social worker's name as Lori Hobbs
- the decision – 'open on duty'.

5.82 The duty manager's action sheet also asked for the details to be logged in and checked. The box marked 'other advice and assistance' was ticked but not the child protection box. Mr Smith therefore logged in the referral under what he understood to be the default classification of a child in need. He did this despite the detailed references to cuts and bruises.

The team manager

5.83 Edward Armstrong was the team manager of the intake duty team at the time Victoria's case was handled by Brent Social Services, and his involvement is of central importance to an understanding of this part of Victoria's story. His evidence merits particular close scrutiny, not least because it is out of line with that of other Brent witnesses on almost every count, and the quality of it leaves much to be desired. Mr Armstrong's memory proved to be highly selective about events of seemingly equal importance and his insistence on how things appeared to be could rarely be substantiated by any rational explanation of why they should be so.

5.84 It was Mr Armstrong's view that there was another referral on 21 June 1999 and that it was this referral, not the 18 June referral taken down by Ms Hunt, that he handled and for which he completed a duty manager's action sheet. This later referral was not a child protection referral. It is Mr Armstrong's evidence that all the papers for this 21 June referral, except the duty manager's action sheet, have gone missing. But he said that a social worker in his team, whom he could no longer identify, did receive a telephone call in relation to a child named 'Anna' in temporary accommodation who was wetting herself. He said the child in this referral was about eight years old. By an extraordinary coincidence, Mr Armstrong claimed that this less serious referral was also not logged onto the system until 6 or 8 July 1999.

5.85 Given that, by his own admission, the papers for the 21 June 1999 referral went missing some time after July 1999, it is almost impossible to accept that Mr Armstrong could have pinpointed so precisely the date of this second referral as well as the date on which it was logged onto the system. Victoria was one of many 'child in need' cases. Indeed, Mr Armstrong stated that his team would hold around 300 cases open. Not surprisingly, Mr Armstrong had no real answer to this point in evidence. Nor did he make any mention of a referral on 21 June in his interview for Brent's Part 8 management review of Victoria's case, nor as part of his own disciplinary process. More importantly, there is no evidence whatsoever that any referral received on 21 June was ever logged onto Brent's client-based system.

5.86 Despite giving vivid accounts of an office in chaos where files went missing and faxes spilled out regularly onto the floor, Mr Armstrong was adamant that the 18 June 1999 referral taken by Ms Hunt was never received in his office. He said that there were three floors in children's social work and that the fax from Ms Hunt could have gone to any of these floors. He said that if he had received that referral he would have discussed it immediately with the child protection team. When asked whether the fact that the fax came through late on Friday afternoon meant that it would have been left to the following Monday 21 June to be dealt with, Mr Armstrong replied that the referral would have been dealt with by his team unless it was received after 5pm, in which case it would have been referred to the out-of-office-hours team. Out-of-office-hours teams are not necessarily staffed by people with expertise in services for children. Since children are not exposed to risk only during normal office hours or at times of administrative convenience, the timing of a referral should not determine the quality of the service provided. I return to the organisation of out-of-office-hours social services at paragraph 6.172.

5.87   To add to the confused picture, Ms Ackah said in evidence that a few days after she spoke to Ms Hunt – she thought less than a week later – she rang Brent Social Services again on exactly the same telephone number. Her reason for doing so was to make "absolutely sure" that social services had taken some action following her earlier call. She spoke to a different person, briefly repeated her story about 'Anna' and was asked to hold on while they went to check. When the person on the other end of the telephone eventually came back to Ms Ackah, she told her that she "thought the first call was received, and probably they [social services] had done something about it". In my view this was no way to respond to a member of the public who had behaved responsibly in contacting the authorities about her concerns for a child.

5.88   I cannot be certain when Ms Ackah made her second telephone call. It could have been on 21 June 1999 and it might have been this second call which was dealt with by someone in Mr Armstrong's team. What is clear is that the call did not trigger a new referral by whoever picked up the telephone in the One Stop Shop and no separate referral was ever logged onto the computer system.

5.89   According to Mr Armstrong, the social worker who took the referral found out that the family had moved from Ealing to Brent and it was Brent's housing department that revealed that Nicoll Road was used by Ealing to place temporary residents. Yet the case file evidence presented to the Inquiry suggests that Brent knew nothing about Ealing's involvement until 14 July 1999. As a result of this referral, Mr Armstrong claimed he made a telephone call to Ealing Social Services to establish whether they had placed a child called 'Anna' in Nicoll Road. Surprisingly, neither he nor anyone else thought to ask Ealing for 'Anna's' surname or, if he did, no surname was recorded at the time. There is no record of this telephone conversation in the Ealing case file for Victoria to support Mr Armstrong's claim.

5.90   Mr Armstrong also said he decided that inquiries should be made to Brent council's housing and health departments, and to the General Medical Practitioner's Board. Those instructions, he said, were put in written form and attached to the case papers, which he claims have now gone missing. Mr Armstrong's initial assessment, based on the information he said he had that the child was wetting herself, was that Victoria was a 'child in need'. As a result, he authorised two unannounced home visits by social workers he could now no longer identify. No records exist of any of these steps being taken, nor of their outcome. The only available recorded instruction by Mr Armstrong are the words "home visit" on the duty manager's action sheet, as noted by Mr Smith when he inputted the details of Ms Hunt's 18 June 1999 referral.

5.91   Asked why it was that a child wetting herself would have of itself justified a 'child in need' label, two unannounced home visits and many inquiries with other agencies, Mr Armstrong replied, "Because a child is wetting herself, and secondly because the culture in Brent at the time was that people who were in temporary accommodation, and came to the borough, we just tried to get them out of the borough for financial reasons."

5.92 This might be thought to be an unconvincing explanation. According to Mr Armstrong, Brent also knew Victoria had been placed by Ealing Social Services. Establishing that Ealing was funding the placement was only a telephone call away.

Contact with Ealing Social Services

5.93 Mr Armstrong recounted a number of telephone conversations that were supposed to have taken place some time after 21 June 1999 between himself and members of his team and Ealing Social Services, all of which it seemed were aimed at shifting responsibility for Victoria's case back to Ealing.

5.94 The first was between Ms Viljoen, a social worker in Mr Armstrong's team, and Godfrey Victor, a social worker at Ealing Social Services, who reportedly said that as the family was living in Brent the case was Brent's responsibility. Mr Armstrong said in evidence that he then rang Mr Victor to press the case for Victoria being transferred back to Ealing but that he was unsuccessful.

Home visits

5.95 Mr Armstrong said that it was at this point he decided that his team should carry out an unannounced visit to the family, pending agreement by Ealing to retake responsibility for the case. He also said that he discussed the case with Ms Roper, the manager of the child protection team, or one of the two seniors in the team, though he could not recall with whom. It was agreed that the case properly belonged to Ealing and should be dealt with as a 'child in need'.

5.96 Within one or two weeks of 21 June 1999, Mr Armstrong said he spoke to John Skinner, assistant director for children's services at Ealing, who accepted that case responsibility rested with Ealing as the family was only temporarily resident in Brent. In the light of his conversation with Mr Skinner, Mr Armstrong said he then contacted Mr Victor again to inform him of the agreed decision. He also said he faxed across the information that Brent held, including details of the two home visits. Rather bizarrely, as Ealing had by now accepted case responsibility according to Mr Armstrong's version of the events, Mr Armstrong said he told Mr Victor that Brent would make an appointment for a home visit to Nicoll Road and report back to him.

5.97 When asked why this was thought necessary when his team could barely cope with the pressures for which they did have responsibility, Mr Armstrong tried to explain his actions by saying, "It's something we do for other boroughs." It seems more than a passing coincidence that the two people Mr Armstrong said he had spoken to at Ealing Social Services were both known to him as former employees of Brent Social Services. Yet neither Mr Victor nor Mr Skinner, nor for that matter Ms Viljoen, Ms Roper or either of her two seniors could recall any of the conversations recounted by Mr Armstrong. There are no records of these conversations or of the fax that Mr Armstrong said he sent to Mr Victor in the Brent file, or more importantly, in the Ealing case file. In short, there is not a shred of written documentation to support any aspect of Mr Armstrong's version of events this far. If Mr Armstrong is to be believed, the implication must be, and Mr Armstrong asserted as much but was unable to point to any evidence to support his allegation, that the papers in both the Brent and Ealing case files relating to just the 21 June 1999 referral must have been tampered with or they were lost in both offices.

5.98 It remains Mr Armstrong's contention that he never saw Esther Ackah's referral of 18 June, but instead dealt with a less serious referral which he appropriately identified and responded to as a 'child in need' case. I find this version of events wholly unbelievable. I am left in no doubt that Mr Armstrong's evidence to this Inquiry in relation to a referral on 21 June 1999 – a referral that I conclude never existed – is an attempt to cover up his team's inept handling of a genuine child protection referral that slipped through the net. The duty manager's action sheet dated 21 July 1999 does not in my opinion support the existence of a new referral, but merely proves the delay in dealing with the referral recorded by Ms Hunt on 18 June. Inevitably, my conclusion as to Mr Armstrong's credibility in relation to this matter will have some impact on the weight to be attached to the rest of his evidence to the Inquiry.

5.99 On 7 July 1999, a computer-generated letter was sent from the duty manager to the occupant of Room 10, 8 Nicoll Road, arranging a home visit for 14 July 1999 at 3pm to discuss the referral about 'Anna'. Although it looked to an inexpert eye suspiciously like his writing, Mr Armstrong denied that he wrote the date 14 July 1999 next to the name "Lori" at the top of the duty manager's action sheet that he signed off on 21 June. Yet Mr Smith was equally clear that, although the administrative staff were responsible for making appointments for social worker visits and recording those on the system (hence the computer-generated letter), they would not have written these dates. Mr Smith assumed that either the duty manager or senior social workers had written the date of 14 July on the action sheet because that was when they wished the visit to take place.

5.100 According to Mr Armstrong, Lori Hobbs, the social worker who had been asked to visit Nicoll Road, went to the address twice on 14 July 1999. On his account, despite knowing that an appointment had been made for 3pm, he said Ms Hobbs inexplicably went to the premises ahead of the appointment time, found no one in and returned to the office. She later went back to Nicoll Road at 3pm in the company of Monica Bridgeman, one of the senior social workers in the duty team.

5.101 Ms Hobbs's recollection, though hazy some two years after the event, was that she made no other visit to Nicoll Road other than in the company of Ms Bridgeman for the 3pm appointment. She explained that she was with Ms Bridgeman only because she did not feel confident to do the visit scheduled immediately after Nicoll Road on her own.

5.102 Ms Hobbs said that the premises they came to looked like houses that had been converted into bedsits. There was no reception area, as Ms Hobbs might have expected of a bed and breakfast, and they found no one who appeared to be in charge. Ms Hobbs said, "There was nothing to indicate that it was anything other than bedsits."

5.103 Ms Bridgeman and Ms Hobbs spoke to a number of people hanging around outside the premises, some of whom were drinking. They asked where Room 10 was, if anybody knew who lived there, and if there was anyone upstairs. The people they spoke to informed them that the family had moved away about a week ago. This was of course true, as Kouao and Victoria had moved in with Manning on or about 6 July 1999. However, Ms Bridgeman agreed in evidence that she should not have relied on this information. They went upstairs to Room 10 and knocked on the door. There was no answer. They asked the people they had spoken to earlier if they had any concerns about the family, but none were raised.

5.104 Ms Hobbs and Ms Bridgeman learned nothing from their abortive visit and they carried out no further investigation while on the premises. The premises did not look like a hostel, so they made no attempts to find out what sort of premises they were in or whether any of the occupants had been placed there by local authorities. Nor did they knock on any other door. It did not occur to them to try to find a manager of the property who would have been the most obvious source of the information they were seeking. Had they pursued any one of these lines of inquiry it might have opened up a fresh trail to Victoria's whereabouts.

5.105   In fact, Ms Bridgeman and Ms Hobbs had come to Nicoll Road with only the haziest idea of the nature of the referral they were supposed to be investigating, a referral which was at least three weeks old judging by the duty manager's action sheet, and without having done any background checks first. They did not even know whether the family was being accommodated by Brent. Ms Bridgeman said she was sure that Ms Hobbs would have done the necessary checks on the address beforehand. She should have checked rather than presumed. Ms Hobbs said in evidence:

> "I do not recall doing any checks prior to the visit, mainly due to the lack of information that was on the form. I probably would have made the decision that it would be more fruitful and economic with my time to do that afterwards, to see if the visit itself brought some light."

5.106   Ms Hobbs thought that before the visit she would have seen the duty manager's action sheet with the instruction to do a home visit, as well as the administrative checks form. There would also have been the referral itself plus anything else that was documented on the computer. But she admitted that she had little to go on. She recalled knowing that the referral was about an eight-year-old girl, she had an address but no surname, no date of birth, no referrer's details and the substance of the referral was about the suitability of the girl's accommodation. This was indeed exactly the issue that Ms Ackah was so keen to stress in her referral to Ms Hunt almost a month earlier. She had no specific memory of a child wetting herself.

5.107   Ms Bridgeman could not assist with any clearer recollection of what she knew when she went to Nicoll Road. However, despite the passage of time, she was "definite" that she knew nothing about a child wetting herself, or references to cuts and bruises or being told the child was not at school. She was clear: "If I was taking a referral like that, the referral details, that would have not gone to Child in Need." If she had seen Ms Hunt's referral sheet she said, "There is no way that I would have taken that on." Like Ms Hobbs, she was not aware of any earlier visits to Nicoll Road by any other social worker. If there had been any unannounced visits she expected they would have come to her attention and they had not.

5.108   If, as seems likely, Ms Hobbs and Ms Bridgeman were in fact responding to the 18 June 1999 referral, then it is deeply troubling that they believed they were dealing with accommodation issues rather then responding to concerns about a child who had been seen with cuts and bruises. It is possible that they are now seeking to minimise the nature of the concerns they were responding to, that they have forgotten, or they were sent out with incomplete information. Nothing on the file allows me to trace what information they had at the time of the visit. What is clear, and admitted by Brent, is that the home visit lacked any sort of social work focus and the inquiries made, such as they were, fell far short of an adequate investigation of a child in need, let alone a child in need of protection. Therefore, I make the following recommendation:

> **Recommendation**
> Social workers must not undertake home visits without being clear about the purpose of the visit, the information to be gathered during the course of it, and the steps to be taken if no one is at home. No visits should be undertaken without the social worker concerned checking the information known about the child by other agencies. All visits must be written up on the case file.

5.109   By the time Ms Hobbs returned to the office after completing the second of the visits scheduled for that afternoon, it was too late to do any further checks. She said that she intended to make some inquiries of the housing department as well as write up a note of her visit the following morning.

5.110 When asked what form her report would take, she replied that it would have been a running case note. She said, "I would have just outlined that a visit was completed with Monica [Bridgeman], that the child was no longer at the address according to the information we received, and that is all I really remember about it."

5.111 She thought she would have passed her note directly to either Ms Bridgeman or Mr Armstrong.

5.112 If indeed such a report of her findings or of any notes of follow-up discussions with her manager existed, they are now all missing. All that is left on the file annotated on the bottom of the 7 July 1999 appointment letter are Ms Hobbs's handwritten notes stating no more than "Not at this address. Have moved." Ms Hobbs disputed that this was the sum total of her recorded note of the visit on 14 July 1999 and Ms Bridgeman agreed. Ms Bridgeman was adamant that she had seen the report prepared by her colleague. The lack of any corroborating evidence, however, suggests the contrary. I am of the opinion that no such report ever existed and that the 'write-up' contained in Ms Hobbs's annotated 7 July appointment letter is all that might have been anticipated, given the vagueness of the referral she and Ms Bridgeman say they were responding to. It is an appalling reflection of Brent's children's social work team that from 18 June to 14 July 1999, the only information additional to the referral was, "Not at this address. Have moved." This was a dreadfully inadequate response to the serious concerns expressed by Ms Ackah and to the needs of Victoria.

The referral from the Central Middlesex Hospital

5.113 Events were then to overtake both Ms Bridgeman and Ms Hobbs. At the time they were making their unsuccessful visit to Nicoll Road, Victoria was admitted to the Central Middlesex Hospital. At 4pm that same day, according to the form she completed at the time, Ms Thrift, a duty social worker in Mr Armstrong's team, received a referral from the Central Middlesex Hospital in respect of a child named 'Anna', about whom the hospital had serious child protection concerns. 'Anna' had been brought to the Central Middlesex Hospital by Avril Cameron, the daughter of 'Anna's' childminder, Priscilla Cameron. 'Anna's' address was said to be 6 or 8 Nicoll Road. Ms Thrift marked the referral as 'child protection' and took down the following details:

> "Anna is a recent arrival in the UK. Her mother lives in a bed and breakfast in Nicoll Road (believed to be housed by Ealing Council – to be checked.) For five weeks Anna has been cared for during the day by a lady named [Priscilla] Cameron (aged 63) ... Avril hadn't seen the child since last Wednesday then mother dropped her off yesterday evening due to problems at the B&B. This morning mother dropped off some items for Anna and said she would return at 7pm today.
>
> Avril noticed bruising on the feet (2–3 days old), arms, legs, buttocks and infected bruises on the fingers. Also noticed Anna's eyes were bloodshot. She took her to the CMH. (Please see fax)
>
> Child currently at the CMH with carer. Will await contact from Brent CSW [children's social work]."

5.114 The referrer was Dr Ajayi-Obe. Ms Thrift was quite clear that all the information that she had taken down by telephone that day, including the suggestion that Kouao had been placed in Brent by Ealing council, must have come from Dr Ajayi-Obe.

Minutes before 4pm, the hospital also faxed across Dr Ajayi-Obe's body map. The body map showed the distribution of marks on Victoria's body as well as her medical report on "a child thought to have suffered abuse".

5.115 At 4.20pm, Ms Thrift passed on the referral, most probably to Mr Armstrong or one of her seniors, who in turn passed it to Ms Hines, a senior social worker in the child protection team. In accordance with the *Brent Child Protection Procedures Manual*, Ms Hines should have consulted with her team manager and the assistant director of child protection on receipt of the referral. Ms Hines said that she attempted to do so, but that her manager, Ms Roper, was at a child protection conference on another case and Mr Charlett, the assistant director for child protection and duty service manager for the duty team and the child protection investigation and assessment team (CPIAT), was not in his office. Ms Roper was adamant that she had arranged for one of the assistant directors to cover her responsibilities, but could not remember whom. Quite clearly it was Ms Roper's job to ensure that proper cover arrangements were in place for her team and that her staff were aware of these, if only so that they could meet the requirements imposed on them by Brent's own child protection procedures. On 14 July 1999, Ms Hines was either unaware of what those cover arrangements were or none had effectively been put in place.

Failure to spot previous referral

5.116 At this stage, or prior to passing the case to Ms Hines, administrative checks on the databases should have been made by a member of the administration team to ascertain whether 'Anna' was known to Brent. Martin Punch believed that he may have inputted the new child protection referral details from the Central Middlesex Hospital. He said, "I think the case came in directly as a child protection case, and I would have done that check." He could not confirm when he did the checks but said that he may have done them on 14 July 1999. Although I cannot rule this out completely, it is, however, more likely these checks were done at the same time as the case was logged onto the database, and a link with the previous referral was made electronically. Scrutiny of the computer printouts supplied by Brent show this in fact occurred the following day, on 15 July, and not on the day when the hospital referral was received. It was on 15 July that the computer system provided Victoria with a second 'unique' reference record number. In fact, during Victoria's brief involvement with Brent Social Services, and partly as a result of the children's social work department running both manual systems and a completely separate client-based computer system from the rest of Brent Social Services, Victoria acquired five different identifier numbers, creating ample scope for information loss and case mismanagement.

5.117 On this occasion, the computer records made on 15 July suggest that a link was made between the Central Middlesex Hospital referral and the 18 June referral taken by Ms Hunt. Against the child protection referral category and description Mr Punch had typed in, the computer printout displayed the following:

"See also URRN 1009966. Carer Avril Cameron noticed bruises on Anna Kouro's body & that she had bloodshot eyes."

5.118 The link was there for anyone who had access to these printouts to see, but it seems likely that as the administrative staff were struggling to cope with the backlog of work at the time, it was simply overlooked. As a result, the link was not at any time drawn to the attention of Ms Roper, the child protection team manager, or either of the seniors. The papers were never brought together and the link was never followed. This had serious consequences for Victoria.

5.119 Ms Hines therefore had to make decisions about Victoria's case without the benefit of information from the previous referral. As far as she was concerned, the family was not known to Brent Social Services at that time. Although she could not recall what happened, Ms Hines said that she could have seen a copy of the computer printout log that specifically said "See also URRN 1009966", but in evidence she confused this reference number as referring to the same Central Middlesex Hospital admission. In any event, she was clear that her attention was not specifically drawn to any earlier referral. Ms Hines accepted that if she had been aware of an earlier child protection referral it would have altered her approach to handling Victoria's case entirely.

5.120 The only witness who gave direct and first-hand evidence that a match was made and recognised between the telephone referral from the Central Middlesex Hospital and the unsuccessful home visit by Ms Hobbs and Ms Bridgeman, was Mr Armstrong. He said that later on 14 July 1999, after Ms Hobbs and Ms Bridgeman returned to the office to report there was nobody present at Nicoll Road, he took the paperwork to Mr Punch who made the match. As a result, Mr Armstrong said he was satisfied that 'Anna' had been identified and her whereabouts were known.

Contact with the Central Middlesex Hospital

5.121 Having received the referral, Ms Hines first telephoned Barnaby ward and was told by Dr Haviland that Victoria had been admitted for what was believed to be non-accidental injury. Although she should have had Dr Ajayi-Obe's body maps and medical report on the file, Ms Hines said in evidence that she never saw these. Despite the reference in Ms Thrift's referral form to "please see fax", Ms Hines never followed this up. Indeed, failure to follow up critical information faxed to Brent Social Services was fast becoming the hallmark of Brent's poor handling of Victoria's case.

5.122 The timing of the Central Middlesex Hospital referral, too, seems to have made a difference to Ms Hines's management of the case, though in practice it should not have done. It was late afternoon when Victoria's case found its way to Ms Hines's desk. She knew that for the moment at least, Victoria was safe in hospital having been taken there by her childminder's daughter. Ms Hines also knew that the hospital had serious child protection concerns but that the whereabouts of the 'mother', who at that stage must have been a prime suspect, was unknown. Ms Hines and her colleague Elzanne Smit then made a number of telephone calls.

Contact with Ealing Social Services

5.123 Ms Smit first made contact with Ealing Social Services at 4.55pm. It is not clear to whom she spoke on this occasion, though she recorded in her contact note a telling comment: "Case was never opened to them in a Social Services capacity." This would seem to illustrate the fact that Ealing viewed Victoria's case as concerning only the family's housing needs.

Placing Victoria under police protection

5.124 In the meantime, at about 5.15pm, Ms Hines, promptly and quite appropriately, telephoned the Brent police child protection team and spoke to PC Rachel Dewar. The decisions taken following the conversation were, however, less than appropriate. Ms Hines told PC Dewar that Victoria's injuries were felt to be serious enough for the hospital to admit her. Together they agreed to take Victoria into police protection, which they did at 5.20pm. Ms Hines colluded in this decision without seeing and speaking to Victoria or her childminder. She did so without making any sort of assessment as to the likelihood of Kouao removing her from the hospital. She did so without ever establishing that the grounds for taking a child into police protection were properly made out. She also did so without authorisation from her senior colleagues. In my view, placing Victoria in police protection was a serious step that could have been safely deferred until, or if, it became necessary. Mr Anderson, who was working that night in the emergency duty team, said he felt confident he could arrange police protection out of hours if it was required.

5.125 Ms Hines admitted that police protection on this occasion was no more than a holding measure designed to keep Victoria in a safe place. However, the practical consequence of this action appears to have been that neither the police nor social services felt they needed to begin their respective inquiries that evening. Instead, Ms Smit briefed Mr Anderson to alert him that Victoria was in police protection and should Kouao turn up at the hospital, she was to be told that Victoria was under police protection and could not be removed.

5.126 Ms Hines said in evidence that she fully intended seeing Victoria the next day. She said:

> "The child was in a safe place, in hospital, all the safeguards had been put in place, we had phoned the emergency duty service ... the police had been informed ... the hospital had been informed that the child was in police protection, so the child was felt to be safe and it was late in the evening and our investigation would have started the following day."

5.127 Looking at the times of the telephone calls made by Ms Hines and Ms Smit that evening, it is doubtful that "late in the evening" could have meant any later than 6pm. Whatever Ms Hines's intentions may have been, the fact was that she failed to see Victoria either that evening or at any time thereafter. I regard prompt action in cases such as this to be vitally important and therefore make the following recommendation:

> **Recommendation**
> Directors of social services must ensure that children who are the subject of allegations of deliberate harm are seen and spoken to within 24 hours of the allegation being communicated to social services. If this timescale is not met, the reason for the failure must be recorded on the case file.

5.128 Ms Hines painted an entirely different picture of how she might have responded if she had received the referral at, for example, 10am. She said she would have tried to make contact with whoever had parental responsibility and seek their permission to speak to the child. If she could not track down that person, or permission to speak to the child was denied, she said she would have discussed the problem with her legal section and possibly sought an emergency protection order. However, Ms Hines did not consider an emergency protection order to be an option in this case because the legal services unit went into answer-phone mode at 5pm every day. Therefore, I make the following recommendation:

> **Recommendation**
> No emergency action on a case concerning an allegation of deliberate harm to a child should be taken without first obtaining legal advice. Local authorities must ensure that such legal advice is available 24 hours a day.

5.129 As well as speaking to PC Dewar, Ms Hines rang Priscilla Cameron. Her purpose in ringing was not to question her about what had happened to Victoria, but instead to ask her to act as a messenger to Kouao. Incredibly, she wanted Mrs Cameron to tell Kouao that Victoria was in police protection and that she was not to be removed from the hospital or the police would be called. In fact, it is a police responsibility to do this.

5.130   Ms Hines agreed that Mrs Cameron was an important source of information in any assessment of Victoria's circumstances and a person she would have interviewed if she had been carrying out inquiries under section 47. However, no such inquiries under section 47 were under way on the evening of 14 July 1999 because the matter had been put on hold until the next day. In the event, Brent never interviewed Mrs Cameron, either as part of the section 47 inquiries or any other inquiries. Indeed, Mrs Cameron was an unregistered childminder, and Brent did not make inquiries about this either.

5.131   As it happens, Kouao was with Mrs Cameron when Ms Hines telephoned, and they spoke over the telephone. Kouao explained to Ms Hines that Victoria's injuries were all self-inflicted. Ms Hines was surprised by this and thought that Kouao sounded "quite cold and matter-of-fact". However, she took the matter no further that evening. As with Victoria and the childminder, Ms Hines did not consider it necessary to interview Kouao there and then. Although Ms Hines agreed that time is of the essence in child protection cases, this was one child protection investigation where time seemed to be anything but of the essence. Instead she gave Kouao an appointment to attend the Brent Social Services office the next morning at 9.30am.

Police protection lifted

5.132   Events were to overtake Ms Hines too, with the result that no section 47 inquiries were ever begun by Brent Social Services the next day, let alone completed. Furthermore, Victoria was placed in, and then taken out of, police protection in less than 24 hours, without ever being seen by either the police or social services. I comment further on the use of police protection in section 13.

5.133   When Kouao failed to turn up at the office on 15 July 1999, Ms Hines telephoned the hospital and spoke to Dr Charlotte Dempster, only to be informed that Kouao was at the hospital. This was her second visit to the ward since Victoria had been admitted and placed under police protection, giving her ample opportunity, if opportunity was needed, to coach Victoria as to how she should respond to questions from a police officer or social worker.

5.134   According to Ms Hines, Dr Dempster told her that Victoria's case "was not child protection at all, and more or less it was not to be seen as child protection, it was actually a child in need". It was for this reason that Ms Hines said she did not feel unduly concerned that Kouao had failed to turn up for her appointment. She presumed that the doctors had already passed this information on to Kouao and this was why Kouao had stayed at the hospital rather than attending the appointment. It was an assumption that she never checked, as she should have done.

5.135   In her contact note at the time, Ms Hines wrote:

> "Dr Schwartz who has now seen the child does not feel that the injuries are non-accidental. Dr Dempster said that the child possibly has scabies and that they would like child protection to withdraw and treat this as a child in need because the family need urgent housing. I advised Dr Dempster that this would be dealt with by our duty team."

5.136   This was a medical diagnosis that was to have important consequences for Victoria, well beyond the confines of this single admission to the Central Middlesex Hospital. That it was Dr Ruby Schwartz who had made the diagnosis appears to have elevated Victoria's case beyond the realm for questioning by social services. As a result, an important opportunity was lost to verify directly Dr Schwartz's true concerns. Subsequently, Dr Schwartz acknowledged that although she had ruled out non-accidental injury, she believed that Victoria must be suffering "other forms" of deliberate harm.

5.137 Ms Hines did nothing to question what factors had been taken into account in the hospital's coming to its diagnosis. She did not speak to Dr Schwartz directly. She said in evidence, "I was told this child was seen by Dr Ruby Schwartz, who is a consultant paediatrician who is highly respected in Brent, she is a member of the ACPC ... I felt that if Dr Schwartz had seen the child, her diagnosis would have been correct, and I did not feel I could have disputed that."

5.138 Yet Ms Hines knew that at the time Victoria was admitted she had been observed to have suffered bruising over her feet, arms, legs and buttocks, to have infected bruises to the fingers and to have bloodshot eyes. All she knew about scabies was that it was some form of skin disease and that it could be caused by unhealthy living conditions. Faced with these glaring discrepancies, however, she was still content to rely completely on what she understood Dr Schwartz's diagnosis to be, as conveyed to her by a third party. She was also content to rely on Dr Schwartz's opinion that there were no longer any child protection issues. This was an opinion that no one in the hospital, including Dr Schwartz, acting on their own, was qualified to give. Social services are charged with the responsibility for investigating and assessing child protection concerns in conjunction with their partner agencies. Therefore, I make the following recommendation:

> **Recommendation**
> The training of social workers must equip them with the confidence to question the opinion of professionals in other agencies when conducting their own assessment of the needs of the child.

5.139 In evidence, Dr Dempster disputed that she had asked social services for the child protection order to be lifted. She said that she did no more than relay Dr Schwartz's diagnosis and outline some concerns about housing and other issues to the duty social worker and to Ms Hines. Ms Viljoen, who was working in the duty team, logged this as a separate 'child in need' referral on 15 July 1999. Dr Dempster was clear that she did not request that child protection be lifted for Victoria, although she kept no record of her conversation. While Ms Viljoen's referral summary makes no mention of child protection, Ms Hines's note completed at that time and the written confirmation subsequently faxed by Dr Dempster to social services, communicated only too clearly that the hospital had ruled out child protection concerns. Whether or not Dr Dempster had also expressly used the term 'child in need', in Ms Hines's mind there was now no longer any other track to pursue.

5.140 This was not the first or only occasion when there were conflicts in the evidence as to who said what between staff working on Victoria's case.

5.141 Ms Hines rang PC Dewar to tell her that the injuries were no longer thought to be non-accidental and the police protection could now be discharged. PC Dewar confirmed: "I was told that they were all as a result of scabies. It was very clear." Victoria was duly discharged from police protection, such as it was, at 10.40am that morning (15 July), without Victoria or her carer ever having been questioned and without any further explanation of the issues that had been deemed important enough, according to both the police and social services, to put Victoria into police protection in the first place.

Communication with the hospital

5.142 Ms Hines spoke to her team manager, Ms Roper, when Ms Roper returned to the office at about midday on 15 July 1999. She fed back to Ms Roper the medical opinion that Victoria's was no longer a child protection case but was now a case about a medical condition. Ms Roper agreed that the section 47 inquiries, which had never got off the ground, could be safely aborted. Although Dr Ajayi-Obe's medical report and body maps had been faxed the day before, Ms Hines said she had not seen them and Ms Roper did not consider these in reaching her decision. Ms Roper said she was not aware of these documents at the time and their existence only came to her attention in 2001. She said she had had difficulty in reading them, but said that even if she had been able to read them, they contained nothing that would have caused her to rethink her decision. This is remarkable given the graphic representation of widespread injuries in Dr Ajayi-Obe's notes. However, Ms Roper was clearly influenced by the information from Dr Dempster, as relayed by Ms Hines and subsequently confirmed in writing from the hospital, that the marks on Victoria's body were caused by scabies. Ms Roper understood that the reportedly self-inflicted marks were the result of Victoria scratching the scabies. She did not query the inconsistency of these reports.

5.143 If the hospital had any other concerns, Ms Roper would have expected the examining doctor to have referred to those in his or her report and they had not, except to mention issues of housing and schooling – neither of which on their own would constitute grounds for continuing with child protection inquiries.

5.144 Ms Roper conceded, however, that it was social services' job, not that of the hospital, to pull together what information existed and ensure that it was properly evaluated as part of any such inquiries. The duty to assess the needs of children is clearly placed on social services. The paediatric assessment notes taken by Dr Rhys Beynon demonstrated that the hospital possessed information that would have been relevant to an assessment of Victoria's needs. Not unreasonably, Ms Roper said she would have expected the hospital to have faxed across a copy of those notes. However, what use she would have made of them had they been sent is questionable.

5.145 Ms Roper said if Brent Social Services had known – and to my mind there can be no doubt whatsoever that it was social services' job to find out – that Kouao had asked Mrs Cameron to look after Victoria for good or that she had suggested that Victoria had cut herself with razor blades, she would have expected her team to have continued with the section 47 inquiries that day. With hindsight, Ms Roper said that a joint visit by a child protection social worker and a duty social worker should have been undertaken before closing the section 47 inquiries. It was, however, her expectation at the time that all the key parties, including Victoria, Kouao and the childminder, would be interviewed as part of a 'child in need' assessment.

5.146 Instead, Ms Roper agreed with Ms Hines that Victoria's case should be re-labelled 'child in need'. The primary focus was once again housing and the case was transferred back to Mr Armstrong's duty team. This illustrates well the dangers which attend the premature classification of 'child in need' and 'child protection'. In my opinion, the correct application of the Children Act 1989 requires a proper assessment to be completed before such a decision is taken.

5.147 Ms Roper wanted to have the hospital's diagnosis in writing. Dr Dempster duly faxed a letter across to the duty team on 15 July 1999, the content of which Dr Schwartz was subsequently to describe as "very superficial". The key passage that was to have such an impact on how Victoria's case was handled not only by Brent Social Services but also by Haringey Social Services thereafter reads as follows:

> "She [Victoria] was admitted to the ward last night with concerns re possible NAI [non-accidental injury]. She had however been assessed by the consultant Dr Schwarz and it has been decided that her scratch marks are all due to scabies. Thus it is no longer a child protection issue."

5.148 Dr Dempster went on to record several social welfare issues that needed to be sorted out urgently, including the fact that Kouao and Victoria were homeless and that Victoria was not attending school.

5.149 Dr Schwartz mentioned for the first time in evidence that she was "almost positive" that she had spoken to someone from social services that morning about her concerns for Victoria, and that possibly it was to Ms Hines. However, Ms Hines firmly denied this. She believed she faithfully recorded in her contact notes the names of all the doctors she had spoken to, together with a brief summary of the conversations. There is no record of any conversation with Dr Schwartz on the Brent case file, nor anything to support Dr Schwartz's claim in the hospital records. In these circumstances, it seems unlikely to me that any such conversation took place. As a result, Brent Social Services were left with Dr Dempster's letter and telephone conversation with Ms Hines, themselves an interpretation by one doctor of a second doctor's notes of Dr Schwartz's evaluation of Victoria, as the final summary of the hospital's concerns.

5.150 Ms Hines passed Victoria's file through to Ms Roper for her to sign off on the morning of 16 July 1999. Owing to a careless error, Ms Roper's own closure summary note would appear to have reduced still further what started out as serious child protection concerns to little more than a minor medical complaint. She wrote:

> "This child has been examined by Dr Dempster and Dr Schwartz. It is not felt to be a child protection case as the marks on the child are noted to be **eczema** [my emphasis]. Dr Dempster has faxed a letter to that effect …
>
> Dr Schwartz wishes the case to be looked into for a child in need assessment particularly as the family are homeless.
>
> Family were originally placed in Brent by Ealing.
>
> Case passed back to duty in order to complete an assessment or agree transfer of case to Ealing."

The internal transfer of case responsibility

5.151 According to Mr Armstrong, Ms Roper had already discussed with him her recommendations to transfer the case back to the duty team the day before, and he had acted on that by telephoning Ealing to agree the transfer of the case to them. It seems an unlikely coincidence that Pamela Fortune at Ealing Social Services should have received a telephone call on the same day, also from a Mr Armstrong, whom she thought worked at the Acton Law Centre. It was her recollection, as recorded in the Ealing case file, that Mr Armstrong had expressed concerns about Kouao's case. However, she said she told him that Ealing had closed the case and that Brent Social Services were dealing with it because they had some concerns about Victoria.

5.152 In evidence, Mr Armstrong relied on Ealing's record of the telephone conversation as support for his claim that he made the telephone call on about 15 July 1999, but his recollection of the outcome of that call was wholly different. It was his contention that Ealing accepted case responsibility, though this, he said, was by verbal agreement with Mr Victor. As a result, Mr Armstrong faxed over the papers to Ealing on 15 or 16 July. Although Brent's duty manager action sheet purports to record that the case was transferred to Ealing on 16 July, there is no other documentation evident in either authority's papers to suggest that a formal transfer of the case was properly executed and recorded. In my judgement, the likelihood is that it was not. If it wasn't for Victoria's later admission to the North Middlesex Hospital and the subsequent involvement of Enfield and Haringey Social Services, concerns about Victoria may well have been left unresolved with neither Brent nor Ealing taking any direct action. This leads me to make the following recommendation to ensure that local authority social services departments are absolutely clear as to who has case responsibility at any one time:

> **Recommendation**
> Directors of social services must ensure that the transfer of responsibility of a case between local authority social services departments is always recorded on the case file of each authority, and is confirmed in writing by the authority to which responsibility for the case has been transferred.

5.153　Quite by chance, Ms Hines saw Kouao and Victoria for the only time when they appeared in reception at social services on 15 or 16 July 1999. By that stage Ms Hines's involvement in the case had already ceased and the case had been, or was in the process of being, transferred back to the duty team. She saw a little girl who was sitting down while Kouao was making a bit of a scene. Ms Hines understood that she had asked for the taxi fare to take her back to Ealing but duty staff refused this. She saw enough of Kouao to observe, as others had done before and were to do again in the future, that she "was very well turned out, dressed up very nicely". Interestingly, Ms Hines could not really say what Victoria looked like, or comment on her demeanour or her clothes.

Kouao's housing application

5.154　A housing application to Brent council was a two-step process, first involving an assessment of a person's eligibility for housing, and second an assessment of points to determine whether an offer of housing can be made.

5.155　Kouao attended Brent's One Stop Shop in Harlesden on 1 September 1999 and put in an application for housing in the borough. Two days later, Faithlyn Anderson, a senior officer in Brent's housing resource centre, received Kouao's application and made the initial assessment of Kouao's eligibility.

5.156　Kouao's application indicated that none of the family suffered from any medical condition, but was in fact accompanied by a nearly two-month-old letter from the Central Middlesex Hospital indicating that Victoria had been treated there for an infection. The letter also stated that Victoria and Kouao were homeless.

5.157　Kouao stated in one section of the form that the people to be included in the application were herself, Victoria, and her son Jean. However, later in the form, when describing her current housing conditions, she stated that only she and Victoria were living in Nicoll Road – an inconsistency that was later picked up by Rachael Green, a transfer and registration officer, when assigning points. Kouao stated on the form that the living conditions at Nicoll Road were very poor and that the family was occupying one room.

5.158 Kouao's application met the local eligibility criteria, but it was judged by Ms Anderson to be non-urgent for the following reasons. Although the letter from the Central Middlesex Hospital indicated that Victoria and Kouao were homeless, Kouao stated on her accompanying application form that she was not homeless and was not expecting to become homeless. Kouao had also waited nearly two months from the date of the letter from the Central Middlesex Hospital to make her application; to qualify for urgent treatment applicants must be threatened with homelessness with 28 days. Ms Anderson stated that applicants often say that they are homeless but are still in accommodation several months later.

5.159 Over the course of the next seven weeks Kouao's application was registered by the finance and systems section – a not unusual delay given the non-urgent nature of the application. Ms Green made the second-stage assessment on receipt of the application on 20 October 1999. She found that Kouao had insufficient points to qualify for housing. A letter to this effect was sent to Kouao on 28 October. At the same time, Ms Green sought clarification about the whereabouts of Kouao's son and about the condition of Nicoll Road. These two issues could potentially affect the number of points Kouao had already been awarded. The letter advised Kouao she would be informed about this at a later stage, presumably after she had provided Brent with the additional requested details. However, as no response to this was received, no further action was taken.

Closing the case

5.160 Brent Social Services closed Victoria's case on 3 September 1999. It might be thought odd that despite the agreed transfer to Ealing Social Services, Mr Armstrong should have marked the case as pending from mid July, a practice that he said was common, particularly if the cases were out of the borough. On his first day back from a month's annual leave, Mr Armstrong marked on the action sheet "Client referred to Ealing" and closed the case.

5.161 There were, in my view, strong grounds for believing that Victoria's needs could and should have been met in Ealing, and I have commented upon this earlier. That did not happen and an opportunity to safeguard and promote her welfare was clearly missed. A second opportunity arose in Brent but once again no assessment was made of Victoria's needs, despite the clear indications that her safety was at risk. Had Brent met their responsibilities to Victoria, it may be that Haringey would not have become involved.

Analysis of practice

5.162 It is plain from the sequence of events that I have just described that the handling of Victoria's case by Brent Social Services is littered with examples of poor practice and a consistent failure to do basic things competently.

5.163 While there can plainly be no excuse for the failure of the front door duty system, it was not helped, in my view, by a structure that was far from conducive to efficient social work intervention. In particular, I regard the following aspects of the system to have contributed to the failure by Brent Social Services ever to undertake a proper assessment of Victoria's needs:

- The taking of referrals by the One Stop Shops
- The lack of efficient IT and administrative support
- The division between 'child protection' and 'child in need' intake teams
- The disproportionate use of agency workers in the duty teams.

I consider each in turn.

The role of the One Stop Shop

5.164 The manner in which social services receive and process information concerning vulnerable children can be critical to the effectiveness of the services that those children eventually receive. The process used to deal with Ms Ackah's referral on 18 June 1999 was unnecessarily complicated and carried with it too great a chance that important information would be lost or misinterpreted.

5.165 Ms Ackah's call was first received by the council's main switchboard, which then passed it on to a One Stop Shop. The One Stop Shop, for these purposes, would seem to have acted as nothing more than a staging-post for such referrals, which were then passed on to the social services duty team.

5.166 The aspect of this system that causes me most concern is that a person in Ms Ackah's position who wishes to pass on information about a child who is potentially in need of protection, speaks, in the first instance, to someone who has little or no training or experience in the taking of referrals concerning vulnerable children. The majority of the work of a One Stop Shop of the type in operation in Brent, will be the handling of routine inquiries about various aspects of the council's work. The handling of sensitive information about a child, perhaps coming from a hesitant referrer, requires skills of a different nature.

5.167 The problem is compounded when, as in Victoria's case, the administrator who takes the call is expected to classify the referral as being of a particular type. Cases involving vulnerable children do not come with convenient labels attached, particularly when the referrer is a member of the public who may have only a sketchy knowledge of the child's circumstances.

5.168 In my view, the solution lies in the establishment of a dedicated 24-hour telephone number manned by specialist staff in children and families' services in accordance with the recommendation I made earlier in paragraph 5.71. I recognise, however, that such arrangements may take time to implement and that even after their implementation, referrals will continue to be made to various points in the local authority network. In such cases, it is vital that proper and efficient use is made of the information provided.

5.169 The fact that the first referral to Brent Social Services concerning Victoria was handled in the first instance by a One Stop Shop, not only caused unnecessary delay in its being picked up by the relevant team within children's services, but it contributed to the fact that the referral was effectively 'lost' afterwards. The management of referrals from members of the public must proceed in accordance with procedures that are simple, clear and universally understood by all front-line workers. The procedures in Brent met none of these criteria. In an effort to ensure that they are met in the future in Brent and elsewhere, I make the following recommendation:

> **Recommendation**
> All front-line staff within local authorities must be trained to pass all calls about the safety of children through to the appropriate duty team without delay, having first recorded the name of the child, his or her address and the nature of the concern. If the call cannot be put through immediately, further details from the referrer must be sought (including their name, address and contact number). The information must then be passed verbally and in writing to the duty team within the hour.

Lack of IT and administrative support

5.170 Once the handling of Ms Ackah's referral got off to a bad start, the prospects of ever redeeming the situation and realising that much still needed to be done to ensure a proper response to the concerns she had highlighted were significantly reduced by the lack of any effective administrative system in operation in Brent at the time.

5.171 The overriding impression I received from the evidence that I heard on this issue was of a lack of any 'system' worthy of the name for the logging and tracking of referrals. I was told, for example, that it took an average of three weeks for a new referral to be logged onto the relevant database, and that a delay of 12 weeks was not unheard of. I also heard evidence of files going missing and faxes containing important information concerning vulnerable children arriving in offices in which there was no system in place for recording their arrival, or distributing them to the correct member of staff.

5.172 The haphazard and chaotic nature of the administrative systems which were supposed to assist Brent's social workers in the efficient discharge of their responsibilities is perhaps most graphically illustrated by the fact that Victoria managed, during the time that her case was open in Brent, to acquire five different 'unique' identification numbers on the various systems that were designed to ensure that the progress of her case was effectively monitored.

Division of teams

5.173 Further confusion was created, in my view, by the division of Brent's intake team into separate 'child in need' and 'child protection' teams. Later in this Report I consider the validity of such a distinction and whether it serves any useful purpose in the safeguarding of children. For the present, it is sufficient simply to observe that the organisation of Brent's intake teams in this manner meant that there was often doubt as to whether a particular case was in the right place. As Ms Roper put it, "What we found ... was that there was a considerable overlap between the two teams and what that meant was that a large number of cases ... were classified as child protection cases when really what was required was a child in need assessment."

5.174 One of the consequences of the overlap she described would seem to have been that children would be transferred between the two teams depending upon the existing view as to the child's appropriate classification. The two most unfortunate side effects of such an approach are risk that important information concerning the case will be lost in the transfer, and the disruption in the continuity of care that will inevitably result when a case is passed between social workers.

5.175 In addition, at times of heavy workload and stretched resources, the temptation to reclassify a case so that responsibility for it could be transferred onto another team could result in social workers being too eager either to downgrade or play up the seriousness of a particular case.

Use of agency staff

5.176 Finally, the effectiveness of the service offered by Brent's front door teams was further undermined, in my view, by the policy to assign the majority of permanent staff to the long-term teams, with the result that there was a disproportionately high number of agency staff working in the duty teams. While I am in no position to judge the general competency of individual agency workers employed by Brent at the time, I was told that many had recently arrived from abroad and were inevitably unfamiliar with local procedures. Regular briefing sessions had to be held in order to familiarise recently arrived agency workers with basic elements of their roles.

5.177   As was pointed out in the SSI May 2000 inspection report, intake work is highly skilled and demanding. Important decisions have to be taken, sometimes in the absence of detailed information about the child concerned, and there can often be limited time available for careful reflection and consideration as to how best to respond to the child's immediate needs. The use of agency staff unfamiliar with basic aspects of the work only increases the chances of mistakes being made and important information being missed.

Impact of structural deficiencies

5.178   Overall, the evidence I heard leads me to the view that the procedures adopted by Brent for the taking of referrals, together with the manner in which its intake teams were structured and resourced, contributed to the chaotic and haphazard manner in which the two referrals concerning Victoria were dealt with and, in particular, the failure to adequately monitor the progress of her case during the period for which it was open in Brent.

5.179   The effective safeguarding of children is a difficult and highly pressurised task. It is rendered virtually impossible if those who are charged with achieving it are not supported by proper systems and structures to work within. I take the view that the chaotic procedures for the monitoring and tracking of cases adopted by Brent Social Services during the period with which I am concerned, contributed greatly to the inadequate response made to both of the referrals they received concerning Victoria.

Poor practice

5.180   Although the front-line staff who came to deal with Victoria's case were not helped in their task by the structure within which they operated they were, in many cases, guilty of inexcusable failures to carry out basic elements of their roles competently. In Brent, as elsewhere, the social workers involved would have needed only to do the simple things properly in order to have greatly increased the chances of Victoria being properly protected.

5.181   Despite the poor quality of the systems in place for the taking, recording and monitoring of referrals in operation in Brent at the time, both of the referrals concerning Victoria eventually came to the attention of staff who should have been in a position to have responded properly to them. With regard to Ms Ackah's referral, for example, two qualified social workers went out to visit Victoria at her home. Properly handled, this visit could have been the first step in the formulation of an effective plan to safeguard and promote Victoria's welfare. In the event, the planning of the visit was so poor that the social workers concerned arrived in Nicoll Road without any real idea of what they were doing there. This, together with their failure to make even the most basic inquiries when they discovered that Kouao and Victoria were not at home, meant that the opportunity to protect Victoria afforded by the visit, and by the referral that prompted it, was squandered.

5.182   Also, basic failures undermined the effectiveness of Brent's response to the second referral. The fact that Victoria was placed under police protection on the evening that the referral was received, clearly demonstrates that the matter was considered to be a serious one that required a positive response. In fact, no assessment of Victoria's needs was ever undertaken in response to this referral. In the first instance, such an assessment would have involved nothing more taxing than speaking to those involved. As it turned out, neither Victoria nor Kouao nor Avril Cameron nor Priscilla Cameron nor the referrer (Dr Ajayi-Obe) were ever spoken to by Brent Social Services for the purpose of gaining an understanding of Victoria's needs and circumstances.

5.183   Time and again the written record of Brent's handling of Victoria's case demonstrates a complete absence of any proper reflection or analysis of the information available to them. Perhaps the most glaring example is provided by the failure to speak to Ms Cameron. Taking another person's child to a hospital and expressing the suspicion that the child is being deliberately harmed is not something that anyone would undertake lightly. It seems inconceivable that anyone who applied their mind to Victoria's case file in any meaningful way could have failed to pick up the fact that the lady who had brought Victoria into hospital in the first place had yet to be spoken to.

5.184   In my view, the proper handling of Victoria's case would have involved at least the following basic steps:

- Victoria should have been seen and spoken to.
- The accommodation in which Victoria and Kouao were living should have been visited and assessed for its suitability.
- Whatever background information was available from Ealing Social Services and the French authorities should have been obtained.
- Legal advice as to Kouao and Victoria's status and the options available to social services in dealing with them should have been sought.
- Avril and Priscilla Cameron should have been spoken to in order to understand why they had come to the view that Victoria had to be taken to hospital.
- Kouao should have been interviewed about the injuries to Victoria and the concerns that had been expressed by the Camerons.
- A multi-agency discussion should then have taken place involving representatives from the Central Middlesex Hospital, Brent Child Protection Team and Ealing Social Services, at which a plan to promote and safeguard Victoria's welfare should have been agreed.

Lack of supervision

5.185   The steps listed above amount to no more, in my view, than standard social work practice of a type that should reasonably be expected in every case of alleged deliberate harm. Their impact on the outcome of Victoria's case is likely to have been very significant indeed. The fact that none of them were taken in Victoria's case is attributable not just to poor practice on the front line, but also, in my view, to a lack of clear managerial direction and, in particular, effective supervision.

5.186   As far as the deficiencies in the supervision offered to those working on Victoria's case is concerned, it is necessary to do little more than observe that her case file was never read thoroughly by any manager for the duration of the time that her case was open in Brent. Effective supervision takes time. It involves reading the case file and applying some thought to the decisions taken on the case. In Brent, such supervision would appear to have been one of the primary casualties of an intake team which was simply unable to cope adequately with the work required of it.

5.187   It is little wonder, therefore, that basic omissions such as the failure to speak to Victoria or Ms Cameron before the case was closed were never picked up and challenged by the managers involved in the case. There can be no excuse for the closure of a case before the basic steps necessary to secure the well-being of the child have been taken. I therefore make the following recommendation:

> **Recommendation**
>
> Directors of social services must ensure that no case that has been opened in response to allegations of deliberate harm to a child is closed until the following steps have been taken:
>
> - The child has been spoken to alone.
> - The child's carers have been seen and spoken to.
> - The accommodation in which the child is to live has been visited.
> - The views of all the professionals involved have been sought and considered.
> - A plan for the promotion and safeguarding of the child's welfare has been agreed.

Low priority of children's services

5.188　A lack of priority was given to the standards of the day-to-day work of front-line social workers by the managers responsible for the operation of the intake teams. This was replicated further up the organisation by the low priority accorded to children's services by Brent's senior officers and elected councillors.

5.189　Despite the efforts of central government to move the protection of children further up the local government agenda through the Quality Protects initiative, I heard much evidence to indicate that children's services in Brent were significantly underfunded at the time that Victoria arrived in the borough. I have set out in detail in paragraphs 5.40–5.41 the extent to which Brent spent less on children's services than the sums allocated to it for that purpose by central government in the Standard Spending Assessments for the periods up to and including the one with which I am primarily concerned. I have also made reference to the various arguments deployed by witnesses from Brent in an effort to persuade me that underspending of this nature should not be interpreted as being indicative of a lack of focus on the protection of children. I do not seek to rehearse those matters here.

5.190　For present purposes I wish simply to record my conclusion on this issue which is that the lack of priority and resources accorded to children's services by Brent over several years leading up to Victoria's arrival in the borough, contributed significantly to the deterioration of the service offered to vulnerable children by the intake teams which handled her case. I found those teams to have been in a deplorable condition in mid 1999. An almost total lack of effective supervision meant that poor practice went unnoticed and unchallenged. A lack of sufficient numbers of staff with the skills and training necessary to perform the tasks required of them, meant that the systems in place were on the verge of collapse.

5.191　As I have already made clear, a lack of resources and management attention cannot provide an excuse for front-line workers for failing to perform basic aspects of the job for which they have been trained and employed. That said, the fact that the teams with which I am concerned were allowed to deteriorate into the state in which I found them during the course of this Inquiry can only be the result of wholly inadequate monitoring by those who were ultimately responsible for the provision of a proper service to vulnerable children in Brent.

5.192　As I stated at the outset of this section of the Report, I have little regard for the concept of what Mr Daniel referred to as "professional distance" between those at the top of the organisation and those working on the front line. It is the job of senior officers and elected councillors to inform themselves about the quality of services being offered by their front-line staff, and to take appropriate action to remedy deficiencies as they are revealed.

5.193 Perhaps the most disturbing aspect of the evidence I heard regarding Brent Social Services was the lack of concern, and even interest, that the senior figures in the council appeared to show in the condition of their children's services intake teams. I regard the regular monitoring of front-line work by senior managers and elected councillors to be an essential component of the effective delivery of services to children. In an effort to ensure that such monitoring takes place, I make the following recommendation:

Recommendation

Chief executives of local authorities with social services responsibilities must make arrangements for senior managers and councillors to regularly visit intake teams in their children's services department, and to report their findings to the chief executive and social services committee.

6 Haringey Social Services

The managerial context

6.1   Victoria spent some 308 days in England. For 211 of them, and in response to a clear child protection referral, she had an allocated social worker from the North Tottenham District Office (NTDO) of Haringey Social Services. Their single responsibility to Victoria throughout this period was to safeguard and promote her welfare in accordance with the Children Act 1989. Their clear and overwhelming failure so to do is the subject of this section.

6.2   As with the other agencies involved in Victoria's care, it is not enough to consider the omissions and failings of individual practitioners in Haringey without considering the context in which they were working at the time. It is also necessary to understand the extent to which the organisation in which they served, and the working practices of the organisations, can, and must, shoulder the blame for serious lapses in individual professional practice. The evidence on this in Haringey is, in my judgement, overwhelming.

6.3   Although the failings in Lisa Arthurworrey's (Victoria's social worker) practice were many and serious, she was badly let down by her managers and the organisation that employed her. In particular, council members and the senior management of Haringey must be held to account for the yawning gap between safe policies and procedures, and poor practice in their children and families' services. As Pauline Bradley, a social worker at Haringey, observed, they "were way out of touch with what was happening at the grass roots and did not really seem to care". Yet Gurbux Singh, chief executive at the time, felt able to distance himself from these failures. He told the Inquiry, "It is absolutely clear that Haringey has messed up and it is absolutely clear that there were fundamental failures ... but I am not clear in my own mind as to where the line of responsibility lies. That is my own dilemma." It is not a dilemma I share, as I have already made clear in respect of Gareth Daniel, chief executive of Brent council. For Mr Singh to seek to hide behind the cloak of corporate responsibility and to say that beyond making sure that effective systems and processes were in place – which they clearly were not as this section will demonstrate – he "could not honestly think of what else I could have done to ensure that the tragedy which happened did not happen" entirely misses the point. As chief executive, Mr Singh carried overall responsibility for the way in which the council operated and performed. If there was a gap between local policies and practice it was exactly his job to know about it, to keep his members informed and to take timely and corrective action.

Haringey

6.4   Haringey is an outer London borough with many of the characteristics and problems of an inner city area. In its 1998 position statement to the Joint Review of Social Services in Haringey Council, Haringey noted that it is the thirteenth most deprived authority in England. A large proportion of its residents were described as experiencing:

> "Severe poverty, unemployment and deprivation, which manifests itself in all areas of their lives, such as the lack of adequate affordable housing, poor levels of educational attainment, poor health and high numbers of children in need."

6.5   I heard evidence that Haringey has one of the most diverse populations in the country, with 160 different languages spoken locally, a long tradition of travellers settling in the borough and a high proportion of asylum seeking families (nine per cent of the total population). The pressure this places on all departments within the local authority is inevitable – none less so than for the children and families' services.

Haringey Children and Families Service

6.6   The NTDO was one of two district offices in the borough accommodating the Haringey Children and Families Service. The other area office was some five miles away in the west of the borough in Hornsey. Based in north Tottenham, in cramped and rather dingy premises, were two investigation and assessment teams (IAT A and IAT B) and four children and families' long-term teams. Members of each of these teams would staff the duty team on a rota basis. It was the duty team that handled in the first instance most of the referrals – including Victoria's – that came into the office, although they operated a completely different system from the duty team in Hornsey.

6.7   Once the social worker on duty had conducted an initial assessment of referrals, cases were transferred to an IAT. It was generally understood, but not made explicit in local guidance, that cases should not be held open for more than three months by an IAT, and usually not beyond a case conference, before being transferred to a long-term team for implementation of a care plan. Despite this, Victoria's case remained throughout her seven-month period in Haringey with the IAT and the social worker to whom it was originally allocated. This adds further weight to the recommendation made in paragraph 4.14 that managers of duty systems must be aware of how many cases are open on duty, what is being done on them and by whom, and when the action needs to be completed. It also demonstrates the need for managers to be aware of when key deadlines in the progress of a case are missed. The fact that a case spends an excessive amount of time open on duty can often indicate that it has been allowed to drift. In an effort to ensure that such signs are not missed, I make the following recommendation:

> **Recommendation**
> Directors of social services must ensure that where the procedures of a social services department stipulate requirements for the transfer of a case between teams within the department, systems are in place to detect when such a transfer does not take place as required.

6.8   Within each IAT there were six social workers and a senior practitioner accountable to a team manager, who was in turn responsible to the commissioning manager for children and families. Until the changes brought about by restructuring in early November 1999 (to which I shall return), Angella Mairs managed team A and her senior practitioner was Rosemarie Kozinos. Carole Baptiste managed team B and her senior practitioner was Barry Almeida. Both team managers reported to David Duncan, commissioning manager, who in turn reported to Carol Wilson, assistant director of children's services and chair of the local Area Child Protection Committee (ACPC). Both team managers took turns managing the duty team. Accordingly, following Victoria's admission to the North Middlesex Hospital in July 1999, it was Ms Baptiste who allocated Victoria's case to Ms Arthurworrey, a social worker in her team.

Induction and training

6.9 At the time she was allocated Victoria's case, Ms Arthurworrey had been employed in Haringey for nine months. Although she told the Inquiry that she was not given "any sort of induction" when she started with Haringey other than to be shown around the building and told to read the department's child protection guidelines, Ms Arthurworrey was not wholly inexperienced because this was her second children's services post since qualifying as a social worker in 1997. Surprisingly, though, she had yet to conduct and see through to completion a joint section 47 inquiry of suspected deliberate harm to a child with the police.

6.10 In Bernard Monaghan's subsequent review of staff involved in Victoria's case, he concluded, "All the staff directly concerned with the VC case had received appropriate training to equip them to deal with the practice matters that arose during their involvement." Mr Monaghan found "no basis to believe that a lack of appropriate training of staff was a contributing factor". Indeed, Ms Arthurworrey told this Inquiry that by June 1999 her training was adequate and it was not a factor relevant to Victoria's case in terms of her conduct of it. I do not share that view. Setting aside Ms Arthurworrey's limited experience in child protection inquiries, she was not trained in the *Memorandum of Good Practice* and could not therefore take a section 47 child protection inquiry through to its conclusion.

6.11 Common sense dictates that before any social worker conducts section 47 inquiries they should:

- be trained in how to complete such an inquiry;
- have had experience in participating in section 47 inquiries while shadowing a more experienced colleague;
- ideally be trained in the *Memorandum of Good Practice*.

6.12 Ultimately it was the responsibility of Ms Wilson to ensure that staff in her department carrying out section 47 inquiries were competent to do so. In order that this happens in future, I make the following recommendation:

> **Recommendation**
> No social worker shall undertake section 47 inquiries unless he or she has been trained to do so. Directors of social services must undertake an audit of staff currently carrying out section 47 inquiries to identify gaps in training and experience. These must be addressed immediately.

Caseloads

6.13 The atmosphere within the NTDO duty and IATs was hectic in 1999. Shanthi Jacob spoke of the "bombardment factor" and Mary Richardson, director of social services in Haringey at the time, stated:

> "Undoubtedly North Tottenham was the busiest social work office. As a consequence of that, by definition staff probably held, on average, slightly more cases than their Hornsey counterparts ... there was regular and fairly unremitting pressure on the north Tottenham office."

6.14 It was an issue recognised by the Joint Review team in early 1999, who referred in their report to potential staff "burn out", which needed to be addressed quickly.

6.15 Ms Arthurworrey told the Inquiry that initially her caseload at Haringey was manageable, but it slowly increased. By the end of August 1999 she was responsible for 19 cases (of which half were child protection). This is seven more cases than the maximum laid out in the *Duty Investigation and Assessment Team Procedures* devised by Ms Mairs. Mr Duncan argued that it was hard to imagine how a social worker could work on more than 12 cases at a time. Yet Ms Arthurworrey said she was unaware of the guidance, and during 1999 Mr Duncan said he knew, though Ms Wilson said she did not, that staff in the NTDO IATs were dealing with a high number of cases and that the average caseload was in excess of the recommended maximum.

6.16   Haringey Social Services admitted that Ms Arthurworrey's caseload in the second half of 1999 was higher than they generally considered desirable, but they argued that this did not affect her ability to deal with Victoria's case. Ms Arthurworrey did not, they said, identify any tasks at the time that she could not carry out because of workload pressures. However, the fact remains that Ms Arthurworrey failed to complete a number of key tasks in relation to Victoria's case, and she worked considerably in excess of her scheduled hours, notching up by the end of 1999 some 52 days of time off in lieu, which could not easily be taken because of workload pressures. It also overlooks entirely the additional need for effective supervision – so demonstrably absent in Victoria's case – when social workers carry active caseloads of this size.

6.17   Ms Bradley, a social worker in one of the long-term teams and a UNISON representative, described the situation as "conveyor belt social work". She said that the "ethos seemed to be particularly about getting the cases through the system and meeting the targets, meeting the statistics, getting them through the system", rather than doing the work that needed to be done.

The management of the IATs

6.18   The personalities of those in charge of the two IATs contributed much to the way the teams worked. Marina Hayes, a social worker in IAT B, recalled that the team was "very divided, and there were a lot of deep conflicts. At times the working environment felt hostile, and it was not a comfortable place to work constructively in". Ms Hayes stated that there seemed to be "two camps in the I and A team. It felt to me that there were insiders and outsiders within the office." Ms Hayes also said, "There were historical conflicts that were just never resolved. Probably nobody knew what they were about. They were just part of the culture. They were part of the dynamic." Ms Hayes found the atmosphere less than supportive, in fact she found work in the NTDO a struggle.

6.19   Similarly, Ms Arthurworrey recalled that there always appeared to be conflict in the IATs. She said it reminded her of a school: "Angella Mairs was the headmistress, Rosemarie Kozinos was the head girl. There were also other head girls [the senior practitioners] and we the social workers were the children." Ms Arthurworrey stated there was a clear division of the team into camps. "The basis of the split was the headmistress and the head girls against the social workers ... It was very difficult to rebel among the schoolgirls because we were regarded as children who should be seen and not heard." Others, including Ms Bradley, agreed.

6.20   I heard different and often conflicting views expressed about Ms Mairs's management style. Ms Arthurworrey and Valerie Robertson, another social worker in IAT B, both considered Ms Mairs a powerful and assertive manager with a reputation for being a bit of a bully. However, Ms Robertson said she felt more comfortable in her social work role once Ms Mairs took over as manager of the combined IAT in November 1999, because she received more and clearer direction. Ms Kozinos, on the other hand, found her an approachable manager and Mr Almeida described her as hard working and loyal.

6.21   Whether or not Ms Mairs's management style verged on the bullying, the evidence suggested that she was a tough, if controlling and autocratic, manager whose reputation was known and valued by Haringey's senior management team and whose skills were considered necessary to run an efficient duty system. Mr Duncan confirmed that twice in the past three or four years Haringey had got itself into a crisis in the management of its duty teams, once in the NTDO and more recently in Hornsey. On both occasions Haringey called on Ms Mairs to pull it out of a tight spot, because she was clear and set up safe, strong systems. According to Mr Duncan, that was one of the things that Ms Mairs was good at. He described her style as "controlling, she wants that team run in her way". In his opinion Ms Mairs would not be everyone's favourite manager, but she may come out on top as being the manager that gives the closest and clearest instructions on what to do. Certainly her management style was to have an influence on relationships between the NTDO IATs and those external agencies that could and should have played a critical role in Haringey's child protection system.

6.22   Relations with health colleagues were, on the whole, reasonable but not without their difficulties. At the time Victoria was admitted to the North Middlesex Hospital, Haringey had no social work presence at the hospital, which raised concerns for hospital staff over gaps in the service provided to Haringey patients. Dr Mary Rossiter, consultant paediatrician at the North Middlesex Hospital, said that prior to Victoria's case there had been occasions when Haringey Social Services had not fully appreciated the paediatric team's concerns or fully respected her views about cases. She felt there were occasions when Haringey Social Services had not reacted properly to her expressions of concern about children that she believed might be the victims of deliberate harm. She said, "It was more that we did not have a good working relationship. I really felt that I had not been able to get through to them to explain my concerns." Dr Rossiter felt social workers were not appreciating her point in more complicated cases. When asked whether race made any difference to the way social workers responded to her concerns, she replied, "Maybe some social workers felt they knew more about black children than I did." The minutes of a meeting between hospital social workers and the North Middlesex Hospital paediatric consultants on 11 February 1998 concluded, "There are a lot of problems with North Tottenham District Office and referring to them (which is done by the clinical staff in some circumstances). This causes negative feelings about social services in general which can be unjustified." It was not a problem that Ann Graham, manager with responsibility for liaison between Haringey Social Services and the North Middlesex Hospital, or more importantly the ACPC on which Dr Rossiter sat, ever properly addressed.

6.23   Tensions also existed between Haringey Social Services and the police. Ms Arthurworrey described a general feeling of hostility towards the police and other agencies, which stemmed from Ms Mairs's view that, "Social services knew best ... we worked the hardest and we knew our procedures. There was just very little consultation." This was not Ms Graham's impression, but this may only serve to highlight the disparity in perception between those on the ground and those operating one step removed. Detective Sergeant Michael Cooper-Bland of the Haringey Child Protection Team summed up relations as a bit like "the curate's egg, partly good and partly bad". He thought that on an individual basis, social worker to police officer, there were many examples of good working relationships. Conversely there were examples of poor working relationships and "in a very few cases, downright rudeness".

6.24   Evidence emerged that the police felt pressurised about their role within child protection inquiries. There were differences of opinion on how cases should proceed, despite the existence of a protocol for inquiries between the police and social services. The police felt social services blocked or frustrated steps that the police wanted to take. Sergeant Alan Hodges did not believe that the work carried out in Victoria's case in July and November 1999, could be said to have been an independent, thorough investigation by the police: "I believe in Haringey the working practices there were difficult for the police officers."

6.25   In a letter to Highgate police staff dated 8 March 2000, Detective Chief Inspector Philip Wheeler mentioned the "difficulty of working with what seems to be an 'aggressive' social services unit". In a report of the same date, DCI Wheeler stated that Haringey Social Services "seems to have its own particular culture and ways of working within the child protection framework. It seems that they are extremely powerful within the protection network and some social workers work hard to actually prevent police involvement". Detective Inspector David Howard said that some of the working relationships were difficult, but relationships had to be maintained and difficulties overcome to prevent a possible total breakdown. Once again the ACPC appeared to have done little to broker good relations between its partner agencies.

Carole Baptiste

6.26   In contrast to Ms Mairs, the main issues arising out of Ms Baptiste's management of IAT B were her lack of availability and her incompetency as a team manager. Ms Baptiste worked two and a half days a week from the end of 1998, following her return from maternity leave, until the summer of 1999. In July 1999, before Victoria's referral to Haringey, the members of IAT B raised a number of persistent and serious concerns with Mr Duncan about Ms Baptiste's management of the team. In particular, the B team felt that Ms Baptiste did not know her cases properly, and care planning suffered as a result of this. Staff also informed Mr Duncan that it was hard to seek Ms Baptiste's advice on cases, given the uncertainty about when she would be in the office.

6.27   As front-line manager of the B team and Ms Arthurworrey's immediate supervisor, the extent to which Ms Baptiste's managerial competency fell short of the mark and was known to be deficient, or ought to have been known to be such by her managers, is of critical importance and deserves careful consideration.

6.28   Ms Baptiste had been temporarily promoted by Haringey as a team manager for at least four and half years. This was not a satisfactory situation but was not unusual according to Joe Heatley, Mr Duncan's predecessor as commissioning manager. He claimed that acting-up managers were not uncommon in the late 1990s. Indeed, most managerial posts were filled that way. He believed this was partly due to the general shortage of experienced social workers at that time.

6.29   While there will always be a need for staff to be temporarily promoted to fill unforeseen vacancies, directors of social services must ensure that such arrangements are subject to routine review at no later than six-monthly intervals, and the reasons for continuation or termination should be recorded on the appropriate personnel file. Therefore, I make the following recommendation:

> **Recommendation**
> When staff are temporarily promoted to fill vacancies, directors of social services must subject such arrangements to six-monthly reviews and record the outcome.

6.30   Prior to joining IAT B, Ms Baptiste had moved to one of the long-term children and families' teams as an acting team manager. Dawn Green (née Cardis), a child protection adviser for the NTDO, recalled Ms Baptiste as being a chaotic manager with lots of files and unallocated cases on her desk. She said Ms Baptiste "presented as not focused and chaotic. She seemed less competent than other managers".

Previous problems

6.31   Mr Heatley, manager for children's services, was equally concerned about Ms Baptiste's lack of management and this came to a head in connection with an under-performing social worker in the children and families' team who was known to this Inquiry as Ms B. Not only had Ms Baptiste failed to pick up Ms B's poor performance, she had failed to respond when asked to deal with it. Ms Wilson was fully aware of the situation and an independent human resources consultant, Alister Prince, was asked to prepare a report into the matter.

6.32   Its terms of reference were extended to consider not only the performance of Ms B but also that of Ms Baptiste, her team manager, as well as that of Mr Heatley because of his handling of the whole affair. Although the report was commissioned in early 1998, the 15-page report was not finally received by Haringey Social Services until March 2001. That was some 21 months after Ms Baptiste joined IAT B as its manager after returning from maternity leave. Given the scope of the report, in particular its focus on the performance of both a first and second tier manager, by any standard this was an unacceptably long delay. Significantly, no decision was made to pursue the findings of the report with any of the individuals concerned.

6.33   Although Ms Baptiste failed to co-operate with Mr Prince's report, it is clear from the evidence given by others including Ms B, a new inexperienced social worker, that supervision with Ms Baptiste closely mirrored the later observations of Ms Arthurworrey and others about their supervision experience with Ms Baptiste in the IAT B. Ms B said that she was an unsupportive and unfocused supervisor and that she would spend supervision sessions talking about feeling oppressed by a sexist and racist department. Ms B said she "felt at sea".

6.34   Mr Prince's report contained a number of other, relevant observations, namely:

- Ms Baptiste had had management responsibility for one of Ms B's cases for in excess of two years and was not aware that the social worker had made only three visits in that time. Mr Prince concluded that Ms B was a problem for Ms Baptiste to manage and consequently a number of children and their families failed to receive a service. Indeed Ms B had presented problems as a social worker from the outset and these had not been vigorously addressed. As with Ms B's caseload, they were allowed to drift. Mr Prince found that even a cursory view of Ms B's files "from her earliest involvement in a case evidences little or no social work input of any meaning, simply gaps exist". It is a comment that could apply equally well to Victoria's file.

- Ms B subsequently transferred to Ms Mairs's IAT and under vigorous management her performance as a social worker turned around. Her new practice manager, Ms Kozinos, "was very positive about her abilities".

- In the face of a near revolt by Ms Baptiste's old children and families' team, she was transferred on return from maternity leave to IAT B team in the NTDO in 1998, but still in an acting-up capacity. Mr Prince was highly critical of the "ostrich like" management response in this regard, and suggested that no consideration was given to returning Ms Baptiste to her substantive grade as a senior practitioner. He argued that the corporate response was in effect to avoid a difficult decision rather than to take positive action. "This lack of positive action meant ... unacceptable 'supervision' of the C&F team by Ms Baptiste and the potential passing on of that particular problem to duty, investigation and assessment workers." It was a telling conclusion.

6.35 The validity of Mr Prince's conclusions was called into question by Haringey. In particular I was told that any subsequent improvements in Ms B's performance were not sustained. Also that it was only one worker from the children and families' team, and not the whole team, who threatened to leave in the summer of 1998 if Ms Baptiste returned to manage that team. Nonetheless, I am firmly of the view that enough was known in 1997, or ought to have been known, about Ms Baptiste's management style for alarm bells to be ringing.

6.36 According to Mr Duncan, Ms Baptiste had recognised the difficulties she had had with the children and families' team and it was she who requested a transfer to the IAT on her return from maternity leave in August 1998. Ms Wilson and Mr Duncan agreed the transfer. According to Mr Duncan, the thinking was to wipe the slate clean and let Ms Mairs, who was considered a strong manager and who had earlier been Ms Baptiste's line manager in another social work team, act as her mentor.

6.37 If this had been the managerial intention, it certainly rendered invalid any notion that the managers of the two IATs in 1999 carried equal responsibility for the running of the teams. Indeed, the overwhelming impression from the evidence of the social workers in Ms Baptiste's team was that Ms Mairs was very much in control. Ms Mairs was equally clear that it was not her understanding that she had any mentoring role for Ms Baptiste. Certainly, no such support was offered by her. Nor was any additional support given to Ms Mairs to take on this task.

Problems with supervision

6.38 The tensions that had featured during Ms Baptiste's time in the children and families' team began to resurface in IAT B. As a result, according to Ms Baptiste, she found it hard to engage some social workers, Ms Arthurworrey included, in the regular supervision so fundamental to good practice. Although Ms Arthurworrey has denied ever refusing supervision when it was offered, there clearly was an issue about the quality and timeliness of the supervision that was provided in Ms Baptiste's team. This was confirmed by the director of social services at the time, Mary Richardson.

6.39 Ms Arthurworrey understood she would get supervision every two to three weeks, "but this never happened". In practice she received supervision about once every seven weeks. "When I asked about drawing up a supervision contract Carole [Baptiste] told me that I was responsible for doing that." Ms Arthurworrey said she experienced serious problems in arranging supervision sessions with Ms Baptiste because of her continued unavailability. Often Ms Baptiste would cancel or rearrange sessions or simply not appear without an explanation.

6.40 Of equal concern, Ms Arthurworrey said she found supervision with Ms Baptiste frustrating because, more often than not, they would start discussing cases and then Ms Baptiste would go off on a tangent. Ms Arthurworrey stated that Ms Baptiste often talked about her experiences as a black woman and her relationship with God. The result was that they would not have time to finish discussing the cases. Ms Arthurworrey said she just tried to manage. Generally it was Ms Baptiste's practice to agree with whatever suggestions Ms Arthurworrey put in front of her. Ms Arthurworrey found this disturbing in the sense that it led her to question Ms Baptiste's knowledge base.

6.41   Two other social workers in Ms Baptiste's team gave evidence as to the irregularity and variable quality of her supervision and complained that she referred to her religious beliefs and gave religious guidance during supervision sessions. However, her senior practitioner Mr Almeida was unaware of any complaints as to the content of Ms Baptiste's supervision sessions, as was Mr Duncan. Ms Baptiste denied using supervision sessions to talk about her own personal religious beliefs saying that any talk of religion "was definitely relevant to the casework". However, she admitted mentioning her religious beliefs during the course of her work because during the period when she was dealing with Victoria's case Ms Baptiste had started attending the Rahema church.

6.42   The extent to which supervision sessions, when they occurred, were preoccupied with talk about religion or matters unrelated to the casework in hand has been difficult to gauge some two years after the event. As pointed out by Haringey council, the record of the meeting with Mr Duncan in July 1999 confined itself to a discussion of Ms Baptiste's poor timekeeping, lack of availability for supervision, poor case management and case allocation. This, together with the assertion by Mr Duncan that he knew nothing of the complaints about the quality of Ms Baptiste's supervision, may suggest that the experience of Ms Arthurworrey and others was not universally shared by other members of the team.

6.43   One outcome of the July meeting was that Ms Baptiste agreed to work full time from July 1999 and it was hoped that this would ease the problem of availability. But, as the restructuring interviews took place throughout the autumn of 1999 and Ms Baptiste's job looked increasingly insecure, her timekeeping became even more erratic. I shall return to the restructuring interviews later at paragraph 6.124.

6.44   Ms Arthurworrey recalled, "Some days she was in the office, most days she was not [and] she did not record her movements in the movement book." Cases would appear on social workers' desks without any guidance from Ms Baptiste about the issues. When she was in the office, Ms Baptiste was not readily available, which became problematic when cases required an urgent response. Ms Arthurworrey said she felt unsupported and isolated at Haringey.

Allocation of cases

6.45   Complaints from IAT B about the lack of any formal allocation system for new cases met with little response. Managers ultimately had discretion as to who was given which cases – a discretion that should have systematically taken into account a social worker's experience and capacity for taking on more work. Typically, cases were just 'plonked' on social workers' desks without prior knowledge, often with very little consideration to a social worker's experience, current commitments or workload. There would be no conversation between manager and social worker as to what work needed to be done on a case. Peter Lewington, assistant branch secretary of Haringey UNISON, stated, "Team managers seemed to be under pressure to get cases allocated and it seemed as if their main priority was just to get a worker's name against a case."

6.46   Once again, Ms Wilson said she was not aware that cases were allocated without the team manager reading the case beforehand or that cases were just left on social workers' desks. Ms Richardson, however, accepted that case allocation was not done in the most rational way and that this may have had an impact on Ms Arthurworrey at the time.

6.47   Following the July 1999 meeting, a new system of case allocation was introduced. Social workers were expected to attend weekly meetings so that cases could be allocated to them involving issues in which they had a particular interest. The experiment was extremely short-lived. Ms Arthurworrey recalled, "One case allocation meeting chaired by Carole [Baptiste] was held in July or August 1999 and this appeared to work quite well. The second meeting was due to be chaired by Carole but was never held because Carole arrived at work late ... and the following week we were informed that the case allocation meetings had been scrapped because there was 'no commitment from the social workers'." Ms Baptiste blamed the social workers for failing to attend and said, "Eventually we reverted to the old system of allocation, as there was simply insufficient commitment to the new system." The problem remained unsolved.

6.48 When Ms Baptiste was not available, Ms Mairs, Mr Almeida and Mr Duncan would provide guidance and supervision to social workers in IAT B. This put additional strain on Ms Mairs and Mr Duncan. Ms Mairs stated that the quality and depth of support she was able to provide would have been less than what would have been available had there been a manager there full time.

6.49 Mr Duncan said he had serious doubts about Ms Baptiste's availability to manage a team after July 1999. Mr Almeida felt that Ms Baptiste could be a capable manager but at the time there were outside factors that affected her capability to a degree. Even more worryingly, Ms Wilson acknowledged that Ms Baptiste "was one of our weaker managers. She was not the weakest".

Restructuring

6.50 At interview in September 1999, Ms Baptiste was deemed unappointable. According to Ms Wilson, "[her] practice responses were not inappropriate and her presentation and performance was just about adequate. In one or two areas she achieved higher marks than other managers. However, she appeared to have little confidence." Ms Wilson admitted, however, in her statement to Mr Monaghan as part of Haringey's own internal inquiry that she became very concerned about Ms Baptiste's performance at interview and said she did not feel that she had a "management grip". Ms Baptiste was subsequently moved from front-line services to Quality Protects funded project work in November 1999. She was formally suspended on 15 February 2000 and made redundant on 25 February (the very day of Victoria's death), though she had been absent on sick leave from 20 December 1999.

6.51 Ms Baptiste's suspension was entirely unrelated to her handling of Victoria's case or to her work in Haringey. However, the issue for this Inquiry is whether the deterioration in Ms Baptiste's mental health culminating in her suspension was one that had been developing in the preceding months and, more particularly, while Ms Baptiste was the team manager responsible for Victoria's case. If so, did it manifest itself in ways that were or should have been noticeable to Ms Baptiste's managers? The evidence on this is far from clear.

6.52 Mr Duncan said that he thought Ms Baptiste's mental state was entirely stable throughout 1999. Further, Mr Duncan stated that he saw Ms Baptiste more than any other manager and he saw no mental or physical symptoms in her. "No more so than any of the other managers." Ms Baptiste was asked whether she was treated or diagnosed with any mental disorder prior to January 2000. Ms Baptiste stated, "not that I am aware of, no". Ms Baptiste advised that she had not been to a doctor about a mental disorder before January 2000 and nobody had diagnosed her as suffering from any mental disorder before January 2000.

6.53 Ms Baptiste stated that she did suffer memory losses during the period August to December 1999 and had discussed this with her manager, Mr Duncan. Ms Baptiste recalled "not being able to conceptualise things ... I was not able to visualise things ... I remember that I found it very difficult to do simple calculations and particularly leading up to the restructuring where it was said that there was going to be … a mathematical exercise … I was really struggling with numbers." Ms Baptiste confirmed that this was around summer 1999. Ms Baptiste spoke to Mr Duncan informally about how she was finding it difficult to remember things and to remember how to do things.

6.54 Asked whether her illness in January came out of the blue, Ms Baptiste said that, "probably in hindsight … I am probably able to say that there was a lot of forgetfulness, absentmindedness, not remembering things, but not being aware that I was not remembering things, which was something that I had mentioned to my manager but it was not something that was taken particularly seriously." Ms Baptiste stated that it was difficult to say whether these early signs were affecting her competence as a team manager during the period from July to November 1999. She confirmed, however, that there was nothing that led her to suspect she might be suffering from any form of mental disorder before January 2000 nor did she report her difficulties to her GP. "I thought at the time it was just because of the additional pressures of what was going on … I did not think it was out of the ordinary."

6.55 Whatever Ms Baptiste's precise mental state may have been during the second half of 1999, it seems clear to me that her managers, in particular Ms Wilson and Mr Duncan, knew enough about her weakness as a manager by the time she left to go on maternity leave in November 1997 to at least seriously question the wisdom of putting her in charge of a pressured investigation and assessment team.

6.56 Indeed, not only were the additional supports entirely absent for Ms Baptiste, but the restructuring process that was to occupy the time of managers throughout so much of 1999 actually limited the capacity of Ms Baptiste's manager to do his job properly.

6.57 Mr Duncan now believes that he may not have dealt sufficiently rigorously with the concerns raised by staff at the July 1999 meeting. In his closing submission he said, "I clearly should have taken a more controlling approach to Carole and her team." As a temporarily promoted manager himself – Mr Duncan was acting commissioning manager for the NTDO from April 1998 to September 1999 – his substantive grade remained that of team manager. As part of the restructuring process, Mr Duncan was expected to compete for both positions – in effect putting him in direct competition with Ms Baptiste, at least for the team manager post. This, he said, may have caused him to take his eye off the ball and led him to feel disempowered in supervising Ms Baptiste from March 1999. While I accept Mr Duncan's evidence as to how he felt at the time, I am of the view that a stronger manager would not have let their acting-up status interfere with the way they did their job. The net effect was that there was no adequate supervision of Ms Baptiste's practice and her supervision at all times.

Local guidance

6.58 This was particularly significant because, at the time, social workers in the NTDO and their first-line managers were simply not following local guidance, and senior managers either knew and condoned this or remained blissfully unaware of its consequence.

6.59 Among the several sets of guidance that IATs were subject to, were the following:

The undated *Child Protection Guidelines*
- These were rewritten in 1997 and outlined the duties and responsibilities of social workers undertaking investigative and assessment work. The introduction states, "It is expected that these will be followed by all staff involved in child protection investigations."

Duty Investigation and Assessment Team Procedures

- These were devised by Ms Mairs in June 1998 and covered "the overall framework for the provision of a Duty Children and Families Service for the North Tottenham District Office [and] work in conjunction with existing procedures". These procedures were intended to operate as a pocketbook enabling social workers to be clear about their duties at a glance. Ms Arthurworrey was aware of the Duty Investigation and Assessment Procedures, which she said influenced her practice. But according to Ms Bradley, "There was a practice manual and other procedures available to social workers. However, social workers were never directed to it and practices developed which were separate to the practice manual. There was a lot of confusion about what the relevant procedures were."

Haringey ACPC handbook

- In addition, there was a handbook prepared by the Haringey ACPC, dated June 1997, outlining each agency's role in the child protection process. These provided a guide to inter-agency procedures and a working tool for professionals involved with children. Ms Arthurworrey, however, had never heard of the ACPC handbook. Likewise, Ms Kozinos said that she had no idea that there were ACPC child protection guidelines to assist her. Ms Mairs said that she had seen the ACPC guidance but she did not think they had much relevance to the day-to-day operation in Haringey. Asked how she expected her team to be able to take into account the ACPC guidelines if she was not familiar with them, she replied that she could not answer. Ms Mairs stated that the guidelines were not something her team would use.

- Not for the first time, senior managers were to express surprise at what they learned during the Inquiry's evidence stage. Speaking about the ACPC guidelines, Ms Richardson said, "I find it difficult to believe that people were not aware of them. They were widely circulated and available in area offices." Ms Richardson said she would expect them to use the guidelines in relation to the inter-agency work that was going on. Ms Wilson advised that copies of the ACPC handbook were available although they were not given out to individual social workers. Further, Ms Wilson said that in January 1999 she "personally spent time in Tottenham and at a large group meeting ... went over each of the relevant plans, documents and procedures which were available to staff, confirmed their existence, accessibility and staff familiarity with them and in relation to procedures and their obligations in law. Managers and social workers concerned in the Inquiry were all members of staff at this time and participated in preparation and review of the services policies and procedures". Ms Wilson said that she was satisfied that the guidelines were available: "I was assured that staff knew they were available. I had feedback through the child protection adviser on reinforcement of access to those guidelines." Ms Wilson said she was very surprised to hear that Ms Kozinos had never even seen a copy of the ACPC guidelines because Ms Wilson had personally seen it on the shelf in that office. While Ms Wilson may well have had grounds for being impressed by the availability of the ACPC guidelines, it is less clear that she had any grounds for being impressed as to their use.

Case Recording Practice Guidelines

- Both Ms Kozinos and Ms Mairs said they had limited familiarity with the *Case Recording Practice Guidelines*, dated January 1998, and that they were not followed because they "did not have the appropriate resource to enable us to follow it." The truth of that statement was all too visible in Victoria's case and more generally as to merit repeated criticism in Social Services Inspectorate (SSI) inspections and the Joint Review of 1999. But senior managers had a different slant on the problem and one that, if correct, needs to be addressed across the social work profession as a whole. Ms Wilson observed, "We had some staff who, although qualified as social workers, did not always appear to achieve that level of literacy on paper." Ms Richardson commented that there was "resistance from some staff in Haringey about using the written word at all".

Supervision policy of Haringey Social Services

- More astonishing still was the admission by Ms Kozinos that they did not follow the supervision policy of Haringey Social Services. Specifically, she claimed that the supervision policy was regarded as having been superseded by the custom and practice in Haringey of not reading the case files. The tragic consequence of this was that nobody in Haringey – not even Ms Arthurworrey – ever read Victoria's case file in its entirety.

Ms Mairs said that while there was a written policy that managers should read files, it was simply not practicable to read every file unless there were concerns about the competence of the social worker. There was a lack of resources to do this and no system in place to facilitate it. Ms Mairs agreed that proper supervision necessitated the reading of case files, if not routinely then at least periodically, and she accepted that it was a rather hopeless system if managers did not look at the files to test the way in which social workers were going about their work.

Mr Duncan knew that managers were not systematically reviewing files, but he claimed he did not know that Ms Mairs was not reading them at the crucial points of supervision. Ms Mairs disputed this, stating that Mr Duncan was aware that managers were not reading files before supervision because it was discussed at team management meetings.

Ms Wilson acknowledged that a manager could not participate fully in supervision unless they had read the file: "I think files were an intricate part of good supervision management." Once again, Ms Wilson was surprised to learn that Ms Mairs's team did not read files or adhere to the supervision policy during 1999. Ms Wilson stated she knew as a certainty that other parts of north Tottenham used the policy and did not accept that was the general practice in the NTDO. I am left questioning just how she could be so certain in the face of the evidence from Duty Investigation and Assessment Team (DIAT) witnesses and the clear failings in practice in Victoria's case. Therefore, I make the following recommendation:

> **Recommendation**
>
> Directors of social services must ensure that the work of staff working directly with children is regularly supervised. This must include the supervisor reading, reviewing and signing the case file at regular intervals.

Child protection advisers

6.60   If local guidance was not routinely being followed in 1999 – and I have no doubt that had it been, the standard of some of the work done in Victoria's case would have been raised substantially – the child protection advisers (CPAs) ought to have provided a necessary and effective safety net. As part of the child protection, quality and review section of children and families' services, they reported direct to Ms Graham and worked independently of the children and families' teams. Petra Kitchman was one of two CPAs that covered the NTDO and had a room in that office, which she used for two days each week.

6.61　Typically, social workers or team managers would invite CPAs to give consultations and advice. CPAs had no case responsibility and would not offer advice in a case unless asked to do so, despite *Child Protection Guidelines* stating that all work in relation to child protection must be carried out in consultation with CPAs.

6.62　It was Ms Wilson's "clear expectation" that "access to a child protection adviser was the right of every social worker who was concerned on a case". It was also her expectation that advice offered by a CPA would be followed, though Ms Kitchman acknowledged that CPAs would not necessarily know whether that was the case or not. Where there was any conflict over the advice offered, it was for the team manager and CPA to resolve, and if necessary, refer the matter up through their respective line managers.

6.63　Ms Arthurworrey's understanding of the role of CPAs was less clear-cut. She acknowledged they were not routinely used in all child protection cases and believed they were only used at the specific direction of team managers. In Ms Arthurworrey's experience, a team manager would involve a CPA if there were issues that could not be resolved in supervision. While Ms Arthurworrey had used CPAs in the past, she did not make regular use of them and she did not initiate contact with Ms Kitchman in Victoria's case. Ms Arthurworrey understood her manager was responsible for her cases and she felt she "needed to get directions from her manager so that she could work in a logical way". This was not a view shared by Ms Baptiste or Ms Mairs.

6.64　Any confusion as to the role of the CPA appeared to extend to what they did when they were consulted. Ms Kitchman advised that she did not have a quality control role in relation to casework, although she acknowledged there was an element of quality assurance in relation to undertaking audits and chairing case conferences. Ms Kitchman said that it was not part of her responsibilities to monitor and evaluate the work of a social worker who approached her for advice or to ensure that they were dealing with the case properly, unless obvious concerns were noted.

6.65　Ms Wilson disagreed. She said CPAs "were an independent audit of good practice". She was quite clear that CPAs had a role in supervising the quality of the work on those cases with which they become involved. In particular, she considered CPAs "had an individual responsibility and accountability in relation to cases and that the service as a whole had a formalised quality assurance role in relation to good practice". CPAs had a "responsibility to determine what was good practice on the case in giving advice. [Ms Wilson] would not expect them to dip in and out unless they were satisfied that the way they had left the position was one of safety".

6.66　Ms Mairs believed there were no politics in using a CPA. Yet Ms Wilson observed that there was opposition to CPA involvement among a number of team managers. CPAs and team managers worked at the same operational level, but Ms Wilson was philosophical about this, stating, "It was something that we recognised as being inherent in the role and that needed to be strongly managed." Those tensions are "built into the role if you have an inspector, but that does not mean you should not have it and that it is not a very important aspect of monitoring practice". According to Ms Wilson, the fact that some team managers were undermining CPAs and that this was causing tension was not a continuous problem. There were individual issues that arose where team managers took a different perspective from a CPA, which was resolved in 95 per cent of the cases, but which needed to be confronted in a small minority of cases.

6.67　If the CPAs' role within Haringey Social Services was less than clearly defined or understood, the position was considerably worse in relation to outside agencies.

6.68　Ms Kitchman was also the link worker with the North Middlesex Hospital. Besides a general duty to liaise with other agencies, there were no established procedures or written documentation setting out what Ms Kitchman's role in relation to the North Middlesex Hospital was to be. As a result, Ms Kitchman thought her role as a link worker to the North Middlesex Hospital was rather tenuous, but believed in practice it amounted to attending liaison meetings at the North Middlesex Hospital with Dr Rossiter, Enfield Social Services and the North Middlesex Hospital social work team manager once every two months. Ms Kitchman saw her relationship with Dr Rossiter as involving liaison over specific cases, for example, at planning meetings.

6.69　Dr Rossiter said she saw Ms Kitchman as the appropriate person in social services with whom she should liaise and to whom she should report concerns. However, Ms Kitchman said she did not see herself as the sole point of contact, nor did she believe that referrals from external agencies should be made to CPAs, in effect bypassing the district offices.

6.70　Ms Mairs thought differently. She advised that CPAs were there as consultants to the public. If agencies wanted to make a referral, they could bypass the district and go straight to the CPAs, but it was important that the CPAs inform the district of that. If a CPA received information on a case that was already in a social work team, Ms Mairs would expect the CPA to discuss it with the social worker and the team manager.

6.71　Ms Green, another CPA, viewed her role as both intra and inter-departmental. Ms Green believed CPAs offered a resource to everybody, including the general public. Anybody could phone up about a child protection concern, including other agencies. Outside agencies, for example paediatricians, would contact the CPAs for advice on child protection issues or because they were concerned a case they had referred to social services was not progressing. If external agencies were frustrated with trying to work things out with social services, CPAs were a safety net and were seen as a centralised team of people who would intervene, hear the case, and make a decision about the best way forward. Sadly no such constructive action was forthcoming when Dr Rossiter sought to involve Ms Kitchman in Victoria's case, nor was it ever likely to be if managers were relying on the flawed and misunderstood guidelines and protocols operating between CPAs and DIAT social workers and CPAs and the North Middlesex Hospital. Therefore, I make the following recommendation:

> **Recommendation**
> Directors of social services must ensure that the roles and responsibilities of child protection advisers (and those employed in similar posts) are clearly understood by all those working within children's services.

Management information

6.72　Haringey's management information system provided managers with very limited help with keeping them up to date with what was going on in their teams in 1999. Its client index system, originally created as a management tool, was later adapted for team managers and service managers to manage caseloads but had yet to achieve its purpose by the time Victoria arrived in Haringey.

6.73　Mr Duncan said that in 1999 the information on the system was often inaccurate. But he accepted that was the fault of the people putting information into the system rather than with the system itself. His business plan for the NTDO, dated February 1999, stated, "Among other things, inaccurate statistics make performance targets hard to set and reach, and plans hard to develop." Dinos Kousoulou, deputy director of housing and social services, who was responsible for the management information system across the directorate, said that he was not aware of this at the time. However, the Joint Review into Haringey in 1999 noted, "The authority is aware that its current client index system is not able to support its service planning and business planning arrangements." Mr Kousoulou could not explain this inconsistency:

> "Certainly if there were these levels of problems then yes I should have been made aware, and if it was to do with the system itself, the IT system rather than the information that was meant to be put into it, then clearly that was my responsibility ... It was for managers like Dave Duncan to make sure that front-line staff used the system effectively that was there. If it was a problem with the actual technology then that should have been brought to my attention."

6.74 Ms Mairs was frustrated with the system and told the Inquiry that she did not rely on the client index system because it was always difficult getting accurate records from it and she had always used a manual system. According to her, there were monthly printouts informing managers what cases the workers had, but she said 9 out of 10 times these were not the cases that were allocated to them, or cases that were closed were still on the system. She thought there were various reasons why the system was not working in terms of the input: "It is a problem that Haringey has had for years and still has." In response, Mr Kousoulou said he was surprised and concerned that Ms Mairs had abandoned the client index system altogether during 1999 and kept some manual system of her own.

6.75 Ms Wilson said she thought the system was improving in 1999 and said, "It was coming into its own as it were in the autumn." Despite Ms Mairs's independent stand, Ms Wilson said she took the view that the client index system was no longer an optional extra: "I took a very firm and clear line that whatever the good bits or the bad bits about the system, it was the one we must use and we must get it as accurate as possible." Ms Richardson thought that, by the time she left Haringey, the client index system was still in a non-user friendly state but it could provide most of the information they had needed up to that point. Mr Kousoulou accepted, however, that the improvements that were put in place at the end of 1999 did not resolve all the difficulties, and that by April/May 2000 Haringey still had a system that was producing inaccurate results and was unable to support service planning.

Unallocated cases

6.76 One performance measure intrinsic to basic, safe, childcare practice and which, if accurate, would have provided Haringey with an instant gauge of the pressures facing its DIATs in 1999 related to its unallocated children's cases.

6.77 In May 1999, Mr Duncan reported that in the NTDO there were 61 unallocated cases and in the Hornsey office there were 48, making a total of 109 unallocated cases for which Haringey had responsibility at the time. The Joint Review from its field work in early 1999 found little evidence of unallocated cases in both district offices, although there were reports of managers holding responsibility for unallocated cases. Ms Wilson stated that it was policy for team managers to assume responsibility for unallocated cases as and when the occasion demanded it, and to delegate work on those cases to social workers where it was appropriate in light of their workloads.

6.78   The state of play on unallocated cases in May 1999 apparently was not known about at the top of office, nor were members apparently kept informed. Gina Adamou was lead member of social services at the time and she thought that the children's service was in good shape. However, Councillor Adamou said she had not seen Mr Duncan's report and she was not informed of this situation: "In May 1999 I just came in after a lapse of two years as a lead member of social services and, no, I could honestly say that I was not told at the time of this [nor did I see] this Report, but there are reports that never come to members."

6.79   Chief executive, Mr Singh, said that the information around unallocated cases was something that was routinely collected through the performance management framework. Had there been a problem he would have picked it up. It was Mr Singh's understanding that unallocated cases was not an issue at that time, further casting doubt on the value of the performance management framework he relied on.

Finances

6.80   Remedying an unreliable and inaccurate management information system was clearly an essential prerequisite to sound business planning for Haringey, particularly in the face of persistent and severe financial pressures. In 1999, these were directly linked to its decision to write off over a 10-year period a sizeable debt expended on the redevelopment of Alexandra Palace, high levels of homelessness and numbers of asylum seekers coupled with pressure from the Government to protect and increase education funding.

6.81   In fact, education had all but taken centre political stage in Haringey in 1999, following a devastating OFSTED review of Haringey's education services, which "completely condemned" the local education authority and suggested the whole of the local education authority function should be externalised.

6.82   As a result, and bowing to Government pressure, by the year 2000/2001 councillors agreed to 'passport' the entire education standard spending assessment (SSA) figure to its education services. It is not for me to judge the merits of Haringey's financial deliberations between its spending departments except to observe that children's services fared badly by comparison. For the years 1997/1998 to 2001/2002, Haringey council spent substantially less than the sum allocated in the SSA for children's social services. In 1998/1999 the gap was approximately £10m, declining thereafter not because of any significant increase in Haringey's spending on children's services, but because of changes in the way the Government estimated children's services SSA across the board. This led to a reduction in Haringey's own children's services assessment figure of just under £8m. The cut was sufficient to prompt Haringey to make complaints to Government ministers about its effect.

6.83   In the evidence of its senior managers, and in their closing submissions, Haringey council was at pains to point out that in the years 1997 to 2000 it did not consider the SSA as a valid assessment of an authority's need to spend, nor that it was a Government instruction to spend at that level. The SSA, it was said, is no more than a formula used by Government to distribute the total national spend on the basis of relative need (allowing for differences in population profiles), which can then be topped up by local authorities from council tax. Its limitations have been recognised by Government, not least the fact that it cannot take account of all the pressures facing a local authority. For example, the SSA formula took no account of the £7m a year Haringey had to spend on its statutory duty to homeless families. Accordingly, the fact that Haringey council spent considerably less than its SSA for the period 1997 to 2000 does not, in the council's view, indicate what priority Haringey council accorded children's services nor does it reveal how well resourced Haringey's children's services were compared with its needs.

6.84   I disagree. While the SSA may not be capable of encompassing all the cost pressures facing a local authority at any one time, it is unlikely to have substantially underestimated these, and certainly not to the extent of £10m for services to children and families. Arguably elements of the SSA should represent no more than the starting points in council budget deliberations, and any departures from these should be justified on the basis of local intelligence about population needs. In my view, any alternative approach to determining children's services budgets has to be at least as good as that offered by the SSA.

6.85   Haringey council claims it had such an alternative approach. The process involved the council's senior social services officers providing information to elected members about local need and local service requirements and ensuring members fully understood the council's statutory responsibilities. To do this, officers held discussions and had extensive contact with service users, other stakeholders in the borough locally, and other agencies, for example, the health service. In Haringey's view, this "local knowledge and discretion" provided a more sophisticated view of need and was therefore a better method than simply following the product of a national formula.

6.86   It would seem that neither the Joint Review of 1999 nor the SSI inspection of children's services in June 2000 agreed. The SSI found that the children and families' services were "poorly resourced in comparison to its equivalent group of councils ... We concluded that the service was underfunded." The SSI commented, "Unless the [children and families'] service is appropriately resourced a difficult situation can only get worse." The Joint Review had also recognised the funding of children and families' services as an issue.

6.87   The 1999/2000 budgetary process was also affected by the publication, in the summer of 1998, of the first Comprehensive Spending Review (CSR), which set the national local government spending totals for the period 1999/2000 to 2001/2002.

6.88   At the time, Haringey council had one of the highest council tax rates in London. In the face of an election manifesto pledge in May 1998 to keep the rate of increases in council tax below the rate of inflation, Haringey council had all but ruled out council tax increases as an extra source of revenue. In any event, the capping regime in place at the time imposed its own level of restraint.

6.89   Instead, Haringey council set a three-year savings target of £26m. In setting savings targets for individual service areas, Haringey council allocated a 'high, medium, low' prioritisation to services. The children's service received a high-priority rating, meaning it should be protected as far as possible.

6.90   According to leader of the council, George Meehan, elected members relied on social services officers to advise them on what the need was and the amount of money to spend. The Inquiry heard conflicting evidence as to whether senior social services officers advised members that Haringey's statutory obligations to children would not be capable of being fulfilled within the budgets set. Councillor Craig Turton recalled that councillors were "consistently advised by senior Haringey Social Services staff" that "The financial allocation made to children's services and to child protection was barely adequate, and unless significant year on year increases were made to the budget, the quality of services provided would inevitably suffer a significant deterioration." However, Councillor Turton acknowledged that these concerns were not recorded in minutes of meetings.

6.91   Haringey council rejected the suggestion that senior officers informed members that the proposed level of spending meant that the council's statutory duties towards children could not be met or were at dangerous levels. Ms Richardson confirmed that she "attempted to get ... the highest level of protection possible" in the 1999/2000 budget for children's services. According to Ms Richardson, the amount of saving in the whole of children's services in proportionate terms was better than the percentage taken out of other services and "the most vulnerable parts of this service we gave the maximum amount of protection to, internally". She stated that while priority was given, she did not feel happy because services were stretched. However, "The reality was that the service was treated better than other services."

6.92 Mr Singh told the Inquiry that while there were expressions of concern about the general tightness of budgets, none of the three directors of social services in post during his tenure advised him that the budgets were insufficient to enable Haringey council to discharge its statutory responsibility in the delivery of children's services. Mr Singh told the Inquiry that if this risk had been drawn to his attention, there would have been some interventions. Likewise, Councillor Meehan advised that if the director had said children's services needed more money, he has no doubt that the council would have provided more money.

6.93 Based on the evidence before me, I accept Haringey council's contention that there was no clear and explicit advice from its senior managers to spend more money on children's services in order to avoid putting at risk Haringey's proper discharge of its statutory duties and avert potential tragedy.

6.94 I do not, however, accept its conclusion that "There is not a shred of evidence that the alleged lack of funding of the children's services had any impact on the way in which Victoria's case was handled ... There was no facility to which she might have been referred to which she was not referred because of lack of funds." Victoria died because those responsible for her care adopted poor practice standards. These were allowed to persist in the absence of effective supervision and monitoring. Corners were cut and resources were fully stretched. There is evidence in plenty to support this. An easing of the financial pressures facing Haringey's children's services could only have had a positive impact on the environment in which Ms Arthurworrey was working in 1999.

Restructuring

6.95 One of the ways Haringey Social Services attempted to ease its financial pressures in 1999 was to restructure its children and families' service. It is to this restructuring exercise that I now turn. It is not the role of this Inquiry to make judgements as to whether Haringey council should have restructured, or when or what form any such restructuring should have taken. It is purely concerned with answering two questions:

- Did the restructuring exercise undertaken by Haringey in 1999 have any adverse impact on the delivery of front-line children's services and, in particular, services to Victoria?
- Could and should those adverse consequences have been foreseen by Haringey's senior management team?

6.96 The overall effect of Haringey's restructuring in 1999 was to produce larger teams with a more streamlined management structure. One of the main changes to emerge in children's services was the reduction in the number of team managers from 12 to six, and the promotion of six out of seven senior practitioners to new practice manager posts with supervisory responsibilities.

6.97 After restructuring, the two NTDO initial assessment teams merged into a single DIAT with Ms Mairs taking up the post of team manager on 8 November 1999. Ms Kozinos and Mr Almeida became two of the three practice managers, supervising their own social workers. On 5 November 1999, Ms Baptiste ceased having a management role.

6.98 In effect, there were two separate restructuring exercises: the children and families restructure, and the redirecting of the work of the housing and social services department restructure, which embraced the whole of the housing and social services department. The latter was influenced by a government agenda to modernise local government. However, Mr Lewington, a UNISON representative, stated that there was no clear indication of how the children and families restructure dovetailed with 'Redirecting the Work of the Department', or how the two separate consultation processes connected with each other.

6.99 'Children and families' was the only front-line service area that underwent any process of restructuring during 1999. Mr Lewington suggested that the thrust behind restructuring the children and families' services appeared to be to rationalise some of the structures more at second and third tier management level. When he received the consultation document, he felt the restructuring proposal was principally aimed at making savings.

6.100 Ms Bradley's perception was that there was an unstated aim to get rid of certain managers whom the council considered were incompetent and wanted to get rid of but whom had not been dealt with directly. Mr Lewington agreed that it became apparent that there was a "clear strategy to weed out those managers regarded as under performing ... To have all these issues underlying a restructuring exercise, particularly having a hidden agenda, was also bound to make this restructure problematic." Mr Duncan did not believe at the time that the restructuring was in part an attempt to get rid of some managers in whom Haringey had lost confidence. However, he told the Inquiry that in hindsight he recognised that was achieved as a by-product of restructuring the whole of children's services.

6.101 Ms Wilson confirmed that the main reasons for restructuring were the modernising agenda of the Government, the need to have a devolved management structure, and the meeting of savings target. In terms of getting rid of managers in whom the council had lost confidence, Ms Wilson acknowledged there were long-standing concerns regarding some front-line management practices, including areas of poor performance. Ms Wilson said, "We had a layer of weak managers who were not making headway in the new agenda."

6.102 In a letter to Ms Wilson dated 26 July 1999, Mr Lewington referred to "restructuring fatigue". Mr Lewington wrote this letter as a result of consultations he had with staff following the announcement of the restructuring proposals. Mr Lewington indicated that restructuring was a common occurrence in Haringey:

> "Many staff are just very tired of these exercises which have been a regular feature of life in this department in recent years. For Children and Families Teams the most recent was last year when they reorganised their front-line duty systems ... People do become stale and exhausted by constant, often ill-thought-out reorganisation. I have often thought about this department that the management approach has tended to be that when there is a problem, rather than address it directly, the response is to have another restructuring."

6.103 Mr Singh agreed that "restructuring can be used for solving ills which in fact should be dealt with through other processes and through other forms of action" because it gives the appearance of activity which may or may not bring with it changes in performance.

6.104   Similarly, Councillor Turton stated, "It seemed to be a sort of annual state of affairs that rather than actually look at a problem in-depth and allow staff to get on and do a job, we would have a cosmetic restructuring state of affairs, which would usually happen from about fourth or first tier officers." Further, Councillor Turton said, "I think it was too often the case that reorganisations are done rather than definitive action ... rather than actually addressing fundamental challenges facing social services." Philip Peatfield, an independent chair of child protection conferences and children looked after reviews, said there was restructuring of some sort or another virtually every year during the mid to late 1990s.

6.105   In response, Ms Richardson stated that, in her experience, "Haringey was a place where myths and rumours were more productive perhaps or non-productive than may be in other places. As far as I can see it was total myth, but it was firmly held from the top to the bottom of the organisation." Senior management and members' perceptions were that there had not been any major restructuring since the early 1990s.

6.106   In terms of the consultation process, a notice of impending redundancies was sent to the trade unions at the end of 1998, advising that the restructuring of the team manager posts was scheduled to take place over the course of 1999/2000. In January 1999, Mr Lewington first had discussions with Ms Wilson. In their meeting Ms Wilson did not discuss what the restructuring might involve but agreed to produce a consultation document within a month. The document was not produced until mid June 1999.

6.107   What was to be a three or four month process took about seven or eight months to effect. The stability and continuity provided by the senior practitioners might have been considered crucial during this period. At the outset, senior management assured staff that the senior practitioners were not going to be affected by the restructuring. However, on 25 June 1999, staff learned for the first time that this process was going to extend to senior practitioners, who were going to have to reapply for their jobs as well.

6.108   Ms Wilson disagreed that staff were not properly consulted. Ms Wilson said there was a very wide process of consultation and dissemination of information via the commissioning managers and the third tier managers, together with supporting material, department-wide meetings, change management seminars, team briefings, and news sheets. In addition, Ms Wilson informed the Inquiry that she regularly met with the trade union representatives, more or less every month. However, in a memorandum to Ms Richardson (copied to Ms Wilson) dated 24 June 1999, the staff in the NTDO wrote, "We would very much welcome an opportunity to discuss these proposals with you directly and therefore be given the opportunity for a true consultation rather than receive information which has already been decided upon." Further, on 7 July 1999 the senior practitioners and team managers wrote to Ms Wilson saying, "Our lack of clarity ... has been borne out of the conflicting information which we have been receiving. All decisions appear to be made and given to us on an ad hoc basis [and] the lack of clarity is beginning to have an impact on the staff morale and service users."

6.109   On 5 November 1999, Mr Lewington wrote to Ms Richardson saying, "I have to inform you that the senior practitioners are quite exasperated with the present situation, as am I. They are now unwilling to do anything further to assist the restructuring." Mr Lewington went on to say that he wanted "unequivocal clarification in writing" and he continued, "I have to say that I am increasingly of the view that many of these difficulties could be resolved by some clear planning and straightforward communication."

6.110 Ms Wilson accepted there were some issues that were much more difficult to resolve and that the goal posts changed throughout the negotiation. However, she did not accept that there was a delay in the process: "I am not trying to pretend it was lovely and it all worked smoothly ... in any process of restructuring it is about accommodation and agreement."

6.111 It is clear from the evidence of a number of witnesses that the restructuring process added considerably to the strain under which staff were working. Mr Almeida said that the NTDO was a stressful place for all social workers and their supervisors. Restructuring in 1999 and the historical restructuring added to people feeling worn down. According to Mr Lewington, the proposal for restructuring "generated a considerable amount of confusion, anger and distress in most quarters".

6.112 In July 1999, the senior practitioners and team managers in the NTDO wrote to Ms Richardson, "to express our dismay and distress at the proposals that are being made to restructure this department". Further, they said that the proposals were "potentially dangerous and detrimental to the people to whom we offer a service" and that the proposals were causing "a great deal of distress to staff across the district". A holding reply was sent on behalf of Ms Richardson, but it appears there was no substantive response to the memorandum.

6.113 Team managers were concerned because they had to apply for their own jobs in competition with colleagues and were being interviewed for a reduced number of team manager positions. For the six months between March 1999 and the end of September 1999, team managers did not know if they would have a job and social workers did not know who their long-term team managers were to be. Again, senior management and members were unaware of the low morale generated as a result of the restructuring. Mr Lewington stated that the consultation process was compressed, meaningless and seemingly inconsequential, thereby creating confusion and anxiety among staff. If Haringey had started the consultation early in the year with a view to creating these changes by September, this would have allowed a reasonably lengthy period to deal with staff concerns and to clarify the process with people. According to Mr Lewington, that did not happen, which contributed substantially to the difficulty of the process.

6.114 There was a feeling from NTDO staff that the low morale was having a knock-on effect on the service to children, and that children might be put in danger, as expressed in a memorandum of 7 July 1999 from the senior practitioners and team managers. The following is an extract from the memorandum:

> "Sadly the workers in this district office have experienced at least two incidences where children have died. The inquiries that have been held subsequent to these deaths have pointed towards issues where improvements could be made in both practice and procedures. We recall very clearly one recommendation that was made from one of these inquiries which stated that any change in the structure of the department should be well organised and should not occur during the summer months. It was envisaged that this would cause least disruption to staff, would prevent low morale and would provide a supportive and safe working environment for practitioners, ensuring that mistakes are not made."

6.115 Mr Duncan stated he would have not put it like that at the time but agreed with it in hindsight. Mr Lewington said that he never received a response from management to the concerns raised in the memorandum.

6.116   I heard evidence that the restructuring had a negative effect on staff members in the NTDO. There was a high turnover of staff during this period and Haringey lost many of its experienced and permanent staff. Recruitment was difficult because of service conditions, in particular poor remuneration, and the fact that there was a national shortage of social workers. Ms Mairs said that towards the end of 1999 experienced staff left and people became very unhappy. It was very stressful and morale was low. People were under pressure to get work done with inadequate numbers of staff. Haringey Social Services had to use agency or newly qualified staff, who were not as experienced as they ought to have been for the caseload.

6.117   Mr Lewington said he thought the restructuring was the final straw for a lot of people: "There was a big exodus of staff around that time, which began in the latter part of 1999 and continued into 2000. Haringey had a real staffing crisis, particularly in the North Tottenham Office."

6.118   Ms Kozinos also stated that there was a high turnover of staff due to the restructuring and that morale was quite low. Ms Kozinos said it was a very uncertain and unsettling time. The restructuring exercise for the DIAT began in May 1999 and was not fully implemented until about February 2000. The demands of the work never changed but the structure did and what was in place afterwards was less resourced than what was in place previously, but it was the same work demands.

6.119   Ms Mairs told the Inquiry that she did not know why Haringey underwent restructuring. She knew what she was told the purpose was, but in terms of the reality at the time, she cannot see how things improved in terms of service delivery or work morale: "The restructuring just brought chaos." Mr Almeida said that the NTDO was a stressful place for all social workers and their supervisors. Mr Duncan confirmed that he took a fairly dim view of the way in which the restructuring was handled by senior management. He advised that the restructuring process was flawed from the outset, although he thought it was acceptable at the time.

6.120   Mr Singh said in evidence that he was unaware there were repeated expressions of serious unhappiness and worries about the direction in which the restructuring proposals were taking the department. Lead member Councillor Adamou never heard any concerns from the trade unions about the restructuring process. But according to Councillor Adamou, there is never going to be universal approval for any restructuring plan and the level of discontent that she picked up from staff was at an acceptable level. Likewise, Councillor Meehan was unaware that there was a particular problem with morale arising out of the restructuring process in mid 1999.

6.121   Ms Richardson accepted the detail about the differences of opinion from staff in the NTDO, but stated, "In terms of the project as a whole, people were almost enthusiastic about it." Ms Richardson did not see the view of NTDO staff as representative of everyone. She noted that the Joint Review team in 1999 was impressed with the willingness of NTDO staff to change. Ms Richardson stated that staff did not raise any informal or formal protest to the restructure of children's services. Indeed, her view was that at the end of the day, the only people who stood to lose in this process were two team managers – and who sought voluntary redundancy rather than accept alternative employment.

6.122   Haringey council submitted: "The fact that most of the problems which the staff now attribute to this restructuring and the stresses which it caused them were not raised at the time, ought to raise doubts in your minds as to whether the picture they are now seeking to paint actually corresponds with the reality." Haringey council stated that the fact that the trade unions did not raise concerns about the restructuring in circumstances where they might have been expected to do so is significant. However, there is evidence to show staff, both collectively and through UNISON, brought concerns to the attention of senior management. Haringey in its own chronology of the reorganisation sets out the various correspondence from staff and Mr Lewington to Ms Wilson.

6.123 Ms Richardson stated that there was more than one side to the picture that was being painted in the evidence. Ms Richardson said she was sure the restructuring process had an effect on the way Victoria's case was handled, but she does not think restructuring on its own was the critical issue.

6.124 Against the backdrop of restructuring, there is plenty of evidence to suggest there was a lack of supervision available in the second half of 1999 because managers were preoccupied with preparing for their interviews. Managers were not totally focused on their duties because they were worried about keeping their jobs and the interviewing process itself.

6.125 Ms Arthurworrey stated that the restructuring created a sense of uncertainty and her morale was very low at that time. Managers had to prepare a presentation for their interviews and this preparation took place during work hours, when otherwise they would have been available to social workers. The atmosphere in the office while this restructuring process was going on was chaotic, busy and very unsettling. There appeared to be no managers available and they "were seeing different faces in the office".

6.126 Ms Baptiste, was one of those who was preparing for an interview, and she was less available than she might otherwise have been. Ms Baptiste prepared for her interview during working hours and in her spare time. Ms Baptiste said that there was not any formal time given by her seniors, nor any formal support that had been identified for staff to have that time. Ms Baptiste agreed that maybe staff should have been doing this preparation in their own time rather than during Haringey's time. With hindsight she accepted it made her less available to those for whom she was responsible. Mr Duncan confirmed there was a lot of revision to do for the interviews but no one approached him to say they needed time to prepare for the interviews or to ask if it could be done during work hours.

6.127 The apparent endorsement of Haringey's restructuring by the Joint Review in early 1999 to which I shall return at paragraph 6.145, helps little, not least because it was early days in the restructuring exercise. As lead reviewer Dennis Simpson reminded the Inquiry, the reviewers knew none of the detail of the restructuring as this had not yet been worked out beyond the top management changes. The imperative was for implementation to an explicit timetable, for it to be consultative with staff and for unnecessary delays to be avoided. The Joint Review team was undoubtedly impressed by what they perceived as the clear sense of direction and vision of the senior management team, which would be fundamental to the delivery of a restructuring with minimum disruption for staff and users alike. What the Joint Review team could not have foreseen was that the driving force behind the restructuring exercise (Ms Richardson) would leave Haringey in March 2000, barely one month after its completion in children's services and before any monitoring and evaluation of its effects could have been undertaken.

6.128 In fact, Ms Richardson was director of social services with Haringey for just under two years in total. Mr Duncan described Ms Richardson's departure as a: "captain deserting a sinking ship". Mr Duncan advised the Inquiry that, "for somebody to be the architect of such a major restructuring, throw all the cards up in the air and then run away before they all fall down" just made morale worse when it was already very low.

6.129 Having heard a considerable amount of evidence on this issue, I am quite satisfied that Haringey's restructuring exercise during 1999, and the problems in its implementation, did occupy the attention of those children's services managers and senior practitioners affected by the process to such an extent that, in Mr Duncan's words, "it may have caused them to take their eye off the ball". This was particularly apparent in the availability of managers to effectively supervise front-line practitioners at a time when real difficulties in recruitment and retention of staff were beginning to emerge and caseloads were undesirably high. More specifically, given the weaknesses already known about in Ms Baptiste's management capability, I am sure that the restructuring process did have an effect on the way Victoria's case was handled which ought to have been foreseen and compensated for as the delays, uncertainties and staff anxieties in the NTDO were making themselves known.

Recruitment and retention

6.130 Restructuring also contributed to the problems of staff recruitment and retention in Haringey. Ms Arthurworrey recalled:

> "During 1999 there was extremely low morale in the social services department. The DIATs had continual problems in recruiting and retaining experienced social workers. Social workers were continually coming and going, which resulted in the high use of locums, temporary and agency staff ... There were a number of permanent posts which were vacant due to the problems with recruitment. It was a chaotic work environment in which relatively inexperienced social workers were carrying high caseloads."

6.131 The minutes of the NTDO management team meeting held on 14 July 1999 noted that the number of vacancies in NTDO was having a major impact on services in terms of the cost of agency fees, the inconsistency of the service offered, and the instability in the staff group. Ms Wilson stated that they always had difficulties – and hence, presumably, these difficulties were predictable – before summer because staff tended to leave at that time of year. Ms Wilson did not think at that time that there were long-term staffing problems. However, towards the end of 1999 a significant number of experienced practitioners left Haringey and there was an impending staffing crisis.

6.132 Ms Baptiste said that during 1999 her team was short of probably one or two social workers, and one of the difficulties she faced as a manager was the number of inexperienced social workers in her team. Ms Mairs said that difficulties in recruiting led to the need to use agency staff and staff who were not as experienced as they ought to have been for the caseload. Ms Kozinos said this put extra pressure on managers who had to supervise them because it resulted in extra guidance, extra training and additional time invested in these people. As a consequence, services were delayed and work often had to be duplicated. There was less stability for team members as well as for service users. In Ms Robertson's view, this affected the quality of the Haringey's initial assessment team service in the second half of 1999, although she hoped that the team tried to do the best it could for service users. In the absence of effective and regular supervision in which case files were read as a matter of routine, this could have amounted to little more than an aspiration.

6.133 Mr Lewington's impression was that the atmosphere in the NTDO was bad, there was inadequate support and supervision, no clear direction from management, and "people just did not feel safe". In addition, pay levels in Haringey had fallen well behind other boroughs.

6.134 Mr Duncan held the view that people left because of restructuring, changes to pay and conditions, and more prospective cuts to the service making working conditions more difficult. According to Mr Duncan, staff leaving "was a consequence that senior management just simply had not foreseen". Ms Wilson said that senior management could not have anticipated the unstable staffing situation at the inception of the restructuring. Yet while front-line managers were clearly concerned at the impact of staffing shortages on service delivery throughout 1999, senior management did not see the problems of staff turnover and agency staffing as particularly acute until the end of 1999.

6.135 In a leader's briefing written by Ms Wilson in January 2000, she reported, "23 social work staff have left children's services since the beginning of December and more resignations are expected." The vacancies were mainly in the front-line teams and in residential work where pressure and stress was highest. In exit interviews offered at the time, two social workers gave restructuring as the reason for leaving the department. Seven expressed resentment at potential terms and conditions changes and expressed the fear of further financial instability as the borough sought to make savings.

6.136 This 'resentment' was to make itself felt in an industrial dispute involving UNISON members, which culminated in strike action in December 1999. At the heart of the dispute were discussions about proposals to implement council wide the single status agreement about terms and conditions.

6.137 In Ms Wilson's opinion, the timing of the council's decision was most unfortunate because staff were in the process of emerging from a very difficult restructuring process only to be faced with a plan to make them work "longer hours for less money". For an authority whose position in the salary league table across London was third from bottom, this would do little to contain a growing social worker recruitment and retention problem.

6.138 Mr Duncan stated, "It was a very strange decision by the council at that time to try to change the terms and conditions of staff because ... the impact in terms of morale was huge. And even if the council had secured the cuts in terms and conditions they wanted, it would not have made that much difference financially to them, so it was really a lose-lose situation for the council." While Mr Singh thought if they had achieved savings of £1m plus it would have been "a success story", Andrew Travers, head of corporate finance, conceded that their discussions about terms and conditions would not have "resulted in significant savings being achieved".

6.139 In the event, the council never made any decision to proceed with the changes to terms and conditions. However, by then the damage had been done. Staff had reacted to the uncertainty around the proposals. It was enough to lead Mr Kousoulou, acting director of social services following Ms Richardson's departure, to describe in a paper to the Policy and Strategy Committee in May 2000, that the difficulties children's services had faced in recruiting staff since the summer of 1999 had "become a haemorrhage from November to December directly linked to the industrial action after which increased numbers of staff tendered their resignation and others noted their intention to seek employment in other authorities".

6.140 In its handling of this issue it is difficult to argue any other conclusion than that Haringey was the author of many of its own misfortunes. It must remain Haringey's right to consider all the means at its disposal for meeting financial pressures. However, to embark on a course of action with the inevitable uncertainty that the prospect of change brings, without first weighing up fully all the likely benefits and costs, was nothing short of irresponsible. It seems clear to me that either no such exercise was done on this occasion, or equally concerning, Haringey council was so out of touch that it entirely misread the impact discussions on changes to terms and conditions would have in particular on its children and families' social work staff.

The Joint Review

6.141 Haringey underwent a Joint Review by the Audit Commission and the Social Services Inspectorate (SSI) in the first part of 1999. Although the fieldwork for the review was completed in February 1999 and the first feedback to managers and lead members was in April, the report of the Joint Review was not finally published until November of that year. By this time Haringey had assumed case responsibility for Victoria for some five months. The only relevance of the Joint Review to this Inquiry is the extent to which it painted a clear and accurate picture of the state of children's services in the months preceding Victoria's arrival in Haringey.

6.142 Lead reviewer Mr Simpson explained that the primary purpose of the Joint Review was to take a strategic overview of the whole of Haringey social service functions, to provide an objective assessment of how well the people of Haringey were being served, and to contribute to any further improvements in those services. Joint Reviews, he said, are to be distinguished from SSI inspections, which typically provide a detailed investigation of one particular service for one particular care group.

6.143 Haringey's Joint Review concluded that the "users of social services are generally well served". In terms of children's services, the reviewers formed the impression "of a working environment that was both challenging and rewarding for staff". The report found, "Overall, this is a service with a strong commitment to good practice, but also one that recognises that there are some inconsistencies that need to be addressed before further improvements can take place." It went on to state, "No single issue emerged during the Review that caused reviewers to have concern about the practice of child protection."

6.144 Of Haringey's senior management, the Joint Review report found:

> "There are clear signs of both management and strategic grip. The Senior Management Team gives obvious leadership, led by a chief officer [presumably Mary Richardson] with a clear sense of purpose and who has quickly gained the respect of her staff since her appointment."

> "The previous history of Haringey is a lack of strategic direction, failure to deal with difficult management issues and solutions found at the 'eleventh hour'. This position has gradually changed as greater political stability has been achieved, supported by senior officers seeking to give the service a clearer sense of purpose and direction, reinforced by the recently appointed Director and supported by the Chief Executive."

6.145 Andrew Webster, the director of Joint Reviews at the time the report was published, was quoted as follows:

> "This review suggests that Haringey has every reason to be optimistic about managing the change programme it has set in place. The council has made, and is continuing to make, positive changes in order to improve the delivery of services. However, while some examples of excellent practice are evident, greater consistency is needed in the direct provision of services. The authority is nevertheless aware of this and generally has strategies in place to take corrective action."

6.146 Haringey's own Joint Review press release was entitled "Praise for Haringey's Social Services". It stated that the report puts Haringey among the leading social services in the country, and that the residents of Haringey were receiving a good service from the council's social services department.

Reaction to the Joint Review

6.147 Not surprisingly, senior management and members were pleased with the report and were reassured by this positive overview. While they saw there were pockets of criticism and areas that needed development, overall the report concluded that Haringey Social Services were heading in the right direction. Ms Richardson said that the reviewers "were finding what we had told them was the problem, that was not news to us". Ms Richardson thought that it was an overstatement to say that many of the positive conclusions reached by the reviewers were based on future promises rather than present actions. However, she accepted that in its assessment the review took into consideration Haringey council's collective ability to take the processes forward – a collective ability that was in fact to all but disappear within 13 months of the report's publication, as the chief executive, director of social services and assistant director of children's services all moved on to presumably better jobs.

6.148 Councillor Adamou, lead member for social services from 17 May 1999 to 15 May 2000, cited the positive report from the Joint Review as the reason she thought children's services were running well. Against a background of council-wide cuts, she agreed that this Joint Review seemed, to Haringey, to be as good as it could get. Councillor Adamou said she was aware that the department had been working towards the Joint Review for a year. Internal audits were taking place in Haringey in order to assess performance. "My view was that preparation for the joint inspection and report had been lengthy and thorough," said Councillor Adamou. Accordingly, she said she knew before the report was released that its conclusions were generally favourable and that where they were not so, steps were being taken to remedy defects. She said that she heard nothing from the senior officers, in particular Ms Wilson and Ms Richardson, which indicated a different picture within social services to the one painted by the Joint Review. Likewise, Councillor Meehan, leader from May 1999, stated that his view of children's services at the end of 1999 was as set out by the Joint Review.

6.149 Others took a very different view. Mr Lewington, a UNISON representative, advised the Inquiry that the Joint Review "still sticks in my mind because it gave Haringey something of a glowing report". According to Mr Lewington, "People clearly were expecting some fairly significant criticism as a result of the Joint Review. They were quite surprised when instead the Joint Review said things were just fine." Mr Lewington stated that he thought "people felt the process had been managed in such a way that they would come up with a good report". Likewise, Mr Peatfield, an independent chair of case conferences and case reviews, said that staff were amazed when the Joint Review gave Haringey a glowing report. Mr Peatfield said he thought the report was "inconsistent with the service to families and children that one felt was being delivered, which was patchy and at times not satisfactory, and one knew the staff were struggling, one knew there were unallocated cases so it really appeared to be one of these sort of dislocations that did not make any sense". He continued, "I think workers were anxious that the department was presenting a picture of managing its task which did not feel to them to be real in terms of their struggle in performing the task."

An alternative view

6.150 In fact, as the evidence I have already referred to in this section makes clear, by November 1999, when the Joint Review was published, children's services were already beginning to become derailed. Senior managers who knew or ought to have known the position did nothing to enlighten the Review team or, it seems, members in the weeks leading up to the formal council feedback sessions in late 1999. As a result, and as events were subsequently to demonstrate all too graphically, the Joint Review's "lasting impression of a service not likely to be blown off course as new service configurations are put in place and management changes are implemented" could not have been more misplaced.

6.151 Two months after Victoria's death in February 2000, an internal review of district cases highlighted serious practice failings verging on the acute and dangerous in the Hornsey office. These included procedures routinely not being followed, an absence of timescales, investigations not being recorded, little evidence of multi-agency planning particularly in family support cases, and cases left to drift.

6.152 Seven months after the Joint Review report came out, there was a detailed inspection of Haringey's children's services by the SSI that was highly critical. I have already referred to its conclusions on Haringey's resourcing of its service. In addition, the SSI found "a service to be seriously understaffed at both practitioner and managerial level". It found:

> "North Tottenham had suffered particularly badly with 47 per cent vacancies overall and 33 per cent of management posts vacant. Although some two-thirds of social worker posts were covered by agency staff this had adversely affected the service. Social workers reported that supervision and support had been compromised when restructuring had initially been implemented ... The situation had improved but there was still a serious shortfall in front-line management availability. This was bound to adversely affect decision making and quality control.

> "The high level of management vacancies coupled with the relative inexperience of many new practice managers was putting enormous strain on the few experienced team managers and the commissioning manager.

> "Morale in the two district teams was reported to be poor and there was a risk that an already difficult staffing situation could spiral downwards. We also had concerns about the quality of some of the practice that we observed.

> "On the other hand we found a significant number of managers and staff who were committed to the service and capable with reasonable resources of seeing the service through its current difficulties."

6.153 The deterioration in Haringey's children and families' service was to culminate in the authority being placed on special measures by the Department of Health on 12 January 2001.

6.154 Inevitably this sequence of events raises a number of questions as to the factors that might account for the change in Haringey's children's services between the perceived 'positive' report of the Joint Review, and the more critical SSI inspection seven months later.

Was the Joint Review wrong?

6.155 Haringey Social Services have repeatedly said that they were entitled to rely on the Joint Review as being an accurate reflection of the state of their children's services in early to mid 1999, but that over the course of the next year or so the service deteriorated, in some areas substantially. They pointed to Victoria's death and huge staff losses during that period, including the director leaving and the effect this had on morale.

6.156 Mr Singh said he depended on external reviews to tell him what was actually happening and "It is perfectly reasonable for me to expect a Joint Review conducted by two reputable bodies, SSI and Audit Commission, to actually be reliable and that gave myself and indeed members of the authority considerable comfort in a very difficult environment that we were operating in."

6.157 Mr Singh went on to state that despite the subsequent poor SSI report, "you cannot simply ignore the positive stuff which came out of the Joint Review as if that also has no bearing on the matter." He continued:

> "Yes, there was a clear condemnation arising out of the children's inspection, but literally a year prior to that there was a glowing response on social services generally. Now that just cannot be disregarded as if it did not happen. That was also a statement about the quality of services which Haringey was providing in the social care area."

Mr Singh said that he did not rely solely on the Joint Review Report as a source of information.

6.158 An alternative explanation could be that the Joint Review simply got it wrong in 1999 and the reality was worse than as portrayed in their report. It was an explanation that John Bolton, head of the Joint Review team, certainly canvassed. Five days after Kouao and Manning were convicted of Victoria's murder and Haringey were placed on special measures, he was quoted in an interview reported for *Community Care* magazine as saying:

> "It is possible that we may have made a mistake and that is a cause for enormous regret. We just don't know ... At the same time, this is a huge tragedy, and we hope that we did not contribute to any complacency in the department."

Reviewing the Joint Review

6.159 In January 2001, unbeknown to Haringey, the Audit Commission and SSI decided to review the processes that had been used by the Haringey Joint Review in order to determine whether there were areas for improvement and to "assist in the governance of both organisations". The authors of the new internal review, David Prince (the auditor's director of operations) and Jennifer Gray (a childcare specialist in the SSI), were quite clear that their task was to "follow in the footsteps" of the Joint Review team and examine how their judgements were reached relative to the evidence they had collected. It was not their role to re-perform the Joint Review's work or second-guess the conclusions of the Joint Review team.

6.160 Mr Prince described it as "a special light-touch quality control review" that focused on the methodology and not the findings of the Joint Review. Special because it had never been done before, light-touch in the sense that it was to be quick and focused on improvements, and quality control to see if anything could be learned from it.

6.161 Nonetheless, whatever their initial brief, both the report of the internal review and the witness statements, particularly of Ms Gray, an inspector with specialist knowledge of childcare practice, called into question some of the initial Joint Review findings and raised potentially concerning aspects of Haringey's children's service, which in Ms Gray's view were not adequately expressed in the Joint Review report. It should be noted they were asked to look only at the children's services, which were only a part of the original Joint Review exercise and report.

6.162   The relevance of this new internal review evidence to the Inquiry (and which was to form the subject matter of the re-opened Phase One hearings) was three-fold:

- First, what additional light did the internal review throw on the state of children's social services in Haringey in early 1999?
- Secondly, what did it suggest Haringey knew or ought to have known about the state of those services – in particular, were Haringey entitled to rely on the Joint Review as an accurate picture of their children's services?
- Thirdly, should the Joint Review have been framed differently and, had it been written differently, would Haringey have changed the way it dealt with cases like Victoria's?

6.163   Mr Prince sought, at the end of his oral evidence, to distance himself from the conclusions of the internal review – a review approved by him and accepted in full by both the SSI and Audit Commission as the sponsoring departments. He did this by asking the Inquiry to disregard any judgements contained in the internal review about the state of Haringey's children's services. This was surprising and in no way reduced the need for this Inquiry to test the validity of the internal review's conclusions.

6.164   In his written and oral evidence, lead joint reviewer Mr Simpson went some way towards accepting the criticism that the Joint Review should have more clearly expressed concerns about practice. At several points in his statement Mr Simpson indicated that, were he writing the report now, he would have placed more emphasis on the need for more consistency in the provision of services, along with the need to improve some services which had fallen below an acceptable standard.

6.165   He also said that the principal deficiency with the Joint Review was that insufficient attention was drawn at the start and the finish of the report to the practice deficiencies. Nonetheless, these were identifiable on a close reading of the body of the report as a whole. Indeed, he felt that the Joint Review report was "encouraging of management, but not to the detriment of dealing with poor monitoring data, poor practice, the need to improve practice guidance to front-line staff, improve case recording, make supervision and performance appraisal more comprehensive, deal with significant budget problems and cope with increased demand for children's services. Hardly a report which shirked from identifying issues related to practice and direct service provision".

6.166   That the Management Action Plan drawn up by Haringey in response to the Joint Review contained 40 action points designed to address deficiencies in practice in children's services was illustrative, according to both Mr Simpson and Haringey Counsel, not only of the fact that the Joint Review had raised these practice deficiencies (and therefore the review could not be said to be overly positive), but that Haringey knew about them and were going to respond to them.

6.167   The most detailed assessment of the state of children's services in early 1999 from Haringey's perspective came from the evidence of Ms Wilson. She, in common with Ms Richardson, had no doubt that there was considerable room for improvement in their children's services at the time. There was, she says, "Still a lot of work to be done."

6.168   Of the extracts from the Joint Reviewers' notebooks on which she commented in her evidence, those concerning the lack of infrastructure, the delays in transferring cases to long-term teams, the pressures faced by the north Tottenham DIATs and the closure of family support cases, were all identified as broadly consistent with her understanding of the state of the service at the time. The findings of the Joint Review, she said, did not come as a surprise to her and reflected much of what Haringey already knew, as identified in the Position Statement prepared in November 1998. Yet despite in Mr Simpson's words the "sack full of work remaining to be done", she submitted that Haringey's children's services in early 1999 were successfully managing their limited resources, and fulfilling their statutory obligations to children and families in the borough contrary to any alternative indication that may have been given by the authors of the internal review.

6.169 Having considered this matter carefully, I come to the view that the internal review, and the evidence of its authors, did little to undermine the conclusions of the original Joint Review Report. As a consequence, the Joint Review, read in its entirety, continues to be the best available evidence as to the state of Haringey's children's services in early 1999. More significantly, I accept Mr Simpson's view that the Joint Review was not as complimentary of the authority as portrayed. While a better balanced report would have emphasised more clearly the service and practice deficiencies in the summary and conclusions, these messages and the actions needed to address them were there in the detail of the report and should have mirrored what Haringey's own management information system was telling them. To that extent, and that extent only, Haringey's senior management and members could justifiably rely on the Joint Review.

6.170 Despite the encouraging headlines, there were substantial detailed criticisms of various aspects of the services in the Joint Review Report. In my view, Haringey did no more than pay lip service to the detail of the report, choosing instead to play to the positive headlines of the Joint Review as was so clearly demonstrated by the evidence of the chief executive and lead members, and by their own press statement. That Haringey listed the concerns raised by the review team in their management action follow-up plan, confirms that they were aware of these issues. The urgency with which those actions were followed through, however, was totally absent. A good illustration of this, and one of particular relevance to Victoria's case, was the potential 'burn out' of staff in north Tottenham to which Haringey's attention was drawn by the Joint Review team as early as April 1999. According to Ms Wilson, this was addressed by a series of 'interim' measures and was still being addressed according to Haringey's management action plan in September 2000, some seven months after Victoria's death. Other concerns raised by the Joint Review were dealt with no more speedily.

6.171 In short, it is my view that those senior managers and lead members could and should have known about the serious deficiencies in Haringey's children's services in early 1999. Furthermore, the gap between the reality for the front-line practitioners in the NTDO children and families' service and the positive impressions of the Joint Review team, were left unchallenged by senior officers. The result was a lack of any real political will and sustained managerial drive to bring about the necessary improvements in the service.

Victoria in Haringey

Referral

6.172 Haringey Social Services first learned of Victoria's admission to the North Middlesex Hospital on Saturday 24 July 1999 – the day she was admitted.

6.173 That evening, it was Luciana Frederick's turn to single-handedly cover the out-of-hours duty for the whole of Haringey Social Services. She started her 12-hour shift at 6.30pm and some time between 8pm and 9pm, according to her report form, she answered a telephone call from Dr Simone Forlee. In fact, the social services duty call log shows that a telephone message from Dr Forlee was taken at 8.42pm and was passed to Ms Frederick as the duty social worker an hour later.

6.174 Ms Frederick does not remember the telephone conversation, but she believes that the report form which she completed at the time – the only record of the telephone conversation that exists – is a concise summary of the information Dr Forlee gave her.

6.175 Ms Frederick noted:

"– child admitted to hospital – concerns about injury caused by hot water poured onto face causing facial burns;
– it appeared to be an accident, however, mother may need support;
– advice given – doctor agreed to discuss case with the hospital social worker the following day;
NFA [no further action]."

6.176 Dr Forlee disagreed with Ms Frederick's summary in one material respect. She did not recollect describing Victoria's injury as appearing to be an accident and believed she told Ms Frederick that she had admitted a child about whom she had concerns.

6.177 We cannot be certain what passed between the two because of the lack of recorded information – indeed in the case of the hospital there was none whatsoever – or whether Ms Frederick simply misunderstood what Dr Forlee was saying. That Dr Forlee had telephoned social services out of hours suggested a degree of concern about Victoria's injuries. This was understandable. Ms Frederick told the Inquiry that she made "concise notes" but admitted it would have been helpful if she had made a full recording specifying Dr Forlee's concerns. Ms Frederick accepted that more detail could have been put in her recording of the conversation, but stated, "The relevant detail is there."

6.178 Both Dr Forlee and Ms Frederick agreed that because Victoria was "safe in hospital" and there appeared to be no immediate risk of her being removed, there was no need that evening for any further investigative action, including seeing Victoria. Dr Forlee was also told to contact the hospital social work team "the following day". Since the referral came in late on Saturday night and there was no hospital social work team working on Sunday, that meant in reality a delay until Monday morning. Ms Frederick admitted that the following day was "probably not appropriate".

6.179 Working from home, Ms Frederick was in no position to do any checks to see if Victoria was known to social services or on the child protection register. She stated that she assumed – though she did not pursue this with Dr Forlee – that these checks would have been done by the hospital, which had access to the names of children on the child protection register and by the hospital social work team, as part of any follow-up.

6.180 Ms Frederick subsequently faxed the report form to the out-of-hours office for filing. She said that if there had been a clear indication of child protection concerns – especially if there had been no other professional involved – she would have made the referral herself direct to the duty team at the NTDO and undertaken whatever was necessary that evening to secure the child's safety. Ms Frederick stated that she had no doubts about what she should do if child protection concerns had been raised.

6.181   As a result of the decision to take no further action and because Victoria's injury "appeared to be an accident", the out-of-hours referral report was consigned to a filing cabinet. No copy was forwarded to the hospital social work team to put them on alert, nor to the local district duty, investigation and assessment team who may have held information about the child and family. Also, there was no system in place to ensure that Dr Forlee made contact with the hospital social work team as advised or that, once in the out-of-hours office filing cabinet, this referral could be automatically linked to any future referral. Ms Frederick accepted that if Dr Forlee had not been on duty on Monday or had forgotten to make the referral to the hospital social worker, the information from Saturday evening may never have got to the hospital social work team or Haringey Social Services. Therefore, I make the following recommendation:

> **Recommendation**
> The chief executive of each local authority with social services responsibilities must ensure that specialist services are available to respond to the needs of children and families 24 hours a day, seven days a week. The safeguarding of children should not be part of the responsibilities of general out-of-office-hours teams.

Contacting the North Middlesex Hospital

6.182   Karen Johns, the hospital social worker, telephoned Caroline Rodgers, the duty social worker at Haringey Social Services, at about 4.30pm. Having accepted the referral, responsibility for Victoria's case transferred to Haringey Social Services at that stage. She recorded key details about Victoria's admission to the North Middlesex Hospital as follows:

- mum brought Anna to the A&E at about 5.25pm on Sat 24th July;
- Anna had burns to head and face;
- mum says Anna has scabies that are being treated by the Central Middlesex Hospital;
- mum heard Anna scream at about 12 noon. She found that Anna had poured hot water over her head (from the tap) to stop the itching on her head;
- next day the nurse who had bathed Anna on Rainbow ward saw old marks on Anna's body;
- until then staff did not suspect physical abuse but they now feel sure the marks are non-accidental;
- Dr Forlee suggests that the marks look like they were done by a belt buckle;
- Anna seems slightly nervous of mum and "seems on edge when mum visits". Ward staff described how she "jumps to attention" when mum appears;
- Anna also wets herself when mum is there;
- on admission Anna appeared unkempt, dirty dress and no underwear. Mum has brought no clean clothes since Anna's admission.

6.183   Ms Rodgers's good sense in following up the referral with a request for full information from the Central Middlesex Hospital is quite clear. She could no longer recall whether she spoke to Dr Schwartz, the consultant in charge of Victoria's case at the Central Middlesex Hospital, or someone else, though her normal practice would have been to go direct to the hospital social worker or possibly to staff in the accident and emergency department.

6.184   Two days later, the Central Middlesex Hospital faxed back several pages of relevant documentation. There is some doubt as to how many pages were faxed across but it is accepted that at the very least the documents seen by Haringey Social Services included a general trauma form dated 14 July 1999, a paediatric assessment record, ongoing communication sheets, a body map and a 'medical report on a child thought to have suffered abuse'.

6.185   However, it is unlikely that Ms Rodgers read any of this material because she said she found it illegible and "could not read it". Regrettably, she made no attempt to ask the Central Middlesex Hospital for help in clarifying its contents. If she had, she would have learned that Victoria had been brought to the hospital by her childminder's daughter, that Kouao was desperate to leave Victoria with the childminder "for good", and that Victoria was not attending school. The medical report identified that there were scars of various sizes and ages all over the body from two days to possibly months old. There were also fresh scars on the face, infected cuts on the fingers and bloodshot eyes. Victoria was said to have cut herself with a razor blade in the past, that she wet herself and that when she arrived at the hospital she was unkempt and had a pungent smell.

6.186   By the time the NTDO received the Central Middlesex Hospital fax – and judging by the date stamp this could have been as late as 2 August 1999 – Ms Jacob, the team manager on duty on 27 and 28 July, had already, though late in the day, arranged a strategy meeting in Victoria's case.

6.187   Having read the details set out in the referral form, Ms Jacob considered that "this could probably have been a child protection case" which needed to be explored further. As was standard practice, she then completed and signed off an action plan on 27 July which included:

- logging the case onto the computer – this was to be done by the duty administrative clerk;
- referring the case to the police child protection team;
- arranging the strategy meeting;
- completing checks with the GP and Central Middlesex Hospital and school, if open.

6.188   Ms Jacob completed the second and third of these herself the following morning. The expectation was that others in the duty team would finish the tasks, in particular that Ms Rodgers would continue her checks of the Central Middlesex Hospital, as she had already made a start on this. Health and education checks were done as a matter of routine – these showed no record of either a GP or a school for Victoria – but no similar checks would have been done of housing unless this had been identified as a problem.

6.189   According to Ms Jacob, once the case was logged, the file would be returned and placed in the specific basket labelled "urgent action". Duty workers were expected to deal with these as a matter of priority and could check with the duty manager if actions still needed to be completed.

The July strategy meeting

6.190   Ms Jacob said in evidence that the decision to call a strategy meeting was reached jointly with the police and the meeting was arranged for 2.30pm on Wednesday 28 July 1999. She was aware that another strategy meeting had already been fixed for 2pm at the NTDO, which the police were expected to attend. She therefore arranged this meeting to follow on directly at the social services office – on the face of it a sensible and convenient arrangement, at least for the police. However, Haringey's local child protection guidelines (known as the Purple Book), clearly stated that "in the event of the child being in hospital the [strategy] meeting must be held in the hospital".

6.191 There is no record of any challenge to Ms Jacob's decision to hold the strategy meeting at the social services office by the police, Ms Rodgers or Ms Johns, though all would, or should, have been familiar with the contents of the Purple Book. However, Ms Johns said that she did question the choice of location on the grounds that the doctors would be unlikely to attend, but that Ms Jacob said, after checking with her manager, that it would not be possible to change the meeting venue. Ms Jacob did not recall this conversation.

6.192 As it happens, the procedures drawn up by Ms Mairs for the day-to-day running of the DIAT in north Tottenham, already prescribed, by agreement with the police, that strategy meetings would take place on Tuesday and Wednesday afternoons and Friday mornings. According to Ms Jacob, the duty team was never fully staffed and rationalising the times when meetings were held was seen as a sensible means of managing the duty system with the resources available. She says there was a presumption that strategy meetings would be held in the office for the same reason but argues that the DIAT procedures did not preclude such meetings taking place in the hospital if necessary, and some did.

6.193 The Purple Book also makes clear that if there is to be any divergence from the procedures, this needs to be endorsed by the team manager and recorded on the file. There is nothing on the case file to suggest that on this occasion an endorsement to hold the strategy meeting outside the hospital was ever sought from, or given by, a manager.

Attendees

6.194 Invited to the strategy meeting on 28 July 1999 were Ms Johns, the initial referrer, and the police from the Haringey Child Protection Team. Ms Jacob said, ideally, she would have wanted the medical staff to attend too, but she cannot recall whether they were invited or indeed whether she asked Ms Johns to do that on her behalf. Ms Johns is clear that had she been asked to issue invitations to the medical staff she would have done so. She did not know who invited Dr Rossiter to the strategy meeting, but she implied in her evidence that it was Haringey.

6.195 In fact, four people attended: Ms Kozinos, a senior practitioner in the DIAT A, who chaired the meeting, Ms Johns from the North Middlesex Hospital social work team, PC Karen Jones from Haringey police Child Protection Team, and Ms Rodgers. None of the nursing or medical staff at the North Middlesex Hospital who had had daily care of Victoria were present, and none of those who were there had seen Victoria, let alone spoken to her, or to Kouao.

6.196 Ms Jacob told the Inquiry that it was her expectation that Ms Johns would represent the hospital and that she would pass on any information that the medical staff wished to share and would bring with her to the meeting the relevant medical reports. She saw nothing unsatisfactory about this arrangement.

Running the meeting

6.197 Ms Kozinos said she was asked to chair the strategy meeting at short notice. She was not on duty that week and would not have expected to chair strategy meetings in new, unallocated cases, and she went into the meeting without first reading the referral completed by Ms Rodgers. Apparently, this was common practice. Ms Kozinos said, "We normally go into strategy meetings cold unless we were the person who took the referral and had knowledge of it on duty." Ms Kozinos expected Ms Rodgers to update those present with any current concerns. These were then recorded, together with the meeting's decisions and recommendations, on a paper strategy meeting record.

6.198   Ms Kozinos was not aware of the substance of Victoria's referral and so could not have realised that the location of the strategy meeting was inappropriate. Once the meeting started, she did not take steps to adjourn the meeting to the hospital so that the medical staff could more easily attend. She told the Inquiry, "I felt we needed to proceed – we had sufficient information and it needed urgent action. There are suggestions of physical abuse, neglect which I felt needed investigating."

6.199   When pressed, Ms Kozinos confirmed that difficulties in getting police to attend strategy meetings had become an issue because, for a variety of reasons, posts in the police child protection team were not being covered. The stacking up of strategy meetings was therefore not unknown.

6.200   Strategy meetings were supposed to be chaired by team managers or child protection advisers. Yet Ms Kozinos told the Inquiry it was common practice at the time for senior practitioners to chair strategy meetings. It is not clear whether what had become common practice in north Tottenham – and was endorsed by north Tottenham's DIAT procedures – was indeed common practice across both district offices. In her evidence to the Inquiry, Ms Wilson, the assistant director for children's services, said this was not her understanding of the position before November 1999, as it was only then that agreement was reached as to the role of the new practice managers, who were to replace the senior practitioners.

6.201   There is some doubt as to exactly what information was available to the strategy meeting on 28 July 1999. It now seems certain that the faxed material from the Central Middlesex Hospital arrived too late. Ms Johns said, and in this she is supported by PC Jones, that she brought along three copies of documents from the North Middlesex Hospital. These included child protection forms, accident and emergency notes and a body map. Ms Rodgers also recalled seeing the body map and Ms Johns giving them copies. However, Ms Kozinos thought Ms Johns had not brought any medical reports with her but could no longer recall what indeed she had brought. By the time Ms Arthurworrey, the social worker allocated to Victoria's case, first received the file on 2 August 1999, she claimed that no such North Middlesex Hospital documentation was included. However, the evidence I shall refer to later suggests otherwise.

Concerns and recommendations

6.202   The sense of the meeting at the end, at least from the social services perspective, was that the cause of Victoria's scalding injuries was uncertain and that this was a child protection case that needed to be investigated thoroughly.

6.203   The strategy meeting recorded the concerns as:

> "Mum – Marie-Therese Kouao brought Anna to North Middlesex Hospital on 24th July at 5.25 saying that the child had poured hot water over her head. Child has scabies and is very itchy and mum said that hot water was supposed to stop itching. Child admitted to Rainbow ward. Nurse noticed old marks on body – Dr Forlee suggests that they look like old belt buckle marks. Skeletal survey carried out – no results as yet. Delay in mother taking child to hospital. Also concerns re neglect, child very unkempt – mother was not."

6.204   It also agreed the following 18 recommendations:

> "i)   Dr Forlee examining paediatrician expressing concerns re previous NAI (shaped like belt buckle). Obtain medical report re their concerns. Also need to state how old injuries are.

ii) Obtain skeletal reports for further information.

iii) Mother to be informed of referral to social services.

iv) Obtain report from hospital social worker re concerns of neglect.

v) Hospital social worker to inform social services when child ready for discharge.

vi) Staff nurses/hospital to monitor contact with mother and child and report back any concerns.

vii) Once we have medical reports arrange joint visit with PCPT and explain fully our child protection procedures to mother.

viii) Need to obtain much more information re scabies – how is this obtained? Is it linked to issues of neglect?

ix) Check with Central Middlesex Hospital for further information.

x) Social services need to carry out a full investigation and assessment.

xi) Social services need to complete checks re schooling and GP.

xii) Hospital social worker to inquire re hospital photographs – can this be given to social services and police.

xiii) Arrange interpreter when completing assessment.

xiv) Interview of mother needs to address – a) recent incident, b) old injuries, and c) neglect issues.

xv) Allocate to DIAT.

xvi) Child to remain in hospital. If mum attempts to take her, hospital to contact us.

xvii) Complete checks in France – international services.

xviii) PCPT to complete immigration checks."

6.205 By the end of the strategy meeting, and in the absence of a clear, written, diagnosis of non-accidental injury by a doctor, no decision was made to proceed to a child protection case conference at that stage. No explicit directions were recorded as to who would carry out the 18 tasks agreed, no timescales were settled, neither was a review date set to monitor progress. Ms Kozinos said that it was understood by all present that tasks not allocated to other agencies would be done by the allocated case worker from the NTDO, though no such person had yet been identified. It was also not the practice in Haringey at the time to hold a review of strategy meetings. The expectation was that decisions and recommendations would be reviewed in supervision between the responsible team manager and allocated social worker – an expectation that was to prove misplaced.

6.206 Ms Kozinos had no further contact with Victoria's case until November 1999.

Allocation of Victoria's case

6.207 On 30 July 1999, Ms Baptiste, the manager for the B investigation and assessment team based at Haringey's NTDO, allocated the case to Ms Arthurworrey, a social worker in her team. In deciding who to allocate the case to, she said she believed

Ms Arthurworrey had space for several more cases but said nothing about her assessment, if any, of Ms Arthurworrey's capacity and experience to tackle such a case.

6.208   In fact, by the time Ms Arthurworrey picked up Victoria's case, she had had 19 months' post-qualification experience and half her caseload was composed of child protection cases. Yet despite this, she had yet to complete a joint section 47 child protection inquiry with the police or a section 47 inquiry about a child in hospital.

6.209   August was also to prove one of Ms Arthurworrey's busiest months. She had a workload of 19 cases, including Victoria's – seven more than the maximum to be held by staff in the investigation and assessment team according to the local procedures handbook. Ms Arthurworrey said that most of these cases were "active" and she "was on the go all day long with no time to reflect".

6.210   Ms Arthurworrey told the Inquiry that she was not on duty the day the case was allocated to her but found the papers on her desk on 2 August 1999. The case file contained:

- the referral of 27 July as recorded by Ms Rodgers;
- the strategy meeting notes;
- a faxed message from Dr Schwartz to Ms Rodgers, dated 28 July requesting that Ms Rodgers contact her urgently;
- a fax from Ms Rodgers to the medical records library;
- a first contact sheet showing no records of a GP or school.

6.211   Although not at the strategy meeting, Ms Arthurworrey did not think she needed to speak to either Ms Rodgers or Ms Kozinos to clarify the decisions they had reached. Nor did she pursue with Ms Rodgers whether she had in fact contacted Dr Schwartz – Ms Rodgers told us she was not aware of ever having seen the fax – or what response if any had been received from the medical records library.

6.212   However, she did speak to her manager, Ms Baptiste, who told her that this was "a case about a child who was in hospital with scabies" and that she should implement the strategy meeting decisions. No date was set to review her progress in completing these tasks, nor did Ms Arthurworrey think it was her job to suggest such a review.

6.213   Ms Arthurworrey said she understood from the outset that she was dealing with a section 47 investigation. She also knew from the papers that Victoria was 'safe' in hospital at the time of the referral the previous week and that the hospital had been asked to notify social services when Victoria was ready for discharge or if Kouao attempted to remove her prematurely.

6.214   In her case file contact sheets, Ms Arthurworrey sets out 11 of the 18 strategy meeting recommendations for completion. These included obtaining a medical report from Dr Forlee, which covered the hospital's concerns regarding previous non-accidental injuries, as well as a report from the hospital of its concerns of any neglect. Both of these, Ms Arthurworrey told us, were necessary before visiting Victoria, "because social services rely on evidence from the hospital into the causes of a child's injuries and we need to know what we are dealing with".

6.215   Ms Arthurworrey makes no mention in the contact sheets of at least four strategy meeting decisions that, on the face of it, she needed to complete. These were to:

- obtain skeletal reports for further information;

- check with the Central Middlesex Hospital for further information;
- obtain more information about scabies; and, most importantly,
- carry out a full investigation and assessment.

6.216 While I accept Ms Arthurworrey's evidence that she was clear when she was allocated the case that she was dealing with a section 47 investigation and that she had to complete the tasks outlined in the strategy meeting, I am far from satisfied with the way she then went about this, and the way Haringey as an organisation allowed her to do so.

6.217 I heard no evidence of what I would term a section 47 inquiry ever being carried out by Haringey Social Services. I deal with the failure of the police to conduct a criminal investigation later in section 14. At the very least, after the strategy meeting, Ms Arthurworrey should have spoken to Ms Kozinos, its chair, to go through the recommendations in detail. I am also surprised that she chose not to speak to Ms Rodgers, especially in light of the 'urgent' message from Dr Schwartz that was on the file. I believe that this initial 'inaction' by Ms Arthurworrey was based on her assumption that Victoria was 'safe' in hospital.

6.218 On 3 August 1999, Ms Johns sent Ms Arthurworrey a note by fax. In it Ms Johns said that she had been informed by the nurse in charge of Rainbow ward (Nurse Isobel Quinn) that Victoria was ready for discharge, and that the ward would like that to happen as soon as possible. The fax also made clear that Victoria's scabies had been successfully treated.

'Fit for discharge'?

6.219 At the time, Ms Arthurworrey says she understood the phrase 'fit for discharge' to mean that the hospital no longer had any concerns about Victoria in the general sense. By contrast, several hospital staff in their evidence to the Inquiry said that 'fit for discharge' meant that Victoria was medically fit to leave and they assumed the social workers would make the necessary inquiries of her home and family before that actually happened.

6.220 In response to Ms Johns's fax, Ms Arthurworrey telephoned Nurse Quinn. It appears to have been a fairly lengthy call. Among other things, Ms Arthurworrey said that she was told by Nurse Quinn (and recorded in her contact sheet for 3 August 1999) about Victoria's behaviour in Kouao's presence ("she appeared to come straight to attention"), that the hospital accepted the explanation that Victoria had sustained the burns by pouring hot water over her own head "from a kettle" to relieve the itching caused by scabies, that there were concerns about a discrepancy between the timing of the incident and Victoria's arrival at hospital, that the hospital had noticed old injuries on Victoria's body, which appeared to be non-accidental, and therefore the hospital had concerns about these as well as Kouao's response to the accident. In evidence Ms Arthurworrey also said that Nurse Quinn mentioned that Dr Rossiter had carried out a ward round, possibly on 1 August, and had noticed signs of deliberate emotional harm – a 'master-servant' relationship between Victoria and Kouao.

6.221 Nurse Quinn's recollection of the telephone conversation is somewhat different in one material respect. Like Dr Forlee, she denied ever saying that the hospital was satisfied with Kouao's explanation for the burns. Rather she claimed to have said precisely the opposite, in other words, that there were remaining concerns about how Victoria received the scalding injuries.

6.222 Nurse Quinn recorded in the critical incident log that she had spoken to Ms Arthurworrey, that Ms Arthurworrey needed to make a home visit before Victoria could go home, and that she had requested Nurse Quinn fax through any concerns the hospital had. Given that on 1 August 1999 Dr Rossiter had already come to the view that Victoria's scalding injuries were self inflicted, it seems highly unlikely that Nurse Quinn, as the nurse in charge of Rainbow ward, did communicate to social services two days later a different hospital view to that of the consultant paediatrician responsible for Victoria. I therefore conclude that, in early August, social services were left with the impression that the hospital had accepted Kouao's explanation for the scalding injuries.

6.223   Nurse Quinn also sent across a fax which Ms Arthurworrey believed would address **all** the hospital's concerns and meet two of the strategy meeting recommendations, namely to obtain a medical report from Dr Forlee and to obtain further information from the hospital regarding neglect.

Nurse Quinn's fax

6.224   Contained in the fax were three of the local child protection forms (CP1, 2 and 3) signed by Dr Forlee, and a letter from Nurse Quinn summarising ward staff observations regarding emotional neglect. Ms Arthurworrey accepts that she did not notice that the date on which the child protection forms had been completed – 24 July 1999 – preceded the strategy meeting and therefore could not possibly be said to meet the strategy meeting recommendation for an updated medical report.

6.225   Moreover, the child protection forms, a body 'diagram' and accident and emergency department notes (all on the Haringey file) were, according to Ms Johns and PC Jones, already available from the strategy meeting. In addition, the Haringey file contained a copy of the North Middlesex Hospital paediatric assessment form. Ms Arthurworrey maintained that she never saw any of the medical material until she received the fax from Nurse Quinn. However, she could not remember how many pages Nurse Quinn sent her. Nurse Quinn told me that the documentation she sent to Ms Arthurworrey consisted of a cover sheet, her handwritten note, child protection form CP1, and probably also child protection forms CP2 and CP3, making a total of six pages in all. If, as seems likely, and contrary to Ms Arthurworrey's earlier evidence, she already had in her possession on 2 August a set of child protection forms, a paediatric assessment form, an accident and emergency department form and a set of body maps, only Nurse Quinn's memo summarising ward staff observations about emotional neglect would have constituted new medical evidence.

6.226   In addition, there was some doubt as to which version of the CP3 form Ms Arthurworrey was sent. Judging from the timing on the fax header sheet, it seems probable that the CP3 form she received was the one confusingly annotated by Dr Rossiter on 1 August 1999 in which she drew an arrow from the box ticked by Dr Forlee 'I wish to await further information before committing myself' to the tick box immediately above 'I consider the incident is likely to be non-accidental' and added the following words "what is uncertain is the category".

6.227   Ms Arthurworrey accepted that it is likely she saw this version but did not recall noticing Dr Rossiter's endorsement which, although unspecific, mentioning neither belt buckle marks nor any suggestion of deliberate physical harm, did at least suggest it was "likely to be non-accidental".

6.228   Ms Arthurworrey told the Inquiry she believed that Nurse Quinn's fax summarised the hospital's concerns in their entirety and, in that sense, superseded the information contained in the initial referral. But even if true, and Ms Arthurworrey had grounds for believing this, by 3 August 1999 she was aware from her conversation with Nurse Quinn that there were unresolved questions about old and possibly non-accidental injuries. Although I conclude that anyone reading the documentation provided by the North Middlesex Hospital would have been very hard pressed to find any indication that the hospital suspected deliberate physical harm, she had been given up-to-date information about the hospital's concerns regarding deliberate emotional harm.

6.229   What she did not have were any medical photographs of Victoria. Ms Johns had already faxed over a memo annotated by Dr Maud Meates, which suggested that although ordered, none had yet been taken, and that if the police wanted copies of them they "should follow the usual procedures". Ms Arthurworrey never pursued with PC Jones whether she understood, let alone followed, the 'usual procedures' and obtained the photographs.

Obtaining information on medical concerns

6.230   To get a better understanding of the medical concerns, Ms Arthurworrey telephoned Dr Rossiter. Dr Rossiter remembered a conversation with Ms Arthurworrey occurring some time that week, but their recollections of what was said are rather different. Ms Arthurworrey said she made a note at the time of what was said. Unfortunately, Dr Rossiter kept no such record.

6.231   Ms Arthurworrey agreed that Dr Rossiter told her Victoria may be subject to emotional harm but said, "I did not know she had grave concerns." She recorded in her notes:

> "[Dr Rossiter] believes she is displaying evidence of anxious attachment. Anna appears to seek attention and praise from all the nursing staff but when mother arrives rushes to her side as if she has been called to attention. Dr Rossiter described that as a master/servant relationship."

6.232   She also mentioned to Ms Arthurworrey, as recorded in Ms Aurthurworrey's notes, Victoria's fear of being undressed and of her being frightened of Kouao's partner, and that Kouao may have over-treated the scabies. But, according to Ms Arthurworrey, Dr Rossiter did not suggest that the marks on Victoria's body were indicative of physical harm. She was "unclear whether these were caused by Victoria scratching herself or infection from the scratching". She also noted two old – and unexplained – thumb marks on Victoria's body.

6.233   In describing her telephone conversation with Dr Rossiter, Ms Arthurworrey said:

> "It was not really a discussion. It was a very factual conversation. It was one-way. Dr Rossiter gave me all this information and I wrote it down at the time ... At the end of the conversation I agreed to update her following the home visit."

6.234   Having made no record of their conversation, Dr Rossiter was not able to dispute Ms Arthurworrey's note of it. (See paragraphs 10.131 – 10.135.)

6.235   Ms Arthurworrey admitted that she never questioned Dr Rossiter as to whether there was any indication of physical harm. Nor did she use the opportunity to systematically explore with Dr Rossiter the possible causes of all the marks found on Victoria's body, or resolve any outstanding concerns – particularly in relation to the belt buckle marks identified by Dr Forlee and the 'new' observations of thumb marks. She said she never asked about the scalding incident because she understood from Nurse Quinn that the hospital was happy with Kouao's explanation. In any event, it was Ms Arthurworrey's view that if Dr Rossiter, as the senior paediatric consultant who had examined Victoria, had had any concerns regarding physical harm she would have communicated those to her directly. I do not consider this an unreasonable view to take. On the other hand, it was Ms Arthurworrey's job to pull together and evaluate all the information available to her and, if by some oversight, she had been given no explanation – or no plausible explanation – for all the marks on Victoria's body, she should have sought one directly.

Failure to make a home visit

6.236 Ms Arthurworrey then discussed the case with her supervisor Ms Baptiste and with PC Jones. Ms Baptiste told her to arrange a home visit before Victoria was discharged from hospital. Accordingly she arranged for PC Jones and herself to visit Somerset Gardens on 4 August 1999.

6.237 By this stage Ms Arthurworrey's concerns about Victoria were beginning to crystallise around emotional abuse and neglect. In her statement to the Inquiry she said that the hospital's "ambivalence" about the marks on Victoria's body "left her with no option but to pursue this as an investigation into social issues". The "ambivalence" ought to have led to Ms Arthurworrey keeping an open mind about the possibility of physical harm while she conducted her inquiry.

6.238 It remains unclear from her evidence just how Ms Arthurworrey expected to resolve this uncertainty or how, given that Victoria was still in hospital and yet to be seen by any social worker, emotional abuse and neglect could be properly assessed by a home visit.

6.239 Ms Arthurworrey said that at the time she had understood that Victoria had contracted scabies from her home address. Her purpose in conducting a home visit was therefore to check that 267 Somerset Gardens was a safe and fit environment for Victoria to be discharged to.

6.240 In the event, the home visit never took place before Victoria's discharge from hospital. PC Jones rang Ms Arthurworrey on 4 August 1999 to report the outcome of a conversation she said she had with the North Middlesex Hospital about scabies. According to Ms Arthurworrey's notes, she was told by PC Jones that scabies was highly infectious and that any contact with the family home would require them to wear protective clothing. PC Jones made it quite clear that she was not prepared to conduct a home visit.

6.241 Ms Arthurworrey did not question the advice given by PC Jones. She updated Ms Baptiste who, according to Ms Arthurworrey, advised that the home visit should be cancelled and Kouao invited to the office for an interview instead. Ms Baptiste claimed to have told Ms Arthurworrey to do no more than speak to the doctor and obtain more information about scabies. Unfortunately the case record shows no evidence to support either version of what was said.

Meeting with Kouao

6.242 Kouao was offered an appointment to attend the NTDO the next day, Thursday 5 August 1999. Ms Arthurworrey also rang the North Middlesex Hospital and found that Kouao had not visited Victoria since Monday morning.

6.243 PC Jones met Ms Arthurworrey about half an hour before the meeting with Kouao was scheduled to start. Neither the police nor any social worker had yet visited Victoria in hospital. In evidence, Ms Arthurworrey relied on Haringey's child protection procedures to explain this. She said, "We needed to interview the carer ... We needed to obtain permission from the carer to interview the child."

6.244 Ms Arthurworrey saw the purpose of the interview with Kouao to explore the recent scalding injury, the old markings and the neglect concerns reported by the hospital as part of her initial assessment. She hoped to use the interview to clear up any ambivalence regarding deliberate physical harm. Little preparation was needed beforehand because, according to Ms Arthurworrey, the topics to be covered were already set out in the strategy meeting recommendations.

6.245 During the course of the interview, Ms Arthurworrey and PC Jones learned, and recorded on a paper initial assessment form, the following:

- Kouao and Victoria came to England from France in March 1999, following the death of Kouao's husband, to try to start over again.
- While in France, Kouao had been in full-time employment as an information assistant at the airport.
- Her purpose in coming to England was to learn English.
- Manning was a close family friend who agreed to help her by offering accommodation to Kouao and Victoria in his studio flat until they had somewhere of their own to live.
- Conditions in the studio flat were cramped. Manning shared the flat with his girlfriend (fiancée); however, their relationship had become rather stressed since Kouao and Victoria moved in.
- A couple of weeks earlier Manning had needed his flat for the weekend so Kouao and Victoria had booked into a bedsit. The conditions were very poor and it was after they had checked out that Victoria had started to scratch herself and scabies was diagnosed at the Central Middlesex Hospital.

6.246 Kouao went on to explain that it was while Victoria was taking a bath she poured a beaker of hot water from the bath tap over her head to reduce the skin irritation, which resulted in the burns and her subsequent admission to the North Middlesex Hospital.

6.247 Although in oral evidence Ms Arthurworrey says she asked Kouao whether she had ever hit Victoria, there is no reference to this in her record of the interview. The only neglect issue she addressed was Victoria's lack of clean clothes while in hospital. Kouao's answer to this was that they had entered the country with few belongings and Victoria had few clothes. In any event the hospital had given Victoria what she needed.

6.248 Ms Arthurworrey (and PC Jones) made a number of observations during the interview. Most significantly they noted that although an interpreter was present, Kouao's command of English was good and she would often reply in English before the interpreter had time to do so. Ms Arthurworrey recorded, "Marie-Therese presented as smart in appearance, proud and a woman who articulated very well." However, her grasp of the English language would fail her whenever she was asked specific child protection questions. Then she appeared not to understand, was evasive and would turn to the interpreter for support.

6.249 Kouao also made clear that she wanted help with housing, finance and finding a school for Victoria and she confirmed – as she had to Ealing and Brent Social Services, the Central Middlesex Hospital and, inadvertently, to the North Middlesex Hospital before – that Victoria had not attended school since her arrival in England.

Hospital visit

6.250 Ms Arthurworrey raised her concerns about Kouao's evasiveness with her manager, Ms Baptiste, who told her to visit Victoria in hospital. Ms Arthurworrey also noted as a further action that she should do a home visit to assess the home situation.

6.251 The next day, Friday 6 August 1999, Ms Arthurworrey and PC Jones travelled together to visit Victoria on the Rainbow ward at the North Middlesex Hospital. They took no interpreter along, despite the fact that Victoria was a seven-year-old child who had arrived in Britain from the Ivory Coast via Paris only four months previously. Ms Arthurworrey says that any doubts she had about Victoria's ability to speak in English were put aside by Kouao's assertion that she spoke good English and by the hospital who had earlier told Ms Arthurworrey that "Victoria had been chatting in English most of the time, all of the time". She also thought that Victoria might find the presence of three adults, rather than two, intimidating. Therefore, I make the following recommendation:

> **Recommendation**
> When communication with a child is necessary for the purposes of safeguarding and promoting that child's welfare and the first language of that child is not English, an interpreter must be used. In cases where the use of an interpreter is dispensed with, the reasons for so doing must be recorded in the child's notes/case file.

6.252 It is important to recall that this was the first meeting between Victoria and anyone from the police or social services in the 13 days since Victoria had been admitted to the North Middlesex Hospital. The interview lasted less than 30 minutes and is summarised in barely a side and a half of handwritten A4 notes on the case file.

6.253 In oral evidence Ms Arthurworrey recalled, "Victoria presented as shy and withdrawn and she was reluctant to answer any of the questions that we were asking her. PC Jones then said a few words to Victoria in French and this seemed to relax and make her more comfortable." In her note of the visit she also commented that Victoria had a very big smile.

6.254 Only two matters were discussed: Victoria's account of the scalding injury which seemed to tally with Kouao's (in PC Jones's words Victoria made 'no allegation of crime'), and when she could go home.

6.255 At no time during the visit did Ms Arthurworrey raise with Victoria the other marks on her body – though she recorded in her notes that Victoria's face "had lots of old dark marks and her hair was very dry and covered with bits of dry scalp". Nor did she explore any of the hospital's concerns about neglect. Although Ms Arthurworrey told the Inquiry "I did not know how to raise the issue of master/servant relationship without sounding offensive," the fact is she believed she already had a plausible explanation from Kouao. She was also beginning to form a view in her mind that the neglect issues needed to be looked at against this family's particular social circumstances – namely a family who appeared to have no fixed abode, who were living temporarily with friends and struggling to find their feet in a new country.

6.256 However, she did observe that Victoria seemed reluctant to talk about her home life, but she put this down to the fact that Victoria had recently lost her father and was in a foreign country, in a strange environment talking to two complete strangers.

6.257 By the end of the interview, Ms Arthurworrey admitted that she had learned precious little other than that Victoria had confirmed Kouao's account of the incident by graphically playing out the actions of pouring hot water over her head.

6.258 Together, she and PC Jones decided there was no evidence of a crime, no grounds for seeking an emergency protection order and that any remaining social issues were a matter for social services alone. As the hospital had told social services that Victoria was ready for discharge and they would like that to happen as soon as possible, Ms Arthurworrey recorded in her notes: "Karen (Jones) and I agreed that the injuries (in particular the scalding injury) were probably accidental and that discharge into the mother's care was appropriate." This appears to be a decision that was endorsed by Ms Baptiste who told Ms Arthurworrey, "OK phone mother, Victoria can go home". Ms Arthurworrey duly phoned Kouao, then the hospital, and Victoria went back to Somerset Gardens later that same day.

Referral to Tottenham Child and Family Centre

6.259 Meanwhile on 5 August 1999, the day of the office interview with Kouao, Ms Arthurworrey spoke to Mr Almeida, a practice manager in the investigation and assessment B team at the NTDO and duty manager for the day, about the health and safety issues raised by doing a home visit at Somerset Gardens. She wanted some advice in the absence of Ms Baptiste but she says she never asked him to undertake any tasks in relation to Victoria's case.

6.260 Nonetheless, it was following this brief conversation that Mr Almeida referred Victoria to the Moira Close Tottenham Child and Family Centre managed by the NSPCC.

6.261 It was an extraordinary referral by any account, because Mr Almeida knew virtually nothing about the case at the time. He said in evidence that his reasons for making the referral were twofold – to obtain advice about the precautions Ms Arthurworrey might take when visiting Somerset Gardens, and secondly to prompt some form of action by the centre directed at Victoria's welfare. However, he was unclear as to what action he expected the centre to take. According to the Tottenham Child and Family Centre records, they understood the purpose of the referral was to provide "help with advisory health/hygiene, meeting Anna's developmental needs and antipathy with the interaction between mother and child". They also told Mr Almeida that it would take up to two months for an assessment to be done.

6.262 Mr Almeida admitted that at the time he made the referral he had not read the file, was not aware that there had been a strategy meeting at which 18 recommendations had been made, and did not know that there were section 47 inquiries under way. Nor did he know that Kouao was coming into the office later that day to talk about the various concerns for the very first time. All he did know was that Victoria was in hospital and that there were ongoing concerns about scabies and possible issues of neglect.

6.263 Mr Almeida passed on Ms Arthurworrey's name as the allocated social worker and assumed that the centre would contact her for more information. Surprisingly, he made no mention of the referral to Ms Arthurworrey, who says she first learned of it after Victoria's death. Although there is a record of the referral signed by Mr Almeida and dated 5 August 1999 on Victoria's file, Ms Arthurworrey believes the contact sheet with the referral details was inserted at a later date. Mr Almeida was not able to tell the Inquiry when he wrote his record. Therefore, I make the following recommendation:

> **Recommendation**
> Directors of social services must ensure that when children and families are referred to other agencies for additional services, that referral is only made with the agreement of the allocated social worker and/or their manager. The purpose of the referral must be recorded contemporaneously on the case file.

Fax from the Central Middlesex Hospital

6.264 On 12 August 1999, Ms Arthurworrey received the faxed information from the Central Middlesex Hospital that had been requested by Ms Rodgers – a fax that was to fundamentally alter Ms Arthurworrey's view of Victoria's case and to provide a crucial turning point in Haringey's whole approach to its handling thereafter.

6.265   The date stamp on the fax shows 2 August 1999, despite being sent on 29 July. I can only assume that because the fax was addressed to Ms Rodgers and she was no longer on duty on 2 August, it first went to her in the long-term children and families' team before being returned to duty and finding its way at a snail's pace to Ms Arthurworrey as the allocated social worker. That an important piece of information should arrive in the childcare office and take 10 days to reach the allocated social worker in the case is quite unacceptable.

6.266   The effectiveness of the 'front door' systems within children's services is of critical importance in the protection of children. The 'loss' of such an important piece of information for some 10 days cannot in my view be down to coincidence alone.

6.267   Like Ms Rodgers before her, Ms Arthurworrey found it very difficult to read the Central Middlesex Hospital material. She read the first page – the handwritten letter from Dr Charlotte Dempster – and flicked through the rest. She registered that Victoria had been in police protection briefly. More importantly Victoria had been assessed by the consultant paediatrician Dr Schwartz and, according to Dr Dempster's letter, "It has been decided that her scratch marks are all due to scabies. Thus it is no longer a child protection issue." However, had she spoken to the doctors at the Central Middlesex Hospital she might have obtained a different picture and one that should have prompted broad new avenues of investigation that would have involved Ealing and Brent Social Services, and exposed the many inconsistencies in the stories Kouao told in explaining the injuries to Victoria.

6.268   Ms Arthurworrey said she relied on Dr Dempster's letter, believing it provided an overview and summary of the Central Middlesex Hospital's involvement with Victoria. It also reinforced the need to address a number of social issues that Ms Arthurworrey had already been made aware of, namely help with housing and a school for Victoria.

6.269   She said she felt reassured by the letter because it seemed to clear up any uncertainty about the old marks on Victoria's body. She also thought it offered a possible explanation for Kouao's avoidance of child protection issues in interview. Since Victoria had previously been in police protection for a short time, it is likely that Kouao had already been questioned about child protection concerns by other agencies and was most likely reluctant to answer these questions again.

6.270   Ms Arthurworrey said she felt annoyed that the Central Middlesex Hospital information had not been made available to the strategy meeting. She recalled 'running' with the fax to Ms Baptiste: "I gave her it, she read the letter, she flicked through the fax, she smiled and she said, 'it is obvious that we made the right decision'."

6.271   Ms Baptiste remembered discussing the Central Middlesex Hospital fax, but she told the Inquiry that in August 1999 she was "confused about the chronology of the concerns" and that she asked Ms Arthurworrey to go back to the doctor and get a letter to confirm what was being said. Again, no record of this management decision appears on the case file.

6.272   The failure of both Ms Arthurworrey and Ms Baptiste to:

- read the Central Middlesex Hospital fax fully;
- seek clarification of the hard-to-read contents from the Central Middlesex Hospital;

- discuss the implications of its contents with staff from both the Central Middlesex Hospital and the North Middlesex Hospital;

is poor social work practice in the extreme. Without doing any of the above, Ms Arthurworrey and Ms Baptiste immediately and wrongly re-framed the case in their eyes to one of 'family support'. At that point, any semblance of urgency was removed.

6.273 Moreover, that the diagnosis provided by the Central Middlesex Hospital could have resolved all the concerns about old marks on Victoria's body raised by her later admission to the North Middlesex Hospital makes absolutely no sense with, or without, hindsight. It clearly could not account, for instance, for injuries that may have been sustained between the two admissions. In her evidence to the Inquiry, Ms Arthurworrey accepted this must be the case.

6.274 She also accepted that Dr Rossiter could not have seen the Central Middlesex Hospital material before the strategy meeting, otherwise it would have been included in the information brought to the meeting by Ms Johns. Nor did she know whether Dr Rossiter had seen it since. Ms Arthurworrey agreed that she should have copied over the notes to Dr Rossiter for her opinion, especially as following their telephone conversation a week or so earlier, Ms Arthurworrey had agreed to get back to Dr Rossiter: "It would have been a perfect time, but it was something that I overlooked due to my other cases." In fact it was not until mid October, some two months later, that Dr Rossiter was finally sent the Central Middlesex Hospital notes.

Dr Rossiter's concerns

6.275 In the meantime, Dr Rossiter had mentioned Victoria's case in passing to Ms Kitchman, a child protection adviser in Haringey Social Services and the designated link worker for the hospital. They had run into each other following a meeting at the North Middlesex Hospital on 17 July 1999. Ms Kitchman says she did not see it as her place to take down the details there and then, nor did she believe that Dr Rossiter was making a referral, which would normally have gone through the duty social worker.

6.276 On 13 August 1999, some four days after Dr Rossiter discovered that Victoria had been discharged, she wrote to Ms Kitchman. If Ms Kitchman had had any doubts before that Dr Rossiter was seeking her assistance with this case, those doubts must have been dispelled on receipt of the letter. It read:

> "Re Anna Kouao.
>
> This is the child I wanted to speak to you about.
>
> I never managed to speak to a social worker face to face (you have heard my concerns about this) and my understanding was that there would be a social assessment prior to an urgent planning meeting and then referral to our child psychiatrist. Unfortunately the ward staff seem to think that social workers can discharge patients who are under the care of a doctor and although I probably would have let the girl go home (she was very eager to do so) at least the consultant should have been informed. I have enormous concerns about this child who is now lost to follow-up somewhere in Haringey. What are you going to do?"

6.277 Perhaps even more unfortunate than the four days it took for that letter to be sent is the fact that it took a further seven days before it was read by its addressee. Ms Kitchman says she saw it for the first time on 20 August 1999. Her immediate response was to telephone Dr Rossiter and record in her 'blue book' the following details:

> "Poured boiling water over her head due to scabies. Inappropriate ... lesions more than scratch marks. Mum turned up to the ward in the middle of the night 10 o'clock. Jumped out of bed and stood to attention. Said if she had another social worker she would leave. Behaviour on ward: anxious attachment, clinging to mum. Poured boiling water on herself due to itching."

6.278   This entry is not dated nor did a copy of the note ever find its way to Victoria's file.

6.279   Ms Kitchman believes she rang the NTDO on the same day and discovered that Victoria's allocated social worker was Ms Arthurworrey. She says she spoke to her on the telephone – although she now has no independent recollection of the phone call – and was told that Ms Arthurworrey and PC Jones were jointly carrying out a section 47 investigation.

6.280   Ms Kitchman relayed this information back to Dr Rossiter by phone and in so doing believed she had addressed the doctor's concerns. Most importantly Victoria was not, as she understood it, "lost to follow-up somewhere in Haringey". She had an allocated social worker and a joint investigation was under way which would include a social work assessment and could result in an urgent planning meeting and a referral to a child psychiatrist. Ms Kitchman told the Inquiry that she had confidence in the management of the duty system in north Tottenham at the time – a confidence that was to prove woefully misplaced – and saw no reason to probe with Ms Arthurworrey whether each of the concerns Dr Rossiter had raised (and that she had recorded in the 'blue book') were being addressed as part of that assessment.

6.281   Ms Kitchman admitted that despite being asked to respond to the "enormous concerns" of a highly regarded paediatrician, she did not ask to check the file for herself. If she had taken the trouble to give even a quick glance at the file she would have quickly discovered that nothing that Dr Rossiter had expected to happen had happened.

6.282   In fact it would have been rather surprising if section 47 investigations were still continuing by 20 August 1999, since the case had already shifted from being child protection to family support on 12 August, after the receipt of the fax from the Central Middlesex Hospital with the scabies diagnosis.

6.283   Ms Arthurworrey is confident that she never told Ms Kitchman either in August or any time afterwards that a joint section 47 investigation was under way. Indeed she can recall no such conversation at all, and in fact was out of the office on 20 August so could not have taken Ms Kitchman's call that day.

6.284   Resolving this conflict of evidence has not been helped by Ms Kitchman's poor note taking. There is certainly no record of a telephone conversation between Ms Arthurworrey and Ms Kitchman in Ms Arthurworrey's contact notes on Victoria's case file. Nor did Ms Kitchman note that conversation in her 'blue book' as she would expect to and as she did with Dr Rossiter. Instead, Ms Kitchman produced in evidence an annotated version of Dr Rossiter's letter in which she believed she noted the following words during her conversation with Ms Arthurworrey: "Central Middlesex, emotionally and physically abused, scabies and Karen Jones CPT."

6.285   However, she could not confirm the source of her information – at least the first three pieces of information could equally well have been provided by Dr Rossiter as Ms Arthurworrey – the date she made these notes or what was their significance.

6.286 Nor did Ms Kitchman use the opportunity when writing to Ms Wilson in August 2000 to correct some factual inaccuracies in the Part 8 review to confirm that she had spoken to Ms Arthurworrey in person. Instead she wrote:

> "I received this letter [Dr Rossiter's] on 20th August. I did telephone North Tottenham District and established that there was an allocated social worker undertaking inquiries under section 47."

6.287 It is my judgement on the basis of the evidence before the Inquiry, and having seen both witnesses, that Ms Kitchman did not discuss Dr Rossiter's letter of 13 August 1999 with Ms Arthurworrey in August, although she may well have received information – some of it misleading – from someone else in the NTDO, which she then fed back to Dr Rossiter.

6.288 I am equally clear that the response Dr Rossiter received to her expression of concerns was significantly less than she could reasonably have expected, particularly from someone in the post of child protection adviser. At the very least I would have expected a face-to-face discussion between Ms Kitchman and Ms Arthurworrey, recorded on the file which should have been read through, reviewed and signed by Ms Kitchman. A full record of the exchanges between herself and Dr Rossiter should also have been entered on the file.

6.289 I am also of the view that it is not unreasonable to have expected Ms Kitchman to have ensured that Ms Arthurworrey, Ms Baptiste, Dr Rossiter and herself met to go through the concerns about the case and agree a course of action. These are the basic steps I would expect any professional to have taken when dealing with concerns raised by another professional about the way a case is being handled in the interests of inter-agency trust, co-operation and the safety of children. Therefore, I make the following recommendation:

> **Recommendation**
> When a professional from another agency expresses concern to social services about their handling of a particular case, the file must be read and reviewed, the professional concerned must be met and spoken to, and the outcome of this discussion must be recorded on the case file.

An announced visit

6.290 On 16 August 1999 – some 10 days after Victoria was discharged home – Ms Arthurworrey visited Kouao, Manning and Victoria at Manning's flat in Somerset Gardens. It was an announced visit and an interpreter was present.

6.291 Ms Arthurworrey said in her statement to this Inquiry that with the benefit of hindsight, she now realises that she was completely "set up" during this visit. She believes that Kouao and Manning purposely presented a positive image of Victoria's home in order to mislead her. Manning told the Inquiry that Victoria had indeed been coached in how to behave during the course of the visit. He also agreed that he and Kouao had deliberately set out to persuade Ms Arthurworrey of certain facts to help to bolster Kouao's housing claim, namely that he was a hard-working, respectable young man with a steady job, a home and a fiancée who was helping Kouao and Victoria out in the short-term until they could find accommodation of their own.

6.292 Whatever story was told by Victoria's killers, the task facing Ms Arthurworrey was clear. Even though the section 47 investigation had been inappropriately closed, this visit was still part of the 'full investigation and assessment' Ms Arthurworrey was expected to undertake under recommendation 10 from the strategy meeting. A golden opportunity for a first home visit had already been missed while Victoria was in hospital, thus increasing the importance of this contact. This visit was also the first contact between Victoria and any of the agencies charged with safeguarding and promoting her welfare since her discharge from hospital. I deal with this in more detail later in this section.

6.293   Ms Arthurworrey observed nothing during the course of her visit that gave her significant cause for concern. She noted that Victoria appeared happy and comfortable. There were toys scattered on the floor and Victoria was playing with a doll. She recalled:

> "Victoria opened the door and I was so struck by her presentation. The last time I had seen Victoria at the North Middlesex Hospital she presented as a shy, withdrawn child. When I saw her on 16 August she was as the nurses have described, like a ray of sunshine. She greeted me. She said 'Hello Lisa'. She had quite a high-pitched voice. She was dressed in a red tartan skirt, a red jumper, she had red socks on, black shoes. She seemed happy and the one thing that I did notice was that her face was heavily moisturised with cocoa butter. I thought Kouao was applying cocoa butter to help to reduce the scarring from the scalds and scabies."

6.294   Ms Arthurworrey saw of Victoria what Kouao had intended her to see. We can only guess at what more Ms Arthurworrey might have learned had she spoken to Victoria on her own. But the fact is she did not speak to Victoria at all during that visit and now "deeply regrets not doing so".

6.295   Ms Arthurworrey accepted that it was her job to test out all the concerns raised and the explanations given and not to make any assumptions, but this she singularly failed to do. Far from keeping an open mind about the possibility of deliberate harm, the superficiality of her questioning on that day went only to confirm her view that she was dealing with a family struggling to find their feet in a new country.

6.296   During the course of the visit, Ms Arthurworrey raised with Kouao just three of the North Middlesex Hospital's concerns around neglect:

- Victoria's bed wetting: Ms Arthurworrey suggested to Kouao that she take Victoria to the next door medical centre for treatment (but subsequently never checked out that Kouao had followed her advice).
- The number of bowls of cereal Victoria had eaten during her stay at the North Middlesex Hospital – Kouao's response was that Victoria had a large appetite anyway. Significantly Ms Arthurworrey recorded that Kouao was cooking in the kitchen at the time of the visit "suggesting Anna was being fed".
- Why Kouao had brought in no clean clothes or treats for Victoria. Kouao told Ms Arthurworrey that finances were tight and she could not afford to buy Victoria treats. She also repeated what she had said in interview on 5 August – that they had entered the country with few belongings and Victoria had few clothes. As the hospital had given Victoria some clothes Kouao saw no need to bring in any more.

6.297   Ms Arthurworrey accepted what she was told:

> "At the time I did not know I was dealing with child killers. I thought Kouao was a respectful adult who was child focused. She had come to this country to make a better life for her and Victoria."

6.298 Ms Arthurworrey's misreading of the Central Middlesex Hospital fax had almost certainly given her a completely false sense of security with respect to Kouao. She admitted, "I was more trusting of Kouao when I went on that visit. I am not a detective. I had no reason to question what I saw and what I was being told at that point." She did not believe that Kouao would harm Victoria in any way.

6.299 Ms Arthurworrey never asked Kouao, let alone Victoria, how she spent the day – a crucial aspect of any child assessment. She did not notice any signs of anxious attachment as reported by Dr Rossiter. She had also been told that Victoria was frightened of Manning but says he was there throughout the visit and Victoria seemed comfortable in his presence.

6.300 However, she did note a sense of formality between Victoria and the two adults but nothing to suggest a master-servant relationship or anything else to cause her concern. She observed Victoria was quiet in the presence of conversing adults and interpreted this as a sign of proper respect. She believed there can often be a sense of formality in the relationship between parent and child in Afro-Caribbean families "because respect and obedience are very important features on the Afro-Caribbean family script".

6.301 With the deliberate harm concerns apparently resolved, the discussion between Ms Arthurworrey and Kouao focused on housing and education and the family's long-term plans. Ms Arthurworrey learned that Kouao had made an application to Haringey housing department on 19 July but had yet to hear anything. Once their housing needs had been resolved, Kouao would enrol Victoria in school.

6.302 In fact, on the housing application Kouao stated she and Victoria had been living at 267 Somerset Gardens since 24 March 1999, and the 'friend' they were staying with had asked them to leave. Although Kouao indicated she was threatened with homelessness, this was not, according to housing registration officer Maria Alexandrou, a "dire emergency that warranted forwarding to the homeless section". Apparently many applicants tick the box indicating they are being asked to leave their accommodation but in fact stay on in it for some time afterwards.

6.303 Ms Arthurworrey observed for herself that the home conditions were "very good" although not big enough for three people. She was told that Victoria's bedwetting was causing difficulties between Manning and his fiancée who had lived with him until Kouao and Victoria had moved in on a temporary basis.

6.304 Ms Arthurworrey said she told Kouao at the time that she thought her housing application would be unsuccessful because, having left her home in France, Kouao appeared to have made herself intentionally homeless. They discussed possible contingency plans and Ms Arthurworrey stressed the importance of Kouao finding a job and perhaps renting in the private sector.

6.305 At the end of the visit, Ms Arthurworrey agreed to chase up Kouao's housing application as a matter of urgency. She believed that unless the accommodation needs were sorted out she could not draw up a care plan for Victoria. She also promised to send the family a copy of *Community Care*, which would provide information on nursing and care-work agencies, as well as sending a separate list of childminders in the borough.

6.306 Ms Arthurworrey said that she then updated Ms Baptiste, informing her that the home visit had not raised any further child protection concerns. She claims she was not advised to do anything else by her manager, although no such endorsement appears on the case file.

Kouao's housing application

6.307 On 25 August 1999, Ms Arthurworrey spoke to Yvonne White, a housing officer in Haringey's housing department, who told her that housing applications can take up to eight weeks to process. She advised Ms Arthurworrey to write to Bambos Kakouratos, the housing registration manager, if she wanted to try to speed up the process.

6.308 Ms Arthurworrey wrote the very same day, explaining that a care plan could not be completed until the housing situation was clarified. This letter was stamped as received by the Haringey housing team on 26 August 1999, and was placed, unacknowledged, on the housing file.

6.309 As a result of Ms Arthurworrey's letter, Kouao's application was passed to Ms Alexandrou for immediate assessment. This was in spite of the fact that Kouao's application would not normally have been considered under Haringey's housing allocation scheme because Kouao had not lived in the borough for six out of the previous 12 months and was, therefore, technically ineligible to go on the housing register. Although this was not communicated to Ms Arthurworrey, Mr Kakouratos said he overlooked the impediment because of the referral from social services.

6.310 Mr Kakouratos said he was quite sure he would have pointed out Ms Arthurworrey's letter to Ms Alexandrou because this explained why the assessment had to be done quickly. However, Ms Alexandrou could not recall discussing the child protection issue with Mr Kakouratos, or whether she read Ms Arthurworrey's letter when making her assessment.

6.311 Ms Alexandrou's initial assessment of Kouao's application resulted in it exceeding the threshold required for the allocation of a two bedroomed property in the borough. Thus a standard letter was sent to Kouao on 1 September 1999 informing her that her application was being taken forward.

6.312 The procedure for taking forward Kouao's application was to make a 'cold call' visit to Manning's flat – a duty allocated by Ms Alexandrou to Karen McGregor (née Brown), a home visitor from Haringey Social Services' housing department. Ms Alexandrou could not recall whether she spoke to Ms McGregor about the child protection aspects of the application before she made her visit. However, Ms McGregor said she was unaware of any urgency relating to Kouao's application and would only be aware of 'complications' if a note were written on the front sheet of the file. However, Ms McGregor admitted she did not always read through files before making home visits.

6.313 During the course of the home visit, Kouao told Ms McGregor that she had left her previous accommodation in France of her own accord. Ms McGregor noted this and as a result, when Kouao's application was reviewed later, she was deemed intentionally homeless and therefore ineligible for housing. This was not communicated to social services. Therefore it was not until Ms Arthurworrey telephoned the housing office on 9 September 1999 to chase up her letter to Mr Kakouratos that she was told the negative outcome of Kouao's application, and that although the housing department would write to Kouao for more information, the decision on the application was unlikely to change.

Care plan

6.314 It was at this stage, armed with the knowledge that Kouao's housing application would most likely fail, that Ms Arthurworrey drafted a care plan. She expressly crossed out sections relating to child protection because she did not consider that any longer to be an issue.

6.315 Although written some time after 9 September 1999 – the care plan is undated – it was due to start on 16 August and had no end or review date. The plan was for ongoing family support, in particular to help Kouao to find accommodation and then to help with schools and a job in that order. The outcome of Ms Arthurworrey's 'assessment' of Victoria was recorded as follows:

"– initial referral received 27 July 1999. CP concerns. Anna admitted to the North Midd hospital with markings to her body;
– concerns investigated jointly with the police and deemed as accidental;
– correspondence also received from the central Midd hospital backing up mother's scabies story;
– case then moved from CP status to family support;
– mother wanting help with housing, however not eligible for housing – made herself intentionally homeless in France;
– assessment completed by housing in September, therefore cannot access services at this stage."

6.316 It is also in the care plan that Ms Arthurworrey suggested for the first time the possibility that the family may have to return to France if Kouao should fail to find suitable housing.

A second letter from Dr Rossiter

6.317 Meanwhile, on 2 September 1999, Dr Rossiter wrote again to Ms Kitchman. She told her she was pleased to hear that Victoria was still at home, had a social worker and appeared to be happy, but she made no mention of the ongoing section 47 investigation. With the letter, Dr Rossiter enclosed the discharge summary from the North Middlesex Hospital dated 13 August 1999. It is a document that repays careful reading. The fourth paragraph reads as follows:

"Noted to be a **very distressed child. Multiple marks on her** not just due to scratching. **Thought possibly due to chastisement eg with looped wire**. Child protection forms completed. Photographs taken, rather belatedly (staffing problems). Discussed in psychosocial ward round. **Child showing anxious attachment, seemed very frightened when mother visited with her boyfriend**, clinging desperately to mother on the short times that she visited alone. **Considered likely to be abused, probable neglect and emotional abuse, less difficult [sic] to prove physical abuse**. Concerns shared with hospital social worker who attended a planning meeting at North Tottenham Social Services. Social worker spoke to Dr Rossiter on the phone who expressed her very clear views as above. Home visit for risk assessment made by social services. On their advice child discharged home by ward staff. **Very worrying case ... the child is emotionally disturbed** ... temporary resident, mother has expressed to the staff that if social services are involved ... she would remove child to France. No GP, not school-time, difficult to follow up the child further." (The emphasis in bold is mine.)

6.318 The letter was received in Ms Kitchman's office on 9 September 1999. As it happened, she was on annual leave at that time and did not see it until 23 September. Ms Kitchman told us she did not know whether anyone covered her post while she was away. She thought that an administration assistant would open her mail and pass it on to her manager, Ms Graham, but that did not happen. When there were specific issues to be dealt with then the child protection advisers would usually make arrangements to cover for each other, but otherwise the likelihood of a post being dealt with while staff were away on leave seemed largely a matter of chance. According to Ms Kitchman, "When people's pigeonholes were quite full someone might walk past and have a look to see what was in there." This is highly unsatisfactory. Therefore, I make the following recommendation:

> **Recommendation**
> Directors of social services must ensure that when staff are absent from work, systems are in place to ensure that post, emails and telephone contacts are checked and actioned as necessary.

6.319   Thus three weeks had already elapsed by the time Ms Kitchman read Dr Rossiter's second letter. She did not attach much urgency to it. It was now one and a half months after Victoria's discharge from the North Middlesex Hospital and she did not see the letter as containing any new information other than the reference to the 'possible' looped wire mark. The fact that Dr Rossiter was now also saying, contrary to an impression she may have given in August when talking to Ms Arthurworrey, that the marks on Victoria's body were not just due to scratching went unheeded.

6.320   On being taken through the discharge summary, Ms Kitchman stated that she did not believe that any of the factors identified by Dr Rossiter, either singly or taken together, put Victoria's case at the top of the risk scale. She admitted, however, that she misread the expression "less difficult to prove physical abuse" as meaning just the opposite. This is in fact what Dr Rossiter had intended, but nonetheless it was a dangerous assumption to make and it needed checking out.

Ms Arthurworrey's and Ms Kitchman's response

6.321   Ms Kitchman waited until her next visit to the NTDO on 28 September 1999 to try to speak to Ms Arthurworrey. In the event, it was not until 1 October – a month after Dr Rossiter wrote the letter – that she discussed the letter with her. At the time, Ms Arthurworrey says she was rather preoccupied in preparing for her first set of care proceedings. Both agree that the conversation was brief – Ms Kitchman estimated maybe 15 to 20 minutes – and that it was not a formal consultation. Ms Kitchman recalled: "Lisa seemed quite keen to get me off her case basically. She was in a hurry and I managed to sit down and talk to her about the case and I thought I would have to be really, really concerned to push the matter further."

6.322   Their accounts of what was said and done during this discussion differ at virtually every turn.

6.323   According to Ms Kitchman, she showed Ms Arthurworrey the discharge summary. They went through it together and Ms Kitchman annotated it as they were talking. She also said in oral evidence, and reiterated in a memo to Ms Wilson dated 16 October 2000, that she is "pretty sure" she photocopied the annotated discharge summary and gave it back to Ms Arthurworrey. Ms Arthurworrey pointed out to her the fax from the Central Middlesex Hospital which Ms Kitchman also took away to photocopy. She then told Ms Athurworrey that she would respond to Dr Rossiter's letter.

6.324   Ms Kitchman's annotation of the discharge summary is barely legible. She deciphered one of the annotations for the Inquiry as "Central Middlesex have investigated" against the reference to the looped wire and also noted "mum has not got a boyfriend".

6.325   Ms Kitchman said she, too, had difficulty reading the Central Middlesex Hospital fax but, like her colleagues before, she did nothing about obtaining a more readable version. She cannot recall whether she saw all 20 pages of the fax – she said what Dr Rossiter received is what she would have seen and sent. However, she does remember seeing Dr Dempster's summary letter, and that Brent Social Services and the police had completed section 47 investigations and concluded that the injuries were accidental.

6.326   Ms Arthurworrey also told her in October that she was undertaking a section 47 investigation and completing a social work assessment. Yet the fact that even according to Ms Kitchman's version of events, this investigation must have been ongoing since early August caused her no particular concerns. She was aware there were still concerns about neglect and emotional harm, which she thought could take slightly longer to assess.

6.327   In evidence, Ms Kitchman accepted that such a delay in assessing Victoria's case was not justified and she admitted that she should have pursued this and probed as to the reasons why. She did not do this.

6.328   Ms Arthurworrey told a very different story. She said that Ms Kitchman had a brief chat with her about Victoria's case on 1 October 1999 and told her that Dr Rossiter had expressed some concerns about the case and wanted to know what was happening. It was at this point that Ms Arthurworrey remembered that she had not updated Dr Rossiter with regard to the earlier section 47 investigation.

6.329   As she was busy preparing another case for care proceedings she said she gave Ms Kitchman Victoria's file to take away, pointing out in particular the correspondence from the Central Middlesex Hospital:

> "I felt that this was a crucial link and I knew that I had not read it, read the fax from page to page, but Dr Rossiter needed to see these notes because she had been ambivalent around the old markings on Victoria's body."

6.330   Ms Arthurworrey said she expected Ms Kitchman to "sit down and read the file and respond back to Dr Rossiter".

6.331   She denied saying to Ms Kitchman in October that she was undertaking a section 47 investigation – that had been completed by 16 August at the latest. She also denied that Ms Kitchman showed her the North Middlesex Hospital discharge summary – in fact she said she did not see this until 28 February 2000, three days after Victoria's death. She said that if she had seen this summary, "I would have run to my manager because it would have meant that the first section 47 investigation I had completed was completely flawed ... this discharge summary was giving me new, different, concerning information."

6.332   Instead Ms Arthurworrey said she was shown the first Dr Rossiter letter dated 13 August 1999. She said she did not raise with Ms Kitchman why it had taken so long to talk to her about it because she was very busy at the time and did not take any specific notice of the date.

6.333   On reading the letter, Ms Arthurworrey said she asked Ms Kitchman why would Dr Rossiter probably have let the girl go home if she had concerns. According to Ms Arthurworrey, Ms Kitchman's response was "I do not know and I do not know why Dr Rossiter is contacting me with this case anyway." Ms Kitchman conveyed a similar sentiment when giving her oral evidence. Despite her role as link worker to the North Middlesex Hospital, Ms Kitchman told us: "Looking at it all now in hindsight I do not think it was a good move for Mary [Rossiter] to have sent me all this information, I think it should have been [sent] directly, and she should have had some direct contact with the team manager."

Ms Kitchman's reply to Dr Rossiter

6.334 Ms Kitchman eventually wrote back to Dr Rossiter on 19 October 1999. Her letter included copies of the Central Middlesex Hospital notes and recorded Ms Arthurworrey's view that Dr Rossiter's concerns about deliberate physical harm and the marks made with looped wire had been satisfactorily addressed because Dr Schwartz, consultant paediatrician at the Central Middlesex Hospital, had found on an earlier occasion that Victoria had suffered from scabies and did not show signs of deliberate physical harm. The letter did not include any hint of an apology for the time taken to reply. On any view it was an extraordinary response.

6.335 She also told Dr Rossiter that:

"– Lisa has undertaken a joint investigation with PC Pauline Ricketts from the police child protection team in relation to the boiling water incident.
– Lisa has visited the family a number of times and established that the mother does not have a boyfriend. She has no concerns about Anna's interaction with her mother.
– The family's legal status in this country is not clear and they are undergoing a habitual residency test. Therefore Anna does not currently have a school place."

6.336 Ms Kitchman asked Dr Rossiter if the hospital could confirm Kouao's explanation for the scalds and whether they could give any more details regarding the emotional abuse and/or neglect they thought Victoria might be experiencing. A copy of her letter also went to Ms Arthurworrey for the file.

6.337 In her reply to Dr Rossiter, Ms Kitchman made no suggestion whatsoever that any of the marks on Victoria's body could postdate the Central Middlesex Hospital admission. Nor did she draw Dr Rossiter's attention to the conflicting medical diagnoses. She told us in evidence that by sending the Central Middlesex Hospital material to Dr Rossiter, she was implicitly passing to her the responsibility to consider the implications. By any stretch of the imagination it is difficult to read her reply in this light. The only impression one could draw was that here was a social worker who had looked at the problems, who was content that everything was in order and was just sending back some documentation for Dr Rossiter's information.

6.338 In the meantime, Ms Arthurworrey told us that the first time she saw Ms Kitchman's letter to Dr Rossiter was the week beginning 15 November 1999, although the date stamp shows it was received in the NTDO on 2 November. She registered that there were a number of inaccuracies in the letter, for example, it was PC Jones, not PC Ricketts, with whom Ms Arthurworrey had undertaken a joint investigation. More significant was the implication that Ms Arthurworrey and Ms Kitchman had worked through the concerns raised by the discharge summary together – but she did nothing to correct these. She did not think it important to do this because the inaccuracies "date back to what I thought were old events".

6.339 Even more important, the letter should have brought to Ms Arthurworrey's attention the existence of a discharge summary, which she had yet to see. She did not make that connection at the time but said in evidence: "I had no idea that the discharge summary would contain information that I did not already know."

Ms Arthurworrey's response to the discharge summary

6.340 If indeed Ms Arthurworrey is telling the truth about the discharge summary, then this would have been the first occasion that she had seen any reference to a looped wire mark on Victoria's body. Yet this did not seem to cause her any undue concern – all the more surprising given that she was reading this information just days after attending a second strategy meeting to investigate allegations made by Kouao that Manning had sexually abused Victoria.

6.341   Ms Arthurworrey told the Inquiry:

> "I saw the reference to the looped wire mark as another pre-diagnosis concern. I knew that there had been a number of pre-diagnosis issues, for example, Dr Rossiter had made mention to thumb marks, there had been mention of a belt buckle mark ... It did not really bother me because I knew that Victoria had been seen by two hospitals."

6.342   It was a view that Ms Arthurworrey had already formed when she spoke to Ms Baptiste about Ms Kitchman's visit. Ms Baptiste had no recollection of Ms Kitchman's involvement in Victoria's case while she had case management responsibility – indeed she said that she thought the case ought to have gone to a child protection adviser but she did not remember whether she passed on this advice to Ms Arthurworrey.

6.343   She recalled that they talked at some stage about Dr Rossiter's concerns. According to Ms Arthurworrey, Ms Baptiste's response was: "Oh, Dr Rossiter, she always gets it wrong, she got it wrong in a child death that I was working on, Baby W1."

6.344   Ms Baptiste denied that she expressed an opinion of this sort or that she had any doubts about Dr Rossiter's professional competence. She believed she implied to Ms Arthurworrey that she needed to be clear about the information and asked her to get Dr Rossiter to put her concerns in writing – presumably the very concerns that Dr Rossiter had put in writing to Ms Kitchman.

6.345   It now seems clear that Ms Arthurworrey did not believe that Dr Rossiter was raising anything new, albeit that she was writing some two and a half weeks after Victoria's discharge. If a looped wire mark had been observed on Victoria's body, she expected that the hospital would have mentioned it, either in the medical report sent by Nurse Quinn, or in the initial referral, or in her conversation with Dr Rossiter on 3 August 1999, and they did not.

6.346   Ms Arthurworrey said she felt reassured by Ms Kitchman's letter because she knew that the Central Middlesex Hospital notes, which she saw as the 'crucial link', had been sent to Dr Rossiter. If the Central Middlesex Hospital fax could explain away the old marks on Victoria's body, then presumably it could also explain away the looped wire mark. If not, then she expected Dr Rossiter or Ms Kitchman would get back to her. Either way, Ms Arthurworrey thought that the enormous concerns that Dr Rossiter had expressed were to do with the fact that she had not updated her on the outcome of the section 47 investigation. Irrespective of Ms Kitchman's covering letter, and the inaccuracies she claims it had, she mistakenly believed that the Central Middlesex Hospital material would fulfil that purpose.

Disagreement of diagnosis

6.347   On 2 November 1999, the same day that a copy of Ms Kitchman's letter to Dr Rossiter arrived at the NTDO, Dr Rossiter endorsed her copy of the letter with the words "we disagreed". She was referring specifically to the comments in Ms Kitchman's letter, which noted that Dr Schwartz at the Central Middlesex Hospital had confirmed that the marks on Victoria were due to scabies.

6.348   Dr Rossiter, in her statement to the Inquiry, said that she communicated this to Ms Kitchman but in evidence thought she may have made a mistake about this and she had no record of any such conversation taking place. Ms Kitchman denied receiving any such telephone call – she said she would have followed it up if she did – and there is no record of one in her diary, notebook or in the team message book.

6.349 It therefore seems unlikely that Dr Rossiter ever made that phone call and Ms Kitchman therefore received no response to her letter. As a result, Haringey Social Services were left in the position of having two diagnoses from two consultant paediatricians, in two different hospitals in relation to two different incidents. The ambiguity around the old markings were anything but resolved. Yet despite the concerns Ms Kitchman said she had about this, and despite asking Dr Rossiter for more information, she did nothing to follow the matter up, nor did she direct Ms Arthurworrey to do so.

6.350 Like Ms Arthurworrey, she was relying on Dr Rossiter to get back to her if she still had concerns. She said:

> "Knowing Mary as I know her ... she would have, if she had been really worried, I do believe that she would have phoned me or spoken to somebody at ACPC or mentioned to me after a case conference or something. She would have been back in touch with me."

Disagreement between Ms Arthurworrey and Ms Kitchman

6.351 Ms Arthurworrey's and Ms Kitchman's accounts of what was said when they met in early October differed profoundly in two key respects. First, as previously discussed, whether or not Ms Arthurworrey told Ms Kitchman that she was engaged in a section 47 investigation – although had she read the file, Ms Kitchman would have realised no such investigation was under way.

6.352 Second, whether or not Ms Kitchman showed and discussed with Ms Arthurworrey the North Middlesex Hospital discharge summary. From all the evidence available, and having heard the witnesses, it is difficult to draw any satisfactory conclusion about this. In Ms Kitchman's letter to Dr Rossiter of 19 October 1999 she wrote, "Although Lisa had not previously seen the discharge summary..." This implied that while Ms Arthurworrey had not seen it before, she had by the time Ms Kitchman came to write her reply. On the other hand, if Ms Kitchman, as she claimed, had photocopied the summary and annotated it before handing it to Ms Arthurworrey, then a copy of the annotated version should have been placed on the Haringey case file. No such copy appears.

6.353 Ms Arthurworrey's brief record of their conversation on the case file assists little. Dated 4 October 1999 – although Ms Arthurworrey confirmed to the Inquiry that the discussion took place on 1 October and Ms Kitchman did not dispute this – it reads as follows:

> "Discussion with Petra – CPA – making inquiries into Anna on behalf of Dr Rossiter who is concerned for Anna. Outcome: informed Petra of current visit. She will now contact Dr Rossiter."

6.354 Ms Kitchman said she made separate notes which she used to draft her response to Dr Rossiter but unfortunately then threw these away. Apart from the 19 October letter itself, no other record of the conversation exists.

6.355 Whether or not Ms Arthurworrey had sight of the discharge summary is important only because it might have affected Haringey's handling of Victoria's case from October 1999. Although Ms Arthurworrey said that if she had seen it, "she would have run to her manager" and steps would have been taken to "refocus Victoria's case", I have to doubt this in the light of her comments to the Inquiry about the looped wire mark and its perceived lack of importance. While Victoria had been a patient in two hospitals, it would appear that receipt of a medical report subsequent to that obtained from the Central Middlesex Hospital, which suggested a rather different cause for Victoria's injury, was disregarded by Haringey social workers who preferred instead to rely on the older diagnosis. On that basis I come to the view that even if Ms Arthurworrey had seen the North Middlesex Hospital discharge summary in October 1999, it would have had little impact on her handling of the case.

6.356   Ms Kitchman agreed that the involvement of a child protection adviser in Victoria's case was of no benefit. Whereas one might have expected a person in such a post to have reacted to some of the many basic casework errors in the management of this case, the sad fact is that Ms Kitchman's involvement merely served to further entrench the authority's woeful misreading of Victoria's situation.

Ms Arthurworrey's supervision

6.357   On 20 September 1999, Ms Arthurworrey had her first supervision session with Ms Baptiste since being allocated Victoria's case at the beginning of August. Among the agenda items they discussed was the considerable amount of time off in lieu (52 hours altogether) that Ms Arthurworrey had accumulated. Ms Baptiste told us, "It was impossible to prevent – the nature of the work and the pressure of the working conditions would often require workers to ... work out of the nine to five."

6.358   Ms Arthurworrey reported to Ms Baptiste a number of cases during the course of that supervision, including Victoria's. Ms Baptiste admitted that she did not read Victoria's file either before or during supervision. But on the basis of a 5 to 10 minute discussion of the case, and Ms Baptiste's earlier recall of the information contained in the Central Middlesex Hospital fax, she agreed with Ms Arthurworrey that the case had been investigated, and endorsed on the file that this was a 'family support' case. That she, too, could have come to the view that Dr Schwartz's diagnosis of Victoria's injuries at the Central Middlesex Hospital could account for the marks observed on Victoria two weeks later at the North Middlesex Hospital is extraordinary – unless she had muddled the chronology of the two hospital admissions and thought that the Central Middlesex Hospital visit came after the North Middlesex Hospital admission. This was a mistake Ms Baptiste admitted to in her oral evidence when she said that she thought that the fax by which the Central Middlesex Hospital notes were sent to Haringey was from the North Middlesex Hospital.

6.359   It was just as important to review each of the 18 recommendations from the July 1999 strategy meeting. Ms Kozinos told the Inquiry she expected this would be done as part of Ms Arthurworrey's regular supervision with her team manager. Ms Baptiste said she started to review the recommendations, but Ms Arthurworrey admits that she never drew them to her manager's attention. It seems clear that the recommendations were simply abandoned when the focus of the case switched from child protection.

6.360   Ms Baptiste's supervision notes on Victoria's case, which she says may have been typical of the quality of her supervision notes at the time, add up to just eight lines of handwritten material:

> "The case identified as family support as CP concerns investigated – NFA. Are issues of housing (Habitual Residence Test). Lisa has given mum a list of childminders. Action:
>
> i)   awaiting response from housing – Lisa to chase up;

> ii) to continue to offer family support until early October."

6.361 Although Ms Baptiste said in her evidence that other decisions were taken and she discussed with Ms Arthurworrey the competing diagnoses of Dr Rossiter and Dr Schwartz and the details of the care plan, there is nothing recorded on the case file to support this. It is my view this did not happen.

6.362 That Ms Baptiste placed much reliance on Ms Arthurworrey's assessment of Victoria is somewhat surprising. She told the Inquiry that she did not think Ms Arthurworrey was particularly diligent in providing feedback and she needed to develop her skills in working with children. She said, "It ... was apparent that she was not always confident in formulating probing questions ... did not appear to be insightful about the situation she was going in to ... not sufficiently analytical ... did not make the right inquiries." Indeed, Ms Baptiste gave in evidence a very different impression to that which might have been gleaned from the competency assessment she completed on Ms Arthurworrey just days before Victoria's case was allocated to her. If true, it should have led Ms Baptiste to rigorously probe Ms Arthurworrey's assessment of Victoria throughout August and September 1999. The supervision session on 20 September provided an obvious but missed opportunity to do just that. I am driven to the conclusion that Ms Baptiste simply failed to apply her mind to the issue. I deal with the practical implications of Ms Arthurworrey's supervision in more detail later in this section of the Report.

A second announced visit

6.363 On 30 September 1999, Ms Alexandrou wrote to Kouao saying that Haringey housing department believed she had given up secure accommodation in France. The letter went on to invite Kouao to put forward, in writing, any special factors or mitigating circumstances to be taken into account before Haringey reached a final decision on her application.

6.364 On 18 October 1999, Ms Arthurworrey telephoned the housing department yet again for information of Kouao's housing application. This telephone call confirmed that what had been anticipated had in fact occurred. Ms Arthurworrey was told that Kouao's application had been unsuccessful because she had made herself intentionally homeless. Ms Arthurworrey was also told that Kouao had the right of appeal, but so far no response had been received from her to the housing department's letter of 30 September explaining this.

6.365 On 28 October 1999, Ms Arthurworrey paid a second, announced, visit to Somerset Gardens. Kouao, Manning and Victoria were all present. In evidence, Ms Arthurworrey described the meeting as "very routine, a very business-type meeting". It had a single purpose, according to the case notes, namely to discuss the options open to the family, given their housing situation.

6.366 Ms Arthurworrey informed Kouao that her housing application had been unsuccessful, although Kouao had already been informed of this by Haringey housing department. As the housing department was still waiting for a response from Kouao to its letter of 30 September, her application was placed in the housing department's 'deferred section' on 30 November while they waited for further contact from Kouao that never materialised. In the event, Ms Arthurworrey discussed with her the possible alternatives. These were threefold:

- to find employment and rent a flat in the private sector;
- to stay as they were;
- to return to France and if there were any financial difficulties here, Haringey Social Services could offer assistance.

6.367 Kouao told Ms Arthurworrey that she had not been able to find a job and that she did not consider the first two options viable. She also told her that she had spoken to friends in France about getting the money together for her and Victoria's fare home – the option that Ms Arthurworrey most favoured at the time as best serving Victoria's interests.

6.368 Ms Arthurworrey says she stressed the importance of Kouao making a decision soon because Victoria had not been in school since March and she needed some stability. She said she would be back in a week's time to see what arrangements Kouao had made. In the meantime, Kouao told Ms Arthurworrey that she would register Victoria at Bruce Grove Primary School, a school round the corner from Somerset Gardens, until the funds from France came through.

6.369 Other than to say "hello", Ms Arthurworrey did not speak to Victoria at all during this meeting. She observed that Victoria was appropriately dressed and seemed bright and happy: "Victoria did not present as a frightful, fearful child; she presented as articulate, she presented as confident."

6.370 Indeed, Manning said in evidence that he could not remember anything being said or done during the course of the visit which would have indicated that Victoria was frightened of him or that the two of them did not get on.

6.371 However, Ms Arthurworrey did refer to one instance of Victoria behaving in a manner which recalled the observation made by some of the staff at the North Middlesex Hospital that the relationship between Kouao and Victoria was one of 'master and servant'. At one point during the visit, according to Ms Arthurworrey, Victoria ran up to Kouao's side 'as if being called to attention'. This did not cause Ms Arthurworrey undue concern because, as she had observed, Victoria "did not present as a fearful child".

6.372 The home appeared perfectly normal – Manning confirmed that the flat had been made especially clean ahead of the visit – and Ms Arthurworrey observed nothing that would indicate a child being deliberately harmed. She said, "There was no evidence of soiling. I did not smell bleach. I did not smell urine. There was no evidence at all."

6.373 Victoria's sleeping arrangements were discussed. According to Manning, Ms Arthurworrey was told that Kouao and Victoria slept on the bed while he had the sofa bed – although by this stage the truth was very different as Victoria had already begun to spend every night in the bath.

6.374 However, Ms Arthurworrey did note that Kouao seemed rather agitated throughout the interview about the outcome of the housing application. She could not understand why social services could not help in finding her a house. At one stage Victoria joined in the conversation. According to Ms Arthurworrey, "She pointed her finger aggressively at me and said, 'You do not respect me, you do not respect my mother, why can you not find us a home?'" It was an outburst that Ms Arthurworrey says she did not expect from a seven-year-old child. She discussed it with Ms Baptiste subsequently, but according to Ms Arthurworrey, she did no more than smile, say "oh yes" and walk off.

6.375 During the course of the conversation Ms Arthurworrey made the point that the council "only accommodated children who were at risk of significant harm" and that Victoria was not, in the council's view, at such risk. It is perhaps no coincidence that the next time Ms Arthurworrey saw Kouao was because of Kouao making allegations, which, if true, would have meant that Victoria was at very real risk.

Sexual harm allegations

6.376 Just four days later at about 9.45am on 1 November 1999, Kouao telephoned the NTDO. It was quite by chance that Ms Arthurworrey answered the call because she was 'on duty' that week and would not normally be answering her ordinary office phone.

6.377 Kouao was in quite a state. According to Ms Arthurworrey, Kouao was shouting and screaming in a mixture of French and English: "I could not really understand what she was saying but I did hear the words 'Carl Manning' and I did hear the words 'sexual abuse'."

6.378 Ms Arthurworrey immediately asked Ms Kozinos, the duty senior that day, for permission to deal with the case – the policy at the time was that duty took priority over a social worker's allocated cases – and for advice. On Ms Kozinos's instructions she telephoned Kouao and told her to come into the office for an interview. She also booked an interpreter for 10.45am.

6.379 Kouao attended the north Tottenham office with Victoria and Manning. Ms Arthurworrey said she first saw them through a glass window in the reception room. Victoria was sitting with her back to Kouao, swinging her legs and watching other children play in the Wendy house. Kouao and Manning sat next to her and appeared to be having a perfectly normal conversation. Ms Arthurworrey told the Inquiry, "I was extremely shocked by that, given Kouao's demeanour earlier on."

6.380 She asked Ms Kozinos to come and have a look. Ms Kozinos told Ms Arthurworrey to ask Manning to leave. Of the three of them, Manning looked the most distressed and he told Ms Arthurworrey, "I did not do what they are saying I did, I do not know why they are saying this." Such was Manning's distress at the situation he now found himself in, that he later wrote in his diary for 5 November 1999 "Judgement day". He expected, according to what he had been told by Kouao or Ms Arthurworrey (although he could no longer recall who told him), that on that day the police would interview him about the allegations. No such interview ever took place on 5 November 1999 or any time thereafter.

6.381 Ms Kozinos also asked Ms Arthurworrey to take down the details of the allegations. She did not, according to Ms Arthurworrey, ask her to carry out a risk assessment, nor did Ms Arthurworrey recall being asked to interview mother and child separately.

The interview

6.382 Once Manning had left, Ms Arthurworrey spoke to Kouao in the presence of Ms Robertson, another social worker in the north Tottenham DIAT B team. In the meantime, Victoria went to play in the reception area.

6.383 According to Ms Robertson, it was a difficult interview because Kouao kept going off on tangents and switching between French and English. Kouao alleged that Manning had sexually harmed Victoria on three separate occasions.

6.384 The first time was around 20 July 1999. Kouao had spent the day in hospital after fainting at home. On her return to Somerset Gardens, Victoria told her that Manning had inserted his finger into her vagina. He then asked her to touch his penis. Victoria described Manning's penis to Kouao and said that she had seen milky liquid coming from the tip. Manning denied the incident when confronted by Kouao and swore on the Bible that he had not touched Victoria. Kouao decided to do nothing about it.

6.385 She claimed that the second occasion was in August 1999. All three of them were at home that day when Victoria came to Kouao in the kitchen. She said that

Manning had been waving his penis at her. Manning again denied this but this time Kouao went to her neighbour for some advice. He told her that Manning could not possibly have done this and again Kouao decided to do nothing about the allegation.

6.386   The third incident apparently happened on the morning of 1 November 1999. Victoria complained to Kouao that while she was having a bath, Manning had walked into the bathroom naked.

6.387   Ms Arthurworrey told the Inquiry that she was "extremely concerned" when she heard these allegations – not least because Haringey Social Services had been involved with the family since July and Kouao had made no mention of them before. She said she told Kouao that she now had considerable doubts about her ability to protect Victoria.

6.388   Kouao's response was that she had accepted Manning's account in relation to the first two occasions but that morning's incident had caused her to reconsider. Regrettably, these events did not prompt Ms Arthurworrey to reflect and reconsider the conclusions she had come to about Victoria's case in August. She said, "With the benefit of hindsight, I believed I had been lulled into a false sense of security and this section 47 investigation was something quite separate to the first section 47 investigation."

6.389   Ms Arthurworrey told Kouao that due to the seriousness of the allegations, the police child protection team would be involved and that Manning would be arrested.

6.390   Ms Arthurworrey and Ms Robertson then spoke to Victoria alone. Kouao was insistent that they should do so and Ms Arthurworrey was anxious to see how she was. In her statement she said she did not want to get a disclosure from Victoria but she did want to gain her perception of how life was at home. Ms Arthurworrey said:

> "I remember she was dressed in a cotton dress, but she had a thick coat and she was wearing thick tights and she had a pair of wellington boots on. She was appropriately dressed and I actually remember thinking that she looked quite cute that day. Although nothing matched, her clothes were clean ... She appeared happy."

6.391   Ms Arthurworrey said she spoke to Victoria in English – she recalled her English as being "very good" but had barely got beyond saying "hello" when Victoria launched straightaway into a graphic disclosure. Ms Arthurworrey stopped the interview when Victoria began to mimic Kouao's gestures in describing one of the sexual harm allegations.

6.392   There is a note at the foot of the fourth page of the record of that interview which was made by Ms Arthurworrey. She wrote: "Noted by both Valerie and myself that Anna's disclosure sounded rehearsed. Sounded as if she had been coached to say the things she did."

6.393   Ms Robertson accepted in evidence that the fact that Victoria's delivery sounded rehearsed did not itself mean that the allegations were untrue. She also recognised at the time that even if the allegations had been fabricated as part of a ploy to get housing, using the child to make up stories of sexual abuse was in itself harmful and needed to be investigated. She thought that she had discussed these concerns with Ms Arthurworrey.

6.394 Ms Arthurworrey told the Inquiry that she stopped her interview with Victoria because she felt she needed a police officer to be present if these disclosures were going to be made. She herself had not been memorandum interview trained, and did not feel she had sufficient experience or the necessary skills to deal with an interview of this kind.

6.395 As Ms Arthurworrey got up to leave, she said Victoria was visibly upset. She was worried that she was not being believed. She was told that she would have a proper chance to explain the incident in more detail next time. Ms Arthurworrey said, "She shouted out, 'I am not lying. I must tell you more. It is true.'"

6.396 Ms Arthurworrey asked Ms Kozinos if she would explain to Kouao about Haringey's child protection procedures because she did not believe Kouao was taking the situation sufficiently seriously. According to Ms Arthurworrey:

> "Her demeanour seemed to suggest that she did not give a damn ... She was telling me that Manning should be punished for what he has done but there was something about her manner, she just was not understanding the seriousness."

Arranging a strategy meeting

6.397 While Ms Kozinos was doing this, Ms Arthurworrey reported the matter to Haringey police Child Protection Team. The referral was taken by Paula Waldron who allocated the task of investigating it to PC Jones the following morning.

6.398 Ms Arthurworrey also set about arranging a strategy meeting – the first sexual harm strategy meeting that she was to attend, despite having eight other cases alleging sexual harm at that time. She said she told Ms Kozinos that she would be out of the office on a training course for the next three days and the first day that she would be available to attend a strategy meeting was Friday 5 November 1999. According to Ms Arthurworrey, Ms Kozinos told her to "go ahead and arrange it for then". This was despite clear local child protection guidelines which call for "a strategy meeting to be convened within 72 hours of receipt of a sexual abuse referral indicating a high level of suspicion or immediately if the sexual abuse had occurred within the past 72 hours". According to Kouao, the most recent incident of sexual harm had occurred that very morning and this should have necessitated an immediate strategy meeting.

6.399 In her oral evidence, Ms Arthurworrey said, "If Rose had told me to arrange the strategy meeting for Tuesday I would have cancelled my training, but she told me to arrange it for Friday when I came back."

6.400 Ms Kozinos disagreed. She said that at the time she knew the allegations were about sexual harm but knew none of the detail – significantly she did not know whether any penetration had been alleged or the dates of the alleged incident(s) – and she did not see Victoria. As the duty senior, and in the absence of Ms Baptiste, she gave advice to Ms Arthurworrey and said she told her to arrange the strategy meeting "as soon as possible". She anticipated that this would be done within 72 hours and by arrangement with Ms Baptiste, who she expected to chair the meeting. She also said it was Ms Baptiste, who, having returned to the office, asked her as a favour to speak to Kouao and explain to her the child protection procedures.

6.401 I accept that Ms Kozinos may not have known the detail of Kouao's allegations and, specifically, whether the threshold for an immediate strategy meeting to be called had been crossed. Nonetheless, as the duty senior it was her job to know and to ensure that the local child protection guidelines were complied with. This she failed to do. The result was that her anticipation was never translated into a clear instruction to Ms Arthurworrey to do as required, namely to convene a strategy meeting literally as soon as possible – even though it might involve cancelling Ms Arthurworrey's training course – and Ms Arthurworrey did not challenge this.

Finding 'safer' accommodation

6.402 On the advice of Ms Kozinos, Ms Arthurworrey told Kouao that she and Victoria could no longer stay with Manning. Kouao suggested that she stay with her friends, the Kimbidimas, and she rang and spoke to Chantal Kimbidima to make the necessary arrangements. Ms Arthurworrey also spoke to Mrs Kimbidima. She explained to her that allegations of sexual harm had been made and that Kouao and Victoria would need to stay with her during the course of their investigations, which she thought would probably take about a month to complete.

6.403 Ms Arthurworrey believed there was no problem with Victoria and Kouao staying with the Kimbidimas, though she only spoke to Mrs Kimbidima. She made no checks at all as to the suitability of the accommodation and whether it would, indeed, provide a 'safe' haven for Victoria. Ms Arthurworrey said in evidence that she had not been advised to do this, and she would have needed advice from Ms Kozinos because her commitments were to the duty team that day.

6.404 Ms Kozinos, as duty senior, was in charge of the duty float and provided the funds when requested to pay for Kouao's taxi fare to the Kimbidimas. She, too, saw no reason to question the suitability of the Kimbidimas' house as a temporary home for Victoria, because she assumed that Ms Arthurworrey would have discussed this with her team manager before Victoria left the social services office.

6.405 Ms Arthurworrey returned to duty that evening and rang the Kimbidimas to check that everything was all right. She said she was told that Victoria was there but that Kouao had returned to Manning's flat to pick up some of their things. Although neither Mr or Mrs Kimbidima remember receiving a second call from social services on 1 November, or any time that week, Mrs Kimbidima confirmed that Kouao did indeed return to Somerset Gardens that evening and it seems unlikely that Ms Arthurworrey could have learned this from anyone else other than the Kimbidimas. What Ms Arthurworrey did not know – and she said she did not learn until 13 December – was that Victoria also returned to live with Kouao in Manning's flat. Significantly, Victoria never spent a single night at the Kimbidimas' home.

6.406 Mr Kimbidima told the Inquiry there had been some misunderstanding. When Kouao told him that Manning was harming her daughter on the morning of 1 November and that she could not stay at Somerset Gardens, he agreed to her leaving her belongings at his home but that was all. He thought he had explained this to his wife, but according to Mr Kimbidima she misunderstood. Therefore, when social services rang to ask if Kouao and Victoria could stay there pending their investigations, Mrs Kimbidima agreed. On his return home, Mr Kimbidima said he made it clear that Victoria and Kouao could not stay. He tried to find them a hotel for the night but when that failed he rang Kouao who told him, "Do not worry, come here anyway. I will explain to you." Mr Kimbidima took Victoria back to Somerset Gardens about 11pm that evening.

6.407 What Kouao wanted to explain to Mr Kimbidima was that Victoria had told her in the taxi back that she had made up the sexual abuse allegations so that Manning would go to prison and she and Kouao would keep his flat.

Retraction of allegations

6.408 On the very next day, 2 November 1999, Kouao returned with Victoria to the NTDO to tell the same story to Ms Kozinos and retract the allegations. Ms Kozinos

was the duty senior that day and Kouao asked to see her after learning that
Ms Arthurworrey was out of the office.

6.409   Ms Kozinos observed that Victoria looked reasonably well and wore clean clothing,
although her hair looked slightly unkempt. She said "hello" to Victoria "who
appeared shy but did say 'hello' back to me. She gave me a big smile".

6.410   This was the last time anyone from any of the statutory agencies was to see
Victoria before her final and fatal admission to the North Middlesex Hospital on
25 February 2000.

6.411   Kouao was keen for Ms Kozinos to hear from Victoria that she had been a "silly
girl" and that she had lied about the sexual allegations. Ms Kozinos said she
observed that Kouao was bullying in her manner to Victoria and she therefore
insisted on speaking to Kouao alone first, while Victoria remained in the reception
area under the care of the receptionist. The interview lasted no more than
10 minutes.

6.412   Kouao's explanations as to why Victoria would make up such stories and why
Kouao had not reported any of the incidents thus far seemed "vague". However,
she was extremely anxious that Manning should not be arrested or spoken to by
the police and described him as a good friend who had treated her and Victoria
well since their arrival in the UK. Ms Kozinos told Kouao she was not satisfied
with the explanation she had been given and that Haringey's child protection
procedures would have to run their course. This was notwithstanding Kouao's story
that she was waiting for funds from France to arrive the following week, and that
as soon as they did she and Victoria planned to return to France. Life had been
problematic for Kouao since their arrival in the UK and she told Ms Kozinos that
she had had enough.

6.413   It seemed to Ms Kozinos that Kouao's priorities were not about Victoria but to keep
Manning out of prison and to resolve her housing needs. Therefore, she could not
be sure of Kouao's ability to protect Victoria. According to her notes of the interview,
Ms Kozinos explained to Kouao there would be a strategy meeting with the police
child protection team, a full family assessment would be completed by the allocated
social worker, and the case would go to case conference. This was a course of action
that Ms Kozinos regarded as inevitable at the time because of the concerns raised
by Kouao's retraction and subsequent explanations. She also told Kouao she would
have to find alternative accommodation and Kouao reassured her that she would go
straight back to the Kimbidimas' house with Victoria and stay there – an option, of
course, that was never in fact open to her – and that she would not allow Manning
contact with Victoria until the investigation had been completed.

After the interview

6.414   Kouao and Victoria did not leave the NTDO immediately. When Ms Kozinos returned
to the reception area to meet another client, she observed Kouao who appeared to
be "coaxing Victoria and telling her something, which she insisted she needed to tell
us. Her manner was bullying and not very sensitive".

6.415   After her interview with Kouao, Ms Kozinos did two things – she updated
Ms Baptiste and wrote up her notes of the interview. Ms Baptiste had no
recollection of their conversation. But according to Ms Kozinos, Ms Baptiste
told her that Ms Arthurworrey had thought that Victoria's answers were totally
rehearsed and that in light of the retraction, Ms Baptiste questioned the rationale
for continuing with the strategy meeting. In fact, she suggested it should
be cancelled. Ms Kozinos quite rightly persuaded her otherwise because she

recognised that the making of such allegations and their withdrawal in such circumstances might be significant in terms of Kouao's relationship with Victoria.

6.416 Ms Kozinos's notes of her 7 to 10 minute conversation with Kouao are detailed, covering three handwritten pages, and appear on the SS5 case forms that are intended for use by Haringey social workers in writing up summaries and interviews between the department and a child or a child's carer. The notes are dated 2 November 1999 and are signed by Ms Kozinos with her correct professional title, senior practitioner, as she was at the time.

6.417 It is Ms Arthurworrey's contention that no such record of the interview with Kouao was written up at that time, in November, and was therefore not available to the strategy meeting on 5 November 1999. She stated in evidence that she only realised the SS5 form was missing from the file after Victoria's final admission to St Mary's Hospital Paddington on 25 February 2000. According to Ms Arthurworrey, she pointed this out to Ms Kozinos who filled a form out in front of her. As the discussion and events surrounding the second strategy meeting on 5 November have some bearing on this particular conflict of evidence, I shall return to this matter later in this Report.

6.418 The strategy meeting took place in the NTDO as arranged at 11am on Friday 5 November 1999. Ms Arthurworrey returned that day from her training course and was told by Ms Kozinos that Kouao had come into the office on the Tuesday and had retracted the allegations, claiming that Victoria had made everything up. Ms Arthurworrey was not surprised, she said, because she "had found the whole circumstances of [Kouao's] disclosure very bizarre". There was no mention, either before or during the strategy meeting, according to Ms Arthurworrey, of Ms Kozinos's observation that Kouao was bullying towards Victoria, or that Victoria had left the office in a withdrawn and subdued state – although both observations appear in Ms Kozinos's note of the interview with Kouao.

6.419 If Ms Kozinos had indeed written up her note on 2 November, then it should have been on the file and available to the strategy meeting on 5 November. As she did not read the file, she was in no position to check this for herself. She believed she conveyed the contents of the note to the meeting but never referred to it directly, nor did she arrange to have it photocopied and distributed to those present, not least because social services would "not normally give things from our file anyway without permission".

6.420 In support of her version of events, Ms Kozinos referred to Ms Arthurworrey's note on the file of the 5 November strategy meeting. Ms Arthurworrey wrote:

> "... informed Marie-Therese had come to the department on Tuesday 2nd November and retracted the allegations. Said Anna had told her she had made everything up. See SS5 for more details."

6.421 The reference to the SS5 refers, according to Ms Kozinos, to the retraction, and must go to show that her note of the interview with Kouao was available at least by 5 November.

6.422 In questioning, Ms Kozinos was asked to consider two other possibilities. First, that Ms Arthurworrey herself had not completed her notes for 5 November until very much later and after Ms Kozinos had completed hers. Second, that Ms Arthurworrey expected Ms Kozinos to complete her note of the interview on an SS5 and, although she did not have it to hand at the time, she anticipated Ms Kozinos would do so at some future date.

6.423 In relation to the first, there has never been any suggestion that Ms Arthurworrey's note of 5 November was not completed at the time, and therefore I discount it as a possibility. In relation to the second, Ms Arthurworrey said in her third statement, written some considerable time after Ms Kozinos gave her oral evidence and therefore after the options had been put, that it was this second option that reflected the truth. She said:

> "I made a cross reference to the SS5 forms for more detail about the retraction because although an SS5 form had not been filled out at the time, I fully expected Rosemarie Kozinos to complete one in accordance with the standard practice. I did not follow up Rosemarie Kozinos nor remind her to fill in an SS5 form."

6.424 If the second option is to carry any weight, Ms Kozinos said she would have expected to see a reference in Ms Arthurworrey's contact note to an expected or 'outstanding' SS5. However, the clear and unambiguous statement "see SS5 for details" implies that the SS5 she wrote already existed. Counsel for Ms Kozinos also suggested that the detailed and comprehensive notes made by Ms Kozinos bore the hallmarks of notes made while events were still fresh in her mind. This argument must carry some weight because Ms Arthurworrey did not say that she saw Ms Kozinos transcribe the notes made during the interview with Kouao from her notebook to the SS5 – which is what Ms Kozinos said she did. Instead, Ms Arthurworrey claimed that when she pointed out the missing note on 25 February, Ms Kozinos simply "took a pen and paper and wrote up that interview from memory". I find I agree with Counsel for Ms Kozinos's suggestion that her notes of her interview with Kouao "do not look like the product of a hurried attempt at a cover up some three months later".

6.425 I also attach weight to the fact that the allegation by Ms Arthurworrey was first raised in her statement to the Inquiry – in particular she makes no reference to it in her statement for the Part 8 review – and the fact that she only provided an explanation for her cross-reference to the SS5 in her contact note after the options had been put to Ms Kozinos.

6.426 I accept that Ms Arthurworrey's allegation in itself probably had little relevance to the events leading to Victoria's death – all the more so if Ms Kozinos did indeed feed back verbally the events of 2 November, although the record of the strategy meeting does not help in this respect as it is singularly deficient in its recording of the actual discussion that took place. However, the allegation plainly impacts on the credibility of both witnesses. It is my view that on this occasion the evidence of Ms Kozinos is to be preferred, and I accept that she had written her note of the interview with Kouao on 2 November or very shortly thereafter.

The November strategy meeting

6.427 The 5 November strategy meeting was chaired by Ms Kozinos as a favour to Ms Baptiste – the second favour of the week. According to Ms Kozinos, she was asked to chair the meeting "possibly within minutes" of the scheduled start time – though Ms Baptiste had no recollection of this. She was also told the case was a family support case, which it clearly no longer was once Kouao had made, and then retracted, the sexual abuse allegations.

6.428 The meeting was attended by Ms Arthurworrey, PC Jones and PC Ricketts. As was the practice at the time, Ms Kozinos again did not read the case file before the strategy meeting began. As a result, she was not aware and did not remember that she had been involved in Victoria's case back in July. In fact, she expected to rely on Ms Arthurworrey and the two police officers to update her. The fact that neither Ms Arthurworrey nor PC Jones brought to her attention that she had chaired the earlier strategy meeting – indeed it was Ms Kozinos who remembered this herself midway through the discussion – did not cause her to question this expectation.

6.429   She did not, as a result of remembering her earlier involvement, ask to see the case file – albeit that the file was in the nearby duty room and would have taken minutes to retrieve – nor did she go through the 18 earlier strategy meeting recommendations to assess the progress made on each. Instead, she continued to rely on what the police and Ms Arthurworrey told her, namely:

> "The allegations had been fully investigated and that there were no concerns, that they had also discussed it with a child protection adviser and they had medical records that showed it was accidental injuries."

6.430   According to Ms Kozinos "the matter had been closed so to speak but it was open as a family support case" and she had "no reason to disbelieve either of them or not to take what they said at face value at the time".

6.431   The strategy meeting identified the following 15 tasks to be completed:

> "i)   PCPT to contact immigration re status; S/W to establish which airport the client came in on;
>
> ii)   S/W to complete a check with France if client previously known. Find out more information re other children;
>
> iii)   Some proof that child is hers;
>
> iv)   Check on Carl Manning by PCPT–S/W to obtain DOB;
>
> v)   Client to give police a statement/or one withdrawing;
>
> vi)   Full assessment on child re neglect issues;
>
> vii)   Discuss case with legal;
>
> viii) Talk to child on her own with mother's permission;
>
> ix)   Need to explore issues of schooling;
>
> x)   Complete check re medical on Anna;
>
> xi)   Explore issues of Anna bedwetting/and bereavement of father;
>
> xii)   Explore Carl and mother's relationship;
>
> xiii) Possible joint home visit with PCPT;
>
> xiv)   Copies of minutes to PCPT;
>
> xv)   Explain child protection procedures to mother and give her copies of leaflets."

6.432   On the face of it this is a sensible and comprehensive list of tasks. The fact that some of them appear to replicate the July strategy meeting recommendations is hardly surprising, given that Victoria's case file was not to hand, as the recommendations were being drawn up and there was no discussion of the progress made with any of the earlier recommendations. As before, no date was set by which any of these new tasks were to be completed, nor was there a review date to check on progress.

6.433   In fact, there is no evidence to suggest that any of the work that this strategy meeting considered important was ever completed. Although Ms Kozinos considered that a case conference was "inevitable", it never took place.

6.434   According to Ms Kozinos, the third strategy meeting recommendation to seek some proof that the child was Kouao's, arose from a feeling she had when Kouao came into the office on 2 November that something was amiss in the interaction and bonding between Kouao and Victoria. She thought it important enough to recommend that Ms Arthurworrey verify their relationship by checking Kouao's documentation. If this check had been completed on Kouao's passport alone, it would almost certainly, according to the police evidence to this Inquiry, have confirmed their suspicions.

6.435   The strategy meeting record also noted that a memorandum interview would not be pursued at that stage. No reasons for this decision appear on the record. Despite the fact that Ms Arthurworrey had already cut short one interview with Victoria on 1 November because she felt that a proper memorandum interview was called for, Ms Kozinos said she believed that Victoria needed to be spoken to again so that the procedures could be explained to her and her views about going ahead with the memorandum interview could be gauged. According to Ms Kozinos, this was a joint decision of the strategy meeting and it was their intention that such an interview would take place shortly after Victoria had been spoken to. It seems more plausible, however, that the decision not to call a memorandum interview straightaway was largely influenced by the feeling of the meeting, conveyed by Ms Arthurworrey, that they simply did not believe the sexual harm allegations were anything other than a ploy by Kouao to obtain housing. The tone of the strategy meeting recommendations would seem to support this.

6.436   Although Victoria was not in school at the time, the strategy meeting record curiously refers to Victoria's school as Bruce Grove Primary School. Ms Arthurworrey accepted that the information was contradictory but that she had told the meeting of Kouao's intention to register Victoria at the school, and the fact that her schooling was still an issue is evident from the strategy meeting recommendations.

6.437   That Victoria was still at the Kimbidimas' house on 5 November 1999 was an assumption made by both Ms Kozinos and Ms Arthurworrey, although PC Jones believed that she had been told by social services that Victoria and Kouao had returned to Manning's flat. In the meantime, Ms Arthurworrey had just returned from a training course and had "no idea" as to whether any checks had been done on Victoria's whereabouts. She said that Ms Kozinos told her that Victoria was with the Kimbidimas. Ms Kozinos, on the other hand, told the Inquiry that she had relied on Kouao's assurance that she and Victoria would stay with the Kimbidimas and that both Ms Arthurworrey and Ms Baptiste were satisfied with the arrangement. Moreover, she was clear that Ms Arthurworrey told her during the strategy meeting that Victoria was with the Kimbidimas, but she did not remember asking Ms Arthurworrey how she knew. In fact, no checks were ever made as to Victoria's whereabouts up to and including 5 November. As a result, social services were inadvertently relying on Kouao's initial intention to stay with the Kimbidimas as evidence that they were staying there.

6.438   According to Ms Kozinos, the strategy meeting also discussed doing a risk assessment that very day, though no note of this appears in the strategy meeting record. The intention was that PC Jones and Ms Arthurworrey would visit Kouao at the Kimbidimas' house to assess her capacity to protect Victoria, though

Ms Kozinos recalled some question as to whether PC Jones could do the visit that day. In Ms Kozinos's mind there was no question as to the need to do a home visit nor its relative urgency as they were approaching the weekend. The use of the word 'possible' in the strategy meeting recommendation referred only to whether the visit would be joint with the police, not whether it should happen at all. She now accepted that that instruction was far from clear – indeed, no such risk assessment was completed on 5 November or any time thereafter.

6.439   Ms Baptiste's management role for the DIAT B team ceased that very day and Ms Mairs assumed responsibility for both A and B teams from 8 November as part of Haringey's restructuring exercise. But this did not deter Ms Kozinos from updating Ms Baptiste after the strategy meeting. She had understood that Ms Baptiste would retain some transitional responsibility through to the new year and would continue to supervise members of her team. Therefore, Ms Kozinos assumed it would fall to her to ensure that any risk assessment was carried out speedily and the strategy meeting recommendations would be met. Yet again, Ms Baptiste said she did not remember this conversation but cannot dispute that it occurred or that she may indeed have still had some team management responsibility at least as of 5 November.

6.440   Ms Arthurworrey accepted that it was her responsibility as the allocated social worker to ensure that all the tasks identified by the strategy meeting were completed. The first task she dealt with was to send a fax to the French consulate welfare department – a task that she should have done in response to the July strategy meeting recommendations and did not – asking whether the family under the misspelled name of 'Kovoa' but giving their correct last known address in Paris were known to French social services. Six days later, according to her contact note, she received a telephone call from the consulate giving her a 'no trace' response.

6.441   This was a relatively simple task. The Inquiry can only speculate as to whether Ms Arthurworrey would have received a different response, and one that might have cast doubt on the viability of Kouao's plan to return to France, if she had at least spelled the family name correctly – a family that she had been working with for the past three months.

6.442   Ms Arthurworrey's understanding of some of the other tasks expected of her was far from clear. She admitted, for example, that she was unsure about what "complete check regarding medical on Anna" actually meant and she did not check with Ms Kozinos exactly what she was required to do. Nor did she see the reference to "a case conference is required" as being definitive. She believed that her role was to carry out an assessment of Victoria, bring the findings back to her team manager for discussion, and only then would a decision to convene a case conference be taken. She told the Inquiry:

> "The case conference was not the focal point of discussion in that strategy meeting. I would have expected that if I were to call a case conference immediately, I would have expected that to be under item one of the work to be undertaken."

6.443   Instead, her intention was to invite Kouao into the office for an interview so that she could update her on the strategy meeting, make arrangements for an assessment to take place, and review the placement with the Kimbidimas.

6.444   Despite an express instruction to the contrary, Ms Arthurworrey did not discuss Victoria's case with Haringey's legal department because she felt she did not have enough information to do so. There had been no mention of initiating care proceedings or taking out an order in respect of Victoria. According to

Ms Arthurworrey, "The last time I saw Victoria she presented as happy, she presented as relaxed. She did not present in my opinion as a child who had been sexually abused."

6.445 It was this impression which undoubtedly contributed to virtual inaction by Ms Arthurworrey and her managers in their handling of Victoria's case from early November onwards. In my view, Haringey allowed this case to drift to its tragic conclusion. Less than four months later, Victoria was dead.

6.446 The next formal opportunity to check on the progress made with Victoria, and in particular how work on the strategy meeting recommendations was progressing, came on 15 November 1999 when Ms Arthurworrey had her second supervision session since being allocated the case. Ms Mairs who had only the previous week taken on responsibility for both the A and B duty and investigation teams initiated and took the supervision.

First supervision with Ms Mairs

6.447 In her new management role, Ms Mairs told the Inquiry that she had gained "maybe seven" additional social workers to supervise, including Ms Arthurworrey, bringing the total to 16. According to Ms Mairs, there was no handover from Ms Baptiste at the time because Ms Baptiste was not around. Ms Baptiste accepted there was no formal handover, as there should have been, but believed she did speak to Ms Mairs about the social workers she had supervised. She could not, however, recall whether each of her supervisee's cases had been discussed, and in the light of her vague evidence on the subject I find it probable that no such discussions did in fact take place.

6.448 Thus it was that Ms Mairs came to the supervision session without prior knowledge from the former team manager about the concerns in Victoria's case. Since it was not the practice to read case files before supervision, she further disadvantaged herself.

6.449 The whole session lasted about one and a half hours, of which about an hour was spent on casework. At the time, Ms Arthurworrey had 16 cases – five were due to close, four were waiting to close, four or five were child protection and the rest were family support. Both agreed that not much more than five minutes were spent discussing Victoria's case.

6.450 Like Ms Kozinos, Ms Mairs believed that Ms Baptiste still retained some supervisory responsibility for her team, so Ms Mairs did not consider that she was initiating a new supervision contract with Ms Arthurworrey. She told the Inquiry: "I was looking at it more from the point of view of reviewing the cases [Ms Arthurworrey] had so she was clear about what actions needed to be done on it and to enable her to get some support."

6.451 Ms Mairs accepted that her supervision of Victoria's case was wholly reliant on Ms Arthurworrey's account of her work. The case had been in hand since July and Ms Arthurworrey had been the social worker throughout. So Ms Mairs said she expected Ms Arthurworrey to be able to update her – albeit that little more than five minutes was set aside for discussion – and she never ascertained if Ms Arthurworrey herself had read everything on the file.

6.452 Not surprisingly, therefore, when Ms Mairs came to give oral evidence concerning what she believed Ms Arthurworrey told her in supervision, she appeared confused. She thought Ms Arthurworrey had received a medical report from the North Middlesex Hospital which made clear that, although an allegation of physical harm had been made, a doctor's examination had concluded that the marks were due to scabies. In fact, that medical report referred to Victoria's first admission to the Central Middlesex Hospital.

6.453 Ms Mairs said she had no reason to doubt what Ms Arthurworrey told her or to check if she could have been mistaken. She appeared to Ms Mairs to be "a very competent and capable social worker" and she was not aware of any concerns about her practice.

6.454 Ms Mairs also accepted at face value Ms Baptiste's decision that the case was 'family support' and, because of what she had been told and the fact that the case had been around since July, she formed the view that the social services investigation was coming to a close. That she could have believed this just days after a strategy meeting to consider allegations of sexual harm in Victoria's case seems extraordinary, unless Ms Mairs's version of events is accurate, namely that Ms Arthurworrey never told her that there had been any allegations of sexual harm, let alone that Kouao had subsequently retracted those allegations and a strategy meeting had followed. According to Ms Mairs, her recorded decisions from the supervision session bear this out and clearly relate only to the July admission to the North Middlesex Hospital.

6.455 Ms Arthurworrey is adamant that Ms Mairs did know about the sexual harm allegations and the 5 November strategy meeting. She admitted that during the supervision she did not draw Ms Mairs's attention to the relevant section of the file, but she had Victoria's file open on her lap and she read from the notes of the November strategy meeting. Ms Mairs wrote down her action points as Ms Arthurworrey was talking.

6.456 Ms Arthurworrey told the Inquiry that as this was the first occasion Ms Mairs had supervised her, and because she had never before discussed Victoria's case with her, she brought Ms Mairs up to date from the beginning of her involvement with the case up to and including the strategy meeting on 5 November 1999.

6.457 Ms Mairs's supervision decisions merit careful consideration. She recorded the following:

"– child protection investigation took place; no further concerns;
– refer to EWO – school;
– permission to interview child on her own;
– discussions bed wetting with GP;
– refer to family centre bereavement counselling;
– closing summary;
– complete care plan;
– complete decisions of strategy meeting;
– work to be completed by 17th December 1999."

6.458 If indeed these decisions related to the July strategy meeting, then an experienced manager such as Ms Mairs ought to have registered and recorded her concerns that almost five months had elapsed and the outstanding work was not now going to be completed before mid December. Moreover, it might have caused her to question her assumption about the competency of Ms Arthurworrey and the need to review the case file. No such record of concern exists and Ms Mairs admitted that she did not remonstrate with Ms Arthurworrey about this. Ms Mairs said she hoped to be able to discuss the case with Ms Baptiste, Ms Arthurworrey's previous manager, but no such opportunity arose.

6.459 Moreover, the second, third, fourth and fifth of Ms Mairs's decisions closely mirror recommendations that emerged from the November strategy meeting.

In particular, the first strategy meeting made no mention of bed wetting or bereavement counselling – factors which arose for Ms Arthurworrey only after her visit to Somerset Gardens in August 1999. The onus on Ms Arthurworrey back in July was simply to complete checks in relation to schooling and not to deal with the issue by way of a referral to the education welfare officer.

6.460   If the decision to speak to Victoria on her own, as Ms Mairs asserted, relates to the July referral then it would have meant that a vital element of a child protection inquiry had yet to happen, nearly five months after the initial referral. This was clearly a grave and unacceptable lapse in professional practice. Further, if Ms Arthurworrey had believed that these decisions related to the first strategy meeting, she would almost certainly have pointed out to Ms Mairs that she had obtained permission to speak to Victoria and did so on the ward in the North Middlesex Hospital on 6 August 1999.

6.461   When asked why, if this was a 'family support' case, Victoria would need to be seen alone and not in the company of Kouao, Ms Mairs told the Inquiry that she associated scabies with neglect and that this was compounded by the bed wetting and the non-school attendance. She said:

> "I considered there may be other things that were going on that wanted further investigation and I made a decision that it was more appropriate to see the child on her own to actually do that because ... once you see a child on their own you do get more from it."

6.462   Ms Mairs admitted that when she told Ms Arthurworrey "to complete the decisions of the strategy meeting" she did not know what those decisions were or how many were outstanding. She said she had the impression they were not "major". In fact, she assumed that as the case was more than four months old, all the major recommendations would have been dealt with. This was an assumption that she was in no position to verify without first reading the case file, and this she did not do.

6.463   Ms Mairs then directed provisional closure of the case provided that no further concerns emerged. She also directed that any outstanding work should be completed by 17 December 1999. Given that Ms Mairs authorised Ms Arthurworrey to take three days off in lieu and two days annual leave, and that she would have had to complete a week on duty during the coming month, in reality Ms Arthurworrey had just two weeks to complete any outstanding tasks. Ms Mairs considered this to be adequate because she believed Ms Arthurworrey was finishing off the earlier July tasks.

Did Ms Mairs know about sexual abuse allegations?

6.464   Ms Mairs has persistently denied that she was ever told about the sexual harm allegations and the 5 November strategy meeting during her only supervision with Ms Arthurworrey about Victoria. In questioning, she did not accept that she could have misunderstood what she had been told. She told the Inquiry that if she had been told she would have written it down, and she would have been far more concerned about the case, and that the decisions that she made in supervision, while valid, would not have gone far enough. Nor could she have expected the work to have been finished by mid December as the case would have had to go to case conference.

6.465   Having reviewed the evidence, I find it hard to accept the accuracy of Ms Mairs's statements in this matter. It seems inconceivable that Ms Arthurworrey would not have updated Ms Mairs about the November sexual abuse allegations, or told her about the second strategy meeting, especially as these events had occurred so recently and Ms Arthurworrey has consistently expressed throughout her evidence the need for confirmation and direction from her managers. I accept that no mention of sexual abuse would have been made if Ms Arthurworrey was simply reading from the November strategy meeting recommendations because those words do not appear. However, Ms Arthurworrey would have had no motive for not mentioning these allegations or that there had been a strategy meeting as recently as 10 days ago.

6.466 It was clearly Ms Mairs's job, as supervisor, to know about the key milestones in the case. Moreover, a number of her supervision decisions mirror almost exactly the recommendations of the second strategy meeting and the concerns they seek to address were not an issue for social services back in July. I am therefore forced to the conclusion that Ms Mairs's supervision decisions could not have referred to the July strategy meeting, and that the reason she took no issue with Ms Arthurworrey about the delay in completing the necessary tasks was because the strategy meeting they were discussing was the November strategy meeting. It follows, therefore, that the unrealistic deadline that she set demonstrated her failure to fully grasp the seriousness of the matters before her, and the opportunity to get a management grip on the case through supervision was lost yet again.

6.467 Ms Arthurworrey told the Inquiry she was not unduly fazed by the December deadline. Indeed, until her supervision with Ms Mairs she had not been given any timetable to complete the work of the November strategy meeting and she thought the deadline was manageable. She said, "We always worked at a fairly cracking pace in north Tottenham." Whether that was true or not, the fact is that by 17 December 1999, Ms Arthurworrey had done little more than make an unsuccessful check with the French consulate.

Losing contact with Kouao and Victoria

6.468 She also wrote to Kouao on 19 November 1999 offering her an office appointment at 2pm on 1 December – a delay she now concedes as being wholly unacceptable. The purpose of the appointment, according to the letter sent by Ms Arthurworrey, was to "discuss her circumstances further" and invite Kouao to contact Ms Arthurworrey should the appointment time prove inconvenient. Hardly, it might be thought, a letter which conveys any sense whatsoever of urgency or seriousness with regard to sexual harm allegations and the outcome of a strategy meeting.

6.469 Ms Arthurworrey addressed the letter to Kouao at Somerset Gardens, and not care of the Kimbidimas, where she said she assumed Kouao and Victoria were staying. Unbeknown to her at the time, she had sent it to the 'right' address. Ms Arthurworrey explained that she was about to take the time off in lieu agreed with Ms Mairs and that she wrote the letter in some haste. It was not until Kouao failed to turn up at the office on 1 December – though it is difficult to infer from the letter any reason that might have persuaded Kouao to attend – that Ms Arthurworrey realised her "mistake".

6.470 She rang Kouao on her mobile phone but there was no reply and she left a message. In evidence, Ms Arthurworrey claimed to have rung Kouao on several occasions although her contact notes only record the first such call made on 1 December. Her next recorded contact note showed she telephoned Manning on 13 December. Again there was no response and she left a message for him to call her back. Perhaps not surprisingly, as he must have still been waiting anxiously for the police or social services to interview him about the sexual harm allegations, he did not do so.

6.471 When asked why she had waited so long to ring Manning, Ms Arthurworrey said that she already formed the impression that Kouao may have moved on, as she said she intended to do the last time Ms Arthurworrey visited Somerset Gardens at the end of October 1999. Ms Arthurworrey accepted that it was a dangerous assumption to make at the time and she should not have done so.

6.472 She also rang the Kimbidimas on 13 December 1999. This, according to Ms Arthurworrey, was the first time she learned that Kouao and Victoria had returned to live with Manning but she did not ask, nor was she told, when they had returned. What is clear is that from 13 December, Ms Arthurworrey ought to have appreciated that arrangements made for keeping Victoria safe after the sexual harm allegations made against Manning had broken down.

6.473 Ms Arthurworrey now had no idea of the whereabouts of the family. She told Ms Kozinos shortly after 1 December that Kouao had failed to turn up for her appointment and was told to "keep on trying" and that they would discuss it in supervision. She also attempted to visit Victoria at Somerset Gardens. Her first two attempts were said to have been in the period between 13 and 23 December 1999, although there is no documentary evidence of either of them.

6.474 It did not occur to Ms Arthurworrey to explore with the legal department the powers open to her – she did not in any event believe that Kouao was deliberately trying to conceal Victoria from social services. However, she said that she told PC Jones on 10 December that she had had no contact with Kouao or Victoria, although again, no record of the conversation appears on the contact sheets.

6.475 As she could not find Kouao and Victoria, Ms Arthurworrey was effectively prevented from taking her investigation and assessment of the family any further forward. The recommendations from the November strategy meeting were, in effect, left to fall by the wayside.

Supervision with Ms Kozinos

6.476 Ms Arthurworrey was to have had another opportunity to discuss Victoria's case in formal supervision, this time with Ms Kozinos, on 14 December. In the event, the meeting was cancelled because of industrial strike action in which both Ms Kozinos and Ms Arthurworrey took part. The supervision session was subsequently rearranged for 23 December.

6.477 Ms Kozinos was to begin her role as practice manager, which carried with it supervisory responsibilities for social workers, the very next day. Although she had never before undertaken formal supervision of social workers, except to provide case direction in the absence of a team manager, she said she felt reasonably confident about taking on the task. Indeed, Ms Arthurworrey had requested that Ms Kozinos should be her supervisor following the restructuring of the DIATs.

6.478 According to Ms Kozinos, this introductory supervision with Ms Arthurworrey took some three hours and covered nine agenda items. Among the decisions agreed upon was that Ms Arthurworrey would be on annual leave from 25 December 1999 to 17 January 2000, and that she would attend a memorandum interview training course in April 2000. Ms Kozinos also noted that Ms Baptiste had completed a performance development review with Ms Arthurworrey but that had "not been handed over". She noted on the record: "I will discuss with Carole next time she is back at work. Need previous supervision and PDR notes. Also need an official handover."

6.479 Ms Kozinos also arranged two further supervision sessions with Ms Arthurworrey for 18 January and 7 February 2000 and a further performance development review for 10 February. According to Ms Kozinos, none of these took place – although Ms Arthurworrey claimed that she had a brief informal supervision with

Ms Kozinos on 18 January in which Victoria's case was mentioned but there was no recorded note.

6.480 Judging by the extreme brevity of Ms Kozinos's action notes of 23 December 1999, discussion of Victoria's case must have been very short indeed. Ms Kozinos admitted that as this was an introductory session, little time was devoted to casework and she estimated that Victoria's case took no more than five minutes to discuss.

6.481 Ms Kozinos recorded the following four lines:

"– Family have left area. No further contact.
– Complete spot visit.
– Complete appropriate paper work then NFA.
– Update PCPT – Karen Jones."

6.482 Ms Arthurworrey's recollection of the session was, as had been her general experience of supervision, that it was not a two-way discussion: "It was myself informing Rose of the situation and then just Rose writing down these actions. There was no discussion."

6.483 Equally, as was the practice, Ms Kozinos did not read the case file either before or during supervision. This is a factor that might have been considered marginally less relevant on this occasion because Ms Kozinos had chaired both the July and November strategy meetings herself. She ought, therefore, to have been aware of the seriousness with which the latter strategy meeting viewed the case, and she might have been expected to recall the general direction of the strategy meeting recommendations, if not the detail.

6.484 However, none of this was evident in the manner in which she dealt with Victoria's case in supervision. Although it is fair to say that Ms Arthurworrey's and Ms Kozinos's evidence about what was said during this meeting conflict with each other, given Ms Kozinos's prior knowledge of the case it is difficult to explain her readiness to accept at face value what she claimed Ms Arthurworrey told her.

6.485 According to Ms Kozinos, Ms Arthurworrey informed her that she had reported to Ms Mairs in supervision on 15 November 1999 – just 10 days after the strategy meeting – that there were no outstanding child protection concerns and that Ms Mairs had recommended case closure. Implicit in this, presumably, was that the concerns had been fully investigated. Ms Arthurworrey's previous managers had also told her not to take Victoria's case to case conference, despite a clear recommendation of the strategy meeting that that was the appropriate course. Indeed, Ms Kozinos's view at the time was that a case conference was inevitable and she had told Kouao the same.

6.486 Ms Kozinos told the Inquiry that she had begun to doubt her own judgement about the case and wondered whether she had been heavy-handed with Kouao. She said:

"I doubted myself and put much more faith in what Lisa told me at face value ... also because of my team manager who I do have faith in, who was very experienced in my view, having recommended to close it, I did not question it."

6.487 Ms Kozinos never asked Ms Arthurworrey about the progress in meeting each of the November strategy meeting recommendations and, more fundamentally, she never asked her whether she had seen Victoria – an essential element of any competent section 47 inquiry – and she regretted not doing so. She simply assumed that such an interview had taken place, whereas a check of the case file would have shown that it had not. She would also have seen that virtually all the 15 tasks identified by the strategy meeting were still outstanding. As to Victoria's whereabouts, Ms Kozinos was adamant that Ms Arthurworrey told her in supervision that the family "had gone ... they have left, gone back to France". But she never asked Ms Arthurworrey how she could have known this.

6.488 At the end of the supervision, Ms Kozinos said she was left with the impression that the majority of Ms Arthurworrey's cases were low-profile family support cases, that she had missed certain deadlines in these cases and that she was going through the process of closing a lot of them. Victoria's case was one of these.

6.489 Ms Arthurworrey, on the other hand, said she told Ms Kozinos that she had not completed any of the strategy meeting recommendations and that she had not had any contact with Victoria since the strategy meeting, despite making a number of telephone calls. She also denied telling Ms Kozinos that her previous line managers had recommended case closure. She also told Ms Kozinos that there was a **possibility** [my emphasis] that the family may have gone back to France because that was what had been discussed in October, but she did not know where they were. Accordingly, Ms Kozinos wrote down the first action note as "'Family have left area, no further contact.'"

6.490 Ms Kozinos explained the reference to "no further contact" as meaning there had been no further contact because the family had returned to France. This, together with her recollection that Ms Arthurworrey had mentioned making some spot visits, confirmed that Ms Kozinos was aware that contact with the family had been lost at some stage.

6.491 Ms Kozinos's second action point – "complete spot visit" – was directed to Manning's flat. Ms Kozinos denied she had been told that Victoria and Kouao had returned there at some point – she said that if she had known this her response would have been very different – and that she had no reason not to accept that the family had left the Kimbidimas and gone to France. However, she wanted to double check. She said:

> "Part of me, with the feelings I got from the visit with the mum, it must have been still something that was niggling at me and I suggested just to be on the safe side, just to be certain, just to make sure, that she has not returned to Manning's."

6.492 Ms Kozinos accepted that a single spot check could hardly prove conclusively that the family had indeed returned to France. She admitted that she did not think it through and did not follow her instinct because she was aware of her manager's decision – a manager who she respected and believed knew better – to close the case, and she did not challenge this.

6.493 In fact, Ms Kozinos's instinct was to prove correct and the consequences for Victoria might have been very different if those instincts had been properly acted upon.

6.494 She recalled that Ms Arthurworrey said she would do several more spot visits because Manning's flat was on her way to work and it would not inconvenience her. However, she denied that this must cast doubt on Ms Arthurworrey's supposed firm belief that the family had returned to France. Ms Kozinos said, "[Ms Arthurworrey] seemed certain ... I think she was going to do this just to reassure me. I think because she said that."

Disagreement over supervision content

6.495 Ms Kozinos's and Ms Arthurworrey's accounts of what was said in supervision on 23 December 1999 differ markedly in a number of key respects and, in particular, whether Ms Kozinos was told that:

- all the concerns had been properly investigated or that none of the strategy recommendations had been completed;
- Victoria had not been seen since the strategy meeting and there had been no contact with the family;
- Victoria and Kouao had returned to Manning's flat at some stage previously;
- the family had definitely or possibly returned to France;
- Ms Arthurworrey's previous line managers had recommended case closure.

6.496 In the absence of any proper record of their discussion, I cannot be certain exactly what Ms Kozinos was told during this supervision session, or whether she misunderstood the information given to her by Ms Arthurworrey. However, having seen and heard both the witnesses, I have come to the conclusion that on this occasion Ms Kozinos's interpretation of what she was told and her direction was almost entirely influenced by her understanding that there had already been a management decision to close the case. Moreover, it seems probable that this understanding could only have come from Ms Arthurworrey, for although Ms Mairs's instruction to prepare a closing summary was recorded on the previous supervision summary and action sheet, both agreed that Ms Kozinos did not read the case file either before or during supervision. As Ms Mairs was a manager highly regarded by Ms Kozinos, she therefore let slide any remaining concerns she may have had and did not properly and systematically apply her mind to these.

Failure to find Kouao and Victoria

6.497 Ms Arthurworrey made one more visit to Somerset Gardens on 6 January 2000 in the hope of catching the family at home. On the first two occasions Ms Arthurworrey did not get beyond the front door of the block of flats. On the third visit she entered the premises and knocked on the door. She said:

> "I remember knocking and I remember thinking it sounds very quiet and then the light time switch [in the hallway] went off and I knocked again. There was no response and then I left."

6.498 She recorded on the contact sheet that the flat was in darkness. In fact, the likelihood is that Victoria was staying at the flat throughout this period and was, at the very least, spending the night there. It is true that she, Kouao and Manning had made three trips to France in late 1999, but it seems likely that she was back from the last trip by the time of Ms Arthurworrey's first spot visit. Manning told the Inquiry that the three of them had made two visits to France, one in early October and one in mid November, and that Kouao and Victoria went alone to France for two weeks in late November/early December. It seems likely but not certain that they were back from that last trip in time for the first attempt by Ms Arthurworrey to visit them in the 10 days between 13 and 23 December.

6.499 On none of the visits did Ms Arthurworrey obtain a response from inside the flat. There are two possible explanations for this. Either Victoria had been taken out by Kouao and Manning, although there is little evidence that at the time she ever went out, except to church, or Victoria was at home unable to get to the door.

6.500 Apart from a couple more unsuccessful phone calls to Kouao and Manning, Ms Arthurworrey made just one more attempt at establishing the whereabouts of Victoria. On 10 January 2000 – more than two months after the November strategy meeting – she telephoned Bruce Grove Primary School. She knew at the end of October that Kouao had intended to register Victoria at the school, so she rang to see whether Victoria had been registered and was attending. No child of that name was on the register or ever had been.

6.501   This was clearly no more than a half-hearted step to locate the family before closing the case. According to Ms Arthurworrey, she had made no checks of the school before January because she had already formed the view that the reason Kouao failed to attend her office appointment on 1 December was because she and Victoria had returned to France. It remained her belief throughout January and February 2000 that the family had moved out of the area.

File closure

6.502   The third direction given in supervision on 23 December was to "complete appropriate paper work then NFA [no further action]". Ms Arthurworrey understood this to mean that she should prepare her closing summary and send out a closing letter. Thus it was on 18 February 2000 she wrote to Kouao at Somerset Gardens. She wrote the following:

> "Dear Marie-Therese
>
> I am writing to inform that as you have failed to maintain contact with this office and your exact whereabouts are unknown, the department will be closing your file.
>
> If you are experiencing any difficulties, please do not hesitate to contact our duty team on the above number.
>
> Yours sincerely
> Lisa Arthurworrey."

6.503   Nobody reading this letter, including Kouao, who almost certainly received it, could have deduced that here was a social services department that had treated at all seriously allegations of sexual harm made as recently as the previous November.

6.504   In Ms Arthurworrey's words, the letter was "very basic". She said she simply did not know how to write the letter. She had asked Ms Kozinos for advice and assistance but she was too busy and quite dismissive. Ms Arthurworrey said, "I came away and I just sat down and thought about it and this is what I came up with."

6.505   Ms Arthurworrey proceeded to close the case in accordance with local guidelines and without any further discussion with either her supervisor, Ms Kozinos, or her team manager, Ms Mairs. She said she prepared a closing summary and recorded on the last contact sheet "file to be closed". She also recorded details of the closing letter that she sent to Kouao and the fact that she had left a message for PC Jones on 18 January 2000 informing her that Haringey Social Services was closing Victoria's file. She believed she handed the file to Ms Kozinos some time between 18 and 25 February 2000 – although Ms Kozinos suggested that she must have been given the file for closure by the latest before her next supervision with Ms Arthurworrey on 21 February, because Victoria's case no longer appears on the February supervision record.

6.506   Both the closing summary and the last contact sheet would have been signed by Ms Kozinos as practice manager. Indeed, Ms Arthurworrey assumed they had been because she found Victoria's file in the "close" basket on 25 February. The closing summary and the last contact sheet would also then have been authorised and countersigned by Ms Mairs.

6.507 The process for closure was described slightly differently by Ms Mairs, who stated that only the closing summary would normally be signed off by the practice manager and then countersigned by the team manager. Yet Ms Arthurworrey recalled seeing both signatures on the last contact sheet on 25 February – a claim that cannot be supported by the documentary evidence as both the contact sheet and closing summary are missing from the file.

6.508 At the final stage in the closure process, Ms Mairs as team manager would have signed off a local children and families' assessment action record, marking it for no further action. This she did. In stark contrast to what she said in her statement to the Inquiry and in her interview with Mr Monaghan as part of Haringey's internal review process, Ms Mairs admitted in oral evidence that she closed Victoria's case on the morning of 25 February 2000, the day Victoria died.

Victoria's final admission to the North Middlesex Hospital and St Mary's Hospital Paddington

6.509 At 3.37am on Friday 25 February Mr Robert Philpotts, the out-of-office-hours social worker for Haringey council, received a telephone call from Dr Pahari at the North Middlesex Hospital. He was ringing to tell social services that a child known as 'Anna' Kouao had been brought to the hospital in an emergency. She was in a coma, with an abnormally low temperature, and was breathing slowly with a slow heart rate. Dr Pahari passed on Kouao's explanation that Victoria had stopped eating the day before she became ill and that Kouao had contacted her church and the church had diagnosed that the child was possessed by an evil spirit. Kouao denied giving Victoria any drugs or potions, only holy water, and that she and the church community had prayed for Victoria. When Victoria failed to improve, she was taken back to the church. From there, Kouao took a minicab to make her way to the hospital, but as Victoria's condition appeared to become critical, the taxi driver stopped at an ambulance station for assistance.

6.510 On examining Victoria, Dr Pahari noticed "several old bruises, scars and ulcers to her wrists and ankles, streaky bruises across her buttocks as if she had been beaten. Anna's face and hands are swollen".

6.511 Kouao denied she had deliberately harmed Victoria. It was also noted that Victoria had no GP, did not attend school and that she had been incontinent since July 1999. Dr Pahari told Mr Philpotts that Victoria was critically ill and was being prepared for transfer to the intensive care unit at St Mary's Hospital Paddington. He asked that a duty social worker follow up the case.

6.512 Mr Philpotts typed up a note of what he had been told on an out-of-office-hours team social work report form, and faxed a copy of it across to the duty team at 5.07am.

Dr Pahari's referral

6.513 Mr Almeida was the duty manager in charge that Friday morning. He received Dr Pahari's referral from the duty clerk first thing in the morning and attached a note to the file at 9.30am, setting out the following actions:

"– check register etc;
– previous concerns;
– family composition etc;
– ring hospital clarify nature of referral;
– injury accidental/non-accidental;
– abuse – physical, sexual, neglect;
– discuss with duty senior **urgently** once the facts have been established."

6.514   Mr Almeida did not recognise the case at the time, nor did he recall that
Ms Arthurworrey, who by chance was also on duty that day, was the allocated social
worker. Instead he gave the case to Ms Hayes to make some urgent telephone calls
to the North Middlesex Hospital and St Mary's Hospital Paddington.

6.515   Ms Hayes told the Inquiry, "When I rang North Middlesex they said they had seen
Anna before and she had been there during the summer for **scabies** [my emphasis].
That is when I realised it was Lisa's case."

6.516   Ms Hayes spoke to the consultant, Dr Lesley Alsford. In addition to what Dr Pahari
had already conveyed to social services, Ms Hayes was told that the hospital
suspected that Victoria might have been poisoned and that tests would be carried
out either there or at St Mary's Hospital. It was thought that cigarette burns might
have accounted for some of the old scars and that the marks on Victoria's arms and
legs suggested that she had been tied bound. Victoria was unable to straighten her
legs. She had ulcerations on both buttocks and lower legs and her feet were red
and swollen. The child was very malnourished. She had low blood protein and it
was thought she may have been starved. Dr Alsford also told Ms Hayes that Victoria
may have AIDS and that she was of the opinion that the child had been neglected.

6.517   At St Mary's Hospital, Ms Hayes spoke to Dr Ivan Dillon who told her that Victoria
was in a critical condition and there was a possibility that she would not survive.
The hospital was unsure of the reasons for Victoria's condition and they were
planning to do a number of tests, including looking at the possibility of HIV/AIDS.
Ms Hayes was told that Kouao was at the hospital and social services should ring
back in the afternoon and speak to Dr Joseph Britto, the consultant on duty, who
might have more information.

6.518   According to Ms Hayes, she then handed over the notes she had made of
her telephone calls to Mr Almeida, who subsequently spoke about the case
to Ms Mairs. In the meantime, Ms Hayes had given a copy of the referral to
Ms Arthurworrey whose case she realised it was.

Immediate reaction to the referral

6.519   Ms Arthurworrey said she went to look for the file and found it in the
administration 'closed file' basket. She said she flicked through it at the time
and noticed that both the last contact sheet and closing summary were on the
file. A decision was made to hold a strategy meeting on 28 February 2000 to
be chaired by Ms Mairs. Ms Mairs also listed a number of action points on the
contact sheet which, given Victoria's critical condition, appear remarkably routine
and demonstrate yet again that she could not have read the details contained in
Dr Pahari's initial referral or any other case file material. She wrote:

"– strategy meeting 28 February;
– request medical report;
– check school if any concerns;
– check GP if any concerns;
– explain child protection procedures to parent;
– detail risk assessment;
– Invite legal, PCPT, SW;
– Up date Dave Duncan;
– Up date me."

6.520   In the event, the strategy meeting held on 28 February 2000 was anything but
routine. Ms Arthurworrey said she heard the news from Ms Kozinos and Ms Mairs
that Victoria had died at about 3.45pm on 25 February. The focus of the strategy

meeting was now no longer a routine child protection case but the death of a child in unexplained circumstances where deliberate harm was strongly suspected.

After Victoria's death

6.521 In the meantime, Ms Green had received a telephone call on 25 February 2000 from Dr Rossiter at the North Middlesex Hospital. Dr Rossiter was critical of social services' involvement in Victoria's case so far and she wondered what they had been doing. She also wanted to alert Ms Green's team to Victoria's second admission to the hospital and her impending transfer to St Mary's Hospital. Ms Green ran an index check on Victoria and having established that Ms Arthurworrey was the allocated social worker she said she contacted her. She also tried unsuccessfully to contact three line managers, none of whom were in work.

6.522 Ms Green was given the name of an assistant director, outside of the children and families' department, who had been named to cover for the absence of the other three. Between them, based on what Ms Arthurworrey and Dr Rossiter had said and the information on the client index system, they agreed that no other children were at risk. On that basis they were content for the strategy meeting to go ahead as planned for the Monday morning.

6.523 Mr Duncan, the commissioning manager for children's services for both district offices, was first alerted to Victoria's death on the Friday afternoon. He was away on leave when Ms Kozinos rang to update him. He was telephoned again in the evening of Sunday 27 February by the out-of-office-hours team to say that Victoria's carers had been arrested and the police wanted to see the social services file. Mr Duncan then sought to contact three people. He left a message for Ms Wilson, assistant director for children's services, on her answer-phone asking her to contact him. He spoke briefly to Ms Graham, commissioning manager child protection, quality and review, to seek advice regarding disclosure of the file and to inform her of Victoria's death. He also spoke to Gerald Lloyd, the principal solicitor dealing with social services matters in Haringey.

6.524 On the following morning, Monday 28 February 2000, according to Mr Duncan, Ms Wilson asked for Victoria's file so that it could be reviewed by senior managers. Ms Wilson recalled telling someone to secure the file and bring it to her office but could not remember whether this was over the telephone to Ms Graham or Ms Green.

6.525 Ms Mairs told the Inquiry that she was instructed by Mr Duncan during a meeting in his room to photocopy Victoria's file and he confirmed in his statement that a copy of the file was retained in the district office.

Removal of documents from Victoria's file

6.526 Exactly what happened during this photocopying session is the subject of several and diverse accounts. According to Ms Arthurworrey, she followed Ms Mairs to the photocopy room and saw her pass the file to an administrative assistant to copy. As Ms Mairs did so, she tore out the last contact sheet saying, "Let us get rid of this" and Ms Arthurworrey believed she screwed it up but cannot be sure. She was unable to recall who the administrative assistant was but said she would not have seen Ms Mairs's actions as she was doing the photocopying and had her back to Ms Mairs. Neither the last contact sheet nor the closing summary appear on the file.

6.527 When asked why she did not protest immediately to Ms Mairs, Ms Arthurworrey said, "Angella Mairs was the headmistress. I was a child who was seen but could not be heard, and I had seen what happened to those who challenged Angella Mairs."

6.528 It might seem extraordinary that Ms Arthurworrey failed to report what she had seen, if true, to anyone in authority. She told the Inquiry that she did not know to whom she could go with this information and feel safe. She had never met either Ms Wilson, the assistant director who had asked for the file, nor Ms Richardson, the director of housing and social services, and she did not think of letting either of them know in writing. Nor did she contact Ms Duncan, the commissioning manager for the NTDO and Ms Mairs's immediate line manager. She said:

> "I did not feel comfortable in discussing this with Dave Duncan. Primarily because I knew I was still in Angella's team and she had made no attempt to hide the fact that she had removed the last contact sheet, she just did that."

6.529 Ms Arthurworrey said her reasons for not making this allegation when interviewed for the Part 8 review was that she found the interview "very oppressive, the line of questioning was accusatory and it was blaming".

6.530 Instead, Ms Arthurworrey chose to tell her friend and colleague Ms Robertson of the incident the day it happened and Ms Robertson confirmed this in evidence. Ms Arthurworrey also spoke about it to another colleague a couple of days later. Ms Robertson told the Inquiry that her conversation with Ms Arthurworrey was brief – both were shortly due to attend the strategy meeting – but that Ms Arthurworrey was visibly upset and did not feel she could trust anybody:

> "Angella was quite powerful and she was quite assertive in her personality so I understand why Lisa felt it might not have been acted upon if it was reported. I can understand her reason."

6.531 In fact, Ms Arthurworrey thought that it was not until December 2000, when she responded in writing to Haringey in connection with the draft Part 8 review report, that she finally made the allegation known to the senior management.

6.532 Ms Green recalled that she was asked by Ms Graham to travel to the NTDO on the Monday morning to retrieve the file. She set off at about 10am. Asked why this did not happen immediately after Victoria's death the previous Friday, she told the Inquiry that none of her line managers was available to give the instruction and the senior manager she had spoken to earlier in the afternoon did not suggest that it was something she should do.

6.533 When Ms Green arrived at the NTDO about half an hour later, Ms Mairs was expecting her and had already begun photocopying the file. Ms Green was not surprised by this, she said, because it was normal practice for the district office to have kept a working copy of the file. She accepted though that on this occasion where there were no other children of the family at risk the practice was entirely devoid of purpose.

6.534 Ms Green reckoned that Ms Mairs and the administrator were halfway through the photocopying by the time she arrived. As the photocopying room was small she went to wait in the DIAT office where she said she found Ms Arthurworrey. She waited a further half an hour before returning to the photocopy room. The task was still not finished and pages of the file were being removed to be photocopied. According to Ms Green, when she asked to have the file Ms Mairs was dismissive. She told her she would get it when it was ready.

6.535 Ms Green did not attempt to seize the file. It needed to be recompiled and she assumed that Ms Mairs had been instructed to copy the file by Mr Duncan, though she never checked this out. Instead, she sought advice by telephone from her line manager, Ms Graham. According to Ms Green, Ms Graham was "incensed" and told Ms Green: "I am not having it, and I will be contacting managers and you will be given the file pronto."

6.536   Ms Green waited another 20 minutes before the file was handed over – the whole photocopying task having taken, by her reckoning, one hour and 20 minutes. During this time, Ms Green said Ms Arthurworrey was working in the DIAT office. She said, "I was not there all of the time because I made a phone call from the next floor up to my manager. But she was in there a lot of the time."

6.537   While Ms Green could not account for what Ms Arthurworrey may have observed prior to her arrival, she was clear, and Ms Arthurworrey confirmed, that nothing was said to her about Ms Mairs removing pages from the file. If the incident had happened she would have expected Ms Arthurworrey to report the facts to her and the opportunity was certainly there for her to do so. Ms Green signed out the file and took it back to Ms Wilson's office at about noon.

6.538   Ms Mairs's version of events that morning differed on a number of counts. She recalled that both Ms Green and Ms Arthurworrey were present while she was photocopying the file, although she acknowledged that Ms Green may have popped out at some time, but not for any lengthy period in her opinion. There may have been an administrative assistant there, too, but she could not remember. She thought that Ms Arthurworrey had been taking out sections of the file to photocopy and then replacing them in the file once they had been photocopied. The whole process, according to her, lasted no more than 45 minutes.

6.539   Ms Mairs denied categorically removing the contact sheet from the file. She told the Inquiry: "I did not do that. I have no reason to do that. It does not serve me any purpose and I would not do that."

6.540   When asked whether the missing papers would have provided documentary evidence that she had instructed there to be no further action in Victoria's case, Ms Mairs said, "I never denied the fact that I closed the case on 25th and that I said I did it."

6.541   While the issue of whether or not Ms Mairs removed the closing summary and last contact sheet from Victoria's case file cannot in any way have impeded Haringey's handling of her case, the allegation that material evidence was deliberately removed is extremely serious and a finding either way must impact on the likely truth of either Ms Arthurworrey's or Ms Mairs's evidence to the Inquiry on other matters.

6.542   In her closing submission, Counsel for Ms Mairs commented that there were opportunities for others to remove papers from the file and that it was Ms Mairs's unchallenged evidence that she did not handle the file between the morning of Friday 25 February – when Ms Arthurworrey said she last saw the papers in question – and the morning of Monday 28 February. Ms Arthurworrey's allegation, however, is not just that the papers were removed from the file but that she saw Ms Mairs do so.

6.543   Ms Mairs has also consistently denied that she had any motive for removing the closing summary and last contact sheet, and that she had always maintained that she closed Victoria's file on 25 February, though she said the decision to do so had been made by Ms Kozinos and Ms Arthurworrey. In fact, this is not the case. In her statement to the Inquiry, Ms Mairs said that although the file had been passed to her, at the time of Victoria's death she had not yet closed the file. Mr Monaghan in his report similarly observed: "[Ms Mairs] maintains that she had not closed the case on 25.2.00. Only the missing documents could verify the status of the case on 25.2.00."

6.544 Counsel for Ms Mairs also suggested that it was inherently unlikely that Ms Mairs, a senior and experienced practitioner, would have behaved in the manner described by Ms Arthurworrey and in full view of her junior colleagues, knowing "that an action of this sort would be likely to lead to consequences of the most serious kind".

6.545 It was Counsel's submission that Ms Arthurworrey's account must be seriously undermined by her failure to report the incident to anyone in authority, either at the time or at the Part 8 investigation. In Counsel's words, "She had no compelling reason for not doing so." It might also be said in support of Ms Mairs that the existence on the file of the children and families' assessment action record, which she also signed on 25 February for no further action, removed any motive for Ms Mairs to lie about when she closed the case and hence would have rendered purposeless the removal of the other documents.

6.546 I am not persuaded by these arguments. That Ms Mairs should have attempted to convey in her statement to this Inquiry and in interview to Mr Monaghan, that she had not closed Victoria's case by the time of her death, when in fact she had, suggests that she did indeed rashly believe that she could hide the truth in February 2000 by removing the closing summary and final contact sheet which bore her signature. It is equally plausible that Ms Mairs simply overlooked the children and families' assessment action record when removing the other documents and, realising that it was still on the file, felt compelled to admit in oral evidence that she had closed Victoria's case on 25 February, a fact which she had previously denied.

6.547 Having seen all the witnesses in connection with this incident, I also attach weight to the evidence of Ms Robertson who confirmed that Ms Arthurworrey had told her immediately what had happened and that she seemed to be visibly upset by the events. That Ms Arthurworrey could and should have immediately reported the incident to her senior managers and did not – she had ample opportunity to mention the incident to Ms Green – was clearly a serious mistake. She had no apparent motive for making up this allegation and it is extremely doubtful that there would have been any reprisals for taking such action. However, both her and Ms Robertson's observations about Ms Mairs's assertive and powerful personality would go some way to explaining Ms Arthurworrey's reluctance in this matter, and it could also account for Ms Mairs's belief she could get rid of material evidence without any attempt to hide her actions and without fear of the consequences.

6.548 Further weight must also be attached to Ms Arthurworrey's version of events, in so far as she and Ms Green corroborate each other as to who was involved in the photocopying, though neither can recall with certainty any details about the administrative assistant who was present. It also seems clear from Ms Green's version that both she and Ms Arthurworrey spent some time in the DIAT office while waiting for Ms Mairs to complete the photocopying and were not, as suggested by Ms Mairs, all standing together for most of the time in the photocopying room.

6.549 Therefore, I am forced to the conclusion that Ms Mairs was responsible for the removal of the closing summary and last contact sheet from Victoria's case file. In the absence of any corroborating testimony, this finding must inevitably cast some doubt on her evidence to the Inquiry on other matters that relate directly to Haringey's handling of Victoria's case and the events leading up to her death.

Analysis of practice

6.550 It is worthwhile at this point to step back from the chronology of events in Haringey to analyse in more detail what that chronology shows to have been the particular deficiencies in the practice of Haringey Social Services in the period with which I am concerned. The value of such an analysis lies in identifying the steps necessary to avoid the same problems arising elsewhere.

6.551 Quite apart from the vast amount of documentation that was provided on the subject, I heard over 20 days of oral evidence concerning the manner in which Haringey discharged its responsibility to safeguard and promote Victoria's welfare. Before commencing a detailed analysis of particular deficiencies in the service offered to Victoria by Haringey Social Services, it is useful to highlight four simple facts which do much to explain how it came to be that Victoria's plight was so disastrously overlooked for so long.

1 During the 211 days that Victoria's case was held by an allocated social worker employed by Haringey Social Services, she was seen by that social worker on only four separate occasions.

2 On none of those occasions did the social worker spend any more than 30 minutes with Victoria.

3 On none of those occasions did the conversation between the social worker and Victoria extend much further than "hello, how are you?"

4 The amount of time that the social worker spent discussing Victoria's case with those who were responsible for supervising her work amounted to no more than 30 minutes in total.

6.552 One's instinctive reaction on hearing the details of a case such as Victoria's, where the most extreme ill-treatment has gone undetected over a substantial period of time, is one of disbelief that nobody would seem to have noticed. The incredulity is increased in those cases in which there has been extensive involvement on the part of professionals whose job it is to protect vulnerable children.

6.553 Victoria's case, for the vast majority of the time that she was known to Haringey, was allocated to a qualified social worker based in an office containing a number of experienced managers. In view of this, it seems inconceivable that so little was done to help her. However, if one bears in mind the four facts listed above, it becomes a little easier to see how important information could have been missed or ignored.

6.554 However, what these facts do not do is explain why the attention that Victoria's case did receive from the staff of Haringey Social Services was so limited and ineffectual. The answer to that question involves looking more closely at a number of specific elements of the practice of the staff concerned. That is the purpose of the section which follows.

6.555 Before turning to consider those particular areas of practice, I wish to make two points.

6.556 The first is that some of what follows may be thought by some to be self-evident or to amount to little more than a call for social workers to do the job they have been trained to do and are paid to carry out. I have some sympathy with this sentiment, as I was often struck during the course of the evidence to this Inquiry by the basic nature of the failures illustrated by Victoria's case.

6.557   I make no apology for labouring these basic points during the analysis that follows. Victoria's case, like several others which have prompted Inquiries of this nature, is one that is characterised by a consistent failure to do basic things properly. In an environment in which time and resources may well be limited, it is of vital importance that sight is not lost of the fundamental aspects of sound social work practice.

6.558   The second point I wish to make at the beginning is that by focusing on specific elements of the practice of those who had direct dealings with Victoria's case, I would not wish to give the impression that I regard those front-line workers as wholly responsible for the deficiencies revealed.

6.559   It is plainly the case that when any member of staff in any organisation fails adequately to carry out a basic element of his or her job, then he or she must shoulder responsibility for that failure. However, where the poor practice concerned is found to be indicative of generally poor standards across the organisation as a whole, or where it is contributed to by the front-line staff being inadequately supported in their roles, then the senior members of that organisation must also accept their share of the blame.

6.560   The evidence I have heard leads me to the view that the manner in which a number of senior managers and elected councillors within Haringey discharged their statutory responsibilities to safeguard and promote the welfare of children living in the borough was an important contributory factor in the mishandling of Victoria's case. As such, the failure to adequately protect Victoria should be seen as a collective failure on the part of those involved with the provision of services to children and families in Haringey to ensure that adequate systems and practices were in place at the time, both to ensure that front-line staff carried out their duties adequately and to detect when they did not.

6.561   Given my views in this regard, I was left unimpressed by the manner in which a number of senior officers and councillors from Haringey sought to distance themselves from the poor practice apparent in Victoria's case. A good illustration of this attitude was provided by the former chief executive of the council, Gurbux Singh, who said:

> "I have personally thought long and hard about what I could have done differently, which could have actually led to a situation where the tragedy of Victoria could not have actually happened. I have thought long and hard about that. I have thought about the sorts of procedures we could have put in place beyond that. But I end up thinking I am not sure that there was a great deal else more that we could have actually done."

6.562   Mr Singh went on to say that, despite it being absolutely clear that Haringey had failed adequately to discharge its duty to safeguard and promote Victoria's welfare, he was not clear in his own mind where the "line of responsibility" for that failure lay.

6.563   As I have already made clear, I do not share his uncertainty. As an organisation charged with the vital task of safeguarding children, Haringey council had a responsibility to ensure that its front-line staff were providing a proper and safe service to vulnerable children in the borough. As chief officer of the organisation, Mr Singh and his senior colleagues had a duty to ensure that such a service was provided.

6.564   A succession of senior managers and councillors from Haringey gave evidence before me and expressed their complete surprise at the state of the council's front-line services as revealed by the evidence given to this Inquiry by social workers and their immediate managers. It is the job of the leaders of any organisation to be aware of conditions on the 'shop floor' and the standard of service provided to its customers. It is their job to identify deficiencies in that service and put them right. Ignorance cannot, in my view, be a legitimate defence. Therefore, I make it clear at the outset that the criticisms of practice, below, are directed not just at the front-line staff concerned but at the senior managers and councillors whose role it was to ensure that Victoria, together with other vulnerable children in the borough, received an adequate service.

6.565   I have set out previously in this section a detailed description of the manner in which Victoria's case was handled by Haringey Social Services during the seven months or so that she was known to them. The occasions on which those involved failed to act in an appropriate and timely manner were numerous and varied. However, there are a number of particular aspects of Haringey Social Services' practice, as illustrated by Victoria's case, which merit more detailed analysis. They are:

- The manner in which the strategy meetings were conducted.
- The way in which the case was allocated to the social worker.
- The decision to authorise Victoria's discharge from hospital.
- The manner in which the home visits were carried out.
- The approach taken to Kouao's credibility.
- The use that was made of Victoria's case file.
- The supervision received by the social worker.
- The manner in which the case was closed.
- The way in which the allegations of sexual harm were dealt with.

I deal with each in turn.

Strategy meetings

6.566   The 1999 version of *Working Together* provides the following guidance as to the circumstances in which it is appropriate to hold a strategy meeting: "Whenever there is reasonable cause to suspect that a child is suffering, or is likely to suffer significant harm, there should be a strategy discussion involving the social services department and the police, and other agencies as appropriate (for example, education and health), in particular any referring agency." As to the format that such discussions should take, the guidance avoids being prescriptive, stating simply, "A strategy discussion may take place at a meeting or by other means (for example, by telephone)."

6.567   The guidance clearly allows for a degree of flexibility as to the precise form that strategy discussions should take. In my view, such flexibility is entirely appropriate because the circumstances in which harm to a child may come to light may be many and varied. In some cases, formal meetings involving all the involved parties may be inappropriate in view of the urgency of the situation.

6.568   An inevitable consequence of the flexibility permitted by the national guidance, however, is that local arrangements and protocols can differ widely. All four sets of strategy meeting guidelines submitted by the social services departments involved in Victoria's case were materially different from each other. In the case of Haringey, I was told that there was even inconsistency between the local ACPC procedures, in this respect, and the custom and practice adopted by front-line staff.

6.569   In my view, Victoria's case demonstrates that the need for flexibility in this area must be balanced against the danger of confusion arising between the partner agencies involved as to the proper manner in which to proceed when first faced with a case of possible deliberate harm. In other words, while circumstances will inevitably dictate the precise procedure to be adopted in any given case, minimum and consistent standards, clearly understood by all the agencies involved, are vital.

6.570 Turning first to the strategy meeting held on 28 July 1999, shortly after Victoria's admission to the North Middlesex Hospital, there are a number of respects in which the perfectly proper decision to have a discussion at this point was undermined by defects in the procedure adopted. The following are clear examples of this:

- The meeting should have been held in the North Middlesex Hospital, as required by the local ACPC procedures. The referral, it will be recalled, had come from the hospital in the first place and, in the four days that Victoria had spent there, a significant amount of relevant information had been collected. It should have been obvious to all concerned that Dr Rossiter's attendance at the meeting was absolutely essential. Her commitments at the hospital meant that she did not have the time to travel to Haringey Social Services offices.

- The meeting was chaired by a senior practitioner, Ms Kozinos, rather than by a team manager. This, again, was contrary to local ACPC procedures. While the competency of the chairmanship is, of course, more important than the identity of the chairman, in my view it is preferable to adopt a clear and consistent approach in this regard. The effective chairing of a strategy meeting can be a challenging task. It is best performed by a manager who is experienced in the work and aware of the responsibilities it carries. Meetings of this nature are a valuable resource which use up a substantial amount of the limited time available to busy professionals. The ad hoc allocation of the chairmanship to whichever manager happens to be free at the time can seriously undermine their effectiveness.

- The danger of inexperienced or inefficient chairmanship is well illustrated by Victoria's case. The 18 action points identified during the course of the meeting were, for the most part, sound. However, the lack of clarity as to precisely who was responsible for what, the absence of any timescales for the completion of the various actions identified, and the failure to circulate copies of the minutes of the meeting to those with responsibility for taking the strategy forward meant that the practical impact of those 18 action points was seriously diminished. Again, this is a defect which adherence to a basic set of procedures could easily have avoided.

- However, of all the deficiencies in the conduct of the strategy meeting, it is the failure to arrange for a review meeting to monitor the progress of the agreed strategy which causes me the greatest concern. The ACPC procedures make reference to the need to "consider" holding such a meeting following a strategy discussion, but no reference at all is made to the practice in the procedures drawn up by Ms Mairs for use in the NTDO. In my view, such meetings are absolutely essential. If one takes Victoria's case as an example, 18 different actions were identified as being necessary and were assigned to a variety of people from a number of different agencies without any specified timescales. To simply assume that all the tasks would be satisfactorily completed, and that it was therefore unnecessary to check, was optimistic to say the least.

6.571 That the deficiencies in the manner in which this first strategy meeting was conducted was not an isolated example of poor practice would seem to be confirmed by the fact that many of the same faults are apparent in the second strategy meeting conducted a little over three months later.

6.572 In particular, a list of 15 generally sensible action points was produced, which, if carried out, may have gone a long to way to establishing the danger that Victoria was in. None of those action points is allocated to a particular individual and none of them has a specified timescale for completion. In view of this, the repeated failure to put in place any form of review mechanism is nothing short of disastrous in the context of Victoria's case.

6.573 The fact that the two strategy meetings in which her case was discussed were so ineffective in safeguarding Victoria's welfare is not explained by any lack of specialist judgement or expertise on the part of the professionals involved. As I have made clear above, the lists of recommended action points produced after each one were detailed, thorough and generally sound. The explanation lies, in my view, in the basic failure to implement simple procedures that would have ensured that the strategies agreed upon at the meetings were put into effect.

6.574 The flexibility afforded by the *Working Together* guidelines would appear to have led, in the case of Haringey at least, to strategy discussions being organised and conducted in a haphazard and ad hoc manner, with the inevitable result that important points were missed.

6.575 Victoria's case leads me to the view that while professionals must be allowed the freedom to tailor their response to individual situations as they see fit, and that it is impossible to lay down a detailed and prescriptive procedure for the conduct of strategy meetings, the time has come for the introduction of a few basic minimum standards. By making the recommendation, I aim to ensure that full value is extracted from strategy meetings and discussions, and that the crucial role they play in the protection of children is not undermined for want of a few basic procedures. Therefore, I make the following recommendation:

Recommendation
Directors of social services must ensure that all strategy meetings and discussions involve the following three basic steps:

- A list of action points must be drawn up, each with an agreed timescale and the identity of the person responsible for carrying it out.
- A clear record of the discussion or meeting must be circulated to all those present and all those with responsibility for an action point.
- A mechanism for reviewing completion of the agreed actions must be specified. The date upon which the first such review is to take place is to be agreed and documented.

Case allocation

6.576 The proper and well-thought-out allocation of cases is a central component of the effective management of a social work team. As with any group of staff, there will be significant variations among a given group of social workers as to their respective levels of experience, training and expertise. Perhaps most important of all, some will have more available time than others by virtue of their current workloads. All of these factors are relevant to the decision of which social worker should be allocated a particular case.

6.577 It is clear that effective management of this nature involves a detailed knowledge on the part of the manager – both of the social workers on his or her team and the precise state of their current workloads. As was explained to me during the course of the evidence, the latter requirement cannot be met effectively by simply maintaining a list of the number of open cases currently held by each social worker on the team. Bare statistics of this sort can mask the fact that some cases require far more time and attention than others, and that a particular case, counted as one for the purposes of such statistics, may involve more than one child in the family.

6.578 It would appear that Victoria's case was allocated to Ms Arthurworrey by Ms Baptiste without any consideration of the sort of factors I have previously described. In the first place, there would seem to have been no assessment of whether Ms Arthurworrey had the requisite capabilities to handle the case. Ms Arthurworrey told me that at the time she found Victoria's case file lying on her desk, she had never completed a section 47 inquiry, never dealt with a child in hospital and never taken a case through to case conference. For present purposes, what concerns me is not whether Ms Arthurworrey was capable of handling Victoria's case in a competent manner, but that no assessment of her capabilities would seem to have been made by her manager before allocating the case to her.

6.579 Nor would there seem to have been any consideration as to whether Ms Arthurworrey's workload at the time allowed her to devote enough time to Victoria's case. The only system for the monitoring of the workload of individual social workers in operation in Ms Baptiste's team at the time was a crude list of the number of open cases held by each social worker, the more obvious limitations of which I have just described. Even on the basis of this unreliable information, Ms Arthurworrey, at the time that she was allocated Victoria's case, was holding more cases than virtually all of her colleagues and seven more than the recommended maximum specified in the office procedures. Again, the issue for present purposes is not whether Ms Arthurworrey had sufficient time to deal adequately with Victoria's case, but rather that no thought would seem to have been given as to whether or not she did.

6.580 Ensuring that a member of staff has the time and ability to undertake a particular task before asking them to do so amounts to no more than basic managerial competence. Therefore, I was greatly surprised to learn not only that this was not done in Victoria's case, but that there was no system in place in the office concerned that suggested it might have been done in respect of other cases. Ms Arthurworrey's experience of returning to the office one morning and finding a new case file sitting on her desk was not, I was concerned to hear, unique.

6.581 With a view to ensuring that such basic lapses in managerial practice are not repeated elsewhere, I make the following recommendation:

> **Recommendation**
> Directors of social services must ensure that no case is allocated to a social worker unless and until his or her manager ensures that he or she has the necessary training, experience and time to deal with it properly.

6.582 However, proper case allocation does not end with the simple identification of the right social worker for the job. It requires the manager to ensure that the social worker understands the work that he or she has been charged with doing. In practical terms, this would involve the manager and the social worker sitting down together with the case file and agreeing on the most appropriate manner in which to take the case forward.

6.583 Nothing of this sort was done in Victoria's case. The only explanation or guidance as to how to proceed with the case given to Ms Arthurworrey by Ms Baptiste would appear to have come in the form of a brief conversation between the two of them after Ms Arthurworrey had glanced through the file. When asked whether she found Ms Baptiste's input on this occasion to be helpful, Ms Arthurworrey replied, "Ms Baptiste just told me that this was a case about a child who was in hospital with scabies. No it was not helpful." Ms Baptiste, she went on to say, did no more than tell her "to implement the strategy meeting recommendations". No indication was given as to when she expected Ms Arthurworrey to have completed those tasks.

6.584   Apart from the factual inaccuracy concerning the reason why Victoria had been admitted to the North Middlesex Hospital (which may have influenced the way in which Ms Arthurworrey approached the case afterwards), there would appear to be a complete absence of any thought on the part of Ms Baptiste as to how best to approach Victoria's case. Consequently, she was unable to offer Ms Arthurworrey anything in the way of meaningful guidance or assistance in taking the case forward.

6.585   Nor would it seem as though manager and social worker read through Victoria's case file at the time of allocation. In addition to gaining a proper understanding of what needs to be done, and by when, this basic step can help to ensure that vital information is not missed at the outset of any investigation of the child's circumstances. An example of such information in Victoria's case is provided by the note on the CP1 form completed by Dr Forlee, which records that Kouao had previously been in contact with social services, who had apparently suggested that she and Victoria be separated. This potentially vital piece of information was never picked up Ms Arthurworrey, despite the inclusion of the document concerned in Victoria's case file.

6.586   I appreciate that in many social services departments up and down the country, the allocation of cases to social workers will routinely follow careful consideration as to who is best placed to handle the case and a thorough discussion between social worker and manager as to what needs to be done and by when. Prior to hearing the evidence to this Inquiry, I would have expected such procedures to be universal. In an effort to ensure that they become so, I make the following recommendation:

> **Recommendation**
> When allocating a case to a social worker, the manager must ensure that the social worker is clear as to what has been allocated, what action is required and how that action will be reviewed and supervised.

6.587   The fact that Victoria had an allocated social worker for the vast majority of the time that she was known to Haringey Social Services meant that she was, in theory at least, better served that many other vulnerable children in the borough.

6.588   During the course of the evidence to this Inquiry there were many references to the problem of open cases which did not have an allocated social worker. By way of an example, my attention was drawn to a report written by Mr Duncan in January 2001 in which he made the worrying observation that there were 100 unallocated cases in the NTDO alone.

6.589   The disadvantages inherent in a case being unallocated are obvious. If there is no particular individual charged with, and responsible for, ensuring that the needs of the child concerned are met, the likelihood of that child failing to receive the service he or she needs is increased enormously. While not of direct impact in Victoria's case, I heard enough evidence, from Haringey and elsewhere, to convince me that the problem of unallocated cases is one that needs urgent attention. I therefore make the following recommendation:

> **Recommendation**
> Directors of social services must ensure that all cases of children assessed as needing a service have an allocated social worker. In cases where this proves to be impossible, arrangements must be made to maintain contact with the child. The number, nature and reasons for such unallocated cases must be reported to the social services committee on a monthly basis.

6.590   However, the mere fact of allocation of a case is not enough to ensure that the child concerned receives the necessary services. The achievement of that objective requires the social worker concerned regularly to see, speak to and work with the child and the child's family. Unless this happens, the fact that the case is recorded as 'allocated' is meaningless. Therefore, in order to ensure that the above recommendation has the positive impact intended, I make the following additional recommendation:

> **Recommendation**
> Directors of social services must ensure that only those cases in which a social worker is actively engaged in work with a child and the child's family are deemed to be 'allocated'.

Discharge from hospital

6.591   The precise sequence of events surrounding Victoria's discharge from the North Middlesex Hospital remains unclear. However, there is no doubt that her discharge was approved by both Ms Arthurworrey and PC Jones following the brief interview of Victoria they conducted on 6 August 1999.

6.592   In my judgement, the decision that it was appropriate for Victoria to go home was taken without any proper consideration of whether it was safe for her to do so. Victoria's discharge from the North Middlesex Hospital is a key event in the story of her case. On the morning of 6 August, she was in a safe place and all her basic needs were being met. By that evening she had been returned to an environment that would eventually bring about her death a little over six months later.

6.593   Given the importance of the decision, the lack of investigation and analysis that preceded it is extremely disappointing. In my view, there were at least 10 important steps that were not taken when considering whether Victoria should have been allowed home. These are:

- No adequate understanding was gained during the course of the interview with Victoria on 6 August of how she spent her days when she was living with Kouao and Manning.
- No attempt was made to seek the views of any of the medical staff who had been involved in Victoria's care, other than Dr Rossiter and Nurse Quinn.
- Victoria's notes were not carefully considered, and the concerns expressed in them were not explored.
- No attempt was made to seek the views of Dr Forlee, the doctor who had made the initial referral.
- No critical analysis was applied to Kouao's account of how Victoria had come by her injuries, and she was not challenged in any meaningful way on the matter.

- No visit was made to the home to which it was proposed to return Victoria.
- No effort was made to gain a proper understanding of the nature and causes of scabies and its links to possible neglect.
- No structured discussion about the case took place between Ms Arthurworrey and her manager, during which the merits of the decision to discharge were properly considered.
- No active consideration was given to convening a case conference, or any other form of multi-agency meeting, in order to explore whether discharge to Manning's flat was in Victoria's best interests.
- No efforts were made to put any community support programme in place for Victoria. For example, the possibility of enrolling her in a summer play scheme was not explored, nor were any attempts made to secure community nursing surveillance.

6.594 In my view, all of the 10 steps should have been taken before deciding that Victoria could return home with Kouao. They are examples of the sort of rigorous consideration that must be undertaken before authorising the removal of a child about whom there have been child protection concerns from a safe place back to the environment in which the concerns first arose. In an effort to encourage the application of careful analysis to decisions of this nature, I make the following recommendation:

> **Recommendation**
> Directors of social services must ensure that no child known to social services who is an inpatient in a hospital and about whom there are child protection concerns is allowed to be taken home until it has been established by social services that the home environment is safe, the concerns of the medical staff have been fully addressed, and there is a social work plan in place for the ongoing promotion and safeguarding of that child's welfare.

Home visits

6.595 Ms Arthurworrey candidly admitted that she was "totally set up" by Kouao and Manning during the two visits she made to Somerset Gardens. The picture of a happy and well-cared for Victoria playing contentedly on the floor with a doll was far removed from the reality of the situation, even at this early stage.

6.596 Although Ms Arthurworrey was by no means the only professional that Kouao deceived into thinking that she had Victoria's best interests at heart, she was the only one who had the opportunity to assess them in their home environment. Home visits of this nature can be extremely valuable sources of information in determining how well a child is cared for. That Ms Arthurworrey came away from both the visits she made to Somerset Gardens without any concern that Victoria might be in danger owes as much to defects in the approach taken to those visits as to any deceit on the part of Kouao or Manning.

6.597 In particular, I consider that the following essential components of a successful home visit were missing on both of the occasions that Ms Arthurworrey went to Victoria's home:

- The proper planning of the visit in advance.
- The maintenance by the social worker of an open mind.
- The review of judgements and assumptions made during the course of the visit.

I consider each in turn.

Proper planning

6.598 There would appear to have been a complete absence of any planning or discussion between Ms Arthurworrey and Ms Baptiste in advance of either of the home visits. There was no consideration of the types of questions that should be asked, the background checks that were necessary before undertaking the visit, the things to look out for in the home, or the manner in which Victoria should be approached and spoken to. All of these, in my view, are matters that should be considered in advance of any home visit of this type.

6.599 The absence of any planning or preparation in advance of the visits also meant that the opportunity was lost to review and, if necessary, challenge the assumptions that Ms Arthurworrey had made about the case. Before the first visit, it will be recalled that she had effectively closed the child protection element of the case. The decision taken with PC Jones at the hospital on 6 August 1999 that Victoria was not a child at risk of significant harm had been reinforced by her interpretation of the material she later received from the Central Middlesex Hospital. Had there been any discussion of the case between Ms Arthurworrey and her manager before the home visit, the deficiencies in her analysis of the case at this point may have been exposed. As it was, she simply turned up at the home with a wholly mistaken view of the sort of case with which she was dealing.

6.600 The same is true of the later visit at the end of October. As the scope of the discussion between Ms Arthurworrey and Kouao illustrates, the prevailing view at this stage would seem to have been that the only issue that needed to be addressed was Kouao's accommodation difficulties. The child protection referral concerning Victoria that had been received three months earlier had turned into a case about an adult with a child who needed better accommodation. Again, had there been any proper planning of this home visit involving a discussion between Ms Arthurworrey and her manager, the point may have been made that it was, in fact, Victoria who was the client in the case. Perhaps then Ms Arthurworrey would have taken the trouble to talk either to or about her during the course of the visit.

Keeping an open mind

6.601 Turning now to the visits themselves, it was suggested to Ms Arthurworrey during the course of her evidence that she showed a "lack of inquisitiveness" during the course of the visits she made in August. Her reply was interesting: "I am a social worker and I work with the facts as they are presented to me. As I have said to you, I was more trusting of Kouao when I went on that visit. I am not a detective. I had no reason to question what I saw and what I was being told at that point."

6.602 While I accept that social workers are not detectives, I do not consider that they should simply serve as the passive recipients of information, unquestioningly accepting all that they are told by the carers of children about whom there are concerns. The concept of "respectful uncertainty" should lie at the heart of the relationship between the social worker and the family. It does not require social workers constantly to interrogate their clients, but it does involve the critical evaluation of information that they are given. People who abuse their children are unlikely to inform social workers of the fact. For this reason at least, social workers must keep an open mind.

6.603 Their managers must also keep an open mind. I have already highlighted the value of discussion between social worker and manager before a home visit takes place so as to test assumptions made about the case thus far. I regard it as equally important for discussion to take place after a visit for the same purpose.

Reviewing judgements and assumptions

6.604 By the time that she had returned to the NTDO after the home visit on 16 August 1999, Ms Arthurworrey had formed the view that Kouao was "a respectful adult who was child focused". This view had been reached without her questioning Victoria about her well-being, establishing how she spent her days or following up any of the concerns expressed by the hospital such as Victoria's unusually large appetite. The second home visit would seem to have served only to reinforce Ms Arthurworrey's view of Kouao, despite the fact that, once again, no attempt was made to establish how Victoria spent her days or how she felt about her current living arrangements.

6.605 These assumptions were never tested in discussion between Ms Arthurworrey and her manager and so, again, the opportunity was lost to discover the lack of analysis that had preceded the assumption being made. Even such simple questions as "How was Victoria?", "What did she say?", or "How does she spend her days?" might have revealed Ms Arthurworrey's failure to focus on the needs of her client. In fact, Ms Baptiste would appear to have restricted herself to being the passive recipient of information given to her by Ms Arthurworrey in the same way that Ms Arthurworrey had been with respect to Kouao.

6.606 The net effect of these deficiencies in practice is that the valuable opportunities to gain an insight into Victoria's situation provided by Ms Arthurworrey's two home visits were completely wasted. That the same deficiencies were apparent in each of the two home visits, and that they were not identified until after Victoria's death, would seem to indicate that bad practice of this nature was not unusual in Haringey at the time. In an effort to ensure that it is not replicated elsewhere, I make the following recommendation:

> **Recommendation**
> Social workers must not undertake home visits without being clear about the purpose of the visit, the information to be gathered during the course of it, and the steps to be taken if no one is at home. No visits should be undertaken without the social worker concerned checking the information known about the child by other child protection agencies. All visits must be written up on the case file.

Working with deceitful people

6.607 One aspect of the manner in which Ms Arthurworrey approached the home visits crops up on numerous occasions during the course of Haringey's handling of Victoria's case and merits further consideration. I refer to the extent to which Ms Arthurworrey was prepared to accept at face value that which she was told by Kouao.

6.608 As recorded earlier, Ms Arthurworrey encouraged me to bear in mind that she was not "a detective" when considering how inquisitive she should have been during the course of her home visits. This point was echoed in Haringey's closing submissions to the Inquiry, in which I was told that social workers "are not used to dealing with wholesale deception" of the type perpetrated by Kouao in this case.

6.609 While I accept that both of these points have some validity, I was struck by the extent to which the information held by Haringey Social Services during the course of their dealings with Victoria revealed clear inconsistencies in Kouao's story, of which the following are some examples:

- The case file records Kouao's date of birth as being "18/07/66", whereas the age of her eldest child is recorded on the CP1 form as being 24. This would have meant that Kouao had her first child at the age of nine or 10. This discrepancy was never explored.
- Kouao's country of birth varies between Zaire, France and the Ivory Coast depending upon which document in the case file one looks at. Similar confusion applied to Victoria. On the record of the 5 November 1999 strategy meeting she is recorded as being a Zairean Catholic.
- The length of time that Kouao intended to spend in the UK is variously recorded as a one-year "leave of absence", "two years to learn English" and "permanent".
- Various dates between January and March are identified for Victoria and Kouao's arrival in the country.
- Several references are made to Manning's "fiancée" but her identity is never established.

6.610   Much was made in the evidence of a number of witnesses to the plausibility of Kouao and how successful she could be at diverting suspicion. In addition to whatever natural talent she may have had in this respect, she would also seem to have used the fact that English was not her first language to good effect. Ms Arthurworrey recalled at one stage that Kouao's English would sometimes deteriorate when certain difficult subjects arose, a tendency that was repeated during the course of her evidence to this Inquiry.

6.611   Nonetheless, it seems to me that a careful review of the available information would have indicated that there were numerous discrepancies in the information that Kouao was giving to social services, which needed to be resolved if an accurate picture of Victoria's situation was to be established. These discrepancies were never properly explored.

6.612   Despite the absence of much in the way of investigation and critical analysis of the available information, it would appear that some of those involved in the case had their suspicions as to the reliability of Kouao's version of events. This is illustrated by the inclusion of the following in the list of 15 action points drawn up at the 5 November strategy meeting: "some proof that the child is hers".

6.613   This note demonstrates that, over three months after the initial referral had been made, there were still doubts as to whether Victoria was Kouao's real daughter. Unfortunately, there is no record of what prompted those suspicions. There are, however, plenty of possibilities including the discrepancy in their appearance and dress, the lack of warmth shown between them, or the infrequency of Kouao's visits to the hospital and failure to bring anything for Victoria when she did visit. Unfortunately, the point is academic in view of the fact that no proof that Victoria was Kouao's daughter was ever sought.

6.614   What the point does illustrate, however, is how significant discrepancies in the account given by the carer can be. If, for example, the suspicion expressed at the strategy meeting on 5 November had been followed up, the first thing that might have been done would have been to look at Kouao's passport which, as the police later discovered, contained the photograph of a little girl who looked different to Victoria. Had such a discovery been made, the outcome of this case may have been different.

6.615   The same might be said in relation to the discrepancies in Kouao's account of her background in France. Quite apart from the inconsistencies set out above, Kouao's decision to leave a well-paid job in France and come to the UK, where she was unable to support herself or find satisfactory accommodation was, on the face of it, curious.

6.616 At the first strategy meeting on 28 July 1999, the need to carry out checks concerning Kouao's and Victoria's background in France was identified – action point 17 states: "complete checks in France – International services." Unfortunately, the notes of the strategy meeting do not specify what checks were necessary or how they should be undertaken.

6.617 This may explain why, by the time of the second strategy meeting over three months later, no such checks had been carried out. Again, the meeting identified the need to contact the French authorities and the following note was made: "s/w to complete a check with France if client is previously known. Find out more information re other children."

6.618 The investigation carried out by the police after Victoria's death revealed that a substantial amount of important information was held by the French authorities concerning Victoria and Kouao. In addition to the discovery that Kouao owed French social services a significant amount of money in respect of improperly claimed benefits, the fact that Victoria had experienced problems with absenteeism at school and had been subject to a child at risk emergency notification was also established. A French social worker had also become involved who had noted a "difficult mother daughter relationship" between Kouao and Victoria.

6.619 The fact that Haringey Social Services proved incapable of discovering this information while Victoria was alive may be attributable to a lack of awareness on the part of the staff concerned as to the proper avenues to explore and procedures to adopt. If that is the case then the situation needs to be addressed. Many social services departments around the country have to deal on a regular basis with children who have arrived in this country from abroad. Even in those cases in which the country of origin of the child concerned is without a developed welfare system, the child may well have passed through such a country on his or her way to the UK. The social services departments of those countries are a potentially valuable source of information. Social workers should be provided with clear guidance and procedures explaining how best to access such information. It is with this objective in mind that I make the following recommendation:

> **Recommendation**
> Directors of social services must ensure that social work staff are made aware of how to access effectively information concerning vulnerable children which may be held in other countries.

Case file management

6.620 During the course of one of his submissions to me, the representative appearing before the Inquiry on behalf of the NHS witnesses informed me that telling medical professionals that they should write better notes was like "pushing at an open door". In doing so, I expect that he intended to convey something of the wearying regularity with which this issue arises in the context of investigations of this nature. Numerous inquiries in the past have called for higher standards of case recording and the more thorough maintenance of case files by professionals from all agencies involved in the welfare of children.

6.621 In view of the regularity with which deficiencies in this regard have been identified, it is disappointing to find them repeated with such regularity throughout Victoria's case. One wonders why, if the problem is so universally acknowledged that to identify it amounts to "pushing at an open door", it has yet to be properly addressed.

6.622   I have dealt elsewhere in this Report with the importance of recording all relevant information concerning a child in his or her case file or notes and have made a general recommendation to this effect directed at all the agencies involved. I do not propose to repeat those matters here, particularly in view of the fact that my concerns regarding the management of Victoria's case file in Haringey are of a slightly different nature.

6.623   The case file is the single most important tool available to social workers and their managers when making decisions as to how best to safeguard the welfare of children under their care. It should clearly and accessibly record the available information concerning the child and the action that has been taken on the case to date. Reference to the case file should be made at every stage of the case and before any significant decision is made.

6.624   My concern regarding the Haringey case file is not that it contained glaring omissions, but rather that so little use would seem to have been made of it by those with responsibility for Victoria's case. As I have mentioned earlier, the case file would not appear to have been read by Ms Baptiste at the time she allocated Victoria's case to Ms Arthurworrey. Nor, it would seem, was any meaningful reference made to the file during the course of the supervision sessions in which Victoria's case was briefly discussed. Most remarkable of all, perhaps, is the fact that the second strategy meeting proceeded in the complete absence of Victoria's case file, despite the fact that it was sitting in the next room at the time.

6.625   The lack of reference to the case file at these and other stages in Victoria's case may go some way to explaining why so many important steps were missed. It is not difficult to envisage how, for example, the review during the course of supervision of the lengthy lists of action points produced after the two strategy meetings would have revealed that there was much outstanding work to be done. It is extremely frustrating to think how important a difference such a basic and self-evident element of good social work practice could have made in Victoria's case. The information contained in Victoria's case file should have been more than sufficient to prompt effective social work intervention in her case. That it was not read at key points is indicative of extremely poor practice and a matter much to be regretted.

6.626   It is impossible for me to form any judgement as to how easy it would have been for a reader of Victoria's case file to have gleaned from it the relevant information at various stages along the way. The reason for this is that by the time that it reached the Inquiry, the case file had been taken apart and copied on several occasions and was no longer in its original order.

6.627   However, it may be that a contributory factor in the failure of various professionals involved in Victoria's case to read the file was that the information was not presented in a sufficiently convenient and accessible way. If only a limited amount of time is available for supervision, for example, the manager concerned may feel it is not worth spending it trying to make sense of a jumble of papers in the file.

6.628   This is one of the reasons why I regard the inclusion in any case file of a clear, comprehensive and up-to-date chronology as absolutely essential. In addition to saving valuable time that would otherwise be spent trying to extract the relevant information from a number of documents, such a chronology would also help to identify actions ordered on the case which had yet to be completed. The discipline of preparing the initial chronology at the outset of the case is also valuable given that it would require the allocated social worker carefully to read the file before embarking upon the assessment.

6.629　If it is to be comprehensive, a chronology will, in many cases, have to take account of the information possessed by other agencies involved and the work they carry out on the case. As the agency best placed to co-ordinate the collection of the relevant information, I regard it as the responsibility of social services to maintain the chronology, seeking the input of other agencies as appropriate. In order to ensure that social services are clear as to their obligations in this regard, I make the following recommendation:

> **Recommendation**
> Directors of social services must ensure that every child's case file includes, on the inside of the front cover, a properly maintained chronology.

Supervision

6.630　There is now a good deal of consensus as to the key features of effective social work supervision. In particular, it is widely recognised that such supervision should be well documented and should include the discussion of individual cases. In addition, supervision provides an opportunity to challenge assumptions and judgements that have been made regarding particular cases and to agree plans of action. All of these elements are present in the supervision policies and guidance in use in Haringey Social Services at the time that they were dealing with Victoria's case.

6.631　Unfortunately, it is very difficult to see these principles reflected in the supervision that was offered to Ms Arthurworrey when she was dealing with Victoria's case.

6.632　The first formal supervision that Ms Arthurworrey received concerning her work on Victoria's case took place on 20 September 1999, some two months or so after the case had first been allocated to her. Although a delay of two months between allocation and first supervision in a case of this nature is unsatisfactory, it is the nature of the supervision when it was provided that causes me most concern.

6.633　As I have noted previously, Victoria's case file was not read by Ms Baptiste either before, during or after the supervision session. Her failure to do so meant that her knowledge of the case was entirely dependent upon what she was told by Ms Arthurworrey. The limitations of such a situation are obvious. If the manager knows only what she is told by the social worker, it will be virtually impossible for her to identify action points that had been missed or to challenge constructively the social worker's understanding. A prime example of the limitations of this approach to supervision provided by Victoria's case is the fact that Ms Baptiste would appear to have been unaware during this supervision session that the majority of the action points identified at the July strategy meeting had yet to be completed.

6.634　In addition to the lack of preparation that preceded it, the supervision session itself was characterised by a complete lack of thoroughness or analysis. The record of the session written by Ms Baptiste on the case file runs to a total of eight handwritten lines which, for the first supervision session in a case referred with child protection concerns, is wholly inadequate.

6.635　The brevity of the record merely reflects the lack of time spent discussing the case which, according to Ms Arthurworrey, did not extend much beyond five minutes. Supervision of this length in a case of the complexity and seriousness of Victoria's can amount to no more than the rubber-stamping of the decisions and judgements already made by the social worker. Overall, one is left with the clear impression that the objective of this first supervision session was simply to get through the cases as quickly as possible, with the manager acting as the passive recipient of whatever information the social worker decided to give her.

6.636   During the seven months or so that she had responsibility for Victoria's case, Ms Arthurworrey participated in a total of four supervision sessions in which it was discussed. The other three would seem to have followed a very similar pattern to the first session, in that the case file was never read and very little in the way of meaningful analysis took place. As a result, whatever mistakes or errors of judgement that Ms Arthurworrey may have made during the course of her handling of Victoria's case went undetected by her immediate managers.

6.637   The nature and extent of the supervision that Ms Arthurworrey received in Victoria's case would seem, from the evidence I heard, to have been typical of the practice in the NTDO at the time. Thorough supervision appears to have been one of the casualties of the inability of some staff to cope with the day-to-day pressures of work in the team. While it may have been possible to record supervision as occurring, and to report as much to senior managers, its quality was extremely poor.

6.638   Effective supervision is the cornerstone of safe social work practice. There is no substitute for it. In particular, the need for such supervision cannot be met by what were referred to as 'corridor conversations' between managers and staff. A number of such conversations regarding Victoria's case took place between Ms Baptiste and Ms Arthurworrey before the first formal supervision session that I have described earlier. A number of extremely important decisions about Victoria's case would seem to have been taken by Ms Baptiste during the course of informal, ad hoc discussions of this nature, of which the following are examples:

- She agreed to the cancelling of the planned home visit prior to Victoria's discharge from hospital.
- She endorsed Ms Arthurworrey's interpretation of the material received from the Central Middlesex Hospital that there were no longer any child protection concerns.
- She accepted Ms Arthurworrey's interpretation of the information obtained during the October home visit that there were still no child protection concerns.
- She decided that the concerns expressed by Dr Rossiter, as relayed via Ms Kitchman, required no further action.

6.639   All of these important decisions were made during the course of informal discussions and without reference to the case file. They illustrate the amateurish way in which the supervision of Victoria's case was approached. The significance of the inadequacy of the supervision given to Ms Arthurworrey cannot be overstated. As with so many aspects of Victoria's case, the faults would have been remedied by the straightforward observance of basic practice standards. In this instance, the outcome for Victoria might have been different if her case file had ever been read by those who were supposed to be supervising Ms Arthurworrey. The recommendation which addresses this is in paragraph 6.59.

Case closure

6.640   The need to thoroughly read the case file before taking any important decision on a case is never more vital than when consideration is being given to closing it. The mechanics of case closure are straightforward – all that is generally considered necessary is that a manager or senior practitioner endorses the view reached by the social worker in charge of the case that there is no reason to keep it open any longer. However, implicit in such a system is the requirement that the manager or senior practitioner concerned carefully reviews the case to ensure that there is not further work for social services still to do.

6.641   Ideally, therefore, a social worker, having carried out all the action identified as necessary on the case, would present that case to a manager who, having verified that this was indeed so, would endorse the decision to close the case. The sequence of events in Victoria's case was very different.

6.642   The strategy meeting held on 5 November added a further 15 action points to those that remained outstanding from the earlier strategy meeting in July. By this stage there were approximately 30 individual steps that had been identified as necessary in Victoria's case, but which had yet to be completed. Despite the fact that all this work remained outstanding, Victoria was never seen again by anyone from Haringey Social Services after 2 November, when she was brought to the NTDO to withdraw the allegation of sexual harm.

6.643   Instead, her case was allowed to limp listlessly towards the point at which those involved would seem simply to have lost interest in doing anything proactive on it. The chronology of what Ms Arthurworrey did in respect of Victoria's case during the four months or so between the November strategy meeting and the decision to close the case makes for depressing reading. A letter was written, a few telephone calls were made and three visits were made to the flat, none of which found anyone at home.

6.644   Therefore, when the case was passed to Ms Mairs for closure, the file should have revealed that, far from the thorough completion of all identified tasks, the preceding four months had witnessed nothing but sporadic and ineffectual attempts to get in contact with the family concerned.

6.645   The last time that this child had been seen she had been making and withdrawing allegations of sexual harm in a manner identified by all those involved at the time as suspicious. As a result, a strategy meeting had been called at which 15 action points had been identified, several of which involved seeing and speaking to Victoria. As even a brief reading of the case file would have revealed, virtually no progress had been made on any of those action points.

6.646   Even if the manager concerned was interested only in whether there were sufficient grounds for safely assuming that Kouao and Victoria had left the borough, the case file would have revealed that there were important steps that had yet to be taken. For example, no checks had been made with the health services to ascertain whether Victoria had received further treatment, no attempt had been made to speak to any of Manning's neighbours to establish who was living at the flat, and no contact had been made with the French authorities in an effort to establish whether Kouao and Victoria had indeed returned to France.

6.647   The closure of a case should be the result of a job well done, not the result of a desire to have one less case to worry about. Victoria's case file shows that there was much still to be done on her case at the time that it was closed. In those circumstances there would appear to be two possibilities. Either the case file was not read before it was signed off for closure, or it was read and the decision to close it was made in the knowledge that there were concerns that had yet to be resolved and important steps that had yet to be taken. Both would amount to very poor practice indeed.

Sexual harm allegation

6.648   Finally, I turn to consider the manner in which Haringey dealt with the allegation made on 1 November 1999 that Manning had sexually harmed Victoria.

6.649   In many respects, an allegation of specific harm done to a child by a named individual is easier to deal with from a social services point of view than a more vague referral of general suspicion. This is not least because of the wealth of procedures and guidance that have been produced in order to assist social workers in identifying the correct steps to take. It was somewhat surprising, therefore, to learn that Haringey's handling of the 1 November allegation was flawed in almost every material respect.

6.650   The crucial error, in my view, was the failure by social work staff, after they had been informed of the allegation and had invited Victoria and Kouao to attend the office, to arrange for a police officer to be present when they arrived. That police officer could then have assisted social services in interviewing both Kouao and Victoria at an early stage. The result of this failure was that when Kouao and Victoria did arrive, they were interviewed in an entirely inadequate manner.

6.651   First, Kouao was spoken to by two social workers – neither of whom had ever been trained in the conduct of interviews of this nature and neither of whom had, by that stage, completed a section 47 investigation. No notes of this interview were taken at the time, although Ms Arthurworrey was able to recall that she told Kouao that the police would be involved and that Manning would be arrested.

6.652   Secondly, Victoria was spoken to by the same inadequately trained social workers. Despite her apparent willingness to talk about what had happened to her she was discouraged from doing so, apparently due to the fact that the social workers realised by this stage that the police should be involved in that process. Had a properly trained child protection officer been involved from the outset, Victoria's account could have been obtained at the time that she seemed anxious to give it. The disadvantages of discouraging a child in Victoria's situation from telling social workers what has happened to her are obvious.

6.653   Only after they had interviewed both Kouao and Victoria did Haringey Social Services contact the police. By this time it was after 4pm and PC Jones, to whom the case was allocated, had gone home for the night. I comment elsewhere in this Report as to the adequacy of the police's response at this stage, but for present purposes it is sufficient to note that had the police been involved from the outset, this particular difficulty would not have arisen.

6.654   Victoria and Kouao were then allowed to leave the office supposedly to stay with the Kimbidimas, a family about which virtually nothing was known. No checks were made as to what the sleeping arrangements would be, how Victoria and Kouao would be fed and looked after or what, if any, connection the Kimbidimas had with Manning, the alleged perpetrator of the harm.

6.655   Thereafter, nothing of any value was done apart from scheduling a strategy meeting for 5 November 1999, some four days after the allegations had first been made. The timing of the strategy meeting is curious to say the least. While an immediate strategy meeting prior to the commencement of a joint investigation may have made sense (as for that matter would a strategy meeting at the end of the initial investigation when all the parties had been interviewed), I can see no logical basis for the decision to call the meeting in the middle of an investigation which had yet to yield any findings.

6.656   To summarise, my view is that when dealing with specific allegations of harm to children, such as the one with which Haringey were presented on 1 November 1999, there a number of steps which must be taken immediately. I set out a list of the immediate action which should have been taken on Victoria's case and which provide a practical template for use in such cases:

- During the same day that the allegations were made, both Victoria and Kouao should have been seen and spoken to at a mutually agreed safe place by a properly trained police officer and social worker.
- Kouao should have been spoken to first and a detailed note made of what she had to say at that time.
- Victoria should then have been interviewed with the use of a video camera.
- If, during the course of that interview, Victoria had made allegations about Manning, he should have been arrested and interviewed by the police. At that point consideration should have been given to obtaining medical and legal advice.
- Social services should then have taken steps to find safe and secure accommodation for Kouao and Victoria. This would involve satisfying themselves that the sleeping arrangements would be adequate and that they would have sufficient means of supporting themselves. Emergency contact details should have been provided.
- Social services and the police should then have reviewed the work they had done and agreed a set of next steps in the investigation.

6.657 All of the steps could and should have been taken on the same day that the allegation was first reported.

7 Tottenham Child and Family Centre

7.1   In drafting this section of the Report I was greatly helped by the closing submissions made by Counsel to the Inquiry. They seem to me to summarise accurately the material evidence, and I have drawn on them heavily in the paragraphs that follow.

7.2   The Tottenham Child and Family Centre was situated in Moira Close, Tottenham, and was one of two centres established under a partnership agreement between Haringey council, Haringey Health Care NHS Trust and the NSPCC.

7.3   The managers of the centres were employees of either the council or the health authority, but they reported to Catriona Scott who was employed by the NSPCC and was responsible for the day-to-day management of the centres. According to Ms Scott, "The main function of the family centres was to provide planned family services relating to health and welfare."

The referral

7.4   On 5 August 1999, Victoria's case was referred to the Tottenham Child and Family Centre by Barry Almeida, a practice manager at the North Tottenham District Office of Haringey Social Services. He had no independent recollection of having made the referral, basing his evidence instead on the handwritten notes he made on the case file, the relevant part of which reads: "Referred to Moira Close Family Centre. They have taken referral but say will take up to two months for assessment."

7.5   Mr Almeida's note also indicates that the family centre was, in fact, the third organisation that he had contacted in an effort to persuade someone to visit Victoria's accommodation. His first port of call would seem to have been the health visiting service that, according to the notes, informed him that they would "not be involved in hygiene assessment of this nature. It would be the school nurse". As Mr Almeida correctly recorded in his notes, this posed something of a problem given the fact that Victoria was not attending school.

7.6   There is nothing to suggest that the point was pushed with the health visiting service. Instead, Mr Almeida tried the environmental health service. His notes indicate that the response he got from them was to be told that people are "allowed to be as squalid as they like in their own home, as long as they do not cause a public health hazard". For this reason, it would seem, they also were not prepared to undertake a visit.

7.7   Having drawn a blank with both the health visiting service and the environmental health service, Mr Almeida decided to try the family centre. In addition to the notes he made on Victoria's case file, the fact that it was indeed Mr Almeida who made the call would seem to be confirmed both by the written evidence of Anna Ieronimou, the family centre officer who took the referral, and by the family centre's own referral sheet, which names Mr Almeida as the referrer.

Reasons for the referral

7.8   However, what is less clear is what Mr Almeida hoped to achieve by making the referral. There would seem to be two possibilities. He initially stated in his oral evidence that the purpose of his call was to obtain advice from the family centre as to what precautions Lisa Arthurworrey should take when visiting Victoria's home in light of the fact that Victoria had previously been diagnosed with scabies. This would appear to contradict the impression given by his statement, which was that he telephoned the family centre because of its ability to carry out parenting assessments and provide family support.

7.9 The discrepancy is plainly an important one. There is a very significant difference between social services telephoning another agency in order to obtain advice as to how to proceed themselves, and seeking to transfer to that other agency some responsibility for the provision of support services to the family concerned.

7.10 Unfortunately, however, when this discrepancy was put to him, Mr Almeida was unable to provide me with much assistance. Instead, he introduced a third possibility by suggesting that his reasons for calling the family centre were in fact a combination of both. In other words, he was concerned both to obtain advice for Ms Arthurworrey and to prompt some form of action by the family centre directed at Victoria's welfare. However, he was unclear as to what action he expected the family centre to take.

7.11 The confusion as to exactly why he telephoned the centre is illustrated by Mr Almeida's admission during the course of his evidence that he did not really think about the referral or whether or not it was appropriate at the time. He accepted that the referral should not have been made until the reasons for it had been carefully thought through, and that the lack of clarity from him probably led to the family centre staff being confused as to what exactly they were supposed to do.

Initial handling of the referral

7.12 Despite the confusion on the part of the referrer as to precisely what he hoped to achieve, the family centre did pick up the referral and log it on their system.

7.13 The 'system' was described by Sylvia Henry, the practice manager, in her evidence. It would seem to have consisted of the recording of the name of the child and the basis for the referral on a sheet of paper. The sheet was then placed into the 'referrals box', the contents of which were checked every Friday at a managers' meeting. During the course of that meeting, each new referral was logged in a book and allocated to a practice manager. The practice manager would then decide whether to deal with the case him or herself, or to pass it on to a family centre officer. Once that decision had been made, the name of the manager or officer to whom the case has been allocated was noted down in the logbook together with an indication of the action required.

Allocation of the referral

7.14 According to Ernell Watson, a practice manager at the family centre, Victoria's case came up for allocation at the managers' meeting on 13 August 1999. Why it was not considered at the first meeting after it had been received, namely Friday 6 August, is unclear. I had originally been led to believe that the reason no meeting took place that day was due to the family centre hosting a party for a group of its users. However, it would appear that there was a meeting, as evidenced by a document that appeared to be the minutes of the 6 August meeting. Ms Watson amended her statement, in light of this document, to remove the reference to the cancellation of the 6 August meeting. She was unable to provide me with any further assistance with the matter, however, due to the fact that, as the minutes confirm, she was not present at that meeting. I am unable to form any conclusion, therefore, as to why Victoria's referral stayed in the family centre's referral box until the following week.

7.15   On 13 August 1999, Victoria's referral was allocated to Ms Henry, a qualified social worker. Ms Henry confirmed in her evidence that, at the time that it was allocated to her, Victoria's case was marked as 'urgent'. There would seem to be little doubt as to whether or not this was the case in view of the fact that Ms Watson made the following note on the family centre's contacts sheet on 13 August 1999: "Case needs to be actioned ASAP."

7.16   Ms Henry explained that, on receipt of a new case, the first thing that she would do would be to determine whether further information was needed from the referrer or whether she could proceed directly to an initial assessment. In Victoria's case she decided that further information from the referrer was needed. She asserted that it would be her usual practice when dealing with urgent cases to make such inquiries as may be necessary within a short time. She could not envisage circumstances where she would have been unable to follow up an urgent referral during the course of the week following its allocation.

7.17   Up to this point, it seems as though the sequence of events can be followed fairly easily. Mr Almeida made a referral to the family centre on 5 August. The family centre had agreed to accept the referral. It was taken by Ms Ieronimou and was placed in the referrals box pending allocation. At the managers' meeting on 13 August the referral was taken out of the referrals box and allocated to Sylvia Henry for urgent action. Ms Henry accepted responsibility for the referral. Having considered the information available at that stage, she decided (unsurprisingly, given Mr Almeida's vagueness as to what he expected the family centre to do) that more information was required from the referrer. She was aware of the need, therefore, to contact Mr Almeida at the earliest available opportunity during the following week.

Ms Henry's note

7.18   It is at this stage, however, that the evidence becomes slightly opaque. The source of the difficulty is the next note which appears on the family centre's contact sheet. It reads: "T/C Barry Almeida. Family now moved out of the borough and case closed." The note is not signed but Ms Henry did not seek to dispute the fact that she made it. Neither, unfortunately, is it dated. This latter omission is significant.

7.19   Ms Henry stated in evidence that her departure from her usual practice of signing and dating all entries on the file can only be explained by her being interrupted at the critical moment. Unfortunately, she seemed to have no recollection of when her conversation with Mr Almeida, in which she was told that the 'family' had moved out of the borough, took place. Mr Almeida was clear in his evidence that the only phone call that he made to the family centre was on 5 August 1999 when he made the initial referral. No written reference to any other telephone call either to or from the family centre can be found in Haringey's case file.

7.20   The most curious aspect of Ms Henry's note, however, is not the fact that it refers to a telephone call (the existence of which is disputed by the other party), but that it records information that is plainly incorrect – Kouao and Victoria never did leave the borough. Therefore, it is surprising that this assertion should have been made by anyone in Haringey Social Services. It is even more surprising if one were to accept Ms Henry's assertion that she would have followed up Victoria's referral promptly after it was allocated to her on 13 August. It is conceivable that someone at the North Tottenham District Office might have formed the view that Victoria and Kouao had left the borough by December 1999 or January 2000 – this was the period during which Lisa Arthurworrey was trying unsuccessfully to contact them. Given that this is the case, it is very hard to see how anyone could have reached this conclusion at any point during the three months or so after Ms Henry assumed responsibility for the case. Furthermore, it would have been readily apparent to anyone in the North Tottenham District Office who took the time to check, that Victoria's case was not closed until 25 February 2000.

Alternative explanations

7.21 In attempting to establish the accurate position in light of these apparent inconsistencies, Counsel to the Inquiry identified four possible versions of events, each of which was put to Ms Henry. They were as follows:

- Ms Henry did not follow up Victoria's referral by calling the North Tottenham District Office until some time after 1 December 1999, the earliest date on which it could even have been suspected by Haringey Social Services that Victoria and Kouao had left the borough. (It was on this date that Kouao failed to attend the North Tottenham District Office for an appointment, without explanation.) If this were true, Ms Henry would have done nothing on this urgent case for at least three and a half months.

- Ms Henry did call the North Tottenham District Office promptly after being allocated Victoria's referral and was given entirely false information by whoever she spoke to at the office. This would mean that despite the fact that Ms Arthurworrey had visited Kouao and Victoria on 16 August 1999, someone at the North Tottenham District Office decided to tell Ms Henry that the family had left the borough and the case was closed.

- The note that Ms Henry made on the family centre's contact sheet was not an accurate reflection of what she was told. In other words, she misheard or misinterpreted what was said and somehow gained the impression that the family had moved. This explanation provides no assistance with the question of when the call was made – such a mistake could have been made at any time up to the date of Victoria's death.

- The entry made by Ms Henry on the contacts sheet was written in after it emerged that Victoria had died, in an effort to explain away the fact that nothing had been done by the family centre in respect of the referral throughout the six months leading up to Victoria's death.

7.22 Having given the matter careful consideration, I am unable to add any further plausible alternatives to Counsel's list. Which of the four scenarios is to be preferred is not an easy question to answer.

7.23 Ms Henry was unable to provide much assistance in respect of this issue. She could not remember the telephone call and she could not say for sure what she was told and when. This is unfortunate because the matter is a significant one. If it is the case that Ms Henry was told relatively soon after she assumed responsibility for Victoria's referral that Victoria and Kouao had moved and their case was closed, the fact that no action was taken on Victoria's case by the family centre may be easily explained.

7.24 Ms Henry refuted the suggestion that she added the entry after Victoria's death in order to attempt to explain her inactivity. She also invited me to reject the conclusion that she did nothing on the case until some time after 1 December 1999. She agreed that there was a possibility that she did not correctly record what she was told during the course of the conversation that she allegedly had with Mr Almeida but invited me to conclude that she did make a call to the North Tottenham District Office before February 2000, during which Mr Almeida told her that the family had moved out of the borough and the case had been closed.

7.25   In attempting to reach a view on this matter I also took into account the fact that Victoria's case was closed on the family centre's computerised information system on 15 March 2000. This may be significant as I was told by Ms Henry that cases tended to be closed on the system within a month or so of them being identified as requiring no further action by family centre staff.

7.26   The fact that the case was closed on 15 March 2000 may indicate, therefore, that Ms Henry was not told that Victoria and Kouao had left the borough until some time in February. Were this to be the case, it might provide an explanation for why she was told that the family had left the borough, as there had been no contact between Kouao and anyone at the North Tottenham District Office for approximately three months. However, it would still not explain why nothing was done in relation to Victoria's case until six months after the referral had first been received by the family centre.

7.27   Having given this matter careful consideration, I am unable to reach a conclusion in which I have any confidence. No satisfactory account of how and when Ms Henry's entry on the contact sheet came to be made has been provided, and I can do no more than speculate as to the true position.

Case recording

7.28   However, what is clear is that the handling of Victoria's case by the family centre provides another example of the importance of adequate record-keeping and supervision of cases. For reasons that it is unnecessary for me to rehearse, the importance of recording and monitoring action taken in response to a referral concerning a vulnerable child cannot be overstated.

7.29   The NSPCC is not one of the agencies covered by the Terms of Reference of this Inquiry. Nonetheless, it is clear that through the work of the family centre for which it was responsible, the NSPCC did have some involvement with Victoria's case, by virtue of which it may have had an opportunity to have made a material difference to its outcome. In view of this, I am grateful for the assistance provided to the Inquiry by the NSPCC.

7.30   That assistance included the making of a closing submission by its director, Mary Marsh. During the course of that closing submission she addressed the issue of the adequacy of the manner in which the handling of Victoria's referral was recorded and supervised by the family centre. In my view, she put the matter very fairly when she made the following statement in relation to the handling of Victoria's case after its allocation to Ms Henry on 13 August 1999:

> "The record thereafter is inadequate and incomplete with no evidence of immediate action despite the recognition of the urgency in the original indication. Regrettably, the only evidence we have is the undated note on the file made by the practice manager, that she was told in a phone call with Haringey Social Services that the family had moved away, with no date recorded or recalled.
>
> There are serious issues here about the inadequate maintenance of records and the supervision and monitoring [of] the progress of cases and referrals, which we recognise and we accept are our fault in this case. It should not have been possible for this referral to have been left without any follow up, apparently for so long."

Uniformity of referrals

7.31 Ms Marsh went on to make a further point in this regard with which I also agree. She explained how a necessary result of the careful and accurate recording of referrals once they have been received by an organisation such as the family centre, is that the referrers themselves act in a consistent and regulated manner. Vague telephone referrals, unconfirmed in writing, such as the one made by Mr Almeida, make the job of all concerned far more difficult than necessary. I also heard evidence to suggest that this was merely one of several ways in which referrals were made to the family centre.

7.32 If the involvement of the family centre in Victoria's case illustrates anything, it is that the valuable work of organisations such as this can be seriously undermined by a lack of basic systems and processes. It is vital that all those involved in the protection of children adopt a rigorous and professional attitude to their work if important opportunities to help children in Victoria's situation are not to be missed.

What should have been done?

7.33 The value of such opportunities was graphically illustrated by the evidence given by Ms Henry and Ms Watson as to what Ms Henry would have done had she followed up Victoria's case in accordance with her usual practice and the family centre's established procedures.

7.34 The family centre's performance indicators required that initial assessments be completed within six weeks of the receipt of the referral. However, both Ms Henry and Ms Watson agreed that a shorter period would be appropriate in cases such as Victoria's, which had been clearly identified as urgent.

7.35 Therefore, at some point well before the end of September, Ms Henry would have carried out an initial assessment of Victoria's situation. I was told that this would have involved the making of further inquiries of social services as to the circumstances of the case, together with a home visit carried out by a member of the family centre's staff. On the basis of the information obtained during the course of such a visit, the family centre staff would have considered how best to support Kouao and Victoria. This may have involved regular home visits or the enrolment of Victoria in some form of daycare activity.

7.36 The potential impact of such support in the context of Victoria's case is self-evident, and it is a matter much to be regretted that she never benefited from the expert attention of either Ms Henry or any other member of the family centre staff.

8 Enfield Social Services

The managerial context

8.1 Enfield Social Services had case responsibility for Victoria for just over 24 hours – from 3.15pm on Monday 26 July 1999, when she was referred to the North Middlesex Hospital social work team, until 4.30pm on Tuesday 27 July 1999, when they transferred responsibility for the case to Haringey Social Services.

8.2 That the local authority of Enfield had any involvement with Victoria at all was largely a matter of history and geography. The North Middlesex Hospital is in the borough of Enfield, just north of the Haringey border and about 12 minutes' walk from Haringey's North Tottenham District Office. Karen Johns, the Enfield hospital social worker allocated to Victoria's case, thought that about 75 per cent of the children admitted to the North Middlesex Hospital came from the borough of Haringey. Yet in 1999, Haringey employed no social workers at the hospital. That has since changed.

8.3 At that time, Haringey had an arrangement with Enfield Social Services whereby Enfield children and families' social workers would provide basic initial services for Haringey children admitted to the hospital before the cases were passed to Haringey. The arrangement was set out inadequately in a two-page minute of a meeting held between the two agencies in July 1996. It was modified following a further meeting in September 1996.

8.4 The location of such a key operational protocol in a set of minutes was not ideal, and I shall return to the content later. The arrangement should have been set out in greater detail as part of Enfield's or the hospital's updated guidelines. At the time, the hospital social work team was expected to follow procedures set out in a variety of written documents, some of which were out of date. These included:

- the *Enfield Child Protection Guide,* published in August 1996, which required that in child protection cases an inter-agency case conference should be held before a case is transferred to the responsible area team;
- the protocol setting out the arrangement between Haringey and Enfield, which although produced at around the same time, envisaged a lesser scale of Enfield involvement;
- the North Middlesex Hospital child protection guidelines of 1998.

8.5 Also available were the Haringey child protection guidelines, which might be thought to have more than a passing relevance to Haringey children admitted to the hospital and referred on to Haringey Social Services. However, according to Ms Johns, these were not followed. Instead the hospital social workers relied on the protocol between the two agencies and the brief and less than adequate North Middlesex Hospital procedures.

8.6 Lesley Moore, the seconded assistant director for children and families from July 2000, did not seek to defend the "poor state of procedures and arrangements". She admitted, "Although staff had access to the right people to give them advice about what should happen and what was in current guidance, it was not readily available to them in the form of accessible written practice, guidance and procedure."

8.7 I would go further and say that the profusion of guidance in various documents relating to the different agencies made it very unclear what was expected of front-line staff. Even worse for Haringey children was the confusion over where Enfield's responsibility ended and Haringey's began. The inadequacy of this arrangement potentially put the safety of children at risk. Therefore, I make the following recommendation:

> **Recommendation**
> Directors of social services must ensure that staff working with vulnerable children and families are provided with up-to-date procedures, protocols and guidance. Such practice guidance must be located in a single-source document. The work should be monitored so as to ensure procedures are followed.

8.8 Although Ms Johns thought that 60 to 70 per cent of the referrals she dealt with were Haringey children, she admitted Enfield responded to them differently from Enfield children. Moreover, when faced with competing pressures in 1999 owing to staff shortages, she sometimes felt obliged to give priority to an Enfield child over a Haringey child. Indeed, Enfield's own management review of Victoria's case found that the issue may not have been about the quality of Ms Johns's practice but about how Enfield social workers at the North Middlesex Hospital regarded Haringey cases at the time. Perhaps not surprisingly, Ms Johns said in evidence that she thought the arrangement with Haringey was "not the best arrangement" and that Haringey should have employed their own social workers at the hospital.

8.9 These were not the only issues of concern for the North Middlesex Hospital social work team in the summer of 1999. There were long-standing staff tensions within the team and there were tensions between the team and the North Middlesex Hospital medical staff, all of which drifted without resolution, in some instances for years. Indeed, the evidence pointed to a complete lack of management grip on any of these issues. As a result, there was a vacuum created by the absence of responsible, managerial decision-making.

Management and accountability

8.10 None of this was helped by the line management and accountability arrangements that existed at the time. Since 1997, there had been two specialist social work divisions within Enfield, one for adults and one for children and families. The hospital social work team had stayed in the adult division as it consisted predominantly of social workers dealing with adults. Therefore, the assistant director for adult services managed all hospital social work.

8.11 The next in command was Lesley Howard, service manager for hospitals and health liaison from April to August 1999. Ms Howard was responsible for the line management of both hospital social work team managers at Chase Farm Hospital and the North Middlesex Hospital. While she was experienced in both adult and children's social work, she had limited experience and training in child protection work. As a result, temporary arrangements were put in place to ensure team leaders and social workers at the hospital could access support and guidance from colleagues in the community children and families' division.

8.12 In July 1999, Lesley Carr was appointed as the new intake and assessment manager for children and families, reporting directly to the assistant director of the children and families' division. Ms Carr was given the specific task of bringing the children and families' hospital social workers at both Chase Farm Hospital and the North Middlesex Hospital within the fold of the children and families' division. Ms Johns was one of only four and a half full-time equivalent hospital social workers specialising in children's work at the time. By the time Ms Carr left her post in October 2000, she had still to complete this task. Indeed, it was not until April 2001 that the hospital social workers specialising in children and families were finally brought under the wing of the children and families' division.

8.13   As a result, during her time in office Ms Carr assumed no management responsibility for children's social work within the two borough hospitals. Her role was "mainly consultancy in terms of service delivery". She would advise on particularly complex childcare cases but only when asked to do so. It was not her job to routinely check case files or to do random samples of the quality of a social worker's work. That was the province of the line managers within the adult division.

8.14   However, this was not a perception shared by Ms Howard. In terms of her own children and families' work, Ms Howard saw her role as being responsible for management and staffing issues. While ultimately responsible for practice issues, she was happy for the team leaders to seek support through "the informal channels that had been put in place". Thus it seemed that there was nobody above team manager who routinely and actively monitored the childcare practice of the hospital social workers.

8.15   I was presented with a number of reasons as to why it took almost two years to move the children and families' social workers. Decisions had yet to be made as to whether the move would be accompanied by a physical move of the social workers away from the hospital site to Edmonton Social Services office. The hospitals did not favour such a move because they saw value in retaining easy face-to-face communication with hospital-based social workers. On the other hand, the alternative solution was the integration of the referral and assessment team. This would have given Enfield greater flexibility in allocating its resources, particularly during periods of staff shortage. Ms Carr told the Inquiry:

> "Part of it was to do with disentangling the bureaucracy around the paying of staff and around the budgets. Part of it was around the fact that we would be taking these staff on with no managers at all. Part of it was linked to the retirement of managers and part of it was linked to not having sufficient managers based in Edmonton and no structure to actually take on the work, and part of it was very much based on concerns the hospitals were raising about moving the hospital children's social workers out of the hospital, the biggest difficulty being if they were based, as they were, in the two hospitals, providing cover between them would have been a very difficult business. There were insufficient numbers to actually do the job properly and that was really what held up a lot of things, was trying to ensure we had enough finances to be able to staff it adequately and run a good service, and it was not something we could actually change overnight, much as I would liked to have."

8.16   Two years could hardly be said to be "overnight". Far more damaging was the admission that the team was insufficiently staffed and had inadequate children and families' team management capacity to do the job properly.

8.17   Ms Carr also suggested the changeover was held up until after budgets could be restructured in April 2000. She acknowledged that budget restructuring was purely an accountancy exercise within the same organisation and did not involve a big transfer of money or a change in conditions of service. However, she had no answer as to why someone with line management responsibility simply did not force the transfer quickly.

8.18   By the time Ms Moore arrived in post, the proposal on the table was to pull the social workers from the hospital and relocate them in the community. She considered this unacceptable and was therefore partly responsible for putting the emerging plans on hold. She felt that the management transfer was slowed because of complex plans to reorganise the whole social services department. She said, "It was not just a question of throwing the hospital teams up in the air and deciding where they may land in a better place, but also all the teams right across the community in adults' and children's services." There were difficulties with senior management agreeing what that structure should look like, although Ms Moore thought these were beginning to resolve themselves by October 2000. At that time, management were "pulled up in [their] tracks by two things". First, the director was taken ill very suddenly and was off sick for a substantial period of time. Second, there was a major financial crisis that occupied senior management's attention. Extreme measures were put in place and eligibility criteria were tightened, with all the associated political issues. According to Ms Moore, "The whole of senior management's group time was taken up in dealing with the practicalities of that and putting straight so that we did not end up without the money to run a service."

8.19   With the appointment of an interim director in January 2001, and the worst of the financial crisis behind them, Enfield's senior management team revisited the structural reorganisation. When it finally came, the decision to relocate the hospital children's social work teams took three months to implement. This, according to Ms Moore, was "as fast as we could humanly function from that point on". Therefore, I make the following recommendation:

> **Recommendation**
> Directors of social services must ensure that hospital social workers working with children and families are line managed by the children and families' section of their social services department.

Lack of attendance at hospital meetings

8.20   The fact that hospital social workers were managed by the 'adults' team within social services led to a lack of clarity as to who was responsible for ensuring hospital social workers attended hospital meetings. Had there been effective line management, this unsatisfactory state of affairs would have been resolved.

8.21   These tensions came to a head over social worker non-attendance at hospital meetings, particularly the Monday afternoon psychosocial meetings. The weekly psychosocial meetings were arranged to be held at the North Middlesex Hospital on Mondays at 2pm. The meetings took, on average, one and a half to two hours and, according to Ms Carr, looked at every child in the ward. Enfield social workers were supposed to attend. Indeed, attendance at multi-agency meetings was an intrinsic and important part of a social worker's role and this expectation was clearly set out in the hospital social workers' job descriptions. The meetings were supposed to be a valuable forum for the exchange of information between medical staff and hospital social workers. Ms Carr said that information exchange "helps to give a more complete picture for the social worker who is doing an assessment". Ms Carr added:

> "It allows a much wider understanding of a range of issues that are going on and certainly helps the social workers to understand the medical perspectives, and it also helps the social worker in interpreting the medical understanding for parents and for supporting other parents and children while in hospital."

8.22   However, by the time Victoria was admitted to the North Middlesex Hospital, Enfield's hospital social workers had long since ceased to attend both the psychosocial meetings and the weekly non-accidental injury forum on Tuesdays. On instruction from the team managers, Cynthia Lipworth and Pat Dale, the hospital social workers ceased attending these hospital meetings as long ago as February 1998. They were not to resume attendance until May 2001, a period of over three years altogether. Hospital medical staff were less than happy with this. The evidence of Nurse Beatrice Norman and Dr Mary Rossiter suggested that the hospital staff placed greater value on these meetings than the social workers did.

8.23   Although the instruction to cease attendance had come from the team managers, it appears to have been driven by the social workers themselves. Evidence from Ms Carr, Ms Lipworth and Ms Johns all suggested that when social workers did attend, they felt deskilled and devalued. They felt their professional expertise was not appreciated, their opinions were not always heard, time was not always provided for their feedback, and meetings were not clearly structured. There was also a concern that the meetings were used to shortcut the formal routes for referrals of work from medical staff to Enfield Social Services.

8.24   Ms Carr felt the problem "should have been resolved and should have been resolved at the beginning", but she also said, "There were a number of what is probably best to describe as difficulties within personalities of the staff involved ... [By July 1999] the position had become pretty intractable and it was not going to be solved overnight." She did not think forced attendance would necessarily have aided communication. Instead she said she tried to work with the consultant paediatricians to formalise the meeting process.

8.25   Ms Carr felt the social and medical staff misunderstood each other's roles, which hindered communication. There were problems getting busy people, particularly Dr Rossiter, to look at the issues closely. Ms Carr scheduled a number of meetings with Dr Rossiter and Dr Naidoo, a consultant child psychiatrist, but they were "occasionally cancelled at short notice" because there were other issues on the agenda and these matters tended to slip down. Ms Carr did have a number of meetings with Dr Rossiter to look at changing working practice as a whole. While the psychosocial meetings were part of those discussions, Dr Rossiter was more concerned about other issues and, according to Ms Carr, those "took up a lot of the discussion time in the early days".

8.26   When pressed, Ms Lipworth agreed that the non-resolution of social work attendance at these hospital meetings had become a big issue. She accepted that it was her responsibility to take the problem up the management chain until it was resolved. Ms Lipworth had attended one of the meetings herself to confirm the social workers' perceptions and she was sure she would have taken the matter up with her line managers, but she could not recall those discussions.

8.27   Ms Moore also partly blamed the organisational structure. Staff from the children and families' division were aware of the issues and had been involved in meetings to resolve the conflict, but because they had no line management responsibility they "pushed the issue across to adults [division] who should have been the ones that made the decision". Ms Moore emphasised the problems that existed within the organisation about decision making:

> "There were certainly more discussions about issues than there were decisions about issues ... and some of the issues did not get resolved. What was needed was a decision. Once I was aware that there was a problem, a decision was made and the meetings have resumed."

Therefore, I make the following recommendation:

> **Recommendation**
> Directors of social services must ensure that hospital social workers participate in all hospital meetings concerned with the safeguarding of children.

Social workers' workload

8.28 According to Ms Johns, by the time Victoria was admitted to the North Middlesex Hospital, workloads were "high but not overwhelming". Others disagreed. With hindsight Ms Moore thought the workload was very high at the time, with caseloads exceeding 12 per worker. As a result, she thought there were some cases "which did not receive speedy enough and adequate enough attention".

8.29 When the specialist children and families' staff were overstretched, adult care workers at the North Middlesex Hospital would provide services to children and families as back-up, as would the hospital social workers at Chase Farm Hospital and the community social workers in the Edmonton Centre. However, as Ms Carr pointed out, back-up staff would then have to adapt to a new environment and new procedures, which was invariably problematic.

8.30 Ms Johns was an experienced social worker who had been with the Enfield hospital social work team for nearly five years. She was one of only two and a half full-time equivalent children and families' social workers in Ms Lipworth's 10-strong team (nine full-time equivalents) at the North Middlesex Hospital. By July 1999, she worked primarily in antenatal, postnatal and general paediatric social work. She had recently returned to work after a month's sick leave from work-related stress caused, she believed, by strife within the team. Ms Johns described difficulties caused by absences and sickness of other full-time staff. Ms Johns also stated that there was "chronic conflict and tension" between staff, including her own line manager Ms Lipworth. As with much else that required managerial resolution in the North Middlesex Hospital social work team, this staffing issue was left unaddressed until June 2000.

8.31 However, Ms Johns was quite clear that these matters in no way influenced her handling of Victoria's case, nor did she rely on work pressures at the time or the availability (or otherwise) of professional advice to explain her actions.

Victoria in Enfield

Referral

8.32 On 26 July 1999, two days after Victoria was admitted to the North Middlesex Hospital, Nurse Sharon Jones of Rainbow ward referred her to the Enfield hospital social work team.

8.33 Ruth Warne took down the details of the referral at 3.15pm and completed an initial contact sheet in the name of 'Anna Kovao' and wrote the address as 267 Somerset Gardens, Creighton Road, London N17. She recorded that Victoria had been admitted on 24 July 1999 with burns. She was suffering from scabies and had poured water on her head to stop the itching. When nurses bathed her they noticed marks on her back and arms. Once child protection forms had been filled out the referral was passed to Ms Johns.

8.34 Had Ms Johns or any of the other hospital social work team attended the weekly psychosocial meeting earlier in the day they would have learned something of the medical team's concerns about Victoria from Dr Rossiter, the consultant paediatrician, and Dr Justin Richardson, the paediatric registrar, even before the referral had been made. The psychosocial notes for that day's meeting question whether the scalding injuries were non-accidental and register the long time delay between the scalding and Victoria's presentation to the accident and emergency department. Certainly, Ms Johns or her colleagues would have had the opportunity to explore those concerns directly and question the extent to which non-accidental injury was suspected. It is possible they would also have seen the body maps, which Dr David Reynders, the paediatric senior house officer, said he prepared in time for the meeting. However, for the reasons already given, Enfield hospital social workers had ceased attending these meetings some 18 months earlier.

8.35   Instead, Ms Johns telephoned Nurse Jones who merely repeated the details recorded by Ms Warne on the initial contact sheet. In her action sheet Ms Johns recorded that following the child protection meeting there was a concern. However, according to Nurse Jones, the completed child protection forms did not specify non-accidental injury.

8.36   This was the first of a number of file notes prepared by Ms Johns in Victoria's case and I give her credit for the quality of her clear, accurate and comprehensive casework recording throughout. Indeed, given the lack of any comparable notes produced at the time by the North Middlesex Hospital, I have placed heavy reliance on Ms Johns's notes and her evidence arising from them to provide an account of the information exchange that took place between the hospital and social services during the first few days of Victoria's admission.

8.37   Ms Johns advised that a doctor speak to Kouao to inform her that a referral was being made to social services and to seek her explanation for the marks on Victoria's body. She also advised that the child protection forms should be reviewed in order to specify whether any of the injuries observed were believed to be non-accidental. She did not consider it appropriate at this stage to go up to the ward to see or speak to Victoria. Had Victoria been an Enfield child, Enfield's child protection procedures state quite clearly the child should be seen by the social workers as a "matter of urgency". However, when asked why the same would not apply to Victoria, Ms Johns said:

> "It would be inappropriate for a social worker to go marching in ... you could not. You would have to ask parents' permission to speak to a child anyway. Talking to a child could prejudice, possibly contaminate evidence that the police may want later for criminal proceedings."

8.38   I do not share Ms Johns's view and these were clearly not concerns that Enfield considered relevant when drafting their own procedures. I return to this issue of speaking to Victoria later in paragraph 8.49 and the wider implications later in this Report.

Contacting Haringey Social Services

8.39   That same afternoon at about 3.45pm, Ms Johns faxed the duty social worker at Haringey's North Tottenham District Office a standard request for any information known about "Anna Kovao". Although Ms Johns was keen for the doctors at the North Middlesex Hospital to firm up their view as to whether Victoria's burns were accidental or not, she certainly had not ruled out non-accidental injury when making her first contact with Haringey Social Services.

8.40   She relayed her reason for the request as follows:

> "Child admitted on 24/7/99 with (?) accidental burns to head and face
> when she poured hot water over her head to stop itching caused by
> scabies. Other marks have been noted on her back and the origin of
> these will be checked out."

8.41   At the time Ms Johns said, "It was the very beginning of a child protection referral
that I saw here." However, she was uncertain whether she had enough information
to convey to Haringey that this case warranted a child protection investigation.
In short, on 26 July1999 Ms Johns said she did not know whether there were
suspected child protection concerns that would have required her to do an initial
assessment of Victoria in accordance with the agreement between Haringey and
Enfield.

8.42   Nonetheless she marked the fax as urgent and asked for a reply "by the next
day, if possible". In fact, according to her file note, Ms Johns received a phone
call from Anil Nair at the North Tottenham District Office, although no copy of
Ms Johns's fax or any record of Haringey's response appears on the Haringey
case file. According to Ms Johns, she was told that "the client" was not known to
Haringey Social Services. This was clearly a mistake for, albeit unknown to Mr Nair,
Dr Simone Forlee had already contacted the out-of-office-hours Haringey social
work team on 24 July 1999 to talk about Victoria's case, and to let Haringey know
that she had been admitted to the hospital.

Obtaining a diagnosis of non-accidental injury

8.43   Early the next morning, 27 July 1999, Ms Johns took a call from Nurse Sue
Jennings who was checking up on the action that social services were taking in
relation to Victoria. Ms Johns explained to Nurse Jennings, as she had previously
to Nurse Jones, that social services would not take any further action, which in
Victoria's case meant making a referral to Haringey, until they had a clear diagnosis
of non-accidental injury and the parents had been informed of social services'
involvement. When questioned, Ms Johns accepted there was in fact no procedural
hurdle that required any such preconditions before she could take action. Nor was
she prevented from doing so because the relevant correct child protection boxes
on the child protection forms had not been ticked. However, it remained her view
the box marked "I wish to await further information before committing myself"
that Dr Forlee had ticked on 24 July was not good enough. She told the Inquiry,
"That should never exist, that box. We can do nothing with that and I have always
had a problem when that box is filled in."

8.44   After updating her team manager, Ms Lipworth, Ms Johns agreed to send a
memorandum to the sister in charge of Rainbow ward and copied it to Dr Maud
Meates, the admitting consultant, repeating the advice she had given to Nurse
Jennings. She delivered the memo to the ward nurse in charge by hand. In support
of what Ms Johns understood to be the correct procedure, she attached to her
memo a copy of the page in the social work department section of the North
Middlesex Hospital child protection procedures. These require the examining
paediatrician to specify whether the case is one of child protection or not, and
to advise the social worker of who has informed the parent(s) that a referral has
been made to social services. However, Ms Johns accepted the procedures did
not suggest, as implied by her memo, that, in the absence of both of these, social
services could do nothing more.

8.45   In her memo she stated she had made preliminary checks and Victoria was not
known to either the hospital social work team or Haringey Social Services. She also
wrote, on the basis of the box on the child protection form ticked by Dr Forlee,

that she understood 'non-accidental' injury had not been suggested in Victoria's case. This observation was to prove remarkably at odds with the observations of Victoria's condition over the previous three days from the staff on Rainbow ward.

8.46   Ms Johns did not have to wait long for the confirmation of non-accidental injury that she was looking for, although it was not in relation to the scalding incident. That same morning, Dr Forlee, the senior house officer who had first admitted Victoria on 24 July, telephoned Ms Johns. Dr Forlee told her that when she (Dr Forlee) had completed the child protection forms she had been unsure whether the facial burns were non-accidental. However, other concerns had emerged. Ms Johns recorded these as follows:

"– Anna has old scars all over her body. A diagram has been made. The marks resemble the shape of a belt buckle
– A skeletal survey has been carried out – results are not yet known
– Concerns regarding interaction with mother. Anna wet herself when mother came even though she had been dry all day (bed wets at night), she seems on edge when mother visits, she was described by the ward staff as seeming to 'jump to attention' when her mother came
– On admission Anna was unkempt in a dirty dress, with no underwear. Mother was well kempt
– Mother has not brought any clean clothes for Anna since her admission."

8.47   Once again Ms Johns said she told Dr Forlee that the child protection forms would need to be amended to reflect these new concerns and that the parents needed to be told that there would be a referral to social services. Dr Forlee agreed to let Ms Johns know when this had happened and she (Dr Forlee) thought most likely it would be the next day.

8.48   By now Ms Johns was clear there were child protection concerns. Ms Johns's understanding of the agreement with Haringey was that she would only be expected to complete an 'initial assessment' of Victoria if Haringey could not respond immediately, and only then by agreement with Haringey.

Failure to speak to Victoria

8.49   Following her phone conversation with Dr Forlee, Ms Johns paid her second visit to Rainbow ward in connection with Victoria's case. Victoria was pointed out to Ms Johns at a distance but Ms Johns did not speak to her, despite what she had learned from Dr Forlee. This was not an oversight. She told the Inquiry, "I made a deliberate decision not to see Victoria". She gave a number of reasons for not doing so:

"For one, there was no parental permission for any social worker to see this child. The parent had not even been told of concerns and also I would not wish to prejudice any investigation given that there was a possibility that a crime had been committed and this little girl was injured."

8.50   She was also aware that English was not Victoria's mother tongue. In her view, "no social worker would have interviewed either the mother or the child without a French-speaking interpreter". Yet again, Ms Johns's decision not to speak to Victoria at the earliest opportunity, and certainly before the referral to Haringey Social Services, was in my opinion fundamentally wrong in principle and practice. I shall return to this at some length later.

8.51   Instead she discussed Victoria's case with Nurse Jennings and read the case notes which she summarised in the social work file. In addition to Kouao's explanation for the scalding injury and the concerns Dr Forlee had already conveyed by phone that morning, Ms Johns also recorded the following facts (without pause for question):

- Kouao's husband had died in June 1994.
- Kouao herself was born in 1966 and yet claimed to have four other children the eldest of whom was 24 [**thus making Kouao nine years old at the time she gave birth to her eldest child**].
- Kouao and Victoria had been in the country four months.
- Kouao had visited Victoria every day but for short periods as she was working.
- Kouao was in the UK on study leave for two years having left behind a job in France as an airport manager.

8.52   Ms Johns updated her team manager and they agreed that she should make a formal referral to Haringey Social Services and that Kouao would have to be interviewed. Ms Johns made the referral by telephone and spoke to Caroline Rodgers in the North Tottenham District Office at around 4.30pm on 27 July 1999.

8.53   It is vitally important that when a social worker from one local authority transfers responsibility for a case in this manner that the receiving authority is clear what its responsibilities are. The Enfield child protection procedures required the manager in Ms Lipworth's position to formally agree the transfer of responsibility with the relevant service manager in Haringey. In Victoria's case this was not done. There is a clear danger when cases are transferred without clear and thorough procedures being followed, that confusion may arise over who is responsible for what. In an effort to avoid such confusion arising in the future, I make the following recommendation:

> **Recommendation**
> Where hospital-based social work staff come into contact with children from other local authority areas, the directors of social services of their employing authorities must ensure that they work to a single set of guidance agreed by all the authorities concerned.

Transferring responsibility to Haringey

8.54   Ms Rodgers's record of what she was told, namely a summary of Victoria's presenting problems on admission and the ward medical team's subsequent concerns for her, appears to be a fair reflection of what Ms Johns knew at the time and was recorded in her own case file notes. Although Ms Johns said she also agreed with Ms Rodgers to await further contact from Haringey before interviewing Kouao, she did not expect to do this now that the case had been formally transferred to Haringey. In fact, Ms Johns expected to do nothing more at all in Victoria's case unless it was by prior negotiation, with Haringey as the lead investigating authority.

8.55   Ms Johns updated both Dr Saji Alexander, the paediatric registrar, and Nurse Jennings about the referral to Haringey Social Services before learning from Shanthi Jacob, duty senior manager at North Tottenham District Office, that a strategy meeting had been arranged for 2.30pm the next day at the social services office, and not the hospital as required by Haringey's own child protection procedures.

Strategy meeting

8.56   In her written statement, Ms Johns said that a hospital social worker would not normally attend Haringey meetings unless a manager thought it essential. When Ms Jacob's invitation arrived Ms Lipworth was not on site. Nonetheless Ms Johns agreed to go without first seeking permission because she said she "felt particularly concerned for Victoria's safety and well-being". She believed she told Ms Jacob words to the effect that she would be lucky to get any medics to attend, although she said it was only later that she learned that Dr Rossiter would not be able to go. According to Ms Johns, that made it "even more crucial that I attend in order to pass all the medical forms to Haringey Social Services".

8.57   Ms Johns said she was not aware it was part of Haringey child protection procedures that strategy meetings involving Haringey children admitted to hospital should be held in the hospital. She simply recollected that Dr Rossiter said she had an agreement with Haringey that it should be so. Ms Johns's lack of awareness of an important requirement of the Haringey procedures highlights the need for a single, clear set of procedures and reinforces the recommendation I made at paragraph 8.7 above.

8.58   In oral evidence, Ms Johns said she asked Ms Jacob if the strategy meeting venue could be changed to the hospital but was told by Ms Jacob, after checking with her manager, that the venue had to stay as planned originally.

8.59   It was Dr Rossiter who told Ms Johns in a telephone conversation that she would not be able to attend the Haringey strategy meeting. According to Ms Johns's note of their conversation they discussed Victoria, and Dr Rossiter queried whether there were signs of anxious attachment. She told Ms Johns she thought at the very least there was neglect, probable emotional abuse and possibly physical abuse. She also mentioned in passing that Kouao visited Victoria late at night and the photographs that had been ordered had now been taken. In fact the photographs were not taken until 29 July 1999. I know of no basis for Dr Rossiter's belief that the photographs had been taken. She also gave Ms Johns the details of Dr Meates, the consultant paediatrician with day-to-day responsibility on the ward but not child protection responsibility. Ms Johns was told that the play therapist on Rainbow ward, Noelle O'Boyce, had also made some observations but Ms Johns did not pursue this as part of any 'initial assessment', either with Dr Rossiter or Ms O'Boyce, because Haringey had accepted responsibility for the case. She said, "All the action was now their action and would have had to be negotiated with me." Dr Rossiter could not recall this conversation but she did not have any note to contradict what Ms Johns recorded as having passed between them.

8.60   Ms Johns believed, though she no longer had any independent recollection of this, that she and Dr Rossiter would have discussed updating the child protection forms. It was not unreasonable for Ms Johns to have focused so much attention on the proper completion of the child protection forms. The child protection forms she had seen on the ward at that time related only to the scalding injuries for which Victoria had been admitted. The hospital medical team was yet to confirm for Ms Johns whether they believed those burns injuries were non-accidental. In addition, the ward staff had now raised new concerns, conveyed to Ms Johns by Dr Forlee, on the basis of marks seen on Victoria's body which appeared to bear no direct relationship to the scalding incident. Ms Johns had yet to see any new child protection forms completed in respect of these concerns and this was the position she found herself in when she attended the strategy meeting at the North Tottenham District Office on 28 July 1999.

8.61   On her way to the meeting, Ms Johns visited Rainbow ward a third time, to collect and photocopy the child protection forms, the accident and emergency card and the body "diagrams". She did not have the skeletal survey results or the photographs because they were not yet available. In fact, contrary to the information she had been given by Dr Rossiter, Ms Johns noted after her visit to the ward that the whole-body photographs had still to be taken. She did not have any of the information from the nurses' critical incident log because she did not know of its existence, nor was she aware of the significance of that document.

8.62   If Ms Johns had looked at the log on this occasion, the only additional information she would have gleaned was that Kouao and a gentleman had visited Victoria at about 10.30pm, had woken Victoria from her sleep and that Kouao kept pointing a finger to her. It was also on the critical incident log that Nurse Jennings observed on 27 July 1999 that 'Anna' would like to communicate and that a French link worker would be a good idea. The important point is that without looking at the log Ms Johns did not know whether she was missing critical pieces of information.

8.63   Apart from the critical incident log, there were significant pieces of information contained elsewhere in Victoria's notes. For example, there was a reference to Victoria's earlier admission to the Central Middlesex Hospital in her ward notes and, on the CP 1 form completed by Dr Forlee, it said that Kouao and Victoria had previously had dealings with an unspecified social services department. Neither of these pieces of information were drawn to the attention of Haringey Social Services in time for the 28 July 1999 strategy meeting.

8.64   While on the ward, Ms Johns said she had been told that Kouao had been informed of the referral to social services but Kouao had not been asked for any explanation of the marks on Victoria's body. Ms Johns did not know why this was but said she noted it down nonetheless.

8.65   Ms Johns expected the child protection forms to have been amended as she had asked and as she thought had been agreed, but they were not. However, despite having no clear, updated medical report from the hospital, she was aware of Dr Forlee's concerns and she conveyed these to the strategy meeting. She also gave each of the participants – Rosemarie Kozinos, Ms Rodgers and PC Karen Jones – a copy of the hospital documentation she brought with her. As a result, by way of written material from the hospital, the strategy meeting had an unresolved view as to whether the scalding incident was non-accidental. They also had a set of body maps showing a series of marks on Victoria's body but no direct written opinion to confirm whether these, too, could possibly be non-accidental injuries.

Action points from the strategy meeting

8.66   Therefore, perhaps not surprisingly, Ms Johns wrote "request medical report regarding skeletal survey and old injuries (dates etc)" in the case file as the first action from the strategy meeting. According to her note, the rest of the action plan was agreed as follows:

"– when medical information is available, undertake joint visit/interview with police child protection team
– if appropriate, interview Anna
– mother to be informed regarding social services intervention
– check scabies and its relationship to possible neglect
– check school attended
– full child protection investigation."

8.67   She took from the meeting the following tasks to perform:

"– seek report from the ward staff regarding neglect
– check with Dr Meates whether photographs can be passed to the police
– alert ward to call the police if attempt to remove Anna from the ward is made
– ask the ward staff to monitor mother/daughter interaction
– keep Haringey Social Services informed of any discharge plans."

8.68   Ms Johns only recorded 12 of the 18 action points that appear in the Haringey case file. That she was not entitled automatically to receive a copy of the minutes of the meeting, according to Haringey's child protection procedures, meant that she was unable to remedy any discrepancy between the two.

8.69   The expectation was that Ms Johns and the chair of the strategy meeting, Ms Kozinos, would jointly undertake the first, second and fifth tasks. In her record of the action plan Ms Kozinos had indicated "hospital social worker" against each of the three tasks. That Ms Johns should have assumed responsibility for the other two tasks, namely to alert the ward to call the police if an attempt was made to remove Victoria, as well as asking the ward staff to monitor mother/daughter interaction, is less than clear, particularly as Ms Kozinos told the Inquiry: "Unless otherwise stated as hospital social worker or police child protection team, it is the social worker from our office that carries the decisions out with the lead agency".

8.70   Given no such 'hospital social worker' indication was made against these two tasks, the scope for confusion was obvious, particularly for Lisa Arthurworrey, to whom the case was subsequently allocated and who had not been present at the strategy meeting.

8.71   On her return to the North Middlesex Hospital, Ms Johns wrote and then delivered a memo for the ward notes addressed to the sister in charge of Rainbow ward. She also updated Nurse Jennings on the outcome of the strategy meeting. In the memo she asked if the ward staff could provide a summary of the observed interaction between Kouao and Victoria that had given cause for concern and if they could continue to monitor and record the interaction between the two. Ms Johns said this was how she interpreted her task from the strategy meeting to seek a report from the ward staff concerning neglect. In terms of the third task that she took from the strategy meeting, Ms Johns advised Nurse Jennings that if Kouao did attempt to remove Victoria from the ward before discharge was **agreed jointly by the hospital and Haringey Social Services**, the police should be alerted immediately and asked to step in. She also gave notice that Haringey would be contacting Dr Meates for further medical information.

8.72   On 29 July 1999, Ms Johns paid her fifth visit to Rainbow ward, to return the original child protection forms she had taken away to photocopy for the strategy meeting and to update Nurse Beatrice Norman. She also tried twice to contact Dr Meates by telephone but she was unavailable. Ms Johns sent her a memo to let her know that Haringey Social Services would be undertaking a child protection investigation in respect of Victoria, and that the duty social worker, Ms Rodgers, would try and contact her in the near future. She also wanted Dr Meates's advice as to the procedure for letting the police have the hospital's medical photographs of Victoria "so as to avoid the need to repeat the procedure twice". According to Ms Johns's statement, Dr Meates replied within two days by annotating Ms Johns's original memo to her – the date stamp suggests it was received by the hospital social work team on 2 August 1999. The reply gave permission for the police to have copies of the photographs provided they followed the procedures. Ms Johns passed on this information to Haringey Social Services.

Victoria is discharged from hospital

8.73   On 2 August 1999, Ms Johns also received a telephone call from Nurse Jennings on Rainbow ward to say that Victoria was fit for discharge. Ms Johns told the Inquiry she was quite clear that fit for discharge meant only that Victoria was 'medically' fit enough to go home or to go elsewhere. Nurse Jennings expressed her view that she would like the discharge to happen as soon as possible. According to Ms Johns it was normal for the ward to say that because they are always in need of beds.

Nurse Jennings also told Ms Johns that the scabies was no longer active. Ms Johns agreed to let North Tottenham District Office know the position.

8.74 For the reasons already noted, Ms Johns did not attend the psychosocial meeting that afternoon. The notes of the meeting, kept in a book in the psychiatry department, identified signs of emotional abuse and noted that Victoria seemed scared of mother's visits with her male friend, though she was not fearful when just mother visited. In fact Victoria seemed "clingy with mother".

8.75 Had Ms Johns attended the psychosocial meeting she may have noticed the inconsistency between this description of Kouao's interaction with Victoria and that contained in Dr Forlee's notes. Dr Forlee's notes revealed concerns regarding Victoria's interaction with Kouao, in particular that Victoria wet herself when her mother visited, Victoria seemed "on edge when her mother visits" and that Victoria seemed to "jump to attention" when Kouao visited. Dr Rossiter did attend the meeting that day and she recalled asking for a psychiatric assessment because of her concerns about emotional abuse. According to Dr Rossiter, the psychiatrist was not prepared to see Victoria without further background information and until she had been assessed by social services. However, as the hospital never wrote to Haringey to pursue this, and partly because Ms Johns did not attend the meeting, this exchange of views never reached Haringey.

8.76 Ms Johns subsequently made four separate telephone calls. First she rang the North Tottenham District Office to speak to Ms Kozinos. Ms Kozinos told her that Victoria's case had been allocated to Ms Arthurworrey. Ms Johns recorded speaking to Ms Arthurworrey that same day and in her oral evidence Ms Arthurworrey said that they probably did have a conversation. Ms Arthurworrey remembered saying she had not yet been given the file but that she would contact Ms Johns when she had it. Ms Johns then left a message for Dr Meates to telephone her. She rang Nurse Jennings on Rainbow ward twice, first to let her know the outcome of her contact with the North Tottenham District Office and then later in the afternoon to say, as she had yet to hear from Ms Arthurworrey, she would fax her and invite her to make contact directly with the ward.

8.77 The next morning, Ms Johns faxed a memo to Ms Arthurworrey letting her know that Victoria was "ready for discharge" and the ward would like this to happen as soon as possible. Ms Johns did not qualify this remark or indicate in any way it was her understanding that although Victoria was medically fit for discharge, discharge should only happen if social services agreed jointly that it was in fact safe for Victoria to be discharged. She indicated to Ms Arthurworrey that she might want to talk to the ward directly to discuss social services' involvement and gave her Nurse Isobel Quinn's details as the nurse in charge for that day. She also mentioned that Victoria's scabies had been successfully treated and was no longer active and she passed on Dr Meates's message for the police with regard to the photographs. She admitted she did not know what the usual procedures were for the police to obtain the photographs but assumed that PC Jones would know.

8.78 Finally, Ms Johns contacted Nurse Quinn to update her and pass on Ms Arthurworrey's contact details. Ms Johns was to have no more involvement in Victoria's case from 3 August 1999. She completed and signed off the necessary paperwork on 9 August, including a brief closing summary. The summary did not address the hospital's view as to whether the scalding incident was non-accidental, the significance of the other marks discovered on Victoria's body and whether there was anything other than a query around possible emotional abuse and neglect. Against the box marked 'risk factors' Ms Johns wrote "N/E" (not established). The reason for this, according to Ms Johns, was that Victoria's case had been transferred to Haringey Social Services and they had accepted responsibility. Therefore, it rested with Haringey to identify the relevant risk factors.

8.79   Ms Lipworth closed Victoria's file in Enfield on 13 September 1999.

Analysis of practice

8.80   Viewed as a whole, Ms Johns's role in Victoria's case was limited to that of a 'postbox' for information passing between the hospital and Haringey Social Services. Ms Johns's description of herself as a "conduit of information" is difficult to challenge and I have to question whether that can be a sensible use of an experienced social worker's time.

8.81   Having heard all the evidence, I fully accept that in her clear and unambiguous referral to Ms Rodgers on 27 July 1999, and in the information she conveyed to the strategy meeting on 28 July, Ms Johns provided Haringey Social Services both orally and in writing with the fullest details she possessed at the time. I am left in no doubt that if Ms Johns had been given the full picture by the North Middlesex Hospital staff, as they described to me in their evidence, she would have recorded it and passed it on to Haringey.

The initial assessment

8.82   The inadequacies in the initial assessment may in part be attributable to the fact that the Enfield-Haringey protocol in place at the time stipulated the following two options in relation to Haringey child protection cases:

- Where there are clear concerns of child protection needs in a case, Enfield hospital social workers find that usually Haringey Social Services respond immediately, whether the case is known to them or not. If they cannot respond immediately they agree a plan of action with the team manager.

- Where child protection needs are not clear but are suspected, if the case is not known to Haringey, the hospital social worker will do an initial assessment in consultation with the duty team manager, ie getting any background information. This assessment will then be discussed with the duty team manager and, if agreed that it is clearly child protection, the district team will continue the work. If hospital social workers feel it is child protection and the district does not, the team leaders of hospital and district need to discuss.

8.83   On 26 July 1999, having established that Victoria was unknown to Haringey, Ms Johns had sufficient information in relation to the scalding incident to firmly put Victoria's case into the second of these two protocol options; in other words child protection needs were not clear but suspected. When asked, Ms Johns accepted that she had responsibility for Victoria from 3.15pm on 26 July – though in her mind the responsibility went no further than seeking to clarify the referral. Counsel to the Inquiry then pressed her as to which child protection protocol option she thought the case fell into at that stage. Ms Johns was less than clear in her response. I have no such doubts.

8.84   Ms Johns had already conceded that she did not, contrary to the advice she gave to the nursing and medical staff on Rainbow ward in her memo, require clear specification by a doctor of non-accidental injury and confirmation that the carers had been told of a referral to social services before she could become involved. Indeed, arguably the whole purpose of the second option, the 'not clear' category, was to kick-start an initial assessment at the earliest opportunity (in conjunction with Haringey) in order to firm up the child protection concerns and assess the risk to Victoria.

8.85 Admittedly, through no fault of Ms Johns, the child protection process had already got off to a false start. Dr Forlee's first discussion with Haringey Social Services on the evening of 24 July 1999 had prompted no immediate investigative action. Ms Johns, however, soon had an opportunity to get matters back on track. In my view, the time she spent from 26 July onwards – reminding hospital staff of the procedures to be followed – would have been better spent talking to Victoria and Kouao and ascertaining the views of the medical and nursing staff responsible for Victoria's care. The only advantage in pressing for the proper completion of the child protection forms with a clear diagnosis of child protection, from Enfield's perspective, was that it would move Victoria's case into the first option, and provided that Haringey accepted the case and could respond immediately, which they did, responsibility for undertaking any assessment would pass to them. As a result, any obligation on an Enfield hospital social worker to do more than the most rudimentary first checks would have disappeared.

8.86 In the 24 hours or so that Victoria's case rested with Ms Johns, and despite there being no clear child protection concerns, Ms Johns did little more social work investigative tasks than check whether Victoria was known to Haringey, speak to medical staff, read Victoria's case notes on the ward and consult with her manager. There were no phone calls to any other agencies. For example, a phone call to the Central Middlesex Hospital would have opened a whole trail of inquiries leading back to Brent and Ealing Social Services. However, Ms Johns thought these were part of the secondary checks that Haringey would perform. The fact they did not is clearly not the responsibility of Enfield Social Services, but once again an opportunity to pull together information known about Victoria by those whose remit it was to do so, and for however short a period, was lost.

8.87 When asked what she thought was meant by an 'initial assessment', Ms Johns was anything but clear because there was no clear definition at the time:

> "At the time ... it was very unclear ... initial assessment could just simply mean gathering the information that was available and clarifying from that what kind of referral there was or was not, or perhaps even interviewing a parent ... You might actually be assessing what kind of case this is, because if child protection needs are not clear, that does need to be clarified at some point. Before the case can be passed to Haringey properly and appropriately, that does need to be clear."

8.88 Both Ms Carr and Ms Lipworth supported Ms Johns's notion that it was sufficient as of 26 July 1999 to do no more than clarify the kind of referral Enfield was dealing with before passing it on to Haringey. Enfield's own management review of Victoria's case took a different view:

> "It must be pointed out that an initial assessment would normally include gathering background information and the Child Protection Guidelines for North Middlesex Hospital state that a hospital should do preliminary checks on all cases."

8.89 However, while the author of that report conceded it was acceptable for those initial checks, which according to the guidelines ought to include health visitor, GP, police child protection team and school if relevant, to be undertaken by Haringey, it was the author's clear opinion that an initial assessment would normally include contact with a parent.

8.90   The doubts expressed by many to the Inquiry about what constitutes an initial assessment will hopefully be remedied with the full-scale implementation of the new National Assessment Framework. For any experienced social worker in the summer of 1999 to believe that undertaking an initial assessment – or as Ms Johns would have it, clarifying the nature of a possible child protection referral – could be done without seeing and speaking to the child, the child's carer and the ward staff who had daily care of the child, is difficult to credit.

8.91   While responsibility for sharing medical information and other observations about Victoria during her stay on the ward clearly rested with the hospital, it seems likely that conversations with the ward and medical staff might have uncovered much that the hospital failed to pass on.

8.92   Enfield accepted that the 'initial assessment' they carried out while Victoria was in hospital was limited, but they submitted that in the circumstances of the case being accepted as a child protection referral by Haringey within 26 hours of Ms Johns receiving the referral and while Victoria was safe in hospital, Ms Johns's actions were quite appropriate. Had Victoria been about to be discharged, or had Haringey responded differently and not accepted the case, Ms Johns said she would have investigated further. I do not accept this. Even at the most basic level Ms Johns did not take the basic steps necessary to ensure that Haringey staff received the fullest information.

Speaking to Kouao

8.93   Enfield has also accepted that none of its social workers spoke to Kouao while Victoria was in hospital, but again claim that the window of opportunity to do so was small and they question what relevance such an interview would have had.

8.94   Ms Johns said in evidence, and the records confirm her understanding of the conversation with Ms Rodgers on 27 July 1999, that she would await contact from Haringey before interviewing Kouao. However, as has been pointed out already in paragraph 8.54, it was not Ms Johns's expectation that she would have to interview Kouao once Haringey had accepted the case, unless this had been negotiated between her and Haringey. In assessing the failure by an Enfield social worker to interview Kouao, the following ought to be borne in mind.

8.95   Although the North Middlesex Hospital guidelines say it is sufficient to discuss with the consultant paediatrician or registrar when the parents/carers should be seen and by whom, the Enfield Area Child Protection Committee guide to inter-agency procedure and practice for professional staff states:

> "Parents need to be clear from the start what procedures are being involved, who makes what decisions, the statutory powers, duties and roles of the agencies involved and their own legal rights. This should all be explained by the social worker."

8.96   By the time of the strategy meeting on 28 July 1999, neither Ms Johns nor any of the medical staff involved in Victoria's care had spoken to Kouao for the purpose of eliciting her explanation for the old marks found on Victoria's body and observing her reaction to the concerns felt by the hospital. Information of this nature may have proved highly valuable for the strategy meeting. Ms Johns was aware, as a result of her dealings with the case so far, that Kouao had yet to be spoken to for these purposes. In my view, she should have done so herself in time for the strategy meeting.

Seeing and speaking to Victoria

8.97   Finally I come to Ms Johns's decision neither to see nor speak to Victoria. Ms Johns visited Rainbow ward on five different occasions but made no attempt to speak to Victoria. She gave several reasons why she did not. Ms Johns was not alone in expressing reservations about speaking to a child in Victoria's circumstances. Several witnesses said they had seen guidance that said they must be cautious about contaminating evidence or forming any kind of relationship with a child. Ms Johns was the person with a vital role in communicating the concerns of the hospital staff to Haringey Social Services in as comprehensive and helpful a manner as possible. In the situation in which Victoria found herself, this was a more important consideration than the possible 'contamination' of any investigative interview that might prove necessary. I note that by this point, in any event, Victoria had already been spoken to by a significant number of other people, including Kouao. In such circumstances, it is difficult to see what further damage to the investigative process Ms Johns might have done.

8.98 It is agreed that, as of 27 July 1999, Haringey had accepted full case responsibility for Victoria and that the ball was firmly in their court when it came to arranging a formal interview, which complied with the Home Office Memorandum of Good Practice (a 'memorandum interview') jointly with the police. That this should be done strictly within the good practice guidelines is not in question. However, those guidelines do not prevent a simple exchange of conversation with the child, the content of which should be properly recorded. Seeing, listening to and observing the child must be an essential element of an initial assessment for any social worker, and indeed any member of staff routinely working with children, and this can be of great importance when dealing with child protection cases.

8.99 Ms Johns should have had such a conversation with Victoria on 26 July 1999, when she had clear case responsibility. She offered two explanations for her failure to do so. First, that she did not wish to "form a relationship" with Victoria. Second, that she did not wish to compromise any future investigation. I reject these. The social worker's role in these circumstances is simply to listen without interruption and to record and evaluate what has been said.

8.100 Enfield went on to suggest that even if Ms Johns had spoken to Victoria, since she had said nothing of significance about her circumstances to the numbers of nurses and others with whom she had had contact on a daily basis in the ward, there was little likelihood of Ms Johns discovering anything of forensic significance. It is a matter of speculation as to whether that is true, but by not seeing and speaking to Victoria Ms Johns passed up an opportunity to form her own impressions about this little girl, and it is these impressions which must go to the core of what a social work assessment is about. Therefore, I make the following recommendation:

> **Recommendation**
> Hospital social workers must always respond promptly to any referral of suspected deliberate harm to a child. They must see and talk to the child, to the child's carer and to those responsible for the care of the child in hospital, while avoiding the risk of appearing to coach the child.

8.101 Finally, Enfield concluded: "The reality is that had Victoria been seen or interviewed by a Haringey social worker on say 29th July no one would be critical of Ms Johns for not seeing her before that."

8.102 Sadly this seems to miss the point entirely. Each individual practitioner must accept accountability for their own practice. They have a job to do and cannot put their trust in what might follow by others to justify their own actions or inaction.

Part three: Health

9 Central Middlesex Hospital

Background to Victoria's admission

9.1   Kouao brought Victoria to Priscilla Cameron's house on 13 July 1999 at about
        8.30pm. She told Mrs Cameron that she had left the Nicoll Road hostel and was
        now living with Manning. She asked Mrs Cameron if she would look after Victoria
        permanently. Mrs Cameron refused, but said that Victoria could stay the night
        with her.

9.2   During the course of the night, both Mrs Cameron and her daughter, Avril
        Cameron, noticed that Victoria had a number of injuries. They decided that she
        had to be taken to hospital.

9.3   The Camerons were concerned not just that Victoria had been injured, but also as
        to how those injuries might have been caused. In order to try and find out, Avril
        Cameron took Victoria the following morning to see Marie Cader, a French teacher
        at her sons' school. She told Ms Cader that she suspected Victoria might have been
        physically abused.

9.4   Ms Cader found Victoria reluctant to talk about her injuries. She also found her
        to be inconsistent in the explanations that she offered for them: "When I referred
        to how she hurt her face she did say to me that she had scratched herself, and
        I looked at her hands at the time, and I noticed that her nails were very short, so
        I asked her if she was sure about having scratched herself, and I explained that her
        nails were short. She then replied, 'I fell.'"

9.5   Ms Cader agreed with Ms Cameron's intention to take Victoria to hospital. She was
        confident that, once Victoria had been placed under the care of the hospital staff,
        "they would carry out the necessary procedure and ensure that the right people
        were contacted in order to help the child". It is clear from what followed that her
        confidence was misplaced.

Central Middlesex Hospital

9.6   On 14 July 1999, Ms Cameron took Victoria to the Central Middlesex Hospital,
        which is situated in north west London within what was then the Brent and Harrow
        Health Authority and is now the North West London Strategic Health Authority.

9.7   The hospital itself formed part of the North West London Hospitals NHS Trust.
        The Trust was formed on 1 April 1999 by the merging of the Central Middlesex
        Hospital NHS Trust with the Northwick Park and St Mark's NHS Trust. The current
        chief executive, John Pope, was appointed shortly after this merger. The current
        medical director, Dr John Riordan, was appointed in July 1999.

Arrival at accident and emergency department

9.8   Victoria was seen at 11.50am on 14 July 1999 by Dr Rhys Beynon, a senior house
        officer in the accident and emergency department. Ms Cameron told him what
        she knew of Victoria's background. He recorded that she had been looked after
        by "a neighbour" for the past month and that "lots of bruises/cuts to face/arms/
        hands" had been noticed. He also noted that, the previous night, Victoria's mother

had asked the Camerons to "look after [Victoria] for good" and that they had noticed "lots of new cuts/bruises/red eyes".

9.9 This history led Dr Beynon to consider it a strong possibility that Victoria's injuries were non-accidental. He was aware of the requirement, laid down in the hospital's child protection guidelines, that cases of suspected abuse had to be referred to a paediatrician. Accordingly, he contacted Dr Ekundayo Ajayi-Obe, the on-call paediatric registrar.

9.10 Dr Ajayi-Obe recalled being paged by Dr Beynon some time after midday. He explained that there was a child in the accident and emergency department whom he suspected to be suffering from non-accidental injury. Dr Ajayi-Obe agreed to take over responsibility for Victoria's care.

Dr Beynon's observations

9.11 Dr Beynon conducted only a very cursory examination of Victoria while she was under his care. His explanation for not being more thorough was as follows: "Given what I was told, she was going to have to be fully examined by the paediatric team. I did not feel any benefit from giving an eight-year-old child two full physical examinations."

9.12 He did, however, notice numerous wounds on Victoria's body. Unfortunately, precisely what he saw is unclear, due to the fact that he did not record his findings. While he accepted that he should have documented all that he saw, Dr Beynon told me that his failure to do so was due, at least in part, to the need for busy casualty officers to manage their time. He was aware that the paediatric team would be taking over Victoria's care and that they would be undertaking a thorough examination at a later stage.

9.13 Despite the brevity of his notes, Dr Beynon said that, had he been informed that Victoria had been scratching excessively prior to her attendance at hospital, he would have recorded this information, as it would have been inconsistent with a diagnosis of non-accidental injury. Furthermore, he did not notice Victoria scratching herself.

9.14 In the context of his role as an accident and emergency senior house officer, I regard the approach that Dr Beynon took to Victoria's care to be appropriate. He described that role as being akin to that of a "switchboard operator", and that his primary responsibility was to refer Victoria on to someone with the requisite specialist knowledge and experience. This is precisely what he did, and in my view, he exhibited sound judgement in his care of Victoria by referring her immediately to a paediatric registrar.

9.15 In the normal course of events, this would be the last contact that a doctor in Dr Beynon's position would expect to have with his patient. However, he was particularly interested in Victoria's case and this led him to go up to the ward before his shift the following day to check on her progress. He was told that the child protection team was aware of Victoria's case and was going to come and assess her.

9.16 Dr Beynon's reasons for taking the time and trouble to find out what was to happen to Victoria after she had been admitted to the ward are instructive. He said that he thought that Victoria had a very interesting history and that, at the time, his concern for her was such that he thought she might end up in care.

9.17   Dr Beynon was an expert neither in paediatrics nor in child abuse – Victoria's was one of only two cases of suspected child abuse that he saw in the six months he spent in the accident and emergency department. Nonetheless, he saw and heard enough, in the brief period during which he was involved in her care, to cause him considerable concern. The obvious implication – namely that Victoria was exhibiting fairly obvious signs of physical abuse on 14 July 1999 – is reinforced by the evidence of Dr Ajayi-Obe who assumed responsibility for her care later that afternoon.

Arrival on Barnaby Bear ward and assessment by Dr Ajayi-Obe

9.18   Victoria was transferred to Barnaby Bear ward. Following her arrival, she was examined by Dr Ajayi-Obe. She found Victoria to be a "jolly child" who was not unduly distressed by what was happening to her at the hospital. Dr Ajayi-Obe felt that, despite the fact that Victoria was able to understand her questions, she was reluctant to talk about how she had come by her injuries. She recorded her as being "a very secretive child".

9.19   Dr Ajayi-Obe's examination of Victoria would seem to have been a thorough one. Of the findings that she recorded in the notes, I consider the following to be of particular significance:

- "Scars of various sizes and ages all over body from about two days to several weeks, possibly months."
- "Relatively fresh scars on the face, corners of mouth. Infected cuts on fingers, bloodshot eyes."
- "A month ago Anna's Mum came knocking on the carer's door ... desperate to leave Anna with somebody for the following Monday."
- "Does not go to school."
- "Pungent smell, unkempt appearance."

9.20   Dr Ajayi-Obe also completed a body map, on which she recorded a number of marks on both sides of Victoria's face, on the top of her right arm, on both hands, on her back and on her buttocks. Precise details of all of these marks were not recorded by Dr Ajayi-Obe, but their location on parts of the body not normally affected by ordinary childhood accidents was sufficient in itself, in my view, to raise a suspicion of physical abuse.

9.21   In addition to their location, the nature of some of the marks was also a cause of concern: for example, the infected cuts that Dr Ajayi-Obe noted to Victoria's fingers. As to the explanation for the cuts given by Kouao to the Camerons, Dr Adjayi-Obe remarked that she had never come across a child who had deliberately cut him or herself with a razor blade. In addition, she considered that Victoria's bloodshot eyes could not have been caused by a cold, or by mere rubbing or crying.

9.22   Nor was Dr Ajayi-Obe satisfied with Victoria's explanation of how she had come by her various injuries. When asked, Victoria indicated that she had caused the injuries herself and demonstrated itching and scratching. However, Dr Ajayi-Obe did not consider this to be credible and told me that, in her opinion, only some of the marks and injuries that she recorded could conceivably have been self-inflicted.

9.23   As to the question of whether Victoria's injuries might have been attributable to scabies, Dr Ajayi-Obe said such a diagnosis did not cross her mind. This was despite the fact that she had seen a number of scabies cases while practising in Lagos.

9.24   In marked contrast to any of the other doctors who saw Victoria, Dr Ajayi-Obe's notes were detailed and comprehensive. She obtained a great deal of information about Victoria's social situation which, together with her examination findings, occupy some seven pages of hospital notes. The examination she gave Victoria was detailed and thorough. As such, her notes provide the best evidence available as to the information available to the hospital staff on the day that Victoria was admitted.

9.25   I am satisfied that this information, viewed as a whole, was sufficient to ground a strong suspicion that Victoria was being physically abused. In particular, the quantity and distribution of marks on Victoria's body added considerable weight to the suspicions expressed by Ms Cameron and the preliminary diagnosis made by Dr Beynon.

9.26   Dr Ajayi-Obe, it would seem, reached the same conclusion. Having examined Victoria and listened to her history, she was "strongly suspicious" that her injuries were non-accidental. She decided that Victoria should be admitted onto the ward.

Initial action by Dr Ajayi-Obe

9.27   Dr Ajayi-Obe then made two telephone calls. The first was to Dr Ruby Schwartz, the 'on-call' consultant who was also the hospital's named doctor for child protection. Dr Schwartz remembers receiving Dr Ajayi-Obe's call while conducting an epilepsy clinic at a local school. She was told that a child was on the ward with suspected non-accidental injuries. Although she made no note of the conversation, Dr Schwartz recalled that her response was to direct Dr Ajayi-Obe to admit Victoria and advise social services of the position. She said that she would come and see the child later that day. Dr Ajayi-Obe never had the opportunity to explain her concerns to Dr Schwartz face to face – she had gone off duty by the time Dr Schwartz arrived at the hospital.

9.28   In accordance with Dr Schwartz's advice, the second call that Dr Ajayi-Obe made was to Brent Social Services, whose records indicate that the referral was received at 4pm. Dr Ajayi-Obe could not recall to whom she spoke but remembers telling someone that she had a child on the ward whom she suspected to be suffering from non-accidental injury.

9.29   At 5.30pm, Nurse Paula Johnson, ward sister and lead child protection nurse at the Central Middlesex Hospital, took a call from Michelle Hines of Brent Social Services. Nurse Johnson recorded in the hospital notes that Victoria had been placed in police protection and that she was not to leave the ward. The note also records that the child protection team preferred Mum not to visit. If she did, she was to be closely supervised.

Nursing records

9.30   At about this time, Ms Cameron left Victoria to go back to her own children. She asked one of the nurses to tell Victoria in French that, although she was leaving, the doctors and nurses would look after her. Far from being reassured, Victoria became "unusually upset" at Ms Cameron's departure and tried desperately to follow her out of the ward. Victoria's reaction was observed by several nurses, but was recorded by none of them.

9.31   In fact, the nursing notes relating to Victoria's time on the ward are bereft of any information that might have been useful in the assessment of whether or not she was the victim of abuse. For example, Nurse Carol Graham, who recalled being told at the time of her admission that there were suspicions about Victoria, was shown marks on Victoria's forearms by one of her colleagues, Nurse Mary Sexton. They both formed the view that the marks were indicative of non-accidental injury. Neither of them made any record of their findings or suspicions.

9.32   Furthermore, the fact that Victoria's admission was related to concerns about abuse is absent from the nursing records. The nursing care plan for Victoria prepared by Nurse Bob Gobin, who was the nurse assigned to Victoria from 7.45pm onwards, makes no mention of any of the child protection concerns that brought Victoria into hospital in the first place, and attributes her admission solely to the fact that she was said to be suffering from scabies.

9.33   If, as Nurse Gobin said, the plan was written after Dr Schwartz's ward round that evening, which I discuss at paragraph 9.36 below, one can understand why the issue of scabies should have featured prominently. Nonetheless, it would plainly have been preferable for the plan to have reflected the concerns relating to possible deliberate harm that had prompted Victoria's admission in the first place, and the further concerns felt by some of the nursing staff during the time that Victoria was on the ward.

9.34   The importance of accuracy applies just as much to nursing records as it does to medical notes. Nurse Johnson shared my surprise that no mention of non-accidental injuries, suspicions of abuse, police protection or concerns about Kouao found their way into the nursing care plan. She told me that this is the first document that a nurse involved in the care of a particular child will look at. In Victoria's case, she would have expected the plan to have consisted of two pages – one dealing with scabies and one relating to the suspicions of abuse which had prompted the admission.

9.35   The observations of nurses during the day-to-day care of children on the ward can be of enormous value in cases of possible deliberate harm. In order for this resource to be most effectively utilised, it is vital that the nursing staff are made aware of which children are the subject of concern. I therefore make the following recommendation:

> **Recommendation**
> When a child is admitted to hospital and deliberate harm is suspected, the nursing care plan must take full account of this diagnosis.

Dr Schwartz's ward round

9.36   Dr Schwartz examined Victoria on the paediatric assessment unit with Dr Anita Modi, an experienced paediatric registrar, at around 8pm. Dr Schwartz said she left Victoria's examination until last because her case was a "complicated one" and she wanted to make sure that she had sufficient time to carry out a full assessment without interruption. Dr Schwartz told me that, prior to examining Victoria, she read all the notes taken since her admission.

9.37   By the time that Dr Schwartz arrived at Victoria's bedside, Kouao was on the ward and the examination was carried out in her presence. Dr Schwartz was not concerned about the way Kouao and Victoria interacted, but she was troubled to hear they were homeless and that Victoria was not attending school. She had a discussion with Kouao (largely in French but using some English words) during the course of which Kouao explained how Victoria had come by her injuries, giving an explanation that Dr Schwartz regarded as plausible.

9.38   Dr Schwartz could not recall whether she spoke directly to Victoria. What is clear, however, is that she did not seek to speak to her alone. With the benefit of hindsight, she accepted this would have been a sensible course of action, but at the time she expected a full investigation to be carried out by social services and was wary of compromising any interview they might wish to conduct.

9.39   I take the view that paediatricians should not be discouraged from speaking directly to a child, or from seeing a child alone, solely on the grounds that this might compromise a future joint investigation. I hold to this view especially when concerns about possible child abuse are presented initially to doctors so that they are the first members of the multi-disciplinary team with an opportunity to evaluate what has happened to a child. I therefore make the following recommendation:

> **Recommendation**
> When the deliberate harm of a child is identified as a possibility, the examining doctor should consider whether taking a history directly from the child is in that child's best interests. When that is so, the history should be taken even when the consent of the carer has not been obtained, with the reason for dispensing with consent recorded by the examining doctor. *Working Together* guidance should be amended accordingly. In those cases in which English is not the first language of the child concerned, the use of an interpreter should be considered.

9.40   When Dr Schwartz finished examining Victoria, she concluded that she had scabies and this had caused her to scratch herself vigorously. She described the findings that led her to this conclusion as follows: "What I found were the marks, particularly on her hands, the scratch marks, the areas that looked as if they had pus in, and the fact that there were scratches on the body as well." She was also influenced by what she considered to be the resemblance between Victoria's symptoms and those of scabies sufferers she had seen in the past.

9.41   As to Dr Ajayi-Obe's alternative interpretation of Victoria's injuries, Dr Schwartz said that, in her judgement, neither the quantity nor the distribution of the marks on Victoria's body were indicative of physical abuse. Furthermore, the marks on Victoria's hands looked to her like superficial scratches rather than cuts inflicted by a razor blade and she noticed nothing significantly abnormal about Victoria's eyes.

9.42   Dr Schwartz could not recall whether she looked at Victoria's fingernails to see if they were long enough to cause the type of marks visible on Victoria's body, nor could she recall asking Victoria whether she scratched herself. In addition, Dr Schwartz found no evidence of the burrows commonly associated with scabies infection.

9.43   Dr Schwartz also accepted that a scabies diagnosis could not account for all of the marks visible on Victoria's body, many of which did not appear in the characteristic sites of scabies in children. However, she took the view that none of these other marks were indicative of physical abuse. She said that, in her view, "Some of them could have been old insect bites, some of them could have been secondary to knocks that she had sustained during the course of play and movement around, some of them could have been things that had occurred prior to her coming to this country. I did not feel that they had the configuration that would worry me of a child that has suffered non-accidental injury."

The merits of Dr Schwartz's diagnosis

9.44   In her evidence before me, Dr Schwartz was unshakeable in her conviction that Victoria had scabies. Although the definitive evidence of scabies provided by sight of the scabies mites or their burrows was not available, she believed that she saw sufficient signs to make her confident of her diagnosis. I was told that the scabies mite and its burrows can often be difficult to detect, particularly in children, and that the fact that Dr Schwartz did not see them in Victoria's case does not demonstrate that her diagnosis was flawed.

9.45   In addition, Dr Ajayi-Obe, even though she herself had not considered a diagnosis of scabies when she examined Victoria, was prepared to accept that such a diagnosis might account for at least some of Victoria's history and presentation.

9.46   While this matter is plainly one that cannot be definitively resolved so long after the event, I heard no compelling evidence to demonstrate that Dr Schwartz was wrong to conclude that Victoria had scabies. In the absence of such evidence, I have decided that the account of this highly experienced paediatrician should be accepted on this point, and that Victoria was suffering from a scabies infection when she was admitted to the Central Middlesex Hospital on 14 July 1999.

9.47   However, the more important question is whether Victoria was suffering from scabies alone or a combination of scabies and physical abuse. In her statement to this Inquiry, Dr Schwartz was clear that, in her judgement, Victoria was not exhibiting signs of physical abuse when she saw her on the evening of 14 July 1999. While she moved slightly from this position during the course of her oral evidence, admitting that she "could not entirely exclude physical abuse", the tenor of her evidence was that there was very little, if any, visible indication that Victoria had been abused when she examined her.

9.48   Having considered all the available material, I reject Dr Schwartz's evidence on this point. I conclude that Victoria was exhibiting visible signs of physical abuse on 14 July 1999 and that Dr Schwartz failed to recognise them. I prefer the conclusions reached by both Dr Beynon and Dr Ajayi-Obe, both of whom took the view, having seen Victoria's injuries and listened to her history, that there was a strong possibility that she had been abused. While this conclusion is based upon the totality of the evidence I heard on the issue, I set out below the specific matters which I found to be of particular relevance.

9.49   Dr Schwartz told me during the course of her oral evidence that the lesions on Victoria's body, which she considered to be compatible with scratching caused by scabies, were to be found "predominantly on her hands and her arms". It is plain from the notes and, in particular, the body map completed by Dr Ajayi-Obe, that Victoria's injuries were by no means restricted to her arms and hands. In fact, Dr Ajayi-Obe recorded that Victoria had scars of varying ages "all over" her body, including on the legs, back, neck and face.

9.50   The only explanation for any of Victoria's injuries that had been provided by the time that she was seen by Dr Schwartz was that she had inflicted them herself, either by scratching or cutting herself with a razor blade. There is nothing to suggest that Kouao put forward any alternative explanation when Dr Schwartz spoke to her at Victoria's bedside. What, then, was Dr Schwartz's diagnosis of the marks on Victoria's body other than those on her hands and arms?

9.51   Her view was that these were the result of old insect bites and ordinary childhood injuries caused by running around and playing. The obvious initial difficulty with this diagnosis is that, as far as can be determined from the notes, nobody had ever suggested that these injuries might have been caused by insect bites or childhood rough and tumble. Therefore, it would appear that Dr Schwartz's diagnosis of these injuries was based upon her assumptions, rather than any information obtained from Victoria or her carer. Nor is there any indication that she took the trouble to test those assumptions by asking them. She certainly did not go through each of the visible injuries and ask Victoria or Kouao how they had been caused.

9.52 Of course, the simple fact that it was based upon untested assumption does not necessarily mean that Dr Schwartz's diagnosis of the marks on Victoria's body was incorrect. However, in my judgement, it is not a diagnosis that withstands close analysis.

9.53 First, the pattern of injuries on Victoria's body is striking. Children who hurt themselves while running around and playing will normally sustain cuts and grazes to their fronts and, particularly, to those parts of their bodies not protected by clothing. When they fall, they tend to fall forwards. However, there is a marked absence of injuries recorded to the front of Victoria's body. The majority of the marks are noted as having been on her back, buttocks and backs of her legs. Therefore, I find that the records completed at the time provide little support for Dr Schwartz's view that a significant proportion of Victoria's injuries could have been caused by childhood rough and tumble.

9.54 Second, Dr Schwartz's theory as to insect bites is substantially undermined by the history taken by Dr Beynon. He recorded that Victoria had arrived in England two to three months earlier, having previously lived in France. Dr Schwartz told me that she had been influenced in her diagnosis by the fact that Victoria had lived "in poor conditions" in the Ivory Coast. She said, "She had lived in poor conditions, I had been informed that she had come from abroad, that she may have had marks from insect bites or the like abroad."

9.55 While I accept that it can sometimes be difficult to accurately assess the age of injuries visible on a child's body, I have no reason to doubt Dr Ajayi-Obe's assessment, recorded in the notes, that the injuries she saw on Victoria ranged in age from "two days to several weeks, possibly months". For any of Victoria's marks to have been attributable to insect bites received in the Ivory Coast, they would have to have been over eight months old. I conclude, in light of Dr Ajayi-Obe's evidence on the point, that the marks she saw on Victoria's body were not that old, and so were not the result of insect bites. I suspect that, had Dr Schwartz taken the trouble to find out how long it had been since Victoria left Africa, she would have reached a similar conclusion.

9.56 The inadequacy of the alternative explanations for Victoria's injuries offered at the time does not, in itself, establish that those injuries were indicative of abuse. In determining what was the correct interpretation of the evidence available to Dr Schwartz, I have found the nature and location of the marks on Victoria's body to be the decisive factor.

9.57 The Central Middlesex Hospital child protection guidelines include a list of factors in a child's presentation and history that should alert a health professional to suspicion of abuse. These include marks to the skin in unusual sites and patterns. As set out above, this was plainly the case with Victoria's marks. She had a number of old and new lesions on her body at sites that could not be explained by either Dr Schwartz's diagnosis of scabies or by the normal rough and tumble of childhood.

9.58 In addition, the guidelines indicate that a lack of supervision by the carer and/or an inappropriate story as to how the injuries might have been sustained can also be suggestive of abuse. The explanation offered as to how Victoria's injuries had been sustained, namely that she had scratched herself and cut her own hands with razor blades, falls in my view into both of those categories. In this regard, Dr Schwartz should also have taken account of the fact that it was the childminder's daughter and not the mother who had actually sought treatment for Victoria's injuries.

9.59   Therefore, I conclude that the marks visible on Victoria's body and the history with which she presented at the hospital were sufficient to ground a strong suspicion of physical abuse of the sort felt by Dr Ajayi-Obe. I also conclude that Dr Schwartz failed properly to assess the evidence available to her at the time in discounting the possibility that some of Victoria's injuries may have been non-accidental.

9.60   It is unclear to what extent Dr Schwartz challenged Kouao on the issues noted by Dr Beynon and Dr Ajayi-Obe because no details of Dr Schwartz's interview with Kouao are recorded. Dr Schwartz said that she should have gone through each of Victoria's injuries and asked Kouao for an explanation, but admitted that she probably did not do this. I consider this a major oversight in Victoria's care. As with any serious medical condition, the proper treatment of deliberate harm requires a thorough and systematic approach so that important matters which might prove crucial to the future welfare of the child are not missed. In order to encourage the use of such an approach, I make the following recommendation:

> **Recommendation**
> When a child has been examined by a doctor, and concerns about deliberate harm have been raised, no subsequent appraisal of these concerns should be considered complete until each of the concerns has been fully addressed, accounted for and documented.

Failure to reconcile differences in medical opinion

9.61   I wish to make one additional point that I consider to be a major factor in determining the outcome of Dr Schwartz's evaluation of Victoria. Dr Schwartz said she was unable to speak to Dr Ajayi-Obe on the evening of 14 July because, by the time she had finished her assessment of Victoria, Dr Ajayi-Obe had gone off duty for the day. Whatever the circumstances that made contact difficult, it is unacceptable that no conversation took place between the two doctors when Dr Schwartz reached such a dramatically different conclusion to Dr Ajayi-Obe as to the cause of Victoria's marks.

9.62   The difference in the diagnoses reached by Dr Schwartz and Dr Ajayi-Obe was plainly of enormous significance to the future management of Victoria's case. Dr Schwartz should have been aware that her diagnosis would have a profound impact on the child protection investigation that had started (albeit ineffectively) that evening. Therefore, it was imperative that, before arriving at the view she did, she ensured that she had a full appreciation of the matters which had led Dr Ajayi-Obe to reach a different view a few hours earlier.

9.63   Although the basis of Dr Ajayi-Obe's concerns was clearly recorded in her notes, finding time to discuss the case with Dr Ajayi-Obe after her own examination might have led Dr Schwartz to reassess her conclusions about the cause of the marks on Victoria's body. At the very least, it might have resulted in a more conscientious attempt by Dr Schwartz to ensure that the concerns that she said she had about Victoria at the time of her examination were clearly reflected in the hospital notes.

9.64 I appreciate that the working practices and shift patterns at the Central Middlesex Hospital at the time could often make contact between two particular doctors difficult to arrange. However, whatever the practical difficulties may have been in this particular case, they do not provide an excuse for the failure of Dr Schwartz to speak to Dr Ajayi-Obe to gain a full understanding of the reasons why she had come to the view that Victoria was likely to be the victim of deliberate harm.

9.65 I conclude that a diagnosis of possible deliberate harm should never be superseded by an alternative diagnosis, without a discussion taking place between the doctors concerned. When major differences of opinion occur, such as in Victoria's case, it is the responsibility of the consultant in charge of the case to make sure that the views of all those concerned are properly taken into account before a conclusion is reached. The diagnosis of deliberate harm is far from an exact science and failure to recognise it can be fatal. In those circumstances, it is imperative that when it is suspected, it is not subsequently ruled out without careful consideration of the alternative view. In an effort to ensure that such consideration takes place, I make the following recommendation:

> **Recommendation**
> When differences of medical opinion occur in relation to the diagnosis of possible deliberate harm to a child, a recorded discussion must take place between the persons holding the different views. When the deliberate harm of a child has been raised as an alternative diagnosis to a purely medical one, the diagnosis of deliberate harm must not be rejected without full discussion and, if necessary, obtaining a further opinion.

Notes of Dr Schwartz's assessment

9.66 The notes of Dr Schwartz's assessment of Victoria were written by Dr Modi and occupy about one-third of a page in the hospital records. Dr Schwartz told me that her normal practice was to write her own notes, particularly in complicated cases such as Victoria's, and her failure to do so on this occasion was likely to have been due to her being called away on an urgent matter.

9.67 As to the quality of the notes, Dr Schwartz told me that they did not reflect the totality of what took place during the course of her examination and assessment of Victoria. In particular, they did not reflect the fact that, although she had ruled out non-accidental injury, she was still concerned that Victoria might be suffering from "other forms" of abuse. She stated that, in light of subsequent events, it was a disaster from her point of view that they did not.

9.68 Dr Modi said that she felt that her notes were adequate, save that she should have written "no physical abuse issues" instead of "no child protection concerns". While it might be possible to criticise Dr Modi for failing to reflect this distinction in the notes, particularly in light of what was to transpire the following day, I take the view that the notes provide a fairly accurate reflection of the conclusions that Dr Schwartz expressed at this point. I am not satisfied that she had pressing "child protection" concerns regarding Victoria, or that she went very much beyond her diagnosis of scabies in her consideration of the case.

9.69 The fact that Dr Schwartz disputed the accuracy of Dr Modi's note illustrates why it is extremely important for consultants, wherever possible, to write their own notes. It is a matter of grave concern that two senior doctors, both of whom were present at the time, were unable to agree as to what was said on a topic of this importance. If the notes confused and misled them, how much more misleading and confusing would they be for others who came to read them later?

9.70   For this reason, I regard it as vitally important that doctors make a full record of their history-taking, observations and findings at the time they are carried out. This is particularly important when dealing with sensitive and potentially contentious issues, such as child protection. Medical opinion is often sought in the context of a multi-agency child protection investigation well after the date on which a child is seen and examined. Medical opinion based on incomplete or imprecise records is virtually worthless.

9.71   In addition, doctors will often have to speak about their concerns for a child in the context of a later strategy meeting, a case conference, or even a criminal trial. In order for them to be able to provide a clear and accurate account of what they saw and thought at the time they examined the child concerned, precise and detailed notes are essential.

9.72   Dr Schwartz was aware that there was likely to be further investigation of Victoria's case by social services, and that she was likely to have role to play in that investigation. I am unable to discern how she could have felt equipped to provide social services with a coherent view of Victoria's circumstances and physical condition without having made her own notes at the time of her interview with Kouao and examination of Victoria. In an effort to avoid the repetition of such a mistake, I make the following recommendation:

> **Recommendation**
> When concerns about the deliberate harm of a child have been raised, doctors must ensure that comprehensive and contemporaneous notes are made of these concerns. If doctors are unable to make their own notes, they must be clear about what it is they wish to have recorded on their behalf.

Further investigations

9.73   Also included in Dr Modi's note were instructions that a skin swab be performed and a dermatology opinion obtained. Dr Modi told me that she considered it to be the responsibility of junior doctors on the ward to ensure that these instructions were carried out and that she delegated this responsibility when she handed over to another junior doctor on the morning of 15 July 1999. Nurse Gobin also recorded "refer to dermatologist and other multidisciplinary team" on the nursing care plan. He said he would have told the nurse in the morning during handover to pass this information on to doctors to ensure it was done.

9.74   The senior house officer on the ward during the morning of 15 July was Dr Charlotte Dempster, a locum. When questioned about the further investigations ordered by Dr Schwartz and recorded in the notes by Dr Modi, she said that she would have expected the skin swab to have been done by a nurse and sent to the laboratory, and that she did not remember whether or not she spoke to a dermatologist in order to seek an opinion. However, what does seem to be clear is that in the event, no skin swab was taken and no dermatology opinion was obtained.

9.75   As to how these unfortunate omissions could have occurred, Dr Schwartz said: "There are many requests that, in this case and in other cases, we ask for that do not appear to occur, and I do not know, in a system where there are so many people, how we can actually prevent these sorts of things from occurring."

9.76   I do not accept Dr Schwartz's assertion that oversights of this nature cannot be prevented. On the contrary, the more people that are involved, the more important it is to devise a system that ensures that requests are followed up. I refuse to accept that failures to follow through important medical requests are somehow either inevitable or excusable. The fact that there would appear to have been no system operating on the ward designed to ensure that requests of this nature were followed up is one, therefore, that causes me considerable concern. I return to the issue of systematic care later in this Report in paragraphs 11.35 and 11.36.

The day after admission

9.77   Dr Dempster first met Victoria and Kouao on the morning ward round on 15 July. She would normally expect to carry out such ward rounds in the company of a consultant or registrar but, on this occasion, she was on her own. This is particularly surprising given that Dr Dempster was a locum working only a single shift in the hospital.

9.78   Dr Dempster based her understanding of Victoria's situation on Dr Modi's notes written the evening before and the information that she was given at the handover when she arrived on the ward. She described that understanding as: "It had been passed over to me that the concerns about non-accidental injury were not a problem any more, so the diagnosis with her was she had scabies."

9.79   Following her ward round, Dr Dempster considered that the priority as far as Victoria was concerned was to contact social services and arrange for them to come and see Victoria. It would normally be the job of a registrar to seek the involvement of social services in cases such as Victoria's but, as she was the only doctor on the ward, Dr Dempster assumed the responsibility for ensuring that this was done.

Dr Dempster's contact with social services

9.80   She rang the number that had been written in the notes on the previous evening but could not remember to whom she spoke or in which department they worked. She refuted the suggestion, made by Ms Hines, that she told social services that the hospital "would like the child protection withdrawn and treat as a child in need, because the family needs urgent housing". Her recollection was that she told social services, "Dr Schwartz's diagnosis from the ward round the night before and … what the concerns were – the problems with the housing and other issues."

9.81   Having listened to Dr Dempster's evidence, I conclude that her recollection of this conversation is to be preferred to that of Ms Hines. The uncertainty she displayed as to the difference between a "child in need of protection" and "a child in need", together with her lack of experience of dealing with social services, causes me to doubt that she expressed herself in the precise and technical way suggested by Ms Hines. As to the lifting of child protection, this was again a matter of which Dr Dempster had little experience. She told me that she would not have known how to go about removing a child from police protection and would not have considered this to be a matter within the authority of a senior house officer. Given her lack of familiarity with the issues involved, I consider that Dr Dempster did little more than relay the conclusion expressed in the notes that there were no longer any "child protection issues".

9.82   Whatever the precise form of words she used, Dr Dempster had some difficulty in securing a satisfactory response from social services. She recalled that she ended up having at least two or three lengthy conversations with social services due to the fact that she was having trouble ascertaining who was going to take responsibility for seeing Victoria. Her impression was that the change in diagnosis from non-accidental injury to scabies meant that a different person was now to take responsibility for the case. She said, "Whoever I talked to made it a lot more complicated, actually, because I thought that whoever I talked to would come in and see her and it would be very straightforward. But it was not."

9.83   In fact, there would appear to have been considerable confusion, not merely as to the identity of the social worker who was to visit Victoria, but whether there was going to be a visit at all.

Dr Dempster's letter

9.84   At some stage during her conversations with social services, Dr Dempster was asked to put the hospital's concerns in writing. In response to this request, she wrote and faxed a letter to the "Duty Social Worker". She expected the letter to be passed to one of the social workers with whom she had been dealing thus far. The letter read as follows:

> "Thank you for dealing with the social issues of Anna Kouao. She was admitted to the ward last night with concerns re: possible NAI [non-accidental injuries]. She has however been assessed by the consultant Dr Schwartz and it has been decided that her scratch marks are all due to scabies. Thus it is no longer a child protection issue. There are however several issues that need to be sorted out urgently: 1) Anna and her mother are homeless. They moved out of their B & B accommodation 3 days ago. 2) Anna does not attend school. Anna and her mother recently arrived from France and do not have a social network in this country. Thank you for your help."

9.85   Dr Dempster said that her intention in writing the letter was to prompt a visit to the hospital by a social worker, rather than to set out every relevant piece of information in the hospital's possession. However, her letter did not contain any such invitation and Dr Dempster explained that it was through the conversations that she had with social workers that she expected someone to come to the ward. She admitted that she could not remember being told outright that a social worker would come to the ward to see Victoria, and agreed that the origin of her understanding was possibly the entry in the hospital notes from the night before that stated: "Michelle Hines will visit ward tomorrow".

9.86   Dr Dempster agreed that, taken at face value, her letter alone was inadequate to ensure a visit, and that it would have been sensible to make explicit her wish that social services come in and see Victoria on the ward before she was discharged. She also accepted not only that she omitted to mention many of the important markers of neglect that were recorded in the hospital notes, but also that she failed to mention these markers verbally to the social workers to whom she spoke. The inevitable result was that social services gained an incomplete picture of the hospital's concerns. As explained above, Dr Dempster thought that these gaps could be filled when the social worker responsible for Victoria's case came to visit the ward. No such visit ever took place.

9.87   Dr Schwartz said that the writing of this letter should not have been left to a locum doctor with little knowledge of the case and that, had she written it herself, its contents and emphasis would have been very different. In particular, she regarded Dr Dempster's letter as constituting only a very "superficial" account of the complex discussion which had taken place the previous evening.

9.88   It is plainly a matter of considerable regret that Dr Dempster's letter did not contain a more thorough account of the information held by the hospital – which was potentially indicative of abuse. However, it is easy to see how Dr Dempster's letter came to be worded in the way that it was. There was little, if anything, in Dr Modi's note of the previous day's ward round which would have indicated to Dr Dempster that Victoria's case was one of particular concern and, by the time that she came onto the ward on the morning of 15 July, the strong suspicions held by Dr Beynon and Dr Ajayi-Obe less than a day earlier had effectively fallen below the horizon.

Victoria's discharge

9.89   How Victoria came to be discharged from Barnaby Bear ward remains a mystery. While Dr Dempster was able to provide me with some assistance as to the discharge procedure that should have been followed, she had no recollection whatsoever of the circumstances of Victoria's departure.

9.90   The decision to discharge, she told me, is normally taken by a senior doctor, following which a discharge letter is written. One copy of the discharge letter should go in the notes, one should go to the patient, and one should go to the GP. The fact that no discharge letter appears in Victoria's notes led Dr Dempster to conclude that she cannot have been involved in the actual discharge itself. In any event, she said that she would not have authorised Victoria's discharge herself, but would have contacted whichever senior doctor was responsible for the ward that day.

9.91   As there was no registrar on duty on 15 July, Dr Dempster thought it likely that she spoke to Dr Schwartz. For her part, Dr Schwartz remembers being paged by Dr Dempster on the morning of 15 July and being told by her that social services were not investigating further.

9.92   Having received this news, Dr Schwartz was "almost positive" that she spoke to someone in social services seeking an assurance that Victoria would not go home without being satisfied that the "significant worries" she felt about her would be addressed. These included, as far as Dr Schwartz was concerned, the concerns about housing and schooling identified in Dr Dempster's letter.

9.93   Unfortunately, there is no note of any conversation between Dr Schwartz and social services in the hospital records and, therefore, no way of knowing if a call took place, to whom Dr Schwartz spoke, or what assurances she received. Nor is there any record of a conversation with Dr Schwartz on the Brent Social Services' case file. Ms Hines was firm in her denial that she spoke to Dr Schwartz and equally firm in her belief that she recorded faithfully in her contact notes details of the doctors she spoke to, together with a brief summary of their conversation.

9.94   In the absence of any objective at evidence from that time that a conversation between Dr Schwartz and social services took place on 15 July, or any convincing explanation of why no record of it was made in either the hospital or social services records, I am driven to conclude that it is unlikely such a conversation occurred. The result of this conclusion is that I reject Dr Schwartz's evidence that she received any assurance, either from Ms Hines or any other Brent social worker, that her concerns regarding Victoria would be addressed before she was discharged.

9.95   The problems caused by such imprecision of recollection are clear. It is understandable that busy professionals dealing with a large number of cases on a daily basis can forget precisely what conversations they may have had about which cases. The result is that cases can proceed on the basis of mistaken assumptions as to what has been done or said. The only solution to this problem lies in the keeping of better notes. I therefore make the following recommendation:

> **Recommendation**
> When concerns about the deliberate harm of a child have been raised, a record must be kept in the case notes of all discussions about the child, including telephone conversations. When doctors and nurses are working in circumstances in which case notes are not available to them, a record of all discussions must be entered in the case notes at the earliest opportunity so that this becomes part of the child's permanent health record.

9.96   Regardless of what her expectations of social services may have been, Dr Schwartz did accept that she should have arranged some form of medical follow-up for Victoria prior to her discharge. She blamed her failure to do so on pressure of time and the fact that there was no "failsafe" mechanism in operation to ensure that children were not discharged before appropriate arrangements had been made for their continuing care.

9.97   Nurse Johnson agreed that appropriate medical follow-up should have been arranged for Victoria and that, as the named child protection nurse, she should have taken responsibility for ensuring that it was. However, the position was complicated by the fact that Victoria was under the care of neither a GP nor a school nurse, who would ordinarily be the hospital's first points of contact. Therefore, once Victoria had left the ward, Nurse Johnson felt that there was nobody she could speak to who was in a position to ensure that Victoria's medical needs were monitored and addressed. In addition, having seen from the notes that Dr Dempster had been in both written and verbal contact with social services, she took the view that 'they' would ensure that Victoria's needs were met. However, she accepted that she should have at least made a telephone call to ascertain why no social worker had ever visited the ward to see Victoria.

9.98   The circumstances of Victoria's discharge illustrate clearly one of the principal concerns I have as to the way that Victoria's case was managed by the Central Middlesex Hospital, namely the marked lack of adequate notes of the important decisions made regarding Victoria's care and the material on which those decisions were based. There is no record of the various conversations that apparently took place between medical staff and social services, or about what was discussed in them. Nor are there any notes which throw any light whatsoever on how Victoria came to be discharged and who took the final decision to let her leave.

9.99   As to this last point, I was very concerned to hear that it was not considered normal practice in the hospital at the time to record the identity of the person who took the decision to discharge a child. I would agree entirely with Dr Schwartz's assessment that this constituted a "worrying state of affairs".

9.100   This lack of adequate record-keeping is indicative, it seems to me, of the amateurish and haphazard manner in which the crucially important decision to discharge Victoria was made. Dr Dempster, a locum working a single shift, was alone on the ward on the morning of 15 July with only Dr Schwartz on the end of a telephone to advise on Victoria's management. Although Dr Dempster had a broad understanding of the role of social services in the protection of children, she was unfamiliar either with the relevant terminology or with the particulars of local child protection arrangements and quickly became confused as to who in social services was dealing with the case and what he or she was proposing to do. In the event, neither she nor any of the other witnesses who appeared before me were able to say how it was that Victoria actually came to leave the ward.

9.101   The unsurprising result of this obviously inadequate approach to Victoria's discharge was that she left hospital without any record of her departure, without a discharge letter, without having been seen by a social worker, and without any arrangements whatsoever being made for any form of medical or nursing follow-up. In the context of her case, these were disastrous omissions. In an effort to ensure that they are not repeated, I make the following recommendations:

> **Recommendation**
> Hospital trust chief executives must introduce systems to ensure that no child about whom there are child protection concerns is discharged from hospital without the permission of either the consultant in charge of the child's care or of a paediatrician above the grade of senior house officer. Hospital chief executives must introduce systems to monitor compliance with this recommendation.

> **Recommendation**
> Hospital trust chief executives must introduce systems to ensure that no child about whom there are child protection concerns is discharged from hospital without a documented plan for the future care of the child. The plan must include follow-up arrangements. Hospital chief executives must introduce systems to monitor compliance with this recommendation.

9.102 I wish to make one further comment concerning Victoria's discharge from hospital that applies equally to the Central Middlesex Hospital and the North Middlesex Hospital, and that is the failure to record a GP for her.

9.103 The uncritical acceptance that Victoria was not registered with a GP, or that her GP was unknown, ensured that no effort was made to identify a GP for Victoria at either the Central Middlesex Hospital or the North Middlesex Hospital. Inevitably, any attempt to follow up Victoria after discharge from hospital, or any attempt to pass on to her GP the very serious concerns that had been identified about her, were severely compromised by this gap in information.

9.104 Registration with a GP is the bedrock of continuity of care in the National Health Service. It is stating the obvious to note the importance of registration with a GP for every child, let alone one in whom there are concerns about deliberate harm. In reality there will be very few children who are not registered with a GP, which is why failure to establish the identity of a GP for Victoria was such a major oversight.

9.105 The discharge of a child from hospital back into the community is as much a transfer of responsibility for a child's care, as is a referral from the community to a hospital consultant. I consider that the importance of continuity of care for all children is such that there needs to be clear responsibility placed on a hospital consultant under whose care a child has been admitted, to ensure that every child is discharged with a registered GP, whether this involves diligently tracking down the GP during admission or, in the rare event of a real lack of a registered GP, registering the child with an appropriate one before discharge. Therefore, I make the following recommendation:

> **Recommendation**
> No child about whom there are concerns about deliberate harm should be discharged from hospital back into the community without an identified GP. Responsibility for ensuring this happens rests with the hospital consultant under whose care the child has been admitted.

10 North Middlesex Hospital

The hospital

10.1   The North Middlesex University Hospital, previously the North Middlesex Hospital, is situated in north east London. It forms part of what was the Barnet, Enfield and Haringey Health Authority and is now the North Central London Strategic Health Authority. It is sited just inside the border of Enfield council. However, despite its location, more than 70 per cent of the children treated in the hospital live in Haringey, with the remainder living in Enfield. In 1999, the approximate combined population of Barnet, Enfield and Haringey councils was over 700,000. The current chief executive of the North Central London Strategic Health Authority is Christine Outram.

Arrival at the hospital

10.2   Kouao took Victoria to the North Middlesex Hospital accident and emergency department on Saturday 24 July 1999 at around 6.15pm. Victoria was seen by a casualty officer who referred her to the paediatric team.

10.3   The on-call paediatric registrar that evening was Dr Olutoyin Banjoko, assisted by a paediatric senior house officer, Dr Simone Forlee. The casualty officer told Dr Forlee over the telephone that a child had been seen with scalds to the head, the explanation for which was that she had poured hot water over herself to relieve the itching caused by scabies.

10.4   Both Dr Banjoko and Dr Forlee thought that this history was unusual and were immediately alert to the possibility that the injuries might be non-accidental. Dr Banjoko decided that Dr Forlee should go and see Victoria.

10.5   On her way there, Dr Forlee collected a set of the hospital's child protection forms on which to record her findings. The individual forms were designed to record specific sorts of information. Form CP1 was for basic administrative data, CP2 was for the history of the presenting complaint, and CP3 was designed to record the medical examination. In addition, CP3 contained a section requiring the doctor concerned to reach a conclusion as to whether the injuries were accidental or non-accidental, or whether further information was required before a conclusion could be reached. Finally, CP5 is an action checklist of things to do to assist with the diagnostic process and with future management.

Dr Forlee's interaction with Kouao and Victoria

10.6   When Dr Forlee saw Victoria, she was "not really in pain" and was "fairly passive". Her scalds were being attended to and, because she did not require immediate medical attention, Dr Forlee concentrated on finding out the details of what had happened from Kouao. During the course of her conversation with Kouao, Dr Forlee made a number of telling observations, the most significant of which are set out below.

10.7   Dr Forlee found Kouao's account of how Victoria had come by her injuries to be inconsistent and unconvincing. That Victoria would pour hot water over herself to ease itching did not "ring true" as far as Dr Forlee was concerned. Nor did she consider the pattern of Victoria's burns to be consistent with her having poured water on her own head in the manner described by Kouao. Furthermore, Kouao seemed unable to provide a consistent account of when the incident occurred – various times were mentioned, ranging from midday to 3pm.

10.8   Of greater concern than Kouao's inability to give a consistent account of when the incident took place was the fact that, on any version, there had been a significant delay before Victoria had been brought to the hospital. Dr Forlee did not ask Kouao to provide an explanation for this delay.

10.9   In addition to her reservations about Kouao's account of how Victoria came by her injuries, Dr Forlee found a number of aspects of the social history recounted by Kouao to be unconvincing. For example, Dr Forlee found Kouao's account of having left a comfortable environment in France to live in awful conditions in England "bizarre", and she was understandably confused when Kouao gave her a date of birth which would have meant that she was seven years old when her first child had been born. Again, Dr Forlee would seem not to have challenged Kouao on these aspects of her story.

10.10   As to her and Victoria's domestic circumstances, Kouao told Dr Forlee that she had been involved with social services in respect of housing, and gave the impression that the accommodation she and Victoria were staying in was substandard. She also mentioned that social workers had spoken about separating her from Victoria, but she did not seem to want to elaborate on this issue. In addition, and of particular concern to Dr Forlee, Kouao said that she was not registered with a GP and indicated that she had no firm plans to send Victoria to school.

10.11   At some point during the course of her discussion with Dr Forlee, Kouao told Victoria in English to "tell the doctor what happened". Dr Forlee recalled that Victoria responded by giving an account of the incident, in broken English, which was broadly consistent with Kouao's. Listening to Victoria give her account, Dr Forlee formed the impression that she had been coached as to what to say.

10.12   Dr Forlee recalled that Victoria was unkempt and smelly and was not wearing any underwear. In contrast, Kouao was immaculately presented. She also observed that there did not seem to be particular warmth between Kouao and Victoria.

10.13   Having listened to Kouao's account and watched the way in which she interacted with Victoria, Dr Forlee felt that Victoria should be spoken to on her own and with the aid of a French interpreter. She said her plan in this regard was to ask a French-speaking member of the nursing staff to obtain a full history from Victoria.

10.14   Unfortunately, however, neither of these entirely appropriate steps was taken. At no point during her stay in the hospital did any doctor speak to Victoria in a formal attempt to find out what had happened to her, either with or without the assistance of an interpreter. I consider this omission to amount to a major oversight in the care with which she was provided by the hospital. I am in no doubt that Victoria should have been spoken to as part of a comprehensive process of gathering information about her condition and circumstances. However, it would seem that the completion of this important task was deferred on the assumption that someone else would do it, or that it would be done at a later date.

10.15   Once she had obtained Kouao's account of how Victoria had come to be injured, Dr Forlee moved on to carry out a brief physical examination of Victoria. She charted the injuries to Victoria's head and checked to see there were no other injuries on her body that required immediate attention. She did not go any further because she had decided that Victoria should be admitted and it would be more appropriate to carry out a detailed examination once she was on the ward under the supervision of a more senior paediatrician. In addition, she was hampered by the poor lighting in the accident and emergency department, together with the fact that much of Victoria's skin was covered in white lotion.

10.16 Dr Forlee was not convinced, on the basis of what she had seen and heard up to this point, that Victoria's injuries were non-accidental. She therefore ticked the box on the CP3 form indicating that more information was required before a firm view as to the nature of the injuries could be taken.

10.17 Having done so, she proceeded to telephone Dr Mary Rossiter, the North Middlesex Hospital's named doctor for child protection and the on-call consultant at the time. She told her about Victoria's injuries and the circumstances in which she had arrived at the hospital. Dr Rossiter agreed with the plan to admit Victoria. In addition to her burns needing attention, she felt that they "needed to get to know her better". Dr Forlee then called Dr Banjoko to tell her what had been decided.

Roles of named and designated professionals

10.18 I have indicated above that Dr Rossiter was the 'named' doctor for child protection. Before I go on to deal with Dr Forlee's referral of Victoria's case to social services, it may help if I pause to explain the nature and extent of the responsibilities of the named and designated healthcare professionals.

10.19 The terms 'designated' and 'named' doctor and nurse for child protection first appeared in the 1991 edition of *Working Together* and were subject to further clarification in 1995 in *Child Protection: clarification of arrangements between the NHS and other agencies*.

10.20 When commissioning child protection services, each health authority must enlist the help of a senior doctor and nurse experienced in child protection to advise on the content of contracts in relation to the protection of children. This is the role of the designated doctor and designated nurse.

10.21 In addition, each NHS organisation concerned with children should have, or be able to call on the services of, a senior doctor and a senior nurse with a high level of expertise in child protection, to perform a number of functions, including identifying the child protection training needs of medical and nursing staff. This ensures that the proper child protection protocols are in place and acts as a reference point for other agencies to ensure that child protection advice is properly co-ordinated. In effect, the named doctor and named nurse are the child protection experts and are expected to lead their colleagues in all matters relating to the protection of children.

Dr Forlee's referral to social services

10.22 Having decided upon a strategy to meet Victoria's immediate medical needs, Dr Forlee contacted Haringey Social Services. The duty social worker on call that evening was Luciana Frederick. Ms Frederick was not immediately available and so Dr Forlee left a message for her at around 8.30pm, their subsequent conversation taking place "a lot later in the evening".

10.23 Dr Forlee's recollection of this conversation was patchy. However, it was sufficient for her to dispute a number of aspects of the note made by Ms Frederick on the Haringey council Out of Hours Social Work Report form, which reads as follows:

"1. Child admitted to hospital – concerns about injury caused by hot water poured onto face causing facial burns. 2. It appeared to be an accident, however mother may need support. 3. Advice given – Doctor agreed to discuss case with hospital s/w the following day. 4. NFA."

10.24 First, and most important, Dr Forlee denied telling Ms Frederick that Victoria's burns appeared accidental. Second, she said that she was told that further action on Victoria's case would have to wait until "normal office hours", which meant that she could not have agreed to talk to the hospital social worker "the following day", because that was a Sunday. Finally, Dr Forlee was certain that she never indicated that "NFA" (meaning no further action) was necessary on the part of Haringey Social Services. As far as Dr Forlee was concerned, it was her responsibility to inform social services of Victoria's case. What they did about it was up to them.

10.25 Before leaving the accident and emergency department and picking up the story of Victoria's treatment at the hospital with her transfer to the ward, there are two aspects of Dr Forlee's involvement with Victoria which require analysis. The first is the standard and contents of her notes. The second is her failure to obtain a copy of the records relating to Victoria's admission to the Central Middlesex Hospital 10 days previously. I deal with each in turn.

Dr Forlee's record keeping

10.26 It is clear from the observations recorded above that, despite the brevity of her physical examination of Victoria, Dr Forlee obtained a large amount of telling information during the course of her interaction with Kouao and Victoria. Even without the benefit of hindsight, there was much that was plainly suspicious in Kouao's account and the manner in which it was given. More importantly, Dr Forlee would appear to have been very perceptive in her assessment of the relationship between Kouao and Victoria.

10.27 Therefore, it is a matter of considerable regret that Dr Forlee chose to record so little of the valuable information she gleaned during the course of her contact with Kouao and Victoria on the child protection forms. In particular, she failed to record the following, vitally important observations that:

- Victoria was living in inadequate and dirty accommodation.
- She suspected that Victoria had been coached to give a consistent account of the manner in which she came by her injuries.
- There was very little warmth in the relationship between Victoria and Kouao.
- She regarded it as appropriate for Victoria to be spoken to alone with the assistance of a French-speaking interpreter.
- The pattern of burns to Victoria's head were inconsistent with Kouao's account of the incident.

10.28 Dr Forlee explained the absence of these observations from her notes by telling me that her role as an on-call senior house officer was to gather information sufficient to ensure a child's safety, before moving on to the next case. In her view, there was simply not the time to produce a comprehensive account of all potentially relevant information. She also explained that when filling in child protection forms, doctors in her position are instructed merely to record and not interpret what they are told, in case it is wrong.

10.29 While I appreciate the considerable burden placed on medical staff in a busy hospital setting, and accept that inexperienced doctors should not act outside their areas of competence, I remain troubled by the fact that so many of Dr Forlee's important observations and insights did not find their way into Victoria's notes. Had they done so, they might have proved very useful in any subsequent child protection investigation.

10.30   The central importance of a detailed history and a complete record of the suspicions and observations of medical staff in the context of a case of possible deliberate harm to a child is self-evident. In many cases, such records can be the most valuable diagnostic tool available to a clinician charged with forming a conclusion as to whether injuries may be non-accidental. I wish doctors to be in no doubt as to their obligations in this regard, and therefore repeat the recommendation made in paragraph 9.72:

> **Recommendation**
> When concerns about the deliberate harm of a child have been raised, doctors must ensure that comprehensive and contemporaneous notes are made of these concerns. If doctors are unable to make their own notes, they must be clear about what it is they wish to have recorded on their behalf.

Failure to obtain the Central Middlesex Hospital notes

10.31   From the outset of her involvement with Victoria, Dr Forlee had what she described as a "vague idea" that she had recently been treated at the Central Middlesex Hospital. It seems most likely that she was given this information by a staff member in the accident and emergency department when she arrived to examine Victoria. Despite this knowledge, Dr Forlee made no attempt either to obtain the Central Middlesex Hospital notes relating to Victoria's previous admission or to telephone the Central Middlesex Hospital in order to speak to a colleague with some knowledge of Victoria's previous problems.

10.32   Her explanation for not doing so seemed to be that sight of the notes would not have made a material difference to her treatment plan. Even without them, she had what she considered to be "sufficient ground to make a reasonably accurate assessment that there was a child at risk", and her decision to admit Victoria "would not have been altered specifically by other information". She also reminded me of the practical difficulties in obtaining notes from other hospitals in the sort of on-call situation in which she was working at the time.

10.33   I agree with Dr Forlee that obtaining the Central Middlesex Hospital notes that evening, and speaking to a doctor who knew Victoria, would not have altered her decision to admit. Furthermore, I appreciate the difficulty associated with obtaining paper-based medical records from other hospitals late in the evening and the constraints on doctors' time in a busy on-call situation. However, I am firmly of the view that, had the doctors at the North Middlesex Hospital seen the Central Middlesex Hospital notes disclosing the possibility of a previous serious assault on Victoria only 10 days previously, the level of concern they felt about her scalding would inevitably have been greater.

10.34   Dr Forlee said that the information contained in the Central Middlesex Hospital notes would have been beneficial "at a later stage". I disagree with her. In my view, the circumstances of Victoria's previous admission was vital information which was relevant from the outset. As it turned out, this step was never taken and the notes relating to Victoria's treatment by the Central Middlesex Hospital were never seen by those treating her at the North Middlesex Hospital.

10.35 In my view, the need to obtain details of other hospital admissions at an early stage in the treatment and management of a child with possible non-accidental injuries is not removed simply because a decision to admit has already been made. Apart from the obvious point that the significance of such further information that may be available cannot be assessed until it has actually been obtained, there may be numerous aspects of the management of the case that may be affected by knowledge of what has happened to the child previously.

10.36 In cases involving possible deliberate harm to a child, it is vital that doctors take their decisions in light of as much relevant information about that child as may be available. The fact that Victoria had been admitted to another hospital 10 days previously with another set of suspected non-accidental injuries was plainly a relevant piece of information in the context of her case. In an attempt to ensure that doctors working in this difficult area have as much relevant information available to them as possible, I make the following recommendation:

> **Recommendation**
> When a child is admitted to hospital and deliberate harm is suspected, the doctor or nurse admitting the child must inquire about previous admissions to hospital. In the event of a positive response, information concerning the previous admissions must be obtained from the other hospitals. The consultant in charge of the case must review this information when making decisions about the child's future care and management. Hospital chief executives must introduce systems to ensure compliance with this recommendation.

10.37 Despite her failure to secure the notes, there was one aspect of Victoria's treatment at the Central Middlesex Hospital of which Dr Forlee was aware. The North Middlesex Hospital casualty card recorded that Victoria had taken "self-discharge" from the Central Middlesex Hospital. I was interested to read this, as it provides a possible explanation as to why there is no record of Victoria's discharge in the Central Middlesex Hospital notes. The fact that a seven-year-old child has discharged "herself" from hospital may also be relevant when assessing whether that child might be the victim of some form of deliberate harm.

Victoria's arrival on Rainbow ward

10.38 At around 10pm, Victoria, still accompanied by Kouao, was moved to Rainbow ward. Shortly after their arrival, they were seen by Dr Banjoko, who explained to Kouao that there was a need to further investigate Victoria's injuries and provide her with appropriate treatment. Dr Banjoko decided not to broach the subject of how Victoria had come by her injuries at this stage.

10.39 Nor did Dr Banjoko consider it appropriate to carry out an examination of Victoria that evening. She was aware from the child protection forms that no proper examination of Victoria's body had yet been carried out but, in view of the late hour, she considered that it would not be "morally right" to conduct a full examination at this stage and that this task was better left to Dr Rossiter who, as she understood it, would be seeing Victoria the next morning.

10.40 In cases where a child presents with possible non-accidental injuries, the importance of a full and thorough examination by a doctor experienced in this area is self-evident. It was, in any event, an express requirement of the hospital's child protection procedures. Therefore, I find it staggering that throughout the two weeks she spent in the hospital, this vital element of her care was overlooked by a succession of doctors who, for the most part, seemed to assume either that it had already been done, or that it could be left to someone else.

10.41 While I am prepared to accept that Victoria's age and her condition at the time may have rendered it inappropriate to conduct a full examination when she first arrived on the ward, I am in no doubt that it should have been done as soon as possible thereafter. I am anxious that doctors receive clear guidance on this important issue, and therefore make the following recommendation:

> **Recommendation**
> Any child admitted to hospital about whom there are concerns about deliberate harm must receive a full and fully-documented physical examination within 24 hours of their admission, except when doing so would, in the opinion of the examining doctor, compromise the child's care or the child's physical and emotional well-being.

Sunday 25 July 1999

10.42 In fact, the first people to examine Victoria the following morning were Nurse Millicent Graham and Nurse Regina Tsiagbe, who had been specifically allocated to take care of her. Nurse Millicent Graham was aware that Victoria had been admitted the previous evening with general suspicions of non-accidental injury and so was on the lookout for anything suspicious from the outset.

10.43 Victoria was the first patient that the two nurses went to see that morning. They went into her cubicle, and Nurse Millicent Graham remembered that Victoria was pretending to be asleep. Nurse Millicent Graham recalled that Victoria had wet the bed overnight and needed a bath, which she and Nurse Tsiagbe proceeded to give her.

10.44 The only entry made by these two nurses in the notes recording what they saw that morning concerns the fact that Victoria had some difficulty in walking to the bathroom and had bruises all over her body. In their evidence before me, however, they were able to recall some more detail. Nurse Millicent Graham, for example, remembered that Victoria's fingernails seemed infected and that she thought some of them might fall off. She also remembered seeing a mark on Victoria's shoulder which looked as if something had been "heated and pressed into her skin". As to the latter observation, she said that although she made no note of it she did bring it to the attention of one of the doctors on the ward at the time.

10.45 This will not be the last time that I remark upon an unfortunate absence in the nursing notes of observations as to Victoria's condition while she was on Rainbow ward that may well have proved to be significant. The failure of the nursing staff to record their observations in the notes, and the consequent discrepancy between the levels of concern they expressed in their oral evidence and that reflected in the records made at the time, was a matter which arose with depressing regularity. In respect of this particular occasion, Nurse Millicent Graham told me that she considered her note taking to have been "absolutely disgusting".

10.46 In view of these discrepancies, each of the nurses who expressed concerns in oral evidence, which they did not record at the time, was asked whether or not their recollections had been coloured by knowledge of what had subsequently happened to Victoria. Perhaps unsurprisingly they all denied that this was the case and assured me that I could confidently rely upon their oral evidence concerning these matters.

10.47 While I do not believe that any of the nursing staff sought deliberately to mislead me during the course of their oral evidence, I have taken into account the fact that recollections can often be influenced by knowledge of later events, particularly when those events are as harrowing as those in Victoria's case. As a result, I have, as far as possible, based the account of events that follows on the documentation made at the time.

Dr Rossiter's initial observations

10.48 Although no written records of it exist, both Dr Forlee and Dr Rossiter clearly recalled conducting a ward round on the morning of Sunday 25 July. Dr Rossiter clearly remembered seeing Victoria during the course of this ward round but her memory of precisely what transpired was "hazy".

10.49 The notes provide some assistance. For example, the fact that Dr Rossiter's signature appears on the CP3 form, and is dated 25 July, would seem to confirm her recollection of having gone through the CP forms with Dr Forlee. In addition, the CP5 form would appear to indicate that Dr Rossiter was correct in her assertion that she directed a skeletal survey to be carried out and a set of photographs of Victoria's injuries to be taken.

10.50 The nature and extent of Dr Rossiter's examination of Victoria on this occasion remains unclear. She thought that she "looked at" Victoria after her bath and noted then that she had injuries that needed to be documented and drawn properly. She remembered considering what may have caused the marks and identified looped wire as a possibility. Unfortunately, no notes were made either of the marks she saw or of her theory as to their possible cause – an omission she regretted but was unable to explain.

10.51 Dr Rossiter's recollection was that she delegated the task of carrying out a full examination of Victoria's body and recording of any marks discovered to Dr David Reynders, the senior house officer who was due to take over from Dr Forlee. Dr Rossiter was confident that Dr Reynders had sufficient experience and ability to be able to perform this task on her behalf.

10.52 If this was indeed Dr Rossiter's plan, there were two problems with it. First, Dr Reynders was not on duty on 25 July and did not arrive on the ward until the following day. Second, Dr Rossiter left no clear instructions in the notes and made no arrangements to ensure that the doctor to whom she had delegated the task had a clear understanding of what was expected of him.

10.53 Dr Rossiter accepted that the arrangements she put in place to ensure that a full examination of Victoria was carried out were "clearly inadequate". In addition to agreeing with her assessment, I would add that her failure to check whether her instructions had been carried out meant that she did not find out until after Victoria's death that no thorough examination of her was ever carried out during the two weeks she was an inpatient at the North Middlesex Hospital.

10.54 Finally, with regard to Dr Rossiter's ward round on 25 July, a note by Nurse Tsiagbe indicates that Dr Rossiter had a conversation with Kouao that morning. Unsurprisingly, the notes record neither the questions put to Kouao by Dr Rossiter nor her responses. Dr Rossiter was unable to assist me any further from her independent recollection. Therefore, I will simply restrict myself to observing that a further opportunity to record potentially useful information for the benefit of those who came later to deal with Victoria's case was squandered.

Visit by Kouao

10.55   The last significant event of 25 July was a visit from Kouao, who arrived on the ward accompanied by a man. Nurse Millicent Graham recalled Kouao behaving towards Victoria in a manner she considered inappropriate, a view apparently shared by Nurse Grace Pereira, who made the following entry in the ward's critical incident log:

> "Mum visited with a gentleman at 10.30pm. Woke Anna up from her sleep. They sat on the chairs whilst Anna stood up in front of mum as they talked. Master servant attitude observed and mum kept pointing a finger at her. They left the room after about 10 mins. Mum went back to the room again to ask her what she needs after a suggestion from nurse and as soon as she entered although Anna had got into bed she got out and stood in front of mum to talk to her."

10.56   The critical incident log was kept in a folder in the ward office and did not form part of the main hospital notes of the child concerned. Its purpose was to record concerns of a child protection nature felt by nurses and, as such, took the place of form CP6, which had been designed for that purpose but was found to be inadequate. The fact that Nurse Pereira chose to record her observations on the critical incident log is an indication that she regarded the interaction between Victoria and Kouao to be relevant in a child protection context.

Monday 26 July 1999

The morning ward round

10.57   The morning ward round on Rainbow ward usually took place between 8.30am and 9.30am. On 26 July 1999, it was conducted by a paediatric registrar, Dr Justin Richardson, who was accompanied by Dr Forlee.

10.58   Dr Richardson recalled being brought up to date with Victoria's case, probably by Dr Forlee. In particular, he remembered being told that there were child protection concerns surrounding Victoria and that marks had been noticed on her body which, it was thought, were attributable to "inappropriate chastisement". Despite being aware of these concerns, Dr Richardson did not look at the child protection forms contained in Victoria's notes to ensure that the concerns and suspicions reported to him were adequately recorded. Nor did he examine the marks on Victoria for himself.

10.59   While I regard a careful review of the notes as one of the key responsibilities of the senior doctor conducting a ward round, I realise that Dr Richardson would probably have been aware that, by the time he saw her, Victoria had been seen by Dr Rossiter, and a plan for her future management had been put into action. In those circumstances, it is perhaps understandable that Dr Richardson should have limited himself to ensuring that Victoria was comfortable rather than taking the child protection issues forward.

10.60   Dr Forlee wrote up the notes at the end of the ward round. In addition to some physical findings she recorded the following: "X-rays; discuss at psychosocial meeting today. Dermatologist. Photographs." As to whose responsibility it was to ensure that these further steps were carried out, Dr Forlee told me that this would have fallen to one of the senior house officers on the ward at the time. However, she did not think that she was responsible on this particular occasion.

10.61   Later the same morning, Nurse Clare Watling and Noelle O'Boyce, the play specialist on Rainbow ward, gave Victoria a bath. At approximately 10.30am, they called over Nurse Beatrice Norman, the lead paediatric nurse at the

North Middlesex Hospital, to show her what they had found. Nurse Norman said that, when she looked, she saw a number of injuries to Victoria's body. She told me that she instructed the nurses to make a note of all they had seen once they had finished bathing Victoria. If that is right then she was disobeyed – the nurses restricted themselves to recording only the fact of Victoria's bath, not what it had revealed.

10.62   The fact that no record was made of Victoria's injuries at this point was quickly rectified, at least in part by Dr Reynders who, at some point during the morning of 26 July, completed a set of body maps upon which he made a detailed record of the marks visible on Victoria's body.

10.63   Dr Reynders would appear to have restricted himself simply to recording the marks on Victoria's body. Despite the fact that he concluded that the shape and distribution of the marks was strongly suggestive of deliberate injury, he did not think that he should be the one to investigate further how they had been caused. That was a task which, in his view, was better left to a more senior clinician working in a controlled environment where any information could be properly recorded.

The psychosocial meeting

10.64   In the afternoon, a routine psychosocial meeting was held. These meetings provided a forum in which any child with possible social or psychological problems could be discussed. Notes of these meetings were recorded in a book stored in the hospital's child psychology department.

10.65   Dr Richardson was at the meeting on 26 July, and Dr Rossiter thought it very probable that she was also there. Neither of them had anything but the vaguest recollection of what was discussed. However, the notes provide some assistance and indicate that Victoria's case was raised. It was recorded that child protection concerns remained and that Dr Rossiter was to carry out an examination of Victoria's injuries.

10.66   When it was put to her, Dr Rossiter was somewhat confused by the note which indicated that she was to carry out an examination. Her recollection was that she was extremely busy that week and could not recall having taken on this responsibility herself. However, whether or not she agreed to do so at the psychosocial meeting, Dr Rossiter agreed that she should have examined Victoria at some point during the days that followed.

10.67   A number of explanations were offered for her failure to do so. First, she speculated that she may have forgotten, and the notes of the psychosocial meeting did not come to the attention of those who might have been in a position to remind her. Second, it was possible that she thought that there was no need to examine Victoria, as this had already been delegated by her to another member of her team. Finally, and to my mind most plausibly, she thought that she may simply have failed to get round to it due to pressure of work and the fact that she was "juggling a lot of cases and trying to prioritise".

Referral to Karen Johns

10.68   It is instructive to pause at this point to consider what, if any, conclusion the hospital had reached as to the cause of Victoria's injuries at this stage. Despite the fact that she had been seen in the bath by five nurses, examined by two doctors and observed by several of the ward staff interacting with her 'mother', no firm view would seem to have been taken as to whether the injuries discovered were likely to be non-accidental.

10.69 This is illustrated by the referral made on the afternoon of 26 July by Nurse Sharon Jones to Karen Johns, a social worker employed by Enfield Social Services. At the time there was an agreement between Enfield and Haringey under which hospital social workers employed by Enfield Social Services would carry out an initial assessment of Haringey children admitted to the North Middlesex Hospital with child protection concerns, and then pass on the case to Haringey Social Services for action.

10.70 Following receipt of the referral, Ms Johns telephoned the ward and spoke to Nurse Jones. Her note of the conversation indicates that she was told by Nurse Jones that the child protection forms did not state that Victoria's injuries were thought to be non-accidental. Nurse Jones's note of the conversation, made in the critical incident log, reads as follows: "S.W. referral made. Spoke with Karen Johns (Hospital Social Worker). Drs and nurses to contact SW dept. again if it is thought that injuries are non-accidental and CP forms have been completed stating this."

10.71 It would seem clear, therefore, that the various suspicions chronicled above were not communicated to Ms Johns on 26 July. As far as she was concerned, the hospital had yet to reach the view that Victoria's injuries were likely to be non-accidental. It would also appear from the note in the critical incident log that she was waiting for such a view to be expressed by the hospital before taking any further action.

10.72 Continuing with Victoria's story, later the same evening, Kouao returned to the ward to visit Victoria. Dr Reynders spoke to her and obtained her consent for the skeletal survey to be carried out and the photographs of Victoria's injuries to be taken.

10.73 There is one aspect of this conversation which causes me some concern. Dr Reynders did not tell Kouao the real reason why the hospital wished to take photographs of Victoria's injuries. Instead of telling her that there were child protection concerns, he said that the photographs were necessary to monitor the healing of the burns. While I understand the reluctance of a junior doctor in Dr Reynders's position to confront a parent about matters of this nature, I regard it as undesirable that an inexperienced clinician be placed in a position where he or she is forced to resort to subterfuge in this way. It is preferable, where possible, to be honest with the parents or carers of a child about whom there are child protection concerns. If that means that difficult conversations are necessary then they should be handled by a senior and experienced doctor. In order to encourage the development of this practice, I make the following recommendation:

> **Recommendation**
> In a case of possible deliberate harm to a child in hospital, when permission is required from the child's carer for the investigation of such possible deliberate harm, or for the treatment of a child's injuries, the permission must be sought by a doctor above the grade of senior house officer.

Observations of Nurse Quinn and Nurse Pereira

10.74 The nurse in charge of the night shift on 26 July was Nurse Isobel Quinn. She allocated Victoria's care to Nurse Pereira. Before settling Victoria down for the night, Nurse Pereira gave her another bath. As she bathed her, Nurse Pereira saw a large number of scars on her body, many of which she considered to be indicative of non-accidental injuries, such as bites and blows with a belt buckle.

10.75 Disturbed by what she had seen, Nurse Pereira called Nurse Quinn to come and look. Nurse Quinn told me that she also saw marks, which she thought may have been caused by a belt buckle. She also noticed that Victoria's arm was bruised and swollen.

10.76 I should state that the first time that either of these two nurses recorded what they saw that evening was in their written evidence to this Inquiry. The only indication in the notes that this incident ever took place was a comment written by Nurse Pereira that, when she bathed Victoria, she found her to be "sore all over her body". There is no mention of the bite marks, the belt buckle mark or the injuries to the arm.

10.77 I have found it very difficult to understand why important observations of this nature were not recorded in the notes. Both Nurse Pereira and Nurse Quinn were aware that Victoria was a child about whom there were child protection concerns, and Nurse Pereira had seen fit the previous evening to make a note in the critical incident log concerning the master-servant relationship between Kouao and Victoria. Nurse Pereira was frank enough to accept that she should have made a note of her observations that night. Nurse Quinn simply told me that she could not account for why she chose not to do so.

10.78 I consider the issue of recording information in more detail in section 11. For present purposes, I wish simply to make the point that this is precisely the sort of information that nurses should record in the notes. They are a vital source of information in the discovery and investigation of child abuse and it should be made clear to anyone who may be in doubt that the recording of suspicious injuries on a child is a fundamental responsibility.

Tuesday 27 July 1999

The morning ward round

10.79 Dr Maud Meates, a consultant paediatrician, conducted the morning ward round on 27 July accompanied by Dr Saji Alexander, a registrar. Both doctors said that they were aware of the fact that there were suspicions that Victoria may have been physically abused. Dr Meates added that discussions she had with other medical staff during the course of her ward round alerted her to possible issues of emotional abuse and neglect as well. At the time, she said the accumulating evidence was "making us much more certain that this was an abusive situation".

10.80 Neither Dr Meates nor Dr Alexander carried out a full examination of Victoria during the course of the ward round. Both doctors apparently assumed that this had already been done. Neither of them sought to confirm this assumption by reading through the notes.

10.81 At the end of the ward round, Dr Alexander recorded an action plan that included referral to the hospital social worker, a request for an opinion about Victoria's right eye that had become swollen, and a further request for photographs and a skeletal survey.

10.82 As to the referral to the hospital social worker, Dr Alexander said that he was "probably" unaware of the fact that Ms Johns had already been informed about Victoria and that she was awaiting a definitive medical opinion as to whether Victoria's injuries were thought to be non-accidental. Dr Meates, it would seem, was similarly ignorant of the current position.

Ms Johns's attempts to obtain a diagnosis

10.83   Dr Meates's ward round appears to have prompted a further call to be made from the ward to Ms Johns. Her records indicate that she received a call from Nurse Sue Jennings concerning Victoria on 27 July. Although Nurse Jennings had no recollection of the conversation, Ms Johns's notes suggest that Ms Johns was asked what action she proposed to take. Ms Johns replied that she intended to take no action until there was a clear diagnosis of non-accidental injury and Victoria's parents had been informed of social services' involvement.

10.84   To reinforce the message, Ms Johns wrote a memo to the "Sister in charge of Rainbow ward", in which she clarified the child protection referral procedures. She explained that, unless and until a paediatrician confirmed that a child was likely to be suffering from non-accidental injury and informed the child's "parents" of that suspicion, social services could do no more than carry out routine checks. Finally, she wrote in the memo that she understood that it had not yet been suggested that Victoria was suffering from non-accidental injury, but that she would retain the papers and await further information.

10.85   Unfortunately, neither Dr Meates nor Dr Rossiter ever saw Ms Johns's memo and so did not take steps to correct her misunderstanding that non-accidental injury had yet to be "suggested". However, even without their intervention, matters started to inch painfully towards the point where Ms Johns felt she had sufficient information to make a child protection referral.

10.86   Although Dr Forlee could not recall doing so, Ms Johns's notes record that Dr Forlee called her on 27 July and explained that fresh concerns had arisen since the child protection forms had originally been completed, and that suspicion was growing that Victoria was the victim of abuse. Ms Johns recorded that she explained to Dr Forlee that the child protection forms would have to be amended to reflect these heightened suspicions and that Victoria's "parents" should be informed.

10.87   Assuming that Ms Johns's note made at the time of her conversation with Dr Forlee is accurate (and I have no reason to doubt it), then Dr Forlee failed to do as she was asked. She made no amendment to the child protection forms herself and could not recall whether or not she reported Ms Johns's request to anyone else. During the course of her oral evidence, Dr Forlee drew my attention to the ad hoc manner in which responsibility for matters of this nature was assumed by doctors on the ward. She told me that "areas that we covered, areas that we had responsibility for changed every day" and that "things happen[ed] fairly haphazardly rather than in an organised, co-ordinated way".

10.88   This is a woeful state of affairs. It combines what appears to me to be an institutionalised lack of any system on the ward for responding to requests and for ensuring the comprehensive and coherent gathering and passing on of information, with a discontinuity of medical care that blurred areas of personal responsibility.

10.89   It is abundantly clear that Ms Johns needed a straightforward, documented statement from ward staff about Victoria's injuries and whether or not these were thought to be non-accidental. She had made a request for this four times: in a conversation with Nurse Jones on 26 July and recorded by her in the critical incident log, in a conversation with Nurse Jennings the following day, in a memorandum to the ward, and in a conversation with Dr Forlee. On each occasion she was clear in her request and in her reasons for it.

10.90   Despite the number and clarity of her requests, she received no satisfactory response from the ward staff. Furthermore, there did not seem to be any system in place on the ward designed to ensure that requests for information from other agencies were dealt with promptly and efficiently. As Dr Rossiter put it, "I think we were in trouble of having a lot of links in the chain most of which are able to break."

Wednesday 28 July 1999

Further action by Ms Johns

10.91   It would appear that Ms Johns eventually decided to take Victoria's case forward, despite the absence of the unambiguous diagnosis she had asked for. Her notes indicate that she spoke to Dr Alexander on 28 July and told him that the referral had been passed on to Haringey Social Services. He told her that the hospital staff would pass on this information to Kouao when they saw her later that day, and a note made by Dr Richardson indicates that this was indeed done.

10.92   Ms Johns's notes further state that she spoke to Nurse Jennings and asked, yet again, if she could remind the doctors either to complete a new CP3 form or amend the existing one to show that non-accidental injury was suspected. Nurse Jennings could not recall what, if anything, she did in response to this request. Whatever it may have been, it certainly did not result either in the amendment of the CP3 form or in the completion of a new version.

10.93   However, it is possible that Ms Johns's call prompted Nurse Jennings to speak to Dr Rossiter concerning Victoria's case and Ms Johns's outstanding queries. This may explain why Dr Rossiter spoke to Ms Johns later the same day. At the end of this conversation, Ms Johns made the following entry in her notes: "Anxious attachment? At least neglect; probable emotional abuse; possible physical abuse."

10.94   Dr Rossiter did not make her own note of the contents of her conversation with Ms Johns and had insufficient recollection of it to enable her to dispute the accuracy of Ms Johns's record. Assuming that the note is an accurate reflection of what Dr Rossiter said, then, in my view, she gave Ms Johns a substantially more equivocal impression of the level of the hospital's concerns regarding physical abuse than the available evidence would have warranted. Nonetheless, Ms Johns considered by this stage that she had sufficient grounds to refer Victoria's case on to Haringey Social Services.

Haringey strategy meeting

10.95   Having received the referral from Ms Johns, Haringey Social Services arranged a strategy meeting for 2.30pm on 28 July at Haringey's offices. No one from the hospital attended. Dr Rossiter said that she was probably aware that the meeting was taking place and would have gone had it been held in the hospital at a time compatible with her other commitments, but that she would not have had time to travel to Haringey's offices on the afternoon in question. Nurse Norman was unaware that the meeting was taking place and none of the ward staff would seem to have been invited.

10.96   Following the strategy meeting, Ms Johns sent a memo to the ward. The memo stated that social services would contact Dr Meates to clarify the medical position and discuss a timetable for intervention (it would seem as though Haringey had yet to realise that Dr Rossiter had assumed responsibility for the child protection aspects of Victoria's case).

10.97   The memorandum ended by asking ward staff to "kindly assist" in the following respects:

"– To provide a brief summary of the observed interactions between Anna and her mother, which led to staff members feeling concerned
– Could staff continue to closely monitor the interaction between mother and daughter and record this
– Should Ms Kovao [sic] attempt to remove Anna from the ward, prior to discharge being agreed jointly by the hospital and Haringey Social Services, the police to be alerted immediately and asked to prevent this."

10.98   The final significant event of 28 July was a visit to the ward by Dr Thomas Mann, a consultant dermatologist. He examined Victoria at around 4.30pm at which point he found no evidence of scabies burrows and concluded that Victoria had been successfully treated and no longer posed a risk of infection. However, he did consider that Victoria's skin may have been irritated by over-treatment with the Derbac lotion that had been prescribed by the Central Middlesex Hospital to treat Victoria's scabies.

Thursday 29 July to Monday 2 August 1999

10.99   The days immediately following the strategy meeting passed uneventfully as far as Victoria was concerned. She would seem to have been well cared for on the ward and her injuries continued to heal. By 2 August, Dr Reynders felt able to write in her notes that Victoria was "much better" and "able for discharge".

10.100 At Dr Rossiter's suggestion, Victoria was befriended by a French-speaking nurse named Lucienne Taub. Nurse Taub would spend some time with Victoria virtually every day and would often take her on little excursions around the hospital, including visits to the neo-natal wards, which Victoria particularly enjoyed.

10.101 While unremarkable from Victoria's perspective, this period witnessed a number of incidents of potential significance to the future management of her case.

Photographs

10.102 The first was the visit of the hospital's photographer, Ian Abernethy, on 29 July. Mr Abernethy took a series of photographs of Victoria's injuries, several of which were shown during the course of the Inquiry's hearings. They constitute a clear and helpful record of the marks visible on Victoria's body at the time.

10.103 Therefore, it is a matter of great concern that they were not seen by anyone until after Victoria's death. Part of the explanation for this unfortunate omission may lie in the fact that the photographs, once developed, were sent to Dr Meates's office rather than Dr Rossiter's office. This was because they had originally been requested in Dr Meates's name. Dr Meates had no recollection of ever having received the photographs. She explained that, if she had received them she would have passed them to Dr Rossiter who, in turn, was clear in her recollection that they never reached her.

10.104 The lack of any adequate system for the proper distribution of the photographs is illustrated by the manner in which Dr Meates dealt with the request, contained in a memo written by Ms Johns on 29 July, for the police to be provided with copies. Dr Meates was prepared to agree to the request, annotated the memo to this effect and sent it back to Ms Johns. Thereafter, nothing was done.

10.105 It is unfortunate that Dr Meates did not share the contents of the memo of 29 July with Dr Rossiter. Given that Dr Rossiter was responsible for the child protection aspects of Victoria's care, her ignorance of it was regrettable. Victoria's case would seem to demonstrate that, unless it is clear to all those concerned exactly which consultant is responsible for the child protection aspects of a particular case, there is the possibility that important information is missed. In order to address this problem, I make the following recommendation:

> **Recommendation**
> When a child is admitted to hospital with concerns about deliberate harm, a clear decision must be taken as to which consultant is to be responsible for the child protection aspects of the child's care. The identity of that consultant must be clearly marked in the child's notes so that all those involved in the child's care are left in no doubt as to who is responsible for the case.

Amendment of CP3

10.106 The second incident of significance happened on 1 August 1999, when Dr Rossiter finally got round to amending the CP3 form originally completed by Dr Forlee over a week earlier. The amendment consisted of an arrow pointing from the conclusion originally ticked by Dr Forlee, "I wish to await further information before committing myself", to the one above which read "I consider the incident is likely to be non-accidental". Next to the arrow Dr Rossiter wrote: "What is uncertain is the category."

10.107 Dr Rossiter explained that the intention of the arrow was to show that her view had changed and that the note beside it was intended to convey that she considered Victoria to be a victim not just of physical abuse but, perhaps just as seriously, emotional abuse and neglect. As to the physical abuse, her view was based not on the scalding injuries to Victoria's head but on the other injuries which had been discovered since her admission. This is significant because Dr Rossiter chose not to amend the 'description of injuries' section on the CP3 form, which continued to refer only to the scalds to Victoria's face.

10.108 In fact, the long-awaited amendment of the CP3 form did little to improve the position as far as social services were concerned. The annotated CP3 form still fell well short of an accurate reflection of the hospital's concerns. In particular, there was no reference to the various marks on Victoria's body which were thought to be indicative of abuse, including those Dr Rossiter thought may have been caused by looped wire. Similarly, there was nothing to indicate that the overall picture of Victoria's circumstances was leading Dr Rossiter to have serious concerns about emotional abuse and neglect.

Psychiatric assessment

10.109 The third incident of significance was when Dr Rossiter decided, during the course of her ward round on 1 August, that Victoria should be subject to a psychiatric assessment. She took the view that a psychiatrist might be able to gain a clearer insight into the difficulties Victoria was facing. Dr Reynders wrote up the notes of that ward round and recorded that the assessment should be done urgently. He also noted that Victoria's case would be discussed at the psychosocial meeting to be held the following day.

10.110 Dr Rossiter attended the psychosocial meeting on 2 August and repeated her instruction that a psychiatric assessment of Victoria should be carried out. In the event, the psychiatrist concerned refused to carry out an assessment until more background information about Victoria's circumstances was available and she had been assessed by social services. Instead of taking steps to provide the psychiatrist with what he needed, matters would seem to have been left there by those responsible for Victoria's care. The result was that no psychiatric assessment was ever carried out and the opportunity it may have provided to gain a valuable insight into Victoria's circumstances was lost.

Tuesday 3 August 1999

Dr Alexander's assessment

10.111 The ward round on the morning of 3 August was carried out by Dr Alexander. He noted that Victoria was "better" and "medically fit for discharge". However, he was concerned that she had yet to provide a satisfactory account of what had happened to her and considered that a proper history was still required.

10.112 In my view, Dr Alexander was undoubtedly right in his assessment of the situation – a proper history was plainly necessary. Unfortunately, this proved to be another example of a member of the hospital staff deciding on an appropriate course of action but failing to follow it through. Dr Alexander did not take the history himself, apparently because he thought that Nurse Taub would do so. However, Nurse Taub said that nobody ever asked her to take a history from Victoria. It would appear, therefore, that Dr Alexander not only failed to take the step that he rightly identified as being necessary, but also omitted to delegate it to someone else.

10.113 Although Dr Alexander considered that Victoria was medically fit for discharge when he saw her on 3 August, he considered that it was still necessary to ensure that it was safe for her to return home. This would have required, in his view, some form of formal investigation or case conference at which the "specific details of further care are discussed". Again, Dr Alexander was plainly correct in his assessment of the situation. It is, therefore, a matter of regret that he did not take the trouble to contact social services to ensure that his expectations in this regard would be met.

Contact between Lisa Arthurworrey and Nurse Quinn

10.114 Later that morning, at around 11.20am, Lisa Arthurworrey, the social worker from Haringey who was responsible for Victoria's case, telephoned the hospital and spoke to Nurse Quinn. Their respective accounts of this conversation differed in a number of critical respects.

10.115 Nurse Quinn said that her conversation with Ms Arthurworrey lasted about 10 minutes, during the course of which she told her about all the concerns the medical staff felt regarding Victoria. These included suspicions that Kouao was not Victoria's real mother and that the scalds to Victoria's head were non-accidental. In addition, Nurse Quinn said that she told Ms Arthurworrey about the inappropriate interaction between Kouao and Victoria that had been observed on the ward.

10.116 According to Nurse Quinn, Ms Arthurworrey appeared to appreciate the hospital's concerns and asked her to fax "details of the nurses' concerns about Victoria's behaviour and interactions with Kouao". Nurse Quinn said that, in response to this request, she faxed to Haringey Social Services a handwritten note along with form CP1 and possibly also forms CP2 and CP3. The fax amounted to six pages in total.

10.117 There is a copy of the note written by Nurse Quinn in the hospital records. It takes the form of a chronology of what Nurse Quinn would seem to have regarded as significant incidents during Victoria's stay on the ward. The following matters were included:

- The 'master and servant' relationship between Kouao and Victoria observed by Nurse Pereira
- The fact that Kouao made no effort to assist Victoria when she wet herself during the course of one of Kouao's visits
- The fact that Kouao never brought any clothes or treats into the hospital for Victoria
- The evidence of 'emotional abuse' recorded by Dr Rossiter during the course of her ward round on 1 August
- The fact that Victoria seemed to simulate crying when Kouao left after a visit on 3 August
- Victoria's large appetite, including the fact that she once ate five bowls of cereal during the course of a single evening.

10.118 There is no indication in the note as to whether it was intended to constitute a comprehensive account of the hospital's concerns, whether the matters included were additional to those discussed over the telephone, or whether they represented a selection of the concerns already discussed. What is clear, however, is that no mention was made of any of the hospital's suspicions about physical abuse.

10.119 For my part, I find it extremely difficult to know what to make of Nurse Quinn's note. Numerous witnesses from the hospital came before me and gave disturbing accounts of the injuries they saw on Victoria's body. I heard a variety of nurses say that they thought Victoria had been bitten, branded and beaten with a belt buckle. Dr Rossiter said that she suspected that some of the marks on Victoria had been caused by chastisement with a looped wire and there were suspicions regarding the serious scalds with which Victoria had originally been admitted. Even if Nurse Quinn is right to say that all the hospital's concerns were covered in her conversation with Ms Arthurworrey prior to the writing of this note, this does not explain why she should have chosen to leave these matters out in favour of a description of how much cereal Victoria ate one morning.

10.120 In addition, the note Nurse Quinn made of her conversation with Ms Arthurworrey in the critical incident log would suggest that she had no justification for being deliberately selective in terms of the concerns she included in her note. Nurse Quinn made a note of the conversation in the critical incident log. The relevant section of the note reads: "She has requested that I fax the CP1 form to her and **any** [my emphasis] concerns we may have."

10.121 The explanation for Nurse Quinn's note may lie in the alternative account of Ms Arthurworrey, whose evidence as to her conversation with Nurse Quinn was bolstered by the fact that she made a detailed note at the time about what was said.

10.122 Critically, Ms Arthurworrey's note contains the following entry: "Hospital are satisfied with the explanation given by Anna's mother re her burns. Explanation was that Anna, who had been suffering from scabies, had poured hot water from a kettle over her head. She did this to relieve the itching."

10.123 Nurse Quinn was adamant that this note was incorrect and said that she told Ms Arthurworrey precisely the opposite. Ms Arthurworrey was equally confident that her note was an accurate reflection of what she was told. The point is plainly one of considerable importance. Deliberately scalding a seven-year-old girl to the extent that she needs two weeks in hospital is a matter of enormous seriousness.

10.124 If the hospital really did suspect that Kouao had injured Victoria in this manner I find it impossible to understand why Nurse Quinn would have chosen not to say so in her note to Ms Arthurworrey which, according to her own record, was supposed to contain "any concerns we may have". The suggestion that one might simply forget to mention the concern that Victoria's mother had deliberately poured boiling water over her head is, to my mind, utterly implausible.

10.125 I find it equally difficult to accept that Ms Arthurworrey could have so disastrously misinterpreted what she was told by Nurse Quinn such that she failed to appreciate that she was being told that the hospital suspected that Kouao had deliberately inflicted very serious injury to Victoria. Ms Arthurworrey's note is detailed and was made at the time. It indicates to me that she was paying close attention to what she was being told by Nurse Quinn.

10.126 Finally, I note that in the letter written by Nurse Quinn to Ms Arthurworrey, the following is included in the list of matters thought by Dr Rossiter to indicate emotional abuse: "self-treatment – boiling water prior to admission and whilst in hospital put Hibisrub on her head". This would seem to indicate that the hospital's concern regarding Victoria's scalds was not that they had been caused by Kouao but that they had been self-inflicted by Victoria. I cannot believe that Nurse Quinn would have written this in her note immediately after telling Ms Arthurworrey that the hospital suspected the scalds to have been caused by Kouao.

10.127 For these reasons I accept Ms Arthurworrey's evidence over that of Nurse Quinn on this issue. I conclude that Nurse Quinn did tell Ms Arthurworrey that the hospital was satisfied with Kouao's explanation for Victoria's scalds, and that it was not considered that they had been caused deliberately.

Old injuries

10.128 Although I have found that Nurse Quinn did not tell Ms Arthurworrey of the hospital's suspicions regarding Victoria's scalds, she did give her other information indicative of possible physical abuse. Ms Arthurworrey's note confirms that she was told by Nurse Quinn that "old injuries" had been discovered on Victoria's body which "appeared to be non-accidental". The question that arises, therefore, is what, if any, information did Nurse Quinn provide regarding these "old injuries", and did it adequately reflect the hospital's concerns about them.

10.129 Nurse Quinn told me that the documentation she sent to Ms Arthurworrey consisted of a cover sheet, her handwritten note, form CP1, and probably also forms CP2 and CP3, making a total of six pages in all. This would seem to be consistent with the entry on the cover sheet stating that the fax consisted of six pages in total. Copies of Nurse Quinn's letter together with forms CP1, CP2 and CP3 are to be found in the Haringey case file, adding further weight to Nurse Quinn's recollection in this regard.

10.130 There is no reference in any of these documents to the "old injuries" about which the hospital was apparently concerned. As set out above, there was no mention of any physical injuries in the letter written by Nurse Quinn, and the only injuries described on the CP forms were the scalds to Victoria's head, briefly described on form CP3. Ms Arthurworrey had asked for the hospital to send information of "any" concerns felt by the medical staff. In the documentation provided in response to this request, the only injury mentioned was the scalding to the head which Nurse Quinn had told Ms Arthurworrey was considered to be accidental. Anyone reading this documentation would be very hard pressed to find any indication that the hospital suspected physical abuse.

Ms Arthurworrey's conversation with Dr Rossiter

10.131 As happened so often during the course of Victoria's tragic case, an opportunity to clear up any confusion presented itself almost immediately. Following receipt of Nurse Quinn's note, Ms Arthurworrey telephoned the hospital and spoke to Dr Rossiter. As far as Dr Rossiter could recall, the purpose of the conversation was to clarify the contents of Nurse Quinn's note.

10.132 Dr Rossiter accepted that she might have played down the issue of physical abuse during her conversation with Ms Arthurworrey. Her explanation for this was that she had previously experienced difficulty in persuading social services to take issues of emotional abuse and neglect sufficiently seriously, and so was trying particularly hard to convey her concerns of this nature to Ms Arthurworrey.

10.133 Dr Rossiter did not regard this discussion as a prelude to Victoria's discharge. As far as she was concerned, she wished to consider the findings and outcome of the section 47 investigation she believed to be under way before deciding whether or not it would be appropriate for Victoria to go home.

10.134 The above account of the events of 3 August illustrates that, despite considerable contact between the hospital and social services during the course of the day, little in the way of clear information demonstrating that the hospital suspected that Victoria was the victim of serious physical abuse was provided to Ms Arthurworrey. Nurse Quinn had made reference to "old injuries" during the course of their telephone conversation, but no reference to these injuries was to be found in the documentation sent by the hospital and little, if any, mention had been made of them by Dr Rossiter when she spoke to Ms Arthurworrey later in the day.

10.135 The concerns that the medical and nursing staff at the hospital told me that they felt about Victoria never, in my view, crystallised into anything resembling a clear, well-thought-through picture of what they suspected had happened to her and that would have helped social services in determining how best to deal with her case.

Friday 6 August 1999

Victoria's discharge

10.136 Following his ward round on the morning of 6 August, Dr Reynders made the following entry in Victoria's notes: "Anna is well. Burns well healed. For home visit today with police. ? D/C [discharge] after that if it is safe."

10.137 Dr Reynders never personally spoke to any social worker handling Victoria's case and was unable to assist me as to how he gained the impression that Victoria's discharge depended on the police and social services deciding that Victoria's home was safe. He said that in marking "discharge" with a question mark in the notes, he intended to convey the following: "If we had received the report back from the social services and the police department that they had established a safe place for her to go to, that she may possibly be discharged." Before any firm decision to discharge was taken, Dr Reynders told me, he would have wanted to discuss the matter with a more senior colleague.

10.138 Unfortunately, while Dr Reynders may have known what his note meant, others did not. Nurse Margaret Ryan, who was the nurse in charge of the ward that day and who accompanied Dr Reynders on his ward round, understood the note to refer not to a possible discharge plan but to a definite one. She thought that if the findings of the home visit proved satisfactory, then Victoria was to go home.

10.139   The last entry in the hospital notes was made later the same day by Nurse Millicent Graham. It reads: "Seen by social worker and police today at 15.30; spoke with Anna, myself also present, Anna happy to go home, started to pack right away. Mum 'phoned to say she was on her way. Picked up Anna at 20.00. Satisfactory day, home with Mum."

10.140   Nurse Millicent Graham told me that by the time they came to the ward to see Victoria on 6 August, she believed Ms Arthurworrey and PC Karen Jones had visited Victoria's home and satisfied themselves that it was safe for her to return. In consequence, she believed that the condition identified by Dr Reynders in his note had been met and that the path was clear for Victoria's discharge. As a result, she updated Nurse Ryan as to the current position and telephoned Kouao to tell her that she could come and collect Victoria.

10.141   For reasons that are set out in detail elsewhere in this Report, Ms Arthurworrey and PC Jones never did make their intended visit to Victoria's home. Nurse Millicent Graham, therefore, was seriously mistaken as to the true position. While she thought (or assumed) that the condition on which Victoria's discharge depended had been met, the reality was precisely the opposite. Nobody had visited Victoria's home to ensure that it was safe for her to return.

10.142   Nurse Ryan was present on the ward at the time Victoria left with Kouao. She also would appear to have been content to let Kouao take Victoria and expressed no reservations as to this course of action at the time.

10.143   I attribute this lack of concern on the part of Nurse Ryan to two misconceptions on her part. The first was that she interpreted Dr Reynders's note as meaning that Victoria's discharge was authorised subject only to a home visit establishing that it was safe for her to return. The second was that she though PC Jones and Ms Arthurworrey had conducted such a home visit and were satisfied with what they found. One can see how the combination of these two misunderstandings would have led Nurse Ryan to believe that it was appropriate for Kouao to leave the hospital with Victoria on the evening of 6 August.

10.144   The discharge from hospital of a child about whom there have been concerns of deliberate harm is a very serious step and one about which there should be no room for confusion. I am firmly of the view that doctors should decide when patients are ready for discharge from hospital. In this regard I agree with the frustration expressed by Dr Rossiter when she commented that Victoria's case illustrates that ward staff appear sometimes to labour under the misapprehension that social workers are entitled to discharge patients who are under the care of a doctor.

10.145   Even if one accepts that Nurse Ryan genuinely believed that a home visit had been carried out and the findings had satisfied both social services and the police, there was still a need, in my opinion, for Dr Rossiter to have been consulted prior to discharge taking place. As I stated in the previous section, I regard the approval of a senior doctor to be an indispensable prerequisite for the discharge from hospital of a child about whom there are concerns of deliberate harm. Therefore, I repeat the recommendation I have made in paragraph 9.101 to this effect:

> **Recommendation**
> Hospital trust chief executives must introduce systems to ensure that no child about whom there are child protection concerns is discharged from hospital without the permission of either the consultant in charge of the child's care or of a paediatrician above the grade of senior house officer. Hospital chief executives must introduce systems to monitor compliance with this recommendation.

10.146 Plainly, before approving the discharge, the senior clinician concerned must be satisfied that the necessary follow-up arrangements have been made to ensure that the child's medical needs continue to be met after he or she leaves the hospital. In an attempt to ensure that the decision to discharge is not taken by the wrong person and that it does not result in the child being returned home with un-addressed health needs, I repeat the following recommendation I have made in paragraph 9.101 to this effect:

> **Recommendation**
> Hospital trust chief executives must introduce systems to ensure that no child about whom there are child protection concerns is discharged from hospital without a documented plan for the future care of the child. The plan must include follow-up arrangements. Hospital chief executives must introduce systems to monitor compliance with this recommendation.

Events following Victoria's discharge

10.147 Dr Rossiter discovered that Victoria had been discharged when she returned to work on 9 August following the weekend. She said the fact that the discharge had taken place and, moreover, that it had happened without her knowledge made her feel "insecure, worried and angry".

10.148 The first thing she did was to dictate a discharge summary that included the following:

> "Noted to be a very distressed child. Multiple marks on her not just due to scratching, thought possibly due to chastisement, eg with looped wire. Child protection forms completed. Photographs taken, rather belatedly (staffing problems). Discussed in psychosocial ward round. Child showing anxious attachment, seemed very frightened when mother visited with her boyfriend, clinging desperately to mother on the short times she visited alone. Considered likely to be abused, probable neglect and emotional abuse, less difficult to prove physical abuse. Social worker spoke to Dr Rossiter on the 'phone who expressed her very clear views as above. Home visit for risk assessment made by social services. On their advice child discharged home by ward staff. Very worrying case."

10.149 While this discharge summary did not record all the concerns identified by the hospital staff and contained several of what Dr Rossiter described as "misconceptions", it was plainly the clearest indication that Victoria was the likely victim of physical and emotional abuse yet committed to paper. It also indicates that Dr Rossiter had grave concerns about Victoria that had not been resolved prior to her discharge.

10.150 Unfortunately, it is impossible to identify to whom this discharge summary was sent at this stage because there is no recipients list attached to the copy of the letter contained in the hospital's medico-legal file. Dr Rossiter's intention in drafting the discharge summary was that it would be sent to Victoria's GP (via the health visitor), and to the social worker dealing with her case. However, Ms Arthurworrey did not see the discharge summary until much later, by which time, as described below, Dr Rossiter's enthusiasm for pursuing the matter had diminished.

10.151 Under normal circumstances it would have been open to Dr Rossiter to seek to arrange some follow-up for Victoria via the liaison health visitor. An ideal opportunity for her to have approached the liaison health visitor would have been at the regular meetings attended by both of them each Tuesday. Unfortunately, these meetings were suspended between 8 June and 14 September due to the excessive commitments of both Dr Rossiter and the liaison health visitor. As a result, Victoria's case did not benefit from this potentially valuable resource.

10.152 Immediately after dictating the discharge summary, Dr Rossiter dictated a letter to Petra Kitchman, a child protection adviser employed by Haringey Social Services. Ms Kitchman was, as far as Dr Rossiter was concerned, the 'link person' between the hospital and social services and so she regarded her as the appropriate person to deal with her concerns and pass them on to whoever had responsibility for Victoria's case.

10.153 The letter reads as follows:

"This is the child I wanted to speak to you about. I never managed to speak to a social worker face to face (you have heard my concerns about this) and my understanding was that there would be a Social Assessment prior to an urgent planning meeting and then referral to a child psychiatrist. Unfortunately the ward staff seemed to think that social workers can discharge patients who are under the care of a doctor and although I would probably have let the girl go home (she was very eager to do so) at least a consultant should have been informed. I have enormous concerns about this child who is now lost to follow up somewhere in Haringey. What are you going to do?"

10.154 Despite being dictated on 9 August, it would appear that Dr Rossiter's letter was not typed until four days later. Ms Kitchman told me that she did not receive it until 20 August, by which time Victoria had been back at Manning's flat for two weeks.

10.155 Shortly after receiving the letter, Ms Kitchman recalls telephoning Dr Rossiter, a fact which would seem to be confirmed by a further letter, written to her by Dr Rossiter dated 2 September, which refers to their conversation. The contents of that letter indicate that Dr Rossiter's concerns had been allayed to a considerable degree by what she had been told by Ms Kitchman. In particular, the following passage would suggest that Dr Rossiter was given the impression that Victoria's welfare was being given close attention: "I was pleased to hear that Anna is still at home, has a social worker and appears to be happy. That is good news."

10.156 Despite being reassured to learn that Victoria's case was receiving attention, Dr Rossiter was not prepared to let the matter rest there. Her letter of 2 September asked that Ms Kitchman ascertain which school Victoria was attending and the identity of her family doctor "so that we can correspond further". Dr Rossiter also enclosed with her letter a copy of the discharge summary she had originally dictated on 9 August.

10.157 Dr Rossiter eventually received a reply to her letter from Ms Kitchman on 19 October. By that stage, Ms Kitchman had discussed the case further with Ms Arthurworrey in light of the matters identified in Dr Rossiter's discharge summary. As for Dr Rossiter's concerns regarding physical abuse, Ms Kitchman wrote: "In terms of your concerns regarding possible physical abuse and the marks made with looped wire, Lisa has advised me that this has already been investigated by Dr Schwartz at the Central Middlesex Hospital who confirmed that the marks on Anna were due to scabies."

10.158 Dr Rossiter accepted that Ms Kitchman's letter demonstrated that social services had entirely misunderstood the nature and significance of the injuries to Victoria which had been discovered while she had been at the North Middlesex Hospital. It was clear that Ms Arthurworrey was labouring under the misapprehension that Dr Rossiter's concerns regarding physical abuse had been adequately addressed by Dr Schwartz's earlier scabies diagnosis.

10.159 As an indication of her dissatisfaction with the contents of Ms Kitchman's letter, Dr Rossiter wrote "we disagreed" next to the paragraph in which it was stated that Dr Schwartz considered that the marks on Victoria were attributable to scabies. She signed the annotation and dated it 2 November 1999. She told me that she wrote it in a "fit of pique" as she was angry and disappointed that her concerns had been misinterpreted and dismissed in this way.

10.160 Unfortunately, Dr Rossiter did nothing to correct the misunderstanding demonstrated by Ms Kitchman's letter. She told me that, to her "shame", she "ran out of steam" at this point. She accepted that this was extremely unfortunate, as had she sought to rectify Ms Arthurworrey's misconception, she may have prompted social services to take some effective action on the case.

10.161 In my view, it is the responsibility of all professionals working in the child protection arena to make sure that the information they provide to their colleagues in partner agencies is properly understood. As Victoria's case illustrates, the nature and significance of medical diagnoses is one area in which misunderstandings can easily arise.

10.162 I consider it unacceptable, therefore, that Dr Rossiter failed to take any steps to contact Ms Kitchman or Ms Arthurworrey to explain why she believed that they were wrong in their conclusion that her concerns had been addressed by Dr Schwartz's scabies diagnosis. While I have some sympathy with her irritation on finding that her views continued to be misinterpreted, there can be no excuse for allowing social services to continue labouring under such a significant misapprehension. I am anxious that doctors should be left in no doubt as to their responsibilities in this regard and therefore make the following recommendation:

> **Recommendation**
> All doctors involved in the care of a child about whom there are concerns about possible deliberate harm must provide social services with a written statement of the nature and extent of their concerns. If misunderstandings of medical diagnosis occur, these must be corrected at the earliest opportunity in writing. It is the responsibility of the doctor to ensure that his or her concerns are properly understood.

10.163 As it turned out, the brief annotation scribbled angrily by Dr Rossiter on Ms Kitchman's letter of 19 October was the last involvement any health professional had in Victoria's case, until she returned to the North Middlesex Hospital on the evening before she died.

11 Health analysis

11.1   In the two preceding sections, I have dealt in some detail with the various deficiencies in the care that Victoria received from the two hospitals in which she was an inpatient during the summer of 1999. As my analysis of the services that Victoria received in the Central Middlesex Hospital and the North Middlesex Hospital went on, I felt it was necessary to expand on two issues in particular.

11.2   The first issue is the way in which information obtained about Victoria while she was in hospital was managed, recorded and shared. The second issue is the status and priority given to child protection in the context of paediatric medicine.

11.3   The regularity with which these issues arose, and their centrality to a proper understanding of what went wrong in the handling of Victoria's case by these two hospitals, mean that these issues are worth separate analysis. That is the purpose of this section.

The information gathered about Victoria

11.4   There was enough information about Victoria readily available to the staff caring for her at the Central Middlesex Hospital and the North Middlesex Hospital for them to have reached a proper appreciation of the danger that she was in. What is more, most if not all of this information came to the attention of at least one of the health professionals concerned. As is clear from the preceding sections, the findings and observations of the doctors and nurses involved in Victoria's care produce a compelling picture of a child at very serious risk. One of the greatest tragedies of Victoria's case is that such ineffective use of this vital information was made at the time.

11.5   There was a consistent failure by doctors and nurses at both hospitals to record information comprehensively, to record and share concerns, and to record and complete the actions that the concerns prompted. Worst of all, nobody noticed when things were not being done.

11.6   I set out below what I consider to be the most glaring examples of poor practice in relation to these aspects of Victoria's care. They are by no means exhaustive and they are not restricted to any particular staff group – senior or junior, doctor or nurse. They demonstrate a generalised failure at both hospitals to appreciate the importance of efficient information management as an integral part of Victoria's care. They also show a failure to recognise that competence in information management is no less critical in cases of deliberate harm to a child, than competence in diagnosis or competence in treatment.

Information was known but not recorded

11.7   The first and most obvious deficiency in the way information was managed by staff at the hospitals was the failure to record their observations and concerns. The periods that Victoria spent in hospital are littered with instances of important information failing to find its way into her notes. Nurse after nurse, from the North Middlesex Hospital in particular, came before me to describe extremely concerning injuries or behaviour about which the records completed at the time are completely silent. Dr Simone Forlee, as discussed in section 10, was extremely perceptive in her initial assessment of Victoria when she was first admitted. But the first time that any of these valuable insights were written down was when she prepared her statement for this Inquiry.

11.8 The wearying regularity with which Counsel to the Inquiry was obliged to ask the simple question "Why did you not record that in the notes?", leads me to conclude that the amount of useful information about Victoria that was recorded by the professionals charged with her care while she was in hospital, is far exceeded by the amount of useful information that was not.

11.9 I express myself in forceful terms on this issue because I wish it to be clearly understood that I regard the keeping of proper notes and the accurate recording of concerns felt about a child as being a fundamental aspect of basic professional competence. At one stage, the representative of the NHS witnesses told me that pointing out to health professionals that they should write better notes "is pushing at an open door". If that was intended to convey that this is a well-recognised problem of which doctors and nurses have long been aware, then it is time that it was addressed.

Recorded information was not shared

11.10 The next information management deficiency illustrated by Victoria's case is that the useful information that was recorded was kept in a variety of different places.

11.11 During the period that Victoria spent on Rainbow ward, information about children was recorded in a number of different locations – the hospital notes, the medico-legal folder containing the child protection forms, the critical incident log, the psychosocial meeting book, and the ward allocation book. Such a fragmented recording system significantly inhibited the sharing of important information.

11.12 The recording of information about a particular child in a number of different places can allow inconsistencies to arise and persist. Chronology is vital in medical records because diagnoses change and more information becomes available. When notes are held in a variety of different places, the difficulties in ensuring that the most up-to-date information is readily obtainable are clear.

11.13 There are many examples in Victoria's hospital care where doctors and nurses did not seek information because they assumed they had a full picture, or were simply ignorant that their knowledge base was incomplete. For example, Dr Justin Richardson did not see the set of completed child protection forms about Victoria in the ward's medico-legal folder when he carried out his ward round on 26 July 1999.

Information was passed verbally and not recorded

11.14 On numerous occasions during the course of the evidence, the answer that was given to the question of why a particular observation or intended action was not recorded in the notes, was that the need to do so had been removed by the fact that the information had been "handed over verbally".

11.15 For example, Dr Forlee felt that Victoria should have been seen in the absence of Kouao and with the aid of a French interpreter. She believed she would have suggested this on her ward round. Unfortunately, the suggested action was not recorded and Victoria never was spoken to alone with the assistance of a French interpreter.

11.16 Similarly, Dr Ekundayo Ajayi-Obe told me that she remembered telling "someone" that she had a child on the ward whom she suspected to be suffering from "non-accidental injury". However, the fact that she did not record to whom she spoke or what she said made it impossible to assess what should have been done as a result of this conversation, or by whom.

11.17   Verbal handovers and referrals, either face-to-face or on the telephone, carry with them a high risk of ambiguous transfer of information and the creation of false confidence that actions have been understood and will be carried out. Such verbal exchanges alone, unsupported by clear documentation, undermine high-quality care.

Actions were agreed without making anyone responsible for carrying them out

11.18   In the context of a busy paediatric ward it may often be the case that a senior doctor will be forced, by virtue of the other calls on his or her time, to delegate a particular task to another member of the medical staff. When such delegation occurs, it is vital that a clear note is made of the identity of the person to whom responsibility for the task has been transferred. The inevitable consequence of not doing so, is that nobody is clear who has responsibility and the task does not get done.

11.19   This was the case with the examination of Victoria while she was in the North Middlesex Hospital. Dr Mary Rossiter believed she delegated the responsibility for documenting the marks on Victoria's body and for a full examination to the senior house officer taking over from Dr Forlee on the morning of 25 July 1999 whom she thought to be Dr David Reynders. As it happened, Dr Reynders was not on duty that day. When Dr Reynders did finally come to see Victoria, he was under the impression that all he was required to do was document Victoria's injuries on a body map.

11.20   The lack of any system on the ward for the proper assigning of responsibility for particular tasks was further illustrated by the evidence of Dr Forlee. When asked how each of the steps in an action plan formulated at a ward round would be taken forward, she explained that the usual procedure was that two senior house officers would be present and that following the ward round "it would be fairly random who wrote in the notes".

11.21   There was apparently no system on Rainbow ward to ensure that actions to be completed were recorded, there was no system for assigning responsibility for carrying out the actions and there was no mechanism to alert anyone if the actions were not completed.

Actions were put off but not completed

11.22   In circumstances in which staff work under severe pressure of time and where a number of different individuals will have responsibility for the care of a particular child during a relatively short period, the dangers of putting off necessary tasks to another day are self-evident. This was illustrated on a number of occasions during the course of Victoria's stay in the North Middlesex Hospital and the Central Middlesex Hospital. The following are good examples:

11.23   First, Dr Forlee decided to defer a full examination of Victoria to a later stage after her admission. She felt that such an examination would best be performed on the ward under the supervision of a more experienced paediatrician than herself.

11.24   Second, later the same day, Dr Olutoyin Banjoko decided that further questioning of Kouao should be done in a more controlled setting where there was a consultant and other members of the child protection team present. She also thought it was not morally right to subject Victoria to an examination that evening, taking into account both the lateness of the hour and the fact that Victoria was to be seen by Dr Rossiter the next day.

11.25   Third, similarly at the Central Middlesex Hospital, Dr Ruby Schwartz put off seeing Victoria alone because she thought a full investigation would be undertaken by social services and she did not want to compromise any interview they might have wanted to have with Victoria. However, she accepted that with hindsight, seeing Victoria alone would have been a sensible thing to do.

11.26 None of the deferred actions set out above subsequently took place. Victoria was never seen alone, Kouao was never interviewed. No thorough examination of Victoria was ever conducted at the North Middlesex Hospital. At least part of the explanation for these omissions lies, in my view, in the fact that the necessary steps were not taken at the time they were identified and, instead, were put off until another day.

11.27 Immediate action may not always be either possible or desirable. Deferring actions either out of consideration for the patient or as a result of clinician workload may be understandable. But failure to record that the action has been deferred and failure to check that the action is completed is virtually guaranteed to ensure it will never get done. Responsibility for the action must remain with the deferring clinician until either the action is completed or until responsibility for the action is handed over unambiguously to another clinician and so documented.

Actions were assumed to be complete but not checked

11.28 Victoria's case contains numerous examples of doctors and nurses making assumptions about either what had already been done or what others were going to do.

11.29 An example of the first is Dr Saji Alexander's assumption, when he conducted his ward round, that a full and thorough examination of Victoria's injuries was unnecessary, given the fact that a record had been made of them on the body maps. The result was that he did not do one himself. He never sought to check his assumption that Victoria had been fully examined. Had he done so, he would have discovered that it was mistaken.

11.30 As to the second, there were a number of instances where medical and nursing staff made assumptions about the steps that social services would take on Victoria's case. For example, Dr Rossiter took no other action following her telephone conversation with Lisa Arthurworrey because she did not think it was a prelude to Victoria's discharge. She thought she would be getting feedback from social services, regrouping at the next psychosocial meeting, and then after that start thinking about Victoria going home. However, her expectations were not realised and Victoria ended up being discharged without her knowledge.

11.31 Presumptions and expectations that others will take appropriate actions may or may not be reasonable in any given situation, but they must always be accompanied by checking that the assumptions are correct and expectations have been met.

Actions were recorded but ignored

11.32 Finally, there were frequent instances when a necessary action was clearly identified in the notes, but simply did not take place afterwards. For example, Dr Reynders wrote up the note following Dr Rossiter's ward round on 1 August 1999, when it was recorded that an urgent psychiatric assessment was needed. No psychiatric assessment ever took place.

11.33 Another example is provided by the note of the psychosocial meeting in the book in the psychiatry department. The note recorded that Dr Rossiter would examine Victoria. This was not done. Dr Rossiter was busy with other commitments that week and was, therefore, puzzled by the note. Even when an action was appropriately recorded, there was no system in place to ensure that the action was completed.

11.34 Many of the criticisms made above deal with the failure to record important information in the notes. They are based upon the assumption that once an action is clearly identified and recorded as necessary, it is more likely to take place. Therefore, it is profoundly disturbing to find instances in Victoria's case which demonstrate that even the clear recording that a particular step was necessary was no guarantee that it would take place.

Systematic care

11.35 In the paragraphs above I have set out some examples of where failure to record and share information, and to record, carry through and check actions, significantly inhibited the efficient management of Victoria's care. The context of these examples was a lack of any system at both hospitals robust enough to have prevented these information management failures from occurring, and resilient enough to have survived the consequences of a human error once it occurred.

11.36 The accurate and efficient recording of information cannot be left solely to the individual diligence of the doctors and nurses concerned. They must be supported by a clear system that minimises the risk of mistakes and provides a mechanism for recognising mistakes when they occur. The greater pressures are on staff, the greater the need for a system to support them. The busier the organisation, the more important it is to have a system that ensures agreed actions are recorded and completed.

Summary

11.37 The management of Victoria's care at the Central Middlesex Hospital and the North Middlesex Hospital was full of inadequate and ambiguous recording of information and actions, deferred actions, assumptions and expectations that things 'would happen' or be done by 'someone' or others 'at a later stage'. There were numerous failures to ensure that things that someone thought 'would happen' did happen. Victoria's case clearly demonstrates the need for doctors and nurses to document information, actions and referrals consistently and unambiguously, to share that information, and to ensure subsequently that what has been agreed is carried through.

11.38 In my view, many of the deficiencies in the way in which information about Victoria was managed by hospital staff could have been avoided if a few basic systems had been in place to provide some logical coherence and clear direction for the way in which information should have been handled. Something as simple as a single action list in Victoria's notes readily available to all those involved in her care may well have ensured that numerous important tasks took place, which, in the event, fell by the wayside.

11.39 Although the evidence that I heard on these matters was restricted to the working practices of the staff at two hospitals only, I am concerned that it is representative of an institutionalised failure within the health services to properly manage information and to give that task the prominence and attention it deserves. In order to address this issue, I make the following recommendations:

> **Recommendation**
> Within a given location, health professionals should work from a single set of records for each child.

Recommendation

During the course of a ward round, when assessing a child about whom there are concerns about deliberate harm, the doctor conducting the ward round should ensure that all available information is reviewed and taken account of before decisions on the future management of the child's case are taken.

Recommendation

When a child for whom there are concerns about deliberate harm is admitted to hospital, a record must be made in the hospital notes of all face-to-face discussions (including medical and nursing 'handover') and telephone conversations relating to the care of the child, and of all decisions made during such conversations. In addition, a record must be made of who is responsible for carrying out any actions agreed during such conversations.

Recommendation

Hospital chief executives must introduce systems to ensure that actions agreed in relation to the care of a child about whom there are concerns of deliberate harm are recorded, carried through and checked for completion.

Recommendation

The Department of Health should examine the feasibility of bringing the care of children about whom there are concerns about deliberate harm within the framework of clinical governance.

Status of child protection

11.40   I turn now to the other issue with which I am particularly concerned, namely the status and priority afforded to child protection within paediatric medicine.

11.41   In the fourth seminar in Phase Two of this Inquiry, Dr Chris Hobbs, a consultant community paediatrician from Leeds, told me that he considers maltreatment to be the single biggest cause of morbidity in children. If he is correct in his assessment (and I am unaware of any statistics which prove or disprove his assertion), then this is a staggering state of affairs. It seems clear that when considering the issue of deliberate harm to children, one must keep in mind that one is dealing not simply with the extreme cases which occasionally prompt Public Inquiries such as this one, but an enormous number of instances in which the health and development of children is impaired by maltreatment.

11.42   Having heard the evidence of a large number of expert practitioners and academics who work in this field, I have no difficulty in accepting the proposition that the scale of this problem is greater than that of what are generally recognised as common health problems in children, such as diabetes or asthma.

11.43   That being so, Dr Hobbs's further statement – that it is difficult to find doctors who wish to work in the field of child protection – is all the more surprising and disturbing. One might have expected that the scale of the problem would act as an inducement to those doctors who wished to make a significant impact on the health and well-being of the child population to enter the field. In such circumstances it is vitally important that those practitioners who do work in the field are adequately equipped to do so effectively.

11.44   The two consultant paediatricians primarily responsible for Victoria's care while she was in hospital, Dr Schwartz at the Central Middlesex Hospital and Dr Rossiter at the North Middlesex Hospital, were both vastly experienced in the child protection field. They were both the named doctor for child protection in their respective hospitals, and Dr Rossiter also filled the role of designated doctor for her health authority, as a result of which she sat on her local Area Child Protection Committee. They both conducted child protection training sessions for the benefit of their junior staff and were used to the multi-disciplinary aspects of the investigation of possible deliberate harm to children.

11.45   In view of their experience and expertise in the field, I was interested to know how they viewed the deliberate harm of a child in comparison with other ailments with which they have to deal as paediatricians. I put it to both doctors that there may be merit in approaching the diagnosis and treatment of deliberate harm in much the same way as one would approach the diagnosis and treatment of any other disease.

11.46   In essence, this would mean taking a history, conducting a thorough examination, carrying out investigations and tests, reaching a differential diagnosis and then determining treatment and management. This sort of systematic and rigorous approach, commonly applied to the treatment of physical disease, contrasts sharply with the rather haphazard manner in which Victoria's case was managed by both hospitals and, I suspect, the manner in which cases of possible deliberate harm are managed in hospitals across the country.

11.47   Dr Schwartz told me that she had never before viewed deliberate harm as a disease process or entity, and thus had never approached its management in the same manner as other childhood ailments with which she would commonly have to deal. However, she thought that there was merit in such an approach, and that it was instructive to compare the management of a case of deliberate harm with the management of a physical disease. Dr Rossiter agreed.

11.48   I was grateful for the evidence of these two experienced clinicians on this matter. It helped reinforce my conclusion that there is no good reason why the rigorous and systematic approach commonly applied by paediatricians to the diagnosis and treatment of physical disease in children, should not be applied to cases of possible deliberate harm. Deliberate harm is a serious and potentially fatal condition. There is no reason, in my view, why it should be approached in any less thorough a manner than physical diseases of equal seriousness.

11.49   It is tempting to question whether Victoria's case would have received the same level of medical concern, and consequently the same level of evaluation and intervention, had she been admitted to either hospital with a presumptive diagnosis of a potentially fatal disease. Nothing I heard in evidence persuaded me that the majority of doctors involved in Victoria's care – including Dr Schwartz and Dr Rossiter – gave anything like the same level of attention to Victoria's condition as they might have done had she been admitted to hospital with, say, a possible brain tumour or a potentially fatal heart condition.

11.50   My firm conviction is that children presenting to doctors with an actual or a presumptive diagnosis of deliberate harm require the rigorous application of the medical model to their evaluation, and that anything less than this is neglectful of their needs and potentially dangerous.

11.51   However, it is not enough to simply state that paediatricians should adopt a more sophisticated and thorough approach to the treatment of deliberate harm to children. It is also necessary that they have the skills to enable them to do so.

11.52   The lead in making sure that paediatricians in a given hospital are adequately trained and instructed in this area must come, in my view, from the named and designated doctors for child protection. These doctors wield a very significant degree of influence within both the hospital and the multi-disciplinary child protection teams. I have recorded numerous instances during the course of Victoria's case where great regard has been shown to the views of the consultant paediatricians concerned, and it will often be the case that their diagnoses determine whether further investigation takes place or not. In those circumstances, it is vital that they have a level of expertise and training equal to their responsibilities. As Victoria's case shows, the proper management of a case of possible deliberate harm to a child can be a very challenging job, even for an experienced paediatrician.

11.53   In order to make sure that cases of possible deliberate harm to children are properly managed by well-qualified paediatricians, I make the following recommendations:

> **Recommendation**
> The investigation and management of a case of possible deliberate harm to a child must be approached in the same systematic and rigorous manner as would be appropriate to the investigation and management of any other potentially fatal disease.

> **Recommendation**
> All designated and named doctors in child protection and all consultant paediatricians must be revalidated in the diagnosis and treatment of deliberate harm and in the multi-disciplinary aspects of a child protection investigation.

> **Recommendation**
> The Department of Health should invite the Royal College of Paediatrics and Child Health to develop models of continuing education in the diagnosis and treatment of the deliberate harm of children, and in the multi-disciplinary aspects of a child protection investigation, to support the revalidation of doctors described in the preceding recommendation.

12 General practice and liaison health visiting

12.1   The diagnosis and management of deliberate harm to children is not the exclusive province of those health professionals who work in hospitals. Others, such as GPs and health visitors have an equally vital role to play in protecting children. During her life in this country, Victoria's case came briefly and sporadically to the attention of a number of such professionals. This section records those occasions and considers ways in which the working practices of GPs and health visitors might be improved in order to provide children with more effective protection against deliberate harm.

General practice

The practice of Dr Indravadan Patel

12.2   On 8 June 1999, Victoria was registered with Dr Indravadan Patel, a single-handed GP whose surgery was situated close to the Nicoll Road hostel in which Victoria and Kouao had been living since the end of April 1999. Dr Patel told me that his practice covered an area of considerable economic and social deprivation and that he was kept extremely busy. He also had to contend with a high patient turnover and many temporary residents.

12.3   Dr Patel's knowledge of and experience in child protection matters was limited at the time Victoria came to be registered with him. Although he made efforts to keep up-to-date with paediatric medicine in general, he had received no training in the medical aspects of child protection or joint working with other agencies. Nor, he told me, had he ever received any child protection policies or guidelines from his local medical committee, or elsewhere.

12.4   Despite this lack of training or guidance, Dr Patel was clear that, were he to consider that a child was or might be in need of protection, he would contact social services and pass on the relevant information. He had never had occasion to do so during the 30 years he had spent in general practice.

12.5   The practice nurse, Grace Moore, undertook Victoria's registration. Nurse Moore was an experienced nurse of 15 years, although she too had had no child protection training.

12.6   Nurse Moore followed the computerised registration protocol used by the practice. The protocol covered such matters as general health, past operations and family history of major diseases. In addition, Victoria was weighed and measured as part of the registration process. Her height and weight were found, according to Dr Patel, to be "within normal guidelines".

12.7   Nurse Moore had no independent recollection of Victoria, basing her evidence on her standard practice and Victoria's patient summary, which consisted of a printout of the computerised registration protocol. However, there was nothing to suggest that the registration process went beyond the basic steps described above. No examination of Victoria was carried out and it would not appear as though Nurse Moore sought to question either Kouao or Victoria about their social circumstances or living conditions.

12.8   Therefore, it is perhaps unsurprising that Nurse Moore did not feel there were any concerns of a child protection nature arising out of her contact with Kouao and Victoria that required any follow-up or report to another agency. Furthermore, as she was told that Victoria had no current health problems, she considered that there was no need to make any further appointment for Victoria to see either her or Dr Patel.

12.9   Dr Patel told me that there was a part-time health visitor attached to his practice. He also indicated he was aware of a 'school contact' to whom he could refer cases involving school-aged children where there might be a problem. Neither the health visitor nor the school contact was informed about Victoria by Nurse Moore.

12.10   Therefore, Victoria's contact with Dr Patel's practice started and ended with the registration appointment on 8 June 1999. The sum total of the information that would appear to have been obtained on this occasion was that Victoria was of unexceptional height and weight, and that she had no current health problems.

The practice of Dr Gurdas Israni

12.11   On 30 June 1999, Kouao registered with Dr Gurdas Israni of the Greenhill Park Medical Centre, which is also located close to the hostel address in Nicoll Road. Dr Israni saw Kouao just once for a routine health check on the occasion of her registration. Kouao wrote on the new patient information card that she had five children aged 23, 20, 18, 16 and seven, but did not give their names. She told Dr Israni that all her children were living in France.

The practice of Dr Martin Lindsay

12.12   On 20 July 1999, Kouao registered with Dr Martin Lindsay at the Somerset Gardens practice. The practice was situated a matter of yards from Manning's flat, which Kouao gave as her address when she registered. Kouao made several visits to this surgery over the course of the next seven months. However, her records contain no family history or mention of any child.

12.13   On 24 November 1999, Victoria was registered with another doctor at the same practice, Dr Wasantha Gooneratne. Information about Victoria was provided in a registration form and a health questionnaire, completed on Victoria's behalf (presumably by Kouao). This information was subsequently entered on the practice computer.

12.14   The registration was completed without anyone at the practice ever actually seeing Victoria. According to Dr Gooneratne, this was not unusual for children over the age of five with no disclosed medical problems. Unsurprisingly, given that Victoria was never seen by anyone at the practice, no child protection concerns were felt and no action was taken.

Victoria's GP records

12.15   Victoria's GP records amount, in total, to two registration cards – one from Dr Patel's practice, the other from Dr Lindsay's practice. Neither contains anything other than the most basic information. In particular, no mention is made of the two occasions on which Victoria was hospitalised, despite the fact that she was registered with Dr Patel at the relevant times.

12.16   Similarly, no reference is made in Victoria's hospital notes to the fact that Dr Patel was her GP. However, there is a reference to the Somerset Gardens practice in Victoria's North Middlesex Hospital notes, which is somewhat surprising given that she was not registered there until four months later.

Suggestions for improvement

12.17   In my view, there are three issues arising out of the limited contact that Victoria had with GPs, which require particular attention. These are:

- The manner in which new child patients are registered with general practitioners
- The information that should be gathered during the registration process and the manner in which that information should be shared
- Training in child protection and knowledge of local policies and procedures.

I deal with each in turn.

The registration of new child patients with GPs

12.18   Dr Patel and Dr Gooneratne followed two different registration procedures. Victoria's registration with Dr Patel required her to have a face-to-face screening interview with Dr Patel's practice nurse. Victoria's registration with Dr Gooneratne was by way of a registration form and health questionnaire, completed on her behalf.

12.19   When Victoria was registered with Dr Patel in June 1999, signs of physical abuse and neglect may not have been of a nature or severity to have been apparent at a screening interview of the type conducted by Nurse Moore. While a child's height and weight may cause concern in some cases, there is nothing to suggest that Victoria's development had been significantly impaired at this stage. Even if Victoria had been subject to a more extensive examination by Nurse Moore, I heard no evidence to indicate that she would have found obvious signs of physical abuse on Victoria's body.

12.20   The same cannot be said about the later registration at the Somerset Gardens practice. This took place three months before Victoria's death and, according to Manning, approximately two months after she had started to spend her nights in the bath. She was also being regularly beaten. If Victoria been seen by a practice nurse on this occasion, it is possible (but by no means certain) that signs of the treatment she was being subjected to may have been apparent. However, as it was, no member of the Somerset Gardens practice staff ever saw Victoria.

12.21   Even the slightly more rigorous approach to registration adopted by Dr Patel's practice would have been unlikely to detect anything but the most glaringly apparent signs of ill-treatment. Nurse Moore was required to do no more than complete the basic registration protocol. Once that had revealed that there were no immediate health concerns, nothing more was required – other than for Dr Patel to include Victoria on his large and rapidly changing list of patients.

12.22   Dr Patel agreed that "it would be nice" to offer a more comprehensive initial screening process, perhaps involving a more thorough examination and a wider questioning of the child and his or her carer, but pointed out that the practice he operated at the time followed the standard health authority protocol, and to do any more than this would take increased resources.

12.23   I understand these practical limitations. However, I regard the skills and experience of GPs as a vital component in any effective scheme of child protection. The registration of child patients with a GP should provide an opportunity to consider their needs over and above their immediate health status.

12.24   I appreciate that in a busy inner-city practice of the type described by Dr Patel, overwhelming workload may make the operation of anything more than a basic registration protocol impractical. However, it is the welfare of children that is at stake, and the occasion of a child patient registration is an opportunity to consider not only factors such as family history of heart disease, but also the wider social and developmental needs of the children concerned.

Information to be gathered and shared

12.25 Of particular relevance in this regard will be information such as whether the child concerned is attending school, how he or she is cared for, and the nature of the accommodation in which the family is living. Had such questions been asked at the time that Victoria registered with Dr Patel (and assuming that they were truthfully answered), he would have learned that Victoria was not attending a school, was living in a potentially unsuitable hostel and that Kouao was about to start a job which would reduce her capacity to look after Victoria during the day.

12.26 It seems to me that there must be a distinct possibility that Dr Patel, if apprised of this information, would have considered that Victoria was a child who needed careful monitoring. In this regard, I do not seek to suggest that GPs should be required to fill the role of social workers – they have neither the time nor the training to do so. However, I do believe that they have a role to play in the distribution of information which might be important in determining whether a child is in need of protection. The health visitor and the 'school contact' to which Dr Patel made reference are examples of the sort of resources available to GPs when they obtain information about a child who causes them concern.

Training in child protection

12.27 I was surprised to hear that an experienced GP such as Dr Patel had never received any training or guidance in child protection matters, particularly in the recognition of possible deliberate harm. As is apparent from the preceding sections, these are difficult and sensitive matters and present a considerable challenge to even the most experienced practitioners. My view is that, in dealing with cases of deliberate harm to children, professionals must have more to rely on than simple common sense. They require training and regularly updated guidelines, and they must be clear as to what constitutes best practice in such situations.

12.28 I appreciate that in a busy general practice environment – particularly a single-handed one – making time to attend training courses is a challenge. With the many educational opportunities available in post-graduate medical centres, choosing how most profitably to spend one's time in training is equally difficult. However, I consider training in child protection not just desirable for GPs, but an essential part of their initial and continuing professional training. Furthermore, I consider that this principle applies with respect to the training of other members of general practice staff where direct contact with children is a routine part of their work.

12.29 I repeat my view that GPs are an extremely important element of the child protection framework. It is crucial that the optimum possible use is made of their skills and experience. With this aim in mind, I make the following recommendations:

> **Recommendation**
> The Department of Health should invite the Royal College of General Practitioners to explore the feasibility of extending the process of new child patient registration to include gathering information on wider social and developmental issues likely to affect the welfare of the child, for example their living conditions and their school attendance.

> **Recommendation**
>
> The Department of Health should seek to ensure that all GPs receive training in the recognition of deliberate harm to children, and in the multi-disciplinary aspects of a child protection investigation, as part of their initial vocational training in general practice, and at regular intervals of no less than three years thereafter.

> **Recommendation**
>
> The Department of Health should examine the feasibility of introducing training in the recognition of deliberate harm to children as part of the professional education of all general practice staff and for all those working in primary healthcare services for whom contact with children is a regular feature of their work.

> **Recommendation**
>
> All GPs must devise and maintain procedures to ensure that they, and all members of their practice staff, are aware of whom to contact in the local health agencies, social services and the police in the event of child protection concerns in relation to any of their patients.

Liaison health visiting

12.30   In drafting this section of the Report, I have derived considerable assistance from the closing submissions made by Counsel to the Inquiry. They seem to me to accurately summarise the material evidence, and I have drawn heavily on them in the paragraphs that follow.

12.31   The purpose of a health visitor in cases where there are concerns of possible child abuse is, according to health visitor Rachel Crowe, to provide "child surveillance" to make sure that the child in question is developing properly and interacting appropriately within the family. In order to carry out that role, regular visiting will be required. She explained that referrals to a health visitor could come from a variety of sources, including the medical and nursing staff on the ward if a child happened to be an inpatient. However, she confirmed that in the majority of cases involving children admitted to hospital, the subsequent involvement of a health visitor will be dependent upon a referral being made by a liaison health visitor.

The liaison health visiting context at the time

12.32   Victoria had the misfortune to be admitted to the North Middlesex Hospital at a time when the post of liaison health visitor with responsibility for the accident and emergency department was vacant. According to the Haringey Primary Care NHS Trust's senior child protection nurse, Liz Fletcher, the post was eventually filled on 4 October 1999 (having been vacant for four months before that).

12.33   In the period during which the post was vacant, cover was provided by health visitors covering the accident and emergency liaison role on a two-week rota basis. This was in addition to their own caseloads, for which they retained responsibility. Ms Crowe was providing cover at the time Victoria was admitted to the North Middlesex Hospital.

12.34   Perhaps unsurprisingly, given the temporary nature of the arrangements, Ms Crowe was unaware of the guidelines that were in force at the time. In particular, she was unaware of the different procedure that was to be followed in non-accidental injury cases, including the requirement that four copies of the accident and emergency front sheet be taken and distributed to the individuals specified.

12.35 She was also unaware of the procedure to be adopted in respect of school-aged children admitted to hospital during the school holidays. This was in spite of a memorandum, dated 22 July 1999, from Bridget Inal, locality nurse manager for north Tottenham, setting out the steps to be taken in such a case.

12.36 It was against this background that Ms Crowe read Victoria's accident and emergency notes on or about 26 July 1999. The fact that she did read them would appear to be indicated by the initials "RC" marked on them, which Ms Crowe confirmed were written by her at the time.

12.37 There are no notes or other records revealing what Ms Crowe did next concerning this referral, and she relied in her evidence solely on her independent recollection of events at what she accepted was a "busy" time for her. However, her memory was helped by the fact that Victoria's referral was something out of the ordinary for her in that it was the only referral of a school-aged child that she made during the period of her cover. Therefore, she told me that she was confident in her recollection of the following sequence of events.

12.38 She went to the accident and emergency department and picked up Victoria's admission card together with her accident and emergency notes. She agreed that there was nothing on Victoria's card that indicated that she had been physically abused. However, it was the accompanying notes made by Dr Forlee that made it clear to her there was a possibility that non-accidental injury had occurred. She then telephoned the ward to establish the current position and remembered being told that Victoria would be on the ward for a while because of the child protection concerns.

12.39 She next telephoned Ms Fletcher to find out what to do with the referral because it concerned a school-aged child admitted during the school holidays. She said that Ms Fletcher's advice was that she should speak to the health visitor responsible for the area in which Victoria lived.

12.40 In accordance with this advice, Ms Crowe telephoned the Lordship Lane Clinic and said she was informed that Launa Brown was the health visitor with responsibility for Victoria's area.

12.41 Ms Crowe said that the two of them then had a telephone conversation during which she told Ms Brown about the child protection concerns surrounding Victoria. She said she told her that Victoria was a school-aged child in her area who would need to be followed up when she was discharged from hospital. There were concerns that Victoria had poured hot water over her face to relieve itching from scabies and it was suspected that the burn injuries to Victoria's head might be non-accidental. She said that Ms Brown indicated that she would follow up the case after Victoria was discharged.

12.42 Again according to Ms Crowe, Ms Brown took down the relevant details and asked for the relevant documentation to be sent to her. In response to this request, Ms Crowe sent her a copy of Victoria's accident and emergency card through the internal post system. She said that she added some handwritten comments to the back of the card before she sent it. Although she could not remember what she wrote, she believed she would have mentioned the concerns that she and Ms Brown had spoken about on the telephone.

12.43   The evidence of Ms Crowe on these matters was both clear and coherent. It was also consistent with the evidence she gave in March 2000 to a locally conducted internal investigation into the Community Nursing Service's involvement with Victoria's case. That investigation concluded that Ms Crowe did make the referral but that "no record can now be found of this action".

12.44   However, Ms Crowe's evidence was directly contradicted by that of Ms Brown, who was equally confident in her recollection that she never received a call from Ms Crowe about Victoria. She also stated that she had no recollection of ever having seen Victoria's accident and emergency card, and that subsequent checks had been unable to find any record of it having arrived at the Lordship Lane Clinic.

Lack of record keeping

12.45   As to this last point, there would seem to have been very little in the way of a system for logging referrals when they arrived at the clinic. If a referral arrived for a health visitor who was not in the office at the time, it would be placed on that health visitor's desk. No record was made of the referral's arrival at the clinic, or of the identity of the health visitor to whom it had been allocated. As a result, Ms Brown accepted that the relevant piece of paper could have gone missing without anyone knowing.

12.46   The absence of any system for the logging of referrals is also relevant to the assertion made by Ms Brown in her statement to the effect that she "checked all the records held at the clinic" and "checked with the other health visitors within the clinic" and could find no reference to Victoria's case.

12.47   Given that there was no logbook or filing system that would have enabled those checking to have identified where the referral should have been, the fact that nobody at the clinic remembered the referral being made amounts to no more than those staff who were questioned being unable to recall what happened to a specific piece of paper some two years after the event. Therefore, the fact that there was no record of the referral having arrived at the clinic and that nobody remembered having seen it, provides me with little help.

12.48   The question of whether or not the referral of Victoria's case was ever made by Ms Crowe to Ms Brown is not an easy one to resolve. Unfortunately, Ms Fletcher was unable to shed any light on the matter as she could not recall having spoken to Ms Crowe about the case and could not say whether or not Ms Crowe had called her to ask how she should deal with Victoria's referral.

12.49   Having carefully considered all the evidence, I have reached the same view as the internal investigation carried out in March 2000. I conclude that Ms Crowe did refer Victoria to Ms Brown.

12.50   In reaching this conclusion I derived considerable assistance from the only piece of documentary evidence available to me – the initialled copy of Victoria's accident and emergency notes. It is clear to me from this that Ms Crowe was indeed aware of Victoria's accident and emergency attendance and I consider it unlikely that, having noted it, the process of onward referral would have stopped at this point. Therefore, I conclude that when Ms Crowe became aware of Victoria, and of the possibility that she had suffered a non-accidental injury, she did indeed take the action she claimed and telephoned the Lordship Lane Clinic to speak to Ms Brown. However, I would emphasise that the lack of reliable evidence on this issue has left me far from confident as to what really happened.

12.51   More important than whether Ms Crowe or Ms Brown is correct in their recollection, is the fact that it was impossible, even in the immediate aftermath of

Victoria's death, to say with any certainty whether or not the referral was made. This points, in my view, to the absence of a reliable system for the recording and tracking of important referrals concerning vulnerable children.

12.52   The assertions of Ms Crowe, and of all the other parties involved in the community nursing aspects of Victoria's care, were unsupported by documentary evidence other than the initialled accident and emergency notes. Neither was there any form of system for recording actions and the onward transmission of information. It is this, and what it represents for the care of vulnerable children, that is a matter of great concern to me.

The role of Rachel Crowe

12.53   A further indication of the unsystematic manner in which referrals of this nature were being handled at the time is given by Ms Crowe's lack of awareness of the procedures that she was supposed to follow when dealing with cases like Victoria's. While I have considerable sympathy for Ms Crowe's individual situation as a busy health visitor having to cover a role with which she was unfamiliar, the fact that she was in this position reinforces, in my view, the need for clear and accessible procedures for her to follow.

The role of Launa Brown

12.54   The importance of the role of the liaison health visitor is illustrated by the description given by Ms Brown of the appropriate steps to be taken in response to a referral concerning a child in Victoria's situation. She said that she would have first made inquiries to see whether the child was registered with a GP and was attending school. She would then have sought to find out where he or she lived and whether there were any siblings. Depending upon the result of those inquiries, it would be decided whether a home visit was necessary.

12.55   Given what we now know to have been Victoria's circumstances at the time and Ms Crowe's claims to have referred her case to Ms Brown, there seems little doubt that, had Ms Brown conducted the inquiries described above, she would have decided that a visit was necessary. One can only speculate as to what she may have discovered during the course of such a visit, but there seems little doubt that the supervision of a health visitor can only have increased the chances of Victoria's abuse being discovered and addressed.

12.56   It is clear, therefore, that the precise circumstances surrounding the alleged referral are of considerably less importance than the fact that no action was taken by the health visiting service in Victoria's case. Her admission to hospital and Ms Crowe's apparent discovery of the concerns of the medical staff provided a valuable opportunity to include Victoria within the provision of primary health services of a type that may well have prevented her death.

12.57   Nothing could illustrate more clearly the need for an efficient and effective referral system for children discharged from hospital about whom there are child protection concerns. In an effort to encourage the development of such systems, I make the following recommendation:

> **Recommendation**
> Liaison between hospitals and community health services plays an important part in protecting children from deliberate harm. The Department of Health must ensure that those working in such liaison roles receive child protection training. Compliance with child protection policies and procedures must be subject to regular audit by primary care trusts.

Part four: The police

13 Brent Child Protection Team

The referral

13.1 Between 4.30pm and 5.15pm on 14 July 1999, PC Rachel Dewar received a telephone call from Michelle Hines, a social worker from Brent Social Services. According to PC Dewar, Ms Hines told her that Victoria was in the Central Middlesex Hospital suffering from bruised feet, arms, legs and buttocks, infected bruises on her fingers, and bloodshot eyes. PC Dewar was told that the medical staff at the hospital considered these to be "serious non-accidental injuries". PC Dewar was also told that Victoria had been taken to hospital by a childminder who had become concerned as to the cause of her injuries.

13.2 PC Dewar happened to pick up the phone when Ms Hines rang, and so it seems this is why she became the officer in the case. There was no formal system within Brent Child Protection Team (CPT) for incoming referrals to be screened and assessed by a supervisor before being allocated to officers. Although Sergeant (Sgt) David Smith said he and Sgt John Gorry checked entries on the crime-recording computer database, CRIS, on a daily basis, an investigation could be well under way before a supervisor became aware of it. It also seemed to be the case that whoever happened to take the initial referral would end up dealing with the case.

13.3 In my view, such a practice carries with it two important disadvantages. First, it may lead to an already overloaded officer taking on more work when a colleague may be better placed to give the referral the required attention. Second, it deprives the team of a mechanism for filtering referrals to make sure valuable police time is not wasted dealing with matters that are not serious enough for police attention.

Accommodation

13.4 At the time it came to deal with Victoria's case, Brent CPT was housed in rather scruffy accommodation in Edgware police station, which it shared with Harrow CPT. The accommodation and the facilities provided for the teams were, like those for many CPTs in London, of a poor standard. Detective Inspector (DI) Michael Anderson, the officer in charge of the team, thought the accommodation was "distinctly bad" when compared with the Metropolitan Police Service (MPS) as a whole, but average for CPTs across the capital. However, I heard no evidence to suggest that the standard of the team's accommodation affected the way Victoria's case was dealt with, and DI Anderson expressly stated that, in his view, it was not responsible for the failings in Victoria's case.

Training and experience of officers

13.5 I heard a great deal of evidence from the MPS witnesses about the training of individual officers and their career profiles before joining the CPTs. I am satisfied that it is highly desirable for officers engaged in child protection investigation work to have some experience in, or knowledge of, criminal investigation. Experience or knowledge would normally be gained by a period of time as a detective in a CID office, but uniformed officers who have worked in, for example, street crime units may also gain the necessary experience. Therefore, it is useful to consider the training and experience of the Brent CPT officers who were directly involved in Victoria's case.

13.6　Brent CPT was made up of one detective inspector, two sergeants and six police constables. The training and career profile of the officers directly involved in Victoria's case are as follows.

Detective Inspector Michael Anderson

13.7　DI Anderson joined the force in 1971. By the time he gave evidence he had retired, but during the relevant period he had 28 years' police service, of which 25 years were spent in various CID roles. He was therefore a 'career detective' and he had been the DI in charge of Brent CPT since 1996. He had received no training specifically in child protection work, but clearly he was a very experienced crime investigator and had attended the CID foundation course. DI Anderson considered Detective Chief Inspector (DCI) Philip Wheeler to be his immediate line manager, even though they rarely saw each other. At the time with which I am concerned, DI Anderson was also the officer in charge of Harrow CPT, also based in Edgware police station.

Sergeant John Gorry

13.8　Sgt Gorry joined the police service in 1975. He has never been a detective but has worked as a uniformed constable in local crime squads and the MPS clubs and vice squad. These roles would have given him some experience of criminal investigation. He said he felt adequately equipped to carry out the role of supervisor, but felt hampered by his lack of training. In particular, the fact he had received little child protection training and no CID training led him to feel ill-equipped to supervise some of the more involved criminal investigations.

Sergeant David Smith

13.9　Sgt Smith has been a police officer since 1980. He spent 10 years as a uniformed constable in various stations, including three years in a district crime squad in Camden. As a sergeant, he spent a period of time in charge of a reactive team dealing with all crime in the Harrow shopping centre. In these two posts he should have gained a reasonable amount of expertise in dealing with and supervising crime investigation. He had attended a two-week child protection course in 1996 but had not undertaken the CID foundation course.

PC Rachel Dewar

13.10　PC Dewar was the officer from Brent CPT designated to investigate the crimes against Victoria. She joined the MPS in 1993 and, after serving for two and a half years as a uniformed beat constable, she successfully applied for a posting with a domestic violence unit. In July 1998, she transferred to Brent CPT. Therefore, by the time she was dealing with Victoria, she had one year's CPT experience and virtually no experience of criminal investigation. She had never attended the CID foundation course and it would appear that her only relevant training was a three-day child protection course in December 1998.

13.11　Despite her job description saying that she should carry out the investigation of crime handed to her, I do not consider that PC Dewar had sufficient training or experience to qualify her to deal with a case of Grievous Bodily Harm (GBH). Her first-line supervisors were slightly better qualified, but with an inexperienced case officer it is vitally important to have first-line supervisors with plenty of experience of the requirements of criminal investigation. This was not the case in Brent CPT. The officer in charge, DI Anderson, was undoubtedly qualified to manage officers engaged in serious crime investigation, but he was expected to control two child protection units, consisting of around 20 officers and support staff.

13.12   When invited to comment on the lack of training received by the officers in his team, Sgt Smith said, "I view it as a failure of the Metropolitan Police to train its officers properly for the most important task they could possibly do." I have considerable sympathy with Sgt Smith's view on this matter, and I conclude that the MPS had indeed failed to ensure that the team charged with the investigation of Victoria's case had sufficient experience in the detection and investigation of serious crime. As a result, Brent CPT was not able to offer an adequate service to victims of child abuse in Brent.

The initial investigation

13.13   After taking the referral, one of the first things that PC Dewar did was to begin an entry on CRIS. In the box that asks for details of the allegation, she entered "assault S.18". This is shorthand for 'Wounding with intent to cause Grievous Bodily Harm', an offence under section 18 of the Offences Against the Person Act 1861. Other than homicide, this is the most serious assault there is, and it is significant that PC Dewar believed it was an offence of this importance that was being reported to her by social services. In her oral evidence, PC Dewar stood by the classification of the offence she made on the basis of the information given to her by Ms Hines. PC Dewar also noted on CRIS that the mother was the likely suspect.

13.14   Therefore, it is apparent that by just after 5pm, PC Dewar knew she was the investigating officer for a serious crime, that the victim was in hospital with multiple injuries, that there was an important witness in the form of the childminder who had taken the child to hospital, and that a suspect had been identified but not accounted for.

13.15   Apart from leaving a message with the police photographic department asking them to take photographs of Victoria's injuries some time in the future, and doing a police database check to see if the family were known, PC Dewar did absolutely nothing to begin investigating the crime before she went off duty at 7pm.

13.16   As a result, vital hours were lost. When a crime comes to the attention of the police, the period immediately afterwards can often be critical to the effectiveness of the investigation. Unless prompt action is taken, forensic evidence can disappear, tracks can be covered and witnesses can be intimidated or coached. When dealing with a possible serious assault against a child, it will never be appropriate, in my view, simply to leave the matter until the following day.

13.17   Having decided against investigating the possible crime committed against Victoria that evening, PC Dewar instead agreed with Ms Hines to place Victoria under police protection. This course of action was taken before Victoria had been seen and before any assessment of her circumstances had been made. In my view, this is a wholly inappropriate way to proceed. Taking a child into police protection is a serious step. It is unthinkable that a proper assessment of the need for protection could be made before the child concerned has been seen and his or her circumstances have been assessed. I therefore make the following recommendation:

> **Recommendation**
> Save in exceptional circumstances, no child is to be taken into police protection until he or she has been seen and an assessment of his or her circumstances has been undertaken.

13.18 One of the requirements of section 46 of the Children Act 1989 is that when a child is taken into police protection, both the child and parent are informed of the reasons why this course of action has been taken. It also requires a 'designated officer' to investigate the circumstances of the case in order to determine whether police protection is appropriate. Neither of these steps would appear to have been taken in Victoria's case. Instead, the hospital was simply informed by means of a faxed 'Form 72' that Victoria was now in police protection and must remain in the hospital as an inpatient. This was an inadequate way of dealing with such a serious matter. It was done without any discussion with a doctor to find out if there was a medical need for her to stay in hospital, or for how long she could stay.

13.19 The use of police protection and the lack of procedures followed in its application in Victoria's case are considered in detail at paragraph 13.67.

Crimes against children

13.20 It is worth spending time to examine what would have happened if the victim of this possible GBH had been an adult, rather than a seven-year-old child. It was clear from listening to the evidence of the MPS senior officers that they believed there should be no difference in the quality or timeliness of a serious crime investigation, just because of the victim's age. Detective Chief Superintendent (DCS) David Cox, head of the North West Crime Operational Command Unit (OCU), was expressly asked what, if any, difference there should be between the investigation of a suspected GBH or serious assault on a child and a similar offence on an adult. He replied, "The police investigations side of it is largely the same. The only other factors would be that it would be a memorandum interview, it would be a joint interview with social services and I believe it would be the child protection plan issues, or those issues that are CPT related. But the actual mechanics of gathering the evidence, preserving the scene, arresting the suspect, getting the forensic evidence, would be much the same."

13.21 His view was echoed by Deputy Assistant Commissioner (DAC) William Griffiths who said, "The basic ingredients of assault are very easy and straightforward to deal with. You want the victim, the victim's account, you want the medical evidence that supports the account, you want to visit the scene and retrieve evidence there and then you move on to suspects, and so on. These are basic steps that are probably taught in lesson two at recruit school: first steps at the report of a crime."

13.22 Finally, DAC Carole Howlett, the current head of SO5 (the new Child Protection Command Unit established in 2000), agreed with her colleagues that there should be no difference in the quality of the investigation of an assault against a child compared with that of an adult. In particular, when asked how quickly she would expect a victim of an assault to be seen by police, she replied, "Within hours, within a couple of hours or whenever. As soon as possible. As soon as practically possible to get there."

13.23 I share the view of the senior officers that a young victim of crime should receive the same prompt and professional service from the police as an adult. It is plainly a cause of serious concern that this does not appear to have been the case with regard to Victoria. On the evening of 14 July 1999, there was every reason to believe that Victoria was a victim of serious crime. Even so, PC Dewar not only went off duty without carrying out a proper investigation, but she also decided to continue with plans to attend a seminar the following day. I find it difficult to believe that this approach would have been adopted if it had been an adult victim of GBH lying in hospital with multiple injuries. Indeed, I was expressly told by PC Dewar that, had she received a referral concerning a case of GBH in the street during her time as a beat officer, she would have visited the hospital to see the victim.

13.24   Such discrepancies in the standards of service provided by the police are, in my view, obviously unacceptable. Crimes against children are every bit as serious as crimes against adults, and they demand the same prompt and efficient response. To address this worrying state of affairs, I make the following recommendation:

> **Recommendation**
> Chief constables must ensure that crimes involving a child victim are dealt with promptly and efficiently, and to the same standard as equivalent crimes against adults.

Deficiencies in the investigation

13.25   The fact that PC Dewar decided to attend the seminar, even though Victoria's case had yet to be investigated, presumably meant that PC Dewar did not anticipate starting the investigation until the following day – nearly 48 hours after Avril Cameron had first raised her concerns at the hospital.

13.26   In fact, an investigation should have begun straight away. Interviews with Ms Cameron, Kouao and Victoria should have been essential elements of the investigation. I deal with each in turn.

Avril Cameron

13.27   When she was asked why she did not urgently seek out and speak to Ms Cameron, PC Dewar replied, "Because I did not think there was anything I needed to urgently speak to Avril Cameron about from the information I had in the referral." When pressed further on the issue, she went on to say, "Well, we would have done but I felt, on the information I had, that Avril Cameron had communicated to the medical staff, that there was nothing in that referral, she did not say who the perpetrator was."

13.28   I have to say that I detect little sense in either of those two answers. When it was pointed out to PC Dewar that perhaps nobody had asked Ms Cameron who the perpetrator of the assaults against Victoria was, she blamed the medical staff at the hospital. She said she would have expected them to have obtained such information from Ms Cameron if it had been available.

13.29   Later, in her evidence to the Inquiry, PC Dewar said she was aware that social services were going to speak to Ms Cameron. If this was indeed her reason for not interviewing Ms Cameron herself, PC Dewar would appear to have been happy to leave the interviewing of the most important witness (other than the victim herself) to hospital staff and social workers, none of whom were trained to ask the right questions in a criminal investigation. This was, in my view, a crucial error of judgement on the part of PC Dewar. Had Ms Cameron been asked the right questions, the police could have obtained the following valuable information, all of which was within Ms Cameron's knowledge:

- Victoria was not attending school.
- Kouao often became very angry towards Victoria and acted aggressively towards her.
- Victoria would regularly wet herself when taking a nap at Priscilla Cameron's house.

- Ms Cameron had asked Kouao about the cuts on Victoria's hands and Kouao had told her that Victoria cut herself with razor blades.
- Kouao had asked Priscilla Cameron to look after Victoria permanently because the man she was staying with did not want Victoria around.
- On the night Kouao dropped Victoria off at the Camerons' house, Ms Cameron noticed that Victoria had a cut above her eye, a healing wound on her cheek, and two bloodshot eyes.
- Ms Cameron had also noticed Victoria's fingers were oozing pus and her face had swollen up.
- Marie Cader told Ms Cameron that Victoria chatted happily about other things, but when asked about her injuries she "went into auto pilot" and became withdrawn.
- While at the hospital, Ms Cameron had seen marks on Victoria's legs, back and arms. She also noticed that Victoria's nails were short and that she held her hand in a half-clenched manner.
- Ms Cameron had seen small circular marks on Victoria which the doctor had told her might have been caused by cigarette burns.
- Ms Cameron had never seen Victoria scratch herself.
- Ms Cameron had taken Victoria to the hospital because she was concerned about the seriousness of the injuries and the possible cause of them.

13.30 If PC Dewar had made proper inquiries, she would probably also have been told of a conversation with somebody called "Nigerian Mary", to the effect that she had asked Mrs Cameron, "What is it you say to Kouao that makes her beat the child each night?"

13.31 In summary, the police would have quickly gained a clear indication that child abuse may have been taking place, and that Kouao was the perpetrator.

Kouao

13.32 In addition to being content for nurses, doctors or social workers to interview Ms Cameron, PC Dewar was prepared to allow social services to speak to Kouao alone. She accepted that Kouao was the main suspect, yet wanted a social worker to speak to Kouao in the first instance in order to "obtain her account" – this being a woman who was suspected of having caused GBH to her seven-year-old child. I find it extremely surprising that PC Dewar should have felt this was an appropriate manner in which to proceed with the investigation, especially given the disadvantages of questioning a suspect in any way but with the Codes of Practice set out in the Police and Criminal Evidence Act 1984.

Victoria

13.33 I am firmly of the view that PC Dewar should have visited Victoria during the evening of 14 July 1999. She was questioned at length about her decision not to do so and gave various answers, of which the following is representative: "I have been told that I should not see the child before the memorandum interview. I knew that Ms Hines would see the child the next day."

13.34 PC Dewar explained that the usual sequence of events in child protection investigations was, as far as she was aware, first to interview the victim and then to carry out any further work depending upon the outcome of the interview. In other words, the investigation should not even start until the child had been spoken to. In order for this approach to have anything other than a seriously damaging effect on the usefulness of the investigation, it is plainly necessary that children who are capable of giving evidence about what has happened to them are seen as soon as possible. Therefore, PC Dewar's suggestion that she would not necessarily have sought to interview Victoria until she was discharged from hospital is extremely worrying.

13.35   I also reject PC Dewar's claim that it would have been inappropriate for her to see Victoria before a memorandum interview had taken place. The established practice in 1999 was that the police, when dealing with suspected crimes against children, would interview the children concerned in a special video interview suite, in accordance with the government guidelines called *The Memorandum of Good Practice*. However, in cases where a child victim is in hospital, a degree of flexibility is necessary. It may have been open to PC Dewar to conclude it was inappropriate to conduct a full interview with Victoria in a hospital setting. However, she should not have made this decision without visiting Victoria and assessing her circumstances with a view to deciding on the appropriate location and timing of the interview. During the course of such an assessment, she should also have considered the chances of recovering forensic evidence from Victoria or from her clothing.

13.36   The Police and Criminal Evidence Act 1984 Codes of Practice (Code C, note 1B) expressly allows the police to speak to any person who can help with their inquiries. However, the MPS *Child Protection Course Training Manual*, dated 1995, advises that, except in urgent cases, interviews with children can only take place with the consent of a parent or guardian. Given this apparent confusion, and assuming that PC Dewar was familiar with the requirements of the manual, it is perhaps not surprising she formed the view that it would be inappropriate for her to see Victoria until she had been given the go ahead to do so by Ms Hines. However, there is no excuse for her failure to interview, and take full statements from, the medical staff involved.

13.37   In addition to interviewing the key witnesses, PC Dewar should also have visited the scene of the possible abuse. By the time Victoria was admitted to the Central Middlesex Hospital, she was living in Manning's flat at 267 Somerset Gardens. One can only guess at what may have been found at the scene if it had been properly searched and examined at this point. However, it is conceivable that some evidence of deliberate harm may have been detected as early as mid July, if the police had tried to look for it. If such evidence had been found, then events may have followed a radically different course.

The end of the investigation

13.38   I turn now to consider why Brent CPT's investigation, such as it was, ended so abruptly.

13.39   At around 10.30am on 15 July 1999, PC Dewar was at the training seminar at Bushey. She said she was expecting a call from Ms Hines to say that social services had spoken to the mother and obtained her account of how Victoria had received her injuries and her permission to speak to Victoria. Plainly, as far as PC Dewar was concerned, the investigation at this stage was in the hands of social services. However, instead of receiving the expected message, PC Dewar was told by Ms Hines that Dr Ruby Schwartz had examined Victoria and concluded that all her injuries were due to scabies.

13.40   However, it is likely that this was an incomplete summary of Dr Schwartz's views, and that if PC Dewar had chosen to question Dr Schwartz, she would have discovered that Dr Schwartz had some lingering concerns about Victoria that she expected to be followed up by social services. More importantly, if Dr Schwartz had been questioned more closely, it would have become clear that she had not satisfactorily accounted for all the marks that had been noted on Victoria's body, so that physical harm remained a possibility.

13.41 I find it remarkable that PC Dewar was prepared to accept, without question, the reported diagnosis of scabies as an explanation for all of Victoria's injuries, particularly because she had described these injuries on CRIS the night before as including multiple bruising on feet, arms, legs and buttocks, infected bruising on her fingers, and bloodshot eyes. If she had applied her mind to the matter, it seems highly likely she would have realised that a scabies diagnosis left several of the reported injuries unexplained.

13.42 The evidence of PC Dewar, together with that of a number of her colleagues, indicated a profound reluctance to challenge the diagnosis of a consultant paediatrician. In order to test the extent of that reluctance, Counsel to the Inquiry asked PC Dewar if she would have accepted a diagnosis of scabies if the child had a broken arm. PC Dewar replied that of course she would not. In re-examination, her Counsel went as far as to say that the analogy was plainly absurd. However, I found it useful because it demonstrated to me that a police officer would feel able to challenge an improbable medical diagnosis. The question raised by PC Dewar's handling of Victoria's case is how improbable that diagnosis would have to be before an officer might be prepared to exercise his or her own independent judgement.

13.43 In my view, social workers and child protection police officers are specialists in child protection. Doctors specialise primarily in dealing with the medical needs of sick children, so they are often able to give child protection investigators opinions as to the cause of injuries. However, the final analysis of the significance and interpretation of those injuries must be made by the practitioners who have the benefit of looking at the whole picture (including the wider family circumstances), any forensic evidence and the experience of the carers.

13.44 It is wrong for social workers or police officers to blindly accept everything they are told by doctors, no matter how important those doctors are, and they must fit the medical evidence in with the other information available before arriving at their own conclusion. It was entirely inappropriate for PC Dewar to completely abandon such a serious investigation because of a third-hand medical report told to her over the telephone.

13.45 Also, PC Dewar had written in the original CRIS entry, "Doctors consider the injuries to be serious non-accidental injuries" and so would have been aware that the reported diagnosis of Dr Schwartz differed from that of the doctors who had examined Victoria the day before. The fact that there was a divergence of medical opinion as to the cause of Victoria's injuries should have led PC Dewar to question Dr Schwartz about her differing opinion.

13.46 However, having received the call from Ms Hines, PC Dewar immediately lifted the police protection and later marked up the CRIS entry as "no crime". Regrettably, she also cancelled the one positive step she had taken the previous evening, which was to arrange for police photographs to be taken of Victoria's injuries. This last action may have been important, because if PC Dewar had kept an open mind and obtained the photographs, then perhaps her supervisor, or one of her social services colleagues, may have seen them and felt suitably concerned to query Dr Schwartz's diagnosis. Certainly, as events were to unfold, the photographs would have been extremely useful a few days later, when a further set of injuries was being pondered over.

Deficiencies in supervision

13.47   Responsibility for failing to undertake any adequate investigation into the possible crime committed against Victoria cannot rest with PC Dewar alone. As I have already indicated, she was a junior officer with very little experience in the investigation of serious crime. In such circumstances, her handling of this referral should have been closely supervised by more senior officers.

13.48   The officer best placed to do so was her first-line manager, Sgt Gorry. Sgt Gorry said that he remembered hearing PC Dewar take the referral concerning Victoria and that she told him it related to a "serious assault, possibly a GBH, on a young girl". He said in evidence, "I remember the call coming in. I remember Rachel's reaction to the phone call and I can remember sort of reacting to it and thinking this is something quite important, quite serious."

13.49   PC Dewar made no mention of any discussion with Sgt Gorry, although she did state that Sgt Gorry gave her permission to work one hour's overtime on the evening in question, perhaps because he knew she had an important referral to deal with.

13.50   However, it would appear that Sgt Gorry took little interest in Victoria's case and did not set down a plan of action for the investigating officer to follow. He was aware that another officer, PC Karen Blackman, was planning to assist PC Dewar with the referral, but despite being on duty throughout the evening, he appears to have left them to their own devices. When Sgt Gorry was asked what he did to satisfy himself that these two junior officers were conducting a proper investigation of this serious offence, he replied, "Other than the fact that I had spoken to them at the initial stages and was aware that they were carrying out the investigation what appeared to be diligently and effectively, nothing more. The reasoning behind that is that I have considerable confidence in the ability of both officers to have come to the right decision."

13.51   Plainly, Sgt Gorry's confidence was misplaced. His explanation for why he failed, the following day, to ask either of the officers what progress they had made in the investigation of the referral was that he was aware that PC Dewar had spoken directly to DI Anderson in the meantime. Sgt Gorry explained, "When I was at the seminar the following day, PC Dewar addressed Detective Inspector Anderson about the matter and it was really not my position to intervene and find out additionally what course of action she was going to take because I assumed, quite reasonably I feel, that the issues would have been covered, discussed and addressed in the conversation that she would have had with Detective Inspector Anderson."

13.52   I am firmly of the view that any referrals of suspected child abuse to the police from social services should be handled at a managerial level, and that a manager from each agency should be involved in discussing how best to take the investigation forward. The danger of doing otherwise is that a junior officer would have to conduct an investigation as he or she sees fit with minimal input from more senior experienced officers. The inevitable risk would be that important decisions are incorrectly taken, causing the whole investigation to be seriously flawed. Such risks can, in my view, be reduced by the involvement of experienced managers in the investigative process. Therefore, I make the following recommendation:

> **Recommendation**
>
> Whenever a joint investigation by police and social services is required into possible injury or harm to a child, a manager from each agency should always be involved at the referral stage, and in any further strategy discussion.

13.53 Sgt Gorry refused to accept that he should bear any blame for failing to supervise any investigation of Victoria's case. I do not share his view. It seems to me that one of the principal functions of a sergeant in a child protection team is to supervise the investigation of crime by more junior officers. I believe Sgt Gorry should have taken a firm grip of this investigation as soon as the referral was taken. He should have agreed with PC Dewar a plan of action that had a clear timescale in which the work should have been carried out. Indeed, it is difficult to see why Sgt Gorry did not take any active part in the inquiry himself, perhaps by visiting the hospital that evening with PC Dewar. He was on duty until l0pm that night, and although he mentioned that he had to make a telephone call to America during the evening, it is hard to imagine that this should have taken precedence over ensuring that such a serious referral was being properly investigated.

13.54 When Sgt Gorry was asked if an "S.18" assault should not have been dealt with by someone more senior than a PC, he replied, "I think in the scheme of the investigations that have been dealt with in Brent, yes it is a serious assault. But initially I think it will be fair to say that there were no complexities about it and, had there been complexities within it, then obviously the supervisor would have overseen it or taken over, but at that initial stage it was something that I personally felt that the combined skills and abilities of PC Dewar and Blackman were able to deal with the initial investigation." I reject Sgt Gorry's assertion that Victoria's case was neither serious or complex enough for him to have become involved, and I was surprised to hear that he continues to think so.

13.55 My view is that the skill and judgement that an experienced officer can bring to an investigation is of vital importance, particularly in making sure that matters get off to a good start. I consider that it should always be the case that such an officer is involved from the outset in investigations involving serious crimes against children. Therefore, I make the following recommendation:

> **Recommendation**
>
> In cases of serious crime against children, supervisory officers must, from the beginning, take an active role in ensuring that a proper investigation is carried out.

13.56 PC Dewar spoke to DI Anderson, but could not remember if it was before or after she received the message from Ms Hines concerning the diagnosis from Dr Schwartz. For his part, DI Anderson was also unable to remember. However, it would seem unlikely that he made a considered assessment of the case before the telephone call from Ms Hines, especially since he told me that, had he known Victoria was in hospital and nothing had been arranged, he would have instructed PC Dewar immediately to formulate a proper strategy with social services and organise for a plan of action to be put in place. Therefore, it is more likely that PC Dewar spoke to DI Anderson after her telephone call with Ms Hines, and presented him with an open and shut case, in as much as she already believed the diagnosis of Dr Schwartz ended the need for a criminal investigation.

13.57   What emerges is a picture of blurred and confused management roles, with nobody taking responsibility for ensuring that an investigation takes place. Sgt Gorry was aware that the referral had come in, but gave no directions as to what action he expected to be taken. Once he knew DI Anderson had been consulted, he ceased to take any active interest.

13.58   When the case was mentioned to him the following day, DI Anderson probably did not grasp how serious the case had been viewed the evening before and, hearing about the scabies diagnosis, thought it was a formality for PC Dewar to lift the police protection and mark the investigation as complete on CRIS. Nonetheless, in my view, DI Anderson should have taken much greater care to explore with PC Dewar the extent to which she had properly investigated the case before lifting police protection. He should also have directed that a written medical opinion be obtained from Dr Schwartz.

13.59   The last occasion on which a supervisor had anything to do with the investigation was on 10 August 1999, when Sgt Smith checked the CRIS report to see if it was ready to close. He said that, having read the contents of the report, he was satisfied that it could be closed. When asked what he understood his role to be in checking the CRIS report before closure, he replied, "I wanted to make sure that the matter had been investigated. I wanted to make sure that the statutory checks had been carried out." When asked whether he was satisfied this had been done after reading this particular report, he replied, "I could see that it had come in initially as a quite serious allegation, that the following day there had been discussions that had taken place between the hospital, the social services, between the officer of the case and the Detective Inspector and that a decision had been made to – I do not want to use the word downgrade – but to change the classification to 'no crime'. When I saw that that had taken place and that there was no further explanation required by police, when I saw that report then I closed it."

13.60   Clearly, Sgt Smith did no serious analysis of the case or any cross-checking to see whether PC Dewar's understanding of the medical evidence was correct. If he had, he would quickly have found out that Dr Schwartz did have ongoing concerns for the child and that there were injuries which could not have been accounted for by scabies. It is also disturbing that a case that started off as being so serious could be closed without a written, detailed, medical report being examined by a supervisor.

13.61   Also, in common with his colleague Sgt Gorry, Sgt Smith placed a lot of importance on the fact that DI Anderson had apparently agreed the decision to "no crime" the case. Therefore, Sgt Smith's input amounted to no more than a 'rubberstamping' exercise, compounding the poor decision-making and supervision of others. Ironically, at the very time that Sgt Smith closed the CRIS entry in Brent, Victoria was being discharged from a hospital in the neighbouring borough, having suffered a further set of serious injuries.

Multi-agency investigation

13.62   In trying to find an explanation for the lack of useful action by Brent CPT, I was helped by another exchange between PC Dewar and her Counsel. He asked her, "In a multi-agency investigation such as this, who did you understand the lead agency to be?" PC Dewar replied that she understood it to be social services.

13.63   This was a view she held in common with several other police officers who gave evidence to the Inquiry. If the impression given by their evidence is representative, it would appear that child protection officers, for some considerable time, have been unsure about exactly where they fit within the *Working Together* system and what their precise responsibilities are in the investigation of the possible deliberate harm of a child.

13.64 The principal function of the police is the prevention and detection of crime. I entirely reject the notion that the police should seek to avoid their responsibility to conduct a swift and thorough criminal investigation by hiding behind the excuse of others being the 'lead agency'. The police are the 'lead agency' in a criminal investigation, and I am concerned that the good intentions of multi-agency decision-making, information sharing and joint working may have now led to a blurring of roles, uncertainty about who should take what action, and a convenient excuse for poor investigation. PC Dewar's view that social services were the lead agency in the investigation of Victoria's case would appear to be reflective of a common view held by child protection officers in the MPS.

13.65 When Victoria came to notice in Brent, social services had an important role to play and should undoubtedly have taken a lead in co-ordinating the various strands of information which were becoming available. However, there should have been a parallel police investigation into the serious crime reported against Victoria, and the evidence gathering exercise for that should have been led, and in large measure conducted, by the police.

13.66 The MPS, and the police service generally, needs seriously to examine its role in child protection investigations. As with other types of crime, it must take responsibility for gathering the necessary evidence. In order to advance this objective, I make the following recommendation:

> **Recommendation**
> The Association of Chief Police Officers must produce and implement the standards-based service, as recommended by Her Majesty's Inspectorate of Constabulary in the 1999 thematic inspection report, *Child Protection*.

Police protection

13.67 Finally, I turn to the issue of police protection. Section 46 of the Children Act 1989 provides a power for a police officer to remove a child into police protection, or cause the child to remain in a safe place such as a hospital, if there is evidence that the child is at risk of significant harm. A crucial safeguard for the child and the family is that an independent supervisory officer, known for these purposes as the 'designated officer', assesses the action taken and ensures that there is a need to remove the child from the control of the carers, and to inform the relative parties why the steps were taken. The Home Office issued guidance to the police service in the form of circular 54/91, which suggested that the designated officer role was most appropriately carried out by an inspector.

13.68 In Victoria's case, PC Dewar acted as the actioning officer as well as the designated officer for the purposes of police protection. It was clear from her evidence to this Inquiry that, when dealing with Victoria's case, she was unaware that the Home Office circular required these roles to be separate and filled by different officers. I heard evidence from senior officers in the MPS to the effect that they had acknowledged their failure to comply with government guidance on this issue and that this had now been corrected. I will therefore restrict myself to urging all police forces to ensure that they operate within Home Office guidelines relating to police protection, that a clear understanding of the designated officer's role is established, and that they comply with the following recommendation:

> **Recommendation**
> Police forces must review their systems for taking children into police protection and ensure they comply with the Children Act 1989 and Home Office guidelines. In particular, they must ensure that an independent officer of at least inspector rank acts as the designated officer in all cases.

13.69   It is doubtful whether there was a need to take Victoria into police protection at all. This is due to the fact that there was no known threat from Kouao that she would seek to remove Victoria from hospital. However, having taken this action, if an independent inspector had been overseeing the case, as laid down in the Children Act 1989 and the Home Office circular, there is a chance that he or she would have spotted the deficiencies in the way the case was being handled, and prevented the police protection from being lifted until a proper investigation had taken place.

13.70   I am also concerned about the fact that Victoria was taken into police protection over the telephone, and with no police officer having been to see her. Examination of the Children Act 1989 and Home Office guidance does not reveal any specific instruction that the child must be seen before taken into police protection. However, I believe it is poor practice for this not to happen. For the police to deny a parent access to their child is a serious step and requires the most searching examination of the need to take such action.

13.71   Whether or not the child needs to be seen, the legislation and guidance is clear that both the child and his or her carer must be told why police protection has been implemented. No attempt was made by any of the officers concerned with this case to explain either to Victoria or to Kouao why this step had been considered necessary.

14 Haringey Child Protection Team

Accommodation

14.1   At the time it came to deal with Victoria's case, Haringey Child Protection Team (CPT) was housed in Highgate police station. The accommodation provided for the team, in common with many CPTs in the capital, was poor quality. In addition, I was told that the team was insufficiently equipped with staff, vehicles and IT equipment.

14.2   I have dealt with my concerns about the priority and resources given to CPTs by the Metropolitan Police Service (MPS) elsewhere in section 13. I will not repeat them here, except to say that I have some sympathy for the view expressed by Sergeant (Sgt) Alan Hodges, one of the officers on the Haringey team. He said, "I do not want to sound pathetic, but it all adds up, and it was just another indication of the way we were treated as a unit." I found no direct link between the standard of the service offered to Victoria by Haringey CPT and the adequacy of its resources, but I believe it would be wrong to discount the corrosive effect that a long period of neglect and under-resourcing can have on the morale and effectiveness of a team like Haringey CPT.

Training and experience of officers

14.3   One of the particular deficiencies in the team that was drawn to my attention was the lack of officers with detective training. In view of the importance that I attach to this issue, I detail the training and experience of the officers who had some direct involvement in Victoria's case.

Detective Inspector Howard

14.4   Detective Inspector (DI) David Howard joined the police service in 1978 and became the officer in charge at Haringey CPT in May 1998. During his 20 years of service before taking up that post, he held a wide range of roles within the uniformed branch. These included beat patrol, public disorder policing, custody sergeant, and management of community beat officers. He had a little experience in mainstream CID work at Kilburn police station, where he was an inspector for about 15 months, but he had never attended the CID foundation course. In 1997, he attended a one-week Management of Serious Crime (MSC) course, which he said was the only investigative training he had received since leaving recruit school. He said, "During my short time in the CID, other than one murder inquiry I really did not investigate fully other crimes. So although I had probably more awareness than some, I certainly did not have the practical skills to really supervise or take on child protection work."

14.5   He had no previous experience in a child protection team, and it was not until he had been in his post a year that he attended a one-week *Working Together* course. That was the only child protection training he ever did. Overall, I do not consider DI Howard to have been sufficiently trained and qualified to manage a group of staff undertaking serious criminal investigations, particularly relating to children.

Sergeant Michael Cooper-Bland

14.6   Sgt Cooper-Bland was, together with Sgt Richard Bird, responsible for the day-to-day supervision of PC Karen Jones at the time the first referral concerning Victoria was received in late July 1999. He joined the police service in 1977 and spent the first 12 years as a uniformed patrol officer. He was promoted to sergeant in 1989 and afterwards worked in various uniformed supervisory roles until 1994 when he joined Haringey CPT. He therefore had no CID experience, nor any training or experience in serious crime investigation. However, by 1999 he had five years of child protection work under his belt and he had attended several courses relating to his child protection work, including a two-week Initial Child Protection course. This made him something of a rarity among the officers from whom I heard evidence.

Sergeant Richard Bird

14.7   Sgt Bird became a police officer in 1977 and spent the first 13 years as a uniformed patrol officer with the Hertfordshire constabulary. He transferred to the MPS in May 1989, and was promoted to sergeant two years later, continuing to serve in uniformed police roles. When he joined Haringey CPT in March 1999, he had no experience of dealing with serious crime investigations, let alone supervising them, and he had received no advanced investigative training. He made the point in his written statement to the Inquiry that, even up to the point of leaving the CPT in 2001, he had still not received any investigative or procedural training for CPT officers, nor any joint investigation training with social services. He said he had specifically asked DI Howard about this, but was told that the training courses had been stopped on the North West Crime Operational Command Unit (OCU) and that there were none now available.

Sergeant Alan Hodges

14.8   Sgt Hodges completes the supervision team at Haringey. He arrived in the team during October 1999, effectively replacing Sgt Cooper-Bland in the middle of the relevant period. Before this, he had 16 years' police service, nine years of which had been as a sergeant. Like his colleagues, Sgt Hodges had never held a detective's post or received any training in serious crime investigation. Just before joining the CPT, he was fortunate enough to attend a five-day *Working Together* course, which at least gave him a basic insight into the main roles of the agencies involved in child protection.

14.9   The level of detective experience among the supervising officers in Haringey CPT is a matter that causes me some concern. In my view, it is extremely important that the first-line supervisors of child protection officers are either fully trained detectives, or have received sufficient training and experience to enable them effectively to oversee serious crime investigations.

14.10   It would seem that my concern was shared by some of the officers themselves. For example, Sgt Bird expressed his feelings rather forcefully when he said, "I applied for a post as police sergeant in the hope that I would gain the knowledge, experience and training to become a detective. There was no training. The *Child Protection Manual* was deemed to be out of date and, even though senior management had been tasked to rewrite and update it, this had not happened by the time I left two years later. I was put in the position of detective sergeant without the experience or the training to prepare me for the seriousness of the investigations I found myself dealing with."

14.11   The situation among the constables was no better. When he arrived on the CPT, Sgt Bird said he was comforted by the fact that there was at least one detective constable on the team in the form of Detective Constable (DC) Braithwaite. However, DC Braithwaite was transferred to other duties in March 1999, which meant that, by the time Victoria arrived in the borough, there were no detectives in Haringey CPT.

PC Karen Jones

14.12   PC Jones was one of the most experienced constables left in the team, and she was to be the investigating officer on each of the two occasions that Victoria was referred to the team. She joined the police force in 1987 and carried out uniformed patrol duties until her appointment to Haringey CPT in 1996. She spent two years with the Clubs and Vice Unit but had never been a detective officer nor undertaken the CID foundation course, nor any other course involving serious crime investigation. However, in 1996, she did undertake the two-week child protection course that was in existence at that time. This course included the identification of possible signs of deliberate harm to a child and the evidence required. Within the first month of her being posted to Harrow CPT, she also attended a Memorandum of Good Practice Interviewing course and a five-day *Working Together* course. Therefore, by August 1999, PC Jones was both experienced in child protection work and, by comparison with other members of the team, was well trained as far as child protection work was concerned.

14.13   Having looked at the background of these officers, the picture which emerges is similar to that of Brent CPT. There were some very experienced police officers on Harrow CPT, but none had any relevant training or experience in dealing with the investigation of serious crimes.

Crimes against children

14.14   Again, a comparison with adult victims of crime is instructive. Sgt Bird said that no officer in his previous posting (the Vulnerable Persons Unit, which deals with domestic violence) would investigate such serious crimes as Grievous Bodily Harm (GBH) or rape, unless they were a detective. Such crimes, he said, would be passed on to CID. However, he confirmed that in Haringey CPT, a crime of equal seriousness committed against a child would be dealt with by an officer with no detective training at all.

14.15   This is a dangerous and illogical approach. It is wrong that victims of crime are disadvantaged in terms of the training and expertise of the investigating officer, simply because they are children. I heard worrying evidence to suggest that the culture of some police forces was such that child protection team work was seen as something less than the investigation of often very serious crimes. In order to address this issue, I make the following recommendation:

> **Recommendation**
> Chief constables must ensure that the investigation of crime against children is as important as the investigation of any other form of serious crime. Any suggestion that child protection policing is of a lower status than other forms of policing must be eradicated.

14.16   Following Victoria's death, Haringey CPT was reviewed. The team was increased to contain three sergeants and eight constables, five of whom were detectives.

The relationship with Haringey Social Services

14.17 In a report written after Victoria's death (to which I return in more detail at paragraph 14.127), Detective Chief Inspector (DCI) Philip Wheeler wrote, "Haringey Social Services itself seems to have its own particular culture and ways of working within the child protection framework. It seems that they are extremely powerful within the protection network and some social workers work hard to actually prevent police involvement." The validity of this comment was tested during the course of the evidence of the officers on the team.

14.18 Sgt Hodges was one of those who thought all was not well. He said that some members of Haringey Social Services were "aggressive" towards the police. In particular, he said that he detected a feeling among a minority of his social services counterparts that the police tended to take too heavy-handed an approach towards joint investigations, seeking to obtain a conviction at all costs rather than focusing on the interests of the child. The result was a feeling that the two agencies were working to different agendas.

14.19 In order to establish the practical effects of this difference in outlook, Sgt Hodges was asked whether he had been held back from doing what he wanted to do in terms of investigating a crime because of the approach of social services. He replied, "Not holding back, no, maybe more delayed, things were a lot slower. We could not just go off and do it, we had to consult with social services before. I remember having arguments over different investigations with different social workers and managers. I would not say I allowed them to dictate totally, but it did present me with a problem of how to progress investigations when they were our main conduit or access to that child or the family."

14.20 Sgt Hodges' perception was echoed to some degree by Sgt Cooper-Bland. When asked to comment on the state of the relationship between Haringey CPT and social services, he replied, "I would say that on an individual basis, social worker to police officer, there were many, many examples of good working relationships. There were, conversely, examples of poor working relationships, and in very few cases downright rudeness. I think the perception that the police are heavy-handed and only interested in securing convictions and not always focusing on the child, is a stereotypical view held by some people in social services. I would say the minority."

14.21 When asked for his views on this issue, DI Howard agreed there were difficulties. Although he thought that DCI Wheeler had exaggerated the problem, he did state that social services were "robust" and "inflexible". He gave an example of this inflexibility by saying, "I made a suggestion, just a suggestion once, that maybe strategy meetings could be held at Highgate [police station]. I felt that would be something that would be progressive, the staff maybe could get to know some of their staff, but it was just a total look of amazement, as if it would take place at the social services offices or nowhere."

14.22 If this was true, and I found no reason to doubt DI Howard, then this is inappropriate behaviour on the part of Haringey Social Services. The strategy meeting ought to be viewed as a shared, multi-agency meeting. It is not a social services meeting to which others are invited, and it should be the cornerstone of a joint investigation. There is absolutely no reason why the other agencies involved in child protection should always go to the social services offices.

14.23 The evidence of Sgt Hodges was illuminating on this issue. He told me, "There was a problem with time delays of having strategy meetings on occasions. Whether it was because of us or because of social services, I think it was a bit of both in many respects, a lot of times we would get phone calls quite late in the day saying, 'We need to have a strategy meeting now', and we would have nobody in the office to actually go all the way to Tottenham to have a strategy meeting. Social services appeared to be loath to have telephone strategy discussions, which maybe would have resolved that problem. On other occasions, you would arrive at the social services for a strategy meeting and then be asked to attend another strategy meeting immediately after. That caused problems because we would not actually know anything about the initial referral, and we would not have had the opportunity to actually do any of our checks as such."

14.24   In her statement to the Inquiry, Rosemarie Kozinos, an acting senior practitioner at Haringey Social Services, said that because there was a difficulty with police attendance, social services would hold strategy meetings one after the other to help the police officers. It does not seem to have occurred to her that it would have been much more convenient to the police if the burden of travelling had been shared more equally between the agencies, perhaps by sometimes holding strategy meetings at police premises where appropriate.

14.25   The strategy meeting should be the forum in which the strategic and operational direction of the criminal investigation is discussed and agreed. It is pointless to ask whichever police officer happens to be at the office for an earlier meeting to attend, just to make up the numbers. For the police to be properly represented at a strategy meeting, the officer who is going to deal with the case, and his or her supervisor, should be present.

14.26   There appeared to me to be no sense of equal partnership between the two agencies. The police must accept criticism for allowing this unhealthy regime to develop without challenging it at the highest level. This is a good example of why the Metropolitan Police Service (MPS) should have ensured it sent a delegate to the Area Child Protection Committee (ACPC) meetings of sufficient rank to challenge such arrangements. This should certainly have been dealt with at superintendent/assistant director level, but it was the practice in the MPS to send the local CPT detective inspector.

14.27   Echoes of this tension were heard in the evidence given by some of the social services witnesses. For example, Lisa Arthurworrey said that Angella Mairs did not like police officers coming into the social services office. When I asked her if there was a general feeling within Haringey Social Services of hostility towards the police or other agencies, she said, "Yes there was."

14.28   The matter was put directly to Ms Mairs, but her response was confused and unhelpful. At one point she stated that she found it difficult to work with some Haringey police officers, citing "institutional racism" as the reason. Later, however, she tried to distance herself from this statement by suggesting that all such problems had long disappeared by the time Victoria's case was being dealt with.

14.29   Ms Mairs aside, I heard enough evidence from other witnesses to conclude that the police in Haringey allowed themselves to be 'led by the nose' by Haringey Social Services. This subservient approach seriously compromised their ability to carry out robust, speedy and effective criminal investigations.

14.30   Obviously, effective multi-agency working will require some give and take by the various agencies involved. However, if the situation in Haringey is representative, it suggests to me that a careful re-evaluation of *Working Together* is needed to make sure that the particular roles and responsibilities of the various agencies involved in child protection are not blurred. In particular, I believe that although there should be a constant and thorough sharing of information between the agencies involved, it is the police who should keep sole responsibility for the evidence-gathering process. This includes the forensic interview (known as a memorandum interview) with a child victim of crime, conducted in accordance with the government guidance *Achieving Best Evidence in Criminal Proceedings* (2001).

14.31 The police should be in no doubt that their primary responsibility is the detection and prevention of crime, and when a crime is suspected, they are responsible for its efficient and prompt investigation. As I set out below, I take the view that Haringey CPT lost sight of the unique and specific role it had to play in dealing with the two referrals concerning Victoria. In doing so, they effectively allowed social services to dictate the speed and depth of the investigations that were carried out. If this type of 'joint working' is being replicated nationally, then new guidelines are urgently needed to ensure that each agency knows precisely the role it is to play in the investigation of possible deliberate harm to a child.

The initial investigation

The referral

14.32 The police in Haringey first became aware of Victoria when Sgt Cooper-Bland received a telephone call from Shanthi Jacob at 11am on 28 July 1999.

14.33 Sgt Cooper-Bland recalled that the information he received concerned a young girl who had been admitted to the North Middlesex Hospital four days earlier with burns to her face and head. He was told that the girl's carer, Kouao, had told medical staff that the girl had poured hot water over herself. Sgt Cooper-Bland also remembers being told that a nurse had noticed old marks on the child's body that resembled belt buckle marks.

14.34 In view of the fact that belt buckle marks were expressly mentioned, Sgt Cooper-Bland must have known that he was being told about possible deliberate harm to a child. It is clear from what he was later to write in the entry on the crime-recording computer database, CRIS, that he also suspected that Victoria's burns had been deliberately caused. According to the CRIS report, his understanding at the time was that Victoria's burns had been caused "by the suspect, as yet unknown, pouring hot water over a child's head". In response to a question from me, he agreed that he was, at that stage, working on the assumption that the burns had been deliberately caused.

14.35 Sgt Cooper-Bland agreed that, in light of this information, the referral constituted a serious case which called for prompt investigation. He classified the allegation on CRIS as "actual bodily harm", an offence under section 47 of the Offences Against the Person Act 1861. Therefore, for the second time in two weeks, a CPT was faced with a clear indication that a serious crime may have been committed against Victoria.

14.36 Sgt Cooper-Bland recalled that Ms Jacob told him that social services had arranged a strategy meeting for 2.30pm on the afternoon of 28 July 1999 and that police attendance was required. It appears that little thought was given by social services as to whether this arrangement was convenient for the police, and this may be an example of social services' inconsiderate action that I criticised above at paragraph 14.24.

Allocation to PC Jones

14.37 Rather than simply informing the police that a strategy meeting was to take place, a social services manager should have spoken to a manager in the CPT to agree whether a strategy meeting was needed. If so, they could then have agreed on an appropriate and mutually convenient time and place for it to be held (which, according to the local procedures in force at the time, should have been in the hospital). In the event, the manner in which the strategy meeting was arranged determined who would represent the police at the meeting.

14.38   Sgt Cooper-Bland said that his original intention had been to allocate the case to PC Sean Mangan, but because that officer was not able to attend the strategy meeting at the time set by social services, the case was given to another officer, PC Jones, who just happened to be at the North Tottenham District Office on that day, attending another meeting.

14.39   In my view, the decision as to which constable is allocated a particular case should be determined according to who is best placed to conduct the necessary criminal inquiry. Once that decision had been made in Victoria's case, Sgt Cooper-Bland should have arranged with his counterpart in social services to hold the strategy meeting at a time which would have enabled that officer to attend. Despite the fact she was not his first choice, Sgt Cooper-Bland considered that PC Jones (as the most experienced officer on the team) would be able to deal with the case properly.

14.40   It is unclear whether Sgt Cooper-Bland, by instructing her to attend the strategy meeting, also expected PC Jones to take responsibility for the investigation. But there was little point in her attending the meeting if that was not to be the case. She certainly received little in the way of briefing from her sergeant before she arrived at the meeting. As Sgt Cooper-Bland put it, "I was not able to give her a detailed briefing at all. It would have been a telephone conversation asking her to attend the strategy meeting, outlining the briefest facts of the case."

PC Jones's understanding of the referral

14.41   This was the unsatisfactory chain of events which led to PC Jones attending the strategy meeting about Victoria at Haringey Social Services' offices on 28 July 1999. At the end of the meeting, it appears that PC Jones assumed that responsibility for the case was to be hers, a state of affairs which plainly found favour with Sgt Cooper-Bland who said, "The following day, I was at Haringey CPT. It appeared that PC Karen Jones had allocated the investigation involving Victoria Climbié to herself. I confirmed with her that this was acceptable and that she was assuming responsibility for the investigation."

14.42   Before dealing in detail with PC Jones's investigation of Victoria's case from this point on, it is helpful to note what she believed herself to be dealing with at the point that she entered the strategy meeting.

14.43   PC Jones told me that she remembered little about her telephone conversation with Sgt Cooper-Bland, but when reminded what he wrote on CRIS, PC Jones said that nothing there was in conflict with her memory of what she had been told. It is safe to assume, therefore, that she knew that Victoria, a seven-year-old girl, had been taken to hospital with burns to her face and head, that she believed the hospital was accepting the explanation given by her 'mother' that Victoria poured the water over herself, and that medical concerns were raised when a nurse found what looked like belt buckle marks on her body. When asked whether it seemed to her to be the sort of case that merited a full investigation, she unhesitatingly answered that it did. She also confirmed that she felt equipped, in terms of training and experience, to deal with it.

14.44   It is important to note that four days had passed between Victoria's admission to hospital and the referral to the police. Wasting time at the outset can seriously damage the effectiveness of a criminal investigation. In this case, it gave Kouao an opportunity to talk to and influence Victoria, for Victoria's injuries to change appearance and for forensic evidence to be lost. Sgt Cooper-Bland did not raise the issue of the delay in bringing Victoria's case to the attention of the police when he took the referral on 28 July 1999. His explanation was worrying: "It is not something I had considered. I have to say that while not common, it was not uncommon for cases to become – to be brought to our notice some time after the suspected offences had occurred."

14.45 In my view, this was an issue that should have been considered, not just by Sgt Cooper-Bland when he took the referral, but also by PC Jones when she entered the strategy meeting. At the forefront of her mind should have been the fact that there was a victim in hospital to whom the main suspect had unrestricted access. She should also have been aware that, somewhere, there might be a belt buckle that matched the marks on Victoria's body. There might also be witnesses able to give helpful evidence.

14.46 PC Jones should have been concerned that there had been a delay of four days between Victoria's admission to hospital and the police being informed that she may have been the victim of deliberate harm. The damaging effect that such a delay could have on the effectiveness of a criminal investigation is obvious. The fact that she would not seem to have raised this issue with her colleagues at the strategy meeting is perhaps indicative of a general approach to investigations of this kind where the police neither receive nor insist upon the immediate notification of potential crimes. In my view, it is vital that the police are involved at the earliest possible opportunity. In order to encourage this practice, I make the following recommendation:

> **Recommendation**
> The guideline set out at paragraph 5.8 of *Working Together* must be strictly adhered to: whenever social services receive a referral which may constitute a criminal offence against a child, they must inform the police at the earliest opportunity.

The July strategy meeting

14.47 In view of the delay that had already occurred since Victoria's admission to hospital, these were all matters which should have been at the forefront of PC Jones's mind when she attended the meeting. She should have left the other participants of the strategy meeting in no doubt that the police needed to try and recover the time lost by the late referral and urgently commence a full investigation. Instead, PC Jones would seem to have done little more than somewhat passively accept a list of tasks from the chairperson at the meeting, who was Ms Kozinos.

14.48 I regard this as wholly unsatisfactory. However competent PC Jones believed Ms Kozinos to be, she was not qualified to direct the course of an investigation into a serious crime. That PC Jones allowed her to do so adds further weight to the recommendation I made at paragraph 13.52 that a police manager should be involved both at the referral stage and in initial strategy discussions in order to make sure, if nothing else, that the investigation gets off on the right foot.

14.49 The strategy meeting lasted half an hour. At the end of the meeting, PC Jones had gained more information, mainly from Karen Johns, a social worker at Enfield. She discovered that Victoria had been presented as unkempt, in a dirty dress and with no underwear, that there were 11 scars in total, including the two buckle marks, and that the injuries caused by the scalding appeared to be "bad". PC Jones should have been in no doubt from this extra information that she was dealing with a serious allegation of crime, as well as a potential case of neglect. PC Jones confirmed the she understood herself to be investigating a possible case of Actual Bodily Harm (ABH).

14.50 The tasks specifically allocated to PC Jones at the strategy meeting were:

- to carry out a check with the immigration service;
- once medical reports had been obtained, to arrange a joint visit with social services to the child's home in order to explain child protection procedures to the mother;
- to take the necessary steps should Kouao attempt to remove Victoria from hospital.

Deficiencies in the investigation

14.51 What concerned me most about the action plan agreed at the strategy meeting was not what the police agreed to do themselves, but what they were content to let others do on their behalf. Two of the most basic steps in investigating this crime should have been the obtaining of statements from the doctors and nurses concerned, and ensuring that Victoria's injuries were photographed.

14.52 PC Jones did neither. In explanation, she told me that she expected Ms Johns to obtain the medical report. This, in my view, is grossly inadequate. PC Jones should have arranged for full witness statements to be obtained from the consultant paediatrician, Dr Mary Rossiter, and the other doctors and nurses who had examined Victoria. A medical report is worthless in a criminal investigation, and someone with PC Jones's experience should have known that proper witness statements were required.

14.53 As to the photographs, although hospital photographs had been ordered (and were eventually taken on 29 July 1999) and arrangements were put in place at the strategy meeting for police and social services to be given a copy, PC Jones should have arranged for a police photographer to record the injuries. A police photographer would approach the matter from an evidential point of view, ensuring that all injuries and marks were photographed, and using special techniques where necessary, such as ultraviolet photography. We now know that the hospital photographer got basic instructions from a doctor about which areas to photograph, by a square being drawn on a body map. The area included the main burn injuries but many of the smaller injuries were not photographed, and the recording of such injuries may have been crucial in a criminal investigation.

14.54 There was a long and depressing exchange between Counsel to the Inquiry and PC Jones when he questioned her on her failure to take positive action at the beginning of what should have been her investigation of the case. Despite the ample evidence of physical abuse and neglect available to her at that stage, she doggedly stuck to her position that, because the doctors believed Kouao's story about the scalding, it must be true. She did not see it as her role to question the doctors' views, or even to check that it was indeed the concluded medical view, given that she had only received this information second-hand from Ms Johns. To discover that an experienced police officer and child protection 'expert' such as PC Jones would not even consider the possibility that Kouao might be lying is incredible. Once again, I repeat that if a competent police manager had been at the strategy meeting, he or she might have applied some independent thought and critical analysis to the available information.

14.55 I believe that there were minimum steps which PC Jones should have informed Ms Kozinos the police would be undertaking:

- The scene of the crime should have been identified and searched for any clues that deliberate harm was taking place, and in particular for the actual belt which matched the buckle marks on Victoria's body.
- Statements should have been arranged and obtained from all doctors and nurses concerned.
- Police photographs should have been obtained, or at the very least the hospital photographs should have been checked to ensure all injuries reported by medical staff had been recorded.
- A full forensic medical examination, by a forensically trained paediatrician or doctor, should have been carried out.
- The likely suspects should have been identified (the prime carers being the most obvious), and a strategy agreed for their arrest and interview in accordance with the Police and Criminal Evidence Act 1984.
- Arrangements should have been made to speak immediately to Victoria, independently of any of the suspects, to allow her to speak freely about what had happened to her. This should have been done with an interpreter and, as far as possible, in accordance with the *Memorandum of Good Practice*.

14.56 I heard no satisfactory explanation from any of the officers from Haringey CPT who gave evidence to the Inquiry as to why these basic investigative steps were not taken. PC Jones's response to the question of why she did not carry out these basic tasks was simply to avoid and refuse to accept even her most obvious failings, saying that medical staff were responsible for identifying the crime scene and that she was not able to speak to Victoria because a doctor needed to examine her. Quite what she thought the doctors had been doing for the previous four days was never established. She even suggested that the police could not really do anything because they had not established that a crime had taken place. It was put to her that surely part of the role of the police is to establish exactly that, but she seemed not to grasp the logic of the argument.

14.57 The fundamental flaw in PC Jones's view of her handling of Victoria's case, and her role as a child protection officer, seems to me to be expressed in the following answer, which is representative of many she gave during the course of her evidence: "Child protection and ordinary policing are completely different things." I believe that they are not different things and that it is absolutely vital that police officers engaged in joint investigations into possible deliberate harm realise that they are responsible for making sure that an effective investigation is carried out. In order to encourage this perception among police officers, I make the following recommendation:

> **Recommendation**
> The *Working Together* arrangements must be amended to ensure the police carry out completely, and exclusively, any criminal investigation elements in a case of suspected injury or harm to a child, including the evidential interview with a child victim. This will remove any confusion about which agency takes the 'lead' or is responsible for certain actions.

14.58 As to the three tasks allocated to her by Ms Kozinos at the strategy meeting, PC Jones said she carried out the immigration check which came back as "no trace" and she decided that no steps were necessary to prevent Kouao removing Victoria from hospital. This left just the 'home visit' to Kouao. As far as she was concerned, this was going to be arranged by the allocated social worker and the timing would be dictated by social services, leaving her to do no more than wait to be told when to turn up at Kouao's home.

14.59 With the exception of the immigration check and a check of the police computer system, PC Jones did nothing more on the case for a further six days. In my view, she neglected her duty as a police officer, and Victoria was let down by this inaction.

The home visit

14.60 On 3 August 1999, PC Jones happened to be at the North Tottenham District Office for meetings in relation to other cases. She said that she saw Lisa Arthurworrey in reception, and that Ms Arthurworrey had got a statement, or statements, back from the hospital indicating that one doctor had described the marks on Victoria's body as belt buckle marks. This was the crucial document which PC Jones said she was waiting for to begin further investigations. This was the confirmation she thought she needed that a crime had taken place. Ms Arthurworrey apparently told PC Jones that she did not have the statement in her possession because she was dealing with another matter at the time, but that she would fax it to the CPT office later. PC Jones said she was not "unduly concerned" that the document was not faxed that day, or indeed the next day.

14.61 Ms Arthurworrey had arranged with PC Jones to carry out the 'home visit' on 4 August 1999. PC Jones said that she saw this visit as being for social services (as the lead agency) to assess whether it was suitable for Victoria to return there. If that is right, then it is unclear why it should have been necessary for PC Jones to attend at all. However, when PC Jones was asked what she thought the purpose of her attendance was, her answer was revealing. She said, "Because of the suspicion there was a crime, somebody had made an allegation."

14.62 Plainly, that was correct. An allegation had been made, a crime was indicated, and Kouao was the principal suspect. That being so, PC Jones, rather than passively attending a social services-led home visit, should have arrested Kouao and interviewed her formally.

14.63 In reality, the home visit never took place. PC Jones recalled that, at the strategy meeting, it had been suggested that Victoria had suffered from scabies. On the day of the proposed home visit, she told me that she telephoned the casualty department at the North Middlesex Hospital and asked for advice relating to scabies. According to her, a casualty nurse (whose name she was unable to supply) warned her to wear protective clothing, not to remain in the infected area for long, and certainly no longer than an hour. She also said that she was advised to destroy her clothing, and wash and shower in disinfectant afterwards. Because of this advice, she said she had concerns for her own family and she therefore telephoned Ms Arthurworrey that morning to say she refused to go to the house.

14.64 The question of whether PC Jones really did receive advice to this effect from a nurse at the North Middlesex Hospital was one which occupied the Inquiry for some time. A number of nurses were asked directly whether they had given such advice. All of them answered "no". Meriel Clarke, lead nurse in the accident and emergency department at the hospital, told me that she had undertaken an investigation among all the nurses in the casualty department. The investigation revealed that none of them could recall a conversation with PC Jones during which advice concerning scabies had been given.

14.65 In any event, it was unequivocally stated by all those medical staff who gave evidence on this issue, that the advice PC Jones claims to have been given was plainly wrong. Ms Clarke said that she could not believe that any of her nurses could have given such advice. In addition, Dr Thomas Mann, a consultant dermatologist at the hospital, said in his statement to the Inquiry that, had he been asked for advice by PC Jones, he would have told her not to worry about scabies because Victoria had been successfully treated by this stage.

14.66 Had PC Jones received the advice that she claims she did and genuinely thought that Victoria's home posed a risk of scabies infection, then plainly she should have objected strongly to Victoria being returned there before the risk had been eliminated. No satisfactory explanation was given as to why she took no such action. I am also left to wonder why PC Jones made no attempt to obtain protective clothing from the police stores, and why she did not consider that meeting Kouao at social services' offices also exposed her to a risk of infection. Finally, I consider that had PC Jones been advised by an individual at the hospital, she would have recorded the name of that person and the exact advice given, particularly bearing in mind her otherwise meticulous note keeping on CRIS.

14.67 On balance, I conclude that there was no conversation between PC Jones and a casualty nurse during which she was advised to take the precautions she claims. I consider it to be more likely that PC Jones decided for herself that she would not attend the home visit, and that she invented the story about seeking advice from the casualty department as a way to avoid criticism.

The views of the medical staff

14.68 On 5 August 1999, PC Jones went to the North Tottenham District Office for the arranged meeting with Kouao. It was at this point that she finally saw the 'statement' that Ms Arthurworrey said she had from a doctor. In fact, this turned out to consist of no more than a letter from Nurse Isobel Quinn. The effect of this letter was to put a stop to the police investigation in the same way that the third-hand report from Dr Schwartz had caused PC Dewar to abandon her investigation a few weeks earlier. The reason for this, according to PC Jones, was that the letter did not specifically say that Dr Rossiter (the named doctor for child protection) thought Victoria had been deliberately physically harmed.

14.69 The only mention of Dr Rossiter was the comment "Dr Rossiter ward round notes, evidence of emotional abuse". This comment was, at best, ambiguous. By no stretch of the imagination did this rule out deliberate physical harm as well. Apart from anything else, the glaring thing that was missing was an explanation for the belt buckle marks. For PC Jones to decide that there was no crime because of this letter was extraordinary.

14.70 The only basis upon which the investigation could properly have been stopped at this point would have been a clear statement from Dr Rossiter to the effect that she was sure that all of the injuries to Victoria, including the belt buckle marks, had innocent explanations. At the outset of her 'investigation', PC Jones had identified the need for a doctor's report. She closed the investigation without ever having received such a report, and without ever having ascertained exactly what the doctor's diagnosis of Victoria's injuries was.

14.71 PC Jones refused to accept that it was her role to make any inquiries herself with the doctors. She maintained the line that it was the doctors who should have told her if there was evidence of deliberate physical harm, and because Nurse Quinn's letter did not address the belt buckle marks at all, PC Jones assumed they were no longer an issue.

14.72 She failed to appreciate, because she never bothered to find out, that the letter from Nurse Quinn was simply a response to the task set at the strategy meeting for social services to get more information on the issue of emotional abuse. It was never intended that this letter should be taken as a full diagnosis of Victoria's condition and, as Dr Rossiter told the Inquiry, she actually thought that Victoria had suffered from "serious and appalling physical abuse", which is what she would have made clear had she been asked directly. Once again, a simple telephone call from a police officer to the doctor concerned may well have cleared up the misunderstanding.

14.73   The parallels with the experience of PC Rachel Dewar in Brent when dealing with the admission of Victoria to the Central Middlesex Hospital are clear. In both cases, there seems to have been an unwillingness by the officers concerned to evaluate the information fed to them concerning the diagnosis of the consultants concerned. The reason may well be a general reluctance, among junior officers in particular, to challenge the diagnoses of what they consider to be eminent medical practitioners. I have already indicated that I regard specialist child protection officers as bringing distinct and invaluable skills to the multi-agency investigation of possible crimes against children. They should not feel inhibited in questioning or challenging the diagnoses of paediatricians. To address this issue, I make the following recommendation:

> **Recommendation**
> Training for child protection officers must equip them with the confidence to question the views of professionals in other agencies, including doctors, no matter how eminent those professionals appear to be.

The meeting with Kouao

14.74   Returning to the meeting with Kouao on 5 August 1999, PC Jones said that the original purpose for her attendance, despite her view that there was no need to carry out a criminal investigation, was to explain to Kouao the child protection procedures and the purpose of police involvement. She said that the meeting, from her perspective, was no more than a "fishing expedition". This would seem to have been contrary to the view of Ms Arthurworrey, who said, "I understood Constable Jones's role as to investigate potential crimes against Victoria." That, of course, is precisely what PC Jones should have been doing.

14.75   In addition to her failure to get to the bottom of the belt buckle marks observed on Victoria's body, PC Jones failed throughout her involvement with the case to address the two to five-hour time delay between Victoria suffering the burns, and her being taken to hospital by Kouao. She told me that she had simply overlooked this important discrepancy – as had Sgt Cooper-Bland when he took the referral on 28 July 1999.

14.76   This was regrettable because, when they met, Kouao repeated to her and Ms Arthurworrey that the scalding incident occurred at 3pm. This would have been the ideal opportunity to ask why they did not arrive at the hospital until after 5pm. Indeed, the CRIS report, which was PC Jones's main working document, said the scalding incident happened at midday, so there was a potential five-hour delay which should have been uppermost in her mind. I got the impression that PC Jones had by now completely closed her mind to the possibility that Victoria had been deliberately harmed, because it seems the meeting with Kouao was conducted in a very passive, non-interrogatory way.

14.77   This seemed to be confirmed by PC Jones when she said of Kouao, "She was not a suspect, she was a lady we were speaking to, to try to find things out about her circumstances, what had happened to her. It was not like a criminal interview, where I would be checking every detail that she said."

14.78 I believe that the police should bring to the child protection arena a healthy scepticism, an open mind and, where necessary, an investigative approach. By the time that she first met her on 5 August 1999, PC Jones seemed to be ready to accept anything she was told by Kouao, which meant that her presence during the interview was worthless. When asked why, during the course of a later home visit, she did not challenge any of the inconsistencies in Kouao's story, Ms Arthurworrey replied, "I am a social worker and I work with the facts as they are presented to me. As I have said to you, I was more trusting of Kouao when I went on that visit. I am not a detective. I had no reason to question what I saw and what I was being told at that point." If the unquestioning acceptance of information given by a carer is undesirable in a social worker, it is unacceptable in a police officer.

Interview with Victoria

14.79 During the interview, Kouao gave permission for PC Jones and Ms Arthurworrey to speak to Victoria. As a result, they went to the North Middlesex Hospital the following afternoon. Their failure to go immediately gave Kouao enough time to visit Victoria and possibly coach her about what to say during the interview. However, given that PC Jones had effectively abandoned any pretence at investigation at this stage, one can well understand why this consideration failed to occur to her.

14.80 PC Jones has little recollection of the questions they asked, and she told the Inquiry that she did not take any notes. In broad terms, she said Victoria's account was similar to that given by Kouao and that she made no allegations of crime. They spent about half an hour with Victoria. Apart from writing up, and 'no-criming' the CRIS entry when she got back to her office, that was the last action PC Jones took in connection with the referral received by the police on 28 July 1999.

14.81 In particular, both she and Ms Arthurworrey did not take any steps to obtain copies of the photographs taken by the hospital, which were so powerful and disturbing when they were shown during Phase One of the Inquiry. This meant that the respective managers in each agency, who should have been reviewing the work carried out by the two front-line staff, were not given the opportunity to see for themselves the extent of Victoria's dreadful injuries, and so possibly challenge some of the assumptions made.

14.82 In my view, PC Jones failed to conduct an adequate investigation of the crime committed against Victoria of which she became aware on 28 July 1999. In the process, she displayed what I consider to be gross incompetence.

The investigation into sexual abuse

Referral and allocation

14.83 At around 4.30pm on 1 November 1999, Paula Waldron, a civilian administration assistant at Haringey CPT, took a referral from Ms Arthurworrey to the effect that Victoria had been indecently assaulted. Ms Waldron began the CRIS entry and recorded that, early that morning, Kouao had telephoned Ms Arthurworrey to allege that Manning had sexually assaulted Victoria. She then allocated the case to PC Jones, because she had dealt with the family before. PC Jones was not on duty at this time, having left the office over an hour earlier. The first time she became aware that she was the investigating officer for this report of crime was the following morning when she came on duty.

Initial investigation

14.84 The following morning, PC Jones discovered that the matter had been allocated to her. She took no action to commence an investigation and, at some point during her shift, was informed by Ms Waldron that Kouao had withdrawn the allegation. Thereafter she did nothing to progress the case until the strategy meeting convened by social services took place.

14.85   When it was put to PC Jones that her entire investigation of the alleged crime committed against Victoria, up to and including 5 November 1999, amounted to no more than her attendance at this strategy meeting, she candidly replied "yes".

The November strategy meeting

14.86   As to the strategy meeting itself, it is worth repeating that this was a vital step in the conduct of the inquiry at which its future management was to be decided. As such, the need for the meeting should have been agreed between the key agencies involved and it should have taken place as soon as reasonably possible.

14.87   However, it appears that the police had no say in the timing or location of the strategy meeting and, once again, they simply turned up at North Tottenham District Office when they were told to. From the point of view of a criminal investigation, this was three days too late. A full inquiry should have been under way by 2 November 1999, if not on the afternoon of 1 November. The meeting was arranged for 5 November because Ms Arthurworrey was on a training course for a few days. This is certainly not a valid reason for holding up an investigation into a possible serious crime, and the police should have objected most strongly to the delay. These issues are discussed further in paragraphs 14.104 and 14.105.

14.88   The strategy meeting was chaired once again by Ms Kozinos. PC Jones again had no manager with her to take the lead in formulating police action, but she was accompanied by PC Pauline Ricketts, who happened to be at the North Tottenham District Office on other business. Ms Kozinos outlined the circumstances of the allegation by Victoria and the fact that Kouao had withdrawn it on Victoria's behalf.

14.89   During the course of the meeting, 15 separate tasks were identified and recorded by Ms Kozinos, of which the following five were assigned to PC Jones:

- Check with immigration.
- Carry out a check on Manning.
- Obtain a police statement from Kouao.
- Speak to Victoria.
- Possibly carry out a joint home visit with social services.

The investigation

14.90   As for speaking to Victoria, the minutes of the strategy meeting record that there was an agreement not to carry out a formal 'memorandum' interview or medical examination with Victoria at that stage. In other words, PC Jones agreed that, despite four days having elapsed since the original allegation, there was to be a further delay of unspecified length before she would have any opportunity to speak to the potential victim.

14.91   As far as the other action points allocated to her are concerned, PC Jones told me that she completed the relevant checks with the immigration service and the police national computer (presumably in respect of Manning) "during the course of the next few days". I would imagine that the work there consisted of two telephone calls.

14.92   She then decided to write to Kouao, in order to arrange an interview. Unbelievably, it was not until 12 January 2000, a period of about nine weeks after the strategy meeting, that this five-line letter inviting her into the office had been translated into French and posted to Kouao. PC Jones fully accepted that the delay was unacceptable and that she should simply have made a telephone call to Kouao or visited her at her house.

14.93   In the event, the nine weeks spent preparing the letter were wasted. Simply inviting Kouao to attend the police station on either 26 or 31 January 2000, was completely inadequate. Unsurprisingly, Kouao failed to keep either appointment and, on 7 February 2000, PC Jones contacted Ms Arthurworrey one last time about the case. She was told that social services had not made any contact with the family either, and so she decided to close the police case completely. The CRIS entry was updated accordingly.

14.94   In respect of this second referral, the suggestion was again made to PC Jones that she should have done more to progress the investigation. In particular, it was put to her that she should have arranged a memorandum interview of Victoria immediately upon hearing of this serious allegation of sexual assault. PC Jones disagreed that this step was appropriate, but I am certain that it was fundamental in establishing what was really going on in Victoria's life.

Deficiencies in supervision

14.95   I heard a large volume of evidence about the supervision, or lack of it, provided to PC Jones during the course of her involvement with Victoria. I was left with a remarkably similar impression to that of Brent CPT, with blurred lines of accountability and managers with little idea as to what their front-line staff were doing.

14.96   The importance of this issue cannot be overstated. Although I have been critical of PC Jones, I believe she was let down completely by her managers. The system of supervision by managers at Haringey CPT was totally ineffective. I address these comments not only in respect of her immediate managers, but also of more senior managers, including DCI Wheeler, Detective Superintendent Susan Akers and Detective Chief Superintendent David Cox. These three senior police officers presided over child protection teams in the north west crime OCU, which lacked proper management systems and where overworked front-line staff were left to muddle through as best they could, sometimes making grave mistakes which were never identified and corrected.

14.97   I feel strongly that, incompetent though they were, both PC Jones (Haringey) and PC Dewar (Brent), have borne the brunt of criticism both in the media and during this Inquiry, much of which should rightfully have been attributed to their line managers. These individual constables would not have been able to make such elementary mistakes if they had been properly supervised and guided by senior officers.

Supervision in Haringey

14.98   I have dealt specifically with the supervision provided in Brent CPT in section 13. I turn now to the situation in Haringey, as revealed by the evidence put before me.

14.99   According to the statement she submitted to the Inquiry, PC Jones reported directly to DI Howard during the period with which I am concerned, calling upon the assistance of whichever sergeant happened to be around as and when necessary.

14.100 I believe this to be an unsatisfactory arrangement. In order for managers to be held accountable, it is important that there is clarity about line management arrangements. It became clear that PC Jones, and presumably her colleagues, would just speak to whoever was around out of the inspector and two sergeants in the team. Obviously, there will be times when immediate advice is needed and it is appropriate to seek it from whoever is most readily available. However, if nobody has 'ownership' of the supervision of a particular officer or case, important issues can be missed and conflicting advice given. In any event, it seems as though there was no 'intrusive supervision' offered to PC Jones at all. In other words, if PC Jones did not ask for advice, she was just left to her own devices.

14.101 Before I deal with each investigation in turn, I want to make the point that, unlike their colleagues at Brent CPT (and, indeed, unlike the majority of managers from all the other agencies involved with Victoria), the inspector and sergeants from Haringey CPT fully accepted that they had badly let down Victoria, her family and PC Jones. Their acceptance of their management failures certainly gives me hope that at least some officers will genuinely learn from this dreadful case and, faced with a similar situation in the future, will take a different course of action. I was impressed by the manner in which they gave their evidence and wish to give them credit for their honesty and frankness before me.

Supervision of first investigation

14.102 On 28 July 1999, Sgt Cooper-Bland received the telephone referral from social services to say that Victoria had been admitted to hospital with serious injuries. I have already expressed my view that it is important that a supervisor is aware of all referrals as they come in and, whether by luck or design, that was the case here.

14.103 However, almost immediately, things started to go wrong. Sgt Cooper-Bland explained his decision to send PC Jones to the July strategy meeting in the following way: "I decided that as PC Jones was already at the social services office on another matter, it would be a sensible use of resources to ask that she attends the strategy meeting."

14.104 I have already indicated that I regard such an approach to be inadequate, and expressed my preference for social services and the police jointly to agree on the location and timing of strategy meetings. In order for such a system to work, there needs to be a relationship of mutual co-operation with social services so that strategy meetings are held at times and in places of mutual convenience. It may well be that the dominant status afforded by the police to Haringey Social Services may have influenced Sgt Cooper-Bland in his decision to send the officer who would enable the strategy meeting to go ahead as scheduled.

14.105 I also repeat my firm belief that all strategy meetings or discussions should include a manager from the key agencies. In this case, either Sgt Cooper-Bland or one of his senior colleagues should have gone with PC Jones to support her, and to ensure that operational decisions were made which would enhance the investigation into this serious crime.

14.106 In effect, PC Jones ended up allocating Victoria's case to herself by virtue of the fact that she happened to be at the North Tottenham District Office at a time convenient for social services. In my view, it is not appropriate for junior officers in PC Jones's position simply to allocate cases to themselves. It must be seen as part of the function of supervising officers in a CPT carefully to allocate work to their junior officers, and afterwards to assume specific and direct responsibility for the supervision of the case. Neither of these key steps were taken in Victoria's case.

14.107 Having instructed PC Jones to attend the strategy meeting on behalf of the police, Sgt Cooper-Bland failed to ask her for an update after the meeting had taken place and he had approved PC Jones's decision to deal with the case herself. In my view, this was a critical omission as it clearly indicates that Sgt Cooper-Bland had no intention of playing any further part in the case from this point onwards. When it was put to him that his inactivity in this regard pointed "to a total lack of supervision in this case", he candidly replied that it did.

14.108 In fact, Sgt Cooper-Bland had brief involvement with Victoria's case on two further occasions. The first was on 4 August 1999, when he recalled having a conversation with PC Jones about a contagious disease and she informed him that she was cancelling a home visit. He would not appear to have questioned or challenged this decision of PC Jones, and he certainly failed to ask the obvious question of why she was prepared to allow Victoria to return to a house that she was not prepared to visit herself.

14.109 Second, on 8 August 1999, Sgt Cooper-Bland endorsed the CRIS entry to indicate that he was content with the way the investigation was progressing. However, in reality he knew nothing about the conduct of the investigation or the fact it had effectively ceased several days previously. Far from constituting supervision, his involvement on this occasion amounted to no more than the unquestioning assumption that all must be well. I agreed entirely with his own assessment of his involvement at this stage when he said, "Regrettably my last supervision occurred at a stage when Karen Jones was still carrying out inquiries into the case. My supervision on that occasion, on 8 August, was not rigorous and I can honestly say that I did not look at the crime in sufficient detail to take in all the information."

14.110 Sgt Bird was also briefly involved in the case on 4 August 1999. Despite the fact that he knew nothing whatsoever about the background to the case, PC Jones apparently expressed concerns to him, as well, about carrying out the home visit as "the child had scabies". Sgt Bird recalled that he advised her to seek advice from the Metropolitan Police occupational health service. Crucially, he said that he "fully expected her to carry out the home visit at some stage in the near future". As subsequent events demonstrated, this assumption was incorrect and would suggest that he should have specifically directed PC Jones to carry out the visit once the appropriate advice had been obtained.

14.111 The next tier of supervision consisted of DI Howard. In his supervision of the first investigation carried out by PC Jones, DI Howard looked at the CRIS entries on 29 July and 9 August 1999. It should have been obvious to him, certainly by 9 August, that this investigation was not being carried out adequately. Nonetheless, he endorsed the CRIS entry in such a way as to indicate he was content. I do not believe he would have done so if he had taken anything more than the most superficial interest in the case. At the very least, he should have spoken to PC Jones about the investigation which, as he understood it, was still ongoing.

14.112 He admitted frankly that his supervision of PC Jones's handling of the first referral concerning Victoria was inadequate. I agree with his assessment.

14.113 I was told that, after DCI Wheeler conducted his review, a new system of supervision was introduced in the team, whereby each sergeant supervises the cases of a particular group of officers. When asked if this was an improvement, Sgt Bird replied, "It is far better because it focuses your mind on that particular officer's investigations. There were also bi-weekly, or fortnightly meetings arranged as well, to sit down with that officer and go through any difficult cases. In practice, we tried to go through all cases. The outcome of that was we took a lot less investigations on ourselves and that freed us up to do the job that we were employed to do, which was supervise."

14.114 I welcome the change and believe its effectiveness illustrates the inadequacy of the arrangements in place when Victoria's case came to be dealt with by Haringey CPT.

Supervision of second investigation

14.115 Turning now to the second referral, in November 1999, I see no reason why an administrative assistant such as Ms Waldron should not have taken the referral and made the initial CRIS entry. However, arrangements should have been in place to ensure that any discussion with social services about the timing of the beginning of the investigation, or the deploying of a particular officer, was carried out by a police manager. The fact that PC Jones had previously dealt with the family was no basis for automatically allocating this case to her. Regardless of the merits of the decision to do so, the decision itself should have been taken by one of the supervising officers following a consideration of all available information.

14.116 It would appear that the first time any supervisor became aware of this investigation was 11 November 1999, when Sgt Hodges carried out a routine check of CRIS. This was now 10 days after the original allegation by Victoria, and five days after the strategy meeting.

14.117 Like his colleagues, Sgt Hodges did nothing but note the CRIS entry, paying no attention to the fact that PC Jones was failing to carry out the tasks allocated to her at the strategy meeting. When asked how his failure to supervise could be explained, he said, "I have to accept responsibility for the actions of my staff. What we did not have at the time was this robust intrusive level of supervision, because the supervisors were relying on the staff to tell them how to do the job and this was a problem for us because we did not have the experience."

14.118 While I accept that there may have been elements of his role that remained unfamiliar to Sgt Hodges at this stage (he had, after all, only been in post for 13 days), he had been a sergeant for nine years. As such, he should have been entirely familiar with the basic principles of good supervision, one of which, in my opinion, is the need to satisfy oneself that the basic steps in an investigation have been taken.

14.119 At some stage, Sgt Hodges recalled that PC Jones expressed concerns about the delay in getting the letter translated into French, and he provided the bland advice that she should "chase up the transcription service". Perhaps if he had inquired more closely, he would have found that the consequence of the letter not being translated was that several weeks had now passed without the victim of possible sexual abuse having been spoken to by the police.

14.120 The final chance for a supervising officer at Haringey CPT to make a difference to Victoria's life was on 5 February 2000, when Sgt Hodges looked at the CRIS entry again. In evidence, he described what happened by saying, "On that occasion I left a message on the CRIS machine for Karen [PC Jones] to update on the result of the meeting that she was meant to have had with Kouao on 31 January. So I was not being robust, but I was asking what was happening, I was trying to progress this investigation. Karen has then replied to that memo two days later. I have not looked at the CRIS report after that. Unfortunately the CRIS report was closed by an officer outside of our department and I had no idea at that time that that investigation had actually been ended." I need not labour the obvious failure of supervision revealed by this explanation.

14.121 Sgt Hodges accepted that he failed to supervise PC Jones's handling of the sexual abuse allegation, but sought to justify this by a lack of training and experience. When asked, "Do you accept that you failed to adequately supervise Police

Constable Jones in the criminal investigation of the sexual abuse allegation?" he replied, "I accept it. I did not have the experience or the training necessary at that time to fully supervise Karen Jones. She was a very experienced child protection team officer, and in many respects I was learning from her. What I did offer was some form of guidance and supervision within my limited capacity at that time."

14.122 As I have already indicated, my view is that little in the way of specialist knowledge of child protection work, or the particular working practices of Haringey CPT, would have been necessary for Sgt Hodges to realise that basic steps in the investigation of this serious allegation had yet to be taken.

14.123 DI Howard was also ineffectual in any supervision of this sexual abuse allegation, and provided no safeguard for the inadequacies of his sergeant. Despite examining CRIS four times, on 29 November 1999, 29 December 1999, 8 January 2000 and 26 January 2000, he did nothing which actually caused PC Jones to carry out the tasks allocated to her. He accepted the proposition, put to him by Counsel to the Inquiry, that these examinations of the CRIS entry should have prompted him to tell PC Jones to "get the investigation moving".

14.124 In addition to the review by DCI Wheeler to which I have already referred, there was another review into Haringey CPT carried out after Victoria's death called *Operation Blue Martin*. When dealing with the supervisory standards at Haringey CPT, the report was scathing. It said, "Put very bluntly, all three sergeants gave no active supervision to the investigating officer." I entirely agree with this judgement and note that these were not newly-promoted officers – each of them had several years' supervisory experience to fall back on. Therefore, I do not excuse them in any way for failing in their basic duty to ensure the crimes committed against Victoria were properly, and professionally, investigated.

Internal police reviews of Haringey CPT

14.125 When Victoria died, the MPS was clearly concerned about the working practices at Haringey CPT, and as a consequence instigated a series of reviews by senior police officers.

14.126 Before I say anything about these reviews, I was surprised that the MPS seemed to overlook the fact that Brent CPT had also failed Victoria by conducting an incompetent investigation earlier, in July 1999. There was never any formal review of Brent practice, and even the internal management review, carried out for the ACPC Part 8 process, was written by the line manager, DI Michael Anderson. Not surprisingly, it contained no criticism of the police. As I am sure has become clear in this Report, I consider the practice in Brent to have also fallen well below acceptable standards, and the MPS should have recognised this at an early stage.

14.127 On 29 February 2000, DCI Graham Sterry from the Westminster CPT was instructed to review the two criminal investigations carried out by Haringey. His report was named *Operation Blue Martin*. DCI Sterry reported that he and his team were hampered by the possibility of disciplinary proceedings because it meant they felt unable to speak to PC Jones directly. I have already made the point that this review was highly critical of the managers, but it also concluded that the CRIS entries showed investigations were incomplete in many areas and caused serious concern. They wrote that the "clear disclosure of sexual abuse had not been investigated by police", and also "a thorough investigation into the allegations of physical abuse was clearly not made by PC Jones, nor is any effective supervision noted".

14.128   At the same time as *Operation Blue Martin* was being completed, Commander Brown, the new Commander (Crime) for the area, commissioned another review to be carried out in Haringey, and this was led by DCI Wheeler. His report was dated 8 March 2000. I am astonished that DCI Wheeler was asked to carry out this task. He had been DI Howard's line manager during the relevant period and could hardly be expected to provide an entirely independent and objective assessment in view of his responsibility for the work of the team.

14.129   Both reviewers found an office lacking in administration systems and management organisation, with poor supervision of cases by the inspectors and sergeants. They both highlighted difficulties with Haringey Social Services, in particular their attitude towards the police and their working practices. What was clearly missing from DCI Wheeler's report, however, was any comment about his own role, or any critical evaluation of the performance of the higher management within the OCU.

14.130   Finally, on 30 March 2000, DCI Wheeler completed a follow-up report to his review. He wrote that he was "somewhat dismayed" to find that some of the remedial action he had requested had not been carried out. He also spoke about a relaxed approach in the office to working hours and continuing problems with supervision.

14.131   I should state that all of the officers from Haringey CPT who were invited to comment on the issue vehemently denied that they took anything other than a responsible approach towards their working hours. In light of their frankness when dealing with other criticisms of them, I have some doubt as to whether DCI Wheeler's comments on this issue are justified. However, many of the problems revealed to me during the course of the evidence were echoed in the reviews of the team conducted in 2000.

14.132   It is a pity that a thorough and competent review of the working practices of Haringey CPT was not conducted soon enough to has helped Victoria. Her Majesty's Inspectorate of Constabulary (HMIC) has an important role in identifying whether police forces are efficient and effective, but its inspectors should also identify any particular elements of an individual force which are failing. There was no evidence that HMIC had identified, during its regular inspections of the MPS, the poor state of the CPIs as they were identified by the internal inspections I have just described. Therefore, I make the following recommendation:

> **Recommendation**
> The Home Office, through Her Majesty's Inspectorate of Constabulary, must take a more active role in maintaining high standards of child protection investigation by means of its regular Basic Commands Unit and force inspections. In addition, a follow-up to the *Child Protection* thematic inspection of 1999 should be conducted.

15 Child protection policing in north west London

15.1 The starting point for my consideration of police involvement in Victoria's case is the firm belief that children should enjoy the same protection from the law, and the same level of service from the police, as adults. 'Child protection policing' is no more or less than the investigation of crime. To treat it otherwise or to remove it from mainstream policing in either philosophy or operational practice is to do a grave disservice to the victims of such crime.

15.2 Therefore, I was very concerned to hear from a large number of officers who gave evidence before me, that child protection teams (CPTs) within the Metropolitan Police Service (MPS) were considered to be somehow 'different' from other police units. In particular, several officers told me that CPTs were the 'poor cousins' or 'Cinderellas' of the force.

15.3 Having listened to a large volume of evidence on this issue, I conclude that the impression gained by these officers as to the priority given to CPTs by the MPS at the time Victoria was alive in this country is accurate. I am firmly of the view that child protection policing in north west London during the second half of 1999 was given neither the attention nor the resources it needed and deserved.

15.4 All of the senior officers who gave evidence to the Inquiry were quick to accept that the work of CPTs is both vitally important and extremely challenging, involving the investigation of some of the most serious crimes. However, I have formed the view that at the time with which this Inquiry is concerned, there was an obvious difference between the priority and attention that these officers said the CPTs should have received, and that which they received, in reality.

15.5 This difference, it seemed to me, was most clearly revealed by the evidence concerning the following four aspects of child protection policing in north west London during the second half of 1999:

- training available to child protection officers
- number of qualified detectives working on child protection teams
- quantity and standard of equipment provided for the teams
- standard of accommodation provided for the teams.

I deal with each in turn.

Training

15.6 Every new recruit who joins the police takes a 15-week initial course followed by a series of two-week training modules during their two-year probationary period. A great deal of this training relates to the investigation of crime. On successful completion of their probation, all constables are expected to be able to deal with the investigation of crimes such as theft, assaults and actual bodily harm.

15.7 Those who wish to can apply to join the CID. As part of the selection process, they undertake a six-week CID foundation course. This is an advanced course for crime investigators, designed to improve an officer's skills in dealing with crimes such as serious assaults and sexual offences, as well as increasing his or her awareness of forensic science techniques, covert surveillance methods and the issues associated with the disclosure of unused material. I believe that some investigations undertaken by CPTs are so serious and complex that it is essential they are handled by officers who have had the benefit of advanced investigative training of this kind. I return to consider this issue in detail at paragraph 15.9.

15.8   However, all police officers should, as a result of their initial training, be aware of the basic principles of effective investigation. It may be unfortunate that neither of the two constables who dealt with Victoria were trained detectives. However, I do not think the almost total lack of effective investigation into any of the three referrals about her can be directly attributed to the fact that neither of them attended the CID foundation course.

Criminal investigation training

15.9   The obvious failures in the police's handling of Victoria's case are recorded in detail in the preceding sections. As Deputy Assistant Commissioner (DAC) William Griffiths memorably said, "In the A to Z of an investigation, that investigation did not get to B." I was also in agreement with Commander Michael Craik when he told the Inquiry "... all officers investigate. Probably any officer with more than two years' service, who has been properly assessed as being competent and has the relevant investigative skills, is capable of starting life working in child protection teams". He went on to say, "It is a cop's job, doing something. Police get called, they start an investigation. The first day a probationer walks out, they could be called to a house where a child has been abused."

15.10   Having listened to these experienced officers, I consider that any constable should be able to take the initial basic steps at the outset of a criminal investigation. As a result, I reject the suggestion made by some of the junior officers involved in Victoria's case that a lack of detective training excused their poor performance. PC Rachel Dewar, for example, told me she felt ill-equipped to deal with serious child abuse because she had only limited experience of criminal investigation, where the most serious level of crime she would deal with would be actual bodily harm. In my judgement, even a basic level of inquiry that would routinely be expected in a case of actual bodily harm could have been enough to discover that Victoria was being abused by her carers.

15.11   However, the MPS should take little comfort from the fact that it provided just enough training for these officers to do the basics. In my view, the organisation should have made sure that there were enough officers on CPTs, particularly those in a supervisory role, who were trained detectives. It seems to me to be self-evident that a child victim of a serious assault is entitled to expect at least the same level of expertise as an adult victim with similar injuries. If adults can expect to have serious assaults against them investigated by trained detectives, so should children in a similar situation.

15.12   During the relevant period, there were hardly any officers working in either Brent CPT or Haringey CPT who had attended the CID foundation course. Certainly none of the officers who worked on, or directly supervised, Victoria's case had done so. Detective Inspector (DI) Michael Anderson was the only manager within either of the CPTs who could properly be regarded as a 'career detective'.

15.13   The explanation for this situation doesn't seem to lie in the failure of local managers to ensure that their staff were appropriately trained. I was told that it is not possible for local managers to instigate CID foundation training. In any event, it would appear that at the time with which I am concerned, such training did not exist. Detective Superintendent (D Supt) Gary Copson told me, "There was no detective training course, there was no junior initial CID course for the

Metropolitan Police for nearly four years [prior to Victoria's death] to the best of my recollection. There was not any." Even if local managers had wanted to put their CPT staff on a CID foundation course in the years leading up to Victoria's death, they would have been unable to do so.

Child protection training

15.14   In addition to generic investigative training, CPT officers should have additional training to deal with the particular requirements of child protection investigation. Sergeant (Sgt) David Smith told me that such training was "vital" to the effective exercise of a CPT officer's duties. With regard to such training, the position within the MPS during the relevant period was haphazard to say the least. Despite having taken a large volume of evidence on the matter, it remains unclear exactly what training was available. Some officers recalled having attended courses ranging from three days to two weeks, but according to DI Anderson, child protection training had been stopped completely by the MPS training department in 1996. If this is right (and DI Anderson appeared confident in his recollection), the inevitable result was that, by 1999, many officers employed in CPTs had received neither CID training nor any form of child protection training.

15.15   The alternative arrangements, described by DI Anderson as "learning on the job", were, in my view, manifestly inadequate. I have formed the view that the officers in the CPTs of north west London at the time Victoria was alive in the area were insufficiently trained to equip them for the difficult job they were required to perform.

15.16   In an effort to ensure that similar deficiencies are avoided in other areas of the country, I make the following recommendation:

> **Recommendation**
> The Home Office, through Centrex and the Association of Chief Police Officers, must devise and implement a national training curriculum for child protection officers as recommended in 1999 by Her Majesty's Inspectorate of Constabulary in its thematic inspection report, *Child Protection*.

Staff levels

15.17   It would appear that, following Victoria's death, some consideration has been given by the MPS to the number of detectives working on CPTs. D Supt Copson expressed shock at what he found. He said, "I do not think I am easily shocked but it certainly shocked me to discover how few there were when I went round looking and counting." These sentiments were echoed by DAC Griffiths, who took over the child protection portfolio from Commander David Kendrick in February 1999. He told me that reading a survey about the distribution of detectives among the CPTs soon after he came into post had been a "shock and revelation" to him.

15.18   However, the problem was shared by other units within the force. I was told that many borough CID offices were also operating with few trained detectives during this period. Much of the explanation for this state of affairs would seem to lie in the combination of an unusually high murder rate in the year in question, and the transfer of a large number of detectives to murder teams following the report of Sir William Macpherson into the death of Stephen Lawrence. Indeed, Commander Carole Howlett, in her statement to the Inquiry, went as far as to say, "Anecdotal information would suggest that following the Macpherson Inquiry into the death of Stephen Lawrence, child protection teams were plundered in order to increase the numbers of personnel on murder investigation teams."

After Victoria's death

15.19 I do not wish to underestimate the scale of the challenges faced by the force in the period with which I am concerned. Nonetheless, the speed and apparent effectiveness of the measures it took to improve child protection policing in London following Victoria's death suggests to me that more could and should have been done at the time.

15.20 I was told that the MPS tried very hard after Victoria's death to improve the practices and composition of CPTs in the capital. Energetic new managers, such as Commander Howlett and Detective Chief Superintendent (DCS) Derrick Kelleher, were given the task of making sweeping changes. As a result, a new department called SO5 (the Child Protection Command Unit) was created, bringing all the CPTs in London under centralised control.

15.21 Much work has also been done to improve the status of child protection work within the force. A number of officers, including D Supt Copson, told me that there was a significant amount of "macho nonsense" in the force concerning the work of CPTs, which were sometimes referred to in a derogatory way such as "cardigan squads". One of the consequences of this low status was that the best detectives would be put off from applying to join these teams.

15.22 Among the initiatives that have been taken to address this problem is the designation of all CPT officers as "branch detectives". I cannot accept the utility of what is basically a cosmetic gesture that fails to address (and may even mask) the lack of real detectives on the teams, but I do welcome the sentiment behind it. Strong efforts must be made throughout the police force to raise the profile and status of child protection work to a level that its importance deserves, thereby encouraging high-calibre officers to apply.

15.23 It may, of course, prove to be the case that even after such efforts have been made, the number of detectives who voluntarily apply for postings on CPTs is insufficient. In those circumstances, I have considerable sympathy with the view of Commander Craik. He told me that in such circumstances, a degree of coercion might be required: "Sorry, you work for the police. We like to have committed volunteers, but if the need was great I would put people in there."

15.24 It is easy to state that there should be some detectives on CPTs, but it is harder to say how many. My view is similar to that shared by DAC Griffiths and Commander Kendrick. They said that a one-to-one ratio of "uniform background" officers against detectives was the aspirational target, but that at least one detective to every two "uniform background" officers was a realistic minimum. Drawing on the considerable experience of these officers, and in light of the evidence in Victoria's case, I make the following recommendation:

> **Recommendation**
> Chief constables must ensure that officers working on child protection teams are sufficiently well trained in criminal investigation, and that there is always a substantial core of fully trained detective officers on each team to deal with the most serious inquiries.

15.25 In addition to containing a suitable number of detectives, it is also important to ensure that CPTs are led by officers of sufficient rank and experience. In this regard, Commander Kendrick told me that, in his view, CPTs ought to be headed-up by detective inspectors. However, he acknowledged that during the period with which

I am concerned, this was not the case in nine out of 28 London CPTs – a situation he considered "unacceptable".

15.26   This is indicative, in my view, of the general state of CPTs in London in 1999, and it shows the priority they were accorded by the MPS as a whole. It would seem that the force was content to allow these teams to perform the vital work of protecting children with, in many cases, insufficient numbers of detectives and inadequately qualified managers.

Equipment

15.27   The Inquiry heard from several witnesses that the CPTs were lacking equipment essential to the proper conduct of their functions. Police vehicles were scarce, computer equipment was outdated and inadequate, and offices were poorly decorated and equipped.

15.28   As to the significance of these deficiencies, I have considerable sympathy with the views of DAC Griffiths who told me, "I do not believe that the lack of provision of resources such as IT, vehicles and so on are actually a reason for not doing your job. Clearly it is desirable for everyone to have the tools they need to do their job but these were not tools that would prevent an officer performing simple, straightforward tasks that are to do with the core role of policing. So whilst I accept the desirability, I do not accept that it is a reason for failing in your duty."

15.29   However, while inadequate facilities may in themselves have had little direct impact on the manner in which Victoria's case was handled, the less tangible effects may have been considerable. I have already expressed the opinion that the CPTs in London were given unacceptably low priority by the MPS as a whole. In addition, the status of the work was low and there was little incentive for high-calibre officers to apply for postings on the teams. The feeling that one's work is not valued or considered important can have a corrosive effect. It damages morale and leads to poor performance. In light of this, and in view of my conclusion that the MPS failed to provide CPTs with adequate equipment of a standard enjoyed by many other branches of the force, I turn briefly to consider the particular deficiencies which were brought to my attention.

Vehicles

15.30   When SO5 was formed in early 2000, the new management team discovered that the 31 CPT sites had only seven police vehicles between them. When one considers that there were approximately 10 staff working from each site, it is clear that this level of provision was inadequate.

15.31   The undesirable consequence of this state of affairs was that officers were obliged, where possible, to use their own cars for police business. In my view, it is wholly inappropriate for officers to be expected to transport detained suspects, or child victims being taken for an interview, in their own private vehicles. Quite apart from the potential insurance difficulties and a lack of necessary equipment (such as child seats), it simply reinforces the impression of a somewhat amateurish and low-priority operation.

15.32   I was very pleased to hear that there are now five times as many vehicles allocated to the CPTs in London as there were in 2000.

Information Technology

15.33   The computer applications used by the MPS at the material time were:

- CRIS – a crime recording system
- OTIS – an office management system
- CRIMINT – a criminal intelligence system.

The evidence I heard indicated that the CPTs were limited in the access they had to all three.

15.34 The problem appears to have been particularly acute with regard to OTIS. Witnesses from all levels of the organisation stated that there were few OTIS terminals readily available to CPT officers. DI Anderson, for example, told me, "What we did not have, unfortunately, was OTIS. You have heard about OTIS, effectively an important telecommunications system within the Metropolitan Police, something which I had asked for personally from the borough we were working for and been refused it, and something which repeated requests I think from all the CPT DIs have been made for, and we were simply assured that yes, we would get it, but the timescale kept getting put back and back."

15.35 A similar picture was painted by Sgt Smith, who said, "I felt very much that we were the poor relations in regard to information technology. A system called OTIS has been mentioned. The OTIS system enables communication throughout London by computers such as email, it allows police notices and orders to be accessible to every police officer in London at the touch of a button. OTIS was introduced in the Metropolitan Police. I know that DI Anderson continued to try to get us access to this, and the information that was fed back to us was that there was a rolling programme and we were at the back end of this rolling programme."

15.36 Even where a particular application was available for use by a CPT, there was no guarantee that it was operationally effective. Sgt Alan Hodges told the Inquiry, "When I arrived at Haringey Child Protection Team they had two computers that were stand-alone systems, very old, liable to break down on a regular basis. The only other system we had was the CRIS system, which was causing us problems at that time, technical problems. We also had access to OTIS but we had one machine in the police station, it was one floor above us, it was not our machine. Again we had link problems with the main server, which virtually made it unusable for our staff."

15.37 When asked about the CRIMINT system, he said, "The problem we had with CRIMINT, it was available to us on that one OTIS machine but it would take 20, 30 minutes to be able to access the system, which was not good enough. We could not spend 20, 30 minutes waiting by a computer waiting for it to warm up."

15.38 PC Karen Jones's experience of using Haringey's CRIS machines was similar. When asked if they were user-friendly, she replied, "No, they would break down. The first one we had was just old, an old machine. The station has stopped using that type of machine. The new one that we got was the newer type that stations were using, but they would still break down, they would often freeze, just lock. You might get the screen and you could not get rid of the screen whatever button you pressed."

15.39 The deficiencies in the IT facilities with which they were provided by the MPS led some CPTs to develop their own individual methods of recording referrals. The most obvious disadvantage of this practice was that it meant that individual CPTs were operating virtually in isolation, unable to share information electronically with their counterparts in other boroughs. Apart from reinforcing the impression of amateurishness surrounding the work of the CPTs, the practical impact of this state of affairs is well illustrated by Victoria's case. None of the officers in Haringey CPT ever became aware, before her death, that Victoria had been the subject of police protection in Brent a mere two weeks before she first came to their attention.

15.40 I was told by Commander Howlett and DCS Kelleher that the MPS is planning to purchase and install systems called PROTECT and MERLIN, which will vastly improve the IT capabilities of the CPTs. I hope that this proves to be the case and that whatever the other advantages of these systems may be, they will facilitate the effective exchange of information between the capital's CPTs. Therefore, I make the following recommendation:

> **Recommendation**
> The Police Information Technology Organisation (PITO) should evaluate the child protection IT systems currently available, and make recommendations to chief constables, who must ensure their police force has in use an effective child-protection database and IT management system.

Accommodation

15.41   The impression I gained of CPTs being neglected by the MPS in the years leading up to Victoria's death was reinforced by the evidence I heard about the accommodation with which they were provided. For example, some teams were based in premises other than police stations. Commander Kendrick said that remoteness from the principal arena of police activity is seen by some as a problem, because it makes CPTs feel "semi-detached". I agree. I have already expressed the view that child protection policing, and the principles that underpin it, should not be viewed as somehow distinct from other forms of policing. It will inevitably prove more difficult to promote this view if the teams are physically separated from the rest of the force.

15.42   However, the simple fact of location within a police station does not appear to be a guarantee of adequate accommodation. Both Brent and Haringey CPTs were located in police-owned buildings and I heard considerable evidence concerning cramped conditions, poor heating systems and difficult access.

15.43   I will not labour the issue because, as I have indicated already, I see no direct correlation between the mishandling of Victoria's case and the accommodation in which the two CPTs concerned were housed. I will simply note that the poor state of the accommodation provided to many CPTs in London adds weight to my conclusion that they had been seriously neglected for some time. No doubt it also added to the feelings of isolation and poor status apparently experienced by many officers working in those teams.

15.44   Overall, the impression I gained from the evidence about the equipping and resourcing of CPTs in London during the period with which I am concerned, is entirely consistent with the findings of the report by DCS Kelleher who, in September 2000, was commissioned to explore what would be needed to bring the CPTs up to a suitable standard. Among his conclusions were the following: "Child protection teams have become the Cinderella of the Metropolitan Police Service ... they have been under-resourced"; and "Child protection teams have suffered ten years of neglect."

15.45   Having heard evidence relating only to CPTs in London, I am unable to comment on the extent to which the problems I have identified above are replicated across the country. In order to ensure that they are not, I make the following recommendation:

> **Recommendation**
> Chief constables must ensure that child protection teams are fully integrated into the structure of their forces and not disadvantaged in terms of accommodation, equipment or resources.

15.46 I heard evidence that suggested that part of the explanation for the long-term neglect of child protection teams, at least in London, may be due to the lack of prominence given to such policing by central government. It is a branch of policing, I was told, which very rarely finds its way onto the list of ministerial priorities. While this should not serve as an excuse for any failure to provide an adequate service to child victims of crime, it would be naïve to underestimate the impact of a strong lead from central government on this issue. With a view to prompting such a lead being given and responded to, I make the following recommendations:

> **Recommendation**
> The Home Office must ensure that child protection policing is included in the list of ministerial priorities for the police.

> **Recommendation**
> Chief constables and police authorities must give child protection investigations a high priority in their policing plans, thereby ensuring consistently high standards of service by well-resourced, well-managed and well-motivated teams.

Accountability

15.47 One of the principal problems I met in seeking to determine who was ultimately accountable for the state of the CPTs in north west London in 1999, was the conflicting evidence of senior officers as to whose job it was to ensure that the teams were adequately staffed and equipped. There would seem to be two potential candidates: the commander of the crime Operational Command Unit (OCU) in whose area the CPT was located, and the 'strategic portfolio holder' with responsibility for maintaining an overview of CPTs across London.

Commander Kendrick

15.48 The portfolio holder up to February 1999 was Commander Kendrick. His evidence did little to convince me that he had much direct knowledge or understanding of the manner in which CPTs were operating during the period he was in post. In 1998, some three years after he assumed responsibility for the CPT, he commissioned an inspection of CPTs across London as a whole. The results echoed many of the findings that I have recorded above: teams were understaffed with poorly trained officers and lacked basic equipment. Prior to this inspection, however, Commander Kendrick told me that he thought that the MPS was providing the CPTs with adequate resources and appropriately trained and qualified staff.

15.49 In my view, Commander Kendrick could not have held this view throughout the three years or so prior to the inspection unless he was anything other than seriously out of touch with the condition of CPTs on the ground. The situation in which they found themselves at the time Victoria's case came to be dealt with was not one which, in my view, could have arisen overnight, and I suspect that the conclusion of DCS Kelleher in his September 2000 report that the CPTs had suffered "ten years of neglect" is sound.

15.50 On the assumption that the deficiencies revealed by his 1998 inspection had been present for some time, Commander Kendrick was asked why there had been no mechanisms in place to bring them to his attention. He replied that mechanisms should have existed within the relevant crime OCUs for identifying and addressing such matters. He told me that he was not seeking to "pass the blame" for the neglect of CPTs to area commanders, but did invite me to conclude that such commanders should be seen as having a degree of "operational responsibility" for the state of the CPTs in their OCU.

Commander Campbell

15.51   For five years leading up to March 1999, the commander (crime) for the OCU which included both Brent and Haringey CPTs was Malcolm Campbell. It was plain from his evidence that he regarded the adequate resourcing and training of CPT officers as the responsibility of Commander Kendrick as the portfolio holder. He told me, "David Kendrick already had meetings, I am not sure of the frequency of these, with the DIs from child protection teams. He was their champion, as it were, to improve their lot, to gain them better resources." When asked if he accepted that he had failed to take sufficient steps to address issues of training and resourcing within the CPTs, he replied, "No, I brought them to the notice of Commander David Kendrick."

15.52   The problem is clear. The two officers who ought to be taking responsibility for ensuring that the CPTs were properly staffed and equipped had inconsistent views as to their respective responsibilities in this regard. Put simply, each thought that the other was doing more than was in fact the case. The inevitable consequence was that not enough was done by either.

15.53   My view is that Commander Campbell, as the commander (crime) for the OCU in which Brent and Haringey CPTs were situated, was responsible for the performance of those teams. As such he should have made sure that he was properly informed about the condition of the teams and the quality of their work. I find that he did not do this, and that he demonstrated precious little understanding of the state of the CPTs in his area or the problems that they faced. This, in my view, amounts to a fundamental gap in the knowledge and awareness of a senior officer in Commander Campbell's position. The work of CPTs is of central importance to all police forces. It is vital that senior officers have an understanding of that work and an appreciation of the challenges faced by the teams. In order to increase that understanding, I make the following recommendation:

> **Recommendation**
> The Home Office, through Centrex, must add specific training relating to child protection policing to the syllabus for the strategic command course. This will ensure that all future chief officers in the police service have adequate knowledge and understanding of the role of child protection teams.

Commander Craik

15.54   Commander Campbell was succeeded in April 1999 by Commander Michael Craik, who held the post of commander (crime) throughout the period that Victoria was alive in Brent and Haringey. The timing of his appointment was such that, even if he had wished to make radical changes to the CPTs, he could have achieved little in time to help Victoria. However, it is fair to say that, whatever the explanation, Commander Craik's level of awareness about the state of the CPTs under his operational command at the time Victoria's case was being dealt with, was little different to that of his predecessor.

15.55   Commander Craik accepted from the outset of his evidence to the Inquiry, that he was responsible for the operational performance of the CPTs in the north west London area during his time in post. When asked by Counsel for the MPS to what extent he personally accepted responsibility for police failures that may have contributed to Victoria's death, Commander Craik candidly replied, "My officers let Victoria and her parents down. I was responsible for those officers. I was the commander. By anybody's definition – you can go through job descriptions as much as you like – I was the boss in the organisation. If they let the family down and Victoria down, I let them down, and I would like to apologise to them for that." This was refreshing to hear. I was impressed by Commander Craik's evidence, and the manner in which he gave it.

15.56   I will say one more thing about Commander Craik, which applies equally to DCS David Cox. Following Victoria's death, it was essential that her killers were identified and successfully prosecuted. The crime OCU managed by these two senior officers, which let Victoria down so badly when she was alive, appears to have carried out a highly professional and detailed murder investigation, which resulted in the conviction of both Kouao and Manning. It is right to give the MPS, and the North West Crime OCU, credit for that successful investigation.

15.57   I recognise the difficulty faced by senior officers in the MPS in maintaining an accurate picture of the standards of work carried out by individual police units operating across the capital. I was reminded during the course of the Inquiry that the MPS is an organisation with 40,000 employees operating from more than 100 sites. One of the principal challenges posed by the management of large organisations such as this, is to be able to retain a feel for life on the 'shop floor'. I do not underestimate the scale of that challenge.

15.58   In order to be able to meet it, it seems to me that senior officers need regular and reliable intelligence from their junior staff. In view of this, I turn now to consider the level of awareness of the condition of the CPTs demonstrated by officers further down the chain of command who gave evidence to the Inquiry.

DCS David Cox

15.59   I start with DCS Cox, who took considerable trouble in both his written and oral evidence to ensure that I was aware of the context in which he and his officers were working in north west London in 1999. Of particular relevance, I was told, was the unusually high murder rate. Put briefly, his area of London had the misfortune to be the scene of 92 murders during the course of that year. This, apparently, is equivalent to the total number of murders dealt with in a typical year by the whole of Greater Manchester Police plus West Midlands Police plus any other county's police force.

15.60   The fact that there were a large number of murders occurring in north west London in 1999 cannot explain or excuse the individual failings of the officers who had direct contact with Victoria's case. However, it may help in understanding why more senior officers in the OCU failed to give the CPTs the attention they deserved. Whatever the explanation, it was clear from his evidence that DCS Cox was not aware of the true state of the CPTs for which he was responsible. Much of his evidence is summarised well by the following answer: "I realised, certainly, the situation on the murder teams was out of control. I do not think I realised the situation on the CPTs was as desperate as it was. I thought they were in better shape."

15.61   Regardless of the murder rate, the CPTs were a critical part of the OCU for which DCS Cox was responsible. Therefore, it was essential that he took the necessary steps to find out whether they were operating in a satisfactory manner. It is plain to me that he either had no mechanisms in place for keeping abreast of the state of his CPTs, or that those mechanisms were inadequate. My overall impression is that DCS Cox, like many of his senior colleagues, actually paid little regard to the CPTs under his command in 1999 because he did not see them as a high priority.

D Supt Susan Akers

15.62 It is possible that DCS Cox drew some comfort from the fact that his deputy, D Supt Akers, was herself a former child protection detective inspector, and appeared to take a keen interest in that side of the work. Of the three detective superintendents working in the crime OCU, she was the one who, for most of the relevant period, had specific responsibility for managing the CPTs. DCS Cox plainly thought that D Supt Akers was keeping a close eye on the teams. He told me, "Child protection was always a topic which Sue had on her lips, so I felt that she was doing that, and she had a good grasp."

15.63 D Supt Akers's view was somewhat different. She said that although she had nominal responsibility for the CPTs, the huge bulk of her work was with the murder squads. Once again, there appears to have been some confusion between senior officers as to the extent to which their colleagues were monitoring and taking responsibility for the work and condition of the CPTs. In my view, this further supports the conclusion that CPTs in the period with which I am concerned had slipped a very long way down the MPS's agenda.

DCI Philip Wheeler

15.64 I deal finally with DCI Wheeler, the most senior officer in the crime OCU who was not heavily engaged in murder inquiries in 1999. As I have stated above, it is vital that senior managers in large organisations of any sort receive accurate intelligence from their subordinates as to the state of affairs on the 'shop floor'. Within the context of the CPTs, someone had to have the job of 'drilling down' into the individual teams to ensure that they were carrying out proper investigations and were adequately equipped for the task.

15.65 All the senior officers to whom this question was addressed were clear in their recollection that the person whose job it was to fulfil this function was DCI Wheeler. Unfortunately, DCI Wheeler did not agree. He told me that he was in no way responsible for the operational management of the CPTs and that his function was an administrative one only. Specifically, when asked if DCS Cox had expressly told him that this was to be the extent of his role, he replied, "He did indeed. I went and spoke to him after one of the reports and he said, 'Do your best, do the best you can' and it is simply administrative, and that is all."

15.66 This seems to me to be a critical matter. Either there was a senior officer responsible for determining whether the CPTs with which I am concerned were doing a good job or there was not. If there was, then he or she will inevitably bear some responsibility for the shortcomings evident in Victoria's case. If not, then one is left facing the remarkable conclusion that nobody in the MPS was charged with the operational management of the north west London area CPTs.

15.67 Furthermore, the practical result of this confusion would seem to be that nobody properly managed the CPTs of Haringey or Brent from within the crime OCU. DCI Wheeler said that he never visited those CPT offices during the relevant period because he did not see it as his role, and the respective detective inspectors confirmed that they hardly ever saw him. This is, frankly, disastrous management on the part of the MPS. For example, had a senior officer taken the trouble to visit Haringey CPT in the months leading up to Victoria's death, there is every chance that he or she would have discovered the same deficiencies in practice highlighted in the two reviews of the team conducted after Victoria's death. Had they done so, then steps could have been taken to remedy the situation in time to have helped Victoria. In view of the seriousness of these matters, I deal with this conflict of evidence in some detail.

15.68 Commander Craik was asked what his understanding of DCI Wheeler's role was in terms of the operational supervision of the CPTs. He replied, "I would expect him to have the capacity to get down and dip sample at that level, as well as checking what the inspector said and checking that the inspector was doing exactly the same thing, looking into the work and quality checking. I would expect him [the inspector] to be able to do some of that himself and verify it. But I would say Mr Wheeler would be the last point in that chain. Mr Wheeler could certainly do it for the number of officers under his command."

15.69 D Supt Akers was equally clear when she was asked if DCI Wheeler had responsibility for operational matters or whether his post was purely concerned with administrative matters. She answered, "both". When informed that DCI Wheeler's evidence was that DCS Cox had assured him that his (DCI Wheeler's) role with regard to the CPTs was purely administrative, D Supt Akers replied, "I find it incredible to believe that Mr Cox would have said that because his view, like my own, was that CPTs needed more than administrative support." When it was put to her that the differences between her and DCI Wheeler on this issue were irreconcilable, and that if her evidence is correct it must mean that DCI Wheeler is lying about what he was told by DCS Cox, D Supt Akers replied, "Yes, I am afraid it does."

15.70 For completeness, I should record that DCS Cox was adamant in his oral evidence that he never told DCI Wheeler that his (DCI Wheeler's) role was restricted to the administrative management of the CPTs and that he fully expected him to take operational responsibility as well.

15.71 I have to make a judgement about whether DCI Wheeler knew he was the operational line manager of the CPTs, or whether, as he put it, he was simply asked to look after their administration. I am satisfied not only that he was the operational line manager for the CPT detective inspectors, but also that he knew his role was to oversee the work of their teams and ensure they were operating to a high standard. He chose not to discharge that function, with the result that the CPTs with which I am concerned operated throughout 1999 without the benefit of any adequate operational supervision.

15.72 In reaching this conclusion, I have been influenced to some degree by the fact that I find it inconceivable that DCS Cox would have said to DCI Wheeler that he was just to act as an administrator. Even if that had happened, I would have expected DCI Wheeler immediately to point out that the result of such an arrangement would be the CPT detective inspectors operating unsupervised – a plainly unsatisfactory state of affairs. When this was put to him, DCI Wheeler replied that he did not do so because he did not see it as part of his function to bring such matters to the attention of his superiors. I reject his evidence in this regard. As a senior officer within the crime OCU it would plainly have been his responsibility to bring any inherent defects in the management structure to DCS Cox's attention. I find it inconceivable that he would have chosen to keep such matters to himself, had he indeed been given the wholly inappropriate role he claims.

15.73 The resolution of this issue has been far from easy but I was assisted to some extent by the insight into DCI Wheeler's working practices provided by D Supt Copson, who took over as his line manager in late 1999. He said of DCI Wheeler, "I think he was hard-working within his own definition and hard-working according to his own priorities, but his priorities were not my priorities, and they are not the priorities he should have had. Phil Wheeler was probably the most difficult supervision case I have had in 23 years' service and I tried hard for a long time to find a way of reaching him and persuading him that he ought to do things differently, and the conclusion I was forced to, was that he did not want to be managed."

15.74   The lack of supervision by DCI Wheeler was, in my view, a crucial factor in Haringey and Brent CPTs being allowed to deteriorate to the state they were in by the time they came to deal with Victoria's case. In the absence of any indication from him to the contrary, it was possible for more senior officers, when they thought about the CPTs at all, to think that all was well. The evidence that I have heard, together with the findings of the reviews of Haringey CPT carried out after Victoria's death, demonstrates precisely the opposite.

15.75   In my view, DCI Wheeler, given his operational responsibility for the CPTs involved, should have been aware that they were struggling to provide an adequate service. He should then have brought this information to the attention of more senior officers so that the deficiencies in the composition, resourcing and practices of the teams could have been addressed. His failure to do so means, in my view, that he must assume a great deal of responsibility for the flawed investigations that were carried out by those under his command.

16 Working with diversity

"There is some evidence to suggest that one of the consequences of an exclusive focus on 'culture' in work with black children and families, is [that] it leaves black and ethnic minority children in potentially dangerous situations, because the assessment has failed to address a child's fundamental care and protection needs."

Ratna Dutt, director, Race Equality Unit

16.1   Victoria was a black child who was murdered by her two black carers. Many of the professionals with whom she came into contact during her life in this country were also black. Therefore, it is tempting to conclude that racism can have had no part to play in her case. But such a conclusion fails to recognise that racism finds expression in many ways other than in the direct application of prejudice.

16.2   One of the ways in which race may play a part in a case involving a child is highlighted by the observation quoted above. This was made by Ratna Dutt, director of the Race Equality Unit, during the course of one of the seminars in Phase Two of this Inquiry. I believe it makes an extremely important point. Several times during this Inquiry I found myself wondering whether a failure by a particular professional to take action to protect Victoria, may have been partly due to that professional losing sight of the fact that her needs were the same as those of any other seven-year-old girl, from whatever cultural background.

The effect of assumptions

16.3   I do not for one moment suggest that the ill-treatment of Victoria by Kouao and Manning was either condoned or deliberately ignored by those responsible for Victoria's case. However, it may be that assumptions made about Victoria and her situation diverted caring people from noting and acting upon signs of neglect or ill-treatment.

16.4   Examples of such assumptions at work may include the following:

- Lisa Arthuworrey said that when she heard of Victoria "standing to attention" before Kouao and Manning she "concluded that this type of relationship was one that can be seen in many Afro-Caribbean families because respect and obedience are very important features of the Afro-Caribbean family script". Victoria's parents, however, made it clear that she was not required to stand in this formal way when she was at home with them. Therefore it seems Ms Arthurworrey's assumption was unfounded, in Victoria's case at least.

- Pastor Pascal Orome told me that he attributed Victoria's potentially concerning behaviour to the fact that she had come "freshly" from Africa. This of course was not the case – Victoria had been in Europe for almost a year by the time she came to his attention.

- On more than one occasion, medical practitioners who noticed marks on Victoria's body considered the possibility that children who have grown up in Africa may be expected to have more marks on their bodies than those who have been raised in Europe. This assumption, regardless of whether it is valid or not, may prevent a full assessment of those marks being made.

16.5   The danger of making assumptions of this kind is clear. Cultural norms and models of behaviour can vary considerably between communities and even families. The concept of Afro-Caribbean behaviour referred to in Victoria's case illustrates the problem. The range of cultures and behavioural patterns it includes is so wide that it would be meaningless to make generalisations, and potentially damaging to an effective assessment of the needs of the child. The wisest course is to be humble when considering the extent of one's own knowledge about different 'cultures' and to take advice whenever it is available.

16.6 Of course, it is impossible to assess after the event the likelihood of a particular step being taken in Victoria's case if she had been a white child. There were so many instances of bad practice in this case that one simply cannot begin to determine which of them may have been influenced by some form of prejudice, and which were due to incompetence or a lack of attention. However, it may well be that, at some point, the focus may have shifted from Victoria's fundamental needs because of misplaced assumptions about her cultural circumstances.

Fear of being accused of racism

16.7 There is another way in which race may have had an impact in Victoria's case. As Counsel to the Inquiry perceptively pointed out in his opening statement to the Inquiry, "Race can affect the way people conduct themselves in other ways. Fear of being accused of racism can stop people acting when otherwise they would. Fear of being thought unsympathetic to someone of the same race can change responses." He urged the Inquiry to keep an open mind on such matters.

16.8 Applying an open mind to the evidence I heard, I detected some hints of the sort of difficulties to which Counsel referred. The evidence of Dr Mary Rossiter provides one example. She said, "I was aware that as a white person I had to be sensitive to the feelings of people of all races and backgrounds, both clinically and with professionals. Maybe some social workers felt they knew more about black children than I did."

16.9 Those involved in the protection of children perform vital and difficult work. They should never feel inhibited from acting in a child's interests on the grounds that they are felt by others to have an insufficient grasp of the child's particular circumstances.

Child safety comes first

16.10 The basic requirement that children are kept safe is universal and cuts across cultural boundaries. Every child living in this country is entitled to be given the protection of the law, regardless of his or her background. Cultural heritage is important to many people, but it cannot take precedence over standards of childcare embodied in law. Every organisation concerned with the welfare and protection of children should have mechanisms in place to ensure equal access to services of the same quality, and that each child, irrespective of colour or background, should be treated as an individual requiring appropriate care.

16.11 There can be no excuse or justification for failing to take adequate steps to protect a vulnerable child, simply because that child's cultural background would make the necessary action somehow inappropriate. This is not an area in which there is much scope for political correctness. In my view, Dr Nnenna Cookey, a participant in the Phase Two seminars and a consultant paediatrician, put the matter very eloquently during the course of one of the seminars. She said, "I do take huge issue with the emphasis that black families should be assessed by or given the opportunity to have a black social worker. For me that detracts from the whole process. A child is a child regardless of colour. I think the social and cultural differences or backgrounds ... of these families is crucial and should be taken into account as part of a general assessment. But I think if we are not careful we'll lose the whole emphasis on the child's welfare. I think if we are not very careful we will send out the very wrong message that non-black social workers do not have the capabilities, the standards and everything that goes with it to assess black families. That would be a mistake, that will be wrong, and I think it does fly in the face of lots of social workers who are Caucasian, or whatever ... who are doing a very good job. I say that not because I want to be anti-establishment. I do not do political correctness when it comes to children. I really do think that these children may be further disadvantaged if we go down that track. I also feel that it means in some ways non-black social workers do not feel able to access the information they need regarding a child's cultural background."

16.12   I agree entirely. A child is a child regardless of his or her colour and he or she must be kept safe. Cultural issues must be considered but the objective is the safety of the child. The success of Ms Ackah and Avril and Priscilla Cameron in identifying the worrying signs that prompted them to seek the intervention of the authorities may have had much to do with the fact that they treated Victoria like any other little girl.

16.13   This was not an Inquiry into racism. But what cannot be ignored is that we live in a culturally diverse society and that safeguards must be in place to ensure that skin colour does not influence either the assessment of need or the quality of services delivered. That is the challenge to us all.

Part five: Learning from experience

17 The seminars

The purpose of the seminars

17.1 The Terms of Reference set for this Inquiry were not restricted to looking back in order to understand and evaluate the reasons for the failure of services to protect Victoria. The Inquiry was also required to look forward and make recommendations on how the safeguards for children might be strengthened in order to prevent a tragedy of this kind happening again.

17.2 To meet this challenge, the Inquiry organised a series of seminars, chaired by Neil Garnham QC. All the seminars were constructed around the essential elements of good childcare practice, and the processes designed to secure the safety and well-being of children.

17.3 An important aspect of the seminars was ensuring that the Inquiry's recommendations would not be based solely on a single tragic case, or on the performance of services in a part of north London. Therefore, those invited to participate were drawn from across the country and from a wide range of professional backgrounds. The wide-ranging experience of participants, and their commitment to serving children and families, was reflected both in the breadth and in the quality of the discussion at each seminar.

17.4 A list of those who contributed can be found in Annex 5. I take this opportunity to thank each one of them, and their employers, for helping the Inquiry. This section cannot do justice to the value of their contributions. Many participants also went to the trouble of submitting written material, which was greatly appreciated. This material and the seminar transcripts can be found on the Inquiry's website (**www.victoria-climbie-inquiry.org.uk**).

17.5 The first half of this section summarises key elements of the discussion under each of the seminar headings. It became apparent that although five topics had been selected for discussion, there was a marked degree of overlap between them. The level of agreement about how to improve services for children and families was striking. In recognition of this, overarching themes for improvement arising from the seminars are taken up in the second half of this section, and recommendations are made in relation to them.

Seminar one: Discovery and inclusion

17.6 The first seminar looked at how we can ensure that every child and their carer receive the full range of services they need and to which they are entitled. Most children and their carers come into contact with various agencies that operate nationally and locally. These include education, health, housing, social services, the police and social security. Discussion in this seminar focused on how to make the most of these opportunities to make sure that no child is lost to the system.

17.7 The mobility of England's population can make keeping track of children more difficult. The problem of discovering the existence of children was felt to be particularly acute in areas where children who have just arrived in the country are settled. These difficulties may be made worse by changes in practice of some services; for example, changes in the organisation of the work of health visitors. In addition, it was noted that some sectors of society feel excluded from, or are hostile to, any form of intervention by those whom they see as representing authority.

Keeping track

17.8   There is a well-developed system for recording the birth of a child and for connecting the child with the health visiting service and other health services. It should be noted, however, that organisational changes have affected the work of health visitors, who can often act as the 'eyes and ears' of the community. In the past, the health visiting service was based on geographical boundaries, but this is no longer the case. Under current arrangements, health visitors are mostly attached to GPs and relate to that GP's patient list, regardless of where the patient lives.

17.9   Once the child reaches school age, the health visitor will usually transfer his or her records to the school nurse. However, a school nurse may not always be available and children do not always attend school. Parents are entitled to educate their children at home. If a child has never attended school, as opposed to those who have been withdrawn once they have started, parents are not legally obliged to notify their local education authority of their child's existence. Families who move home are not obliged to inform the authorities of their movements. If parents do not do this, or do not then register the child with the authorities at their new address, it is particularly difficult to keep track of the child. Records held by the local health authority will not necessarily be transferred if the child's new address is not known and, as stated above, parents do not have to enrol their child at school. Therefore, there is no guarantee of successfully keeping track of all children, and there is likely always to be a small number of children who either remain unknown, or become 'lost' to the system.

New arrivals to the country

17.10   The problem in respect of children newly arrived in this country is perhaps more acute. The immigration service takes steps to ensure that information in relation to unaccompanied children arriving in this country is passed to the relevant authorities. An unaccompanied child seeking asylum is referred to the children's panel of the Refugee Council, which then provides support and advice to the child throughout the asylum process. They also ensure that the child is 'plugged into' the social and health services. Some local authorities have established teams that have direct links with the immigration service.

17.11   The situation is rather less satisfactory where children arrive in the UK as part of a 'family'. If a child arrives in the UK with people who appear to be his or her parents, and the immigration officer is satisfied that the family's documentation is genuine and their reason for entering the UK is acceptable, they will be given leave to enter and pass through immigration control. 'Families' who are EU citizens will be subject to only minimal scrutiny, if any at all. In such circumstances, no notification of the child's arrival in the UK is made to health, education or social services. One participant estimated that some 90 million people enter Britain each year, of which about 75 million do so as EU citizens.

Private fostering

17.12   Under current regulations, prospective foster parents must tell the local authority of private foster care arrangements. There is also an obligation on parents who are involved in having a child privately fostered. There is no duty, however, to approve or register private foster parents. It has to be recognised that a large number of children who are privately fostered do not become known to the authorities.

17.13   For children who live with their parents but go to a childminder every day, the position is different. Local authorities must keep a register of childminders and the registration system is based on the person being "fit" to look after children.

The local authority must also inspect the premises annually. It is an offence to provide daycare for children without being registered.

17.14   There was general agreement – with which I concur – that this inconsistency in the law should be removed. These issues were fully reported by Sir William Utting in the document *People Like Us*.

Hostility and exclusion

17.15   It was recognised that children may hesitate or be too frightened to approach agencies who may be able to provide help and support. Indeed, they may go out of their way to avoid identification by such agencies. It was agreed that ways must be found to make it easier for children experiencing difficulties to approach the agencies.

17.16   A number of participants agreed that there would be value in introducing a process whereby all practitioners who come across a child for the first time should, as a matter of routine, make sure they obtain basic information about the child and his or her family. This would include:

- the name of the child
- age
- address
- relationship to the primary carer
- whether he or she is registered with a GP and if so who
- if he or she is of school age, whether or not he or she is enrolled at and attending school.

17.17   This practice should be put into operation across all key agencies and include services such as housing and social security. If the response to any or all of these questions gives rise to concern it should trigger further inquiries. This may appear to be a rather simple suggestion to a complex problem, but on reflection I concluded that it would be yet another easy-to-operate safeguard, and if it secures the well-being of even a handful of children it will have justified itself.

Seminar two: Identification

17.18   The second seminar looked at ways of identifying, at the earliest possible stage, those children who may be in need of help or, if necessary, protection. It also considered how agencies can best work together to ensure a consistent approach.

Common thresholds

17.19   The seminar attempted to reach an understanding of what it was that we should be aiming to achieve for children. The responses supported the common objective of ensuring that each child is able to reach his or her maximum potential. While it is plainly the case that different agencies will have particular areas of responsibility, and that the broad objective of reaching maximum potential comprises a whole range of elements, it was encouraging to learn that there was this degree of agreement.

17.20   Participants considered whether it was possible to achieve the desired consistency of outcome in the absence of common thresholds of intervention. In other words, are common definitions of need necessary in order to ensure that all children receive the help they need to reach their potential?

17.21   This is important because it is clear that there are marked variations in both the understanding and the application of thresholds, not only across the country, but also between different services of the same authority. There would seem to be a number of reasons for this, of which the most significant was said to be the availability of resources. It was claimed that the only way in which services can work within the limited resources allocated to them is to apply eligibility criteria so as to control the number of children coming through the 'front door'. In particular, one unintended consequence of social services departments using thresholds in this way is that other agencies, seeking to refer a child, will often frame the referral in such a way as to prompt a response.

17.22 By acting in this way, the operation of the system becomes distorted. Instead of responding creatively to the particular needs of the individual child in an effort to achieve agreed outcomes, professionals become preoccupied by the categorisation of children in light of eligibility criteria. This means that not only do fewer children receive help of an early, preventive nature, but that also the degree of danger is sometimes exaggerated in order to secure action.

Identification of need in the local population

17.23 Some services have a better picture of both the problems and strengths of their local community than others. But it was clear from the discussion that there would be considerable benefit to be gained from all the services knowing their local communities better and by services being more accessible to the communities they serve. Key services could do this directly themselves or involve community-based organisations, such as voluntary and charitable organisations. Each local authority needs to develop a strategy to achieve this and to ensure that it happens in practice.

17.24 The benefits of such an approach are clear. If the analysis and strategic planning are done effectively, then the resources of the agencies involved can be targeted at the sections of the population with the greatest potential need. There is also the possibility that by using such an approach, the different agencies will be able to complement, rather than duplicate, each other's work.

Identification of individual children

17.25 After considering how need could better be identified on a community-wide level, the discussion turned to the identification of individual children. A number of participants explained their approach in identifying children potentially in need of services. It appeared that often there is considerable variation in the way guidance is applied to individual children – even between staff in the same agency.

17.26 In light of the high level of variability illustrated by this discussion, the seminar explored how greater consistency might be achieved in identifying children who may need a greater level of help. Four areas in particular received detailed consideration:

- the possibility of a 'common language' being developed by those working with children and families;
- whether a common referral form could be used by agencies when referring cases to social services;
- the question of whether a common assessment format could be developed for use by those working with children and families;
- whether common elements could be incorporated in the training of all staff working with children and families. At present it seems that such training is developed independently by each agency.

Sharing information and issues of confidentiality

17.27 The discussion then turned to the critical issue of how information collected could best be shared between agencies so that an accurate picture of the entirety of the child's situation could be formed.

17.28 Central to this question is the issue of confidentiality. Some participants had developed practical approaches to this issue, but many said there was confusion among professionals as to when they were allowed to share information with each other without the consent of the child or of his or her carers. The general view seemed to be that many professionals found that current guidelines rely too much on individual judgement and would be assisted by clear, central guidance on these issues, to which reference could be made by staff on a day-to-day basis.

Involving other groups

17.29 Having considered how best to use the information gained by practitioners as a result of their contact with children, alternative sources of information were discussed. The discussion was concerned with obtaining information from the children themselves, from voluntary and community organisations, and from the community-at-large.

17.30 There was general agreement that improvements are necessary in the way that staff in the different services talk to children and how staff use the information given. A range of suggestions was made. However, a point that was returned to time and time again was the need for a relationship of trust between practitioner and child. Clearly, some children tend to react badly to authority and, as said at paragraph 17.15, tend to be fearful of the consequences of confiding in someone in a position of authority. It was suggested that this distrust of authority means that voluntary and community organisations are particularly important when identifying need among children. The potential contribution of the general public was discussed, and the general view was that the 'eyes and ears' of the community are not used enough in the identification of children potentially in need. It was felt that efforts should be made to encourage more members of the public to come forward with their concerns.

Seminar three: Determining requirements

17.31 Having identified children and families in need of extra help and support from the agencies, the third seminar went on to explore how a thorough assessment of their needs should be carried out, and how an appropriate plan of action could be put in place to meet those needs.

Essential elements of a good assessment

17.32 The seminar began by examining what constitutes a good assessment of a child's needs and what commonly prevents a good assessment from taking place.

17.33 There was general agreement that the essential prerequisite of good assessment is clearly defined and agreed objectives. Without a clear idea of what the assessment is attempting to achieve, the staff involved will inevitably face considerable difficulty in conducting it in a practical and focused way. The basic aim of any assessment of a child should be to understand the child in his or her social situation.

17.34 A number of participants were also able to draw on their experience of the assessment process to provide a number of helpful pieces of practical guidance for general use. Some of the most useful suggestions were:

- allowing sufficient time in the assessment process to listen to the views of the child concerned, as well as to those of the family;
- information that the assessment will be based on should be collected in a systematic way;

- those conducting the assessment must be prepared not just to record information, but to analyse it and consider its potential significance;
- conclusions that are reached must be recorded so that those who come to deal with a case at a later stage are aware of the analysis that has already been made.

Obstacles to a good assessment

17.35　Three obstacles were identified as particularly significant.

17.36　First, the limited resources within which all the relevant agencies are required to operate, and the resulting need to prioritise the provision of services, means that in some cases, assessments are focused on identifying immediate risk to the child, rather than his or her needs.

17.37　Second, there is a tendency among many social workers to assess cases as either section 17 or section 47 at an early stage of the assessment process. The purpose of drawing such a distinction is to attempt to ensure that the available resources are targeted at the most serious cases. However, there are two principal problems with such an approach. First, the majority of section 47 cases start off as section 17 cases, and so only dealing with them when they become serious represents false economy for social services. Second, the rigid classification is insufficiently flexible to deal with the wide variety of cases with which social services has to deal. The result is that some children may not receive the services they need because they do not fit neatly into one specific category.

17.38　Third, as a result of the prioritisation of cases, other services find themselves tempted to present information to social services in a misleading way. If it is known to the referrer that social services are unlikely to act or to provide a service to a child about whom they are concerned unless it is perceived that the child is at risk of harm, then the temptation is to overstate the risks they consider the child is facing.

17.39　Assessment does not exist in a vacuum, nor is it a 'once and for all time' process. The needs of the child and the family may not be catered for in the current range of available services. It is frustrating to assess a child as being in need of a particular service if that service is then unavailable to them. Where resources are limited, the temptation is understandably to assess children according to availability of services, rather than according to their need.

Identifying the roles of the agencies involved

17.40　The seminar then turned to consider the respective roles of the different agencies concerned with the care and protection of children in the assessment process, in order to explore the extent to which assessment is purely a social services function. While there may be general agreement that 'assessment is everybody's business', and should be viewed as such, it would appear that the situation on the ground is different.

17.41　The reality appeared to be that assessment was seen as the business of social services, who could call for the input of other agencies as appropriate. It seems there is sometimes a lack of enthusiasm among the other agencies to adopt a more active approach to assessment with a view to establishing whether they could meet the needs of a particular child from their own resources, without the need for a referral or as partners in a plan of action.

17.42　Part of the explanation for this may be that many people outside social services view the process of assessing a child and his or her family as a complicated one, requiring specialist skills. This may be true quite often, but there has been considerable success experienced in some areas of the country by introducing a basic initial assessment tool, which can be used by a wide range of services that come into contact with children.

National Assessment Framework

17.43 The seminar considered whether a basic multi-agency assessment tool might be used more widely. In particular, consideration was given to the question of whether the initial assessment components of the National Assessment Framework were suitable for use across the agencies. While a number of minor criticisms were made regarding its length and complexity, there was strong support for the National Assessment Framework, which was described variously as "a huge move forward" and "a major achievement". However, while the breadth of support was impressive, it was somewhat disappointing to hear of the extent to which the National Assessment Framework was seen by the other agencies as almost exclusively a social services tool.

17.44 In order for a variety of agencies to participate effectively in the assessment process and make consistent use of a common tool to assist them, some form of common training would seem to be highly desirable.

Confidentiality and the exchange of information

17.45 There was clear evidence that staff in a whole range of agencies felt inhibited from freely exchanging information relating to children and families due to concerns about alleged legal restrictions on doing so. The need for clarity was emphasised with several participants calling for a nationally devised protocol setting out precisely what information can be shared and in what circumstances. In addition, wherever possible, professionals should ensure that they are passing on material that has been validated. The indiscriminate sharing of unchecked information can have the counterproductive effect of presenting a misleading picture to the receiving agency, as well as swamping it with more information than it can process effectively. This issue was also discussed in seminar two. See paragraphs 17.27 and 17.28 for more details.

Seminar four: Service provision and delivery

17.46 Despite a national regulatory framework for children's services, the organisation and delivery of those services, both in and across agencies, is not consistent. The fourth seminar examined the current issues that influence service provision and service delivery.

17.47 It was said that when work with children goes well it is because staff with different expertise know and trust each other. But there were competing views about what it was that damaged trust and co-operation. Some thought that agencies other than social services often did not give enough priority to their work in relation to protecting children. Others said that social services had become the dominant agency rather than the lead agency, and to an unhealthy degree.

17.48 For some, the problem lay in society's attitude to children. Children were not sufficiently valued and some level of violence towards them was tolerated. The solution would be nationally agreed outcomes for children, which everyone involved could work to.

17.49 For many of the participants, inadequacies in the level and quality of staffing had an immediate effect on service provision. Front-line staff in all the services were said to be under pressure because of increasing workloads, high vacancy rates, inadequate information technology and administrative systems, and inadequate training.

Structural reform

17.50 A number of the papers received for this seminar suggested that the deficiencies in the child protection system could only be addressed properly by structural reform. The main suggestions were:

- a national child protection agency
- a national supervising agency
- a national network of multi-agency teams, based on the Youth Offending Team model
- child safeguarding teams
- reform of Area Child Protection Committees (ACPCs)
- a 'virtual' child protection team.

National child protection agency

17.51 The suggested creation of a national child protection agency would be a freestanding, independent agency, staffed by qualified social workers, police officers, medical practitioners, and other professionals. It would investigate and respond to all cases where there were grounds to suspect the ill-treatment of a child.

National supervising agency

17.52 The Metropolitan Police Service proposed an alternative arrangement. It was suggested that the current agency structures should be retained but that a new national supervising agency should be superimposed. The agency would be responsible for policy, inspection and review, training and investigative standards, and the setting of standard operating procedures across the country.

National network of multi-agency teams

17.53 The Youth Offending Team model brings together the important agencies without divorcing them from their local management. This model was considered by some participants as providing a useful model for child protection work.

Child safeguarding teams

17.54 The NSPCC, in their written submission, had developed detailed proposals for greatly strengthened multi-disciplinary teams. During the seminar, they expanded on their call for the establishment of child safeguarding teams involving all the main agencies in the delivery of initial investigation and assessment of children.

Reform of ACPCs

17.55 Proposals for reforming ACPCs received wide support. Although many do good work, they seemed widely to be regarded as lacking 'teeth'. They had no real authority over their constituent agencies and did not provide the strategic leadership needed.

17.56 There were several proposals on how ACPCs could be made more effective. These included:

- placing them on a statutory footing
- strengthening their executive powers
- requiring them to engage independent chairs
- making them directly accountable to the local authority chief executive or to the National Care Standards Commission
- giving them power to require financial contributions from the other agencies
- adding to their membership representatives of housing authorities or local social security offices or Jobcentres
- giving them a strategic responsibility.

'Virtual' child protection team

17.57 The creation of a 'virtual' child protection team with the aid of modern technology and the electronic sharing of information was also discussed, and such a model was described. The model described did not remove the apparent legal restrictions on data sharing, but it did appear to provide a sensible way of managing large amounts of information from different sources.

Improving performance

17.58 There was much discussion about the means by which performance in the delivery of services might be improved, and what the barriers to such improvement would be.

17.59 It was suggested it was important that practice should be governed by professional judgement, and not by rules and procedures. While regulation had its place, it could not be a substitute for reflection and judgement. There was also much discussion about the importance of high-quality supervision and clear lines of accountability.

17.60 A really serious matter is the recruitment and retention of good-quality staff, which is a prerequisite to improving performance. It was considered essential that means are found to acknowledge the importance of child protection and support work for children and families, and to value staff who do this work. The 'blame culture', that was said to have developed, has to be replaced by a 'responsibility culture' to discourage the present tendency of defensive practice.

17.61 Unsurprisingly, training was regarded as critical to improving performance. Training had to be of high quality, not only before qualification, but also during practice. Continuing training for social workers had to be more systematic, and it was suggested by some that training of medical staff in the safeguarding of children should become compulsory at all levels. Risk assessment and risk management training were seen as essential for both medical and social care staff. Child protection training for the police needs to be more detailed.

17.62 Finally, the discussion turned to look at the way in which agencies decide what services to provide. There appeared to be a widely held view that in practice, social work tends to be service-led rather than needs-led. The majority of service users tend to receive the services that are available, not necessarily the services they require. This is the result of limited resources, administrative convenience, and the failure to recognise the need for individual assessment to determine the service to be provided.

17.63 The difficulty in adopting a needs-led approach was said to be due both to the shortage of skilled staff and to the substantial capital investment involved in providing certain services that demanded their subsequent use. Nonetheless, there should be the expectation that all agencies ought to be providing services that meet the needs of their clients rather than seeking users that can take advantage of their services.

Seminar five: Monitoring performance

17.64 Monitoring performance plays a vital role in delivering good outcomes for children and their families. Robust systems that monitor what is actually taking place and its effectiveness is critical. The fifth and final seminar addressed the question of how the performance of the agencies involved in protecting children should be evaluated.

17.65 There was no doubt that the work of each of the key agencies supporting children and families should be rigorously monitored. In the past, the tendency has been to concentrate on the measurement of inputs; for example, the size of the budget, the number of staff, or the range of equipment used. This approach is of limited value and does not address the more important question of what is actually being achieved, and whether the lives of children and families are being improved by the investment.

17.66 In recent years, some progress has been made in correcting this deficiency. However, it was said that, in general, performance measurements remain crude. Often what emerges from their analysis is still more information about the quantity of activity, rather than about the quality and effectiveness of the work delivered. Meaningful and informative outcome measurements in the field of child and family support are notoriously difficult to achieve. However, this should not deter efforts being made to refine the current arrangements for the evaluation of services.

17.67 For monitoring to be effective it has to be conducted against a predetermined set of standards. The development of the National Assessment Framework for children was seen as a means of bringing together what had previously been the fragmented and uncoordinated provision of services for children. Although still at an early stage of development, it was seen to be capable of providing the sort of outcome-based standards seen as desirable.

Internal monitoring

17.68 It was said that there is a marked variation in the quality of internal monitoring among social services departments and police forces. In social services, performance and measurement had to be made relevant to outcomes for children and families. What matters is that such measures continue to strengthen what is best for children and families, and are not diverted from this by undue attention being centred on targets set by central government. Performance management among the police was described as "at best, ad hoc". As regards child protection, it was said that until the protection of children features in the Home Secretary's 'Police Priorities' list, it was unlikely that steps would necessarily be taken at a local level to improve the quality of police child protection teams.

17.69 It is intended that introducing clinical governance will make a significant difference throughout the health service, but little was heard to suggest that the monitoring of performance in relation to the protection of children at a local level in the NHS has been much developed so far. There was much discussion in general terms about the need to develop a culture of self-audit – "empowering the front line" – and providing mechanisms for medical practitioners to talk about outcomes, and develop the ones that they regard as important.

17.70 A healthy culture begins with high-quality leadership by senior managers willing to 'walk the talk' and who are anxious to understand the issues facing front-line staff. It grows once people are willing to analyse their individual practice and contemplate change. That in turn requires management being willing to adopt, not a blame-free culture, but a learning culture. Individual responsibility had to be recognised, but there needed to be a willingness to accept that it was possible for teams and individuals to fail, to learn from their mistakes, and to start again. In that context, performance measurements become a means of self-improvement.

Multi-agency monitoring

17.71 There was a good deal of support in the papers received for the idea that multi-agency working should be monitored on a multi-agency basis. This is already an established feature of current practice. In particular, in response to the Government's White Paper *Modernising Social Services*, fieldwork is presently being undertaken to prepare a report on the state of child safeguards. That involves joint working by eight different inspectorates. This report has now been published. This approach appears, for good reason, to be widely welcomed. There was support for its extension so that, for example, it covered regular inspection of police forces by such 'outsiders' at both senior and grass-roots levels.

17.72 The possibility of changes to the role of multi-agency bodies in monitoring performance was considered.

17.73 There was considerable debate on the best way to learn from child deaths. I was told that often Part 8 reviews carried out under the auspices of ACPCs concentrate on organisational rather than practice issues. There was said to be a lack of uniformity across the country as to when Part 8 reviews are ordered. It was felt that benefit could be gained by taking steps to ensure that practice lessons are learned not just locally, but nationally too. Work on analysing the effectiveness of Part 8 reviews has already been done in Wales and is currently being done in England.

17.74 There was some discussion about the possibility of adapting the Department of Health's 'Confidential Inquiry' system. This is used, for example, in cases of maternal deaths and child protection cases. The NSPCC's proposal for child death review teams was also considered.

17.75 There are clear advantages in ensuring that every death or serious deliberate harm to a child known to social services is investigated. It would remove the stigma attached to Part 8 reviews, it would ensure that no cases were missed, and it would assist in the development of preventive strategies more generally. Others thought such an arrangement might be expensive and bureaucratic, adding further systems and processes to those already in place.

External monitoring

17.76 The current arrangements for external inspection of children's services are changing. It was said that the Social Services Inspectorate (SSI) is moving from thematic inspections to a rolling programme of inspections and is revising its methodologies. Joint reviews in their present form between the SSI and the Audit Commission are to end next year. A new Police Standards Unit is being established in the Home Office. However, it must be recognised that the government inspectorates operate annual programmes which are designed to ensure that over the years, each of the key responsibilities of the services have been inspected. This being so, it may well be that several years will elapse between the inspection of the services dealing with the safety of children. Something more than this is required.

17.77 In the week before seminar five, the Government announced the establishment of two new inspectorates – a social care inspectorate (the National Social Care Inspectorate) and a health inspectorate (the Commission for Health Audit and Inspection). The two are to have similar duties, powers and responsibilities and be placed under statutory duties to co-operate with each other.

17.78 I hope these changes strengthen inspection and secure a more effective way of monitoring the co-operation between agencies.

Seminar conclusions

17.79 These seminars proved to be of great value to this Inquiry. They provided the opportunity to consider, in a wider forum, many of the issues raised in evidence during Phase One. It was disturbing to hear that many of the weaknesses in the safeguarding of children I heard about in Phase One were reflected in the seminar discussions. However, it was reassuring that there was support for the legislative framework provided by the Children Act 1989. Concerns were primarily about the way agencies worked together and standards of practice.

17.80 It is obvious that the focus of the work of each of the services must be on securing the well-being of children. The challenge is to ensure that this is translated into day-to-day practice. This requires staff in each of the services being properly trained for their different tasks, and each person having the ability and the will to work flexibly across organisational boundaries.

17.81 In order to avoid either drift or confusion, the decision-making processes must be clearly defined, generally understood, and always put into operation. This is never more important than when the safety of a child is at stake.

17.82 The recommendations that follow are not intended to restrict the imaginative ways in which children can be helped and safeguarded. They are intended to create more freedom, but this freedom must be exercised in a system which is consistent and well organised. Success in safeguarding children and families depends in large measure on each of the key services being properly managed and financed. The outcomes for children and families should be closely monitored so that lessons can be learned within each service with a view to securing constant improvements in practice. All staff working with children and families should be required to undertake regular training to ensure that practice is kept up to date.

17.83 It should be noted that this Inquiry is the latest in a long list of inquiries following the tragic death or deliberate serious harm to a child known to the services. Even during the course of this Inquiry, tragic cases of a similar nature have appeared before the courts.

17.84 The concerns expressed about the way in which the Children Act 1989 is being put into practice highlighted the need for greater certainty about the operational and practice standards in each of the services. I am in no doubt that it must be possible to provide more effective means of supporting families and children – not just for those children for which there is concern for their safety. To achieve this, local authorities should encourage and support the work of independent agencies. Many voluntary organisations have demonstrated an ability to help children and families to overcome their reluctance to either seek or accept help. These agencies can be both innovative and flexible in responding to the needs of children and families. The value of the services they provide should be acknowledged and ways should be found to enable them to contribute to the responsibilities of the proposed local Management Board for Children and Families referred to in the recommendation below.

The need for change

A new management and accountability structure

17.85 What is needed most of all is a structure in which there is no ambiguity about the decision-making process for the quality of services to children and families. The performance of managers and their effectiveness should be judged against the efficiency, reliability and standards of services delivered to vulnerable children and families, rather than in the maintenance of bureaucratic procedures, which may have limited relevance to the safety of children.

17.86 Both Parliament and the public must have confidence in the effectiveness and efficiency of these arrangements. This Inquiry heard too much evidence of

organisational confusion and 'buck passing' for me to believe that the safety of
a child can be achieved simply through issuing more guidance.

17.87   The evidence to this Inquiry indicates there is an urgent need to ensure that the
numerous policies, procedures, protocols and strategies for children and families
are translated into coherent action at the point at which services are delivered.

17.88   In recent years, the Government has announced several initiatives aimed at
reducing the impact of organisational boundaries and securing better joint working
between staff in key agencies. It is clear that what is now needed is a structure
which is reinforced by statute, and which has at its centre a clear process for both
decision making and monitoring of performance; for example, it should not be
possible for multi-agency plans to safeguard children to be drawn up and then left
solely for social services to implement.

17.89   It is unrealistic to expect that it will ever be possible to eliminate the deliberate
harm or death of a child – indeed, no system can achieve this. However, there is
great scope for services to be operated more efficiently and effectively. This will
require action at all levels, ranging from agreed outcomes for children to having
a well-managed, properly-resourced and adequately-trained workforce.

17.90   At present, the gap between intention and achievement is unacceptably large.
The delivery of services is too unpredictable and the co-operation between staff of
the key agencies relies too heavily on personal inclination. The need to work across
ever-changing geographical boundaries has created the danger that too much time
is being spent on the bureaucratic aspects of inter-agency working and too little on
actually helping children and families in need.

17.91   Over the years, preventive work with families has been declining. As a result, the
absence of a timely supportive intervention has allowed more family problems
to deteriorate to the point of crisis. This trend has to be reversed. This can only
be achieved if a higher priority is given to services working jointly in supporting
families and helping them to overcome their difficulties. These arrangements need
to be properly funded.

17.92   The support and protection of children cannot be achieved by a single agency.
It is best achieved when the statutory services work in close association with
community-based groups, whether they are independent agencies, charities or
self-help groups.

17.93   None of this will be possible unless the statutory agencies become more
outward-looking and more flexible in the way they work and use their resources.
This cannot be confined to the enthusiasts. Every service has to play its part.
All staff must have placed upon them the clear expectation that their primary
responsibility is to the child and his or her family. The changes recommended in
this section of the Report are based on the following eight principles. The service
must be:

- child and family centred;
- responsive to local needs and opportunities;
- adequately resourced;
- capable of delivering an agreed set of measurable, national outcomes for children;
- clear in its accountability from the top to the bottom of the organisation;
- transparent in its work and open to scrutiny;
- clear and straightforward to understand;
- placed on a statutory footing, with the powers to deliver the desired outcomes.

It is with these principles in mind that I make the recommendations set out below.

Structural change

17.94 The evidence I heard in both Phase One and Phase Two of this Inquiry leads me to the conclusion that the structures within which the services to children and families in need is organised are inefficient and need to be changed; for example, I heard that ACPC arrangements had become removed from day-to-day practice and lack any statutory powers. In many parts of the country, the lack of overlap of the boundaries in the key services has resulted in local arrangements being thought to be bureaucratic and with little impact on delivery of services. The safety of children should not be placed in jeopardy because of the absence of machinery to ensure the co-operation of the different services.

Serious case reviews

17.95 During this phase of the Inquiry there was considerable variation in the evidence relating to the number of deaths and serious injury caused deliberately to children in this country. I do not propose to comment on this beyond saying that it would be valuable if information on the topic was collected on the basis of an agreed definition. One estimate is that 90 serious case reviews (Part 8 reviews) are conducted each year by ACPCs. However, there is no certainty that this figure is a true reflection of the other times when, with proper intervention, the well-being of a child could have been safeguarded.

17.96 A fundamental weakness of the current system is the variability of the circumstances under which a review must be taken. In fact, it could be said that there are considerable incentives against undertaking such reviews, not least because of the amount and complexity of the work involved, and the extent of service failures that may be exposed. I conclude that this procedure is inadequate and must now be replaced by a system which is both more robust and more consistent.

17.97 The new arrangements must retain the ability to look beyond child deaths caused intentionally, and to examine cases where children have been deliberately harmed, but not killed. This is an essential way to learn lessons and promote examples of good practice. Therefore, I make the following recommendations:

Recommendation
With the support of the Prime Minister, a ministerial Children and Families Board should be established at the heart of government. The Board should be chaired by a minister of Cabinet rank and should have ministerial representation from government departments concerned with the welfare of children and families.

Recommendation
The chief executive of a newly established National Agency for Children and Families will report to the ministerial Children and Families Board. The post of chief executive should incorporate the responsibilities of the post of a Children's Commissioner for England.

Recommendation

The newly established National Agency for Children and Families should have the following responsibilities:

- to assess, and advise the ministerial Children and Families Board about, the impact on children and families of proposed changes in policy;
- to scrutinise new legislation and guidance issued for this purpose;
- to advise on the implementation of the UN Convention on the Rights of the Child;
- to advise on setting nationally agreed outcomes for children and how they might best be achieved and monitored;
- to ensure that legislation and policy are implemented at a local level and are monitored through its regional office network;
- to report annually to Parliament on the quality and effectiveness of services to children and families, in particular on the safety of children.

Recommendation

The National Agency for Children and Families will operate through a regional structure which will ensure that legislation and policy are being implemented at a local level, as well as providing central government with up-to-date and reliable information about the quality and effectiveness of local services.

Recommendation

The National Agency for Children and Families should, at their discretion, conduct serious case reviews (Part 8 reviews) or oversee the process if they decide to delegate this task to other agencies following the death or serious deliberate injury to a child known to the services. This task will be undertaken through the regional offices of the Agency with the authority vested in the National Agency for Children and Families to secure, scrutinise and analyse documents and to interview witnesses. I consider it advisable that these case reviews are published, and that additionally, on an annual basis, a report is produced collating the Part 8 review findings for that year.

Recommendation

Each local authority with social services responsibilities must establish a Committee of Members for Children and Families with lay members drawn from the management committees of each of the key services. This Committee must ensure the services to children and families are properly co-ordinated and that the inter-agency dimension of this work is being managed effectively.

Recommendation

The local authority chief executive should chair a Management Board for Services to Children and Families which will report to the Member Committee referred to above. The Management Board for Services to Children and Families must include senior officers from each of the key agencies. The Management Board must also establish strong links with community-based organisations that make significant contributions to local services for children and families. The Board must ensure staff working in the key agencies are appropriately trained and are able to demonstrate competence in their respective tasks. It will be responsible for the work currently undertaken by the Area Child Protection Committee.

Recommendation

The Management Board for Services to Children and Families must appoint a director responsible for ensuring that inter-agency arrangements are appropriate and effective, and for advising the Management Board for Services to Children and Families on the development of services to meet local need. Furthermore, each Management Board for Services to Children and Families should:

- establish reliable ways of assessing the needs and circumstances of children in their area, with particular reference to the needs of children who may be at risk of deliberate harm;
- identify ways of establishing consultation groups of both children and adult users of services.

Recommendation

The budget contributed by each of the local agencies in support of vulnerable children and families should be identified by the Management Board for Services to Children and Families so that staff and resources can be used in the most flexible and effective way.

Recommendation

As part of their work, the government inspectorates should inspect both the quality of the services delivered, and also the effectiveness of the inter-agency arrangements for the provision of services to children and families.

Recommendation

The Government should review the law regarding the registration of private foster carers.

Recommendation

Front-line staff in each of the agencies which regularly come into contact with families with children must ensure that in each new contact, basic information about the child is recorded. This must include the child's name, address, age, the name of the child's primary carer, the child's GP, and the name of the child's school if the child is of school age. Gaps in this information should be passed on to the relevant authority in accordance with local arrangements.

Improvements in practice and operation of services to children and families

17.98   Changes to the structure need to be reinforced and supported by improvements in the practice and operation of services to children and families. This includes the way in which referral of a child is managed by social services, training, exchange of information between professionals, and a database for children. I refer to each in turn.

Social services' response to a referral of a child

17.99   Throughout this Inquiry, I repeatedly heard evidence which caused me great concern about the way in which social services departments interpret their responsibilities under sections 17 and 47 of the Children Act 1989. Section 17 of the Act places a general duty on the local authority "to safeguard and promote the welfare of children" in need in their area. Section 47 places a duty on the local authority to "make or cause to be made, such inquiries as they consider necessary" if they "have reasonable cause to suspect that a child ... in their area is suffering, or is likely to suffer, significant harm ... the purpose of which being to establish whether they need to take any action to safeguard or promote the child's welfare". The evidence I heard of a potentially harmful debate around sections 17 and 47 of the Children Act 1989 appears to have a number of serious implications for practice, but the most significant of these are as follows.

17.100 Professional confusion exists about what inquiries can be made into concerns about children without parental permission being first sought and granted. I was repeatedly told that if a case fell short of a clear section 47 child protection label, and was therefore categorised as section 17, **no dialogue** could take place between the protective agencies until the child's carer had been informed and their permission given. Furthermore, if their permission was not given, the nature of any intervention would have to be reconsidered, and it could well stop there and then.

17.101 It was often suggested that if social services respond under section 17, then only in exceptional circumstances might a child be spoken to by a social worker without parental permission having first been sought and granted. Also, if a case attracted a section 17 'label', its status was automatically lowered and it soon slipped down the priority list.

17.102 I also heard evidence that the downgrading of cases to the status of section 17, and afterwards closure, was becoming an attractive option to childcare teams struggling to deal with what they perceived to be an ever-increasing number of child protection referrals, case conferences and registrations. In response to social services downgrading referrals under section 17, partner agencies either tended not to make referrals or to re-frame concerns about children in a way which would attract a section 47 response. They saw the latter as the only way to access services for children they were worried about.

17.103 This approach to the use of sections 17 and 47 can only be described as dangerous. It is at odds with my understanding of the aspirations of the Children Act 1989. These factors were clearly evident in the failure to protect Victoria in the four different local authorities, the two hospitals, and the one police force.

17.104 It was clear from a number of witnesses that there is uncertainty about taking any preventive action under section 17 without parental consent. I believe that parents of most children in this country would expect the protective agencies to communicate with each other and check the information they have about the child as soon as possible before deciding on any further action.

17.105 Clearly, the co-operation of parents or carers must always remain a vital consideration of any plan to safeguard and promote the welfare of a child. Parents or carers must continue to be fully involved as soon as possible in circumstances that fall short of a section 47 label. The attempt to secure parental permission should not block the initial information gathering and sharing exercise, which must also include talking to the child, as appropriate.

17.106 Child protection cases do not always come labelled as such. At the point of referral, the social worker can never be sure what the degree of potential harm to the child may be. Good communication, checking with partner agencies at the point of referral, and talking to the child as appropriate, must be the main way to decide how best to safeguard and promote a child's welfare.

17.107 The Department of Health's evidence to the Inquiry was that the seeking of parental permission and the sharing of information between agencies is a matter for local negotiation. In my view, this is unacceptable. Existing *Working Together* guidance and national assessment framework guidance must be clearer on this issue.

17.108 In my view, the main task facing all the agencies is to jointly agree a response following the identification of concerns about a child. This response must meet both the immediate needs of the child and promote the child's welfare. Under this approach, sections 17 and 47 of the Children Act 1989 are used simply to identify the part of the Act which is being used and is not a justification for inactivity.

17.109 To achieve this, consideration should be given to unifying the *Working Together* guidance and the National Assessment Framework guidance into a single document, which sets out clearly how these sections of the Children Act 1989 should be applied. A clear direction should be given for the action to be taken under both section 17 and section 47 of the Act.

17.110 I was told that staff feel under pressure to reduce the number of section 47 inquiries. As a result, there is widespread practice of driving down child protection case conferences and the number of children whose names are placed on the child protection register. Therefore, the value of the local register has reduced. I recognise that including the name of a child on a register does not add to the safeguarding of that child. Indeed, there is the danger that other agencies may make unwarranted assumptions of the level of help and support being given to a child whose name is on the register. It is for this reason that I now have considerable doubt about the usefulness of these registers in the safeguarding of children.

17.111 Therefore, I make the following recommendation:

> **Recommendation**
> The Department of Health should amalgamate the current *Working Together* and the National Assessment Framework documents into one simplified document. The document should tackle the following six aspects in a clear and practical way:
>
> - It must establish a 'common language' for use across all agencies to help those agencies to identify who they are concerned about, why they are concerned, who is best placed to respond to those concerns, and what outcome is being sought from any planned response.
> - It must disseminate a best practice approach by social services to receiving and managing information about children at the 'front door'.
> - It must make clear in cases that fall short of an immediately identifiable section 47 label that the seeking or refusal of parental permission must not restrict the initial information gathering and sharing. This should, if necessary, include talking to the child.
> - It must prescribe a clear step-by-step guide on how to manage a case through either a section 17 or a section 47 track, with built-in systems for case monitoring and review.
> - It must replace the child protection register with a more effective system. Case conferences should remain, but the focus must no longer be on whether to register or not. Instead, the focus should be on establishing an agreed plan to safeguard and promote the welfare of the particular child.
> - The new guidance should include some consistency in the application of both section 17 and section 47.

Training

17.112 It is clear that the safeguarding of children will continue to depend upon services such as health, education, housing, police and social services working together. Each of these services has its own training organisation dedicated to its core functions and the specific responsibilities they carry. It may be neither desirable nor possible to change the fundamentals of these arrangements, but proper recognition must be paid to the importance of effective joint working between the staff of these services. The National Agency for Children and Families should require the training bodies of each of the key agencies to demonstrate how inter-agency working fits into the curricula of the training they authorise. Furthermore, each training body should be required to promote training specifically designed to bring together staff from different agencies on topics where joint working is essential, such as working with children and families.

17.113 The key national training bodies should be required to produce a National Framework for Joint Training to which they are each committed. It is important that the organisations with a specific responsibility to promote professional training give a strong lead on this. The skills involved in working successfully across organisational boundaries must be given proper recognition in both the basic training and in the continuing training of staff. It cannot be left only to those individuals who have the motivation to do it. Working across boundaries should be an expectation placed on all staff, and it must be reflected in training programmes.

17.114 It is now generally recognised that training is not confined to the beginning of professional life, but must be a life-long process. Each service must ensure that training opportunities are available throughout the career of staff. Individual staff should be required to take responsibility for keeping their practice up to date by demonstrating they have satisfactorily completed appropriate training courses. The ACPC arrangement lacked the authority to ensure this happened at local level. The new Management Board for Services to Children and Families must have the power to fill this gap and ensure that training is provided. Its performance in this should be evaluated as part of the inspections to be undertaken jointly by the relevant government inspectorates. Therefore, I make the following recommendations:

> **Recommendation**
>
> The National Agency for Children and Families should require each of the training bodies covering the services provided by doctors, nurses, teachers, police officers, officers working in housing departments, and social workers to demonstrate that effective joint working between each of these professional groups features in their national training programmes.

> **Recommendation**
>
> The newly created local Management Boards for Services to Children and Families should be required to ensure training on an inter-agency basis is provided. The effectiveness of this should be evaluated by the government inspectorates. Staff working in the relevant agencies should be required to demonstrate that their practice with respect to inter-agency working is up to date by successfully completing appropriate training courses.

Exchange of information between professionals

17.115 Throughout this Inquiry it was said repeatedly that when there is professional concern about the welfare of a child, the free exchange of information is inhibited by the Data Protection Act 1998, the Human Rights Act 1998, and common law rules on confidentiality. The evidence put to the Inquiry was that unless a child is deemed to be in need of protection, information cannot be shared between agencies without staff running the risk that their actions are unlawful. This either deters information sharing, or artificially elevates concern about the need for protection – each of which is not compatible with serving well the needs of children and families. Clearly these matters are complicated. There must be a balance struck between the protection of a child and the right to privacy.

17.116 I heard evidence that professionals working with children and families in these circumstances would be assisted by clear guidance on the related issues of confidentiality and the exchange of information. Therefore, I make the following recommendation:

> **Recommendation**
>
> The Government should issue guidance on the Data Protection Act 1998, the Human Rights Act 1998, and common law rules on confidentiality. The Government should issue guidance as and when these impact on the sharing of information between professional groups in circumstances where there are concerns about the welfare of children and families.

A national database for children

17.117 Seminar one was about 'discovery and inclusion'. It focused on the means by which we can be sure that every child is included in the general provision of services to which they are entitled. Several of the participants in this seminar recounted their personal experiences of individual children having 'slipped through the net' or having disappeared without any of the services knowing where they had gone. The potential for this to happen seems to be greater in urban areas. It is contributed to by an increasing number of homeless families, changes in traditional family group structures, and a mobile population. Several factors, therefore, suggest that it is much easier now than in the past for children to be 'lost in the system'. In addition to this, adults who wish to exploit the vulnerability of children, or who harm them in outbursts of temper, often go to great lengths to ensure that their children are kept out of sight.

17.118 One suggestion that attempts to overcome these factors, is for the Government to establish a national database for children. I was advised that there are no technical reasons why every child could not be registered shortly after birth, or upon arrival in this country, and then 'tracked' throughout their childhood. There are bigger and more complex systems in operation, for example, the national vehicle licence system and systems operated by the Passport Office and the Inland Revenue.

17.119 I realise this suggestion should not be made lightly. Indeed, it is likely to be countered by concerns about personal privacy expressed by those who oppose the use of national identity cards. Therefore, it will be a matter of judgement about where the balance is struck between providing a possible greater safeguard for children and what may be felt by some to be an intrusion into privacy.

17.120   Strict controls would need to be in place to ensure against the unauthorised access of information held in a database for children. Such a system would also need to be easy to use, effective in the maintenance of contact with children and families, and value for money.

17.121   The support expressed by participants for a national children's database persuaded me of the potential worth of such a facility. However, only a feasibility study will reveal whether this is a practical proposition. Therefore, I make the following recommendation:

Recommendation

The Government should actively explore the benefit to children of setting up and operating a national children's database on all children under the age of 16. A feasibility study should be a prelude to a pilot study to explore its usefulness in strengthening the safeguards for children.

Recommended new structure

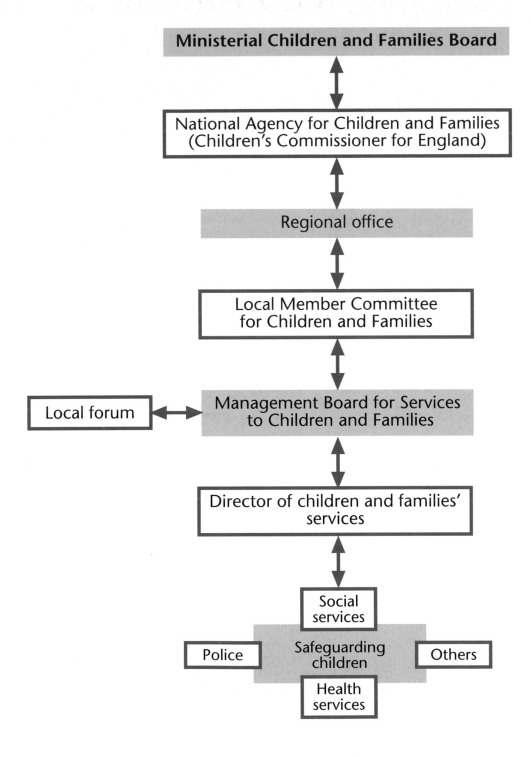

Part six: Recommendations

18 Recommendations

This section brings together the recommendations that are to be found in the Report. The way in which local authorities name committees and officers can vary. For ease of reference, the recommendations are expressed in the terms of the Local Authorities Personal Social Services Act 1970. To the left of each recommendation is an indication of the timescale for action:

1 means the recommendation should be implemented within three months.

2 means the recommendation should be implemented within six months.

3 means the recommendation should be implemented within two years.

Of the 108 recommendations in this Report, 46 are under '1' and a further 36 are under '2'. This means that some 82 of the recommendations could be acted upon within six months.

The paragraph numbers that follow the recommendations are cross-references to the paragraphs in this Report in which they can be found.

General recommendations

3   **Recommendation 1** With the support of the Prime Minister, a ministerial Children and Families Board should be established at the heart of government. The Board should be chaired by a minister of Cabinet rank and should have ministerial representation from government departments concerned with the welfare of children and families. (paragraph 17.97)

3   **Recommendation 2** The chief executive of a newly established National Agency for Children and Families will report to the ministerial Children and Families Board. The post of chief executive should incorporate the responsibilities of the post of a Children's Commissioner for England. (paragraph 17.97)

3   **Recommendation 3** The newly established National Agency for Children and Families should have the following responsibilities:

- to assess, and advise the ministerial Children and Families Board about, the impact on children and families of proposed changes in policy;
- to scrutinise new legislation and guidance issued for this purpose;
- to advise on the implementation of the UN Convention on the Rights of the Child;
- to advise on setting nationally agreed outcomes for children and how they might best be achieved and monitored;
- to ensure that legislation and policy are implemented at a local level and are monitored through its regional office network;
- to report annually to Parliament on the quality and effectiveness of services to children and families, in particular on the safety of children. (paragraph 17.97)

3   **Recommendation 4** The National Agency for Children and Families will operate through a regional structure which will ensure that legislation and policy are being implemented at a local level, as well as providing central government with up-to-date and reliable information about the quality and effectiveness of local services. (paragraph 17.97)

3   **Recommendation 5** The National Agency for Children and Families should, at their discretion, conduct serious case reviews (Part 8 reviews) or oversee the process if they decide to delegate this task to other agencies following the death or serious deliberate injury to a child known to the services. This task will be undertaken through the regional offices of the Agency with the authority vested in the National Agency for Children and Families to secure, scrutinise and analyse documents and to interview witnesses. I consider it advisable that these case reviews are published, and that additionally, on an annual basis, a report is produced collating the Part 8 review findings for that year. (paragraph 17.97)

2   **Recommendation 6** Each local authority with social services responsibilities must establish a Committee of Members for Children and Families with lay members drawn from the management committees of each of the key services. This Committee must ensure the services to children and families are properly co-ordinated and that the inter-agency dimension of this work is being managed effectively. (paragraph 17.97)

2   **Recommendation 7** The local authority chief executive should chair a Management Board for Services to Children and Families which will report to the Member Committee referred to above. The Management Board for Services to Children and Families must include senior officers from each of the key agencies. The Management Board must also establish strong links with community-based organisations that make significant contributions to local services for children and families. The Board must ensure staff working in the key agencies are appropriately trained and are able to demonstrate competence in their respective tasks. It will be responsible for the work currently undertaken by the Area Child Protection Committee. (paragraph 17.97)

3   **Recommendation 8** The Management Board for Services to Children and Families must appoint a director responsible for ensuring that inter-agency arrangements are appropriate and effective, and for advising the Management Board for Services to Children and Families on the development of services to meet local need. Furthermore, each Management Board for Services to Children and Families should:

- establish reliable ways of assessing the needs and circumstances of children in their area, with particular reference to the needs of children who may be at risk of deliberate harm;
- identify ways of establishing consultation groups of both children and adult users of services. (paragraph 17.97)

2   **Recommendation 9** The budget contributed by each of the local agencies in support of vulnerable children and families should be identified by the Management Board for Services to Children and Families so that staff and resources can be used in the most flexible and effective way. (paragraph 17.97)

2   **Recommendation 10** As part of their work, the government inspectorates should inspect both the quality of the services delivered, and also the effectiveness of the inter-agency arrangements for the provision of services to children and families. (paragraph 17.97)

3   **Recommendation 11** The Government should review the law regarding the registration of private foster carers. (paragraph 17.97)

1   **Recommendation 12** Front-line staff in each of the agencies which regularly come into contact with families with children must ensure that in each new contact, basic information about the child is recorded. This must include the child's name, address, age, the name of the child's primary carer, the child's GP, and the name of the child's school if the child is of school age. Gaps in this information should be passed on to the relevant authority in accordance with local arrangements. (paragraph 17.97)

3   **Recommendation 13** The Department of Health should amalgamate the current *Working Together* and the National Assessment Framework documents into one simplified document. The document should tackle the following six aspects in a clear and practical way:

- It must establish a 'common language' for use across all agencies to help those agencies to identify who they are concerned about, why they are concerned, who is best placed to respond to those concerns, and what outcome is being sought from any planned response.
- It must disseminate a best practice approach by social services to receiving and managing information about children at the 'front door'.
- It must make clear in cases that fall short of an immediately identifiable section 47 label that the seeking or refusal of parental permission must not restrict the initial information gathering and sharing. This should, if necessary, include talking to the child.
- It must prescribe a clear step-by-step guide on how to manage a case through either a section 17 or a section 47 track, with built-in systems for case monitoring and review.
- It must replace the child protection register with a more effective system. Case conferences should remain, but the focus must no longer be on whether to register or not. Instead, the focus should be on establishing an agreed plan to safeguard and promote the welfare of the particular child.
- The new guidance should include some consistency in the application of both section 17 and section 47. (paragraph 17.111)

3   **Recommendation 14** The National Agency for Children and Families should require each of the training bodies covering the services provided by doctors, nurses, teachers, police officers, officers working in housing departments, and social workers to demonstrate that effective joint working between each of these professional groups features in their national training programmes. (paragraph 17.114)

2   **Recommendation 15** The newly created local Management Boards for Services to Children and Families should be required to ensure training on an inter-agency basis is provided. The effectiveness of this should be evaluated by the government inspectorates. Staff working in the relevant agencies should be required to demonstrate that their practice with respect to inter-agency working is up to date by successfully completing appropriate training courses. (paragraph 17.114)

3   **Recommendation 16** The Government should issue guidance on the Data Protection Act 1998, the Human Rights Act 1998, and common law rules on confidentiality. The Government should issue guidance as and when these impact on the sharing of information between professional groups in circumstances where there are concerns about the welfare of children and families. (paragraph 17.116)

3   **Recommendation 17** The Government should actively explore the benefit to children of setting up and operating a national children's database on all children under the age of 16. A feasibility study should be a prelude to a pilot study to explore its usefulness in strengthening the safeguards for children. (paragraph 17.121)

Social care recommendations

1   **Recommendation 18** When communication with a child is necessary for the purposes of safeguarding and promoting that child's welfare, and the first language of that child is not English, an interpreter must be used. In cases where the use of an interpreter is dispensed with, the reasons for so doing must be recorded in the child's notes/case file. (paragraph 6.251)

1   **Recommendation 19** Managers of duty teams must devise and operate a system which enables them immediately to establish how many children have been referred to their team, what action is required to be taken for each child, who is responsible for taking that action, and when that action must be completed. (paragraph 4.14)

2   **Recommendation 20** Directors of social services must ensure that staff in their children and families' intake teams are experienced in working with children and families, and that they have received appropriate training. (paragraph 4.16)

1   **Recommendation 21** When a professional makes a referral to social services concerning the well-being of a child, the fact of that referral must be confirmed in writing by the referrer within 48 hours. (paragraph 4.59)

1   **Recommendation 22** If social services place a child in temporary accommodation, an assessment must be made of the suitability of that accommodation and the results of that assessment must be recorded on the child's case file. If the accommodation is unsuitable, this should be reported to a senior officer. (paragraph 4.77)

1   **Recommendation 23** If social services place a child in accommodation in another local authority area, they must notify that local authority's social services department of the placement. Unless specifically agreed in writing at team manager level by both authorities or above, the placing authority must retain responsibility for the child concerned. (paragraph 4.82)

1   **Recommendation 24** Where, during the course of an assessment, social services establish that a child of school age is not attending school, they must alert the education authorities and satisfy themselves that, in the interim, the child is subject to adequate daycare arrangements. (paragraph 4.143)

1   **Recommendation 25** All social services assessments of children and families, and any action plans drawn up as a result, must be approved in writing by a manager. Before giving such approval, the manager must ensure that the child and the child's carer have been seen and spoken to. (paragraph 4.152)

1   **Recommendation 26** Directors of social services must ensure that no case involving a vulnerable child is closed until the child and the child's carer have been seen and spoken to, and a plan for the ongoing promotion and safeguarding of the child's welfare has been agreed. (paragraph 4.183)

2   **Recommendation 27** Chief executives and lead members of local authorities with social services responsibilities must ensure that children's services are explicitly included in their authority's list of priorities and operational plans. (paragraph 5.4)

2   **Recommendation 28** The Department of Health should require chief executives of local authorities with social services responsibilities to prepare a position statement on the true picture of the current strengths and weaknesses of their 'front door' duty systems for children and families. This must be accompanied by an action plan setting out the timescales for remedying any weaknesses identified. (paragraph 5.9)

2   **Recommendation 29** Directors of social services must devise and implement a system which provides them with the following information about the work of the duty teams for which they are responsible:

- number of children referred to the teams;
- number of those children who have been assessed as requiring a service;
- number of those children who have been provided with the service that they require;
- number of children referred who have identified needs which have yet to be met. (paragraph 5.24)

1   **Recommendation 30** Directors of social services must ensure that senior managers inspect, at least once every three months, a random selection of case files and supervision notes. (paragraph 5.27)

2   **Recommendation 31** Directors of social services must ensure that all staff who work with children have received appropriate vocational training, receive a thorough induction in local procedures and are obliged to participate in regular continuing training so as to ensure that their practice is kept up to date. (paragraph 5.30)

3   **Recommendation 32** Local authority chief executives must ensure that only one electronic database system is used by all those working in children and families' services for the recording of information. This should be the same system in use across the council, or at least compatible with it, so as to facilitate the sharing of information, as appropriate. (paragraph 5.46)

3   **Recommendation 33** Local authorities with responsibility for safeguarding children should establish and advertise a 24-hour free telephone referral number for use by members of the public who wish to report concerns about a child. A pilot study should be undertaken to evaluate the feasibility of electronically recording calls to such a number. (paragraph 5.71)

2   **Recommendation 34** Social workers must not undertake home visits without being clear about the purpose of the visit, the information to be gathered during the course of it, and the steps to be taken if no one is at home. No visits should be undertaken without the social worker concerned checking the information known about the child by other child protection agencies. All visits must be written up on the case file. (paragraphs 5.108 and 6.606)

1   **Recommendation 35** Directors of social services must ensure that children who are the subject of allegations of deliberate harm are seen and spoken to within 24 hours of the allegation being communicated to social services. If this timescale is not met, the reason for the failure must be recorded on the case file. (paragraph 5.127)

1   **Recommendation 36** No emergency action on a case concerning an allegation of deliberate harm to a child should be taken without first obtaining legal advice. Local authorities must ensure that such legal advice is available 24 hours a day. (paragraph 5.128)

2   **Recommendation 37** The training of social workers must equip them with the confidence to question the opinion of professionals in other agencies when conducting their own assessment of the needs of the child. (paragraph 5.138)

1   **Recommendation 38** Directors of social services must ensure that the transfer of responsibility of a case between local authority social services departments is always recorded on the case file of each authority, and is confirmed in writing by the authority to which responsibility for the case has been transferred. (paragraph 5.152)

1   **Recommendation 39** All front-line staff within local authorities must be trained to pass all calls about the safety of children through to the appropriate duty team without delay, having first recorded the name of the child, his or her address, and the nature of the concern. If the call cannot be put through immediately, further details from the referrer must be sought (including their name, address and contact number). The information must then be passed verbally and in writing to the duty team within the hour. (paragraph 5.169)

1   **Recommendation 40** Directors of social services must ensure that no case that has been opened in response to allegations of deliberate harm to a child is closed until the following steps have been taken:

- The child has been spoken to alone.
- The child's carers have been seen and spoken to.
- The accommodation in which the child is to live has been visited.
- The views of all the professionals involved have been sought and considered.
- A plan for the promotion and safeguarding of the child's welfare has been agreed. (paragraph 5.187)

2   **Recommendation 41** Chief executives of local authorities with social services responsibilities must make arrangements for senior managers and councillors to regularly visit intake teams in their children's services department, and to report their findings to the chief executive and social services committee. (paragraph 5.193)

1   **Recommendation 42** Directors of social services must ensure that where the procedures of a social services department stipulate requirements for the transfer of a case between teams within the department, systems are in place to detect when such a transfer does not take place as required. (paragraph 6.7)

2   **Recommendation 43** No social worker shall undertake section 47 inquiries unless he or she has been trained to do so. Directors of social services must undertake an audit of staff currently carrying out section 47 inquiries to identify gaps in training and experience. These must be addressed immediately. (paragraph 6.12)

1   **Recommendation 44** When staff are temporarily promoted to fill vacancies, directors of social services must subject such arrangements to six-monthly reviews and record the outcome. (paragraph 6.29)

1   **Recommendation 45** Directors of social services must ensure that the work of staff working directly with children is regularly supervised. This must include the supervisor reading, reviewing and signing the case file at regular intervals. (paragraph 6.59)

1   **Recommendation 46** Directors of social services must ensure that the roles and responsibilities of child protection advisers (and those employed in similar posts) are clearly understood by all those working within children's services. (paragraph 6.71)

3 **Recommendation 47** The chief executive of each local authority with social services responsibilities must ensure that specialist services are available to respond to the needs of children and families 24 hours a day, seven days a week. The safeguarding of children should not be part of the responsibilities of general out-of-office-hours teams. (paragraph 6.181)

1 **Recommendation 48** Directors of social services must ensure that when children and families are referred to other agencies for additional services, that referral is only made with the agreement of the allocated social worker and/or their manager. The purpose of the referral must be recorded contemporaneously on the case file. (paragraph 6.263)

1 **Recommendation 49** When a professional from another agency expresses concern to social services about their handling of a particular case, the file must be read and reviewed, the professional concerned must be met and spoken to, and the outcome of this discussion must be recorded on the case file. (paragraph 6.289)

1 **Recommendation 50** Directors of social services must ensure that when staff are absent from work, systems are in place to ensure that post, emails and telephone contacts are checked and actioned as necessary. (paragraph 6.318)

1 **Recommendation 51** Directors of social services must ensure that all strategy meetings and discussions involve the following three basic steps:

- A list of action points must be drawn up, each with an agreed timescale and the identity of the person responsible for carrying it out.
- A clear record of the discussion or meeting must be circulated to all those present and all those with responsibility for an action point.
- A mechanism for reviewing completion of the agreed actions must be specified. The date upon which the first such review is to take place is to be agreed and documented. (paragraph 6.575)

2 **Recommendation 52** Directors of social services must ensure that no case is allocated to a social worker unless and until his or her manager ensures that he or she has the necessary training, experience and time to deal with it properly. (paragraph 6.581)

1 **Recommendation 53** When allocating a case to a social worker, the manager must ensure that the social worker is clear as to what has been allocated, what action is required and how that action will be reviewed and supervised. (paragraph 6.586)

2 **Recommendation 54** Directors of social services must ensure that all cases of children assessed as needing a service have an allocated social worker. In cases where this proves to be impossible, arrangements must be made to maintain contact with the child. The number, nature and reasons for such unallocated cases must be reported to the social services committee on a monthly basis. (paragraph 6.589)

1 **Recommendation 55** Directors of social services must ensure that only those cases in which a social worker is actively engaged in work with a child and the child's family are deemed to be 'allocated'. (paragraph 6.590)

1   **Recommendation 56** Directors of social services must ensure that no child known to social services who is an inpatient in a hospital and about whom there are child protection concerns is allowed to be taken home until it has been established by social services that the home environment is safe, the concerns of the medical staff have been fully addressed, and there is a social work plan in place for the ongoing promotion and safeguarding of that child's welfare. (paragraph 6.594)

2   **Recommendation 57** Directors of social services must ensure that social work staff are made aware of how to access effectively information concerning vulnerable children which may be held in other countries. (paragraph 6.619)

1   **Recommendation 58** Directors of social services must ensure that every child's case file includes, on the inside of the front cover, a properly maintained chronology. (paragraph 6.629)

2   **Recommendation 59** Directors of social services must ensure that staff working with vulnerable children and families are provided with up-to-date procedures, protocols and guidance. Such practice guidance must be located in a single-source document. The work should be monitored so as to ensure procedures are followed. (paragraph 8.7)

2   **Recommendation 60** Directors of social services must ensure that hospital social workers working with children and families are line managed by the children and families' section of their social services department. (paragraph 8.19)

1   **Recommendation 61** Directors of social services must ensure that hospital social workers participate in all hospital meetings concerned with the safeguarding of children. (paragraph 8.27)

2   **Recommendation 62** Where hospital-based social work staff come into contact with children from other local authority areas, the directors of social services of their employing authorities must ensure that they work to a single set of guidance agreed by all the authorities concerned. (paragraph 8.53)

1   **Recommendation 63** Hospital social workers must always respond promptly to any referral of suspected deliberate harm to a child. They must see and talk to the child, to the child's carer and to those responsible for the care of the child in hospital, while avoiding the risk of appearing to coach the child. (paragraph 8.100)

Healthcare recommendations

1   **Recommendation 64** When a child is admitted to hospital and deliberate harm is suspected, the nursing care plan must take full account of this diagnosis. (paragraph 9.35)

2   **Recommendation 65** When the deliberate harm of a child is identified as a possibility, the examining doctor should consider whether taking a history directly from the child is in that child's best interests. When that is so, the history should be taken even when the consent of the carer has not been obtained, with the reason for dispensing with consent recorded by the examining doctor. *Working Together* guidance should be amended accordingly. In those cases in which English is not the first language of the child concerned, the use of an interpreter should be considered. (paragraph 9.39)

1   **Recommendation 66** When a child has been examined by a doctor, and concerns about deliberate harm have been raised, no subsequent appraisal of these concerns should be considered complete until each of the concerns has been fully addressed, accounted for and documented. (paragraph 9.60)

2   **Recommendation 67** When differences of medical opinion occur in relation to the diagnosis of possible deliberate harm to a child, a recorded discussion must take place between the persons holding the different views. When the deliberate harm of a child has been raised as an alternative diagnosis to a purely medical one, the diagnosis of deliberate harm must not be rejected without full discussion and, if necessary, obtaining a further opinion. (paragraph 9.65)

1   **Recommendation 68** When concerns about the deliberate harm of a child have been raised, doctors must ensure that comprehensive and contemporaneous notes are made of these concerns. If doctors are unable to make their own notes, they must be clear about what it is they wish to have recorded on their behalf. (paragraphs 9.72 and 10.30)

1   **Recommendation 69** When concerns about the deliberate harm of a child have been raised, a record must be kept in the case notes of all discussions about the child, including telephone conversations. When doctors and nurses are working in circumstances in which case notes are not available to them, a record of all discussions must be entered in the case notes at the earliest opportunity so that this becomes part of the child's permanent health record. (paragraph 9.95)

2   **Recommendation 70** Hospital trust chief executives must introduce systems to ensure that no child about whom there are child protection concerns is discharged from hospital without the permission of either the consultant in charge of the child's care or of a paediatrician above the grade of senior house officer. Hospital chief executives must introduce systems to monitor compliance with this recommendation. (paragraphs 9.101 and 10.145)

2   **Recommendation 71** Hospital trust chief executives must introduce systems to ensure that no child about whom there are child protection concerns is discharged from hospital without a documented plan for the future care of the child. The plan must include follow-up arrangements. Hospital chief executives must introduce systems to monitor compliance with this recommendation. (paragraphs 9.101 and 10.146)

1   **Recommendation 72** No child about whom there are concerns about deliberate harm should be discharged from hospital back into the community without an identified GP. Responsibility for ensuring this happens rests with the hospital consultant under whose care the child has been admitted. (paragraph 9.105)

2   **Recommendation 73** When a child is admitted to hospital and deliberate harm is suspected, the doctor or nurse admitting the child must inquire about previous admissions to hospital. In the event of a positive response, information concerning the previous admissions must be obtained from the other hospitals. The consultant in charge of the case must review this information when making decisions about the child's future care and management. Hospital chief executives must introduce systems to ensure compliance with this recommendation. (paragraph 10.36)

1   **Recommendation 74** Any child admitted to hospital about whom there are concerns about deliberate harm must receive a full and fully-documented physical examination within 24 hours of their admission, except when doing so would, in the opinion of the examining doctor, compromise the child's care or the child's physical and emotional well-being. (paragraph 10.41)

1   **Recommendation 75** In a case of possible deliberate harm to a child in hospital, when permission is required from the child's carer for the investigation of such possible deliberate harm, or for the treatment of a child's injuries, the permission must be sought by a doctor above the grade of senior house officer. (paragraph 10.73)

1   **Recommendation 76** When a child is admitted to hospital with concerns about deliberate harm, a clear decision must be taken as to which consultant is to be responsible for the child protection aspects of the child's care. The identity of that consultant must be clearly marked in the child's notes so that all those involved in the child's care are left in no doubt as to who is responsible for the case. (paragraph 10.105)

1   **Recommendation 77** All doctors involved in the care of a child about whom there are concerns about possible deliberate harm must provide social services with a written statement of the nature and extent of their concerns. If misunderstandings of medical diagnosis occur, these must be corrected at the earliest opportunity in writing. It is the responsibility of the doctor to ensure that his or her concerns are properly understood. (paragraph 10.162)

1   **Recommendation 78** Within a given location, health professionals should work from a single set of records for each child. (paragraph 11.39)

1   **Recommendation 79** During the course of a ward round, when assessing a child about whom there are concerns about deliberate harm, the doctor conducting the ward round should ensure that all available information is reviewed and taken account of before decisions on the future management of the child's case are taken. (paragraph 11.39)

1   **Recommendation 80** When a child for whom there are concerns about deliberate harm is admitted to hospital, a record must be made in the hospital notes of all face-to-face discussions (including medical and nursing 'handover') and telephone conversations relating to the care of the child, and of all decisions made during such conversations. In addition, a record must be made of who is responsible for carrying out any actions agreed during such conversations. (paragraph 11.39)

2   **Recommendation 81** Hospital chief executives must introduce systems to ensure that actions agreed in relation to the care of a child about whom there are concerns of deliberate harm are recorded, carried through and checked for completion. (paragraph 11.39)

2   **Recommendation 82** The Department of Health should examine the feasibility of bringing the care of children about whom there are concerns about deliberate harm within the framework of clinical governance. (paragraph 11.39)

2   **Recommendation 83** The investigation and management of a case of possible deliberate harm to a child must be approached in the same systematic and rigorous manner as would be appropriate to the investigation and management of any other potentially fatal disease. (paragraph 11.53)

3   **Recommendation 84** All designated and named doctors in child protection and all consultant paediatricians must be revalidated in the diagnosis and treatment of deliberate harm and in the multi-disciplinary aspects of a child protection investigation. (paragraph 11.53)

3 **Recommendation 85** The Department of Health should invite the Royal College of Paediatrics and Child Health to develop models of continuing education in the diagnosis and treatment of the deliberate harm of children, and in the multi-disciplinary aspects of a child protection investigation, to support the revalidation of doctors described in the preceding recommendation. (paragraph 11.53)

3 **Recommendation 86** The Department of Health should invite the Royal College of General Practitioners to explore the feasibility of extending the process of new child patient registration to include gathering information on wider social and developmental issues likely to affect the welfare of the child, for example their living conditions and their school attendance. (paragraph 12.29)

3 **Recommendation 87** The Department of Health should seek to ensure that all GPs receive training in the recognition of deliberate harm to children, and in the multi-disciplinary aspects of a child protection investigation, as part of their initial vocational training in general practice, and at regular intervals of no less than three years thereafter. (paragraph 12.29)

3 **Recommendation 88** The Department of Health should examine the feasibility of introducing training in the recognition of deliberate harm to children as part of the professional education of all general practice staff and for all those working in primary healthcare services for whom contact with children is a regular feature of their work. (paragraph 12.29)

2 **Recommendation 89** All GPs must devise and maintain procedures to ensure that they, and all members of their practice staff, are aware of whom to contact in the local health agencies, social services and the police in the event of child protection concerns in relation to any of their patients. (paragraph 12.29)

2 **Recommendation 90** Liaison between hospitals and community health services plays an important part in protecting children from deliberate harm. The Department of Health must ensure that those working in such liaison roles receive child protection training. Compliance with child protection policies and procedures must be subject to regular audit by primary care trusts. (paragraph 12.57)

Police recommendations

1 **Recommendation 91** Save in exceptional circumstances, no child is to be taken into police protection until he or she has been seen and an assessment of his or her circumstances has been undertaken. (paragraph 13.17)

1 **Recommendation 92** Chief constables must ensure that crimes involving a child victim are dealt with promptly and efficiently, and to the same standard as equivalent crimes against adults. (paragraph 13.24)

1 **Recommendation 93** Whenever a joint investigation by police and social services is required into possible injury or harm to a child, a manager from each agency should always be involved at the referral stage, and in any further strategy discussion. (paragraph 13.52)

1 **Recommendation 94** In cases of serious crime against children, supervisory officers must, from the beginning, take an active role in ensuring that a proper investigation is carried out. (paragraph 13.55)

3   **Recommendation 95** The Association of Chief Police Officers must produce and implement the standards-based service, as recommended by Her Majesty's Inspectorate of Constabulary in the 1999 thematic inspection report, *Child Protection*. (paragraph 13.66)

2   **Recommendation 96** Police forces must review their systems for taking children into police protection and ensure they comply with the Children Act 1989 and Home Office guidelines. In particular, they must ensure that an independent officer of at least inspector rank acts as the designated officer in all cases. (paragraph 13.68)

2   **Recommendation 97** Chief constables must ensure that the investigation of crime against children is as important as the investigation of any other form of serious crime. Any suggestion that child protection policing is of a lower status than other forms of policing must be eradicated. (paragraph 14.15)

1   **Recommendation 98** The guideline set out at paragraph 5.8 of *Working Together* must be strictly adhered to: whenever social services receive a referral which may constitute a criminal offence against a child, they must inform the police at the earliest opportunity. (paragraph 14.46)

3   **Recommendation 99** The *Working Together* arrangements must be amended to ensure the police carry out completely, and exclusively, any criminal investigation elements in a case of suspected injury or harm to a child, including the evidential interview with a child victim. This will remove any confusion about which agency takes the 'lead' or is responsible for certain actions. (paragraph 14.57)

3   **Recommendation 100** Training for child protection officers must equip them with the confidence to question the views of professionals in other agencies, including doctors, no matter how eminent those professionals appear to be. (paragraph 14.73)

3   **Recommendation 101** The Home Office, through Her Majesty's Inspectorate of Constabulary, must take a more active role in maintaining high standards of child protection investigation by means of its regular Basic Commands Unit and force inspections. In addition, a follow-up to the *Child Protection* thematic inspection of 1999 should be conducted. (paragraph 14.132)

3   **Recommendation 102** The Home Office, through Centrex and the Association of Chief Police Officers, must devise and implement a national training curriculum for child protection officers as recommended in 1999 by Her Majesty's Inspectorate of Constabulary in its thematic inspection report, *Child Protection*. (paragraph 15.16)

3   **Recommendation 103** Chief constables must ensure that officers working on child protection teams are sufficiently well trained in criminal investigation, and that there is always a substantial core of fully trained detective officers on each team to deal with the most serious inquiries. (paragraph 15.24)

3   **Recommendation 104** The Police Information Technology Organisation (PITO) should evaluate the child protection IT systems currently available, and make recommendations to chief constables, who must ensure their police force has in use an effective child-protection database and IT management system. (paragraph 15.40)

2   **Recommendation 105** Chief constables must ensure that child protection teams are fully integrated into the structure of their forces and not disadvantaged in terms of accommodation, equipment or resources. (paragraph 15.45)

2   **Recommendation 106** The Home Office must ensure that child protection policing is included in the list of ministerial priorities for the police. (paragraph 15.46)

2   **Recommendation 107** Chief constables and police authorities must give child protection investigations a high priority in their policing plans, thereby ensuring consistently high standards of service by well-resourced, well-managed and well-motivated teams. (paragraph 15.46)

2   **Recommendation 108** The Home Office, through Centrex, must add specific training relating to child protection policing to the syllabus for the strategic command course. This will ensure that all future chief officers in the police service have adequate knowledge and understanding of the roles of child protection teams. (paragraph 15.53)

Annex 2 Witnesses

The following is a list of witnesses who were asked to give evidence to this Inquiry.

Those who gave written evidence are marked with a "W" and those who gave oral evidence in addition to written evidence are marked with an "O". The exception is Kouao, who gave oral evidence but did not provide a written statement.

The witnesses' positions and job titles are those held at the time the individual or their organisation was involved with Victoria, or other relevant period, as appropriate.

Abernethy, I	Senior medical photographer, North Middlesex Hospital	W
Ackah, E	Relative of Kouao	O
Adamou, G	Councillor, Haringey council, lead member for social services	O
Addington, L	Hospital teacher, Brent Education Support Service	W
Agyarko, K	Acquaintance of Kouao	W
Ajayi-Obe, E	Locum paediatric registrar, Central Middlesex Hospital	O
Akers, S	Detective Superintendent, North West Crime Operational Command Unit, Metropolitan Police Service	O
Alexander, S	Specialist registrar in paediatrics, North Middlesex Hospital	O
Alexandrou, M	Housing registration officer, Haringey Social Services	O
Almeida, B	Senior practitioner, Haringey Social Services	O
Alsford, L	Consultant paediatrician, North Middlesex Hospital	O
Anderson, F	Senior re-housing officer, Brent Social Services	O
Anderson, M	Detective Inspector, Brent and Harrow Child Protection Teams, Metropolitan Police Service	O
Anderson, P	Social worker, Brent Social Services	O
Ani, C	Paediatric senior house officer, North Middlesex Hospital	W
Armstrong, E	Team manager, Brent Social Services	O
Arnold, L	Councillor, Haringey council	W
Arthurworrey, L	Social worker, Haringey Social Services	O
Atherton, DJ	Consultant paediatric dermatologist, Great Ormond Street Children's Hospital	W
Austin, C	Senior social worker, Brent Social Services	O
Bainbridge, A	Manager, First Capital Bus Company	W
Bamford, B	Assistant director finance and administration, Brent Social Services	O
Banjoko, O	Community paediatric registrar, North Middlesex Hospital	O
Baptiste, C	Team manager, Haringey Social Services	O
Barnett, P	GP, Somerset Gardens Family Healthcare Centre	W

Bell, P	Staff nurse, accident and emergency department, North Middlesex Hospital	W
Benjamin, L	Detective Superintendent, Serious Crime Group West, Metropolitan Police Service	W
Beynon, R	Senior house officer, accident and emergency department, Central Middlesex Hospital	O
Bird, R	Sergeant, Haringey Child Protection Team, Metropolitan Police Service	O
Bishop, M	Bursar, Harlesden Primary School	W
Blackman, K	Police Constable, Brent Child Protection Team, Metropolitan Police Service	O
Boafoa, C	Nurse, Rainbow ward, North Middlesex Hospital	W
Bolton, J	Director of joint reviews, Audit Commission	W
Boyd, A	Detective Constable, Serious Crime Group East, Metropolitan Police Service	W
Boyle, M	Director, Brent Social Services	O
Bradley, P	Social worker, Haringey Social Services, and UNISON trade union representative	O
Brandon, R	Police Sergeant, Metropolitan Police Service	W
Bridgeman, M	Senior social worker, Brent Social Services	O
Bristow, A	Director, Haringey Social Services	O
Britto, J	Consultant paediatrician, paediatric intensive care unit, St Mary's Hospital Paddington	W
Brown, DA	Temporary Area Detective Chief Inspector, Metropolitan Police Service	W
Brown, L	Team leader in health visiting, Haringey NHS Primary Care Trust	O
Cader, M	French teacher	O
Cameron, A	Daughter of Priscilla Cameron, Victoria's childminder	O
Cameron, Patrick	Son of Priscilla Cameron, Victoria's childminder	O
Cameron, Priscilla	Victoria's childminder	O
Campbell, M	Commander, North West Crime Operational Command Unit, Metropolitan Police Service	O
Carey, N	Home Office accredited pathologist, Guy's Hospital	O
Carr, L	Team manager, Enfield Social Services	O
Charlett, D	Team manager, Brent Social Services	O
Chauhan, S	Accident and emergency department nurse, Central Middlesex Hospital	W
Choufani, O	Translator/interpreter, language services, Ealing council, London	W
Clarke, M	Lead accident and emergency department nurse, North Middlesex Hospital	O

Climbié, F	Victoria's father	O
Clitheroe, H	Finance and systems manager, Housing Resource Centre, Brent council	W
Cooper-Bland, M	Detective Sergeant, Haringey Child Protection Team, Metropolitan Police Service	O
Copson, G	Detective Superintendent, North West Crime Operational Command Unit, Metropolitan Police Service	O
Corrigan, J	Deputy domestic manager, Gardiner Merchant Food and Management Services	W
Cox, DM	Detective Chief Superintendent, North West Crime Operational Command Unit, Metropolitan Police Service	O
Craik, M	Commander, North West Crime Operational Command Unit, Metropolitan Police Service	O
Crego, J	Director of learning technologies, Metropolitan Police Service	W
Cribbin, M	Councillor, Brent council, lead member for social services	O
Crowe, R	Health visitor, Haringey Primary Care NHS Trust	O
Cuddihy, B	Operational services manager, North Middlesex Hospital	O
Cussons, PD	Consultant in burns and plastic surgery, Mount Vernon Hospital	W
Daniel, G	Chief executive, Brent council	O
Davidson, T	Staff nurse on Rainbow ward, North Middlesex Hospital	O
Dempster, C	Locum paediatric senior house officer, Central Middlesex Hospital	O
Deveney, L	Head of homelessness and advice, Ealing council, London	W
Dewar, R	Police Constable, Brent Child Protection Team, Metropolitan Police Service	O
Dickinson, D	Detective Constable, Serious Crime Group West, Metropolitan Police Service	W
Dillon, I	Doctor, paediatric intensive care, St Mary's Hospital Paddington	W
Doncaster, S	Sister, accident and emergency department, North Middlesex Hospital	W
Doyle, B	Classroom assistant, Brent Education Support Service	W
Duncan, D	Commissioning manager, Haringey Social Services	O
Edwards, B	Designated doctor for child protection, Central Middlesex Hospital	O
Emes, A	Forensic scientist	W
Eminowicz, M	Senior education officer, Brent Social Services	O
Ezekwe, AM	Paediatric senior house officer, North Middlesex Hospital	W
Featherstone, L	Leader of the opposition, Haringey council	W
Finlay, J	Senior commissioning manager, Ealing Social Services	O

Fletcher, E	Senior nurse for child protection, Haringey Primary Care NHS Trust	O
Forlee, S	Senior house officer in paediatrics, North Middlesex Hospital	O
Forrest, P	Leader of the Conservative group, Haringey council	W
Fortune, P	Social worker, Ealing Social Services	O
Frederick, L	Team manager, Haringey Social Services	O
Fysh, R	Forensic scientist, Metropolitan Police Service	O
Gallagher, A	Operational service manager, North Middlesex University Hospital NHS Trust	O
Gallagher, S	Sister, accident and emergency department, North Middlesex Hospital	W
Garner, K	Bank nurse, North Middlesex Hospital	W
Gaunt, D	Social worker, Ealing Social Services	O
Geraghty, D	Police Constable, Metropolitan Police Service	W
Gibb, R	Chief executive of North Middlesex University Hospital NHS Trust	O
Gilbert, C	Acquaintance of Manning	W
Gobin, B	Staff nurse, Barnaby Bear ward, Central Middlesex Hospital	O
Golding, E	Information officer, Haringey Education Services	W
Goodall, J	Director, Brent Social Services	O
Goodman, D	Director of primary care development, Haringey Primary Care NHS Trust	W
Gooneratne, W	GP, Somerset Gardens Family Healthcare Centre	W
Gorry, J	Detective Sergeant, Brent Child Protection Team, Metropolitan Police Service	O
Graham, A	Commissioning manager, child protection quality and review, Haringey Social Services	O
Graham, B	Director of education and community services, NSPCC	W
Graham, C	Staff nurse, Barnaby Bear ward, Central Middlesex Hospital	O
Graham, M	Staff nurse, Rainbow ward, North Middlesex Hospital	O
Gray, J	Social services inspector	O
Green, D (née Cardis)	Child protection adviser, Haringey Social Services	O
Green, R	Transfer and registration officer, Brent Social Services	O
Griffin, M	Housing assessments manager, Haringey housing services	W
Griffiths, J	The Benefits Agency	W
Griffiths, W	Deputy Assistant Commissioner, Metropolitan Police Service	O
Harris, T	Leader, Haringey council	W
Hartley-Martin, A	Assistant to the Pastors at the Universal Church of the Kingdom of God	O

Haviland, J	Paediatrics registrar, Central Middlesex Hospital	W
Hayes, M	Social worker, Haringey Social Services	O
Heatley, J	Commissioning manager, Haringey Social Services	O
Henry, S	Practice manager, Tottenham Child and Family Centre, NSPCC	O
Hinds, L	Staff nurse, Rainbow ward, North Middlesex Hospital	O
Hines, M	Senior social worker, Brent Social Services	O
Hitchen, C	Assistant director, Brent Social Services	W
Hobbs, L	Social worker, Brent Social Services	O
Hodges, A	Police Sergeant, Haringey Child Protection Team, Metropolitan Police Service	O
Howard, D	Detective Inspector, Haringey Child Protection Team, Metropolitan Police Service	O
Howard, L	Service manager, Enfield Social Services	W
Howlett, C	Commander in the serious crime group, Metropolitan Police Service	O
Hunt, N	Director of child protection, NSPCC	W
Hunt, S	Customer services officer, One Stop Shop, Brent	O
Ieronimou, A	Family centre officer, Tottenham Child and Family Centre, NSPCC	W
Inal, B	Primary care manager (Haringey), Haringey Primary Care NHS Trust	O
Irwin, J	Deputy leader, Haringey council	W
Israni, GK	GP, Greenhill Park Medical Centre	W
Jackson, A	Paediatric senior house officer, North Middlesex Hospital	W
Jacob, S	Senior practitioner, Haringey Social Services	O
Jennings, S	Senior staff nurse, Rainbow ward, North Middlesex Hospital	O
John, A	Deputy leader, Brent council	O
Johns, J	Director of Mobile Radiography Services LTD	W
Johns, K	Social worker, Enfield Social Services	O
Johnson, P	Ward manager, Barnaby Bear ward, Central Middlesex Hospital	O
Jones, K	Police Constable, Haringey Child Protection Team, Metropolitan Police Service	O
Jones, L	Social worker, Ealing Social Services	O
Jones, S	Service manager, surgery and paediatrics services, Central Middlesex Hospital	W
Joseph, P	Assistant lawyer, Ealing Social Services	O
Junior, C	Pastor, Universal Church of the Kingdom of God	W
Kakouratos, B	Housing registration manager, Haringey Social Services	O
Keating, C	Senior paediatics staff nurse, Rainbow ward, North Middlesex Hospital	O

Kelleher, D	Detective Chief Superintendent, Paddington Green Division, City of Westminster, Metropolitan Police Service	O
Kendrick, D	Commander (Crime and Criminal Justice) North East London, Metropolitan Police Service	O
Kimbidima, C	Acquaintance of Kouao	O
Kimbidima, J	Acquaintance of Kouao	O
Kitchman, P	Child protection adviser, Haringey Social Services	O
Konigsberg, M	Assistant director, Brent Social Services	O
Kouao, MT	Convicted of the murder of Victoria Climbié	O
Kousoulou, D	Deputy director, Haringey Social Services	O
Kozinos, R	Senior practitioner, Haringey Social Services	O
Lachman, P	Clinical director for women and children services, directorate of North West London Hospitals NHS Trust	O
Lally, M	Director of adult and child community health services, Haringey Primary Care NHS Trust	W
Lampe, C	Nursery nurse, North Middlesex Hospital	W
Lapeze, J	Secretary, private letting agency	W
Laudat, J	Senior assessment officer, Haringey housing services	W
Lawrence, S	Senior practitioner, Ealing Social Services	O
Lewin, D	Forensic odontologist and registered dental surgeon	W
Lewington, P	Assistant branch secretary (Haringey), UNISON	O
Lima, A	Pastor, Universal Church of the Kingdom of God	O
Lindsay, MS	GP, Somerset Gardens Family Healthcare Centre	W
Lipworth, C	Team manager, Enfield Social Services	O
Lloyd, G	Principal social services solicitor, Haringey Social Services	W
Ludgate, R	Acting director, Brent Social Services	O
Mairs, A	Team manager, Haringey Social Services	O
Makar, S	Paediatric senior house officer, North Middlesex Hospital	W
Makwana, C	Product development manager, Metropolitan Police Service	W
Mallia, J	Detective Constable, Metropolitan Police Service	W
Mandic, R	Proprietor of bed and breakfast accommodation used by Victoria and Kouao	W
Mann, T	Consultant dermatologist, North Middlesex Hospital	W
Manning, C	Convicted of the murder of Victoria Climbié	O
Marques, T	Assistant Pastor, Universal Church of the Kingdom of God	W
Marsh, M	Director and chief executive, NSPCC	W
Martin, A	Team manager, Haringey Social Services	W
Martin, W	Social worker, Ealing Social Services	O
McColl, B	Radiographer, North Middlesex Hospital	W

McDougall, M	Service unit manager, Brent Social Services	W
McFarlane, C	Neighbour of Kouao	W
McGregor, K (née Brown)	Home visitor (housing), Haringey Social Services	O
McKennan, A	Interpreter	W
McMahon, A	Paediatrics senior house officer, Central Middlesex Hospital	W
McTigue, J	Chief inspector, inspection unit, Brent Social Services	W
Mead, S	Assistant review director, Audit Commission	W
Meates, MA	Consultant paediatrician, North Middlesex Hospital	O
Meehan, G	Leader, Haringey council	O
Mensah, P	Minister, Joy Baptist Church, Harlesden	O
Millard, T	Radiographer, North Middlesex Hospital	W
Miran, M	Lecturer, School of Oriental and African Studies	W
Modi, A	Specialist registrar in paediatrics, Central Middlesex Hospital	O
Moore, G	Registered nurse, the surgery of Dr IP Patel	W
Moore, L	Interim assistant director, Enfield Social Services	O
Mooruth, K	Staff nurse, paediatrics, Central Middlesex Hospital	W
Niven, K	Detective Inspector, North West Area Major Incident Team, Metropolitan Police Service	O
Norman, B	Lead nurse, Paediatrics, North Middlesex Hospital	O
Nottage, A	Deputy chief inspector, social services inspectorate	W
O'Boyce, N	Hospital play specialist, North Middlesex Hospital	O
Orome, P	Pastor, Mission Ensemble Pour Christ	O
Pandelli, P	Employee, Star Estates and Lettings	W
Park, K	Detective Inspector, Serious Crime Group, Metropolitan Police Service	W
Patel, I	General family practitioner, The Surgery, London	O
Patel, R	Service development manager, Brent Social Services	W
Peatfield, P	Independent chair of child protection case conferences, Haringey Social Services	O
Pereira, G	Registered nurse, Rainbow ward, North Middlesex Hospital	O
Phillips, P	Senior social worker, Brent Social Services	W
Philpotts, R	Social worker, Haringey Social Services	W
Pinarbasi, S	Minicab driver, Lord Cars Minicab Office	W
Pollock, T	Homestay agency manager, central London	W
Prince, D	Director of operations, Audit Commission	O
Punch, M	Team administration support officer, Brent Social Services	O
Quansah, G	Daughter of Esther Ackah, distant relative of Kouao	W

Quinn, I	Senior staff nurse, Rainbow ward, North Middlesex Hospital	O
Raimundo, P	Pastor, Universal Church of the Kingdom of God	W
Reynders, D	Paediatric senior house officer, North Middlesex Hospital	O
Richardson, J	Paediatric registrar, North Middlesex Hospital	O
Richardson, M	Director, Haringey Social Services	O
Ricketts, P	Police Constable, Haringey Child Protection Team, Metropolitan Police Service	W
Riordan, J	Executive medical director, North West London Hospitals NHS Trust	O
Robertson, V	Social worker, Haringey Social Services	O
Rodgers, C	Social worker, Haringey Social Services	O
Roper, T	Team manager, Brent Social Services	O
Rossiter, MA	Consultant paediatrician, North Middlesex Hospital	O
Routis, JJ	Social services officer, Department of Social Services, Villepinte and Tremblay-en-France, France	W
Ryan, M	Staff nurse, Rainbow ward, North Middlesex Hospital	O
Sanders, C	Solicitor, Ealing Social Services	W
Schwartz, R	Consultant paediatrician and named doctor for child protection, Central Middlesex Hospital and St Mary's Hospital Paddington	O
Scott, C	Service manager, Tottenham Child and Family Centre, NSPCC	O
Selby, A	Ambulance technician, London Ambulance Service	W
Sexton, M	Staff nurse, Central Middlesex Hospital	W
Shirsalkar, N	Ophthalmology senior house officer, North Middlesex Hospital	W
Simpson, D	Joint review team, Audit Commission	O
Singh, G	Chief executive, Haringey council	O
Sivanandam, P	Office manager, private letting agency	W
Skinner, J	Assistant director, Ealing Social Services	O
Small, L	Customer services officer (housing), Brent Social Services	W
Smit, E	Social worker, Brent Social Services	O
Smith, D	Police Sergeant, Brent Child Protection Team, Metropolitan Police Service	O
Smith, J	Staff nurse, accident and emergency department, Central Middlesex Hospital	W
Smith, R	Group administration officer, Brent Social Services	O
Spicer, J	Paramedic, London Ambulance Service	W
Stinson, A	Clinical facility manager/Senior Nurse, accident and emergency department, Central Middlesex Hospital	O
Stollard, S	Team manager, Ealing Social Services	O
Stoneham, P	Detective Sergeant, Metropolitan Police Service	W

Strugnell, S	Criminal intelligence analyst, Metropolitan Police Service	W
Sulaiman, T	Deputy lead member for social services, Haringey council	W
Sy, R	Sessional interpreter, Haringey	W
Tachakra, S	Clinical director of accident and emergency services, Central Middlesex Hospital	W
Tall, S	Partnerships and commissioning services manager	W
Taub, L	Sister, special care baby unit, North Middlesex Hospital	O
Teodorski, H	Ambulance technician, London Ambulance Service	O
Thrift, K	Social worker, Brent Social Services	O
Travers, A	Head of corporate finance, Haringey council, London	O
Tsiagbe, R	Nursery nurse, North Middlesex Hospital	W
Tudor-Williams, G	Consultant microbiologist, St Mary's Hospital Paddington	W
Turnbull, A	Assistant director, Haringey Social Services	W
Turton, C	Chair, social services committee, Haringey council	O
Tutt, N	Director, Ealing Social Services	O
Tyrrell, K	Joint reviewer, Audit Commission	W
Tyrrell, V	Specialist child protection nurse, Brent and Harrow Health Authority	O
Victor, G	Social worker, Ealing Social Services	O
Viljoen, Y (née Hurter)	Locum social worker, Haringey Social Services	O
Wakelin, S	Consultant dermatologist, St Mary's Hospital Paddington	W
Watling, C	Staff Nurse, North Middlesex Hospital	W
Watson, C	Diagnostic radiographer, North Middlesex Hospital	W
Watson, ED	Practice manager, Tottenham Child and Family Centre, NSPCC	O
Webster, A	Director of public services research, Audit Commission	W
Weithers, E	Lead clinician, accident and emergency department, North Middlesex Hospital	W
Wheeler, P	Detective Chief Inspector, North West Crime Operational Command Unit, Metropolitan Police Service	O
White, Y	Housing registration officer, Haringey housing services	W
Wilkin, B	Group support assistant, Ealing Social Services	O
Wilson, C	Assistant director, Haringey Social Services	O
Wilson, E	Student nurse, Central Middlesex Hospital	W
Winter, J	Homeless persons officer, Ealing Social Services	O
Young, M	Family liaison officer, Metropolitan Police Service	W

Annex 3 Inquiry staff

The size and composition of the team varied according to the various stages of the Inquiry. The following is a list of all staff who worked on the Inquiry.

Secretary to the Inquiry

Mandy Jacklin

Solicitor to the Inquiry

Michael Fitzgerald

Counsel to the Inquiry

Neil Garnham QC

Caroline Gibson

Neil Sheldon

Secretariat

Tara Lawson Mean (Deputy Secretary, February – August 2001)

Maria Butler

Sarah Connelly

Dawn Cumberbatch Worrall

Hannah Fitzgerald

Emily Forder White

Susan Goodwin

Legal team

Fiona Loveridge (Assistant Solicitor, April – August 2001)

Lyndon Branfield

Edward Brown

Simon Catherall

Steve Condie

Jane Herschell

Richard Moule

Philip Perrins

Kathleen Price

Charlotte Reynolds

Jessica Skinns

Marianne Thorbro

Sarah Watson

Special advisers

Dr Valerie Brasse

Dr Susan Shepherd

Communications

Paul Rees (Communications Director)

Lara Williams

Contractors

ICL/CSC

Michael Aremu

David Johnson

Haris Kazazic

Smith Bernal

Jacqueline Gleghorn

Chanelle Piper

Claire Stanley

Ailsa Williams

Sound

Jean-Raphael Dedieu

This Report was prepared for publication by COI Communications.

Annex 4 Legal representatives

Interested Parties and their representatives before the Inquiry

Interested Parties	Representatives
Mr and Mrs Climbié	Margo Boye-Anawoma and Joanna Dodson QC, instructed by Imran Khan & Partners solicitors, and Bhatt Murphy solicitors from July 2002
Ealing council	Vera Mayer, instructed by Director of Legal and Democratic Services, London Borough of Ealing
Enfield council	Alex Verdan, instructed by Solicitor to the Council, London Borough of Enfield
Brent council	David Turner QC and Joy Okoye, instructed by Borough Solicitor, London Borough of Brent
Haringey council	Elizabeth Lawson QC and James Presland, instructed by Borough Solicitor, London Borough of Haringey
North West London Hospitals NHS Trust	David Mason of Capsticks solicitors
North Middlesex University Hospital Trust	David Mason of Capsticks solicitors
Haringey Primary Care NHS Trust	David Mason of Capsticks solicitors
Barnet, Enfield and Haringey Health Authority	David Mason of Capsticks solicitors
Metropolitan Police Service	Ronald Thwaites QC and Vince Williams, instructed by Directorate of Legal Services, Metropolitan Police Service
Detective Inspector Howard	Patrick Gibbs, instructed by Reynolds Dawson solicitors
Police Sergeants Hodges, Bird and Cooper-Bland	Gareth Rees, instructed by Russell Jones & Walker solicitors
PC Karen Jones	Maura McGowan QC, instructed by Russell Jones & Walker solicitors
Detective Inspector Anderson, Detective Sergeant Smith and Detective Constable Dewar	Michael Egan, instructed by Reynolds Dawson solicitors

Lisa Arthurworrey — Jane Hoyal and Michael Paget, instructed by Employment Rights Unit, UNISON

NSPCC — Peter Downey of Hempsons solicitors

Witnesses and their representatives before the Inquiry

Witnesses	Representatives
Ackah, E	Imran Khan & Partners solicitors
Akers, S	Rowe Cohen solicitors
Armstrong, E	Thompsons solicitors
Baptiste, C	Fisher Meredith solicitors
Cameron, A	Imran Khan & Partners solicitors
Cameron, Patrick	Imran Khan & Partners solicitors
Cameron, Priscilla	Imran Khan & Partners solicitors
Copson, G	Rowe Cohen solicitors
Cox, D	Rowe Cohen solicitors
Gorry, J	Venters Reynolds solicitors
Gray, J	Solicitor to the Department of Health
Kitchman, P	Mullinger Banks solicitors
Kouao, MT	Chesham & Co. solicitors
Kozinos, R	Reynolds Porter Chamberlain solicitors
Mairs, A	Irwin Mitchell solicitors
Prince, D	Solicitor to the Audit Commission
Simpson, D	Solicitor to the Audit Commission
Teodorski, H	Legal Services department for London Ambulance
Wheeler, P	Illiffes Booth Bennett solicitors
Wilson, C	Bates Wells & Braithwaite solicitors

Annex 5 Seminar participants

Seminar one: Discovery and inclusion

Name	Title	Organisation
Antoniou, G	Homestart scheme manager	Enfield and Haringey Health Authority
Baderman, H	Accident and emergency consultant	
Bowen, R	Assistant director of children's services	Southwark Social Services
Clarke, B	Chair	Community Practitioners' and Health Visitors' Association
Cloke, C	Head of child protection awareness and advocacy	NSPCC
Coaker, L	Housing assessment manager	Harrow council
Dutt, R	Director	Race Equality Unit
Ellery, S	Policy officer	West Sussex Social Services
Gibb, M	Executive director of housing and social services	Kensington and Chelsea council
Jones, R	Assistant chief inspector	Social Services Inspectorate
Khan, R	Duty assessment team manager	Birmingham Social Services
Lammy, D	MP for Tottenham	House of Commons
Macaulay, S	Senior education welfare officer	Education Welfare Service, Wandsworth
Mason, R	Social worker	Portsmouth Social Services
McCallum, D	Detective Sergeant, child protection expert	Avon and Somerset Constabulary
McCullough, A	Project leader	Safe in the City, Manchester
McEwan, Y	GP and GP tutor	Essex Health Authority
McGrath, B	Private fostering co-ordinator	Gloucestershire Social Services
McQuarrie, R	Practice nurse	Hertfordshire
Morgan, P	Deputy director of operational support	Immigration Services, Home Office
Palmer, T	Principal policy and practice officer	Barnardo's
Parton, N	Director, Centre for Applied Childhood Studies	University of Huddersfield
Pritchard, C	Professor of psychiatric social work	University of Southampton
Sanderson, J	Caller care manager	Samaritans
Shiyabola, T	Director	African Women's Welfare Association
Tomkins, B	Designated nurse for child protection	East Kent Community NHS Trust

Seminar two: Identification

Name	Title	Organisation
Amamoo, N	Director	African Families Foundation
Ariyo, MD	Co-ordinator	Africans Unite Against Child Abuse
Barker, J	Senior practitioner	Norfolk Social Services
Booth, L	School improvement officer	Manchester
Carthigesan, S	Consultant community paediatrician and named doctor for child protection	Medway Maritime Hospital
Cheal, S	Chief executive	The Who Cares? Trust
Emberson, M	Principal child care manager	Reading Social Services
Fletcher, T	Project leader, First Stop Project	The Children's Society
Hayler, T	Detective Superintendent	Avon and Somerset Constabulary
Hogg, J	Detective Sergeant, child protection unit	Northumbria Police
Holmes-Smith, J	Consultant paediatrician	Surrey Hampshire Borders NHS Trust
Jones, R	Assistant chief inspector	Social Services Inspectorate, Manchester
Little, M	Researcher	Dartington Social Research Unit
Munro, E	Lecturer in social policy	London School of Economics and Political Science
Pearson, D	Director	Churches' Child Protection Advisory Service
Peel, M	Director of the national open learning programme	Open University
Pell, K	Named nurse for child protection	Children's Centre, City Hospital, Nottingham
Plant, A	Team manager	Dudley Social Services
Tapsfield, R	Chief executive	Family Rights Group
Williams, J	Director	Cheshire Social Services
Wilson, R	Consultant paediatrician	Royal College of Paediatrics and Child Health

Seminar three: Determining requirements

Name	Title	Organisation
Anderson, B	Assistant director, commissioning and planning	East Kent Social Services
Atkinson, I	Senior practitioner	Peterborough Education and Children's Services
Banks, R	Principal for the Standards and Qualifications Framework	Training Organisation for Personal and Social Services (TOPSS)
Basker, D	Principal child care manager	North Lincolnshire Social and Housing Services
Begley, P	IT consultant	ISISS Ltd
Bowman, A	Strategic director, social care and health	Brighton and Hove council
Butler, C	Acting chief executive	South West London and St George's NHS Trust
Cookey, N	Consultant paediatrician	North Durham NHS Trust
Davies, O	National officer for social services	UNISON
Davies, R	Assistant commissioner for Wales, policy and services evaluation	National Assembly for Wales
Evans, D	Child protection co-ordinator	Swindon Social Services
Hampson, P	Chief Constable	West Mercia Constabulary
Held, J	Director	Camden Social Services
Hendry, E	Head of child protection training and consultancy	NSPCC
Jones, D	Consultant child, adolescent and family psychiatrist	Park Hospital for Children, Oxford
Jones, R	Assistant chief inspector	Social Services Inspectorate, Manchester
Lynch, M	Professor of community paediatrics	Guy's, King's and St Thomas's School of Medicine
Marlow, K	Detective Inspector	South Wales Police
Rundle, M	Director of social services	Wandsworth Social Services
Ryan, H	Child care manager	Northamptonshire Social Services
Spicer, D	Honorary secretary	British Association for the Study and Prevention of Child Abuse and Neglect
Thorpe, D	Professor of applied social science	Lancaster University
Tunstill, J	Professor of social work	Royal Holloway, University of London
Webster, D	Principal educational psychologist	Lancashire council

Seminar four: Service provision and delivery

Name	Title	Organisation
Barnett, A	Assessment team manager, children and families' services	Middlesbrough Social Services
Bates, R	Manager, policy performance and commissioning (children)	Bradford Social Services
Blom-Cooper QC, Sir L		Independent
Brook, G	Clinical nurse specialist	Birmingham Children's Hospital NHS Trust
Cooper, A	Professor of social work	Tavistock Clinic and University of East London
Dawson, H	MP for Lancaster and Wyre	House of Commons
Hobbs, C	Consultant community paediatrician	Leeds Teaching Hospitals' NHS Trust
Hopwood, M	Detective chief inspector	West Yorkshire Police
Hutchinson, R	Director of social services	Portsmouth Social Services, Chair of Association of Directors of Social Services Children and Families' Committee
Johnston, I	Director	British Association of Social Workers
Kings, A	Detective Constable, family support unit	Greater Manchester Police
Mason, G	Assistant chief inspector	Social Services Inspectorate
Peynser, P	Head of children and families' services	Sheffield Social Services
Ransford, J	Director of education and social policy	Local Government Association
Ross, J	Chief executive, primary care trust and director of social services	Barking and Dagenham council
Shephard, G	MP for Norfolk South West	House of Commons
Simpson, V	Chartered forensic and counselling psychologist, child protection specialist	Independent
Skinner, J	Senior social worker	Kensington and Chelsea council
Stone, R	Policy adviser	NSPCC
Sturge, M	General director	African and Caribbean Evangelical Alliance
Thoburn, J	Professor of social work	University of East Anglia, Norwich
Thomas, I	Detective Superintendent	Metropolitan Police Service
Tucker, C	Assistant director for children, families and youth offending services	Brighton and Hove Social Services
Utting, Sir W	Former chief inspector of social services	
York, A	Consultant child and adolescent psychiatrist	Child and Adolescent Mental Health Service, Richmond, Surrey
Young, F	Named nurse for child protection	Maidstone and Tunbridge Wells NHS Trust

Seminar five: Monitoring performance

Name	Title	Organisation
Aynsley-Green, A	National clinical director for children and chair of the children's taskforce	Department of Health
Conlon, M	Primary care lead	NHS Clinical Governance Support Team
Cooling, R	Clinical director	Sutton and Merton Primary Care Trust
Donkor, E	Clinical governance manager	University Hospital Lewisham NHS Trust
Foster, Sir A	Controller	Audit Commission
Frater, M	Chief executive	Telford and Wrekin council
Fry, M	Head of clinical quality, ethics and genetics division	Department of Health
Grange, T	Chief Constable	Dyfed-Powys Police Service
Grindrod, K	Senior practitioner	Manchester city council
Hallsworth, K	Detective Inspector	South Liverpool Family Support Unit
Herbert, B	Programme director	Office of Children's Rights, Commissioner of London
Hollis, T	Assistant Inspector of constabulary with lead for crime	Her Majesty's Inspectorate of Constabulary
James, A	Team manager	Leeds Social Services
Leadbetter, M	Director	Essex County Social Services
Logan, L	Chief Inspector and chairman	Black Police Association
Pinnock, M	Social services performance manger	North Lincolnshire Social Services
Platt, D	Chief inspector	Social Services Inspectorate
Renouf, C	Director of inspection services	NSPCC
Rigg, G	Head of children and families' services	Lancashire Social Services
Robertson, D	Lead officer for child protection	West Kent Health Authority
Robertson, L	Regional development officer	Training Organisation for Personal and Social Services (TOPSS)
Street, B	Assistant director	Bridgend Social Services
Webster, A	Director of public services research department	Audit Commission

Printed in the UK by The Stationery Office Limited
on behalf of the Controller of Her Majesty's Stationery Office
Id 135253 03/03 77240